ACCOUNTING
INFORMATION
SYSTEMS

ELEVENTH EDITION

ACCOUNTING INFORMATION SYSTEMS

ELEVENTH EDITION

Marshall B. Romney
Brigham Young University

Paul John Steinbart
Arizona State University

PEARSON

Prentice
Hall

Pearson Education International

AVP/Editor-in-Chief: Eric Svendsen
Product Development Manager: Ashley Santora
Editorial Project Manager: Kierra Kashickey
Editorial Assistant: Mauricio Escoto
Senior Marketing Manager: Jodi Bassett
Associate Director, Production Editorial: Judy Leale
Production Project Manager: Kerri Tomasso
Permissions Coordinator: Charles Morris
Senior Operations Supervisor: Arnold Vila
Operations Specialist: Michelle Klein
Cover Designer: Kevin Kall
Cover Image Creation: Kevin Kall
Cover image: Jaime Chard/Digital Vision/ Getty Images
Composition/Full-Service Project Management: Ann Courtney, GGS Book Services,
 Atlantic Highlands
Printer/Binder: Courier/Kendallville
Typeface: 10.5/12. Times.

Credits and acknowledgments borrowed from other sources and reproduced, with permission, in this textbook appear on appropriate page within text.

Microsoft® and Windows® are registered trademarks of the Microsoft Corporation in the U.S.A. and other countries. Screen shots and icons reprinted with permission from the Microsoft Corporation. This book is not sponsored or endorsed by or affiliated with the Microsoft Corporation.

If you purchased this book within the United States or Canada you should be aware that it has been wrongfully imported without the approval of the Publisher or the Author.

Pearson Education LTD., London
Pearson Education Singapore, Pte. Ltd
Pearson Education, Canada, Ltd
Pearson Education–Japan
Pearson Education Australia PTY,
 Limited
Pearson Education North Asia Ltd
Pearson Educación de Mexico, S.A. de C.V.
Pearson Education Malaysia, Pte. Ltd.
Pearson Education, Upper Saddle River,
 New Jersey

10 9 8 7 6 5 4 3 2 1
ISBN-13: 978-0-13-500937-6
ISBN-10: 0-13-500937-5

BRIEF CONTENTS

CONTENTS

PREFACE

To the Student

The eleventh edition of *Accounting Information Systems* is designed to prepare you for a successful accounting career in public practice, industry, or government. All of you will be users of accounting information systems. As such, you should participate in the design of those systems. Doing so effectively, however, requires that you have a sound understanding of how they work. In addition to being users, some of you will become managers. Others will become internal and external auditors, and some of you will become consultatnts. All of these roles need to understand how accounting information systems work in order to effectievly measure how cost-effectively they perform, to assess their reliability and that of the information produced, or to lead the redesign and implementation of new and better systems. Mastering the material presented in this text will give you the foundational knowledge you need in order to excel at all those tasks.

This text discusses important new IT developments, such as the widespread deployment of wireless networking and the move to replace bar code technologies with radio frequency identification (RFID) tags because such developments affect business processes and often cause organizations to redesign their accounting systems to take advantage of new capabilities. The focus, however, is not on IT for the sake of IT, but on how IT affects business processes and controls. Indeed, new IT developments not only bring new capabilities, but also often create new threats and affect the overall level of risk. This text will help you understand these issues so that you can properly determine how to modify accounting systems controls to effectively address those new threats and accurately assess the adequacy of controls in those redesigned systems. We also discuss the effect of recent regulatory developments, most notably the Sarbanes-Oxley Act, on the design and operation of accounting systems.

In addition to technology- and regulatory-driven changes, companies are responding to the increasingly competitive business environment by reexamining every internal activity in an effort to reap the most value at the least cost. As a result, accountants are being asked to do more than simply report the results of past activities. They must take a more proactive role in both providing and interpreting financial and non-financial information about the organization's activities. Therefore, throughout this text we discuss how accountants can improve the design and functioning of the accounting information system (AIS) so that it truly adds value to the organization.

Key Learning Objectives

When you finish reading this text, you should understand the following key concepts:

- The business activities performed in the major business cycles
- The collection and processing of data about an organization's business activities
- The use of the latest IT developments to improve the efficiency and effectiveness of business activities
- How to design an AIS to provide the information needed to make key decisions in each business cycle
- The fundamentals of e-business and how they affect modern accounting information systems
- The motives and techniques used to perpetrate fraud

- Internal control objectives and the effects of IT on these objectives, as well as the specific controls used to achieve those objectives

- The COSO and COSO-ERM models for internal control and risk management

- Computer and information security

- The Control Objectives for Information and Related Technology (COBIT) Framework for the effective governance and control of information systems

- The AICPA's Trust Services framework for ensuring systems reliability by developing procedures to protect the confidentiality of proprietary information, maintain the privacy of personally-identifying information collected from customers, assure the availability of information resources, and provide for information processing integrity

- Goals, objectives, and methods for auditing information systems

- Fundamental concepts of database technology and data modeling and their effect on an AIS

- The tools for documenting AIS work, such as REA diagrams, data flow diagrams, and flowcharting

Features to Facilitate Learning

To help you understand these concepts the text includes the following features:

1 **Each chapter begins with an integrated case that introduces that chapter's key concepts and topics and identifies several key issues or problems that you should be able to solve after mastering the material presented in that chapter.** The case is referenced throughout the chapter and the chapter summary presents solutions to the problems and issues raised in the case.

2 **Focus Boxes and real-world examples** to help you understand how companies are using the latest IT developments to improve their AIS.

3 **Hands-on Excel and Access exercises in many chapters** to help you hone your computer skills. Many of these exercises are based on "how-to" tutorials that appeared in recent issues of the Journal of Accountancy.

4 **Numerous problems in every chapter** provide additional opportunities for you to demonstrate your mastery of key concepts. Many problems were developed from reports in current periodicals. Other problems were selected from the various professional examinations, including the CPA, CMA, CIA, and SMAC exams. **Each chapter also has one or more cases** that require more extensive exploration of specific topics.

5 **Chapter quizzes** at the end of each chapter enable you to self-assess your understanding of the material. We also provide detailed explanations about the correct answer to each quiz question.

6 **Extensive use of Graphics.** The text contains hundreds of figures, diagrams, flowcharts, and tables that illustrate the concepts taught in the chapters.

7 **Numerous References.** On the Web site is an extensive bibliography, organized by chapter. This list contains references to the real-world examples used in each chapter and provides you with a starting point for further research.

8 A **comprehensive glossary** located at the back of the book makes it easy to look up the definition of the various technical terms used in the text.

9 **Extensive on-line support** at Prentice-Hall's content-rich, text-supported Web site at *www.prenhall.com/romney*.

Content and Organization

This text is divided into five parts, each focused on a major theme.

Part I: Conceptual Foundations of Accounting Information Systems

Part I consists of four chapters which present the underlying concepts fundamental to an understanding of AIS. Chapter 1 introduces basic terminology and discusses how an AIS can add value to an organization. It also discusses basic strategies and the strategic positions that firms can pursue, so that you can understand how IT can be used to help organizations achieve their goals. Chapter 2 provides an overview of AIS topics, focusing on understanding basic business processes. It introduces transaction processing in automated systems, presenting basic information processing and data storage concepts. You will see the wide range of data that must be collected by the AIS. This information helps you to understand what an AIS does; as you read the remainder of the book, you will see how advances in IT affect the manner in which those functions are performed. Chapter 3 covers two of the most important tools and techniques used to understand, evaluate, design, and document information systems: data flow diagrams and flowcharts. Chapter 4 introduces the topic of databases, with a particular emphasis on the relational data model and creating queries in Microsoft Access.

Part II: Control and Audit of Accounting Information Systems

The five chapters in Part II focus on threats to the reliability of AIS and applicable controls for addressing and mitigating the risks associated with those threats. Chapter 5 discusses the threats to an AIS and why they are growing. It also defines fraud and explains how and why it occurs, with special emphasis on computer fraud. Chapter 6 uses the COSO framework, including the expanded entripres risk management (COSO-ERM) model, to discuss the basic concepts of control. Chapter 7 addresses information security and discusses the COBIT framework for effective governance and control of information systems. It introduces the fundamental concepts of defense-in-depth and the time-based approach to security. The chapter provides a broad survey of a variety of security topics including access controls, firewalls, encryption, and incident detection and response. Chapter 8 discusses the many specific computer controls used in business organizations to achieve the objectives of ensuring privacy, confidentiality, availability, and integrity of processing. Chapter 9 reviews principles and techniques for the audit and evaluation of internal control in a computer-based AIS and introduces the topic of computer-assisted auditing.

Part III: Accounting Information Systems Applications

Part III focuses on how a company's AIS provides critical support for its fundamental business processes. Most large and many medium-sized organizations use enterprise resource planning (ERP) systems to collect, process, and store data about their business processes, as well as to provide information reports designed to enable managers and external parties to assess the organization's efficiency and effectiveness. To make it easier to understand how an ERP system functions, Part III consists of five chapters, each focusing on a particular business process. Chapter 10 covers the revenue cycle, including sales, billing, accounts receivable, and cash receipts. Chapter 11 covers the expenditure cycle, including purchasing, receiving, accounts payable, and cash disbursements. Chapter 12 covers the production cycle, with a special focus on the implications of recent cost accounting developments, such as activity-based costing, for the

design of the production cycle information system. Chapter 13 discusses the human resources management/payroll cycle and explores the ways in which these two systems can be integrated. Chapter 14 focuses on the general ledger and reporting activities in an organization. XBRL, the balanced scorecard, and data warehousing are also covered. Each of these five chapters explains the three basic functions performed by the AIS: efficient transaction processing, provision of adequate internal controls to safeguard assets (including data), and preparation of information useful for effective decision making.

Part IV: The REA Data Model

Part IV consists of three chapters that focus on the REA data model, which provides a conceptual tool for designing and understanding the database underlying an AIS. Chapter 15 introduces the REA data model and how it can be used to design an AIS database. The chapter focuses on modeling the revenue and expenditure cycles. It also demonstrates how the REA model can be used to develop an AIS that can not only generate traditional financial statements and reports but can also more fully meet the informatoin needs of management. Chapter 16 explains how to implement an REA data model in a relational database system. It also shows how to query a relational database in order to produce various financial statements and management reports. Chapter 17 presents how to develop REA data models of the production, HR/payroll, and financing cycles. It also discusses a number of advanced modeling issues, such as the acquisition and sale of intangible products and services and rental transactions.

Part V: The Systems Development Process

Part V consists of three chapters that cover various aspects of the systems development process. Chapter 18 introduces the systems development life cycle and discusses the introductory steps of this process (systems analysis, feasibility, and planning). Particular emphasis is placed on the behavioral ramifications of change. Chapter 19 discusses an organization's many options for acquiring or developing an AIS (e.g., purchasing software, writing software, end-user–developed software, and outsourcing) and for speeding up or improving the development process (business process reengineering, prototyping, and computer-assisted software engineering). Chapter 20 covers the remaining stages of the systems development life cycle (conceptual design, physical design, implementation, and operation and maintenance) and emphasizes the interrelationships among the phases.

To the Instructor

This book is intended for use in a one-semester course in accounting information systems at the undergraduate or graduate level. Introductory financial and managerial accounting courses are suggested prerequisites, and an introductory information systems course that covers a computer language or software package is helpful. The book can also be used as the main text in graduate or advanced undergraduate management information systems courses. Indeed, the topics covered in this text provide information systems students with a solid understanding of transaction processing systems that they can then build on as they pursue more in-depth study of specific topics such as databases, data warehouses and data mining, networks, systems analysis and design, computer security, and information system controls.

Enhancements in the Eleventh Edition

The eleventh edition has been revised and rewritten to incorporate recent developments, while retaining the features that have made prior editions easy to use. Every chapter has been updated to include up-to-date examples of important concepts. Specific changes include:

1 Increased focus on the COSO-ERM model.

2 More coverage of the COBIT framework.

3 Updated discussion of computer fraud techniques.

4 Update discussion of information security countermeasures.

5 Additional Excel and Access exercises.

6 New end-of-chapter discussion questions and problems.

7 Movement of the Any Company case to the web site. In prior editions, the Any Company case, which is an ongoing case designed to provide students with the opportunity to apply their knowledge to the specific problems and challenges faced by a business in their local area, was subdivided by topics and appeared in every chapter. However, this made it difficult to appreciate the full potential for use as the basis for a comprehensive semester-long case. Therefore we consolidated all the requirements into one place and located it on the web site.

Customize this Text

You can easily customize this text via Prentice Hall Custom Business Resources. PHCBR offers you the flexibility to select specific chapters from this text to create a customized book to exactly match your course needs. In addition, you may choose alternate versions of Chapters 15–17 using Batini style notation instead of the crows feet notation featured in this book. When you customize a book with PHCBR, your book will have the chapters in the order that matches your syllabus with sequential pagination. All cross references to other chapters will be removed. You even have the option to add your own material or third party content!

To receive your free evaluation copy, please fill out the order form in the beginning of the text, build your book online: www.prenhall.com/custombusiness, contact your Pearson representative or contact us directly at Pearson Custom Publishing. E-mail: dbase.pub@pearsoncustom.com Ph: 1-800-777-6872. You can expect your evaluation copy to arrive within 7–10 business days.

Supplemental Resources

As with prior editions, our objective in preparing this eleventh edition has been to simplify the teaching of AIS by enabling you to concentrate on classroom presentation and discussion, rather than on locating, assembling, and distributing teaching materials. To assist you in this process, the following supplementary materials are available to adopters of the text:

- *Solutions Manual* prepared by William Henniger at Brigham Young University.

- *Instructors Manual/Test Item File* prepared by Richard Barrett at Simpson College.

- *Test Item File* prepared by Robert F. Brooker at Gannon University.

- *TestGen testing software,* a computerized test item file.

- *Instructor's Resource CD* includes electronic versions of key supplements.

- *VangoNotes.* Study on the go with *VangoNotes*—chapter reviews from your text in downloadable mp3 format. *VangoNotes* are flexible; download all the material directly to your player, or only the chapters you need. And they're efficient. Use them in your car, at the gym, walking to class, or wherever. So get yours today. And get studying. *VangoNotes.com.*

- *PowerPoint Presentation* slides developed by Steve Harrast at the University of Northern Iowa. The 11th edition includes an entirely new set of PowerPoint slides that make extensive use of high-quality graphics to illustrate key concepts. The slides do not merely consist of bullet points taken verbatim from the text, but instead are designed to help students notice and understand important relationships among concepts. In addition, many chapters include over 100 slides, providing instructors a great deal of flexibility in choosing which topics they wish to emphasize in class.

In addition, you can access these supplements from the protected instructor area of www.pearsonhighered.com. Free online course support is also available on Blackboard and CourseCompass platforms. CourseCompass is Prentice Hall's nationally hosted solution.

We recognize that you may also wish to use specific software packages when teaching the AIS course. Contact your local rep to learn about bundling options with software packages such as Peachtree or other texts such as *Peachtree Computerized Practice Set: Comprehensive Assurance and Systems Tool (CAST); Manual AIS Practice Set: Comprehensive Assurance and Systems Tool (CAST); or CAST: Auditing Simulation,* all written by Frank A. Buckless, Laura R. Ingraham, and J. Gregory Jenkins, all at North Carolina State University.

Acknowledgments

We wish to express our appreciation to all supplements authors for preparing the various supplements that accompany this edition. We thank Martha M. Eining of the University of Utah and Carol F. Venable of San Diego State University for preparing the comprehensive cases included on our Web site. We are also grateful to Iris Vessey for her contributions to the problem material. Perhaps most importantly, we are indebted to the numerous faculty members throughout the world who have adopted the earlier editions of this book and who have been generous with their suggestions for improvement. We are especially grateful to the following faculty who participated in reviewing the eleventh edition throughout various stages of the revision process:

Chih-chen Lee, *Northern Illinois University*
Keith Harrison, *Truman State University*
Rose Martin, *Cal Poly Pomona University*
Jim Menshing, *Cal State Chico University*
Nancy Jones, *Cal State Chico University*
Janet Bear Wolverton, *Oregon Tech*

Kurt Fanning, *Grand Valley State University*
Robert Booker, *Gannon University*
Steve Harrast, *Northern Iowa University*
Margarita Lenk, *Colorado State University*
Robert Conway, *Wisc-Plateville University*
Debra M. Cosgrove, *University of Nebraska Lincoln*

We are grateful for permission received from four professional accounting organizations to use problems and unofficial solutions from their past professional examinations in this book. Thanks are extended to the American Institute of Certified Public Accountants for use of the CPA Examination materials, to the Institute of Certified Management Accountants for use of CMA Examination materials, to the Institute of Internal Auditors for use of CIA Examination materials, and to the Society of Management Accountants of Canada for use of SMAC Examination materials.

Of course, any errors in this book remain our responsibility. We welcome your comments and suggestions for further improvement.

Finally, we want to thank our wives and families for their love, support, and encouragement. We also want to thank God for giving us the ability to start and complete this book.

— Marshall B. Romney
Provo, Utah

— Paul John Steinbart
Tempe, Arizona

Conceptual Foundations of Accounting Information Systems

CHAPTER 1

LEARNING OBJECTIVES

After studying this chapter, you should be able to:

● Distinguish between data and information, discuss the characteristics of useful information, and explain how to determine the value of information.

● Explain what an accounting information system (AIS) is and describe the basic functions it performs.

● Discuss why studying accounting information systems is important.

● Explain the role an AIS plays in a company's value chain and discuss how the AIS can add value to a business.

● Discuss how an AIS can provide management with information for decision making.

● Compare and contrast the basic strategies and strategic positions that a business can adopt.

Accounting Information Systems: An Overview

INTEGRATIVE CASE S&S, INC.

After working for several years as a regional manager for a national retailing organization, Scott Parry decided to open his own business. Susan Gonzalez, one of his district managers, had also wanted to go into business for herself. Together they formed S&S, Inc., to sell appliances and consumer electronics devices. Scott and Susan decided to pursue a "clicks and bricks" strategy. They began by renting a large and attractive building in a busy part of town but planned to add an electronic storefront as well.

Scott and Susan each contributed enough money to see them through the first six months of business. They estimated that they needed to hire 10 to 15 employees—3 or 4 to stock the shelves, 3 or 4 customer sales representatives, and 4 to 7 checkout clerks. They plan to begin hiring these employees within the next two weeks.

Scott and Susan plan to hold the grand opening of S&S in five weeks. As they review what remains to be done to meet that deadline, they realize that they have not yet made the following important decisions:

1 How should they organize their accounting records so that the financial statements their banker requires can be easily produced?
2 How can they design a set of procedures to ensure that they meet all of their government obligations, such as remitting sales, income, and payroll taxes?

3 How should they price their products to be competitive yet earn a profit?

4 Should they extend credit, and if so, on what terms? How can they accurately track what customers owe and have paid?

5 How should they hire, train, and supervise their employees? What compensation and benefits packages should they offer, and how should they process payroll?

6 How can they track cash inflows and outflows so that S&S is not caught in a cash squeeze?

7 What is the appropriate product mix and quantities to carry, given S&S's limited showroom space?

8 What functionality should be provided on S&S's Web site?

Although Scott and Susan could make many of these decisions on the basis of an educated guess or "gut feel," they know they will make better decisions if they obtain additional information. A well-designed *accounting information system (AIS)* **can solve some of these issues. Moreover, if properly designed, the AIS can provide most of the information needed to make the remaining decisions.**

Introduction

We begin this chapter by defining several terms, such as *system, data*, and *information*. We then explain what an accounting information system (AIS) is. Next we discuss why the AIS is an important topic to study. Then we describe the role of the AIS in the value chain and how an AIS adds value to an organization. Then we discuss how the AIS can provide information for decision making. We conclude by describing the basic strategies and strategic positions that organizations can pursue.

Systems, Data, and Information

A **system** is a set of two or more interrelated components that interact to achieve a goal. Systems are almost always composed of smaller subsystems, each performing a specific function important to and supportive of the larger system of which it is a part. For example, the college of business is a system composed of various departments, each of which is a subsystem. Yet the college itself is a subsystem of the university.

Each subsystem is designed to achieve one or more organizational goals. When the **systems concept** is used in systems development, changes in subsystems cannot be made without considering the effect on other subsystems and the system as a whole. **Goal conflict** occurs when a decision or action of a subsystem is inconsistent with the goals of another subsystem or the system as a whole. **Goal congruence** is achieved when a subsystem achieves its goals while contributing to the organization's overall goal. Subsystems should maximize organizational goals, even if subsystem goals are not maximized. The larger the organization and the more complicated the system, the more difficult it is to achieve goal congruence.

The systems concept also encourages **integration**, which eliminates duplicate recording, storage, reporting, and other processing activities in an organization. For example, companies that used to have separate programs to prepare customer statements, collect cash, and maintain accounts receivable records now combine these functions into a single application.

Data are facts that are collected, recorded, stored, and processed by an information system. Data usually represent observations or measurements of business activities that are of importance to information system users. Several kinds of data need to be collected in businesses, such as:

- Facts about the activities that take place
- The resources affected by the activities
- The people who participate in the activity

For example, data need to be collected about a sales event (e.g., the date of the sale, total amount), the resource being sold (e.g., the identity of the goods or services, the quantity sold, unit price), and the people who participated in the sale (e.g., the identity of the customer and the salesperson).

Information is data that have been organized and processed to provide meaning to a user. Users typically need information to make decisions or to improve the decision-making process. As a general rule, users can make better decisions as the quantity and quality of information increase.

However, there are limits to the amount of information the human mind can effectively absorb and process. **Information overload** occurs when those limits are passed. Information overload is costly, because decision-making quality declines while the costs of providing that information increase. Consequently, information system designers must consider how advances in information technology (IT) can help decision makers more effectively filter and condense information, thereby avoiding information overload. For example, Wal-Mart has over 500 terabytes (trillions of bytes) of data in its data warehouse. That is equivalent to 2000 miles of bookshelves or about 100 million digital photos. Wal-Mart has invested heavily in technology so that it can effectively collect, store, and manage these data. Most important, it has spent a great deal of time and money figuring out how to turn all of these data into useful information.

The **value of information** is the benefit produced by the information minus the cost of producing it. The major benefits of information are a reduction of uncertainty, improved decisions, and a better ability to plan and schedule activities. The costs are the time and resources spent collecting, processing, and storing data, as well as distributing information to decision makers. Unfortunately, determining the value of information is not easy. Information costs and benefits can be difficult to quantify, and it is difficult to determine the value of information before it has been produced and utilized. Nevertheless, the expected value of information should be calculated as effectively as possible so information is not produced whose costs exceed its benefits.

To illustrate the value of information consider the case of 7-Eleven. The Japanese licensed the 7-Eleven name in 1973 from Southland Corp. after the 7-Eleven convenience store was already a big success. 7-Eleven Japan felt that information about its customers and products had value and invested heavily in IT. The U.S. stores did not make the IT investment.

Each 7-Eleven store in Japan was given a computer that:

- Keeps track of the 3,000 items sold in each store and determines what products are moving, at what time of day, and under what weather conditions.
- Keeps track of customers (what and when they buy). If their best customers are single men, for example, the store makes sure it has the fresh rice dishes they purchase on their lunch hour and at the end of the workday.
- Orders sandwiches and rice dishes from suppliers automatically. Orders are placed and filled three times a day so stores can always have fresh food. Since food orders take as many as 12 hours to prepare, 7-Eleven allows its suppliers to access sales data in their computers so they can forecast demand.
- Coordinates deliveries with suppliers. This allows the stores to reduce the number of deliveries from 34 to 12 a day, resulting in less clerical receiving time.
- Prepares a color graphic display that indicates which store areas contribute the most to sales and profits.

The information produced by this system has a great deal of value. Average daily sales of 7-Eleven Japan were 30% higher and its operating margins almost double those of its closest competitor. And what of Southland and its 7-Eleven stores in the United States? Profits declined and Southland eventually had to file for bankruptcy. Who came to the company's rescue? 7-Eleven Japan and its parent company, who purchased 64% of Southland. 7-Eleven Japan obviously made a wise choice in assessing the value of information about their stores, products, and customers.

Table 1-1 presents seven characteristics that make information useful and meaningful for decision making.

Information can be provided to both internal and external users. The information supplied to external users is either **mandatory information** required by a governmental entity (such as a report to the IRS on taxable income and withholdings) or **essential information** required to conduct business with external parties (such as purchase orders and customer billings). Most internal information is **discretionary information**, since choices must be made regarding what information should be made available, to whom, and how frequently. The primary consideration in producing mandatory and essential information is to minimize costs while meeting minimum standards of reliability and usefulness and meeting regulatory requirements. The primary consideration in producing discretionary information is that its benefits exceed its costs. Internal reporting is more difficult than external reporting because most managerial decisions demand more detailed information than does external reporting and there are more ways to report information to internal users than to external users.

What Is an AIS?

An **accounting information system (AIS)** is a system that collects, records, stores, and processes data to produce information for decision makers. This is illustrated in Figure 1-1.

An AIS can be a very simple paper-and-pencil-based manual system, a very complex system using the very latest in computers and information technology, or something between these two extremes. Regardless of the approach taken, the process is the same. The AIS and the people who use it must still collect, enter, process, store, and report data and information. The paper and pencil or the computer hardware and software are merely the tools used to produce the information.

There are six components of an AIS:

1 The *people* who operate the system and perform various functions
2 The *procedures and instructions*, both manual and automated, involved in collecting, processing, and storing data about the organization's activities

Table 1-1
Characteristics of Useful Information

Relevant	Information is relevant if it reduces uncertainty, improves decision makers' ability to make predictions, or confirms or corrects their prior expectations.
Reliable	Information is reliable if it is free from error or bias and accurately represents the events or activities of the organization.
Complete	Information is complete if it does not omit important aspects of the underlying events or activities that it measures.
Timely	Information is timely if it is provided in time for decision makers to make decisions.
Understandable	Information is understandable if it is presented in a useful and intelligible format.
Verifiable	Information is verifiable if two knowledgeable people acting independently would each produce the same information.
Accessible	Information is accessible if it is available to users when they need it and in a format they can use.

Figure 1-1
An AIS Processes Data to Produce Information for Decision Makers

3 The *data* about the organization and its business processes
4 The *software* used to process the organization's data
5 The *information technology infrastructure*, including computers, peripheral devices, and network communications devices used to collect, store, process, and transmit data and information
6 The *internal controls and security measures* that safeguard the data in the AIS

Together, these six components enable an AIS to fulfill three important business functions:

1 Collect and store data about organizational activities, resources, and personnel. These topics are covered in greater detail in Chapter 2.
2 Transform data into information that is useful for making decisions so management can plan, execute, control, and evaluate activities, resources, and personnel. Decision making is discussed in greater detail later in this chapter.
3 Provide adequate controls to safeguard the organization's assets, including its data, to ensure that the assets and data are available when needed and the data are accurate and reliable. Control concepts are discussed in detail in Chapters 5–9.

Why Study Accounting Information Systems?

This section explains several reasons why a student's knowledge of accounting is not complete without an understanding of accounting information systems.

Study of the AIS Is Fundamental to Accounting

In *Statement of Financial Accounting Concepts No. 2*, the Financial Accounting Standards Board defined accounting as being an information system. It also stated that the primary objective of accounting is to provide information useful to decision makers. Therefore, it is not surprising that the Accounting Education Change Commission recommended that the accounting curriculum should emphasize that accounting is an information identification, development, measurement, and communication process. The commission suggested that the accounting curriculum should be designed to provide students with a solid understanding of three essential concepts:

1 The use of information in decision making
2 The nature, design, use, and implementation of an AIS
3 Financial information reporting

The other accounting courses you take (financial, managerial, tax, and auditing) focus on your role as a user or provider of information (making journal entries, preparing or reading financial statements or other reports, etc.). It is assumed that you have

access to certain data and can address questions about how to account for, report, or audit the information. For example, a managerial accounting class may discuss how to use information to make decisions but never discuss how information is collected, stored, or made available to the decision maker. The question of where the information comes from is often not even asked in these classes. The answer is that the AIS provides the information. In contrast, the AIS course focuses on understanding how the accounting system works: how to collect data about an organization's activities and transactions; how to transform that data into information that management can use to run the organization; and how to ensure the availability, reliability, and accuracy of that information. Thus, the AIS course complements the other accounting courses you take.

The accounting information systems class is unlike most other accounting classes. It is not a number-crunching course—the course is more concept driven than numbers driven. Some students feel the AIS course is more ambiguous than other accounting courses because there often are no numbers to crunch to get the "one right answer." Instead, there may be two or three or more "right answers." There are choices among alternative ways to develop an AIS or gather data and process it to produce information. Each alternative will work, but each has pros and cons. The developer must select the best mix of advantages and disadvantages to solve a problem or achieve a desired result.

AIS Skills Are Important to Your Career Success

You may intend to pursue a career in public accounting. Auditors need to evaluate the accuracy and reliability of information produced by the AIS. To do so they must understand how a system is developed, how it operates, and how it can be properly controlled. They must be able to evaluate and understand the strengths and weaknesses of an AIS. This course provides you with that knowledge; indeed, that is why many universities make the AIS course a prerequisite to the auditing course. If you specialize in tax, you need to understand enough about your client's AIS to be confident that the information used for tax planning and compliance work is complete and accurate.

Many students work in private industry or for not-for-profit organizations. Accounting systems work is one of the most important activities performed by corporate accountants. Other important activities include designing internal control systems, business process improvements, and long-term strategic planning.

A third career option is management consulting. One of the fastest-growing types of consulting services entails the design, selection, and implementation of a new AIS. Indeed, the American Institute of Certified Public Accountants (AICPA) has recently created a new credential, the Certified Information Technology Professional (CITP), to provide CPAs with a means of documenting their systems expertise (see Focus 1-1). The AIS course provides an introduction to that body of knowledge.

The AIS Course Complements Other Systems Courses

Many systems courses help you develop specialized skills in such areas as the design and implementation of information systems, databases, expert systems, and telecommunications. The AIS course differs from these information systems courses in its focus on accountability and control. These issues are important because in most large businesses the managers are not the owners. Instead, the owners have entrusted management with assets and hold them accountable for their proper use. Data and information are some of an organization's most valuable assets. To see why, consider what would happen if an organization lost all information about customers' balances, or if a competitor obtained a list of its most profitable customers. Clearly, the AIS must include controls to ensure the safety and availability of the organization's data. Controls are also needed to ensure that the information produced from that data is both reliable and accurate. These topics usually receive little attention in other systems courses. Thus, the AIS course complements other systems courses you may take and is an important part of the information systems curriculum.

1-1 FOCUS CITP—A New Specialty Designation for CPAs

The AICPA offers several specialty designations that CPAs can earn. One of these is the Certified Information Technology Professional (CITP). The CITP designation identifies CPAs who possess a broad range of technological knowledge and understand how organizations use information technology to achieve their business objectives. The new CITP designation reflects the AICPA's recognition of the importance of information technology and its interrelationship with accounting.

To be awarded the CITP, a CPA must earn 100 points in the areas of business experience, lifelong learning, and an optional exam. Candidates must earn a minimum of 15 points, and a maximum of 75 points, in the area of business experience. The number of points awarded depends on the number of hours spent working in the following areas in the three-year period preceding application for the CITP designation:

- Information Technology Strategic Planning
- Information Systems Management

- Systems Architecture
- Business Applications and E-Business
- Security, Privacy, and Contingency Planning
- Systems Development, Acquisition, and Project Management
- Systems Auditing and Internal Control
- Databases and Database Management

A candidate for the CITP designation must also earn a minimum of 30 points, up to a maximum of 70 points, in the category of lifelong learning. Lifelong learning includes continuing education, additional degrees, and obtaining or maintaining other technology-related certifications during the three-year period preceding application for the CITP designation.

An optional exam is also available for candidates who have earned at least 60 points in the areas of business experience and lifelong learning. Candidates can earn 40 points by passing an exam that covers the eight topical areas listed in the preceding discussion of work experience.

AIS Topics Are Tested on the New CPA Exam

The computerized uniform CPA Exam is a four section, 14-hour exam. A new section, Business Environment & Concepts, was added in April 2004. About 25% of the new section deals with information technology implications in the business environment. The AICPA Board of Examiners has approved and adopted content specification outlines for each of the four sections. All of the information technology concepts on the approved content specification outlines are covered in this text. Therefore, studying accounting information systems using this text is a good way to prepare for the CPA Exam.

The Impact of the AIS on Corporate Strategy and Culture

Figure 1-2 shows three factors that influence the design of an AIS: developments in information technology (IT), business strategy, and organizational culture. The business press frequently report ways IT is changing the way accounting and other business activities are performed. Because this impact is likely to continue, throughout this book we will focus on understanding how IT can be used to improve the performance of an AIS.

The AIS course, however, is more than a "computer course." To be sure, your professor will likely assign out-of-class projects designed to help you refine and improve your computer skills. Nevertheless, you also need to know how to evaluate the costs and benefits of new IT developments. This requires developing a basic understanding of business strategies and how IT can be used to implement them, as well as how new IT developments create an opportunity to modify those strategies (note the arrow from IT to strategy in Figure 1-2). These topics are introduced in this chapter and will continue to be discussed throughout the text.

Because an AIS functions within an organization, it should be designed to reflect the values of that organization's culture. Thus, Figure 1-2 shows that organizational culture influences AIS design. Note that the arrow between organizational culture and the AIS is bidirectional. Although the organization's culture should influence the design of its AIS,

Figure 1-2
Factors Influencing Design
of the AIS

it is important to recognize that the design of the AIS can also influence the organization's culture by controlling the flow of information within the organization. For example, an AIS that makes information easily accessible and widely available is likely to increase pressures for more decentralization and autonomy. Throughout this text we discuss the potential behavioral ramifications of making changes to a company's AIS.

The Role of the AIS in the Value Chain

The objective of most organizations is to provide value to their customers.[1] This requires performing a number of different activities. Figure 1-3 shows that those activities can be conceptualized as forming a **value chain**.

An organization's value chain consists of five **primary activities** that directly provide value to its customers:

1 **Inbound logistics** consists of receiving, storing, and distributing the materials an organization uses to create the services and products it sells. For example, receiving, handling, and storing steel, glass, and rubber are some of the inbound logistics activities of an automobile manufacturer.
2 **Operations** activities transform inputs into final products or services. For example, assembly-line activities at an automobile manufacturer convert raw materials into a finished car.
3 **Outbound logistics** activities distribute finished products or services to customers. For example, shipping automobiles to car dealers is an outbound logistics activity.
4 **Marketing and sales** activities help customers buy the organization's products or services. Advertising is an example of a marketing and sales activity.
5 **Service** activities provide post-sale support to customers. Examples include repair and maintenance services.

Support activities allow the five primary activities to be performed efficiently and effectively. They are grouped into four categories:

1 **Firm infrastructure** is the accounting, finance, legal, and general administration activities that allow an organization to function. The AIS is part of the firm infrastructure.

[1]This section is based on Michael E. Porter and Victor E. Millar, "How Information Gives You Competitive Advantage" *Harvard Business Review,* (July–August 1985), pp. 149–160.

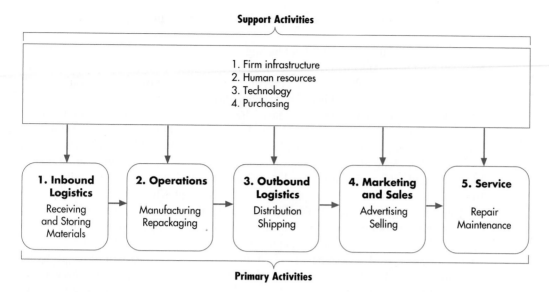

Figure 1-3
The Value Chain

2 Human resources activities include recruiting, hiring, training, and providing employee benefits and compensation.

3 Technology activities improve a product or service. Examples include research and development, investments in new information technology, Web site development, and product design.

4 Purchasing activities procure raw materials, supplies, machinery, and the buildings used to carry out the primary activities.

Primary and support activity systems have multiple activities. For example, the sales and marketing system includes market research, calling on customers, order processing, and credit approval activities.

Information technology can be used to redesign supply chain systems, yielding tremendous benefits and large cost savings. For example, Tennessee Valley Authority, a power generator, reengineered its supply chain and created an enterprisewide system that provides up-to-the-minute information, rather than the "current once a day" system that it replaced. The new system replaced 20 smaller and often incompatible systems and reduced head count by 89 people. The redesigned system is expected to save $54 million in its first five years of existence.

The primary and support activity systems are subsystems of the value chain system. In addition, an organization's value chain is itself a part of a larger system called a **supply chain**. As shown in Figure 1-4, a manufacturing organization interacts with its suppliers and distributors.

By paying attention to the interorganizational linkages in its supply chain, a company can improve its performance by helping the other organizations in the supply chain to improve their performance. In the opening case, for example, S&S can improve its purchasing and inbound logistics activity by implementing a just-in-time inventory management system. S&S's costs are reduced because its purchasing and inbound logistics activities are performed more efficiently and because less of its capital is tied up in inventory. S&S can reap additional benefits if it links its new systems with its suppliers to help them perform some of their primary value chain activities more efficiently and effectively. For example, by providing more detailed and timely information about its inventory needs, S&S can help its suppliers more efficiently plan their production schedules to meet S&S's needs. This reduces their costs,

Figure 1-4
The Supply Chain

and part of that reduction is likely to be passed on to S&S in the form of lower product costs.

The problems that result from not having a good supply chain system are illustrated by examining what happened to Limited Brands. Limited experienced explosive growth, including acquisitions of other retail companies, such as Lane Bryant, Victoria's Secret, Lerner, and Abercrombie & Fitch. These acquisitions left Limited with a tangled web of over 60 incompatible information systems. This complexity caused significant problems with its supply chain system. The problems came to a head one night when 400 trailers converged on a distribution center parking lot that could only fit 150 trailers. The trailers blocked traffic along all the highways around the distribution center and caused countless traffic and community problems. No one in Limited knew where all the trailers came from, what the merchandise was, or where it was to be sent. Chaos reigned for sometime until the merchandise could be routed to stores and other distribution centers.

Limited is working to solve its information systems problems. It is replacing its older, incompatible systems with a new, integrated system that will greatly improve its supply chain processes and technologies. Limited hopes the new systems will result in higher sales, more flexibility in responding to market demands, and automated logistics tasks so employees can focus on selling products instead of ordering them. Developing the system will not be easy. Limited has over a thousand suppliers and sells its merchandise using various platforms, including retail stores, the Internet, catalogs, and third-party retailers.

How an AIS Can Add Value to an Organization

As a support activity, the AIS adds value by providing accurate and timely information so the five primary value chain activities can be performed more effectively and efficiently. A well-designed AIS can do this by:

1 **Improving the quality and reducing the costs of products or services.** For example, an AIS can monitor machinery so operators are notified immediately when performance falls outside acceptable quality limits. This helps maintain product quality. It also reduces the amount of wasted materials and the costs of having to rework anything.

2 **Improving efficiency.** A well-designed AIS can make operations more efficient by providing more timely information. For example, a just-in-time manufacturing approach requires constant, accurate, up-to-date information about raw materials inventories and their locations.

3 **Sharing knowledge.** A well-designed AIS can make it easier to share knowledge and expertise, perhaps thereby improving operations and even providing a competitive advantage. For example, the largest public accounting firms all use their information systems to share best practices and to support communication between people located at different offices. Employees can search the corporate database to identify the relevant experts to provide assistance for a particular client; thus, all of a public accounting firm's accumulated international expertise can be made available to service any local client.

4 **Improving the efficiency and effectiveness of its supply chain.** For example, allowing customers to directly access the company's inventory and sales order entry systems can reduce the costs of sales and marketing activities. Moreover, if such access reduces customers' costs and time of ordering, both sales and customer retention rates may increase.

5 **Improving the internal control structure.** Security, control, and privacy are important issues in today's world. An AIS with the proper internal control structure can protect systems from problems such as fraud, errors, equipment and software failures, and natural and political disasters.

6 **Improving decision making.** Because improved decision making is so important it is discussed more fully in the next section.

Focus 1-2 discusses how information technology added value to UPS.

1-2 FOCUS

The Use of Technology by UPS

Up until the early 1980s, UPS invested heavily in training its employees to perform tasks in less time but spent comparatively little money on new information technology (IT). Back then, when you wanted to ship something you called UPS, scheduled a pickup, and waited until you were notified that the shipment had arrived at its destination.

Today, UPS is among the leaders in IT spending (over $1 billion a year) because of the value IT adds to its business. It has 4,700 employees devoted to developing and maintaining proprietary software and a Web site that almost 19 million people visit each day. It has fifteen huge mainframe computers and almost 9,000 servers. This technology allows UPS customers to control each shipment (15 million a day) from the time a delivery order is initiated to the time it arrives at its destination. Here is how the system works:

- Customers use UPS software or go to the UPS Web site to initiate a delivery. They create labels containing detailed information on the sender, as well as the time the shipment should arrive at its designated destination. They print the labels and attach them to their shipment.
- They schedule a pickup time electronically.
- The UPS system routes the label information to the distribution center closest to the shipment's destination.
- At the distribution center, proprietary software uses the shipment's destination, desired arrival time, traffic and weather conditions, and street information (such as one-way streets) to create the most efficient delivery route. Drivers have handheld computers with a global-positioning system (GPS) that guide them on their routes.
- The system creates a label that specifies where to put the shipment on the delivery truck so the earliest shipments are nearest the driver. Drivers average 100 pickups and deliveries a day, and boxes loaded out of order can delay the driver for as long as 30 minutes.
- Customers can log onto the UPS Web site and reroute or track their shipment. The GPS allows UPS to predict accurately the approximate arrival time of the shipment.
- The handheld computer is programmed to beep at the driver if a shipment is delivered to the wrong address or forgotten.

UPS's commitment to IT has produced dramatic results. The most recent system improvements have allowed drivers to make seven to nine more stops each day, have reduced the number of miles UPS drives each year by 1.9 million, and save over $600 million per year in operating costs.

However, UPS is not sitting back congratulating itself on how well it has used IT to improve its business. The UPS system is a work in progress. UPS continues to innovate and find ways to use IT to become even more efficient and better serve the customer.

Source: Corey Dade, "How UPS Went from Low-Tech to an IT Power— and Where It's Headed Next," *The Wall Street Journal,* July 24, 2006, R4.

Providing Information for Decision Making

Decision making is a complex, multistep activity: identify the problem, collect and interpret information, evaluate ways to solve the problem, select a solution methodology, and implement the solution. An AIS can provide assistance in all phases of decision making. Reports can help to identify potential problems. Different decision models and analytical tools can be provided to users. Query languages can facilitate the gathering of relevant data upon which to make the decision. Various tools, such as graphical interfaces, can help the decision maker interpret decision model results and evaluate and choose among alternative courses of action. In addition, the AIS can provide feedback on the results of actions.

Information can improve decision making in several ways:

- It identifies situations requiring management action. For example, a cost report with a large variance might stimulate management to investigate and, if necessary, take corrective action.
- It provides a basis for choosing among alternative actions by reducing uncertainty. For example, information is used to set prices and determine credit policies.

- Information about the results of previous decisions provides valuable feedback that can be used to improve future decisions. For example, if a particular marketing strategy is tried and the information gathered indicates that it did not succeed, a different marketing strategy is selected.
- An AIS can improve decision making by providing accurate information in a timely manner. For example, Wal-Mart has created an enormous database that contains detailed information about sales transactions at each of its stores. It uses this information to optimize the amount of each product carried at each store. It also analyzes the data to discover patterns of items that seem to be purchased together, and it uses such information to improve the layout of merchandise to encourage additional sales of related items. In a similar vein, Amazon.com uses its database of sales activity to suggest additional books that customers may want to purchase.

The degree to which an AIS can support decision making depends, however, on the type of decision being made. Decisions can be categorized either in terms of the degree of structure that exists or by their scope.

Decision Structure

Decisions vary in terms of the degree to which they are structured. **Structured decisions** are repetitive, routine, and understood well enough that they can be delegated to lower-level employees in the organization. For example, the decision about extending credit to established customers only requires knowledge about the customer's credit limit and current balance. Structured decisions can often be automated.

Semistructured decisions are characterized by incomplete decision making rules and the need for subjective assessments and judgments to supplement formal data analysis. An example is setting a marketing budget for a new product. Although such decisions usually cannot be fully automated, they are often supported by computer-based decision aids.

Unstructured decisions are nonrecurring and nonroutine. Examples include choosing the cover for a magazine, hiring senior management, and selecting basic research projects to undertake. No framework or model exists to solve such problems. Instead, they require considerable judgment and intuition. Nevertheless, unstructured decisions can be supported by computer-based decision aids that facilitate gathering information from diverse sources.

Decision Scope

Decisions vary in terms of their scope. **Operational control** relates to the effective and efficient performance of specific tasks. Examples include decisions relating to inventory management and extending credit.

Management control relates to the effective and efficient use of resources for accomplishing organizational objectives. Examples include decisions relating to budgeting, developing human resource practices, and deciding on research projects and product improvements.

Strategic planning relates to establishing organizational objectives and policies for accomplishing those objectives. Examples include decisions relating to setting financial and accounting policies, developing new product lines, and acquiring new businesses.

A correspondence exists between a manager's level in an organization and his or her decision-making responsibilities. Top management faces unstructured and semistructured decisions involving strategic planning issues. Middle managers deal with semistructured decisions involving management control. Lower-level supervisors and employees face semistructured or structured decisions involving operational control.

The AIS and Corporate Strategy

There are many opportunities to invest in IT to improve decision making. Most organizations, however, do not have unlimited resources to invest in improving their information systems. Therefore, it is important to identify which potential AIS improvements are likely to yield the greatest return. Making this decision wisely requires an understanding of the organization's overall business strategy. To illustrate this, consider the results of a "State of the CIO" survey conducted by *CIO* magazine. Five hundred Chief Information Officers were asked to identify the three most important skill sets for a CIO. Over 75% of the respondents put strategic thinking and planning on their list.

Strategies and Strategic Positions

Michael Porter, world-renowned professor of business at Harvard, argues that there are two basic business strategies that companies can follow:[2]

1 A **product differentiation strategy** entails adding features or services not provided by competitors to a product so you can charge customers a premium price.
2 A **low-cost strategy** entails striving to be the most efficient producer of a product or service.

Sometimes a company can succeed in both producing a better product than its competitors and doing so at costs below its industry average. Usually, however, companies must choose between the two basic strategies. If they concentrate on being the lowest-cost producer, they will have to forego some value-added features that might differentiate their product. If they focus on product differentiation, they most likely will not have the lowest costs in their industry. Thus, a business strategy involves making choices.

Porter argues that the fundamental choice companies must make involves selecting a specific strategic position they wish to adopt. He describes three basic strategic positions:

1 A **variety-based strategic position** involves producing or providing a subset of the industry's products or services. For example, Jiffy Lube International focuses on oil changes and lubrication services rather than a wide range of automotive repair services.
2 A **needs-based strategic position** involves trying to serve most or all of the needs of a particular group of customers in a target market. For example, AARP focuses on retirees.
3 An **access-based strategic position** involves serving a subset of customers who differ from other customers in terms of factors such as geographic location or size, which creates different requirements for serving those customers. For example, the stock brokerage offices of Edward Jones are located primarily in smaller towns and cities not served by the larger brokerage houses.

Porter explains that these three basic strategic positions are not mutually exclusive and, indeed, often overlap. For example, Southwest Airlines employs a variety-based strategic position because it only offers a subset of the products provided by the airline industry (no first-class seating, no meals, no international flights). Southwest also employs a needs-based strategic position in that it has identified a specific target market (price-sensitive leisure travelers) for which it designs its services. Finally, Southwest employs an access-based strategic position because it does not service all markets.

[2]The material in this section is based on Michael E. Porter, "What Is Strategy?" *Harvard Business Review* (November–December 1996), pp. 61–78.

Choosing a strategic position is important because it enables a company to focus its efforts; otherwise it risks trying to be everything to everybody. Porter argues that the specific strategic position an organization selects is not important. What is important is to design the organization's activities so they mutually reinforce one another in filling the selected strategic position and in implementing the business strategy. This results in **synergy**, wherein the entire system of organizational activities is greater than the sum of each individual part. This makes it difficult for competitors to successfully imitate, because they must do more than just mimic specific procedures. Indeed, companies that have achieved a high degree of fit among their activities often do not worry about keeping their processes secret from competitors because they know that they cannot be adopted piecemeal.

Information Technology and Business Strategy

As shown in Figure 1-2, IT developments can affect business strategy. The growth of the Internet is a classic illustration. It has profoundly affected the way many value chain activities are performed. For example, the Internet enables organizations to significantly streamline their inbound and outbound logistics activities. The Internet also significantly affects both strategy and strategic positioning. For example, the Internet dramatically cuts costs, thereby helping companies to implement a low-cost strategy. If every company in a given industry, however, uses the Internet to adopt a low-cost strategy, then the effects may be problematic. Indeed, one possible outcome may be intense price competition among firms, with the likely result that most of the cost savings provided by the Internet get passed on to the industry's customers, rather than being retained in the form of higher profits. Moreover, because every company can use the Internet to streamline its value chain activities, it is unlikely that any particular company will be able to use the Internet to gain a sustainable long-term competitive advantage vis-à-vis its competitors. Therefore, once the majority of companies in an industry begin to fully integrate the Internet into their value chains, the effect may be to encourage companies to shift from following primarily a low-cost strategy toward adopting some form of product differentiation strategy.

The Internet may also affect the relative desirability of following the three strategic positions described previously. For example, by drastically reducing or eliminating geographic barriers, the Internet makes a company's products available almost anywhere. Consequently, it may be more difficult to establish and maintain an access-based strategic position.

As Focus 1-3 explains, the Internet alters many fundamental characteristics of industry structure, thereby requiring companies to carefully reconsider their overall business strategy.

Many other technological advances affect company strategy and provide an opportunity to gain a competitive advantage. An example is **predictive analysis**, which uses data warehouses and complex algorithms to forecast future events, based on historical trends and calculated probabilities. Predictive analysis provides an educated guess of what one may expect to see in the near future, allowing companies to make better business decisions and improve their processes. FedEx uses predictive analysis to predict, with 65% to 90% accuracy, how customers respond to price changes and new services. Blue Cross Blue Shield of Tennessee uses a neural-based predictive model to predict the health care that specific patients will need, the severity of illnesses, and organ failures. Stock market analysts are using predictive analysis to predict short-term trends in the stock market.

An organization's AIS plays an important role in helping it adopt and maintain a strategic position. Achieving a close fit among activities requires that data be collected about each activity. It is also important that the information system collect and integrate both financial and nonfinancial data about the organization's activities.

The authors of this text believe that the disciplines of accounting and information systems have much in common and should be closely integrated. Therefore, we do not try to distinguish between an AIS and other types of information systems. Instead, we

1-3 FOCUS The Internet Makes Strategy More Important Than Ever

The Internet has changed the way many business processes are performed. It has also dramatically affected the five characteristics that determine the profitability of an entire industry: the bargaining power of buyers, the bargaining power of suppliers, barriers to entry, the threat of substitute products or services, and the level of rivalry among existing competitors.

Unfortunately for companies in most industries, the development of the Internet has tended to increase the relative power of one or more of these five factors, thereby decreasing the overall profitability of the average firm in a given industry. The Internet has reduced barriers to entry in many industries by reducing or eliminating the need to invest in and develop specific assets, such as a dedicated sales force. It increases the power of buyers by reducing switching costs and simplifying detailed comparisons across products and services. The

Internet creates new methods of performing basic business processes, thereby creating new substitute products and services. It enables suppliers to bypass intermediaries and sell directly to end consumers. Finally, because the Internet decreases the level of variable costs relative to fixed costs, it increases pressures to compete more on price.

As a result of these factors, many companies find that although the Internet has made them more efficient and effective, they are unable to retain much of those benefits in the form of increased profits. In fact, if a company is not careful, it can find itself drawn into a vicious level of price competition that benefits only consumers. The only way companies can avoid that trap is to define a strategy and stake out a strategic position that effectively differentiates themselves from their competitors. Thus, the most important effect of the development of the Internet is the increased importance of strategy.

adopt the viewpoint that the AIS can and should be the primary information system of an organization and that it will provide users with the information they need to perform their jobs.

SUMMARY AND CASE CONCLUSION

Scott and Susan require a well-designed AIS to provide the information they need to effectively plan, manage, and control their business. S&S's AIS must be able to process data about sales and cash receipts, purchasing and paying for merchandise and services, payroll and tax-related transactions, and acquiring and paying for fixed assets. The company's AIS must also provide the information needed to prepare financial statements.

Fortunately, there are many computer-based accounting packages available for the retail industry. As they begin looking at various popular software packages, however, Scott and Susan quickly learn that considerable accounting knowledge is required to choose the one that will best fit their business. Because neither has an accounting background, Scott and Susan decide that their next task will be to hire an accountant.

KEY TERMS

system 26	information 27	accounting information system (AIS) 28
systems concept 26	information overload 27	
goal conflict 26	value of information 27	value chain 32
goal congruence 26	mandatory information 28	primary activities 32
integration 26	essential information 28	support activities 32
data 27	discretionary information 28	supply chain 33

AIS IN ACTION

CHAPTER QUIZ

1 Data differ from information in which way?
 a. Data are output and information is input.
 b. Information is output and data are input.
 c. Data are meaningful bits of information.
 d. There is no difference.

2 Which of the following is not a characteristic that makes information useful?
 a. It is reliable.
 b. It is timely.
 c. It is inexpensive.
 d. It is relevant.

3 Which of the following is a primary activity in the value chain?
 a. purchasing
 b. accounting
 c. post-sales service
 d. human resource management

4 Top management continually emphasizes and supports investments designed to improve the efficiency of the manufacturing process. Such a focus most likely reflects the pursuit of which type of strategy?
 a. product differentiation
 b. low-cost
 c. needs-based
 d. variety-based

5 Which of the following is not a means by which information improves decision making?
 a. increasing information overload
 b. reducing uncertainty
 c. providing feedback about the effectiveness of prior decisions
 d. identifying situations requiring management action

6 In the value chain concept, upgrading IT is considered what kind of activity?
 a. primary activity
 b. support activity
 c. service activity
 d. structured activity

7 Lower-level management employees are most likely to make which of the following decisions?
 a. structured decisions involving strategic planning
 b. unstructured decisions involving managerial control
 c. structured decisions involving operational control
 d. unstructured decisions involving strategic planning

8 Which of the following is a function of an AIS?
 a. reducing the need to identify a strategy and strategic position
 b. transforming data into useful information
 c. allocating organizational resources
 d. automating all decision making

9 A firm, its suppliers, and its customers collectively form which of the following?
 a. supply chain
 b. value chain
 c. ERP system
 d. AIS

10 A company that focuses its marketing efforts on a specific subset of the population (e.g., college students) is probably pursuing which type of strategic position?
 a. variety-based
 b. needs-based
 c. access-based
 d. low-cost

DISCUSSION QUESTIONS

1.1 Apply the value chain concept to S&S, Inc. Explain how it performs the various primary and support activities.

1.2 The value of information equals the difference between the benefits realized from using that information and the costs of producing it. Would you, or any organization, ever produce information if its expected costs exceeded its benefits? If so, provide some examples. If not, why not?

1.3 One function of the AIS is to provide adequate controls to ensure the safety of organizational assets, including data. Many people, however, often view control procedures as "red tape." Discuss how controls can improve overall efficiency and effectiveness.

1.4 One interesting property of digital assets is that they can be reproduced and distributed via the Internet at very little cost. What are some of the implications of having a product with a marginal cost close to zero?

1.5 Figure 1-2 shows that organizational culture and the design of an AIS influence one another. What does this imply about the degree to which an innovative system developed by one company can be transferred to another company?

1.6 Figure 1-2 shows that developments in IT affect both an organization's strategy and the design of its AIS. How can a company determine whether it is spending too much, too little, or just enough on IT?

1.7 To what extent can all the characteristics of useful information listed in Table 1-1 be simultaneously met?

1.8 Information technology enables organizations to easily collect large amounts of information about employees. Discuss the following issues:
 a. To what extent should management monitor employees' e-mail?
 b. To what extent should management monitor which Web sites employees visit?
 c. To what extent should management monitor employee performance by, for example, using software to track keystrokes per hour or some other unit of time? If such information is collected, how should it be used?
 d. Should companies use software to electronically "shred" all traces of e-mail?
 e. Under what circumstances and to whom is it appropriate for a company to distribute information it collects about the people who visit its Web site?

PROBLEMS

1.1 Write a two-page report explaining the two basic strategies that S&S, Inc. can pursue and the three different strategic positions that it can adopt. Include in your report a discussion and examples of how IT can be used to support the different strategies and strategic positions.

1.2 Decision scope categorizes decisions into three broad areas of managerial decision making. These three areas are operational control, management control, and strategic planning. In your own words, define operational control, management control, and strategic planning in relation to managerial decision making. Based on your experience working at a summer job or part-time job during the school year, provide two examples of operational control, management control, and strategic planning decisions that you or your manager would make.

1.3 Information technology is continually changing the nature of accounting and the role of accountants. Write a two-page report describing what you think the nature of the accounting function in a large company will be like in the year 2020.

1.4 The annual report is considered by some to be the single most important printed document that companies produce. In recent years, annual reports have become large documents. They now include such sections as letters to the stockholders, descriptions of the business, operating highlights, financial review, management discussion and analysis, a discussion of company internal controls, segment reporting, and inflation data, as well as the basic financial statements. The expansion has been due in part to a general increase in the degree of sophistication and complexity in accounting standards and disclosure requirements for financial reporting.

The expansion also is reflective of the change in the composition and level of sophistication of users. Current users include not only stockholders but also financial and securities analysts, potential investors, lending institutions, stockbrokers, customers, employees, and, whether the reporting company likes it or not, competitors. Thus a report that was originally designed as a device for communicating basic financial information now attempts to meet the diverse needs of an ever-expanding audience.

Users hold conflicting views on the value of annual reports. Some argue that they fail to provide enough information, whereas others believe that disclosures in annual reports have expanded to the point where they create information overload. Others argue that the future of most companies depends on acceptance by the investing public and by its customers; therefore, companies should take this opportunity to communicate well-defined corporate strategies.

Required

 a. Identify and discuss the basic factors of communication that must be considered in the presentation of the annual report.

 b. Discuss the communication problems a corporation faces in preparing the annual report that result from the diversity of the users being addressed.

 c. Select two types of information found in an annual report, other than the financial statements and accompanying footnotes, and describe how they are helpful to the users of annual reports.

 d. Discuss at least two advantages and two disadvantages of stating well-defined corporate strategies in the annual report.

 e. Evaluate the effectiveness of annual reports in fulfilling the information needs of the following current and potential users:

 1. Shareholders

 2. Creditors

3. Employees

4. Customers

5. Financial analysts

f. Annual reports are public and accessible to anyone, including competitors. Discuss how this affects decisions about what information should be provided in annual reports.

(CMA Examination, adapted)

1.5 Research the programming language XBRL and write a two-page report about its effect on financial reporting via the Internet.

1.6 United Services Automotive Association (USAA) grew to become the fourth-largest insurer of homes and the fifth-largest insurer of automobiles during its first fifteen years. One reason for its success was the use of IT to lower costs and improve customer service. USAA spent almost $150 million on computer and imaging technologies over a 25-year period.

USAA uses its extensive database to keep track of minute details, such as which auto parts are fixed most frequently. It also uses its database to find ways to reduce claims costs. For example, USAA discovered that repair shops would rather charge up to $300 to replace a windshield with punctures than to charge $40 to repair it. USAA began offering to waive the deductible if the owners would repair the windshield rather than replace it.

USAA spent extensively to develop an image-processing system that digitizes all paper documents sent in by claimants (over 25 million a year). It only takes a few keystrokes for a policy service representative to retrieve pictures of all the documents in a customer's file. The system can sort and prioritize documents so that employees are always working on the most important and urgent tasks.

Required

a. Why should USAA collect data on which auto parts are getting fixed most frequently? What could it do with this data?

b. Even though USAA offered to waive the deductible, the repair shops still managed to convince 95% of the owners to replace rather than repair their damaged windshields. How could USAA use its AIS to persuade more shop owners to repair rather than replace their windows?

c. How does the image-processing system at USAA add value to the organization?

1.7 Matching

Match the description listed in the right column with the information characteristic listed in the left column.

___ **1.** Relevant	**a.** The report was carefully designed so that the data contained in the report became information to the reader.
___ **2.** Reliable	**b.** The manager was working one weekend and needed to find some information about production requests for a certain customer. He was able to find the report on the company's network.
___ **3.** Complete	**c.** The data in a report was checked by two clerks working independently.
___ **4.** Timely	**d.** An accounts receivable aging report included all customer accounts.
___ **5.** Understandable	**e.** A report was checked by three different people for accuracy.
___ **6.** Verifiable	**f.** An accounts receivable aging report is used in credit granting decisions.
___ **7.** Accessible	**g.** An accounts receivable aging report was received before the credit manager had to make a decision whether to extend credit to a customer.

1.8 The Howard Leasing Company is a privately held, medium-size business that purchases school busses and leases them to school districts, churches, charitable organizations, and other businesses. To better serve its customers and, more importantly, to protect its investment in the busses, Howard operates a large maintenance facility to maintain and repair leased vehicles and vehicles available for lease. Howard's annual sales for last year were $37 million with a net income of $2.9 million. Howard employs approximately 150 people.

After graduating with a degree in accounting, you were recently hired as a staff accountant for Howard and are eager to prove your worth to the company. Your supervisor just called you into her office and asked you to prepare an accounts receivable aging report as of the end of the year for use in the upcoming audit of the company's financial statements.

Required

a. What is an accounts receivable aging report?
b. Why is an accounts receivable aging report needed for an audit?
c. What is an accounts receivable aging report used for in normal company operations?
d. What data will you need to prepare the report?
e. Where will you collect the data you need to prepare the report?
f. If the data are maintained on paper, how will you collect the necessary data?
g. If the data are in machine-readable form, how will you collect the data?
h. What will the report look like (i.e., how will you organize the data collected to create the information your supervisor needs for the audit)? Prepare an accounts receivable aging report in Excel or another spreadsheet package.
i. How will you distribute the report? How many copies will you make? Who should receive the copies? What security features will you implement?

1.9 Based on Wal-Mart's success in the United States, many expected the company to dominate the British market after it bought the Asda grocery chain in 1999. That has not happened; Wal-Mart's market share in groceries is only half that of its biggest competitor, Tesco. Tesco's sales and net income are rising significantly while Wal-Mart's sales and net income are increasing at a much slower rate.

Wal-Mart is finding Tesco to be a formidable worldwide competitor. Tesco operates almost 2,400 stores in Britain in four different formats. It has a very successful operation in Central Europe. Tesco has plans to expand to the United States. In Korea, Tesco's 39 stores are thriving while Wal-Mart gave up after an eight-year effort to succeed and sold its 16 stores.

One of the biggest reasons for Tesco's success is its use of technology. In 1995, Tesco started a loyalty card program, called Clubcard, and 80% of Tesco customers are now members. Shoppers fill out an application in the store and receive a plastic card in the mail that is scanned before they make a purchase. Tesco gathers massive amounts of data about its customers' 15 million purchases each week. Sales data are analyzed and turned into information that provides Tesco with a significant competitive advantage.

As traditional advertising loses effectiveness, these large stores of data allow Tesco to find new and creative ways to market its products.

Required

a. What kind of information do you think Tesco gathers?
b. How do you think Tesco has motivated over 12 million customers to sign up for its Clubcard program?
c. What can Tesco accomplish with the Clubcard data it collects? Think in terms of strategy and competitive advantage.
d. What are some of the disadvantages to the Clubcard program?

1.10 Have you ever imagined having one electronic device that does everything you would ever need? Mobile phone makers in Japan have gone beyond the imagining phase.

Cell phones in Japan are becoming more versatile than ever. Newer models of cell phones contain a myriad of applications and can do many of the things that a personal computer (PC) can do. PCs are also able to function as phones. DualCor Technologies offers a handheld Windows XP PC that also comes with a built-in cell phone. The PC comes with a 1.5 GHz processor, 1 GB of memory, and a 40 GB hard drive that it shares with the cell phone component. The PC is 6.5 inches long, 3.3 inches wide, 1.2 inches thick, has a 5-inch diagonal screen, and costs around $1,500. A small but growing number of professionals are trading in their laptops for BlackBerrys and other handheld computers.

Required

a. What commercial activities can be done with a cell phone/PC combination device?
b. How can businesses utilize this technology to attract more customers, sell more products, advertise their products, facilitate the sale of products, and conduct and manage their businesses more efficiently and effectively?
c. What are some problems or drawbacks you can see with using this device in business?

CASE 1-1 Any Company, Inc. An Ongoing Comprehensive Case

The Web case at the end of each chapter is an assignment that allows you to apply key concepts to a local company. This case, then, may become an ongoing case study on which you work throughout the term. The Any Company Case can be found on the Web site for this book.

CASE 1-2 Ackoff's Management Misinformation Systems

The Web site for this book contains an adaption of Russell L. Ackoff's classic article "Management Misinformation Systems" from *Management Science*. In the article, Ackoff identified five common assumptions about information systems and then explained why he disagreed with them.

Required

Read the five assumptions, contentions, and Ackoff's explanations. For each of the five assumptions, decide if you agree or disagree with Ackoff's contentions. Prepare a report in which you defend your stand and explain your defense.

AIS IN ACTION SOLUTIONS

 QUIZ KEY

1 Data differ from information in which way?
 a. Data are output and information is input. [Incorrect. Data are facts and figures that once organized can become information. Therefore, data are inputs and information is output.]
 ✔ b. Information is output and data are input. [Correct.]
 c. Data are meaningful bits of information. [Incorrect. Information is organized and processed data that provide meaning.]

 d. There is no difference. [Incorrect. There is a difference. Data are unorganized facts and figures. Information is meaningful, organized, and processed data.]

2 Which of the following is <u>not</u> a characteristic that makes information useful?
 a. It is reliable. [Incorrect. This is one of the information characteristics listed in Table 1-1 on page 28.]
 b. It is timely. [Incorrect. This is one of the information characteristics listed in Table 1-1 on page 28.]
 ✔ **c.** It is inexpensive. [Correct. This is not one of the information characteristics listed in Table 1-1 on page 28.]
 d. It is relevant. [Incorrect. This is one of the information characteristics listed in Table 1-1 on page 28.]

3 Which of the following is a primary activity in the value chain?
 a. purchasing [Incorrect. This is a support activity.]
 b. accounting [Incorrect. This is a firm infrastructure support activity.]
 ✔ **c.** post-sales service [Correct. Service is a primary activity.]
 d. human resource management [Incorrect. This is a support activity.]

4 Top management continually emphasizes and supports investments designed to improve the efficiency of the manufacturing process. Such a focus most likely reflects the pursuit of which type of basic business strategy?
 a. product differentiation [Incorrect. This strategy adds new features and services not provided by competitors.]
 ✔ **b.** low-cost [Correct. Seeking to improve manufacturing efficiency is part of a low-cost strategy.]
 c. needs-based [Incorrect. This strategy focuses on serving most of the needs of a particular group of customers in a target market.]
 d. variety-based [Incorrect. This strategy focuses on producing or providing a subset of the industry's products or services.]

5 Which of the following is <u>not</u> a means by which information improves decision making?
 ✔ **a.** increasing information overload [Correct. Decision makers receiving too much information have difficulty incorporating all of the information into their decision framework and as a result decision quality can be reduced rather than improved.]
 b. reducing uncertainty [Incorrect. More reliable information leads to less uncertainty and thus better decisions.]
 c. providing feedback about the effectiveness of prior decisions [Incorrect. Knowledge of effective and ineffective decisions can lead to better decisions in the future.]
 d. identifying situations requiring management action [Incorrect. Identifying the need for management action can lead to improved decision making.]

6 In the value chain concept, upgrading IT is considered what kind of activity?
 a. primary activity [Incorrect. Investing in IT is a support activity.]
 ✔ **b.** support activity [Correct. Technology activities, including investing in IT, are considered a support activity.]
 c. service activity [Incorrect. The value chain includes only primary and support activities. A service activity is a type of primary activity.]
 d. structured activity [Incorrect. The value chain includes only primary and support activities. A structured activity is neither a primary nor a secondary activity.]

7 Lower-level management employees are most likely to make which of the following decisions?
 a. structured decisions involving strategic planning [Incorrect. Strategic planning decisions are made at the executive level.]

b. unstructured decisions involving managerial control [Incorrect. Mid-level managers are typically involved in managerial control decisions.]

✔ **c.** structured decisions involving operational control [Correct. Everyday operational decisions are made by lower-level managers.]

d. unstructured decisions involving strategic planning [Incorrect. Strategic planning decisions are made at the executive level.]

8 Which of the following is a function of an AIS?

a. reducing the need to identify a strategy and strategic position [Incorrect. An AIS does not reduce the need to identify a strategy. It provides information to executives for the purpose of making strategic decisions.]

✔ **b.** transforming data into useful information [Correct. This is one of the primary functions of an AIS.]

c. allocating organizational resources [Incorrect. Decision makers allocate resources, and the purpose of the AIS is to provide information to the decision makers so they can make the allocation.]

d. automating all decision making [Incorrect. The AIS provides information to decision makers; it is not designed to automate all decision making.]

9 A firm, its suppliers, and its customers collectively form which of the following?

✔ **a.** supply chain [Correct. The supply chain is comprised of the firm, its suppliers, and customers.]

b. value chain [Incorrect. The value chain is comprised of primary and support activities within the firm.]

c. ERP system [Incorrect. An ERP system integrates all aspects of an organization's activities into one system.]

d. AIS [Incorrect. The AIS is comprised of the human and capital resources within an organization that are responsible for collecting and processing transactions and preparing financial information.]

10 A company that focuses its marketing efforts on a specific subset of the population (e.g., college students) is probably pursuing which type of strategic position?

a. variety-based [Incorrect. This strategy focuses on providing a subset of an industry's products or services.]

✔ **b.** needs-based [Correct. This strategy focuses on serving most of the needs of a particular group of customers, such as college students.]

c. access-based [Incorrect. This strategy focuses on serving a subset of customers based on geographic location or size.]

d. low-cost [Incorrect. This strategy focuses on providing products and services at the lowest cost.]

CHAPTER 2

LEARNING OBJECTIVES

After studying this chapter, you should be able to:

- Explain the basic activities companies engage in, the types of decisions they must make, and the types of information they need to make those decisions.

- Identify the major internal and external parties that an AIS interacts with and the type of information it provides each user.

- Describe the major transaction cycles present in most companies.

- Describe the four major steps in the data processing cycle and the major activities in each.

- Describe the documents and procedures used in an AIS to collect and process transaction data.

- Describe the ways information is stored in computer-based information systems.

- Discuss the types of information that an AIS can provide.

Overview of Business Processes

INTEGRATIVE CASE S&S, INC.

The grand opening of S&S, Inc. is two weeks away. Scott Parry and Susan Gonzalez are working long hours to make the final arrangements for the store opening. Most of the employees have already been hired; training is scheduled for next week.

Susan has ordered what she thinks will be an adequate amount of inventory for the first month. The store is being remodeled and will have a bright, cheery decor. All seems to be in order—all, that is, except the accounting records.

Like many entrepreneurs, Scott and Susan have not given as much thought to their accounting records as they have to other parts of their business. They recognize that they need qualified accounting help and have hired a full-time accountant, Ashton Fleming. Scott and Susan think Ashton is perfect for the job because of his three years of experience with a national CPA firm. Ashton is looking forward to working for S&S because he has always wanted to be involved in building a company from the ground up.

During Ashton's first day on the job, Susan shows him where she stored the invoices for the inventory she purchased. Scott explains that the sales staff is paid a fixed salary plus commissions and that all other employees are paid hourly rates. Employees are paid every two weeks, with their first paychecks due next week. Susan then pulls out several folders and hands them to Ashton. One contains the documentation on their bank loan, with the first payment due several days after the grand opening. The other folders contain information on rental payments, utilities, and other expenses. Susan tells Ashton that she and Scott know little about accounting

and are relying on him to help them decide how to run the accounting end of S&S. She adds that the only thing they have done so far is to open a checking account for S&S and that they have kept the check register updated to monitor their cash flow.

Ashton asks Scott what accounting software the company is using. Scott replies that with all the challenges they have had in opening up S&S, he and Susan have not had time to tackle that aspect yet. Scott adds that he and Susan did begin to look at some of the popular packages but quickly realized that they did not know enough about accounting to make an intelligent choice. Scott then tells Ashton that his first task should be to purchase whatever accounting software he thinks will be best for S&S.

After Scott leaves, Ashton feels both excited and a little nervous about his responsibility for creating an AIS for S&S. Although Ashton has audited many companies, he has never organized a company's books and is unsure how to go about it. A million questions run through his head. Here are just a few of them:

1 How am I going to organize things? Where do I start? What information do Scott and Susan need to run S&S effectively? What external entities will S&S interact with, and what information do they need? What kinds of information do management and other employees need? How can all that information be provided?

2 How am I going to collect and process data about all the types of transactions in which S&S will engage?

3 How do I organize all the data that will be collected?

4 How should I design the AIS so that the information provided is reliable and accurate?

Introduction

This chapter is divided into two major sections. The first major section discusses the basic business activities an organization engages in, the key decisions that must be considered when managing those activities, and the information needed to make those decisions. It also discusses the types of interactions that an organization's AIS has with both internal and external parties. It concludes with a description of the major transaction cycles common to most organizations. In discussing these things, we show that the nature and objectives of an organization affect the design of its AIS.

The second major section discusses the data processing cycle and its role in organizing business activities and providing information to users. It explains how organizations capture and enter data about business activities into their AIS. It explains how companies process data and transform it into useful information. It also discusses basic data storage concepts, showing how data are stored for further use. Finally, information output is discussed, including the different ways information is provided to users and the different purposes for which information is provided.

A small section at the end of the chapter discusses the role of the information system in modern organizations and introduces the concept of an enterprise resource planning system (ERP). An ERP can help integrate all aspects of a company's operations with its traditional AIS. In other words, an ERP integrates financial data with nonfinancial operating data.

Information Needs and Business Activities

Ashton decides he must understand how the company functions before he can select an accounting package. This will help him identify the information Scott and Susan need to manage S&S effectively. Then Ashton can determine the types of data and procedures that will be needed to collect and produce that information.

Information Needs

Ashton created Table 2-1 to summarize part of his analysis. In the left column he lists S&S's basic business activities or processes. In the middle column, he lists some of the key decisions that will need to be made for each of these processes. Finally, in the right column, he lists helpful information that Scott and Susan will need to make these decisions.

Table 2-1
Overview of S&S's Business Processes, Key Decisions, and Information Needs

Business Processes	Key Decisions	Information Needs
Acquire capital	How much? Find investors or borrow funds? If borrow, best terms?	Cash flow projections Pro-forma financial statements Loan amortization schedule
Acquire building and equipment	Size of building? Amount of equipment? Rent or buy? Location? How to depreciate?	Capacity needs Building and equipment prices Market study Tax tables and depreciation regulations
Hire and train employees	Experience requirements? How to assess integrity and competence of applicants? How to train employees?	Job descriptions Applicant job history and skills
Acquire inventory	What models to carry? How much to purchase? How to manage inventory (store, control, etc.)? Which vendors?	Market analyses Inventory status reports Vendor performance
Advertising and marketing	Which media? Content?	Cost analyses Market coverage
Sell merchandise	Markup percentage? Offer in-house credit? Which credit cards to accept?	Pro-forma income statement Credit card costs Customer credit status
Collect payments from customers	If offer credit, what terms? How to handle cash receipts?	Customer account status Accounts receivable aging report Accounts receivable records
Pay employees	Amount to pay? Deductions and withholdings? Process payroll in-house or use outside service?	Sales (for commissions) Time worked (hourly employees) W4 forms Costs of external payroll service
Pay taxes	Payroll tax requirements Sales tax requirements	Government regulations Total wage expense Total sales
Pay vendors	Whom to pay? When to pay? How much to pay?	Vendor invoices Accounts payable records Payment terms

Ashton realizes that the list is not exhaustive, but he is satisfied it provides a good overview of S&S. He also recognizes that not all the information needs listed in the right-hand column will be produced internally by S&S's AIS. Information about payment terms for merchandise purchases, for example, will be provided by vendors. Thus the AIS must be able to effectively integrate external data with internally generated data so that Scott and Susan can use both types of information to run S&S.

Interaction with External and Internal Parties

The AIS at S&S will interact with many external parties, such as customers, vendors, creditors, and governmental agencies as well as with internal parties such as management and employees. To get a better handle on the more important interactions with these parties, he prepared Figure 2-1.

Business Processes

Next, Ashton decides to reorganize the business processes listed in Table 2-1 into groups of related transactions. A **transaction** is an agreement between two entities to exchange goods or services or any other event that can be measured in economic terms by an organization. Examples include selling goods to customers, buying inventory from suppliers, and paying employees. The process that begins with capturing transaction data and ends with an informational output such as the financial statements is called **transaction processing**.

From his audit experience, Ashton knows that many business activities are pairs of events involved in a **give-get exchange**.[1] Most organizations engage in a

Figure 2-1
Interactions Between S&S and
External and Internal Parties

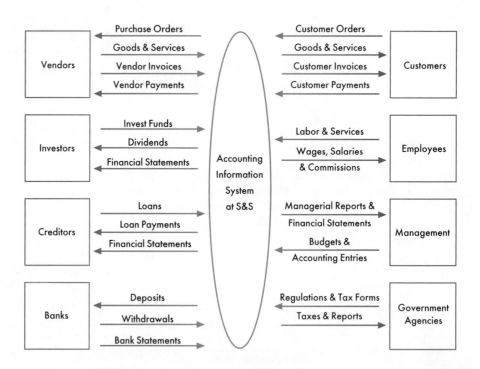

[1]The idea of modeling an AIS as a set of "Give and Take" exchanges was developed in Cheryl L. Dunn and William E. McCarthy, "Conceptual Models of Economic Exchange Phenomena: History's Third Wave of Accounting Systems," *Collected Papers of the Sixth World Congress of Accounting Historians*, Vol. 1, Kyoto, Japan. pp. 133–164; and in Guido Geerts and William E. McCarthy, "Modeling Business Enterprises as Value-Added Process Hierarchies with Resource-Event-Agent Object Templates," *Business Object Design and Implementation: OOPSLA 1995 Workshop Proceedings* (October 16, 1995), Austin, TX: Springer.

small number of give-get exchanges, but each type of exchange happens many times. For example, S&S has thousands of sales to customers every year in exchange for cash. Likewise, S&S will continuously buy inventory from suppliers in exchange for cash.

These basic exchanges can be grouped into five major **business or transaction cycles**:

- The **revenue cycle**, where goods and services are sold for cash or a future promise to receive cash.
- The **expenditure cycle**, where companies purchase inventory for resale or raw materials to use in producing products in exchange for cash or a future promise to pay cash.
- The **production cycle**, where raw materials are transformed into finished goods.
- The **human resources/payroll cycle**, where employees are hired, trained, compensated, evaluated, promoted, and terminated.
- The **financing cycle**, where companies sell shares in the company to investors and borrow money and where investors are paid dividends and interest is paid on loans.

These cycles process a few related transactions over and over again. For example, most revenue cycle transactions are either selling goods or services to customers or collecting cash for those sales. Figure 2-2 shows the main transaction cycles and the give-get exchange inherent in each cycle.

These basic give-get exchanges are supported by a number of other business activities. For example, S&S may need to answer a number of customer inquiries and check inventory levels before it can make a sale. Likewise, it may have to check customer credit before a credit sale is made. Accounts receivable will have to be increased each time a credit sale is made and decreased each time a customer payment is received. Table 2-2 lists the major activities in each transaction cycle.

Notice that the last activity listed in Table 2-2 for each transaction cycle is "send appropriate information to the other cycles." Figure 2-2 shows how these various transaction cycles relate to one another and interface with the **general ledger and reporting system**, which is used to generate information for both management and external parties.

In many accounting software packages, the various transaction cycles are implemented as separate modules. Every organization does not need to implement every module. Retail stores like S&S, for example, do not have a production cycle and would not implement that module. Moreover, some types of organizations have unique requirements. Financial institutions, for example, have demand-deposit and installment-loan cycles that relate to transactions involving customer accounts and loans, respectively. In addition, the nature of a given transaction cycle differs across different types of organizations. For example, the expenditure cycle of a service company, such as a public accounting or a law firm, does not involve processing transactions related to the purchase, receipt, and payment for merchandise that will be resold to customers.

Each transaction cycle can include many different business processes or activities. Each business process can be relatively simple or quite complex. Focus 2-1 shows how Toyota's attention to continuously improving its business processes has helped it become the largest and most profitable automobile manufacturer in the world.

After preparing Tables 2-1 and 2-2 and Figures 2-1 and 2-2, Ashton believes that he understands S&S well enough to begin shopping for an accounting package that would serve as the core of its AIS. He recalled, however, several audits in which clients had several separate information systems, because their basic accounting software was not designed to accommodate the information needs of all managers. Ashton also vividly recalled attending one client's board meeting where he

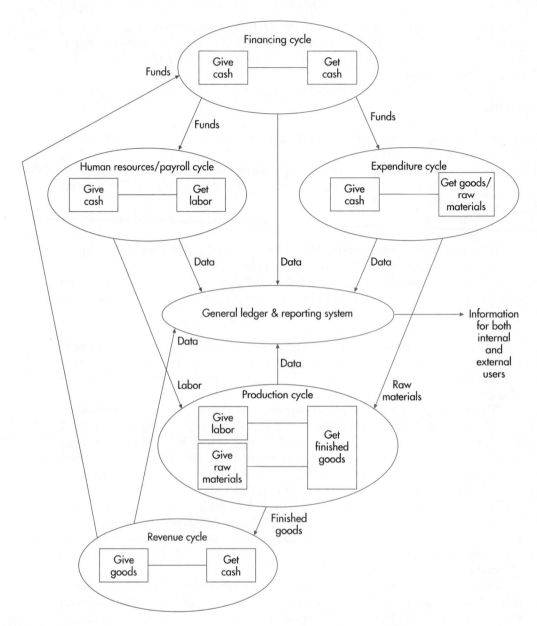

Figure 2-2
The AIS and Its Subsystems

Source: Adapted from classroom materials originally developed by Julie Smith David at Arizona State University and based on ideas developed in the sources listed in footnote 1.

witnessed the negative effects of having multiple systems. The head of marketing had one report on year-to-date sales by product, the production manager had a different report that contained different sales figures, and the controller's report, which was produced by the general ledger system, had yet a third version of year-to-date sales. Over an hour had been wasted trying to reconcile those different reports! Ashton vowed that he would make sure that S&S did not ever find itself in such a mess. He would make sure that any accounting software package he selected would have the capability to integrate both financial and nonfinancial data about S&S's various business processes so that everyone could pull information from the same system.

Transaction Cycle	Major Activities in the Cycle
Revenue	Receive and answer customer inquiries
	Take customer orders and enter them into the AIS
	Approve credit sales
	Check inventory availability
	Initiate back orders for goods out of stock
	Pick and pack customer orders
	Ship goods to customers or perform services
	Bill customers for goods shipped or services performed
	Update (increase) Sales and Accounts Receivable
	Receive customer payments and deposit them in the bank
	Update (reduce) Accounts Receivable
	Handle sales returns, discounts, allowances, and bad debts
	Prepare management reports
	Send appropriate information to the other cycles
Expenditure	Request goods and services be purchased
	Prepare, approve, and send purchase orders to vendors
	Receive goods and services and complete a receiving report
	Store goods
	Receive vendor invoices
	Update (increase) accounts payable
	Approve vendor invoices for payment
	Pay vendors for goods and services
	Update (reduce) accounts payable
	Handle purchase returns, discounts, and allowances
	Prepare management reports
	Send appropriate information to the other cycles
Human Resources/ Payroll	Recruit, hire, and train new employees
	Evaluate employee performance and promote employees
	Discharge employees
	Update payroll records
	Collect and validate time, attendance, and commission data
	Prepare and disburse payroll
	Calculate and disburse taxes and benefit payments
	Prepare employee and management reports
	Send appropriate information to the other cycles
Production	Design products
	Forecast, plan, and schedule production
	Request raw materials for production
	Manufacture products (transform raw materials and labor into finished goods)
	Store finished products
	Accumulate costs for products manufactured
	Prepare management reports
	Send appropriate information to the other cycles
Financing	Forecast cash needs
	Sell stock/securities to investors
	Borrow money from lenders
	Pay dividends to investors and interest to lenders
	Retire debt
	Prepare management reports
	Send appropriate information to the other cycles

Table 2-2
Common Cycle Activities

2-1 FOCUS — Improving Business Processes Helps Drive Toyota's Success

Toyota's Georgetown, Kentucky, manufacturing plant, its largest in North America, is the size of 156 football fields, employs 7,000 people, and produces a new car every 55 seconds. Because Toyota produces a higher-quality car at a lower cost than its competitors, it is now the largest automobile manufacturer in the world, a title General Motors had for almost a hundred years.

A major factor in its success is Toyota Production System (TPS); a set of philosophies, principles, and business processes supported by information technology. Its goal is to continually improve so Toyota has the most effective and most efficient manufacturing and business processes possible. Toyota willingly shares TPS and its manufacturing and business processes with its suppliers to help them improve their quality and efficiency. It also shares TPS with its competitors, knowing that by the time they duplicate it Toyota will have greatly improved TPS.

Some of the principles and business processes on which TPS is built and that Toyota's information systems must support and enable are these:

- Performance monitoring software warns assembly line workers of equipment problems. Workers stop production whenever necessary to prevent or correct defects.
- Their just-in-time (JIT) inventory system is one of the most sophisticated in the world. Driverless carts take parts to assembly stations at the time they are needed so inventory does not pile up. Suppliers must meet rigid delivery standards. For example, four hours before they are needed Toyota software electronically notifies Johnson Controls exactly what kind of car seats are needed for each car and the exact order in which they must be shipped.

- Continuous improvement is a critical and ongoing process. No process or detail is too small or insignificant to improve. Technology is especially important in the continuous improvement process. This emphasis on continuous improvement creates a culture that values continuous learning and embraces change.
- Electronic displays, many connected directly to the manufacturing equipment, help workers monitor the assembly line. Information is communicated by light colors (green means the process is operating correctly, yellow shows a problem is being investigated, and red shows the assembly line has stopped) and by printed messages (which machine malfunctioned, its speed and temperature when it broke down, and who was operating the machine.)
- Electronic quality control devices, such as an electronic sensor on a tool or a beam of light, monitor a process. These devices let a computer know when a tool is not used or a required part is not picked up and used at the appropriate time.
- More than half of Toyota's information systems employees work in operations at its plants so they can accompany executives, team leaders, and factory workers when they go to solve assembly line problems.

In summary, Toyota has a very clear and in-depth understanding of the business processes that make it successful, continuously improves those process, and understands the role information systems play in managing, supporting, and facilitating those processes.

Source: Mel Duvall, "What's Driving Toyota?" *Baseline Magazine,* September 5, 2006.

Transaction Processing: The Data Processing Cycle

Accountants have a significant role to play in the data processing cycle. For example, they must interact with systems analysts to help answer questions such as these: What data should be entered and stored by the organization, and who should have access to them? How should the data be organized, updated, stored, accessed, and retrieved? How can both scheduled and unanticipated information needs be met? To answer these and related questions, accountants must understand the data processing concepts explained in this chapter.

One important function of the AIS is to efficiently and effectively process data about a company's transactions. In manual (non-computer-based) systems, data are entered into journals and ledgers maintained on paper. In computer-based systems, data are entered into computers and stored in files and databases. The operations

performed on data to generate meaningful and relevant information are referred to collectively as the **data processing cycle**. As shown in Figure 2-3, this process consists of four steps: data input, data storage, data processing, and information output.

Data Input

The first step in processing transactions is to capture the data for each transaction that takes place and enter them into the system. The data capture process is usually triggered by the occurrence of a business activity. Data must be collected about three facets of each business activity:

1 Each activity of interest
2 The resource(s) affected by each activity
3 The people who participate in each activity

For example, the most frequent transaction in the revenue cycle is a sale, either for cash or on credit. S&S may find it useful to collect the following data about a sales transaction:

- Date and time of day the sale occurred
- Employee who made the sale and the checkout clerk who processed the sale
- Checkout register where the sale was processed
- Item(s) sold
- Quantity of each item sold
- List price and actual price of each item sold
- Total amount of the sale
- For credit sales: deiivery instructions, customer bill-to and ship-to addresses, customer name.

Historically, most businesses used paper **source documents** to collect data about their business activities. They later transferred that data into the computer. Table 2-3 lists some common transaction cycle activities and the name of the source document or form used to capture data about that event. Examples of many of these documents can be found in Chapters 10 through 13. For example, a purchase order, used to request merchandise from suppliers, is shown in Figure 11-5 on page 445 in Chapter 11.

Today it is more common for data about business activities to be recorded directly through computer data entry screens. The data entry screen often retains the same name as the paper source document it replaced.

If paper documents are exchanged with customers or suppliers, data input accuracy and efficiency are improved by using **turnaround documents**, which are records of company data sent to an external party and then returned to the system as input. Turnaround documents are prepared in machine-readable form to facilitate their subsequent processing as input records. An example is a utility bill that is sent to the customer, returned with the customer's payment, and read by a special scanning device when it is returned.

Figure 2-3
The Data Processing Cycle

Table 2-3
Common Business Activities
and Source Documents

Business Activity	Source Document
Revenue Cycle	
Take customer order	Sales order
Deliver or ship order	Delivery ticket or bill of lading
Receive cash	Remittance advice or remittance list
Deposit cash receipts	Deposit slip
Adjust customer account	Credit memo
Expenditure Cycle	
Request items	Purchase requisition
Order items	Purchase order
Receive items	Receiving report
Pay for items	Check
Human Resources Cycle	
Collect employee withholding data	W4 form
Record time worked by employees	Time cards
Record time spent on specific jobs	Job time tickets or time sheet

Source data automation is yet another means to improve the accuracy and efficiency of data input. Source data automation devices capture transaction data in machine-readable form at the time and place of their origin. Examples include ATMs used by banks, point-of-sale (POS) scanners used in retail stores, and bar code scanners used in warehouses.

The second step in processing transactions is to make sure captured data are accurate and complete. One way to increase accuracy and completeness is to use well-designed turnaround documents and data entry screens, as well as source data automation. Control is improved either by purchasing prenumbered source documents or by having the system automatically assign a sequential number to each new transaction. Prenumbering simplifies verifying that all transactions have been recorded and that none of the documents has been misplaced. (Imagine trying to balance a checkbook if the checks were not prenumbered.)

Well-designed paper forms and data entry screens improve accuracy and completeness by providing instructions or prompts about what data to collect, grouping logically related pieces of information close together, using checkoff boxes or pulldown menus to present the available options, and using appropriate shading and borders to clearly separate data items. Data input screens are usually preformatted such that they list all the data the user needs to enter. Sometimes these screens resemble source documents and users fill out the screen the same way they would a paper source document.

It is also important for control purposes that certain transactions be verified by the system. For example, S&S would not want to sell goods to a customer who was not paying his bills or to sell an item for immediate delivery that was out of stock. These kinds of problems could be prevented by programming the system to check a customer's credit limit and payment history, as well as inventory status, before confirming a sale to a customer.

Data Storage

A company's data are one of its most important resources. However, the mere existence of relevant data does not guarantee that they are useful. An organization must have ready and easy access to its data to function properly. Therefore, accountants need to understand how data are organized and stored in an AIS and how they can be accessed. In essence, they need to know how to manage data for maximum corporate use.

Imagine how difficult a textbook would be to read if it were not organized into chapters, sections, paragraphs, and sentences. Now imagine how hard it would be for S&S to find an invoice if all documents were randomly dumped into file cabinets. Fortunately, most textbooks and company files are organized for easy retrieval.

Likewise, information in an AIS is organized for easy and efficient access. This section explains basic data storage concepts and definitions, such as ledgers, journals, coding techniques, chart of accounts, and computer-based storage concepts.

Ledgers

In an AIS, the files used to store cumulative information are called ledgers. Ashton decided that S&S, like most companies, should have both a general ledger and a set of subsidiary ledgers. The **general ledger** contains summary-level data for every asset, liability, equity, revenue, and expense account of the organization. A **subsidiary ledger** records all the detailed data for any general ledger account that has many individual subaccounts. For example, the general ledger contains an accounts receivable account that summarizes the total amount owed to the company by all customers. The subsidiary accounts receivable ledger has a separate record for each individual customer, each of which contains detailed information (name, address, purchases, payments, account balance, credit limit, etc.) about a particular customer. Subsidiary ledgers are commonly used for items such as accounts receivable, inventory, fixed assets, and accounts payable.

The general ledger account corresponding to a subsidiary ledger is called a **control account**. The relationship between the general ledger control account and the individual account balances in the subsidiary ledger plays an important role in maintaining the accuracy of the data stored in the AIS. Specifically, the sum of all entries in the subsidiary ledger should equal the amount in the corresponding general ledger control account. For example, the inventory subsidiary ledger would contain dollar balances for each inventory item carried by S&S. The sum of all the dollar balances in the inventory subsidiary ledger should equal the total dollar balance in the inventory control account in the general ledger. Any discrepancy between the total of the subsidiary ledger and the balance in the corresponding general ledger control account indicates that an error in the recording process has occurred.

Coding Techniques

The data stored in ledgers must be organized in a logical fashion. The most common way to do that is to use coding techniques. **Coding** is the systematic assignment of numbers or letters to items to classify and organize them. Many different types of codes are used in business and accounting applications.

- With **sequence codes**, items are numbered consecutively to ensure that there will be no gaps in the sequence. This enables the user to account for all the items, because any missing items will cause a gap in the numerical sequence. Examples include prenumbered checks, invoices, and purchase orders.
- With a **block code**, blocks of numbers within a numerical sequence are reserved for categories having meaning to the user. For example, S&S could reserve a specific range of code numbers for major product categories, as shown here:

Product Code	Product Type
1000000–1999999	Electric range
2000000–2999999	Refrigerator
3000000–3999999	Washer
4000000–4999999	Dryer

 Users familiar with the code can readily identify the type and model of item by code number alone. Other examples include ledger account numbers (blocked by account type), employee numbers (blocked by department), and customer numbers (blocked by region).
- **Group codes** are often used in conjunction with the block code. In group codes two or more subgroups of digits are used to code the item. If S&S uses

a seven-digit product code number, for example, the group coding technique might be applied as follows.

Digit Position	Meaning
1–2	Product line, size, style
3	Color
4–5	Year of manufacture
6–7	Optional features

There are four subcodes within the product code, each conveying a different meaning. This type of code allows one to sort, summarize, and retrieve information by using one or more of the subcodes. This technique is often applied to general ledger account numbers.

In designing a coding system, the following guidelines will result in a better coding system:

- The code should be consistent with its intended use, which requires the code designer to determine the types of system outputs desired by users prior to selecting the code.
- Make sure the code allows for growth in the number of items to be coded. For example, don't choose a three-digit employee code for a fast growing company with 950 employees.
- Make the coding system as simple as possible in order to minimize costs, facilitate memorization and interpretation of coding categories, and ensure employee acceptance.
- Make sure the coding system is consistent (1) with the company's organizational structure and (2) across the different divisions of an organization.

Chart of Accounts

Perhaps the best example of coding in organizations is the chart of accounts. Each general ledger account is assigned a specific number, and the **chart of accounts** is a list of all general ledger accounts an organization uses. Since the codes are account numbers, they allow transaction data to be coded, classified, and entered into the proper accounts.

The structure of the chart of accounts is an important aspect of an AIS because it affects the preparation of financial statements and reports. Data stored in individual accounts can easily be summed for presentation in reports, but data stored in summary accounts cannot be easily analyzed and reported in more detail. Consequently, it is important that the chart of accounts contain sufficient detail to meet an organization's information needs.

To illustrate, consider the consequences if S&S were to use only one general ledger account for all sales transactions. It would be easy to produce reports showing the total amount of sales for a given time period, but it would be very difficult to prepare reports separating cash and credit sales. Indeed, the only way to produce these latter reports would be to go back to the source documents or electronic record of the sale to identify the nature of each sales transaction. Clearly, this approach is not practical. If, however, S&S used separate general ledger accounts for cash and credit sales, then reports showing both types of sales could be easily produced. Total sales could also be easily reported by summing each type of sale.

Table 2-4 shows the initial chart of accounts Ashton developed for S&S. Each account number is three digits long, with each digit serving a specific purpose. The first digit represents the major account categories as they appear on S&S's financial statements: current assets, noncurrent assets, liabilities, equity accounts, revenues, expenses, and summary accounts. Notice that each major category is assigned a separate block of numbers, which corresponds with the sequence in which that category appears in the financial statements. Thus all current assets are numbered in the 100s, noncurrent assets are numbered in the 200s, and so on.

Table 2-4
Sample Chart of Accounts for S&S

Account Code	Account Name	Account Code	Account Name
100–199	**Current Assets**	**400–499**	**Equity Accounts**
101	Checking Account	400	Common Stock
102	Savings Account	410	Retained Earnings
103	Petty Cash		
120	Accounts Receivable	**500–599**	**Revenues**
125	Allowance for Doubtful Accounts	501	Cash Sales
130	Notes Receivable	502	Credit Sales
150	Inventory	510	Sales Returns & Allowances
160	Supplies	511	Sales Discounts
170	Prepaid Rent	520	Interest Revenue
180	Prepaid Insurance	530	Miscellaneous Revenue
200–299	**Noncurrent Assets**	**600–799**	**Expenses**
200	Land	600	Cost of Goods Sold
210	Buildings	611	Wages Expense
215	Accumulated Depreciation—Buildings	612	Commissions Expense
230	Equipment	613	Payroll Tax Expense
235	Accumulated Depreciation—Equipment	620	Rent Expense
		630	Insurance Expense
240	Furniture & Fixtures	640	Supplies Expense
245	Accumulated Depreciation—Furniture & Fixtures	650	Bad Debt Expense
		701	Depreciation Expense—Buildings
250	Other Assets	702	Depreciation Expense—Equipment
		703	Depreciation Expense—Furniture & Fixtures
		710	Income Tax Expense
300–399	**Liabilities**		
300	Accounts Payable		
310	Wages Payable		
321	Employee Income Tax Payable	**900–999**	**Summary Accounts**
322	FICA Tax Payable	910	Income Summary
323	Federal Unemployment Tax Payable		
324	State Unemployment Tax Payable		
330	Accrued Interest Payable		
360	Other Liabilities		

The second digit in each account code represents the primary financial subaccounts within each category. Again, the accounts are assigned numbers to match the order of their appearance in financial statements (in order of decreasing liquidity). Thus account 120 represents accounts receivable and account 150 represents inventory.

The third digit identifies the specific account to which the transaction data will be posted. For example, account 501 represents cash sales, and account 502 represents credit sales. Similarly, accounts 101 through 103 represent the various cash accounts used by S&S.

It is important to realize that the chart of accounts will differ, depending on the nature and purpose of the organization it represents. For example, the sample chart of accounts for S&S reflects the fact that the company is a corporation. In contrast, the chart of accounts for a partnership would include separate capital and drawing accounts for each partner, instead of common stock and retained earnings. Likewise,

because S&S is a retail organization, it has only one type of general ledger inventory account. A manufacturing company, in contrast, would have separate general ledger accounts for raw materials, work in process, and finished goods inventories.

Notice that Ashton left a number of gaps in S&S's chart of accounts to allow for later insertion of additional accounts. For example, S&S does not currently have enough excess cash to invest in marketable securities. Later, when it can do so, a new general ledger account for marketable securities can be created and assigned the number 110. Ashton also knows that Scott and Susan hope to open additional stores in the future. When this occurs, he plans to add two more digits to the chart of accounts to represent each store in the chain, so that S&S can track sales, expenses, inventory, and other items in each individual store.

Accounts in the subsidiary ledgers often have longer account codes than those used in the general ledger. For example, Ashton plans that each individual account receivable will have a seven-digit code. The first three digits are 120, the code for accounts receivable in the general ledger. The additional four digits provide a means for identifying up to 10,000 individual customers. The accounts payable and inventory subsidiary ledgers will be organized in a similar manner.

Journals

Transaction data are often recorded in a journal before they are entered into a ledger. Understanding the process of entering data into journals and then in ledgers is important. This section briefly explains that process.

A journal entry is made for each transaction showing the accounts and amounts to be debited and credited. A **general journal** is used to record infrequent or nonroutine transactions, such as loan payments and end-of-period adjusting and closing entries. A **specialized journal** is used to simplify the process of recording large numbers of repetitive transactions such as credit sales, cash receipts, purchases on account, and cash disbursements.

Table 2-5 is an example of a sales journal. Notice that the sales journal has only one column to record the transaction amount because the sales journal is used only for recording credit sales. Consequently, every entry represents a debit to accounts receivable and a credit, for the same amount, to sales revenue. This also means that there is no need to write an explanation of each entry, as would be the case if credit sales were recorded in the general journal. Instead, all the information about the transaction is recorded in one line: the date, invoice number, name and account number of the customer, and the amount of the sale. When you consider the number of sales transactions likely to occur every day, the time saved by recording these transactions in a sales journal, rather than in the general journal, is considerable.

The column in the sales journal, titled Post Ref, is used to indicate when transactions are posted to the appropriate ledgers. Ledgers are used to summarize the financial

Table 2-5
Sample Sales Journal

SALES JOURNAL					PAGE 5
Date	**Invoice Number**	**Account Debited**	**Account Number**	**Post Ref.**	**Amount**
Oct.15	151	Brown Hospital Supply	120-035	✓	798.00
15	152	Greenshadows Hotel Suites	120-122	✓	1,267.00
15	153	Heathrow Apartments	120-057	✓	5,967.00
15	154	LMS Construction	120-173	✓	2,312.50
15	155	Gardenview Apartments	120-084	✓	3,290.00
15	156	KDR Builders	120-135	✓	1,876.50
		TOTAL	120/502		15,511.00

status, including the current balance, of individual accounts. In a manual system, ledgers are actually books; hence, the phrase "keeping the books" refers to the process of maintaining the ledgers.

Figure 2-4 shows how to journalize and post sales transactions. As shown in the top portion of the figure, each credit sale is first recorded in the sales journal. Each individual entry in the sales journal is then posted to the appropriate customer's account in the accounts receivable subsidiary ledger (note the arrow at the top of Figure 2-4 linking the $1,876.50 sale to KDR Builders in the sales journal to the debit for $1,876.50 in the accounts receivable subsidiary ledger at the bottom of the figure). The same process is followed for credit sales to all other customers. Periodically, the total of all entries recorded in the sales journal is then posted to the general ledger (note the debit of $15,511.00, representing total sales on October 15, linked by the arrow to the accounts receivable general ledger account in the middle of

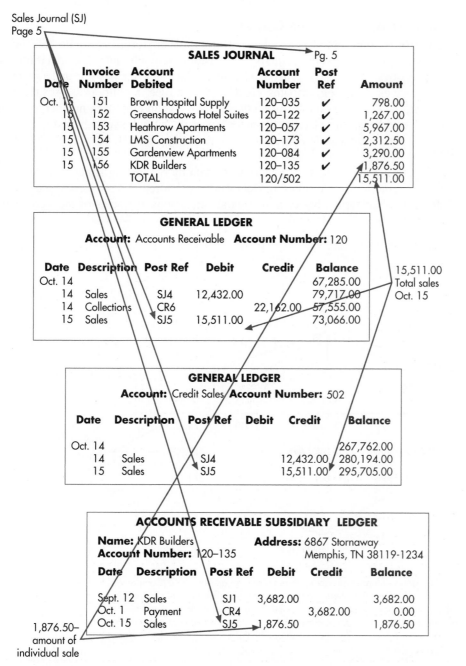

Figure 2-4
Recording and Posting a Credit Sale

Figure 2-4 and to the corresponding credit to the general ledger sales account for the same amount).

Audit Trail

Figure 2-4 also shows how the posting references and document numbers provide what is known as an **audit trail**. An audit trail provides a means to check the accuracy and validity of ledger postings. To illustrate this, observe that the posting reference for the $15,511 credit to the sales account in the general ledger, SJ5, refers back to page 5 of the sales journal. By checking page 5 of the sales journal, it is possible to verify that $15,511 represents the total credit sales recorded on October 15. Similarly, the posting reference for the $1876.50 debit to the KDR Builders' account in the subsidiary accounts receivable ledger also refers to page 5 of the sales journal as the source of that entry. Furthermore, note that the sales journal lists the invoice numbers for each individual entry. This provides the means for locating and examining the appropriate source documents in order to verify that the transaction did occur and was recorded accurately.

Computer-Based Storage Concepts

An **entity** is something about which information is stored. Examples of entities include employees, inventory items, and customers. Each entity has **attributes**, or characteristics of interest, that need to be stored. An employee pay rate and a customer address are examples of attributes. Generally, each type of entity possesses the same set of attributes. For example, all employees possess an employee number, pay rate, and home address. The specific values for those attributes, however, will differ among entities. For example, one employee's pay rate might be $10.00, whereas another's might be $10.25.

Figure 2-5 shows that computers store data by organizing smaller units of data into larger, more meaningful ones. Data values are stored in a physical space called a **field**. The set of fields that contain data about various attributes of the same entity

Figure 2-5
Data Storage Elements

This accounts receivable file stores information about three separate entities: XYZ Company, ABC Company, and QRS Company. As a result, there are three records in the file. Five separate attributes are used to describe each customer: customer number, customer name, address, credit limit, and balance. There are, therefore, five separate fields in each record. Each field contains a data value that describes an attribute of a particular entity (customer). For example, the data value 19283 is the customer number for the XYZ Company.

forms a **record**. In Figure 2-5, each row represents a different record and each column represents an attribute, or field. Thus, each intersecting row and column in Figure 2-5 is a field within a record, the contents of which are called a **data value**.

Related records are grouped to form a **file**. Two basic types of files exist. A **master file** is conceptually similar to a ledger in a manual AIS. Master files store cumulative information about an organization's resources and the agents with whom it interacts. For example, the inventory and equipment master files store information about important organizational resources. Similarly, the customer, supplier, and employee master files store information about important agents with whom the organization interacts.

Master files are permanent; they exist across fiscal periods. Individual records within a master file, however, are frequently changed. The most common type of change made to records in master files involves updating the data to reflect the effect of specific transactions. For example, the account balances of individual customer accounts in the customer master file are updated to reflect new sales transactions and payments received. Periodically, new records may also be added to a master file, and sometimes individual records may even be deleted.

The second basic type of file is called a **transaction file**, which is conceptually similar to a journal in a manual AIS. Transaction files contain records for the individual business transactions that occur during a specific fiscal period. For example, S&S, Inc. would have a transaction file containing records of sales events and another transaction file containing records of customer payments. Both of these files would be used to update individual customer account balances in the customer master file. Transaction files are not permanent but are usually only maintained online for one fiscal period.

A set of interrelated, centrally coordinated files is referred to as a **database**. For example, the accounts receivable file might be combined with customer, sales analysis, and related files to form a customer database. Databases are so important that Chapter 4 is devoted to a discussion of database technology.

Data Processing

Once data about a business activity have been collected and entered into the system, they must be processed. This processing helps keep the data stored in files or databases current. There are four different types of data processing. These basic activities are often referred to as CRUD, an acronym derived from the first letter of the four activities.

1 **Creating** or adding new data records, such as adding a new employee to the payroll master file or database after they have been hired.
2 **Reading,** retrieving or viewing existing data.
3 **Updating** data previously stored about the activity, the resources affected by the activity, or the people who performed the activity. Figure 2-6 is an example of file updating and depicts the steps required to update an accounts receivable record with a sales transaction. The two records are matched using the account number. The sale amount ($360) is added to the account balance ($1500) to get a new current balance ($1860).
4 **Deleting** data, such as purging the vendor master file of all vendors that the company no longer does business with.

Updating can be done periodically, such as daily, or immediately as each transaction occurs. Periodic updating of data is referred to as **batch processing**. Updating as each transaction occurs is referred to as **online, real-time processing**. Batch processing is a legacy method that continues to be used for some applications, such as payroll, that naturally occur at fixed time periods.

The obvious disadvantage of batch processing is that stored data are only current and accurate immediately after the periodic batch updating process. Consequently, most companies are switching to online, real-time processing for most applications.

Figure 2-6

The Accounts Receivable File
Update Process

Online data entry is more accurate than periodic batch input because the system can refuse incomplete or erroneous entries. In addition, because the data are being entered at the time the transaction occurs, any errors can be easily corrected. Real-time processing ensures that stored information is always current, thereby increasing its usefulness for making decisions. A combination of the two approaches is online batch processing, where transaction data are entered into the system as they occur. Batch and online, real-time processing are summarized in Figure 2-7.

Many companies use online, real-time processing because of the competitive advantages it offers. For example, a few years ago Federal Express updated its mission statement to include the phrase "Positive control of each package will be maintained by utilizing real-time electronic tracking and tracing systems." The company's online real-time system tells the exact location of each package and estimates its arrival time. Federal Express also provides customers with software that allows them to track their parcels.

This concludes our description of the documents and procedures commonly used to record, process, and store data about transactions. In a small company like S&S, it will be Ashton's responsibility not only to design and manage the AIS but also to perform most of the procedures we have just described. Ashton would also likely be responsible for keeping abreast of technology developments and how they affect both business operations and employee responsibilities.

Information Output

The final step in the data processing cycle is information output. In this section you will learn about the format, purpose, and user responsibilities associated with output.

Forms of Information Output

Information is usually presented in one of three forms: a document, a report, or a response to a query. **Documents** are records of transaction or other company data. Some, such as checks and invoices, are transmitted to external parties. Others, such as receiving reports and purchase requisitions, are used internally. Documents generated at the end of transaction processing activities are called **operational documents** to distinguish them from source documents, which are used at the beginning of the process.

Documents can be printed out or they can be stored as electronic images in a computer. For example, Toys 'R' Us uses electronic data interchange to communicate with

Figure 2-7
Batch and Online Processing

Batch Processing

Group source documents into batches. Generate control totals.

Enter batches at predetermined times or batch sizes. Sort file and edit data as appropriate.

Store data in temporary file.

Process all batches. Update old master files with transaction data, creating new master file.

Print desired output. Also print error reports, transaction reports, control total reports.

Online Batch Processing

Enter transactions into system as they occur.

Store data in temporary file.

Process temporary file at predetermined time. Update old master files with transaction data, creating new master file.

Print desired output.

Online Real-Time Processing

Enter transactions into system as they occur.

Process transactions as they occur. Update master files with transaction data.

Print desired output.

its suppliers. Every year it processes over half a million invoices electronically, thereby eliminating paper documents and dramatically reducing costs and errors. This has resulted in higher profits and more accurate information.

Reports are prepared for both internal and external users. Reports are used by employees to control operational activities and by managers to make decisions and to design strategies for the business. External users need reports for a wide variety of reasons, such as to evaluate company profitability, to judge creditworthiness, or to comply

with regulatory requirements. For example, Eli Lilly, a large drug manufacturer, has applications that automatically gather, process, and display IT data in any form, such as text, spreadsheets, or easy-to-understand graphs or charts. When the Food and Drug Administration (FDA) mandated that it receive certain information electronically, Eli Lilly programmed its system to gather the needed data from its different systems, organize them, and submit them electronically to the FDA.

Some reports, such as financial statements and sales analyses, are produced on a regular basis. Others are produced on an exception basis to call attention to unusual conditions. For example, S&S could have its system produce a report to indicate when product returns exceed a certain percentage of sales. Reports can also be produced on demand. For example, Susan could produce a report to identify the salesperson who sold the most items during a specific promotional period.

It is important to periodically reassess the need for each report a company produces. All too often, reports continue to be prepared long after the need for them disappears, wasting time, money, and computer resources. For example, a team at a regional Bell Telephone Company interviewed the preparers and users of every report. It found many duplicate and unnecessary reports, including a 25-page report that took five days to prepare and sat unread. In the end, 6 million pages of reports were eliminated, a stack four times higher than the company's 41-story headquarters building. Another example is the finance and administrative side of NCR Corporation, which used to produce 1200 customized reports. After carefully reexamining the system, the company was able to reduce the number to just over 100.

Increasingly, information needs cannot be satisfied strictly by documents or periodic reports. Instead, problems and questions constantly arise that need rapid action or answers. To respond to this problem, personal computers or terminals are used to **query** the system. A user enters a request for a specific piece of information. When the information is found, it is retrieved, displayed, or analyzed as requested. Since many queries are repetitive, users will usually have a predetermined set of queries available to them. To shorten the time required to develop the queries and to improve their efficiency, these repetitive queries are often developed by information systems (IS) specialists. Any unusual or one-time queries are usually developed by the users themselves. When displayed on a monitor, output is referred to as "soft copy." When printed on paper, it is referred to as "hard copy."

Companies have even made it possible for their suppliers to query their databases. For example, Wal-Mart allows many suppliers to access any information in their databases that will help them better serve Wal-Mart's needs, excluding any data about their competitors. This allows the suppliers to gauge how well a product is selling in every Wal-Mart store in the world. Wal-Mart and its suppliers can maximize sales by stocking and promoting items that are selling well. Customers are satisfied because the items they want are almost always available.

Purpose of the Output

Whether presented in the form of paper reports or displayed on a computer screen, information is typically produced for a specific purpose. Two of the more important categories of financial information are financial statements and managerial reports. External users are provided with financial statements to meet stewardship requirements and to provide the information needed to make decisions, such as whether to loan money to an organization or invest in it. Internal users also use the financial statements produced by the AIS. We do not discuss financial statements as your other accounting and finance courses focus on financial statements in great detail.

An organization's AIS must also provide managers with detailed operational information to plan, manage, control, and evaluate company performance. For planning purposes, management needs information about such things as inventory status, relative profitability of products, sales forecasts, and new product revenue and cost estimates. They also need **budgets**, which are formal expressions of goals in financial terms. One of the most common and important types of budgets is the **cash budget**

that shows projected cash inflows and outflows. This information is especially important to a small business, because cash flow problems are a principal cause of small-business failures. A cash budget can provide advance warning of cash flow problems in time to permit corrective action to be taken.

To help effectively manage day-to-day operations, management needs information on business matters such as production and delivery schedules, open purchase orders, and inventory stock status reports.

For control purposes, an organization must constantly monitor its progress so that problems can be corrected as soon as possible. Often, monitoring is done using **performance reports** that compare standard, or expected, performances with actual performance. Since budgeted amounts are estimates, there are almost certain to be variances for each item in the performance report. Therefore, the principle of management by exception is used to interpret those variances. If actual performance is at or near budgeted figures, a manager can assume the item is under control and no action is needed. On the other hand, significant deviations from budgeted amounts signal the need to investigate the cause of the discrepancy and take whatever action is appropriate to correct the problem. Examples of performance reports include comparisons of standard and actual production rates, materials use, labor efficiency, profitability, and sales.

For evaluation purposes, it is important for the AIS to store information about both traditional financial measures and operational data. To improve the evaluation process, corporate accountants must know how to organize existing internal company data and present them in a manner that sheds new light on operational results. They must also collect important data from external sources. For example, companies regularly survey their customers or hire market research firms to collect that data. It is important to design the AIS so that such externally generated data are integrated with internally generated measures in a manner that facilitates the preparation of reports based on both kinds of data. Examples of evaluation reports are comparisons of the relative performance of each salesperson, data on how well an organization meets its delivery commitments, and how satisfied its customers are.

Behavioral Implications of Managerial Reports

Employees focus their efforts primarily on those tasks that are measured and evaluated. This can be either good or bad, depending on the nature of the relationship between the behavior being measured and the organization's overall goals. To illustrate, consider the task of customer complaint resolution. The organization wants to satisfy its customers to the greatest extent possible, at the lowest possible cost. If customer service representatives are evaluated solely in terms of the number of complaints resolved per unit of time, however, two types of problems may arise: the customer service representatives may be so focused on quickly resolving each complaint in the store's favor that they alienate some customers in the process, or customer service representatives may "give away the store" just to appease and please every customer with a complaint.

Budgets can often result in dysfunctional behavior. For example, if a budget does not include all the funds required to purchase the equipment needed to meet performance goals, then managers may be tempted to rent the equipment. This solution might allow them to meet their performance targets and remain within budget but may end up costing the company more than it would have spent to purchase the equipment outright.

Indeed, the budgeting process itself can be dysfunctional. Management may expend a great deal of effort in "number crunching," trying to get the budget numbers to turn out as desired, rather than focusing on how to accomplish the organization's mission and goals.

We have presented several examples of how reports produced by the AIS can unintentionally result in dysfunctional behavior. The key point to remember is that the AIS does not "neutrally" report on employee performance. Rather, it directly affects behavior.

Role of the AIS

Traditionally, the AIS has been referred to as a transaction processing system because its only concern was financial data and accounting transactions. For example, when a sale took place, the AIS would record a journal entry showing only the date of the sale, a debit to either cash or accounts receivable, and a credit to sales. Other potentially useful nonfinancial information about the sale, such as the time of day that it occurred, would traditionally be collected and processed outside of the AIS. Consequently, many organizations developed additional information systems to collect, process, store, and report information not contained in the AIS. Unfortunately, the existence of multiple systems creates numerous problems and inefficiencies. Often the same data must be captured and stored by more than one system, which not only results in redundancy across systems but also can lead to discrepancies if data are changed in one system but not in others. In addition, it is difficult to effectively integrate data from the various systems.

Enterprise resource planning (ERP) systems are designed to overcome these problems as they integrate all aspects of a company's operations with its traditional AIS. Thus, when the sales force enters an order, the effect of the transaction automatically flows to all affected parts of the company. Inventory is updated, production schedules are adjusted, and purchase orders are initiated to acquire any needed raw materials and supplies. Moreover, important nonfinancial data, such as the time the activity occurred, is collected and stored in the same system.

A key feature of ERP systems is the integration of financial with other nonfinancial operating data. The value of such integration suggests that there may be strategic benefits to more closely linking the traditionally separate functions of information systems and accounting, and many organizations are beginning to combine these two functions. The importance of this trend is reflected in the fact that some universities have merged their accounting and information systems departments.

 ## SUMMARY AND CASE CONCLUSION

Ashton reflected on the steps he had followed to guide his selection of accounting software. He had begun by obtaining an understanding of S&S's basic business activities and of the key decisions that Scott and Susan would need to make to operate the business effectively. He followed that with an analysis of the internal and external parties that the AIS would have to interact with and the information the AIS would have to provide them.

Since S&S is a retail merchandising company, its business processes could be described in terms of four basic transaction cycles:

1 The *revenue cycle* encompasses all transactions involving sales to customers and the collection of cash receipts for those sales.
2 The *expenditure cycle* encompasses all transactions involving the purchase of and payment for the merchandise sold by S&S, as well as other services it consumes, such as rent and utilities.
3 The *human resources/payroll cycle* encompasses all the transactions involving the hiring, training, and payment of employees.
4 The *financing cycle* encompasses all transactions involving the investment of capital in the company, borrowing money, payment of interest, and loan repayments.

These four cycles interface with the *general ledger and reporting system*, which consists of all activities related to the preparation of financial statements and other managerial reports.

Ashton knew that Scott and Susan planned to open additional stores in the near future and also wanted to develop a Web site to conduct business over the Internet. Based on this information, Ashton will select an accounting package that will satisfy

S&S's current and anticipated future needs. The software should be able to take care of all data processing and data storage tasks. Ashton will also make sure that the software can interface with the source data automation devices he wants to use to capture most data input. The software must be capable of producing a full set of financial reports and be flexible enough to produce other useful information the company will need to be successful. Finally, Ashton realized his next step would be to select the software and produce some documentation of how the system worked.

KEY TERMS

transaction 52
transaction processing 52
give-get exchange 52
business or transaction
 cycle 52
revenue cycle 53
expenditure cycle 53
production cycle 53
human resources/payroll
 cycle 53
financing cycle 53
general ledger and
 reporting system 53
data processing cycle 57
source documents 57
turnaround documents 57
source data
 automation 58

general ledger 59
subsidiary ledger 59
control account 59
coding 59
sequence code 59
block code 59
group code 59
chart of accounts 60
general journal 62
specialized journal 62
audit trail 64
entity 64
attribute 64
field 64
record 65
data value 65
file 65
master file 65

transaction file 65
database 65
batch processing 65
online, real-time
 processing 65
document 66
operational document 66
report 67
query 68
budget 68
cash budget 68
performance reports 69
enterprise resource
 planning (ERP)
 systems 70

AIS IN ACTION

CHAPTER QUIZ

1 Which transaction cycle includes interactions between an organization and its suppliers?
 a. revenue cycle
 b. expenditure cycle
 c. human resources/payroll cycle
 d. general ledger and reporting system

2 All of the information (name, GPA, major, etc.) about a particular student is stored in which of the following?
 a. file
 b. record
 c. attribute
 d. field

3 Which of the following would contain the total value of all inventory owned by an organization?
 a. source document
 b. general ledger
 c. cash budget

4 Which of the following is most likely to be a general ledger control account?
 a. accounts receivable
 b. petty cash
 c. prepaid rent
 d. retained earnings

5 Which of the following is the most useful for projecting the need for short-term borrowing?
 a. income statement
 b. performance report
 c. cash budget
 d. balance sheet

6 What report expresses goals in financial terms?
 a. performance report
 b. financial statement
 c. budget
 d. chart of accounts

7 How does the chart of accounts list general ledger accounts?
 a. alphabetical order
 b. chronological order
 c. size order
 d. the order in which they appear in financial statements

8 In which cycle does a company ship goods to customers?
 a. production cycle
 b. financing cycle
 c. revenue cycle
 d. expenditure cycle

9 What are records of company data sent to an external party and then returned to the system as input called?
 a. turnaround documents
 b. source data automation documents
 c. source documents
 d. external input documents

10 Recording and processing information about a transaction at the time it takes place is referred to as which of the following?
 a. batch processing
 b. online, real-time processing
 c. captured transaction processing
 d. chart of accounts processing

DISCUSSION QUESTIONS

2.1 Examine Table 2-1 and discuss how the various information needs would be collected and reported by a company's AIS.

2.2 Many restaurants use customer checks with prenumbered sequence codes. Each food server is given a packet of these checks on which to write up customer orders. Food servers are told not to destroy any customer checks; if a mistake is made, they are to void that check and write a new one. All voided checks are to be turned in to the manager daily. How does this policy help the restaurant control cash receipts?

2.3 How does an organization's line of business affect the design of its AIS? Give several examples of how differences among organizations are reflected in their AISs.

2.4 At most movie theaters, one employee is usually responsible for issuing tickets and collecting cash while another person collects those tickets when patrons enter the theater. What is the reason for this practice?

2.5 Some individuals argue that accountants should focus on producing financial statements and leave the design and production of managerial reports to information systems specialists. What are the advantages and disadvantages of following this advice? To what extent should accountants be involved in producing reports that include more than just financial measures of performance? Why?

PROBLEMS

2.1 The chart of accounts must be tailored to an organization's specific needs. Discuss how the chart of accounts for the following organizations would differ from the one presented for S&S in Table 2-4.
 a. university
 b. bank
 c. government unit (city or state)
 d. manufacturing company
 e. expansion of S&S to a chain of 23 stores

2.2 Ollie Mace has recently been appointed controller of S. Dilley & Company, a family-owned manufacturing firm founded 28 years ago. The firm manufactures automotive parts. Its four major operating divisions are heat treating, extruding, small parts stamping, and machining. Last year's sales from each division ranged from $150,000 to over $3,000,000. Each division is physically and managerially independent, except for the constant surveillance of S. Dilley, the firm's founder.

The accounting system for each division has evolved according to its needs and the abilities of its accounting staff. Mace is the first controller in the firm's history to have responsibility for overall financial management. Dilley expects to retire in a few years and wants Mace to improve the AIS before he retires so that it will be easier to monitor performance in each division.

Mace decides to redesign the financial reporting system to include the following features:
 ● It should give managers uniform, timely, and accurate reports of business activity. Monthly reports should be uniform across divisions and be completed by the fifth of the following month to provide enough time to take corrective actions to affect the next month's performance. Company-wide financial reports should be available at the same time.
 ● Reports should provide a basis for measuring the return on investment for each division. Thus, in addition to revenue and expense accounts, reports should show assets assigned to each division.
 ● The system should generate meaningful budget data for planning and decision-making purposes. Budgets should reflect managerial responsibility and show costs for major product groups.

Mace believes that a new chart of accounts is required to accomplish these goals. He wants to divide asset accounts into six major categories, such as current assets and plant and equipment. He does not foresee a need for more than 10 control accounts within each of these categories. From his observations to date, 100 subsidiary accounts are more than adequate for each control account.

No division now has more than five major product groups. Mace foresees a maximum of six cost centers within any product group, including both the operating and nonoperating groups. He views general divisional costs as a non-revenue-producing product group. Altogether, Mace estimates that approximately 44 expense accounts plus 12 specific variance accounts would be adequate.

Required

Design a chart of accounts for S. Dilley & Company. Explain how you structured the chart of accounts to meet the company's needs and operating characteristics. Keep total account code length to a minimum, while still satisfying all of Mace's desires.

(CMA Examination, adapted)

2.3 An audit trail enables a person to trace a source document to its ultimate effect on the financial statements or work back from amounts in the financial statements to source documents. Describe in detail the audit trail for the following:
 a. Purchases of inventory
 b. Sales of inventory
 c. Employee payroll

2.4 Assume that you have purchased a small retail nursery. Your nursery sells various types and sizes of trees, bedding plants, vegetable plants, and shrubs. It also sells fertilizer and potting soil. Based on what you have learned from the chapter, design a coding scheme for your nursery.

2.5 Search popular business magazines (*Business Week, Fortune, Forbes*) for an article that describes a dysfunctional behavior resulting from a poorly designed managerial reporting and performance evaluation system. Write a two-page report summarizing the problem and explaining how the managerial report led to the unplanned (and undesired) behavior.

2.6 Shauna Washington started a business to sell art supplies and related curricula to home school families. The business grew quickly, with sales doubling three times during a five-year period. At that point, she sold the business because it had grown too large to manage from her home. Under the new owners, sales doubled again during the next two years. Profits, however, did not keep pace with sales. In addition, the firm had borrowed heavily to open a warehouse. Inventory costs and operating expenses at the warehouse were higher than anticipated, and the monthly payments on the loan were proving to be burdensome. Recently, the number and amount of past due accounts have risen dramatically. Together, these problems have created a severe cash flow problem. If the cash flow situation does not improve quickly, the firm may have to declare bankruptcy, even though sales are continuing to increase.

Required

Describe some of the information that a good AIS could have provided for this firm and that, if provided in a timely manner, could have helped it avoid some of its problems.

2.7 Classify each of the following items as belonging in the revenue, expenditure, human resources/payroll, production, or financing cycle.
 a. Purchase raw materials
 b. Pay off mortgage on a factory
 c. Hire a new assistant controller
 d. Establish a $10,000 credit limit for customer XYZ Company
 e. Pay for raw materials
 f. Disburse payroll checks to factory workers
 g. Record goods received from vendor
 h. Update the allowance for doubtful accounts

 i. Decide how many units to make next month
 j. Complete picking ticket for goods ordered by a customer
 k. Record factory employee timecards
 l. Sell concert tickets
 m. Draw on line of credit
 n. Send new employees to a business ethics course
 o. Pay utility bills
 p. Pay property taxes on office building
 q. Pay federal payroll taxes
 r. Sell DVD player
 s. Collect payment on customer accounts
 t. Obtain a bank loan
 u. Pay sales commissions
 v. Send an order to a vendor
 w. Put purchased goods into the warehouse

2.8 Identify whether the following transactions belong in a master file or a transaction file.
 a. Update customer address change
 b. Update unit pricing information
 c. Record daily sales
 d. Record payroll checks
 e. Change employee pay rates
 f. Record production run variances
 g. Record sales commissions
 h. Change employee office location
 i. Update accounts payable balance
 j. Update the accounts receivable balance
 k. Change vendor payment discount terms
 l. Record purchases

2.9 You have been hired to assist Ashton Fleming in designing an accounting system for S&S. Ashton has developed a list of the journals, ledgers, reports, and documents that he thinks S&S needs (see Table 2-6). He asks you to complete the following tasks:
 1 Specify what data you think should be collected on each of the following documents:
 a. sales invoice
 b. purchase order
 c. receiving report
 d. employee time card
 2 Design a report to manage inventory.
 3 Design a report to assist in managing credit sales and cash collections.
 4 Visit a local office supply store and identify what types of journals, ledgers, and blank forms for various documents (sales invoices, purchase orders, etc.) are available. Describe how easily they could be adapted to meet S&S's needs.

2.10 On the following Web sites you will find several online demonstrations for the SAP and Oracle ERP systems. Visit these Web sites and explore their content by doing the following:
 a. The SAP Web site is www.sap.com/solutions. Watch the video and explore any of the other enterprise applications of interest. Click on mySAP ERP and watch one or more of the video demos and read several of the articles, such as the customer successes. Click on mySAP ERP Financials and watch one or more of the demos and read several of the articles.
 b. The Oracle Web site is www.oracle.com/solutions/mid/demo.html. Explore the Web site like you explored the SAP site.

Table 2-6

Documents, Journals, and Ledgers for S&S

Title	Purpose
Documents	
Sales Invoice	Record cash and credit sales of merchandise
Service Invoice	Record sales of repair services
Delivery Ticket	Record delivery of merchandise to customers
Monthly Statement	Inform customers of outstanding account balances
Credit Memo	Support adjustments to customer accounts for sales returns & allowances and sales discounts; also support write-off of uncollectible accounts
Purchase Order	Order merchandise from vendors
Receiving Report	Record receipt of merchandise from vendors, indicating both quantity and condition of items received
Time Card	Record time worked by employees
Specialized Journals	
Sales	Record all credit sales
Cash Receipts	Record cash sales, payments from customers, and other cash receipts
Purchases	Record all purchases from vendors
Cash Disbursements	Record all cash disbursements
General Journal	Record infrequent, nonroutine transactions; also record adjusting and closing entries.
Subsidiary Ledgers	
Accounts Receivable	Maintain details about amounts due from customers
Accounts Payable	Maintain details about amounts due to vendors
Inventory	Maintain details about each inventory item
Fixed Assets	Maintain details about each piece of equipment and other fixed assets
General Ledger	Maintain details about all major asset, liability, equity, revenue, and expense accounts

Required

After viewing the Web sites and based on your reading of the chapter, describe how an ERP can connect and integrate the revenue, expenditure, human resources/payroll, and financing cycles of a business.

2.11 For each of the following scenarios identify which data processing method (batch or online, real-time) would be the most appropriate.

 a. Make an airline reservation

 b. Register for a university course

 c. Prepare biweekly payroll

 d. Process an order through an e-commerce Web site

 e. Prepare a bank deposit

 f. Prepare customer bills for a local utility

 g. Accumulate costs from a production run of a single automobile part

 h. Identify the replacement drill bit size for a drill bit broken during a recent production run

Additional problems for this Chapter are available at the Web Site for this book. The Any Company Case can also be found on at the Web Site.

CASE 2-1 Bar Harbor Blueberry Farm

The Bar Harbor Blueberry Farm is a family-owned, 200-acre farm that grows and sells blueberries to grocery stores along the central coast, blueberry wholesalers, and small roadside stands. Bar Harbor has 25 full-time employees and usually hires 150 to 200 seasonal workers for the harvest.

For the past six summers, you have picked berries for Bar Harbor during the summer breaks from high school and college. Now that you have graduated with a degree in accounting, you were recently hired full-time as the farm accountant/office manager for Bar Harbor. Until now, Bar Harbor kept most of its accounting records in a big file box. Jack Phillips, the owner, would like a more organized approach to the farm's accounting records. He asked you to establish a proper set of books for the farm. Your first day on the job you find a stack of invoices from suppliers that need to be recorded. You decide to start by establishing appropriate journals and ledgers for these transactions.

The following are a set of vendor invoices and a few partially completed journals and ledgers. Your job is to record these transactions and update the appropriate ledgers. Be sure to leave a proper audit trail. You may also choose to use Excel, Great Plains, Peachtree, QuickBooks or another accounting software package of your choosing to complete this problem.

Vendor Invoices

DATE	SUPPLIER INVOICE	SUPPLIER NAME	SUPPLIER ADDRESS	AMOUNT
March 7	AJ34	Bud's Soil Prep, Inc.	PO Box 34	$2,067.85
March 11	14568	Osto Farmers Supply	45 Main	$ 67.50
March 14	893V	Whalers Fertilizer, Inc.	Route 34	$5,000.00
March 21	14699	Osto Farmers Supply	45 Main	$3,450.37
March 21	10102	IFM Package Wholesale	587 Longview	$4,005.00
March 24	10145	IFM Package Wholesale	587 Longview	$ 267.88

Purchases Journal

PAGE 1

DATE	SUPPLIER	SUPPLIER INVOICE	ACCOUNT NUMBER	POST REF	AMOUNT
March 7	Bud's Soil Prep, Inc.	AJ34			$2,067.85

General Ledger

ACCOUNTS PAYABLE				ACCOUNT NUMBER: 300	
DATE	DESCRIPTION	POST REF	DEBIT	CREDIT	BALANCE
March 1	Balance Forward				$18,735.55

General Ledger

PURCHASES					ACCOUNT NUMBER: 605
DATE	**DESCRIPTION**	**POST REF**	**DEBIT**	**CREDIT**	**BALANCE**
March 1	Balance Forward				$54,688.49

Accounts Payable Subsidiary Ledger

ACCOUNT NO: 23	BUD'S SOIL PREP, INC.	PO BOX 34		TERMS: 2/10, NET 30
DATE	**DESCRIPTION**	**DEBIT**	**CREDIT**	**BALANCE**

ACCOUNT NO: 24				TERMS: 2/10, NET 30
DATE	**DESCRIPTION**	**DEBIT**	**CREDIT**	**BALANCE**

ACCOUNT NO: 36				TERMS: 2/10, NET 30
DATE	**DESCRIPTION**	**DEBIT**	**CREDIT**	**BALANCE**

ACCOUNT NO: 38				TERMS: 2/10, NET 30
DATE	**DESCRIPTION**	**DEBIT**	**CREDIT**	**BALANCE**

AIS IN ACTION SOLUTIONS

1 Which transaction cycle includes interactions between an organization and its suppliers?
 a. revenue cycle [Incorrect. The revenue cycle involves interactions between an organization and its customers.]
 ✔ **b.** expenditure/payroll cycle [Correct.]
 c. human resources/payroll cycle [Incorrect. The human resources/payroll cycle involves interactions between an organization and its employees, government, and potential hires.]
 d. general ledger and reporting system [Incorrect. The general ledger and reporting system receives summary information from all cycles.]

2 All of the information (name, GPA, major, etc.) about a particular student is stored in which of the following?
 a. file [Incorrect. A file is designed to include information about many students.]
 ✔ **b.** record [Correct. A record should include all information maintained by the system about a particular entity such as a student.]
 c. attribute [Incorrect. An attribute is a descriptor or a characteristic of an entity—in this example the student's major is an attribute.]
 d. field [Incorrect. A field represents a data storage space—in this example an accounting student would have "Accounting" stored in the major field.]

3 Which of the following would contain the total value of all inventory owned by an organization?
 a. source document [Incorrect. A source document contains data about a particular event or transaction.]
 ✔ **b.** general ledger [Correct. The general ledger maintains summary information on inventory and every other general ledger account.]
 c. cash budget [Incorrect. A cash budget only provides information on projected cash inflows and outflows.]

4 Which of the following is most likely to be a general ledger control account?
 ✔ **a.** accounts receivable [Correct. Accounts receivable is typically comprised of many individual customer accounts maintained in a subsidiary ledger. The total of all individual customer accounts in the subsidiary ledger is maintained in the accounts receivable control account in the general ledger.]
 b. petty cash [Incorrect. Petty cash is comprised of only one account.]
 c. prepaid rent [Incorrect. A subsidiary ledger containing multiple prepaid rent accounts is usually not necessary.]
 d. retained earnings [Incorrect. Retained earnings is typically comprised of only one account.]

5 Which of the following is the most useful for projecting the need for short-term borrowing?
 a. income statement [Incorrect. The income statement measures earnings over a period of time irrespective of cash inflows and outflows.]
 b. performance report [Incorrect. A performance report measures outcomes according to prescribed criteria.]
 ✔ c. cash budget [Correct. The cash budget forecasts cash inflows and outflows and thus can be used to determine when outflows are likely to exceed inflows and require short-term borrowing.]
 d. balance sheet [Incorrect. The balance sheet presents the status of the permanent accounts as of a certain date.]

6 What report expresses goals in financial terms?
 a. performance report [Incorrect. A performance report measures outcomes according to prescribed criteria.]
 b. financial statement [Incorrect. The financial statement presents actual financial performance.]
 ✔ c. budget [Correct. A budget presents goals in financial terms.]
 d. chart of accounts [Incorrect. The chart of accounts is a listing of all general ledger accounts.]

7 How does the chart of accounts list general ledger accounts?
 a. alphabetical order [Incorrect. General ledger accounts are listed in the order they appear in the financial statements, not in alphabetical order.]
 b. chronological order [Incorrect. General ledger accounts are listed in the order they appear in the financial statements, not according to the date they were created.]
 c. size order [Incorrect. General ledger accounts are listed in the order they appear in the financial statements, not according to their size.]
 ✔ d. the order in which they appear in financial statements [Correct.]

8 In which cycle does a company ship goods to customers?
 a. production cycle [Incorrect. The production cycle involves the transformation of raw materials into finished goods.]
 b. financing cycle [Incorrect. The financing cycle deals with interactions between an organization and its lenders and owners.]
 ✔ c. revenue cycle [Correct. The revenue cycle involves interactions between an organization and its customers, such as shipping them goods.]
 d. expenditure cycle [Incorrect. The expenditure cycle involves interactions between an organization and its suppliers.]

9 What are records of company data sent to an external party and then returned to the system as input called?
 ✔ a. turnaround documents [Correct. Documents like a utility bill are sent to a customer, who then returns the bill with payment.]
 b. source data automation documents [Incorrect. Source data automation is capturing input data in machine readable form.]
 c. source documents [Incorrect. Source documents collect data about business activities.]
 d. external input documents [Incorrect. These documents originate from external sources.]

10 Recording and processing information about a transaction at the time it takes place is referred to as which of the following?

 a. batch processing [Incorrect. Batch processing involves processing transactions in groups or batches all at the same time.]

✔ **b.** online, real-time processing [Correct. Online, real-time processing involves processing transactions as they occur.]

 c. captured transaction processing [Incorrect. This is not a recognized transaction processing method.]

 d. chart of accounts processing [Incorrect. The chart of accounts, although typically updated every so often, is not a transaction processing method.]

CHAPTER 3

LEARNING OBJECTIVES

After studying this chapter, you should be able to:

- Prepare and use data flow diagrams to understand, evaluate, and design information systems.

- Prepare and use flowcharts to understand, evaluate, and design information systems.

Systems Development and Documentation Techniques

INTEGRATIVE CASE S&S, INC.

What a hectic few months it has been for Ashton Fleming! He has helped S&S get started, helped get S&S through its weeklong grand opening, and was swamped processing all the transactions from the highly successful opening. Because of its rapid growth, S&S has outgrown the initial rudimentary AIS that Ashton selected. Lacking time and expertise, Ashton has engaged Computer Applications (CA), a systems consulting firm, to help S&S select and install a new and more powerful AIS.

During Ashton's first meeting with Kimberly Serra, CA's manager, she asked about S&S's system requirements and management's expectations. Ashton had yet to think through these issues, so he could not answer her specifically. When she asked how S&S's system worked, Ashton plunged into a discussion about the use of various company documents, but Kimberly seemed unable to fully absorb his detailed explanations. Ashton thought that part of his discussion was helpful, but overall it was irrelevant to the issue at hand.

Ashton came away impressed by CA and Kimberly. He also realized the need to understand S&S's information requirements more clearly. From his days as an auditor, Ashton knew the value of good system documentation in assisting unfamiliar users with both understanding and evaluating a system. Good system documentation would be a big help to him and Kimberly, as well as to Scott and Susan as they evaluate the current and proposed systems.

After sharing his conclusions with Susan and Scott, Ashton's plan to document the current and proposed systems was well received. They supported his taking a leadership role in moving toward a new system and were especially interested in diagrams or charts that would help them understand how the system worked. Scott and Susan gave Ashton the following assignment:

1 What types of tools and techniques should S&S use to document its existing system so it is easy to understand and evaluate?
2 What development tools and techniques should S&S use to design its new computer-based information system?

Introduction

Documentation encompasses the narratives, flowcharts, diagrams, and other written materials that explain how a system works. This information covers the who, what, when, where, why, and how of data entry, processing, storage, information output, and system controls. Popular means of documenting a system include diagrams, flowcharts, tables, and other graphical representations of information. These are supplemented by a **narrative description** of the system, a written step-by-step explanation of system components and interactions. In this chapter we explain data flow diagrams and flowcharts, the most common systems documentation tools. These tools save an organization both time and money.

Depending on your job function, documentation tools are important on one or more of the following levels:

1 At a minimum, you must be able to *read* documentation to determine how the system works.
2 You may be required to *evaluate* internal control systems documentation to identify control strengths and weaknesses and recommend improvements. Alternatively, you may have to evaluate the documentation for a proposed system to determine if the system meets the company's needs.
3 The greatest amount of skill is needed to *prepare* documentation. If you are a member of a team that is developing a new system, then you must prepare documentation to show how both the existing and the proposed systems operate. Perhaps you will document your understanding of a company's system of internal controls for others to review.

This chapter discusses the following documentation tools:

1 **Data flow diagram (DFD),** a graphical description of the source and destination of data that shows data flow within an organization, the processes performed on the data, and how data are stored
2 **Document flowchart,** a graphical description of the flow of documents and information between departments or areas of responsibility within an organization
3 **System flowchart,** a graphical description of the relationship among the input, processing, and output in an information system
4 **Program flowchart,** a graphical description of the sequence of logical operations that a computer performs as it executes a program

Documentation techniques are used extensively by accountants. Statement on Auditing Standards (SAS) 94, "The Effect of Information Technology on the Auditor's Consideration of Internal Control in a Financial Statement Audit," requires that independent auditors understand the automated and manual internal control

procedures an entity uses. One of the best ways to gain this understanding is to use flowcharts to document the internal control system, as weaknesses and strengths are more easily spotted from such graphic portrayals.

The passage of the Sarbanes-Oxley Act (SOX) in 2002 made documentation skills even more important. The Sarbanes-Oxley Act requires management of public companies to include in its annual report an internal control report that (1) states that management is responsible for establishing and maintaining an adequate internal control structure and (2) assesses the effectiveness of the company's internal controls. SOX also specifies that a company's auditor must evaluate management's assessment of the company's internal control structures and attest to its accuracy. The auditor's attestation should include a specific notation about any significant defects or material noncompliance found during the internal control tests. In other words, both the company and its auditors have to document and test the company's internal controls. This means that company employees as well as auditors must be able to prepare, evaluate, and read different types of documentation, such as flowcharts.

These documentation tools are also used extensively in the systems development process. According to Microsoft, systems development is an extremely complex process, one that is far more complicated than building a Boeing 747. These tools are used to create order from chaos and complexity. In addition, the team members who develop information systems applications often change, and these documentation tools help the new team members get up to speed quickly.

According to one study, data flow diagrams and flowcharts are the two most frequently used systems development documentation tools. The study shows that 62.5% of information professionals use DFDs and that 97.6% use flowcharts. Over 92% of users were satisfied with the use of both DFDs and flowcharts and use both.

Both DFDs and flowcharts are easy to prepare and revise when a DFD or flowcharting software package is used. These packages are easier to use, in fact, than most word processors. Once a few basic commands are mastered, users can quickly and easily prepare, store, revise, and print presentation-quality DFDs or flowcharts. To create a flowchart, the user selects the appropriate symbol, indicates where it should be placed, enters the appropriate text, and moves to the next symbol. Editing a flowchart is easy; users merely click on the appropriate symbol and edit, delete, or move it.

The documentation tools explained in this chapter are used throughout the book. They are also tested on professional examinations—as you can see by noting the number of questions in this book that are adapted from these exams. Learning about these tools will better prepare you for these examinations.

Data Flow Diagrams

A **data flow diagram (DFD)** graphically describes the flow of data within an organization.[1] It is used to document existing systems and to plan and design new ones. There is no ideal way to develop a DFD, because different problems call for different methods.

Elements in a Data Flow Diagram

A DFD is composed of four basic elements: data sources and destinations, data flows, transformation processes, and data stores. Each is represented on a DFD by one of the symbols shown in Figure 3-1.

These four symbols are combined to show how data are processed. For example, the DFD in Figure 3-2 shows that the input to process C is data flow B, which comes from data source A. The outputs of process C are data flows D and E. Data flow E is

[1]Parts of this discussion are based on Tom DeMarco, *Structured Analysis and System Specification* (Upper Saddle River, NJ: Prentice Hall, 1979). DeMarco has been at the forefront of structural analysis and design techniques and is a well-respected authority on the subject.

Figure 3-1
Data Flow Diagram Symbols

Symbol	Name	Explanation
☐	Data sources and destinations	The people and organizations that send data to and receive data from the system are represented by square boxes. Data destinations are also referred to as data sinks.
↗	Data flows	The flow of the data into or out of a process is represented by curved or straight lines with arrows.
◯	Transformation processes	The processes that transform data from inputs to outputs are represented by circles. They are often referred to as bubbles.
──	Data stores	The storage of data is represented by two horizontal lines.

sent to data destination J. Process F uses data flows D and G as input and produces data flows I and G as output. Data flow G comes from and returns to data store H. Data flow I is sent to data destination K. Figure 3-3 assigns specific titles to each of the processes depicted in Figure 3-2. Figures 3-2 and 3-3 will be used to examine the four basic elements of a DFD in more detail.

Data Sources and Destinations

A source or destination symbol on the DFD represents an organization or individual that sends or receives data that the system uses or produces. An entity can be both a source and a destination. **Data sources** and **data destinations** are represented by squares, as illustrated by items A (customer), J (bank), and K (credit manager) in Figure 3-3.

Data Flows

A **data flow** represents the flow of data between processes, data stores, and data sources and destinations. Data that pass between data stores and either a data source or a destination must go through some form of data processing—that is, through a transformation process. Data flow arrows are labeled to indicate the type of data being passed. Thus, the reader knows exactly what information is flowing; no inferences are required. The only exception to this is data flows between a process and a data store, such as data flow G in Figure 3-3, because the data flow is usually obvious. In data flow G, for example, data from the accounts receivable file is retrieved, updated, and

Figure 3-2
Basic Data Flow Diagram
Elements

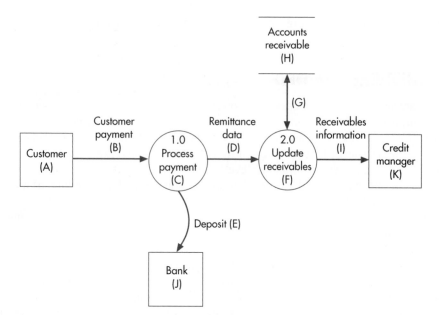

Figure 3-3
Data Flow Diagram of
Customer Payment Process

stored back in the file. Other data flows in Figure 3-3 are items B (customer payment), D (remittance data), E (deposit), and I (receivables information).

A data flow can consist of one or more pieces of datum. For example, data flow B (customer payment) consists of two parts: a payment and remittance data. Process 1.0 (process payment) splits these two data elements and sends them in different directions. The remittance data (D) flows to another process, where it is used to update accounts receivable records, and the payment (E) is sent to the bank with a deposit slip.

Because data flows may consist of more than one data element, the designer must determine the number of lines to show. The determining factor is if the data elements always flow together. For example, if customers sometimes send inquiries about the processing of their payments, the DFD could be revised as shown in Figure 3-4. The figure shows two lines because customer inquiries (L), although interacting with the same elements of the DFD, do not always accompany a payment. The two data elements have different purposes, and customer inquiries occur less frequently. If represented by the same data flow, the separate elements would be obscured, and the DFD would be more difficult to interpret.

Processes

Processes represent the transformation of data. Figure 3-3 shows that process payment (C) takes the customer payment and splits it into the remittance data and the deposit (which includes the check and deposit slip created within process payment). The update receivables (F) process takes the remittance data (D) and the accounts receivables file (H) data and produces an updated receivables record and sends receivables information to the credit manager.

Data Stores

A **data store** is a temporary or permanent repository of data. DFDs do not show the physical storage medium (such as disks and paper) used to store the data. As with the other DFD elements, data store names should be descriptive. As shown in Figure 3-3,

Figure 3-4
Splitting Customer Payments
and Inquiries

item H, data stores are represented by horizontal lines, with the respective name recorded inside.

Subdividing the DFD

DFDs are subdivided into successively lower levels to provide ever-increasing amounts of detail, because few systems can be fully diagrammed on one sheet of paper. Users have differing needs, so a variety of levels can better satisfy these requirements.

The highest-level DFD is referred to as a **context diagram**. A context diagram provides the reader with a summary-level view of a system. It depicts a data processing system and the external entities that are the sources and destinations of the system's inputs and outputs.

Figure 3-5 is the context diagram that Ashton Fleming drew when he was analyzing the payroll processing procedures at S&S. It shows that the payroll processing system receives time card data from different departments and employee data from the human resources department. When these data are processed, the system produces (1) tax reports and payments for governmental agencies, (2) employee pay checks, (3) a deposit in the payroll account at the bank, and (4) payroll information for management.

Ashton also wants to diagram the system's details, so he decides to decompose the context diagram into successively lower levels, each with an increasing amount of detail. In preparation, he wrote the narrative description of S&S's payroll processing procedures contained in Table 3-1. Take a few minutes to read this description and determine the following:

● How many major data processing activities are involved?
● What are the data inputs and outputs of each activity (ignoring all references to people, departments, and document destinations)?

Based on Ashton's description, you should have identified approximately five data processing activities. You may have noted more or fewer, depending on how you identified the activities. The first activity is updating the employee/payroll master file (first paragraph of the narrative). The second activity is handling employee compensation (second, fifth, and sixth paragraphs). Later in this chapter, you will see a breakdown of this activity into smaller parts in a lower-level DFD. A third activity is generating

Figure 3-5
Context Diagram for S&S
Payroll Processing

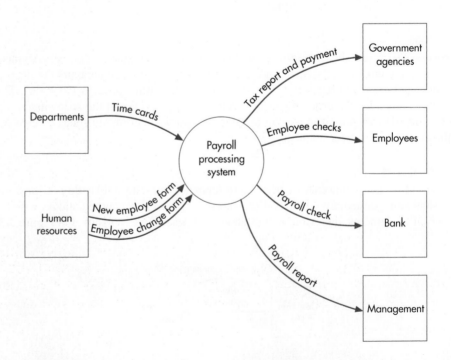

Table 3-1
Narrative Description of
Payroll Processing at S&S

When employees are hired, they complete a new-employee form. When a change to an employee's payroll status occurs, such as a raise or a change in the number of exemptions, human resources completes an employee change form. A copy of these forms is sent to payroll. These forms are used to create or update the records in the employee/payroll file and are then stored in the file. Employee records are stored alphabetically.

Some S&S employees are paid a salary, but most are hourly workers who record their time on time cards. At the end of each pay period, department managers send the time cards to the payroll department. The payroll clerk uses the time card data, data from the employee file (such as pay rate and annual salary), and the appropriate tax tables to prepare a two-part check for each employee. The clerk also prepares a two-part payroll register showing gross pay, deductions, and net pay for each employee. The clerk updates the employee file to reflect each employee's current earnings. The original copy of the employee paychecks is forwarded to Susan. The payroll register is forwarded to the accounts payable clerk. The time cards and the duplicate copies of the payroll register and paychecks are stored by date in the payroll file.

Every pay period the payroll clerk uses the data in the employee/payroll file to prepare a payroll summary report for Susan so that she can control and monitor labor expenses. This report is forwarded to Susan, with the original copies of the employee paychecks.

Every month the payroll clerk uses the data in the employee/payroll file to prepare a two-part tax report. The original is forwarded to the accounts payable clerk, and the duplicate is added to the tax records in the payroll file. The accounts payable clerk uses the tax report to prepare a two-part check for taxes and a two-part cash disbursements voucher. The tax report and the original copy of each document are forwarded to Susan. The duplicates are stored by date in the accounts payable file.

The accounts payable clerk uses the payroll register to prepare a two-part check for the total amount of the employee payroll and a two-part disbursements voucher. The original copy of each document is forwarded to Susan, and the payroll register and the duplicates are stored by date in the accounts payable file.

Susan reviews each packet of information she receives and approves and signs the checks. She forwards the cash disbursements vouchers to Ashton, the tax reports and payments to the appropriate governmental agency, the payroll check to the bank, and the employee checks to the employees. She files the payroll report chronologically.

Ashton uses the payroll tax and the payroll check cash disbursement vouchers to update the general ledger. He then cancels the journal voucher by marking it "posted" and files it numerically.

management reports (third paragraph). A fourth activity is paying taxes (fourth paragraph), and a fifth is posting entries to the general ledger (last paragraph). All data inflows and outflows, and the five activities, form the basis of the DFD as summarized in Table 3-2.

Using this information, Ashton exploded his context diagram and created the Level 0 DFD (called level 0 because there are zero meaningful deci mal points—1.0, 2.0, etc.) shown in Figure 3-6. Notice that some data inputs and outputs have been excluded from this DFD. For example, in process 2.0, the data inflows and outflows that are not related to an external entity or to another process are not depicted (tax tables and payroll register in this case). These data flows are internal to the "pay employees" activity and are shown on the next DFD level.

Not fully satisfied with the level of detail he had captured, Ashton exploded process 2.0 (pay employees) to create a Level 1 DFD (so called because it has one meaningful decimal place—2.1, 2.2, etc.). Figure 3-7 provides more detail about the data processes involved in paying employees, and it includes the tax rates table and the payroll register data flow omitted from Figure 3-6. In a similar fashion, each of the processes shown in Figure 3-6 could be exploded, using a Level 1 DFD, to show a greater level of detail.

Some general guidelines for developing DFDs are shown in Focus 3-1.

Table 3-2
Activities and Data Flows in
Payroll Processing at S&S

Activities	Data Inputs	Data Outputs
Update employee/ payroll file	New employee form Employee change form Employee/payroll file	Updated employee/payroll file
Pay employees	Time cards Employee/payroll file Tax rates table	Employee checks Payroll register Updated employee/payroll file Payroll check Payroll cash disbursements voucher
Prepare reports	Employee/payroll file	Payroll report
Pay taxes	Employee/payroll file	Tax report Tax payment Payroll tax cash disbursements voucher Updated employee/payroll file
Update general ledger	Payroll tax cash disbursements voucher Payroll cash disbursements voucher	Updated general ledger

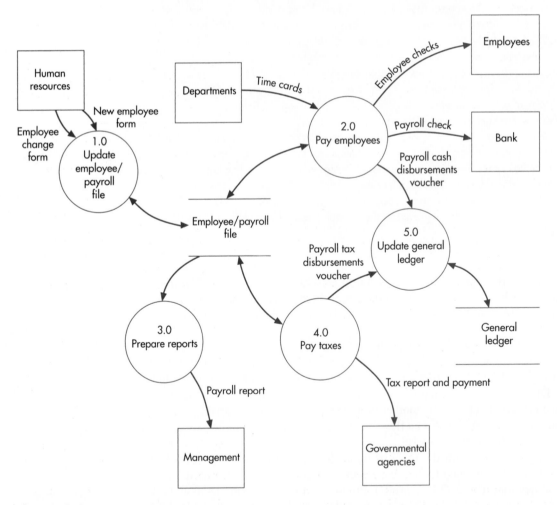

Figure 3-6
Level 0 DFD for S&S payroll processing

Guidelines for Drawing a DFD

1 **Understand the system.** To understand how the system works, observe the flow of information through an organization and interview the individuals who use and process the data.

2 **Ignore certain aspects of the system.** The purpose of a DFD is to diagram the origins, flow, transformation, storage, and destinations of data. Therefore, all control processes and control actions should be ignored. Only very important error paths should be included in the DFD. The details of unimportant error paths should be ignored. Determining how the system starts and stops is usually deferred to a later stage in the development process.

3 **Determine system boundaries.** Determine what to include in and exclude from the system. Include all relevant data elements in the DFD, because excluded items will not be considered during system development. When in doubt about an element's importance, include it until a definitive decision can be made to discard it.

4 **Develop a context diagram.** A context diagram is a good way of depicting system boundaries. In the diagram's center is a circle; inside of it is displayed the system of concern. The outside entities, with which the system interacts directly, are in boxes on either side, connected by data flows depicting the data passed between them. (See Figure 3-5 and its attendant discussion.) DFDs are prepared, in successively more detail, to depict data flows in the system.

5 **Identify data flows.** Identify all data flows entering or leaving the system's boundary, including where the data originate and the final destination. Any significant movement of information is usually a data flow. All data flows come from and go to either a transformation process, a data store (file), or a data source or destination. As each of these is identified, it should be connected to the appropriate data flow. Data flows can move in two directions, shown as a line with arrows on both ends (see G in Figure 3-3).

6 **Group data flows.** A data flow can consist of one or more pieces of datum. Data elements that always flow together should be grouped together and shown as one data flow until they are separated. If the data elements do not always flow together, then they should be shown as two separate data flows.

7 **Identify transformation processes.** Place a circle wherever work is required to transform one data flow into another. All transformation processes should have one or more incoming and outgoing data flows.

8 **Group transformation processes.** Transformation processes that are logically related or occur at the same time and place should be grouped together. Never combine unrelated items into a single transformation process. If data are not processed together, or are sometimes processed differently, then separate them.

9 **Identify all files or data stores.** Data are stored temporarily or permanently in most systems. Each data repository, and each data flow into and out of it, should be identified.

10 **Identify all data sources and destinations.** All sources and destinations of data should be identified and included on the DFD.

11 **Name all DFD elements.** Except for data flows into or out of data stores (the data store name is usually sufficient to identify the data flow), data elements should be given unique and descriptive names representing what is known about them. This makes a DFD easier to read and understand as it provides the reader with key information. Naming data flows first forces the developer to concentrate on the all-important data flows, rather than on the processes or stores. Once data flows have been labeled, naming the processes and data stores is usually easy, because they typically take their names from the data inflows or outflows. Choose active and descriptive names, such as "update inventory" and "validate transaction," rather than "input data" or "update process." Process names should include action verbs such as update, edit, prepare, reconcile, and record.

12 **Subdivide the DFD.** A cluttered DFD is hard to read and understand. If you have more than five to seven processes on a single page, then use higher-level and lower-level DFDs. Decompose the context diagram into high-level processes, and then explode these high-level processes into successively lower-level processes. This process is explained in greater detail in this chapter.

13 **Give each process a sequential number.** In a completed DFD, as shown in Figures 3-6 and 3-7, each process is given a sequential number that helps readers move back and forth between the different DFD levels. Data flows should usually go from lower-numbered to higher-numbered processes.

14 **Repeat the process.** DFD developers must work through organization data flows several times. Each subsequent pass helps refine the diagram and identify the fine points. As you refine the DFD, organize it to flow from top to bottom and from left to right.

15 **Prepare a final copy.** Draw a final copy of the DFD. Do not allow data flow lines to cross over each other; if necessary, repeat a data store or destination. Place the name of the DFD, the date prepared, and the preparer's name on each page.

Figure 3-7
Level 1 DFD for Process 2.0 in
S&S Payroll Processing

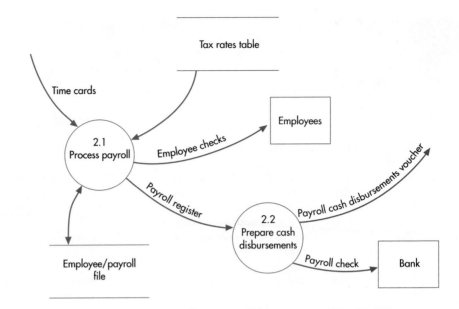

Flowcharts

A **flowchart** is an analytical technique used to describe some aspect of an information system in a clear, concise, and logical manner. Flowcharts use a standard set of symbols to describe pictorially the transaction processing procedures a company uses and the flow of data through a system.

Flowchart Symbols

The symbols used to create flowcharts are shown in Figure 3-8. Each symbol has a special meaning that is easily conveyed by its shape. The shape indicates and describes the operations performed and the input, output, processing, and storage media employed.

Flowcharting was introduced by industrial engineers in the 1950s as a way of (1) recording how business processes are performed and documents flow and (2) analyzing how to improve processes and document flows. Soon internal auditors began using flowcharts in operational audits to understand better their company's business processes. Later, external auditors began using flowcharts to evaluate their clients' internal controls. Good controls are relied upon to produce accurate numbers and allow auditors to reduce the number of transactions they audit.

The Sarbanes-Oxley Act requires companies to document their business processes and internal controls. Most companies use flowcharting to do this because it provides significant advantages. A flowchart is a pictorial representation that is much easier to understand than a narrative description. It is also likely to be more complete, as flows have to be evident and accounted for. Both the auditor and the business owner can also use the flowchart as a working tool during discussions. For an experienced flowcharter using a computerized drawing tool, flowcharts provide an easy way to capture and record data during interviews and can be easily and quickly revised.

Flowcharts do have some disadvantages. Some people do not like or understand them. Many are poorly drawn and therefore not as helpful as they should be. They are time-consuming to prepare if the flowcharter is not trained properly.

In the early days of flowcharts, the symbols were drawn using a **flowcharting template**, a piece of hard, flexible plastic on which the shapes of symbols have been die cut. Most flowcharts are now drawn using a software program. An example is Visio, a drawing package based on the green plastic flowchart templates. Flowcharts can also be drawn using Microsoft Word, Excel, or PowerPoint.

Flowcharting symbols can be divided into the following four categories, as shown in Figure 3-8:

1 **Input/output symbols** represent devices or media that provide input to or record output from processing operations.

Figure 3-8
Common flowcharting symbols

Symbol	Name	Explanation
Input/output symbols		
	Document	A document or report.
	Multiple copies of one document	Illustrated by overlapping the document symbol and printing the document number on the face of the document in the upper right corner
	Input/output; Journal/ledger	Any input or output function on a program flowchart. Also used to represent accounting journals and ledgers in a document flowchart
	Display	Information displayed by an online output device such as a terminal, monitor, or screen
	Online keying	Data entry by online devices such as a terminal or personal computer
	Terminal or personal computer	The display and online keying symbols are used together to represent terminals, personal computers, and other electronic devices capable of both input and output.
	Transmittal tape	Manually prepared control totals; used for control purposes to compare to computer-generated totals
Processing Symbols		
	Computer processing	A computer-performed processing function; usually results in a change in data or information
	Manual operation	A processing operation performed manually
	Auxiliary operation	A processing function performed by a device that is not a computer
	Off-line keying	An operation utilizing an off-line keying operation device (e.g., key to disk, cash register)
Storage Symbols		
	Magnetic disk/drive	Data stored on a magnetic disk or drive
	Magnetic tape	Data stored on a magnetic tape

(continued)

Figure 3-8
(continued)

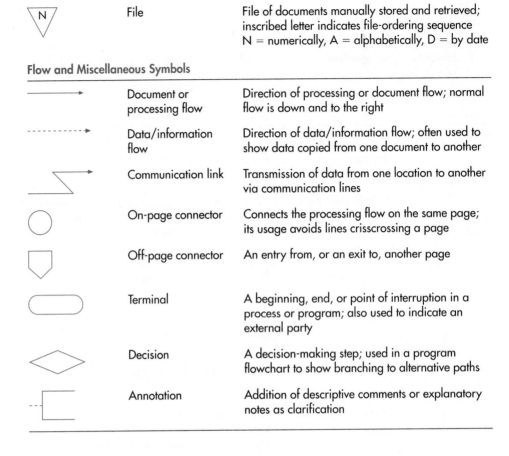

| | File | File of documents manually stored and retrieved; inscribed letter indicates file-ordering sequence N = numerically, A = alphabetically, D = by date |

Flow and Miscellaneous Symbols

	Document or processing flow	Direction of processing or document flow; normal flow is down and to the right
	Data/information flow	Direction of data/information flow; often used to show data copied from one document to another
	Communication link	Transmission of data from one location to another via communication lines
	On-page connector	Connects the processing flow on the same page; its usage avoids lines crisscrossing a page
	Off-page connector	An entry from, or an exit to, another page
	Terminal	A beginning, end, or point of interruption in a process or program; also used to indicate an external party
	Decision	A decision-making step; used in a program flowchart to show branching to alternative paths
	Annotation	Addition of descriptive comments or explanatory notes as clarification

2 **Processing symbols** either show what type of device is used to process data or indicate when processing is performed manually.

3 **Storage symbols** represent the device used to store data that the system is not currently using.

4 **Flow and miscellaneous symbols** indicate the flow of data and goods. They also represent such operations as where flowcharts begin or end, where decisions are made, and when to add explanatory notes to flowcharts.

Document Flowcharts

A **document flowchart** illustrates the flow of documents and information among areas of responsibility within an organization. Document flowcharts trace a document from its cradle to its grave. They show where each document originates, its distribution, the purposes for which it is used, its ultimate disposition, and everything that happens as it flows through the system.

A document flowchart is particularly useful in analyzing the adequacy of control procedures in a system, such as internal checks and segregation of functions. Document flowcharts that describe and evaluate internal controls are often referred to as **internal control flowcharts**. The document flowchart can reveal weaknesses or inefficiencies in a system, such as inadequate communication flows, unnecessary complexity in document flows, or procedures responsible for causing wasteful delays. Document flowcharts also can be prepared as part of the systems design process and should be included in the documentation of an information system.

The document flowchart that Ashton developed for the payroll process at S&S, as described in Table 3-2, is shown in Figure 3-9.

General guidelines for preparing flowcharts that are readable, clear, concise, consistent, and understandable are presented in Focus 3-2 (see page 95).

.3-2 FOCUS Guidelines for Preparing Flowcharts

1 Understand a system before flowcharting it. Interview users, developers, auditors, and management, or have them complete a questionnaire. Read through a narrative description of the system, or walk through system transactions.

2 Identify the entities to be flowcharted, such as departments, job functions, or external parties. Identify documents and information flows in the system, as well as the activities or processes performed on the data. (For example, when reading a description of the system, the preparer could draw a box around the entities, a circle around the documents, and a line under the activities.)

3 When several entities, such as departments or functions, need to be shown on a flowchart, divide the flowchart into columns with a label for each. Flowchart the activities of each entity in its respective column.

4 Flowchart only the normal flow of operations, ensuring that all procedures and processes are in the proper order. Identify exception procedures by using the annotation symbol.

5 Design the flowchart so that flow proceeds from top to bottom and from left to right.

6 Give the flowchart a clear beginning and ending. Designate where each document originated, and show the final disposition of all documents so there are no loose ends that leave the reader dangling.

7 Use the standard flowcharting symbols, and draw them with a template or a computer.

8 Clearly label all symbols. Write a description of the input, process, or output inside the symbol. If the description will not fit, use the annotation symbol. Print neatly, rather than writing in cursive.

9 When using multiple copies of a document, place document numbers in the top right-hand corner of the symbol. The document number should accompany the symbol as it moves through the system.

10 Each manual processing symbol should have an input and an output. Do not directly connect two documents, except when moving from one column to another. When a document is moved to another column, it is often best to show the document in both.

11 Use on-page connectors to avoid excess flow lines, which results in a neat-looking page. Use off-page connectors to move from one flowchart page to another. Clearly label all connectors to avoid confusion.

12 Use arrowheads on all flow lines. Do not assume that the reader will know the direction of the flow.

13 If a flowchart cannot fit on a single page, clearly label the pages 1 of 3, 2 of 3, and so on.

14 Show documents or reports first in the column in which they are created. They can then be shown moving to another column for further processing. A manual process is not needed to show documents being forwarded.

15 Show all data entered into or retrieved from a computer file as passing through a processing operation (a computer program) first.

16 Draw a line from a document to a file to indicate that it is being filed. A manual process is not needed to show a document entering a file.

17 Draw a rough sketch of the flowchart as a first effort. Be more concerned with capturing content than a perfect drawing. Few systems can be flowcharted in a single draft.

18 Redesign the flowchart to avoid clutter and a large number of crossed lines.

19 Verify the flowchart's accuracy by reviewing it with the people familiar with the system. Be sure all uses of flowcharting conventions are consistent.

20 Draw a final copy of the flowchart. Place the name of the flowchart, the date, and the preparer's name on each page.

System Flowcharts

System flowcharts depict the relationships among the input, processing, and output of an AIS. A system flowchart begins by identifying the inputs that enter the system and their origins. The input can be new data entering the system, data stored for future use, or both. The input is followed by the processing portion of the flowchart—that is, the steps performed on the data. The logic the computer uses to perform the processing task is shown on a program flowchart. The resulting new information is the output component, which can be stored for later use, displayed on a screen, or printed on paper. In many instances, the output from one process is an input to another.

The sales processing system flowchart in Figure 3-10 represents Ashton's proposal to capture sales data using state-of-the-art sales terminals. These terminals will edit the sales data and print a customer receipt. All sales data will be stored in a sales

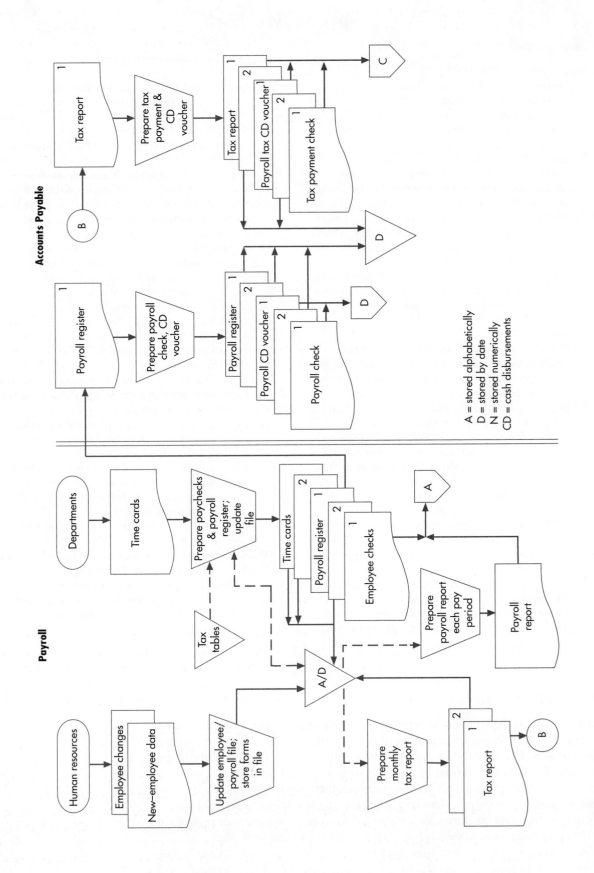

Figure 3-9
Document Flowchart of Payroll Processing at S&S

Figure 3-9
(continued)

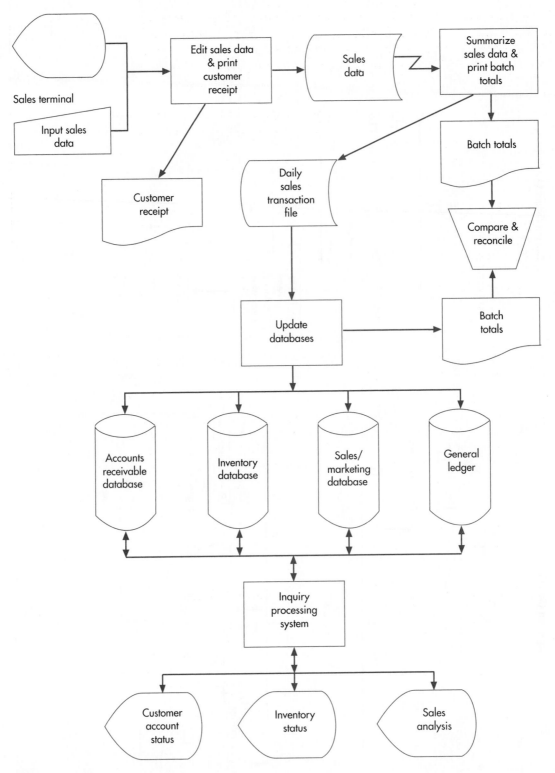

Figure 3-10
System Flowchart of Sales Processing at S&S

data file on a disk. At the end of each day, the data will be forwarded to S&S's computers, where it will be summarized and batch totals will be printed. A batch total is the sum of a numerical item contained in each transaction being processed. An example is total sales for all sales transactions. The summary data will then be processed, and batch totals will again be generated and printed. These amounts will be compared

with the batch totals generated prior to processing, and all errors and exceptions will be reconciled. The accounts receivable, inventory, and sales marketing databases and the general ledger will be updated. Users can access the files at any time by using an inquiry processing system. This system will produce standard reports and allow users to access the data needed for special analyses.

System flowcharts are an important systems analysis, design, and evaluation tool. They are universally employed in systems work and provide an immediate form of communication among workers. The system flowchart is an excellent vehicle for describing information flows and procedures within an AIS.

Program Flowcharts

A **program flowchart** illustrates the sequence of logical operations performed by a computer in executing a program. The relationship between system and program flowcharts is shown in Figure 3-11. A program flowchart describes the specific logic to perform a process shown on a system flowchart.

Program flowcharts employ a subset of the symbols shown in Figure 3-8. Once designed and approved, the program flowchart serves as the blueprint for coding the computer program.

SUMMARY AND CASE CONCLUSION

Ashton prepared the DFDs and flowcharts of S&S's payroll processing system (Figures 3-6, 3-7, and 3-9) to document and explain the operation of the existing system. He was pleased to see that Scott and Susan were able to grasp the essence of the system from this documentation. The DFDs indicated the logical flow of data and the flowcharts illustrated the physical dimensions of the system: The origin and final disposition and the interworkings of the documents in each department were clear.

Susan and Scott agreed that Ashton should document the remainder of the system. The documentation would help all of them understand the current system.

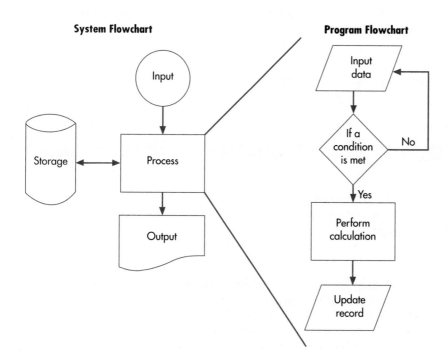

Figure 3-11
Relationship Between System and Program Flowcharts

It would also help Ashton and the consultants design the new system. In fact, the payroll documentation had already helped them identify a few minor changes they wanted to make in their system. Using the information from Figure 3-9, Susan now understands why the payroll clerk sometimes had to borrow the only copy of the payroll report that was prepared. She thus recommended that a second copy be made and kept in the payroll department. Susan also questioned the practice of keeping all the payroll records in one employee/payroll file. To keep the file from becoming unwieldy, she recommended that it be divided into three files: personal employee data, pay period documentation, and payroll tax data. A discussion with the payroll clerk verified that this approach would make payroll processing easier and more efficient.

Over the next few weeks, Ashton documented the remaining accounting cycles. This process helped him identify inefficiencies and unneeded reports. He also found that some system documents were inadequately controlled. In addition, he got several ideas about how an automated system could help him reengineer the business processes at S&S. By substituting technology for human effort, outdated processes and procedures could be eliminated to make the system more effective.

When Ashton completed his analysis and documentation of the current system, Susan and Scott asked him to continue his work in designing a new system using a relational database. To do that, Ashton must thoroughly understand the information needs of the various employees in the company. Then he can design a new system using the tools, such as DFDs and flowcharts, that were examined in this chapter (systems development is discussed in Chapters 18 through 20). He also has to learn more about database technology so that he can make sure that the software he selects uses the most up-to-date technology.

KEY TERMS

documentation 84
narrative description 84
data flow diagram
 (DFD) 85
data source 86
data destination 86

data flow 86
process 87
data store 87
context diagram 88
flowchart 92
flowcharting template 92

document flowchart 94
internal control
 flowchart 94
system flowchart 95
program flowchart 99

AIS IN ACTION

CHAPTER QUIZ

1 A DFD is a representation of which of the following?
 a. relationship among modules, data, and programs of an AIS
 b. flow of data in an organization
 c. decision rules in a computer program
 d. computer hardware configuration

2 Documentation methods such as DFDs and flowcharts save both time and money, adding value to an organization.
 a. True
 b. False

3 Which of the following statements is false?
 a. Flowcharts make use of many symbols.
 b. A flowchart emphasizes the flow of documents or records containing data.
 c. DFDs help convey the timing of events.
 d. Both a and b are false.

4 A DFD consists of the following four basic elements: data sources and destinations, data flows, transformation processes, and data stores. Each is represented on a DFD by a different symbol.
 a. True
 b. False

5 Which of the following is *not* one of the guidelines that should be followed in naming DFD data elements?
 a. Process names should include action verbs such as *update, edit, prepare*, and *record*.
 b. Make sure the names describe all the data or the entire process.
 c. Name only the most important DFD elements.
 d. Choose active and descriptive names.

6 The understanding of documentation skills that accountants require varies with their job function. However, they should at least be able to do which of the following?
 a. Read documentation to determine how the system works.
 b. Critique and correct documentation that others prepare.
 c. Prepare documentation for a newly developed information system.
 d. Teach others how to prepare documentation.

7 Which of the following statements is false?
 a. A flowchart is an analytical technique used to describe some aspect of an information system in a clear, concise, and logical manner.
 b. Flowcharts use a standard set of symbols to describe pictorially the flow of documents and data through a system.
 c. Flowcharts are easy to prepare and revise when the designer utilizes a flowcharting software package.
 d. A system flowchart is a narrative representation of an information system.
 e. A program flowchart shows the logic used in computer programs.

8 Which of the following flowcharts illustrates the flow of information among areas of responsibility in an organization?
 a. program flowchart c. system flowchart
 b. computer configuration chart d. document flowchart

9 Which of the following is *not* one of the recommended guidelines for making flowcharts more readable, clear, concise, consistent, and understandable?
 a. Divide the flowchart into columns with labels.
 b. Flowchart all information flows, especially exception procedures and error routines.
 c. Design the flowchart so that flow proceeds from top to bottom and from left to right.
 d. Show the final disposition of all documents to prevent loose ends that leave the reader dangling.
 e. Each manual processing symbol should have an input and an output.

10 Data sources and destinations are represented in a data flow diagram as:
 a. a square d. two parallel lines
 b. a curved arrow e. none of the above
 c. a circle

COMPREHENSIVE PROBLEM

Accuflow Cash Disbursements Process

SoftData, a vendor, sends an invoice to Accuflow for data warehousing support services. The invoice is sent directly to Megan Waters, the accounts payable clerk, who manually records the invoice in the accounts payable subsidiary ledger. Once the invoice is recorded it is forwarded to Stan Phillips, the cash disbursements clerk, for processing. Stan prepares a check to pay the invoice and sends the check and invoice to John Sterling, the company treasurer. John approves and signs the check and cancels the invoice. John then mails the check back to SoftData and returns the canceled invoice to Stan for recording in the cash disbursements journal and filing. Once a week, Megan manually posts disbursements from the cash disbursements journal to the accounts payable subsidiary ledger.

Required

Prepare a document flowchart, context diagram, level 0 data flow diagram, and a level 1 data flow diagram for the Accuflow cash disbursement process. To maximize learning from this problem, do your best to solve it before looking at the solution at the end of the chapter.

DISCUSSION QUESTIONS

3.1 Identify the DFD elements in the following narrative: A customer purchases a few items from a local grocery store. Jill, a salesclerk, enters the transaction in the cash register and takes the customer's money. At closing, Jill gives both the cash and the register tape to her manager.

3.2 Do you agree with the following statement: "Any one of the systems documentation procedures, such as a DFD, can adequately document a given system"? Explain.

3.3 Compare the guidelines for preparing flowcharts and DFDs. What general design principles and limitations are common to both documentation techniques?

3.4 Your classmate asks you to explain flowcharting conventions using real-world examples. Draw each of the major flowchart symbols from memory, placing them into one of four categories: input/output, processing, storage, and flow and miscellaneous. For each symbol, suggest several uses.

PROBLEMS

3.1 Prepare systems flowcharting segments for each of the following operations:
 a. processing transactions stored on magnetic tape to update a master file stored on magnetic tape
 b. processing transactions stored on magnetic tape to update a database stored on a disk
 c. converting source documents off-line to magnetic tape using an optical character reader (OCR)
 d. processing OCR documents online to update a database on magnetic disk
 e. reading data from a disk file into the computer to be printed on a report
 f. keying data from source documents to a file stored on a disk

g. manually sorting and filing invoices

h. processing a source document online using a terminal from a remote location, which is connected to a central computer system for updating and recording source data in a database stored on magnetic disk

i. a scheduled automatic backup of an internal hard drive to an external hard drive

j. query customer sales data maintained on disk

k. enter employee hours worked data (recorded on time cards) to the payroll transaction file maintained on disk and match to wage data maintained on the payroll master file

l. access a price list maintained on disk to complete a purchase order. An electronic copy of the purchase order is sent to the vendor and a backup copy is printed and filed by vendor name

m. update an airline reservation on a Web-based airline reservation system from a home computer

3.2 The Happy Valley Utility Company uses turnaround documents in its computerized customer accounting system. Meter readers are provided with preprinted computer forms, each containing the account number, name, address, and previous meter readings. Each form also contains a formatted area in which the customer's current meter reading can be marked in pencil. After making their rounds, meter readers turn in batches of these documents to the computer data preparation department, where they are processed by a mark-sense document reader that transfers their contents to magnetic tape.

This magnetic tape file is used as input for two computer runs. The first run sorts the transaction records on the tape into sequential order by customer account number. On the second run, the sorted transaction tape is processed against the customer master file, which is stored on a magnetic disk. Second-run outputs are (1) a printed report listing summary information and any erroneous transactions detected by the computer and (2) customer bills printed in a special OCR-readable font. Bills are mailed, and customers are requested to return the stub portion along with payment.

Customer payments are received in the mail room and checked for consistency against the returned stubs. Checks are then sent to the cashier's office. The mail room provides the computer data preparation department with three sets of records: (1) stubs with compatible amounts, (2) stubs with differing amounts, and (3) a list of amounts received from customers, without stubs. For the latter two types of records, data preparation personnel use a special typewriter to prepare corrected stubs. An OCR document reader then reads all the stubs and the computer updates the customer master file to post the payment amounts. Two printed outputs from this second process are (1) reports listing erroneous transactions and summary information and (2) past-due customer balances.

Required

a. Draw a system flowchart of the billing operations, commencing with the computer preparation of the meter reading forms and ending with the mailing of customer bills.

b. Draw a system flowchart depicting customer payments processing, starting with the mail room operations and ending with the two printed reports.

3.3 The Dewey Construction Company processes its payroll transactions to update both its payroll master file and its work-in-process master file in the same computer run. Both the payroll master file and the work-in-process master file are maintained on disk and accessed directly.

Job time tickets are keyed onto a tape using a key-to-tape encoder. The tape is then processed to update the files. This processing run also produces a payroll register on magnetic tape, employee paychecks and earnings statements, and a printed report listing error transactions and summary information.

Required

Prepare a system flowchart of the process described.

3.4 Prepare a document flowchart to reflect how ANGIC Insurance Company processes its casualty claims. The process begins when the claims department receives a notice of loss from a claimant. Claims prepares and sends the claimant four copies of a proof-of-loss form on which the claimant must detail the cause, amount, and other aspects of the loss. Claims also initiates a record of the claim, which is sent with the notice of loss to the data processing department, where it is filed by claim number.

The claimant must fill out the proof-of-loss forms with an adjuster's assistance. The adjuster must concur with the claimant on the estimated amount of loss. The claimant and adjuster each keep one copy of the proof-of-loss form. The claimant sends the two remaining copies to the claims department. Separately, the adjuster submits a report to the claims department, confirming the estimates on the claimant's proof-of-loss form.

The claims department authorizes a payment to the claimant, forwards a copy of the proof-of-loss form to data processing, and files the original proof-of-loss form and the adjuster's report alphabetically. The data processing department prepares payment checks and mails them to the customers, files the proof-of-loss form with the claim record, and prepares a list of cash disbursements, which it transmits to the accounting department.

3.5 Beccan Company is a discount tire dealer operating 25 retail stores in the metropolitan area. Beccan sells both private-brand and name-brand tires. The company operates a centralized purchasing and warehousing facility and employs a perpetual inventory system. All purchases of tires and related supplies are placed through the company's central purchasing department to optimize quantity discounts. The tires and supplies are received at the central warehouse and distributed to the retail stores as needed. The perpetual inventory system at the central facility maintains current inventory records, designated reorder points, and optimum order quantities for each type and size of tire and other related supplies. Beccan uses the following five documents in its inventory control system.

- **Retail stores requisition.** The retail stores submit this document to the central warehouse when they need tires or supplies. The shipping clerks in the warehouse department fill the orders from inventory and authorize delivery to the stores.
- **Purchase requisition.** The inventory control clerk in the inventory control department prepares this document when the quantity on hand for an item falls below the designated reorder point. It is then forwarded to the purchasing department.
- **Purchase order.** The purchasing department prepares this document when items need to be ordered. It is then submitted to an authorized vendor.
- **Receiving report.** The warehouse department prepares this document when ordered items are received from vendors. The receiving clerk completes the document by indicating the vendor's name and the date and quantity of the shipment received.
- **Invoice.** An invoice is received from vendors, specifying the amounts Beccan owes.

The following departments are involved in Beccan's inventory control system:

- **Inventory control department.** Responsible for the maintenance of all perpetual inventory records for all stock items. This inventory includes current quantity on hand, reorder point, optimum order quantity, and quantity on order for each item carried.
- **Warehouse department.** Maintains the physical inventory of all items carried in stock. All orders from vendors are received (receiving clerk) and all distributions to retail stores are filled (shipping clerks) in this department.

- **Purchasing department.** Places all orders for items needed by the company.
- **Accounts payable department.** Maintains all open accounts with vendors and other creditors, in addition to processing payments.

Required

Prepare a document flowchart that indicates the interaction and use of these documents among all departments at Beccan Company's central facility. It should provide adequate internal control over the receipt, issuance, replenishment, and payment of tires and supplies. You may assume that there is a sufficient number of document copies to ensure that the perpetual inventory system has the necessary basic internal controls.

(CMA Examination, adapted)

3.6 As the internal auditor for No-Wear Products of Hibbing, Minnesota, you have been asked by your supervisor to document the company's current payroll processing system. Based on your documentation, No-Wear hopes to develop a plan for revising the current information system to eliminate unnecessary delays in paycheck processing. Your best explanation of the system came from an interview with the head payroll clerk:

> *The payroll processing system at No-Wear Products is fairly simple. Time data are recorded in each department using time cards and clocks. It is annoying, however, when people forget to punch out at night and we have to record their time information by hand. At the end of the period, our payroll clerks enter the time card data into a payroll file for processing. Our clerks are pretty good—though I've had to make my share of corrections when they mess up the data entry.*
>
> *Before the payroll file is processed for the current period, human resources sends us data on personnel changes, such as increases in pay rates and new employees. Our clerks enter this information into the payroll file so it is available for processing. Usually, when mistakes get back to us, it's because human resources is recording the wrong pay rate or an employee has left and the department forgets to remove the record.*
>
> *The data are then processed and individual employee paychecks are generated. Several important reports are also generated for management—though I don't know exactly what they do with them. In addition, the government requires regular federal and state withholding reports for tax purposes. Currently, the system generates these reports automatically, which is nice.*

Required

a. Prepare a context diagram and level 0 DFD to document the payroll processing system at No-Wear Products.
b. Prepare a document flowchart to document the payroll processing system at No-Wear Products.

3.7 Ashton Fleming has decided to analyze the accounts payable process at S&S. His intent is to document how the present system works so the transition to a computerized system will be easier. He also hopes to improve any weaknesses he discovers in the system. In the following narrative, Ashton explains what happens at S&S:

> *Before S&S pays a vendor invoice, the invoice must be matched against the purchase order used to request the goods and the receiving report that the receiving department prepares. Because all three of these documents enter the accounts payable department at different times, a separate alphabetical file is kept for each type of document. The purchase orders that are forwarded from purchasing are stored in a purchase order file. The receiving reports are stored in a receiving report file. When vendor invoices are received, the accounts payable clerk records the amount due in the accounts payable file and then files the invoices in the vendor invoice file.*
>
> *S&S's policy is to make sure all accounts are paid within 30 days to take advantage of the early-payment discounts that suppliers offer. When it comes time to pay a particular bill, the accounts payable clerk retrieves the vendor invoice and attaches the purchase*

order and the receiving report. These matched documents are forwarded to Ashton Fleming.

Ashton reviews the documents to ensure they are complete and prepares a two-part check. The checks and the other three documents are forwarded to Susan for her approval and signature. Ashton records the check amount in the cash disbursements journal.

Susan reviews the documents to ensure they are valid payables and then signs the checks. She forwards the check to the vendor and returns the documents and the second copy of the check to the accounts payable clerk. The clerk files the documents alphabetically in a paid invoice file. At the end of every month, the accounts payable clerk uses information from the accounts payable ledger to prepare an accounts payable report. This report is forwarded to Susan for her review. After she is finished with the report, Susan files it chronologically.

Required

a. Prepare a context diagram and a level 0 DFD to document accounts payable processing at S&S.

b. Prepare a document flowchart to document accounts payable processing at S&S.

3.8 Since opening its doors in Hawaii two years ago, Oriental Trading has enjoyed tremendous success. As a wholesaler, Oriental Trading purchases textiles from Asian markets and resells them to local retail shops. To keep up with the strong demand for textiles in the Hawaiian Islands, Oriental Trading is expanding its local operations. At the heart of the expansion is the introduction of a new information system to handle the tremendous increase in purchases.

You have conducted several interviews with department supervisors who interact with the acquisition/payment system. The following is a summary of your discussions:

A purchase requisition is sent from the inventory system to Sky Ishibashi, a clerk in the purchasing department. Sky prepares a purchase order from information in the vendor and inventory files and mails it to the vendor. The vendor returns a vendor acknowledgment to Sky indicating receipt of the purchase order. Sky then sends a purchase order notification to Elei Mateaki, a clerk in the accounts payable department.

When the receiving department accepts vendor goods, the inventory system notifies Elei by sending him a receiving report. Elei also receives invoices from the various vendors. He matches the invoices with the purchase order notification and the receiving report and updates the accounts payable master file. Elei then sends a payment authorization to the accounting department. There, Andeloo Nonu prepares and mails a check to the vendor. When the check is issued, the system automatically updates the accounts payable master file and the general ledger.

Required

a. Develop a context diagram and a level 0 DFD of the acquisition/payment system at Oriental Trading.

b. Prepare a document flowchart to document the acquisition/payment system at Oriental Trading.

3.9 Ashton Fleming has worked furiously for the past month trying to document the major business information flows at S&S. Upon completing his personal interviews with cash receipts clerks, Ashton asks you to develop a comprehensive DFD for the cash receipts system. Ashton's narrative of the system follows:

Customer payments include cash received at the time of purchase and account payments received in the mail. At day's end, the treasurer endorses all checks and prepares a deposit slip for the checks and the cash. A clerk then deposits the checks, cash, and deposit slip at the local bank each day.When checks are received as payment for accounts due, a remittance slip is included with the payment. The remittance slips are used to update the accounts receivable file at the end of the day. The remittance slips are stored in a file drawer by date.

Every week, a cash receipts report and an aged trial balance are generated from the data in the accounts receivable ledger. The cash receipts report is sent to Scott and Susan. A copy of the aged trial balance by customer account is sent to the credit and collections department.

Required

 a. Develop a context diagram and a level 0 DFD for the cash receipts system at S&S.

 b. Prepare a document flowchart to document the cash receipts system at S&S.

3.10 A mail-order skin and body care company advertises in magazines. Magazine subscribers initiate most orders by completing and sending coupons directly to the company. The firm also takes orders by phone, answers inquiries about products, and handles payments and cancellations of orders. Products that have been ordered are sent either directly to the customer or to the company's regional offices that handle the required distribution. The mail order company has three basic data files, which contain customer mailing information, product inventory information, and billing information based on invoice number. During the next few years, the company expects to become a multimillion-dollar operation. Recognizing the need to computerize much of the mail order business, the company has begun the process by calling you.

Required

Draw a context diagram and at least two levels of DFDs for the preceding operations.

3.11 The local community college requires that each student complete a registration request form and mail or deliver it to the registrar's office. A clerk enters the request into the system. First, the system checks the accounts receivable subsystem to ensure that no fees are owed from the previous quarter. Next, for each course, the system checks the student transcript to ensure that he or she has completed the course prerequisites. Then the system checks class position availability and adds the student's Social Security number to the class list.

The report back to the student shows the result of registration processing: If the student owes fees, a bill is sent and the registration is rejected. If prerequisites for a course are not fulfilled, the student is notified and that course is not registered. If the class is full, the student request is annotated with "course closed." If a student is accepted into a class, then the day, time, and room are printed next to the course number. Student fees and total tuition are computed and printed on the form. Student fee information is interfaced to the accounts receivable subsystem. Course enrollment reports are prepared for the instructors.

Required

 a. Prepare a context diagram and at least two levels of DFDs for this operation.

 b. Prepare a document flowchart to document this operation.

3.12 Charting, Inc., a new audit client of yours, processes its sales and cash receipts documents in the following manner:

 1 Payment on account. Each morning a mail clerk in the sales department opens the mail. The mail clerk prepares a remittance advice (showing customer and amount paid) if one is not received. The checks and remittance advices are then forwarded to the sales department supervisor, who reviews each check and forwards the checks and remittance advices to the accounting department supervisor.

The accounting department supervisor, who also functions as credit manager in approving new credit and all credit limits, reviews all checks for payments on past-due accounts and then forwards the checks and remittance advices to the accounts receivable clerk, who arranges the advices in alphabetical order. The remittance advices are posted directly to the accounts receivable ledger cards. The checks are endorsed by stamp and totaled. The total is posted to the cash receipts journal. The remittance

advices are filed chronologically. After receiving the cash from the previous day's cash sales, the accounts receivable clerk prepares the daily deposit slip in triplicate. The third copy of the deposit slip is filed by date, and the second copy and the original accompany the bank deposit.

2 Sales. Sales clerks prepare sales invoices in triplicate. The original and second copy are presented to the cashier. The sales clerk retains the third copy in the sales book. When the sale is for cash, the customer pays the sales clerk, who presents the money to the cashier with the invoice copies.

The cashier approves a credit sale from an approved credit list after the sales clerk prepares the three-part invoice. After receiving the cash or approving the invoice, the cashier validates the original copy of the sales invoice and gives it to the customer. At the end of each day, the cashier recaps the sales and cash received and forwards the cash and the second copy of the sales invoices to the accounts receivable clerk.

The accounts receivable clerk balances the cash received with cash sales invoices and prepares a daily sales summary. The credit sales invoices are posted to the accounts receivable ledger, and then all invoices are sent to the inventory control clerk in the sales department for posting to the inventory control cards. After posting, the inventory control clerk files all invoices numerically. The accounts receivable clerk posts the daily sales summary to the cash receipts and sales journals and files the sales summaries by date.

The cash from cash sales is combined with the cash received on account to make up the daily bank deposit.

3 Bank deposits. The bank validates the deposit slip and returns the second copy to the accounting department, where the accounts receivable clerk files it by date.

Monthly bank statements are reconciled promptly by the accounting department supervisor and filed by date.

Required

You recognize weaknesses in the existing system and believe a document flowchart would be beneficial in evaluating this client's internal control in preparing for your examination of the financial statements.

 a. Complete the flowchart given in Figure 3-12, for sales and cash receipts of Charting, Inc., by labeling the appropriate symbols and indicating information flows.

 b. Using the guidelines for preparing flowcharts in Focus 3-2 and the flowcharting symbols shown in Figure 3-8, critique the flowchart shown in Figure 3-12. List the ways the flowchart violates the guidelines or uses improper symbols.

(CPA Examination, adapted)

3.13 A partially completed flowchart appears in Figure 3-13. The flowchart depicts the credit sales activities of the Bottom Manufacturing Corporation.

A customer's purchase order is received, and a six-part sales order is prepared therefrom. The six copies are initially distributed as follows:

 Copy 1—Billing copy, to billing department
 Copy 2—Shipping copy, to shipping department
 Copy 3—Credit copy, to credit department
 Copy 4—Stock request copy, to credit department
 Copy 5—Customer copy, to customer
 Copy 6—Sales order copy, file in sales order department

When each copy of the sales order reaches the appropriate department or destination, it calls for specific internal control procedures and related documents. Some procedures and related documents are indicated on the flowchart; others are labeled by the letters *a* to *r*.

Required

 a. List the procedures or the internal documents that are labeled letters *c* to *r* in the flowchart of Bottom Manufacturing Corporation's charge sales system.

Figure 3-12
Charting, Inc. Flowchart for Sales and Cash Receipts

Figure 3-13
Bottom Manufacturing Corporation Flowchart of Credit Sales Activities

110

Organize your answer as follows (Note that the explanations of the letters *a* and *b* in the flowchart are entered as examples):

Flowchart Symbol Letter	Procedures or Internal Document
a	Prepare six-part sales order.
b	File by order number.

b. Using the guidelines for preparing flowcharts in Focus 3-2 and the flowcharting symbols shown in Figure 3-8, critique the flowchart shown in Figure 3-13. List the ways the flowchart violates the guidelines or uses improper symbols.

(CPA Examination, adapted)

3.14 Prepare a context diagram and a level 0 data flow diagram for each of the following situations.
 a. Prepare and file a tax return with the tax owed to the Internal Revenue Service.
 b. A customer pays an invoice with a check. Accounts receivable is updated to reflect the payment. The check is recorded and deposited into the bank.
 c. A customer places an online order to purchase merchandise. The order is approved, filled, and sent to the customer with an invoice.
 d. An inventory request is received by the purchasing department. The purchasing department prepares and sends a purchase order to the appropriate vendor.
 e. A vendor invoice is received, reviewed, and compared against the appropriate purchase order, then paid and filed.
 f. A bill of lading for ordered inventory is received from a vendor, recorded, checked against the appropriate purchase order, and filed.

3.15 Melanie is doing a study on various weight loss plans and needs to determine an individual's weight status by calculating his body-mass index. To calculate a person's body-mass index Melanie requires that height be measured in meters and weight be measured in kilograms. The index is calculated by dividing a person's weight by the square of his height. The person's index is then compared to the following scale to determine his weight status: Below 18.5 = underweight, 18.5–24.5 = normal, over 25.0 = overweight. Five hundred people have agreed to participate in Melanie's study. With so many calculations to perform, she would like a computer program that will do this calculation for her. She decides to prepare a flowchart to help her properly design the computer program.

Required

Prepare a program flowchart to help Melanie program this process.

3.16 Match the flowchart, context diagram, or data flow diagram segments in the right column to an appropriate description in the left column.

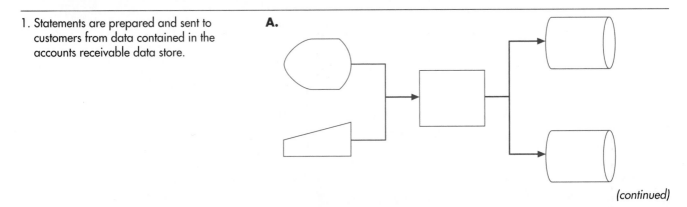

1. Statements are prepared and sent to customers from data contained in the accounts receivable data store.

A.

(continued)

2. A customer sends a sales invoice to the accounts payable process.

B.

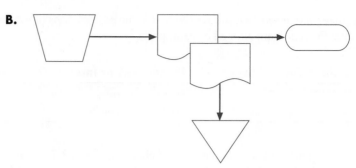

3. A check is manually prepared from data on a vendor invoice.

C.

4. The cash receipt process updates the cash receipts data store.

D.

5. A sales invoice is manually prepared and sent to a customer.

E.

6. A report is prepared from data stored on magnetic tape.

F.

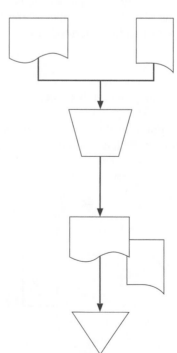

7. Billing data are entered online and used to update the sales order file and the customer master file.

G.

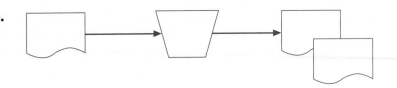

8. Data from a cancelled invoice are used to update the cash disbursements ledger.

H.

9. A sales order is prepared manually. Copy 1 is sent to the warehouse and copy 2 is filed.

I.

10. An accounts receivable aging report is prepared from the accounts receivable master file and the cash receipts master file, both stored on disk.

J.

11. An error listing and batch total are compared and filed.

K.

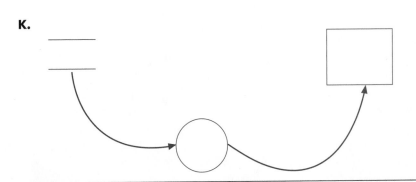

3.17 Replicate the following flowchart in Visio, Microsoft Word, Microsoft Excel, or some other documentation software package.

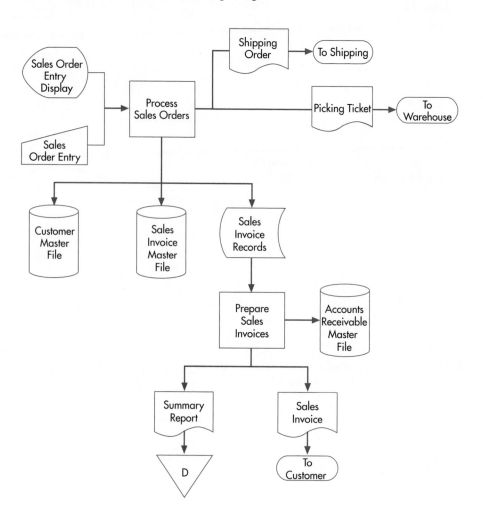

3.18 Replicate the following data flow diagram in Visio, Microsoft Word, Microsoft Excel, or some other documentation software package.

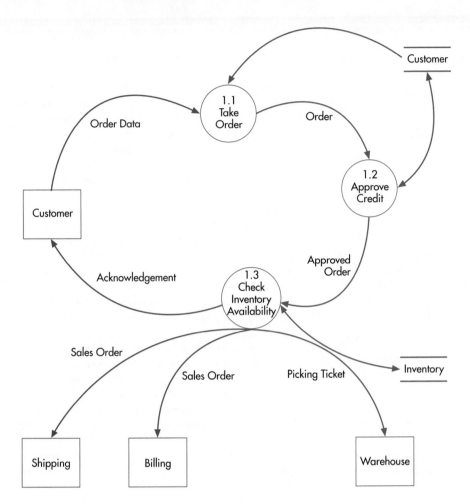

CASE 3-1 Dub 5

You are the systems analyst for the Wee Willie Williams Widget Works (also known as Dub 5, which is a shortened version of 5 Ws). Dub 5 produces computer keyboard components. It has been producing keyboards for more than 20 years and has recently signed an exclusive 10-year contract to provide the keyboards for all Dell personal computers. As the systems analyst, you have been assigned the task of developing a level 0 DFD for Dub 5's order processing system. You have finished gathering all the information you need to develop the first-pass DFD and now want to complete the diagram.

Customer orders, which are all credit sales, arrive via e-mail and by phone. When an order is processed, a number of other documents are prepared. You have diagrammed the overall process and the documents produced, as shown in the context diagram Figure 3-14.

The following documents are created:

- Order processing creates a packing slip, which is then used by the warehouse to fill the order.
- A customer invoice is prepared and sent once the goods have been shipped.
- When orders are not accepted, an order rejection is sent to the customer, explaining why the order cannot be filled.
- A receivables notice, which is a copy of the customer invoice, is sent to the accounting department so accounts receivable records can be updated.

After reviewing your notes, you write the following narrative summary:

When an order comes in, the order processing clerk checks the customer's credit file to confirm credit approval and ensure that the amount falls within the credit limit. If either of these conditions is not met, the order is sent to the credit department. If an order meets both conditions, the order processing clerk enters it into the system on a standard order form. The information on the form is used to update the company's customer file (in which the name, address, and other information are stored), and the form is then placed in the company's open order file.

When the credit department receives a rejected order, the credit clerk first determines why the order has been rejected. If the credit limit has been exceeded, the customer is notified that his or her credit limit has been exceeded and that the merchandise will be shipped as soon as Dub 5 receives payment. If the customer has not been approved for credit, a credit application is sent to the customer along with a notification that the order will be shipped as soon as credit approval is granted.

Before preparing a packing slip, the system checks the inventory records to determine if the company has the products ordered on hand. If the items are in stock, a packing slip is prepared and sent to the warehouse.

Once notification of shipped goods has been received from the warehouse, a customer invoice is prepared. A copy is filed by the order processing department, another is sent to the customer, and another is sent to the accounting department so that accounts receivables can be updated. A note is placed in the customer file indicating that the invoice has been sent.

From the information presented, complete a Level 0 DFD for order processing and a Level 1 DFD for the credit review process for Dub 5.

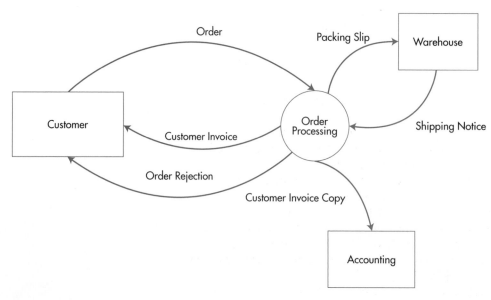

Figure 3-14
Context Diagram for Dub 5

AIS IN ACTION SOLUTIONS

QUIZ KEY

1 A DFD is a representation of which of the following?
 a. relationship among modules, data, and programs of an AIS [Incorrect. A
 flowchart represents the relationship among modules, data, and programs.]
✔ **b.** flow of data in an organization [Correct.]
 c. decision rules in a computer program [Incorrect. A DFD is a graphical repre-
 sentation of how data move through an organization. Decision rules are
 objective statements specific to computer programs.]
 d. computer hardware configuration [Incorrrect. This relates to how various
 parts of a computer fit together.]

2 Documentation methods such as DFDs and flowcharts save both time and
 money, adding value to an organization.
✔ **a.** True [Correct. A picture is worth 1,000 words. An individual may learn
 more and learn it quicker by studying the DFD or flowchart of a system than
 by reading a text-based description of the same system.]
 b. False [Incorrect]

3 Which of the following statements is false?
 a. Flowcharts make use of many symbols. [Incorrect. The statement is true. See
 Figure 3-8 for an illustration of the many symbols used in flowcharts.]
 b. A document flowchart emphasizes the flow of documents or records contain-
 ing data. [Incorrect. The statement is true. The reason it is called a document
 flowchart is because it shows the flow of documents or records containing
 data.]
✔ **c.** DFDs help convey the timing of events. [Correct. The statement is false.
 DFD's show data movement but not necessarily the timing of the
 movement.]
 d. Both a and b are false. [Incorrect. As explained above, a and b are true
 statements.]

4 A DFD consists of the following four basic elements: data sources and destina-
 tions, data flows, transformation processes, and data stores. Each is represented
 on a DFD by a different symbol.
✔ **a.** True [Correct. The four elements of DFDs are illustrated in Figure 3-1.]
 b. False [Incorrect]

5 Which of the following is *not* one of the guidelines that should be followed in
 naming DFD data elements?
 a. Process names should include action verbs such as *update, edit, prepare*, and
 record. [Incorrect. This is a true statement. Action verbs should be used to
 name process data elements. See item 11 in Focus 3-1.]
 b. Make sure the names describe all the data or the entire process. [Incorrect.
 This statement is true. Data element names should reflect what is known
 about the element. See item 11 in Focus 3-1.]
✔ **c.** Name only the most important DFD elements. [Correct. This statement is
 false. All data elements should be named with the exception of data flows
 into data stores, when the inflows and outflows make naming the data store
 redundant. See item 11 in Focus 3-1.]
 d. Choose active and descriptive names. [Incorrect. This is a true statement.
 Active and descriptive names should be used in naming data elements. See
 item 11 in Focus 3-1.]

6 The understanding of documentation skills that accountants require varies with their job function. However, all accountants should at least be able to do which of the following?

✔ **a.** Read documentation to determine how the system works. [Correct. All accountants should at least be able to read and understand system documentation.]

b. Critique and correct documentation that others prepare. [Incorrect. Although senior accountants may critique and correct documentation prepared by junior accountants, at a minimum all accountants need to be able to read and understand documentation.]

c. Prepare documentation for a newly developed information system. [Incorrect. Some accountants may need to develop documentation, but system developers and analysts normally prepare systems documentation.]

d. Teach others how to prepare documentation. [Incorrect. Most accountants will not be asked to teach documentation skills.]

7 Which of the following statements is false?

a. A flowchart is an analytical technique used to describe some aspect of an information system in a clear, concise, and logical manner. [Incorrect. This is a true statement. This is the bolded definition of a flowchart given previously in the text.]

b. Flowcharts use a standard set of symbols to describe pictorially the flow of documents and data through a system. [Incorrect. This is a true statement. The symbols used for flowcharting are shown in Figure 3-8.]

c. Flowcharts are easy to prepare and revise when the designer utilizes a flowcharting software package. [Incorrect. This is a true statement. There are a number of good flowcharting software packages that make it easy to draw and modify flowcharts.]

✔ **d.** A system flowchart is a narrative representation of an information system. [Correct. This statement is false. A flowchart is a graphical rather than a narrative representation of an information system.]

e. A program flowchart shows the logic used in computer programs. [Incorrect. This is a true statement. A program flowchart illustrates program logic and the structure of the program.]

8 Which of the following flowcharts illustrates the flow of information among areas of responsibility in an organization?

a. program flowchart [Incorrect. A program flowchart documents a computer program.]

b. computer configuration chart [Incorrect. A computer configuration chart illustrates how computer hardware is arranged and implemented.]

c. system flowchart [Incorrect. A system flowchart illustrates the relationship among inputs, processes, and outputs of a system, not areas of responsibility.]

✔ **d.** document flowchart [Correct. A document flowchart traces the life of a document from its cradle to its grave as it works its way through the areas of responsibility within an organization.]

9 Which of the following is *not* one of the recommended guidelines for making flowcharts more readable, clear, concise, consistent, and understandable?

a. Divide the flowchart into columns with labels. [Incorrect. This is a correct statement. Dividing the flowchart into columns helps make it more readable, clear, concise, consistent, and understandable. See item 3 in Focus 3-2.]

✔ **b.** Flowchart all information flows, especially exception procedures and error routines. [Correct. Including all exception procedures and error routines clutters the flowchart and makes it difficult to read and understand. See item 4 in Focus 3-2.]

c. Design the flowchart so that flow proceeds from top to bottom and from left to right. [Incorrect. This is a correct statement. Flowcharts should be prepared so that they are read like a book. See item 5 in Focus 3-2.]

 d. Show the final disposition of all documents to prevent loose ends that leave the reader dangling. [Incorrect. This is a correct statement. All documents should be placed either in a file or sent to another entity. See item 6 in Focus 3-2.]

 e. Each manual processing symbol should have an input and an output. [Incorrect. This is a correct statement. A manual process must have an input and an output. Without an input nothing can be processed and without an output there is no evidence of processing. See item 10 in Focus 3-2.]

10 Data sources and destinations are represented in a data flow diagram as:

 ✔ **a.** a square [Correct. See Figure 3-1.]

 b. a curved arrow [Incorrect. A curved arrow represents a data flow. See Figure 3-1.]

 c. a circle [Incorrect. A circle represents a process. See Figure 3-1.]

 d. two parallel lines [Incorrect. Two parallel lines represent a data store. See Figure 3-1.]

 e. none of the above [Incorrect. Option a is correct.]

COMPREHENSIVE PROBLEM SOLUTION

Flowchart

In preparing a document flowchart the first item of business is to become familiar with the problem. The next step is to identify the primary actors or major players in the problem. In this problem there are three major players: Megan Waters (accounts payable clerk), Stan Phillips (cash disbursement clerk), and John Sterling (treasurer). Since we are documenting Accuflow's cash disbursement process, we are not interested in the internal workings of the vendor, SoftData. As a result we do not include it as one of our major players. Now that we have identified the major players we can list their functions in Table 3-3. Note that forwarding and receiving to/from the next major player is not considered a function in preparing document flowcharts.

 We will now explain, step by step, how to create the document flowchart solution for Accuflow shown in Figure 3-15. To document the functions of the three major players, divide the document flowchart into three columns, one for each player. It is usually best to arrange the columns in the order they occur and use the primary function of the major player as the column name. Since the accounts payable clerk receives the invoice from the vendor, we place her in the first column. After the accounts payable clerk records the invoice, she sends it to the cash disbursements clerk who prepares a check and sends it to the treasurer. Therefore, the cash disbursements clerk should be in the second column and the treasurer should be in the last column, as illustrated in Figure 3-15.

 Since the process begins with an invoice from an external party (a vendor), a terminal symbol with the term "From Vendor" is placed in the upper left portion of the Accounts Payable Clerk column. Next, a document symbol with the words "Vendor Invoice" printed inside it is placed below the terminal symbol. An arrow representing the document's flow and the order of operations connects the two symbols.

Table 3-3
Accuflow's Table of Functions

Accounts Payable Clerk (Megan Waters)	Cash Disbursements Clerk (Stan Phillips)	Treasurer (John Sterling)
Receives invoice	Prepares check	Approves and signs check
Records invoice	Records cash disbursement	Cancels invoice
Posts cash disbursement	Files cancelled invoice	Mails check

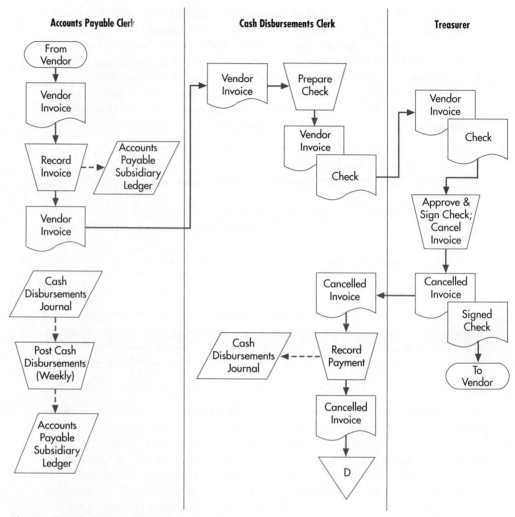

Figure 3-15
Accuflow's Document Flowchart

According to the narrative, Megan manually records the invoice in the accounts payable subsidiary ledger. Thus, a manual process symbol with the words "Record Invoice" is placed below the invoice document symbol and the two symbols are connected with an arrow. Then, a journal/ledger symbol, also called an input/output symbol, is placed to the side of the manual process. Since only information from the invoice is used to update the accounts payable subsidiary ledger, a dotted arrow is used to connect the two symbols. A new vendor invoice symbol is drawn below the record invoice symbol.

Because the vendor invoice moves from the accounts payable clerk to the cash disbursements clerk, the vendor invoice symbol is placed at the top of the cash disbursements column with an arrow connecting the two representations of the same document. We redraw the vendor invoice symbol in the cash disbursements clerk column to make the flowchart easier to read.

To show that the cash disbursement clerk prepares a check to pay the vendor invoice, a manual process symbol with "Prepare Check" inside it is placed next to the vendor invoice (we could have placed it below the invoice symbol but put it beside it to save space) and two document symbols are placed below the manual process for the vendor invoice and the newly prepared check.

The cash disbursements clerk then sends the invoice and check to the treasurer. As a result, the vendor invoice and check appear in the treasurer's column. A manual symbol with "Approve & Sign Check; Cancel Invoice" inside is used to show that the check is signed and the invoice is cancelled. The documents are again shown in the flowchart, this time with new titles (Cancelled Invoice and Signed Check) to show the changed

nature of the documents. The treasurer sends the signed check to the vendor, which is illustrated using a terminal symbol with words "To Vendor" written in it.

The cancelled invoice is used to record the cash disbursement in the cash disbursements journal so it is sent back to the middle column (Cash Disbursements). A manual process symbol with "Record Payment" inside it and a dotted arrow are used to show that the disbursement is recorded in the cash disbursements journal, represented by a journal/ledger symbol. To illustrate that the cancelled invoice is filed by date, it is shown, using appropriate arrows, as exiting the record payment manual process and entering a file. A "D" is placed in the file symbol to indicate that the documents are filed by date.

Each week the accounts payable clerk manually posts entries from the cash disbursements journal to the accounts payable subsidiary ledger. To show this, the cash disbursements journal symbol is reproduced in the accounts payable clerk column, and a manual process symbol with the words "Post Cash Disbursements (Weekly)" is placed under it. Dotted arrows show information from this journal being entered into the accounts payable subsidiary ledger.

This completes the document flowchart for the Accuflow Company's cash disbursements process.

Context Diagram

A context diagram is an overview of the information process being documented. As such, a context diagram includes a single transformation process (circle or bubble) and the data sources and data destinations that send or receive data directly from the transformation process. Thus, the first step in preparing a context diagram is to draw a single circle or bubble and then label it with a name that best describes the process being documented. In this case, "Cash Disbursements System" effectively describes the process (see Figure 3-16).

The next step is to draw and label squares for the entities that either send data to the cash disbursements process or receive data from the cash disbursements process. In this example, there is a single entity, the vendor, that acts as both a source and destination of data to/from the cash disbursements process. In other processes, an outside entity could also be just a source or a destination of data and there could be more than one source or destination of data.

The last step is to connect the process (circle) with the source/destination (square) with arrows representing data flows. In this case, we have two arrows representing an invoice sent to Accuflow's cash disbursement process and a check sent to the vendor from Accuflow.

Level 0 Data Flow Diagram

In the context diagram, we saw the entire cash disbursements process in one bubble. In a level 0 DFD, we break down the cash disbursements process into its major functions. In reading the narrative, we find the following five primary steps in the cash disbursements process at Accuflow:

1 Receive vendor invoice and record payable
2 Prepare the check
3 Sign and send the check and cancel the invoice
4 Record the cash disbursement
5 Post the cash disbursements to the accounts payable ledger

Each of these processes is represented by a circle or bubble in Figure 3-17. Since this is the level 0 DFD, we assign each of these processes a real number with the first digit after the decimal point being a zero. We also place the circles in the order that the

Figure 3-16
Accuflow's Context Diagram

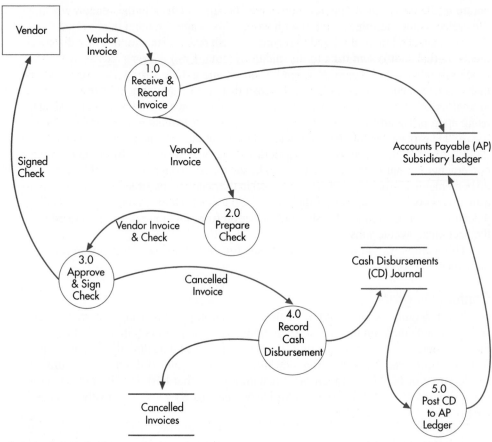

Figure 3-17
Accuflow's Level 0 Data Flow Diagram

data should flow in the process. As a result, receive and record invoice is assigned process 1.0, prepare check is assigned process 2.0, approve and sign check is 3.0, record cash disbursement is 4.0, and post cash disbursement to accounts payable ledger is 5.0. This numbering system allows us to decompose these processes into more detailed subprocesses and still keep a consistent numbering system. Thus, if we needed to decompose process 3.0 to a more detailed level we could assign subprocess bubbles as 3.1, 3.2, 3.3, etc. We can even provide greater detail by decomposing process 3.1 into subprocesses 3.1.1, 3.1.2, 3.1.3, etc.

Next, we place the data sources and data destinations on the level 0 DFD. Since we had only one data source and destination (i.e., the vendor), we draw a square and label it "Vendor." It is very important that we reconcile back to the context diagram when we prepare the different levels of DFDs. That is, the same data sources and destinations that appeared on the context diagram must also appear on the level 0 DFD. No new data sources and destinations may appear on the level 0 DFD. If, when preparing the level 0 DFD, you discover that a data source/destination is necessary to properly document the system, then you must revise the context diagram with the new data source/destination because the context diagram should represent the entire process.

Once the data source/destinations and processes are drawn, we then connect them by drawing the arrows between the appropriate symbols. These arrows represent the data moving or flowing from one process to another and from one source or destination to or from a particular process. Accordingly, we have a vendor invoice moving from the vendor to the receive and record invoice process and from that process to the prepare check process. The vendor invoice and a check move from the prepare check process to the approve and sign check process. We also have arrows leaving process 3.0 to represent the signed check being sent to the vendor and the cancelled invoice going to process 4.0, record cash disbursements.

Some processes require that data be stored. As a result, we also draw any necessary files or data stores. The level 0 DFD is the first time data stores appear in a DFD set. (Note: Data stores should not be represented on a context diagram.) Data store labels should identify the data being sent to or from it. As a result, labeling the data flows to or from data stores is normally unnecessary. Data stores are prepared by drawing two parallel lines and inserting the name of the data store between the parallel lines.

In Figure 3-17 we have three data stores: the cash disbursements journal, accounts payable subsidiary ledger, and the cancelled invoices data store. Since the cash disbursements journal is updated in process 4.0, a data flow is sent from the process 4.0 circle to the cash disbursements journal data store. To show that the accounts payable ledger is updated when invoices are received (process 1.0), an arrow is drawn from that process to the accounts payable ledger. To show that accounts payable is updated with data from the cash disbursements journal (process 5.0), a data flow arrow is drawn from the cash disbursements data store to process 5.0 and another data flow arrow is drawn from process 5.0 to the accounts payable subsidiary ledger data store. The update takes place weekly, but unlike document flowcharts, a DFD does not indicate the timing of data flows.

Level 1 Data Flow Diagram

When additional detail is needed to adequately document data flows, a process bubble may be decomposed further. As indicated in Focus 3-1, to keep a DFD clear, understandable, and easy to read a DFD should contain no more than seven process bubbles. In the Accuflow example, we broke the company's data flows into five main processes. Each of these five processes can be further decomposed. To illustrate this, we will decompose process 3.0. The narrative indicates that the treasurer approves and signs the prepared check, sends it to the vendor, and cancels the invoice to prevent duplicate payments. Therefore we will break down process 3.0 into process 3.1 (approve and sign check), 3.2 (send check to vendor), and 3.3 (cancel invoice). To display the three processes, we draw three circles and label them as shown on Figure 3-18. We also draw the data flows and label them. Notice that the vendor data source/destination is not needed on the level 1 DFD since it is already shown on level 0. Since it would clutter the DFD, and because we are showing greater detail on the level 1 than on the level 0 for one particular process, we do not replicate all of the processes and data stores in the level 0 DFD.

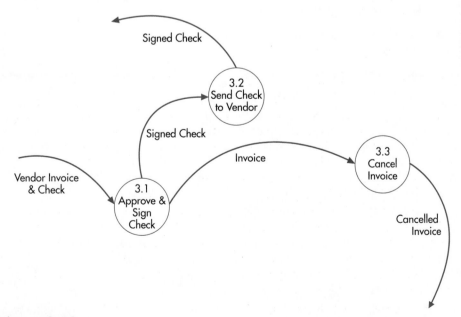

Figure 3-18
Accuflow's Level 1 Data Flow Diagram

CHAPTER 4

 LEARNING OBJECTIVES

After completing this chapter, you should be able to:

● Explain the importance and advantages of databases, as well as the difference between database and file-based legacy systems.

● Explain the difference between logical and physical views of a database.

● Explain fundamental concepts of database systems such as DBMS, schemas, the data dictionary, and DBMS languages.

● Describe what a relational database is and how it organizes data.

● Create a set of well-structured tables to properly store data in a relational database.

● Perform simple queries using the Microsoft Access database.

Relational Databases

INTEGRATIVE CASE S&S, INC.

S&S, Inc., has been very successful and now operates five stores and a popular Web site. Ashton Fleming believes that it is time to upgrade S&S's AIS so that Susan Gonzalez and Scott Parry can have easy access to the information they need to run their business. Most new AISs are based on a relational database. Ashton knows, however, that Scott and Susan are likely to have questions about the new system and whether a relational database is really appropriate for S&S. Therefore, he decides to prepare a brief report that explains why S&S's new AIS should be a relational database system. He organizes his report by addressing the following questions:

1. What is a database system, and how does it differ from file-oriented systems?
2. What is a *relational* database system?
3. How do you design a well-structured set of tables in a relational database?

Introduction

Relational databases underlie most modern integrated AISs. This chapter and Chapters 15 through 17 in Part IV explain how to participate in the design and implementation of a database AIS. This chapter defines the concept of a database. The emphasis is on understanding the structure of a relational database system, which is the most popular type of database used for transaction processing. Chapter 15 introduces two specific tools accountants use to facilitate database design—Entity-Relationship diagramming and REA data modeling—and demonstrates how to use these tools to build a data model of an AIS. Chapter 16 explains how to implement an REA data model in a database and how to produce the information needed to effectively manage an organization. Chapter 17 discusses a number of advanced data modeling and database design issues.

Files Versus Databases

To fully appreciate the power of databases, it is important to understand some basic principles about how data are stored in computer systems. Figure 4-1 shows the basic elements of data hierarchy. Information about the attributes of an entity, such as a customer's name and address, are stored in fields. All the fields containing data about one entity (e.g., one customer) form a record. A set of related records, such as all customer records, forms a file (e.g., the customer file). A set of interrelated, centrally coordinated files forms a database.

Database systems were developed to address the problems associated with the proliferation of master files. For many years companies created new files and programs each time an information need arose. The result was a significant increase in the number of master files. For example, Bank of America at one time had 36 million customer accounts in 23 separate systems. One governmental agency had data stored in 22 separate systems.

This proliferation of master files created problems. Often, the same data were stored in two or more separate master files, as shown in Figure 4-2. This made it difficult to effectively integrate data stored in different files and to obtain an organization-wide view of the data. It also created problems because the specific data values stored in the different files may not have been consistent. For example, a customer's address

Figure 4-1
Basic Elements of Data Hierarchy

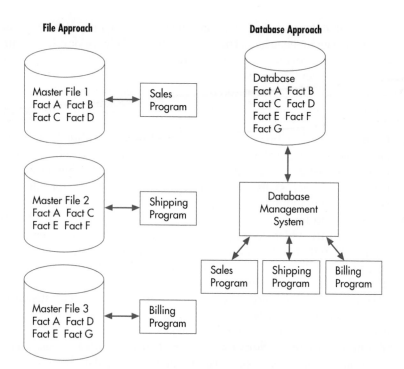

Figure 4-2
File-Oriented Versus Database Systems

may have been correctly updated in the master file used to ship merchandise, but the old address may still be stored in the master file used for billing.

As explained in Chapter 2, a database is a set of interrelated, centrally coordinated files. Figure 4-2 illustrates the differences between file-oriented and database systems. The database approach treats data as an organizational resource that should be used by and managed for the entire organization, not just the originating department or function. A **database management system (DBMS)** acts as an interface between the database and the various application programs. The combination of the database, the DBMS, and the application programs that access the database through the DBMS is referred to as the **database system**. The person responsible for the database is the **database administrator (DBA)**.

As technology improves, many companies are developing very large databases called **data warehouses**. For example, Bank of America created a customer information database to provide customer service, marketing analysis, and managerial information. At the time it was created, it was the largest in the banking industry, with over 600 billion characters of data. It contained copies of all bank data on checking and savings accounts; real estate, consumer, and commercial loans; ATMs; and bank cards. Although it cost the bank $14 million a year, it was well worth the cost. Queries that used to average two hours took only five minutes. Minutes after Los Angeles suffered an earthquake, the bank sorted its $28 billion mortgage loan portfolio by Zip code and identified the real estate loans in the earthquake area and calculated its potential loan loss. Hewlett-Packard is in the process of replacing 784 isolated databases with a single companywide data warehouse. Data warehouses and **data mining**, the process of analyzing data repositories for new knowledge about the company's data and business processes, are discussed in greater detail in Chapter 14.

The Importance and Advantages of Database Systems

Database technology is everywhere, and everyone is or will be affected by it. Most new AISs are implemented using a database approach. Virtually all mainframe computer sites use database technology, and database use in personal computers is growing rapidly.

Most accounting students will audit or work for a company that uses database technology to store, process, and report accounting transactions. Many accountants

work directly with databases since they are directly involved in entering, processing, and querying the data in databases. They are also responsible for developing and evaluating the internal controls necessary to ensure database integrity. Some will become involved as designers and managers of databases.

Database technology is widespread because it provides organizations with the following benefits:

- **Data integration** Integration is achieved by combining master files into larger "pools" of data that many application programs can access. An example is an employee database that consolidates data formerly contained in payroll, personnel, and job skills master files. This makes it easier for information to be combined in unlimited ways.
- **Data sharing** Integrating data makes it easier to share data with all authorized users. The FBI, which does a good job of collecting data but a poor job of sharing it with authorized users who need it, is planning to spend eight years and up to $400 million on a new database system that integrates data from many different systems throughout the bureau.
- **Reporting flexibility** Reports can be revised easily and generated as needed, and the database can be easily browsed to research a problem or obtain detailed information underlying a summary report.
- **Minimal data redundancy and data inconsistencies** Because data items are usually stored only once, data redundancy and data inconsistencies are minimized.
- **Data independence** Because data and the programs that use them are independent of each other, each can be changed without having to change the other. This makes programming easier and simplifies data management.
- **Central management of data** Data management is more efficient because a database administrator is responsible for coordinating, controlling, and managing data.
- **Cross-functional analysis** In a database system, relationships, such as the association between selling costs and promotional campaigns, can be explicitly defined and used in the preparation of management reports.

The Importance of Good Data

While database systems provide many advantages, bad or incorrect data stored in the database can lead to bad decisions, embarrassment, and angry users of the data. For example:

- For quite some time, a company sent half its catalogs to incorrect addresses. A manager finally investigated the large volume of returns and customer complaints and corrected the customer address problem in the database. He saved the company $12 million a year.
- The city of Valparaiso, Indiana, used the county database to develop its tax rates. After the tax notices had been mailed, a huge error was discovered. A $121,900 home had somehow been valued at $400 million. As a result of the $3.1 million property tax revenue shortfall, the city, the local school district, and various governmental agencies had to make severe budget cuts.

The problem with bad data is not going away.

The Data Warehousing Institute estimates that each year dirty data costs businesses well over $600 billion due to unnecessary postage and marketing costs, as well as lost customer credibility. One consulting firm estimates that over 25% of the data businesses use is inaccurate or incomplete. According to a recent survey, 53% of 750 IT professionals and business said their companies had experienced problems because of poor-quality data, up from 44% four years earlier. Further complicating the problem is that managing data gets harder every year because the quantity of data businesses

generate and store doubles every 18 months. And the problem with bad data spreads as more businesses share information with outside partners and customers.

To avoid outdated, incomplete, or erroneous data, management needs policies and procedures that ensure clean, or "scrubbed," data. Clean data is especially important to top executives as the Sarbanes-Oxley Act states that they can face jail time if they do not have the company's financial data in order. Preventing and detecting bad data are discussed in more detail in Chapters 5 through 9.

Database Systems

Logical and Physical Views of Data

In file-oriented systems, programmers must know the physical location and layout of records used in an application program. Figure 4-3 shows a **record layout** of an accounts receivable file. Suppose a programmer wants a credit report showing the customer number, credit limit, and current balance. To write the program, the programmer must understand the location and length of the fields needed (i.e., record positions 1 through 10 for customer number) and the format of each field (alphanumeric or numeric). The process becomes more complex if data from several files are used.

Database systems overcome this problem by separating the storage and use of data elements. The database approach provides two separate views of the data: the physical view and the logical view. The **logical view** is how the user or programmer conceptually organizes and understands the data. For example, a sales manager may conceptualize all information about customers as being stored in the form of a table. The **physical view** refers to how and where the data are physically arranged and stored in the computer system. Separating the logical and physical views of data facilitates developing new applications because programmers can concentrate on coding the application logic (what the program will do) and do not need to focus on how and where the various data items are stored or accessed.

As shown in Figure 4-4, database management system (DBMS) software handles the link between the way data are physically stored and each user's logical view of that data. Thus, the DBMS controls the database so that users can access, query, or update it without reference to how or where the data are physically stored. The user is responsible only for defining the logical data requirements of the application. Separating the logical and physical views of data also means that users can change their conceptualization about relationships among data items (their logical view of the task) without making changes in the way those data are physically stored. Likewise, the database administrator can change the physical storage of the data to improve system performance without affecting users or application programs.

Schemas

A **schema** describes the logical structure of a database. There are three levels of schemas: the conceptual, the external, and the internal. Figure 4-5 shows the relationships among these three levels.

The **conceptual-level schema** is the organizationwide view of the *entire* database. It lists all data elements and the relationships among them. The **external-level schema**

Customer number N	Customer name A		Address A	Credit limit N	Balance N
1 10	11 30	31	60	61 68	69 76

A = alphanumeric field
N = numeric field

Figure 4-3
Accounts Receivable File Record Layout

Figure 4-4
Function of the DBMS: to
Support Multiple Logical Views
of Data

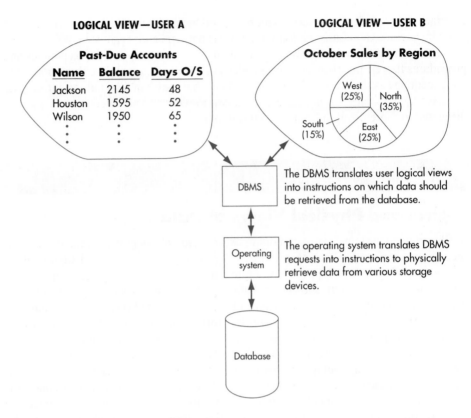

Figure 4-5
Three Levels of Schemas

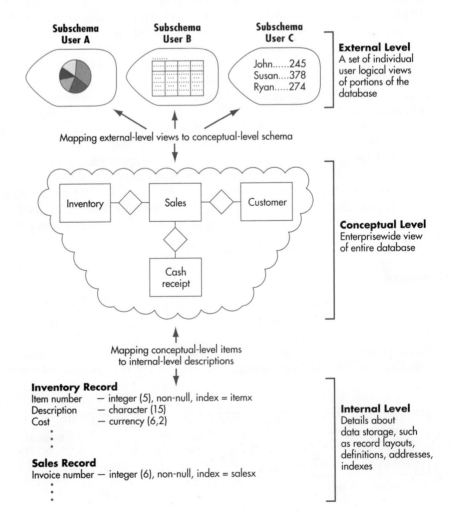

consists of a set of individual user views of portions of the database, each of which is also referred to as a **subschema**. The **internal-level schema** provides a low-level view of the database. It describes how the data are actually stored and accessed, including information about record layouts, definitions, addresses, and indexes. Figure 4-5 connects each of these levels with bidirectional arrows, which represent the mappings between the schemas. The DBMS uses these mappings to translate a user's or an application program's request for data (expressed in terms of logical names and relationships) into the corresponding indexes and addresses needed to physically access the data.

Accountants are frequently involved in developing the conceptual- and external-level schemas, so it is important to understand the difference between the two. Consider the revenue cycle for S&S. The conceptual schema for the revenue cycle database would contain information about customers, sales, cash receipts, sales personnel, cash, and inventory. At the external level, a number of subschemas could be derived from this schema, each tailored to the needs of different users or application programs. Each subschema would also be designed to prevent access to those portions of the database that are not relevant to a particular user's job. For example, the external-level subschema for the sales order entry staff would include information about customer credit limits and current balances as well as inventory quantities and prices. However, it would probably not include information about the costs of inventory or current company bank account balances. The external-level subschema for the delivery staff would include information about the customer's address but would probably not include information about each customer's credit limit or employee pay rates. Additional subschemas would define the relevant portions of the database that other employees must access to perform their jobs.

The Data Dictionary

A key component of a DBMS is the **data dictionary**, which contains information about the structure of the database. For each data element stored in the database, such as the customer number, there is a corresponding record in the data dictionary describing it. Table 4-1 shows examples of the kind of information the data dictionary contains about each data element. Accountants often participate in the development of the data dictionary because they understand the data elements that exist in a business organization, where they originate, and where they are used.

The DBMS usually maintains the data dictionary. In fact, this is often one of the first applications of a newly implemented database system. Inputs to the data dictionary include records of any new or deleted data elements, as well as changes in names, descriptions, or uses of existing data elements. Outputs include a variety of reports useful to programmers, database designers, and users of the information system. Sample reports include (1) a list of all programs in which a data item is used, (2) a list of all synonyms for the data elements in a particular file, (3) a list of all data elements used by a particular user, and (4) a list of all output reports in which a data element is used. These reports are useful in the design and implementation of a database system, provide documentation of the system, and can become part of the audit trail.

DBMS Languages

Every DBMS must provide a means of performing the three basic functions of creating, changing, and querying the database. The set of commands used to perform these functions are referred to as the data definition, data manipulation, and data query languages, respectively.

The **data definition language (DDL)** is used to (1) build the data dictionary, (2) initialize or create the database, (3) describe the logical views for each individual user or programmer, and (4) specify any limitations or constraints on security imposed on database records or fields.

Table 4-1
Example of a Data Dictionary

Data Element Name	Description	Records in Which Contained	Source	Field Length	Field Type	Programs in Which Used	Outputs in Which Contained	Authorized Users	Other Data Names
Customer number	Unique identifier of each customer	A/R record, customer record, sales analysis record	Customer number listing	10	Numeric	A/R update, customer file update, sales analysis update, credit analysis	A/R aging report, customer status report, sales analysis report, credit report	No restrictions	None
Customer name	Complete name of customer	Customer record	Initial customer order	20	Alphanumeric	Customer file update, statement processing	Customer status report, monthly statement	No restrictions	None
Address	Street, city, state, and Zip code	Customer record	Credit application	30	Alphanumeric	Customer file update, statement processing	Customer status report, monthly statement	No restrictions	None
Credit limit	Maximum credit that can be extended to customer	Customer record, A/R record	Credit application	8	Numeric	Customer file update, A/R update, credit analysis	Customer status report, A/R aging report, credit report	D. Dean R. Dalebout H. Heaton	CR_limit
Balance	Balance due from customer on credit purchases	A/R record, sales analysis record	Various sales and payment transactions	8	Numeric	A/R update, sales analysis update, statement processing, credit analysis	A/R aging report, sales analysis report, monthly statement, credit report	G. Burton B. Heninger S. Summers	Cust_bal

The **data manipulation language (DML)** is used for data maintenance, which includes such operations as updating, inserting, and deleting portions of the database.

The **data query language (DQL)** is used to interrogate the database. Whereas the DML is used to change the contents of the database, the DQL retrieves, sorts, orders, and presents subsets of the database in response to user queries. Most DQLs contain a fairly powerful, but easy to use, set of commands that enable users to satisfy many of their information needs without a programmer's assistance.

Many DBMSs also include a **report writer**, which is a language that simplifies report creation. Typically, users need only specify which data elements they want printed and how the report should be formatted. The report writer then searches the database, extracts the specified data items, and prints them out according to the user-specified format.

All users generally have access to both the DQL and the report writer. Access to the DDL and DML, however, should be restricted to those employees with administrative and programming responsibilities. This helps to limit the number of people who can make changes to the database.

Relational Databases

A DBMS is characterized by the type of logical data model on which it is based. A **data model** is an abstract representation of the contents of a database. Most new DBMSs are called relational databases because they use the relational data model developed by Dr. E. F. Codd in 1970. Therefore, this chapter focuses primarily on relational databases.

The **relational data model** represents everything in the database as being stored in the form of tables like the one shown in Table 4-2. Technically, these tables are called **relations** (hence the name *relational* data model), but we will use the two words interchangeably. Moreover, keep in mind that the relational data model only describes how the data appear in the conceptual- and external-level schemas. The data are not actually stored in tables but rather in the manner described in the internal-level schema.

Each row in a relation, called a **tuple** (which rhymes with *couple*), contains data about a specific occurrence of the type of entity represented by that table. For example, each row in the inventory table in Table 4-2 contains data about a particular inventory item that S&S carries. Similarly, each row in a customer table would contain information about a specific customer. Each column in a table contains information

Table 4-2
Sample Inventory Table for S&S

Item Number	Description	Color	Vendor Number	Quantity on Hard	Price
1036	Refrigerator	White	10023	12	1199
1038	Refrigerator	Almond	10023	7	1299
1039	Refrigerator	Hunter Green	10023	5	1499
2061	Range	White	10011	6	799
2063	Range	Black	10011	5	999
3541	Washer	White	10008	15	499
3544	Washer	Black	10008	10	699
3785	Dryer	White	10019	12	399
3787	Dryer	Almond	10019	8	499

Record: 10 of 10

about one specific attribute of that entity. For example, each column in the inventory table in Table 4-2 contains data about specific inventory attributes, such as description, color, and price. Similarly, each column in a customer table would contain information about customer attributes, such as customer name and customer address.

Types of Attributes

Tables in a relational database have several types of attributes. A **primary key** is the attribute, or combination of attributes, that uniquely identifies a specific row in a table. For example, the primary key for the inventory table in Table 4-2 is Item Number. Each different merchandise item that S&S sells can be uniquely identified by its item number. Usually, the primary key is a single attribute. In some tables, however, two or more attributes jointly form the primary key. For example, the primary key of the Sales-Inventory table in Table 4-5 (see page 138) is the combination of Sales Invoice # and Item #.

A **foreign key** is an attribute in a table that is a primary key in another table. Foreign keys are used to link tables. An example is the attribute Customer # in Table 4-5. It is the primary key in the Customer table and, as a foreign key in the Sales table, it is used to link the data about a particular customer in the Sales table to the Customer table (see arrows connecting tables).

Other nonkey attributes in each table store important information about that entity. For example, the inventory table in Table 4-2 also contains information about the description, color, vendor number, quantity on hand, and price of each item S&S carries.

Designing a Relational Data Base for S&S, Inc.

In a manual accounting system, S&S would capture sales information on a preprinted paper form called a sales invoice. This hard-copy document provides both a logical and physical view of the data collected. Physical storage of sales invoice data is simple: S&S retains one or more copies of the invoice in a file cabinet. For example, one copy could be stored by invoice number to provide a chronological record of all sales and another could be filed by customer name to facilitate analysis of specific customer accounts.

Storing the same data in a computer is a little more complex. Suppose, for example, that S&S had five sales invoices (numbered from 101 to 105) that it wanted to store electronically. On several of these invoices, a customer purchases more than one item (a television and a refrigerator, for example). Let us look at the effects of several potential ways of storing this information.

Option 1: Store All Data in One Uniform Table. S&S could store all its sales data in one table, as illustrated in Table 4-3, but this approach has two disadvantages. First, it creates a great deal of redundancy in terms of stored data. For example, examine sales invoice number 102 in Table 4-3. Since there are three separate inventory items sold, the invoice and customer data (columns 1–9) are recorded three times. Likewise, inventory descriptions and unit prices are repeated each time an item is sold. Because sales volume can be fairly high in a retail store (remember, Table 4-3 represents only five invoices), such redundancy can make file maintenance unnecessarily time-consuming and error-prone.

Several problems can occur when you try to store all the sales invoice data in one table. The first is called an **update anomaly**, because changes (updates) to data values are not correctly recorded. For example, changing a customer's address in our example would require searching the entire table and changing every occurrence of that customer's address. Overlooking even one row would create an inconsistency in the database, because multiple addresses would then exist for the same customer. This could result in unnecessary duplicate mailings and other types of errors.

The other two types of problems associated with the approach depicted in Table 4-3 are caused by the fact that customer, salesperson, and inventory data are not maintained

Table 4-3
Example of Storing All Sales Data for S&S in One Table

Sales Invoice #	Date	Salesperson	Customer #	Invoice Total	Customer Name	Street	City	State	Item #	Quantity	Description	Unit Price	Extended Amount
101	10/15/2008	J. Buck	151	1447	D. Ainge	123 Lotus Lane	Phoenix	AZ	10	2	Television	499	998
101	10/15/2008	J. Buck	151	1447	D. Ainge	123 Lotus Lane	Phoenix	AZ	50	1	Microwave	449	449
102	10/15/2008	S. Knight	152	4394	G. Kite	40 Quatro Road	Mesa	AZ	10	1	Television	499	499
102	10/15/2008	S. Knight	152	4394	G. Kite	40 Quatro Road	Mesa	AZ	20	3	Freezer	699	2097
102	10/15/2008	S. Knight	152	4394	G. Kite	40 Quatro Road	Mesa	AZ	30	2	Refrigerator	899	1798
103	10/15/2008	S. Knight	151	898	D. Ainge	123 Lotus Lane	Phoenix	AZ	50	2	Microwave	449	898
104	10/15/2008	J. Buck	152	789	G. Kite	40 Quatro Road	Mesa	AZ	40	1	Range	789	789
105	11/14/2008	J. Buck	153	3994	F. Roberts	401 Excel Way	Chandler	AZ	10	3	Television	499	1497
105	11/14/2008	J. Buck	153	3994	F. Roberts	401 Excel Way	Chandler	AZ	20	1	Freezer	699	699
105	11/14/2008	J. Buck	153	3994	F. Roberts	401 Excel Way	Chandler	AZ	30	2	Refrigerator	899	1798

Record: 11 of 11

independently of sales invoice data. The second problem that can occur is referred to as an **insert anomaly**, because there is no way to store information about prospective customers until they actually make a purchase. For example, if information about a prospective customer was entered before a purchase is made, the Sales Invoice # column would be blank. However, the sales invoice number is the primary key for Table 4-3 and cannot be blank, as it uniquely identifies the record.

The third problem is called a **delete anomaly**, because unintended results occur when deleting a row in the table. For example, if a customer has made only one purchase, consisting of a single item, deleting that row from the table in Table 4-3 would result in the loss of all information about that customer.

Option 2: Vary the Number of Columns. An alternative to the data storage scheme depicted in Table 4-3 is to record the sales invoice and customer information just once within the first nine columns and then add additional columns to record each item sold. Table 4-4 illustrates this approach.

Although this approach does reduce some of the data redundancy and some of the anomalies associated with the data storage scheme illustrated in Table 4-3, it still has its drawbacks. S&S would have to decide in advance how many item numbers to leave room for in each row (that is, how many columns to put in the table; note in Table 4-4 that to store each additional item requires five additional columns—Item, Quantity, Description, Unit Price, and Extended Amount). If room is left for only four items (20 columns), how would information about a sale involving eight items (requiring 40 columns) be stored? If room is left for eight items, however, there will be a great deal of wasted space, as is the case for sales invoices 103 and 104.

The Solution: A Set of Tables. The problems associated with the data storage schemes from Tables 4-3 and 4-4 can be solved using what is called a **relational database**. The set of tables depicted in Table 4-5 represent a well-structured relational database. The guidelines used to develop a properly structured relational database are now discussed.

Basic Requirements of a Relational Database

1 Every column in a row must be single valued. In a relational database there is one, and only one, value in any given cell. At S&S, each sales transaction can involve more than one inventory item. For example, on sales invoice number 102, the customer bought a television, a freezer, and a refrigerator. If Item # was included as an attribute in the sales table, it would have to take on more than one value (item numbers 10, 20, and 30). To solve this problem, a sales-inventory table was created that lists each item sold on an invoice. Note that the third line in the sales-inventory table in Table 4-5 shows invoice number 102 and item number 10 (television). The fourth line shows invoice number 102 and item number 20 (freezer). The fifth line shows invoice number 102 and item number 30 (refrigerator). This table allows the invoice number to be repeated as often as needed to show all the different items purchased on any one sales invoice.

Table 4-4
Example of Storing S&S Sales Data by Adding Columns for Each Additional Item Sold

Sales Invoice #	Columns 2-9	Item #	Quantity	Description	Unit Price	Extended Amount	Item #2	Quantity2
101	Same 8	10	2	Television	499	998	50	1
102	columns	10	1	Television	499	499	20	3
103	as in	50	2	Microwave	449	898		
104	Table 4-3	40	1	Range	789	789		
105	above	10	3	Television	499	1497	20	1

Record: ◄ ◄ | 6 | ► ►► ►* | of 6

2 Primary keys cannot be null. The primary key is the attribute, or combination of attributes, that uniquely identifies a specific row in a table. For this to be true, the primary key of any row in a relation cannot be null (blank), for then there would be no way to uniquely identify that row and retrieve the data stored there. A non-null value for the primary key indicates that a specific object exists and can be identified by reference to its primary key value. This is referred to as the **entity integrity rule**, because it ensures that every row in every relation must represent data about some specific object in the real world. Note in the Sales-Inventory table in Table 4-5 that there is no single field that uniquely identifies each row. However, the Sales Invoice # and Item # columns, taken together, do uniquely identify each row. Therefore, both attributes are combined to form the primary key.

3 Foreign keys, if not null, must have values that correspond to the value of a primary key in another table. Foreign keys are used to link rows in one table to rows in another table. (See the lines and arrows in Table 4-5.) For example, the Customer # is a foreign key in the sales table in Table 4-5, and links each sales transaction with the customer who participated in that event. This is only possible, however, if the customer number values in the sales table correspond to actual customer numbers in the customer table. This constraint is referred to as the **referential integrity rule** because it ensures the consistency of the database. Foreign keys can contain null values, however. For example, some customers pay cash and for privacy reasons do not want to give S&S any way to identify and track them. Therefore, for such cash sales, the Customer # field in the sales table would be blank.

4 All nonkey attributes in a table should describe a characteristic about the object identified by the primary key. Most tables contain other attributes in addition to primary and foreign keys. Consider the sales table shown in Table 4-5. Sales Invoice # is the primary key. Both Customer # and Salesperson are foreign keys, although the salesperson table is not shown. The remaining attribute (Date) is an important fact about the sales event. Details about the customer or salesperson who participated in that transaction, or about the items purchased, however, are stored in those tables, not in the sales table.

These four constraints produce a well-structured (normalized) database in which data are consistent and redundancy is minimized and controlled. Notice how the relational database tables illustrated in Table 4-5, with a table for each separate entity of interest, avoids the problems discussed previously. First, notice that redundancy is greatly reduced. For example, all nonkey attributes, such as customer addresses and unit prices, are stored just once. This avoids the potential of update anomaly problems. Note that redundancy is not entirely eliminated, however. Certain items, such as Sales Invoice # and Item #, appear in more than one table. These attributes appear more than once only when they function as foreign keys, however. Consequently, the referential integrity rule ensures that there will be no update anomaly problems with the foreign keys.

Description2	Unit Price2	Extended Amou	Item #3	Quantity3	Description3	Unit Price3	Extended Amount3
Microwave	449	449					
Freezer	699	2097	30	2	Refrigerator	899	1798
Freezer	699	699	30	2	Refrigerator	899	1798

of 6

Table 4-5
Set of Relational Tables for
Storing S&S Sales Data

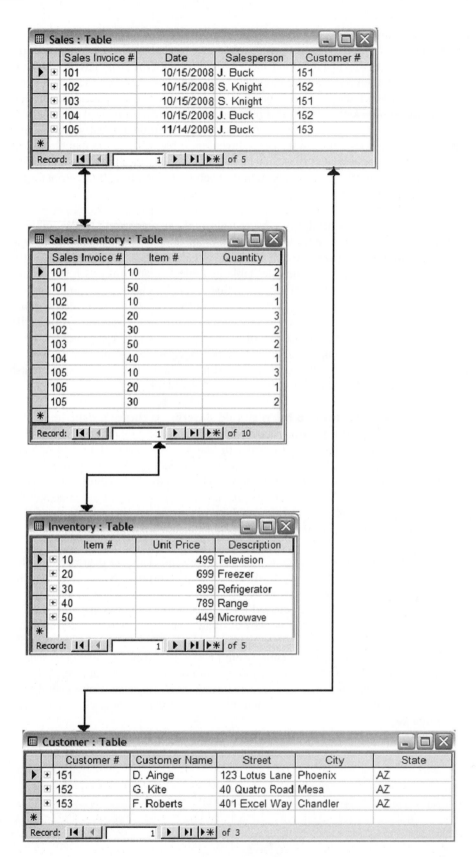

Sales : Table

	Sales Invoice #	Date	Salesperson	Customer #
+	101	10/15/2008	J. Buck	151
+	102	10/15/2008	S. Knight	152
+	103	10/15/2008	S. Knight	151
+	104	10/15/2008	J. Buck	152
+	105	11/14/2008	J. Buck	153

Record: 1 of 5

Sales-Inventory : Table

Sales Invoice #	Item #	Quantity
101	10	2
101	50	1
102	10	1
102	20	3
102	30	2
103	50	2
104	40	1
105	10	3
105	20	1
105	30	2

Record: 1 of 10

Inventory : Table

	Item #	Unit Price	Description
+	10	499	Television
+	20	699	Freezer
+	30	899	Refrigerator
+	40	789	Range
+	50	449	Microwave

Record: 1 of 5

Customer : Table

	Customer #	Customer Name	Street	City	State
+	151	D. Ainge	123 Lotus Lane	Phoenix	AZ
+	152	G. Kite	40 Quatro Road	Mesa	AZ
+	153	F. Roberts	401 Excel Way	Chandler	AZ

Record: 1 of 3

An important feature of the schema depicted in Table 4-5 is that data about various things of interest (customers, inventory, and sales transactions) are stored in separate tables. This makes it easier to add new data to the system. For example, information about prospective customers can be stored simply by adding another row in the customer table. Thus, the set of tables depicted in Table 4-5 avoids the problem of an insert anomaly.

The schema shown in Table 4-5 also simplifies the deletion of information. For example, deleting sales invoice 105, representing the only sale to customer 153 (F. Roberts), would not result in the loss of all information about that customer, because information about each customer is stored in the customer table. Thus, the set of tables depicted in Table 4-5 is free from delete anomalies.

Another benefit of the schema depicted in Table 4-5 is that space is used efficiently. The sales-inventory table contains a row for each item sold on each invoice. There are no blank rows, yet all data about each sale are recorded. In contrast, the schema depicted in Table 4-4 results in much wasted space.

Two Approaches to Database Design

There are two basic ways to design well-structured relational databases like the one depicted in Table 4-5. One approach, called **normalization**, starts with the assumption that everything is initially stored in one large table. A set of rules is then followed to decompose that initial table into a set of normalized tables. The objective is to produce a set of tables in what is called third normal form (3NF), because such tables are free of the types of update, insert, and delete anomaly problems described previously. The details of the normalization process are beyond the scope of this book but can be found in any database textbook.

An alternative way to design well-structured relational databases involves semantic data modeling. Under this approach, the database designer uses knowledge about how business processes typically work and about the information needs associated with transaction processing to draw a graphical picture of what should be included in the database. The resulting figure can then be directly used to create a set of relational tables that are in 3NF.

Semantic data modeling has two significant advantages over simply following the rules of normalization. First, because it makes use of the system designer's knowledge about business processes and practices, it facilitates the efficient design of transaction processing databases. Second, because the resulting graphical model explicitly represents information about the organization's business processes and policies, it facilitates communicating with the intended users of the system. Such communication is extremely important in ensuring that the resulting system meets the actual needs of users. Chapter 15 introduces two semantic data modeling tools that accountants and business systems professionals use to design transaction processing databases, namely E-R (entity-relationship) diagramming and the REA data model.

Creating Relational Database Queries

Databases store data for people and organizations. To retrieve the stored information, a database and its attendant set of tables are queried. This section of the chapter provides a brief introduction to database queries using Microsoft Access. If you want to follow along and personally create the queries illustrated, download the S&S In-Chapter Database from the text's Web site.

When the database is opened and the Queries tab or view is selected, the screen will appear as shown in the top half of Table 4-6. There are two ways to query (question) the database to extract information: create a query in Design view or utilize the wizard. In the text, the design view is used to create the queries. Double-clicking on "Create query in Design View" produces the Show Table window shown in the bottom half of Table 4-6. This screen allows the user to select the tables needed to query the database. The user

Table 4-6
Creating Queries in the
Microsoft Access Database

should only select the tables that are necessary to produce the needed information; if more tables than necessary are selected, the query may not run properly.

To illustrate how to query an Access database, we will walk you through the steps needed to create and run five separate queries. This section is not intended to make you experts in querying an Access database but rather to show you how you can produce useful information from a database. We will explain enough about querying Access to help you generate these five queries.

Query 1

Query 1 answers two questions: What are the invoice numbers of all sales made to D. Ainge, and who was the salesperson for each sale?

The first step in creating a query is to determine which of the tables in Table 4-5 contain the needed information. We need three pieces of information to satisfy our query: Sales Invoice #, Salesperson, and Customer Name. The first two items are in the Sales table, and the last item is in the Customer table.

Next, we select the two tables we need using the Show Table window shown in the bottom half of Table 4-6. We select the Sales and then the Customer table by double-clicking on their names or by single-clicking on the table and clicking the Add button. When tables are selected, they will appear as shown in the top half of Table 4-7. A line connects the common fields (the primary key Customer # in the Customer table and the foreign key Customer # in the Sales table) in the two tables. The 1 and ∞ symbols attached to the lines indicates that each Sale is to only one customer and each customer can be associated with many (the ∞ symbol) sales. We are done with the Show Table window; so we click on Close to make it disappear.

We need to populate the bottom half of the Select Query screen, as shown in Table 4-7. Select Sales Invoice # and Salesperson from the Sales table by double-clicking on them or by dragging and dropping them into the Field row. Do the same for Customer Name from the Customer table. Access automatically puts a check mark in the box in the Show line so the item will be shown when the query is run.

Table 4-7
Completed Query 1

Since we only want sales to D. Ainge, we type that value in the criteria line of the Customer Name column, (see Table 4-7). To run our query we click on the red ! (exclamation) mark on the Access toolbar or click the Query option on the toolbar and then the Run command. The tables used, the primary-foreign key relationship between the tables, and the query answer are shown in Table 4-8. If you are working along with the text, note that your query does not have the title "Ainge Sales" as shown at the bottom of Table 4-8. To assign the query a name, you must first save the query and then

Table 4-8
Query 1 Relationships and Query Answer

rerun it. We save queries by selecting File from the Access menu, then Save As, and then entering "Ainge Sales" in the first line of the Save As window. When you rerun the query again, the query title will be shown as in the bottom of Table 4-8.

Query 2

Query 2 answers this question: How many televisions were sold in October? We create this query in the Design view. By referring to Table 4-5, we determine that the dates needed for this query are in the Sales table, the Inventory Description is in the Inventory table, and the Quantity sold is in the Sales-Inventory table.

Accordingly, we again click on "Create query in Design view" (see Table 4-6) and select the Sales, Sales-Inventory, and Inventory tables. We select the Date field from the Sales table, the Description field from the Inventory table, and the Quantity field from the Sales-Inventory table, as shown in Table 4-9.

Since we want only the quantity of televisions sold in October, we add the criteria "Between #10/1/2005# And #10/31/2005#" to the Date field and "Television" to the Description field.

Access uses several phrases, or operators, for specifying criteria, including "Between," "And," "Or," and such. An "And" operator returns the data that meets *all* the criteria linked by "And" operators. The "Between" operator allows us to find or select all the data in October of 2005; that is, between and including the first and last days of the month. If the Between operator was not used and the "Or" operator replaced the "And" operator in our criteria statement, all the televisions sold either on

Table 4-9
Completed Query 2 and Answer

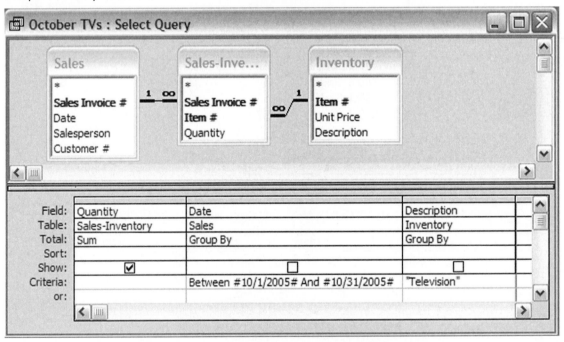

Query Answer

10/1/2005 or on 10/31/2005 would be located. Access uses the "#" symbol to tell the program that it is looking for a date rather than some other type of text.

Since we are looking for the total television sales in October, the Date field will not be meaningful in our query answer (there may be various dates in October when televisions are sold). Therefore, in the Show line we uncheck the box in the Date column. To generate total sales, right-click in the Quantity field. From the pop-up menu that appears, select Totals. A new line, called Total, will appear on the screen (compare Tables 4-7 and 4-9). Left-click on the cell that is the intersection of the Totals line and the Quantity column. Click on the down-arrow symbol that appears. From the pop-up menu that appears, select Sum. The remaining two fields in the Total line will stay as Group By.

We are now ready to run the query shown in Table 4-9. Again, select the red exclamation point on the Access menu. The answer shown in the bottom half of Table 4-9 appears.

Query 3

Query 3 answers this question: What are the names and addresses of the customers buying televisions in October? This is the type of query management might ask as a follow-up to Query 2. It also illustrates the use of all four tables in our example.

To answer this query, we need the Date field from the Sales table (so we can select the October sales), the Description field from the Inventory table (so we can restrict the query to televisions), and the Customer Name, Street, City, and State fields from the Customer table (the information we want to display). We also need to select the Sales-Inventory table, as the only way to move between the Sales table and the Inventory table is through the Sales-Inventory table. (See Table 4-5.) We use the same criteria we used in Query 2. The date and description data are not needed in the query answer, so the boxes in the Show line are unchecked.

Selecting all four tables and the needed data produces the Select Query screen shown in the top half of Table 4-10. Running the query produces the answer shown at the bottom of Table 4-10.

Table 4-10
Completed Query 3 and Answer

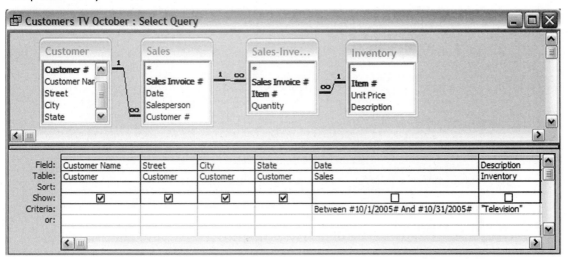

Query Answer

Query 4

Query 4 answers this question: What are the sales invoice numbers, dates, and invoice totals for all sales in October, arranged in descending order by amount of the sale? Since the database does not contain an Invoice Total column, we must calculate it. This is a two-step process.

1 Calculate, for each invoice, the total sales price of each item sold by multiplying the Quantity sold field in the Sales-Inventory table by the Unit Price field in the Inventory table. For example, we see in the Sales-Inventory table in Table 4-5 that three items were sold on Sales Invoice 102 (items 10, 20, and 30). For item 20, we multiply the quantity (3) by the Unit Price of 699, which comes from the Inventory table. The total is 2,097. We do the same for items 10 and 30.

2 Add the three subtotals together to get an invoice total.

Query 4 requires the Sales table (the Date and Sales Invoice #), Sales-Inventory table (the Quantity sold), and the Inventory table (the Unit Price). However, not all of these fields will appear in columns on the Select Query window. We will only display three columns: Sales Invoice #, Date, and the Invoice Total we will calculate. The other fields are used in the Total Invoice calculations. The tables and fields selected will appear on the screen as shown in the top half of Table 4-11.

To create the Invoice Total column, we type "Invoice Total:" in the first blank Field cell, right-click in the cell, and select Build from the pop-up menu that appears. An Expression Builder window (see Table 4-12) appears on the screen. We will use this screen to build the formula needed to calculate the total for each invoice. To do so, we type "Sum()". Then, with the cursor between the parentheses, double-click on the + sign in front of the Tables folder. The four tables in the database appear. Click on the Sales-Inventory folder, and the fields in the Sales-Inventory table appear. Double-click on Quantity to put this field in the expression. Note in Table 4-11 or 4-12 that the expression shows the table name and the field name, separated by an exclamation

Table 4-11
Completed Query 4 and Answer

Query Answer

Table 4-12
Expression Builder for Query 4

point. Since we want to multiply Quantity by Unit Price, we type an * (the multiplication symbol) and select the Inventory table and the Unit Price field. Our formula is now complete, and the screen will appear as shown in Table 4-12. To place the expression in the Select Query window (shown in Table 4-11), click on OK.

To complete Query 4, right-click in any cell and add the Total line. Click on the down arrow in the intersection of the Total row and Invoice Totals column and select Expression from the pop-up menu. This tells Access to calculate the indicated expression for all items with the same sales invoice number and date. In the same column, click on the down arrow in the Sort row and select Descending so that the answer is show in descending Invoice Total order. In the criteria section of the Date column, use the Between operator to specify the month of October. Query 4 is now complete, and running it produces the answer shown in the bottom half of Table 4-11.

Query 5

Query 5 will answer this question: What are total sales by salesperson? This query is similar to Query 4, except that we total invoices by salesperson rather than by invoice number. We are also not confining our query to the month of October. Try coming up with the query by yourself. The completed query and the answer are shown in Table 4-13.

Database Systems and the Future of Accounting

Database systems may profoundly affect the fundamental nature of accounting. For instance, database systems may lead to the abandonment of the double-entry accounting model. The basic rationale for the double-entry model is that the redundancy of recording the amount of a transaction twice provides a check on the accuracy of data processing. Every transaction generates equal debit and credit entries, and the equality of debits and credits is checked and rechecked at numerous points in the accounting process. Data redundancy, however, is the antithesis of the database concept. If the

Table 4-13
Query 5

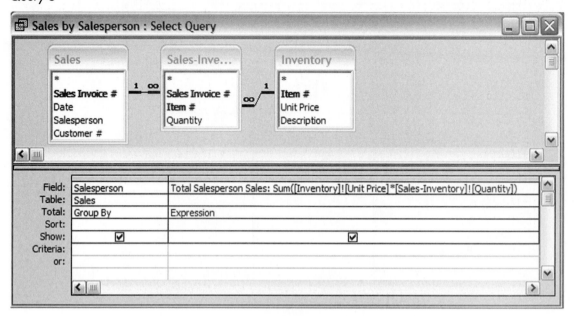

Query Answer

amounts associated with a transaction are entered into a database system correctly, then it is necessary to store them only once, not twice. Computer data processing is sufficiently accurate to make unnecessary the elaborate system of checks and double checks that characterizes the double-entry accounting model.

Database systems also have the potential to significantly alter the nature of external reporting. Considerable time and effort are currently invested in defining how companies should summarize and report accounting information to external users. Why not simply make a copy of the company's financial database and make it available to external users in lieu of the traditional financial statements? Users would then be free to manipulate and analyze the raw data in whatever manner they see fit. Focus 4-1 discusses this possibility in more detail.

Perhaps the most significant effect of database systems will be in the way accounting information is used in decision making. The difficulty of formulating ad hoc queries in accounting systems based on traditional files or nonrelational DBMSs meant that accountants acted, in effect, as information gatekeepers. Financial information was readily available only in predefined formats and at specified times. Relational databases, however, provide query languages that are powerful and easy to use. Thus, managers need not get bogged down in procedural details about how to retrieve information. Instead, they can concentrate solely on specifying what information they want. As a result, financial reports can be easily prepared to cover whatever time periods managers want to examine, not just the time frames accountants traditionally use.

Relational DBMSs can also accommodate multiple views of the same underlying phenomenon. For example, tables storing information about assets can include columns not only for historical costs but also for current replacement costs and market values. Thus, managers will no longer be forced to look at data in ways predefined by accountants.

4-1 FOCUS · Databases or Financial Statements?

 lthough information technology has dramatically changed the way that business is conducted, it has had relatively little effect on external reporting. Companies still produce periodic (quarterly and annual) financial reports of past activities based on historical costs. Moreover, they present that information at a highly aggregated level. It is estimated that the average financial database of a typical large company is on the order of 100 gigabytes. Yet annual reports contain, on average, only about 100 kilobytes of data. Consequently, users of annual reports see only a small portion of the data about the organization. In addition, the information is presented in a predefined format (the financial statements).

Why not replace the annual report with a copy of the company's financial database? Many companies already give their suppliers and customers limited access to their internal databases. Suppliers, for example, may be given access to inventory data so that they can plan production and deliveries to replenish shortages. They are not, however, given access to human resource or payroll data.

Companies could similarly define a view of their database that excluded data too sensitive to be allowed to fall into the hands of competitors. This view of the database could be placed on CD-ROMs or made available over the Internet to investors, creditors, and other external users.

The technical capability for providing such database access exists. The computing power of current PCs makes processing such a database feasible for a wide range of users. External users would get a fuller picture of the organization's performance, and the information would also be more timely.

In such a system, the company's primary financial reporting function would involve the definition of data elements and database structure. Users would then be free to aggregate and classify that information using whatever decision model they believed to be appropriate.

Source: Robert K. Elliot, "Confronting the Future: Choices for the Attest Function," *Accounting Horizons* (September 1994): 106–124.

Finally, relational DBMSs provide the capability of integrating financial and operational data. For example, data about customer satisfaction, collected by surveys or interviews, could be stored in the same database used to store information about current account balances and credit limits. Managers would thus have access to a richer set of data for making tactical and strategic decisions.

In all these ways, relational DBMSs have the potential to increase the use and value of accounting information for making the tactical and strategic decisions involved in running an organization. Accountants, however, must become knowledgeable about database systems so that they can participate in designing the accounting information systems of the future. Such participation is important for ensuring that adequate controls are included in those systems to safeguard the data and ensure the reliability of the information produced.

SUMMARY AND CASE CONCLUSION

Ashton prepared a report for Scott and Susan summarizing what he knew about database systems in general and the relational data model in particular. His report explained that a database management system (DBMS) is the software that makes a database system work. A DBMS is based on a logical data model, which determines how users perceive the data as being stored.

Many DBMSs are based on the relational data model. This model represents data as being stored in the form of tables, which are called relations. Every row in a relational table has only one data value in each column. Neither row nor column position is significant. These properties support the use of simple, yet powerful, query languages for interacting with a relational database. Users need specify only what data they want

and need not be concerned with how the data are retrieved. The DBMS functions as an intermediary between the user and the database, thereby hiding the complex addressing schemes actually used to retrieve and update the information stored in the database.

After reading Ashton's report, Scott and Susan agreed that it was time to upgrade S&S's AIS. They agreed with Ashton's suggestion that S&S hire a consulting firm to help guide the selection and installation of the new system. They also asked him to be involved in the design process to ensure that the new system meets their needs.

KEY TERMS

database management
 system (DBMS) 127
database system 127
database administrator
 (DBA) 127
data warehouse 127
data mining 127
record layout 129
logical view 129
physical view 129
schema 129
conceptual-level
 schema 129

external-level
 schema 129
subschema 131
internal-level schema 131
data dictionary 131
data definition language
 (DDL) 131
data manipulation
 language (DML) 133
data query language
 (DQL) 133
report writer 133
data model 133

relational data model 133
relation 133
tuple 133
primary key 134
foreign key 134
update anomaly 134
insert anomaly 136
delete anomaly 136
relational database 136
entity integrity rule 137
referential integrity
 rule 137
normalization 139

AIS IN ACTION

CHAPTER QUIZ

1 The relational data model portrays data as being stored in
 a. hierarchies
 b. tables
 c. objects
 d. files

2 How a user conceptually organizes and understands data is referred to as the
 a. physical view
 b. logical view
 c. data model view
 d. data organization view

3 What is each row in a relational database table called?
 a. relation
 b. attribute
 c. anomaly
 d. tuple

4 Which of the following is an individual user's view of the database?
 a. conceptual-level schema
 b. external-level schema
 c. internal-level schema
 d. logical-level schema

5 Which of the following would managers most likely use to retrieve information about sales during the month of October?
 a. DML
 b. DSL
 c. DDL
 d. DQL

6 Which of the following attributes would most likely be a primary key?
 a. supplier name
 b. supplier number
 c. supplier Zip code
 d. supplier account balance

7 Which of the following is a software program that runs a database system?
 a. DQL c. DML
 b. DBMS d. DDL

8 The constraint that all primary keys must have non-null data values is referred to as which of the following?
 a. referential integrity rule c. normalization rule
 b. entity integrity rule d. relational data model rule

9 The constraint that all foreign keys must have either null values or the value of a primary key in another table is referred to as which of the following?
 a. referential integrity rule c. foreign key value rule
 b. integrity entity rule d. null value rule

10 Which of the following attributes in the Cash Receipts table (representing payments received from customers) would most likely be a foreign key?
 a. cash receipt number c. customer number
 b. customer check number d. cash receipt date

COMPREHENSIVE PROBLEM

The Butler Financing Company runs a mortgage brokerage business in which it matches lenders with borrowers. Table 4-14 lists a small portion of the data that Butler maintains on its clients (borrowers) and lenders. The data are maintained on a spreadsheet and must be manually updated each time a new client is engaged, a new lender is listed, or a new mortgage is prepared. This manual updating is error prone, and on more than one occasion business has been hurt by spreadsheet errors. In addition, the spreadsheet has to be sorted in many different ways to retrieve the necessary data.

Create a database from Butler's spreadsheet that does not have any of the data anomalies presented in the chapter. To test the database, prepare a query to show which borrowers (both borrower number and name) took out loans from Excel Mortgage and who the appraiser was for each loan.

DISCUSSION QUESTIONS

4.1 A database allows two distinct views of data: a logical view and a physical view. Contrast the two views, and discuss why separate views are necessary in database applications. Describe which perspective is most useful for each of the following employees: a programmer, a manager, and an internal auditor. How will understanding logical data structures assist accountants in designing and using database systems?

4.2 The relational data model represents data as being stored in tables. Spreadsheets are another tool that accountants use to employ a tabular representation of data. What are some similarities and differences in the way that both of these tools use tables? How might an accountant's familiarity with the tabular representation of spreadsheets facilitate or hinder learning how to use a relational DBMS?

4.3 The text explained how database technology may eliminate the need for double-entry accounting. This creates three possibilities: (1) the double-entry model will be

Table 4-14
Butler Financing Company Spreadsheet

Borrower Number	Last Name	First Name	Current Address	Requested Mortgage Amount	Lender Number	Lender Name	Lender Office Address	Property Appraiser Number	Property Appraiser Name
450	Adams	Jennifer	450 Peachtree Rd.	$245,000	13	Excel Mortgage	6890 Sheridan Dr.	8	Advent Appraisers
451	Adamson	David	500 Loop Highway	$124,688	13	Excel Mortgage	6890 Sheridan Dr.	9	Independent Appraisal Service
452	Bronson	Paul	312 Mountain View Dr.	$345,000	14	CCY	28 Buckhead Way	10	Jones Property Appraisers
453	Brown	Marietta	310 Loop Highway	$ 57,090	15	Advantage Lenders	3345 Lake Shore Dr.	10	Jones Property Appraisers
454	Charles	Kenneth	3 Commons Blvd.	$ 34,000	16	Capital Savings	8890 Coral Blvd.	8	Advent Appraisers
455	Coulter	Tracey	1367 Peachtree Rd.	$216,505	13	Excel Mortgage	6890 Sheridan Dr.	8	Advent Appraisers
456	Foster	Harold	678 Loop Highway	$117,090	12	National Mortgage	750 16 St.	9	Independent Appraisal Service
457	Frank	Vernon	210 Bicayne Blvd.	$ 89,000	12	National Mortgage	750 16 St.	10	Jones Property Appraisers
458	Holmes	Heather	1121 Bicayne Blvd.	$459,010	16	Capital Savings	8890 Coral Blvd.	10	Jones Property Appraisers
459	Johanson	Sandy	817 Mountain View Dr.	$ 67,900	15	Advantage Lenders	3345 Lake Shore Dr.	9	Independent Appraisal Service
460	Johnson	James	985 Loop Highway	$ 12,000	12	National Mortgage	750 16 St.	10	Jones Property Appraisers
461	Jones	Holly	1650 Washington Blvd.	$ 67,890	15	Advantage Lenders	3345 Lake Shore Dr.	9	Independent Appraisal Service

abandoned; (2) the double-entry model will not be used directly, but an external-level schema based on the double-entry model will be defined for accountants' use; or (3) the double-entry model will be retained in database systems. Which alternative do you think is most likely to occur? Why?

4.4 Relational DBMS query languages provide easy access to information about the organization's activities. Does this mean that online, real-time processing should be used for all transactions? Does an organization need real-time financial reports? Why or why not?

PROBLEMS

4.1 The following data elements comprise the conceptual-level schema for a database:

billing address
cost
credit limit
customer name
customer number
date
description
invoice number
item number
price
quantity on hand
quantity sold
shipping address
terms

Required

 a. Identify three potential users and design a subschema for each. Justify your design by explaining why each user needs access to that data element.
 b. Using any relational database product, such as Microsoft Access, create the set of tables to implement your schema. Specify the primary key(s) and foreign key(s) for each table. Learn how to enforce referential integrity, and test your model by entering sample data in each table.

4.2 Most DBMS packages contain a data definition language, a data manipulation language, and a data query language. For each of the following examples, indicate which language would be used and why.
 a. A database administrator defines the logical structure of the database.
 b. The controller requests a cost accounting report containing a list of all employees being paid for more than 10 hours overtime in a given week.
 c. A programmer develops a program to update the fixed-assets records stored in the database.
 d. The human resources manager requests a report noting all employees who are retiring within five years.
 e. The inventory serial number field is extended in the inventory records to allow for recognition of additional inventory items with serial numbers containing more than 10 digits.
 f. A user develops a program to print out all purchases made during the past two weeks.
 g. An additional field is added to the fixed-asset records to record the estimated salvage value of each asset.

4.3 Ashton wants to store the following data about S&S's purchases of inventory:

item number
date of purchase
vendor number
vendor address
vendor name
purchase price
quantity purchased
employee number

employee name
purchase order number
description
quantity on hand
extended amount
total amount of purchase

Required

 a. Design a set of relational tables to store this data. Do all of the data items need to be stored in a table? If not, which ones do not need to be stored and why do they not need to be stored?
 b. Identify the primary key for each table.
 c. Identify the foreign keys needed in the tables to implement referential integrity.
 d. Implement your tables using any relational database product to which you have access.
 e. Test your specification by entering sample data in each table.
 f. Create a few queries to retrieve or analyze the data you stored.

4.4 Retrieve the S&S In-Chapter Database (in Microsoft Access format) from the text's Web site (or create the set of relational tables in Table 4-5 in any relational DBMS product to which you have access). Write queries to answer the following questions. *Note*: For some of these questions you may have to create two queries—one to calculate a total such as invoice total and the second to answer the question asked.
 a. How many different kinds of inventory items does S&S sell?
 b. How many sales were made during October?
 c. What were total sales in October?
 d. What was the average amount of a sales transaction?
 e. Which salesperson made the largest sale?
 f. How many units of each product were sold?
 g. Which product was sold most frequently?

4.5 Implement the set of relational tables shown in Table 4-15 in a relational DBMS package to which you have access. Write queries to answer the following questions. *Note*: For some of these questions you may have to create two queries—one to calculate a total such as invoice total and the second to answer the question asked.
 a. Which customers (show their names) made purchases from Martinez?
 b. Who has the largest credit limit?
 c. How many sales were made in October?
 d. What were the item numbers, price, and quantity of each item sold on invoice number 103?
 e. How much did each salesperson sell?
 f. How many customers live in Arizona?
 g. How much credit does each customer still have available?
 h. How much of each item was sold? (Include the description of each item in your answer.)
 i. Which customers still have more than $1,000 in available credit?
 j. For which items are there at least 100 units on hand?

4.6 The BusyB Company wants to store data about its employees' skills. Each employee may possess one or more specific skills. In addition, several employees may have the same skill. The following facts need to be included in the database:

date hired
date of birth
date skill acquired
employee name
employee number
pay rate

Table 4-15

Customer : Table

Customer Numt	Name	City	State	Credit Limit
1000	Smith	Phoenix	AZ	2500
1001	Jones	St. Louis	MO	1500
1002	Jeffries	Atlanta	GA	4000
1003	Gilkey	Phoenix	AZ	5000
1004	Lankford	Phoenix	AZ	2000
1005	Zeile	Chicago	IL	2000
1006	Pagnozzi	Salt Lake City	UT	3000
1007	Arocha	Chicago	IL	1000

Record: 9 of 9

Inventory : Table

Item Number	Description	Unit Cost	Unit Price	Quantity on Hand
1010	Blender	14	29.95	200
1015	Toaster	12	19.95	300
1020	Mixer	23	33.95	250
1025	Television	499	699.95	74
1030	Freezer	799	999.95	32
1035	Refrigerator	699	849.95	25
1040	Radio	45	79.95	100
1045	Clock	79	99.95	300

Record: 9 of 9

Sales-Inventory : Table

Invoice Number	Item Number	Quantity	Extension
101	1025	1	699.95
101	1035	1	849.95
102	1045	3	299.85
103	1010	1	29.95
103	1015	1	19.95
103	1025	2	1399.90
104	1025	1	699.95
104	1045	1	99.95
105	1035	1	849.95
106	1045	1	99.95
107	1030	1	999.95
107	1035	1	849.95
107	1040	2	159.90
107	1045	2	199.90
108	1025	1	699.95
108	1045	1	99.95

Record: 17 of 17

Sales : Table

Invoice Number	Date	Salesperson	Customer Number	Amount
101	10/3/2008	Wilson	1000	1549.90
102	10/5/2008	Mahomet	1003	299.95
103	10/5/2008	Jackson	1002	1449.80
104	10/15/2008	Drezen	1000	799.90
105	10/15/2008	Martinez	1005	849.95
106	10/16/2008	Martinez	1007	99.95
107	10/29/2008	Mahomet	1002	2209.70
108	11/3/2008	Martinez	1000	779.90

Record: 9 of 9

skill name
skill number
supervisor

Required

a. Design a set of relational tables to store these data.

b. Identify the primary key for each table, and identify any needed foreign keys.

c. Implement your schema using any relational DBMS to which you have access. Specify primary and foreign keys, and enforce referential integrity. Demonstrate the soundness of your design by entering sample data in each table.

4.7 You want to extend the schema depicted in Table 4-16 (see next page) to include information about payments from customers. Customers can make installment payments on each invoice. They may also write one check to pay for several different invoices. Ashton specifically wants to store the following information:

amount applied to a specific invoice
cash receipt number
customer name
customer number
date of receipt
employee processing payment
invoice payment applies to
total amount received

Required

a. Modify the set of relational tables in Table 4-16 to store this additional data.

b. Identify the primary key for each new table you created in step a.

Table 4-16
Database That Needs
to Be Extended

Inventory Table (Item number is primary key)

Customer Table (Customer number is primary key)

Sales Table (Invoice Number is primary key)

Sales-Inventory Line Items Table (Combination of Invoice Number and Item Number forms primary key)

c. Implement your schema using any relational DBMS package available to you. Indicate which attributes are primary and foreign keys, and enter sample data in each table you create.

4.8 Using only the data in Table 4-17, create a set of relational tables that solve the update, insert, and delete anomalies.

Table 4-17
Invoice table

Invoice #	Date	Order Date	Customer ID	Customer Name	Item #	Description	Quantity
52	6-19-08	5-25-08	201	Johnson	103	Trek 9000	5
52	6-19-08	5-25-08	201	Johnson	122	Nimbus 4000	8
52	6-19-08	5-25-08	201	Johnson	10	Izzod 3000	11
52	6-19-08	5-25-08	201	Johnson	71	LD Trainer	12
57	6-20-08	6-01-08	305	Henry	535	TR Standard	18
57	6-20-08	6-01-08	305	Henry	115	NT 2000	15
57	6-20-08	6-01-08	305	Henry	122	Nimbus 4000	5

4.9 Using only the data in Table 4-18, create a set of relational tables that solve the update, insert, and delete anomalies.

Table 4-18
Purchase Order (PO) Table

Purchase Order #	Purchase Date	Order Part #	Description	Unit Price	Quantity Ordered	Vendor #	Vendor Name	Vendor Address
2	3/9/08	334	XYZ	$30	3	504	KL Supply	75 Stevens Dr.
2	3/9/08	231	PDQ	$50	5	504	KL Supply	75 Stevens Dr.
2	3/9/08	444	YYM	$80	6	504	KL Supply	75 Stevens Dr.
3	4/5/08	231	PDQ	$50	2	889	Oscan Inc	55 Cougar Cir.

4.10 From the database created in the comprehensive problem, perform queries based on the tables and query grid shown in Table 4-19.
 a. Which borrowers use Advent Appraisers?
 b. What is the average amount borrowed from National Mortgage?
 c. List all of the property appraisers.
 d. List all of the lenders.
 e. List the lenders that lent more than $100,000.
 f. Which borrower requested the largest mortgage?
 g. Which borrower requested the smallest mortgage?

Table 4-19
Select Query Screen for Chapter Comprehensive Problem

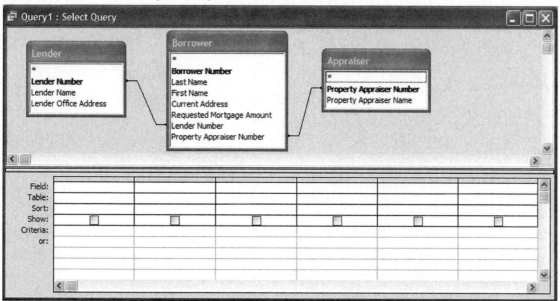

CASE 4-1 Research Projects

As in all areas of information technology, DBMSs are constantly changing and improving. Research how businesses are using DBMSs, and write a report of your findings. Address the following issues:

1 Which popular DBMS products are based on the relational data model?

2 Which DBMS products are based on a logical model other than the relational data model?

3 What are the relative strengths and weaknesses of the different types (relational versus other logical models) of DBMSs?

AIS IN ACTION SOLUTIONS

QUIZ KEY

1 The relational data model portrays data as being stored in
 a. hierarchies (Incorrect. A hierarchical database portrays data as being stored in hierarchies.)
 ✔ b. tables (Correct. The relational data model portrays data as being stored in a table or relation format.)
 c. objects (Incorrect. An object-oriented data base portrays data as being stored as objects.)
 d. files (Incorrect. The file-based data model portrays data as being stored in files.)

2 How a user conceptually organizes and understands data is referred to as the
 a. physical view (Incorrect. The physical view shows how and where data are physically stored.)
 ✔ b. logical view (Correct. The logical view shows how a user conceptually organizes and understands data.)
 c. data model view (Incorrect. This is not a typical database view.)
 d. data organization view (Incorrect. This is not a typical database view.)

3 What is each row in a relational database table called?
 a. relation (Incorrect. A relation is a table in a relational database.)
 b. attribute (Incorrect. Each column in a relational data base is an attribute that describes some characteristic of the entity about which data are stored.)
 c. anomaly (Incorrect. An anomaly is a problem in a database, such as an insert anomaly or a delete anomaly.)
 ✔ d. tuple (Correct. A tuple is also called a row in a relational database.)

4 Which of the following is an individual user's view of the database?
 a. conceptual-level schema (Incorrect. A conceptual-level schema is the organizationwide view of the entire database.)
 ✔ b. external-level schema (Correct. The external-level schema represents an individual user's view of the database.)
 c. internal-level schema (Incorrect. The internal-level schema represents how the data are actually stored and accessed.)
 d. logical-level schema (Incorrect. This is not a schema mentioned in the text.)

5 Which of the following would managers most likely use to retrieve information about sales during the month of October?
 a. DML (Incorrect. DML—data manipulation language—is used for data maintenance.)
 b. DSL (Incorrect. DSL is not a DBMS language.)
 c. DDL (Incorrect. DDL—data definition language—is used to build the data dictionary, create a database, describe logical views, and specify any limitations or constraints on security.)
 ✔ d. DQL (Correct. DQL—data query language—is used to retrieve information from a database.)

6 Which of the following attributes would most likely be a primary key?
 a. supplier name (Incorrect. The primary key must be unique. The same name could be used by multiple entities.)
 ✔ b. supplier number (Correct. A unique number can be assigned as a primary key for each entity.)
 c. supplier Zip code (Incorrect. The primary key must be unique. More than one supplier could reside in the same Zip code.)

d. supplier account balance (Incorrect. The primary key must be unique. The same account balance, such as a $0.00 balance, could be maintained by multiple entities.)

7 Which of the following is a software program that runs a database system?
 a. DQL (Incorrect. DQL—data query language—is used to retrieve information from a database.)
✔ **b.** DBMS (Correct. A DBMS—database management system—is a software program that acts as an interface between a database and various application programs.)
 c. DML (Incorrect. DML—data manipulation language—is used for data maintenance.)
 d. DDL (Incorrect. DDL—data definition language—is used to build the data dictionary, create a database, describe logical views, and specify any limitations or constraints on security.)

8 The constraint that all primary keys must have non-null data values is referred to as which of the following?
 a. referential integrity rule (Incorrect. The referential integrity rule stipulates that foreign keys must have values that correspond to the value of a primary key in another table or be empty.)
✔ **b.** entity integrity rule (Correct. Every primary key in a relational table must have a non-null value.)
 c. normalization rule (Incorrect. This term was not discussed in the text.)
 d. relational data model rule (Incorrect. The text does not discuss a relational data model rule.)

9 The constraint that all foreign keys must have either null values or the value of a primary key in another table is referred to as which of the following?
✔ **a.** referential integrity rule (Correct.)
 b. entity integrity rule (Incorrect. This rule states that every primary key in a relational table must have a non-null value.)
 c. foreign key value rule (Incorrect. The text does not discuss a foreign key value rule.)
 d. null value rule (Incorrect. The text does not discuss a null value rule.)

10 Which of the following attributes in the Cash Receipts table (representing payments received from customers) would most likely be a foreign key?
 a. cash receipt number (Incorrect. A cash receipt number is a good candidate for the primary key of the Cash Receipts table.)
 b. customer check number (Incorrect. Since there is no reason to store customer check numbers in a separate table, it is not a good candidate for a foreign key.)
✔ **c.** customer number (Correct. Customer number would be a foreign key in the Cash Receipts table and would link the Cash Receipts table to the Customer Table.)
 d. cash receipt date (Incorrect. Dates usually are not good candidates for foreign keys. The cash receipt date would likely be an attribute in the Cash Receipts table.)

COMPREHENSIVE PROBLEM SOLUTION

An analysis of Table 4-14 shows that lender and appraiser data are repeated throughout the spreadsheet and that there are update, insert, and delete anomalies present. To create an effective relational database from the spreadsheet shown in Table 4-14, we must break down the spreadsheet into smaller tables in such a way that there will be no anomaly problems. The spreadsheet contains data about three separate entities: borrowers,

lenders, and appraisers. Therefore, we can significantly reduce the redundant information and avoid anomalies by creating a table for borrowers (Table 4-20), lenders (Table 4-21), and appraisers (Table 4-22).

Borrower number, lender number, and appraiser number are chosen as the primary keys for the three tables since each uniquely identifies the rows in their respective tables. The primary keys from the Lender and Appraiser tables are added to the Borrower table as foreign keys so that the Lender and Appraiser tables will have a direct link to the Borrower table.

Creating the smaller tables with their respective primary and foreign keys solves the three anomaly problems.

- The insert anomaly is solved because a new lender and appraiser can be added without requiring a borrower.
- The delete anomaly is solved because if a borrower decides not to pursue a mortgage, and the row is deleted, the information pertaining to the lender and appraiser is not lost.
- The update anomaly is solved because if a lender moves and changes its address, there is only one row in one table to update, instead of changing the spreadsheet in all rows that store the lender address.

After the data are entered into the Microsoft Access tables, we can query the database.

Table 4-20
Borrower Table

Borrower Number (Primary Key)	Last Name	First Name	Current Address	Requested Mortgage Amount	Lender Number (Foreign Key to Lender Table)	Property Appraiser Number (Foreign Key to Appraiser Table)
450	Adams	Jennifer	450 Peachtree Rd.	$245,000	13	8
451	Adamson	David	500 Loop Highway	$124,688	13	9
452	Bronson	Paul	312 Mountain View Dr.	$345,000	14	10
453	Brown	Marietta	310 Loop Highway	$ 57,090	15	10
454	Charles	Kenneth	3 Commons Blvd.	$ 34,000	16	8
455	Coulter	Tracey	1367 Peachtree Rd.	$216,505	13	8
456	Foster	Harold	678 Loop Highway	$117,090	12	9
457	Frank	Vernon	210 Bicayne Blvd.	$ 89,000	12	10
458	Holmes	Heather	1121 Bicayne Blvd.	$459,010	16	10
459	Johanson	Sandy	817 Mountain View Dr.	$ 67,900	15	9
460	Johnson	James	985 Loop Highway	$ 12,000	12	10
461	Jones	Holly	1650 Washington Blvd.	$ 67,890	15	9

Table 4-21
Lender Table

Lender Number (Primary Key)	Lender Name	Lender Office Address
12	National Mortgage	750 16 St.
13	Excel Mortgage	6890 Sheridan Dr.
14	CCY	28 Buckhead Way
15	Advantage Lenders	3345 Lake Shore Dr.
16	Capital Savings	8890 Coral Blvd.

Property Appraiser Number (Primary Key)	Property Appraiser Name
8	Advent Appraisers
9	Independent Appraisal Service
10	Jones Property Appraisers

Table 4-22
Appraiser Table

To find which borrowers took out loans from Excel Mortgage and who the appraiser was, the query in Table 4-23 is created as follows:

- From the Query menu option, select Create Query in Design View.
- Add all three tables to your Query Design. Access automatically links the primary and foreign keys.
- Select the following fields: Borrower Number, Last Name, First Name (all from the Borrower table), Lender Name (from the Lender table), and Property Appraiser Name (from the Appraiser table).
- Specify "Excel Mortgage" as the criteria in the Lender Name column.
- Run the query.

Table 4-23
Borrowers with Loans from Excel Mortgage

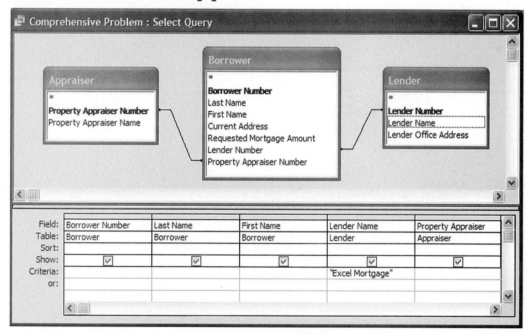

Part II

Control and Audit of Accounting Information Systems

CHAPTER 5

Computer Fraud
and Abuse

After completing his bachelor's degree in accounting at Idaho State, Jason Scott was hired as an internal auditor for Northwest Industries, a diversified forest products company. A few years later, on the last Sunday of March, he finished his tax return. Before sealing the envelope, he reviewed his return for a final time. Jason quickly compared the documents used to prepare his return with the actual numbers. Everything was in order except his withholding amount. For some reason, the federal income tax withholdings on his final paycheck totaled $5 more than on his W-2 form. He decided to use the W-2 amount and made a note to check with the payroll department to find out what happened to the other $5. The next day was a typical Monday at Northwest Industries, and Jason was swamped. After reviewing his to-do list, he decided to dismiss the $5 difference because the amount was immaterial.

At lunch on April 16, several people were joking about their last-minute attempts to complete their tax returns. In the course of the conversation, one of Jason's coworkers grumbled about the company taking out $5 more from his check than he was given credit for on his W-2. No one followed up on the comment, and it was not until after lunch that the coincidence hit Jason: He was not the only one to have a $5 discrepancy between his withholdings and his W-2 statement. After obtaining the appropriate clearances, Jason began to investigate.

By the end of the following day, Jason was worried. All of the 1,500 company employees had a $5 discrepancy between their reported withholdings and the

actual amount withheld. Interestingly enough, the W-2 of Don Hawkins, a programmer in charge of the payroll system, showed that thousands of dollars more in withholdings had been reported to the IRS than had been withheld from his paycheck.

It certainly looked to Jason like Northwest had a serious problem. He knew that when he reported the situation, management was going to ask the following questions:

1 What constitutes a fraud, and is the withholding problem a fraud?
2 If this is indeed a fraud, how was it perpetrated? What motivated Don to commit it?
3 Why did the company not catch these mistakes earlier? Was there a breakdown in controls?
4 What can the company do to detect and prevent fraud?
5 Just how vulnerable are computer systems to fraud?

Introduction

Our society has become increasingly dependent on accounting information systems, which have grown increasingly more complex to meet our escalating needs for information. As system complexity and our dependence on systems increase, companies face the growing risk of their systems being compromised. For example, recent surveys show that 67% of companies had a security breach, over 45% were targeted by organized crime, and 60% reported financial losses.

The four types of threats a company faces are explained here and summarized in Table 5-1.

AIS Threats

Natural and political disasters—such as fires, floods, earthquakes, hurricanes, tornados, blizzards, war, and attacks by terrorists—can destroy an information system and cause a company to fail. When a disaster strikes, many companies are affected at the same time. Examples of these disasters include the following:

- The two terrorist attacks on the World Trade Center in New York City and the attack on the Federal Building in Oklahoma City destroyed or disrupted all the systems in those buildings.
- A flood in Chicago destroyed or damaged 400 data processing centers. Hurricanes Charley, Frances, Ivan, and Jeanne destroyed many computer systems in Florida.
- Unrelenting rains caused the Mississippi and Missouri Rivers to overflow and flood parts of eight states. Many organizations lost their systems, including Des Moines, Iowa, whose computers were buried under eight feet of water.
- Earthquakes in Los Angeles and San Francisco destroyed numerous systems and severed communication lines. Other systems were damaged by falling debris, water from ruptured sprinkler systems, and dust.

Threats	Examples
Natural and political disasters	Fire or excessive heat
	Floods
	Earthquakes and landslides
	Hurricanes, tornados, and high winds
	Blizzards, snowstorms, and freezing rain
	War and attacks by terrorists
Software errors and equipment malfunctions	Hardware or software failures
	Software errors or bugs
	Operating system crashes
	Power outages and fluctuations
	Undetected data transmission errors
Unintentional acts	Accidents caused by human carelessness, failure to follow established procedures, and poorly trained or supervised personnel
	Innocent errors or omissions
	Lost, erroneous, destroyed, or misplaced data
	Logic errors
	Systems that do not meet company needs or are incapable of handling their intended tasks
Intentional acts (computer crimes)	Sabotage
	Misrepresentation, false use, or unauthorized disclosure of data
	Misappropriation of assets
	Financial Statement fraud
	Corruption
	Computer fraud – attacks, social engineering, malware, etc.

Table 5-1
Threats to Accounting
Information Systems

- The Defense Science Board predicts that attacks on government information systems by foreign countries, espionage agents, and terrorists will soon be widespread. Military contractors and businesses are also expected to be targets.

A second threat includes software errors and equipment malfunctions. Examples include software errors, operating system crashes, hardware failures, power outages and fluctuations, and undetected data transmission errors. Of especial concern are the vulnerabilities in Microsoft Windows software; in one recent survey, 30% of companies had moved some systems off Windows to reduce security risks.

A federal study estimated yearly economic losses due to software bugs at almost $60 billion a year. More than 60% of companies studied had significant software errors in the previous year. For example,

- Bugs in a tax accounting system were to blame for California's failure to collect $635 million in business taxes.
- Massive power failures caused by defective software have left hundreds of thousands of people and businesses without power.
- A software bug in Burger King's software resulted in a $4,334.33 debit card charge for four hamburgers. The cashier accidentally keyed in the $4.33 charge twice, resulting in the overcharge.

A third threat, unintentional acts such as accidents or innocent errors and omissions, results in the greatest risk to information systems and the greatest dollar losses.

The Computing Technology Industry Association estimates that human errors cause 80% of security problems. Forrester Research estimates that employees unintentionally create legal, regulatory, or financial risks in 25% of their outbound e-mails.

These unintentional acts usually are caused by human carelessness, failure to follow established procedures, and poorly trained or supervised personnel. Users lose or misplace data and accidentally erase or alter files, data, and programs. Computer operators and users enter the wrong input or erroneous input, use the wrong version of a program or the wrong data files, or misplace data files. Systems analysts develop systems that do not meet company needs or that leave them vulnerable to attack, or develop systems incapable of handling their intended tasks. Programmers make logic errors. Examples include the following:

- In Japan, a data entry clerk at Mizuho Securities mistakenly keyed in a sale for 610,000 shares of J-Com for 1 yen instead of the sale of 1 share for 610,000 yen. The error cost the company $250 million.
- A bank programmer mistakenly calculated interest for each month using 31 days. During the 5 months before the mistake was discovered, over $100,000 in excess interest was paid.
- An error in a Fannie Mae spreadsheet resulted in a $1.2 billion misstatement of its earnings.
- UPS lost a cardboard box with computer tapes containing information, such as names, Social Security numbers, account numbers, and payment histories on 3.9 million Citigroup customers.
- The U. S. Treasury sent a letter informing purchasers of its direct-purchase securities program that they would receive a substantial interest check. However, someone at the Treasury department transposed the interest rate to 8.67% from the correct rate of 6.87%. Fortunately, sharp-eyed investors caught the error and notified the Treasury department before they sent out checks overpaying investors by over $14 million.

A fourth threat is intentional acts, typically referred to as computer crimes. The most frequent type of computer crime is fraud, where the intent is to steal something of value. This threat can also take the form of **sabotage**, in which the intent is to destroy or harm a system or some of its components. Information systems are increasingly vulnerable to attack. In a recent three-year period, the number of networks that were compromised rose 700%. That is just the tip of the iceberg, as experts believe the actual number of incidents is as much as six times higher due to companies not reporting security breaches.

Consider the case of OpenTable, a restaurant reservation service that did not properly design its **cookie** (data that Web sites store on your computer to identify their Web sites to your computer and to identify you to the Web site so you do not have to log on each time you visit the site). At OpenTable, the customer number stored in the cookie was very easy to change. An experienced programmer opened an account at OpenTable and, in less than an hour, wrote a program that cycled through all the customer numbers and downloaded most of the company's database. Many other companies, such as Gateway, Kohl's, Iomega, and Saks Fifth Avenue, have had problems with the same type of system vulnerability.

The five chapters in Part II focus on control concepts. Fraud is the topic of this chapter. Chapter 6 explains general principles of control in business organizations and describes a comprehensive business risk and control framework. Chapter 7 introduces five basic principles that contribute to systems reliability and then focuses on security, the foundation on which the other four principles rest. The chapter discusses basic security concepts, as well as specific technologies and procedures used to implement security. Chapter 8 discusses the other four principles of systems reliability: confidentiality, privacy, processing integrity, and availability. Chapter 9 examines the processes and procedures used in auditing computer-based systems.

This chapter discusses fraud in five main sections: an introduction to fraud, why fraud occurs, approaches to computer fraud, computer fraud techniques, and how to deter and detect computer fraud.

Introduction to Fraud

Fraud can be defined as gaining an unfair advantage over another person. Legally, for an act to be fraudulent there must be:

1 A *false statement, representation, or disclosure*
2 A *material fact*, which is something that induces a person to act
3 An *intent to deceive*
4 A *justifiable reliance;* that is, the person relies on the misrepresentation to take an action
5 An *injury or loss* suffered by the victim

No one knows the total losses to fraud each year, but organizations have estimated them:

- The Association of Certified Fraud Examiners estimates total fraud losses in the United States to be over $660 billion a year.
- Income tax fraud (the difference between what taxpayers owe and what they pay) is estimated to be over $350 billion dollars a year.
- Fraud in the health care industry is estimated to exceed $100 billion a year.

An estimated 75% to 90% of computer crimes are perpetrated by knowledgeable insiders with the requisite access, skills, and resources. Because employees understand a company's system and its weaknesses, they are better able to commit and conceal a fraud. The controls used to protect corporate assets make it more difficult for an outsider to steal from a company. Fraud perpetrators are often referred to as **white-collar criminals**.

According to Statement on Auditing Standards (SAS) No. 99, fraud takes two forms: misappropriation of assets and fraudulent financial reporting.

Misappropriation of Assets

Misappropriation of assets, often referred to as **employee fraud**, is the theft of company assets. Examples include the fraud discovered by Jason Scott in the introductory story and the following:

- Albert Miano, a manager at *Reader's Digest* responsible for processing bills, embezzled $1 million over a five-year period. Miano forged the signature of a superior on invoices for services never performed, submitted them to accounts payable, forged the endorsement on the checks, and deposited them in his own account. Milano used the stolen funds to buy an expensive home, five cars, and a boat.
- A bank vice president approved $1 billion in bad loans in exchange for $585,000 in kickbacks. The loans cost the bank $800 million and helped trigger its collapse.
- A manager at a Florida newspaper went to work for a competitor after he was fired. Before long, the first employer realized its reporters were constantly being scooped. An investigation revealed the manager still had an active account and password and regularly browsed its computer files for information on exclusive stories.

A typical employee fraud has a number of important elements or characteristics:

- The perpetrator gains the trust or confidence of the person or company being defrauded.
- Instead of using a weapon or physical force, a fraud perpetrator uses trickery, cunning, or false or misleading information.
- Perpetrators hide their tracks by falsifying records or other information.
- Few frauds are terminated voluntarily. Instead, they continue due to perpetrator need or greed or because terminating the fraud will lead to detection. Often perpetrators come to depend on the "extra" income and cannot afford to stop. Other times they move to a higher lifestyle that requires even greater amounts of money. Some frauds are self-perpetuating. If perpetrators stop, their actions are discovered and they are caught. For these reasons, there are no small frauds—only large ones that are detected early.
- Fraud perpetrators spend their ill-gotten gains, usually on an extravagant lifestyle. Rarely do they save or invest the money they take.
- Many perpetrators become greedy and take ever-larger amounts of money at more frequent intervals. Larger amounts are more prone to scrutiny, and a scheme that might otherwise go undetected is uncovered because the amount taken at any one time rises to a noticeable level.
- As time passes, many perpetrators grow careless or overconfident, make a mistake, and are caught.
- In time, the sheer magnitude of the fraud leads to its detection. For example, at an auto repair shop, the accountant, a lifelong friend of the shop's owner, embezzled ever-larger sums of money from the shop over a seven-year period. In the last year of the fraud, when the embezzler took over $200,000, the owner, facing bankruptcy, eventually had to lay off the accountant and have his wife take over the bookkeeping. When the company immediately began doing better, the wife investigated and uncovered the fraud.
- The most significant contributing factor in most employee frauds is the absence of internal controls and/or the failure to enforce existing internal controls.

Fraudulent Financial Reporting

The National Commission on Fraudulent Financial Reporting (the Treadway Commission) defined **fraudulent financial reporting** as intentional or reckless conduct, whether by act or omission, that results in materially misleading financial statements. Financial statements are falsified to deceive investors and creditors, increase a company's stock price, meet cash flow needs, or hide company losses and problems. The Treadway Commission studied 450 lawsuits against auditors and found undetected fraud to be a factor in half of them.

In recent years, a number of highly publicized financial statement frauds have been widely reported including Enron, WorldCom, Tyco, Adelphia, HealthSouth, Global Crossing, and Xerox. In each case, company executives misrepresented the company's financial statements, leading to huge financial losses for investors and, in some cases, bankruptcy for the companies involved.

The most frequent way executives "cook the books" is by inflating revenues fictitiously. Other common ways are holding the books open (recognizing revenues before they are earned), closing the books early (delaying current period expenses to a later period), overstating inventories or fixed assets, and concealing losses and liabilities.

The Treadway Commission recommended four actions to reduce the possibility of fraudulent financial reporting:

1 Establish an organizational environment that contributes to the integrity of the financial reporting process
2 Identify and understand the factors that lead to fraudulent financial reporting
3 Assess the risk of fraudulent financial reporting within the company

4 Design and implement internal controls to provide reasonable assurance that fraudulent financial reporting is prevented

A study by the Association of Certified Fraud Examiners found that misappropriation of assets is more than 17 times more likely than fraudulent financial reporting. They also discovered that the average misappropriation of assets fraud is much smaller than the average fraudulent financial reporting fraud. Because employee frauds are smaller and less likely to be material to the financial statements, auditors are generally more concerned with the risks associated with not discovering fraudulent financial reporting fraud than they are with asset misappropriation fraud. On the other hand, as employee fraud is much more likely to occur, internal auditors, chief financial officers, and other members of management are much more likely to have to deal with a misappropriation of assets than with a financial statement fraud. The following section discusses auditors' responsibility for detecting material fraud.

SAS No. 99: The Auditor's Responsibility to Detect Fraud

SAS No. 82, *Consideration of Fraud in a Financial Statement Audit*, was adopted in 1997 to clarify the auditor's responsibility to detect fraud. It was revised as SAS No. 99, with the same title, and became effective in December 2002. SAS No. 99 requires auditors to:

- **Understand fraud.** Since auditors cannot effectively audit something they do not understand, they must gain an understanding of fraud.
- **Discuss the risks of material fraudulent misstatements.** While planning the audit, team members should discuss among themselves how and where the company's financial statements might be susceptible to fraud.
- **Obtain information.** The audit team must gather evidence about the existence of fraud by looking for fraud risk factors; testing company records; and asking management, the audit committee of the board of directors, and others if they know of any past or current fraud. Since many frauds involve revenue recognition, special care should be exercised in examining revenue accounts.
- **Identify, assess, and respond to risks.** Auditors use the information they gather to identify, assess, and respond to fraud risks. Auditors can respond by varying the nature, timing, and extent of their auditing procedures and evaluating more carefully the risks related to management overriding internal controls.
- **Evaluate the results of their audit tests.** When an audit is completed, auditors must evaluate whether any identified misstatements indicate the presence of fraud. If they do, the auditor must determine the impact of this on the financial statements and the audit.
- **Document and communicate findings.** Auditors must document their findings and communicate them to management, the audit committee, and others.
- **Incorporate a technology focus.** SAS No. 99 recognizes the impact technology has on fraud risks and provides commentary and examples specifically recognizing this impact. It also notes the opportunities the auditor has to use technology to design fraud-auditing procedures.

Who Perpetrates Fraud and Why It Occurs

Researchers have compared the psychological and demographic characteristics of three groups of people: white-collar criminals, violent criminals, and the general public. They found significant differences between violent and white-collar criminals and few differences between white-collar criminals and the public. White-collar criminals

mirror the public in education, age, religion, marriage, length of employment, and psychological makeup. Some fraud perpetrators are disgruntled and unhappy with their jobs and are seeking revenge against their employers. Others are regarded as ideal employees who are dedicated, hard working, and trusted. Many have no previous criminal record; they were honest citizens who were valued and respected members of their communities.

Perpetrators of computer fraud tend to be younger and possess more computer knowledge, experience, and skills. Some hackers and computer fraud perpetrators are motivated by curiosity, a quest for knowledge, the desire to learn how things work, and the challenge of "beating the system." They view their actions as a game rather than as dishonest behavior. Others commit computer fraud to gain stature in the hacking community.

However, a very large and growing number of computer fraud perpetrators want to profit financially. Malicious software is a big business and a huge profit engine for the criminal underground, especially for digitally savvy hackers in Eastern Europe. They break into financial accounts and steal money. They sell data to spammers, organized crime, hackers, and the intelligence community. They market malware, such as virus-producing software, to others. Some work with organized crime. In essence, they do anything they can to turn their actions into money. For example, a recently convicted hacker was paid $150 for every 1000 computers he could infect with his adware and was making hundreds of thousands of dollars a year.

Cyber-criminals are now the FBI's third-highest priority, behind terrorists and spies, because many computer fraud perpetrators have moved from isolated and uncoordinated attacks to organized fraud schemes targeted at specific individuals and businesses. The perpetrators use online payment companies to launder their ill-gotten gains and take advantage of the lack of coordination between law enforcement organizations in different countries to hide their money.

The Fraud Triangle

Research shows that three conditions are present when fraud occurs: a pressure, an opportunity, and a rationalization. This is referred to as the fraud triangle and is shown as the middle triangle in Figure 5-1

Pressures

A **pressure** is a person's incentive or motivation for committing fraud. Three common types of pressures that lead to employee fraud are shown in the Employee Pressure Triangle in Figure 5-1 and summarized in Table 5-2.

Figure 5-1
Fraud Triangles

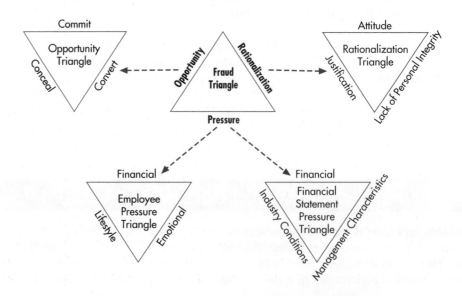

Table 5-2
Pressures That Can Lead to Employee Fraud

Financial	Emotional	Lifestyle
Living beyond means	Greed	Gambling habit
High personal debt/expenses	Performance not recognized	Drug or alcohol
"Inadequate" salary/income	Job dissatisfaction	addiction
Poor credit ratings	Fear of losing job	Sexual relationships
Heavy financial losses	Need for power or control	Family/peer pressure
Bad investments	Excessive pride or ambition	
Tax avoidance	Overtly, deliberately	
Unreasonable quotas/goals	nonconformist	
	Envious or resentful of others	
	Cannot abide or respect rules	
	Challenge of beating the system	

One type of pressure motivating misappropriation of assets, or employee fraud, is financial in nature. Examples include living beyond one's means, having heavy financial losses, or high personal debt. Often, the perpetrator feels such pressures cannot be shared with others and believes fraud is the only or the best way out of a difficult situation. For example, Raymond Keller worked his way up from driving a coal truck to owning a grain elevator. He made money by trading on commodities and built a lavish house overlooking the Des Moines River. His financial situation declined, and Raymond had a severe cash shortage and went deeply into debt. He asked some farmers to wait for their money, and he gave others bad checks. Finally, the seven banks to which he owed over $3 million began to call in their loans, so Raymond began to sell grain that did not belong to him (he stored it for local farmers) to cover his losses. When a state auditor showed up at his door unexpectedly, Raymond chose to take his life rather than face the consequences of his fraud.

A second type of employee pressure is related to emotional feelings or problems. Many employees are motivated by greed. Some employees turn to fraud because they have strong feelings of resentment or believe they were treated unfairly. They may feel that their pay is too low, that their contributions to the company are not appreciated sufficiently, or that the company is taking advantage of them. In one case, an accountant in California, who was passed over for a raise, increased his salary by 10%, the amount of an average raise. When apprehended, he defended his actions by saying he was only taking what was rightfully his. When asked how he would have felt if he had increased his salary by 11% he responded that he would have been stealing 1%. Other people are motivated by the challenge of "beating the system" or subverting system controls and breaking into a system. In one case, a company boasted in its advertisements that its new information system was so secure that outsiders would not be able to break into it. Within 24 hours of the system's implementation, a team of individuals had broken into the system and left a message that the impenetrable system had just been compromised.

A third type of employee pressure is related to a person's lifestyle. These include the need for funds to support a gambling habit (or pay off gambling debts) or support an addiction or problem with drugs or alcohol. Some people commit fraud to keep pace financially with other family members. For example, one plastic surgeon, making up to $800,000 a year, defrauded his clinic of over $200,000 so that he could compete with family members who engaged in a game of financial one-upmanship.

The three types of organizational pressures that motivate management to misrepresent their financial statements are shown in the Financial Statement Pressure triangle in Figure 5-1. The more important pressures or indicators of financial statement fraud in each of these three classifications are listed in Table 5-3. The most prevalent financial

Table 5-3
Pressures That Can Lead to Financial Statement Fraud

Management Characteristics	Industry Conditions	Financial
Questionable management ethics, ability, management style, and track record	Declining industry	Intense pressure to meet or exceed earnings expectations
Unduly aggressive earnings forecasts, performance standards, accounting methods, or incentive programs	Industry or technology changes leading to declining demand, product obsolescence	Significant cash flow problems; unusual difficulty collecting receivables, paying payables
Significant incentive compensation based on achieving unduly aggressive goals	New regulatory requirements that impair financial stability or profitability	Heavy losses, high or undiversified risk, high dependence on debt, or unduly restrictive debt covenants
Management actions or transactions with no clear business justification	Significant competition or market saturation, with declining margins	Heavy dependence on new or unproven product lines
Overly sensitive to the effects of alternative accounting treatments on EPS	Significant tax changes or adjustments	Severe inventory obsolescence or excessive inventory buildup
Strained relationship with past auditors		Economic conditions (inflation, recession)
Not correcting errors on a timely basis, leading to even greater problems		Litigation, especially management vs. shareholders
High management/employee turnover		Impending business failure or bankruptcy
Unusual/odd related-party relationships		Problems with regulatory agencies
		High vulnerability to rise in interest rates
		Poor or deteriorating financial position
		Unusually rapid growth/profitability compared to companies in same industry
		Significant estimates involving highly subjective judgments or uncertainties

pressure is a need to meet or exceed earnings expectations to keep a stock price from falling. Managers can also create significant pressure for themselves with unduly aggressive earnings forecasts that they then feel they have to meet. They can also create unrealistic performance standards or incentive programs that motivate themselves and others to falsify financial results to keep their jobs or to receive stock options and other incentive payments. Also, industry conditions such as new regulatory requirements or significant market saturation with declining margins can motivate fraud.

Opportunities

As shown in the Opportunity Triangle in Figure 5-1, **opportunity** is the condition or situation that allows a person or organization to do three things:

1 Commit the fraud. The theft of assets, such as cash, inventory, tools, supplies, information, and computer time and services, is the most common type of employee fraud. Most fraudulent financial reporting consists of the overstatement of assets or revenues, the understatement of liabilities, or the failure to disclose information.

2 Conceal the fraud. When assets are stolen or overstated, the only way to balance the accounting equation is to inflate other assets or to decrease liabilities or equity. Unless perpetrators find some way to keep the accounting equation in balance, their theft or financial statement misrepresentation can be discovered. Concealment often takes more effort and time and leaves behind more evidence than the actual theft or misrepresentation. For example, taking cash requires only a few seconds, whereas altering records to hide the theft can be more challenging and time-consuming.

A common and effective way to hide a theft is to charge the stolen item to an expense account. The perpetrator's exposure is limited to a year or less, because the expense accounts are zeroed out at the end of the year. On the other hand, perpetrators

who hide a theft by affecting a balance sheet account must continue the concealment. One way to hide a decrease in assets is a **lapping** scheme, in which the perpetrator steals the cash or check that customer A mails in to pay its accounts receivable. Funds received at a later date from customer B are used to pay off customer A's balance. Funds from customer C are used to pay off customer B, and so forth. Because the theft involves two asset accounts (cash and accounts receivable) the cover-up must continue indefinitely unless the money is replaced because the theft will be uncovered if the scheme is stopped.

In a check **kiting** scheme, the perpetrator creates cash by taking advantage of the timing lag between depositing a check and the check clearing the bank. For example, suppose a fraud perpetrator opens checking accounts in banks A, B, and C. The perpetrator can "create" cash by depositing a $1,000 check from bank A into bank B and withdrawing the funds. If it takes two days for his check to clear bank A, he has created $1,000 for two days. After two days, since there are insufficient funds in bank A to cover the $1,000 check, the perpetrator deposits a $1,000 check from bank C to bank A. He has covered the creation of the $1,000 for another two days. Since bank C also has insufficient funds, $1,000 must be deposited to bank C before the check to bank A clears. The check to bank C is written from bank B, which also has insufficient funds. The scheme continues, writing checks and making deposits as needed to keep the checks from bouncing.

3 Convert the theft or misrepresentation to personal gain. In employee fraud, all fraud perpetrators go through the conversion phase unless they steal actual cash that can be spent or use the asset personally. For example, employees who steal inventory and equipment must sell them or otherwise convert them to cash. When financial statements are falsified, the perpetrators convert their actions to personal gain through indirect benefits: they keep their jobs, their stock rises, they receive pay raises and promotions, or they gain more power and influence.

The list of opportunities that make fraud easy to commit and conceal is almost endless. Table 5-4 lists some of the more frequently mentioned opportunities that permit employee and financial statement fraud.

As shown in the first column of Table 5-4, opportunities for fraud often stem from internal control factors. For example, a perpetrator may be able to commit and conceal a fraud because the company did not implement proper controls, such as proper authorization procedures, clear lines of authority, adequate supervision, adequate documents and records, a system to safeguard assets, or independent checks on performance. Likewise, there may be no separation of duties among the authorization, custodial, and record-keeping functions. Management may allow fraud to occur by not getting involved in designing or enforcing the system of internal control or through inattention or carelessness. Alternatively, management may commit the fraud by overriding internal controls or using their position of power to compel subordinates to carry out the fraud. However, the most prevalent opportunity for fraud results from a company's failure to *enforce* its system of internal controls.

A control feature many companies lack is a background check on all potential employees. This would have saved one company from the "phantom controller." In that case, the company president stopped by the office one night, saw a light on in the controller's office, and went to see why he was working so late. He was surprised to find a complete stranger at work. An investigation showed the controller was not an accountant and had been fired from three of his previous five jobs over the prior eight years. Because he was unable to do the accounting work, he had hired someone to come in at night to do his work for him. Before his scam was discovered, the controller defrauded the company of several million dollars.

The second column in Table 5-4 summarizes other factors that provide an opportunity to commit and conceal fraud, such as large, unusual, or complex transactions; numerous adjusting entries at year-end; questionable accounting practices; pushing accounting principles to the limit; or related-party transactions. Other factors include incompetent personnel, inadequate staffing, rapid turnover of key employees, lengthy tenure in a key job, and lack of training. Other opportunities arise when the company

Table 5-4
Opportunities Permitting Employee and Financial Statement Fraud

Internal Control Factors	Other Factors
Failure to enforce/monitor internal controls	Large, unusual, or complex transactions
Management not involved in control system	Numerous adjusting entries at year-end
Management override of controls	Related-party transactions
Managerial carelessness, inattention to details	Accounting department understaffed, overworked
Dominant and unchallenged management	Incompetent personnel
Ineffective oversight by board of directors	Rapid turnover of key employees
No effective internal auditing staff	Lengthy tenure in a key job
Infrequent third-party reviews	Overly complex organizational structure
Insufficient separation of authorization, custody, and record-keeping duties	No code of conduct, conflict-of-interest statement, or definition of unacceptable behavior
Too much trust in key employees	Frequently changing auditors, legal counsel
Inadequate supervision	Operating on a crisis basis
Unclear lines of authority	Close association with suppliers/customers
Lack of proper authorization procedures	Assets highly susceptible to misappropriation
No independent checks on performance	Questionable accounting practices
Inadequate documents and records	Pushing accounting principles to the limit
Inadequate system for safeguarding assets	Unclear company policies and procedures
No physical or logical security system	Failing to teach and stress corporate honesty
No audit trails	Failure to prosecute dishonest employees
Failure to conduct background checks	Low employee morale and loyalty
No policy of annual vacations, rotation of duties	

has unclear policies and procedures, fails to teach and stress corporate honesty, and fails to prosecute those who perpetrate fraud.

Many frauds arise when employees build mutually beneficial personal relationships with customers or suppliers. For example, a buyer could agree to purchase goods at an inflated price in exchange for a kickback from the vendor. Fraud can also occur when a crisis arises and the company disregards its normal control procedures. For instance, one Fortune 500 company was hit with three multimillion-dollar frauds in the same year. All three took place when the company was trying to resolve a series of crises and failed to follow the standard internal control procedures.

Rationalizations

The third element of the fraud triangle is a **rationalization** that allows perpetrators to justify their illegal behavior. As shown on the Rationalization Triangle in Figure 5-1, this rationalization can take the form of a justification of one's actions ("I only took what they owed me"), an attitude ("The rules do not apply to me"), or a lack of personal integrity ("Having what I want is more important than being honest"). In other words, perpetrators rationalize that they are not actually being dishonest, that honesty is not required of them, or that their reasons for committing fraud are more compelling than honesty and integrity. Some perpetrators rationalize that they are not hurting a real person; it is just a faceless and nameless computer system that is affected or a large, impersonal company that will not miss the money. For example, one perpetrator took pains to steal no more than $20,000, which was the maximum that the insurance company would reimburse the company for losses.

The list of rationalizations people use is lengthy. These are some of the most frequent:

- I am only "borrowing" the money (or asset) and will repay my "loan."
- You would understand if you knew how badly I needed it.
- What I did was not that serious.
- It was for a good cause. (The Robin Hood syndrome: robbing from the rich to give to the poor.)

- I occupy a very important position of trust. I am above the rules.
- Everyone else is doing it, so it is not that wrong.
- No one will ever know.
- The company owes it to me, and I am taking no more than is rightfully mine.

Fraud occurs when people have high pressures, an opportunity to commit and conceal the fraud and convert the action to personal gain, and the ability to rationalize away their personal integrity. Fraud is less likely to occur when people have few pressures, little opportunity, and high personal integrity. Usually all three elements of the fraud triangle must be present to some degree before a person commits fraud.

Likewise, fraud can be prevented by eliminating or minimizing one or more of the fraud triangle elements. While companies can do some things to reduce or minimize pressures and rationalizations, their greatest opportunity to prevent fraud lies in reducing or minimizing the opportunity to commit fraud. This is typically done by implementing a good system of internal controls, which is discussed in Chapters 6 through 9.

Computer Fraud

The U.S. Department of Justice defines **computer fraud** as any illegal act for which knowledge of computer technology is essential for its perpetration, investigation, or prosecution. More specifically, it includes the following:

- Unauthorized theft, use, access, modification, copying, and destruction of software or data
- Theft of money by altering computer records
- Theft of computer time
- Theft or destruction of computer hardware or software
- Use or conspiracy to use computer resources to commit a felony
- Intent to illegally obtain information or tangible property through the use of computers

Using a computer, fraud perpetrators are able to steal more of something in much less time and with much less effort. For instance, they can steal millions of dollars in less than a second and leave little or no evidence. Therefore, computer fraud is often much more difficult to detect than other types of fraud.

The Rise in Computer Fraud

Computer systems are particularly vulnerable to computer crimes for the following reasons:

- Billions of characters of data are stored in company databases. People who manage to break into these databases can steal, destroy, or alter massive amounts of data in very little time.
- Organizations want employees, customers, and suppliers to have access to their system. The number and variety of these access points significantly increase the risks.
- Computer programs only need to be modified once without permission for the system to operate improperly for as long as the system is in use.
- Modern systems utilize personal computers (PCs), which are inherently more vulnerable to security risks. It is difficult to control physical access to each networked PC. In addition, PCs and their data can be lost, stolen, or misplaced. Adequate segregation of duties is difficult because PCs are located in user departments, and one

person may be responsible for both development and operations. Also, PC users are generally less aware of the importance of security and control. The more legitimate users there are, the greater the risk of an attack on the network.

● Computer systems face a number of unique challenges: reliability (i.e., accuracy, completeness), equipment failure, environmental dependency (i.e., power, damage from water or fire), vulnerability to electromagnetic interference and interruption, eavesdropping, and misrouting.

As early as 1979, *Time* labeled computer fraud a "growth industry." Organizations that track computer fraud estimate that most U.S. businesses have been victimized by at least one incident of computer fraud. During a one-year period, the estimated dollar losses from unauthorized employee abuses in the United States increased 15-fold, from $181,400 to $2.81 million per incident. A few years ago it was estimated that computers at the U.S. Defense Department were attacked more than a half million times per year and that the number of incidents was increasing 50% to 100% per year. Defense Department staffers and outside consultants made 38,000 "friendly hacks" on their networks to evaluate security. Almost 70% were successful, and the Defense Department detected only 4% of the attacks; the others went unnoticed. At the Pentagon, which has the U.S. government's most advanced hacker-awareness program, only 1 in 500 break-ins was detected and reported.

The number of incidents, the total dollar losses, and the sophistication of the perpetrators and the schemes used to commit computer fraud are increasing rapidly due to the following reasons:

1 Not everyone agrees on what constitutes computer fraud. For example, many people do not believe that making an unlicensed copy of software constitutes computer fraud. Software publishers think otherwise and prosecute those who make illegal copies. Similarly, some people do not think it is a crime to browse through someone else's computer if they do not harm the organization or its data. Companies whose data are browsed view those actions much differently.

2 Many computer frauds go undetected. At one time, the FBI estimated that only 1% of all computer crime is detected; other estimates are between 5% and 20%.

3 A high percentage of uncovered frauds is not reported. The most commonly cited reason for this is fear that adverse publicity would result in copycat fraud and a loss of customer confidence, which could cost more than the fraud itself.

4 Many networks have a low level of security. Dan Farmer, who wrote SATAN (a network security testing tool), tested 2,200 high-profile Web sites at government institutions, banks, and newspapers. Only three of the sites detected him and contacted him to find out his intentions.

5 Many Internet pages give step-by-step instructions on how to perpetrate computer crimes and abuses. For instance, an Internet search found more than 17,000 matches for "denial of service," a common form of computer abuse.

6 Law enforcement is unable to keep up with the growing number of computer frauds. The FBI is only able to investigate 1 in 15 computer crimes due to the lack of funding and staff with the necessary skills.

7 The total dollar value of losses is difficult to calculate. It is difficult to calculate losses when information is stolen, Web sites are defaced, and viruses shut down entire computer systems.

The increase in computer fraud and abuse has lead to the need for investigative specialists, or cybersleuths. This is discussed in more depth in Focus 5-1.

5-1 FOCUS Cybersleuths

Hired to investigate suspected fraud, two forensic experts, disguised as repairmen, entered the company's offices after hours. They took a digital photograph of three employees' desks and then made a copy of each employee's hard drive. Then they used the digital photo to make sure everything on the desks was left as found. The copy of the hard drive was taken to their forensics lab where it was analyzed. They found evidence of a fraud and notified the company that hired them. The company turned the case over to law enforcement officials for investigation and prosecution.

So, who were the forensic experts breaking into companies and copying data? Employed by one of the Big Four accounting firms, they are accountants, turned cybersleuths, who specialize in catching fraud perpetrators. Cybersleuths come from a variety of backgrounds, including accounting, government, law enforcement, the military, banking, and information systems. Some of the skills cybersleuths need are these:

- **The ability to follow a trail, think analytically, and be thorough.** Fraud perpetrators leave tracks, and a cybersleuth must be able to think analytically to follow paper and electronic trails and uncover fraud. They must also be thorough so that they do not miss or fail to follow up on clues.
- **A good understanding of information technology.** Cybersleuths need to understand data communications, how data are stored, and how to retrieve hidden or deleted files and e-mails.
- **The ability to think like a fraud perpetrator.** Cybersleuths must understand how fraud

perpetrators think and what motives them as well as the schemes perpetrators use to commit and conceal fraud.
- **The ability to use hacking tools and techniques.** Cybersleuths need to understand the tools that computer criminals use to perpetrate their fraud and abuse.

Another way investigative firms are fighting crime is by developing software that examines bank or accounting records for suspicious transactions. Companies have developed pattern recognition software to search millions of bank, brokerage, and insurance accounts and review trillions of dollars worth of transactions each day. Some companies, such as PayPal, have used the software to significantly lower their fraud rates.

This software is based on a mathematical principle know as Benford's Law. In the 1920s, Benford discovered that you could predict the first or second digit in a set of numerical data with surprising accuracy. Benford found that the number 1 will appear as the first digit 31% of the time, compared to only 5% for the number 9. Today, software companies are applying this law in pattern recognition software to root out possible accounting fraud through the examination of company databases and transaction records.

So, what does all this mean to students seeking to find their niche in life? Probably the most important thing is simply awareness that a career as a cybersleuth is a viable option with big potential for growth as the world becomes ever more reliant on technology. If playing James Bond sounds appealing, then maybe a career as a computer forensics expert is the way to go.

Computer Fraud Classifications

As shown in Figure 5-2, one way to categorize computer fraud is to use the data processing model.

Input Fraud

The simplest and most common way to commit a fraud is to alter or falsify computer input. It requires little if any computer skills. Instead, perpetrators need to understand only how the system operates so they can cover their tracks. For example, about 7 cents per $100 (7 basis points) of all credit card purchases are fraudulent charges.

A man opened an account at a New York bank, then had a printer prepare blank bank deposit slips. The slips were similar to those available in bank lobbies, except that his account number was encoded on them. Early one morning he replaced all the deposit slips in the bank lobby with his forged ones. For three days, all bank deposits using the forged slips went directly into the perpetrator's account. After three days, the perpetrator withdrew the money and disappeared. Because he used an alias, his identity was never uncovered, nor was he ever found.

One perpetrator used desktop publishing to prepare fraudulent bills for office supplies that were never ordered and mailed them to companies across the country. The

Figure 5-2
Computer Fraud Classifications

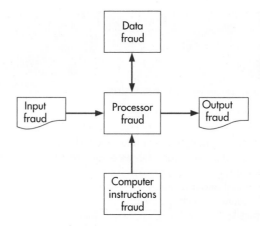

perpetrator kept the dollar amount below $300 so companies did not bother to require purchase orders or approvals. A high percentage of the companies paid the bills.

A Milwaukee woman used computers at her home and the public library to electronically file over $13,000 of federal and state income tax refund claims for 10 fictitious people. She received over $6,000 before she was caught and convicted. An employee at the Arizona Veteran's Memorial Coliseum sold customers full-price tickets, entered the sales as half-price tickets, and pocketed the difference. Several railroad employees entered data into the company's system to show that more than 200 railroad cars were scrapped or destroyed. They removed the cars from the railway system, then repainted and sold them.

Processor Fraud

Computer fraud can be committed through unauthorized system use, including the theft of computer time and services. For example, after a large insurance company installed software to detect abnormal system activity, it found computers hidden under the floor of its data center. Further investigation revealed that several employees were using the computers and the insurance company's system to run an illegal gambling Web site. In another fraud, two accountants without the appropriate access rights were able to get into Cisco's system that manages stock option disbursements. They forged the forms needed to authorize and transfer more that $6.3 million of Cisco stock to their personal brokerage accounts. They then sold the stock and used part of the funds to support an extravagant lifestyle, including a $52,000 Mercedes-Benz, a $44,000 diamond ring, and a $20,000 Rolex watch.

Computer Instructions Fraud

Computer fraud can be accomplished by tampering with the software that processes company data. This may include modifying the software, copying software illegally, using software in an unauthorized manner, or developing software to carry out an unauthorized activity. This approach to computer fraud used to be one of the least common because it required specialized knowledge about computer programming that was beyond the scope of most users. Today, such frauds are much more frequent because of the many Web pages that instruct users on how to create viruses and other computer-based schemes.

Data Fraud

The greatest exposure to data fraud comes from employees with access to the data. The exposure to outsiders is very real but much less likely to occur. The most frequent type of data fraud is the illegal use of company data, typically by copying it, using it, or searching it without permission. In a recent survey, one in six companies reported having lost equipment containing company data in the prior one-year period. However, companies do not have to have equipment stolen to lose data. For example, an employee using a small flash drive or an iPod can steal large amounts of data and remove it without being

detected. In today's world, you can even buy wristwatches with a USB port and internal memory. The following are some recent examples of stolen data:

- The office manager of a Wall Street law firm found information about prospective mergers and acquisitions in the firm's Word files. He sold the information to friends and relatives, who made several million dollars trading the securities illegally.
- A 22-year old Kazakhstan man broke into Bloomberg's network and stole account information, including that of Michael Bloomberg, the mayor of New York and the founder of the financial news company. He demanded $200,000 in exchange for not using or selling the information. He was arrested in London when accepting the ransom.
- A software engineer tried to steal Intel's plans for a new microprocessor. Because he could view but not copy or print the manufacturing plans, he photographed them screen by screen late at night in his office. Unbeknownst to him, one of Intel's controls was to notify security when the plans were viewed after hours. He was caught photographing the plans.
- Cyber-criminals used sophisticated hacking and identity theft techniques to hack into seven major online brokerage firm accounts. They sold the securities in those accounts and used the cash to pump up the price of 15 low-priced, thinly traded public companies they already owned. They then dumped the 15 stocks in their personal accounts for huge gains. E-trade lost $18 million and Ameritrade $4 million in similar pump-and-dump schemes.
- The U.S. Department of Veterans Affairs was sued because an employee laptop that contained the records of 26.5 million veterans was stolen, exposing them all to identity theft. Soon thereafter, another laptop with the records of 38,000 people disappeared from a subcontractor's office.

Data can also be changed, damaged, destroyed, or defaced. For example, in numerous situations disgruntled employees have scrambled, altered, or destroyed data files. Vandals broke into the NCAA's Web site just before the basketball tournament pairings were announced and posted swastikas, racial slurs, and a white-power logo. The U.S. Air Force, CIA, and NASA have also been the victims of high-profile Web site attacks. An analyst at the Computer Security Institute described the problem as "cyberspace vandals with digital spray cans."

Data also can be lost due to negligence or carelessness. Particularly good sources of confidential data are the hard drives of used computers donated to charity or resold. One professor at a major university bought 10 used computers for his computer forensics class. Using commercially available software, his students found and easily read highly confidential data on 8 of the 10 hard drives.

Deleting files does not erase them. Even reformatting a hard drive often does not erase files or wipe the drive clean. To erase a hard drive completely, special software must be used. When disposing of used computers, the best way to prevent data crooks from buying and mining recycled hard drives is to destroy the hard drive.

Output Fraud

Computer output, displayed on monitors or printed on paper, can be stolen or misused. Unless properly safeguarded, output is subject to prying eyes and unauthorized copying. A study by a Dutch engineer shows that some computer monitors emit a television-like signal that can be picked up, restructured with the help of some inexpensive electronic gear, and displayed on a standard television screen. Under ideal conditions these signals can be picked up from terminals as far away as two miles. During one experiment, the engineer was able to set up his equipment in the basement of an apartment building and read the screen on a computer located on the eighth floor.

Fraud perpetrators also can use computers and output devices to forge authentic-looking outputs. For example, most companies use a laser printer to prepare paychecks. A fraud perpetrator could use a personal computer and a scanner to scan in a company's

paycheck and then use desktop publishing software to erase the payee and amount and then print as many fictitious paychecks as desired on check paper sold in office supply stores. Losses to check fraud in the United States total more than $20 billion a year.

Computer Fraud and Abuse Techniques

Over time perpetrators have devised many ways to commit fraud and abuse using the computer or other electronic devices. This section discusses some of the more common techniques, as summarized alphabetically in Table 5-5. The fraud and abuse techniques

Table 5-5
Computer Fraud and Abuse Techniques

Technique	Description
Adware	Using software to collect web-surfing and spending data and forward it to advertising or media organizations. It also causes banner ads to pop up on computer monitors as the Internet is surfed.
Bluebugging	Taking control of someone else's phone to make calls, send text messages, listen to their phone calls, or read their text messages.
Bluesnarfing	Stealing contact lists, images, and other data using Bluetooth.
Botnet, bot herders	A network of hijacked computers. Hackers, called bot herders, that control the hijacked computers, called zombies, use them in a variety of Internet attacks.
Chipping	Planting a chip that records transaction data in a legitimate credit card reader.
Click fraud	Clicking online ads numerous times to inflate advertising bills.
Cyber-extortion	Requiring a company to pay a specified amount of money to keep the extortionist from harming the company electronically.
Data diddling	Changing data before, during, or after they are entered into the system.
Data leakage	Copying company data, such as computer files, without permission.
Denial-of-service attack	Sending e-mail bombs (hundreds of messages per second) from randomly generated false addresses. The recipient's Internet service provider e-mail server is overloaded and shuts down.
Dictionary attack	Using software to guess company addresses and send them blank e-mails. Unreturned messages are valid addresses that are added to spammer e-mail lists.
Eavesdropping	Listening to private voice or data transmissions, often using a wiretap.
Economic espionage	The theft of information, trade secrets, and intellectual property.
E-mail threats	Sending a threatening message asking the recipient to do something that makes it possible to defraud them.
Evil twin	A wireless network with the same name as a local wireless access point. The hacker disables the legitimate access point, users unknowingly reconnect to the evil twin, and hackers monitor the traffic looking for useful information.
Hacking	Accessing and using computer systems without permission, usually by means of a personal computer and a telecommunications network.
Hijacking	Gaining control of someone else's computer to carry out illicit activities without the owner's knowledge.
Identity theft	Assuming someone's identity, usually for economic gain, by illegally obtaining confidential information such as a Social Security number.
Internet misinformation	Using the Internet to spread false or misleading information.
Internet terrorism	Using the Internet to disrupt communications and electronic commerce.
Key logger	Using spyware to record a user's keystokes.
Logic and time bombs	Software that sits idle until a specified circumstance or time triggers it, destroying programs, data, or both.
Malware	Software that can be used to do harm.
Masquerading/ impersonation	Accessing a system by pretending to be an authorized user. The impersonator enjoys the same privileges as the legitimate user.
Packet sniffing	Using a computer to find confidential information as it travels the Internet and other networks.
Password cracking	Penetrating system defenses, stealing valid passwords, and decrypting them so they can be used to access system programs, files, and data.

Table 5-5 (*continued*)

Pharming	Redirecting traffic to a spoofed Web site to gain access to personal and confidential information.
Phishing	Sending e-mails requesting recipients to visit a Web page and verify data or fill in missing data. The e-mails and Web sites look like legitimate companies, primarily financial institutions.
Phreaking	Attacking phone systems and using telephone lines to transmit viruses and to access, steal, and destroy data.
Piggybacking	1. The clandestine use of someone's Wi-Fi network. 2. Tapping into a telecommunications line, latching on to a legitimate user, and accompanying the perpetrator into the system. 3. Bypassing physical security controls by entering a secure door when an authorized person opens it.
Posing	Creating a seemingly legitimate business, collecting personal information while making a sale, and never delivering the item sold.
Pretexting	Acting under false pretenses to gain confidential information.
Rootkit	Software that conceals processes, files, network connections, and system data from the operating system and other programs.
Round-down	Truncating interest calculations at two decimal places. The truncated fraction of a cent is placed in an account controlled by the perpetrator.
Salami technique	Stealing tiny slices of money over time. An example is increasing expenses by a fraction of a percent and placing those funds in a perpetrator-controlled dummy account.
Scavenging/dumpster diving	Searching for confidential corporate or personal information by searching trash cans or scanning the contents of computer memory.
Shoulder surfing	Watching people or listening as they enter or give confidential information.
Skimming	Double-swiping a credit card or covertly swiping it in a card reader that records the data for later use.
Social engineering	Techniques that trick a person into disclosing confidential information.
Software piracy	Illegally copying computer software.
Spamming	E-mailing an unsolicited message to many people at the same time.
Splog	A spam blog that promotes affiliated Web sites to increase their Google PageRank (how often a Web page is referenced by other Web pages).
Spyware	Using software to monitor computing habits and send that data to someone else, often without the computer user's permission.
Spoofing	Making an e-mail message look as if someone else sent it.
Steganography	Hiding data from one file inside a host file such as a large image or sound file.
Superzapping	Using special software to bypass system controls and perform illegal acts.
Trap door	Entering a system using a back door that bypasses normal system controls.
Trojan horse	Unauthorized code in an authorized and properly functioning program.
Typosquatting/URL hijacking	Setting up Web sites with names similar to real Web sites so users making typographical errors entering Web site names are sent to a site filled with malware.
Virus	A segment of executable code that attaches itself to software, replicates itself, and spreads to other systems or files. Triggered by a predefined event, it damages system resources or displays a message on the monitor.
Vishing	Voice phishing, where e-mail recipients are asked to call a phone number where they are asked to divulge confidential data.
War dialing	Dialing thousands of phone lines searching for idle modems that can be used to enter the system, capture the attached computer, and gain access to the network(s) to which it is attached.
War driving/rocketing	Looking for unprotected wireless networks using a car or a rocket.
Worm	Similar to a virus, but a program rather than a code segment hidden in a host program. Copies and actively transmits itself directly to other systems. It usually does not live very long but is quite destructive while alive.
Zero-day attack	An attack between the time a new software vulnerability is discovered and a software patch that fixes the problem is released.

are discussed in three subsections: computer attacks, social engineering, and malware. These classifications are not clean, in that there is a lot of blurring between the categories. For example, social engineering methods are often used to launch computer attacks. However, these classifications do serve as a way of organizing the techniques.

Computer Attacks

All companies that use the Web, especially those with important trade secrets or valuable IT assets, are under constant attack from disaffected employees, industrial spies, foreign governments, hackers, terrorist groups, and competitors. Preventing attacks is a constant battle. On a busy day, large Web hosting farms suffer millions of attack attempts. This section describes some of the more common techniques used to attack a system.

Hacking is the unauthorized access and use of computer systems, usually by means of a personal computer and a telecommunications network. Most hackers break into systems using known flaws in operating systems or application programs, or as a result of poor access controls. One company that monitors software flaws estimated that over 7,000 known flaws are present in new software released in any given year. The following examples illustrate hacking attacks and the damage they cause:

- Several years ago, Russian hackers broke into Citibank's system and stole $10 million from customer accounts.
- During Operation Desert Storm, Dutch hackers broke into computers at 34 different military sites and extracted confidential information. Among the information stolen were the troop movements and weapons used in the Iraq war. The group offered to sell the information to Iraq, but the government declined, probably because it feared it was a setup.
- A 17-year-old hacker, nicknamed Shadow Hawk, was convicted of electronically penetrating the Bell Laboratories national network, destroying files valued at $174,000, and copying 52 proprietary software programs worth $1.2 million. He published confidential information—such as telephone numbers, passwords, and instructions on how to breach AT&T's computer security system—on underground bulletin boards. He was sentenced to nine months in prison and given a $10,000 fine. Like Shadow Hawk, many hackers are fairly young, some as young as 12 and 13.

A hacker also can access a company's system by breaking into the system of a customer or supplier that has privileged access to the company's system. For example, a hacker penetrated the computer of a custom-software supplier who was doing some work for a large financial services company. The hacker used the "open pipe" that the supplier used to communicate with the bank to install a powerful Trojan horse in the bank's computer.

Hackers who search for dial-up modem lines by programming computers to dial thousands of phone lines are **war dialing**. Hackers can enter through the idle modem, capture the PC attached to the modem, and gain access to the network to which the computer is connected. This approach got its name from the movie *War Games*. Much more problematic in today's world are rogue wireless access points that are not properly controlled. **War driving** is driving around looking for unprotected wireless networks. Some war drivers draw chalk symbols on sidewalks to mark unprotected wireless networks, a practice referred to as **war chalking**. One enterprising group of researchers went **war rocketing**. They sent rockets into the air that let loose wireless access points, each attached to a parachute. As the parachutes decended, the access points detected unsecured wireless networks in a 50-square-mile area.

A **botnet**, short for robot network, is a network of hijacked computers. **Hijacking** is gaining control of someone else's computer to carry out illicit activities without the user's knowledge. The hacker installs the bot software (typically some kind of malware)

3 An unauthorized person passing through a secure door when an authorized person opens it, thereby bypassing physical security controls such as keypads, ID cards, or biometric identification scanners.

Data diddling is changing data before, during, or after it is entered into the system to delete, alter, add, or incorrectly update key system data. For example, a clerk for a Denver brokerage altered a transaction to record 1,700 shares of Loren Industries stock worth about $2,500 as shares in Long Island Lighting worth more than $25,000.

Data leakage is the unauthorized copying of company data. Ten employees compromised the Social Security Administration system and stole 11,000 Social Security numbers (and other identifying information, such as the mother's maiden name), which they sold to identity theft fraudsters.

A fraud perpetrator can use the **salami technique** to embezzle large sums of money a "salami slice" at a time from many different accounts. For example, a disgruntled employee programmed the company computer to systematically increase all production costs by a fraction of a percent and place the excess in the account of a dummy vendor he controlled. Every few months the fraudulent costs were raised another fraction of a percent. Because all expenses were rising together, no single account or expense would call attention to the fraud. The accountant was caught when an alert teller failed to recognize the payee name on a check the perpetrator was trying to cash and brought it to the company's attention. The salami scheme was part of the plot line in several films, including *Superman III, Hackers*, and *Office Space*. One salami technique has been given a name. In a **round-down fraud**, all interest calculations are truncated at two decimal places and the excess decimals put into an account the perpetrator controls. No one is the wiser, since all the books balance. Over time, these fractions of a cent add up to a significant amount, especially when interest is calculated daily.

Phreaking is attacking phone systems to obtain free phone line access. One telephone company lost $4.5 million in three days when its system was compromised and details on how to use its phone lines were published on the Internet. Phreakers also use the telephone lines to transmit viruses and to access, steal, and destroy data. Phreakers break into voice mail systems, as the New York Police Department learned. The hackers changed the voice mail greeting to say that officers were too busy drinking coffee and eating doughnuts to answer the phone and to call 119 (not 911) in case of an emergency. The owner of two small voice-over-IP (VoIP) phone companies hacked into a larger VoIP provider and routed over $1 million of calls through one of his two systems. To keep the rerouting from being discovered, they broke into a New York firm's system, set up a server, and made it look like the calls came from many third parties. Other hackers have hijacked calls, rerouted them to their own call centers, and asked callers to identify themselves by divulging confidential information.

Economic espionage is the theft of information, trade secrets, and intellectual property. It increased by 323% during one five-year period. The U.S. Department of Justice estimates that intellectual property theft losses total $250 billion a year. Almost 75% of these losses are to an employee, former employee, contractor, or supplier. At any point in time, the FBI is investigating about 800 separate incidents of economic espionage. One noteworthy example was the allegation that Reuters Analytics broke into the computers of its competitor, Bloomberg, and stole lines of code that enable financial institutions to analyze historical stock market data. In another case, Toshiba had to pay $465 million in damages to Lexar Media as compensation for the theft of trade secrets provided by a member of Lexar's board of directors.

A growing problem is **cyber-extortion**, in which fraud perpetrators threaten to harm a company if it does not pay a specified amount of money. For example, the owner of a small company that processed credit cards for online businesses received an unsolicited e-mail listing the names of his clients, as well as the names and credit card numbers of customers the client had done business with over the weekend. The e-mail told him to pay $50,000 in six equal payments or the data would be sent to his

clients. An investigation showed that his system had been successfully attacked and customer data had been copied. Not believing the attacker would carry out his threat, he did nothing. The extortionists released the data, and he spent the next several days trying to calm and reassure his very irate customers. His efforts were futile; his customers abandoned him, and within six months he had to shut down his business.

Internet terrorism occurs when hackers use the Internet to disrupt electronic commerce and to destroy company and individual communications. For example, a Massachusetts man hired hackers to attack the Web site of WeaKnees.com, an online retailer, because WeaKnees turned down a proposed business deal with him. The six-week-long attack was carried out using a botnet of 5,000 to 10,000 hijacked computers and caused over $2 million in damage. Internet terrorism is also conducted on a more personal level. Diana DeGarmo, the American Idol runner-up from season three, and her family and friends were stalked and terrorized by an obsessive fan who wanted to "become" Diana. The fan broke into Diana's MySpace account, stole her identity, and sent e-mails to her friends and fans. The fan phoned, e-mailed, and text messaged Diana more than a hundred times a day. In an attempt to get rid of her, Diana finally asked her what she wanted. Her reply was $1 million.

Internet misinformation is using the Internet to spread false or misleading information about people or companies. This can be done using Web sites, blogs, chat rooms, instant messages, and e-mails. For example, McDonald's spent seven years fighting false accusations spread using Web sites. After 313 days of testimony and an expenditure of $16 million, McDonald's won the case and was awarded $94,000. A Web site immediately mocked the verdict, called its campaign against McDonald's "unstoppable," and set up shop under a new name. Another form of Internet misinformation is people pretending to be someone they are not. They often post messages to Internet newsgroups or online bulletin boards with the intent to harm the reputation of the impersonated person. Even more subtle are the cases in which bogus information is entered in legitimate news stories. For example, one young man broke into Yahoo's news pages and replaced the name of an arrested hacker with that of Microsoft chairman Bill Gates.

Perpetrators also send unsolicited **e-mail threats**. For example, Global Communications sent a message to many people threatening legal action if an unspecified overdue amount was not paid within 24 hours. The message stated that court action could be avoided by calling Mike Murray at an 809 area code (the Caribbean). People who called got a clever recording that sounded like a live person and responded to the caller's voice. The responses were designed to keep callers on the phone as long as possible because they were being billed at $25 per minute.

Many companies advertise online and pay based on how many users click on ads that take them to the company's Web site. Advertisers pay from a few cents to over $10 for each click. **Click fraud** is intentionally clicking on these ads numerous times to inflate advertising bills. Competitors click on a company's ad to drive up their advertising costs. A Web-page owner, who gets a commission to host a pay-per-click ad, can repeatedly click on the ad to boost commissions. Ad agencies can inflate the number of clicks to make an ad campaign appear more effective. To reduce the cost of perpetrating the fraud, companies can pay workers in poor nations to sit at a computer all day and click on ads or use software that automatically clicks ads and uses different IP addresses to simulate random users. It is estimated that as many as 30% of all clicks are not legitimate.

Software piracy is copying software without the publisher's permission. It is estimated that for every legal software sale, between seven and eight illegal copies are made. Within days of being released, most new software is on the Internet and available free to those who want to download it illegally. An estimated 26% of software used in the United States is pirated. In some countries, this figure is over 90%. The software industry estimates the economic losses of piracy at $20 billion a year.

Piracy is such a serious problem that the Software Publishers Association (SPA) files lawsuits against companies and individuals. In one case, the Business Software Alliance found 1,400 copies of unlicensed software at an adult vocational school in

the Los Angeles School District and claimed $5 million in damages. Individuals convicted of software piracy are subject to fines of up to $250,000 and jail terms of up to five years. However, the SPA often negotiates more creative punishments. For example, a Puget Sound student caught distributing copyrighted software over the Internet was required to write a 20-page paper on the evils of software piracy and copyright infringement. He also had to perform 50 hours of community service that consisted of wiring schools for Internet usage. Failure to comply with either item would have subjected him to a $10,000 fine and resulted in a lawsuit for copyright infringement.

Social Engineering

Social engineering refers to techniques used to obtain confidential information, often by tricking people. The information is used to break into computer systems and commit identity theft. **Identity theft** is assuming someone's identity, usually for economic gain, by illegally obtaining and using confidential information, such as a Social Security, bank account, or credit card number. Identity thieves empty the victim's bank accounts, apply for credit cards, run up large debts, and take out mortgages and other loans. If the identity thief is careful to cover his tracks and makes sure all bills and notices are sent to an address he controls, rather than to the victim's address, the scheme can be prolonged because the victim will usually not know what is happening until considerable damage has been caused. Victims can usually prove they are not responsible for the debts or missing funds, but they usually have to spend a significant amount of time cleaning up their credit records and restoring their reputations.

In one case, a convicted felon incurred $100,000 of credit card debt, took out a home loan, purchased homes and consumer goods, and then filed for bankruptcy in the victim's name. While doing this, he telephoned his victim and mocked him because he could do nothing about it as identity theft was not a crime at the time. Sadly, the victim and his spouse spent over four years and $15,000 to restore their credit and reputation. The identity thief served a brief sentence for lying while buying a gun and did not have to make restitution to his victim. This and similar cases resulted in Congress making identity theft a federal offense in 1998.

Quite a few different types of social engineering have been used over time.

In **pretexting**, people act under false pretenses to gain confidential information. For example, they might conduct a security survey and lull the person into disclosing confidential information by asking 10 innocent questions before asking the confidential ones. They also call help desks and claim to be an employee who has forgotten a password, or they call users and say they are testing the system and need a password. They pose as buyers, prospective employees, or salespeople to get plant tours and obtain information that may help them break into the system. Some pretexters use voice-changing devices to make a male voice sound like a female voice or use spoofing devices to make it appear they are phoning from the intended victim's phone number. In a famous recent case, the chairwoman of Hewlett-Packard was forced to resign after H-P hired a private investigator to catch H-P directors who had leaked confidential information to reporters. The private investigator pretended to be someone that he was not to get private phone records and other confidential information of directors and journalists. As a result, Congress passed a bill making the use of pretexting to obtain a person's phone records illegal. In another famous case, a man was able to access some undetermined portion of ChoicePoints's files on 19 billion people by claiming in writing and on the telephone to be someone he was not.

Posing is creating a seemingly legitimate business, collecting personal information while making a sale, and never delivering a product. Fraudsters have been known to employ the same technique with Internet job listing sites. Consumers submit résumés, sometimes with birth dates and Social Security numbers, which the fraudster uses to commit identity fraud.

Phishing is sending an e-mail, instant message, or text message pretending to be a legitimate company, usually a financial institution, and requesting information. The recipient is asked to respond to the e-mail request, visit a Web page and submit data, or respond to a text message. The request is bogus, and the information gathered is used to commit identity fraud. Some phishing e-mails secretly install software that spies on or hijacks the user's computer. For example, the software could capture log-on names or take pictures of the user's screen when he logs into his financial institution. In the early days of phishing, each e-mail resulted in tens of thousands of calls to financial service company call centers, disrupted business, and hundreds of thousand of dollars of extra expense as the deluge of calls was handled.

It is relatively easy to launch a phishing attack as hackers sell phishing-in-a-box kits that lead people step by step through the process. A surprisingly high number of Internet users reply to the messages. ITT Corporation has estimated that more than 2 million Americans have been fooled by phishing scams to the tune of over $2 billion in losses.

Less sophisticated phishing attacks can be spotted in several ways: an urgent message or threat, such as your account being closed, that tries to motivate you to act; no link to the legitimate company's home page; and grammatical errors in the e-mail. However, phishers are becoming more skilled at making the e-mails and Web sites look professional—like they come from legitimate companies—by including company logos, familiar graphics, phone numbers, and Internet links that appear to be those of the victimized company; such links, however, are not to the legitimate company's site but to a site controlled by the phisher.

The IRS is such a favorite of phishers that it has set up a Web site and an e-mail address (phishing@irs.gov) where people can forward for investigation suspicious e-mails that purport to be from the IRS. A recent IRS phishing attack told the e-mail recipients they were due a refund and directed them to a Web site where they could claim the refund. The bogus Web site looked just like the IRS Web site and had forms that looked just like IRS forms. To "claim" the refund, however, you had to enter personal and confidential information that facilitated identity theft. The claimed refund was, of course, never sent.

The simplest way to avoid being phished is to realize that financial institutions and government agencies such as the IRS never ask for sensitive personal information via e-mail. Any e-mails that request Social Security numbers, IDs, passwords, or account numbers should be ignored.

In voice phishing, or **vishing**, e-mail recipients are asked to call a specified phone number, where a recording tells them to enter confidential data. The perpetrators use Voice over Internet Protocol (VoIP) technology to detect the telephone keystrokes. Identity thieves spoofed an e-mail from PayPal containing an account compromise warning and asking the recipients to call a phone number. An automated system told PayPal users to enter their credit card data and even asked them to reenter data that was not correct.

Phished (and otherwise stolen) credit card numbers can be bought and sold, which is called **carding**. Scores of underground Web sites facilitate carding, with some rating the reliability of sellers the same way eBay does. Other sites have created software to automate the collection of stolen credit cards, card verification numbers (the three-digit number on the back of a credit card), and PIN numbers. Organized gangs of cyber-criminals run many of the sites.

Pharming is redirecting a Web site's traffic to a bogus (spoofed) Web site, usually to gain access to personal and confidential information. So, how does pharming work? If you do not know someone's phone number, you look it up in a phone book. If you could change XYZ Company's number in the phone book to your phone number, people calling XYZ Company would reach you instead. You could then ask them to divulge information only they would know to verify their identity.

Each Web site has a unique IP (Internet) address (four groupings of numbers separated by three periods), and there is a Domain Name System (think phone book) that converts a domain (Web site) name to an IP address. Pharmers change the IP address in the Domain Name System (DNS) to an IP address they control. They then collect the

personal and private information of everyone who visits the spoofed Web site. Compromised DNS servers are referred to as "poisoned."

An alternative pharming approach is to use malware to change a computer's host file (think internal DNS) or an Internet service provider's internally maintained list of common IP addresses. Once these files are poisoned, all subsequent requests to visit that Web site are directed to the spoofed site. Because most PCs are not well controlled, they are often better targets for pharming than Internet servers are.

Pharming is difficult to detect because the user's browser shows the correct Web site. As a result, pharming is a major concern to businesses hosting e-business and online banking Web sites. Antivirus and spyware removal software are currently ineffective protections against pharming. Instead, complicated anti-pharming techniques are required. This has made pharming a very popular social engineering tool for hackers. It is also very popular because pharming allows scammers to target many people at a time through domain spoofing rather than one at a time with phishing e-mails.

An **evil twin** is when a hacker sets up a wireless network with the same name (called *Service Set Identifier*, or *SSID*) as the wireless access point at a local hot spot or a corporation's wireless network. The hacker disrupts or disables the legitimate access point by disconnecting it, directing a denial-of-service against it, or creating radio frequency interference around it. Users are unaware that they reconnect to the evil twin, and hackers monitor the traffic to that device looking for useful information, such as passwords and credit card numbers. Hackers also use evil twins to unleash a wide variety of malware and to install software to attack other computers.

Typosquatting, also called URL hijacking, is setting up Web sites with names very similar to real Web sites so when users make mistakes, such as typographical errors, in entering a Web site name the user is sent to an invalid site. For example, typing goggle.com instead of google.com might lead you to a site set up by a cyber-squatter. The typosquatter's site may do the following:

- Trick the user into thinking she is at the real site by using a copied or a similar logo, Web site layout, or content. These sites often contain advertising that would appeal to the person looking for the real domain name. The typosquatter might also be a competitor.
- Send the user to a site very different from what was wanted. In one famous case, a typosquatter sent people looking for sites that appealed to children to a pornographic Web site.
- Use the false addresses to distribute viruses, adware, spyware, or other malware.

To stop typosquatting, companies may need to send a cease-and-desist letter to the offender, purchase the Web site address from the typosquatter, or file a lawsuit against the offending site or individual. To prevent it, a company tries to obtain all the Web names similar to theirs and to redirect people to the correct site. It also uses software that scans the Internet and finds domains that appear to be typosquatting. Parents can use the same software to restrict access to sites that squat on typos of children's Web sites.

Scavenging or **dumpster diving** is gaining access to confidential information by searching corporate or personal records. Some identity thieves search garbage cans, communal trash bins, and city dumps to find documents or printouts with confidential company or personal information that allows them to assume an identity. Oracle Corporation was embarrassed a few years ago when investigators it hired were caught going through the trash of companies that supported its rival Microsoft. The investigators had obtained the trash by paying building janitors $1,200.

In another case, Jerry Schneider noticed a trash bin full of papers on his way home from high school. Rummaging through it he discovered operating guides for Pacific Telephone computers. Over time his scavenging activities resulted in a technical library that later allowed him to steal $1 million worth of electronic equipment. In a

case in South America, a man attached a video camera to a car battery, hid it in some bushes, and pointed it at the company president's computer that was visible through a first-floor window. A significant business acquisition almost fell through as a result of the information on the videotape.

Shoulder surfing is watching or listening to people give out confidential information. Some fraudsters use simple card trapping devices, such as plastic sleeves inserted in ATM machines, to trap an ATM card. Perpetrators approach the helpless victim and pretend to help, tricking the person into entering her PIN. Once the victim gives up, the thief removes the card and records the PIN that goes with it.

Skimming is double-swiping a credit card in a legitimate terminal or covertly swiping a credit card in a small, hidden, handheld card reader that records credit card data for later use. Commonly committed in retail outlets such as restaurants and carried out by employees with a legitimate reason to possess the victim's cards, these schemes exceed $1 billion per year.

Chipping is posing as a service engineer and planting a small chip in a legitimate credit card reader. The chip records transaction data and the person returns at a later date to remove the chip containing the valuable data.

Eavesdropping enables perpetrators to observe private communications or transmissions of data. One way to intercept signals is by setting up a wiretap. The equipment needed to wiretap an unprotected communications line is readily available at local electronics stores. One alleged wiretapping fraud involved Mark Koenig, a 28-year-old telecommunications consultant, and four associates. Federal agents say they pulled personal identification numbers and other crucial information about Bank of America customers from telephone lines and used the data to make 5,500 fake ATM cards. Koenig and his friends allegedly intended to use the cards over one long weekend to withdraw money from banks all over the country. Authorities were tipped off, however, and the criminals were apprehended before they could use the cards.

Malware

This section describes **malware**, which is any software that can be used to do harm.

Spyware software secretly collects personal information about users and sends it to someone else without the user's permission. The information is gathered by logging keystrokes, monitoring computing habits such as Web sites visited, and scanning documents on the computer's hard disk. Spyware can also hijack your browser, replacing your computer's home page with a page chosen by the spyware—a page with links that the spyware creator wants you to visit. Unless the spyware is removed, resetting your browser home page only lasts until your computer is rebooted. Spyware can also hijack search requests, returning results chosen by the spyware rather than the results desired.

Spyware infections, of which users are usually unaware, come from the following:

- Downloads such as file sharing programs, system utilities, games, wallpaper, screensavers, music, and videos.
- Web sites that secretly download spyware when they are visited. This is called *drive-by downloading*.
- A hacker using security holes in Web browsers and other software.
- Programs masquerading as anti-spyware security software.
- A worm or virus.
- Public wireless networks. For example, users receive a message they believe is from the coffee shop or hotel where they are using wireless technology. Clicking on the message inadvertently downloads a Trojan horse or spyware application. At Kinko's in Manhattan, an employee gathered the data needed to open bank accounts and apply for credit cards in the names of the people using Kinko's wireless network.

Spyware is especially problematic for companies that have employees who telecommute or dial into the network from remote locations using laptop computers. Spyware on these computers records the user's interaction with the network and corporate data and may even introduce spyware to the entire organization. One of the largest sources of spyware is adult-oriented sites. The computers of people who visit those sites are infected, and when they log onto their corporate systems those infections are passed into their employer's internal network.

Adware (short for *advertising supported software*) is a type of spyware that causes banner ads to pop up on a monitor as users surf the net, to collect information about the user's Web-surfing and spending habits, and to forward it to the company gathering the data. Adware companies charge advertisers and media organizations for each computer showing its ads. To increase the number of computers with their software, adware companies pay shareware authors and developers to bundle the adware with their software. This allows the shareware developers to make money without charging for their software.

Computers are infected with adware the same way they are infected with spyware. For example, one music and digital content sharing company offers users a $30 version or a free "ad-supported" version. The license agreement for the free software discloses the adware (hence making it "legal" spyware), but most users do not read the agreement and are unaware of its installation. Reputable adware companies claim that sensitive or identifying data are not collected. However, there is no way for users to effectively control or limit the data collected and transmitted. Adware is not illegal if its installation is disclosed in the license agreement, but many privacy-conscious users object to its use.

In a recent survey, 55% of companies had experienced a spyware, adware, or some other malware infection. In larger organizations, the average cost of getting rid of spyware is over $1.5 million a year. Recently, an antispyware vendor surveyed 2 million consumer computers and found that 81% of them were infected. The best protection against spyware and adware is a good antispyware software package that neutralizes or eliminates it and prevents its installation. One downside is that after the spyware or adware is erased the free software that was its host may not work.

Some malware developers intentionally make their software difficult to uninstall. Malware companies sometimes battle each other over whose software will infect a computer. Some of them have developed **torpedo software** that destroys competing malware, resulting in "malware warfare" between competing developers.

Key logger software records computer activity, such as a user's keystokes, e-mails sent and received, Web sites visited, and chat session participation. Parents use the software to monitor their children's computer usage, and businesses use it to monitor employee activity. Fraud perpetrators use the software to capture confidential information and send it to the perpetrator by e-mail. There are over 10,000 unique key logging software programs; most are free or very cheap and are widely available in underground chat rooms. Computers are infected with key logging software when they visit corrupt Web sites or download free software. One enterprising student was able to install key logging software on his teacher's computer and recorded her typed answers to her exams. He decoded the keystrokes and was caught trying to sell exam answers to other students.

A **Trojan horse** is a set of malicious computer instructions in an authorized and otherwise properly functioning program. The programs that launch denial-of-service attacks are often Trojan horses. Some Trojan horses give the creator the power to remotely control the victim's computer. Unlike viruses and worms, the code does not try to replicate itself. Most trojan horse infections occur when a user is tricked into running an infected program received in an e-mail or instant message or by visiting a Web site. Trojan horses are often placed in software billed as helpful add-ons to popular software programs. For example, several thousand America Online subscribers were sent messages containing an offer of free software. Users who opened the attachments unknowingly unleashed a Trojan horse that secretly copied the subscriber's

account name and password and forwarded them to the sender. In Israel, companies were sent business proposals on floppy disks that contained the Trojan. In another case, visitors to an adult site were told to download a special program to see the pictures. This program also contained embedded code that disconnected users from their Internet service providers and connected them to a service that billed them $2 a minute until they turned off their computers. Over 800,000 minutes were billed, with some phone bills as high as $3,000, before the scam was detected.

Time bombs and **logic bombs** are Trojan horses that lie idle until triggered by a specified time or circumstance. Once triggered, the bomb goes off, destroying programs, data, or both. Company insiders, typically disgruntled programmers or other systems personnel who want to get even with their company, write many bombs. System administrator Roger Duronio was convicted of setting off such a bomb at USB PaineWebber after he did not receive the bonus or the new contract he felt he deserved. He anticipated not getting the money and planted the Trojan horse time bomb on USB's system some months before the compensation dispute. Several weeks after he left the firm, the trigger date of March 4 arrived. The approximately 60 lines of malicious code he wrote attacked the 2,000 servers in the company's system and deleted company files just as the stock market began trading. The effects were catastrophic. Brokers' computers were out of commission for days or weeks, depending on how badly the machines were damaged and the existence of branch backup tapes. Some 20% of the computers had no backup tapes, and some servers were never fully restored. Over 400 company employees and 200 consultants from IBM worked feverishly, at a cost of $3.1 million, to restore the system. Duronio cashed out his IRA and sold UBS stock short, figuring to make a killing when the stock plunged. It never did, and he lost money on his short sale.

A **trap door**, or back door, is a way into a system that bypasses normal system controls. Programmers use trap doors to modify programs during systems development and normally remove them before the system is put into operation. When a trap door is not removed before the program is implemented, anyone who discovers it can enter the program and commit a fraud. Programmers can also insert trap doors before they are terminated, allowing them access to the system after they leave. BackOrifice, Netbus, and SubSeven are tools intruders use to gain remote, back door access to systems with Windows software.

Packet sniffers are programs that capture data from information packets as they travel over the Internet or company networks. Captured data are sifted to find confidential information, such as user IDs and passwords, and confidential or proprietary information that can be sold or otherwise used.

Steganography programs hide data from one file inside a host file, such as a large image or sound file. There are more than 200 different steganographic software programs available on the Internet. The software merges the two files by removing scattered bytes from the host file and replacing them with data from the hidden file. The steganography program password protects the merged file, and the only way to reassemble the hidden file is to key the password into the same steganography program. The host file can still be heard or viewed because human visual and auditory senses are not good enough to pick up the slight decrease in image or sound quality that the hidden file causes. Company employees can merge confidential information with a seemingly harmless file and send it anywhere in the world, where the confidential information is reassembled.

A **rootkit** is software that conceals processes, files, network connections, memory addresses, systems utility programs, and system data from the operating system and other programs. Rootkits often modify parts of the operating system or install themselves as drivers. A rootkit can also be used to hide a hacker's presence from the system. A rootkit can be used to hide the presence of trap doors, sniffers, and keyloggers; to conceal software that originates a denial-of-service or an e-mail spam attack; and to access user names and log-in information. Unlike viruses and worms, rootkits do not spread to other systems.

Rootkit software also is readily available on the Internet. Several vendors sell programs that detect rootkits, and security vendors are beginning to include rootkit detection in their antivirus products. When a rootkit is detected, it is usually better to reinstall the operating system from scratch than to spend the time and effort to try to delete it from the system. Perhaps the most famous rootkit use was the Sony BMG CD copy protection scandal. Unbeknownst to users, their music CDs secretly placed a rootkit on Microsoft Windows PCs when the CDs were played on computers.

Superzapping is the unauthorized use of special system programs to bypass regular system controls and perform illegal acts, all without leaving an audit trail. The technique derives its name from a software utility, called Superzap, developed by IBM to handle emergencies, such as restoring a system that has crashed.

A computer **virus** is a segment of self-replicating, executable code that attaches itself to a file or program. During its replication phase, the virus spreads to other systems when the infected file or program is downloaded or e-mailed and opened by the recipient. Newer viruses can mutate each time they infect a computer, making them much more difficult to detect and destroy. Many viruses lie dormant for extended periods without causing any specific damage, except to propagate themselves. In one survey, almost 90% of the respondents said their company was infected with a virus within the prior 12 months.

During the attack phase, triggered by some predefined event, viruses destroy or alter data or programs, take control of the computer, destroy the hard disk's file allocation table, delete or rename files or directories, reformat the hard disk, change the content of files, or keep users from booting the system or accessing data on a hard disk. A virus can intercept and change transmissions, print disruptive images or messages on the screen or change its color, or cause the screen image to disappear. Many viruses can automatically send e-mail, faxes, or text messages with the victim's name as the alleged source. As the virus spreads, it takes up space, clogs communications, and hinders system performance. For example, a particularly bad virus attack shut down a bank with 200 servers and 10,000 desktop computers for four days. During the downtime, the bank was locked out of its system and customer accounts could not be accessed. A firm that specializes in fixing virus attacks eventually restored the system.

Symptoms of a computer virus include computers that will not start or execute; unexpected read or write operations; an inability to save files; long program load times; abnormally large file sizes; slow systems operation; and unusual screen activity, error messages, or file names.

The Sobig virus, written by Russian hackers, infected an estimated 1 of every 17 e-mails several years ago. The virus took months to write and was released in ever-improving versions. A year later, the MyDoom virus infected 1 in 12 e-mails and did $4.75 billion in damages. It is estimated that viruses and worms cost businesses over $20 billion a year.

Virus creators send an estimated 1 billion e-mail messages containing a virus every day. The creators are getting good at making them look authentic. For example, one virus comes in an e-mail that appears to come from Microsoft—the Microsoft logo and copyright are even included in the message window launched by the virus. The e-mail tells the recipient to use the attached patch to fix a security flaw in either Microsoft Internet Explorer or Outlook. Instead, opening the attachment downloads malicious software from a remote Web site that installs a back door into the compromised computer. The perpetrator can then control the computer using the back door.

A computer system can be protected from viruses by following the guidelines listed in Focus 5-2.

Most viruses attack computers, but all devices connected to the Internet or that are part of a communications network run the risk of being infected. Recent viruses have attacked cell phones and personal digital assistants. These devices are infected through text messages, Internet page downloads, and Bluetooth wireless technology.

Flaws in Bluetooth applications have opened up the system to attack. **Bluesnarfing** is stealing (snarfing) contact lists, images, and other data from other

5-2 FOCUS

Keeping Your Computers Virus-Free

Here are some practical suggestions for protecting computers from viruses:

- Install reliable antivirus software that scans for, identifies, and destroys viruses.
- Make sure that the latest versions of the antivirus programs are used. National City Bank in Cleveland, Ohio, installed some new laptops. The manufacturer and the bank checked the laptops for viruses but did not use the latest antivirus software. A virus spread from the laptop hard drives to 300 network servers and 12,000 workstations. It took the bank over two days to eradicate the virus from all bank systems.
- Scan all incoming e-mail for viruses at the server level rather than when it hits users' desktops.
- All software should be certified as virus-free before loading it into the system. Be wary of software from unknown sources, as they may be virus

bait—especially if their prices or functionality sound too good to be true.
- Deal with trusted software retailers.
- Some software suppliers use electronic techniques to make tampering evident. Ask if the software you are purchasing has such protection.
- Check new software on an isolated machine with virus detection software. Software direct from the publisher has been known to have viruses.
- Have two backups of all files. Data files should be backed up separately from programs to avoid contaminating backup data.
- If you use flash drives, diskettes, or CDs, do not put them in strange machines as they may become infected. Do not let others use those storage devices on your machine. Scan all new files with antiviral software before any data or programs are copied to your machine.

devices using Bluetooth. **Bluebugging** is taking control of someone else's phone to make calls or send text messages, or to listen to phone calls and monitor text messages received. The bills for the calls and text messages appear on the attacked phone's bill. These attacks will become increasingly popular as phones are used to make payments electronicaly for items purchased. Think about the possibilities for a fraudster. When he wants something, all he has to do is bluebug a nearby phone and charge that phone for the purchase. To prevent these attacks, a bluetooth device can be set to make it hard for other devices to recognize it. Antivirus software is also being developed for phones to deal with such problems.

In the future, many other devices—such as home security systems, home appliances, automobiles, and elevators—will be connected to the Internet and will also become the target of viruses.

A computer **worm** is a self-replicating computer program similar to a virus except for the following three differences:

1 A virus is a segment of code hidden in or attached to a host program or executable file, while a worm is a stand-alone program.
2 A virus requires a human to do something (run a program, open a file, etc.) to replicate itself, whereas a worm does not and actively seeks to send copies of itself to other devices on a network.
3 Worms harm networks (if only by consuming bandwidth), whereas viruses infect or corrupt files or data on a targeted computer.

Worms often reside in e-mail attachments, which, when opened or activated, can damage the user's system. Worms often reproduce by mailing themselves to the recipient's mailing list, resulting in an electronic chain letter. Some recent worms have completely shut down e-mail systems at a number of firms. Worms are not confined to personal computers. Hundreds of thousands of worms infect cell phones each year by jumping from phone to phone over wireless networks.

A worm usually does not "live" very long, but it is quite destructive while "alive." It takes little technical knowledge to create a worm or virus. In fact, several Web sites

provide unsophisticated users with an application that enables them to create worms. One such application has been downloaded more than 20,000 times.

One of the earliest and more destructive worms, written by Robert T. Morris, affected 6,000 computers in a very short time. Focus 5-3 details the impact of this worm on systems across the country.

More recently, MySpace had to go offline to disable a worm that added over 1 million friends to the hacker's site in less than a day. MySpace profiles were also infected by a worm after viewing a QuickTime video containing malicious software that replaced the links in the user's page with links to a phishing site. The malware also embedded a copy of the malicious code in the QuickTime video on the user's site so that users who visited the infected profile had their own profile infected.

Many viruses and worms exploit known software vulnerabilities than can be corrected with a software patch. Therefore, one of the best defenses against them is making sure that all software patches are installed as soon as they become available.

Preventing and Detecting Computer Fraud and Abuse

Because fraud and other security issues are serious problems, organizations must create a climate that makes fraud less likely, increases the difficulty of committing a fraud, improves detection methods, and reduces the amount of loss if a fraud occurs. These measures are listed in Table 5-6 and discussed in Chapters 6 through 8.

5-3 FOCUS A Worm Run Amok

Scientists at Berkeley's Experimental Computing Facility noticed a rash of unknown users trying to log on to their system. Within minutes, the program brought Berkeley's mammoth system to a halt. Within 30 minutes, it was clear that the program was not limited to the Berkeley system. Within hours, computer experts discovered it was invading the *entire* Internet. While scientists attempted to stop the worm, law enforcement officials and the press investigated it. Information on the perpetrator was scarce until an unidentified phone caller tipped a *New York Times* writer by inadvertently referring to him as "RTM."

Robert Tappan Morris acquired a passion for computer security issues while working with his father, a scientist at Bell Labs. At Harvard, he received extensive recognition for projects that improved Bell Systems Internet operations and its operating system, UNIX. At age 20, Robert's skills in UNIX security were so extensive that he gave an address on computer security to both the National Security Agency and the Naval Research Laboratory.

While Robert was attending graduate school at Cornell University, the first computer viruses were receiving national media attention. This sparked Robert's interest in developing an undetectable worm that would reach as many computers as possible. With Robert's background in UNIX security issues and his unlimited access to the Cornell computer system, developing a worm was easy. Using a bug in the UNIX Sendmail subprogram, Robert developed a worm capable of entering a given system without authorization.

When the worm was finished, Robert illegally logged on to an artificial intelligence lab computer at MIT from his system at Cornell and released his creation. After dinner, Robert attempted to log on, but the computer did not respond. He immediately knew something was wrong. After several attempts to remedy the problem, Robert realized he had made a fatal programming error that allowed the worm to replicate out of control throughout the Internet. Cleaning out the Internet system and recreating the files that the worm destroyed took several months.

Robert was arrested and charged with a felony for his unauthorized computer access. In 1990, he was convicted of computer crime and sentenced to three years probation, 400 hours of community service, and a $10,000 fine.

Table 5-6
Summary of Ways to Prevent and Detect Computer Fraud

Make Fraud Less Likely to Occur

- Create an organizational culture that stresses integrity and commitment to ethical values and competence.
- Adopt an organizational structure, management philosophy, operating style, and appetite for risk that minimizes the likelihood of fraud.
- Require oversight from an active, involved, and independent audit committee of the board of directors.
- Assign authority and responsibility for business objectives to specific departments and individuals, encourage them to use initiative to solve problems, and hold them accountable for achieving those objectives.
- Identify the events that lead to increased fraud risk and take steps to prevent, avoid, share, or accept that risk.
- Develop a comprehensive set of security policies to guide the design and implementation of specific control procedures and communicate them effectively to company employees.
- Implement human resource policies for hiring, compensating, evaluating, promoting, and discharging employees that send messages about the required level of ethical behavior and integrity.
- Effectively supervise employees, including monitoring their performance and correcting their errors.
- Train employees in integrity and ethical considerations, as well as security and fraud prevention measures.
- Require annual employee vacations, periodically rotate the duties of key employees, and require signed confidentiality agreements.
- Implement formal and rigorous project development and acquisition controls, as well as change management controls.
- Increase the penalty for committing fraud by prosecuting fraud perpetrators more vigorously.

Increase the Difficulty of Committing Fraud

- Develop a strong system of internal controls.
- Segregate the accounting functions of authorization, recording, and custody.
- Implement a proper segregation of duties between systems functions.
- Restrict physical and remote access to system resources to authorized personnel.
- Require transactions and activities to be authorized by appropriate supervisory personnel. Have the system authenticate the person, and their right to perform the transaction, before allowing the transaction to take place.
- Use properly designed documents and records to capture and process transactions.
- Safeguard all assets, records, and data.
- Require independent checks on performance, such as reconciliation of two independent sets of records, where possible and appropriate.
- Implement computer-based controls over data input, computer processing, data storage, data transmission, and information output.
- Encrypt stored and transmitted data and programs to protect them from unauthorized access and use.
- When disposing of used computers, destroy the computer's hard drive to keep crooks from buying and mining recycled hard drives.
- Fix known software vulnerabilities by installing the latest updates to operating systems, as well as security and application programs.

Improve Detection Methods

- Create an audit trail so that individual transactions can be traced through the system to the financial statements and financial statement data can be traced back to individual transactions.
- Conduct periodic external and internal audits, as well as special network security audits.
- Install fraud detection software.
- Implement a fraud hotline.
- Employ a computer security officer, computer consultants, and forensic specialists as needed.
- Monitor system activities, including computer and network security efforts, usage and error logs, and all malicious actions. Use intrusion detection systems to help automate the monitoring process.

Reduce Fraud Losses

- Maintain adequate insurance.
- Develop comprehensive fraud contingency, disaster recovery, and business continuity plans.
- Store backup copies of program and data files in a secure off-site location.
- Use software to monitor system activity and recover from fraud.

⬤ SUMMARY AND CASE CONCLUSION

Jason Scott believed Don Hawkins had committed a fraud, but he needed more details to support that conclusion. In preparation for his meeting with management, he expanded the scope of his investigation. A week later, Jason presented his findings to the president of Northwest. To introduce the problem and to make it hit a little closer to home, Jason presented the president with a copy of his own withholding report filed with the IRS and pointed out the president's withholdings. Then he showed him a printout of withholdings from the payroll records and pointed out the $5 difference, as well as the difference of several thousand dollars in Don Hawkins's withholdings. This immediately got the president's attention, and Jason proceeded to tell him how he believed a fraud had been perpetrated.

During the latter part of the prior year, the payroll system had undergone some minor modifications. Don had been in charge of the project. Due to pressing problems with several other projects, the payroll project had been completed without the usual review by other systems personnel. Jason arranged for a member of the audit staff, who was a former programmer, to review the code changes. She found a few lines of unusual code in the program for generating the withholdings report for the IRS. The code subtracted $5 from employees' withholdings and added it to Don's withholdings. Don got his hands on the money when the IRS sent him a huge refund check.

It appeared that Don intended to use the scheme every year, as he had not removed the incriminating code. He must have been fairly confident of his scheme, because he had not tried to modify the company's copy of the withholdings report. Somehow he knew there was no reconciliation of withholdings from the payroll records with the IRS report. It was a simple plan, and it could have gone undetected for years if Jason had not overheard someone in the cafeteria talk about a $5 difference.

Jason quietly investigated Don and found he had a reputation for being disgruntled. He had been passed over the previous year for a managerial position in the programming department and had been unhappy ever since. He made numerous comments to coworkers about favoritism and unfair treatment. He even mentioned getting even with the company somehow. Don had also recently purchased a fairly expensive sports car. No one knew where he got the money, but Don had mentioned that he had made a sizable down payment when he bought the car in April.

When the president asked how the company could prevent this type of fraud from happening again, Jason suggested the following guidelines:

1 Conduct a review of the company's internal controls to analyze their effectiveness in preventing fraud. One control that already existed—reviewing program changes—could have prevented Don's scheme had it been followed. As a result, Jason suggested a stricter enforcement of the existing controls.
2 Put new controls into place to detect fraud. For example, Jason suggested a reconciliation of the withholdings on the IRS report with those on the payroll records.
3 Train employees in fraud awareness, security measures, and ethical issues.

Jason also urged the president to prosecute the case. The president was reluctant to do so because of the adverse publicity and the problems it would cause for Don's wife and children. Jason's supervisor tactfully suggested that if other employees found out that Don was not prosecuted, it would send the wrong message to the rest of the company. The president finally conceded to prosecute if the company could prove that Don was guilty. The president agreed to hire a forensic accountant to build a stronger case against Don and try to get him to confess.

KEY TERMS

sabotage 166
cookie 166
fraud 167
white-collar criminal 167
misappropriation of
 assets 167
employee fraud 167
fraudulent financial
 reporting 168
pressure 170
opportunity 172
lapping 173
kiting 173
rationalization 174
computer fraud 175
hacking 182
war dialing 182
war driving 182
war chalking 182
war rocketing 182
botnet 182
hijacking 182
bot herder 183
zombie 183
denial-of-service
 attack 183
spamming 183
dictionary attack 183

blog 184
splog 184
spoofing 184
zero-day attack 184
patch 184
password cracking 184
masquerading/
 impersonation 184
piggybacking 184
data diddling 185
data leakage 185
salami technique 185
round-down fraud 185
phreaking 185
economic espionage 185
cyber-extortion 185
Internet terrorism 186
Internet
 misinformation 186
e-mail threats 186
click fraud 186
software piracy 186
social engineering 187
identity theft 187
pretexting 187
posing 187
phishing 188
vishing 188

carding 188
pharming 188
evil twin 189
typosquatting 189
scavenging/dumpster
 diving 189
shoulder surfing 190
skimming 190
chipping 190
eavesdropping 190
malware 190
spyware 190
adware 191
torpedo software 191
key logger 191
Trojan horse 191
time bomb/logic
 bomb 192
trap door 192
packet sniffers 192
steganography
 programs 192
rootkit 192
superzapping 193
virus 193
Bluesnarfing 193
Bluebugging 194
worm 194

AIS IN ACTION

CHAPTER QUIZ

1 Which of the following is a fraud in which later payments on account are used to pay off earlier payments that were stolen?
 a. lapping
 b. kiting
 c. Ponzi scheme
 d. salami technique

2 Which type of fraud is associated with as many as 50% of all lawsuits against auditors?
 a. kiting
 b. fraudulent financial reporting
 c. Ponzi schemes
 d. lapping

3 Which of the following statements is false?
 a. The psychological profiles of white-collar criminals differ from those of violent criminals.
 b. The psychological profiles of white-collar criminals are significantly different from those of the general public.
 c. There is no difference between computer fraud perpetrators and other types of white-collar criminals.
 d. Computer fraud perpetrators often do not view themselves as criminals.

4 Which of the following conditions is/are usually necessary for a fraud to occur? (There may be more than one right answer.)
 a. pressure
 b. opportunity
 c. explanation
 d. rationalization

5 Which of the following is *not* an example of computer fraud?
 a. theft of money by altering computer records
 b. obtain information illegally through use of a computer
 c. failure to perform preventive maintenance on a computer
 d. unauthorized modification of a software program

6 A set of instructions to increase a programmer's pay rate by 10% is hidden inside an authorized program. It changes and updates payroll files. What is this computer fraud technique called?
 a. virus
 b. worm
 c. trap door
 d. Trojan horse

7 What is the computer fraud technique called that involves a set of instructions hidden inside a calendar utility that copies itself each time the utility is enabled and until memory is filled and the system crashes?
 a. logic bomb
 b. trap door
 c. virus
 d. Trojan horse

8 Which of the following control procedures is most likely to deter lapping?
 a. encryption
 b. continual update of the access control matrix
 c. background check on employees
 d. periodic rotation of duties

9 Which of the following is the most important, basic, and effective control to deter fraud?
 a. enforced vacations
 b. logical access control
 c. segregation of duties
 d. virus protection controls

10 Which of the following is/are methods of reducing fraud losses once fraud has occurred? (There may be more than one right answer.)
 a. insurance
 b. regular backup of data and programs
 c. contingency plan
 d. segregation of duties

DISCUSSION QUESTIONS

5.1 Do you agree that the most effective method of obtaining adequate system security is to rely on the integrity of company employees? Why or why not? Does this seem ironic? What measures should a company take to ensure the integrity of its employees?

5.2 You are the president of a multinational company. One of your senior executives confessed to kiting $100,000. Explain what kiting is and what your company can do to prevent it. How would you respond to your employee's confession? What issues must you consider before pressing formal charges?

5.3 One morning, the computers at U.S. Leasing Company began acting sluggish. Computer operators were relieved when a software troubleshooter from IBM called several hours later. They were more than happy to let him help correct the problem they were having. The troubleshooter asked for a phone number for the computers as well as a log-on number and password.

The next morning, the computers were worse. A call to IBM confirmed U.S. Leasing's suspicion: Someone had impersonated an IBM repairman to gain unauthorized access to the system and destroy the database. U.S. Leasing was also concerned that the intruder had devised a program that would let him get back into the system even after all the passwords were changed.

What techniques might the impostor have employed to breach U.S. Leasing's internal security? What could U.S. Leasing do to avoid these types of incidents in the future?

5.4 A few days after the inventory control system for Revlon, the cosmetics giant, went down, officials discovered that Logisticon, a software developer, caused the downtime. Seven months earlier, Revlon had signed an agreement to have Logisticon install a real-time invoice and inventory processing system. Prior to completion of phase 1 of the project, Revlon discovered a series of programming bugs. Revlon proceeded to withhold any additional payment on the contract to Logisticon, who contended that the software was fine but that the computer hardware was faulty. When Revlon refused payment, Logisticon sought repossession: It used a telephone dial-in feature in the software to make a disabling phone call and render the system unusable.

After a three-day standoff, Logisticon reactivated Revlon's inventory system. Revlon filed suit in California Superior Court, charging Logisticon with trespassing, breach of contract, and misappropriation of trade secrets (use of Revlon passwords). Logisticon filed a countersuit for breach of contract. Revlon and Logisticon later settled out of court.

Would Logisticon's actions be classified as sabotage or repossession? Why? Would you find the company guilty of committing a computer crime? Be prepared to defend your position to the class.

5.5 Improved computer security measures create their own set of problems: user antagonism, sluggish response time, and hampered performance. Many professionals believe that the most effective way to promote computer security is to educate users about good moral conduct. According to Richard Stallman, a computer activist, software licensing is antisocial because it prohibits the growth of technology by keeping information away from the neighbors. He believes high school and college students should have unlimited access to computers without security measures so they can learn constructive and civilized behavior. He states that a protected system is a puzzle and, because it is human nature to solve puzzles, eliminating computer security so that there is no temptation to break in would reduce hacking.

Do you agree with Stallman's statements? Do you agree that software licensing is antisocial? Is ethical teaching the solution to computer security problems? Would the removal of computer security measures reduce the incidence of computer fraud? Why or why not?

5.6 Discuss the following statement by Roswell Steffen, a convicted embezzler: "For every foolproof system, there is a method for beating it." Do you believe a completely secure computer system is possible? Explain. If internal controls are less than 100% effective, why should they be employed at all?

5.7 What motives do people have for hacking? Why has hacking become so popular in recent years? Do you regard it as a crime? Explain your position.

PROBLEMS

5.1 An experienced senior auditor was assigned to investigate a possible fraudulent situation characterized by extremely high, unexplained merchandise shortages at one location of the company's department store chain. During the course of the investigation, the auditor determined the following:

 a. The supervisor of the receiving department was the owner and operator of a small boutique carrying many of the same labels as the chain store. The chain store's general manager was unaware of the ownership interest.
 b. The receiving supervisor signed receiving reports showing that the total quantity shipped by a supplier had been received. A total of 5% to 10% of each shipment was diverted to the boutique.
 c. The chain's buyers were unaware of the short shipments because the receiving supervisor would enter the correct quantity on the move ticket accompanying the merchandise to the sales areas.
 d. The chain's accounts payable department paid vendors for the total quantity shown on the receiving report.
 e. Based on the supervisor's instructions, quantities on the move tickets were not compared with those on the receiving report.

Required

Classify each of the five situations as a fraudulent act, an indicator of fraud, or an event unrelated to the investigation. Justify your answers.

(CIA Examination, adapted)

5.2 A small but growing firm has recently hired you to investigate a potential fraud. The company heard through its hot line that the purchases journal clerk periodically enters fictitious acquisitions. The nonexistent supplier's address is given as a post office box, which the clerk rents. He forwards notification of the fictitious purchases for recording in the accounts payable ledger. Payment is ultimately mailed to the post office box. He then deposits the check in an account established in the name of the nonexistent supplier.

Required

 a. Define fraud, fraud deterrence, fraud detection, and fraud investigation.
 b. List four red-flag indicators (personal as opposed to organizational) that might point to the existence of fraud in this example.
 c. List two procedures you could follow to uncover the fraudulent behavior of the purchases journal clerk in this situation.

(CIA Examination, adapted)

5.3 Most experts maintain that the computer frauds that are publicly revealed represent only the tip of the iceberg. Although the major threat to computer security is perceived by many to be external, the more dangerous threats come from insiders. Management must recognize these problems and develop and enforce security programs to deal with the many types of computer fraud.

Required

Explain how each of the following six types of fraud is committed. Using the format provided, also identify a different method of protection for each, and describe how it works.

Type of Fraud	Explanation	Identification and Description of Protection Methods
a. Input manipulation		
b. Program alteration		
c. File alteration		
d. Data theft		
e. Sabotage		
f. Theft of computer time		

(CMA Examination, adapted)

5.4 Fraudulent financial reporting usually occurs as the result of environmental, institutional, or individual pressures and opportune situations. These pressures and opportunities, present to some degree in all companies, motivate individuals and companies to engage in fraudulent financial reporting. The prevention and detection of fraudulent financial reporting require that these pressures and opportunities be identified and evaluated in terms of the risks they pose to a company. These risk factors include internal ethical and control factors, as well as external environmental conditions.

Required

 a. Identify two company situational pressures that would increase the likelihood of fraud.
 b. Identify three corporate opportunities that make fraud easier to commit and detection less likely.
 c. For each of the following, identify the external environmental factors that should be considered in assessing the risk of fraudulent financial reporting:
 ● The company's industry
 ● The company's business environment
 ● The company's legal and regulatory environment
 d. What can top management do to reduce the possibility of fraudulent financial reporting?

(CMA Examination, adapted)

5.5 The impact of employee and management fraud is staggering both in terms of dollar costs and the effect on the victims. For each of the following independent cases of employee fraud, describe the recommendations internal auditors should make to prevent similar problems from occurring in the future.
 a. A retail store that was part of a national chain experienced an abnormal inventory shrinkage in its audiovisual department. The internal auditors, noting this shrinkage, included an in-depth evaluation of the department in the scope of their store audit. During their review the auditors learned from an employee that a particular customer bought a large number of small electronic components and that the customer always went to a certain cashier's checkout line. The auditors' work revealed that the cashier and the customer had colluded to steal a number of electronic components. The cashier did not record the sale of several items the customer took from the store.
 b. During an unannounced visit to a large hospital, internal auditors discovered a payroll fraud when they observed the distribution of paychecks. The supervisors of each department distributed paychecks to employees and were supposed to return unclaimed checks to the payroll department. When the auditors took control of, and followed up on, an unclaimed paycheck for an employee in the food

service department, they discovered that the employee had quit four months previously. The employee and the supervisor had had an argument, and the employee had simply left and never returned. The supervisor had continued to turn in a time card for the employee and had taken the unclaimed checks and cashed them.

c. While performing an audit of cash disbursements at a manufacturing firm, internal auditors discovered a fraud committed by an accounts payable clerk. She made copies of supporting documents and used them to support duplicate payments to a supplier of manufacturing materials. The clerk, who had opened a bank account in a name similar to that of the supplier, took the duplicate checks and deposited them in her bank account.

(CMA Examination, adapted)

5.6 Rent-A-Wreck's policy requires a "sealed bid" to sell motor vehicles that are no longer efficient. In reviewing the sale of some vehicles that had been declared obsolete, the auditor found that management had not always complied with the stated policy. Records indicated that several vehicles on which major repairs had recently been performed were sold at negotiated prices. Management assured the auditor that by performing limited repairs and negotiating with knowledgeable buyers, better prices had been obtained for the salvaged vehicles than had the required sealed-bid procedures been followed. The auditor suspected that there might be more involved than management indicated. Further investigation revealed that the vehicles had been sold to employees at negotiated prices well below market value. The auditor's work eventually resulted in three managers and five other employees pleading guilty to criminal charges and making restitution to the organization.

Required

a. Based on this scenario, outline the symptoms or indications of possible fraud that would have aroused the auditor's suspicion.
b. Suggest audit procedures that the auditor could have employed to establish the fact that fraud had in fact occurred.

(CIA Examination, adapted)

5.7 A few years ago, news began circulating about a computer virus named Michelangelo that was set to "ignite" on March 6, the birthday of the famous Italian artist. The virus attached itself to the computer's operating system boot sector. On the magical date, the virus would release itself, destroying all of the computer's data. When March 6 arrived, the virus did minimal damage. Preventive techniques limited the damage to isolated personal and business computers. Though the excitement surrounding the virus was largely illusory, Michelangelo helped the computer-using public realize its systems' vulnerability to outside attack.

Required

a. What is a computer virus? Cite at least three reasons why no system is completely safe from a computer virus.
b. Why do viruses represent a serious threat to information systems? What damage can a virus do to a computer system?
c. How does a virus resemble a Trojan horse?
d. What steps can individuals and companies take to prevent the spread or propagation of a computer virus?

5.8 The auditor of a bank is called to a meeting with a senior operations manager because of a customer's report that an auto loan payment was not credited. According to the customer, the payment was made at a teller's window using a check drawn on an account in that bank. The payment was made on its due date, May 5. On May 10, the customer decided to sell the car and called the bank for a payoff on the loan. The payment had not been credited to the loan. The customer came to the bank on May 12 to inquire about the payment and meet with the manager. The manager found that the

payment had been credited the night before the meeting (as of May 11); the customer was satisfied because no late charge would have been assessed until May 15. The manager asked if the auditor was comfortable with this situation.

The auditor located the customer's paid check in the deposit department and found that it had cleared as of May 5. The auditor traced the item back through the computer records and found that the teller had processed the check as being cashed. The auditor traced the payment through the entry records of May 11 and found that the payment had been made with cash instead of a check.

Required

What type of embezzlement scheme does this appear to be, and how does that scheme operate?

(CIA Examination, adapted)

5.9 It was a typical Wednesday on the UCLA campus when everything began going wrong in the student computer lab. The computer lab was filled to capacity as the end of the semester neared. Nearly 70 students were logged in to the UCLA computer network when the system came to a halt. Students tried running software without success, and many students could not even log in.

System directors initially suspected a cable break or an operating system failure as the culprit, but diagnostics revealed nothing. After several frustrating hours, a staff member began running a virus detection program and uncovered a virus on the lab's main server. The virus was eventually traced to the computers of unsuspecting UCLA students. When staff workers used the infected computers to gain supervisor access to the operating system, the virus spread.

The virus cost UCLA about 25 person-hours and disrupted the lives of frantic students preparing for finals. Later that evening, the system was brought back online after infected files were replaced with backup copies.

Required

a. What conditions made the UCLA system a potential breeding ground for the virus?
b. What symptoms indicated that a virus was present?
c. What advice would you give UCLA's director of computing to prevent the same incident from recurring?

5.10 The following e-mail with an authentic looking e-mail address and logo was received by the controller of a small business:

From: *Big Bank [antifraud@bigbank.com]*
To: *Justin Lewis, Controller, Small Business USA*
Subject: *Official Notice for all users of Big Bank!*

Due to the increased incidence of fraud and identity theft, we are asking all bank customers to verify their account information on the following Web page: www.antifraudbigbank.com
 Please confirm your account information as soon as possible. Failure to confirm your account information will require us to suspend your account until confirmation is made.

A week later, the following e-mail was delivered to the controller:

From: *Big Bank [antifraud@bigbank.com]*
To: *Justin Lewis, Controller, Small Business USA*
Subject: *Official Notice for all users of Big Bank!*

Dear Client of Big Bank,
Technical services at Big Bank is currently updating our software. Therefore, we kindly ask you to follow the reference given below to confirm your data. Otherwise your access to the system may be blocked.
 web.da-us.bigbank.com/signin/scripts/login2/user_setup.jsp
 We are grateful for your cooperation.

Required

 a. What should Justin do about these e-mails?

 b. What should Big Bank do about these e-mails?

 c. Identify the computer fraud and abuse technique illustrated.

5.11 The following e-mail was received by a purchasing department at a small manufacturing and distribution firm.

Dear Accounts Payable Clerk,

You can purchase everything you need online—including peace of mind—when you shop using Random Account Numbers (RAN). RAN is a free service for Big Credit Card customers that substitutes a random credit card number in place of your normal credit card number when you make online purchases and payments. This random number provides you with additional security. Before every online purchase, simply get a new number from RAN to use at each new vendor.

 Sign up for an account at www.bigcreditcard.com. Also, take advantage of the following features:

- *Automatic Form automatically completes a vendor's order form with the RAN and its expiration date, your shipping address, and your billing address.*
- *Set the spending limit and expiration date for each new RAN.*
- *Use RAN once or use it for recurring payments for up to one year.*

Required

Explain which computer fraud and abuse techniques could be prevented using a random account number that links to your corporate credit card.

5.12 The Jamison Cardstock Company did not spend a lot of time or money instituting proper internal controls over its cash transactions. The following information reflects Jamison's cash position as of June 30:

- The cash recorded on Jamison's accounting records revealed a balance of $18,901.62 that also included undeposited cash receipts.
- A credit of $100 on the bank statement was not recorded in the company's accounting records.
- The balance on the bank statement was $15,550.
- Outstanding checks:

Check Number	Amount
62	$116.25
183	$150.00
284	$253.25
8621	$190.71
8623	$206.80
8632	$145.28

The company cashier embezzled all undeposited cash receipts in excess of the $3,794.41 listed on the bank reconciliation that she prepared, as shown next.

Balance, per books, June 30			$18,901.62
Add: Outstanding Checks:			
No. 8621	$190.71		
No. 8623	$206.80		
No. 8632	$145.28	442.79	
			$19,344.41
Subtract: Undeposited Receipts			3,794.41
Balance per bank, June 30			$15,550.00
Subtract: Unrecorded Credit			100.00
True Cash, June 30			$15,450.00

Required

 a. Prepare a schedule showing how much the cashier embezzled.

 b. Describe how the cashier attempted to hide the theft.

<div align="right">

(AICPA, adapted)

</div>

5.13 An accountant employed by the organizing committee for the Atlanta Summer Olympic Games was charged with embezzling approximately $60,000. The money allegedly was used to purchase a used Mercedes-Benz automobile and to invest in a certificate of deposit.

 Police reports indicate that Steve Council wrote about $60,000 in Olympic Committee checks and deposited them into a bogus bank account. Council is a Brown University honors graduate who supervisors stated was a very trusted and loyal employee. Police report that Council allegedly created fictitious invoices from International Protection Consulting, as well as Languages Services. Both had contracts with the Olympic Committee. He allegedly deposited $44,500 into an account he opened under the name of one of the companies. Police have also discovered substantial additional losses. Council cooperated with police to the extent of telling them of the bogus bank account and the 1990 Mercedes-Benz.

1 How does Council fit the profile of a fraudster? In what ways does Council not fit the profile?

2 What fraud scheme did Council use to perpetrate his fraud?

3 What controls could have prevented Council's fraud?

4 What controls could have detected Council's fraud?

5.14 Computer Fraud and Abuse Techniques.

Match the internet related computer fraud and abuse technique in the left column with the scenario in the right column. Terms may be used once, more than once, or not at all.

_____ 1 Adware	a. Software that monitors and reports a user's computing habits
_____ 2 Botnet	b. A program stored in a Web page that is executed by a Web browser.
_____ 3 Bot herder	c. Sending an e-mail instructing the recipient to do something or they will suffer adverse consequences
_____ 4 Click fraud	d. Using the Internet to pass off the work of another as your own
_____ 5 DOS	e. E-mailing an unsolicited message to many people at the same time
_____ 6 E-mail threats	f. Creating Web sites with names similar to real Web sites so users making errors while entering a Web site name are sent to a site filled with malware
_____ 7 Hijacking	g. An e-mail warning regarding a virus that, in reality, does not exist
_____ 8 Internet misinformation	h. A spam blog that promotes affiliated Web sites to increase their Google PageRank
_____ 9 Internet terrorism	i. Software used to collect consumer surfing and purchasing data
_____ 10 Key logger	j. E-mails that look like they came from a legitimate source but are actually from a hacker who is trying to get the user to divulge personal information
_____ 11 Pharming	k. Making an e-mail look like it came from someone else
_____ 12 Phishing	l. Gaining control, often by means of a Trojan horse, of a computer to carry out illicit activities without the owner's knowledge.
_____ 13 Spamming	m. Using the Internet to disrupt communications and e-commerce

_____ 14 Splog

_____ 15 Spyware

_____ 16 Spoofing

_____ 17 Typosquatting

n. Diverting traffic from a legitimate Web site to a different Web site controlled by a hacker in order to gain access to personal and confidential information

o. A network of hijacked computers

p. Using a legion of compromised computers to launch a coordinated attack on an Internet site

q. Use of spyware to record a user's keystrokes

r. Hackers that control hijacked computers

s. Circulating lies or misinformation using the world's largest network

t. Overloading an Internet service provider's e-mail server by sending hundreds of e-mail messages per second from randomly generated false addresses

u. Inflating advertising revenue by clicking online ads numerous times

5.15 Computer Fraud and Abuse Techniques.
Match the data communications-related computer fraud and abuse technique in the left column with the scenario in the right column. Terms may be used once, more than once, or not at all.

_____ 1 Bluebugging

_____ 2 Bluesnarfing

_____ 3 Eavesdropping

_____ 4 Evil twin

_____ 5 Packet sniffing

_____ 6 Phreaking

_____ 7 Piggybacking

_____ 8 Vishing

_____ 9 War dialing

_____ 10 War driving

a. Intercepting Internet and other network transmissions

b. E-mails instruct a user to call a phone number where they are asked to divulge personal information

c. The search for unprotected wireless networks

d. Gaining access to a protected system by latching on to a legitimate user

e. Decodes and organizes captured network data

f. Intercepting and/or listening in on private voice and data transmissions

g. Deep packet filtering

h. Searching for modems on unprotected phone lines in order to access the attached computer and gain access to the network(s) to which it is attached

i. Making phone calls and sending text messages using another user's phone without physically holding that phone

j. Using telephone lines to transmit viruses and to access, steal, and destroy data

k. Capturing data from devices that use Bluetooth technology

l. Devices that hide IP addresses

m. A wireless access point masquerading as a legitimate wireless access point

5.16 Computer Fraud and Abuse Techniques.
Match the data related computer fraud and abuse technique in the left column with the scenario in the right column. Terms may be used once, more than once, or not at all.

_____ 1 Chipping

_____ 2 Data diddling

_____ 3 Data leakage

_____ 4 Identity theft

_____ 5 Round-down

_____ 6 Salami technique

a. Illegally obtaining confidential information, such as a Social Security number, about another person so that it can be used for financial gain

b. Searching through garbage for confidential data

c. Covertly swiping a credit card in a card reader that records the data for later use

d. Embezzling small fractions of funds over time

e. Inserting a chip that captures financial transaction data in a legitimate credit card reader

f. Copying company data, such as computer files, without permission

_____ 7 Scavenging

 g. Concealing data within a large MP3 file
 h. Use of spyware to record a user's keystrokes
 i. Altering data during the IPO (Input-Process-Output) cycle
 j. Placing truncated decimal places in an account controlled by the perpetrator

5.17 Computer Fraud and Abuse Techniques.
Match the data security computer fraud and abuse technique in the left column with the scenario in the right column. Terms may be used once, more than once, or not at all.

Term		Scenario
_____	1 Dictionary attack	a. Special software used to bypass system controls
_____	2 Hacking	b. A segment of executable code that attaches itself to software
_____	3 Logic bomb	c. Capturing and decrypting passwords to gain access to a system
_____	4 Malware	d. Malicious computer code that specifically targets a computer's start-up instructions
_____	5 Masquerading	e. Using a wireless network without permission
_____	6 Password cracking	f. Covertly swiping a credit card in a card reader that records the data for later use
_____	7 Piggybacking	g. Concealing data within a large MP3 file
_____	8 Posing	h. An attack between the time a new software vulnerability is discovered and a software patch that fixes the problem is released
_____	9 Pretexting	i. Entering a system using a back door that bypasses normal system controls
_____	10 Rootkit	j. Using software to guess company addresses and send them blank e-mails; unreturned messages are valid addresses that are added to spammer e-mail lists
_____	11 Shoulder surfing	k. Unauthorized code in an authorized and properly functioning program
_____	12 Skimming	l. Software used to do harm
_____	13 Social engineering	m. A program that can replicate itself and travel over networks
_____	14 Software piracy	n. Pretending to be a legitimate user, thereby gaining access to a system and all the rights and privileges of the legitimate user
_____	15 Steganography	o. Special code or password that bypasses security features
_____	16 Superzapping	p. Making an illegal copy of software that you did not purchase
_____	17 Trap door	q. Software that conceals processes, files, network connections, and system data from the operating system and other programs
_____	18 Trojan horse	r. Methods used to trick someone into divulging personal information
_____	19 Virus	s. Malware that requires a trigger to activate
_____	20 Worm	t. The act of duplicating software, music, or movies
_____	21 Zero-day attack	u. Acting under false pretenses to gain confidential information
		v. Observing or listening to users in the hope that they divulge personal information
		w. Gaining access to a computer system without permission
		x. Creating a seemingly legitimate business, collecting personal information while making a sale, and never delivering the item sold

5.18 On a Sunday afternoon in 2005 at a busy hospital in the Pacific Northwest, computers started running slower and documents would not print. By Monday morning, the situation became worse as more employees returned to work and logged on to their computers. Even stranger things started happening, such as operating-room doors stopped opening, pagers wouldn't work, and computers in the intensive care unit shut down. By 10:00 A.M., all 50 people in the hospital's information-technology department were summoned, but their efforts made little difference.

As the hospital's information-technology staff discovered, the hospital was under attack by a botnet, a network of computers infected with malware that was controlled by three hackers. The trio exploited a flaw in the Microsoft Windows operating systems that let them install pop-up ads on the hospital's computers. They got access to the first computer on Sunday and then started spreading the infection to other computers through the hospital's network. As each computer became infected, it turned into another bot or zombie, which would in turn scan the hospital's network looking for new victims to infect. As a result, the network became clogged with zombie traffic and hospital communications began to break down. Initially, the hospital's technology staff tried to halt the attack by shutting off the hospital from the Internet, but by then it was too late. The bots were inside the hospital's computer systems and infecting other computers faster than they could be cleaned.

By Monday afternoon, the IT department figured out which malware the bots were installing on computers and wrote a script, which was pushed out hourly, directing computers to remove the bad code. The script helped to slow the bots down a bit.

(*Reference:* Gage, D., *Baseline Security,* February 6, 2007)

Required

a. What could the hospital do to stop the attack and contain the damage?
b. Which computer fraud and abuse technique did the hackers use in their attack on the hospital?
c. What steps should the hospital have taken to prevent the damage caused by the attack?

CASE 5-1 David L. Miller: Portrait of a White-Collar Criminal

There is an old saying in crime-fighting circles: Crime doesn't pay. However, for David Miller crime has paid rich dividends. It paid for two Mercedes-Benz sedans; a $280,000 suburban house; a condominium at Myrtle Beach, South Carolina; $500 suits; and $75 tailored and monogrammed shirts. It also paid for diamond, sapphire, ruby, and emerald rings for his wife and a new car for his father-in-law. Though Miller has confessed to embezzling funds from six different employers over a 20-year period, he has never been prosecuted and has never been incarcerated. In large part, his freedom is the result of the fear that companies have about turning in employees who defraud them.

Miller's first employer was also his first victim. After 10 months of selling insurance in Wheeling, West Virginia, Miller was fired for stealing $200. After holding an assortment of odd jobs, he moved to Ohio and worked as an accountant for a local baker. Miller was caught embezzling funds and paid back the $1,000 he had stolen. Again, he was not reported to the authorities and was quietly dismissed.

Miller returned to Wheeling and went to work for Wheeling Bronze, Inc., a bronze-castings maker. A number of months later, the president of Wheeling Bronze discovered that several returned checks were missing and that there was a $30,000 cash shortfall. After an extensive search, workers uncovered a number of canceled checks with forged signatures in an outdoor sandpile. Miller was questioned and confessed to the scheme. He was given the choice of paying back the stolen amount or going to jail. Miller's parents took out a mortgage on their home to pay back the

stolen money. No charges were ever filed, and Miller was dismissed.

Several months later, Miller found a job in Pennsylvania working for Robinson Pipe Cleaning. When Miller was caught embezzling funds, he again avoided prosecution by promising to repay the $20,000 he had stolen.

Miller's next job was at Crest Industries, where he was hired as an accountant. Miller proved to be the ideal employee and was quickly promoted to the position of office manager. He was very dedicated, worked long hours, and did outstanding work. Soon after his promotion he purchased a new home, a new car, and a new wardrobe.

Two years later, Miller's world unraveled again when Crest's auditors discovered that $31,000 was missing. Once again there was a tearful confession and a promise to repay all money stolen. Miller confessed that he had written several checks to himself and had then recorded payments to suppliers on the carbon copies of the checks. To cover his tracks, he intercepted and altered the company's monthly bank statements. He had used the money he had stolen to finance his lifestyle and to repay Wheeling Bronze and Robinson Pipe Cleaning.

Miller claimed in his confession that he had never before embezzled funds. He showed a great deal of remorse, so much so that Crest even hired a lawyer for him. He gave Crest a lien on his house, and he was quietly dismissed. Because the president of Crest did not want the publicity to harm Miller's wife and three children, Crest never pressed charges against him.

Miller next took a job as an accountant in Steubenville, Ohio, with Rustcraft Broadcasting Company, a chain of radio and television stations. When Rustcraft was acquired by Associated Communications, Miller moved to Pittsburgh to become Associated's new controller.

Miller immediately began dipping into Associated's accounts. Over a six-year period, Miller embezzled approximately $1.36 million, $445,000 of that after he was promoted to CFO. Miller used various methods to embezzle the money. One approach to circumvent the need for two signatures on every check was to ask another executive who was leaving on vacation to sign several checks "just in case" the company needed additional cash while he was gone. Miller used most of these checks to siphon funds to his personal account. To cover the theft, Miller retrieved the canceled check from the bank reconciliation and destroyed it. The amount stolen was then charged to a unit's expense account to balance the company's books.

While working at Associated, Miller was able to lead a very comfortable lifestyle. He bought a new house and several expensive cars. He bought vacation property and an extravagant wardrobe, and he was generous with tips and gifts. His $130,000 salary could not have supported this lifestyle, yet no one at Associated ever questioned the source of his conspicuous consumption.

Miller's lifestyle came crashing down while he was on vacation. A bank officer called to inquire about a check written to Mr. Miller. An investigation ensued, and Miller confessed to embezzling funds. As part of the out-of-court settlement with Miller, Associated Communications received most of Miller's personal property.

Miller cannot explain why he was never prosecuted. He always insisted that he was going to pay the company back. Such statements would usually satisfy his employers and get him off the hook. He believes that these agreements actually contributed to his subsequent thefts. For example, one rationale for starting to steal from a new employer was to pay back the former one.

After leaving Associated, Miller was hired by a former colleague. Miller underwent therapy and believes he has resolved his problem with compulsive embezzlement.

When interviewed about his past activities, Miller thought his problem with theft was an illness, just like alcoholism or compulsive gambling. The illness was driven by a subconscious need to be admired and liked by others. He thought that by spending money, others would like him. Ironically, he was universally well liked and admired at each job, and it had nothing to do with money. In fact, one coworker at Associated was so surprised at the news of the thefts that he said it was like finding out that your brother was an ax murderer. In the interview, Miller also claimed that he is not a bad person. He says he never intended to hurt anyone, but once he got started, he just could not stop.

1 How does Miller fit the profile of the average fraud perpetrator? How does he differ? How did these characteristics make him difficult to detect?

2 Discuss how Miller accomplished the three elements of the opportunity triangle (commit, conceal, convert) in embezzling funds from Associated Communications. What specific concealment techniques did Miller use?

3 What pressures motivated Miller to embezzle? How did Miller rationalize his actions?

4 Miller had a framed T-shirt in his office that said, "He who dies with the most toys wins." What does this tell you about Miller? What lifestyle red

flags could have tipped off the company to the possibility of fraud?

5 Identify several reasons why companies hesitate in prosecuting white-collar criminals. What are the problems with these reasons? What could law enforcement officials do to encourage more rigorous prosecution of white-collar criminals?

6 Identify the primary action each of the victimized companies could have taken to prevent Miller's embezzlement. What other controls could help in preventing future fraud?

Source: Based on Bryan Burrough, "David L. Miller Stole from His Employer and Isn't in Prison," *The Wall Street Journal* (September 19, 1986): 1.

CASE 5-2 Lexsteel Corporation

Lexsteel Corporation is a leading manufacturer of steel furniture. The company has manufacturing plants and distribution facilities throughout the United States, but the purchasing, accounting, and treasury functions are centralized at corporate headquarters in Fresno, California.

While discussing a recent management letter with the external auditors, Ray Landsdown, controller of Lexsteel, became aware of potential problems with the accounts payable system. The auditors had to perform additional audit procedures to attest to the validity of accounts payable and cutoff procedures. The auditors have recommended a detailed study of current procedures to assess the company's exposure to embezzlement and fraud and to identify ways to improve internal controls.

Landsdown has assigned the study to Dolores Smith, a new accountant in the department. Because Smith could not find adequate documentation of the accounts payable procedures, she interviewed those employees involved and constructed a flowchart of the current system. This flowchart is shown in Figure 5-3, and descriptions of the current procedures follow.

COMPUTER RESOURCES

The host computer mainframe at corporate headquarters is linked to the computers at each branch location. Data entry occurs at the source and is transmitted to an integrated database maintained on the host computer. Data transmission occurs over leased telephone lines between the branch offices and the host computer. The software allows flexibility for managing user access and editing data input.

PROCEDURES FOR PURCHASING RAW MATERIALS

The host computer at corporate headquarters generates production orders and appropriate bills of material. From

these bills of material, purchase orders for raw materials are generated by the centralized purchasing function and either e-mailed or mailed directly to the vendors. Each purchase order instructs the vendor to ship the materials directly to the appropriate manufacturing plant. Assuming that the necessary purchase orders have been issued, the manufacturing plants proceed with the production orders received from corporate headquarters.

Upon receipt of goods, the manufacturing plant examines and verifies the count against the packing slip and transmits the receiving data to accounts payable at corporate headquarters. In the event that raw material deliveries fall behind production, each branch manager is given the authority to order materials and issue emergency purchase orders directly to the vendors. Data about the emergency orders and verification of materials receipt are e-mailed to accounts payable at corporate headquarters. Since the company employs a cost-effective computerized perpetual inventory system, physical counts of raw materials are not performed.

ACCOUNTS PAYABLE PROCEDURES

Vendor invoices are either e-mailed or mailed directly to corporate headquarters and entered by accounts payable personnel when received. This often occurs before the branch offices transmit the receiving data. The final day the invoice can be paid is entered as the payment due date. Using information listed on the invoice, the data entry person often must calculate this due date.

Once a week, invoices due the following week are printed in chronological entry order on a payment listing, and the corresponding checks are drawn. The checks and the payment listing are sent to the treasurer's office for signature and mailing to the payee. The check number is printed by the computer, displayed on the check and the payment listing, and validated as the checks are

Figure 5-3
Accounts Payable Procedures at Lexsteel

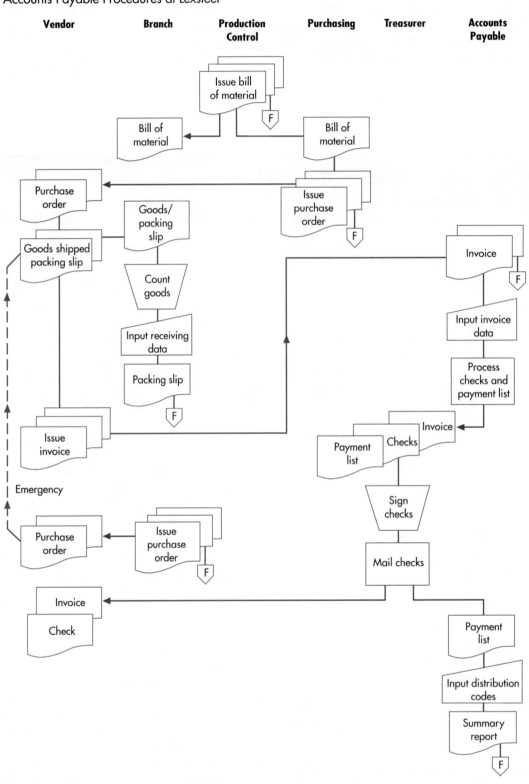

signed. After the checks are mailed, the payment listing is returned to accounts payable for filing. When there is insufficient cash to pay all the invoices, the treasurer retains certain checks and the payment listing until all checks can be paid. When the remaining checks are mailed, the listing is then returned to accounts payable. Often, weekly check mailings include a few checks from the previous week, but rarely are there more than two weekly listings involved.

When accounts payable receives back the payment listing from the treasurer's office, the expenses are distributed, coded, and posted to the appropriate plant/cost center accounts. Accounts payable processes weekly summary performance reports for each cost center and branch location reflecting all data entry to that point.

1 Identify and discuss three areas where Lexsteel Corporation may be exposed to fraud or embezzlement due to weaknesses in the procedures described. Recommend improvements to correct these weaknesses.

2 Describe three areas where management information could be distorted due to weaknesses in Lexsteel's procedures. Recommend improvements to correct these weaknesses.

3 Identify three strengths in Lexsteel's procedures, and explain why they are strengths.

(CMA Examination, adapted)

CASE 5-3 Shadowcrew

On October 26, 2004, at 9:00 P.M., Andrew Mantovani, cofounder of the group Shadowcrew, received a knock at his door while chatting on his computer. For Mantovani and 27 others, that knock marked the end of their illicit organization.

SHADOWCREW

Shadowcrew was an organization that provided online marketplaces and discussion forums for identity thieves. Shadowcrew members used the organization's Web site to traffic in stolen Social Security numbers, names, e-mail addresses, counterfeit driver's licenses, birth certificates, foreign and domestic passports, and also to share "best practices" for carrying out fraudulent activity. By the time the organization was shut down, Shadowcrew had trafficked in at least 1.7 million credit cards and was responsible for more than $4.3 million in direct losses to consumers, businesses, and government.

SHADOWCREW OPERATION

Shadowcrew, considered by many to be the online equivalent of the mob or Russian Mafia, operated as a highly sophisticated and hierarchical organization. All users operated under aliases, never revealing their true names or other personal information. Operations and communications were conducted through the use of proxy servers that hid the location and identity of the users. Shadowcrew users were divided into five different roles: administrators, moderators, reviewers, vendors, and members.

Administrators Shadowcrew administrators were the heads of the organization.

Moderators About a dozen people worked as moderators and controlled the flow of information. Moderators were chosen from the general membership based on proven skill in fraudulent activity.

Reviewers Reviewers tested the quality of illicit goods (credit cards, passports, etc.) trafficked on the Shadowcrew site. For example, reviewers would run a test called a "dump check" on credit card numbers by hacking into a retailer's cash register system. The fraudster accessed the system through back doors used by technical support personnel to remotely perform maintenance or repairs. The reviewer would then enter a trivial charge of $1 or $2 to see if the charge was approved. Reviewers would then write up and post detailed descriptions of the credit cards or other merchandise tested.

Vendors Vendors managed the sale of products or stolen data. Prices for goods would either be posted, or products could be sold using an auction forum much like eBay. Payments were usually processed via Western Union money transfers or some form of electronic currency and were generally made using a fraud victim's stolen data.

General Members Thousands of people accessed the Shadowcrew Web site as general members. These individuals would gather and share

information on committing identity fraud. Shadowcrew practiced open registration, but more sensitive discussion areas were password protected, and members needed another trusted member to vouch for them in order to join the forum.

Members could be "promoted" up the organization by providing quality products or by sharing new or unique tips or techniques for committing fraud. Shadowcrew also punished acts of disloyalty among the ranks. For instance, one group member who was accused of being disloyal had his actual name, address, and phone number posted on the Web site for all to see.

THE BREAKUP

Shadowcrew's demise began with a tip to the United States government from MasterCard International, Inc., that reported on about a hundred such Web sites that exist to promote identity fraud activity. The United States Secret Service covertly infiltrated the organization. Acting as trusted members, agents set up a Virtual Private Network (VPN) over which Shadowcrew leaders could conduct illicit business. The VPN allowed the Secret Service to track the organization's doings and discover the legitimate identities and locations of Shadowcrew users.

The covert operation prepared the Secret Service to launch Operation Firewall on October 26, 2004. Agents initiated an online discussion forum on undisclosed subject matter that enticed the operation targets to join. It was vital that all arrests occur simultaneously, since any one of the targets could instantly warn the others via the discussion forum.

With the help of the United States Justice Department, the United States Homeland Security Department, the Royal Canadian Mounted Police, Europol, and local police departments, authorities simultaneously knocked on the suspects' doors at precisely 9:00 P.M.

The operation led to 28 arrests, 21 in the United States. Rather than immediately deactivating the Web site, investigators replaced the home page for a few days with the following warning: "Activities by Shadowcrew members are being investigated by the United States Secret Service." Under a picture of hands clutching bars of a jail cell, agents listed the criminal charges that Shadowcrew members faced and called on visitors to turn themselves in: "Contact your local United States Secret Service field office before we contact you!!!"

(Reference: J. McCormick and D. Gage, Baseline Security, March 7, 2005.)

1 What were some of the methods by which Shadowcrew members concealed their true identities? What are ways that average citizens can protect their identities while interacting online?

2 In what ways has the Internet made detecting and identifying identity fraudsters difficult?

3 What are some of the most common electronic means of stealing personal information?

4 What is the most common way that fraudsters use personal data?

5 What measures can consumers take to protect against the online brokering of their personal data?

6 What are the most effective means of detecting identity theft?

7 What pieces of personal information are most valuable to identity fraudsters?

AIS IN ACTION SOLUTIONS

QUIZ KEY

1 Which of the following is a fraud in which later payments on account are used to pay off earlier payments that were stolen?

✔ a. lapping (Correct.)

b. kiting (Incorrect. In a kiting scheme, the perpetrator creates cash by transferring money between banks.)

c. Ponzi scheme (Incorrect. The Ponzi scheme works on the "rob-Peter-to-pay-Paul" principle. Money from new investors is used to pay off earlier investors.)

d. salami technique (Incorrect. The salami technique steals tiny slices of money over a period of time.)

2 Which type of fraud is associated with as many as 50% of all lawsuits against auditors?

 a. kiting (Incorrect. Kiting is a fraud scheme involving bank transfers. It does not result in large-enough losses to be associated with 50% of all lawsuits against auditors.)

✔ **b.** fraudulent financial reporting (Correct. A large percentage of lawsuits is against auditors for attesting to fraudulent financial statements.)

 c. Ponzi schemes (Incorrect. The Ponzi scheme is a type of investment fraud in which money from new investors is used to pay off earlier investors. It does not result in large-enough losses to be associated with 50% of all lawsuits against auditors.)

 d. lapping (Incorrect. Lapping, where the fraud perpetrator uses later payments on account to pay off earlier payments that were stolen, does not result in large-enough losses to be associated with 50% of all lawsuits against auditors.)

3 Which of the following statements is false?

 a. The psychological profiles of white-collar criminals differ from those of violent criminals. (Incorrect. This is a true statement.)

✔ **b.** The psychological profiles of white-collar criminals are significantly different from those of the general public. (Correct. This is false because the psychological profile of white-collar criminals is similar to that of the general public.)

 c. There is no difference between computer fraud perpetrators and other types of white-collar criminals. (Incorrect. This is a true statement. While there are many similarities, computer fraud perpetrators are sometimes motivated by different things than other types of white-collar criminals.)

 d. Computer fraud perpetrators often do not view themselves as criminals. (Incorrect. This is a true statement. Computer fraud perpetrators often do not view what they do as wrong.)

4 Which of the following conditions is/are usually necessary for a fraud to occur? (There may be more than one right answer.)

✔ **a.** pressure (Correct. A pressure is one of the three elements of the fraud triangle. See Figure 5-1.)

✔ **b.** opportunity (Correct. An opportunity is one of the three elements of the fraud triangle. See Figure 5-1.)

 c. explanation (Incorrect. An explanation is not one of the three elements of the fraud triangle. See Figure 5-1.)

✔ **d.** rationalization (Correct. A rationalization is one of the three elements of the fraud triangle. See Figure 5-1.)

5 Which of the following is *not* an example of computer fraud?

 a. theft of money by altering computer records (Incorrect. Altering computer records to steal money is computer fraud.)

 b. obtain information illegally through use of a computer (Incorrect. Using a computer to illegally acquire information is computer fraud.)

✔ **c.** failure to perform preventive maintenance on a computer (Correct. Failure to perform preventive maintenance is poor management of computer resources but is not computer fraud.)

 d. unauthorized modification of a software program (Incorrect. Modifying software without proper authorization is computer fraud.)

6 A set of instructions to increase a programmer's pay rate by 10% is hidden inside an authorized program. It changes and updates payroll files. What is this computer fraud technique called?

 a. virus (Incorrect. A virus damages systems using a segment of executable code that attaches itself to software, replicates itself, and spreads to other systems or files.)

 b. worm (Incorrect. A worm is a program that is hidden in a host program and copies and actively transmits itself directly to other systems.)

 c. trap door (Incorrect. A trap door is entering a system using a back door that bypasses normal system controls.)

✔ **d.** Trojan horse (Correct. Placing unauthorized computer instructions, such as fraudulently increasing an employee's pay, in an authorized and properly functioning program is an example of a Trojan horse.)

7 What is the computer fraud technique called that involves a set of instructions hidden inside a calendar utility that copies itself each time the utility is enabled and until memory is filled and the system crashes?

 a. logic bomb (Incorrect. A logic bomb sabotages a system using a program that lies idle until some specified circumstance or a particular time triggers it.)

 b. trap door (Incorrect. A trap door is entering the system using a back door that bypasses normal system controls.)

✔ **c.** virus (Correct. A virus damages systems using a segment of executable code that attaches itself to software, replicates itself, and spreads to other systems or files.)

 d. Trojan horse (Incorrect. Placing unauthorized computer instructions, such as fraudulently increasing an employee's pay, in an authorized and properly functioning program is an example of a Trojan horse.)

8 Which of the following control procedures is most likely to deter lapping?

 a. encryption (Incorrect. Encryption is used to code data in transit so it cannot be read unless it is decoded. It cannot stop employees from lapping accounts receivable payments.)

 b. continual update of the access control matrix (Incorrect. The access control matrix specifies what computer functions employees can perform and what data they can access. It cannot stop employees from lapping accounts receivable payments.)

 c. background check on employees (Incorrect. A background check can help screen out dishonest job applicants, but it cannot stop employees from lapping accounts receivable payments.)

✔ **d.** periodic rotation of duties (Correct. Lapping requires a constant and ongoing cover-up to hide the stolen funds. Rotating duties such that the perpetrator does not have access to the necessary accounting records will result in the fraud's discovery.)

9 Which of the following is the most important, basic, and effective control to deter fraud?

 a. enforced vacations (Incorrect. Enforced vacations will prevent or deter some, but not all, frauds.)

 b. logical access control (Incorrect. Logical access controls will prevent or deter some, but not all, frauds.)

✔ **c.** segregation of duties (Correct. When duties are segregated among different employees, it is difficult for any single employee to both commit and conceal a fraud.)

 d. virus protection controls (Incorrect. Virus protection controls will help prevent computer-related losses, but are unlikely to deter much fraud.)

10 Which of the following is/are methods of reducing fraud losses once fraud has occurred? (There may be more than one right answer.)

✔ **a.** insurance (Correct. Insurance is used to compensate for fraud losses.)

✔ **b.** regular backup of data and programs (Correct. Regular backup
allows the injured party to recover lost or damaged data and programs.)

✔ **c.** contingency plan (Correct. A contingency plan helps the injured party restart
operations on a timely basis.)

d. segregation of duties (Incorrect. Segregation of duties is an effective method
of deterring fraud but does not help a company recover from fraud once it
occurs.)

CHAPTER 6

Control and Accounting Information Systems

INTEGRATIVE CASE SPRINGER'S LUMBER & SUPPLY

Jason Scott, an internal auditor for Northwest Industries, was assigned to audit Springer's Lumber & Supply, Northwest's building materials outlet in Bozeman, Montana. His supervisor, Maria Pilier, asked him to trace a sample of purchase transactions from purchase requisition to cash disbursement to verify that proper control procedures were followed. By midafternoon, Jason is frustrated with this task, and for good reasons:

- ► The purchasing system is poorly documented.
- ► He keeps finding transactions that have not been processed as Ed Yates, the accounts payable manager, said they should be.
- ► Purchase requisitions are missing for several items that had been personally authorized by Bill Springer, the purchasing vice president.
- ► Some vendor invoices have been paid without supporting documents, such as purchase orders and receiving reports.
- ► Prices charged for some items seem unusually high, and there are a few discrepancies in item prices between the vendor invoice and the corresponding purchase order.

Yates seemed to have a logical answer for every question Jason raised. Yates ended the discussion by advising Jason that the real world is not always as tidy as

the world portrayed in college textbooks. When Jason discussed his findings with Maria, he learned that she also has some concerns.

▶ Springer's is the largest supplier in the area and has a near monopoly.

▶ Management authority is held by the company president, Joe Springer, and his two sons, Bill (the purchasing vice president) and Ted (the controller). Several relatives and friends are on the payroll. Together, the Springers own 10% of the company.

▶ Lines of authority and responsibility within the company are loosely defined and confusing.

▶ Maria believes that Ted Springer may have engaged in "creative accounting" to make Springer's one of Northwest's best-performing retail outlets.

After talking to Maria, Jason ponders the following issues:

1 Because Ed Yates had a logical explanation for every unusual transaction, should Jason describe these transactions in his report?

2 Is a violation of proper control procedures acceptable if management has authorized it?

3 Maria's concerns about Springer's loosely defined lines of authority and possible use of creative accounting are matters of management policy. With respect to Jason's control procedures assignment, does he have a professional or an ethical responsibility to get involved?

Introduction

Why AIS Threats Are Increasing

In today's world, controlling the security and integrity of computer systems is an important issue. Control risks have increased in the last few years as studies show that more than 60% of organizations have recently experienced a major control failure. Among the reasons for the increase in security problems are the following:

● Increasing numbers of information systems mean that information is available to an unprecedented number of workers. Computers and servers are everywhere. Chevron, for example, has over 35,000 PCs.

● Distributed computer networks are harder to control than centralized mainframe systems. At Chevron, information is distributed among many systems and thousands of employees working all over the world.

● Wide area networks are giving customers and suppliers access to each other's systems and data, making confidentiality a major concern. For example, Wal-Mart allows certain vendors to access particular information in its computers as a condition of their alliance. Imagine the potential confidentiality problems if these vendors also formed alliances with Wal-Mart competitors.

Historically, many organizations have not adequately protected their data due to the following:

- Computer control problems have been underestimated and downplayed, and companies viewed the loss of crucial information as a distant, unlikely threat. For example, the number of participants in an Ernst & Young study that thought computer security was an extremely important issue declined from 35% to 25% over a one-year period.
- The control implications of moving from centralized, host-based computer systems to a networked or Internet-based system have not been fully understood.
- Many companies have not realized that data security is crucial to their survival. Information is a strategic resource, and protecting it must be a strategic requirement. For example, one company lost millions of dollars over a period of several years because it did not protect its data transmissions. A competitor tapped into its phone lines and obtained faxes of new product designs sent to an offshore plant.
- Productivity and cost pressures have motivated management to forgo time-consuming control measures.

Any potential adverse occurrence or unwanted event that could be injurious to either the AIS or the organization is referred to as a **threat** or an event. The potential dollar loss should a particular threat become a reality is referred to as the **exposure** or **impact** of the threat, and the probability that the threat will happen is the **likelihood** associated with the threat.

Why Control and Security Are Important

Fortunately, companies are taking positive steps to better control companies and increase computer control and security. They are devoting full-time staff to security and control concerns and educating their employees about control measures. Many are establishing and enforcing formal information security policies. They are making controls a part of the applications development process and are moving sensitive data to more secure environments.

As an accountant, you must understand how to protect systems from the threats they face. You must also have a good understanding of IT and its capabilities and risks. This knowledge can help you use IT to achieve an organization's control objectives.

Achieving adequate security and control over information resources should be a top management priority. Although internal control objectives remain the same regardless of the data processing method, a computer-based AIS requires different internal control policies and procedures. For example, although computer processing reduces the potential for clerical errors, it may increase the risks of unauthorized access to or modification of data files. In addition, segregating the authorization, recording, and asset custody functions within an AIS must be achieved differently, as computer programs may be responsible for one or more of these functions. Fortunately, computers also provide opportunities for an organization to enhance its internal controls.

One of the primary objectives of an AIS is to control a business organization. The accountant can help achieve this objective by designing effective control systems and by auditing or reviewing control systems to ensure their effectiveness. Management expects accountants to (1) take a proactive approach to eliminating system threats and (2) detect, correct, and recover from threats when they occur.

It is much easier to build controls into a system at the initial design stage than to add them after the fact. For that reason, accountants and other control experts should be important members of the team that develops or modifies an information system.

Overview of Control Concepts

In today's dynamic business environment, companies must react quickly to changing conditions and markets. One good way to do this is to hire creative and innovative employees and give them the power and flexibility to satisfy changing customer demands, pursue new opportunities to add organizational value, and implement process improvements. At the same time, companies need control systems so they are not exposed to excessive risk or behaviors that might harm their reputation for honesty and integrity.

Internal control is the process implemented by the board of directors, management, and those under their direction to provide reasonable assurance that the following control objectives are achieved:

- Safeguarding assets, including preventing or detecting, on a timely basis, the unauthorized acquisition, use, or disposition of material company assets
- Maintaining records in sufficient detail to accurately and fairly reflect company assets
- Providing accurate and reliable information
- Providing reasonable assurance that financial reporting is prepared in accordance with GAAP
- Promoting and improving operational efficiency, including making sure company receipts and expenditures are made in accordance with management and directors' authorizations
- Encouraging adherence to prescribed managerial policies
- Complying with applicable laws and regulations

Internal control is a process because it permeates an organization's operating activities and is an integral part of basic management activities. Internal control provides reasonable, rather than absolute, assurance, because providing complete assurance is difficult to achieve and prohibitively expensive. In addition, all internal control systems have inherent limitations, such as being susceptible to simple errors and mistakes, faulty judgments and decision making, being overridden by management, or two or more employees colluding with each other.

Internal control purposes are sometimes at odds with each other. For example, many people are pushing for radical business process reengineering so they can have better and faster information and improve operational efficiency. Others resist those changes because they impede the safeguarding of company assets and require significant changes in managerial policies.

Internal controls perform three important functions. **Preventive controls** deter problems before they arise. Hiring highly qualified personnel; appropriately segregating employee duties; and effectively controlling physical access to assets, facilities, and information are effective preventive controls. Because not all control problems can be prevented, **detective controls** are needed to discover problems as soon as they arise. Examples include duplicate checking of calculations and preparing bank reconciliations and monthly trial balances. **Corrective controls** remedy control problems that have been discovered. They include procedures taken to identify the cause of a problem, correct resulting errors or difficulties, and modify the system so that future problems are minimized or eliminated. Examples include maintaining backup copies of transaction files and master files and adhering to procedures for correcting data entry errors, as well as those for resubmitting transactions for subsequent processing.

Internal controls are often segregated into two categories: general controls and application controls. **General controls** are designed to make sure an organization's control environment is stable and well managed. They apply to all sizes of systems, from large and complex mainframe systems to client/server systems to desktop and laptop computer systems. Some of the more important general controls are

information systems management controls; security management controls; IT infrastructure controls; and software acquisition, development, and maintenance controls. **Application controls** prevent, detect, and correct transaction errors and fraud. They are concerned with the accuracy, completeness, validity, and authorization of the data captured, entered into the system, processed, stored, transmitted to other systems, and reported.

An effective system of internal controls should exist in all organizations to help them achieve their missions, as well as their performance and profitability goals, while minimizing surprises along the way. An effective internal control system can also help companies deal with rapidly changing economic and competitive environments and shifting customer demands and priorities. Regrettably, not all companies—even those that should know better—have an effective system of internal controls. For instance, an inspector general report indicated that the FBI is plagued by IT infrastructure vulnerabilities and security problems, some of which were identified in an audit 13 years previously. Specific areas of concern were security standards, guidelines, and procedures; segregation of duties; access controls, including password management and usage; backup and recovery controls; and software development and change controls.

The Sarbanes–Oxley and Foreign Corrupt Practices Acts

In 1977, shock waves reverberated through the accounting profession when Congress incorporated language from an AICPA pronouncement into the **Foreign Corrupt Practices Act**. The primary purpose of the act was to prevent the bribery of foreign officials in order to obtain business. A significant effect of the act, however, was to require corporations to maintain good systems of internal accounting control. Unfortunately, the resultant improvement in internal control systems was not sufficient to prevent further problems.

The airwaves and print media in the late 1990s and early 2000s were full of news of accounting frauds and problems at Enron, WorldCom, Xerox, Tyco, Global Crossing, Adelphia, and other companies. When Enron, with $62 billion in assets, declared bankruptcy in December 2001, it was the largest bankruptcy in U.S. history. In June 2002, Arthur Andersen, once the largest CPA firm, collapsed. The Enron bankruptcy was dwarfed when WorldCom, with over $100 billion in assets, filed for bankruptcy in July 2002. In response to these problems, Congress passed the **Sarbanes–Oxley Act** of 2002 (SOX). SOX applies to publicly held companies and their auditors and was intended to prevent financial statement fraud, make financial reports more transparent, provide protection to investors, strengthen the internal controls at public companies, and punish executives who perpetrate fraud.

SOX has had a material impact on the way boards of directors, management, and accountants of publicly held companies operate. In fact, many people believe that SOX is the most important and influential business-oriented legislation in the last 70 years. It has also had a dramatic impact on CPAs of publicly held companies and the audits of those companies. Some of the most important aspects of SOX are:

- **Public Company Accounting Oversight Board.** SOX created a five-member **Public Company Accounting Oversight Board (PCAOB)** to control the auditing profession. The SEC appoints PCAOB members and oversees their activities. In effect, nonaccountants now regulate the auditing profession, as three PCAOB members cannot be CPAs. Mandatory fees for public companies, as well as registration and annual fees for auditing firms, fund the PCAOB. The PCAOB sets and enforces auditing, quality control, ethics, independence, and other standards relating to audit reports.
- **New rules for auditors.** Auditors must report specific information to the company's audit committee, such as critical accounting policies and practices,

alternative GAAP treatments, and auditor-management disagreements. Audit partners must be rotated periodically. SOX prohibits auditors from performing certain nonaudit services such as bookkeeping, information systems design and implementation, internal audit outsourcing services, management functions, and human resource services. Any permissible nonaudit services have to be preapproved by the board of directors and periodically disclosed to investors. Audit firms cannot provide services to publicly held companies if top management was previously employed by the auditing firm and worked on the company's audit in the preceding 12 months.

- **New roles for audit committees.** Audit committee members must be on the company's board of directors and be independent of the company. One member of the audit committee must be a financial expert. The audit committee hires, compensates, and oversees the auditors, who report directly to them.

- **New rules for management.** SOX requires the CEO and CFO to certify that financial statements and disclosures are fairly presented, were reviewed by management, and are not misleading. In addition, they must certify that they are responsible for internal controls and that the auditors were told about all material internal control weaknesses and fraud. If management willfully and knowingly violates the certification, they can be imprisoned for up to 20 years and fined up to $5,000,000. In addition, management and directors cannot receive loans that those outside the company cannot get. Finally, companies must disclose, in plain English, material changes to their financial condition on a rapid and current basis.

- **New internal control requirements.** Section 404 of SOX requires publicly held companies to issue a report accompanying the financial statements that states management is responsible for establishing and maintaining an adequate internal control structure and appropriate control procedures. The report must also contain management's assessment of the company's internal controls and attest to their accuracy, including notations of significant defects or material noncompliance found during their internal control tests. SOX also specifies that a company's auditor must attest to, as well as report on, management's internal control assessment. Each audit report must describe the scope of the auditor's internal control tests. Large companies indicate that it costs them millions of dollars to comply with Section 404 requirements.

After SOX was passed, the SEC mandated that management must:

- Base its evaluation on a recognized control framework. The most likely frameworks, formulated by COSO, are discussed later in this chapter.
- Disclose any and all material internal control weaknesses.
- Conclude that a company does not have effective internal controls over financial reporting if there are any material weaknesses.

Levers of Control

Many people feel there is a basic conflict between creativity and controls. Robert Simons, a Harvard business professor, has espoused four levers of control to help companies reconcile this conflict. The first is a concise **belief system** that communicates company core values to employees and inspires them to live by them. It should draw attention to how the organization creates value and help employees understand the direction management wants the company to take. It has to be broad enough to appeal to employee groups at all organizational levels.

A **boundary system** helps employees act ethically by setting limits beyond which an employee must not pass. Employees are not told exactly what they must do, in the form of rules and standard operating procedures, as this can discourage initiative and creativity and often does not result in empowered, entrepreneurial employees. Instead,

employees are encouraged to think and act creatively to solve problems and meet customer needs as long as they operate within certain limits, such as meeting minimum standards of performance, shunning activities that are off-limits, and avoiding courses of action that would damage the company's reputation.

To ensure the efficient and effective achievement of important goals, a **diagnostic control system** measures company progress by comparing actual performance to planned performance. Planned performance often takes the form of budgets or performance goals such as those for sales, profitability, or revenue per employee. A diagnostic control system helps managers track critical performance outcomes and monitor the progress of individuals, departments, or locations as they strive to achieve strategically important goals. The control system provides feedback that allows management to adjust and fine-tune inputs and processes so future outputs will more closely match goals.

An **interactive control system** helps top-level managers with high-level activities that demand frequent and regular attention, such as developing company strategy, setting company objectives, understanding and assessing threats and risks, monitoring changes in competitive conditions and emerging technologies, and developing responses and action plans to proactively deal with these high-level issues. The system also helps managers focus the attention of their subordinates on key strategic issues and to be more involved in their decisions. Data generated by an interactive system are best interpreted and discussed in face-to-face meetings of superiors, subordinates, and peers.

Control Frameworks

A number of control frameworks have been developed to help companies develop good internal control systems. In this section, we discuss three of the most important.

COBIT Framework

The Information Systems Audit and Control Foundation (ISACF) developed the **Control Objectives for Information and related Technology (COBIT)** framework. COBIT is a framework of generally applicable information systems security and control practices for IT control. The framework allows (1) management to benchmark the security and control practices of IT environments, (2) users of IT services to be assured that adequate security and control exist, and (3) auditors to substantiate their opinions on internal control and to advise on IT security and control matters.

The framework addresses the issue of control from three vantage points, or dimensions:

1 **Business objectives.** To satisfy business objectives, information must conform to criteria called business requirements for information. The criteria are divided into seven categories that map into the COSO (see next section) objectives: effectiveness (relevant, pertinent, and timely), efficiency, confidentiality, integrity, availability, compliance with legal requirements, and reliability.

2 **IT resources.** This includes people, application systems, technology, facilities, and data.

3 **IT processes.** These are broken into four domains: planning and organization, acquisition and implementation, delivery and support, and monitoring and evaluation.

COBIT, which consolidates standards from 36 different sources into a single framework, is having a big impact on the information systems profession. It is helping managers learn how to balance risk and control in an information system environment. It provides users with assurance that the security and IT controls provided by internal

and third parties are adequate. It guides auditors as they substantiate their opinions and as they provide advice to management on internal controls.

COSO's Internal Control Framework

The **Committee of Sponsoring Organizations (COSO)** is a private-sector group consisting of the American Accounting Association, the AICPA, the Institute of Internal Auditors, the Institute of Management Accountants, and the Financial Executives Institute. In 1992, COSO issued the **Internal Control—Integrated Framework**, which defines internal controls and provides guidance for evaluating and enhancing internal control systems. The report is widely accepted as the authority on internal controls and is incorporated into policies, rules, and regulations that are used to control business activities.

The study from which the control framework was derived took three years and involved hundreds of people and tens of thousands of hours of research, discussion, analysis, and due process. COSO's internal control integrated framework model has five crucial components, which are summarized in Table 6-1 and discussed in greater depth later in this chapter. These five components are also a part of COSO's newer Enterprise Risk Management framework.

COSO's Enterprise Risk Management Framework

Nine years after COSO issued the internal control integrated framework, it began investigating how to effectively identify, assess, and manage risk so organizations could improve the risk management process. The result was an enhanced corporate governance document, called **Enterprise Risk Management—Integrated Framework (ERM)**. ERM expands on the elements of the internal control integrated framework and provides an all-encompassing focus on the broader subject of enterprise risk management. The intent is to achieve all the goals of the control framework and help the organization to:

- Provide reasonable assurance that company objectives and goals are achieved and problems and surprises are minimized.
- Achieve its financial and performance targets.

Table 6-1
Five Interrelated Components of COSO's Internal Control Model

Component	Description
Control environment	The core of any business is its people—their individual attributes, including integrity, ethical values, and competence—and the environment in which they operate. They are the engine that drives the organization and the foundation on which everything rests.
Control activities	Control policies and procedures must be established and executed to help ensure that the actions identified by management as necessary to address risks and achieve the organization's objectives are effectively carried out.
Risk assessment	The organization must be aware of and deal with the risks it faces. It must set objectives so that the organization is operating in concert. It must also establish mechanisms to identify, analyze, and manage the related risks.
Information and communication	Surrounding the control activities are information and communication systems that enable the organization to capture and exchange the information needed to conduct, manage, and control its operations.
Monitoring	The entire process must be monitored, and modifications made as necessary so the system can react dynamically and change as conditions warrant.

- Assess risks continuously and identify the steps to take and the resources to allocate to overcome or mitigate risk.
- Avoid adverse publicity and damage to the entity's reputation.

The ERM framework defines enterprise risk management as "a process, affected by an entity's board of directors, management and other personnel, applied in strategy setting and across the enterprise, designed to identify potential events that may affect the entity, and manage risk to be within its risk appetite, to provide reasonable assurance regarding the achievement of entity objectives."

The basic principles behind enterprise risk management are:

- Companies are formed to create value for their owners.
- Company management must decide how much uncertainty it will accept as it creates value.
- Uncertainty results in risk, which is the possibility that something will occur to affect adversely the company's ability to create value or to erode existing value.
- Uncertainty can also result in an opportunity, which is the possibility that something will occur to affect positively the company's ability to create or preserve value.
- The ERM framework helps management manage uncertainty, and its associated risk and opportunity, so it can build and preserve value.

COSO developed the model shown in Figure 6-1 to illustrate the elements of ERM. The columns at the top of the figure represent the four types of objectives that management must meet to achieve company goals. **Strategic objectives** are high-level goals that are aligned with and support the company's mission. **Operations objectives** deal with the effectiveness and efficiency of company operations, such as performance and profitability goals and safeguarding assets. **Reporting objectives** help ensure the accuracy, completeness, and reliability of internal and external company reports, of both a financial and nonfinancial nature. They also improve decision making and monitor company activities and performance more efficiently. **Compliance objectives** help the company comply with all applicable laws and regulations. Parties external to the organization often set compliance rules, and companies in the same industry often have similar compliance concerns.

ERM can provide reasonable assurance that reporting and compliance objectives will be achieved because companies have control over them. However, strategic and operations objectives are sometimes at the mercy of external events the company is unable to control. Therefore, the only reasonable assurance ERM can provide is that

Figure 6-1
COSO's Enterprise Risk
Management Model

company management and directors are informed on a timely basis of the progress the company is making in achieving them.

The columns on the right side of Figure 6-1 represent the company's units: the entire company, or a division, business unit, or subsidiary of the company.

The horizontal rows are the eight interrelated risk and control components of COSO. A brief explanation of those components follows:

1 **Internal environment.** This is the tone or culture of a company and helps determine how risk conscious employees are. It is the foundation for all other ERM components, providing discipline and structure. It is essentially the same thing as the control environment in the internal control integrated framework.

2 **Objective setting.** ERM ensures that company management puts into place a process to formulate strategic, operations, reporting, and compliance objectives that support the company's mission and that are consistent with the company's tolerance for risk. The strategic objectives are set first, as a foundation for the other three. The various objectives provide guidance to companies as they identify the events that give rise to the risks the company faces and as they assess and respond to those risks.

3 **Event identification.** ERM requires management to identify events that may affect the company's ability to implement its strategy and achieve its objectives. Management must then determine whether these possible events represent risks (negative-impact events requiring assessment and response) or opportunities (positive-impact events that influence the strategy and objective-setting processes).

4 **Risk assessment.** Identified risks are assessed to determine how to manage them and how they affect the company's ability to achieve its objectives. Qualitative and quantitative methods are used to assess risks in several different ways: likelihood, positive and negative impact, individually and by category, their effect on other organizational units, and on an inherent and a residual basis. There is a corresponding risk assessment element in COSO's internal control integrated framework.

5 **Risk response.** To align identified risks with the company's tolerance for risk, management can choose to avoid, reduce, share, or accept the risks. To select a response, management must take an entity-wide, or portfolio, view of risk and assess risk likelihood and impact, as well as the costs and benefits of the alternative responses.

6 **Control activities.** To implement management's risk responses, control policies and procedures are established and implemented throughout the various levels and functions in the organization. There is a corresponding control activities element in COSO's internal control integrated framework.

7 **Information and communication.** Information about the company and the various ERM components must be identified, captured, and communicated so employees can fulfill their responsibilities. To be communicated effectively, information must have a means of flowing through all levels and functions in the company and to and from all external parties. There is a corresponding information and communication element in COSO's internal control integrated framework.

8 **Monitoring.** To remain effective, ERM processes must be monitored on an ongoing basis and modified as needed. Monitoring is accomplished with ongoing management activities and separate evaluations. Deficiencies in ERM processes are reported to management. There is a corresponding monitoring element in COSO's internal control integrated framework.

The ERM model is three-dimensional. This means that each of the eight risk and control elements applies to each of the four objectives in the entire company and/or one of its subunits. For example, XYZ Company could look at the control activities for the operations objectives in its Pacific Division.

The ERM Framework Versus the Internal Control Framework

The internal control integrated framework has been widely adopted as the principal way to evaluate internal controls, as required by the Sarbanes–Oxley law. However, it has too narrow a focus. Examining controls without first examining the purposes and risks of business processes provides little context for evaluating the results, making it hard to know which control systems are most important, whether they adequately deal with risk, and whether important control systems are missing. Focusing on controls first also has an inherent bias toward past problems and concerns. Long-standing internal control systems often have multiple layers of controls to protect against items that are no longer risks or are no longer important.

COSO recognized this and developed the more comprehensive ERM framework, which takes a risk-based, rather than a controls-based, approach to the organization that is oriented toward the future and constant change. ERM incorporates, rather than replaces, COSO's internal control framework and is more comprehensive than its predecessor. ERM contains three additional elements: setting objectives, identifying positive and negative events that may affect the company's ability to implement its strategy and achieve its objectives, and developing a response to assessed risk. As a result, controls are flexible and relevant because they are linked to current organizational objectives. Another key change is that the ERM model recognizes that risk, in addition to being controlled, can be accepted, avoided, diversified, shared, or transferred.

Because it is more comprehensive, it is anticipated that as time passes the ERM model will become the most widely adopted risk and control model. As a result, the eight components of the ERM Framework are the topic of the remainder of the chapter.

The Internal Environment

The **internal environment** is the most important component of the ERM and internal control frameworks. It influences how organizations establish strategies and objectives; structure business activities; and identify, assess, and respond to risk. A weak or deficient internal control environment often results in risk management and control breakdowns. An internal environment consists of items such as the following:

1 Management's philosophy, operating style, and risk appetite
2 The board of directors
3 Commitment to integrity, ethical values, and competence
4 Organizational structure
5 Methods of assigning authority and responsibility
6 Human resource standards
7 External influences

Enron is an example of how an ineffective internal environment can result in financial failure and a ruined public image. Enron appeared to have an effective ERM system: an exciting and new strategy; a board of directors composed of high-powered and influential people; competent and well-regarded management; an efficient AIS; a policies and procedures manual; and an internal control system that included supervision, reconciliations, and other internal checks. Unfortunately, its internal environment turned out to be defective. Management engaged in risky and dubious business practices, which the board of directors never questioned. Management misrepresented the company's financial condition, lost the confidence of shareholders as the stock price dwindled to almost nothing, and finally filed for bankruptcy.

Management's Philosophy, Operating Style, and Risk Appetite

Collectively, an organization's management has a philosophy, or shared beliefs and attitudes, about risk. This affects everything the organization does, from setting strategy, to conducting daily business, to influencing the organization's values, operating style, and culture. It is reflected in policies, procedures, oral and written communications, and the decisions that are made. Companies also have a **risk appetite**, which is the amount of risk a company is willing to accept in order to achieve its goals and objectives. To avoid undue risk, and to maximize the company's ability to achieve its objectives, risk appetite must be in alignment with company strategy.

The more responsible management's philosophy and operating style and the more clearly they are communicated, the more likely employees will behave responsibly. If management shows little concern for internal controls and risk management, then employees are less diligent and effective in achieving control objectives. For example, Maria Pilier found that lines of authority and responsibility at Springer's were loosely defined, and she suspected that management may have engaged in creative accounting to show its performance in the best light. Meanwhile, Jason Scott found evidence of poor internal control practices in the purchasing and accounts payable function. It is quite possible that these two conditions are related. In other words, management's loose attitude may have contributed to the purchasing department's inattentiveness to good internal control practices.

Management's philosophy, operating style, and risk appetite can be assessed by answering questions such as these:

- Does management take undue business risks to achieve its objectives, or does it assess potential risks and rewards prior to acting?
- Does management attempt to manipulate such performance measures as net income so that its performance can be seen in a more favorable light?
- Does management pressure employees to achieve results regardless of the methods, or does it demand ethical behavior? In other words, does management believe the ends justify the means?

The Board of Directors

An active and involved board of directors plays an important internal control role in organizations. The board should oversee management and scrutinize its plans, performance, and activities; approve company strategy; review financial results; annually review the company's security policy; and interact with internal and external auditors. Directors should possess management, technical, or other expertise; knowledge and experience so they can provide counsel and advice; and a willingness to represent shareholders and serve as a necessary check and balance on management by questioning, scrutinizing, and overseeing its activities. At least a majority of directors should be independent, outside directors. An independent director is one who does not receive any fees (other than board of director fees) from the company and is not affiliated with the company or any subsidiary thereof.

Section 301 of the Sarbanes–Oxley Act requires all public companies to have an **audit committee** composed entirely of outside (nonemployee), independent directors. The audit committee is responsible for overseeing the corporation's internal control structure, its financial reporting process, and its compliance with related laws, regulations, and standards. The committee works closely with the corporation's external and internal auditors. In fact, the Sarbanes–Oxley Act requires audit committees to be responsible for hiring, compensating, and overseeing the auditors and for auditors to report all critical accounting policies and practices to the audit committee. One of the committee's responsibilities is to provide an independent review of the actions of corporate managers on behalf of company shareholders. This review serves as a check on

management integrity and increases the confidence of the investing public in the propriety of financial reporting. In order to perform their responsibilities, audit committee members must understand their business and its objectives and processes, be able to recognize risk, and understand risk management and internal controls.

Commitment to Integrity, Ethical Values, and Competence

It is important to create an organizational culture that stresses integrity and commitment to both ethical values and competence. Well-managed companies know that ethics pays and that ethical standards of behavior are good business. Integrity starts at the top, and the CEO and other members of management must set the example because company employees tend to adopt top management's attitudes about risks and controls. A powerful message is sent when the CEO is confronted with a difficult decision and makes the ethically correct choice.

Companies endorse integrity as a basic operating principle by actively teaching and requiring it. For example, management should make it clear that honest reports are more important than favorable ones. Management should avoid unrealistic expectations, incentives, or temptations that motivate employees to engage in dishonest, illegal, or unethical acts. These include an attitude of revenue or earnings at any price, overly aggressive sales practices, unfair or unethical negotiation tactics, implied kickback offers, and bonuses excessively based on reported financial results.

Management should consistently reward and encourage honesty and give verbal labels to honest and dishonest behavior. If companies simply punish or reward honesty without labeling it as such or explaining the principle, or if the standard of honesty is inconsistent, then employees will most likely be inconsistent in their moral behavior.

Management should develop clearly stated policies that explicitly describe honest and dishonest behaviors, often in the form of a written code of conduct, and communicate them to employees. These policies should cover issues such as conflicts of interest and the acceptance of gifts. For example, most purchasing agents would agree that accepting a $5,000 bribe from a supplier is dishonest, but a weekend vacation at a hunting cabin is not as clear-cut. A major cause of dishonesty comes from rationalizing unclear situations and allowing the criterion of expediency to replace the criterion of right versus wrong. Companies should document that employees have read and understand the code of conduct.

Companies should require employees to report any dishonest, illegal, or unethical acts and discipline employees who knowingly fail to report violations. All dishonest acts should be thoroughly investigated, and dishonest employees should be dismissed and prosecuted to send the message that such behavior will not be allowed.

Companies need to make a commitment to competence, and this begins with having competent employees. Competence varies for each job and is a factor of knowledge, experience, training, and skills.

The levers of control discussed previously, particularly beliefs and boundaries systems, can be used to create the kinds of commitment to integrity that the organization wants. For these systems to be effective, they require more than lip service and forms, such as requiring annual sign-offs indicating that an employee has read the ethics statement. Instead, they must be systems in which top management actively participates to demonstrate their importance. Active participation by management also helps employees to buy into the system and goes a long ways toward creating a team spirit.

Organizational Structure

An organizational structure defines lines of authority, responsibility, and reporting. It provides the overall framework for planning, directing, executing, controlling, and

monitoring operations. Important aspects of organizational structure include the following:

- Centralization or decentralization of authority
- Assignment of responsibility for specific tasks
- Whether there is a direct reporting relationship or more of a matrix structure
- Organization by industry, product line, geographical location, or by a particular distribution or marketing network
- The way responsibility allocation affects management's information requirements
- The organization of the accounting and information system functions
- The size and the nature of company activities

An overly complex or unclear organizational structure may indicate more serious problems. ESM, a brokerage company dealing in government securities, used a multilayered organizational structure to hide a $300 million fraud. Company officers funneled cash to themselves and hid it in their financial statements by reporting a fictitious receivable from a related company.

In today's business world, drastic changes are occurring in management practices. Hierarchical organizational structures, with many layers of management personnel who supervise and control the work of those under them, are disappearing. They are being replaced with flat organizations that have self-directed work teams. Team members are empowered to make decisions without seeking multiple layers of approval to complete their work. The emphasis is on continuous improvement rather than on the periodic reviews and appraisals characteristic of earlier evaluations. These changes have an enormous impact on a company's organizational structure and on the nature and type of controls used.

Methods of Assigning Authority and Responsibility

Management should make sure employees understand the entity's objectives, assign authority and responsibility for business objectives to specific departments and individuals, encourage them to use initiative to solve problems, and then hold them accountable for achieving those objectives. It is especially important for management to identify who is responsible for designing and implementing the company's information security policy.

Authority and responsibility are assigned through formal job descriptions; employee training; operating plans, schedules, and budgets; a formal company code of conduct; and a written **policy and procedures manual**. The manual explains proper business practices, describes the knowledge and experience needed by key personnel, spells out management policy for handling specific transactions, and documents the systems and procedures employed to process those transactions. It includes the organization's chart of accounts and sample copies of forms and documents. The manual is a helpful on-the-job reference for employees and a useful tool in training new employees.

Human Resources Standards

Many controls consultants claim that the most effective method of obtaining adequate system security is to rely on the integrity of company employees. At the same time, research shows that current and former employees commit the most fraud. Thus, employees can be both the greatest control strength and weakness.

Organizations can implement human resource policies and practices with respect to hiring, training, compensating, evaluating, counseling, promoting, and discharging employees that send messages to employees about the level of expertise, competence,

ethical behavior, and integrity that are required. Policies governing working conditions, job incentives, and career advancement can also be a powerful force in encouraging efficiency and loyal service. These policies and practices also affect an organization's ability to minimize threats, risks, and exposures. The following policies and procedures are important

Hiring. To obtain the most qualified and ethical employees, hiring should be based on educational background, relevant work experience, past achievements, honesty and integrity, and how well potential employees meet written job requirements. Potential employees should undergo a formal, in-depth employment interview. Resumes, reference letters, and thorough background checks are important means of evaluating the qualifications of job applicants.

A thorough **background check** includes verifying educational and work experience, talking to references, checking for a criminal record, and checking credit records. Studies show that as many as half of all applicants include false information in their applications or on their resumes. For example, Philip Crosby Associates (PCA) hired John Nelson, an MBA and CPA, without conducting a background check. In reality, the CPA and the glowing reference from Nelson's former employer were phony. Nelson was actually Robert W. Liszewski, who had recently served an 18-month jail sentence for embezzling $400,000 from an Indiana bank. By the time PCA discovered this fact, Liszewski had embezzled $960,000 using wire transfers to a dummy corporation, supported by forged signatures on contracts and authorization documents.

Many firms hire companies that specialize in conducting background checks because applicants are becoming more aggressive in trying to fool potential employers. Some applicants buy phony academic degrees from Web site operators who also "validate" the bogus educational background when called by potential employers. Some applicants increase their credibility and embellish their resumes by paying hackers to break into legitimate educational institution databases and enter fake graduation dates and data.

Because they are not subjected to normal hiring practices such as background checks, some people intent on breaking into systems pose as janitors or temporary employees to gain access to the company's site and its information system. Once they have legitimate access to the building or the system, they can use any number of techniques to commit fraud or sabotage the system. For this reason, all company personnel, including cleaning crews and temporary employees, should be subject to all hiring and firing policies.

Compensating. It is important to pay employees a fair and competitive wage. Poorly compensated employees are more likely to feel the resentment and financial pressures that might lead to fraud. Appropriate bonus incentives can help motivate and reinforce outstanding employee performance.

Training. Training programs should familiarize new employees with their responsibilities; expected levels of performance and behavior; and the company's policies and procedures, history, culture, and operating style. Ongoing training is needed to help employees tackle new challenges, stay ahead of the competition, adapt to changing technologies, and deal effectively with the evolving environment. Since companies that shortchange training are more likely to have fraud and security breaches, employee training and education are important elements of fraud prevention and security programs. Fraud training is discussed in this section of the chapter, and security training is discussed in more depth in Chapter 7.

Fraud is much less likely to occur in an environment where employees believe security is everyone's business. An ideal corporate culture exists when employees are proud of their company, are protective of its assets, and believe they have a responsibility to report fraud because what harms the company harms them. This culture does

not just happen. It has to be created, taught, and practiced. Therefore, a company should provide the following training on fraud and ethics:

- **Fraud awareness.** Employees should be made aware of fraud's prevalence and its dangers. They should be taught why people commit fraud and how to deter and detect it.
- **Ethical considerations.** Acceptable and unacceptable behavior should be defined because some business practices fall into a gray area between right and wrong, especially in the computer industry. For example, many computer professionals see nothing wrong with using corporate computer resources for personal use or gaining unauthorized access and browsing another company's databases. When arrested for unauthorized browsing, one programmer was shocked because he believed his activities were a common industry practice.
- **Punishment for fraud and unethical behavior.** Employees should be informed of the consequences of unethical behavior (reprimands, dismissal, and prosecution). For example, employees should be informed that using a computer to steal or commit fraud is a federal crime and anyone doing so faces immediate dismissal and/or prosecution.

Employees can be trained by conducting informal discussions and formal meetings, issuing periodic departmental memos, distributing written guidelines and codes of professional ethics, circulating reports of unethical behavior and its consequences, and promoting security and fraud training programs.

Evaluating and Promoting. Employees should be given periodic performance appraisals that help them understand their strengths and weaknesses. Promotions should be based on performance and how well-qualified employees are for the new position.

Discharging. A company should take care when firing employees. To prevent sabotage or copying confidential data before they leave, dismissed employees should be removed from sensitive jobs immediately and denied access to the information system. One employee, after learning he had been terminated, lit a butane lighter under a smoke detector located just outside the computer room. It set off a sprinkler system that ruined most of the computer hardware in the room.

Managing Disgruntled Employees. Some employees who commit fraud are seeking revenge for a perceived wrong done to them. Hence, companies should have procedures for identifying disgruntled employees and either helping them resolve their feelings or removing them from jobs where they might be able to harm the organization or perpetrate a fraud. Grievance channels and employee counseling, where someone outside the normal chain of command can help employees resolve their problems, can decrease the number of dissatisfied employees. This is often not easy to accomplish, because most employees fear that airing their feelings could have negative consequences for their careers.

Vacations and rotation of duties. Many fraud schemes, such as lapping and kiting, require the ongoing attention of the perpetrator. Many of these employee frauds are discovered when the perpetrator is suddenly forced, by illness or accident, to take time off. Periodically rotating the duties of key employees, where their job functions are performed by other staff members, can achieve the same results. If mandatory vacations are coupled with the temporary rotation of duties, such ongoing fraud schemes would fall apart.

For example, when federal investigators raided an illegal gambling establishment, they found that Roswell Steffen, who earned $11,000 a year, was betting up to

$30,000 a day at the racetrack. Investigators at Union Dime Savings Bank discovered he had embezzled and gambled away $1.5 million of the bank's money over a three-year period. A compulsive gambler, Steffen began by borrowing $5,000 to place a bet on a sure thing that did not pan out. He embezzled ever-increasing amounts in an effort to win back the original money he had "borrowed." Steffen committed his fraud by transferring money from inactive accounts to his own account. If the owner of an inactive account complained, Steffen, the chief teller who had the power to resolve these types of problems, replaced the money by taking it from another inactive account. After being caught and asked how the fraud could have been prevented, he said the bank could have coupled a two-week vacation period with several weeks of rotation to another job function. That would have made his embezzlement, which required his physical presence at the bank and his constant attention, almost impossible to cover up.

Confidentiality agreements and fidelity bond insurance. All employees, suppliers, and contractors should be required to sign and abide by a nondisclosure or confidentiality agreement. Fidelity bond insurance coverage of key employees protects companies against losses arising from deliberate acts of fraud by bonded employees.

Prosecute and incarcerate hackers and fraud perpetrators. Most fraud cases and hacker attacks go unreported and are not prosecuted for several reasons:

1 Companies are reluctant to report computer crimes and intrusions—a recent study showed only 36% reporting intrusions—because a highly visible fraud is a public relations disaster. Fraud also can reveal information system vulnerabilities, possibly attracting more fraud or hacker attacks.
2 Law enforcement officials and the courts are so busy with violent crimes that they have little time for computer crimes in which no physical harm occurs.
3 Fraud is difficult, costly, and time-consuming to investigate and prosecute.
4 Many law enforcement officials, lawyers, and judges lack the computer skills needed to investigate, prosecute, and evaluate computer crimes.
5 When fraud cases are prosecuted and a conviction is obtained, the sentences received are often light. For example, Judge John Lord, when sentencing convicted white-collar criminals, stated they were God-fearing, highly civic-minded men who had spent their lifetimes in sincere and honest dedication and service to their families, churches, country, and communities. He said he could never send them to jail. One investigator noted that the average sentence for a fraud perpetrator was one year in jail for every $10 million stolen. One of the most famous cases of a light sentence involved C. Arnoldt Smith, former owner of the San Diego Padres, who was named Mr. San Diego of the Century. Smith was very involved in the community and made large political contributions. When investigations showed that he had stolen $200 million from his bank, he pleaded no contest. His sentence was four years of probation. He was fined $30,000, to be paid at the rate of $100 a month for 25 years, with no interest. Mr. Smith was 71 at the time. The embezzled money was never recovered.

External Influences

External influences that affect an organization's control environment include requirements imposed by stock exchanges, the Financial Accounting Standards Board (FASB), the Public Company Accounting Oversight Board (PCAOB), and the Securities and Exchange Commission (SEC). They also include regulatory agency requirements, such as those for banks, utilities, and insurance companies. An example is an audit of financial institutions delete by the Federal Deposit Insurance Corporation (FDIC).

Objective Setting

Objective setting is the second ERM component because it must precede the other six components. For example, management must set objectives before it can identify the events that affect the company's ability to achieve those objectives. Likewise, event identification must precede assessing the risks related to the events.

Top management, with board approval, needs to articulate why the company exists and what it hopes to achieve. This is often referred to as the corporate vision or mission. The company uses its mission statement as a base from which it sets and prioritizes corporate objectives, which need to be easy to understand and measure. Objectives are set at the corporate level and linked to and integrated with a cascading series of ever more specific subobjectives set in the various subunits in a company. For each set of objectives, critical success factors (things that must go right to achieve the objectives) must be determined and performance measures established to determine whether the objectives are met.

Strategic objectives, which are high-level goals that support the company's mission and are intended to create shareholder value, must be set first. To meet these strategic objectives, management should identify alternative ways of accomplishing the objectives, identify and assess the risks and implications of each alternative, formulate a corporate strategy, and set operations, compliance, and reporting objectives. As a rule, a company's mission and strategic objectives are stable. However, its strategy and other objectives are more dynamic and must be adjusted for changing conditions and realigned with strategic objectives.

Operations objectives, which are a product of management preferences, judgments, and style, may vary significantly among entities. For example, one company decides to be an early adopter of new technology, another chooses to adopt technology as soon as it is proven, and a third elects to adopt a technology only after it has matured and is generally accepted. Operations objectives are influenced by and must be relevant to the company's industry, economic conditions, and competitive pressures. Understandable operations objectives give clear direction as to how to allocate resources and are a key factor in corporate success.

Most compliance objectives, and many reporting objectives, are imposed by external entities due to laws or regulations. For example, some entities must comply with requirements to submit information to government agencies, such as the Internal Revenue Service. Others, such as publicly traded companies, have to send reports to securities regulators. A company's reputation can be impacted significantly by how well it meets its compliance and reporting objectives.

Event Identification

The third ERM component is event identification. COSO defines an **event** as "an incident or occurrence emanating from internal or external sources that affects implementation of strategy or achievement of objectives. Events may have positive or negative impacts or both." By their nature, events represent uncertainty. An event may or may not occur. If it does occur, it is hard to know when it will occur. Until it occurs, it may be difficult to determine its impact on the company. When it occurs, it may trigger another event. Events may occur individually or concurrently. Therefore, management must anticipate all possible events, whether positive or negative, that might affect the company. It must also determine which events are most and least likely to occur, and it must understand the interrelationship of events.

Table 6-2 lists some of the many internal and external factors that COSO indicated could influence events and affect a company's ability to implement its strategy and achieve its objectives. Lists like these help management identify factors, evaluate their

Table 6-2
COSO's Nine ERM Event Categories

EVENT CATEGORIES	
External Factors	**Internal Factors**

ECONOMIC
- Availability of capital; lower or higher costs of capital
- Lower barriers to competitive entry, resulting in new competitors
- Price movements upward or downward
- Ability to issue credit and possibility of default
- Concentration of competitors, customers, or vendors
- Presence or absence of liquidity
- Movements in the financial markets or currency fluctuations
- Rising or declining unemployment rates
- Mergers or acquisitions
- Potential regulatory, contractual, or criminal legal liability

NATURAL ENVIRONMENT
- Natural disasters such as fires, floods, or earthquakes
- Emissions and waste
- Energy restrictions or shortages
- Restrictions limiting development

POLITICAL
- Election of government officials with new political agendas
- New laws and regulations
- Public policy, including higher or lower taxes
- Regulation affecting the company's ability to compete

SOCIAL
- Changing demographics, social mores, family structures, and work/life priorities
- Consumer behavior that changes demand for products and services or creates new buying opportunities
- Corporate citizenship
- Privacy
- Terrorism
- Human resource issues causing production shortages or stoppages

TECHNOLOGICAL
- New e-business technologies that lower infrastructure costs or increase demand for IT-based services
- Emerging technology
- Increased or decreased availability of data
- Interruptions or downtime caused by external parties

INFRASTRUCTURE
- Inadequate access to or poor allocation of capital
- Availability and capability of company assets
- Complexity of systems

PERSONNEL
- Employee skills and capability
- Employees acting dishonestly or unethically
- Workplace accidents, health or safety concerns
- Strikes or expiration of labor agreements

PROCESS
- Process modification without proper change management procedures
- Poorly designed processes
- Process execution errors
- Suppliers cannot deliver quality goods on time

TECHNOLOGY
- Insufficient capacity to handle peak IT usages
- Security breaches
- Data or system unavailability
- Inadequate data integrity
- Poor systems selection/development
- Inadequately maintained systems

importance, and examine those that can affect objectives. Identifying events at the activity and entity levels allows companies to focus their risk assessment on major business units or functions and helps align the company's risk tolerance and risk appetite.

As an example of event identification, consider an organization that is implementing an electronic data interchange (EDI) system to provide instantaneous communication and eliminate paper documents. An EDI system allows the company to create electronic documents, transmit them over private networks or the Internet to their customers' and suppliers' computers, and receive electronic responses in return. A few of the events, or threats, that the company will face are these:

1 **Choosing an inappropriate technology.** The companies might move to EDI before their customers and suppliers are ready. They may also choose to use EDI when there is a more effective means of communicating with their customers and suppliers electronically.
2 **Unauthorized system access.** Hackers can break into the system and steal data or sabotage the system.
3 **Tapping into data transmissions.** Hackers can eavesdrop on a data transmission and copy the transmission, distort it, or prevent it from arriving at its destination.
4 **Loss of data integrity.** Errors may be introduced into the data due to employee or software errors, erroneous input, faulty transmissions, and so forth.
5 **Incomplete transactions.** The receiving computer may not receive all the data from the sending computer.
6 **System failures.** Hardware or software problems, power outages, sabotage, employee mistakes, or other factors may cause the EDI system to fail or be inaccessible for a time.
7 **Incompatible systems.** Some companies have difficulty interacting with other systems because of incompatible computer systems.

Some of the more common techniques companies use to identify events follow. Often, two or more of these techniques are used together.

- **Use comprehensive lists of potential events.** These lists are often produced by special software that allows a company to tailor the list to a specific industry, activity, or process.
- **Perform an internal analysis.** An internal committee is organized to analyze events. It contacts the appropriate insiders, including internal audit, and appropriate outsiders such as business partners, customers, and vendors.
- **Monitor leading events and trigger points.** Appropriate transactions, activities, and events are monitored and compared to predefined criteria to determine when action is needed.
- **Conduct workshops and interviews.** The knowledge and expertise of employees are gathered during structured discussions or individual interviews.
- **Perform data mining and analysis.** Data on prior events are carefully examined to identify trends and causes that help identify possible events.
- **Analyze business processes.** The internal and external factors that affect inputs, processes, and outputs are analyzed to identify events that might help or hinder the process.

Risk Assessment and Risk Response

The fourth and fifth components of COSO's ERM model are risk assessment and risk response. COSO indicates that there are two types of risk. The risk that exists before management takes any steps to control the likelihood or impact of a risk is **inherent**

risk. The risk that remains after management implements internal controls, or some other response to risk, is **residual risk**. Companies should assess inherent risk, develop a response, and then assess residual risk. The ERM model indicates that there are four ways to respond to risk:

- **Reduce.** The most effective way to reduce the likelihood and impact of risk is to implement an effective system of internal controls.
- **Accept.** Accept the likelihood and impact of the risk by not acting to prevent or mitigate it.
- **Share.** Share some of the risk or transfer it to someone else. For example, buy insurance, outsource an activity, or enter into hedging transactions.
- **Avoid.** Risk is avoided by not engaging in the activity that produces the risk. This may require the company to sell a division, exit a product line, or not expand as anticipated.

Accountants play an important role in helping management design effective control systems to reduce inherent risk. They also evaluate internal control systems to ensure that they are operating effectively. Accountants can assess and reduce inherent risk using the risk assessment and response strategy shown in Figure 6-2. We will walk through the major steps in this strategy. The first step, event identification, has already been discussed.

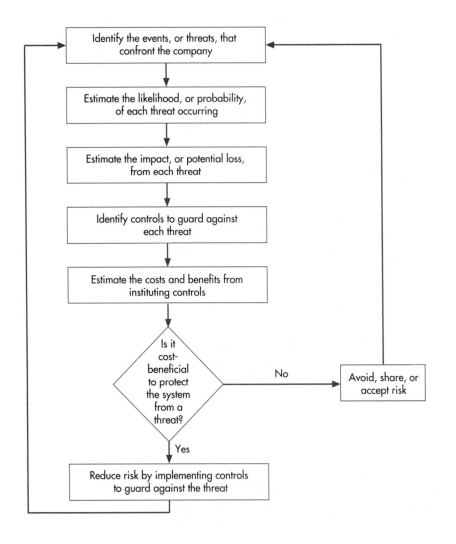

Figure 6-2
Risk Assessment Approach to Designing Internal Controls

Estimate Likelihood and Impact

Some events pose a greater risk because the probability of their occurrence is more likely. For example, a company is more likely to be the victim of a fraud than of an earthquake, and employees are more likely to make unintentional errors than they are to commit fraud. The likelihood of an earthquake may be small, but the impact can be enormous. It could completely destroy a company and force it into bankruptcy. The impact from a fraud is usually not as great, as most frauds do not threaten a company's existence. The impact from unintentional errors has a broad range of effects, depending on the nature of the error and how long it persists. Likelihood and impact must be considered together. As either increases, both the materiality of the event and the need to protect against it rise.

Software tools have been developed to help automate the risk assessment and response process. For example, Blue Cross Blue Shield of Florida uses an ERM software system that lets managers enter a perceived risk. Then, using a rules engine built around risk assessment, all managers affected by the perceived risk are prompted to think through the risk—its nature, likelihood, and impact—and eventually assign it a numerical rating. By aggregating the rankings of all the managers, a companywide assessment of the risk is developed.

Identify Controls

Management must identify one or more controls that will protect the company from each event. In evaluating the benefits of specific internal control procedures, management should consider their effectiveness and timing. All other factors being equal, a preventive control is superior to a detective one. However, if preventive controls fail, detective controls are essential for discovering the problem, and corrective controls help recover from the problem. Thus, preventive, detective, and corrective controls complement each other, and a good internal control system should employ all three. Similarly, a company should make use of the four levers of control discussed previously in this chapter.

Estimate Costs and Benefits

No internal control system can provide foolproof protection against all events, as the cost would be prohibitive. In addition, because many controls negatively affect operational efficiency, too many controls slow the system and make it inefficient. Therefore, the objective in designing an internal control system is to provide, at an affordable cost and without unduly slowing the system, reasonable assurance that events and other control problems do not take place.

The benefits of an internal control procedure must exceed its costs. Benefits, which can be hard to quantify, include increased sales and productivity, reduced losses, better integration with customers and suppliers, increased customer loyalty, competitive advantages, and lower insurance premiums. Costs are usually easier to measure than benefits. The primary cost element is personnel, including the time to perform control procedures, the costs of hiring additional employees to achieve effective segregation of duties, and the costs of programming controls into a computer system.

One way to estimate the value of internal controls involves **expected loss**, the mathematical product of impact and likelihood:

$$\text{Expected loss} = \text{Impact} \times \text{Likelihood}$$

The value of a control procedure is the difference between the expected loss with the control procedure(s) and the expected loss without it.

Determine Cost/Benefit Effectiveness

After estimating benefits and costs, management determines if the control is cost beneficial. For example, at Atlantic Richfield data errors occasionally required an entire payroll to be reprocessed at a cost of $10,000. Management determined that a data validation step would reduce the likelihood of this event from 15% to 1%, at a cost of $600 per pay period. The cost/benefit analysis that management used to determine if the validation step should be employed is shown in Table 6-3.

If the proposed payroll validation procedure is not utilized, then the expected loss to the company is $1,500. Because the expected loss with the validation step is $100, the control provides an expected benefit of $1,400. After deducting the control costs of $600, the validation step provides a net benefit of $800. Clearly it should be implemented.

In evaluating internal control costs and benefits, management must consider factors other than those in the expected benefit calculation. For example, if an event threatens an organization's existence, it may be worthwhile to spend more than indicated by the cost/benefit analysis to minimize the possibility that the organization will perish. This extra cost can be viewed as a catastrophic loss insurance premium.

Implement Control or Avoid, Share, or Accept the Risk

When controls are cost-effective, they should be implemented so that risk can be reduced. Risks that are not reduced must be accepted, shared, or avoided. Companies typically accept risk when it is within the company's risk tolerance range. An example would be a risk with a very small likelihood of occurring and whose impact is small. A reduce or share response is used to bring residual risk into an acceptable risk tolerance range. An avoid response is typically only used when there is no way to cost-effectively bring risk into an acceptable risk tolerance range.

Control Activities

The sixth component of COSO's ERM model is **control activities**, which are policies, procedures, and rules that provide reasonable assurance that management's control objectives are met and the risk responses are carried out. It is management's responsibility to develop a secure and adequately controlled system. Controls are much more effective when placed in the system as it is built, rather than as an afterthought. As a result, managers need to involve systems analysts, designers, and end users when designing computer-based control systems.

Management must also establish a set of procedures to ensure control compliance and enforcement. The corporate information security officer and the operations staff are typically responsible for ensuring that control procedures are followed.

	Without Validation Procedure	With Validation Procedure	Net Expected Difference
Cost to reprocess entire payroll	$10,000	$10,000	
Risk of payroll data errors	15%	1%	
Expected reprocessing cost ($10,000 × risk)	$1,500	$100	$1,400
Cost of validation procedure	$0	$600	$(600)
Net expected benefit of validation procedure			$800

Table 6-3
Cost/Benefit Analysis of Payroll Validation Procedure

It is especially important to ensure that control activities are in place during the end-of-the-year holiday season. Research shows that a disproportionate amount of computer fraud and security break-ins takes place during this time. Some reasons for this are (1) extended employee vacations and fewer people to "mind the store," (2) students out of school with more time on their hands, and (3) counterculture hackers getting lonely this time of year and increasing their attacks on systems.

Generally, control procedures fall into one of the following categories:

1 Proper authorization of transactions and activities
2 Segregation of duties
3 Project development and acquisition controls
4 Change management controls
5 Design and use of documents and records
6 Safeguarding assets, records, and data
7 Independent checks on performance

Focus 6-1 discusses how a violation of specific control activities, combined with internal environment factors, resulted in fraud within a Midwestern school district.

Proper Authorization of Transactions and Activities

Employees perform tasks and make decisions that affect company assets. Because management lacks the time and resources to supervise each activity and decision, it establishes policies for employees to follow and then empowers them to perform them

6-1 FOCUS — Control Problems in a School District

The director of finance for a Midwestern school district with 42 schools hired a CPA firm to audit the school district's books. The completed audit report was accompanied by a report showing that the district's system had some serious internal control deficiencies. The director, a former auditor, set out to improve the control system. The district (1) selected a new software package that all sites would use, (2) standardized accounting and bookkeeping procedures, (3) instituted consistent purchase order procedures, (4) implemented a separation of duties, and (5) created a control system for student vending machine cash and inventory.

As the changes were being made, the director noted that book collection fees for the middle school were low. He asked the district's internal auditor to investigate. The auditor contacted the middle school secretary, who was responsible for making daily deposits of all student fees and writing checks to the central office for book fees. The secretary said the low amount was due to the increase in the number of fees waived by the principal for students who qualified for free or reduced lunches.

The principal denied that he was waiving the fee. The principal, the auditor, and the director examined the fee cards for each child. Their investigation showed that the daily deposits into the activity checking account did not agree with the dates stamped paid on the student fee cards. A search of the premises revealed no uncashed

checks. So where did the money go, and how did the secretary manage to take it when most of the fees were paid with checks made out to the school?

They finally discovered that the secretary was also in charge of the faculty welfare and vending machine receipts fund. The district was not responsible for the fund, and so it was never audited or examined. Nor was the fund subject to the newly implemented system of internal controls. Deposits to the welfare fund were checks from the faculty and cash from the vending machines.

An examination of the available records revealed how the $20,000 fraud took place. The secretary stole all cash received from the vending machines. She also wrote and recorded checks to vendors, and on some checks she erased the name of the payee and replaced it with her name. She deposited student fees into the faculty welfare fund to cover up the stolen money.

The secretary was immediately discharged for improper bookkeeping practices. Because the secretary was bonded, the district was able to recover all of its missing funds.

The school district made changes to strengthen its control. Internal auditors now examine all funds at the schools. The control of faculty welfare funds was transferred to a faculty member. The investigation also revealed that the secretary had a prior criminal record. As a result, a background check was required for all future hires.

accordingly. This empowerment, called **authorization**, is an important part of an organization's control procedures. Authorizations are often documented by signing, initializing, or entering an authorization code on a transaction document or record. Computer systems are now capable of recording a **digital signature**, a means of signing a document with a piece of data that cannot be forged. Digital signatures are discussed in more depth in Chapter 7.

Employees who process transactions should verify the presence of the appropriate authorization(s). Auditors review transactions to verify proper authorization, as their absence indicates a possible control problem. For example, when reviewing purchases, Jason Scott discovered that some did not have a purchase requisition. Instead, they had been "personally authorized" by Bill Springer, the purchasing vice president. In addition, Jason found that some vendor invoice payments had been authorized without proper supporting documents, such as purchase orders and receiving reports. These findings raise questions about the adequacy of Springer's internal control procedures.

Certain activities or transactions may be of such consequence that management grants **specific authorization** for them to occur. For example, management review and approval may be required for sales in excess of $20,000, capital expenditures in excess of $10,000, or uncollectible write-offs in excess of $5,000. In contrast, management can authorize employees to handle routine transactions without special approval, a procedure known as **general authorization**. Management should have written policies on both specific and general authorization for all types of transactions.

Segregation of Duties

Good internal control requires that no single employee be given too much responsibility over business transactions or processes. An employee should not be in a position to commit *and* conceal fraud. Segregation of duties is discussed in two separate sections: segregation of accounting duties and segregation of systems duties.

Segregation of Accounting Duties

As shown in Figure 6-3, effective **segregation of accounting duties** is achieved when the following functions are separated:

- **Authorization**—approving transactions and decisions
- **Recording**—preparing source documents; entering data into online systems; maintaining journals, ledgers, files or databases; preparing reconciliations; and preparing performance reports
- **Custody**—handling cash, tools, inventory, or fixed assets; receiving incoming customer checks; writing checks on the organization's bank account

If two of these three functions are the responsibility of a single person, then problems can arise. For example, the former city treasurer of Fairfax, Virginia, was convicted of embezzling $600,000 from the city treasury. When residents used cash to pay their taxes, she would keep the currency. She recorded tax collections on the property tax records but did not report them to the city controller. Eventually, she made an adjusting journal entry to bring her records into agreement with those of the controller. When the treasurer received cash to pay for business license fees or court fees, she recorded these transactions on a cash register and deposited this money daily. She stole some of this cash and made up discrepancies in the bank deposit by substituting miscellaneous checks received in the mail that would not be missed when they went unrecorded. Because the treasurer was responsible for both the *custody* of cash receipts and the *recording* of those receipts, she was able to steal cash receipts and falsify the accounts to conceal the theft.

Figure 6-3
Separation of Duties

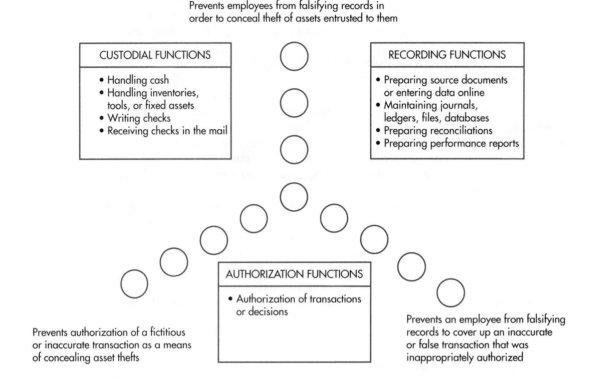

The utilities director of Newport Beach, California, who was responsible for *authorizing* transactions and had *custody* of cash, was charged with embezzling $1.2 million. He forged invoices or easement documents (the right to pass through a person's land) authorizing payments to a real or fictitious property owner. Finance department officials gave him the checks to deliver to the property owners. He forged signatures, endorsed the checks to himself, and deposited them in his own account. Because he was given physical custody of checks relating to transactions that he had authorized, he was able to authorize fictitious transactions and steal the payments.

The payroll director of the Los Angeles Dodgers, who was responsible for both authorization and recording functions, pleaded guilty to embezzling $330,000 from the team. He credited employees for hours not worked and then received a kickback of 50% of their extra compensation. He also added fictitious names to the Dodgers payroll and cashed the paychecks. The fraud was discovered when the payroll director became ill and another employee took over his duties. Since the perpetrator was responsible for both *authorizing* the hiring of new employees and for *recording* employee hours worked, he did not need to prepare or handle the actual paychecks. The club treasurer would simply mail the checks to an address specified by the payroll director.

In modern information systems, the computer often can be programmed to perform one or more of the already mentioned functions—in essence, replacing employees. The principle of separating duties remains the same; the only difference is that the computer, not a human, performs the function. For example, gas stations use pumps that allow customers to insert a credit card to pay for their gas. The computer performs both the custody of the "cash" and the recording function. In addition to improving internal controls, these machines better serve the customer by increasing convenience and eliminating lines to pay for the gas.

In a system that incorporates an effective separation of duties, it should be difficult for any single employee to commit embezzlement successfully. Detecting fraud where two or more people are in **collusion** to override the preventive aspect of the internal control system is more difficult. When two or more people work together, it is much easier for perpetrators to conceal the fraud. For example, two women employed by a credit card company colluded to steal funds. One woman was authorized to set up credit card accounts, the other to write off unpaid accounts of less than $1,000. The first woman created a new account for each of them using fictitious data. When the amounts outstanding neared the $1,000 limit, the woman in collections wrote them off. The first woman would then create two new cards, and the process would be repeated. The women were caught when the jilted boyfriend of one of them sought revenge. He called the credit card company and disclosed the fraudulent scheme.

Employees can collude with other employees or with the company's customers or vendors. The most frequent forms of employee/vendor collusion include billing at inflated prices, performing substandard work and receiving full payment, payment for nonperformance, duplicate billings, and improperly funneling more work to, or purchasing more goods from, a colluding company. The most frequent forms of employee/customer collusion include unauthorized loans or insurance payments, receipt of assets or services at unauthorized discount prices, forgiveness of amounts owed, and unauthorized extension of due dates.

Segregation of Systems Duties

In a highly integrated information system, procedures once performed by separate individuals are combined. Therefore, any person who has unrestricted access to the computer, its programs, and live data could perpetrate and conceal fraud. To combat this threat, organizations must implement control procedures such as the effective **segregation of systems duties** within the information system function. Authority and responsibility must be divided clearly among the following functions:

1 **Systems administration. Systems administrators** are responsible for ensuring that the different parts of an information system operate smoothly and efficiently.

2 **Network management. Network managers** ensure that all applicable devices are linked to the organization's internal and external networks and that the networks operate continuously and properly.

3 **Security management. Security management** ensures that all aspects of the system are secure and protected from all internal and external threats.

4 **Change management.** These individuals manage all changes to an organization's information system to ensure they are made smoothly and efficiently and to prevent errors and fraud.

5 **Users.** Users record transactions, authorize data to be processed, and use system output.

6 **Systems analysis. Systems analysts** help users determine their information needs and then design an information system to meet those needs.

7 **Programming. Programmers** take the design provided by systems analysts and create an information system by writing the computer programs.

8 **Computer operations. Computer operators** run the software on the company's computers. They ensure that data are input properly and correctly processed and needed output is produced.

9 **Information system library.** The information system librarian maintains custody of corporate databases, files, and programs in a separate storage area called the **information system library**.

10 **Data control.** The **data control group** ensures that source data have been properly approved, monitors the flow of work through the computer, reconciles

input and output, maintains a record of input errors to ensure their correction and resubmission, and distributes systems output.

It is important that different people perform these functions. Allowing a person to do two or more jobs exposes the company to the possibility of fraud. For example, if a programmer for a credit union was allowed to use actual data to test her program, she could erase her car loan balance while conducting the test. Likewise, if a computer operator has access to programming logic and documentation, he might, while processing the company payroll program, be able to increase his salary.

In addition to adequate segregation of duties, organizations should ensure that the people who design, develop, implement, and operate the company's information system are qualified and well trained. The same holds true for those in charge of system security.

Project Development and Acquisition Controls

It is important to have a formal, appropriate, and proven methodology to govern the development, acquisition, implementation, and maintenance of information systems and related technologies. The methodology should contain appropriate controls for management review and approval, user involvement, analysis, design, testing, implementation, and conversion. The methodology also should make it possible for management to trace information inputs from their source to their final disposition or from their final disposition back to the original source (the audit trail). The methodologies used to develop or acquire systems are discussed in more detail in Chapters 18 through 20.

Examples abound of poorly managed projects that have wasted large sums of money because project management controls were ignored. For example, the Oklahoma State Insurance Fund terminated a software development contract when the project fell several months behind schedule and went $1 million over budget.

To minimize failures and reduce cost overruns, while substantially improving system efficiency and effectiveness, the following principles of control should be applied to systems development:

1 **Strategic master plan.** To align an organization's information system with its business strategies, a multiyear **strategic master plan** is developed and updated yearly. It shows the projects that must be completed to achieve long-range company goals and addresses the company's hardware, software, personnel, and infrastructure requirements.

2 **Project controls.** A **project development plan** shows how a project will be completed, including the modules or tasks to be performed and who will perform them, the dates they should be completed, and project costs. The plan should specify **project milestones**—or significant points when progress is reviewed and actual and estimated completion times are compared. Each project should be assigned to a manager and team who should be held responsible for the success or failure of the project. A **performance evaluation** of project team members should be prepared as each project is completed.

3 **Data processing schedule.** To maximize the use of scarce computer resources, all data processing tasks should be organized according to a **data processing schedule**.

4 **Steering committee.** A **steering committee** should be formed to guide and oversee systems development and acquisition.

5 **System performance measurements.** For a system to be evaluated properly, it must be assessed using **system performance measurements**. Common measurements include **throughput** (output per unit of time), **utilization** (percentage of time the system is being productively used), and **response time** (how long it takes the system to respond).

6 Postimplementation review. After a development project is completed, a **post-implementation review** should be performed to determine if the anticipated benefits were achieved.

To simplify and improve systems development, some companies hire a **systems integrator**, a vendor who uses common standards and manages a cooperative systems development effort involving its own development personnel and those of the client and other vendors. These third-party systems development projects are subject to the same cost overruns and missed deadlines as systems developed internally. For example, Westpac Banking Corporation began a five-year, $85 million systems development project to decentralize Westpac's information systems, generate new financial products, and downsize its internal AIS department. Three years and nearly $150 million later, no usable results had been attained and it was clear the scheduled completion date would not be met. With a runaway on its hands, Westpac fired IBM, the primary software developer, and brought in Accenture to review the project and develop recommendations for salvaging it.

When using systems integrators, companies should use the same basic rules of project management and control as on internal projects. In addition, they should do the following:

- **Develop clear specifications.** Before third parties bid on a project, clear specifications must be developed, including exact descriptions and definitions of the system, explicit deadlines, and precise acceptance criteria. Suffolk County, New York, spent 12 months and $500,000 preparing detailed specifications for a new $16 million criminal justice information system before accepting bids. Only 6 of the 22 integrators that had originally expressed interest bid on the project due to the county's rigorous cost and quality standards. County officials believe their diligent up-front efforts helped ensure their new system's success and saved the county $3 million.
- **Monitor the systems integration project.** Companies should establish formal procedures for measuring and reporting the status of the project. The best approach is to divide the project into manageable tasks, assign responsibility for each task, and then meet at least monthly to review progress and assess quality.

Change Management Controls

Organizations constantly modify their information systems to reflect new business practices and to take advantage of advances in information technology. **Change management** is the process of making sure changes do not negatively affect systems reliability, security, confidentiality, integrity, and availability. Change management controls are discussed in Chapter 8.

Design and Use of Documents and Records

The proper design and use of electronic and paper documents and records help ensure the accurate and complete recording of all relevant transaction data. Their form and content should be kept as simple as possible to promote efficient record keeping, minimize recording errors, and facilitate review and verification. Documents that initiate a transaction should contain a space for authorizations. Those used to transfer assets to someone else should have a space for the receiving party's signature. To reduce the likelihood of documents being used fraudulently, they should be sequentially prenumbered so each can be accounted for. A good audit trail facilitates tracing individual transactions through the system, the correction of errors, and the verification of system output. Document, form, and input screen design are discussed in more detail in Chapter 20.

Safeguard Assets, Records, and Data

In addition to safeguarding cash and physical assets such as inventory and equipment, a company needs to protect its information. For example, a Reuters reporter noticed that Intentia, a Swedish software developer, released its first and second quarter earnings reports on Web sites with nearly identical Web addresses. When he typed in his guess for the third-quarter Web address, he found the company's as yet unreleased numbers and ran a story on the disappointing third-quarter results. Upset at the premature release of its numbers, Intentia filed criminal hacking charges against Reuters that were dismissed eventually. The Swedish Stock Exchange censored Intentia for placing its financial information on an unprotected and public Web site, thereby not providing adequate protection of its financial information.

Many people mistakenly believe that the greatest risks companies face are from outsiders. However, studies show that company employees are a much greater risk when it comes to loss of data, as they know the system and its weakness better and are therefore better able to hide their illegal acts. In a recent poll, almost 50% of the companies reported that insiders had accessed data without the proper authorization. Often they do more than just access the data. For example, a software engineer at America Online was arrested and charged with stealing and selling 92 million e-mail addresses. The engineer allegedly used the ID and password of one of the AOL employees authorized to access the company's confidential customer database. Authorities claim the engineer sold the names to the owner of an Internet gambling business, who used them to help his company increase earnings by $10,000 to $20,000 a day. The alleged data theft was not uncovered for almost a year, until an anonymous tipster informed authorities that the gambling business owner was reselling the names to spammers selling herbal male enhancement products.

There are other, less intentional threats to company data from insiders, such as accidentally deleting company data, letting viruses loose by opening virus-laden e-mail attachments, or trying to fix hardware or software without the appropriate expertise. These can result in crashed networks, corrupt data, and hardware and software malfunctions.

Companies also face significant risks from customers and vendors that have access to company data. For example, Scott Levine was accused of perpetrating one of the largest data thefts in history. Levine worked for a company that did business with Acxiom, a company that gathers data about almost everyone in America. Acxiom created very powerful data analysis software to provide data to consumers such as insurers, direct marketers, banks, and credit bureaus. When needed, Acxiom provided customers and vendors with user IDs and passwords so they could interface with its database. Levine was accused of misusing a legitimate ID and password to secretly download millions of names, e-mail and home addresses, and personal and financial information such as income, employment data, home value, type of car driven, and the number of people in the household. He allegedly used the data at his company, called Snipermail, to mail advertisements for his customers.

Many steps can be taken to safeguard both information and physical assets from theft, unauthorized use, and vandalism. Chapters 7 and 8 discuss the many computer-based controls that can be put into place to safeguard assets. In addition, it is important to

- **Create and enforce appropriate policies and procedures.** The first step in safeguarding assets is to develop appropriate policies and procedures. Unfortunately, all too often they are created but not adequately enforced. For example, a laptop containing the names, Social Security numbers, and birth dates of 26.5 million people was stolen from the home of a Veteran Affairs (VA) Department analyst. The VA did not enforce its policy that this sensitive data not leave VA offices. Nor did it enforce its policy that this sensitive data be encrypted. The cost to taxpayers of

notifying all 26.5 million people and buying them a credit-checking service was $100 million. Two years prior to the theft, an inspector general report identified the inadequate control of sensitive data as a weakness, but it had never been addressed.

- **Maintain accurate records of all assets.** Periodically reconcile the recorded amounts of company assets such as inventory, equipment, cash, and securities to physical counts of those assets.
- **Restrict access to assets.** Restricted storage areas are used to protect inventories and equipment. Cash registers, safes, lockboxes, and safety deposit boxes limit access to cash, securities, and paper assets. Over $1 million was embezzled from Perini Corp. because of poor controls. Blank checks were kept in an unlocked storeroom. Employees simply took a check, made it out to a fictitious vendor, ran it through the check-signing machine, which was left unlocked, and cashed the check.
- **Protect records and documents.** Fireproof storage areas, locked filing cabinets, backup files, and off-site backup locations are effective means of protecting records and documents. Access to blank checks and documents should be limited to authorized personnel. In Inglewood, California, a janitor was charged with stealing 34 blank checks while cleaning the city finance office. He forged the names of city officials on the checks and cashed them in amounts ranging from $50,000 to $470,000.

Independent Checks on Performance

Internal checks to ensure that transactions are processed accurately are another important control element. These checks should be independent, because they are more effective if performed by someone other than the person who is responsible for the original operation. The following independent checks are typically used in businesses:

- **Top-level reviews.** Management at all levels should monitor company results and periodically compare actual company performance to (a) planned performance, as shown in budgets, targets, and forecasts; (b) prior period performance; and (c) the performance of competitors.
- **Analytical reviews.** An **analytical review** is an examination of the relationships between different sets of data. For example, as credit sales increase, so should accounts receivable. In addition, there are relationships between sales and other accounts such as cost of goods sold, inventory, and freight out. Management should periodically analyze and review these relationships to detect fraud and other business problems.
- **Reconciliation of two independently maintained sets of records.** One way to check the accuracy and completeness of records is to reconcile them with other records that should have the same balance. For example, a bank reconciliation verifies that company checking accounts agree with bank statements. Another example is comparing the accounts receivable subsidiary ledger total with the accounts receivable total in the general ledger.
- **Comparison of actual quantities with recorded amounts.** Periodically count significant assets and reconcile the count to company records. The cash in a cash register drawer at the end of each clerk's shift should be the same as the amount recorded on the cash register tape. All inventories should be counted at least annually and the results compared with inventory records. High-dollar-value items, such as jewelry, should be counted more frequently.
- **Double-entry accounting.** The maxim that debits must equal credits provides numerous opportunities for internal checks. For example, debits in a payroll entry may be allocated to numerous inventory and/or expense accounts

by the cost accounting department. Credits are allocated to several liability accounts for wages and salaries payable, taxes withheld, employee insurance, union dues, and so on by the payroll department. At the conclusion of these two complex operations, the comparison of total debits with total credits provides a powerful check on the accuracy of both processes. Any discrepancy indicates the presence of one or more errors.

- **Independent review.** After one person processes a transaction, a second person sometimes reviews the work of the first. The second person checks for proper authorization signatures, reviews supporting documents, and checks the accuracy of crucial data items such as prices, quantities, and extensions.

Information and Communication

The seventh component of COSO's ERM model is information and communication. The primary purpose of an AIS is to gather, record, process, store, summarize, and communicate information about an organization. This means accountants must understand how (1) transactions are initiated, (2) data are captured in machine-readable form or converted from source documents to machine-readable form, (3) computer files are accessed and updated, (4) data are processed, and (5) information is reported to internal users and external parties. Accountants must also understand the accounting records and procedures, supporting documents, and specific financial statement accounts involved in processing and reporting transactions. These items make it possible for the system to have an audit trail. An **audit trail** exists when individual company transactions can be traced through the system from where they originate to where they end up on the financial statements. Likewise, the numbers on the financial statements can be traced back through the system to the individual transactions making up the balance.

According to the AICPA, an AIS has five primary objectives:

1 **Identify and record all valid transactions.** For example, if a company intentionally records a fictitious sale, it can overstate revenues and net income. If a company forgets to record some expenses at the year's end, expenses are understated and net income is overstated.
2 **Properly classify transactions.** For example, improperly classifying an expense as an asset overstates assets and net income.
3 **Record transactions at their proper monetary value.** For example, an account receivable that becomes uncollectible should be written off.
4 **Record transactions in the proper accounting period.** For example, recording 2006 sales in 2005 overstates sales and net income for 2005 and has the opposite effect for 2006.
5 **Properly present transactions and related disclosures in the financial statements.** For example, failing to disclose a lawsuit or a contingent liability could mislead the reader of a financial statement.

Accounting systems generally consist of several accounting subsystems, each designed to process transactions of a particular type. Although they differ with respect to the type of transactions processed, all accounting subsystems follow the same sequence of procedures. These procedures are referred to as accounting cycles. The five major accounting cycles and their related control objectives and procedures are detailed in Chapters 10 through 14.

Monitoring

The eighth component of COSO's ERM model is monitoring company performance. Monitoring can be accomplished with a series of ongoing events or by separate evaluations. Key methods of monitoring performance are now discussed.

Perform ERM Evaluations

ERM effectiveness can be measured by conducting an ERM evaluation, either through a formal evaluation or through a self-assessment process. A special group can be assembled to conduct the evaluation, or it can be turned over to internal auditing.

Implement Effective Supervision

Effective supervision involves training and assisting employees, monitoring their performance, correcting errors, and safeguarding assets by overseeing employees who have access to them. Supervision is especially important in organizations that cannot afford elaborate responsibility reporting or are too small to have an adequate segregation of duties.

Use Responsibility Accounting

Responsibility accounting systems include budgets, quotas, schedules, standard costs, and quality standards; performance reports that compare actual with planned performance and highlight significant variances; and procedures for investigating significant variances and taking timely action to correct the conditions leading to such variances.

Monitor System Activities

Risk analysis and management software packages are available to review computer and network security measures, detect illegal entry into systems, test for weaknesses and vulnerabilities, report weaknesses found, and suggest improvements. Cost parameters can be entered to balance acceptable levels of risk tolerance and cost-effectiveness. Software is also available to monitor and combat viruses, spyware, adware, spam, phishing, and other inappropriate e-mails. They also block pop-up ads and prevent browsers from being hijacked. Software can also validate a phone caller's identity by comparing the caller's voice to a previously recorded voiceprint. Software can also help companies recover from frauds and malicious actions. One such software package helped a company recover from a rampage caused by a disgruntled employee who had received a negative performance evaluation. The perpetrator ripped cards and cables out of PCs, changed the inventory control files, and edited the password file to stop people from logging on to the network. Shortly after the incident, the software identified the corrupted files and flashed an alert to company headquarters. The damage was undone by issuing simple commands to the utility software, which restored the corrupted file to its original status.

All system transactions and activities should be recorded in a log that indicates who accessed what data, when, and from which online device. These logs should be reviewed frequently to monitor system activity and trace any problems to their source. The data collected can be used to evaluate employee productivity, control company costs, fight corporate espionage and other attacks, and comply with legal requirements. For example, one company used the data it collected to analyze why one particular employee had almost zero productivity. An analysis of his computer usage showed that he spent six to seven hours a day visiting Internet pornography sites.

The Privacy Foundation estimated that one-third of all American workers with access to computers are monitored, and that number is expected to increase.

Companies who monitor system activities need to make sure they do not violate employee privacy. One way to do that is to have written policies that employees agree to in writing and indicate the following:

- The technology employees use on the job belongs to the company.
- E-mails received on company computers are not private and can be read by supervisory personnel. This policy allowed a large pharmaceutical company to electronically monitor employee e-mails to identify, and then terminate, the employee who was e-mailing confidential drug-manufacturing data outside the company.
- Employees should not use technology in any way to contribute to a hostile work environment.

Track Purchased Software and Mobile Devices

The Business Software Alliance (BSA) is very aggressive in tracking down and fining companies that violate software license agreements. To comply with copyrights and protect themselves from software piracy lawsuits, companies should periodically conduct software audits. Of key concern is making sure there are enough licenses for all users and that the company is not paying for more licenses than are needed. Employees should be informed of the consequences of using unlicensed software.

An increasing number of mobile devices are able to access company networks. These devices need to be tracked and monitored, as the loss of a laptop or other device could represent a substantial exposure to a company. Among the items that must be tracked are who has mobile devices, what devices they have, what tasks they perform with those devices, what built-in security features the devices have, and what software needs to be installed to maintain adequate system and network security.

Conduct Periodic Audits

One way to monitor risk and detect fraud and errors is to conduct periodic external and internal audits, as well as special network security audits. Care must be exercised to make sure employees' privacy rights are not violated during the audits. Informing employees that auditors will conduct a random surveillance not only helps resolve the privacy issue but also significantly deters computer crime and reduces errors. Auditors should regularly test system controls and periodically browse system usage files looking for suspicious activities. For example, during a security audit at a West Coast health care company, auditors pretending to be computer support staff persuaded 16 of 22 employees to reveal their user IDs and passwords. They also found that employees testing a new system had inadvertently left the company's network exposed to outside attacks. Systems auditing is explained in more depth in Chapter 9.

Internal auditing involves reviewing the reliability and integrity of financial and operating information and providing an appraisal of internal control effectiveness. It also involves assessing employee compliance with management policies and procedures and applicable laws and regulations as well as evaluating the efficiency and effectiveness of management. For example, internal audits can detect excess overtime, underused assets, obsolete inventory, padded travel expense reimbursements, excessively loose budgets and quotas, poorly justified capital expenditures, and production bottlenecks. Objectivity and effectiveness require that the internal audit function be organizationally independent of accounting and operating functions. For example, the head of internal auditing should report to the audit committee of the board of directors, rather than to the controller or chief financial officer.

One alert internal auditor noted that a department supervisor took the entire office staff out to lunch in a limousine on her birthday. During the remainder of the audit, he noted other evidences of an extravagant lifestyle. Questioning if her salary could support her lifestyle, he began a more in-depth investigation. He found that she had set up several fictitious vendors, sent the company invoices from these vendors, and then

cashed the checks when they were mailed to her. Over a period of several years, she had embezzled over $12 million.

Employ a Computer Security Officer, a Chief Compliance Officer, and Computer Consultants

A **computer security officer (CSO)** is in charge of AIS security and should be independent of the information system function and report to the chief operating officer (COO) or the CEO. Prior to SOX, the chief financial officer (CFO) usually handled financial compliance and the COO and others handled other types of compliance. The overwhelming number of new tasks related to SOX and other forms of compliance has led many larger companies to delegate all compliance issues to a **chief compliance officer** (CCO). In addition, many companies use outside computer consultants or in-house teams to test and evaluate their security procedures and computer systems. The use of a CSO and computer consultants is discussed in greater depth in Chapter 7.

Engage Forensic Specialists

Forensic accountants specialize in fraud detection and investigation. Forensic accounting is one of the fastest-growing areas of accounting due to the Sarbanes–Oxley law, new accounting rules such as SAS No. 99, and boards of directors demanding that forensic accounting be an ongoing part of the financial reporting and corporate governance process. Most forensic accountants are CPAs, and many have received specialized training with the FBI, the IRS, or other law enforcement agencies. Some of the forensic accountants in greatest demand are those with the necessary computer skills to ferret out and combat today's fraud perpetrators, who are using sophisticated technology to commit complex frauds and accounting scams. A professional certification program, the Certified Fraud Examiner (CFE), was developed by the Association of Certified Fraud Examiners. To become a CFE, candidates must pass a two-day exam. Currently there are over 25,000 CFEs worldwide.

Management may also need to call on **computer forensics specialists** for help. Computer forensics is discovering, extracting, safeguarding, and documenting computer evidence such that its authenticity, accuracy and integrity will not succumb to legal challenges. Some have likened computer forensics to performing an autopsy on a computer system to determine if a computer crime was committed and who committed it and then marshalling the evidence that lawyers need to prove it in court. Some of the more common things investigated are improper Internet usage; fraud; sabotage; the loss, theft, or corruption of data; retrieving information from e-mails and databases that users thought they had erased; and figuring out who performed certain actions on a computer. For example, a Deloitte & Touche forensics team uncovered evidence that was instrumental in the conviction of a Giant Supermarket purchasing manager who accepted over $600,000 in supplier kickbacks.

Install Fraud Detection Software

People who commit fraud tend to follow certain patterns and leave behind clues, such as things that do not make sense. Software has been developed to uncover these fraud symptoms. For example, a health insurance company could use fraud detection software to review how often procedures are performed, if a diagnosis and the procedures performed fit a patient's profile, how long a procedure takes, and how far patients live from the doctor's office. ReliaStar Financial used a fraud detection package from IBM to detect the following:

- Hundreds of thousands of dollars in fraudulent claims from a Los Angeles chiropractor. The software noticed that all of the chiropractor's patients lived more than 50 miles from the doctor's office, so it flagged the bills for investigation.

- A Long Island doctor who submitted bills weekly for a rare and expensive procedure that is normally done only once or twice in a lifetime.
- A podiatrist who saw four patients and then billed ReliaStar for almost 500 separate procedures.

Other companies have **neural networks** (programs that mimic the brain and have learning capabilities), which are quite accurate in identifying suspected fraud. For example, the Visa and MasterCard operation at Mellon Bank uses neural network software to track 1.2 million accounts. Its neural network can spot the illegal use of a credit card and notify the owner shortly after it is stolen. The software can also spot trends before bank investigators do. For example, one investigator learned about a new fraud from another bank. When he went to the system to have it check for the fraud, he noticed that the neural network had already identified the fraud and had printed out a list of transactions that fit its pattern. The software cost Mellon Bank less than $1 million and paid for itself in six months. These and other recent advances in fraud detection software have reduced the incidence of credit card fraud to less than 0.06% of all transactions.

Implement a Fraud Hotline

People witnessing fraudulent behavior are often torn between two conflicting feelings. They want to protect company assets and report fraud perpetrators, yet they are uncomfortable in the whistle-blower role and find it easier to remain silent. This reluctance is even stronger if they are aware of whistle-blowers who have been ostracized or persecuted by their coworkers or superiors or have had their careers damaged.

The Sarbanes–Oxley law mandates that companies set up mechanisms for employees to report abuses such as fraud. An effective way to comply with the law and resolve whistle-blower conflict is to provide employees with **fraud hotlines** so they can anonymously report fraud. In one study, researchers found that 33% of the 212 frauds studied were detected through anonymous tips. The insurance industry set up a hotline to control an estimated $17 billion a year in fraudulent claims. In the first month, more than 2,250 calls were received; 15% of these resulted in investigative action. The downside of hotlines is that many of the calls are not worthy of investigation. Some are made seeking revenge, others are vague reports of wrongdoing, and others have no merit.

A potential problem with a hotline is that those who operate it may report to people who are involved in top-management fraud. Using a fraud hotline set up by a trade organization or commercial company can overcome this threat. This company can pass reports of management fraud directly to the board of directors.

SUMMARY AND CASE CONCLUSION

After three days in Bozeman, Jason and Maria returned to Northwest's main office and filed their audit report. One week later, they were summoned to the office of Roger Sawyer, Northwest's director of internal auditing, to explain their findings. Shortly thereafter, a high-level internal audit team was dispatched to Bozeman to take a closer look at the situation.

When the audit team returned, Jason and Maria inquired about their findings and were told the situation was still under investigation. Six months later, a company newsletter included an announcement that the Springer family had sold its remaining 10% interest in the Bozeman business to Northwest and had resigned from all

management positions. Two Northwest executives were transferred in to replace them. Still, there was no word on the audit findings.

Two years later, Jason and Maria were assigned to a job supervised by Frank Ratliff, a member of the high-level internal audit team. After hours, Frank told them the story. Based on Jason and Maria's reports, the investigation team had examined a large sample of purchasing transactions and all employee timekeeping and payroll records for a 12-month period. The team had also taken a detailed physical inventory. The investigators discovered that the problems identified by Jason—including missing purchase requisitions, purchase orders, and receiving reports, as well as excessive prices—were widespread. They found that these problems occurred almost exclusively in transactions with three large vendors from whom Springer's had purchased several million dollars' worth of inventories and supplies. The team discussed the unusually high item prices with the vendors but did not receive a satisfactory explanation. However, a check of the county business-licensing bureau revealed that Bill Springer held a majority ownership interest in each of these three companies. By authorizing excessive prices to companies he owned, Springer had earned a significant share of several hundred thousand dollars of excessive profits, all at the expense of Northwest Industries.

The investigation team also found evidence that several of Springer's employees were paid for more hours than documented by timekeeping records. Finally, the team determined that Springer's inventory account was materially overstated. The physical inventory revealed that a significant portion of recorded inventory did not exist and that other portions were obsolete. The adjusting journal entry reflecting Springer's real inventory wiped out much of the outlet's profits over the past three years.

When confronted, the Springers vehemently denied any laws had been broken. Northwest considered going to the authorities for a formal fraud investigation but were concerned its case was not strong enough to prove in court. Northwest also worried that adverse publicity might damage the company's position in Bozeman. After months of negotiation, the Springers agreed to the settlement reported in the newsletter. Part of the settlement was that no public statement would be made about any alleged fraud or embezzlement involving the Springers. According to Frank, this policy was not unusual. In many cases of fraud, settlements are reached quietly, with no legal action taken, so the company can avoid adverse publicity.

KEY TERMS

threat 221
exposure 221
impact 221
likelihood 221
internal control 222
preventive control 222
detective control 222
corrective control 222
general control 222
application control 223
Foreign Corrupt Practices
 Act 223
Sarbanes–Oxley Act
 (SOX) 223
Public Company
 Accounting
 Oversight Board
 (PCAOB) 223

belief system 224
boundary system 224
diagnostic control
 system 225
interactive control
 system 225
Control Objectives for
 Information and related
 Technology
 (COBIT) 225
Committee of Sponsoring
 Organizations
 (COSO) 226
Internal Control—
 Integrated
 Framework 226
Enterprise Risk
 Management—

Integrated Framework
 (ERM) 226
strategic objective 227
operations objective 227
reporting objective 227
compliance objective 227
internal environment 229
risk appetite 230
audit committee 230
policy and procedures
 manual 232
background check 233
event 236
inherent risk 238
residual risk 239
expected loss 240
control activities 241
authorization 243

AIS IN ACTION

CHAPTER QUIZ

1 COSO identified five interrelated components of internal controls. Which of the following is *not* one of those five?
 a. risk assessment
 b. internal control policies
 c. monitoring
 d. information and communication

2 In the ERM model developed by COSO, there are four types of objectives that management must meet to achieve company goals. Which of the following is *not* one of those types?
 a. responsibility objectives
 b. strategic objectives
 c. compliance objectives
 d. reporting objectives
 e. operations objectives

3 Which of the following statements is true?
 a. The COSO report on enterprise risk management is narrow in scope and is limited to financial controls.
 b. COSO's internal control integrated framework report has been widely accepted as the authority on internal controls.
 c. The Foreign Corrupt Practices Act had no impact on internal accounting control systems.
 d. It is easier to add controls to an already designed system than to include them during the initial design stage.

4 All other things being equal, which of the following is true?
 a. Detective controls are superior to preventive controls.
 b. Corrective controls are superior to preventive controls.

c. Preventive controls are equivalent to detective controls.

d. Preventive controls are superior to detective controls.

5 Which of the following statements about the control environment is false?

a. Management's attitudes toward internal control and ethical behavior have little impact on employee beliefs or actions.

b. An overly complex or unclear organizational structure may be indicative of more serious problems.

c. A written policy and procedures manual is an important tool for assigning authority and responsibility.

d. Supervision is especially important in organizations that cannot afford elaborate responsibility reporting or are too small to have an adequate separation of duties.

6 To achieve effective segregation of duties, certain functions must be separated. Which of the following is the correct listing of the accounting-related functions that must be segregated?

a. control, recording, and monitoring

b. authorization, recording, and custody

c. control, custody, and authorization

d. monitoring, recording, and planning

7 Which of the following is not an independent check?

a. bank reconciliation

b. periodic comparison of subsidiary ledger totals to control accounts

c. trial balance

d. re-adding the total of a batch of invoices and comparing it with your first total

8 Which of the following is a control procedure relating to both the design and use of documents and records?

a. locking blank checks in a drawer

b. reconciling the bank account

c. sequentially prenumbering sales invoices

d. comparing actual physical quantities with recorded amounts

9 Which of the following is the correct order of the risk assessment steps discussed in this chapter?

a. Identify threats, estimate risk and exposure, identify controls, and estimate costs and benefits.

b. Identify controls, estimate risk and exposure, identify threats, and estimate costs and benefits.

c. Estimate risk and exposure, identify controls, identify threats, and estimate costs and benefits.

d. Estimate costs and benefits, identify threats, identify controls, and estimate risk and exposure.

10 Your current system is deemed to be 90% reliable. A major threat has been identified with an impact of $3,000,000. Two control procedures exist to deal with the threat. Implementation of control A would cost $100,000 and reduce the likelihood to 6%. Implementation of control B would cost $140,000 and reduce the likelihood to 4%. Implementation of both controls would cost $220,000 and reduce the likelihood to 2%. Given the data, and based solely on an economic analysis of costs and benefits, what should you do?

a. Implement control A only.

b. Implement control B only.

c. Implement both controls A and B.

d. Implement neither control.

DISCUSSION QUESTIONS

6.1 Answer the following questions about the audit of Springer's Northwest Lumber & Supply.
- **a.** What deficiencies existed in the internal environment at Springer's?
- **b.** Do you agree with the decision to settle with the Springers rather than prosecute them for fraud and embezzlement? Why or why not?
- **c.** Should the company have told Jason and Maria the results of the high-level audit? Why or why not?

6.2 Effective segregation of duties is sometimes not economically feasible in a small business. What internal control elements do you think can help compensate for this threat?

6.3 Some people believe that, instead of producing tangible benefits, business controls create resentment and loss of company morale. Discuss this position.

6.4 In recent years, Supersmurf's external auditors have given clean opinions on its financial statements and favorable evaluations of its internal control systems. Discuss whether it is necessary for this corporation to take any further action to comply with the Sarbanes–Oxley Act.

6.5 When you go to a movie theater, you buy a prenumbered ticket from the cashier. This ticket is then handed to another person at the entrance to the movie. What kinds of irregularities is the theater trying to prevent? What controls is it using to prevent these irregularities? What remaining risks or exposures can you identify?

PROBLEMS

6.1 You are an audit supervisor who has recently been assigned to a new client, Go-Go Corporation, which is listed on the New York Stock Exchange. You recently visited Go-Go's corporate headquarters to become acquainted with key personnel and to conduct a preliminary review of the company's accounting policies and systems. During this visit, the following events occurred:
- **a.** You met with Go-Go's audit committee, which consists of the corporate controller, treasurer, financial vice president, and budget director.
- **b.** You recognized the treasurer as a former aide to Ernie Eggers, who was convicted of fraud several years ago.
- **c.** Management explained its plans to change accounting methods for depreciation from the accelerated to the straight-line method. Management implied that, if your firm does not concur with this change, Go-Go will employ other auditors.
- **d.** You learned that the financial vice president manages a staff of five internal auditors.
- **e.** You noted that all management authority seems to reside with three brothers, who serve as chief executive officer, president, and financial vice president.
- **f.** You were told that the performance of division and department managers is evaluated on a subjective basis, because Go-Go's management believes that formal performance evaluation procedures are counterproductive.
- **g.** You learned that the company has reported increases in earnings per share for each of the past 25 quarters; however, earnings during the current quarter have leveled off and may decline.

h. You reviewed the company's policy and procedures manual, which listed policies for dealing with customers, vendors, and employees.

i. Your preliminary assessment is that the accounting systems are well designed and employ effective internal control procedures.

j. Some employees complained that some managers would, on occasion, contradict the instructions of other managers regarding proper data security procedures.

k. After a careful review of the budget for data security enhancement projects, you feel it appears to be adequate.

l. The new information systems project for an enhanced network firewall appeared to be on a very aggressive implementation schedule. The manager for IT mentioned that even if he put all of his personnel on this project for the next five weeks, he still would not be able to complete the project in time. The manager has mentioned this to company management, which seems unwilling to modify the schedule.

m. Several new employees have had trouble completing some of their duties, and they do not appear to know who to ask for help.

n. Go-Go's strategy is to achieve consistent growth for its shareholders. However, its policy is to not invest in any project unless its payback period is no more than 48 months and yields an internal rate of return that exceeds its cost of capital by 3%.

o. You observe that company purchasing agents wear clothing and exhibit other paraphernalia from major vendors. Also, while interviewing the purchasing department manager, you notice a picture on his desk of him holding a big fish on the deck of a very nice fishing boat that has the logo of a major Go-Go vendor painted on its wheelhouse.

Required

The information you have obtained suggests potential problems relating to one or more elements of Go-Go's internal environment. Identify the problems and explain them in relation to the internal environment concepts discussed in this chapter.

6.2 Explain how the principle of separation of duties is violated in each of the following situations. Also suggest one or more procedures to reduce the risk and exposure highlighted in each example.

a. A payroll clerk recorded a 40-hour work week for an employee who had quit the previous week. He then prepared a paycheck for this employee, forged her signature, and cashed the check.

b. While opening the mail, a cashier set aside, and subsequently cashed, two checks payable to the company on account.

c. A cashier prepared a fictitious invoice from a company using his brother-in-law's name. He wrote a check in payment of the invoice, which the brother-in-law later cashed.

d. An employee of the finishing department walked off with several parts from the storeroom and recorded the items in the inventory ledger as having been issued to the assembly department.

e. A cashier cashed a check from a customer in payment of an account receivable, pocketed the cash, and concealed the theft by properly posting the receipt to the customer's account in the accounts receivable ledger.

f. Several customers returned clothing purchases over a week's time. Instead of putting the returned clothing into a return bin to be put back on the rack, a clerk put the clothing in a separate bin under some cleaning rags. After her shift, she transferred the clothes to a gym bag and took them home.

g. A receiving clerk noticed that four cases of MP3 players were included in a shipment when only three were ordered. The clerk put the extra case aside and took it home after his shift ended.

h. An insurance claims adjuster had check signing authority of $6,000. The agent created three businesses that subsequently billed the insurance company for

work not performed on legitimate insurance claims. The agent signed the checks for the invoices. The invoices never exceeded $6,000.

i. An accounts receivable clerk recorded invoices received from a company that he and his wife own and authorized their payment.

j. A cashier created false purchase return vouchers to hide his theft of several thousand dollars from his cash register.

k. A purchasing agent received a 10% kickback of the invoice amount for all purchases made from a specific vendor.

6.3 The following description represents the policies and procedures for agent expense reimbursements at Excel Insurance Company.

Agents submit a completed expense reimbursement form to their branch manager at the end of each week. The branch manager reviews the expense report to determine if the claimed expenses are reimbursable based on the company's expense reimbursement policy statements and reasonableness of amount. Company policy states that agents are to document any questionable expense item and the branch manager must approve in advance expenditures exceeding $500.

After the expenses are approved, the branch manager sends the expense report to the home office, where accounting records the transaction and cash disbursements prepares the expense reimbursement check. Cash disbursements sends the expense reimbursement checks to the branch manager, who distributes them to the agents.

To receive cash advances for anticipated expenses, agents must complete a Cash Advance Approval form. The branch manager reviews and approves the Cash Advance Approval form and sends a copy to accounting and another to the agent. The agent submits the copy of the Cash Advance Approval form to the branch office cashier to obtain the cash advance.

At the end of each month, internal audit at the home office reconciles the expense reimbursements. It adds the total dollar amounts on the expense reports from each branch, subtracts the sum of the dollar totals on each branch's Cash Advance Approval form, and compares the net amount to the sum of the expense reimbursement checks issued to agents. Internal audit investigates any differences.

- Identify the internal control strengths and weaknesses in Excel's expense reimbursement process.

(CMA Examination, adapted)

6.4 The Gardner Company, a client of your firm, has come to you with the following problem: It has three clerical employees who must perform the following functions:

a. Maintain the general ledger
b. Maintain the accounts payable ledger
c. Maintain the accounts receivable ledger
d. Prepare checks for signature
e. Maintain the cash disbursements journal
f. Issue credits on returns and allowances
g. Reconcile the bank account
h. Handle and deposit cash receipts

Assuming equal abilities among the three employees, the company asks you to assign the eight functions to them to maximize internal control. Assume that these employees will perform no accounting functions other than the ones listed.

Required

a. List four possible unsatisfactory pairings of the functions.
b. State how you would distribute the functions among the three employees. Assume that with the exception of the nominal jobs of the bank reconciliation and the issuance of credits on returns and allowances, all functions require an equal amount of time.

(CPA Examination, adapted)

6.5 During a recent review, ABC Corporation discovered that it has a serious internal control problem. It is estimated that the impact associated with this problem is $1 million and that the likelihood is presently 5%. Two internal control procedures have been proposed to deal with this problem. Procedure A would cost $25,000 and reduce likelihood to 2%; procedure B would cost $30,000 and reduce likelihood to 1%. If both procedures were implemented, likelihood would be reduced to one-tenth of 1%.

Required

 a. What is the estimated expected loss associated with ABC Corporation's internal control problem before any new internal control procedures are implemented?

 b. Compute the revised estimate of expected loss if procedure A were implemented, if procedure B were implemented, and if both procedures were implemented.

 c. Compare the estimated costs and benefits of procedure A, procedure B, and both procedures combined.

 d. Considering only the estimates of cost and benefit, which procedure(s) should be implemented? What other factors might be relevant to the decision?

6.6 The management at Covington, Inc., recognizes that a well-designed internal control system provides many benefits. Among the benefits are reliable financial records that facilitate decision making and a greater probability of preventing or detecting errors and fraud. Covington's Internal Auditing Department periodically reviews the company's accounting records to determine internal control effectiveness. In its latest review, the internal audit staff found the following eight conditions:

 1 Daily bank deposits do not always correspond with cash receipts.

 2 Bad debt write-offs are prepared and approved by the same employee.

 3 There are occasional discrepancies between physical inventory counts and the perpetual inventory records.

 4 The auditor noticed alterations to physical inventory counts and perpetual inventory records.

 5 There is a high percentage of customer refunds and credits.

 6 Many original documents are missing or lost. However, there are substitute copies of all missing originals.

 7 An unexplained decrease in the gross profit percentage has occurred.

 8 Many documents are not approved.

Required

For each of the eight conditions detected by the Covington internal audit staff:

 a. Describe a possible cause of the condition.

 b. Recommend actions to be taken and/or controls to be implemented that would correct the condition.

(CMA, adapted)

6.7 Consider the following two situations:

 1 Many employees of a firm that manufactures small tools pocket some of the tools for their personal use. Since the quantities taken by any one employee are immaterial, the individual employees do not consider the act as fraudulent nor detrimental to the company. The company is now large enough to hire an internal auditor. One of the first things she did was to compare the gross profit rates for industrial tools to the gross profit for personal tools. Noting a significant difference, she investigated and uncovered the employee theft.

 2 A manufacturing firm's controller created a fake subsidiary. He then ordered goods from the firm's suppliers, told them to ship the goods to a warehouse he rented, and approved the vendor invoices for payment when they arrived. The controller later sold the diverted inventory items, and the proceeds were deposited to the controller's personal bank account. Auditors suspected something was wrong when they could not find any entries regarding this fake subsidiary office

in the property, plant, and equipment ledgers or a title or lease for the office in the real-estate records of the firm.

Required

For the situations presented, describe the recommendations the internal auditors should make to prevent similar problems in the future.

(CMA, adapted)

6.8 Tralor Corporation manufactures and sells several different lines of small electric components. Its internal audit department completed an audit of the expenditure cycle for the company. Part of the audit involved a review of the internal accounting controls for payables, including the controls over the authorization of transactions, accounting for transactions, and the protection of assets. The auditors noted the following items:

1 Routine purchases are initiated by inventory control notifying the purchasing department of the need to buy goods. The purchasing department fills out a prenumbered purchase order and gets it approved by the purchasing manager. The original of the five-part purchase order goes to the vendor, a copy is retained in purchasing, a copy is sent to the user department, a copy is sent to receiving to be used as a receiving report, and a copy is sent to accounts payable in the accounting department.

2 For efficiency and effectiveness, purchases of specialized goods and services are negotiated directly between the user department and the vendor. Company procedures require that the user department and the purchasing department approve invoices for any specialized goods and services before making payment.

3 Accounts payable maintains a list of employees who have purchase order approval authority. The list was last updated two years ago and is seldom used by accounts payable clerks.

4 All vendor invoices are recorded in an invoice register. The register indicates the receipt date, any invoices dealing with special orders, when those special orders are sent to the requesting department for approval, and when they are returned. Review of the register indicated that there were seven open invoices for special purchases, which had been forwarded to operating departments for approval over 30 days ago and had not yet been returned.

5 Prior to making entries in accounting records, the accounts payable clerk checks the mathematical accuracy of the transaction, makes sure that all transactions are properly documented (the purchase order matches the signed receiving report and the vendor's invoice), and obtains any departmental approval of invoices for special purchases.

6 All approved invoices are filed alphabetically. Invoices are paid on the 5th and 20th of each month, and all cash discounts are taken regardless of the terms.

7 The treasurer signs the checks and cancels the supporting documents after they are paid. An original document is required for a payment to be processed.

8 Prenumbered blank checks are kept in a locked safe accessible only to the cash disbursements department. Other documents and records maintained by the accounts payable section are readily accessible to all persons assigned to the section and to others in the accounting function.

Required

Review the eight items listed and decide whether they represent an internal control strength or weakness.

 a. For each internal control strength identified, explain how the described procedure helps achieve good authorization, accounting, or asset protection control.

 b. For each internal control weakness identified, explain why it is a weakness and recommend a way to correct the weakness.

(CMA, adapted)

6.9 Lancaster Company makes electrical parts for contractors and home improvement retail stores. After their annual audit, Lancaster's auditors commented on the following items regarding internal controls over equipment:

1 The operations department that needs the equipment normally initiates a purchase requisition for equipment. The department supervisor discusses the proposed purchase with the plant manager. If there are sufficient funds in the requesting department's equipment budget, a purchase requisition is submitted to the purchasing department once the plant manager is satisfied that the request is reasonable.

2 Upon receiving a purchase requisition, the purchasing department manager selects an appropriate supplier and sends a formal purchase order to the supplier. When the equipment arrives, the user department installs it.

3 The property, plant, and equipment control accounts are supported by schedules organized by year of acquisition. The schedules are used to record depreciation using standard rates, depreciation methods, and salvage values for each type of fixed asset. These rates, methods, and salvage values were set 10 years ago during the company's initial year of operation.

4 When equipment is retired, the plant manager notifies the accounting department so that the appropriate entries can be made in the accounting records.

5 There has been no reconciliation since the company began operations between the accounting records and the equipment on hand.

Required

Identify the internal control weaknesses in Lancaster's system and recommend ways to correct them.

(CMA, adapted)

6.10 The Langston Recreational Company (LRC) manufactures ice skates for racing, figure skating, and hockey. The company is located in Kearns, Utah, so it can be close to the Olympic Ice Shield where many Olympic speed skaters train.

Given the precision required to make skates, tracking manufacturing costs is very important to management so it can price the skates appropriately. To capture and collect manufacturing costs, the company acquired an automated cost accounting system from a national vendor. The vendor provides support, maintenance, and data and program backup service for LRC's system.

LRC operates one shift, five days a week. All manufacturing data are collected and recorded by Saturday evening so the prior week's production data can be processed. One of management's primary concerns is how the actual manufacturing process costs compare with planned or standard manufacturing process costs. As a result, the cost accounting system produces a report that compares actual costs with standards costs and provides the difference, or variance. Management focuses on significant variances as one means of controlling the manufacturing processes and calculating bonuses.

Occasionally, errors occur in processing a week's production cost data, which requires the entire week's cost data to be reprocessed at a cost of $34,500. The current risk of error without any control procedures is 8%. LRC's management is currently considering the addition of a set of cost accounting control procedures that is estimated to reduce the risk of the data errors from 8% to 3%. This data validation control procedure is projected to cost $1,000 per week.

Required

a. Perform a cost/benefit analysis of the data validation control procedures.

b. Based on your analysis, make a recommendation to management regarding the control procedure.

c. The current risk of data errors without any control procedures is estimated to be 8%. The data control validation procedure costs $1,000 and reduces the risk to 3%. At some point between 8% and 3% is a point of indifference—that is, Cost of reprocessing the data without controls = Cost of processing the data with the controls + Cost of controls. Use a spreadsheet application such as Excel Goal Seek to find the solution.

6.11 Spring Water Spa Company is a 15-store chain in the Midwest that sells hot tubs, supplies, and accessories. Each store has a full-time, salaried manager and an assistant manager. The sales personnel are paid an hourly wage plus a commission based on sales volume. The company uses electronic cash registers to record each transaction. The salesperson rings up the order by scanning the item's bar code card, which then displays the item's description and unit price. The salesperson enters the quantity sold as well as his or her employee number. The cash register automatically assigns a consecutive number to each transaction. The cash register prints a sales receipt that shows the total, any discounts, the sales tax, and the grand total. The salesperson then collects payment from the customer, gives the receipt to the customer, and either directs the customer to the warehouse to collect the items purchased or makes arrangements with the shipping department for delivery. If the customer wishes to purchase on credit, the salesperson is also responsible for credit approval on credit card sales and approving sales paid by check. Sales returns are handled in exactly the reverse manner, with the salesperson issuing a return slip when necessary.

At the end of each day, the cash registers print a sequentially ordered list of sales receipts and provide totals for cash, credit card, and check sales, as well as cash and credit card returns. The assistant manager reconciles these totals to the cash register tapes, the total of the consecutively numbered sales invoices, and the return slips. The assistant manager prepares a daily reconciled report for the store manager's review.

Cash sales, check sales, and credit card sales are reviewed by the manager, who prepares the daily bank deposit. The manager physically makes the deposit at the bank and files the validated deposit slip. At the end of the month, the manager performs the bank reconciliation. The cash register tapes, sales invoices, return slips, and reconciled report are electronically forwarded daily to corporate headquarters to be processed with files from all the other stores. Corporate headquarters returns a weekly Sales and Commission Activity Report to each store manager for review.

Required

Please respond to the following questions about Spring Water Spa Company's operations based on the preceding narrative:
a. The fourth component of the COSO ERM framework is risk assessment. What risk(s) does Spring Water face?
b. Identify control strengths in Spring Water's sales/cash receipts system.
c. The sixth component of the COSO ERM framework deals with control activities. What control activities do these strengths fall under?
d. What problems were avoided or risks mitigated by the controls identified in question b.
e. How might Spring Water improve its system of controls?

6.12 PriceRight Electronics Inc. (PEI) is a wholesale discount supplier of a wide variety of electronic instruments and parts to regional retailers. PEI processes its records manually except for stand-alone automated inventory and accounts receivable systems. The driving force of PEI's business is its deep discount, short-term (three-day) delivery reputation, which allows retailers to order materials several times during the month to minimize in-store inventories. PEI's management has decided to

finish automating its operations, but because of cash flow considerations this needs to be accomplished on a step-by-step basis.

It was decided that the next function to be automated should be sales order processing to enhance quick response to customer needs. PEI's systems consultants implemented and modified a commercially available software package to meet PEI's operations. In an effort to reduce the number of slow-paying or delinquent customers, PEI's consultants installed Web-based software that links to a commercial credit rating agency Web site to check customer credit at the time of purchase. The following are the new sales order processing system modules:

- **Marketing.** Sales orders are received by telephone, fax, e-mail, or standard mail and entered into the sales order system by the Marketing department. Customer orders are automatically compared to the credit rating Web site to determine credit limits. If credit limits are met, the system generates multiple copies of the sales order.

- **Credit.** On a daily basis, the credit manager reviews new customer applications for creditworthiness, establishes credit limits, and enters them into the customer database. The credit manager also reviews the calendar month-end accounts receivable aging report to identify slow-paying or delinquent accounts for potential revisions to or discontinuance of credit. In addition, the credit manager issues credit memos for merchandise returns based on requests from customers and forwards copies of credit memos to Accounting for appropriate account receivable handling.

- **Warehousing.** Warehouse personnel update the inventory master file for purchases and disbursements, confirm availability of materials to fill sales orders, and establish back orders for sales orders that cannot be completed from stock on hand. Warehouse personnel assemble and forward materials with corresponding sales orders to Shipping and Receiving. They also update the inventory master file for merchandise returns that are received by Shipping and Receiving.

- **Shipping and receiving.** Shipping and Receiving accepts materials and sales orders from Warehousing, packs and ships the order with a copy of the sales order as a packing slip, and forwards a copy of the sales order to Billing. Merchandise returns received from customers are unpacked, sorted, inspected, and sent to Warehousing.

- **Accounting.** Billing prices all sales orders received, which takes approximately 5 days after the order ships. To spread the work effort throughout the month, customers are segregated and placed in six 30-day billing cycles. Monthly statements, prepared by Billing, are sent to customers during the cycle billing period. Outstanding carry-forward balances reported by Accounts Receivable and credit memos prepared by the credit manager are included on the monthly statement. Billing also prepares electronic sales and credit memos for each cycle. Electronic copies of invoices and credit memos are forwarded to Accounts Receivable for entry into the accounts receivable master file by customer account. An aging report is prepared at the end of each month and forwarded to the credit manager. The General Accounting office staff access the accounts receivable master file reflecting total charges and credits processed through the accounts receivable system for each cycle. General Accounting runs a query to compare this information to the electronic sales and credit memo and posts the changes to the general ledger master file.

Required

 a. Identify any internal control strengths that you find in PEI's system.

 b. Identify any internal control weaknesses that you find in PEI's system, and suggest ways PEI's system control weaknesses may be corrected.

On a Saturday afternoon, Nino Moscardi received an anonymous note in his mail. Moscardi, president of Greater Providence Deposit & Trust, was shocked to read that an employee of the bank was putting through bogus loans. On the following Monday, Moscardi directed the bank's internal auditors to investigate certain transactions detailed in the note. The investigation led to James Guisti, manager of a North Providence branch office and a trusted 14-year employee who had once worked as one of the bank's internal auditors. Later, Guisti was charged with embezzling $1.83 million from the bank through 67 phony loans taken out over a three-year period.

Court documents revealed numerous details of Guisti's embezzlement scheme. For example, the first bogus loan was written for $10,000. The loans were 90-day notes requiring no collateral and ranging in amount from $10,000 to $63,500. Guisti originated the loans; when each one matured, he would take out a new loan, or rewrite the old one, to pay the principal and interest due. Some loans had been rewritten five or six times.

The 67 loans were taken out by Guisti in various names, including his wife's maiden name, his father's name, and the names of two of his friends. These people denied they received any stolen funds or knew anything about the embezzlement. In addition, one loan was in the name of James Vanesse, who police said did not exist. The Social Security number on Vanesse's loan application was issued to a female, and the phone number belonged to a North Providence auto dealer.

Court records also disclosed the details of police interviews with bank employees to determine how the loan money was dispensed. According to Lucy Fraioli, a customer service representative who cosigned checks to the five names to which Guisti had originated loans, Guisti was her supervisor and she thought nothing was wrong with the checks, though she did not know any of the five people. Marcia Perfetto, head teller at the branch, told police that she had cashed checks for Guisti made out to four of the five persons. Asked if she gave the money to Guisti when he gave her the checks to cash, she answered, "Not all of the time," though she could not recall ever having given the money directly to any of the four, whom she did not know.

According to news reports, Guisti was authorized to make consumer loans up to a certain dollar limit without loan committee approvals, which is a standard industry practice. Guisti's lending limit was $10,000 until it was increased to $15,000 then increased again to $25,000. Some of the loans, however, including the one for $63,500, far exceeded his lending limit. In addition, all loan applications should have been accompanied by a report on the applicant's credit history, purchased from an independent credit rating firm. The loan taken out in a fictitious name would not have had a credit report and

should have been flagged by a loan review clerk at the bank's headquarters.

News reports raised several questions about why the fraud had not been detected earlier. State regulators had examined the bank's books and the bank's own internal auditors failed to detect the fraud. In checking for bad loans, however, bank auditors do not examine all loans and generally focus on loans much larger than the ones in question. In addition, Greater Providence had recently dropped its computer services arrangement with a local bank in favor of an out-of-state bank, and this changeover may have reduced the effectiveness of the bank's control procedures. Finally, the bank's loan review clerks were rotated frequently, making follow-up on questionable loans more difficult.

Court records indicate that Guisti was a frequent gambler and used the proceeds of the embezzlement to pay gambling debts. The bank's losses totaled $624,000. Its bonding company covered the loss, which was less than the $1.83 million in bogus loans, because Guisti used a portion of the borrowed money to repay some loans as they came due.

According to financial reports, the bank had assets of $220 million, outstanding loans of $184 million, and earned a record $1.6 million. It had eight branches in the Providence area.

The bank experienced other adverse publicity during that period. The bank was fined $50,000 after pleading guilty to failure to report a series of cash transactions exceeding $10,000, which is a felony. Its current owners took the bank private, but only after a lengthy public battle with State Attorney General Arlene Violet. The state charged that the bank had inflated its assets and overestimated its capital surplus to make its balance sheet look stronger. The bank denied this charge.

1 Discuss how Greater Providence Deposit & Trust might improve its control procedures over the disbursement of loan funds to minimize the risk of this type of fraud. In what way does this case indicate a lack of proper segregation of duties?

2 Discuss how Greater Providence might improve its loan review procedures at bank headquarters to minimize its fraud risk. Was it a good idea to rotate the assignments of loan review clerks? Why or why not?

3 Discuss whether Greater Providence's auditors should have been able to detect this fraud.

4 Are there any indications that the control environment at Greater Providence may have been deficient? If so, how could it have contributed to this embezzlement?

Source: John Kostrezewa, "Charge: Embezzlement," *Providence Journal-Bulletin* (July 31, 1988): F-1.

AIS IN ACTION SOLUTIONS

QUIZ KEY

1 COSO identified five interrelated components of internal controls. Which of the following is *not* one of those five?

 a. risk assessment (Incorrect. Risk assessment is one of COSO's five components of internal control. The organization must be aware of and deal with the risks it faces.)

 ✔ **b.** internal control policies (Correct. Internal control policies are not one of COSO's five components of internal control.)

 c. monitoring (Incorrect. Monitoring is one of COSO's five components of internal control. The entire internal control process must be monitored, and modifications made as necessary.)

 d. information and communication (Incorrect. Information and communication is one of COSO's five components of internal control. The primary purpose of an AIS is to process and communicate information about an organization, and these activities are an essential part of an internal control system.)

2 In the ERM model, COSO specified four types of objectives that management must meet to achieve company goals. Which of the following is *not* one of those types?

 ✔ **a.** responsibility objectives (Correct. Responsibility objectives are not one of the objectives in COSO's ERM model.)

 b. strategic objectives (Incorrect. Strategic objectives are high-level goals aligned with the company's mission and are one of the objectives in COSO's ERM model.)

 c. compliance objectives (Incorrect. Compliance objectives help the company comply with all applicable laws and regulations and are one of the objectives in COSO's ERM model.)

 d. reporting objectives (Incorrect. Reporting objectives help ensure the accuracy, completeness, and reliability of internal and external reports and are one of the objectives in COSO's ERM model.)

 e. operations objectives (Incorrect. Operations objectives deal with the effectiveness and efficiency of operations and are one of the objectives in COSO's ERM model.)

3 Which of the following statements is true?

 a. The COSO report on enterprise risk management is narrow in scope and is limited to financial controls. (Incorrect. The scope of the COSO report on ERM incorporates all kinds of internal controls, not just financial controls, and provides an all-encompassing focus on the broader subject of enterprise risk management.)

 ✔ **b.** COSO's internal control integrated framework report has been widely accepted as the authority on internal controls. (Correct. The internal control integrated framework is the accepted authority on internal controls and is incorporated into policies, rules, and regulations that are used to control business activities.)

 c. The Foreign Corrupt Practices Act had no impact on internal accounting control systems. (Incorrect. The Foreign Corrupt Practices Act specifically requires corporations to maintain good systems of internal accounting control.)

 d. It is easier to add controls to an already designed system than to include them during the initial design stage. (Incorrect. The opposite is true. It is easier to include internal controls at the initial design stage than after the system is already designed.)

4 All other things being equal, which of the following is true?
 a. Detective controls are superior to preventive controls. (Incorrect. The reverse is true—preventive controls are superior to detective controls. Preventive controls keep an error or irregularity from occurring. Detective controls uncover an error or irregularity after the fact.)
 b. Corrective controls are superior to preventive controls. (Incorrect. The reverse is true—preventive controls are superior to corrective controls. Preventive controls keep an error or irregularity from occurring. Corrective controls fix an error after the fact.)
 c. Preventive controls are equivalent to detective controls. (Incorrect. Preventive controls keep an error or irregularity from occurring. Detective controls uncover an error or irregularity after the fact.)
 ✔ **d.** Preventive controls are superior to detective controls. (Correct. With respect to controls, it is always of utmost importance to prevent errors from occurring.)

5 Which of the following statements about the control environment is false?
 ✔ **a.** Management's attitudes toward internal control and ethical behavior have little impact on employee beliefs or actions. (Correct. This statement is false because management attitude toward internal control is critical to the organization's effectiveness and success.)
 b. An overly complex or unclear organizational structure may be indicative of more serious problems. (Incorrect. This is a true statement. Management may intentionally build overly complex or unclear organizational structures to hide fraud or errors.)
 c. A written policy and procedures manual is an important tool for assigning authority and responsibility. (Incorrect. This is a true statement. A written policy and procedures manual explains proper business practices, describes the knowledge and experience needed by key personnel, and lists the resources provided to carry out specific duties.)
 d. Supervision is especially important in organizations that cannot afford elaborate responsibility reporting or are too small to have an adequate separation of duties. (Incorrect. This is a true statement. In many organizations, effective supervision takes the place of more expensive controls. Effective supervision involves training and assisting employees, monitoring their performance, correcting errors, and safeguarding assets by overseeing employees who have access to them.)

6 To achieve effective segregation of duties, certain functions must be separated. Which of the following is the correct listing of the accounting-related functions that must be segregated?
 a. control, recording, and monitoring (Incorrect. See Figure 6-3.)
 ✔ **b.** authorization, recording, and custody (Correct. See Figure 6-3.)
 c. control, custody, and authorization (Incorrect. See Figure 6-3.)
 d. monitoring, recording, and planning (Incorrect. See Figure 6-3.)

7 Which of the following is not an independent check?
 a. bank reconciliation (Incorrect. A bank reconciliation is an internal check, as are top-level reviews, analytical reviews, reconciling two independently maintained sets of records, comparisons of actual quantities with recorded amounts, double-entry accounting, and independent reviews.)
 b. periodic comparison of subsidiary ledger totals to control accounts (Incorrect. A periodic comparison of subsidiary ledger totals to control accounts is an internal check, as are top-level reviews, analytical reviews, reconciling two independently maintained sets of records, comparisons of actual quantities with recorded amounts, double-entry accounting, and independent reviews.)
 c. trial balance (Incorrect. A trial balance is an internal check, as are top-level reviews, analytical reviews, reconciling two independently maintained sets of records, comparisons of actual quantities with recorded amounts, double-entry accounting, and independent reviews.)

✔ **d.** re-adding the total of a batch of invoices and comparing it with your first total (Correct. A person performing the same procedure twice using the same documents, such as re-adding invoice batch totals, is not an independent check because it does not involve a second person, a second set of documents or records, or a second process.)

8 Which of the following is a control procedure relating to both the design and use of documents and records?

a. locking blank checks in a drawer (Incorrect. Locking blank checks in a drawer is not a control procedure related to the design of documents.)

b. reconciling the bank account (Incorrect. Reconciling the bank account is not a control procedure related to the design of documents.)

✔ **c.** sequentially prenumbering sales invoices (Correct. Designing documents so that they are sequentially prenumbered and then using them in order is a control procedure relating to both the design and use of documents.)

d. comparing actual physical quantities with recorded amounts (Incorrect. Comparing actual quantities to recorded amounts is not a control procedure related to the design of documents.)

9 Which of the following is the correct order of the risk assessment steps discussed in this chapter?

✔ **a.** Identify threats, estimate risk and exposure, identify controls, and estimate costs and benefits. (Correct. See Figure 6-2.)

b. Identify controls, estimate risk and exposure, identify threats, and estimate costs and benefits. (Incorrect. See Figure 6-2.)

c. Estimate risk and exposure, identify controls, identify threats, and estimate costs and benefits. (Incorrect. See Figure 6-2.)

d. Estimate costs and benefits, identify threats, identify controls, and estimate risk and exposure. (Incorrect. See Figure 6-2.)

10 Your current system is deemed to be 90% reliable. A major threat has been identified with an impact of $3,000,000. Two control procedures exist to deal with the threat. Implementation of control A would cost $100,000 and reduce the likelihood to 6%. Implementation of control B would cost $140,000 and reduce the likelihood to 4%. Implementation of both controls would cost $220,000 and reduce the likelihood to 2%. Given the data, and based solely on an economic analysis of costs and benefits, what should you do?

a. Implement control A only. (Incorrect. Procedure A only provides a benefit of $20,000, whereas control procedure B provides a net benefit of $40,000.)

✔ **b.** Implement control B only. (Correct. Control procedure B provides a net benefit of $40,000. Procedure A and the combination of A and B only provide a benefit of $20,000.)

c. Implement both controls A and B. (Incorrect. The combination of procedures A and B only provides a benefit of $20,000, whereas control procedure B provides a net benefit of $40,000.)

d. Implement neither control. (Incorrect. Both controls provide a net benefit. Control procedure B provides a net benefit of $40,000. Procedure A and the combination of A and B each provide a benefit of $20,000.)

Expected loss = Impact × Likelihood ($300,000 = $3,000,000 × 10%)

Control Procedure	Likelihood	Impact	Revised Expected Loss	Reduction in Expected Loss	Cost of Control(s)	Net Benefit (Cost)
A	0.06	$3,000,000	$180,000	$120,000	$100,000	$20,000
B	0.04	$3,000,000	$120,000	$180,000	$140,000	$40,000
Both	0.02	$3,000,000	$ 60,000	$240,000	$220,000	$20,000

CHAPTER 7

 LEARNING OBJECTIVES

After studying this chapter, you should be able to:

- **Explain how information security affects systems reliability.**

- **Identify the four criteria that can be used to evaluate the effectiveness of an organization's information security.**

- **Explain the time-based model of security and the concept of defense-in-depth.**

- **Describe the various types of preventive, detective, and corrective controls used to provide information security.**

- **Explain how encryption contributes to security and how the two basic types of encryption systems work.**

Information Systems Controls for Systems Reliability—Part 1: Information Security

INTEGRATIVE CASE NORTHWEST INDUSTRIES

Jason Scott's next assignment is to review Northwest Industries' existing information systems controls. To ensure compliance with the requirements of the Sarbanes–Oxley Act, management wants an assessment of the reliability of the company's systems. Several competitors have recently experienced costly security breaches, and top management is concerned about the risk of similar problems occurring at Northwest Industries.

Jason decides to use the COBIT framework to guide his review because it not only specifies control objectives but also provides detailed audit guidelines. He quickly becomes overwhelmed, however, by COBIT's complexity. A friend who is an independent consultant suggests that Jason should examine the Trust Services framework developed by the AICPA and the Canadian Institute of Chartered Accountants. The Trust Services framework focuses only on a subset of the matters covered by COBIT, specifically those that directly affect the reliability of financial reporting systems. Jason visits the AICPA Web site to download the most recent version of the Trust Services Framework. After reviewing it, he decides to begin by focusing on the quality of Northwest's

information system security controls. He writes down the following questions to guide his investigation:

1 What techniques can be used to prevent unauthorized access to the company's information systems resources?

2 How can successful and unsuccessful attempts to compromise the company's systems controls be detected in a timely manner?

3 What steps can management take to be prepared to effectively respond to security incidents?

Introduction

One basic function of an accounting information system is to provide information useful for decision making. To be useful, the information produced by the AIS—such as financial statements and various managerial reports—must provide an accurate, complete, and timely picture of the organization's activities. Moreover, that information must be available whenever needed. Further, the information and the system itself must be protected from loss, compromise, and theft. In short, to provide information that is useful for decision making, an organization's AIS must be reliable.

Figure 7-1 shows five fundamental principles that contribute to the overall objective of systems reliability. Note the importance of information security. Security procedures restrict system access to authorized users only, thereby protecting the confidentiality of sensitive organizational data and the privacy of personal identifying information collected from customers. Security procedures provide for processing integrity by preventing submission of unauthorized or fictitious transactions as well as preventing unauthorized changes to stored data or programs. Finally, security procedures provide protection against a variety of attacks, including viruses and worms, thereby ensuring that the system is available when needed. Thus, as Figure 7-1 shows, information security is the foundation of systems reliability. Consequently, this chapter focuses on information security. Chapter 8 discusses controls relevant to the other four principles underlying systems reliability: confidentiality, privacy, integrity of processing, and availability.

The press is replete with stories about how information security incidents affect both organizations and individuals: denial-of-service attacks that disrupt business activities, fraud, loss of trade secrets, and identity theft. Clearly, it is important for accountants and information systems professionals to understand the basic principles of information

Figure 7-1
Relationships Among
Components of Systems
Reliability

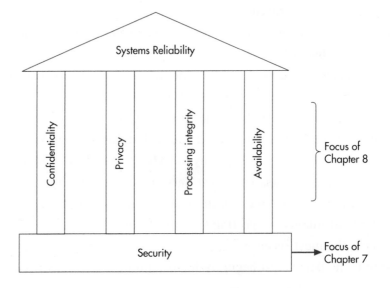

security so that they can help reduce the risks to both the organizations for which they work and to themselves. This chapter, however, provides only a broad *introduction* to the topic of information systems security. Anyone interested in a career in information systems security will need to undertake additional detailed study. Indeed, entire courses exist to enable information systems professionals to become certified in many of the individual topics, such as firewalls and intrusion detection systems, which are discussed in this chapter.

The COBIT and Trust Service Frameworks

Figure 7-2 presents a high-level overview of the Control Objectives for Information and related Technology (COBIT) framework, which as Chapter 6 noted, provides comprehensive guidance for effectively controlling and managing information systems. It shows that achieving the organization's business and governance objectives requires adequate controls over IT resources to ensure that information provided to management satisfies seven key criteria:

1 Effectiveness—the information must be relevant and timely.
2 Efficiency—the information must be produced in a cost-effective manner.
3 Confidentiality—sensitive information must be protected from unauthorized disclosure.
4 Integrity—the information must be accurate, complete, and valid.
5 Availability—the information must be available whenever needed.
6 Compliance—controls must ensure compliance with internal policies and with external legal and regulatory requirements.
7 Reliability—management must have access to appropriate information needed to conduct daily activities and to exercise its fiduciary and governance responsibilities.

Figure 7-2 shows 34 generic IT processes that must be properly managed and controlled in order to produce information that satisfies the seven criteria listed above. Those processes are grouped into four basic management activities, which COBIT refers to as domains:

1 Plan and Organize (PO). Figure 7-2 lists ten important processes for properly planning and organizing an organization's information systems.
2 Acquire and Implement (AI). Figure 7-2 lists seven fundamental processes that pertain to the acquisition and implementation of technology solutions.
3 Deliver and Support (DS). Figure 7-2 lists 13 critical processes for effectively and efficiently delivering the information management needs to run the organization.
4 Monitor and Evaluate (ME). Figure 7-2 lists four essential processes for monitoring and evaluating an organization's information systems.

The COBIT framework also specifies detailed control objectives that exist for each of the 34 IT processes in Figure 7-2.

Note the circle of arrows in Figure 7-2, which indicates that effective operation, control, and governance of an information system is an ongoing process. Management develops plans to organize information resources to provide the information it needs. It then authorizes and oversees efforts to acquire (or build internally) the desired functionality. Management then performs a number of activities to ensure that the resulting system actually delivers the desired information. Finally, there is a need for constant monitoring and evaluation of performance against the established criteria. The entire cycle constantly repeats, as management modifies existing plans and procedures or develops new ones in order to respond to changes in business objectives and new developments in information technology.

COBIT specifies 210 detailed control objectives for effectively managing an organization's information resources. It also describes specific audit procedures for assessing

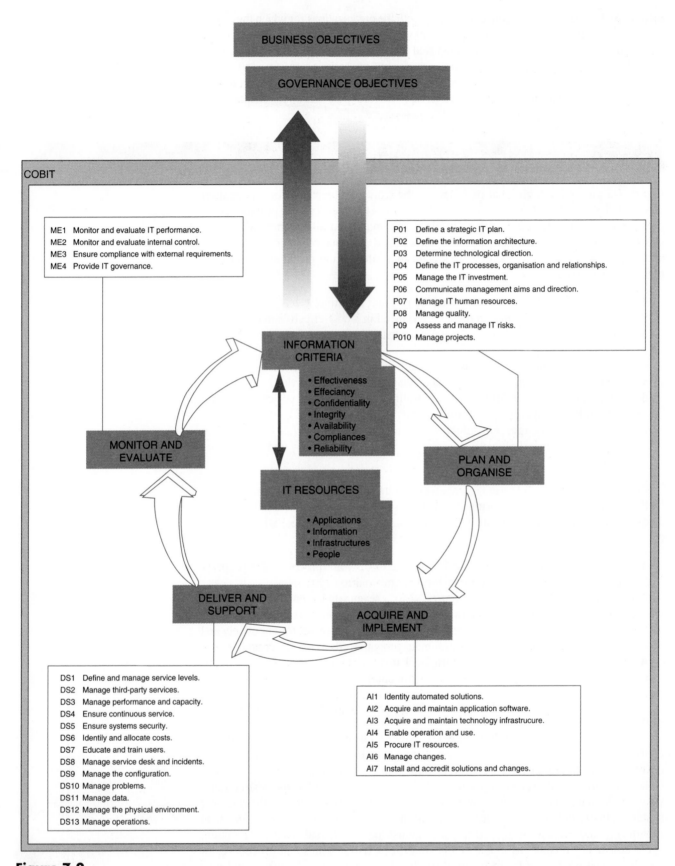

Figure 7-2
COBIT Framework

(*Source:* Figure 23 in COBIT 4.1, Excerpt, Executive Summary Framework, IT Governance Institute, p. 26)

the effectiveness of those controls and suggests metrics that management can use to evaluate performance. This comprehensiveness is one of the strengths of COBIT and explains its growing international acceptance as a framework for managing and controlling information systems. Oftentimes, however, auditors may only be concerned with a subset of the issues covered by COBIT. For example, the Sarbanes–Oxley (SOX) Act specifically addresses the issue of systems reliability as it pertains to the accuracy of an organization's financial statements. The Trust Services Framework developed jointly by the AICPA and the Canadian Institute of Chartered Accountants focuses specifically on five aspects of information systems controls and governance that most directly pertain to systems reliability:

1 Security—access to the system and its data is controlled and restricted to legitimate users.
2 Confidentiality—sensitive organizational information (e.g., marketing plans, trade secrets, etc.) is protected from unauthorized disclosure.
3 Privacy—personal information about customers is collected, used, disclosed and maintained only in compliance with internal policies and external regulatory requirements.
4 Processing Integrity—data is processed accurately, completely, in a timely manner, and only with proper authorization.
5 Availability—the system and its information is available to meet operational and contractual obligations.

The Trust Services framework is not a substitute for COBIT, because it only addresses a subset of the issues covered by COBIT. We adopt it to guide our discussion of IT controls in this text, however, because it provides a useful means for consolidating COBIT's control objectives to focus on a specific aspect of IT governance that has become especially relevant because of SOX: systems reliability. For example, the various audit issues and control objectives pertaining to information security occur in all four COBIT domains (PO, AI, DS, and ME) and the same holds true for confidentiality, privacy, processing integrity, and availability. We believe that accounting students, and auditors, can benefit from using the Trust Services framework to identify those sections of the COBIT framework that are most directly related to systems reliability. Therefore chapters 7 and 8 are organized in terms of the five principles of system reliability depicted in Figure 7-1. We will refer to specific sub-sections of the COBIT framework that pertain to the topics discussed in the text, using COBIT's two-letter (PO, AI, DS, or ME) domain abbreviations. For example, information security is one of the 13 generic processes in the Delivery and Support (DS) domain. DS 5, the process of providing information security, itself has 11 detailed control objectives, each of which is referenced by the format DS 5.n. To illustrate, DS 5.5 is the detailed control objective of regularly testing the effectiveness of information security controls. This chapter focuses on the Trust Services principle of information security because, as Figure 7-1 shows, information security is the foundation of systems reliability. Chapter 8 discusses the controls and audit issues related to the principles of confidentiality, privacy, processing integrity, and availability.

Three Fundamental Information Security Concepts

1 Security Is a Management Issue, Not a Technology Issue

Although information security is a complex technical subject, it is important to recognize that security is first and foremost a management issue, not an information technology issue. Management is responsible for the accuracy of the various internal

reports and financial statements produced by the organization's information systems. In fact, Section 302 of SOX requires the CEO and the CFO to certify that the financial statements fairly present the results of the company's activities. Section 302 also requires the CEO and CFO to certify that they have evaluated the effectiveness of the organization's internal controls. In addition, Section 404 of SOX requires annual reports to include a report on the company's internal controls in which management acknowledges its responsibility for designing and maintaining internal controls and its assessment of the effectiveness of those controls. Security is a key component of internal control and system reliability. As explained in Chapter 6, the COSO framework identifies the critical importance of top management's philosophy and operating style in creating an effective control environment. Thus, top management plays a critical role in information security.

The Trust Services framework identifies four essential criteria for successfully implementing each of the five principles that contribute to systems reliability:

1 Developing and documenting policies
2 Effectively communicating policies to all authorized users
3 Designing and employing appropriate control procedures to implement policies
4 Monitoring the system and taking corrective action to maintain compliance with policies

Top-management involvement and support is necessary to satisfy each of these criteria. COBIT section PO 6 identifies the Chief Information Officer (CIO) as being both responsible and accountable for ensuring that information policies and controls are defined and communicated to all employees.

Policy Development

It has been said that fighting fires is exciting, preventing them is boring. Yet, fire prevention is more cost-effective fire fighting. The same is true of information security: Planning is more effective than reacting. Management needs to develop a comprehensive set of security policies before designing and implementing specific control procedures. Otherwise, it will most likely end up purchasing a mishmash of security products that do not protect every information system resource.

Developing a comprehensive set of security policies begins by taking an inventory of information system resources. This includes not only hardware but also software and databases. Many organizations are surprised at what they find the first time that they undertake such an inventory.

Once the organization's information systems resources have been identified, they need to be valued in order to select the most cost-effective control procedures. This is not always easy, particularly in the case of information itself. Top-management involvement is essential because only it possesses the breadth of understanding of the organization's mission and goals to accurately assess the likely impact of a security incident that would involve the loss or disclosure of specific information resources. That is why DS 5.1, the first detailed control objective pertaining to information security in the COBIT framework, stresses the importance of managing information security at the highest appropriate level in order to ensure that the organization's security policies adequately address all aspects of operations and strategy.

Effective Communication of Policies

COBIT control objective DS 5.2 stresses that security policies must be communicated to and be understood by employees, customers, suppliers, and other authorized users. To be effective, this communication must involve more than just handing people a written document and asking them to sign an acknowledgement that they received and read it. Instead, users must receive regular, periodic reminders about security policies and training in how to comply with them. Only the active support and involvement of

top management can ensure that such training and communication is taken seriously. Moreover, for security policies to be effective, there need to be sanctions associated with their violation. Only top management can provide the necessary support for enforcing sanctions against users who violate security policies.

The Design and Employment of Appropriate Control Procedures

Control frameworks, such as COBIT and Trust Services, identify a variety of specific control procedures and tools that can be used to mitigate various security threats. The various options differ in terms of both implementation cost and effectiveness. Determining the optimal level of investment in security, therefore, involves evaluating the cost/benefit trade-offs of alternative control procedures. This requires knowledge not only of the technical merits of each potential security investment but also the risks of various threats and the potential costs of different types of incidents. Systems professionals possess the requisite technical knowledge, but only senior management can ensure that all relevant organizational factors are considered so that adequate funds are invested in security. That is why COBIT section PO 9 stresses that both the CEO and CFO are accountable for ensuring that the organization has implemented a thorough risk assessment program and regularly monitors the effectiveness of the actions taken to address identified risks. This is important because, as Focus 7-1 discusses, the consequences of inadequate investments in security are increasing.

7-1 FOCUS Information Security Threats Could Also Cost in Court

Many CIOs are bracing themselves for what may be a deluge of liability lawsuits for information security breaches. The threat is that companies could be held responsible for damages suffered by their customers as a result of a security incident. For example, some of Qwest's customers in the state of Washington who were without DSL phone coverage for 10 days because of an Internet worm attack complained to their state attorney general's office. Although Qwest insisted that it was not at fault for an attack made by somebody else, the attorney general's office asked that the company issue a refund to its customers.

It is likely only a matter of time before judges and juries will have to decide if companies are legally responsible for insufficient security. Even though no legal precedents have been set as yet, corporate officers could be held personally liable for breaches of security. Therefore, management has a personal stake in ensuring the adequacy of their organization's security procedures. Sarah D. Scalet, in an article in CIO magazine, offers managers the following tips for avoiding successful lawsuits:

- *"Establish and implement an in-house security policy."* Develop a definite policy for how the company safeguards data and make sure the policy is well documented.
- *"Have a security audit done."* Ensure that the company is adhering to its information security policy by contracting a third person to test it. Having a third and unbiased party review a company's information security can help prove that the company is actively seeking to stay abreast of potential security risks.
- *"Remember security in contracts."* When outsourcing, a company must be sure the other company has in place and is following adequate security procedures.
- *"Don't make promises you can't keep."* A company should never promise faultless security, but rather appropriate security measures. Making big promises can leave you at risk for breach of contract lawsuits.
- *"Pay attention to regulations affecting your industry."* Countries sometimes have laws on the protection of customer information. Make sure the company is aware of the laws in the countries where it is doing business.
- *"Consider purchasing e-commerce insurance."* Cyber insurance covers online risks not covered by basic business insurance. Cyber insurance covers such occurrences as attacks involving denial of service, malicious code, and inappropriate Web content.
- *"Pay attention to what similar companies are doing."* Keep track of what other companies are doing so that you can prove that you are doing as much as anybody else for security.

Monitoring and Taking Remedial Action

Finally, it is important to understand that security is a moving target. Advances in information technology create new threats and alter the risks associated with existing threats. Therefore, effective control over information systems involves a continuous cycle of developing policies to address identified threats, communicating those policies to all employees, implementing specific control procedures to mitigate risk, monitoring performance, and taking corrective actions in response to identified problems. Often, the necessary corrective actions involve the modification of existing policies and the development of new ones, thereby beginning the entire cycle anew (refer to Figure 7-2). Senior management needs to be involved in this process to ensure that security policies remain consistent with and support the organization's business strategy.

2 The Time-Based Model of Security

Auditors have long recognized that preventive controls can never provide 100% protection. Given enough time and resources, any preventive control can be circumvented. Consequently, effective control requires supplementing preventive procedures with methods for detecting incidents and procedures for taking corrective remedial action. Moreover, the detection and corrective actions must be timely. This is especially important for information security, because once preventive controls have been breached, it takes little time to destroy, compromise, or steal the organization's economic and information resources.

The **time-based model of security** focuses on the relationship between preventive, detective, and corrective controls. All three types of controls are necessary. The role of preventive controls is to limit actions to those in accord with the organization's security policy and to not allow undesired actions. The role of detective controls is to identify when preventive controls have been breached. The role of corrective controls is to repair damage from any problems that occurred and to improve the functioning of both preventive and detective controls in order to reduce the likelihood of future problems.

The time-based model of security evaluates the effectiveness of an organization's security by measuring and comparing the relationship among the following three variables:

P = the time it takes an attacker to break through the organization's preventive controls

D = the time it takes to detect that an attack is in progress

C = the time it takes to respond to the attack

Those three variables are then evaluated as follows: If $P > D + C$, then the organization's security procedures are effective. Otherwise, security is ineffective.

The time-based model of security provides a means for management to identify the most cost-effective approach to improving security by comparing the effects of additional investments in preventive, detective, or corrective controls. For example, management may be considering the investment of an additional $100,000 to enhance security. One option might be the purchase of a new firewall that would increase the value of P by 10 minutes. A second option might be to upgrade the organization's intrusion detection system in a manner that would decrease the value of D by 12 minutes. A third option might be to invest in new methods for responding to information security incidents so as to decrease the value of C by 30 minutes. In this example, the most cost-effective choice would be to invest in additional corrective controls that enable the organization to respond to attacks more quickly.

Although the time-based model of security provides a sound theoretical basis for evaluating and managing an organization's information security practices, it is difficult to directly apply. One problem is that it is hard, if not impossible, to derive accurate reliable measures of the parameters P, D, and C. In addition, even when those

parameter values can be reliably calculated, their validity is often quickly lost due to new IT developments. For example, discovery of a major new vulnerability can effectively reduce the value of P to zero. Consequently, the time-based model of security is best used as a high level framework for strategic analysis. For tactical and daily management of security, most organizations follow the principle of defense-in-depth.

3 Defense-in-Depth

The idea of **defense-in-depth** is to employ multiple layers of controls in order to avoid having a single point of failure. Redundancy increases effectiveness because even if one procedure fails or is circumvented, another may function as planned. The use of overlapping, complementary and redundant controls also buys time for the organization to detect and react to attacks. For example, banks use a combination of locked doors, bars on windows, security guards, and safes to provide multiple preventive controls designed to restrict physical access to cash. Similarly, information security involves the use of a combination of firewalls, passwords, and other preventive procedures to restrict access to information systems. Redundancy also applies to detective and corrective controls.

Understanding Targeted Attacks

Before discussing the preventive, detective, and corrective controls that can be used to mitigate the risk of systems intrusions, it is helpful to understand the basic steps used by criminals to attack an organization's information system:

1 *Reconnaissance*. Bank robbers usually do not just drive up to a bank and attempt to rob it. Instead, they first study their target's physical layout to learn about the controls it has in place (alarms, number of guards, placement of cameras, etc.). Computer attackers similarly begin by collecting information about their target. Much valuable information can be obtained by perusing an organization's financial statements, SEC filings, Web site, and press releases. The objective of this initial reconnaissance is to learn as much as possible about the target and to identify potential vulnerabilities.

2 *Attempt social engineering*. Why go through all the trouble of trying to break into a system if you can get someone to let you in? Attackers will often try to use the information obtained during their initial reconnaissance to socially engineer (i.e., "trick") an unsuspecting employee into granting them access. Social engineering can take place in countless ways, limited only by the creativity and imagination of the attacker. Attacks often take place over the telephone. One common technique is for the attacker to impersonate an executive who cannot obtain remote access to important files. The attacker calls a newly-hired administrative assistant and asks that person to help them obtain the critical files. Another common ruse is for the attacker to pose as a clueless temporary worker who cannot log onto the system and who calls the help desk for assistance. Social engineering attacks can also take place via email. An attack known as "spear phishing" involves sending emails purportedly coming from someone else in the organization whom the victim knows, or should know. The email asks the victim to click on an embedded link which contains a Trojan horse program that enables the attacker to obtain access to the system. Yet another social engineering tactic is to spread USB drives in the targeted organization's parking lot. An unsuspecting or curious employee who picks up the drive and plugs it into their computer will load a Trojan horse program that enables the attacker to gain access to the system.

3 *Scan and map the target*. If an attacker cannot successfully penetrate the target system via social engineering, the next step is to conduct more detailed reconnaissance

Table 7-1
Summary of Types of Security Controls

Type of Control	Examples
Preventive	• Authentication controls (passwords, tokens, biometrics, MAC addresses) • Authorization controls (access control matrices and compatibility tests) • Training • Physical access controls (locks, guards, biometric devices) • Remote access controls—IP packet filtering by border routers and firewalls using access control lists; intrusion prevention systems; authentication of dial-in users; wireless access controls • Host and application hardening procedures—firewalls, antivirus software, disabling of unnecessary features, user account management, software design (e.g., to prevent buffer overflows) • Encryption
Detective	• Log analysis • Intrusion detection systems • Managerial reports • Security testing (vulnerability scanners, penetration tests, and war dialing)
Corrective	• Computer emergency response teams • Chief Information Security Officer (CISO) • Patch management

to identify potential points of remote entry. The objective is to identify computers that can be remotely accessed and the types of software they are running. A number of automated tools, like nmap, are used to identify computers accessible from the Internet. Those same tools are then used to perform a "port scan" of each potential target, sending a series of messages that reveal the specific programs that are running on that machine, including information about its operating system.

4 *Research.* Once the attacker has identified specific targets and knows what versions of software are running on them, the next step is to conduct research to find known vulnerabilities for those programs and how to take advantage of those vulnerabilities.

5 *Execute the attack* and obtain unauthorized access to the system.

6 *Cover tracks.* After penetrating the victim's information system, most attackers will try to cover their tracks and create "back doors" that can be used to obtain access in the event that their initial attack is discovered and controls are implemented to block that method of entry.

Now that we have a basic understanding of how criminals attack an organization's information system, we can proceed to discuss methods for mitigating the risk that such attacks will be successful. The following sections discuss the major types of preventive, detective, and corrective controls listed in Table 7-1 that can be used to provide information security through defense-in-depth.

Preventive Controls

The objective of preventive controls is, as their name implies, to prevent security incidents from happening. This section discusses the seven major types of preventive controls listed in Table 7-1.

Authentication Controls

Authentication focuses on verifying the identity of the person or device attempting to access the system. The objective of authentication controls is to ensure that only legitimate users can access the system.

Users can be authenticated by verifying

1 Something they know, such as passwords or personal identification numbers (PINs)
2 Something they have, such as smart cards or ID badges
3 Some physical characteristic (referred to as a **biometric identifier**), such as their fingerprints or voice

Passwords are probably the most commonly used authentication method, and also the most controversial. Focus 7-2 (on page 282) discusses some of the requirements for creating strong passwords as well as the on-going debate about their continued use in the future.

Individually, each authentication method has its limitations. Passwords can be guessed, lost, written down, or given away. Physical identification techniques (cards, badges, USB devices, etc.) can be lost, stolen, or duplicated. Thus, neither passwords nor physical devices provide 100% assurance that only legitimate users are obtaining access to the system. Biometric techniques are expensive and often cumbersome to use. In addition, they are not yet 100% accurate, sometimes rejecting legitimate users (for example, voice recognition systems may not recognize an employee who has a cold and handprint readers may reject someone wearing a new ring) and sometimes allowing access to unauthorized people. Moreover, some biometric techniques, such as fingerprints, carry negative connotations that may hinder their acceptance. There are also security concerns about storage of the biometric information itself. Biometric templates, such as the digital representation of an individual's fingerprints or voice, must be stored somewhere. The compromising of those templates would create serious, lifelong problems for the donor since biometric characteristics, unlike passwords or tokens, cannot be replaced or changed.

Although none of the three basic authentication methods, by itself, is foolproof, the use of two or all three methods in conjunction, a process referred to as **multifactor authentication**, is quite effective. For example, requiring a user to both insert a smart card in a card reader and enter a password provides much stronger authentication than using either method alone.

Authorization Controls

Authorization restricts access of authenticated users to specific portions of the system and specifies what actions they are permitted to perform. For example, an employee in the marketing department may not be authorized to access the payroll system. In addition, that employee may be permitted to only read, but not change, the prices of inventory items.

Authorization controls are implemented by creating an **access control matrix**, which is a table specifying which portions of the system users are permitted to access and what actions they can perform (see Figure 7-3). Then, when an employee attempts to access a particular information systems resource, the system performs a **compatibility test** that matches the user's authentication credentials against the access control matrix to determine whether that employee should be allowed to access that resource and perform the requested action. It is important to regularly update the access control matrix to reflect changes in job duties due to promotions or transfers. Otherwise, over time an employee may accumulate a set of rights and privileges that are incompatible with proper segregation of duties.

Authentication and authorization can, and should, be applied not only to users but also to devices. Every workstation, printer, or other computing device needs a network interface card (NIC) to connect to the organization's internal network. Each NIC has a unique identifier, referred to as its media access control (MAC) address. Therefore, it

7-2 FOCUS The Debate over Passwords

To be effective, passwords must satisfy a number of requirements:

- **Length.** The strength of a password is directly related to its length. Most security experts recommend that strong passwords include at least eight characters.
- **Multiple character types.** Password strength is greatly increased by using a mixture of upper- and lowercase alphabetic, numeric, and special characters.
- **Randomness.** Passwords should not be words found in dictionaries. Nor should they be words with either a preceding or following numeric character (such as 3Diamond or Diamond3). They must also not be related to the employee's personal interests or hobbies, because special-purpose password-cracking dictionaries can be found on the Internet that contain the most common passwords related to various topics. For example, the password Ncc1701 appears, at first glance, to fit the requirements of a strong password: It contains a mixture of upper- and lowercase characters and numbers. But any Star Trek fan will instantly recognize it as the designation of the starship enterprise. Consequently, Ncc1701 and many variations on it (changing which letters are capitalized, replacing the number 1 with the ! symbol, etc.) are included in most password-cracking dictionaries and, therefore, are quickly broken.
- **Changed frequently.** Passwords should be changed at regular intervals. Most users should change their passwords at least every 90 days; users with access to sensitive information should change their passwords more often, possibly every 30 days.

Most important, passwords must be kept secret to be effective. However, a problem with strong passwords, such as dX%m8K#2, is that they are not easy to remember. Consequently, when people do follow the requirements for creating strong passwords they tend to write those passwords down. This weakens the value of the password by changing it from something they know to something they have—which can then be stolen and used by anyone.

These problems have led some information security experts to conclude that the attempt to enforce the use of strong passwords is counterproductive. They note that a major component of help desk costs is associated with resetting passwords that users forgot. Consequently, they argue for abandoning the quest to develop and use strong passwords and to rely on the use of dual-factor authentication methods, such as a combination of a smart card and a simple PIN, instead.

Other information security experts disagree. They note that operating systems can now accommodate passwords that are longer than 15 characters. This means that users can create strong, yet easy-to-remember, passphrases, such as Ilove2gosnorkelinginHawaiidoU?. Such long passphrases dramatically increase the effort required to crack them by brute-force guessing of every combination. For example, an eight-character password consisting solely of lower- and uppercase letters and numerals has 62^8 possible combinations, but a 20-character passphrase has 62^{20} possible combinations. This means that passphrases do not need to be changed as frequently as passwords. Therefore, some information security experts argue that the ability to use the same passphrase for long periods of time, coupled with the fact that it is easier to remember a long passphrase than a strong password, should dramatically cut help desk costs while improving security. However, it remains to be seen whether users will balk at having to enter long passphrases, especially if they need to do so frequently because they are required to use passphrase-protected screen savers.

is possible to restrict network access to only those devices that have recognized MAC addresses. There exists software, however, that can be used to change a device's MAC address, thereby enabling malicious users to "spoof" their device's identity. Therefore, a stronger way to authenticate devices involves the use of digital certificates that employ encryption techniques to assign unique identifiers to each device. It is also possible to use MAC addresses and digital certificates for authorization. For example, including MAC addresses or digital certificates in the access control matrix makes it possible to restrict access to the payroll system and payroll master files to only payroll department employees and only when they log in from their desktop or assigned laptop computer. After all, why would a payroll clerk need to log in from a workstation located in the warehouse or attempt to establish dial-in access from another country? The application of authentication and authorization controls to both humans and devices is another example of how defense-in-depth increases security.

User	Files			Programs			
User ID	A	B	C	1	2	3	4
NHale	0	0	1	0	0	0	0
JPJones	0	2	0	0	0	0	1
BArnold	1	1	0	1	1	0	0
....

Codes for File Access:
0 = No Access
1 = Read/display only
2 = Read/display and update
3 = Read/display, update, create, and delete

Codes for Program Access:
0 = No Access
1 = Execute

Figure 7-3
Example of an Access Control Matrix

Training

People play a critical role in information security. The effectiveness of specific control procedures depends on how well employees understand and follow the organization's security policies. Thus, training is a critical preventive control. Indeed, its importance is reflected in the fact that one of the 34 top-level control processes in the COBIT framework, DS 7, focuses exclusively on the need to train both users and systems professionals.

All employees should be taught why security measures are important to the organization's long-run survival. They also need to be trained to follow safe computing practices, such as never opening unsolicited e-mail attachments, using only approved software, not sharing or revealing passwords, and taking steps to physically protect laptops. Training is especially needed to educate employees about **social engineering** attacks, which use deception to obtain unauthorized access to information resources. For example, employees should be trained to never divulge passwords or other information about their accounts or their workstation configurations to anyone who contacts them by telephone, e-mail, or instant messaging and claims to be part of the organization's information systems security function. Employees also need to be trained not to allow other people to follow them through restricted access entrances. This social engineering attack, called *piggybacking*, can take place not only at the main entrance to the building but also at any internal locked doors, especially to rooms that contain computer equipment. Piggybacking may be attempted not only by outsiders but also by other employees who are not authorized to enter a particular area. Piggybacking often succeeds because many people feel it is rude to not let another person come through the door with them and they want to avoid confrontations. Role-playing exercises are particularly effective for increasing sensitivity to and skills for dealing with social engineering attacks.

Training of information security professionals is also important. New developments in technology continuously create new security threats and make old solutions obsolete. Therefore, it is important for organizations to support continuing professional education for their security specialists. Unfortunately, surveys indicate that many organizations fail to adequately invest in such training.

Keeping abreast of recent hacking developments is especially useful. So-called "white-hat" organizations monitor hackers and their activities and then publish the findings on Web pages. These pages explain how to perpetrate all known hacking activities. The sites then explain how network administrators can protect themselves from each hacking approach, and they provide information systems managers with a valuable way to learn about the latest security threats and how to protect themselves from those threats. Underground journals, books, and cracker Web sites are another source for information on how to break into systems. Details on how to take advantage of newly discovered security holes are published almost daily. It is important to

monitor these sites and find postings that pertain to systems that your company uses so they can be protected from hacker attacks.

Finally, top-management support for training is critical. In addition to providing the funding to conduct such training, management needs to demonstrate that it supports employees who follow prescribed security policies. This is especially important for combating social engineering attacks, because countermeasures may sometimes create embarrassing confrontations with other employees. For example, a systems professional at a major bank refused to allow a person who was not on the list of authorized employees to enter the room housing the servers that contained the bank's key financial information. The person denied entry happened to be a new executive who was just hired. Instead of reprimanding the employee, the executive demonstrated the bank's commitment to and support for strong security by writing a formal letter of commendation for meritorious performance to be placed in the employee's performance file. It is this type of visible top management support for security that enhances the effectiveness of all security policies. Top management also needs to support the enforcement of sanctions, up to and including termination, against employees who willfully violate security policies. Doing so not only sends a strong message to other employees but may sometimes lessen the consequences to the organization if the employee had engaged in illegal behavior.

Controlling Physical Access

Physical access controls are another important layer of preventive controls. In fact, controlling physical access to the system is absolutely essential to achieve any degree of information security. A skilled attacker needs only a few minutes of unsupervised direct physical access in order to bypass existing information security controls. For example, an attacker with unsupervised direct physical access can install a keystroke logging device that captures a user's authentication credentials, thereby enabling the attacker to subsequently obtain unauthorized access to the system by impersonating a legitimate user. Someone with unsupervised physical access could also insert special "boot" disks that provide direct access to every file on the computer and then copy sensitive files to a portable device like a USB drive. Alternatively, an attacker with unsupervised physical access could simply remove the hard drive or even steal the entire computer. Given this wide range of potential threats associated with unsupervised physical access, it should not be surprising that another of COBIT's 34 top-level control objectives, DS 12, focuses specifically on physical security.

Physical access control begins with entry points to the building itself. Ideally, there should only be one regular entry point that is unlocked during normal office hours. Fire codes usually require additional emergency exits, but these should not permit entry from the outside and should be connected to an alarm system that is automatically triggered whenever the fire exit is opened. In addition, either a receptionist or a security guard should be stationed at the main entrance to verify the identity of employees and to require that all visitors sign in and be met by an employee, who escorts them wherever they go in the building.

Once inside the building, physical access to rooms housing computer equipment must also be restricted. These rooms should be securely locked and all entry/exit monitored by closed circuit television systems. Multiple failed access attempts should trigger an alarm. Rooms housing servers that contain especially sensitive data should supplement regular locks with stronger technologies such as card readers, numeric keypads, or various biometric devices such as iris or retina scanners, fingerprint readers, or voice recognition. Focus 7-3 describes an especially elaborate set of physical access controls referred to as a man-trap.

Access to the wiring used in the organization's LANs also needs to be restricted in order to prevent wiretapping. That means that cables and wiring should not be exposed in areas accessible to casual visitors. Wall jacks not in current use should be physically disconnected from the network to prevent someone from just plugging in their laptop and attempting to access the network. Wiring closets containing telecommunications

7-3
FOCUS
Controlling Physical Access with Man-Traps

Financial institutions, defense contractors, and various intelligence agencies store especially valuable data. Therefore, they often need to employ much more elaborate physical access control measures than those used by most other organizations. One such technique involves the use of specially designed rooms called man-traps. These rooms serve as an entryway to the data center. They typically contain two doors, each of which uses multiple authentication methods to control access. For example, entry to the first door may require both insertion of an ID card or smart card into a reader as well as entering an identification code into a keypad. Successful authentication opens the first door and provides access to the entrance room. Once inside the room, the first door automatically closes behind the person, locks, and cannot be opened from inside the room. The other door, which opens into the data center, is also locked. Thus, the person is now trapped in this small room (hence the name *man-trap*). The only way out is to successfully pass a second set of authentication controls that restrict access through the door leading to the data center. Typically, this involves multifactor authentication that include using a biometric device. Failure to pass this second set of tests leaves the person in the room until members of the security staff arrive. Man-traps are effective, but expensive. Therefore, they are only used to protect extremely valuable assets.

equipment need to be securely locked as well. If wiring closets are shared with other tenants of an office building, the organization should place its telecommunications equipment inside locked steel cages to prevent unauthorized physical access by anyone else with access to that wiring closet.

Physical access security must be cost-effective. This requires top-management involvement in planning physical access security controls to ensure that all information system resources are properly valued and that the nature and combination of access controls reflect the value of the assets being protected.

Laptops, cell phones, and PDA devices require special attention. Laptop theft is a large problem. The major cost is not the price of replacing the laptop, but the loss of the confidential information it contains and the costs of notifying those affected. For example, when a laptop of a Wells Fargo Bank employee containing personal account information was stolen, the company incurred the costs of notifying thousands of customers about the potential compromise of their personal information and the costs associated with assisting them to change passwords and account information. GMAC Insurance experienced a similar problem when two laptops were stolen from an employee's car in Atlanta.

To deal with the threat of laptop theft, employees should be trained to always lock their laptops to an immovable object. This is necessary even when in the office, as there have been cases where thieves disguised as cleaning crews have stolen laptops and other equipment during working hours. In addition, sensitive data should be stored only on removable media, not the hard drive, and special care should be taken to restrict access to the removable storage media. Several government research labs, including Los Alamos, Sandia, and Lawrence Livermore, have had to suspend work because of the disappearance or theft of such removable media containing classified information. Consequently, because of the possibility of theft, security experts suggest that any confidential or sensitive data be encrypted during storage to minimize the likelihood that a thief will be able to access it. Some organizations are also installing special software on laptops so that if one is stolen, it will automatically dial a toll-free number and reveal its current location when the thief attempts to use it to connect to the Internet.

Cell phones and PDAs also increasingly store confidential information and therefore need the same types of controls that are used for laptops. It is also important to restrict access to network printers, because they often store document images on their hard drives. There have been cases where intruders have stolen the hard drives in those printers, thereby gaining access to sensitive information.

Controlling Remote Access

Most organizations provide employees, customers, and suppliers with remote access to their information systems. Usually this access occurs via the Internet, but some organizations still maintain proprietary WANs or provide direct dial-up access by modem. Many organizations also provide wireless access to their systems. We now discuss the various methods that can be used to satisfy COBIT control objective DS 5.10 to control remote access to information resources.

Perimeter Defense: Routers, Firewalls, and Intrusion Prevention Systems

Figure 7-4 shows the relationship between an organization's information system and the Internet. A device called a **border router** connects an organization's information system to the Internet. Behind the border router is the main **firewall**, which is either a

Figure 7-4
Example Organizational
Network Architecture

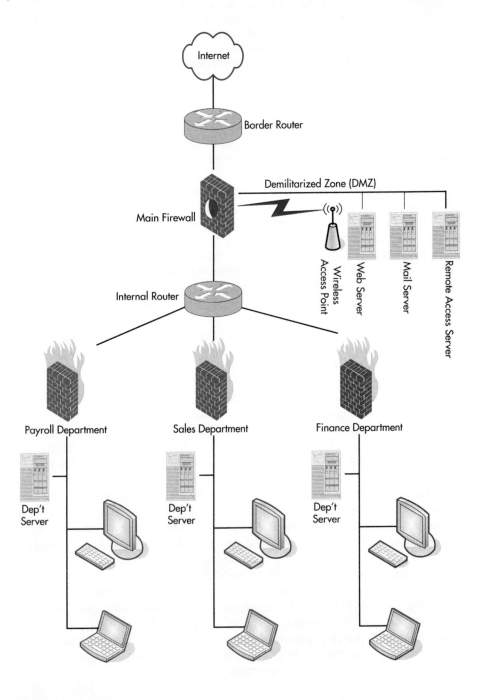

special-purpose hardware device or software running on a general-purpose computer. The **demilitarized zone (DMZ)** is a separate network that permits controlled access from the Internet to selected resources, such as the organization's e-commerce Web server. Together, the border router and firewall act as filters to control which information is allowed to enter and leave the organization's information system. To understand how they function, it is first necessary to briefly discuss how information is transmitted on the Internet.

Overview of TCP/IP and Routers. Information traverses the Internet and internal local area networks in the form of packets. Thus, the documents and files on your computer are not sent intact to a printer or a colleague. Instead, they are first divided into packets and those packets are then sent over the local area network and, perhaps, the Internet, to their destination. The device receiving those packets must then reassemble them in order to recreate the original document or file. Well-defined rules and procedures called protocols dictate how to perform all these activities. Figure 7-5 (see next page) shows how two important protocols, referred to as TCP/IP, govern the process for transmitting information over the Internet. The **Transmission Control Protocol (TCP)** specifies the procedures for dividing files and documents into packets to be sent over the Internet and the methods for reassembly of the original document or file at the destination. The **Internet Protocol (IP)** specifies the structure of those packets and how to route them to the proper destination.

The structure of IP packets facilitates their efficient transmission over the Internet. Every IP packet consists of two parts: a header and a body. The header contains the packet's origin and destination addresses, as well as information about the type of data contained in the body of the packet. The IP protocol prescribes the size of the header and the sequence of information fields in it. For example, in IP version 4, which is still commonly used in North America, the 13th through 16th bytes in the header *always* contain the IP address of the source of the packet, and the 17th through 20th bytes *always* contain the destination address. This well-defined structure makes it easy for computers to decide where to send each packet that arrives.

Special-purpose devices called **routers** are designed to read the destination address fields in IP packet headers to decide where to send (route) the packet next. The current version of the IP protocol, IPv4, uses 32-bit-long addresses. Those addresses consist of four 8-bit numbers separated by periods. When users type a URL in their browser, that name is translated into the appropriate address. For example, the Acme Manufacturing Company's publicly accessible Web server might have an IP address of 135.22.74.10, but anyone wishing to visit the site can enter the URL of www.acme.com in their browser instead of that IP address. An organization's border router checks the contents of the destination address field of every packet it receives. If the address is not that of the organization, the packet is forwarded on to another router on the Internet. If the destination address matches that of the organization, the packet undergoes one or more tests before being allowed in.

Filtering Packets. A set of rules, called an **access control list (ACL)**, determines which packets are allowed entry and which are dropped. Border routers typically perform what is called **static packet filtering**, which screens individual IP packets based solely on the contents of the source and/or destination fields in the IP packet header. For example, a border router's ACL usually contains rules that specify that the following packets should not be allowed further entry into the organization's information system:

- Packets with illegal source addresses. Certain IP addresses have been reserved for internal use only and are not supposed to be routed over the Internet:
 10.0.0.0–10.255.255.255
 172.16.0.0–172.31.255.255
 192.168.0.0–192.168.255.255

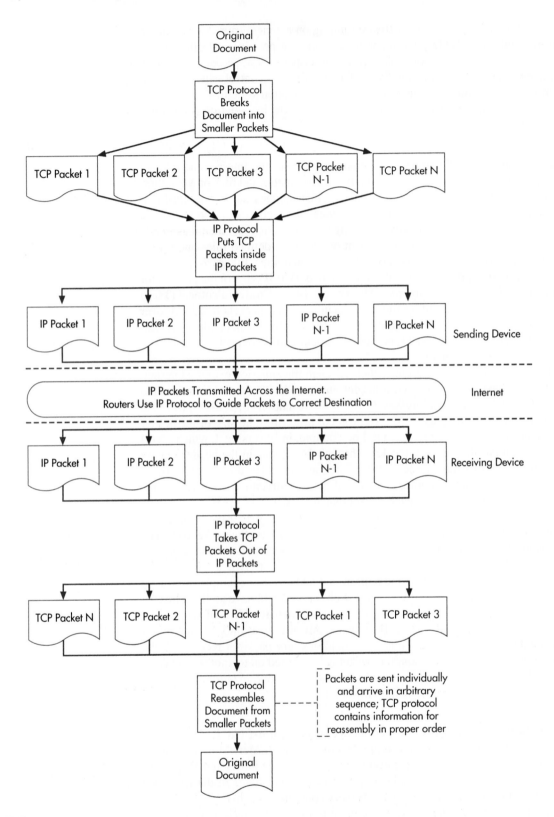

Figure 7-5
Functions of TCP/IP Protocols

If a packet arriving over the Internet at a border router has one of these source addresses, it is either the result of an error or more likely is a specially crafted attack packet intended to deceive the recipient about its source of origin. In either case, the packet should not be allowed entry.

● Packets with the organization's IP address as the source address. IP packets sent from one internal employee to another usually do not need to be routed over the Internet. Thus, any packet arriving from the Internet with an internal address in the source IP address field likely represents an attempt to spoof the recipient about its origin and, therefore, should not be allowed entry.

Border router ACLs often contain several additional rules that specify other types of packets that should be denied entry. The function of the border router is to quickly identify and drop certain types of packets and to pass all other packets to the firewall, where they will be subjected to more detailed testing before being allowed to enter the organization's internal network. Thus, most rules in the border router's ACL focus on dropping packets. The last rule in the ACL, however, usually specifies that any packet not dropped because of the preceding rules should be passed on to the firewall.

Like the border router, firewalls use ACLs to determine what to do with each packet that arrives. A major difference, however, is that firewalls are designed to only permit packets that meet specific conditions to pass. Thus, unlike border routers, the final rule in a firewall ACL usually specifies that any packet not allowed entry by a previous rule should be dropped. Note, however, that firewalls do not block *all* traffic, but only filter it. That is why all the firewalls in Figure 7-4 have holes in them—to show that certain kinds of traffic can pass through.

Firewalls use more sophisticated techniques than border routers do to filter packets. For example, most firewalls employ what is called stateful packet filtering. Whereas static packet filtering examines each IP packet in isolation, **stateful packet filtering** maintains a table that lists all established connections between the organization's computers and the Internet. The firewall consults this table to determine whether an incoming packet is part of an ongoing communication initiated by an internal computer. This information enables the firewall to reject specially crafted attack packets that would have passed a simple static packet filter by pretending to be a response to an internally initiated request, when in fact no such preceding request occurred.

Deep Packet Inspection. Stateful packet filtering is still limited to examining only information in the IP packet header, however. Essentially, this is the same thing as trying to screen mail simply by looking at the destination and return addresses on the envelope. Such a process is fast and can catch patently undesirable packages (e.g., businesses may not want to accept mail from casinos or pornographic magazines), but its effectiveness is limited. Undesirable mail can get through if the return address is not on the list of unacceptable sources. Clearly, control over incoming mail would be more effective if each envelope or package were opened and inspected. Similarly, firewalls that examine the data in the body of an IP packet can provide more effective access control than those that look only at information in the IP header. Such a process is called **deep packet inspection**. The added control provided by deep packet inspection, however, comes at the cost of speed: It takes more time to examine the body of an IP packet, which could contain more than a thousand bytes of data, than to examine only the 20 bytes in the header of an IPv4 packet.

Deep packet inspection is the heart of a new type of filter called **intrusion prevention systems (IPS)**, which are designed to identify and drop packets that are part of an attack. IPSs use several techniques to identify undesirable packets. One involves checking packet contents against a database of patterns (signatures) of known attack methods. Another involves developing a profile of "normal" traffic and using statistical analysis to identify packets that do not fit that profile. Most promising is the use of rule bases that specify acceptable standards for specific types of traffic and that drop all packets that do not conform to those standards. The beauty of this approach is that

it blocks not only known attacks, for which signatures already exist, but also any new attacks that violate the standards.

Although IPSs are a promising addition to the arsenal of security products, they are relatively new and, therefore, not without problems. As mentioned earlier, deep packet inspection slows overall throughput. In addition, IPSs are prone to false alarms, which results in rejecting legitimate traffic. Nevertheless, a great deal of research is being undertaken to improve the intelligence of IPSs and they are likely to become an important part of an organization's security toolkit. IPSs will not, however, replace the need for firewalls. Instead, they are a complementary tool and provide yet another layer of perimeter defense.

Defense-in-depth. The use of multiple perimeter filtering devices is actually more efficient than trying to use only one device. Thus, border routers quickly filter out obviously bad packets and pass the rest to the main firewall. The firewall does more detailed checking, allowing in only those packets purporting to contain specific types of data for specific types of programs and dropping all others. The IPS then performs deep packet inspection on the packets passed by the firewall to verify that the data they contain does indeed conform to the organization's security policies.

Figure 7-4 illustrates one other dimension of the concept of defense-in-depth: the use of a number of internal firewalls to segment different departments within the organization. Recall that many security incidents involve employees, not outsiders. These internal firewalls help to restrict what data and portions of the organization's information system particular employees can access. This not only increases security but also strengthens internal control by providing a means for enforcing segregation of duties.

An especially effective way to achieve defense-in-depth is to integrate physical and remote access control systems. For example, if an organization uses keypads, card or badge readers, or biometric identifiers to control and log physical access to the office, that data should be considered when applying remote access controls. This would identify situations likely to represent security breaches, such as when the same employee supposedly is inside the office and yet simultaneously trying to log into the system remotely from another geographically distant location.

Dial-up Connections

Many organizations still permit employees to remotely access the organizational network by dialing in with a modem. It is important to verify the identity of users attempting to obtain dial-in access. The **Remote Authentication Dial-In User Service (RADIUS)** is a standard method for doing that. Dial-in users connect to a remote access server and submit their log-in credentials. The remote access server passes those credentials to the RADIUS server, which performs compatibility tests to authenticate the identity of that user. Note that Figure 7-4 shows the remote access server located in the DMZ. Thus, only *after* the user has been authenticated is access to the internal corporate network granted. This subjects dial-in users to the same controls applied to traffic coming in from the untrusted Internet.

Modems, however, are cheap and easy to install, so employees are often tempted to install them on their desktop workstations without seeking permission or notifying anyone that they have done so. This creates a huge hole in perimeter security, because the incoming connection is not filtered by the main firewall. Moreover, when employees install modems they seldom configure any strong authentication controls. Consequently, a single unauthorized ("rogue") modem connected to an employee's desktop workstation creates a "back door" through which attackers can often easily compromise an otherwise well-protected system. Therefore, either information security or internal audit staff should periodically check for the existence of rogue modems. This is most efficiently and effectively accomplished by using **war dialing** software, which calls every telephone number assigned to the organization to identify those which are connected to modems. (Hackers do this also, to identify targets). Any rogue modems discovered by

war dialing should be disconnected, with sanctions applied to the employees responsible for installing them.

Wireless Access

Many organizations also provide wireless access to their information systems. Wireless access is convenient and easy. This ease of access provides another venue for attack and extends the perimeter that must be protected. For example, a number of companies have experienced security incidents in which intruders used a laptop equipped with a wireless NIC to access the corporate network while sitting in a car parked outside the building. It is not enough to monitor the parking lot because wireless signals can often be picked up miles away.

To secure wireless access, Figure 7-4 shows that all wireless access points (the devices that accept incoming wireless communications and permit the sending device to connect to the organization's network) should be located in the DMZ. This treats all wireless access as if it was coming in from the Internet and forces all wireless traffic to go through the main firewall and any intrusion prevention systems that are used to protect the perimeter of the internal network. In addition, the following procedures need to be followed to adequately secure wireless access:

- Turn on available security features. Most wireless equipment is sold and installed with these features disabled. For example, the default installation configuration for most wireless routers does not turn on encryption.
- Authenticate all devices attempting to establish wireless access to the network *before* assigning them an IP address. This can be done by treating incoming wireless connections as dial-in access attempts and routing them first through a RADIUS server or other authentication device.
- Configure all authorized wireless NICs to operate only in infrastructure mode, which forces the device to connect only to wireless access points. (Wireless NICs can also be set to operate in ad hoc mode, which enables them to communicate directly with any other device that has a wireless NIC. This is a security threat because it creates peer-to-peer networks with little or no authentication controls.)
- Use noninformative names for the access point's address, which is called a service set identifier (SSID). SSIDs like "payroll," "finance," or "R&D" are more obvious targets to attack than devices with generic SSIDs like "A1," or "X2."
- Predefine a list of authorized MAC addresses and configure wireless access points to only accept connections if the device's MAC address is on the authorized list.
- Reduce the broadcast strength of wireless access points to make unauthorized reception off-premises more difficult.
- Locate wireless access points in the interior of the building and use directional antennas to make unauthorized access and eavesdropping more difficult.

Finally, as is the case with modems, it is easy and inexpensive for employees to set up unauthorized wireless access points in their offices. Therefore, information security or internal audit staff should periodically test for the existence of such rogue access points, disable any that are discovered, and appropriately discipline the employees responsible for installing them.

Host and Application Hardening

Routers, firewalls, and intrusion prevention systems are designed to protect the network perimeter. However, just as many homes and businesses supplement exterior door locks and alarm systems with locked cabinets and safes to store valuables, information system security is enhanced by supplementing preventive controls on the network perimeter with additional preventive controls on the workstations, servers,

printers, and other devices (collectively referred to as **hosts**) that comprise the organization's network. Three areas deserve special attention:

1 Host configuration
2 User accounts
3 Software design

1 Host Configuration

Hosts can be made more secure by modifying their configurations. Default configurations of most devices typically turn on a large number of optional settings that are seldom, if ever, used. Similarly, default installations of many operating systems turn on many special-purpose programs, called services, that are not essential. Turning on unnecessary features and extra services maximizes the likelihood of successful installation without the need for customer support. This convenience, however, comes at the cost of creating security weaknesses. Every program running on a host represents a potential point of attack because it probably contains flaws, called **vulnerabilities**, that can be exploited to either crash the system or take control of it. Therefore, any optional programs and features that are not used should be disabled. Tools like the Microsoft Baseline Security Analyzer and vulnerability scanners can be used to identify unused and, therefore, unnecessary programs that represent potential security threats. This process of turning off unnecessary features is called **hardening**.

In addition to hardening, every host needs to be running antivirus and firewall software that is regularly updated. Moreover, COBIT control objective DS 5.7 states that it is especially important to harden and properly configure every device used to protect the network (e.g., firewalls, IPS, routers, etc.), to make them resistant to tampering.

2 Managing User Accounts and Privileges

COBIT control objective DS 5.4 stresses the need to carefully manage all user accounts, especially those accounts that have unlimited (administrative) rights on that computer. Administrative rights are needed in order to install software and alter most configuration settings. These unlimited capabilities make accounts with administrative rights prime targets for attackers. Therefore, users who need administrative powers on a particular computer should be assigned two accounts: one with administrative rights and another that has only limited privileges. Users should log in under their limited account to perform routine daily duties, and only log in to their administrative account when they need to perform some action, such as installing new software, that requires administrative rights. It is especially important to use a limited regular user account when browsing the Web or reading e-mail. This way, if the user visits a compromised Web site or opens an infected e-mail, the attacker will only acquire limited rights on the machine. COBIT control objective DS 5.4 also stresses the importance of periodically reviewing all accounts and their associated privileges.

3 Software Design

As organizations have increased the effectiveness of their perimeter security controls, attackers have increasingly targeted vulnerabilities in application programs. Buffer overflows, SQL injection, and cross-site scripting are common examples of attacks against the software running on Web sites. These attacks all exploit poorly written software that does not thoroughly check user-supplied input prior to further processing. Consider the common task of soliciting user input such as name and address. Most programs set aside a fixed amount of memory, referred to as a buffer, to hold user input. However, if the program does not carefully check the size of data being input, an attacker may enter many times the amount of data that was anticipated and overflow the buffer. The excess data may be written to an area of memory normally used to store and execute commands. In such cases, an attacker may be able to take control of the machine by sending carefully crafted commands in the excess data. Similarly, SQL injection attacks occur whenever Web application software that interfaces with a database server does not filter user input,

thereby permitting an attacker to send SQL commands and execute them on the database server. Cross-site scripting attacks occur if web application software does not carefully filter user input before returning any of that data to the browser, in which case the victim's browser will execute any embedded malicious script.

The common theme in all of these attacks is the failure to "scrub" user input to remove potentially malicious code. Programmers must be trained to treat all input from external users as untrusted and to carefully check it before performing further actions. Poor programming techniques occur in both internally created code and in software purchased from third parties. The gravity of this threat is reflected in the fact that several sections of the COBIT framework are devoted to control objectives for application software. Section AI 2 specifies the need to carefully design security into all new applications. Section AI 7 stresses the importance of thoroughly testing new applications before deployment. Sections DS 1 and DS 2 enumerate specific control objectives appropriate when contracting with vendors.

Encryption

Encryption is the final layer of preventive controls. Encrypting sensitive data while it is stored provides one last barrier that must be overcome by an intruder who has obtained unauthorized access to that information resource. Encryption also strengthens authentication procedures and plays an essential role in ensuring and verifying the validity of e-business transactions. Therefore, it is important for accountants, auditors, and systems professionals to understand encryption.

Encryption is the process of transforming normal text, called **plaintext**, into unreadable gibberish, called **ciphertext**. **Decryption** reverses this process, transforming ciphertext back into plaintext. Figure 7-6 shows that both a key and an algorithm

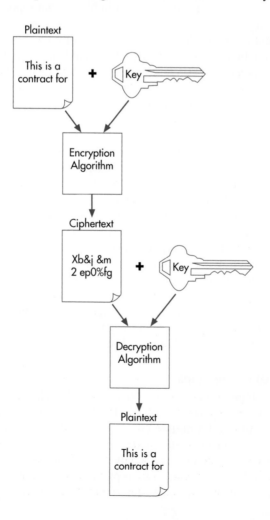

Figure 7-6
Encryption and Decryption Process

are used to encrypt plaintext into ciphertext and to decrypt the ciphertext back into plaintext. Computers represent plaintext and ciphertext as a series of binary digits (0s and 1s). The key is also a string of binary digits of a fixed length; for example, a 128-bit key consists of a string of 128 0s and 1s. The algorithm is a formula for combining the key and the text. Most documents are longer than the key, so the computer first divides the plaintext or ciphertext into blocks, each block being of equal length to the key. It then applies the algorithm to each block of text. For example, if a 128-bit key was being used, the computer first divides the document or file into 128-bit-long blocks and then combines each block and the key in the manner specified by the algorithm (for example, by adding them). This produces a ciphertext version of the document or file, equal in size to the original. To reproduce the original document, the computer first divides the ciphertext into 128-bit blocks and then applies the decryption key to each block.

Encryption Strength

Three important factors determine the strength of any encryption system:

1 Key length
2 Key management policies
3 Nature of the encryption algorithm

Longer keys provide stronger encryption by reducing the number of repeating blocks of ciphertext. This makes it harder to spot patterns in the ciphertext that reflect patterns in the original plaintext. For example, *the* is one of the most common three-letter words in English. Each character in English is represented by an 8-bit code. Thus, a 24-bit encryption key would create ciphertext in blocks that represent three consecutive English language characters. Such a short key is weak because it provides an opportunity to identify commonly recurring blocks of ciphertext likely to represent common words, thereby enabling the analyst to "break" the encryption code.

COBIT control objective DS 5.8 identifies important control objectives related to the management of cryptographic keys. Indeed, this is often the most vulnerable aspect of encryption systems. No matter how strong an encryption algorithm is, if the keys have been compromised, the encryption can be easily broken. Therefore, access to encryption keys must be tightly controlled. Organizations must also have a way to decrypt the data in the event that the employee who encrypted it leaves. The best way to do this is to use encryption software that creates a built-in master key that can be used to decrypt anything encrypted by that software. A second-best alternative is a process called **key escrow**, which involves making copies of all encryption keys used by employees and storing those copies securely. Key escrow is less desirable than using built-in master keys because the organization now has to protect both the original and duplicate copies of the encryption keys.

A third factor affecting encryption strength concerns the nature of the algorithm. A strong algorithm is difficult, if not impossible, to break by using brute-force guessing techniques. Secrecy is not necessary for strength. Indeed, the procedures used by the most accepted and widely used encryption algorithms are publicly available. Their strength is due not to their procedures being secret, but to the fact that they have been rigorously tested and demonstrated to resist brute-force guessing attacks.

Types of Encryption Systems

There are two basic types of encryption systems. **Symmetric encryption systems** use the same key both to encrypt and to decrypt. DES and AES are examples of symmetric encryption systems. **Asymmetric encryption systems** use two keys. One key, called the **public key**, is widely distributed and available to everyone; the other, called the **private key**, is kept secret and known only to the owner of that pair of keys. Either the public or private key can be used to encrypt, but only the other key can decrypt the ciphertext. RSA and PGP are examples of asymmetric encryption systems.

Symmetric encryption is much faster than asymmetric encryption, but it has several problems. First, both parties (sender and receiver) need to know the shared secret key. This means that the two parties need to have some method for securely exchanging the key. E-mail is not a solution, because anyone who can intercept the e-mail would know the secret key. A second problem is that separate secret keys need to be created for use with each different party with whom encryption is going to be used. Otherwise, anyone possessing the common secret key could decrypt any encrypted documents to which access is obtained, legitimately or illegitimately, whether intended for that person or not. The number of secret keys required grows quickly, becoming difficult to manage if encryption is desired with thousands of other entities. Third, because both parties using symmetric encryption must know the same secret key, there is no way to prove who created a specific document. Each party could claim that the other used the shared secret key in an attempt to defraud. Thus, symmetric encryption provides no way to create legally binding agreements.

Asymmetric encryption systems solve these three problems. It does not matter who knows the public key, because any text encrypted with it can only be decrypted by using the corresponding private key. Therefore, the public key can be distributed by e-mail or even be posted on a Web site so that anyone who wants to can send encrypted information to the owner of that public key. Also, any number of parties can use the same public key to send encrypted messages because only the owner of the corresponding private key can decrypt the messages. Finally, information can be encrypted with the private key and then decrypted with the corresponding public key. Since the private key is possessed by only one party, this makes it possible to prove who created a document, thereby providing a means for creating legally binding electronic agreements.

The main drawback to asymmetric encryption systems is speed. Asymmetric encryption is much (thousands of times) slower than symmetric encryption. Thus, asymmetric encryption is too slow to be used to exchange large amounts of data over the Internet. Consequently, e-business uses both types of encryption systems. Symmetric encryption is used to encode most of the data being exchanged. Asymmetric encryption is used to safely send the symmetric key to the recipient for use in decrypting the ciphertext. As discussed later, asymmetric encryption is also used in combination with a process called hashing to create digital signatures.

Hashing

Hashing is a process that takes plaintext of any length and transforms it into a short code called a **hash**. For example, the SHA-256 algorithm creates a 256-bit hash, regardless of the size of the original plaintext. Hashing differs from encryption in two important aspects. First, as Table 7-2 shows, encryption always produces ciphertext similar in length to the original plaintext, but hashing always produces a hash that is of a fixed short length, regardless of the length of the original plaintext. The second difference is that encryption is reversible, but hashing is not. Given the decryption key and the algorithm, ciphertext can be decrypted back into the original plaintext. In contrast, it is not possible to transform a hash back into the original plaintext, because hashing throws away information. For example, using SHA-256 to hash a 20,000-word document produces a 256-bit hash. There is no way to convert that short string of bits back into the original document.

Length of Input	Length of Encrypted Output	Length of Output Hashing (SHA-256 algorithm)
1 sentence	1 sentence	256 bits
1 page	1 page	256 bits
10 pages	10 pages	256 bits

Table 7-2
Comparison of Encryption and Hashing

Digital Signatures

Asymmetric encryption and hashing are used to create digital signatures. A **digital signature** is information encrypted with the creator's private key. Information so encrypted can only be decrypted using the corresponding public key. Therefore, successful decryption with an entity's public key proves that the message could only have been created by using the corresponding private key. By definition, that private key is known only to its owner. Consequently, only the entity owning the pair of public and private keys could have created that message.

Remember that asymmetric encryption is slow. Therefore, digital signatures are not normally created by using the private key to encrypt the entire contract, purchase order, or other document being exchanged. Instead, the document is first run through a hashing algorithm. The resulting hash is then encrypted using the sender's private key to create the digital signature.

Using a hash of the original plaintext to create a digital signature not only is efficient but also provides a means for establishing that the message decrypted by the recipient is exactly the same as the message created by the sender. Hashing algorithms use every bit in the original plaintext to calculate the hash value. Therefore, changing any character in the document being hashed, such as replacing a 1 with a 7, will produce a different hash value. This property of hashing algorithms provides a means to verify that the contents of a message have not been altered. The recipient can use the sender's public key to decrypt the digital signature, which produces a hash of the original document. After decrypting the encrypted document, the recipient can then run the plaintext through the same hashing algorithm used by the sender. If the resulting hash matches the digital signature, the recipient is assured that the plaintext document received and decrypted is exactly what the sender originally created.

One question still remains, however. Successfully using a public key to decrypt a document or file proves that it was created by the entity possessing the corresponding private key. But, how can the recipient be sure of that entity's identity? For example, how can a consumer know that a file purportedly created by a financial institution really was created by that financial institution and not by someone who created a pair of public and private keys and uses them to masquerade as that financial institution? For that matter, how does the recipient obtain the sender's public key? Having the sender provide its public key directly to the recipient would not provide any protection against impersonation. The answers to these questions involve the use of digital certificates and the creation of a public key infrastructure.

Digital Certificates and Public Key Infrastructure

A **digital certificate** is an electronic document, created and digitally signed by a trusted third party, that certifies the identity of the owner of a particular public key. In fact, the digital certificate contains that party's public key. Digital certificates can be stored on Web sites. Browsers are designed to automatically obtain a copy of that digital certificate and use the public key contained therein to communicate with the Web site. (You can manually examine the contents of a Web site's digital certificate by double-clicking on the lock icon that appears in your browser window when you visit a Web site.) Thus, digital certificates provide an automated method for obtaining an organization's or individual's public key.

The term **public key infrastructure (PKI)** refers to the system and processes used to issue and manage asymmetric keys and digital certificates. The organization that issues public and private keys and records the public key in a digital certificate is called a **certificate authority**. Digital certificates intended for e-business use are typically issued by commercial certificate authorities, such as Thawte and VeriSign. The certificate authority hashes the information stored on a digital certificate and then encrypts that hash with its private key. That digital signature is then appended to the digital certificate, which provides the means for validating the authenticity of the certificate.

Organizations can also create their own digital certificates for internal use. Although it is unlikely that other parties would trust such certificates for business

transactions, they do enable the organization to use public and private keys to provide stronger authentication of users. Each organization configures the browsers on employee workstations with a list of trusted certificate authorities. (In Internet Explorer, you can view the list of certificate authorities trusted by your browser by opening your browser, selecting Internet Options on the Tools menu, then moving to the Content tab and then clicking the "Publishers" button.) Thus, the entire PKI system hinges on trusting the certificate authority.

The AICPA's Trust Services framework contains a list of criteria that can be used to evaluate the overall reliability of a particular certificate authority. One important factor concerns the procedures the certificate authority uses to verify the identity of an applicant for a digital certificate. Several classes of digital certificates exist. The cheapest, and least trustworthy, may involve nothing more than verifying the applicant's e-mail address. The most expensive certificates may require verification of the applicant's identity through use of credit reports and tax returns. Digital certificates, like driver licenses and passports, are valid for only a specified period of time. Thus, a second important criterion for assessing the reliability of a certificate authority is the procedures it uses to update certificates and revoke expired digital certificates.

Illustrative Example: The Role of Encryption and Hashing in E-Business

Figure 7-7 uses the example of Northwest Industries submitting a competitive bid to provide services to a local government agency to illustrate how hashing, symmetric encryption, and asymmetric encryption techniques are all used together in an e-business transaction. The example assumes that both Northwest Industries and the government agency have previously acquired digital certificates from a mutually trusted certificate authority.

Step 1 A Northwest Industries employee connects to the government agency's Web site and clicks on the button for submitting bids on open contracts. *The browser moves to a secure Web page displaying the familiar lock icon. The browser software on the employee's computer obtains the Web site's digital certificate, verifies its validity, and opens it to get the agency's public key. The government Web site software follows similar steps to acquire Northwest Industries' public key.*

Step 2 The employee clicks a button to attach and submit the company's bid. *Behind the scenes, the encryption software performs the following actions:*
 (a) Uses a hashing algorithm, such as SHA-256, to create a hash of the bid.
 (b) Encrypts the hash using Northwest Industries' private key. This creates a digital signature for the bid.
 (c) Encrypts the bid using the AES symmetric key algorithm. This protects the confidentiality of the bid, as only someone who knows the AES key can decrypt it.
 (d) Uses the government agency's public key to encrypt the AES key used in step 2c. This ensures that only the intended recipient (the government agency) will be able to decrypt the AES key needed to decrypt the bid.

Step 3 The encrypted bid (created in step 2c), the AES key needed to decrypt that bid (created in step 2d), and Northwest Industries' digital signature (created in step 2b) are all sent over the Internet to the government agency.

Step 4 The government agency's computer receives the package of information and performs the following steps:
 (a) Uses Northwest Industries' public key, obtained in step 1, to decrypt the digital signature created in step 2b. This yields the hash of the original bid that was created by the sender.
 (b) Uses its private key to decrypt the AES key sent by Northwest Industries in step 2d.
 (c) Uses the AES key from step 4b to decrypt the encrypted bid produced in step 2c. This produces a plaintext version of Northwest Industries' bid.

Figure 7-7
Use of Encryption and Hashing
for E-business

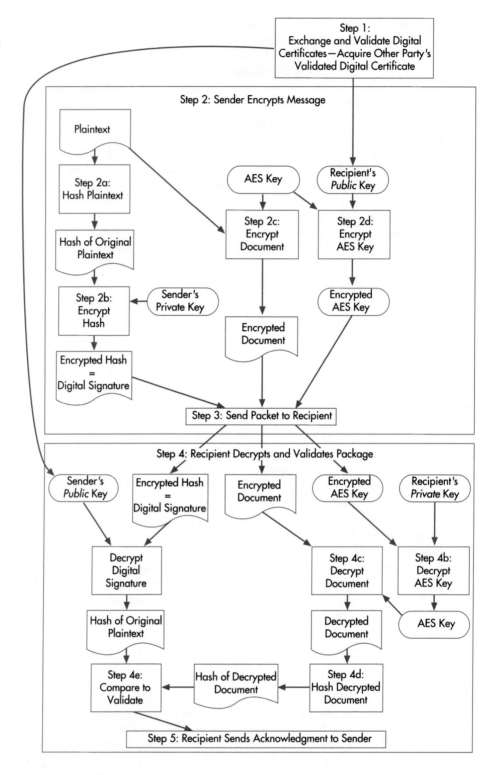

(d) Uses the same hashing algorithm used by Northwest Industries in step 2a to hash the plaintext copy of the bid created in step 4c.

(e) Compares the hash created in step 4d to that produced by step 4a. If the two match, the government agency knows that (1) the copy of the bid it re-created in step 4c was created by Northwest Industries, and (2) the bid has not been altered or garbled during transmission.

Step 5 The agency sends Northwest Industries an acknowledgement that its bid has been received.

Sidebar: Digital Signatures versus E-signatures

Digital signatures use asymmetric encryption to create legally-binding electronic documents. Web-based e-signatures are an alternative mechanism for accomplishing the same objective. An **e-signature** is a cursive-style imprint of a person's name that is applied to an electronic document. Users must first register with a company that provides Web-based e-signature services, a process that includes getting a password. When the user wants to affix their e-signature to a document, they visit the Web site of the e-signature company, log in and answer a series of authentication questions, and then click on the location on the document where they want their "signature" to appear. The software then affixes a cursive imprint of the user's name. Note that the user does not actually "sign" the document, as you do when using credit card readers at many stores. Instead, the software just attaches their name in a cursive font of the user's choice. Nevertheless, e-signatures are legally-binding, just as if the user had really "signed" a paper copy of the document.

Effects of Encryption on other Layers of Defense

Although encryption provides many benefits, it also creates problems for other security procedures. For example, firewalls function by inspecting the contents of packets but cannot effectively screen packets that are encrypted. Some organizations address this problem by having the firewall route encrypted packets to a computer in the DMZ that decrypts them; that computer then sends the decrypted packets back through the firewall for filtering before being allowed into the internal network. Although this approach allows the firewall to screen all incoming packets, it makes the decrypted packets vulnerable to sniffing attacks on the internal network. On the other hand, configuring the main firewall to allow encrypted packets to enter the internal network protects the confidentiality of sensitive information until it reaches the appropriate destination but creates potential holes in access controls because the packets are not filtered by the firewall. Thus, organizations must choose which security objective is more important: confidentiality or access control. Unfortunately, this type of dilemma is not unique to firewalls; antivirus programs and intrusion detection systems also have difficulty in dealing with encrypted packets. This necessity of trading off one aspect of security against another is one reason that designing and implementing comprehensive information security procedures is so difficult.

Detective Controls

Preventive controls are never 100% effective in blocking all attacks. Therefore, COBIT control objective DS 5.5 stresses that organizations also need to implement controls designed to detect intrusions in a timely manner. Detective controls enhance security by monitoring the effectiveness of preventive controls and detecting incidents in which preventive controls have been successfully circumvented.

Some security procedures function as both preventive and detective controls. For example, COBIT control objective DS 5.3 prescribes the use of authentication and authorization controls as preventive controls designed to implement the organization's policies governing access to the system and limiting the actions that can be performed by authorized users. The audit trail created by those authentication and authorization controls is itself a detective control that can be examined to determine whether actual system use is in compliance with those policies. The remainder of this section discusses the four types of detective controls listed in Table 7-1: log analysis, intrusion detection systems, managerial reports, and security testing.

Log Analysis

Most systems come with extensive capabilities for logging who accesses the system and what specific actions each user performed. These logs form an audit trail of system access. Like any other audit trail, logs are of value only if they are routinely examined. **Log analysis** is the process of examining logs to monitor security.

Figure 7-8 is an example of a portion of security log from a computer running the Windows operating system. It shows that a user named "rjones" unsuccessfully tried to log onto computer named "payroll server." The person analyzing the log must seek to determine the reason for this failed log-on attempt. It may be that rjones is a legitimate user who forgot the password. Another possibility is that rjones is a legitimate user but is not authorized to access the payroll server. Yet another possibility is that the user ID is itself invalid, in which case this may represent an attempted attack by an external intruder.

Log analysis needs to be done regularly in order to detect problems in a timely manner. This is not easy, because logs can quickly grow in size. Consequently, system administrators use a number of software tools to efficiently strip out routine log entries so that they can focus their attention on anomalous behavior that might represent signs of an intrusion. In addition, most organizations are supplementing log analysis with software tools, called intrusion detection systems, to automate the monitoring process.

Intrusion Detection Systems

A major weakness of log analysis is that it is labor-intensive and prone to human error. Intrusion detection systems represent an attempt to automate part of the monitoring function. **Intrusion detection systems (IDS)** create logs of network traffic that was permitted to pass the firewall and then analyze those logs for signs of attempted or successful intrusions. The most common method of analysis used by IDSs is to compare their logs to a database containing patterns of traffic associated with known attacks, just as antivirus (A-V) software compares code to a database of known viruses. An alternative technique used by more sophisticated IDSs first builds a model representing "normal" network traffic and then uses various statistical techniques to identify unusual or anomalous behavior.

IDS sensors are usually located in several places. The most common location is just inside the main firewall. Some organizations place additional IDSs inside each internal firewall to monitor the effectiveness of policies concerning employee access to information resources. IDS sensors are also sometimes located just outside the main firewall. This provides a means to monitor the number of attempted intrusions successfully blocked by the firewall and can provide early warning signals that the organization is being targeted. IDSs can also be located on individual hosts to provide warnings of attempts to compromise that system.

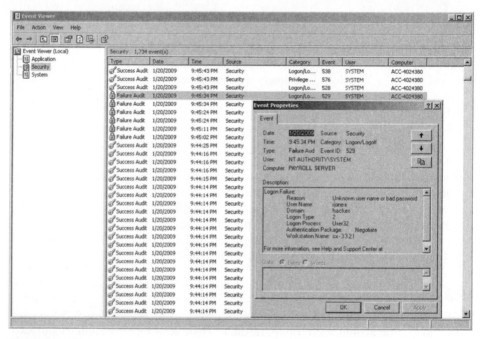

Figure 7-8
Example of System Log

Managerial Reports

Management reports are another important detective control. The COBIT Framework provides management guidelines that identify critical success factors associated with each objective and suggests key performance indicators that management can use to monitor and assess control effectiveness. For example, the COBIT management guidelines suggest that key performance indicators relevant to DS 5, information security, include

1 Number of incidents with business impact
2 Percent of users who do not comply with password standards
3 Percent of cryptographic keys compromised and revoked

Thus, management could use COBIT materials to develop a scorecard for monitoring the effectiveness of existing security measures.

COBIT sections ME 1 and ME 2 address the need for management to monitor and evaluate both system performance and controls. Nevertheless, although regular review of periodic performance reports, including analyses of trends in key performance indicators, can help ensure that security controls are adequate, surveys indicate that many organizations fail to regularly monitor security. This is clearly an area where accountants can help by participating in the design of security effectiveness scorecards and encouraging management to regularly review such reports.

Security Testing

As noted earlier, COBIT control objective DS 5.5 stresses the need to periodically test the effectiveness of existing security procedures. One way to do this is to perform **vulnerability scans**, which use automated tools designed to identify whether a given system possesses any well-known vulnerabilities. In addition, there exist a number of information security Web sites such as the Center for Information Security (www .cisecurity.org), that provide benchmarks for security best practices and tools that can be used to measure how well a given system conforms to those benchmarks.

Penetration testing provides a more rigorous way to test the effectiveness of an organization's information security. A **penetration test** is an authorized attempt by either an internal audit team or an external security consulting firm to break into the organization's information system. Several of the largest accounting firms have more than 1,000 computer risk management specialists, and more than half of their chargeable hours are spent on security matters. Large financial organizations, such as the Federal Reserve Bank of New York, have internal staff whose full-time job is to test the organization's information system for weaknesses. These teams try everything possible to compromise a company's system. To get into offices to locate passwords or access computers, they masquerade as janitors, temporary workers, or confused delivery personnel. They also use sexy decoys to distract guards, climb through roof hatches, and drop through ceiling panels. Some outside consultants claim that they can get into 90% or more of the companies they attack by using such techniques!

Corrective Controls

Detection of attempted and successful intrusions is not enough. Therefore, the AICPA Trust Services Framework specifies the need for procedures to react to incidents and to take corrective actions on a timely basis. Many corrective controls, however, rely on human judgment. Consequently, their effectiveness depends to a great extent on proper planning and preparation. That is why COBIT control objective DS 5.6 prescribes the need to define and communicate characteristics of security incidents to facilitate their proper classification and treatment. In addition, COBIT sections DS 8 and DS 10 outline specific control objectives for effectively managing incidents and problems.

Three key components that satisfy these criteria are

1 Establishment of a computer emergency response team
2 Designation of a specific individual with organization-wide responsibility for information security
3 An organized patch management system

Computer Emergency Response Team

A key component to being able to respond to security incidents promptly and effectively is the establishment of a **computer emergency response team (CERT)**, sometimes referred to as a Computer Incident Response Team (CIRT), responsible for dealing with major incidents. The CERT should include not only technical specialists but also senior operations management, because some potential responses to security incidents have significant economic consequences. For example, it may be necessary to temporarily shut down an e-commerce server. The decision to do so is too important to leave to the discretion of IT security staff; only operations management possesses the breadth of knowledge to properly evaluate the costs and benefits of such an action, and only it should have the authority to make that decision.

The CERT team should lead the organization's incident response process through the following four steps:

1 *Recognition* that a problem exists. Typically, this occurs when an IDS signals an alert or as a result of log analysis by a systems administrator.
2 *Containment* of the problem. Once an intrusion is detected, prompt action is needed to stop it and to contain the damage.
3 *Recovery*. Damage caused by the attack must be repaired. This may involve restoring data from backup and reinstalling corrupted programs. Backup and disaster recovery procedures are discussed in more detail in Chapter 8.
4 *Follow-up*. Once recovery is in process, the CERT should lead the analysis of how the incident occurred. Steps need to be taken to modify existing security policy and procedures to minimize the likelihood of a similar incident occurring in the future. An important decision that needs to be made is whether to attempt to catch and punish the perpetrator. If the organization decides that it wants to prosecute the attacker(s), it needs to immediately involve forensic experts to ensure that all possible evidence is collected and maintained in a manner that makes it admissible for use in court.

Communication is vital to all four steps in the incident response process. Therefore, multiple methods of notifying members of the CERT are necessary. For example, IDSs might be configured to send e-mail alerts. However, if the system goes down or is compromised, the e-mail alerts may not work. Traditional telephones and cell phones provide good alternative channels for sending the initial alerts and subsequent communications.

It is also important to practice the incident response plan, including the alert process. It is much better to discover a gap in the plan during a practice run than when a real incident occurs. Regular practice helps identify the need for change in response to technological changes. For example, some organizations are switching from a traditional telephone system to one based on voice over IP (VoIP). This can save considerable money, but it also means that if the computer network goes down, so, too, does the phone system. This side effect may not be noticed until the incident response plan is practiced.

Chief Information Security Officer (CISO)

COBIT control objective PO 4.8 specifies that responsibility for information security be assigned to someone at an appropriate senior level. One way to satisfy this objective is to create the position of a chief information security officer (CISO) who should

be independent of other information systems functions and should report to either the chief operating officer (COO) or the CEO. The CISO must understand the company's technology environment and work with the CIO to design, implement, and promote sound security policies and procedures. The CISO should also be an impartial assessor and evaluator of the IT environment. Accordingly, the CISO should conduct vulnerability and risk assessments, as well as audit the security measures implemented by the CIO. The CISO disseminates information about fraud, errors, security breaches, and other improper system uses and their consequences.

It is especially important that the CISO work closely with the person in charge of building security, because unauthorized physical access can allow an intruder to bypass the most elaborate logical access controls. To facilitate this integration, some organizations have created a new position, the chief security officer (CISO), who is responsible for integrating both physical and information security.

Patch Management

COBIT control objective DS 5.9 stresses the need to fix known vulnerabilities by installing the latest updates to both security programs (e.g., antivirus and firewall software) and to operating systems and other applications programs in order to protect the organization from viruses and other types of malware. This is important because, the number of reported vulnerabilities rises each year. A primary cause of the rise in reported vulnerabilities is the ever-increasing size and complexity of software. Many widely used programs now contain millions of lines of code. This means that even if 99.99% of the code is "bug-free," there are still 100 possible vulnerabilities for each million lines of code. Hackers and security consulting firms constantly search for vulnerabilities in widely used software. Once a vulnerability has been identified, the next step is to explore how to take advantage of it. Hackers usually publish the instructions for doing so on the Internet. The set of instructions for taking advantage of a vulnerability is called an **exploit**. Although the discovery of an exploit takes considerable skill, once published on the Internet it can be automatically executed by anyone who runs that code. Security consultants refer to attackers who execute such programmed exploits as "script kiddies."

The ease of automatically running many exploits makes it important for organizations to take steps to quickly correct known vulnerabilities in software they use. A **patch** is code released by software developers that fixes a particular vulnerability. **Patch management** is the process for regularly applying patches and updates to all software used by the organization. This is not as straightforward as it sounds. Patches represent modifications to already complex software. Consequently, patches sometimes create new problems because of unanticipated side effects. Therefore, organizations need to carefully test the effect of patches prior to deploying them; otherwise, they run the risk of crashing important applications. Further complicating matters is the fact that there are likely to be multiple patches released each year for each software program used by an organization. Thus, organizations may face the task of applying hundreds of patches to thousands of machines every year. This is an area where intrusion prevention systems (IPS) hold great promise. If an IPS can be quickly updated with the information needed to respond to new vulnerabilities and block new exploits, the organization can deploy the IPS to buy the time needed to thoroughly test patches before applying them.

SUMMARY AND CASE CONCLUSION

Jason Scott finished his review of the company's information systems security procedures and prepared an interim report for his supervisor. The report began by explaining that security was one of five principles of systems reliability. Because absolute security is not practical, the report noted that Northwest Industries' goal should be to adopt the time-based model of security and employ a combination of detective and

corrective controls such that it could detect and respond to attacks in less time than it would take an intruder to break through the company's preventive controls and successfully attack the system. In addition, the report pointed out the value of deploying redundant, overlapping controls to provide layers of defense-in-depth.

Jason's report then described and evaluated the various security procedures in place at Northwest Industries. Physical access to the company's office was limited to one main entrance, which was staffed at all times by a security guard. All visitors had to sign in at the security desk and were escorted at all times by an employee. Access to rooms with computing equipment required insertion of an employee badge in a card reader plus entry of a PIN in a keypad lock on the door. Remote access controls included a main firewall that performed stateful packet filtering and additional internal firewalls that segregated different business functions from one another. The information security staff regularly scanned all equipment for vulnerabilities and made sure that every employee's workstation was running a current version of the company's A-V software as well as a personal firewall. Important files were encrypted while in storage, and all business information exchanged via the Internet was encrypted while in transit. To improve security awareness, all employees attended monthly hour-long workshops that covered a different current security issue each month. The company used intrusion detection systems, and top management received monthly reports on system security effectiveness. Corrective controls included the formation of a computer emergency response team and the development and practicing of an incident response plan.

Jason's report concluded by emphasizing that information security is primarily a management issue, not an IT issue. Jason explained how management's attitude and philosophy about security are critical determinants of an organization's overall security. When top management considers information security to be an integral part of the organization's processes, similar to quality, security is likely to be more proactive and effective. In contrast, if top management considers information security to be primarily an issue of compliance with regulatory requirements, security is likely to be more reactive in nature and less effective.

Jason's supervisor was pleased with his interim report. She asked Jason to continue his review of the company's information systems by examining the other four principles of systems reliability in the AICPA's Trust Services framework: confidentiality, privacy, processing integrity, and availability.

KEY TERMS

time-based model of
 security 278
defense-in-depth 279
authentication 281
biometric identifier 281
multifactor
 authentication 281
authorization 281
access control matrix 281
compatibility test 281
social engineering 283
border router 286
firewall 286
demilitarized zone
 (DMZ) 287
Transmission Control
 Protocol (TCP) 287
Internet Protocol(IP) 287

routers 287
access control list
 (ACL) 287
static packet filtering 287
stateful packet
 filtering 289
deep packet
 inspection 289
intrusion prevention
 systems (IPS) 289
Remote Authentication
 Dial-In User Service
 (RADIUS) 290
war dialing 290
hosts 292
vulnerabilities 292
hardening 292
encryption 293

plaintext 293
ciphertext 293
decryption 293
key escrow 294
symmetric encryption
 systems 294
asymmetric encryption
 systems 294
public key 294
private key 294
hashing 295
hash 295
digital signature 296
digital certificate 296
public key infrastructure
 (PKI) 296
certificate authority 296
e-signature 299

AIS IN ACTION

CHAPTER QUIZ

1 Which of the following statements is true?
a. The concept of defense-in-depth reflects the fact that security involves the use of a few, sophisticated technical controls.
b. Information security is primarily a management issue.
c. The time-based model of security can be expressed in the following formula: $P < D + C$.
d. Symmetric encryption is slower than asymmetric encryption.

2 Firewalls are an example of
a. preventive controls
b. detective controls
c. corrective controls
d. reactive controls

3 The control procedure designed to verify a user's identity is called
a. authorization
b. authentication
c. compatibility test
d. intrusion detection

4 A weakness that an attacker can take advantage of to either disable or take control of a system is called a(n)
a. exploit
b. patch
c. vulnerability
d. hash

5 Which of the following techniques involves the creation and use of a pair of public and private keys?
a. hashing
b. asymmetric encryption
c. symmetric encryption
d. key escrow

6 Which of the following is a preventive control?
a. penetration testing
b. patch management
c. training
d. log analysis

7 The approach to perimeter defense that involves examining only information in the packet header of each individual IP packet is referred to as
a. deep packet inspection
b. static packet filtering
c. stateful packet filtering
d. deep packet filtering

8 In order to create a digital signature
a. the sender encrypts a hash using the recipient's public key
b. the sender encrypts a hash using the sender's private key
c. the sender encrypts a hash using the recipient's public key
d. the sender encrypts a hash using the sender's public key

9 Which of the following is an authorization control?
a. fingerprint reader
b. compatibility test
c. encryption
d. log analysis

10 Modifying default configurations to improve security is called
a. encryption
b. patching
c. hardening
d. war dialing

DISCUSSION QUESTIONS

7.1 Explain how each of the following security procedures can increase system reliability:

1 Encryption
2 Employee security awareness training
3 Firewalls
4 IDS
5 VPNs

7.2 What are the advantages and disadvantages of having the person responsible for information security report directly to the chief information officer (CIO), who has overall responsibility for all aspects of the organization's information systems?

7.3 How much knowledge about information security do internal and external auditors need to be effective?

7.4 Is it possible to provide absolute security for an organization's information system? Why or why not?

7.5 What are the limitations, if any, of relying on the results of penetration tests to assess the overall level of security?

7.6 Security awareness training is necessary to teach employees "safe computing" practices. The key to effectiveness, however, is that it changes employee behavior. How can organizations maximize the effectiveness of their security awareness training programs?

7.7 In what ways can the quest for information security be compared to striving for total quality?

7.8 What are the advantages and disadvantages of biometric security devices, such as fingerprint readers, in comparison with other security measures such as passwords and locked doors?

PROBLEMS

7.1 Which preventive, detective, and/or corrective controls would best mitigate the following threats?

 a. An employee's laptop was stolen at the airport. The laptop contained personally identifying information about the company's customers that could potentially be used to commit identity theft.

 b. A salesperson successfully logged into the payroll system by guessing the payroll supervisor's password.

 c. A criminal remotely accessed a sensitive database using the authentication credentials (user ID and strong password) of an IT manager. At the time the attack occurred, the IT manager was logged into the system at his workstation at company headquarters.

d. An employee received an email purporting to be from her boss informing her of an important new attendance policy. When she clicked on a link embedded in the email to view the new policy, she infected her laptop with a keystroke logger.

e. The director of R&D quit abruptly after an argument with the CEO. The company cannot access any of the files about several new projects because the R&D director had encrypted them before leaving.

f. A company wrote custom code for the shopping cart feature on its Web site. The code contained a buffer overflow vulnerability that could be exploited when the customer typed in the ship-to address.

g. A company purchased the leading "off-the-shelf" e-commerce software for linking its electronic storefront to its inventory database. A customer discovered a way to directly access the back-end database by entering appropriate SQL code.

h. Attackers broke into the company's information system through a wireless access point located in one of its retail stores. The wireless access point had been purchased and installed by the store manager without informing central IT or security.

i. An employee picked up a USB drive in the parking lot and plugged it into their laptop to "see what was on it," which resulted in a keystroke logger being installed on that laptop.

j. A competitor intercepted the company's bid for a lucrative contract that was emailed to the local government's Web site. The competitor used the information contained in the email to successfully underbid and win the contract.

k. When an earthquake destroyed the company's main data center, the CIO spent half a day trying to figure out who in the organization needed to be contacted in order to implement the company's cold site agreement.

l. Although logging was enabled, the information security staff did not review the logs early enough to detect and stop an attack that resulted in the theft of information about a new strategic initiative.

m. To facilitate working from home, an employee installed a modem on his office workstation. An attacker successfully penetrated the company's system by dialing into that modem.

n. An attacker gained access to the company's internal network by installing a wireless access point in a wiring closet located next to the elevators on the fourth floor of a high-rise office building that the company shared with seven other companies.

7.2 EXCEL Problem
Objective: learn how to protect spreadsheets.

Required:

a. Read the article "Keeping Secrets: How to protect your computer from snoops and spies," by Theo Callahan in the July 2007 issue of the *Journal of Accountancy* (available at the AICPA's Web site: www.aicpa.org).

b. Create a new workbook that contains two individual worksheets. On the first worksheet, just enter your name, course number, date, and name of your instructor. On the second worksheet, create the refinancing worksheet as depicted in Exhibit 5 of the *Journal of Accountancy* article.

c. Implement the following controls on the spreadsheet that you created in step b:
 a. Password to open
 b. Password to modify
 c. Apply passwords to each individual worksheet
 d. Encrypt the data
 e. Set the workbook to be Read-only
 f. Protect the appropriate cells in the refinancing worksheet so that they cannot be altered.

 d. Write a brief memo discussing your experience implementing these data protection controls (how easy to create, how they worked when you attempted to reopen the workbook, what happens if you did not enter one of the passwords, etc.).
 e. Turn in your report and an electronic copy of your workbook.

7.3 You are the chief information security officer for a small company. You are asked to design appropriate controls for the payroll and inventory management systems. Following is a list of users and the types of activities each group wants to be able to perform:

User Group	Desired Privileges
Sales	Read records in the inventory master file
Inventory control	Read, create, modify, and delete inventory file records
Payroll clerk	Read and modify payroll file records
HR manager	Read, create, modify, and delete payroll file records
Payroll programmer	Process payroll records; read payroll file and payroll transaction file records
Inventory programmer	Process inventory records; read both inventory file and inventory transaction file records
Yourself	Perform all possible actions on all files

Required

 a. Create an access control matrix that gives each user group its desired level of access to the following five items: payroll master file, payroll program, inventory master file, inventory update program, and the system log files. Use the following codes for access rights:
 0 = no access
 1 = read only
 2 = read and modify
 3 = read, modify, create, and delete
 b. What changes should the internal auditor recommend be made to the access control matrix to improve internal control?

7.4 Install and run the Microsoft Security Baseline Analyzer on your home computer or laptop. Write a report explaining any weaknesses identified and how to best correct them. Attach a copy of the tools' output to your report.

7.5 Visit the Web sites listed here and write a report describing the information provided on each site about information security that would be most useful to an auditor:
 ● The SANS Institute (www.sans.org)
 ● The National Security Agency (www.nsa.gov)
 ● Information Systems Audit and Control Association (www.isaca.org)
 ● Information Systems Security Association (www.issa.org)
 ● CERT (www.cert.org)
 ● American Institute of Certified Public Accountants (www.aicpa.org)
 ● National Institute of Standards (www.nist.gov)
 ● Computer Crime and Intellectual Property Section of the U.S. Department of Justice (www.cybercrime.gov)

7.6 Visit the Center for Internet Security Web site (www.cisecurity.org) and download the appropriate scoring tool for your computer. Run the tool to assess how well

your computer conforms to the center's benchmarks. Write a brief report explaining the results of your test. Attach a printout copy of the scoring tool's results to your report.

7.7 **a.** Apply the following data to evaluate the time-based model of security for the XYZ Company. Does the XYZ Company satisfy the requirements of the time-based model of security? Why?
- Estimated time for intruder to successfully penetrate system = 25 minutes
- Estimated time to detect an intrusion attempt and notify appropriate security staff = 5 minutes in best-case scenario; 10 minutes in worst-case scenario
- Estimated time to analyze detected intrusion attempts and implement corrective actions: best-case scenario = 6 minutes; worst-case scenario = 20 minutes

b. Which of the following security investments would you recommend? Why? If you could do only one, which would you recommend? Why?
- Invest $50,000 to increase the estimated time to successfully penetrate the system by 10 minutes
- Invest $40,000 to reduce the time to detect an intrusion attempt and notify appropriate security staff to 1 minute in best-case scenario, 4 minutes in worst-case scenario
- Invest $60,000 to reduce the time required to analyze detected intrusion attempts and implement corrective actions to 4 minutes under the best-case scenario and 10 minutes under the worst-case scenario

7.8 Use your operating system's built-in capability to encrypt a file. Store the encrypted file in a folder that can be shared with other users on that computer. Then create a new user account. Assign it a password.

Required

a. Log out of your normal account and log in as the new user account you created. Search for the file that you encrypted. Which of the following actions can you perform?
1 Open the file
2 Copy the file to another location on the hard drive
3 Copy the file to a USB drive
4 Move the file to another location on the hard drive
5 Move the file to a USB drive
6 Rename the file
7 Delete the file
8 Restore the file and then try to open it

b. Log out of the new user account you used in step a and log back in using your normal account. Create another file and encrypt it. What happens when you try to perform all the actions listed under step a?

7.9 Create a table about the password policies enforced at the following:
a. Your school's network
b. Your school's email system
c. Your personal email account (at Yahoo, Gmail, etc.)
d. Your financial institution

Your table should include information about the following issues:

a. Password length (minimum and maximum)
b. Types of characters that can be used

 c. Frequency of mandatory changes

 d. Password history (i.e., does the system prevent you from retyping your old password as your new password?)

Why do you think these different systems impose different requirements for passwords?

7.10 The chapter briefly discussed the following three common attacks against applications

 a. Buffer overflows

 b. SQL injection

 c. Cross-site scripting

Required

Research each of these three attacks and write a report that explains in detail how each attack actually works and that describes suggested controls for reducing the risks that these attacks will be successful.

7.11 Physical security is extremely important. List and describe the physical security controls that should be used to protect the data center of a financial institution. Read the article "19 Ways to Build Physical Security into a Data Center," which appeared in the CSO Magazine November 2005 (you can find the article at www.csoonline.com/read/110105/datacenter.html). Which methods would you expect to find used by almost any major corporation? Which might likely only be justified at a financial institution?

CASE 7.1 Costs of Preventive Security

Firewalls are one of the most fundamental and important security tools. You are likely familiar with the software-based host firewall that you use on your laptop or desktop. Such firewalls should also be installed on every computer in an organization. However, organizations also need corporate-grade firewalls, which are usually, but not always, dedicated special-purpose hardware devices. Conduct some research to identify three different brands of such corporate-grade firewalls and write a report that addresses the following points:

1. Cost
2. Filtering capability (packet-filters, deep-packet inspection, other)
3. Other security features
4. Ease of configuration
5. Ease of use

CASE 7.2 Developing an Information Security Checklist

Design a checklist for assessing information security controls. The checklist should be organized as follows:

- Three major categories: preventive, detective, and corrective controls.
- Appropriate subcategories for each major topic discussed in this chapter.

- For each subcategory, develop individual questions about the existence of specific control procedures discussed in this chapter. Each question should have three possible answers: Yes, No, Not Applicable.

AIS IN ACTION SOLUTIONS

1 Which of the following statements is true?
 a. The concept of defense-in-depth reflects the fact that security involves the use of a few, sophisticated technical controls. (Incorrect. The concept of defense-in-depth is based on the idea that, given enough time and resources, any single control, no matter how sophisticated, can be overcome—therefore, the use of redundant, overlapping controls maximizes security.)
 ✔ **b.** Information security is primarily a management issue. (Correct.)
 c. The time-based model of security can be expressed in the following formula: $P < D + C$. (Incorrect. The formula is $P > D + C$.)
 d. Symmetric encryption is slower than asymmetric encryption. (Incorrect. Symmetric encryption is faster than asymmetric encryption.)

2 Firewalls are an example of
 ✔ **a.** preventive controls (Correct. Firewalls are designed to prevent problems by filtering which packets are allowed to enter and leave a system.)
 b. detective controls (Incorrect. Firewalls use access control lists to filter packets, thus serving to prevent access.)
 c. corrective controls (Incorrect. Firewalls do not take steps to remedy any control violations.)
 d. reactive controls (Incorrect. There is no such category of controls.)

3 The control procedure designed to verify a user's identity is called
 a. authorization (Incorrect. Authorization is the process of controlling what actions—read, write, delete, etc.—a user is permitted to perform.)
 ✔ **b.** authentication (Correct. Authentication is the process of verifying a user's identity.)
 c. compatibility test (Incorrect. A compatibility test is an authorization control to limit what actions an authenticated user can perform.)
 d. intrusion detection (Incorrect. Intrusion detection is a detective control that identifies when an attack has occurred.)

4 A weakness that an attacker can take advantage of to either disable or take control of a system is called a(n)
 a. exploit (Incorrect. An exploit is the code for taking advantage of a weakness.)
 b. patch (Incorrect. A patch is code designed to fix a weakness.)
 ✔ **c.** vulnerability (Correct. A vulnerability is any weakness that can be used to disable or take control of a system.)
 d. hash (Incorrect. A hash is a digital summary of a document or file.)

5 Which of the following techniques involves the creation and use of a pair of public and private keys?
 a. hashing (Incorrect. Hashing is a one-way algorithm that produces a digital summary of a document or file.)
 ✔ **b.** asymmetric encryption (Correct. Asymmetric encryption uses two keys: The public key is available to anyone; the private key is secret and known only to its owner. Either key can be used to encrypt, but only the other key can be used to decrypt that message.)

 c. symmetric encryption (Incorrect. Symmetric encryption uses the same secret key to both encrypt and decrypt.)

 d. key escrow (Incorrect. Key escrow involves storing a copy of the encryption keys in a safe location.)

6 Which of the following is a preventive control?

 a. Penetration testing (Incorrect. Penetration testing is a detective control designed to identify weaknesses.)

 b. DES (Incorrect. DES is a symmetric encryption algorithm that can be used to both encrypt and decrypt information.)

✔ **c.** Training (Correct. Training users about security enhances the effectiveness of security procedures and increases the likelihood that users will comply with security policies.)

 d. Log analysis (Incorrect. Log analysis is a detective control used to understand prior activity.)

7 The approach to perimeter defense that involves examining only information in the packet header of each individual IP packet is referred to as

 a. deep packet inspection (Incorrect. Deep packet inspection examines the contents of the data in the body of the IP packet.)

✔ **b.** static packet filtering (Correct. Static packet filtering examines the headers of individual IP packets.)

 c. stateful packet filtering (Incorrect. Stateful packet filtering examines not only the headers of individual IP packets but also a state table to determine whether incoming packets are part of an already established connection.)

 d. intrusion prevention systems (IPS) (Incorrect. An IPS uses attack signatures and statistical models of normal traffic to automatically identify and respond to suspected intrusions.)

8 In order to create a digital signature

 a. the sender encrypts a hash using the recipient's (Incorrect. The sender does not know the recipient's private key.)

✔ **b.** the sender encrypts a hash using the sender's private key (Correct. Only the sender know the sender's private key. Therefore if the recipient can successfully decrypt the hash using the sender's public key, that proves that the sender must have created and sent the hash.)

 c. the sender encrypts a hash using the recipient's public key (Incorrect. This ensures that only the recipient can decrypt the hash but because everyone knows the recipient's public key there is no way to prove who used it to encrypt the hash.)

 d. the sender encrypts a hash using the sender's public key (Incorrect. Anyone can encrypt a message with someone's public key, so there is no way to prove who created the message.)

9 Which of the following is an authorization of control?

 a. fingerprint reader (Incorrect. Biometric tools like fingerprint readers are an authentication control used to verify the identify of someone attempting to access the system.)

✔ **b.** compatibility test (Correct. A compatibility test uses an access control matrix to determine what actions an authenticated user is allowed to perform.)

 c. encryption (Incorrect. Encryption is a preventive control that preserves the confidentiality of sensitive information.)

 d. log analysis (Incorrect. Log analysis is a detective control that can be used to identify unauthorized actions taken by users.)

10 Modifying default configurations to improve security is called

 a. encryption (Incorrect. Encryption protects the confidentiality of information by encoding it so that it is unreadable without the decryption key.)

b. patching (Incorrect. Patching is the process of applying vendor-supplied code to correct existing vulnerabilities.)

✔ **c.** hardening (Correct. This is the definition of hardening.)

d. war dialing (Incorrect. War dialing is a process used to identify modems.)

CHAPTER 8

LEARNING OBJECTIVES

After studying this chapter, you should be able to:

- Identify and explain controls designed to protect the confidentiality of sensitive corporate information.

- Identify and explain controls designed to protect the privacy of customers' personal information.

- Identify and explain controls designed to ensure processing integrity.

- Identify and explain controls designed to ensure systems availability.

Information Systems Controls for Systems Reliability—Part 2: Confidentiality, Privacy, Processing Integrity, and Availability

INTEGRATIVE CASE NORTHWEST INDUSTRIES

Jason Scott was preparing for his meeting with the company's chief information officer. Although Jason was satisfied that Northwest Industries' computer security policies and procedures provided the company with adequate protection against intrusions, he was concerned about other aspects of systems reliability. In particular, he wanted to learn what Northwest Industries was doing to address the following four issues:

1 Protecting the confidentiality of sensitive corporate information, such as marketing plans

2 Protecting the privacy of personal information collected from customers

3 Ensuring that information about business activities was processed accurately, completely, and in a timely manner

4 Ensuring that information systems resources would always be available whenever management needed access to them

Jason planned to use his interview with the CIO to obtain a general understanding of the company's information systems controls. He would then follow up by collecting evidence about the effectiveness of those controls.

Introduction

Chapter 7 discussed information security, which is the fundamental principle of systems reliability. This chapter covers the other four principles of reliable systems: confidentiality, privacy, processing integrity, and availability. We conclude with a discussion of the importance of controlling changes to systems to ensure that the new system satisfies all five principles of systems reliability.

Confidentiality

Reliable systems maintain the confidentiality of sensitive information. Satisfying this principle requires first that management identify which information is sensitive and needs to be protected from unauthorized disclosure. Although each organization will develop its own definitions of what information needs to be protected, most definitions are likely to include business plans, pricing strategies, client and customer lists, and legal documents. COBIT control objective PO 2.3 specifies the need to not only identify potentially senstitive information, but also to properly label it, assign responsibility for its protection, and implement appropriate controls. Table 8-1 summarizes the key controls designed to protect the confidentiality of such information.

Table 8-1 shows that encryption is a fundamental control procedure for protecting the confidentiality of sensitive information. Note that confidential information should be encrypted both while it is stored and whenever transmitted to trusted parties. The Internet provides an inexpensive way to transmit information to others. Doing so does not protect the confidentiality of sensitive information, however, because it is easy to intercept information sent over the Internet. Encryption solves this problem. Encrypting information before sending it over the Internet creates what is called a **virtual private network (VPN)**, so named because it provides the functionality of a privately owned network, while using the Internet. Using VPN software to encrypt information while it is in transit over the Internet in effect creates private communication channels, often referred to as tunnels, which are accessible only to those parties possessing the appropriate encryption and decryption keys. VPNs also include controls to authenticate the parties exchanging information and to create an audit trail of

Table 8-1
Summary of Key Controls to Protect Confidentiality and Privacy

Situation	Controls
In storage	Encryption and access controls
During transmission	Encryption and access controls
Disposal	Shredding, thorough erasure, physical destruction
Overall	Categorization to reflect value and training in proper work practices

the exchange. Thus, VPNs satisfy COBIT control objective DS 5.11, which specifies controls over the electronic exchange of sensitive information. The cost of the VPN software is much less than the cost of leasing or buying the infrastructure (telephone lines, satellite links, communications equipment, etc.) needed to create a privately owned secure communications network. It is also much cheaper and easier to reconfigure VPNs to include new sites than it is to add or remove the corresponding physical connections in a privately owned network.

It is especially important to encrypt any sensitive information stored in laptops, personal digital assistants (PDAs), cell phones, and other portable devices because they are so easily lost or stolen. Although organizations may have policies against storing sensitive data on such devices, many employees admit in surveys that they did keep valuable organizational data on their laptops and PDA devices.

Encryption alone, however, is not sufficient to protect confidentiality. Access controls are also needed. Otherwise, unauthorized parties may be able to obtain copies of the encrypted data. Given enough time and resources, many encryption schemes can be broken. Access controls are also important because it is not always possible to encrypt all confidential information while it is stored. In such cases, strong authentication techniques are necessary to ensure that only authorized individuals have access to the information. In addition, strong authorization controls should be used to limit the actions (read, write, change, delete, copy, etc.) that authorized users can perform when accessing confidential information.

It is also important to control access to system outputs. Useful control procedures for doing so include the following:

- Do not allow visitors to roam through buildings without supervision, to prevent them from seeing sensitive information on workstation displays or picking up and reading printed reports.
- Require employees to log out of any applications prior to leaving their workstation unattended, so that other employees do not have unauthorized access to the information in that application. All workstations should also use password-protected screen savers that automatically engage whenever there is no activity after a specified period of time.
- Restrict access to rooms housing printers and fax machines.
- Code reports to reflect the importance of the information contained therein, and train employees to not leave reports containing sensitive information in plain view on their desktops when they are not physically present.

It is especially important to control the *disposal* of information resources. In fact, COBIT control objective DS 11.4 specifically addresses the need to define and implement procedures governing the disposal of sensitive data and any hardware on which those data were stored. Printed reports and microfilm containing sensitive information should be shredded before being thrown out. Special procedures are needed to destroy information stored on magnetic and optical media. Using built-in operating system commands to delete that information is insufficient, because many utility programs have been developed to recover deleted files. For example, the British company Pointsec Mobile Technologies purchased 100 hard drives from an online auction site and found that it could recover data from 70% of them. Proper disposal of computer media requires use of special software designed to "wipe" the media clean by repeatedly overwriting the disk with random patterns of data. Alternatively, magnetic disks and tapes can be run through devices that demagnetize them. Physical destruction of magnetic and optical disks prior to disposal may be the safest alternative for devices that have been used to store extremely sensitive data.

Controls designed to protect confidentiality must be continuously reviewed and modified to respond to new threats created by technological advances. For example, the incorporation of digital cameras in cell phones makes it possible for visitors to surreptitiously capture confidential information. Consequently, many organizations now

prohibit visitors from using cell phones while touring manufacturing facilities or other areas likely to contain confidential information. Because camera phones are so easy to hide, some organizations also use jamming devices to deactivate the imaging systems in the phones while on company premises. Telephone conversations are another area affected by advances in technology. In the past, wiretaps were the only serious threat to the confidentiality of telephone conversations, and the difficulty of setting them up meant that the risk of that threat was relatively low. The use of voice-over-the-Internet (VoIP), however, means that telephone conversations are now routed as packets over the Internet. This means that VoIP telephone conversations are as vulnerable to interception as any other information sent over the Internet. Therefore VoIP conversations about sensitive topics should be encrypted.

Employee use of e-mail and instant messaging (IM) probably represents two of the greatest threats to the confidentiality of sensitive information. It is virtually impossible to control the subsequent distribution of any information contained in e-mail or IM messages once the intended recipient has that information. Therefore, organizations need to develop comprehensive policies governing the appropriate and allowable use of these technologies for business purposes. Employees need to be trained concerning what kinds of information they can, and cannot, share. Training is needed, especially with IM, because the real-time nature of an IM conversation makes it easy to disclose confidential information without realizing it. In addition, as the number of e-mail and IM users increases, so too does the probability that two or more users of a given system have identical first names, middle initials, and last names. Therefore, employees need to be trained to carefully double-check the identity of the person to whom they are sending confidential information.

Privacy

The Trust Services framework privacy principle is closely related to the confidentiality principle, differing primarily in that it focuses on protecting personal information about customers rather than organizational data. Thus, as indicated in Table 8-1, the key controls related to the protection of privacy are the same that pertain to protecting confidentiality.

COBIT control objective DS 11.2 which addresses the management of data, specifies the need to comply with regulatory requirements. A number of regulations, including the Health Insurance Portability and Accountability Act (HIPAA) and the Financial Services Modernization Act (commonly referred to as the Gramm–Leach–Bliley Act, representing the names of its three Congressional sponsors), require organizations to protect the privacy of their customers' personal information. To address these myriad requirements, the AICPA/CICA Trust Services Privacy framework lists 10 internationally recognized best practices for protecting the privacy of customers' personal information:

1 **Management.** The organization establishes a set of procedures and policies for protecting the privacy of personal information it collects and assigns responsibility and accountability for those policies to a specific person or group of employees.

2 **Notice.** The organization provides notice about its privacy policies and practices at or before the time it collects personal information from customers, or as soon as practicable thereafter.

3 **Choice and consent.** The organization describes the choices available to individuals and obtains their consent to the collection and use of their personal information. Note that the choices offered differ across countries. In the United States, the default policy is called opt-out, which allows organizations to collect personal information about customers unless the customer explicitly objects. In contrast, the default policy in Europe is opt-in, meaning that organizations cannot

collect personally identifying information unless customers explicitly give them permission to do so.

4 **Collection.** The organization collects only that information needed to fulfill the purposes stated in its privacy policies. One particular issue of concern is the use of cookies on Web sites. A **cookie** is a text file created by a Web site and stored on a visitor's hard disk. Cookies store information about what the user has done on the site. Most Web sites create multiple cookies per visit in order to make it easier for visitors to navigate to relevant portions of the Web site. Browsers can be configured to not accept cookies, but doing so is likely to cause many Web sites to not function properly. It is important to note that cookies are text files, which means that they cannot "do" anything besides store information. Nevertheless, some people are worried that the information collected in cookies violates their privacy.

5 **Use and retention.** The organization uses its customers' personal information only in the manner described in its stated privacy policies and retains that information only as long as it is needed.

6 **Access.** The organization provides individuals with the ability to access, review, correct, and delete the personal information stored about them.

7 **Disclosure to third parties.** The organization discloses customers' personal information to third parties only in the situations and manners described in its privacy policies and only to third parties who provide equivalent protection of that information.

8 **Security.** The organization takes reasonable steps to protect customers' personal information from loss or unauthorized disclosure. One sometimes overlooked issue concerns the disposal of computer equipment. It is important to follow the suggestions presented in the section on protecting confidentiality for properly erasing all information stored on computer media. Perhaps one of the most famous incidents of failing to properly erase information on a hard drive involved the disposal of an obsolete personal computer by a British bank. It was sold at an auction; the buyer found that it contained personal information about the financial affairs of Paul McCartney. E-mail presents a second threat vector to consider. For example, in 2002 drug manufacturer Eli Lilly sent an e-mail about its antidepressant drug Prozac to 669 patients. The e-mail, however, also identified all the recipients to whom it was sent. A third often overlooked area concerns the release of electronic documents. Just as special procedures are used to black out (redact) personally identifiable information on paper documents, similar procedures are needed to remove such information on electronic documents in a manner that it cannot be recovered by the recipient of the document.

9 **Quality.** The organization maintains the integrity of its customers' personal information.

10 **Monitoring and enforcement.** The organization assigns one or more employees to be responsible for assuring compliance with its stated privacy policies and periodically verifies compliance with those policies. It also provides procedures for responding to customer complaints, which includes the use of a third-party dispute resolution process.

As is the case for confidential information, encryption and access controls are the two basic mechanisms for protecting consumers' personal information. Indeed, it is common practice to use SSL to encrypt all personal information transmitted between individuals and the organization's Web site. However, SSL only protects the information while it is in transit over the Internet. Consequently, strong authentication controls need to be used to restrict Web site visitors' access to individual accounts. After all, what good is it if the information you send to a Web site is encrypted in transit, but anyone visiting the site can easily obtain access to your account and read, and possibly change, the information the Web site stores about you?

Organizations should also consider encrypting customers' personal information in storage. In fact, such encryption may be economically justified. A California law (SB 1386), for example, requires any business with customers in that state to personally notify

every customer following a security incident involving access to the databases containing customer personal information. Of course, most businesses that have customers in California also have customers in other states. Those customers would likely be very upset if they were not also notified about security incidents that could have exposed their personal information to unauthorized parties. Thus, California SB 1386 effectively requires companies to notify *all* their customers whenever a security incident may have led to the compromise of personally identifiable information. This can be expensive for businesses with hundreds of thousands of customers. The law's costly notification requirement is waived, however, if the information was encrypted while in storage.

Organizations also need to train employees on how to manage personal information collected from customers. This is especially important for medical and financial information. Obviously, intentional misuse of such information can have serious negative economic consequences, including significant declines in stock prices. Unintentional disclosure of such personal information can also create costly problems, however. For example, someone denied health or life insurance because of improper disclosure of personal information is likely to sue the organization that was supposed to restrict access to that data.

Incidents involving the unauthorized disclosure of customers' personal information, whether intentional or accidental, can be costly. For example, Spain levies fines of up to $600,000 per privacy violation and France imposes jail sentences of up to three years. Governments may also restrict daily business operations. For example, in November 2003, after Citibank's online credit card application in Taiwan was hacked and personal customer data compromised, the government imposed a one-month moratorium on issuing new credit cards and a three-month suspension of the online application, until Citibank's online security could be independently verified.

Concerns about privacy appear to be increasing. For example, Google received a great deal of criticism when it announced that it planned to use software to scan the subject field in e-mail headers as well as the body of messages in order to select specific pop-up ads likely to be of interest to the recipient.

A related concern involves the ever-increasing amount of spam. The volume of unsolicited e-mail that contains either advertising or offensive content is overwhelming many e-mail systems. Not only does spam reduce the efficiency benefits of e-mail but it is also a source of many viruses, worms, spyware programs, and other types of malware. To deal with this problem, the U.S. Congress passed the Controlling the Assault of Non-Solicited Pornography and Marketing (CAN-SPAM) Act in 2003. CAN-SPAM provides both criminal and civil penalties for violations of the law. CAN-SPAM applies to commercial e-mail, which is defined as any e-mail that has the primary purpose of advertising or promotion. This covers much of the legitimate e-mail sent by many organizations to their customers, suppliers, and, in the case of nonprofit organizations, their donors. Thus, organizations need to be sure to follow CAN-SPAM's guidelines or risk sanctions. Key provisions include the following:

- The sender's identity must be clearly displayed in the header of the message.
- The subject field in the header must clearly identify the message as an advertisement or solicitation.
- The body of the message must provide recipients with a working link that can be used to opt out of future e-mail. After receiving an opt-out request, organizations have 10 days to implement steps to ensure they do not send any additional unsolicited e-mail to that address. This means that organizations need to assign someone responsibility for processing opt-out requests.
- The body of the message must include the sender's valid postal address. Although not required, best practice would be to also include full street address, telephone, and fax numbers.
- Organizations should not send commercial e-mail to randomly generated addresses, nor should they set up Web sites designed to "harvest" e-mail addresses of potential customers. Experts recommend that organizations redesign their own Web sites to include a visible means for visitors to opt in to receive e-mail, such as checking a box.

8-1 FOCUS **Protecting Yourself from Identity Theft**

Identity theft is a growing problem. Victims often spend much time and money to recover. Fortunately, there are a number of simple steps you can take to minimize your risk of becoming a victim of identity theft.

- Shred all documents that contain personal information, especially unsolicited credit card offers. Cross-cut shredders are much more effective than strip-cut shredders.
- Never send personally identifying information in unencrypted e-mail.
- Beware of e-mail, telephone, and print requests to "verify" personal information that the requesting party should already possess. For example, credit card companies will never need to ask you for the three- or four-digit security code on your card. Similarly, the IRS will never e-mail you asking you to send personally identifying information in response to an audit. The number of these types of fake requests, referred to as phishing, dramatically increased in the spring of 2004. One especially newsworthy incident involved a forged e-mail purportedly soliciting contributions to the Kerry–Edwards campaign. The e-mail included a link to a site in India designed to collect personal information that could be used to commit identity theft. Fortunately, this scam was quickly detected and stopped. The Kerry campaign Webmaster noticed that the attack included a reference to a photo on the legitimate campaign Web site; the Webmaster quickly replaced the photo with a message warning people about the hoax. Thus, the fraudster's e-mail message ended up including a warning that the message was a scam!

- Do not carry your Social Security card with you. Be wary of requests to reveal the last four digits of your Social Security number. The first three and middle two digits are assigned based on the location and date you applied for a Social Security number, but the last four digits are assigned randomly.
- Print only your initials and last name, rather than your full name, on checks. This prevents a thief from knowing how you sign your name.
- Limit the amount of other information (address and phone number) preprinted on checks, and consider totally eliminating such information.
- Do not place outgoing mail containing checks or personal information in your mailbox for pickup.
- Do not carry more than a few blank checks with you.
- Use special software to thoroughly clean any digital media prior to disposal, or physically destroy the media. It is especially important to thoroughly erase or destroy hard drives prior to donating or disposing of obsolete equipment because it likely contains information about online financial transactions.
- Monitor your credit reports regularly.
- File a police report as soon as you discover that your purse or wallet was stolen.
- Make photocopies of driver's licenses, passports, and credit cards. Store this information, along with the telephone numbers of all your credit cards, in a safe location to facilitate notifying appropriate authorities in the case that those documents are lost or stolen.
- Immediately cancel any stolen or lost credit cards.

One privacy-related issue that is of growing concern is identity theft. Focus 8-1 discusses the steps that individuals should take to minimize the risk of becoming a victim of identity theft. Organizations also have a role to play in preventing identity theft. Customers entrust them with personally identifying information. Organizations economically benefit from having access to that information. Therefore, organizations have an ethical and moral obligation to implement controls to protect those databases that contain their customers' personal information.

Processing Integrity

COBIT control objective DS 11.1 addresses the need for controls over the input, processing, and output of data to ensure data are accurately and completely processed in a timely manner so that the system provides the information needed by management. The COBIT framework identifies six categories of application controls (AC) that can

Table 8-2
Summary of Key Controls to
Ensure Processing Integrity

Process Stage and COBIT Category	Threats/Risks	Controls
Input: • AC1—Source Data Preparation and Authorization • AC2—Source Data Collection and Entry • AC3—Accuracy, Completeness, and Authenticity Checks	Data that is: • Invalid • Unauthorized • Incomplete • Inaccurate	Forms design, cancellation and storage of documents, authorization and segregation of duties controls, visual scanning, data entry controls
Processing: • AC4—Processing Integrity and Validity	Errors in output and stored data	Data matching, file labels, batch totals, cross-footing and zero-balance tests, write-protection mechanisms, database processing integrity controls
Output: • AC5—Output Review, Reconciliation and Error Handling • AC6—Transaction Authenticity and Integrity	• Use of inaccurate or incomplete reports • Unauthorized disclosure of sensitive information • Loss, alteration, or disclosure of information in transit	Reviews and reconciliations, encryption and access controls, parity checks, message acknowledgement techniques

be used to satisfy that objective. Table 8-2 groups these six categories of application controls according to whether they apply to the input, processing, or output of data.

Input Controls

The phrase "garbage in, garbage out" highlights the importance of data quality. If the data entered into a system is inaccurate or incomplete, the output will be too. Therefore, controls over the quality of data that is collected about business activities and entered into the information system are vital. Companies must establish control procedures to ensure that all source documents are authorized, accurate, complete, properly accounted for, and entered into the system or sent to their intended destination in a timely manner. The following source data controls regulate the integrity of input:

● **Forms design.** Source documents and other forms should be designed to help ensure that errors and omissions are minimized. Two particularly important controls involve sequentially prenumbering source documents and using turnaround documents. Prenumbering forms improves control by making it possible to verify that none is missing. (To understand this, consider the difficulty you would have in balancing your checking account if none of your checks were numbered.) When sequentially prenumbered source data documents are used, the system should be programmed to identify and report missing or duplicate form numbers. A turnaround document is a record of company data sent to an external party and then returned by the external party to the system as input. Turnaround documents are prepared in machine-readable form to facilitate their subsequent processing as input

records. An example is a utility bill that a special scanning device reads when the bill is returned with a payment. Because turnaround documents are system outputs that come back as machine-readable input records, they are much more accurate than input records prepared manually. Chapter 18 discusses forms design in more detail.

- **Cancellation and storage of documents.** Documents that have been entered into the system should be canceled so they cannot be inadvertently or fraudulently reentered into the system. Paper documents should be defaced, for example, by stamping them "paid." Electronic documents can be similarly "canceled" by setting a flag field to indicate that the document has already been processed. *Note:* Cancellation does *not* mean disposal. Original source documents (or their electronic images) should be retained for as long as needed to satisfy legal and regulatory requirements.
- **Authorization and segregation of duties.** Source documents should be prepared only by authorized personnel acting within their authority. Employees authorized to prepare source documents should not be assigned other incompatible functions.
- **Visual scanning.** Source documents should be scanned for reasonableness and propriety before being entered into the system.

Data Entry Controls

Common tests used to validate input data include:

- A **field check** determines if the characters in a field are of the proper type. For example, a check on a field, such as a U.S. Zip code, that is supposed to contain only numeric values, would indicate an error if it contained alphabetic characters.
- A **sign check** determines if the data in a field have the appropriate arithmetic sign. For example, the quantity-ordered field should never be negative.
- A **limit check** tests a numerical amount to ensure that it does not exceed a predetermined value. For example, the regular hours-worked field in weekly payroll input must be less than or equal to 40 hours. Similarly, the hourly wage field should be greater than or equal to the minimum wage.
- A **range check** is similar to a limit check except that it has both upper and lower limits.
- A **size check** ensures that the input data will fit into the assigned field. For example, the value 458,976,253 will not fit in an eight-digit field.
- A **completeness check** on each input record determines if all required data items have been entered. For example, sales transaction records should not be accepted for processing unless they include the customer's complete address.
- A **validity check** compares the ID code or account number in transaction data with similar data in the master file to verify that the account exists. For example, if a sale to customer 65432 is entered, the computer must verify the existence of customer 65432 in the customer database to confirm that the sale was indeed made to a valid customer.
- A **reasonableness test** determines the correctness of the logical relationship between two data items. For example, a $1,000 monthly salary increase is reasonable for an executive with a current salary of $15,000 per month but not for a data entry clerk making $1,500 per month.
- **Check digit verification**. Authorized ID numbers (such as an employee number) can contain a **check digit** that is computed from the other digits. For example, the system could assign each new employee a nine-digit number, then calculate a tenth digit from the original nine and append that calculated number to the original nine to form a ten-digit ID number. Data entry devices

can be programmed to perform **check digit verification** by using the first nine digits to calculate the tenth digit each time an ID number is entered. If an error is made in entering any of the ten digits, the calculation made on the first nine digits will not match the tenth, or check digit.

The preceding tests are used for both batch processing and online real-time processing. Additional data input controls differ for the two processing methods.

Additional Batch Processing Data Entry Controls

- Batch processing works correctly only if the transactions are presorted to be in the same sequence as records in the master file. A **sequence check** tests if a batch of input data is in the proper numerical or alphabetical sequence.
- Information about data input or data processing errors (date they occurred, cause of the error, date corrected and resubmitted) should be entered in an **error log**. Errors should be investigated, corrected, and resubmitted on a timely basis (usually with the next batch of transactions) and reedited using the same input validation routine. Periodically, the error log should be reviewed to ensure that all errors have been corrected and then used to prepare an error report that summarizes errors by record type, error type, cause, and disposition.
- **Batch totals** that summarize key values for a batch of input records should be calculated. Three commonly used batch totals are
 1. A **financial total** sums a field that contains dollar values, such as the total dollar amount of all sales for a batch of sales transactions.
 2. A **hash total** sums a nonfinancial numeric field, such as the total of the quantity ordered field in a batch of sales transactions.
 3. A **record count** sums the number of records in a batch.

 These batch totals are calculated and recorded when data is entered. They will be used later to verify that all input was processed correctly.

Additional Online Data Entry Controls

Whenever possible, the system should automatically enter transaction data, which saves keying time and reduces errors. For example, the system can determine the next available document number and enter it into the transaction record. The system also can generate new ID numbers that satisfy the check digit algorithm and do not duplicate existing numbers and then enter them into the input record. Other online processing data entry controls include

- **Prompting**, in which the system requests each input data item and waits for an acceptable response. This ensures that all necessary data are entered (i.e., an on-line completeness check).
- **Preformatting**, in which the system displays a document with highlighted blank spaces and waits for the data to be entered.
- **Closed-loop verification** checks the accuracy of input data by using it to retrieve and display other related information. For example, if a clerk enters an account number, the system could retrieve and display the account name so that the user could verify that the correct account number had been entered.
- Creation of a **transaction log** that includes a detailed record of all transaction data; a unique transaction identifier; the date and time of entry; terminal, transmission line, and operator identification; and the sequence in which the transaction was entered. If an online file is damaged, the log can be used for reconstruction purposes. If a malfunction temporarily shuts down the system, the log can be used to ensure that transactions are not lost or entered twice.
- Error messages should indicate when an error has occurred, which item is in error, and what the operator should do to correct it.

Processing Controls

Controls are also needed to ensure that data is processed correctly. Important processing controls include the following:

- **Data matching.** In certain cases, two or more items of data must be matched before an action can take place. For example, the system should verify that information on the vendor invoice matches that on both the purchase order and the receiving report before paying a vendor.

- **File labels.** File labels need to be checked to ensure that the correct and most current files are being updated. Both external labels that are readable by humans and internal labels that are written in machine-readable form on the data recording media should be used. Two important types of internal labels are header and trailer records. The **header record** is located at the beginning of each file and contains the file name, expiration date, and other identification data. The **trailer record** is located at the end of the file and contains the batch totals calculated during input.

- **Recalculation of batch totals.** Batch totals can be recomputed as each transaction record is processed and compared to the values in the trailer record. Any discrepancies indicate a processing error. Often, the nature of the discrepancy provides a clue about the type of error that occurred. For example, if the recomputed record count is smaller than the original, one or more transaction records were not processed. Conversely, if the recomputed record count is larger than the original, either additional unauthorized transactions were processed or some transaction records were processed twice. If a financial or hash total discrepancy is evenly divisible by 9, the likely cause is a **transposition error**, in which two adjacent digits were inadvertently reversed (e.g., 46 instead of 64). Transposition errors may appear to be trivial but can have enormous financial consequences. For example, consider the effect of misrecording the interest rate on a loan as 6.4% instead of 4.6%.

- **Cross-footing and zero-balance tests.** Often totals can be calculated in multiple ways. For example, in spreadsheets a grand total can often be computed either by summing a column of row totals or by summing a row of column totals. These two methods should produce the same result. A **cross-footing balance test** compares the results produced by each method to verify accuracy. A **zero-balance test** applies this same logic to control accounts. For example, the payroll clearing account is debited for the total gross pay of all employees in a particular time period. It is then credited for the amount of all labor costs allocated to various expense categories. The payroll clearing account should have a zero balance after both sets of entries have been made; a nonzero balance indicates a processing error.

- **Write-protection mechanisms.** These protect against the accidental writing over or erasing of data files stored on magnetic media. Many businesses are replacing bar-codes and manual tags with radio frequency identification (RFID) tags that can store up to 128 bytes of data. It is important to ensure that these tags are write-protected. Otherwise, unscrupulous customers can change the price information on merchandise.

- **Database processing integrity procedures.** Database systems use database administrators, data dictionaries, and concurrent update controls to ensure processing integrity. The administrator establishes and enforces procedures for accessing and updating the database. The data dictionary ensures that data items are defined and used consistently. **Concurrent update controls** protect records from errors that occur when two or more users attempt to update the same record simultaneously. This is accomplished by locking out one user until the system has finished processing the update entered by the other.

Output Controls

Careful checking of system output provides additional control over processing integrity. Important output controls include:

- **User review of output.** Users should carefully examine system output for reasonableness, completeness, and that they are the intended recipient.
- **Reconciliation procedures.** Periodically, all transactions and other system updates should be reconciled to control reports, file status/update reports, or other control mechanisms. In addition, general ledger accounts should be reconciled to subsidiary account totals on a regular basis. For example, the inventory control account balance in the general ledger should equal the sum of the item balances in the inventory database. The same is true for the accounts receivable, capital assets, and accounts payable control accounts.
- **External data reconciliation.** Database totals should periodically be reconciled with data maintained outside the system. For example, the number of employee records in the payroll file can be compared with the total from human resources to detect attempts to add fictitious employees to the payroll database.

COBIT application control objective AC6 addresses the need to protect the authenticity and integrity of data during transmission. Encryption techniques, such as using SSL for e-commerce transactions and VPNs for providing remote access to the corporate network, satisfy this objective.

In addition to using encryption to protect the confidentiality of information transmitted from one location to another, organizations need to implement controls designed to minimize the risk of data transmission errors. Whenever the receiving unit detects a data transmission error, it requests the sending unit to retransmit that data. Generally, the system will do this automatically and the user is unaware that it has occurred. Occasionally, the system may not be able to accomplish automatic retransmissions and the sender must manually retransmit the data. Parity checking and message acknowledgement techniques are two basic types of data transmission controls.

Parity Checking

Computers represent characters as a set of binary digits (bits). When data are transmitted, some bits may be lost or received incorrectly due to media disruptions or failures. To detect these types of errors, an extra digit, called a **parity bit**, is added to every character. For example, the digits 5 and 7 can be represented by the seven-bit patterns 0000101 and 0000111, respectively. An eighth bit could be added to each character to serve as the parity bit. Two basic schemes are referred to as *even parity* and *odd parity*. In even parity, the parity bit is set so that each character has an even number of bits with the value 1; in odd parity, the parity bit is set so that an odd number of bits in the character have the value 1. Thus, in the preceding example, an even parity system would set the parity bit for 5 to 0, so that it would be transmitted as 00000101 (which has an even number of bits with the value 1). The parity bit for 7 would be set to 1 so that it would be transmitted as 10000111 (which has an even number of bits set with the value 1). The receiving device performs **parity checking**, which entails verifying that there are the proper number of bits set to the value 1 in each character received. Additional accuracy can be provided by using more complex parity schemes.

Message Acknowledgment Techniques

A number of message acknowledgment techniques can be used to let the sender of an electronic message know that a message was received:

- **Echo check.** When data are transmitted, the system calculates a summary statistic such as the number of bits in the message. The receiving unit performs the same calculation—a procedure known as an **echo check**—and sends the

result to the sending unit. If the counts agree, the transmission is presumed to be accurate.

- **Trailer record.** The sending unit stores control totals in a trailer record. The receiving unit uses that information to verify that the entire message was received.
- **Numbered batches.** If a large message is transmitted in segments, each can be numbered sequentially so that the receiving unit can properly assemble the segments.

Example: Credit Sales Processing

Many of the processing integrity controls described in this section can be illustrated using a credit sale as an example. The following transaction data are used: sales order number, customer account number, inventory item number, quantity sold, sale price, and delivery date. If the customer purchases more than one product, there will be multiple inventory item numbers, quantities sold, and prices associated with each sales transaction. Processing these transactions includes the following steps: (1) entering and editing the transaction data; (2) updating the customer and inventory records (the amount of the credit purchase is added to the customer's balance; for each inventory item, the quantity sold is subtracted from the quantity on hand); and (3) preparing and distributing shipping and/or billing documents. We will now discuss the use of processing controls in both batch and online processing of sales transactions.

Batch Processing Integrity Controls

Processing credit sales transactions in a batch processing mode includes the following steps:

1 **Prepare batch totals.** These totals are recorded on batch control forms added to each group of sales documents.
2 **Deliver the transactions to the computer operations department for processing.** There each batch is checked for proper authorization and recorded in a control log.
3 **Enter the transaction data into the system.** Data entry errors generally fall into one of two types. Operator errors arise when an operator reads a source document incorrectly or accidentally strikes the wrong key. These errors are generally benign and can be corrected immediately after being detected. Incorrect source data, such as an unauthorized sales transaction or an invalid account number, are more problematic and should be returned to the sales department for correction.
4 **Sort and edit the transaction file.** Either before or after the sales transaction file is sorted into customer number sequence, a program performs several input validation checks. Rejected transactions are listed on a control report with the computed batch totals. Data control reconciles the batch totals, investigates and corrects any errors, and submits the corrected transactions for processing.
5 **Update the master files.** The sales transaction file is processed against customer (accounts receivable) and inventory databases or master files. If the databases or master files are stored off-line, care must be taken to ensure that the correct file copies are retrieved from the file library and loaded onto the system. The operator must check the file name and processing date on the external labels before loading the files. The file update program checks the internal label (header record) before processing begins. Each file has a trailer record containing a record count and other file totals. These are checked and updated during the file updating run.
6 **Prepare and distribute output.** Outputs include billing and/or shipping documents and a control report. The control report contains batch totals accumulated during the file update run and a list of transactions rejected by the update program.
7 **User review.** Users in the shipping and billing departments perform a limited review of the documents for incomplete data or other obvious deficiencies.

Figure 8-1
Flowchart of Sales Order Processing and Related Control Procedures (continues on next page)

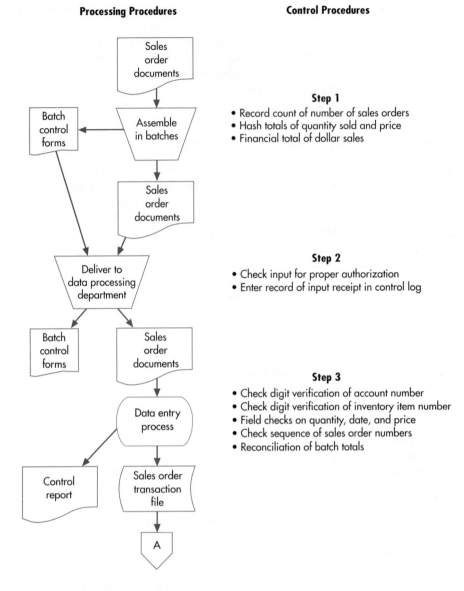

Processing Procedures

Control Procedures

Step 1
- Record count of number of sales orders
- Hash totals of quantity sold and price
- Financial total of dollar sales

Step 2
- Check input for proper authorization
- Enter record of input receipt in control log

Step 3
- Check digit verification of account number
- Check digit verification of inventory item number
- Field checks on quantity, date, and price
- Check sequence of sales order numbers
- Reconciliation of batch totals

Figure 8-1, above and on page 329 illustrates these seven steps and identifies the application controls that should be utilized at each stage.

Online Processing Integrity Controls

Online real-time processing records each credit sales transaction as it occurs. As the following example shows, it also makes it easier and faster to detect and correct errors.

Online Data Entry Controls

- When a user accesses the online system, logical access controls confirm the identity of the data entry device (personal computer, terminal) and the validity of the user's ID number and password.
- A compatibility test is performed on all user interactions to ensure that only authorized tasks are performed.
- The system automatically assigns the transaction the next sequential sales order number and the current date as the date of the invoice.
- To assist authorized personnel in entering sales data, the system prompts for all required input (completeness test). After each prompt, the system waits for a response.

Processing Procedures **Control Procedures**

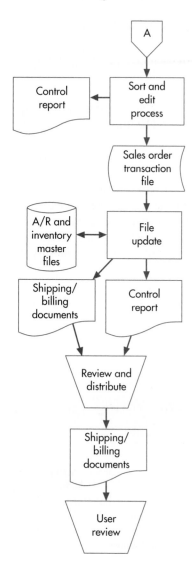

Step 4
- Sequence check on account number
- Limit checks on quantity and price
- Range check on delivery date
- Completeness test on entire record
- Reconciliation of batch totals
- Review errors identified by edit checks
- Investigation and correction of erroneous input

Step 5
- Security of master files in file library
- Protection of master files with file labels
- Maintenance of backup copies of master files
- Validity check of customer account number
- Validity check of inventory item number
- Sign check of inventory quantity on hand
- Limit check of sale amount versus credit limit
- Range check on sale price
- Reasonableness test of quantity ordered
- Redundant data check on customer data
- Redundant data check on inventory data

Step 6
- Reconciliation of batch totals
- Review of errors identified by edit checks
- Investigation and correction of erroneous input
- Distribution of billing and shipping documents
- Recording of output distribution in control log
- Return of master files to file library

Step 7
- Visual inspection of output
- Reconciliation of batch totals

- Each response is tested using one or more of the following controls: validity checks (valid customer and inventory numbers), field and sign checks (only positive, numeric characters in the quantity, date, and price fields), and limit or range checks (delivery date versus current date).
- When the customer number is entered, the system retrieves the corresponding customer name from the database and displays it on the screen (closed-loop verification). The operator visually examines the customer name. If it matches the name on the sales order document, the operator signals the system to proceed with the transaction. If not, the operator rechecks the customer number and enters the correct value.
- When the inventory item number is entered, the system and the operator go through the same procedures as they do with the customer number.

Online Processing Controls. Because the file update program accesses the customer and inventory database records, it performs additional input validation tests by comparing data in each transaction record with data in the corresponding database record. These tests often include the following:

- Validity checks on the customer and inventory item numbers
- Sign checks on inventory-on-hand balances (after subtracting quantities sold)

- Limit checks that compare each customer's total amount due with the credit limit
- Range checks on the sale price of each item sold relative to the permissible range of prices for that item
- Reasonableness tests on the quantity sold of each item relative to normal sales quantities for that customer and that item

Online Output Controls. Outputs of this process include billing and/or shipping documents and a control report. Output controls that can be utilized are as follows:

- Billing and shipping documents are forwarded electronically to only pre-authorized users.
- Users in the shipping and billing departments perform a limited review of the documents by visually inspecting them for incomplete data or other obvious errors.
- The control report is sent automatically to its intended recipients, or they can query the system for the report. If they query the system, logical access controls confirm the identity of the device making the query and the validity of the user's ID number and password.

Processing integrity controls are important to nonbusiness systems, too. Focus 8-2 discusses some of the issues involving the use of electronic voting machines.

8-2 FOCUS Assuring the Processing Integrity of Electronic Voting

Electronic voting may eliminate some of the types of problems that occurred in Florida in the November 2000 election. For example, voting software could use completeness checks to ensure that voters made choices in all races (this would eliminate the "hanging chad" problem created by failing to completely punch out the hole on a paper ballot). Similarly, limit checks could identify and prevent voters from attempting to select more candidates than permitted in a particular race. In addition, the ability to supplement printed choices with audio information may make it easier for people with visual disabilities to vote.

Nevertheless, there are concerns about electronic voting, particularly its audit trail capabilities. For example, in early 2004 the government of Ireland decided to postpone allowing the use of electronic voting machines until their ability to create auditable records was demonstrated. Similarly, in May 2004 the California secretary of state banned the use of Diebold's touch-screen voting machines because they did not provide an adequate paper audit trail. In June 2004, the state of Ohio approved the use of AccuPoll Inc.'s touch-screen voting machines because they did create a paper audit trail.

At issue is the ability to verify that only properly registered voters did indeed vote and voted only once. Although no one disagrees with the need for such authentication, there is debate over whether electronic voting machines can create adequate audit trails without risking the loss of voters' anonymity. There is also debate about the overall security and reliability of electronic voting. Some security experts suggest that election officials adopt the methods used by the state of Nevada to ensure that electronic gambling machines operate honestly and accurately, which include the following:

- The Gaming Control Board keeps copies of all software. It is illegal for casinos to use any unregistered software. For electronic voting, the government should keep copies of the source code.
- Frequent on-site spot checks of the computer chips in gambling machines are made to verify compliance with the Gaming Control Board's records. Similar tests should be done to voting machines.
- Extensive tests are conducted of the machine's physical security, such as how it reacts to stun guns and large electric shocks. Voting machines should be similarly tested.
- All gambling machine manufacturers are carefully scrutinized and are registered. Similar checks should be performed on voting machine manufacturers, and software developers.

Nevertheless, even with adoption of such controls, most experts agree that the presence of trained poll workers to identify and respond to problems on the spot will continue to be critical to fair elections.

Availability

The loss of system availability can cause significant financial losses, especially if the system affected is essential to e-commerce. Consequently, COBIT section DS 4 addresses the important issue of ensuring that systems and information are available for use whenever needed in order to perform business processes. Threats to system availability originate from many sources, including:

- Hardware and software failures
- Natural and man-made disasters
- Human error
- Worms and viruses
- Denial-of-service attacks and other acts of sabotage

It is impossible to entirely eliminate the risk of all these threats. Therefore, the primary objective is to maximize availability by minimizing system downtime. Preventive controls, however, are not sufficient. Organizations also need to develop comprehensive disaster recovery and business continuity plans to enable them to quickly resume normal operations after such an event. Table 8-3 (see below) summarizes the key controls related to these two availability objectives.

Minimizing Risk of System Downtime

Organizations can take a variety of steps to minimize the risk of system downtime. COBIT control objective DS 13.5 identifies the need for preventive maintenance, such as cleaning disk drives and properly storing magnetic and optical media, to reduce the risk of hardware and software failure. The use of redundant components, such as dual processors and arrays of multiple hard drives, provides **fault tolerance**, enabling a system to continue functioning in the event that a particular component fails.

COBIT control objectives DS 12.1 and 12.4 address the importance of locating and designing the rooms housing mission-critical servers and databases so as to minimize the risks associated with natural and man-made disasters. Raised floors provide protection from damage caused by flooding. Installation of fire detection and suppression devices can reduce the likelihood of fire damage. Adequate air-conditioning systems

Objective	Threats/Risks	Applicable Controls
Minimizing system downtime	System outages or failure that interrupts critical business operations; loss or destruction of important information due to natural disasters, mistakes, worms and viruses, and deliberate attacks	Preventive maintenance; fault tolerance; physical location and design of rooms housing computing resources; Uninterruptible Power Supply (UPS); training; installing, running, and keeping antivirus software current; security measures
Recovery	Loss of access to mission critical information systems resources; inability to perform essential business operations	Backup procedures; disaster recovery and business continuity plans, including the documentation and periodic testing of those plans

Table 8-3
Summary of Key Controls to Ensure System Availability

can reduce the likelihood of damage to computer equipment due to overheating or humidity. Cables with special plugs that cannot be easily removed reduce the risk of system damage due to someone accidentally unplugging the device. Surge protection devices provide protection against temporary power fluctuations that might otherwise cause computers and other network equipment to crash. An **uninterruptible power supply (UPS)** system provides protection in the event of a prolonged power outage, using battery power to enable the system to operate long enough to back up critical data and safely shut down.

Training is especially important. Well-trained operators are less likely to make mistakes and will know how to recover with minimal damage from errors they do commit. That is why COBIT control objective DS 13.1 stresses the importance of defining and documenting operational procedures and ensuring that operations staff understand their responsibilities. Security awareness training, particularly concerning safe e-mail and Web-browsing practices, is also important because it can reduce the risk of infection by viruses and worms. It is also important to install, run, and keep antivirus software current. E-mail should be scanned for viruses both at the server level and at the desktop. Newly acquired software and any diskettes, CDs, or DVDs brought into the organization should always be scanned and tested on a machine that is isolated from the main network.

Finally, the physical and logical access controls discussed in Chapter 7 can reduce the risk of successful denial-of-service attacks. In addition, good computer security reduces the risk of system downtime due to the theft or sabotage of information system resources.

Disaster Recovery and Business Continuity Planning

Disaster recovery and business continuity plans are essential if an organization hopes to survive a major catastrophe. Being without an information system for even a short period of time can be quite costly; some companies report losses as high as $500,000 per hour of downtime. Moreover, experience suggests that companies that have had a major disaster resulting in loss of use of their information system for more than a few days have a greater than 50% chance of going out of business. Focus 8-3 describes how a thorough disaster recovery and business continuity plan enabled Nasdaq to survive the complete destruction of the World Trade Center on September 11, 2001. Focus 8-4 discusses how disaster recovery and business continuity plans helped two banks survive the effects of a catastrophic fire.

In light of such experiences, it is incredible that surveys indicate that many large U.S. companies do not have adequate disaster recovery and business continuity plans. The objectives of a disaster recovery and business continuity plan are to (1) minimize the extent of the disruption, damage, and loss; (2) temporarily establish an alternative means of processing information; (3) resume normal operations as soon as possible; and (4) train and familiarize personnel with emergency operations. The following sections discuss the key components of effective disaster recovery and business continuity plans: data backup procedures, provision for access to replacement infrastructure (equipment, facilities, phone lines, etc.), thorough documentation, and periodic testing. In addition, organizations should attempt to acquire adequate insurance coverage to defray part or all of the expenses associated with implementing their disaster recovery and business continuity plans.

Data Backup Procedures

Data need to be backed up regularly and frequently. A **backup** is an exact copy of the most current version of a database, file, or software program. A backup provides fault tolerance, being intended for use in the event of a hardware or software failure. The process of installing the backup copy for use is called **restoration**.

Several different backup procedures exist. A *full backup* is an exact copy of the entire database. Full backups are time-consuming, so most organizations only do full

8-3 FOCUS How NASDAQ Recovered from September 11

Thanks to an effective disaster recovery plan, NASDAQ was up and running six days after the September 11, 2001 terrorist attack that destroyed the twin towers of the World Trade Center. NASDAQ'S headquarters was located on the 49th and 50th floors of One Liberty Plaza, just across the street from the World Trade Center. When the first plane hit, NASDAQ'S security guards immediately evacuated personnel from the building. Most of the employees were out of the building by the time the second plane crashed into the other tower. Although employees were evacuated from the headquarters and the office in Times Square had temporarily lost telephone service, NASDAQ was able to relocate to a backup center at the Marriott Marquis. Once there, NASDAQ executives went through their list of priorities: first, their employees; next, the physical damage; and lastly, the trading industry situation.

Effective communication became essential in determining the condition of these priorities. NASDAQ attributes much of its success in communicating and coordinating with the rest of the industry to its dress rehearsals for Y2K. While preparing for the changeover, NASDAQ had regular nationwide teleconferences with all the exchanges. This helped the company organize similar conferences after the attack. NASDAQ had already planned for one potential crisis, and this proved helpful in recovering from another unexpected crisis. By prioritizing

and teleconferencing, the company was able to quickly identify problems and the traders who would need extra help before NASDAQ could open the market again.

NASDAQ'S extremely redundant and dispersed systems also helped the company quickly reopen the market. Each trader is linked to two NASDAQ connection centers, and there are 20 connection centers in the United States. The centers are connected to each other using two separate paths and sometimes two distinct vendors. Servers are kept in different buildings and have two network topologies. Even with the electricity out in Lower Manhattan, NASDAQ'S systems were relatively unaffected.

When employees could no longer occupy the Manhattan office and phone lines were out in the Times Square office, NASDAQ still had offices in Maryland and Connecticut, which allowed it to monitor the regulatory processes. This also lessened the risk of losing all NASDAQ'S senior management. Even if large numbers of people had been lost in One Liberty Plaza, the company still would have had members of its senior management in other locations.

NASDAQ also took such precautions as having its executives carry more than one mobile phone in case one service provider went down. It also invested in interruption insurance to help defer the costs of closing the market. Planning and foresight saved NASDAQ from losing what could have been tens of millions of dollars.

backups weekly and supplement them with daily partial backups. Two types of partial backups are possible:

1 An **incremental backup** involves copying only the data items that have changed since the last backup. This produces a set of incremental backup files, each containing the results of one day's transactions. Restoration involves first loading the last full backup and then installing each subsequent incremental backup in the proper sequence.

2 A **differential backup** copies all changes made since the last full backup. Thus, each new differential backup file contains the cumulative effects of all activity since the last full backup. Consequently, except for the first day following a full backup, daily differential backups take longer than incremental backups. Restoration is simpler, however, because the last full backup needs to be supplemented with only the most recent differential backup, instead of a set of daily incremental backup files.

Many organizations make incremental and differential backups daily. The optimal frequency of backups depends upon an organization's business needs and management's risk tolerance. Data about any transactions that occurred between the time of the last backup and a disaster will have to be reentered, if source documents exist. If there are no source documents, all transactions that occurred since the last backup will be lost. Thus, management must establish a **recovery point objective (RPO)**, which represents the maximum length of time for which it is willing to risk the possible loss of transaction data.

FOCUS 8-4 How Planning Enabled Banks to Survive a Fire

On Thanksgiving Day, a huge fire swept through the offices of Northwest National Bank of Minneapolis, destroying bank transaction records and data processing facilities. It was described as one of the worst fires in the city's history. Yet the following Monday, bank employees were back on the job in new quarters—handling deposits, withdrawals, investments, loans, and other routine bank transactions. The fire could have threatened the bank's ability to remain in business, but it did not, thanks to a detailed disaster recovery plan. Because a record of nearly every bank transaction was stored elsewhere in computers or on microfilm, the bank lost few, if any, important records. The day after the fire, computers at a local service bureau were hard at work making new copies of the destroyed records. The recovery plan provided bank executives with a detailed blueprint for lining up new office space, replacing computer equipment and supplies, procuring new office equipment, and making other arrangements essential to the continuation of Northwest's banking operations.

Northwest's experiences helped the Bank of the Sierra in Porterville, California, survive the effects of an early morning fire that destroyed its corporate offices and melted its mainframe computer. Although the facility was seemingly well protected by a sprinkler system and a halon-gas fire-extinguishing system, this fire burned through the building's roof, which collapsed, crushing the sprinkler system and releasing the halon gas into the air. The bank's central databases and related records, including all personal and mortgage loan records, credit card records, and unprocessed checks, were lost.

Using a 150-page disaster recovery plan grounded in Northwest National Bank's experience, Bank of the Sierra officials quickly identified team members, crucial tasks, and required equipment and began an overnight effort to restore bank services. By 10:00 A.M. the following morning, nine hours after the fire started, backup files were online and tellers were conducting business at branch windows as if nothing had happened. For processing of the bank's 25,000 to 40,000 daily transactions, a data processing hot site in nearby San Ramon was used. Updated files were downloaded from the hot site to a mainframe computer, provided by a Denver company, from which printouts were flown back to Porterville daily. Within six days after the fire, the bank had cleaned up its transaction processing backlog and its customer accounts were current.

An alternative to these traditional backup methods that almost entirely eliminates the risk of losing any data is called real-time mirroring. **Real-time mirroring** involves maintaining two copies of the database at two separate data centers at all times and updating both copies in real-time as each transaction occurs. In the event that something happens to one data center, the organization can immediately switch all daily activities to the other. Real-time mirroring is expensive, but it is a business necessity for some organizations, such as financial institutions and airlines, that cannot function without access to their information systems and cannot afford to lose any transactions data.

Regardless of the organization's RPO, most mission-critical database systems make multiple temporary backups of the database several times throughout the day. This entails making a copy of the database at a point in time, called a **checkpoint**, and storing it on backup media. If a hardware or software fault interrupts processing, the checkpoint is used to restart the system and only the transactions that occurred after the last checkpoint was created need to be reprocessed.

No matter which backup procedure is used, multiple backup copies should be created. One copy can be stored on-site, for use in the event of minor incidents like failure of a hard drive. In the event of a major disaster, such as a fire or flood, any backup copies stored on-site will likely be destroyed or inaccessible. Therefore, a second backup copy needs to be stored off-site. These backup files can be transported to the remote storage site either physically (e.g., by courier) or electronically. In either case, the same security controls need to be applied to backup files as are used to protect the original copy of the information. This means that backup copies of sensitive data should be encrypted both in storage and during electronic transmission. Access to backup files also needs to be carefully controlled and monitored.

Backups are retained for only a fixed period of time. An **archive** is a copy of a database, master file, or software that will be retained indefinitely as an historical record, usually to satisfy legal and regulatory requirements. As with backups, multiple

copies of archives should be made and stored in different locations. Appropriate security controls should also be used to restrict access to archive files.

What media should be used for backups and archives, tape or disk? Disk backup is faster and disks are less easily lost. Tape, however, is cheaper, easier to transport, and more durable. Consequently, many organizations use both media. Data is first backed up to disk, for speed, and then transferred to tape. Archives are usually stored on tape.

Special attention needs to be paid to e-mail, because it has become an important repository of organizational behavior and information. Access to archived e-mail is especially important when it contains information relevant to lawsuits. It may be tempting for an organization to adopt a policy of periodically deleting all e-mail, to prevent a plaintiff's attorney from finding a "smoking gun." Most experts, however, advise against such policies. For starters, there are likely to be copies of the e-mail stored in archives outside the organization. In addition, it means that the organization will not be able to tell its side of the story; instead, the court (and jury) will only read the e-mail created by the other party to the dispute. Moreover, the courts have sanctioned companies for failing to provide timely access to e-mail. For example, an investment bank was penalized because it had lost e-mail relevant to a sex discrimination lawsuit filed by an ex-employee. Consequently, security experts recommend that organizations include e-mail in their backup and archive procedures.

Infrastructure Replacement

Major disasters can totally destroy an organization's information processing center, or at least make it inaccessible. Therefore, a second key component of disaster recovery and business continuity plans includes provisions for replacing the necessary computing infrastructure: computers, network equipment and access, telephone lines, other office equipment (e.g., fax machines), and supplies. It may even be necessary to hire temporary staff. For example, companies affected by the September 11, 2001 attack on the World Trade Center, such as American Express, had to hire temporary replacements to assist in resuming operations in New Jersey because bridge closures made it impossible for some regular employees to commute there.

Earlier, we discussed the importance of establishing a recovery point objective. A second critical business decision concerns how long management thinks the organization can function without access to its information system. The **recovery time objective (RTO)** represents the time following a disaster by which the organization's information system must be available again. Figure 8-2 depicts the relationship and differences between the recovery time objective (RTO) and the recovery point objective (RPO).

Organizations have three basic options for replacing computer and networking equipment. The least expensive approach is to create reciprocal agreements with another organization that uses similar equipment to have temporary access to and use of their information system resources. Reciprocal agreements can be effective

This gap represents RPO = the length of time for which data may be lost

This gap represents RTO = the length of time for which the system is down

Time of Last Backup

Time of Incident

Time system restored

Figure 8-2
Relationship of RTO and RPO

solutions to disasters of limited duration and magnitude, especially for smaller organizations. Major disasters, however, such as the September 11, 2001 destruction of the World Trade Center, are likely to affect both parties to the agreement. Another problem is that the "host" organization must use its information system resources, too. Consequently, most organizations use more elaborate and expensive methods of arranging for access to alternative information systems infrastructure. One solution involves purchasing or leasing a **cold site**, which is an empty building that is prewired for necessary telephone and Internet access, plus a contract with one or more vendors to provide all necessary computer and other office equipment within a specified period of time. Note that a cold site still leaves the organization without the use of its information system for a period of time. A more expensive solution is to create what is referred to as a hot site. A **hot site** is a facility that is not only prewired for telephone and Internet access but also contains all the computing and office equipment the organization needs to perform its essential business activities. Thus, a hot site is essentially a backup infrastructure designed to provide fault tolerance in the event of major disasters. In fact, hot sites enable organizations to employ the real-time mirroring approach to backup.

Documentation

Documentation is an important, but often overlooked, component of disaster recovery and business continuity planning. The plan itself, including instructions for notifying appropriate staff and the steps to take to resume operations, needs to be well documented. Assignment of responsibility for various actions needs to be clearly delineated. Vendor documentation of all hardware and software must be available. It is especially important to document the numerous modifications made to default configurations, so that the replacement system has the same functionality as the original. Failure to do so can create substantial costs and delays in implementing the recovery process. Detailed operating instructions are also needed, especially if temporary replacements have to be hired. Finally, copies of all documentation need to be stored both on-site and off-site so that it is available when needed.

Testing

Periodic testing and revision is probably the most important component of effective disaster recovery and business continuity plans. Most plans fail their initial test because it is impossible to fully anticipate everything that could go wrong. The time to discover such problems is not during an actual emergency, but rather in a setting in which weaknesses can be carefully and thoroughly analyzed and appropriate changes in procedures made.

Disaster recovery and business continuity plans need to be tested on at least an annual basis to ensure that they accurately reflect recent changes in equipment and procedures. It is especially important to test the procedures involved in executing either reciprocal agreements or the transfer of actual operations to cold or hot sites. Backup restoration procedures also require regular practice to verify that they function correctly.

Brainstorming sessions involving mock scenarios can be effective in identifying gaps and shortcomings. More realistic and detailed simulations or drills should also be performed, although it is not necessary to incur the expense of completely performing every activity. For example, it is sufficient to test the notification process up to the point where key staff members arrive at the airport but without actually flying to the designated recovery sites. Experts also recommend testing individual components of disaster recovery plans separately, because it is too complex and costly to simulate and effectively analyze every aspect of a plan simultaneously. Finally, disaster recovery and business continuity documentation needs to be updated to reflect any changes in procedures made in response to problems identified during tests of those plans.

Change Management Controls

Organizations constantly modify their information systems to reflect new business practices and to take advantage of advances in information technology. Controls are needed to ensure that such changes do not negatively affect systems reliability. It is also necessary to modify existing controls related to the principles of security, confidentiality, privacy, processing integrity, and availability to maintain their effectiveness after implementing changes to the underlying technology and operating procedures. For example, change management controls need to ensure that modifications to the organizational structure and the adoption of new software for performing business activities maintain adequate segregation of duties.

Important change management controls include the following:

- All change requests should be documented and follow a standardized format that clearly identifies the nature of the change, the reason for the request, the date of the request, and so on.
- All changes should be approved by appropriate levels of management. Approvals should be clearly documented to provide an audit trail. Managers should consult with the CISO or other IT managers about the effects of the proposed changes on systems reliability.
- Changes should be thoroughly tested prior to implementation. This includes assessing the impact of the change on all five principles of systems reliability. As data from old files and databases are entered into new data structures, conversion controls are needed to ensure that the new data storage mediums are free of errors. The old and new systems should be run in parallel at least once and the results compared to identify discrepancies. All testing should take place in a separate, nonproduction environment, not the system actually used for daily business processes. Internal auditors should review data conversion processes for accuracy.
- All documentation (program instructions, systems descriptions, backup and disaster recovery plans, etc.) should be updated to reflect authorized changes to the system.
- "Emergency" changes or deviations from standard operating policies must be documented and subjected to a formal review and approval process as soon after implementation as practicable. Log all such actions to provide an audit trail.
- Develop "backout" plans for reverting to previous configurations in case approved changes need to be interrupted or abandoned.
- User rights and privileges need to be carefully monitored *during* the change process to ensure that proper segregation of duties is maintained.

Probably the *most important* change management control is adequate monitoring and review by top management to ensure that proposed and implemented changes are consistent with the organization's multiyear strategic plan. The objective of this oversight is to make certain that the organization's information system continues to effectively support its strategy. Many organizations create IT steering committees to perform this monitoring function.

SUMMARY AND CASE CONCLUSION

Jason Scott reviewed what he had learned about Northwest Industries' information systems controls. He noted that confidential information, such as new marketing initiatives and detailed cost analyses, was encrypted both in storage and whenever it was

transmitted over the Internet. He had also learned that access to such sensitive information was carefully controlled and monitored and that access control matrices were reviewed and updated regularly to reflect the effects of transfers, promotions, and new hires. In addition, similar controls existed to protect the privacy of information Northwest Industries collected from its customers.

Jason also had observed and verified the effectiveness of controls designed to ensure processing integrity. To minimize data entry, and the opportunity for mistakes, Northwest Industries mailed turnaround documents to customers, which were returned with their payments. All data entry was done online, with extensive use of input validation routines to ensure the accuracy of the information entering the system. Output was reviewed for reasonableness by knowledgeable recipients, and the accuracy of key components of financial reports was regularly cross-validated with independent sources. For example, inventory was counted quarterly and the results of the physical counts were reconciled to the quantities stored in the system.

Jason was concerned about the effectiveness of controls designed to ensure systems availability, however. He noted that although Northwest Industries had developed a disaster recovery and business continuity plan in the fall of 2001, it had not been reviewed or updated since then. Of even greater concern was the fact that many portions of the plan, including arrangements for a cold site located in California, had never been tested. Jason's biggest concern, however, related to backup procedures. All files were backed up weekly, on Saturdays, onto DVDs, and incremental backups were made each night. No one had ever practiced restoring the data, however. In addition, the backups were not encrypted and one copy was stored on-site in the main server room on a shelf by the door.

Jason concluded his report with specific recommendations for improving the weaknesses he had identified in controls pertaining to systems availability. He felt confident that once those recommendations were implemented, management could be reasonably assured that Northwest Industries' information systems had satisfied the AICPA's Trust Services framework criteria and principles for systems reliability.

KEY TERMS

virtual private network (VPN) 316
cookie 319
field check 323
sign check 323
limit check 323
range check 323
size check 323
completeness check 323
validity check 323
reasonableness test 323
check digit 323
check digit verification 324
sequence check 324
error log 324
batch totals 324
financial total 324

hash total 324
record count 324
prompting 324
preformatting 324
closed-loop verification 324
transaction log 324
header record 325
trailer record 325
transposition error 325
cross-footing balance test 325
zero-balance test 325
concurrent update controls 325
parity bit 326
parity checking 326
echo check 326

fault tolerance 331
uninterruptible power supply (UPS) 332
backup 332
restoration 332
incremental backup 333
differential backup 333
recovery point objective (RPO) 333
real-time mirroring 334
checkpoint 334
archive 334
recovery time objective (RTO) 335
cold site 336
hot site 336

AIS IN ACTION

1 Which of the following measures the potential amount of data that might be lost due to a system disaster?
a. checkpoint
b. restoration
c. RTO
d. RPO

2 Which data entry application control would detect and prevent entry of alphabetic characters as the price of an item in the inventory master file?
a. field check
b. limit check
c. completeness check
d. reasonableness test

3 Which of the following statements is true?
a. Encrypting data is sufficient to protect confidentiality and privacy.
b. Cookies are text files that only store information and cannot do anything.
c. A hot site is an empty facility that is prewired for telephone and Internet access.
d. Verifying that a customer is of legal age to purchase alcohol is an example of a reasonableness test.

4 Which of the following is designed to identify entry of a nonexistent customer account number?
a. sequence check
b. field check
c. completeness check
d. validity check

5 A batch total that is calculated by summing the part numbers sold in a batch of 50 sales invoices is called a
a. financial total
b. hash total
c. record count
d. part count

6 Which of the following is an example of an output control?
a. size check
b. encryption
c. cross-footing balance check
d. forms design

7 Which infrastructure replacement option involves purchasing or leasing a physical site, prewiring it for telephone and Internet access, and contracting with one or more vendors to have computers and other equipment delivered to the site within 12–24 hours?
a. reciprocal agreement
b. hot site
c. cold site
d. real-time mirroring

8 Which backup method is the fastest?
a. full daily backup
b. incremental daily backup
c. differential daily backup
d. complete daily backup

9 A copy of the state of a database at a specific point in time during the middle of a normal business day is called a(n)
a. archive
b. cookie
c. checkpoint
d. restoration

10 Which of the following statements is true?
a. Concurrent update controls are designed to facilitate restoration of backups.
b. Use of a VPN protects the confidentiality of information while it is being transmitted over the Internet.

 c. Cross-footing balance tests are an effective method for detecting entry of invalid account numbers.

 d. "Emergency" changes to information systems do not need to be formally approved and documented.

DISCUSSION QUESTIONS

8.1 What are the advantages and disadvantages to the opt-in versus the opt-out approaches to collecting personal information from the viewpoint of the customer? From the viewpoint of the organization desiring to collect such information?

8.2 Theoretically, a control procedure should only be implemented if the benefits it provides exceed its costs. How can you estimate the costs and benefits of the following controls:

 a. segregation of duties

 b. data backup procedures

 c. input validation routines

8.3 Discuss the relative advantages and disadvantages of doing daily partial backups versus daily full backups versus real-time mirroring. How does each option affect RPO and RTO?

8.4 Use the numbers 10–19 to show why transposition errors are always divisible by 9.

8.5 Segregation of duties is essential to good internal control. Increasingly, computer systems automatically authorize and record transactions, such as generating purchase orders whenever the quantity on hand of an inventory item falls below its reorder point. Does this violate segregation of duties? Why (or why not)?

8.6 What risks, if any, does offshore outsourcing of various information systems functions pose to satisfying the principles of confidentiality and privacy?

8.7 Should organizations permit personal use of e-mail systems by employees during working hours?

8.8 What privacy concerns might arise from the use of biometric authentication techniques? What about the embedding of RFID tags in products such as clothing?

PROBLEMS

8.1 Cost-effective controls to provide confidentiality require valuing the information that is to be protected. This involves classifying information into discrete categories. Propose a minimal classification scheme that could be used by any business, and provide examples of the type of information that would fall into each of those categories.

8.2 Excel Problem

 Enter the data in Table 8-4 into a spreadsheet and perform the following tasks:

Employee Number	Pay Rate	Hours Worked	Gross Pay	Deductions	Net Pay
121	6.50	38	$247	25.50	221.50
123	7.25	40	290	60	230
125	6.75	90	607.5	450	57.5
122	67.5	40	2700	500	2200

Table 8-4
Data for Problem 8.2

Required

a. Calculate an example of these batch totals:
- a hash total
- a financial total
- a record count

b. For each of the following controls, give a specific example from the four records in Table 8-4 of an error or probable error that the control would detect or prevent. Identify the error, do not merely describe it.
- field check
- sequence check
- limit check
- reasonableness test
- cross-footing balance test

c. Create a control procedure that would either prevent, or at least detect, each of the types of errors listed in step b.

8.3 Excel Problem

The Moose Wings Cooperative Flight Club owns a number of airplanes and gliders. It serves fewer than 2,000 members, who are numbered sequentially from the founder, Tom Eagle (0001), to the newest member, Jacques Noveau (1368). Members rent the flying machines by the hour, and all must be returned on the same day. The following six records were among those entered for the flights taken on November 1, 2009:

Member #	Flight Date DDMMYY	Plane Used	Takeoff Time	Landing Time
1234	311109	G	0625	0846
4111	011109	C	0849	1023
1210	011109	P	0342	0542
0023	011109	X	0159	1243
012A	011109	P	1229	1532
0999	011109	L	1551	1387

*G = Glider; C = Cessna; P = Piper Cub; L = Lear Jet

Required

a. For each of the five data fields, suggest one or more input edit controls that could be included in the program for detecting possible errors.

b. Identify and describe any errors in the records.

c. Enter the data in a spreadsheet, and create appropriate controls to prevent the input of erroneous data.

8.4 The first column in Table 8-5 lists transaction amounts that have been summed to obtain a batch total. Assume that all data in the first column are correct. Columns a through d contain batch totals computed from the same amounts after these transaction amounts were processed in a subsequent processing step. One processing error occurred during each of the four cases.

Table 8-5
Data for Problem 8.4

Transaction amounts	a	b	c	d
$ 3,630.62	$ 3,630.62	$ 3,630.62	$ 3,630.62	$ 3,630.62
1,484.86	1,484.86	1,484.86	1,484.86	1,484.86
2,164.67	2,164.67	2,164.67	2,164.67	2,164.67
946.43	946.43	946.43	946.43	946.43
2,626.28	−2,626.28	2,626.28	2,626.28	2,626.28
969.97	969.97	969.97	969.97	969.97
2,772.42	2,772.42	2,772.42	3,772.42	2,772.42
934.25	934.25	934.25	934.25	934.25
1,620.94	1,620.94	1,620.94	1,620.94	1,620.94
4,566.86	4,566.86	4,656.86	4,566.86	4,566.86
1,249.32	1,249.32	1,249.32	1,249.32	1,249.32
1,070.27	1,070.27	1,070.27	1,070.27	1,070.27
2,668.51	2,668.51	2,668.51	2,668.51	2,668.51
1,762.62	1,762.62	1,762.62	1,762.62	873.26
873.26	873.26	873.26	873.26	
$29,341.28	$24,088.72	$29,431.28	$30,341.28	$27,578.66

Required

For each case, you are to do the following:

 a. Compute the difference between the batch total obtained after processing and the correct batch total shown in the first column.

 b. Explain specifically how this difference is helpful in discovering the processing error.

 c. Identify the processing error.

8.5 Taibert Corporation hired an independent computer programmer to develop a simplified payroll application for its newly purchased computer. The programmer developed an online data entry system that minimized the level of knowledge required by the operator. It was based on keying answers to input cues that appeared on the terminal's viewing screen. Examples of the cues follow:

 a. Access routine:
 1. Operator access number to payroll file?
 2. Are there new employees?
 b. New employees routine:
 1. Employee name?
 2. Employee number?
 3. Social Security number?
 4. Rate per hour?
 5. Single or married?
 6. Number of dependents?
 7. Account distribution?
 c. Current payroll routine:
 1. Employee number?
 2. Regular hours worked?
 3. Overtime hours worked?
 4. Total employees this payroll period?

The independent auditor is attempting to verify that certain input validation (edit) checks exist. The checks should ensure that errors resulting from omissions, invalid entries, or other inaccuracies are detected as soon as the answers to the input cues are entered.

Required

1. Identify the various types of input validation (edit) checks an auditor would expect to find in this system. Describe the assurances provided by each identified validation check. Do not discuss the review and evaluation of these controls.

2. Use Microsoft Access or other database management software package to create a set of tables to store the data listed and a form to enter that data. Design the form and tables to include the edit checks identified in part 1.

8.6 The headquarters of Gleicken Corporation, a private company with $3.5 million in annual sales, is located in California. For its 150 clients, Gleicken provides an online legal software service that includes data storage and administrative activities for law offices. The company has grown rapidly since its inception three years ago, and its data processing department has mushroomed to accommodate this growth. Because Gleicken's president and sales staff spend a great deal of time out of the office soliciting new clients, planning the computing facilities has been left to the information technology professionals.

Gleicken recently moved its headquarters into a remodeled warehouse on the outskirts of the city. While remodeling the warehouse, the architects retained much of the original structure, including the wooden-shingled exterior and exposed wooden beams throughout the interior. The company's hardware is situated in a large open area with high ceilings and skylights. This openness makes the computer operations area accessible to the rest of the staff and encourages a team approach to problem solving. Before Gleicken began to occupy its new facility, city inspectors declared the building safe (adequate fire extinguishers, sufficient exits, etc.).

Gleicken wanted to provide further protection for its large database of client information. Therefore, it instituted a tape backup procedure that automatically backs up the database every Sunday evening to avoid interrupting daily operations and procedures. All the tapes are labeled and carefully stored on shelves in the data processing department reserved for this purpose. The departmental operator's manual has instructions on how to use these tapes to restore the database should the need arise. In the event of an emergency, there is a home-phone list of the individuals in the data processing department. Gleicken has recently increased its liability insurance for data loss from $500,000 to $1,000,000.

This past Saturday, the Gleicken headquarters building was completely destroyed by fire. The company must now inform its clients that all their information has been destroyed.

Required

a. Describe the control weaknesses present at Gleicken Corporation that made it possible for a disastrous data loss to occur.

b. List the components that should have been included in the disaster recovery plan at Gleicken Corporation in order to ensure computer recovery within 72 hours.

c. What factors, other than those included in the plan itself, should a company consider when formulating a disaster recovery plan?

d. What threats, other than the fire, should Gleicken have protected itself from?

8.7 Visit the SANS Institute Web site (www.sans.org) and navigate to the page with sample policies. Download the SANS Institute's sample template for e-mail retention (or whichever other policy template your instructor chooses). Obtain a copy of your university's version of that policy. Compare the two and write a memo that analyzes any differences between the two documents. If your university does not have a comparable written policy, develop one.

8.8 Download the mortgage prepayment Excel spreadsheet on the textbook Web site. Create the following controls:

- Field check to ensure that only numeric data is entered in the "Life of loan in years" field.
- Range check to ensure that annual interest rates must be between 4% and 9%, inclusive.
- Limit check to verify that "Amount of loan" is less than $300,000.

- Reasonableness test: amount of extra principal payment cannot be greater than 50% of the initial total monthly payment.
- Cross-footing balance checks to verify that total amount paid in principal plus extra principal over the life of the loan equals original loan amount.
- Conditional limit check to calculate the final "Extra principal" payment so that it does not reduce the outstanding balance below zero.
- Format the amounts in the first row and last row (totals) to display $ signs.
- Format all other rows to only show two digits after the decimal point, but no $ sign.

8.9 Use the following data to calculate the effects of different backup approaches. Which approach would you recommend? Why? Consider the time required to backup, the amount of media that must be dedicated to backup and retained to enable complete restoration, and the time required for restoration.

 a. Full daily backup:
 - time to backup = 60 minutes
 - size of backup = 50 GB
 - time to restore = 60 minutes
 b. Weekly full backup on Fridays plus daily incremental backup:
 - time to backup = 60 minutes for full backup, 10 minutes for incremental
 - size of backup = 50 GB for full backup, 8 GB on average for incremental backup
 - time to restore = 60 minutes for full backup, 5 minutes for each incremental backup day
 c. Weekly full backup on Fridays plus daily differential backup:
 - time to backup = 60 minutes for full backup, 15 minutes for differential
 - size of backup = 50 GB for full backup, 6–30 GB for differential backups depending on how many days since last backup
 - time to restore = 60 minutes for full backup, 8 minutes on average for differential backup

8.10 Visit the Information Systems Audit and Control Association's (ISACA) Web site (www.isaca.org) to review the COBIT framework (version 4.1). Complete the following matrix to show how the 34 high-level control objectives in the COBIT framework map to the five Trust Services principles of system reliability (you will need to add 31 rows for the remaining COBIT Control Objectives not listed in the table below). Fill in the matrix by placing an "X" in each column affected by that COBIT control. Some COBIT control objectives may affect multiple Trust Services Framework principles.

TRUST SERVICES FRAMEWORK PRINCIPLE

COBIT Control Objective	Security	Confidentiality	Privacy	Processing Integrity	Availability
PO 1 Define a strategic IT plan					
PO 2 Define the information architecture					
...					
...					
ME 4 Provide IT governance					

8.11 Which control(s) would best mitigate the following threats?

a. The time worked field in a payroll transaction record contained the value 400 instead of 40. As a result, the employee received a paycheck for $6,257.24 instead of $654.32.

b. The accounts receivable file was destroyed because it was accidentally used to update accounts payable.

c. During processing of customer payments, the digit 0 in a payment of $204 was mistakenly typed as the letter "O." As a result, the transaction was not processed correctly and the customer erroneously received a letter that the account was delinquent.

d. A salesperson mistakenly entered an online order for 50 laser printers instead of 50 laser printer toner cartridges.

e. A 20-minute power brownout caused a mission-critical database server to crash, shutting down operations temporarily.

f. A fire destroyed the data center, including all backup copies of the accounts receivable files.

g. After processing sales transactions, the inventory report showed a negative quantity on hand for several items.

h. A customer order for an important part did not include the customer's address. Consequently, the order was not shipped on time and the customer called to complain.

i. When entering a large credit sale, the clerk typed in the customer's account number as 45982 instead of 45892. That account number did not exist. The mistake was not caught until later in the week when the weekly billing process was run. Consequently, the customer was not billed for another week, delaying receipt of payment.

j. A visitor to the company's Web site entered 400 characters into the five-digit Zip code field, causing the server to crash.

k. Two traveling sales representatives accessed the parts database at the same time. Salesperson A noted that there were still 55 units of part 723 available and entered an order for 45 of them. While salesperson A was keying in the order, salesperson B, in another state, also noted the availability of 55 units for part 723 and entered an order for 33 of them. Both sales reps promised their customer next-day delivery. Salesperson A's customer, however, learned the next day that the part would have to be back-ordered. The customer canceled the sale and vowed to never again do business with the company.

l. The warranty department manager was upset because special discount coupons were mailed to every customer who had purchased the product within the past 3 years, instead of to only those customers who had purchased the product within the past 3 months.

m. The clerk entering details about a large credit sale mistakenly typed in a nonexistent account number. Consequently, the company never received payment for the items.

n. A customer filled in the wrong account number on the portion of the invoice being returned with payment. Consequently, the payment was credited to another customer's account.

o. A batch of 73 time sheets was sent to the payroll department for weekly processing. Somehow, one of the time sheets did not get processed. The mistake was not caught until payday, when one employee complained about not receiving a paycheck.

p. A competitor intercepted the company's bid submitted by e-mail and used the information to underbid and win the contract.

q. Sunspot activity resulted in the loss of some data being sent to the regional office. The problem was not discovered until several days later when managers attempted to query the database for that information.

8.12 MonsterMed Inc. (MMI) is an online pharmaceutical firm. MMI has a small systems staff that designs and writes MMI's customized software. Until recently, MMI's transaction data were transmitted to a service bureau for processing on its hardware.

MMI has experienced significant sales growth as the cost of prescription drugs has increased and medical insurance companies have been tightening reimbursements in order to restrain premium cost increases. As a result of these increased sales, MMI has purchased its own computer hardware. The computer center is installed on the ground floor of its two-story headquarters building. It is behind large plate glass windows so that the state-of-the-art computer center can be displayed as a measure of the company's success and to attract customer and investor attention. The computer area is equipped with halon-gas fire suppression equipment and an uninterruptible power supply system.

MMI has hired a small computer operations staff to operate this computer center. To handle MMI's current level of business, the operations staff works a two-shift schedule, five days per week. MMI's systems and programming staff, now located in the same building, has access to the computer center and can test new programs and program changes when the operations staff is not available. Since the systems and programming staff is small and the work demands have increased, systems and programming documentation is developed only when time is available. Backups occur periodically as time allows. MMI backs up its programs and data files, storing them at an off-site location.

Unfortunately, due to several days of heavy rains, MMI's building recently experienced serious flooding that reached several feet into the first-floor level and destroyed not only the computer hardware but also the data and program files that were on-site.

Required

 a. Describe at least four computer security weaknesses that existed at MonsterMed Inc. prior to the flood occurrence.

 b. Describe at least five components that should be incorporated in a formal disaster recovery plan in order that MMI can become operational within 72 hours after a disaster affects its computer operations capability.

(CMA, adapted)

CASE 8-1 The State Department of Taxation

The department of taxation in your state is developing a new computer system for processing individual and corporate income-tax returns. The new system features direct data input and inquiry capabilities. Identification of taxpayers is provided by using the Social Security number for individuals and federal tax identification number for corporations. The new system should be fully implemented in time for the next tax season.

The new system will serve three primary purposes:

1 Data will be input directly into the system from tax returns using computer terminals located at central headquarters.

2 The returns will be processed using the main computer facilities at central headquarters. Processing will include four steps:
 a. Verifying mathematical accuracy
 b. Auditing the reasonableness of deductions, tax due, and so on, through the use of edit routines, which also include a comparison of current and prior years' data.

 c. Identifying returns that should be considered for audit by department revenue agents
 d. Issuing refund checks to taxpayers

3 Inquiry service will be provided to taxpayers upon request through the assistance of tax department personnel at five regional offices. A total of 50 terminals will be placed at each regional office. A taxpayer will be allowed to determine the status of his or her return or get information from the last three years' returns by calling or visiting one of the department's regional offices.

The state commissioner of taxation is concerned about data security during input and processing, over and above protection against natural hazards such as fire and flood. This includes protection against the loss or damage of data during data input and processing as well as the improper input or processing of data. In addition, the tax commissioner and the state attorney general have discussed the general problem of data confidentiality

that may arise from the nature and operation of the new system. Both individuals want to have potential problems identified before the system is fully developed and implemented so that the proper controls can be incorporated into the new system.

Required

1 Describe the potential confidentiality problems that could arise in each of the following three areas of processing, and recommend the corrective action(s) to solve each problem identified:

a. Data input
b. Processing of returns
c. Data inquiry

2 The state tax commission wants to incorporate controls to provide data security against the loss, damage, improper input, or use of data during data input and processing. Identify the potential problems (outside of natural hazards such as fire or floods) for which the department of taxation should develop controls, and recommend the possible controls for each problem identified.

AIS IN ACTION SOLUTIONS

QUIZ KEY

1 Which of the following measures the potential amount of data that might be lost due to a system disaster?
 a. checkpoint (Incorrect. A checkpoint is a temporary, intra-day copy of a database at a point in time.)
 b. restoration (Incorrect. Restoration is the process of installing backups.)
 c. RTO (Incorrect. The RTO, or recovery time objective, represents the length of time to recover and have the system backup and running after a disaster.)
 ✔ d. RPO (Correct. The RPO, or recovery point objective, represents the amount of time between the last backup and the time of a system disaster.)

2 Which data entry application control would detect and prevent entry of alphabetic characters as the price of an item in the inventory master file?
 ✔ a. field check (Correct. A field check could be used to limit entry of data into the price field to be only numeric characters.)
 b. limit check (Incorrect. A limit check could be used to set a maximum price for an item.)
 c. completeness (Incorrect. A completeness check could be used to ensure that the price is not left blank, but it would not check the values entered in the price field.)
 d. reasonableness test (Incorrect. A reasonableness test verifies the correctness of one data item being entered by comparing it to the value of another data item.)

3 Which of the following statements is true?
 a. Encrypting data is sufficient to protect confidentiality and privacy. (Incorrect. Access to encrypted data must also be controlled because, given enough time, any encryption scheme can be broken.)
 ✔ b. Cookies are text files that only store information and cannot do anything. (Correct. Cookies are text files that store information, not programs capable of performing any functions.)
 c. A hot site is an empty facility that is prewired for telephone and Internet access. (Incorrect. This is the definition of a cold site.)
 d. Verifying that a customer is of legal age to purchase alcohol is an example of a reasonableness test. (Incorrect. This is an example of a limit check. A reasonableness test involves verifying the accuracy of one data item by comparing it to the value of another.)

4 Which of the following is designed to identify entry of a nonexistent customer account number?

 a. sequence check (Incorrect. A sequence check is used to identify missing records.)

 b. field check (Incorrect. A field check verifies whether the data input into a particular field is of the proper type, such as numeric.)

 c. completeness check (Incorrect. A completeness check verifies that data are not missing.)

 ✔ **d.** validity check. (Correct. A validity check compares input data to a master file to verify that the record being referenced does indeed exist.)

5 A batch total that is calculated by summing the part numbers sold in a batch of 50 sales invoices is called a

 a. financial total (Incorrect. A financial total is a dollar amount.)

 ✔ **b.** hash total (Correct. The sum of part numbers does not mean anything but can be used to verify processing integrity.)

 c. record count (Incorrect. A record count records the number of records in a batch; in this case, it would equal 50.)

 d. part count (Incorrect. There is no such input validation control.)

6 Which of the following is an example of an output control?

 a. size check (Incorrect. A size check is an input control designed to prevent errors during data entry. It can also be used to prevent a buffer overflow attack.)

 ✔ **b.** encryption (Correct. Encryption provides away to protect sensitive data during transmission.)

 c. cross-footing balance check (Incorrect. A cross-footing balance check is a processing control designed to ensure accurate transaction processing.)

 d. forms design (Incorrect. Forms design is an input control designed to reduce the risk of error during data entry.)

7 Which infrastructure replacement option involves purchasing or easing a physical site, prewiring it for telephone and Internet access, and contracting with one or more vendors to have computers and other equipment delivered to the site within 12–24 hours?

 a. reciprocal agreement (Incorrect. A reciprocal agreement is a solution that provides use of another company's up-and-running data center.)

 b. hot site (Incorrect. A hot site contains all the equipment needed to function as an alternative data center.)

 ✔ **c.** cold site (Correct. A cold site contains everything but the actual computers and other equipment necessary to function as an alternative data center.)

 d. real-time monitoring (Incorrect. Real-time monitoring is a backup strategy that makes us of a hot site.)

8 Which backup method is the fastest (quickest time to make the backup copy)?

 a. full daily backup (Incorrect. Full backup takes the longest because it copies the entire file, which is why it is seldom done on a daily basis.)

 ✔ **b.** incremental daily backup (Correct. Incremental backups only back up the portions of the file that changed as a result of that day's transactions.)

 c. differential daily backup (Incorrect. Differential daily backups back up all portions of the file that have changed since the last full backup, not just that one day's changes—exception: differential and incremental backups are the same on the first day following a full backup.)

 d. complete daily backup (Incorrect. This is the same as a full backup, which takes the longest because it copies the entire file.)

9 A copy of the state of a database at a specific point in time during the middle of a normal business day is called a(n)

 a. archive (Incorrect. An archive is a backup copy kept for historical purposes to fulfill legal and regulatory requirements.)

b. cookie (Incorrect. A cookie is a text file used to facilitate browsing Web sites.)

✔ **c.** checkpoint (Correct. This is the definition of a checkpoint.)

d. restoration (Incorrect. Restoration is the process of installing a backup copy of a file or database to recover from damage or loss of the original.)

10 Which of the following statements is true?

a. Concurrent update controls are designed to facilitate restoration of backups. (Incorrect. Concurrent update controls prevent errors that can arise when two or more users simultaneously attempt to change the same item in a database.)

✔ **b.** Use of a VPN protects the confidentiality of information while it is being transmitted over the Internet. (Correct. VPNs use encryption to create protected tunnels through which information can be sent confidentially over the Internet.)

c. cross-footing balance tests are an effective method for detecting entry of invalid account numbers. (Incorrect. Cross-footing balance tests provide a check on processing integrity by comparing two alternative ways of calculating the same sum.)

d. "Emergency" changes to information systems do not need to be formally approved and documented. (Incorrect. Although emergency changes are usually made without being approved and documented due to the need to respond quickly to a problem, they should be reviewed and documented as soon as practicable.)

CHAPTER 9

LEARNING OBJECTIVES

After studying this chapter, you should be able to:

- Describe the scope and objectives of audit work, and identify the major steps in the audit process.

- Identify the objectives of an information system audit, and describe the four-step approach necessary for meeting these objectives.

- Design a plan for the study and evaluation of internal control in an AIS.

- Describe computer audit software, and explain how it is used in the audit of an AIS.

- Describe the nature and scope of an operational audit.

Auditing Computer-Based Information Systems

INTEGRATIVE CASE SEATTLE PAPER PRODUCTS

Shortly after learning how to use a computer audit software package, Jason Scott was assigned to a project at Seattle Paper Products (SPP). The company is modifying its sales department payroll system to change the way it calculates sales commissions. Under the old system, commissions were a fixed percentage of dollar sales. The new system is considerably more complex, with commission rates varying according to the product sold and the total dollar volume of sales.

Jason's assignment is to use the audit software to write a parallel simulation test program to calculate sales commissions and compare them with those generated by the new system. Jason obtained the necessary payroll system documentation and the details on the new sales commission policy. After a few days his program was ready to run.

Jason obtained the file containing sales transaction data from the last payroll period and used it to run his program. To his surprise, his calculations were $5,000 less than those produced by SPP's new program; in fact, individual differences existed for about half of the company's salespeople. Jason double-checked his program code but could not locate any errors. He selected a salesperson for whom there was a discrepancy and recalculated the commission by hand. The result agreed with his program. He reviewed the new commission policy with the sales manager, line by line, and concluded that he understood the new policy completely. Jason is now convinced that his program is correct and that the error

lies with the new program. Based on this conclusion, he ponders the following questions:

1 How could a programming error of this significance be overlooked by experienced programmers who thoroughly reviewed and tested the new system?
2 Is this an inadvertent error, or could it be a fraud?
3 What can be done to find the error in the program?

Introduction

This chapter focuses on the concepts and techniques used in auditing an AIS. Auditors are employed for a wide range of tasks and responsibilities. Many organizations in the United States employ internal auditors to evaluate company operations. The General Accounting Office and state governments employ auditors to evaluate management performance and compliance with legislative intent in government departments. The Department of Defense employs auditors to review the financial records of companies with defense contracts. Publicly held companies hire external auditors to provide an independent review of their financial statements.

This chapter is written primarily from the perspective of the internal auditor. Internal auditors are directly responsible for helping management improve organizational effectiveness and efficiency, including assisting in the design and implementation of an AIS that contributes to the organization's goals. In contrast, external auditors are primarily responsible to corporate shareholders and investors and are only indirectly concerned with the effectiveness of a corporate AIS. Despite this distinction, many of the internal audit concepts and techniques discussed in this chapter apply to external audits.

The first section of this chapter provides an overview of auditing, the scope and objectives of internal audit work, and the steps in the auditing process. The second section describes a methodology and set of techniques for evaluating internal controls in an AIS and conducting an information system audit. The third section discusses the computer software and other techniques for evaluating the reliability and integrity of information in an AIS. Finally, operational audits of an AIS are reviewed.

The Nature of Auditing

The American Accounting Association has formulated the following general definition of **auditing**: "Auditing is a systematic process of objectively obtaining and evaluating evidence regarding assertions about economic actions and events to ascertain the degree of correspondence between those assertions and established criteria and communicating the results to interested users."[1]

Auditing requires a step-by-step approach characterized by careful planning and judicious selection and execution of appropriate techniques. Auditing involves the collection, review, and documentation of audit evidence. In developing recommendations, the auditor uses established criteria, such as the principles of management and control described in previous chapters, as a basis for evaluation.

Auditors used to audit around the computer and ignore the computer and its programs. They examined the system's printed records and output, thinking that if output was correctly obtained from system input, then processing must be reliable. The current approach, auditing through the computer, uses the computer to check the

[1]Committee on Basic Auditing Concepts, *A Statement of Basic Auditing Concepts* (Sarasota, FL: American Accounting Association, 1973), 2.

adequacy of system controls, data, and output. In fact, SAS No. 94 requires external auditors to evaluate how audit strategy is affected by an organization's use of information technology (IT). It also states that auditors may need specialized skills to (1) determine how the audit will be affected by IT, (2) assess and evaluate IT controls, and (3) design and perform both tests of IT controls and substantive tests.

Internal Auditing Standards

According to the Institute of Internal Auditors (IIA), the purpose of an internal audit is to evaluate the adequacy and effectiveness of a company's internal control system and determine the extent to which assigned responsibilities are actually carried out. The IIA's five audit scope standards outline the internal auditor's responsibilities:

1 Review the reliability and integrity of operating and financial information and how it is identified, measured, classified, and reported.
2 Determine if the systems designed to comply with operating and reporting policies, plans, procedures, laws, and regulations are actually being followed.
3 Review how assets are safeguarded, and verify the existence of assets as appropriate.
4 Examine company resources to determine how effectively and efficiently they are used.
5 Review company operations and programs to determine if they are being carried out as planned and if they are meeting their objectives.

Today's organizations use a computerized AIS to process, store, and control company information. To achieve the preceding five objectives, an internal auditor must be qualified to examine all elements of the computerized AIS and to use the computer as a tool to accomplish these auditing objectives. In other words, computer expertise is essential to conducting an internal audit.

Types of Internal Auditing Work

Three different types of audits are commonly performed:

1 The **financial audit** examines the reliability and integrity of accounting records (both financial and operating information) and correlates with the first of the five scope standards.
2 The **information systems**, or **internal control**, **audit** reviews the controls of an AIS to assess its compliance with internal control policies and procedures and its effectiveness in safeguarding assets. Its scope roughly corresponds to the IIA's second and third standards.
3 The **operational**, or **management**, **audit** is concerned with the economical and efficient use of resources and the accomplishment of established goals and objectives. Its scope corresponds to the fourth and fifth standards.

An Overview of the Auditing Process

All audits follow a similar sequence of activities and may be divided into four stages: planning, collecting evidence, evaluating evidence, and communicating audit results. Figure 9-1 presents an overview of the auditing process, specifying many of the procedures typically performed within each of these stages. This section discusses the four auditing stages and activities in greater detail.

Audit Planning

The purpose of audit planning is to determine why, how, when, and by whom the audit will be performed. The first step in audit planning is to establish the scope and objectives of the audit. For example, a publicly held corporation is audited to determine if its financial

Figure 9-1
Overview of the Auditing
Process

```
┌─────────────────────────────────────────┐
│            Audit Planning                │
│       Establish scope and objectives     │
│           Organize audit team            │
│   Develop knowledge of business operations│
│         Review prior audit results       │
│           Identify risk factors          │
│           Prepare audit program          │
└─────────────────────────────────────────┘
                     │
                     ▼
┌─────────────────────────────────────────┐
│        Collection of Audit Evidence      │
│     Observation of operating activities  │
│          Review of documentation         │
│         Discussions with employees       │
│              Questionnaires              │
│        Physical examination of assets    │
│       Confirmation through third parties │
│        Reperformance of procedures       │
│         Vouching of source documents     │
│             Analytical review            │
│               Audit sampling             │
└─────────────────────────────────────────┘
                     │
                     ▼
┌─────────────────────────────────────────┐
│        Evaluation of Audit Evidence      │
│      Assess quality of internal controls │
│       Assess reliability of information  │
│         Assess operating performance     │
│     Consider need for additional evidence│
│           Consider risk factors          │
│        Consider materiality factors      │
│           Document audit findings        │
└─────────────────────────────────────────┘
                     │
                     ▼
┌─────────────────────────────────────────┐
│      Communication of Audit Results      │
│         Formulate audit conclusions      │
│    Develop recommendations for management│
│            Prepare audit report          │
│      Present audit results to management │
└─────────────────────────────────────────┘
```

statements are presented fairly. In contrast, an internal audit may examine an entire division, a specific department, or a computer application. It may focus on internal controls, financial information, operating performance, or some combination of the three.

An audit team with the necessary experience and expertise is formed. Team members become familiar with the auditee by conferring with supervisory and operating personnel, reviewing system documentation, and reviewing the findings of prior audits.

An audit should be planned so that the greatest amount of audit work focuses on the areas with the highest risk factors. There are three types of risk when conducting an audit:

1 **Inherent risk** is the susceptibility to material risk in the absence of controls. For example, a system that employs online processing, networks, database software, telecommunications, and other forms of advanced technology has more inherent risk than a batch processing system.

2 **Control risk** is the risk that a material misstatement will get through the internal control structure and into the financial statements. A company with weak internal controls has a higher control risk than one with strong controls. Control risk can be determined by reviewing the control environment, testing internal controls, and considering control weaknesses identified in prior audits and evaluating how they have been rectified.

3 **Detection risk** is the risk that auditors and their audit procedures will not detect a material error or misstatement.

To conclude the planning stage, a preliminary audit program is prepared to show the nature, extent, and timing of the procedures necessary for achieving audit objectives and minimizing audit risks. A time budget is prepared, and staff members are assigned to perform specific audit steps.

Collection of Audit Evidence

Most audit effort is spent collecting evidence. The following are among the most commonly used methods of collecting audit evidence:

- *Observation* of the activities being audited (e.g., watching how employees enter the computer site or how data control personnel handle data processing work as it is received).
- *Review of documentation* to understand how a particular AIS or internal control system is supposed to function.
- *Discussions* with employees about their jobs and how they carry out certain procedures.
- *Questionnaires* that gather data about the system.
- *Physical examination* of the quantity and/or condition of tangible assets such as equipment, inventory, or cash.
- *Confirmation* of the accuracy of certain information, such as customer account balances, through communication with independent third parties.
- *Reperformance* of selected calculations to verify quantitative information on records and reports (e.g., the auditor could recalculate the annual depreciation expense).
- *Vouching* for the validity of a transaction by examining all supporting documents, such as the purchase order, receiving report, and vendor invoice supporting an accounts payable transaction.
- *Analytical review* of relationships and trends among information to detect items that should be further investigated. (For example, an auditor for a chain of dress shops discovered that at one shop the ratio of accounts receivable to sales was far too high. An investigation revealed that the manager had diverted funds from collections to her personal use.)

Because many audit tests and procedures cannot feasibly be performed on the entire set of activities, records, assets, or documents under review, they are often performed on a sample basis. A typical audit will usually be a mix of audit procedures. For example, an audit designed to evaluate internal controls would make greater use of observation, review of documentation, discussions with employees, and reperformance of control procedures. An audit of financial information would focus on physical examination, confirmation, vouching, analytical review, and reperformance of account balance calculations.

Evaluation of Audit Evidence

The auditor evaluates the evidence gathered in light of the specific audit objective and decides if it supports a favorable or unfavorable conclusion. If inconclusive, the auditor plans and executes additional procedures until sufficient evidence is obtained to reach a definitive conclusion.

Materiality and reasonable assurance are important when deciding how much audit work is necessary and when evaluating evidence. Because errors are bound to exist in any system, auditors focus on detecting and reporting those that have a significant impact on management's interpretation of the audit findings. Determining **materiality**, what is and is not important in a given set of circumstances, is primarily a matter of judgment. Materiality is generally more important to external audits, when the overall emphasis is on the fairness of financial statement presentation, than to internal audits, when the focus is on determining adherence to management's policies.

The auditor seeks **reasonable assurance** that no material error exists in the information or process audited. Because it is prohibitively expensive to seek complete assurance, the auditor must be willing to accept some risk that the audit conclusion is incorrect. It is important to realize that when inherent or control risk is high, the auditor must obtain greater assurance to offset the greater uncertainty and risks.

At all stages of the audit, findings and conclusions are carefully documented in audit working papers. Documentation is especially important at the evaluation stage, when final conclusions must be reached and supported.

Communication of Audit Results

The auditor prepares a written (and sometimes oral) report summarizing the audit findings and recommendations, with references to supporting evidence in the working papers. This report is presented to management, the audit committee, the board of directors, and other appropriate parties. After the audit results are communicated, auditors often perform a follow-up study to ascertain if recommendations have been implemented.

The Risk-Based Audit Approach

The following four-step approach to internal control evaluation, referred to as the risk-based audit approach, provides a logical framework for carrying out an audit:

1 Determine the threats (fraud and errors) facing the AIS.
2 Identify the control procedures implemented to minimize each threat by preventing or detecting the fraud and errors.
3 Evaluate the control procedures. Reviewing system documentation and interviewing appropriate personnel to determine if the necessary procedures are in place is called a **systems review**. Then **tests of controls** are conducted to determine if these procedures are satisfactorily followed. These tests include activities such as observing system operations; inspecting documents, records, and reports; checking samples of system inputs and outputs; and tracing transactions through the system.
4 Evaluate weaknesses (fraud and errors not covered by control procedures) to determine their effect on the nature, timing, or extent of auditing procedures and client suggestions. This step focuses on the control risks and if the control system as a whole adequately addresses them. If a control deficiency is identified, the auditor asks about **compensating controls**, or procedures that compensate for the deficiency. Control weaknesses in one area may be acceptable if they are compensated for by control strengths in other areas.

The risk-based approach to auditing provides auditors with a clear understanding of the fraud and errors that can occur and the related risks and exposures. This understanding provides a sound basis for developing recommendations to management on how the AIS control system should be improved.

Information Systems Audits

The purpose of an information systems audit is to review and evaluate the internal controls that protect the system. When performing an information systems audit, auditors should ascertain that the following objectives are met:

1 Security provisions protect computer equipment, programs, communications, and data from unauthorized access, modification, or destruction.
2 Program development and acquisition are performed in accordance with management's general and specific authorization.
3 Program modifications have management's authorization and approval.
4 Processing of transactions, files, reports, and other computer records is accurate and complete.

5 Source data that are inaccurate or improperly authorized are identified and handled according to prescribed managerial policies.

6 Computer data files are accurate, complete, and confidential.

Figure 9-2 depicts the relationship among these six objectives and information systems components. Each of these objectives is discussed in detail in the following sections. Each description includes an audit plan to accomplish each objective, as well as the techniques and procedures to carry out the plan.

Objective 1: Overall Security

Table 9-1 contains a framework for auditing computer security. It shows the following:

1 Types of security errors and fraud faced by companies. These include accidental or intentional damage to system assets; unauthorized access, disclosure, or modification of data and programs; theft; and interruption of crucial business activities.

2 Control procedures to minimize security errors and fraud. These include developing an information security/protection plan, restricting physical and logical access, encrypting data, protecting against viruses, implementing firewalls, instituting data transmission controls, and preventing and recovering from system failures or disasters.

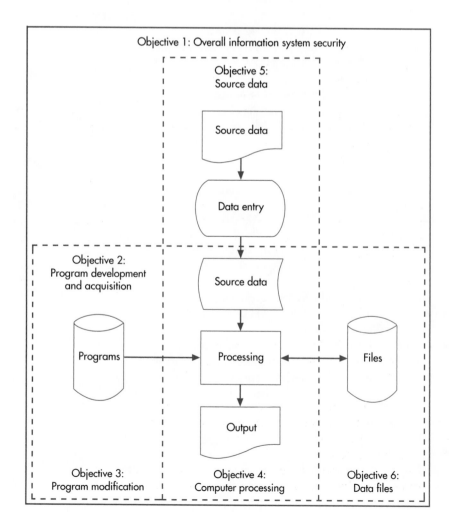

Figure 9-2
Information Systems Components and Related Audit Objectives

Table 9-1
Framework for Audit of Overall Computer Security

TYPES OF ERRORS AND FRAUD
- Theft of or accidental or intentional damage to hardware and files
- Loss or theft of or unauthorized access to programs, data files, and other system resources
- Loss or theft of or unauthorized disclosure of confidential data
- Unauthorized modification or use of programs and data files
- Interruption of crucial business activities

CONTROL PROCEDURES
- Information security/protection plan
- Restrictions on physical access to computer equipment
- Logical access controls based on password protection and other authentication procedures
- Data storage and transmission controls such as encryption
- Virus protection procedures
- File backup and recovery procedures
- Fault-tolerant systems design
- Disaster recovery plan
- Preventive maintenance
- Firewalls
- Information systems insurance

AUDIT PROCEDURES: SYSTEM REVIEW
- Inspect computer sites
- Review the information security/protection plan
- Interview information system personnel about security procedures
- Review physical access policies and procedures
- Review logical access policies and procedures
- Review file backup and recovery policies and procedures
- Review data storage and transmission policies and procedures
- Review procedures employed to minimize system downtime
- Review vendor maintenance contracts
- Examine system access logs
- Examine disaster recovery plan
- Examine information system casualty insurance policies

AUDIT PROCEDURES: TESTS OF CONTROLS
- Observe computer site access procedures
- Observe the preparation and off-site storage of backup files
- Review records of password assignment and modification
- Investigate how unauthorized access attempts were dealt with
- Verify the extent and effectiveness of data encryption use
- Verify the effective use of data transmission controls
- Verify the effective use of firewalls
- Verify the effective use of virus protection procedures
- Verify the use of preventive maintenance and uninterruptible power supply
- Verify amounts and limitations on insurance coverage
- Examine the results of test simulations of the disaster recovery plan

COMPENSATING CONTROLS
- Sound personnel policies
- Effective user controls
- Segregation of incompatible duties

3 **Systems review audit procedures.** These include inspecting computer sites; interviewing personnel; reviewing policies and procedures; and examining access logs, insurance policies, and the disaster recovery plan.

4 **Tests of controls audit procedures.** Auditors test security controls by observing procedures, verifying that controls are in place and work as intended, investigating errors or problems to ensure they were handled correctly, and examining any tests previously performed. For example, one way to test logical access controls is to try to break into a system. During a U.S. government agency security audit, auditors used agency terminals to gain unauthorized access to its computer system, disable its security-checking procedures, and control the system from the terminal. The security breakdown was possible because of poor administrative controls and inadequate security software.

5 **Compensating controls.** If security controls are seriously deficient, the organization faces substantial risks. Sound personnel policies and effective segregation of incompatible duties can partially compensate for poor computer security. Good user controls will also help, if user personnel can recognize unusual system output. Because it is unlikely these controls can compensate indefinitely for poor computer security, auditors should strongly recommend that security weaknesses be corrected.

Objective 2: Program Development and Acquisition

Two things can go wrong in program development: (1) inadvertent errors due to misunderstanding of system specifications or careless programming and (2) unauthorized instructions deliberately inserted into the programs. These problems can be controlled by requiring management and user authorization and approval, thorough testing, and proper documentation.

The auditor's role in systems development should be limited to an independent review of systems development activities. To maintain the objectivity necessary for performing an independent evaluation function, auditors should not be involved in developing the system. During the systems review, auditors should gain an understanding of development procedures by discussing them with management, system users, and information system personnel. They should also review the policies, procedures, standards, and documentation listed in Table 9-2.

To test systems development controls, auditors should interview managers and system users, examine development approvals, and review the minutes of development team meetings. The auditor should review thoroughly all documentation relating to the testing process and ascertain that all program changes were tested. The auditor should examine the test specifications, review the test data, and evaluate the test results. If unexpected test results were obtained, the auditor should ascertain how the problem was resolved. Strong processing controls (see objective 4) sometimes can compensate for inadequate development controls. If auditors rely on compensatory processing controls, they should obtain persuasive evidence of compliance, using techniques such as independent processing of test data. If this type of evidence cannot be obtained, they may have to conclude that a material weakness in internal control exists and that the risk of significant errors or fraud in application programs is unacceptably high.

Table 9-2 provides a framework for reviewing and evaluating the program development process.

Objective 3: Program Modification

Table 9-3 presents a framework for auditing application program and system software changes. The same errors and fraud that can occur during program development can happen during program modification. For example, one programmer assigned to modify his company's payroll system inserted a command to erase all company files if a termination notice was ever entered into his own payroll record. When the programmer was fired, his termination notice caused the system to crash and erase key files.

Table 9-2
Framework for Audit of
Program Development

TYPES OF ERRORS AND FRAUD
- Inadvertent programming errors
- Unauthorized program code

CONTROL PROCEDURES
- Review software license agreements
- Management authorization for program development and approval of programming specifications
- Management authorization of software acquisition
- User approval of programming specifications
- Thorough testing of new programs
- User acceptance testing
- Complete systems documentation, including approvals

AUDIT PROCEDURES: SYSTEM REVIEW
- Independent and concurrent review of the systems development process
- Review systems development/acquisition policies and procedures
- Review systems authorization and approval procedures
- Review programming evaluation standards
- Review program documentation standards
- Review program testing and test approval procedures
- Review procedures for ensuring all acquired software has a proper copyright license agreement
- Discuss systems development procedures with management, system users, and information system personnel
- Review final application system documentation

AUDIT PROCEDURES: TESTS OF CONTROLS
- Interview users about their involvement in systems acquisition/development and implementation
- Review minutes of development team meetings for evidence of involvement
- Verify management and user sign-off at milestone points in the development process
- Review test specifications, test data, and results of systems tests
- Review software license agreements

COMPENSATING CONTROLS
- Strong processing controls
- Independent processing of test data by auditor

When a program change is submitted for approval, a list of all required updates should be compiled and approved by management and program users. All program changes should be thoroughly tested and documented. During the change process, the developmental version of the program must be kept separate from the production version. After the modified program has received final approval, the change is implemented by replacing the production version with the developmental version.

During systems review, auditors should gain an understanding of the change process by discussing it with management and user personnel. The policies, procedures, and standards for approving, modifying, testing, and documenting the changes should be examined. A complete set of final documentation materials for recent program changes, including test procedures and results, should be reviewed. Finally, the auditor should review the procedures used to restrict logical access to the developmental version of the program.

An important part of an auditor's tests of controls is to verify that program changes were identified, listed, approved, tested, and documented. This step requires that the auditor observe how changes are implemented to verify that separate development and production programs are maintained and that changes are implemented by

Table 9-3
Framework for Audit of
Program Modifications

TYPES OF ERRORS AND FRAUD
- Inadvertent programming errors
- Unauthorized program code

CONTROL PROCEDURES
- List program components that are to be modified
- Management authorization and approval of program modifications
- User approval of program change specifications
- Thorough testing of program changes, including user acceptance test
- Complete program change documentation, including approvals
- Separate development, test, and production versions of program
- Changes implemented by personnel independent of users and programmers
- Logical access controls

AUDIT PROCEDURES: SYSTEM REVIEW
- Review program modification policies, standards, and procedures
- Review documentation standards for program modification
- Review program modification testing and test approval procedures
- Discuss program modification policies and procedures with management, system users, and information systems personnel
- Review final documentation of program modifications
- Review test specifications, test data, and results of systems tests
- Review logical access control policies and procedures

AUDIT PROCEDURES: TESTS OF CONTROLS
- Verify user and information system management approval for program changes
- Verify that program components to be modified are identified and listed
- Verify that program change test procedures comply with standards
- Verify that program change documentation complies with standards
- Verify that logical access controls are in effect for program changes
- Observe program change implementation and verify that
 (1) separate development, test, and production versions are maintained and
 (2) changes are not implemented by either user or programming personnel
- To test for unauthorized or erroneous program changes, use a source code comparison program, reprocessing, and parallel simulation

COMPENSATING CONTROLS
- Independent audit tests for unauthorized or erroneous program changes
- Strong processing controls

someone independent of the user and programming functions. The auditor should review the development program's access control table to verify that only those users assigned to carry out the modification had access to the system.

To test for unauthorized program changes, auditors can use a source code comparison program. After auditors thoroughly test a newly developed program (objective 2), they keep a copy of its source code. At any subsequent time, the auditor may use the comparison program to compare the current version of the program with the original source code. If no changes have been authorized, these two versions should be identical. Therefore, any unauthorized differences should result in an investigation. If the difference represents an authorized change, the auditor can refer to the program change specifications to ensure that the changes were authorized and correctly incorporated.

Two additional techniques detect unauthorized program changes. The **reprocessing** technique also uses a verified copy of the source code. On a surprise basis, the auditor uses the program to reprocess data and compare that output with the company's output. Discrepancies in the two sets of output are investigated to ascertain their cause.

Parallel simulation is similar to reprocessing except that the auditor writes a program instead of saving a verified copy of the source code. The auditor's results are compared with the company's results, and any differences are investigated. Parallel simulation can be used to test a program during the implementation process. For example, Jason used this technique to test a portion of SPP's new sales department payroll system.

Auditors should observe the testing and implementation, review related authorizations and documents, and, if necessary, perform independent tests for each major program change. If this step is skipped and program change controls are subsequently determined to be inadequate, it may not be possible to rely on program outputs. In addition, auditors should always test programs on a surprise basis as a precaution against unauthorized program changes being inserted after the examination is completed and then removed just prior to the next scheduled audit.

If internal controls over program changes are deficient, a compensating control is source code comparison, reprocessing, or parallel simulation performed by the auditor. In addition, the presence of sound processing controls, independently tested by the auditor, can partially compensate for such deficiencies. However, if the deficiencies are caused by inadequate restrictions on program file access, the auditor should strongly recommend actions to strengthen the organization's logical access controls.

Objective 4: Computer Processing

Table 9-4 provides a framework for auditing computer processing controls. The focus of the fourth objective is the processing of transactions, files, and related computer records to update files and databases and to generate reports.

During computer processing, the system may fail to detect erroneous input, improperly correct input errors, process erroneous input, or improperly distribute or disclose output. Table 9-4 shows the control procedures to detect and prevent these errors and the systems review and tests of control procedures the auditor employs. The purpose of these audit procedures is to gain an understanding of the controls, evaluate their adequacy, and observe operations for evidence that the controls are in use.

Auditors must periodically reevaluate processing controls to ensure their continued reliability. If processing controls are unsatisfactory, user and source data controls may be strong enough to compensate. If not, a material weakness exists and steps should be taken to eliminate the control deficiencies.

Several specialized techniques allow the auditor to use the computer to test processing controls. They include processing test data, using concurrent audit techniques, and analyzing program logic. Each of the techniques has its own advantages and disadvantages, which means that they are more appropriate in some situations and less appropriate in others. No one technique is good for all circumstances. Auditors should not disclose which technique they use, as that may lessen the effectiveness of the audit test. Each of these procedures is now explained.

Processing Test Data

One way to test a program is to process a hypothetical series of valid and invalid transactions. The program should process all of the valid transactions correctly and identify and reject all of the invalid ones. All logic paths should be checked for proper functioning by one or more of the test transactions. Examples of invalid data include records with missing data, fields containing unreasonably large amounts, invalid account numbers or processing codes, nonnumeric data in numeric fields, and records out of sequence.

The following resources are helpful when preparing test data:

- A listing of actual transactions
- The test transactions the programmer used to test the program
- A **test data generator program**, which automatically prepares test data based on program specifications

Table 9-4
Framework for Audit of
Computer Processing Controls

TYPES OF ERRORS AND FRAUD

- Failure to detect incorrect, incomplete, or unauthorized input data
- Failure to properly correct errors flagged by data editing procedures
- Introduction of errors into files or databases during updating
- Improper distribution or disclosure of computer output
- Intentional or unintentional report inaccuracies

CONTROL PROCEDURES

- Computer data editing routines
- Proper use of internal and external file labels
- Reconciliation of batch totals
- Effective error correction procedures
- Understandable operating documentation and run manuals
- Competent supervision of computer operations
- Effective handling of data input and output by data control personnel
- File change listings and summaries prepared for user department review
- Maintenance of proper environmental conditions in computer facility

AUDIT PROCEDURES: SYSTEM REVIEW

- Review administrative documentation for processing control standards
- Review systems documentation for data editing and other processing controls
- Review operating documentation for completeness and clarity
- Review copies of error listings, batch total reports, and file change lists
- Observe computer operations and data control functions
- Discuss processing and output controls with operators and information system supervisory personnel

AUDIT PROCEDURES: TESTS OF CONTROLS

- Evaluate adequacy of processing control standards and procedures
- Evaluate adequacy and completeness of data editing controls
- Verify adherence to processing control procedures by observing computer operations and the data control function
- Verify that selected application system output is properly distributed
- Reconcile a sample of batch totals, and follow up on discrepancies
- Trace disposition of a sample of errors flagged by data edit routines to ensure proper handling
- Verify processing accuracy for a sample of sensitive transactions
- Verify processing accuracy for selected computer-generated transactions
- Search for erroneous or unauthorized code via analysis of program logic
- Check accuracy and completeness of processing controls using test data
- Monitor online processing systems using concurrent audit techniques
- Recreate selected reports to test for accuracy and completeness

COMPENSATING CONTROLS

- Strong user controls
- Effective source data controls

In a batch processing system, the company's program and a copy of relevant files are used to process the test data. The results are compared with the predetermined correct output; discrepancies indicate processing errors or control deficiencies that should be thoroughly investigated.

In an online system, auditors enter test data using a data entry device, such as a personal computer or a terminal, and observe and log the system's response. If the system accepts erroneous or invalid test transactions, the auditor reverses the effects of the transactions, investigates the problem, and corrects the deficiency.

Although processing test transactions is usually effective, it does have the following disadvantages:

1 The auditor must spend considerable time developing an understanding of the system and preparing an adequate set of test transactions.
2 Care must be taken to ensure that test data do not affect the company's files and databases. The auditor can reverse the effects of the test transactions or process the transactions in a separate run using a copy of the file or database. However, a separate run removes some of the authenticity obtained from processing test data with regular transactions. Also, since the reversal procedures may reveal the existence and nature of the auditor's test to key personnel, it can be less effective than a concealed test.

Concurrent Audit Techniques

Millions of dollars of transactions can be processed in an online system without leaving a satisfactory audit trail. In such cases, evidence gathered after data processing is insufficient for audit purposes. In addition, because many online systems process transactions continuously, it is difficult or impossible to stop the system to perform audit tests. Thus, the auditor uses **concurrent audit techniques** to continually monitor the system and collect audit evidence while live data are processed during regular operating hours. Concurrent audit techniques use **embedded audit modules**, which are segments of program code that perform audit functions. They also report test results to the auditor and store the evidence collected for the auditor's review. Concurrent audit techniques are time-consuming and difficult to use but are less so if incorporated when programs are developed.

Auditors commonly use five concurrent audit techniques. An **integrated test facility (ITF)** technique places a small set of fictitious records in the master files. The records may represent a fictitious division, department, or branch office or a customer or supplier. Processing test transactions to update these dummy records will not affect the actual records. Because fictitious and actual records are processed together, company employees usually remain unaware that this testing is taking place. The system must distinguish ITF records from actual records, collect information on the effects of the test transactions, and report the results. The auditor compares processing with expected results to verify that the system and its controls are operating correctly.

In a batch processing system, the ITF technique eliminates the need to reverse test transactions and is easily concealed from operating employees. ITF is well suited to testing online processing systems, because test transactions can be submitted on a frequent basis, processed with actual transactions, and traced throughout every processing stage. All this can be accomplished without disrupting regular processing operations; however, care must be taken not to combine dummy and actual records during the reporting process.

The **snapshot technique** examines the way transactions are processed. Selected transactions are marked with a special code that triggers the snapshot process. Audit modules in the program record these transactions and their master file records before and after processing. Snapshot data are recorded in a special file and reviewed by the auditor to verify that all processing steps have been properly executed.

System control audit review file (SCARF) uses embedded audit modules to continuously monitor transaction activity and collect data on transactions with special audit significance. The data are recorded in a SCARF file or **audit log**. Transactions recorded in a SCARF file include those exceeding a specified dollar limit, involving inactive accounts, deviating from company policy, or containing write-downs of asset values. Periodically, the auditor receives a printout of the SCARF file, examines the information to identify any questionable transactions, and performs any necessary follow-up investigation.

Audit hooks are audit routines that flag suspicious transactions. For example, internal auditors at State Farm Life Insurance determined that their policyholder system was vulnerable to fraud every time a policyholder changed his or her name or address and then

subsequently withdrew funds from the policy. State Farm devised a system of audit hooks to tag records with a name or address change. The internal audit department is now notified when a tagged record is associated with a withdrawal and can appropriately investigate the transaction for fraud. When audit hooks are used, auditors can be informed of questionable transactions as they occur. This approach, known as **real-time notification**, displays a message on the auditor's terminal. Additional information about State Farm's use of audit hooks, including how a major fraud was detected, is contained in Focus 9-1.

Continuous and intermittent simulation (CIS) embeds an audit module in a database management system (DBMS). The CIS module examines all transactions that update the database using criteria similar to those of SCARF. If a transaction has special audit significance, the module independently processes the data (in a manner similar to parallel simulation), records the results, and compares them with those obtained by the DBMS. If any discrepancies exist, the details are written on an audit log for subsequent investigation. If serious discrepancies are discovered, the CIS may prevent the DBMS from executing the update process.

Analysis of Program Logic

If an auditor suspects that a particular application program contains unauthorized code or serious errors, then a detailed analysis of the program logic may be necessary. This process is time-consuming and requires programming language proficiency, so it should be used only as a last resort. To perform the analysis, auditors refer to systems and program flowcharts, data flow diagrams, program documentation, and a listing of the program source codes. The following software packages serve as aids in this analysis:

- **Automated flowcharting programs**, which interpret program source code and generate a corresponding program flowchart.
- **Automated decision table programs**, which generate a decision table representing the program logic.

9-1 FOCUS — Using Audit Hooks at State Farm Life Insurance Company

The State Farm Life Insurance Company computer system has a host computer in Bloomington, Illinois, and smaller computers in regional offices. In the regional offices, more than 1,500 terminals and personal computers are used to update over 4 million individual policyholder records in the host computer. The system processes more than 30 million transactions per year and keeps track of policyholder funds valued at more than $7 billion.

This online, real-time system updates files and databases as transactions occur. Paper audit trails have virtually vanished, and documents supporting changes to policyholder records have been virtually eliminated or are only held a short time before disposition.

Since anyone with access and a working knowledge of the system could potentially commit fraud, the internal audit staff was given the challenge of identifying all the ways fraud was possible. To accomplish this task, the internal auditors brainstormed ways to defraud the system and interviewed various system users who provided extremely valuable insights.

Auditors implemented 33 embedded audit hooks to monitor 42 different types of transactions. One audit hook monitors unusual transactions in transfer accounts, which are clearing accounts for temporarily holding funds that are to be credited to multiple accounts.

The audit hooks have been very successful. One employee fraudulently obtained cash by processing a loan on her brother's life insurance policy. She then forged her brother's endorsement and cashed the check. To cover up the fraud, she had to repay the loan before the annual status report was sent to her brother. To do so, she used a series of fictitious transactions involving a transfer account. The fraud was uncovered almost immediately when the transfer account audit hook recognized the first of these fictitious transactions and notified the auditor. Within a month of the notification, the case had been investigated and the employee terminated.

Source: Linda Marie Leinicke, W. Max Rexroad, and John D. Ward, "Computer Fraud Auditing: It Works," *Internal Auditor* (August 1990).

- **Scanning routines**, which search a program for occurrences of a specified variable name or other character combinations.
- **Mapping programs**, which identify unexecuted program code. This software could have uncovered the program code that an unscrupulous programmer inserted to erase all computer files when he was terminated.
- **Program tracing**, which sequentially prints all application program steps executed during a program run. This list is intermingled with regular output so auditors can observe the precise sequence of events that unfold during program execution. Program tracing helps auditors detect unauthorized program instructions, incorrect logic paths, and unexecuted program code.

Objective 5: Source Data

Auditors use an **input controls matrix**, such as the one depicted in Figure 9-3, to document the review of source data controls. The matrix shows the control procedures applied to each field of an input record.

Auditors should make sure that the data control function is independent of other functions, maintains a data control log, handles errors, and ensures the overall efficiency of operations. It is usually not economically feasible for small businesses and PC installations to have an independent data control function. To compensate, user department controls must be stronger over data preparation, batch control totals, edit programs, restrictions on physical and logical access to the system, and error-handling procedures. These procedures should be the focus of the auditor's systems review and tests of controls when there is no independent data control function.

Figure 9-3
Input Controls Matrix

Record Name: Employee Weekly Time Report

Field Names:

Input Controls	Employee number	Last name	Department number	Transaction code	Week ending (date)	Regular hours	Overtime hours	Comments
Financial totals					✓	✓		
Hash totals	✓							
Record counts								Yes
Cross-footing balance								No
Visual inspection								All fields
Check digit verification	✓							
Prenumbered forms								No
Turnaround document								No
Edit program								Yes
Sequence check	✓							
Field check	✓		✓		✓	✓		
Sign check								
Validity check	✓		✓	✓	✓			
Limit check						✓	✓	
Reasonableness test						✓	✓	
Redundant data check	✓	✓	✓					
Completeness check				✓	✓	✓	✓	
Overflow procedure								
Other:								

Although source data controls may not change often, the strictness with which they are applied may. Therefore, auditors should test them on a regular basis. The auditor tests the system by evaluating samples of source data for proper authorization. A sample of batch controls should be reconciled. A sample of data edit errors should be evaluated to check that they were resolved and resubmitted into the system.

If source data controls are inadequate, user department and computer processing controls may compensate. If not, the auditor should strongly recommend steps to correct the source data control deficiencies.

Table 9-5 shows the internal controls that prevent, detect, and correct inaccurate or unauthorized source data. It also shows the system review and tests of control procedures that auditors use for evaluation. In an online system, the source data entry and processing functions are one operation. Therefore, source data controls, such as proper authorization and editing data input, are integrated with processing controls.

Table 9-5
Framework for Audit of Source Data Controls

TYPES OF ERRORS AND FRAUD
- Inaccurate source data
- Unauthorized source data

CONTROL PROCEDURES
- Effective handling of source data input by data control personnel
- User authorization of source data input
- Preparation and reconciliation of batch control totals
- Logging of the receipt, movement, and disposition of source data input
- Check digit verification
- Key verification
- Use of turnaround documents
- Computer data editing routines
- File change listings and summaries prepared for user department review
- Effective procedures for correcting and resubmitting erroneous data

AUDIT PROCEDURES: SYSTEM REVIEW
- Review documentation about responsibilities of data control function
- Review administrative documentation for source data control standards
- Review methods of authorization and examine authorization signatures
- Review accounting systems documentation to identify source data content, processing steps, and source data controls
- Document accounting source data controls using an input control matrix
- Discuss source data control procedures with data control personnel, as well as system users and managers

AUDIT PROCEDURES: TESTS OF CONTROLS
- Observe and evaluate data control department operations and specific data control procedures
- Verify proper maintenance and use of data control log
- Evaluate how items recorded in the error log are dealt with
- Examine samples of accounting source data for proper authorization
- Reconcile a sample of batch totals and follow up on discrepancies
- Trace disposition of a sample of errors flagged by data edit routines

COMPENSATING CONTROLS
- Strong user controls
- Strong processing controls

Objective 6: Data Files

The sixth objective concerns the accuracy, integrity, and security of data stored in machine-readable files. Data storage risks include the unauthorized modification, destruction, or disclosure of data. Many of the controls discussed in Chapter 8 are used to protect the system against these risks. If file controls are seriously deficient, especially with respect to physical or logical access or to backup and recovery procedures, then the auditor should strongly recommend they be rectified.

The auditing-by-objectives approach is a comprehensive, systematic, and effective means of evaluating internal controls in an AIS. It can be implemented using an audit procedures checklist for each objective. The checklist should help the auditor reach a separate conclusion for each objective and suggest compensating controls when an objective is not fully achieved. A separate version of the checklist should be completed for each significant application.

Auditors should review system designs while there is still time to adopt their suggestions for control and audit features. Techniques such as ITF, snapshot, SCARF, audit hooks, and real-time notification should be incorporated into a system during the design process, rather than as an afterthought. Similarly, most application control techniques are easier to design into the system than to add after the system is developed. Table 9-6 summarizes the errors, controls, and audit procedures for this objective.

Computer Software

A number of computer programs, called **computer audit software (CAS)** or **generalized audit software (GAS)**, have been written especially for auditors. Two of the most popular are Audit Control Language (ACL) and IDEA. In essence, CAS is a computer program that, based on the auditor's specifications, generates programs that perform the audit functions. CAS is ideally suited for examination of large data files to identify records needing further audit scrutiny. For example, Focus 9-2 describes how the U.S. government uses CAS to battle the federal budget deficit. Table 9-7 contains a list of CAS functions and one or more audit examples for each function.

9-2 FOCUS Battling Federal Budget Deficits with Audit Software

The U.S. government is finding that computer audit software is a valuable tool in its attempts to reduce massive federal budget deficits. For example, the software is being used to identify fraudulent Medicare claims and pinpoint excessive charges by defense contractors.

A computer audit by the General Accounting Office (GAO) cross-checked figures with the IRS and discovered that thousands of veterans lied about their income to qualify for pension benefits. The audit revealed that 116,000 veterans receiving pensions on the basis of need failed to disclose $338 million in income from savings accounts, stock dividends, or rents. More than 13,600

veterans underreported their income, and one did not report income of over $300,000.

Before the computer check was instituted, the Veterans Administration (VA) relied on the vets for accurate income reports. Once the VA notified beneficiaries that their income would be verified with the IRS and the Social Security Administration, the pension rolls dropped by more than 13,000, at a savings of $9 million a month, the GAO reported.

The VA plans to use the same system for checking income levels of those applying for medical care. If their income is found to be above a certain level, patients will be required to make copayments.

Table 9-6
Framework for Audit of Data
File Controls

TYPES OF ERRORS AND FRAUD
- Destruction of stored data due to errors, hardware or software malfunctions, and intentional acts of sabotage or vandalism
- Unauthorized modification or disclosure of stored data

CONTROL PROCEDURES
- Secure file library and other restrictions on physical access to data files
- Logical access controls using passwords and an access control matrix
- Proper use of file labels and write-protection mechanisms
- Concurrent update controls
- Use of data encryption for highly confidential data
- Use of virus protection software
- Maintenance of backup copies of all data files in an off-site location
- Use of checkpoint and rollback to facilitate system recovery

AUDIT PROCEDURES: SYSTEM REVIEW
- Review documentation for file library operation
- Review logical access policies and procedures
- Review operating documentation to determine prescribed standards for:
 - use of file labels and write-protection mechanisms
 - use of virus protection software
 - use of backup data storage
 - system recovery, including checkpoint and rollback procedures
- Review systems documentation to examine prescribed procedures for:
 - use of concurrent update controls and data encryption
 - control of file conversions
 - reconciling master file totals with independent control totals
- Examine disaster recovery plan
- Discuss data file control procedures with systems managers and operators

AUDIT PROCEDURES: TESTS OF CONTROLS
- Observe and evaluate file library operations
- Review records of password assignment and modification
- Observe and evaluate file-handling procedures by operations personnel
- Observe the preparation and off-site storage of backup files
- Verify the effective use of virus protection procedures
- Verify the use of concurrent update controls and data encryption
- Verify completeness, currency, and testing of disaster recovery plans
- Reconcile master file totals with separately maintained control totals
- Observe the procedures used to control file conversion

COMPENSATING CONTROLS
- Strong user controls
- Effective computer security controls
- Strong processing controls

Figure 9-4 shows how CAS is used. The auditor's first step is to decide on audit objectives, learn about the files and databases to be audited, design the audit reports, and determine how to produce them. This information is recorded on specification sheets and entered into the system via a data entry program. This program creates specification records that the CAS uses to produce one or more auditing programs. The auditing programs process the source files and perform the auditing operations needed to produce the specified audit reports. Frequently, an initial CAS computer run is performed to extract key auditing information and place it in an audit work file.

Table 9-7
General Functions of Computer Audit Software

Function	Explanation	Examples
Reformatting	Read data in different formats and data structures and convert it into a common format and structure	Read inventory records from a purchasing database and convert them to an inventory file usable by the CAS program
File manipulation	Sort records into sequential order; merge files sequenced on the same sort key	Sort inventory records by location; merge customer transaction files with the receivables master file
Calculation	Perform the four basic arithmetic operations: add, subtract, multiply, and divide	Recalculate total of client accounts receivable file; recalculate client inventory valuation; recalculate client depreciation; sum employee payroll by department
Data selection	Review data files to retrieve records meeting specified criteria	Identify customer accounts having a balance exceeding the credit limit; select all purchase transactions in excess of a specified dollar amount
Data analysis	Examine records for errors or missing values; compare fields in related records for inconsistencies	Perform data editing of client files; compare personnel and payroll files to verify consistency
File processing	Provide programming capability for file creation, updating, and downloading to a personal computer	Use parallel simulation to verify that client gross pay calculations are correct; download sample of client inventory records to personal computer for further analysis to support inventory test counts
Statistics	Stratify file records by item valuation; select statistical samples; analyze statistical sampling results	Stratify customer accounts by size of account balance and select a stratified sample of accounts for audit confirmation
Report generation	Format and print reports and documents	Prepare analysis of financial statement ratios and trends; prepare accounts receivable aging schedule; prepare audit confirmations

Additional audit reports and analyses are generated by subsequent computer runs that use the audit work file as input.

The following case illustrates the value of audit software. In a small New England town, a new tax collector was elected, defeating the incumbent. The new tax collector requested an audit of the city's tax collection records. Using CAS, the auditor accessed the tax collection records for the past four years, sorted them by collection date, summed the amount of taxes collected monthly, and prepared a four-year summary report of monthly tax collections. The analysis revealed that tax collections during January and July, the two busiest months, had declined by 58% and 72%, respectively. Auditors used the CAS to compare the tax collection records, one by one, with the city's property records. The ensuing report identified several discrepancies, including one case where the former tax collector used another taxpayer's payment to cover her own delinquent tax bills. The former tax collector was arrested and charged with embezzlement.

The primary purpose of CAS is to assist the auditor in reviewing and retrieving information in computer files. When the auditor receives the CAS reports, most of the audit work still remains to be done. Items on exception reports must be investigated, file totals must be verified against other sources of information such as the general ledger, and audit samples must be examined and evaluated. Although the advantages of using CAS are numerous and compelling, CAS cannot replace the auditor's judgment or free the auditor from other phases of the audit.

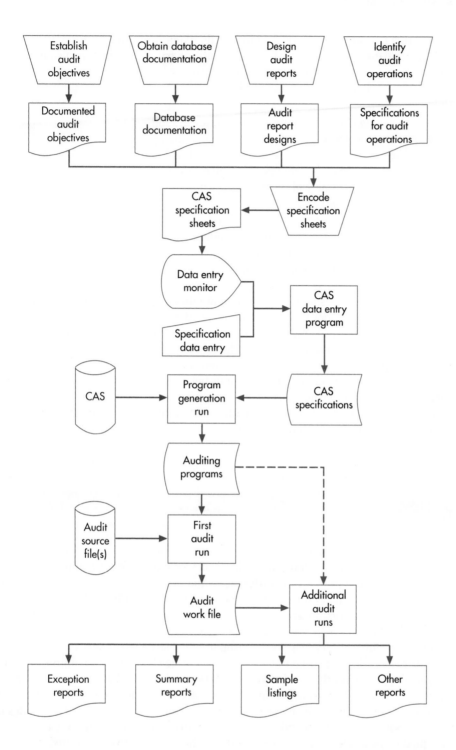

Figure 9-4
Overview of GAS Processing

Operational Audits of an AIS

The techniques and procedures used in operational audits are similar to audits of information systems and financial statements. The basic difference is that the scope of the information systems audit is confined to internal controls, whereas the scope of the financial audit is limited to systems output. In contrast, the scope of the operational audit is much broader, encompassing all aspects of information systems management. In addition, operational audit objectives include evaluating such factors as effectiveness, efficiency, and goal achievement.

The first step in an operational audit is audit planning, during which the scope and objectives of the audit are established, a preliminary review of the system is performed, and a tentative audit program is prepared.

Evidence collection includes the following activities:

- Reviewing operating policies and documentation
- Confirming procedures with management and operating personnel
- Observing operating functions and activities
- Examining financial and operating plans and reports
- Testing the accuracy of operating information
- Testing controls

At the evidence evaluation stage, the auditor measures the actual system against an ideal one, a system that follows the best principles of systems management. One important consideration is that the results of management policies and practices are more significant than the policies and practices themselves. That is, if good results are achieved through policies and practices that are theoretically deficient, then the auditor must carefully consider whether recommended improvements would substantially improve results. In any event, the auditor should thoroughly document the findings and conclusions and communicate the audit results to management.

Being a good operational auditor requires some degree of management experience. Those with strong auditing backgrounds but weak or no management experience often lack the perspective necessary to understand the management process. Thus, the ideal operational auditor is a person with audit training and experience and a few years' experience in a managerial position.

SUMMARY AND CASE CONCLUSION

Jason is trying to determine how his parallel simulation program generated sales commission figures that differed from those of SPP's program. When he studied the figures, he noticed that in all the differences, the sales commission was higher than average. This meant there might have been a systematic error in one of the programs. After verifying that his program was correct, he asked to review a copy of SPP's program.

The program was very lengthy, so Jason used the scanning technique to search the code for a specified set of characters. Under the new policy, the commission rate changes when sales for the period exceed \$40,000. Jason searched the code for occurrences of "40000," which directed him to the place where the commission rate structure resides. To his astonishment, he discovered a commission rate of 0.085 for sales in excess of \$40,000, while the policy called for only 0.075. Some quick calculations confirmed this was the source of the differences between the two programs.

Jason reported the findings to his supervisor, who called the audit manager. They arranged a meeting between the audit manager and the head of the systems development team. The meeting was quite embarrassing for the team head and her staff, but the coding error was acknowledged and corrected.

The audit manager called Jason to congratulate him and informed him that if the programming error had gone undetected, SPP would have paid over \$100,000 per year in excess sales commissions. Jason was grateful to receive the manager's praise, but he also took the opportunity to point out deficiencies in the programming practices employed by the development team. First, the commission rate table had been embedded in the program code; good programming practice would require that it be stored in a separate table to be used by the program when needed. Second, he suggested that the incident called into question the quality of SPP's program development and testing practices. Jason

asked if a more extensive operational audit of those practices might be appropriate. The audit manager agreed that this might be worth examining, and he promised to raise the issue at his next meeting with Northwest's director of internal auditing.

KEY TERMS

auditing 352
financial audit 353
information systems
audit 353
internal control audit 353
operational audit 353
management audit 353
inherent risk 354
control risk 354
detection risk 354
materiality 355
reasonable assurance 356
systems review 356
tests of control 356
compensating
controls 356

reprocessing 361
parallel simulation 362
test data generator
program 362
concurrent audit
techniques 364
embedded audit
modules 364
integrated test facility
(ITF) 364
snapshot technique 364
system control audit
review file
(SCARF) 364
audit log 364
audit hooks 364

real-time notification 365
continuous and
intermittent simulation
(CIS) 365
automated flowcharting
programs 365
automated decision table
programs 365
scanning routines 366
mapping programs 366
program tracing 366
input controls matrix 366
computer audit software
(CAS) 368
generalized audit software
(GAS) 368

AIS IN ACTION

CHAPTER QUIZ

1 Which of the following is a characteristic of auditing?
 a. Auditing is a systematic, step-by-step process.
 b. Auditing involves the collection and review of evidence.
 c. Auditing involves the use of established criteria to evaluate evidence.
 d. All of the above are characteristics of auditing.

2 Which of the following is *not* a reason an internal auditor should participate in internal control reviews during the design of new systems?
 a. It is more economical to design controls during the design stage than to do so later.
 b. It eliminates the need for testing controls during regular audits.
 c. It minimizes the need for expensive post-system-implementation modifications.
 d. It permits the design of audit trails while they are economical.

3 Which type of audit involves a review of general and application controls, with a focus on determining if there is compliance with policies and adequate safeguarding of assets?
 a. information systems audit
 b. financial audit
 c. operational audit
 d. compliance audit

4 At what step in the audit process do the concepts of reasonable assurance and materiality enter into the auditor's decision process?
 a. planning
 b. evidence collection
 c. evidence evaluation
 d. They are important in all three steps.

5 What is the four-step approach to internal control evaluation that provides a logical framework for carrying out an audit called?
 a. inherent risk analysis c. tests of controls
 b. systems review d. risk-based approach to auditing

6 Which of the following procedures is *not* used to detect unauthorized program changes?
 a. source code comparison c. reprocessing
 b. parallel simulation d. reprogramming code

7 Which of the following is a concurrent audit technique that monitors all transactions and collects data on those that meet certain characteristics specified by the auditor?
 a. integrated test facility c. SCARF
 b. snapshot techniques d. audit hooks

8 Which of the following is a computer technique that assists an auditor in understanding program logic by identifying all occurrences of specific variables?
 a. mapping program c. automated flowcharting
 b. program tracing d. scanning routine

9 Which of the following is a computer program written especially for audit use?
 a. GAS c. ITF
 b. CAAT d. CIS

10 The focus of an operational audit is on which of the following?
 a. reliability and integrity of financial information
 b. all aspects of information systems management
 c. internal controls
 d. safeguarding assets

DISCUSSION QUESTIONS

9.1 Auditing an AIS effectively requires that an auditor have some knowledge of computers and their accounting applications. However, it may not be feasible for every auditor to be a computer expert. Discuss the extent to which auditors should possess computer expertise to be effective auditors.

9.2 Should internal auditors be members of systems development teams that design and implement an AIS? Why or why not?

9.3 Berwick Industries is a fast-growing corporation that manufactures industrial containers. The company has a sophisticated AIS that uses advanced technology. Berwick's executives have decided to pursue listing the company's securities on a national stock exchange, but they have been advised that their listing application would be stronger if they were to create an internal audit department.

At present, no Berwick employees have auditing experience. To staff its new internal audit function, Berwick could (a) train some of its computer specialists in auditing, (b) hire experienced auditors and train them to understand Berwick's information system,

(c) use a combination of the first two approaches, or (d) try a different approach. Which approach would you support, and why?

9.4 The assistant finance director for the city of Tustin, California, was fired after city officials discovered that she had used her access to city computers to cancel her daughter's $300 water bill. An investigation revealed that she had embezzled a large sum of money from Tustin in this manner over a long period. She was able to conceal the embezzlement for so long because the amount embezzled always fell within a 2% error factor used by the city's internal auditors. Should Tustin's internal auditors have discovered this fraud earlier? Discuss.

9.5 Lou Goble, an internal auditor for a large manufacturing enterprise, received an anonymous note from an assembly-line operator who has worked at the company's West Coast factory for the past 15 years. The note indicated that on the payroll there are some fictitious employees and some employees who have left the company. He offers no proof or names. What computer-assisted audit technique could Lou use to help him substantiate or refute the employee's claim?

(CIA Examination, adapted)

PROBLEMS

9.1 You are the director of internal auditing at a university. Recently, you met with Issa Arnita, the manager of administrative data processing, and expressed the desire to establish a more effective interface between the two departments. Issa wants your help with a new computerized accounts payable system currently in development. He recommends that your department assume line responsibility for auditing suppliers' invoices prior to payment. He also wants internal auditing to make suggestions during system development, assist in its installation, and approve the completed system after making a final review.

Required

Would you accept or reject each of the following? Why?
 a. The recommendation that your department be responsible for the preaudit of suppliers' invoices.
 b. The request that you make suggestions during development of the system.
 c. The request that you assist in the installation of the system and approve the system after making a final review.

(CIA Examination, adapted)

9.2 As an internal auditor for the Quick Manufacturing Company, you are participating in the audit of the company's AIS. You have been reviewing the internal controls of the computer system that processes most of its accounting applications. You have studied the company's extensive documentation of its systems and have interviewed the MIS manager, operations supervisor, and other employees to complete your standardized computer internal control questionnaire.

You report to your supervisor that the company has designed a successful set of comprehensive internal controls into its computer systems. He thanks you for your efforts and asks for a summary report of your findings for inclusion in a final overall report on accounting internal controls.

Required

Have you forgotten an important audit step? Explain. List five examples of specific audit procedures that you might recommend before reaching a final conclusion.

9.3 As an internal auditor, you have been assigned to evaluate the controls and operation of a computer payroll system. To test the computer systems and programs, you are to submit independently created test transactions with regular data in a normal production run.

Required

> **a.** List four advantages of this technique.
>
> **b.** List two disadvantages of this technique.

(CIA Examination, adapted)

9.4 You are involved in the internal audit of accounts receivable, which represent a significant portion of the assets of a large retail corporation. Your audit plan requires the use of the computer, but you encounter the following reactions:

> **a.** The computer operations manager says that the company's computer is running at full capacity for the foreseeable future and that the auditor will not be able to use the system for any audit tests.
>
> **b.** The computer scheduling manager suggests that your computer program be cataloged into the computer program library (on disk storage) so that it can be run when computer time becomes available.
>
> **c.** You are refused admission to the computer room.
>
> **d.** The systems manager tells you that it will take too much time to adapt the auditor's computer audit program to the computer's operating system and that company programmers will write the programs needed for the audit.

Required

For each of the four situations described, state the action the auditor should take to proceed with the accounts receivable audit.

(CIA Examination, adapted)

9.5 You are a manager for the regional CPA firm of Dewey, Cheatem, and Howe (DC&H). You are reviewing your staff's working papers of an audit of the state welfare agency. You find that the test data concept was used to test the agency's computer program that maintains accounting records. Specifically, your staff obtained a duplicate copy of the program, the welfare accounting data file from the manager of computer operations, and the test transaction data file used by the welfare agency's programmers when the program was written. These were processed on DC&H's home office computer. A copy of the edit summary report that listed no errors was included in the working papers, with a notation by the audit senior that the test indicates good application controls.

You note that the quality of the audit conclusions obtained from this test is flawed in several respects, and you decide to ask your subordinates to repeat the test.

Required

Identify three existing or potential problems with the way this test was performed. For each problem, suggest one or more procedures that might be performed during the revised test to avoid flaws in the audit conclusions.

9.6 You are auditing the financial statements of Aardvark Wholesalers, Inc. (AW), a wholesaler with operations in 12 western states and total revenues of about $125 million. You are carrying out an information system audit to evaluate internal controls in AW's computer system.

From an AW manual, you have obtained the following job descriptions for key personnel:

> *Director of information systems:* Reports to Chief Information Officer (CIO). Responsible for defining the mission of the information systems division and for planning, staffing, and managing a department that optimally executes this mission.
>
> *Manager of systems development and programming:* Reports to director of information systems. Responsible for managing a staff of systems analysts and

programmers whose mission is to design, program, test, implement, and maintain cost-effective data processing systems. Also responsible for establishing and monitoring documentation standards.

Manager of operations: Reports to director of information systems. Responsible for cost-effective management of computer center operations, for enforcement of processing standards, and for systems programming, including implementation of operating system vendor upgrades.

Data entry supervisor: Reports to manager of operations. Responsible for supervision of data entry operations and monitoring of data preparation standards.

Operations supervisor: Reports to manager of operations. Responsible for supervision of computer operations staff and monitoring of processing standards.

Data control clerk: Reports to manager of operations. Responsible for logging and distributing computer input and output, monitoring source data control procedures, and custody of program and data files.

Required

a. Prepare an organizational chart for AW's information systems division.
b. Name two positive and two negative aspects (from an internal control standpoint) of this organizational structure.
c. What additional information, if any, would you require before making a final judgment on the adequacy of AW's separation of functions in the information systems division?

9.7 Robinson's Plastic Pipe Corporation uses a computerized inventory data processing system. The basic input record to this system has the format shown in Table 9-8. You are performing an audit of source data controls for this system, and you have decided to use an input controls matrix for this purpose.

Required

Prepare an input controls matrix using the same format and listing the same controls as shown in Figure 9-3; however, replace the field names shown in Figure 9-3 with those of the inventory transaction file shown in Table 9-8. Place checks in the cells of the matrix that represent input controls you might expect to find for each field.

9.8 As an internal auditor for the state auditor's office, you have been assigned to review the implementation of a new computer system in the state welfare agency. The agency is installing an online computer system to maintain the state's database of welfare recipients. Under the old system, state residents applying for welfare assistance completed a form giving their name, address, and other personal data, plus details about their income, assets, dependents, and other data needed to establish their eligibility. The data on these forms are checked by welfare examiners to verify their authenticity. The welfare examiners then certify the applicant's eligibility for assistance and determine the form and amount of aid.

Under the new system, welfare applicants will provide their case data to clerks, who will simultaneously enter the data into the system using online terminals. Each applicant record will be assigned a "pending" status until a welfare examiner can verify the authenticity of the crucial data used in determining eligibility for assistance. When this verification process has been completed, the welfare examiner will enter a change in the

Field Name	Field Type
Item number	Numeric
Transaction date	Date
Transaction type	Alphanumeric
Document number	Alphanumeric
Quantity	Numeric
Unit cost	Monetary

Table 9-8
Parts Inventory Transaction File

status code from "pending" to "approved," and then the system will execute a program to calculate the appropriate amount of aid.

Periodically, the circumstances (income, assets, dependents, etc.) of welfare recipients change and the database must be updated accordingly. Welfare examiners will enter these change transactions into the system as soon as their accuracy has been verified. The system will then immediately recalculate the recipient's welfare benefit. At the end of each month, checks are generated and mailed to all eligible welfare recipients.

Welfare assistance in your state amounts to several hundred million dollars annually. You are concerned about the possibilities of fraud and abuse.

Required

 a. Describe how you could employ concurrent audit techniques within this system to reduce the risks of fraud and abuse.

 b. Describe how computer audit software could be used to review the work of welfare examiners in verifying applicant eligibility data. For this purpose, you may assume that the state auditor's office has access to computerized databases maintained by other state and local government agencies.

9.9 You are an internal auditor for the Military Industrial Company. You are presently preparing test transactions for the company's weekly payroll processing program. Each input record to this program contains the following data items:

 Social Security number
 Pay code (1 = hourly; 2 = salaried)
 Wage rate or salary
 Hours worked, in tenths
 Number of exemptions claimed
 Year-to-date gross pay, including cents
 Employee name and address

The program performs the following edit checks on each input

- Field checks to identify any records that have nonnumeric characters in the fields for wage rate/salary, hours, exemptions, and year-to-date gross pay
- A validity check of the pay code
- A limit check to identify any hourly employee records with a wage rate higher than $40
- A limit check to identify any hourly employee records with hours worked greater than 70 hours
- A limit check to identify any salaried employee records with a weekly salary greater than $4,000 or less than $100

Records that do not pass these edit checks are listed on an error report. For those that pass the edit checks, the program performs a series of calculations. First, the employee's gross pay is determined. Gross pay for a salaried employee is equal to the salary amount contained in the wage rate field. Gross pay for an hourly employee is equal to the wage rate times the number of hours up to 40, plus 1.5 times the wage rate times the number of hours in excess of 40 hours.

The program computes federal withholding tax for each employee by multiplying gross pay times a tax rate determined from Table 9-9. The program next computes state withholding tax for each employee by multiplying gross pay times a tax rate determined from Table 9-10.

The program next computes the employee's pension contribution, which is 3% of gross pay for hourly employees and 4% of gross pay for salaried employees. Finally, the program computes the employee's net pay, which is gross pay minus tax withholdings and pension contribution. Once these calculations have been completed for one employee record, the program prints that employee's paycheck and summary earnings statement and then proceeds to the next employee input record to perform edit checks and payroll calculations, continuing this cycle until all input records have been processed.

Table 9-9
Computation of Federal
Withholding Tax

Number of Exemptions	GROSS PAY RANGE			
	$0–$99.99	$100–$249.99	$250–$499.99	Over $500
0–1	0.06	0.12	0.18	0.24
2–3	0.04	0.10	0.16	0.22
4–5	0.02	0.08	0.14	0.20
Over 5	0.00	0.06	0.12	0.18

Table 9-10
Computation of State
Withholding Tax

Number of Exemptions	GROSS PAY RANGE	
	$0–$499.99	Over $500
0–3	0.03	0.05
Over 3	0.01	0.03

Your short-term goal is to prepare a set of test transactions containing one of each possible type of error and another set of test transactions that will test each of the computational alternatives one at a time. Transactions to test for multiple errors in one record, or to test for multiple combinations of logic paths, are to be developed later.

The test transactions you prepare need not include a Social Security number or an employee name and address.

Required

a. Prepare a set of test transactions; each transaction should contain one of the errors tested for by the edit checks. Determine the expected results of processing for each of these test transactions.

b. Prepare a set of test transactions that tests every possible way gross pay may be calculated. Determine the expected gross pay for each of these transactions.

c. Prepare a set of test transactions that tests every possible way federal withholding tax may be computed. Determine the expected value of the federal withholding tax for each of these test transactions.

d. Prepare a set of test transactions that tests every possible way state withholding tax may be computed. Determine the expected value of the state withholding tax for each of these test transactions.

e. Prepare a set of test transactions that tests every possible way the pension contribution may be computed. Determine the expected value of the pension contribution for each of these test transactions.

9.10 The internal audit department of Sachem Manufacturing Company is considering the purchase of computer software that will aid the auditing process. Sachem's financial and manufacturing control systems use a large mainframe computer. Melinda Robinson, the director of internal auditing, believes that Sachem should acquire computer audit software to assist in the financial and procedural audits that her department conducts. Robinson is considering the following types of software packages:

- A generalized audit software package that assists in basic audit work such as the retrieval of live data from large computer files. The department would review this information using conventional audit investigation techniques. More specifically, the department could perform criteria selection, sampling, basic computations for quantitative analysis, record handling, graphical analysis, and the printing of output (i.e., confirmations).

- An ITF package that uses, monitors, and controls dummy test data as they are processed by existing programs. It also checks the programs and the existence and adequacy of program data entry and processing controls.
- A flowcharting package that graphically presents the flow of information through a system and pinpoints control strengths and weaknesses.
- A parallel simulation and modeling package that uses actual data to conduct the same tests using another program, a computer logic program developed by the auditor. The package can also be used to seek answers to difficult audit problems (involving many comparisons) within statistically acceptable confidence limits.

Required

 a. Without regard to any specific computer audit software, identify the general advantages of using computer audit software to assist with audits.

 b. Describe the audit purpose facilitated and the procedural steps to be followed by the internal auditor in using the following:
- Generalized audit software package
- Integrated test facility package
- Flowcharting package
- Parallel simulation and modeling package

(CMA Examination, adapted)

9.11 The Thermo-Bond Manufacturing Company maintains its fixed-asset records on its computer. The fixed-asset master file includes the following data items:

Asset number	Date of retirement*
Description	Depreciation method code
Type code	Depreciation rate
Location code	Useful life (years)
Date of acquisition	Accumulated depreciation at beginning of year
Original cost	Year-to-date depreciation

Required

Refer to Table 9-7, which describes the general functions of computer audit software. Then explain several ways such software could be used by an auditor in performing a financial audit of Thermo-Bond's fixed assets.

9.12 An auditor is conducting an examination of the financial statements of a wholesale cosmetics distributor with an inventory consisting of thousands of individual items. The distributor keeps its inventory in its own distribution center and in two public warehouses. It maintains an inventory computer file on a computer disk, and at the end of each business day it updates the file. Each record of the inventory file contains the following data:

Item number	Cost per item
Description of item	Date of last purchase
Quantity-on-hand	Date of last sale
Location of item	Quantity sold during year

The auditor will use audit software to examine inventory data as of the date of the distributor's physical inventory count. The auditor will perform the following audit procedures:

 1 Observe the distributor's physical count of inventories as of a given date, and test a sample for accuracy.

 2 Compare the auditor's test counts with the inventory records.

 3 Compare physical count data with the inventory records.

 4 Test the mathematical accuracy of the distributor's final inventory valuation.

 5 Test inventory pricing by obtaining item costs from buyers, vendors, or other sources.

*For assets still in service, the retirement date is assigned the value 99/99/99.

6 Examine inventory purchase and sale transactions on or near the year-end date to verify that all such transactions were recorded in the proper accounting period.

7 Ascertain the propriety of inventory items located in public warehouses.

8 Analyze inventory for evidence of possible obsolescence.

9 Analyze inventory for evidence of possible overstocking or slow-moving items.

10 Test the accuracy of individual data items listed in the distributor's inventory master file.

Required

Describe how the use of the audit software package and a copy of the inventory file data might be helpful to the auditor in performing each of these auditing procedures.

(AICPA Examination, adapted)

9.13 Which of the following functions should have the primary responsibility to detect and correct data processing errors? Explain why that function should have primary responsibility and why the others should not.

a. The data processing manager

b. The computer operator

c. The corporate controller

d. The independent public accountant

(CPA Examination, adapted)

CASE 9-1 Preston Manufacturing Company

You are performing a financial audit of the general ledger accounts of the Preston Manufacturing Company. At the beginning of the current fiscal year, the company converted its general ledger accounting from a manual to a computer-based system. The new system uses two computer files.

Each day, as detailed transactions are processed by Preston's other computerized accounting systems, summary journal entries are accumulated; at the end of the day, they are added to the general ledger file. At the end of each week and each month, the general journal file is processed against the general ledger control file to compute a new current balance for each account and to print a trial balance.

The following resources are available as you complete the audit:

- Your firm's generalized computer audit software package, which can perform the general functions listed in Table 9-7
- A complete copy of the general journal file for the entire year
- A copy of the general ledger file as of the fiscal year-end (current balance = year-end balance)
- A printout of Preston's year-end trial balance listing the account number, account name, and balance of each account on the general ledger control file

GENERAL JOURNAL

Field Name	Field Type
Account number	Numeric
Amount	Monetary
Debit/credit code	Alphanumeric
Date (MM/DD/YY)	Date
Reference document type	Alphanumeric
Reference document number	Numeric

GENERAL LEDGER CONTROL

Field Name	Field Type
Account number	Numeric
Account name	Alphanumeric
Beginning balance/year	Monetary
Beg-bal-debit/credit code	Alphanumeric
Current balance	Monetary
Cur-bal-debit/credit code	Alphanumeric

Create an audit program for Preston Manufacturing. For each audit step, list the audit objectives and the procedures you would use to accomplish the audit program step.

AIS IN ACTION SOLUTIONS

QUIZ KEY

1 Which of the following is a characteristic of auditing?
 a. Auditing is a systematic, step-by-step process. (Incorrect. Auditing is a systematic, step-by-step process, but this is not the only correct answer.)
 b. Auditing involves the collection and review of evidence. (Incorrect. Auditing does involve the collection and review of evidence, but this is not the only correct answer.)
 c. Auditing involves the use of established criteria to evaluate evidence. (Incorrect. Auditing does use established criteria to evaluate evidence, but this is not the only correct answer.)
 ✔ d. All of the above are characteristics of auditing. (Correct. Auditing is a systematic, step-by-step process that involves the collection and review of evidence and uses established criteria to evaluate evidence.)

2 Which of the following is *not* a reason an internal auditor should participate in internal control reviews during the design of new systems?
 a. It is more economical to design controls during the design stage than to do so later. (Incorrect. Internal audit should participate in internal control reviews because it is far less expensive to design controls during systems design than to try and implement controls after the system has been designed.)
 ✔ b. It eliminates the need for testing controls during regular audits. (Correct. Even if internal audit participates in internal control reviews, controls will still have to be tested during every regular audit to determine if they are in place and working as intended.)
 c. It minimizes the need for expensive post-system-implementation modifications. (Incorrect. Internal audit should participate in internal control reviews because it reduces the likelihood of post-system-implementation modifications.)
 d. It permits the design of audit trails while they are economical. (Incorrect. Internal audit should participate in internal control reviews because their participation in systems design does facilitate the design of effective audit trails.)

3 Which type of audit involves a review of general and application controls, with a focus on determining if there is compliance with policies and adequate safeguarding of assets?
 ✔ a. information systems audit (Correct. An information systems audit reviews general and application controls, with a focus on determining if there is compliance with policies and adequate safeguarding of assets.)
 b. financial audit (Incorrect. A financial audit examines the reliability of accounting records.)
 c. operational audit (Incorrect. An operational audit is concerned with the efficient use of resources and the accomplishment of entity objectives.)
 d. compliance audit (Incorrect. A compliance audit is concerned with reviewing whether an entity is meeting prescribed policies, rules, and laws.)

4 At what step in the audit process do the concepts of reasonable assurance and materiality enter into the auditor's decision process?
 a. planning (Incorrect. Although materiality and reasonable assurance enter into the auditor's decision process during planning, they are also important in other steps in the audit process.)
 b. evidence collection (Incorrect. Although materiality and reasonable assurance enter into the auditor's decision process during evidence collection, they are also important in other steps in the audit process.)

c. evidence evaluation (Incorrect. Although materiality and reasonable assurance enter into the auditor's decision process during evidence evaluation, they are also important in other steps in the audit process.)

✔ **d.** They are important in all three steps. (Correct. Materiality and reasonable assurance are important when planning an audit and when collecting and evaluating evidence.)

5 What is the four-step approach to internal control evaluation that provides a logical framework for carrying out an audit called?

a. inherent risk analysis (Incorrect. Inherent risk is the susceptibility to material risk in the absence of controls.)

b. systems review (Incorrect. Systems review involves reviewing system documentation and interviewing appropriate personnel to determine if the necessary procedures are in place.)

c. tests of controls (Incorrect. Tests of controls are conducted to determine if control policies and procedures are satisfactorily followed.)

✔ **d.** risk-based approach to auditing (Correct. The risk-based audit approach is a four-step approach to carrying out an audit. The four steps are determining threats, identifying control procedures, evaluating control procedures, and evaluating weaknesses.)

6 Which of the following procedures is *not* used to detect unauthorized program changes?

a. source code comparison (Incorrect. Source code comparison is used to detect unauthorized program changes by thoroughly testing a newly developed program and keeping a copy of its source code.)

b. parallel simulation (Incorrect. To use parallel simulation to detect unauthorized program changes, an auditor writes a version of the program, reprocesses the company's data, compares the results to the company's results, and investigates any differences.)

c. reprocessing (Incorrect. To use reprocessing to detect unauthorized program changes, the auditor verifies the integrity of an application program, saves it, and on a surprise basis uses the program to reprocess data and compare that output with the company's output.)

✔ **d.** reprogramming code (Correct. Reprogramming code is not used to test for unauthorized program changes.)

7 Which of the following is a concurrent audit technique that monitors all transactions and collects data on those that meet certain characteristics specified by the auditor?

a. integrated test facility (Incorrect. An integrated test facility inserts a dummy company or division into a computer system to test transaction data without affecting real data.)

b. snapshot techniques (Incorrect. The snapshot technique records the content of both a transaction record and a related master file record before each processing step.)

✔ **c.** SCARF (Correct. System control audit review file is a concurrent audit technique that embeds audit modules into application software to continuously monitor all transaction activity.)

d. audit hooks (Incorrect. An audit hook is a concurrent audit technique that embeds audit routines into application software to flag certain kinds of transactions that might be indicative of fraud.)

8 Which of the following is a computer technique that assists an auditor in understanding program logic by identifying all occurrences of specific variables?

a. mapping program (Incorrect. Mapping programs are activated during regular processing and provide information as to which portions of the application program were not executed.)

 b. program tracing (Incorrect. Program tracing is a technique used to determine application program logic in order to test program controls.)

 c. automated flowcharting (Incorrect. Automated flowcharting interprets source code and generates a flowchart of that program.)

✔ **d.** scanning routine (Correct. Scanning routine software programs search for particular variable names or specific characters.)

9 Which of the following is a computer program written especially for audit use?

✔ **a.** GAS (Correct. Generalized audit software is a software program written especially for audit uses such as testing data files. Examples are ACL and IDEA.)

 b. CAAT (Incorrect. Computer-assisted audit techniques is the name given to all techniques used to audit computers.)

 c. ITF (Incorrect. An integrated test facility places a small set of fictitious records in master files. Transactions are processed for these records, and the actual and expected results are compared.)

 d. CIS (Incorrect. Continuous and intermittent simulation embeds an audit module in a DBMS that examines all transactions that update the database.)

10 The focus of an operational audit is on which of the following?

 a. reliability and integrity of financial information (Incorrect. A financial audit examines the reliability and integrity of financial information.)

✔ **b.** all aspects of information systems management (Correct. An operational audit is concerned with all aspects of information systems management.)

 c. internal controls (Incorrect. The focus of an operational audit is much broader than just internal controls.)

 d. safeguarding assets (Incorrect. The focus of an operational audit is much broader than just safeguarding assets.)

Accounting Information Systems Applications

T he five chapters in Part III describe in detail how a company's AIS provides critical support for fundamental business processes. Most large and many medium-sized organizations use enterprise resource planning (ERP) systems to collect, process, and store data about their business processes, as well as to provide information reports designed to enable managers and external parties to assess the organization's efficiency and effectiveness. As shown in Figure III-1, a properly configured ERP system uses a centralized database to share information across business processes. An ERP system is designed to enable efficient and effective coordination of activities. This is important because an activity that is part of one business process often triggers a complex series of activities throughout many different parts of the organization. For example, a customer order may necessitate scheduling additional production to meet the increased demand. In turn, this may trigger an order to purchase more raw materials. In addition, it may also be necessary to schedule overtime or hire temporary help. A well-designed ERP system provides management with easy access to up-to-date information about all of these activities

Figure III-1
Integrated ERP System

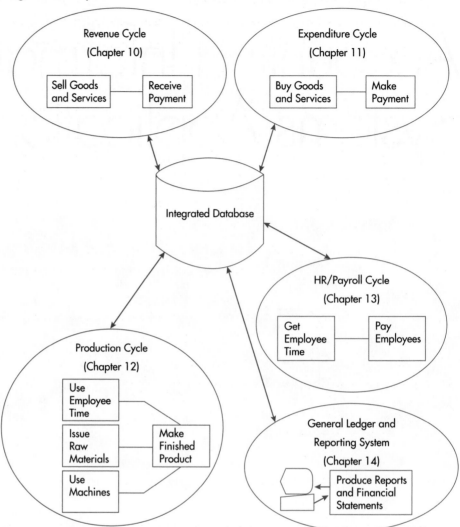

(Adapted from classroom materials created by Julie Smith David at Arizona State University)

in order to efficiently and effectively plan, control, and evaluate the performance of the organization's business processes.

The centralized database underlying ERP systems also provides an integrated, enterprise-wide single view of the organization's financial situation. This improves efficiency and effectiveness in several ways. One common benefit is an overall reduction in inventory levels because of more timely information about actual needs. In addition, organizations often find that ERP systems facilitate the standardization of procedures across business units. This can be especially valuable in organizations that have grown through mergers and acquisitions, because the various business units may each have retained their preacquisition HR and payroll systems. An ERP system provides the opportunity to replace those disparate systems with a single, unified process.

Reaping the potential benefits of ERP systems, however, requires conscious effort and involvement by top management. ERP systems inherently change basic business processes. This means that employees must not only be trained in new procedures but also must be convinced of the value of changing how they do their jobs. This is not always easy, and employee resistance is a major reason why many ERP implementations fail to fully realize their potential benefits. Top-management involvement in, commitment to, and support for the necessary changes greatly increases the chances of success.

ERP systems typically provide the following modules:

- System Tools—tools for establishing master file data, specifying flow of information, and so on
- Financials—accounting tasks (accounts receivable, accounts payable, general ledger, fixed assets, budgeting, and preparation of various managerial reports and financial statements)
- Human Resources and Payroll—payroll, employee benefits, training, and government reporting
- Distribution/Logistics—includes sales order entry, shipping, purchasing, receipt of inventory, inventory management, and warehouse management
- Manufacturing—includes production scheduling, bill of materials, work-in-process, and other production-related activities

Most managers and employees only see and have access to a small portion of the system, however. One reason for this is related to the principle of segregating duties to provide sound internal control: specifically, the importance of separating responsibility for custody of assets, the authorization of activities

that affect those assets, and the recording of information about the performance of those activities and the status of organizational assets. In addition, because ERP systems integrate so many different business activities, they are very complex. Usually, it takes considerable training and experience to enable individual employees and managers to master the portions of the system relevant to their specific job functions.

The importance of sound internal controls in an ERP cannot be overstated. The integrated nature of ERP systems means that unless every data item is validated and checked for accuracy at time of initial entry, errors will automatically propagate throughout the system. Thus, data entry controls and access controls are essential. In addition, because many processes automatically trigger additional actions in other modules, proper configuration is essential. This requires a sound understanding of all major business processes and their interactions.

To make it easier to understand how an ERP system functions and to reflect the limited access provided to most employees, we divide our coverage of ERP systems into five chapters, each focusing on a particular business process. We begin with the revenue cycle (Chapter 10), which consists of all of the activities associated with the basic economic exchange of selling goods or services and collecting cash from customers for those goods or services. Next we describe the expenditure cycle (Chapter 11), which involves the activities associated with acquiring and paying for goods and services. Then we discuss the production cycle (Chapter 12), which consists of the activities associated with using labor and equipment to transform raw materials into finished goods. The fourth chapter focuses on the human resources/payroll cycle (Chapter 13), addressing issues associated with the effective development and management of employees and their skills. In the final chapter we look at the general ledger and reporting system (Chapter 14), examining issues associated with providing management with timely and accurate financial and nonfinancial information about the effectiveness and efficiency with which the organization executes its various business activities.

Each chapter has three main objectives. The first is to provide a thorough understanding of how organizations perform basic business processes and how they can use new developments in information technology to do so more efficiently and effectively. The second is to explain the control procedures that can be used to mitigate the most common threats that occur when performing various business activities. The third objective is to understand the information management needs in order to make key decisions related to a particular business process.

The text's Web site provides detailed examples of the separate, stand-alone systems that companies used in the past. As you read each of the following chapters, you may find it helpful to compare and contrast the way in which modern ERP systems support business processes with those old (legacy) systems to better understand and appreciate the benefits provided by a centralized and integrated database.

CHAPTER 10

LEARNING OBJECTIVES

After studying this chapter, you should be able to:

- Describe the basic business activities and related information processing operations performed in the revenue cycle.

- Discuss the key decisions that need to be made in the revenue cycle, and identify the information needed to make those decisions.

- Document your understanding of the revenue cycle.

- Identify major threats in the revenue cycle, and evaluate the adequacy of various control procedures for dealing with those threats.

The Revenue Cycle: Sales to Cash Collections

INTEGRATIVE CASE ALPHA OMEGA ELECTRONICS

Alpha Omega Electronics (AOE) manufactures a variety of inexpensive consumer electronic products, including calculators, digital clocks, radios, pagers, toys, games, and small kitchen appliances. AOE's primary customers are retail stores, but the company has recently begun selling in bulk to mail-order firms that advertise in catalogs and magazines. Figure 10-1 (see page 392) shows a partial organization chart for AOE.

Linda Spurgeon, president of AOE, called an executive meeting to discuss two pressing issues. First, AOE has been steadily losing market share for the past three years. Second, cash flow problems have necessitated increased short-term borrowing. At the executive meeting, Trevor Whitman, vice president of marketing, explained that one reason for AOE's declining market share is that competitors are apparently providing better customer service. When Linda asked for specifics, however, Trevor admitted that his opinion was based on recent conversations with two major customers. He also admitted that he could not readily identify AOE's 10 most profitable customers. Linda then asked Elizabeth Venko, the controller, about AOE's cash flow problems. The most recent accounts receivable aging schedule indicated a significant increase in the number of past-due customer accounts. Consequently, AOE has had to increase its short-term borrowing because of delays in collecting customer payments. In addition, the Best Value Company, a retail chain that has been one of AOE's major customers, recently went bankrupt. Elizabeth admitted that she is unsure if AOE will be able to collect the large balance due from Best Value.

Figure 10-1
Partial Organization Chart for AOE

Linda was frustrated with the lack of detailed information regarding both issues. She ended the meeting by asking Elizabeth and Trevor to work with Ann Brandt, vice president of information systems, to develop improved reporting systems so that AOE could more closely monitor and take steps to improve both customer service and cash flow management. Specifically, Linda asked Elizabeth, Trevor, and Ann to address the following issues:

1 How could AOE improve customer service? What information does marketing need to perform its tasks better?
2 How could AOE identify its most profitable customers and markets?
3 How can AOE improve its monitoring of credit accounts? How would any changes in credit policy affect both sales and uncollectible accounts?
4 How could AOE improve its cash collection procedures?

As the AOE case indicates, deficiencies in the information system used to support revenue cycle activities can create significant problems for an organization. As you read this chapter, think about how AOE's information system can be redesigned to provide more efficient and effective support of its revenue cycle activities.

Introduction

The **revenue cycle** is a recurring set of business activities and related information processing operations associated with providing goods and services to customers and collecting cash in payment for those sales (see Figure 10-2). The primary external exchange of information is with customers. Information about revenue cycle activities also flows to the other accounting cycles (via the centralized database, which is not

Figure 10-2
The Context Diagram of the Revenue Cycle

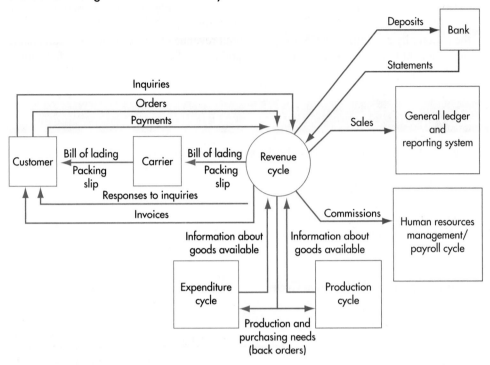

shown in Figure 10-2 to reduce clutter). For example, the expenditure and production cycles use information about sales transactions to initiate the purchase or production of additional inventory to meet demand. The human resources management/payroll cycle uses information about sales to calculate sales commissions and bonuses. The general ledger and reporting function uses information produced by the revenue cycle to prepare financial statements and performance reports.

The revenue cycle's primary objective is to provide the right product in the right place at the right time for the right price. To accomplish that objective, management must make the following key decisions:

- To what extent can and should products be customized to individual customers' needs and desires?
- How much inventory should be carried, and where should that inventory be located?
- How should merchandise be delivered to customers? Should the company perform the shipping function itself or outsource it to a third party that specializes in logistics?
- What are the optimal prices for each product or service?
- Should credit be extended to customers? If so, what credit terms should be offered? How much credit should be extended to individual customers?
- How can customer payments be processed to maximize cash flow?

In addition, management must monitor and evaluate the efficiency and effectiveness of revenue cycle processes. This requires easy access to detailed data about the resources employed in the revenue cycle, the events that affect those resources, and the agents who participate in those events. Moreover, to be useful and relevant for decision making, that data must be accurate, reliable, and timely.

This chapter examines the three basic functions of the AIS in the revenue cycle: capturing and processing data about business activities, storing and organizing that data to support decision making, and providing controls to ensure the reliability of data and the safeguarding of organizational resources. We begin by describing the

basic business activities performed in the revenue cycle. Then we examine the methods used to collect, store, and process data about revenue cycle activities. Next, we examine the major control objectives in the revenue cycle and discuss how to design the AIS to mitigate the threats associated with revenue cycle activities. We conclude the chapter by examining various reports about revenue cycle activities that can enable management to better make key decisions and more effectively monitor performance.

Revenue Cycle Business Activities

Figure 10-3 shows the four basic business activities performed in the revenue cycle:

1 Sales order entry,
2 Shipping,
3 Billing,
4 Cash collections.

Figure 10-3
Level 0 Data Flow Diagram of the Revenue Cycle

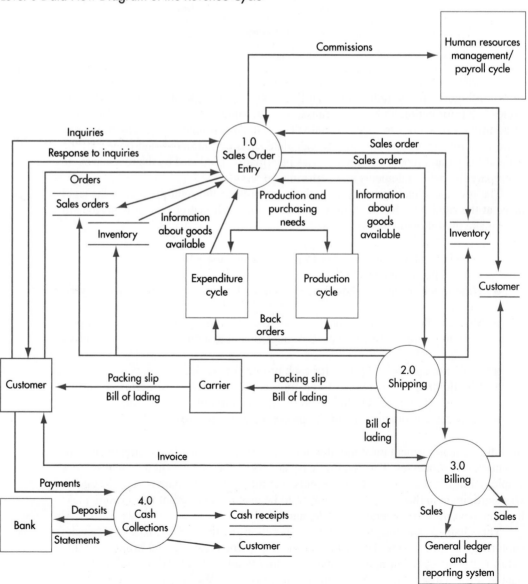

Sales Order Entry

The revenue cycle begins with the receipt of orders from customers. The sales order department, which reports to the vice president of marketing (refer back to Figure 10-1), performs the sales order entry process. Figure 10-4 (see below) shows that the sales order entry process entails three steps: taking the customer's order, checking and approving customer credit, and checking inventory availability. Figure 10-4 also includes an important related event that may be handled either by the sales order department or by a separate customer service department (which typically also reports to the vice president of marketing), that of responding to customer inquiries.

Taking Customer Orders

Customer order data are recorded on a sales order document. The document is usually an electronic form displayed on a computer monitor screen. As shown in Figure 10-5 (see page 396), the **sales order** contains information about item numbers, quantities, prices, and other terms of the sale.

Customer orders can be received in many different ways: in store, by mail, by phone, over a Web site, or by a salesperson in the field. In recent years, organizations have discovered a number of ways to use IT to improve the efficiency and effectiveness of the sales order entry process. One way to improve sales order entry efficiency is by allowing customers to enter sales order data themselves. For example, many retail stores and mail-order firms have customers mark item numbers and quantities on preprinted order forms that an optical character recognition (OCR) device can read.

Web sites provide another way to automate sales order entry. Online order information can be automatically routed to the warehouse to generate picking and shipping instructions. This improves efficiency and cuts costs by eliminating the need for

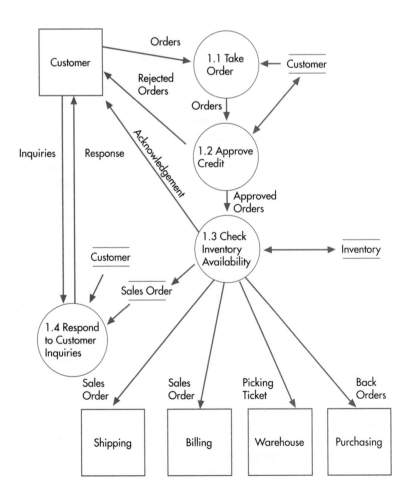

Figure 10-4
Level 1 Data Flow Diagram: Sales Order Entry

Figure 10-5
Sample AOE Sales Order

				SALES ORDER			**12345**
				Alpha Omega Electronics			
				2431 Bradford Lane			
				St. Louis, MO 63105–2311			

Sold To: Hardware City
35 Appliance Way
Phoenix, AZ 85201

Ship To: Hardware City
6742 Mesa Dr.
Mesa, AZ 85284

Date:	Customer Purchase Order No.	Salesperson	Shipping Instructions:
March 17, 2009	7291	JKL	Rush

Quantity Ordered	Quantity Shipped	Quantity Back Ordered	Item Number	Description	Unit Price	Amount
100	100		2741	Calculator	17.95	1795.00
50	50		3315	Pager	49.95	2497.50

Thank You!

human involvement in the sales order entry process. Besides cutting costs, Web sites also provide opportunities to increase sales. One technique, used by many Internet retailers, is to use sales history information to create marketing messages tailored to the individual customer. For example, once an Amazon.com customer selects a book, the Web site suggests related books that other customers have purchased when they bought the one the customer has already selected. Amazon.com and other Internet retailers also use sales history data to create customized electronic coupons that they periodically send to customers to encourage additional purchases. Another technique involves the use of interactive sales order entry systems, called **choiceboards**, to allow customers to customize products to meet their exact needs. For example, visitors to Dell Computer's Web site can try numerous combinations of components and features until they find a configuration that meets their needs at a price they can afford. Many other companies also use choiceboards. In addition to increasing sales, choiceboards improve a company's cash flow in two ways. First, because many sales are built-to-order, less capital needs to be tied up in carrying a large inventory of finished goods. Second, the build-to-order model allows companies to collect all or part of the payment in advance, possibly even before they have to pay for the raw materials, thereby improving cash flow.

Yet another way to improve the sales order entry process involves using electronic data interchange (EDI) to link directly with customers. With EDI, retail stores would send their orders directly to AOE's sales order system in a format that would eliminate the need for data entry. Implementing EDI over the Internet (EDINT) avoids the costs associated with proprietary EDI, making it possible to extend the use of EDI to any business that can afford an Internet connection. Some manufacturers and distributors even use EDI to assume responsibility for managing a retail customer's inventory, an arrangement referred to as **vendor-managed inventory (VMI)**. With VMI, the retailer provides the supplier with access to data from the retailer's point-of-sale (POS) system. The POS

system tracks what inventory is sold. The supplier uses that data to monitor inventory levels and automatically initiates replenishment when inventory falls to specified levels. VMI arrangements benefit both parties. Retailers save money by outsourcing the costs associated with inventory management and by reducing the likelihood of stockouts (lost sales). Manufacturers and distributors benefit because more accurate sales forecasts enable them to optimize production and delivery schedules, and the reduced likelihood of retailer stockouts increases total sales.

Information technology also provides many opportunities to improve sales force efficiency and effectiveness, a process referred to as sales force automation. Storing promotional information online is cheaper than printing and mailing those materials to sales representatives. E-mail and instant messaging (IM) reduce the costs and time it takes to inform sales staff of pricing changes and sales promotions. Both techniques also can be used to provide sales staff with "last-minute" reminders about a particular customer's special needs and interests and to enable management to quickly approve special deals. E-mail and IM also reduce the need for salespeople to return to the home office, thereby increasing the proportion of time they can spend with customers. Technology also enhances the quality of sales presentations. Laptop computers enable salespeople to make multimedia presentations, which improves their ability to demonstrate and explain the capabilities and features of complex technical products. Increasing sales is not the only way that technology improves the efficiency and effectiveness of the sales process. Focus 10-1 describes how sophisticated software can be used to optimize selling prices.

Online sales order entry also increases accuracy by reducing the number of data items that must be manually entered. For example, Figure 10-6 depicts a typical sales order entry screen. In the header section (the shaded area at the top of the screen), the user need only enter the name of the customer in the sold-to and ship-to fields and the system pulls the rest of the information from the customer master file. In the detail section (the lower unshaded portion of the figure), the user need enter only the item number and quantity ordered, and the rest of the information is pulled from the inventory master file.

Credit Approval

Most business-to-business sales are made on credit. Credit sales should be approved before they are processed. For existing customers with well-established payment histories, a formal credit check for each sale is usually unnecessary. Instead, order takers have general authorization to approve orders from customers in good standing, meaning those without past-due balances. This usually is accomplished by establishing a **credit limit** (maximum allowable account balance) for each customer based on the customer's past credit history and ability to pay. In such cases, approving customer credit involves checking the customer master file to verify the account exists, identifying the customer's credit limit, and verifying that the amount of the order plus any

10-1 FOCUS Using Price Optimization to Increase Total Revenues

Manufacturers have traditionally used a cost-plus model for pricing their products: calculating the total costs to make a product and then marking it up by a fixed percentage. That price is then adjusted only for volume discounts. Although simple, this approach can result in lost profits because of under pricing. Price-optimization software uses detailed sales data (e.g., sales volume by customer, by region, competitor prices, etc.) and sophisticated marketing models to identify fast-moving products for which customers might be willing to pay more. The software also identifies which sets of optional features appeal to specific subsets of customers. The travel industry has used price-optimization techniques for many years to wring extra revenue out of every sale. Thanks to integrated ERP systems, which make it easier to pull together the necessary information, manufacturers are now beginning to use the same approach in an attempt to transform what has long been the "art" of pricing into a science.

Figure 10-6
Sample Sales Order Entry
Input Screen

Copyright © 2004 PeopleSoft, Inc.
All Rights Reserved.

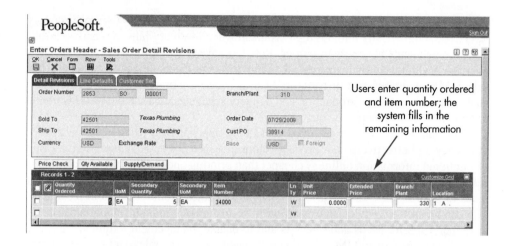

current account balance does not exceed this limit. Figure 10-7 shows the information typically available for this purpose: the customer's credit limit, current balance, and age of any outstanding unpaid invoices. Note that this process can itself be automated, thereby increasing efficiency and reducing the opportunity for errors.

The preceding credit approval process applies to existing customers with good credit. Specific authorization for approving credit is used for new customers, when an order exceeds the customer's credit limit, or when the customer has outstanding past-due balances. These situations require specific authorization by the credit manager.

Checking Inventory Availability

The next step is to determine if there is sufficient inventory available to fill the order, so that customers can be informed of the expected delivery date. Figure 10-8 (see page 399) shows an example of the information typically available to the sales order entry clerk: quantity on hand, quantity already committed to other customers, and quantity

Figure 10-7
Sample Inquiry Screen for
Checking Customer Credit

Copyright © 2004 PeopleSoft, Inc.
All Rights Reserved.

available. If sufficient inventory is available to fill the order, the sales order is completed and the quantity-available field in the inventory file for each item ordered is reduced by the amount ordered. The shipping, inventory control, and billing departments are then notified of the sale, and an acknowledgment may be sent to the customer. If there is not sufficient inventory on hand to fill the order, a **back order** for those items must be created. In manufacturing companies, creating a back order involves notifying the production department to initiate the production of the requested items. In retail companies, the purchasing department would be notified about the need to order the required items.

Once inventory availability has been determined, the system then creates a **picking ticket** that lists the items, and quantities of each item that the customer ordered. The picking ticket authorizes the inventory control function to release merchandise to the shipping department. Although traditionally a paper document, picking tickets today are often electronic forms that may be displayed on portable handheld devices or on monitors built into forklifts. To further improve efficiency, the picking ticket often lists the items by the sequence in which they are stored in the warehouse, rather than in the order listed on the sales order.

The accuracy of inventory records is important because customers may become justifiably upset when unexpected delays occur in filling their orders. Maintaining accurate and current inventory records requires careful data entry during performance of several tasks in the revenue cycle. Shipping and sales clerks must correctly record the items delivered to customers. This task is particularly error-prone in retail establishments. For example, when customers purchase multiple items with the same price, such as different flavors of yogurt or soft drinks, the checkout clerks at supermarkets may scan only one item and then enter the total quantity purchased. Although this will generate the correct total sales amount, it will introduce errors into the inventory records. The recorded quantity-on-hand for the one item that was physically scanned will be too low, and the recorded quantity-on-hand for the other flavors of that item will be too high. Proper handling of sales returns is another task that contributes to inaccurate inventory records, particularly in retail establishments. In clothing stores, for example, when a customer returns the wrong-size item and exchanges it for another, the clerks should enter the exchange into the system. Often, especially during extremely busy sales periods, the clerks simply make the exchange and put the returned item back on the shelf but fail to make the proper entry in the system. Consequently, the system's records for both items are inaccurate.

Responding to Customer Inquiries

Besides processing customer orders, Figure 10-4 shows that the sales order entry process also includes responding to customer inquiries. Sometimes these inquiries precede an order, and often they occur after orders have been placed. In either case, responding to customer inquiries is extremely important. Indeed, the quality of customer service provided is often key to a company's success.

Customer service is so important that many companies use special software packages, called customer relationship management (CRM) systems, to support this vital process. CRM systems help organize detailed information about customers to facilitate more efficient and more personalized service. For example, information about customer preferences and transaction history can be used to suggest other products the customer may want to consider. Detailed data about customer requirements and business practices can also be used to proactively contact customers about the need to reorder.

The goal of customer relationship management is to retain customers. This is important because a general marketing rule of thumb is that it costs at least five times as much to attract and make a sale to a new customer as it does to make a repeat sale to an existing customer. Retention requires more than merely satisfying customers. It requires creating loyalty. Research indicates that if customer satisfaction is rated on a 1-to-5 scale, with 5 representing completely satisfied and 1 representing completely dissatisfied, customers who rated their satisfaction level at 5 were many times more likely to make repeat purchases than were customers who rated their satisfaction level only at 4. Moreover, that same research indicates that the key to generating total satisfaction, and thereby retaining customers, is the quality and nature of the postsale customer contacts. Therefore, CRM systems should not be viewed as a way to keep customers at arm's length and reduce, or totally automate, all interaction with them. Instead, CRM systems should be seen as tools to improve the level of customer service provided. The goal is to turn satisfied customers into loyal customers by *enriching* the relationship.

Transaction processing technology can also be used to improve customer relationships. For example, many commercial POS systems can link not only with the inventory file but also with the customer master file. This not only automatically updates accounts receivable balances but provides an opportunity to print customized coupons and personal messages on each sales receipt. Printing a simple "Thank you, Joe, we appreciate your business" message on a sales receipt can increase customer loyalty. In addition, printing targeted coupons for items related to the current transaction, such as offering a discount on the customer's next purchase of pretzels whenever the current sales transaction includes soda or beer, is likely to generate more sales than mass-mailing the same coupon to everyone living in a given zip code.

Many customer inquiries are routine, however. Consequently, companies can and should use IT to automate the response to common requests, such as questions about account balances and order status, so that sales order and customer service representatives can concentrate their time and effort on handling the more complex, nonroutine inquiries. For example, Web sites provide a cost-effective alternative to traditional toll-free telephone customer support, automating that process with a list of frequently asked questions (FAQs). Discussion boards can also be provided so that customers can share information and useful tips with one another. Web sites also enable customers to use PINs to directly access their account information and to check on the status of orders. These techniques can significantly reduce customer service costs. Wells Fargo, for example, found that customers with online access to their accounts made 40% fewer calls to the customer service department than did customers without such access. It is impossible, however, to anticipate every question customers may ask. Therefore, Web sites designed to provide customer service should probably include an instant messaging or chat feature to enable customers to obtain real-time expert assistance and advice for dealing with special issues the FAQ list does not satisfactorily address.

The effectiveness of a Web site depends largely on its design. Companies should regularly review records of customer interaction on their Web sites to quickly identify potential problems. A hard-to-use Web site may actually hurt sales by frustrating customers and creating ill will. Conversely, a well-designed Web site can provide insights that may lead to increased sales. For example, National Semiconductor analyzes which products receive the most attention from visitors to its Web site. When sales managers noticed the increased interest in new heat sensors, they were able to revise their sales forecasts and ramp up production early enough to satisfy a marked increase in orders for that product. Without the advance warning provided by analyzing Web site traffic, National Semiconductor would not have been prepared for the upsurge in customer demand and probably would have lost some of those new orders to competitors.

Shipping

The second basic activity in the revenue cycle (circle 2.0 in Figure 10-3) is filling customer orders and shipping the desired merchandise. As shown in Figure 10-9 (see below), this process consists of two steps: (1) picking and packing the order and (2) shipping the order. The warehouse and shipping departments perform these activities, respectively. Both functions include custody of inventory and, as shown in Figure 10-1, report ultimately to the vice president of manufacturing.

Pick and Pack the Order

The picking ticket printed by sales order entry triggers the pick and pack process. Warehouse workers use the picking ticket to identify which products, and the quantity of each product, to remove from inventory. Warehouse workers record the quantities of each item actually picked, either on the picking ticket itself if a paper document is used or by entering the data into the system if electronic forms are used. The inventory is then transferred to the shipping department.

AOE, like many companies, has made significant investments in automated warehouse systems consisting of computers, bar-code scanners, conveyer belts, and communications technology. The goals are to reduce the time and cost of moving inventory into and out of the warehouse while also improving the accuracy of perpetual inventory systems. Wireless technology can increase warehouse productivity by eliminating the need for workers to repeatedly return to a centralized dispatch center to receive printed instructions. For example, JC Penney equips its forklifts with radio-frequency data communication (RFDC) terminals to provide drivers with information

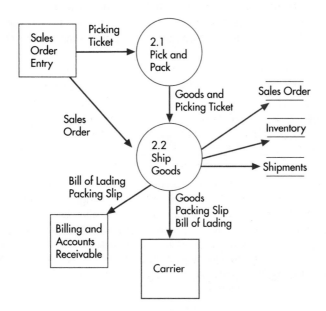

Figure 10-9
Level 1 Data Flow Diagram: Shipping

about which items to pick next and where they are located. At Corporate Express, an office supplies distributor in Broomfield, Colorado, warehouse workers wear headsets and listen to computer-synthesized voice instructions. The company reports that the oral instructions result in fewer mistakes than occur when trying to read a small terminal screen in dim light. Wireless technology also improves the efficiency and accuracy of tracking inventory movement. With bar codes, the item or box must be positioned properly so that the bar code can be read by the scanner. Replacing the bar code with a radio-frequency identification (RFID) tag eliminates this need to align items with scanners; instead, the tags can be read as the inventory moves throughout the warehouse. In addition, each RFID tag can store up to 128 bytes of detailed information to facilitate properly storing and routing the inventory item. For companies that handle large volumes of merchandise, like Federal Express and UPS, RFID's ability to reduce by even a few seconds the time it takes to process each package can field enormous cost savings. Focus 10-2 discusses how RFID can even help companies improve revenues.

Automated warehouse systems not only cut costs and improve efficiency in handling inventory but can also enable more customer-responsive shipments. For example, manufacturers can use bar code and RFID systems in their warehouses to facilitate packing and shipping related items (e.g., matching shirts and ties) together. The cartons can then be either bar-coded or RFID-tagged so that retailers can quickly check in the merchandise and move it to the selling floor. These services not only save retailers time and money but also help improve turnover thereby increasing the manufacturer's sales.

Ship the Order

The shipping department compares the physical count of inventory with the quantities indicated on the picking ticket and with the quantities indicated on the copy of the sales order that was sent directly to shipping from sales order entry. Discrepancies can arise either because the items were not stored in the location indicated on the picking ticket or the perpetual inventory records were inaccurate. In such cases, the shipping department needs to initiate the back ordering of the missing items and enter the correct quantities shipped on the packing slip.

After the shipping clerk counts the goods delivered from the warehouse, the sales order number, item number(s), and quantities are entered using online terminals. This process updates the quantity-on-hand field in the inventory master file. It also produces a packing slip and multiple copies of the bill of lading. The **packing slip** (it may be a copy of the picking ticket) lists the quantity and description of each item included in the shipment. The **bill of lading** is a legal contract that defines responsibility for the goods in transit. It identifies the carrier, source, destination, and any special shipping instructions, and it indicates who (customer or vendor) must pay the carrier (see Figure 10-10 on page 403). A copy of the bill of lading and the packing slip accompany the shipment. If the customer is to pay the shipping charges, this copy of the bill

10-2 FOCUS RFID to Increase Revenues

Manufacturers are finding that they can use RFID to increase sales. Typically, manufacturers of consumer products send retailers displays and promotional items designed to be placed on the floor the day a new advertising campaign begins. However, retailers receive the displays days or sometimes weeks in advance and must store them in their warehouses until the target date. The problem is that often those materials may get "lost" in storage, with the result that a significant percentage of retailers fail to display the items on the promotion launch day. The result of such failures is lost sales and wasted advertising. By embedding RFID tags in the promotional displays, manufacturers make it easier for retailers to locate them when needed. This increases sales for both the retailer and manufacturer.

Figure 10-10
Sample Bill of Lading

STRAIGHT BILL OF LADING — SHORT FORM	Not Negotiable.

Shipper's No.

Carrier **Carrier's No.**

RECEIVED, subject to the classifications and tariffs in effect on the date of the issue of this Bill of Lading.

at_____20_____ from _____

the property described below, in apparent good order, except as noted (contents and condition of contents of packages unknown), marked, consigned, and destined as indicated below, which said carrier (the word carrier being understood throughout this contract as meaning any person or corporation in possession of the property under the contract) agrees to carry to its usual place of delivery at said destination, if on its route, otherwise to deliver to another carrier on the route to said destination. It is mutually agreed, as to each carrier of all or any of said property over all or any portion of said route to destination, and as to each party at any time interested in any or all of said property, that every service to be performed hereunder shall be subject to all terms and conditions of the Uniform Domestic Straight Bill of Lading set forth (1) in Uniform Freight Classification in effect on the date hereof, if this is a rail or a rail-water shipment, or (2) in the applicable motor carrier classification or tariff if this is a motor carrier shipment.

Shipper hereby certifies that he is familiar with all the terms and conditions of the said bill of lading, including those on the back thereof, set forth in the classification or tariff which governs the transportation of this shipment, and the said terms and conditions are hereby agreed to by the shipper and accepted for himself and his assigns.

Consigned to _____

(Mail or street address of consignee — For purposes of notification only.)

Destination _____ State _____ Zip Code _____ County _____

Delivery Address ★ _____

(★ To be filled in only when shipper desires and governing tariffs provide for delivery thereat.)

Route _____

Delivering Carrier Car or Vehicle Initials No.

No. Packages	Kind of Package, Description of Articles, Special Marks, and Exceptions	*Weight (Sub. to Cor.)	Class or Rate	Check Column	Subject to Section 7 of Conditions of applicable bill of lading, if this shipment is to be delivered to the consignee without recourse on the consignor, the consignor shall sign the following statement.
					The carrier shall not make delivery of this shipment without payment of freight and all other lawful charges.
					(Signature of Consignor.)
					If charges are to be prepaid, write or stamp here, "To Be Prepaid."

*If the shipment moves between two ports by a carrier by water, the law requires that the bill of lading shall state whether it is "carrier's or shipper's weight."

NOTE—Where the rate is dependent on value, shippers are required to state specifically in writing the agreed or declared value of the property.

The agreed or declared value of the property is hereby specifically stated by the shipper to be not exceeding

Received $ _____ to apply in prepayment of the charges on the property described hereon.

_____ per

Agent or Cashier

†"The fiber boxes used for this shipment conform to the specifications set forth in the box maker's certificate thereon, and all other requirements of Uniform Freight Classification."

†Shipper's imprint in lieu of stamp; not a part of bill of lading approved by the Interstate Commerce Commission.

Per _____

amount prepaid.)

Charges advanced:
$

_____ Shipper, per _____ Agent, Per _____

Permanent post office address of shipper, _____ _____ _____

of lading may serve as a *freight bill*, to indicate the amount the customer should pay to the carrier. In other cases, the freight bill is a separate document.

The shipping department keeps a second copy of the bill of lading to track and confirm the transfer of goods to the carrier. Another copy of the bill of lading and the packing slip are sent to the billing department to indicate that the goods have been shipped and that an invoice should be prepared and mailed. The carrier also retains a copy of the bill of lading for its records.

One major decision that needs to be made when filling and shipping customer orders concerns the choice of delivery method. Traditionally, many companies have maintained their own truck fleets for deliveries. Large companies such as GM have even assigned entire departments to this function. Increasingly, however, manufacturers are outsourcing this function to commercial carriers such as Ryder System, Inc., Roadway Services, Inc., and Schneider National Company. Outsourcing deliveries reduces costs and allows manufacturers to concentrate on their core business activity (the production of goods). Selecting the proper carrier, however, requires collecting and monitoring information about carrier performance (e.g., percentage of on-time deliveries and damage claims).

Another important decision concerns the location of distribution centers. Increasingly, many customers are asking suppliers and manufacturers to deliver products only when needed. Consequently, suppliers and manufacturers must use logistics software tools to identify the optimal locations to store inventory in order to minimize the total amount of inventory carried and to meet each customer's delivery requirements. Logistics software also helps optimize daily activities, such as how to most efficiently use 17 available trucks to make 300 deliveries to various locations in one metropolitan area.

Globalization adds complexity to outbound logistics. The efficiency and effectiveness of different distribution methods, such as trucking or rail, differ around the world. Taxes and regulations in various countries can also affect distribution choices. Therefore, an organization's AIS must include logistics software that can maximize the efficiency and effectiveness of its shipping function.

RFID systems can provide real-time information on shipping status and thus provide additional value to customers. For example, if the seller learns that a shipment is going to be late, prompt notification can help that customer revise its plans accordingly. The cost of providing such notifications is minimal, especially if done via e-mail or IM, but the effort is likely to significantly improve customer satisfaction and loyalty.

Billing

The third basic activity in the revenue cycle (circle 3.0 in Figure 10-3) involves billing customers. Figure 10-11 shows that this involves two separate, but closely related tasks: invoicing and updating accounts receivable, which are performed by two separate units within the accounting department.

Invoicing

Accurate and timely billing for shipped merchandise is crucial. The billing activity is just an information processing activity that repackages and summarizes information

Figure 10-11
Level 1 Data Flow Diagram: Invoicing and Accounts Receivable

from the sales order entry and shipping activities. It requires information from the shipping department identifying the items and quantities shipped and information about prices and any special sales terms from the sales department.

The basic document created in the billing process is the **sales invoice** (see Figure 10-12), which notifies customers of the amount to be paid and where to send payment. Like many companies, AOE still prints paper invoices that it mails to many of its smaller customers. Larger customers, however, receive invoices via EDI. Information technology provides opportunities to reduce the costs associated with billing. Sending invoices to businesses via EDI is faster and cheaper than mailing paper documents. For example, Sonoco Products Company estimates that EDI saves it 70 to 80 cents per invoice over processing of paper invoices. The Grocery Manufacturers of America and the National Association of Convenience Stores found that switching from paper to electronic invoices cut the time it took a convenience store manager to process each invoice from 5 minutes to 30 seconds. Over the course of a year, this could save over $100,000 in labor costs. Increasingly, companies are also providing their business customers with access to a Web site at which they can view their accounts and make electronic payments. Doing so cuts costs by eliminating many routine customer service calls and often increases customer satisfaction. Businesses that sell to end consumers can reap similar advantages by convincing their customers to sign up for online billing and payment using the Internet. EDI invoices and online bill payment also benefit customers by reducing their time and costs (including postage) associated with processing paperwork.

A well-designed AIS can entirely eliminate the need to create and store invoices, at least with customers that have sophisticated systems of their own. To understand

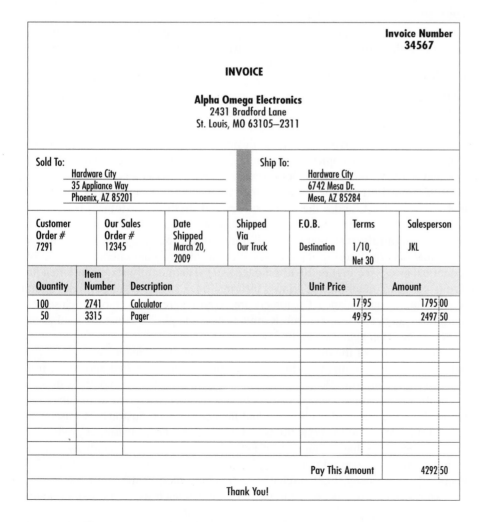

Figure 10-12
Sample AOE Sales Invoice

						Invoice Number 34567

INVOICE

Alpha Omega Electronics
2431 Bradford Lane
St. Louis, MO 63105–2311

Sold To:
Hardware City
35 Appliance Way
Phoenix, AZ 85201

Ship To:
Hardware City
6742 Mesa Dr.
Mesa, AZ 85284

Customer Order #	Our Sales Order #	Date Shipped	Shipped Via	F.O.B.	Terms	Salesperson
7291	12345	March 20, 2009	Our Truck	Destination	1/10, Net 30	JKL

Quantity	Item Number	Description	Unit Price	Amount
100	2741	Calculator	17 95	1795 00
50	3315	Pager	49 95	2497 50
			Pay This Amount	4292 50

Thank You!

this concept, reexamine the information included in a typical sales invoice (see Figure 10-12). The invoice indicates the quantity of each item sold and the price charged for that item; but the price is usually set at the time the order is placed, and the actual quantity sold is known at the time the merchandise is shipped to the customer. Thus, the selling company's AIS already contains all the information needed to calculate the amount of the sale at the time the goods are shipped. Indeed, invoices are often printed in a batch process without any manual data entry. Conversely, the buyer knows the price at the time the order is placed and knows the quantity purchased when the goods are received. Consequently, if both companies have accurate online systems, it may be possible to establish an agreement in which the buyer will automatically remit payments within a specified number of days after receiving the merchandise. The seller sends an electronic notification, usually via e-mail, when the goods are shipped and the customer sends an electronic acknowledgment when the goods are received. Ford is just one of many companies that have established such relationships with their major suppliers. Note that the seller can still monitor and determine accounts receivable by reconciling shipments to customer remittances: Accounts receivable represents all shipments that have yet to be paid. The attraction of such invoiceless billing is that it saves both the seller and buyer considerable amounts of time and money by eliminating the need to perform a traditional business process (invoicing) that does not provide any new information.

An integrated AIS also provides the opportunity to merge the billing process with the sales and marketing function by using data about a customer's past purchase history to send information about related products and services with the monthly statement. Such customized advertising may generate additional sales with little if any incremental costs.

Maintain Accounts Receivable

The accounts receivable function, which reports to the controller, performs two basic tasks: It uses the information on the sales invoice to debit customer accounts and subsequently credits those accounts when payments are received. The two basic ways to maintain accounts receivable are the open-invoice and the balance-forward methods. The two methods differ in terms of when customers remit payments, how those payments are applied to update the accounts receivable master file, and the format of the monthly statement sent to customers.

Under the **open-invoice method**, customers typically pay according to each invoice. Usually, two copies of the invoice are mailed to the customer, who is requested to return one copy with the payment. This copy is a turnaround document called the **remittance advice**. Customer payments are then applied against specific invoices. In contrast, under the **balance-forward method**, customers typically pay according to the amount shown on a monthly statement, rather than by individual invoices. A **monthly statement** lists all transactions, including both sales and payments, that occurred during the past month and informs customers of their current account balances (see Figure 10-13 on page 407). The monthly statement often has a tear-off portion containing preprinted information, including the customer's name, account number, and balance. Customers are asked to return this stub, which serves as a remittance advice, with payment. Remittances are applied against the total account balance, rather than against specific invoices.

One advantage of the open-invoice method is that it is conducive to offering discounts for prompt payment, as invoices are individually tracked and aged. It also results in a more uniform flow of cash collections throughout the month. A disadvantage of the open-invoice method is the added complexity required to maintain information about the status of each individual invoice for each customer. Consequently, the open-invoice method is typically used by business whose customers are primarily other businesses, so that the number of individual transactions is relatively small and the dollar value of those transactions is high. Companies with large numbers of customers who make many small purchases each month, such as utility companies, credit card issuers like Citibank, or national retail chains such as Sears and JC Penney,

MONTHLY STATEMENT Alpha Omega Electronics 2431 Bradford Lane St. Louis, MO 63105–2311						March 2009

Hardware City

35 Appliance Way

Phoenix, AZ 85201

Invoice Number	Date	Current	Past Due 1–30	Past Due 31–60	Past Due 61–90	Past Due Over 90
34567	3/20/2009	4292.50				
34591	3/27/2009	2346.50				
	Totals	6639.00				
		Total Amount Due	6639.00			

Please detach here and return with remittance

Pay To: AOE
PO Box 7341
St. Louis, MO 63112-7341

Bill date	03/31/2009
Account number	73256
Payment due	04/10/2009
Total amount due	6639.00
Amount enclosed	

Figure 10-13
Sample AOE Monthly Statement

typically use the balance-forward method. For them, this method is more efficient and reduces costs by avoiding the need to process cash collections for each individual sale. It is also more convenient for the customer to make one monthly remittance.

To obtain a more uniform flow of cash receipts, many of these companies use a process called cycle billing to prepare and mail monthly statements to their customers. Under **cycle billing**, monthly statements are prepared for subsets of customers at different times. For example, the customer master file might be divided into four parts, and each week monthly statements would be prepared for one-fourth of the customers. Cycle billing produces a more uniform flow of cash collections throughout the month and reduces the time that the computer system is dedicated to printing monthly statements. Cycle billing can significantly affect processing requirements. Consider the case of a utility company serving several million customers in a large metropolitan area. If it prepared monthly statements for all its customers at the same time, and it took 10 seconds to print out each one, its printers would be tied up for several days.

Image processing technology can improve the efficiency and effectiveness of managing customer accounts. The digital images of customer remittances and accounts can be stored electronically and be easily retrieved, manipulated, and integrated with other images and data to produce various types of output. Doing so provides employees fast access to all documents relating to a customer and eliminates the time wasted searching through file cabinets for lost paperwork. If a customer needs a duplicate copy of a monthly statement or an invoice to replace a lost original, it can be retrieved, printed, and faxed while talking to the customer on the phone. Image processing also can facilitate resolving customer complaints, because the same image can be viewed simultaneously by more than one person. Thus, a customer account representative and a credit manager could both review an image of a document in question while discussing the

problem with the customer on the telephone. Finally, image processing reduces the space and cost associated with storing paper documents. The savings in this area can be substantial: One optical disk can store up to 20,000 documents, in a fraction of the space.

Exceptions: Account Adjustments and Write-offs

Adjustments to a customer's account are sometimes necessary. For example, customer accounts may be credited to reflect either the return of items or allowances granted for damaged goods. To credit a customer's account for returned goods, the credit manager must obtain information from the receiving dock that the goods were actually returned and placed back in inventory. Upon notification from the receiving department that the goods have been returned, the credit manager issues a **credit memo** (see Figure 10-14 on below), which authorizes the crediting of the customer's account. If the damage to the goods is minimal, the customer may agree to keep them for a price reduction. In such cases, the credit manager issues a credit memo to reflect the amount that should be credited to the customer's account. A copy of the credit memo is sent to accounts receivable to authorize an adjustment to the customer's account balance; another copy is sent to the customer.

After repeated attempts to collect payment have failed, it may be necessary to write off a customer's account. In such cases, the credit manager issues a credit memo to authorize the write-off. Unlike the cases involving damaged or returned goods, however, a copy of the credit memo used to authorize the write-off of an account is not sent to the customer.

Figure 10-14
Sample AOE Credit Memo

11121

CREDIT MEMORANDUM

Alpha Omega Electronics
2431 Bradford Lane
St. Louis, MO 63105–2311

Credit To:	Hardware City			Date	April 7, 2009
	35 Appliance Way				
	Phoenix, AZ 85201			Salesperson	FRM

| Apply To Invoice Number 34603 | | Date April 1, 2009 | Customer's Order No. 7413 |

Quantity	Item Number	Description	Unit Price	Amount
3	4120	PCS	85.00	255 00

Reason Credit Issued: Units damaged during shipment. Returned on April 6, 2009

| Received By: ALZ | Authorized By: PJS |

| **We Credit Your Account For This Amount** | 255 00 |

Cash Collections

The final step in the revenue cycle is cash collections (circle 4.0 in Figure 10-3). The cashier, who reports to the treasurer (see Figure 10-1), handles customer remittances and deposits them in the bank.

Because cash and customer checks can be stolen so easily, it is important to take appropriate measures to reduce the risk of theft. As discussed more fully in the section on controls, this means that the accounts receivable function, which is responsible for recording customer remittances, should not have physical access to cash or checks. Yet, the accounts receivable function must be able to identify the source of any remittances and the applicable invoices that should be credited. One solution involves mailing the customer two copies of the invoice and requesting that one be returned with the payment. This remittance advice is then routed to accounts receivable and the actual customer payment is sent to the cashier. If the remittance advice also contains a space for the customer to indicate the amount being remitted, an OCR machine can scan in the remittance data, thereby eliminating the potential for mistakes during data entry. An alternative solution is to have mailroom personnel prepare a **remittance list**, which is a document identifying the names and amounts of all customer remittances, and send it to accounts receivable. In place of a remittance list, some companies photocopy all customer remittances and send the copies to accounts receivable while forwarding the actual remittances to the cashier for deposit. Focus 10-3 describes how imaging technology can be used to improve the efficiency of processing customer payments.

The preceding discussion assumes that customer remittances are sent directly to the company. Another way to safeguard customer remittances is to set up a lockbox arrangement with a bank. A **lockbox** is a postal address to which customers send their remittances. The participating bank picks up the checks from the post office box and deposits them to the company's account. The bank then sends the remittance advices, an electronic list of all remittances, and photocopies of all checks to the company. Using a lockbox not only prevents theft of customer remittances by employees but also improves cash flow management. Having customers send payments to a lockbox eliminates the delay associated with processing customer remittances before depositing them. Cash flow also is improved by selecting several banks around the country to maintain lockboxes, with the locations chosen to minimize the time customer checks are in the mail. Similarly, establishing lockbox arrangements with foreign banks reduces the time it takes to collect payments from sales to international customers. Information technology can provide additional efficiencies in the use of lockboxes. Under an **electronic lockbox** arrangement, the bank electronically sends the company information about the customer account number and the amount remitted as soon as it

10-3 FOCUS Using Technology to Speed Cash Collections

Image-scanning software can improve the efficiency of the internal processing of customer payments and reduce the time it takes to access those funds. Scanners can detect the presence of any metal objects such as coins or staples in envelopes containing payments from customers. Envelopes without such items can be opened mechanically and their contents (customer checks) run through a high-speed imaging device that automatically applies remittances to the corresponding customer account. Only envelopes containing staples or coins need to be processed manually.

Remote Deposit Capture software reduces the time it takes to get access to funds remitted by customers. The software creates an encrypted file of customer checks that have been scanned. Then, instead of physically depositing the customer checks with its bank, the company electronically transmits the encrypted file of check images. The bank decrypts the file and notifies the company electronically when the checks have cleared. This process shaves at least one day off the clearing process and also saves the company the time and expense associated with physically depositing the checks.

receives and scans those checks. This method enables the company to begin applying remittances to customer accounts before the photocopies of the checks arrive.

Lockbox arrangements, however, only eliminate the delays associated with internal processing of remittances mailed directly to the company. Electronic funds transfer provides the opportunity to reduce other causes of delay in obtaining access to customer funds. With **electronic funds transfer (EFT)** and electronic bill payment services, customers send their remittances electronically to the company's bank and thus eliminate the delay associated with the time the remittance is in the mail system. Eliminating this check-clearing time also reduces the time lag before the bank makes the deposited funds available to the company. EFT is usually accomplished through the banking system's Automated Clearing House (ACH) network.

EFT only involves the transfer of funds. To properly credit customer accounts, companies also need additional data about each remittance, such as invoice numbers and discounts taken. Although every bank can do EFT through the ACH system, not every bank possesses the EDI capabilities necessary to process the related remittance data. Consequently, many companies have had to separate the EFT and EDI components of processing customer payments, as shown in the top panel of Figure 10-15. This complicates the seller's task of properly crediting customer accounts for payments because information about the total amount of funds received arrives separately from information about the invoices that payment should be applied against. Similarly, the customer's task is complicated by the need to send information about the payment to two different parties.

Financial electronic data interchange (FEDI) solves these problems by integrating the exchange of funds (EFT) with the exchange of the remittance data (EDI). As shown in the lower panel of Figure 10-15, the customer sends both remittance data and funds transfer instructions together. Similarly, the seller receives both pieces of information simultaneously. Thus, FEDI completes the automation of both the billing and cash collections processes. To fully reap the benefits of FEDI, however, requires

Figure 10-15
FEDI versus EFT

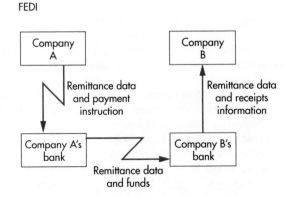

that both the selling company and its customers use banks that are capable of providing EDI services.

When dealing with customers who are not FEDI capable, or with individual consumers, companies can also speed the collection process by accepting credit cards or procurement cards (a special type of credit card discussed in Chapter 11). Accepting such payment methods speeds collection, because the card issuer usually transfers the funds within two days of the sale. These benefits must be weighed against the costs of accepting such cards, which typically range from 2% to 4% of the gross sales price.

This concludes our discussion of basic revenue cycle business activities. The next section describes how the AIS can be designed to efficiently collect and process data about those activities.

Information Processing Procedures

In response to the Y2K crisis, AOE, like many other organizations, replaced its existing AIS with an integrated ERP (enterprise resource planning) system. Figure 10-16 depicts the portion of AOE's new ERP system that supports its revenue cycle activities. The fundamental characteristics of AOE's new revenue cycle system are the sharing of data between activities and the increased integration that results.

Figure 10-16a
Integrated Revenue Cycle System for AOE: Sales Order Entry

Figure 10-16b
Cash Receipts

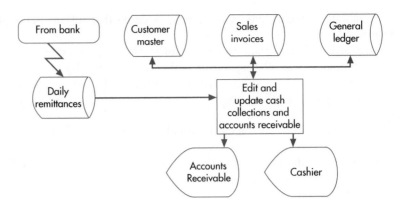

AOE's online sales order processing system handles customer orders, via the Internet, as well as orders via the sales force. Using their laptops, salespeople can enter orders directly in the field, or the sales department can enter customer orders received over the telephone or by mail. Regardless of how the order is initially received, the system quickly verifies customer creditworthiness, checks inventory availability, and notifies the warehouse and shipping departments about the approved sale.

Wireless technology improves efficiency of warehouse and shipping operations. Warehouse and shipping employees enter data about their activities as soon as they are performed, thereby updating information about inventory status in real time. Bar codes and RFID tags facilitate tracking the movement of inventory. Nightly, the invoice program runs in batch mode, generating paper or electronic invoices for customers who require invoices. At any time, different departments can use the inquiry processing system to ascertain the status of orders and plan their future activities. The easy access to up-to-date accurate information also improves customer service.

Cash receipts processing also is largely automated. AOE's customers either send checks to one of six regional banks with which AOE has established electronic lockboxes or remit their payments to those banks via EFT. Each day, the bank sends AOE a file containing remittance data, which are then used to update customer accounts and cash.

In summary, AOE's integrated ERP system improves the efficiency and effectiveness of its revenue cycle activities in the following ways:

1 Real-time order entry detects errors, such as missing data, as the order is being entered, and when it is easiest to correct those errors.
2 Credit approval decisions can be made at the time the customer places the order. If special approval is required, the credit manager is notified by e-mail or IM and can immediately make that decision.
3 Inventory records are more accurate and timely, enabling sales order entry staff to provide customers accurate information about expected delivery dates.
4 The warehouse and shipping departments can better plan activities to minimize the time required to fill customer orders.
5 The system compares data that the shipping department entered with the sales order file, thereby detecting and facilitating correction of any errors prior to shipment.
6 Cash receipts are processed more quickly, improving cash flow.
7 Reports and performance measures are timelier, enhancing management's ability to monitor and improve efficiency and effectiveness.

To fully appreciate these benefits, you may want to compare the process illustrated in Figures 10-16a and 10-16b with those AOE followed in its old (legacy) systems that are described on the Web site for this text. To fully realize these benefits

provided by an integrated ERP system, however, presupposes that adequate controls exist to ensure that the information in the system is available, accurate, secure, and maintainable. The next section discusses applicable control procedures to achieve those objectives.

Control Objectives, Threats, and Procedures

In the revenue cycle, a well-designed AIS should provide adequate controls to ensure that the following objectives are met:

1 All transactions are properly authorized.
2 All recorded transactions are valid (actually occurred).
3 All valid, authorized transactions are recorded.
4 All transactions are recorded accurately.
5 Assets (cash, inventory, and data) are safeguarded from loss or theft.
6 Business activities are performed efficiently and effectively.

The documents and records described in the previous sections play an important role in achieving these objectives. Simple, easy-to-complete documents with clear instructions facilitate the accurate and efficient recording of transaction data. The inclusion of appropriate application controls, such as validity checks and field (format) checks, further increases the accuracy of data entry when using electronic documents. Providing space on paper and electronic documents to record who completed and who reviewed the form provides evidence that the transaction was properly authorized. Prenumbering documents facilitates checking that all transactions have been recorded. Restricting access to blank documents, if paper documents are still used, and to programs that create documents reduces the risk of unauthorized transactions.

Table 10-1 lists the major threats in the revenue cycle and the appropriate control procedures that should be in place to mitigate them. Every company, regardless of its line of business, faces these threats. Therefore, it is important to understand how the AIS can be designed to counter them. This discussion is organized around the four stages of the revenue cycle: sales order entry, shipping, billing and accounts receivable, and cash collections. This section concludes with a discussion of general control issues that apply to all revenue cycle activities.

Sales Order Entry

The primary objectives of the sales order entry process are to accurately and efficiently process customer orders, ensure that the company gets paid for all credit sales and that all sales are legitimate, and to minimize the loss of revenue arising from poor inventory management. Threats 1 through 4 in Table 10-1 relate to these objectives.

Threat 1: Incomplete or Inaccurate Customer Orders

A basic threat during sales order entry is that important data about the order will be either missing or inaccurate. Not only does this create inefficiencies due to the need to call back the customer and reenter the order in the system but it also may negatively affect customer perceptions and, thereby, adversely affect future sales. A variety of data entry edit controls can mitigate this threat. For example, completeness checks can ensure that all required data, such as both shipping and billing addresses, are entered. Automatic lookup of reference data, such as customer addresses, already stored in the customer master file, prevents errors by eliminating data entry. Reasonableness tests should compare the quantity ordered with item numbers and past sales history. Validity checks of customer and item numbers are also needed to ensure accuracy. These data entry edit controls are also needed on Web sites to ensure that customers accurately and completely enter all required data.

Table 10-1
Threats and Controls in the Revenue Cycle

Process/Activity	Threat	Applicable Control Procedures
Sales order entry	1. Incomplete or inaccurate customer orders	Data entry edit checks
	2. Credit sales to customers with poor credit.	Credit approval by credit manager, not by sales function; accurate records of customer account balances
	3. Legitimacy of orders	Signatures on paper documents; digital signatures and digital certificates for e-business
	4. Stockouts, carrying costs, and markdowns	Inventory control systems; sales forecasts; periodic physical inventory counts
Shipping	5. Shipping errors: Wrong merchandise Wrong quantities Wrong address	Reconciliation of sales order with picking ticket and packing slip; bar code scanners; data entry application controls
	6. Theft of inventory	Restrict physical access to inventory; documentation of all internal transfers of inventory; periodic physical counts of inventory and reconciliation of counts with recorded amounts; RFID and barcode technology
Billing and account receivable	7. Failure to bill customers	Separation of shipping and billing functions; prenumbering of all shipping documents and periodic reconciliation with invoices; reconciliation of picking tickets and bills of lading with sales orders
	8. Billing errors	Data entry edit controls; price lists
	9. Posting errors in updating accounts receivable	batch totals; reconciliation of subsidiary accounts receivable ledger with general ledger; monthly statements to customers
Cash collections	10. Theft of cash	Segregation of duties; minimization of cash handling; lockbox arrangements; prompt endorsement and deposit of all receipts; periodic reconciliation of bank statement with records by someone not involved in cash receipts processing
General control issues	11. Loss, alteration, or unauthorized disclosure of data	Backup and disaster recovery procedures; access controls (physical and logical); proper systems configuration; encryption; data transmission controls
	12. Poor performance	Preparation and review of performance reports

Threat 2: Credit Sales to Customers with Poor Credit

A second threat in sales order entry is the possibility of making sales that later turn out to be uncollectible. Requiring proper authorization for each credit sale diminishes this threat. In general, this is accomplished by setting credit limits for each customer and granting sales staff general authorization to approve additional credit sales to existing customers provided that such sales do not increase the customer's total account balance beyond the approved credit limit. Limit checks can be used to flag orders that require specific authorization because they exceed a customer's preapproved credit limit. For cases requiring specific authorization, such as new customers or the extension of additional credit to existing customers, someone other than the sales representative should grant approval, especially if the sales staff is paid on commission. The organization chart for AOE (see Figure 10-1) shows this segregation of duties: The credit manager, who sets credit policies and approves the extension of credit to new customers and the raising of credit limits for existing customers, is independent of the marketing function. To enforce this segregation of duties in integrated online systems, sales order entry clerks should be granted read-only access to information about

individual customer credit limits. To be effective, however, credit approval must occur prior to releasing the goods from inventory. It is also important to maintain accurate and current records of customer account balances and credit limits so that automated controls, such as limit checks, will function correctly.

Threat 3: Legitimacy of Orders

Another threat concerns the legitimacy of orders. Traditionally, legitimacy of customer orders is established by receipt of a signed purchase order from the customer. Digital signatures and digital certificates provide similar control for electronic business transactions.

Threat 4: Stockouts, Carrying Costs, and Markdowns

Yet another threat in the sales order entry process is that sales will be lost due to stockouts. Conversely, excess inventory increases carrying costs and may even require significant markdowns. To address these problems, companies need accurate inventory control and sales forecasting systems. Online AISs, as depicted in Figure 10-16, facilitate the use of the perpetual inventory method, thereby ensuring that records about the quantity of inventory available for sale are accurate. Periodic physical counts of inventory also help to verify the accuracy of recorded amounts. Sales forecasts should be regularly reviewed for accuracy and revised frequently. Therefore, the AIS needs to collect such information and make it available to management on a timely basis.

Shipping

The primary objectives of the shipping function are to fill customer orders efficiently and accurately and to safeguard inventory. Threats 5 and 6 in Table 10-1 relate to these objectives.

Threat 5: Shipping Errors

Shipping the wrong items or quantities of merchandise and shipping to the wrong location are serious errors because they can significantly reduce customer satisfaction and thus future sales. They may also result in the loss of assets if customers do not pay for goods erroneously shipped. Online systems as depicted in Figure 10-16 can reduce the risk of shipping errors if shipping personnel are required to enter the quantities of items being sent before the goods are shipped. This enables detecting, and then correcting, any mistakes before the merchandise leaves the premises by comparing the shipment data with the sales order. The use of bar-code scanners and RFID tags to record the picking and shipping of inventory can virtually eliminate data entry errors. At companies where data entry is still performed manually, the use of application controls, such as field checks and completeness tests, can significantly reduce errors. Only after the system has verified that the shipment is correct should the packing slip and bill of lading be printed.

Threat 6: Theft of Inventory

Another threat in the shipping stage of the revenue cycle involves the theft of inventory. Theft losses can be extremely large and the perpetrators can be either outsiders or employees. For example, Exide, Inc., a battery manufacturer, reported a loss of $3.5 million worth of batteries due to employee theft. Theft while inventory is in transit is also a concern, with losses estimated to be approximately $10 billion each year. In addition to a loss of assets, theft also makes inventory records inaccurate, which can lead to problems in filling customer orders.

Several control procedures can reduce the risk of inventory theft. First, inventory should be kept in a secure location to which physical access is restricted. Second, all inventory transfers within the company should be documented. Inventory should be released to shipping employees based only on approved sales orders. In addition, both warehouse and shipping employees should sign the document accompanying the goods (or make the appropriate acknowledgment of the transfer online) at the time the goods

are transferred from inventory to shipping. This procedure facilitates tracking the cause of any inventory shortages. In addition, such accountability encourages employees to prepare and maintain accurate records. In addition, the use of wireless communications technologies and RFID tags can provide real-time tracking of inventory in transit, which may help reduce theft. Finally, recorded amounts of inventory should be periodically reconciled with physical counts of inventory on hand, and the employees responsible for inventory custody should be held accountable for any shortages.

Billing and Accounts Receivable

The primary objectives of the billing and accounts receivable functions are to ensure that customers are billed for all sales, that invoices are accurate, and that customer accounts are accurately maintained. Threats 7 through 9 in Table 10-1 relate to these objectives.

Threat 7: Failure to Bill Customers

Failure to bill customers for items shipped results in the loss of assets and erroneous data about sales, inventory, and accounts receivable. Segregating the shipping and billing functions can diminish this threat. Otherwise, an employee performing both functions could ship merchandise to friends without billing them. Sales orders, picking tickets, packing slips, and sales invoices should be sequentially numbered and then periodically accounted for. Any sales orders or packing slips that cannot be matched to a sales invoice represent shipments that have not been billed, and corrective action should then be taken. When invoices are not generated (e.g., invoiceless systems), it is especially important to ensure that every shipment is entered into the computer system.

Threat 8: Billing Errors

Billing errors, such as pricing mistakes and billing customers for items not shipped or on back order, represent another potential threat. Overbilling can result in customer dissatisfaction, and underbilling results in the loss of assets. Pricing mistakes can be avoided by having the computer retrieve the appropriate data from the inventory master file. Mistakes involving quantities shipped can be caught by reconciling the quantities listed on the packing slips with those on the sales order.

Threat 9: Errors in Maintaining Customer Accounts

Errors in maintaining customer accounts can lead to the loss of future sales and also may indicate possible theft of cash. The following edit checks should be used to ensure accuracy in updating customer accounts:

1. Validity checks on the customer and invoice numbers,
2. Closed-loop verification to ensure that the proper account is being credited,
3. A field check to ensure that only numeric values are entered for payment amounts.

Customer payments are often processed in batches, so batch totals can provide an additional means to detect posting errors. Specifically, the sum of all customer payments processed should equal the change to the total of all customer account balances. It is also important to reconcile the subsidiary accounts receivable records with the general. After processing customer payments, the sum of all individual customer account balances (the accounts receivable subsidiary file) should equal the total balance of the accounts receivable control account in the general ledger. If the two are not equal, an error in posting has probably occurred and all transactions just entered should be reexamined. To ensure that all remittances were processed, the number of customer accounts updated should be compared with the number of checks received. These reconciliations should be performed by someone other than the individual involved in processing the original transactions

because (1) it is easier to catch someone else's mistakes than your own and (2) it provides a means to identify irregularities. The Sarbanes–Oxley Act requires that unless companies can prove that their internal controls would have found the error, they must report most errors found by the external auditor as material misstatements or material weaknesses. Thus, it is important to perform account reconciliations on a timely basis. Finally, mailing monthly account statements to every customer provides an additional independent review of posting accuracy because customers will complain if their accounts have not been properly credited for payments they remitted.

Cash Collections

The primary objective of the cash collections function is to safeguard customer remittances. Threat 10 in Table 10-1 relates to this objective.

Threat 10: Theft of Cash

Special control procedures must be utilized because cash is so easy to steal. Segregation of duties is the most effective control procedure for reducing theft. Employees who have physical access to cash should not have responsibility for recording or authorizing any transactions involving its receipt. Specifically, the following pairs of duties should be segregated:

1 **Handling cash or checks and posting remittances to customer accounts.** A person performing both of these duties could commit the special type of embezzlement called lapping.
2 **Handling cash or checks and authorizing credit memos.** A person performing both of these duties could conceal theft of cash by creating a credit memo equal to the amount stolen.
3 **Issuing credit memos and maintaining customer accounts.** A person performing both of these duties could write off as uncollectible amounts owed by friends.

In general, the handling of money and checks within the organization should be minimized. The optimal methods are a bank lockbox arrangement or the use of EFT or FEDI for customer payments. The costs of these arrangements must be weighed against the benefits of reduced internal processing costs and faster access to customer payments. If customer payments must be processed internally, prompt documentation of remittances is crucial, because the risk of loss is greatest at the time of first receipt. Thus, a list of all checks received should be prepared immediately after opening the mail. The checks should also be restrictively endorsed at that time. To minimize the risk of misappropriating any cash or checks received, two people should open all incoming mail.

Segregating the recording and custody functions as follows provides additional control: Only the remittance data should be sent to the accounts receivable department, with customer payments being sent to the cashier. Such an arrangement establishes two mutually independent control checks. First, the total credits to accounts receivable recorded by the accounting department should equal the total debit to cash representing the amount deposited by the cashier. Second, the copy of the remittance list that is sent to the internal audit department can be compared with the validated deposit slips and bank statements to verify that all checks the organization received were deposited. Finally, the monthly statements mailed to customers provide another layer of control, because customers would notice the failure to properly credit their accounts for payments remitted.

Retail stores and organizations that receive cash directly from customers should use cash registers that automatically produce a written record of all cash received. In these situations, customers also can play a role in controlling cash collections. For example, many stores use signs to inform customers that their purchase is free if they fail to get a receipt or that receipts marked with a red star entitle them to a discount.

Such policies encourage customers to watch that employees actually ring up the cash sale and do so correctly.

All customer remittances should be deposited, intact, in the bank each day. Daily deposits reduce the amount of cash and checks at risk of theft. Depositing all remittances intact, and not using any of them for miscellaneous expenditures, facilitates reconciliation of the bank statement with the records of sales, accounts receivable, and cash collections.

Finally, the employee who reconciles the bank statements should be independent of all other activities involved in handling or recording the receipt of cash. This separation of duties provides an independent check on the cashier and prevents manipulation of the bank statement to conceal the theft of cash.

General Control Issues

Two general objectives pertaining to all revenue cycle activities are that accurate data be available when needed and that all activities be performed efficiently and effectively. Threats 11 and 12 in Table 10-1 are general threats that affect all phases of the revenue cycle.

Threat 11: Loss, Alteration, or Unauthorized Disclosure of Data

A significant general threat in the revenue cycle is loss or alteration of data about customer accounts. Loss of all accounts receivable data could threaten a company's continued existence. Accurate customer account and inventory records are important not only for external and internal reporting purposes but also for responding to customer inquiries. Unauthorized disclosure of confidential business data, such as marketing plans, can jeopardize the company's competitiveness. Unauthorized disclosure of personal customer information is not only likely to lead to loss of customer loyalty and future sales but may also result in fines and other sanctions. Therefore, companies must protect revenue cycle information.

The master accounts receivable, sales, and cash receipts files must be backed up regularly. Two backup copies of key files, such as the accounts receivable master file, should be made. One should be kept on-site and the other stored off-site. Backup copies of the most recent transaction file also should be made. All disks and tapes should have both external and internal file labels to reduce the possibility of accidentally erasing important files.

Access controls are also important. Unauthorized access increases the risk of damage to important data files and of disclosure of sensitive information. A system of passwords and user IDs should be used to limit employees' access to files and allowable operations on files. For example, only sales staff should be allowed to create sales orders. Moreover, sales staff should have read-only access to customer credit limits and current account balances. Access controls also should exist for individual terminals. For example, the system should be programmed to reject any attempts to enter sales orders from a terminal located at the shipping dock. Finally, logs of all activities, especially any actions involving managerial approval (e.g., extending credit limits), should be recorded and maintained for later review as part of the audit trail.

It is important to point out that enforcing proper access controls and segregation of duties requires that the controller or CFO review and suggest appropriate configuration of user rights in integrated AIS packages and ERP systems. The default installation of such systems typically provides every user with far too much power. For example, consider the situation where a sales order entry clerk types in the name of a customer who is not currently in the customer database. The default configurations of most integrated AIS packages and ERP systems would respond by asking whether the clerk wants to create a new customer. This violates segregation of duties by permitting the person who does the recording (sales order entry) to also authorize the creation of new accounts. Similarly, the default configurations of many systems permit sales order entry staff to not only read the prices of various products and current customer account

balances but also to change the values of those data items. These examples are just some of the many areas that the controller or CFO needs to review to ensure that various users are assigned only those privileges necessary to perform their specified job duties. Properly configuring an ERP requires both a sound understanding of proper segregation of duties for different business processes and knowledge of the default manner in which those processes are configured in a particular ERP system.

Access and processing integrity controls are also needed to ensure the confidentiality and accuracy of revenue cycle data transmissions. Sensitive data, such as price lists, marketing promotions, and personal information collected from customers, should be encrypted both while in storage and during transmission over the Internet. One way to do this is to establish VPNs with major trading partners. Web sites should use SSL to provide secure communications with individual customers. Parity checks and acknowledgment messages should also be used to ensure the accuracy of data transmissions. In addition, various control totals, such as the total amount of sales or customer payments plus record counts indicating the number of individual sales or customer payment transactions about which information is being sent, should be used to verify the accuracy of information exchanged between various offices.

Threat 12: Poor Performance

In addition to ensuring accuracy and safeguarding assets, another objective of internal controls is to encourage efficient and effective performance of duties. Preparing and reviewing reports provides a basis for assessing the efficiency and effectiveness of revenue cycle activities and for diminishing the threat of substandard performance. The nature and quality of the reports produced by an AIS determine how effectively it fulfills its function of providing management with information useful for decision making. The next section discusses some of the key revenue cycle decisions and the information that the AIS must provide to enable management to make optimal choices.

Revenue Cycle Information Needs

Effective management of revenue cycle activities requires timely access to accurate information. Operational data are needed to monitor performance and to perform the following recurring tasks:

- Respond to customer inquiries about account balances and order status,
- Decide whether to extend credit to a particular customer,
- Determine inventory availability,
- Select methods for delivering merchandise.

In addition, current and historical information is needed to enable management to make the following strategic decisions:

- Setting prices for products and services,
- Establishing policies regarding sales returns and warranties,
- Deciding what types of credit terms to offer,
- Determining the need for short-term borrowing,
- Planning new marketing campaigns.

Furthermore, the AIS must also supply the information needed to evaluate performance of critical revenue cycle processes. Key metrics include:

- Response time to customer inquiries; percentage of customer issues satisfactorily resolved customer inquiries
- Time required to fill and deliver orders;
- Percentage of sales that required back orders;

- Customer satisfaction rates and trends;
- Analyses of market share and sales trends;
- Profitability analyses by product, customer, and sales region;
- Sales volume in both dollars and number of customers;
- Effectiveness of advertising and promotions;
- Sales staff performance;
- Bad-debt expenses;
- Days receivables outstanding;
- Remittances processed daily.

Notice that both financial and operating information are needed to manage and evaluate revenue cycle activities. For example, evaluating the efficiency and effectiveness of sales order entry requires data not only about sales volumes but also about order processing time. Evaluating the overall effectiveness of all revenue cycle activities also requires information from external sources, such as measures of customer satisfaction. Traditionally, the AIS has provided the internally generated financial measures of performance and managers have turned to other sources for the internal operating and external information they need. This situation is costly, inefficient, and no longer necessary. Database technology makes it possible to redesign the AIS to capture and store both financial and operating data about revenue cycle transactions and to integrate that internally generated data with information from external sources.

The potential number of informational reports that can be generated is limited only by management's choice about what activities are important to monitor and control. For example, sales order entry efficiency can be monitored by preparing periodic reports of sales orders processed per individual in a given time period. The efficiency and effectiveness of the sales force can be assessed by **sales analysis reports**, which break down the sales by salesperson, region, or product (see Figure 10-17). Further insights about overall marketing performance can be provided by preparing **profitability analysis reports**, which break down the marginal profit contribution made by each territory, customer, distribution channel, salesperson, product, or other basis (see Figure 10-18 on page 421). For retail stores, the use of POS systems can automatically generate much of the data needed for these types of reports.

Reports on the frequency and size of back orders provide insight about the effectiveness of inventory management policies in satisfying customer demands. Similarly, reports that identify slow-moving products help to avoid excessive stockpiling.

The preceding internally focused dimensions of performance provide only one view of success in meeting customer satisfaction goals. Organizations also need to

Figure 10-17
Sample Sales Analysis Report

Period Ending: October 31, 2009 **Territory: East Texas**

Salesperson	Period	Actual Sales	Prior Year Sales	Percent Change	Sales Quota	Percent Variance from Quota
Benjamin, H.L.	This month	$ 50,000	$ 40,000	+25	$ 48,000	+4
	Year to date	120,000	115,000	+4	125,000	−4
Carlton, J.C.	This month	40,000	38,000	+5	45,000	−11
	Year to date	105,000	110,000	−5	130,000	−19
.
.
.
.
Territory totals	This month	$300,000	285,000	+5	$350,000	−14
	Year to date	850,000	840,000	+1	950,000	−11

Figure 10-18
Sample Profitability Analysis by Product

	A	B	C	D	E	F	G
1							
2				For the Month of January 2009			
3							
4			Unit	Total	Variable	Contribution	Margin
5	Product Class		Volume	Revenue	Cost	Margin	Percent
6	Calculators		164500	$ 259,750	$ 184,500	$ 75,250	28.97
7	Digital clocks		109750	$ 318,500	$ 220,500	$ 98,000	30.77
8	Radios		128750	$ 335,400	$ 230,200	$105,200	31.37
9	Small appliances		142200	$ 382,900	$ 251,500	$131,400	34.32
10	Pagers		56800	$ 246,700	$ 144,800	$101,900	41.31
11	Toys and games		124500	$ 253,200	$ 121,400	$131,800	52.05
12	Totals		726500	$1,796,450	$1,152,900	$643,550	35.82

capture and integrate internally generated measures of process efficiency with externally generated data about customer attitudes. Thus, Trevor wants Ann to redesign AOE's AIS to be able to track and store trends in customer satisfaction ratings.

Cash flow problems are a major reason why many businesses fail. Therefore, a **cash budget** (see Figure 10-19), which provides precise estimates of cash inflows (projected collections from sales) and outflows (outstanding payables), is essential. It can alert an organization to a pending short-term cash shortage, thereby enabling it to plan ahead to secure short-term loans at the best possible rates. Conversely, an organization that knows a surplus of cash is pending can take steps to invest those excess funds to earn the best possible returns. A cash budget could have helped AOE better manage its short-term borrowing needs.

Projected cash receipts from customers are a key component of a cash budget. Consequently, careful monitoring of accounts receivable is extremely important. A useful report for doing this is an **accounts receivable aging schedule**, which lists customer account balances by length of time outstanding (see Figure 10-20). Aging based on the invoice print date (usually the date of the sale) provides information useful for projecting the timing of future cash inflows related to sales. Aging based on the invoice due date provides information useful for deciding whether to increase the credit limit for specific customers and for estimating bad debts. Management needs to regularly review the accounts receivable aging schedule because prompt attention to customers who fall behind in their payments can minimize losses. Such a report could have enabled AOE to spot problems with the Best Value Company earlier, so that it could have stopped making additional credit sales that are unlikely to be paid for.

	January	February	March	April
Beginning Balance	10,000	11,000	8,000	8,000
Projected Cash Receipts:				
Cash Sales	7,000	8,500	8,000	9,000
Collections on Account	26,000	29,000	28,000	30,000
Total Cash Available (A)	43,000	48,500	44,000	47,000
Projected Cash Disbursements (B)	(32,000)	(41,000)	(39,000)	(36,000)
Projected Ending Cash Balance (C = A − B)	11,000	7,500	5,000	11,000
Desired Minimum Balance (D)	8,000	8,000	8,000	8,000
Amount Needed to Borrow	0	500	3,000	0
Ending Balance	11,000	8,000	8,000	11,000

Figure 10-19
Sample Cash Budget

10-4 FOCUS

Revenue Margin: A New Metric for Evaluating Revenue Cycle Performance

Companies have long focused on revenue trends as a performance indicator. A better metric for evaluating the quality of growth, however, may be revenue margin. Revenue margin equals gross margin minus all selling costs: payroll, commissions, salesforce travel-expense reimbursements, customer service and support costs, warranty expenses, marketing and advertising expenses, and distribution and delivery expenses.

The value of revenue margin as a metric is that it integrates the effects of changes in sales, pricing, and the costs associated with generating sales on overall company operating profits. Although a financial number, revenue margin reflects such nonfinancial factors as productivity, reputation, and market position strength. Thus, trends in revenue margin provide useful insights for management about the revenue cycle activities' overall performance. Growth in revenue margin indicates that customers are satisfied, productivity is increasing, or both. Conversely, a declining trend indicates potential problems with customer retention, productivity, or pricing pressures due to competition.

Revenue margin is a nontraditional performance metric. It is one example of the kinds of new measures developed by accountants to help managers more effectively control business practices.

Figure 10-20
Sample Accounts Receivable Aging Report

Customer	Amount	Current	1–30 Days Past Due	31–60 Days Past Due	61–90 Days Past Due	Over 90 Days Past Due
Able						
Invoice 221	$ 3,450	$ 3,450				
Invoice 278	2,955	2,955				
Total	$ 6,405	$ 6,405				
Baker						
Invoice 178	$ 4,500			$ 4,500		
Invoice 245	2,560	2,560				
Total	$ 7,060	$ 2,560		$ 4,500		
Other Accounts	$ 185,435	$ 137,935	$ 28,500	$ 5,500	$ 2,500	$ 11,000
Totals	$ 198,900	$ 146,900	$ 28,500	$ 10,000	$ 2,500	$ 11,000

Accountants should continually think of ways to refine and improve performance reports. This requires developing a better understanding of the underlying business processes. Focus 10-4 discusses one example of a new type of metric designed specifically to provide a leading indicator of revenue cycle performance.

SUMMARY AND CASE CONCLUSION

The four basic activities in the revenue cycle are sales order entry, shipping, billing and accounts receivable, and cash collections. The AIS should be designed to maximize the efficiency with which each of these functions is performed. The AIS must also incorporate adequate internal control procedures to mitigate threats such as

uncollectible sales, billing errors, and lost or misappropriated inventory and cash. Control procedures also are needed to ensure that the information provided for decision making is both accurate and complete. Finally, to facilitate strategic decision making, the AIS should be designed to accommodate the integration of internally generated data with data from external sources.

At the next executive meeting, Elizabeth summarized the proposals that she, Trevor, and Ann developed to provide the information needed to better manage customer relationships and cash flows. Among the recommendations were the following:

1 Equip the sales force with wireless-enabled pen-based laptop computers. Trevor Whitman, vice president of marketing, believes that AOE will still need its sales staff to visit existing customers to identify which additional products can be profitably carried. Sales staff also will continue to make cold calls on prospective customers to try to convince them to carry AOE's products. As they walk down store aisles, sales representatives can check off the items that need to be restocked and then write in the appropriate quantities. When the order is complete, they can transmit the order back to headquarters. The system can check the customer's credit status and inventory availability and confirm orders within minutes, including an estimated delivery date. After the customer approves the order, the system will immediately update all affected files so that current information about inventory status is available to other sales representatives.

2 Improve warehouse and shipping efficiency by replacing bar-code scanners with RFID devices.

3 Improve billing process efficiency by increasing the number of customers who agree to participate in invoiceless sales relationships and, when possible, by using EDI to transmit invoices to those customers who still require them.

4 In an effort to improve customer service, work with major customers to obtain access to their POS data so that AOE can help them better manage their product inventory.

5 Periodically survey customers about their satisfaction with AOE's products and performance.

6 Improve the efficiency of cash collections by encouraging all customers to use EFT. In addition, encourage EDI-capable customers to move to FEDI so that AOE receives both the funds and remittance data together.

Linda Spurgeon approved these proposals. She then asked Elizabeth and Ann to turn their attention to solving several problems related to AOE's expenditure cycle business activities.

KEY TERMS

revenue cycle 392
sales order 395
choiceboards 396
vendor managed inventory (VMI) 396
credit limit 397
back order 399
picking ticket 399
packing slip 402
bill of lading 402
sales invoice 405

open-invoice method 406
remittance advice 406
balance-forward method 406
monthly statement 406
cycle billing 407
credit memo 408
remittance list 409
lockbox 409
electronic lockbox 409

electronic funds transfer (EFT) 410
financial electronic data interchange (FEDI) 410
sales analysis reports 410
profitability analysis reports 410
cash budget 411
accounts receivable aging schedule 411

AIS IN ACTION

CHAPTER QUIZ

1 Which activity is part of the sales order entry process?
 a. setting customer credit limits
 b. preparing a bill of lading
 c. checking customer credit
 d. approving sales returns

2 Which document often accompanies merchandise shipped to a customer?
 a. picking ticket
 b. packing slip
 c. credit memo
 d. sales order

3 Which method is most likely used when a company offers customers discounts for prompt payment?
 a. open-invoice method
 b. balance-forward method
 c. accounts receivable aging method
 d. cycle billing method

4 Which of the following techniques is the most efficient way to process customer payments and update accounts receivable?
 a. EFT
 b. VMI
 c. FEDI
 d. ACH

5 Which of the following revenue cycle activities can potentially be eliminated by technology?
 a. sales order entry
 b. shipping
 c. billing
 d. cash collections

6 Which report would be most useful for estimating likely bad debts?
 a. accounts receivable aging schedule
 b. profitability analysis
 c. sales analysis
 d. cash budget

7 Which document is used to authorize the release of merchandise from inventory control (warehouse) to shipping?
 a. picking ticket
 b. packing slip
 c. shipping order
 d. sales invoice

8 Which of the following provides a means to both improve the efficiency of processing customer payments and also enhance control over those payments?
 a. VMI
 b. lockboxes
 c. aging accounts receivable
 d. EDINT

9 For good internal control, who should approve credit memos?
a. credit manager c. billing manager
b. sales manager d. controller

10 For good internal control over customer remittances, the mailroom clerk should separate the checks from the remittance advices and send the customer payments to which department?
a. billing c. cashier
b. accounts receivable d. sales

 DISCUSSION QUESTIONS

10.1 Customer relationship management systems hold great promise, but their usefulness is determined by the amount of personal data customers are willing to divulge. To what extent do you think concerns about privacy-related issues affect the use of CRM systems?

10.2 Some products, like music and software, can be digitized. How does this affect each of the four main activities in the revenue cycle?

10.3 Many retailers have installed point-of-sale (POS) systems to better manage their inventory and to save time and cut costs associated with ringing up customer sales. How should employees be trained to operate these POS systems in order to ensure that inventory records are indeed more timely and accurate?

10.4 Many companies use accounts receivable aging schedules to project future cash inflows and bad-debt expense. Review the information typically presented in such a report (see Figure 10-20). Which specific metrics can be calculated from those data which might be especially useful in providing early warning about looming cash flow or bad-debt problems?

10.5 Airlines have long used database technology to monitor capacity and maximize revenue by charging different prices to almost every passenger on a given flight. To what extent can other industries adopt similar "smart" pricing strategies? What are the risks of doing so?

10.6 Invoiceless pricing has been adopted by some large businesses for B2B transactions. What are the barriers, if any, to its use in B2C commerce?

10.7 The use of some form of electronic "cash" that would provide the same kind of anonymity for e-commerce that cash provides for traditional physical business transactions has been discussed for a long time. What are the advantages and disadvantages of electronic cash to customers? To businesses? What are some of the accounting implications of using electronic cash?

10.8 Why not use copies of the sales order as the picking ticket, packing list, and sales invoice?

 PROBLEMS

10.1 Modify Table 10-1 web site for to indicate whether each control listed there is preventive, detective, or corrective in nature.

10.2 Table 10-1 suggests that restricting physical access to inventory is one way to reduce the threat of theft. Describe specific ways to use information technology to accomplish that objective.

10.3 What internal control procedure(s) would provide protection against the following threats? If more than one control procedure could be used to solve a problem, rank the alternatives in terms of their effectiveness.

 a. Theft of goods by the shipping dock workers, who claim that the inventory shortages reflect errors in the inventory records.

 b. Posting the sales amount to the wrong customer account because a customer account number was incorrectly keyed into the system.

 c. Making a credit sale to a customer who is already four months behind in making payments on his account.

 d. Authorizing a credit memo for a sales return when the goods were never actually returned.

 e. Writing off a customer's accounts receivable balance as uncollectible to conceal the theft of subsequent collections.

 f. Billing customers for the quantity ordered when the quantity shipped was actually less due to back ordering of some items.

 g. Theft of checks by the mailroom clerk, who then endorsed the checks for deposit into the clerk's personal bank account.

 h. Theft of funds by the cashier, who cashed several checks and did not record their receipt.

 i. Theft of cash by a waiter who destroyed the customer sales ticket for customers who paid cash.

 j. Shipping goods to a customer but then failing to bill that customer.

 k. Lost sales because of stockouts of several products for which the computer records indicated there was adequate quantity on hand.

 l. Unauthorized disclosure of buying habits of several well-known customers.

 m. Loss of all information about amounts owed by customers in New York City because the master database for that office was destroyed in a fire.

 n. The company's Web site was unavailable for seven hours because of a power outage.

 o. Interception and theft of customers' credit card numbers while being sent to the company's Web site.

 p. A sales clerk sold a $7,000 wide-screen TV to a friend and altered the price to $700.

 q. A shipping clerk who was quitting to start a competing business copied the names of the company's 500 largest customers and offered them lower prices and better terms if they purchased the same product from the clerk's new company.

 r. The company's main server crashed and destroyed all the files on the hard disk. Backup copies were used to restore the database on a new server, but the backup did not contain information about any sales made during the past three days.

 s. A fire in the office next door damaged the company's servers and all optical and magnetic media in the server room. The company immediately implemented its disaster recovery procedures and shifted to a backup center several miles away. The company had made full daily backups of all files and stored a copy at the backup center. However, none of the backup copies were readable.

10.4 EXCEL PROJECT. (Hint: For help on steps b and c, see the article "Dial a Forecast," by James A. Weisel, in the December 2006 issue of the *Journal of Accountancy*. The *Journal of Accountancy* is available in print or online at the AICPA's Web site: www.aicpa.org).

 a. Create a 12-month cash budget in Excel using the following assumptions:
- Initial sales of $5,000,000 with forecasted monthly growth of 1%
- 40% of each month's sales for cash; 30% collected the following month; 20% collected 2 months later; 8% collected 3 months later; and 2% never collected
- Initial cash balance of $350,000

b. Add a "spinner" to your spreadsheet that will enable you to easily change forecasted monthly sales growth to range from 0.5% to 1.5% in increments of 0.1%.

c. Add a scroll bar to your spreadsheet that will let you modify the amount of initial sales to vary from $4,000,000 to $6,000,000 in increments of $100,000.

d. Design appropriate data entry and processing controls to ensure spreadsheet accuracy.

10.5 The following documents are used in the revenue cycle:
- Customer order
- Sales order
- Sales invoice
- Credit memo
- Picking ticket
- Packing slip
- Bill of lading
- Monthly statement
- Remittance advice
- Remittance list

Required

a. Identify which of these documents are internally generated and which are externally generated.

b. For each internally generated document, how many copies are needed? What is the purpose of each copy? Where does each copy go?

c. Describe the application controls that should be in place if each of these paper documents were replaced by electronic forms.

10.6 Create a questionnaire checklist that can be used to evaluate controls for each of the four basic activities in the revenue cycle (sales order entry, shipping, billing, and cash collections).

Required

a. For each control issue, write a Yes/No question such that a "No" answer represents a control weakness. For example, one question might be "Are customer credit limits set and modified by a credit manager with no sales responsibility?".

b. For each Yes/No question, write a brief explanation of why a "No" answer represents a control weakness.

10.7 The Quality Building Supplies Company operates six wholesale outlets that sell roofing materials, electrical and plumbing supplies, lumber, and other building materials to general contractors in a large metropolitan area. The company is studying the feasibility of introducing a guaranteed same-day delivery plan, under which it would guarantee delivery within four hours for orders received from approved customers by noon of that day. For orders received in the afternoon, delivery would be guaranteed by 8 A.M. the next day. The company believes that this system would give it a substantial competitive advantage relative to other regional building wholesalers because it would enable contractors to maintain smaller inventories yet still be assured of having building supplies when needed.

You have been asked to help design the proposed system. It will be designed to receive customer orders by phone so that contractors can call from the construction site. Customers will be billed monthly for all purchases. You want to streamline the processing of cash collections and minimize the time it takes to deposit those funds in the company's bank account.

Required

a. Specify the factors needed to qualify customers for this new service.

b. Identify the input transactions that this system must process and the output documents (excluding reports) that it should produce.

c. Describe several reports that would be useful to management's implementation of the new credit sales policy. What data need to be collected to produce these reports? What application controls should be in place to ensure that these reports contain complete, accurate, and valid information?

d. Draw a systems flowchart of your proposed system.

e. Describe possible threats to the system and the control procedures required in the new system to address those threats.

10.8 O'Brien Corporation is a midsize, privately owned, industrial instrument manufacturer supplying precision equipment to manufacturers in the Midwest. The corporation is 10 years old and operates a centralized AIS. The administrative offices are located in a downtown building and the production, shipping, and receiving departments are housed in a renovated warehouse a few blocks away. The shipping and receiving areas share one end of the warehouse.

The marketing department consists of four sales representatives. Upon obtaining an order over the telephone, a salesperson manually prepares a prenumbered, two-part sales order. One copy of the order is filed by date and the second copy is sent to the shipping department. All sales are on credit, FOB destination. Because of the recent increase in sales, the sales representatives have not had time to check credit histories. As a result, 15% of credit sales are either late collections or uncollectible.

The shipping department receives the sales orders and packages the goods from the warehouse, noting any items that are out of stock. The terminal in the shipping department is used to update the perpetual inventory records of each item as it is removed from the shelf. The packages are placed near the loading dock door in alphabetical order by customer name. A shipping clerk signs the sales order, indicating that the order is filled and ready to send.

The sales order is forwarded to the billing department, where a two-part sales invoice is prepared. The sales invoice is prepared upon receipt of the sales order from the shipping department so that the customer is billed only for the items that were sent, not for back orders. Billing sends the customer's copy of the invoice back to shipping, and shipping then inserts it into a special envelope on the package in order to save postage.

The carrier of the customer's choice is then contacted to pick up the goods. In the past, goods were shipped within two working days of receipt of the customer's order; however, shipping dates now average six working days. One reason for this slippage is that two new shipping clerks are still undergoing training. Because these clerks have fallen behind, the two experienced clerks in the receiving department have been assisting them.

The receiving department is located adjacent to the shipping dock, and many different carriers deliver merchandise daily. The receiving clerks share a computer terminal with the shipping department. The date, vendor, and number of items received are entered upon receipt to keep the perpetual inventory records current.

Hard copies of the changes in inventory (additions and shipments) are printed monthly. The receiving supervisor checks that the additions are reasonable and forwards the printout to the shipping supervisor, who is responsible for checking the reasonableness of the deductions from inventory (shipments). The inventory printout is stored in the shipping department by date. A complete inventory list is printed only once a year when the entire inventory is counted.

Figure 10-21 presents the document flows employed by O'Brien Corporation.

Required

a. Identify at least five weaknesses in O'Brien Corporation's marketing, shipping, billing, and receiving information system. Describe the exposure resulting from each weakness. Recommend control procedures that should be added to the system to correct the weakness. Format your answer as follows:

 Weakness Threat Recommended Control Procedure(s)

b. Discuss how O'Brien Corporation could use IT to improve both control and efficiency during sales order processing.

(CMA Examination, adapted)

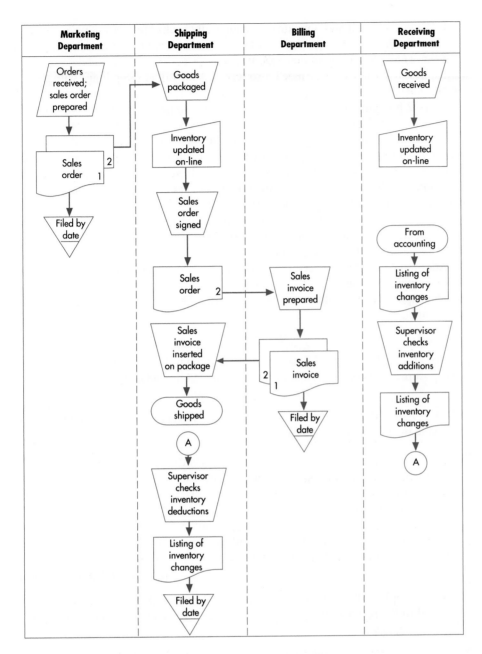

Figure 10-21
Revenue Cycle Activities for
O'Brien Corporation

10.9 Parktown Medical Center, Inc. is a small health care provider owned by a publicly held corporation. It employs seven salaried physicians, ten nurses, three support staff, and three clerical workers. The clerical workers perform such tasks as reception, correspondence, cash receipts, billing, and appointment scheduling. All are adequately bonded.

Most patients pay for services rendered by cash or check on the day of their visit. The clerical staff does not approve credit. The physician who is to perform the respective services approves credit based on an interview. When credit is approved, the physician files a memo with the billing clerk (clerk 2) to set up the receivable from data the physician generates.

The servicing physician prepares a charge slip that is given to clerk 1 for pricing and preparation of the patient's bill. Clerk 1 transmits a copy of the bill to clerk 2 for preparation of the revenue summary and for posting in the accounts receivable subsidiary ledger.

The cash receipts functions are performed by clerk 1, who receives cash and checks directly from patients and gives each patient a prenumbered cash receipt.

Clerk 1 opens the mail and immediately stamps all checks "for deposit only" and lists cash and checks for deposit. The cash and checks are deposited daily by the office manager. The list of cash and checks, with the related remittance advices, are forwarded by clerk 1 to clerk 2. Clerk 1 also serves as the office receptionist with general correspondence duties.

Clerk 2 prepares and sends monthly statements to patients with unpaid balances. He also prepares the cash receipts journal and is responsible for the accounts receivable subsidiary ledger. No other clerical employee is permitted access to the accounts receivable subsidiary ledger. Clerk 2 writes off uncollectible accounts only after the physician who performed the respective services believes the account will not pay and communicates the write-off to the office manager. The office manager then issues a write-off memo, which clerk 2 processes.

The office manager supervises the clerks, issues write-off memos, schedules appointments for the doctors, makes bank deposits, reconciles bank statements, and performs general correspondence duties.

Additional services are performed monthly by a local accountant who posts summaries prepared by the clerks to the general ledger, prepares income statements, and files the appropriate payroll forms and tax returns. The accountant reports directly to the parent corporation.

Required

Identify at least four control weaknesses at Parktown. Describe the potential threat and exposure associated with each weakness, and recommend how to best correct them.
(CPA Examination, adapted)

10.10 Figure 10-22 (see pages 432–433) depicts the activities performed in the revenue cycle by the Newton Hardware Company.

Required

1 Identify the weaknesses in Newton Hardware's revenue cycle. Explain the resulting threat and suggest methods to correct the weakness. Organize your answer as follows:
 Weakness Threat Recommended Improvement
2 Identify ways to use IT to streamline Newton's revenue cycle activities. Describe the control procedures required in the new system.
(CPA Examination, adapted)

10.11 Complete the cell entries in Table 10-2, which lists the various activities performed in the revenue cycle and the journal entries, documents, data, and control issues associated with them.

10.12 Match threats in the first column to appropriate control procedures in the second column.

Threat	Control Procedure
1. Sending incorrect merchandise	a. Perform a completeness check
2. Crediting customer payment to wrong account	b. Credit sales approved by credit manager
3. Giving goods away for free	c. Reconcile sales orders to packing slips
4. Corrupted data files	d. Use a sales forecasting system
5. Data entry errors by warehouse employees	e. Use bar-code scanners
6. Theft of customer payments	f. Document inventory transfers
7. Charging the wrong price	g. Segregate shipping and billing functions
8. Inventory shrinkage due to theft by employees	h. Maintain an updated inventory master file
9. Missing or incomplete order data	i. Closed-loop verification
10. Inept operations	j. Employ a bank lockbox
11. Sales made to customers with poor credit	k. Off-site data storage of backup files
12. Excess inventory	l. Prepare and review performance reports

Table 10-2
Overview of Revenue Cycle Business Activities

	Contact Customer	Customer Agrees to Sale	Approve Credit	Transfer Goods	Bill Customer	Receive Remittance	Credit Accounts Receivable	Deposit Cash
				REVENUE CYCLE				
Accounting transaction				Sale				
Journal entry							Dr. Cash Cr. A/R	
Documents		Purchase order from customer						
Data collected	Name Address Contact person							
Department						Accounting		
Control issues			Only approved customers get credit					
Information required								
Information generated								
Effect of automation								

Source: Adapted from teaching materials developed by Martha Eining, University of Utah.

10.13 The Family Support Center is a small charitable organization. It has only four full-time employees: two staff, an accountant, and an office manager. The majority of its funding comes from two campaign drives, one in the spring and one in the fall. Donors make pledges over the telephone. Some donors pay their pledge by credit card during the telephone campaign, but many prefer to pay in monthly installments by check. In such cases, the donor pledges are recorded during the telephone campaign and they are then mailed pledge cards. Donors mail their contributions directly to the charity. Most donors send a check, but occasionally some send cash. Most donors return their pledge card with their check or cash donation, but occasionally the Family Support Center receives anonymous cash donations.

The procedures used to process donations are as follows:

Sarah, one of the staff members who has worked for the Family Support Center for 12 years, opens all mail. She sorts the donations from the other mail and prepares a list of all donations, indicating the name of the donor (or anonymous), amount of the donation, and the pledge number (if the donor returned the pledge card). Sarah then sends the list, cash, and checks to the accountant.

The accountant enters the information from the list into the computer to update the Family Support Center's files. The accountant then prepares a deposit slip (in duplicate) and deposits all cash and checks into the charity's bank account at the end of each day. No funds are left on the premises overnight. The validated deposit slip is then filed by date.

Figure 10-22
Newton Hardware Company Revenue Cycle Procedures

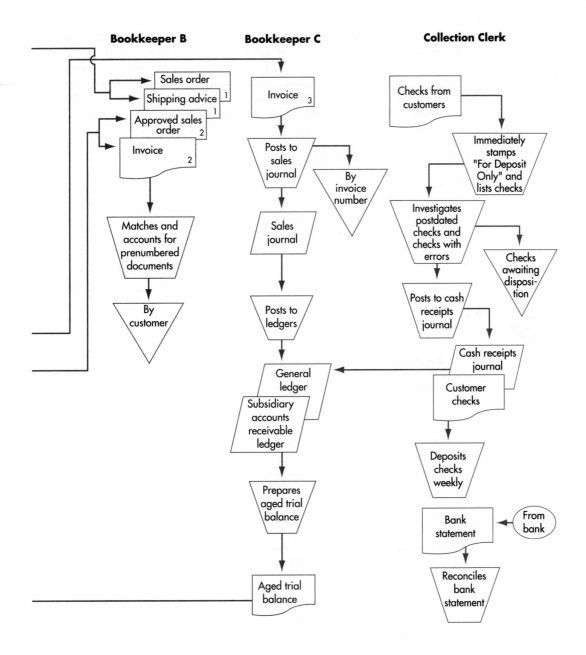

The accountant also mails an acknowledgment letter thanking each donor. Monthly, the accountant retrieves all deposit slips and uses them to reconcile the Family Support Center's bank statement. At this time, the accountant also reviews the pledge files and sends a follow-up letter to those people who have not yet fulfilled their pledges.

Each employee has a computer workstation that is connected to the internal network. Employees are permitted to surf the Web during lunch hours. Each employee has full access to the charity's accounting system, so that anyone can fill in for someone else who is sick or on vacation. Each Friday, the accountant makes a backup copy of all computer files. The backup copy is stored in the office manager's office.

Required

a. Identify two major control weaknesses in the Family Support Center's cash receipts procedures. For each weakness you identify, suggest a method to correct that weakness. Your solution must be specific—identify which specific employees should do what. *Assume that no new employees can be hired.*

b. Describe the IT control procedures that should exist in order to protect the Family Support Center from loss, alteration, or unauthorized disclosure of data.

10.14 EXCEL PROJECT.

a. Create a spreadsheet with the following data:

Product	Sales ($)	Division
Widgets	245000	A
Widgets	74000	B
Widgets	178944	C
Gadgets	123678	A
Gadgets	163888	B
Gadgets	201999	C
Gizmos	178000	A
Gizmos	123456	B
Gizmos	198346	C
Wingdings	158255	A
Wingdings	273050	B
Wingdings	95000	C
Dohingeys	333000	A
Dohingeys	144357	B
Dohingeys	188500	C
Thingamabobs	184750	A
Thingamabobs	222000	B
Thingamabobs	100000	C
Whatchamacallits	278000	A
Whatchamacallits	200000	B
Whatchamacallits	129905	C
Round2its	103000	A

Number of products
 with sales >200,000
Total sales all products
 for Division A

Division to sum
Total sales all products
 in that division

b. Write a function to display the number of products with more than $200,000 in sales. Display the answer in the cell to the right of that statement.

c. Write a function to display total sales for division A. Display the answer in the cell to the right of that statement.

d. Write a function that will display the total sales for the division that the user inputs in the cell to the right of the statement "Division to sum." Display the

answer in the cell to the right of the statement "Total sales all products in that division."

e. Use conditional formatting to highlight all three cells in red in any row in which sales are less than $100,000. (Hint: you may need to use different formulas for each cell.)

CASE 10-1 Elite Publishing Company

Elite Publishing Company has established Business Book Club, Inc. (BBC), a subsidiary that operates as follows: BBC's editors select from among recently published business books those they believe will be most interesting to businesspeople. BBC will purchase these books in large quantities at approximately 40% of list price and then sell them to their club members at approximately 75% of list price.

Both direct mail and advertisements in selected publications are used to solicit new customers. The advertisements offer an introductory membership bonus whereby new members who purchase one book will receive four free titles. Each month, club members receive a list of new selections and a book order form. For every four books they purchase, members earn one free book.

You have been called upon to design a computerized billing and book inventory system for BBC. The advertising

manager wants to know which advertising media are most effective, the credit manager wants to know which accounts are more than 90 days past due, and the editors want to know which books are best-sellers for the club.

Required

1 Identify the input transactions that this system must process and the output documents and reports that the system should be designed to produce.
2 Describe how IT can be used to maximize efficiency of sales order entry, shipping, billing, and cash collections. Draw a systems flowchart of your proposal.
3 Describe the control procedures that should be included in this system.

CASE 10-2 Frontier Floors

Frontier Floors is a manufacturer and distributor of carpet and vinyl floor coverings. The home office is located in Baton Rouge, Louisiana. Carpet mills are located in Helen, Georgia, and the vinyl floor covering plant is in Weston, Florida. Total sales from the last fiscal year were just under $175 million. Frontier makes 350 different varieties of commercial and residential carpet that it sells under six different brand names. There are as many as seven product lines under each brand. The various lines represent differing levels of quality and color. In addition, Frontier offers 330 vinyl floor coverings for commercial and residential use that are listed under five different brand names with twelve different patterns and eight color styles for each pattern. Frontier sells to over 500 wholesale customers and many large construction companies. In addition, there are outlet stores at each plant that sell overruns, seconds, and discontinued items direct to the public. The company maintains 10 sales regions and each region is divided into 15 sales areas with one salesperson stationed in each area.

Frontier's management wants to better use the Internet to streamline its revenue cycle activities. Specifically, it is considering adding a Web site on which customers can place orders and adopting both EDI and EFT.

Required

a. Identify the advantages and disadvantages of Frontier implementing an electronic data interchange (EDI) system with its wholesale customers.
b. What control procedures should Frontier design into its Web site? Explain the purpose of each recommended control.
c. Design reports that would enable Frontier's management to effectively manage revenue cycle activities. Explain the purpose of each report and the source of the data used to create each report.
d. What other recent information technology developments should Frontier consider implementing? Why?

AIS IN ACTION SOLUTIONS

QUIZ KEY

1 Which activity is part of the sales order entry process?
 a. setting customer credit limits (Incorrect. The credit department, not the sales department, sets credit limits.)
 b. preparing a bill of lading (Incorrect. This occurs as part of the shipping process.)
 ✔ **c.** checking customer credit (Correct. Checking customer credit and inventory availability are two key parts of the sales order entry process.)
 d. approving sales returns (Incorrect. Someone outside of the sales department should approve all returns.)

2 Which document often accompanies merchandise shipped to a customer?
 a. picking ticket (Incorrect. The picking ticket is used by warehouse workers to fill the order. If a copy of the picking ticket is used as a packing slip, it is referred to as a packing slip.)
 ✔ **b.** packing slip (Correct. This document specifies what is being shipped.)
 c. credit memo (Incorrect. A credit memo is used to adjust a customer's account balance for sales returns, allowances, or write-offs.)
 d. sales order (Incorrect. This is a source document created during sales order entry.)

3 Which method is most likely used when a company offers customers discounts for prompt payment?
 ✔ **a.** open-invoice method (Correct. The open-invoice method provides a means to offer discounts because it facilitates aging each invoice to verify whether a discount should be granted.)
 b. balance-forward method (Incorrect. The balance-forward method does not facilitate tracking the age of individual invoices and thus is difficult to use to offer discounts for early payment of individual invoices.)
 c. accounts receivable aging method (Incorrect. Aging of accounts receivable is a control measure.)
 d. cycle billing method (Incorrect. Cycle billing is a method of smoothing the timing of cash receipts by billing different subsets of the customer file each week.)

4 Which of the following techniques is the most efficient way to process customer payments and update accounts receivable?
 a. EFT (Incorrect. EFT only deals with the transfer of funds. It does not include remittance information necessary to update accounts receivable.)
 b. VMI (Incorrect. VMI stands for vendor-managed inventory.)
 ✔ **c.** FEDI (Correct. FEDI integrates EFT, for processing customer payments, with EDI, for processing related remittance data to update accounts receivable.)
 d. ACH (Incorrect. ACH stands for Automated Clearing House, the private communications network used by financial institutions to transfer funds.)

5 Which of the following revenue cycle activities can potentially be eliminated by technology?
 a. sales order entry (Incorrect. IT may change how sales orders are entered, but the sales process must always begin with taking the customer's order.)
 b. shipping (Incorrect. The product must always be shipped to the customer. The manner may change, particularly for products that can be digitized, but there is still a shipping process.)
 ✔ **c.** billing (Correct. The use of integrated AIS (or ERPs) makes printing invoices superfluous, since both the seller and customer already know all the information included in the invoice. Some large manufacturers have already moved to invoiceless systems with their major suppliers.)

d. cash collections (Incorrect. IT may change how the funds are received, but sellers will always need to collect payments from customers.)

6 Which report would be most useful for estimating likely bad debts?

✔ **a.** accounts receivable aging schedule (Correct. One of the primary purposes of aging accounts receivable is to identify accounts that are way overdue and, therefore, may not be collected.)

b. profitability analysis (Incorrect. A profitability analysis helps identify how product lines and business units are performing.)

c. sales analysis (Incorrect. A sales analysis helps identify how product lines and business units are performing.)

d. cash budget (Incorrect. A cash budget is an important tool for managing cash.)

7 Which document is used to authorize the release of merchandise from the inventory control (warehouse) to shipping?

✔ **a.** picking ticket (Correct. A picking ticket is generated by sales order entry to authorize removal of inventory to be shipped to the customer.)

b. packing slip (Incorrect. The packing slip accompanies the shipment and lists the contents of the shipment.)

c. shipping order (Incorrect. A shipping order is an internal document used to record what was shipped when the shipping function is performed in-house; a bill of lading serves the same purpose when using a third-party common carrier to deliver merchandise.)

d. sales invoice (Incorrect. A sales invoice documents the terms of the sale and requests payment.)

8 Which of the following provides a means to both improve the efficiency of processing customer payments and also enhance control over those payments?

a. VMI (Incorrect. VMI stands for vendor-managed inventory and is a process used to improve inventory management.)

✔ **b.** lockboxes (Correct. The use of lockboxes eliminates the delays involved in processing customer payments and then depositing them. It also improves control because customer payments are not directly handled by any employees.)

c. aging accounts receivable (Incorrect. Aging accounts receivable is an important control for managing customer accounts, but not for processing payments.)

d. EDINT (Incorrect. EDINT stands for EDI over the Internet. It is used to exchange documents, but not to process customer payments.)

9 For good internal control, who should approve credit memos?

✔ **a.** credit manager (Correct. This is the credit manager's function.)

b. sales manager (Incorrect. The same person who authorizes sales should not also authorize credit memos to adjust customer accounts for those sales.)

c. billing manager (Incorrect. The billing manager is in charge of invoicing customers and should not have authority to reduce accounts receivable by issuing credit memos.)

d. controller (Incorrect. The controller is responsible for the recording function and should not also be able to authorize changes to accounts via credit memos.)

10 For good internal control over customer remittances, the mailroom clerk should separate the checks from the remittance advices and send the customer payments to which department?

a. billing (Incorrect. Billing creates invoices but should not be involved in processing payments from customers.)

b. accounts receivable (Incorrect. Accounts receivable performs the recording function and should not also have physical custody of assets.)

✔ **c.** cashier (Correct. This is the cashier's job. The cashier function has custody of cash accounts.)

d. sales (Incorrect. Sales authorizes release of merchandise and should not also have custody of assets.)

CHAPTER 11

LEARNING OBJECTIVES

After studying this chapter, you should be able to:

● Describe the basic business activities and related information processing operations performed in the expenditure cycle.

● Discuss the key decisions to be made in the expenditure cycle, and identify the information needed to make those decisions.

● Document an understanding of the expenditure cycle.

● Identify major threats in the expenditure cycle, and evaluate the adequacy of various control procedures for dealing with those threats.

The Expenditure Cycle: Purchasing to Cash Disbursements

INTEGRATIVE CASE ALPHA OMEGA ELECTRONICS

Although AOE's new integrated AIS has enabled it to slash its costs associated with purchasing and accounts payable, Linda Spurgeon, AOE's president, is convinced that additional improvements are needed. She is particularly concerned about issues recently raised by LeRoy Williams, vice president of manufacturing for AOE. LeRoy is upset because several production runs were delayed at the Wichita plant due to components that AOE's inventory records indicated as being in stock but that actually were not on hand. There were also delays at the Dayton plant because suppliers either did not deliver components on time or delivered substandard products.

Linda asked Elizabeth Venko, the controller, and Ann Brandt, AOE's vice president of information systems, for some recommendations on how AOE's AIS could help solve these problems. Specifically, she asked Elizabeth and Ann to address the following issues:

1 What must be done to ensure that AOE's inventory records are current and accurate and to avoid unexpected components shortages like those experienced at the Wichita plant?
2 How could the problems at the Dayton plant be avoided in the future? What can be done to ensure timely delivery of quality components?
3 Is it possible to reduce AOE's investment in materials inventories?
4 How could the AIS provide better information to guide planning and production?
5 How could IT be used to further reengineer expenditure cycle activities?

As this case suggests, deficiencies in the information system used to support expenditure cycle activities can create significant financial problems for an organization. The availability of current and accurate information about inventories, suppliers, and the status of outstanding purchase orders is crucial for managing the expenditure cycle effectively. As you read this chapter, think about how changes in AOE's AIS could improve the effectiveness and efficiency of its expenditure cycle activities.

Introduction

The **expenditure cycle** is a recurring set of business activities and related information processing operations associated with the purchase of and payment for goods and services (see Figure 11-1). This chapter focuses on the acquisition of raw materials, finished goods, supplies, and services. Chapters 12 and 13 address two other special types of expenditures: the acquisition of fixed assets and labor services, respectively.

In the expenditure cycle, the primary external exchange of information is with suppliers (vendors). Within the organization, information flows to the expenditure cycle from the revenue and production cycles, inventory control, and various departments about the need to purchase goods and materials. Once the goods and materials arrive, notification of their receipt flows back to those sources from the expenditure cycle. Expense data also flow from the expenditure cycle to the general ledger and reporting function for inclusion in financial statements and various management reports.

The primary objective in the expenditure cycle is to minimize the total cost of acquiring and maintaining inventories, supplies, and the various services the organization needs to function. To accomplish such an objective, management must make the following key decisions:

- What is the optimal level of inventory and supplies to carry?
- Which suppliers provide the best quality and service at the best prices?
- Where should inventories and supplies be held?
- How can the organization consolidate purchases across units to obtain optimal prices?
- How can IT be used to improve both the efficiency and accuracy of the inbound logistics function?
- Is sufficient cash available to take advantage of any discounts suppliers offer?
- How can payments to vendors be managed to maximize cash flow?

Figure 11-1
Context Diagram of the
Expenditure Cycle

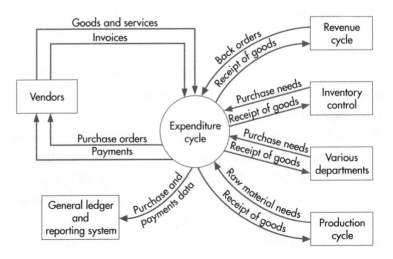

In addition, management must be able to monitor and evaluate the efficiency and effectiveness of expenditure cycle processes. That requires easy access to detailed data about the resources employed in the expenditure cycle, the events that affect those resources, and the agents who participate in those events. Moreover, to be useful and relevant for decision making, the data must be accurate, reliable, and timely.

This chapter examines the three basic functions of the AIS in the expenditure cycle: capturing and processing data about business activities, storing and organizing the data to support decision making, and providing controls to ensure the reliability of data and the safeguarding of organizational resources. We begin by describing the basic business activities performed in the expenditure cycle. Then we examine the methods used to collect, store, and process data about those activities. Next, we examine the major control objectives in the expenditure cycle and discuss how to design the AIS to mitigate the threats associated with those activities. We conclude the chapter by discussing how an AIS can enable management to make key decisions and effectively monitor performance.

Expenditure Cycle Business Activities

One function of the AIS is to support the effective performance of the organization's business activities by efficiently processing transaction data. Figure 11-2 shows the three basic business activities in the expenditure cycle:

1 Ordering goods, supplies, and services;
2 Receiving and storing goods, supplies, and services;
3 Paying for goods, supplies, and services.

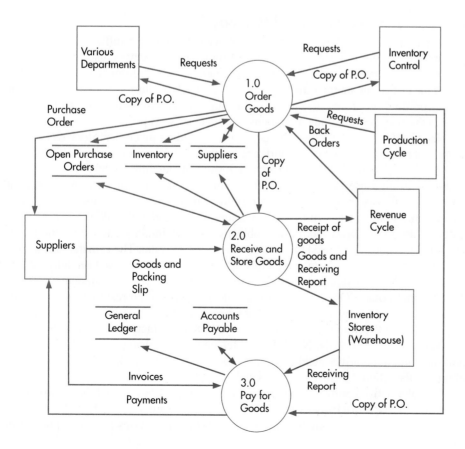

Figure 11-2
Level 0 Data Flow Diagram for the Expenditure Cycle

Notice that these activities in the expenditure cycle are mirror images of the basic activities performed in the revenue cycle:

- The order goods activity generates the purchase order that serves as the customer input to the sales order entry process.
- The receive goods activity handles the goods sent by the supplier's shipping function.
- The pay for goods activity generates the payments that are processed by the supplier's cash collection activity.

As we will see, these close linkages between the buyer's expenditure cycle activities and the seller's revenue cycle activities have important implications for AIS design. Specifically, by applying new IT developments to reengineer expenditure cycle activities, companies create opportunities for suppliers to reengineer their revenue cycle activities. Conversely, using IT to redesign a company's revenue cycle can create opportunities for customers to modify their own expenditure cycles. In many cases, the changes in one company's operations may *necessitate* changes in the AIS of other companies with which it does business. For example, the major automobile manufacturers and many large retailers, like Wal-Mart, require their suppliers to transmit invoices via EDI, or they will not do business with them.

Order Goods

The first major business activity in the expenditure cycle (circle 1.0 in Figure 11-2) is ordering inventory or supplies. The key decisions made in this initial step are identifying what, when, and how much to purchase, as well as identifying from which supplier to purchase. Weaknesses in the inventory control function can create significant problems, as the introductory AOE case demonstrated. Specifically, inaccurate inventory records caused AOE's inventory shortages at the Wichita plant that led to the failure to purchase needed components in a timely manner.

Alternative Inventory Control Methods

The traditional approach to managing inventory is to maintain sufficient stock so that production can continue without interruption even if inventory use is greater than expected or if suppliers are late in making deliveries. This traditional approach is often called the **economic order quantity (EOQ)** approach because it is based on calculating an optimal order size to minimize the sum of ordering, carrying, and stockout costs. *Ordering costs* include all expenses associated with processing purchase transactions. *Carrying costs* are those associated with holding inventory. *Stockout costs* are those that result from inventory shortages, such as lost sales or production delays.

Actual application of the EOQ approach varies depending on the type of item. For high-cost or high-use items, such as the computer chips and displays AOE uses, all three types of costs are included in the formula. For low-cost or low-usage items, such as the screws and springs AOE uses to assemble its products, ordering and carrying costs are usually ignored and the sole objective is to maintain sufficient inventory levels. The EOQ formula is used to calculate *how much* to order. The **reorder point** specifies *when* to order. Companies typically set the reorder point based on delivery time and desired levels of safety stock to handle unexpected fluctuations in demand.

The traditional EOQ approach to inventory control often results in carrying significant amounts of inventory. The money invested in carrying inventory earns nothing. Consequently, in recent years many large U.S. manufacturing companies, including Xerox, Ford, Motorola, NCR, Intel, McDonnell Douglas, and Delco Electronics, have adopted alternative methods of inventory control that seek to minimize or even eliminate the amount of inventory on hand.

One alternative approach to managing inventory is called **materials requirements planning (MRP)**. MRP seeks to reduce required inventory levels by improving the accuracy of forecasting techniques to better schedule purchases to satisfy production

needs. For example, the production planning department of a company using MRP would prepare a detailed schedule specifying the quantities of each finished product to manufacture in a specified time period, such as the next three months, based on sales forecast data. This schedule and the engineering specifications for each product identify the quantities of raw materials, parts, and supplies needed in production and the point in time when they will be needed. Thus, MRP systems reduce uncertainties about when raw materials are needed and therefore enable companies to carry less inventory.

A **just-in-time (JIT) inventory system** is another alternative approach to managing inventory. JIT systems attempt to minimize, if not totally eliminate, carrying inventory by only purchasing and producing goods in response to actual, rather than forecasted, sales. Therefore, JIT systems are characterized by frequent deliveries of small amounts of materials, parts, and supplies directly to the specific locations that require them when they are needed, rather than by infrequent bulk deliveries to a central receiving and storage facility. Thus, a factory using a JIT system will have multiple receiving docks, each assigned to accept deliveries of items needed at nearby work centers.

A major difference between MRP and JIT systems is production scheduling. MRP systems schedule production to meet forecasted sales, thereby creating a stock of finished goods inventory. JIT systems schedule production in response to customer demands, thereby virtually eliminating finished goods inventory. Both MRP and JIT systems can reduce costs and improve efficiency. Choosing between them depends, in part, on the types of products a company sells. MRP systems are more effectively used with products that have predictable patterns of demand, such as consumer staples. For such items, companies can plan purchases to minimize stockouts (with the resultant lost sales) while simultaneously minimizing the risk of overstocking and the subsequent costs of marking down or scrapping the excess inventory. In contrast, JIT inventory systems are especially useful for products that have relatively short life cycles and for which demand cannot be accurately predicted, such as toys associated with specific movies. In such cases, it is important to be able to quickly speed up production to meet unanticipated demand as well as to quickly stop production to avoid accumulating large inventories that must be marked down for clearance because the product is no longer in demand.

Purchase Requests

The request to purchase goods or supplies is triggered either by the inventory control function or by employees noticing a shortage of materials. The advanced inventory control systems used in large manufacturing companies, such as IBM and Ford, automatically generate purchase requests when the quantity of an item on hand falls below its reorder point. In small companies, however, the employees who use the items note when stock is running low and request that it be reordered. Moreover, even in large companies, office supplies such as copier paper and pencils are often ordered by the employees who use those items when they notice that stock is running low.

Regardless of its source, the need to purchase goods or supplies often results in the creation of a purchase requisition. The **purchase requisition** (Figure 11-3) is a document, or electronic form, that identifies the requisitioner; specifies the delivery location and date needed; identifies the item numbers, descriptions, quantity, and price of each item requested; and may suggest a supplier. The person approving the purchase requisition indicates the department number and account number to which the purchase should be charged.

Figure 11-4 shows a typical purchase requisition data entry screen used in ERP systems. As with sales order entry, both efficiency and accuracy are improved by minimizing the amount of data that must be manually entered. Thus, in Figure 11-4 the employee initiating the purchase request needs to complete only the supplier and ship-to fields in the header section (the shaded portion at the top of the screen) and the item number and quantity requested in the details section. The system then pulls up all the other relevant information from the related master files. It is also instructive to compare Figure 11-4 to Figure 10-6. Notice the similarity in overall design. This is intentional, in order to make it easier for employees to learn how to perform new job duties arising from promotions or transfers.

Figure 11-3
Sample AOE Purchase
Requisition (items in bold are
preprinted)

ALPHA OMEGA ELECTRONICS				
PURCHASE REQUISITION			No. 89010	
Date Prepared: 07/02/2009	**Prepared by:** Harold Brown *H B*		**Suggested Vendor:** Best Office Supply	
Deliver To: Copy Center		**Attention:** Harold Brown	**Date Needed:** 7/15/2009	

Item Number	Quantity	Description	Price/Unit
32047	15 boxes	Xerox 4200 paper, 20 wt., 10 ream box	$33.99
80170	5 boxes	Moore 2600 continuous form, 20 lb	$31.99
81756	20 boxes	CD cases, box of 10	$ 6.49
10407	100	700 MB CDs, 1 box	$19.99

Approved by: Susan Chen	Department: Admin. Services	Date Approved: 07/02/2009	Account No.: 91887

Generating Purchase Orders

Purchasing agents (sometimes called buyers) within the purchasing department usually perform the purchasing activity. In manufacturing companies such as AOE, the purchasing function is closely related to the production cycle. Consequently, Ryan McDaniel, the head of the purchasing department at AOE, reports directly to LeRoy Williams, the vice president of manufacturing. The crucial operating decision in the purchasing activity is selecting suppliers for inventory items. Several factors should be considered in making this decision:

- Price,
- Quality of materials,
- Dependability in making deliveries.

Figure 11-4
Purchase Requisition Data
Entry Screen

Copyright © 2004 PeopleSoft, Inc. All
rights reserved.

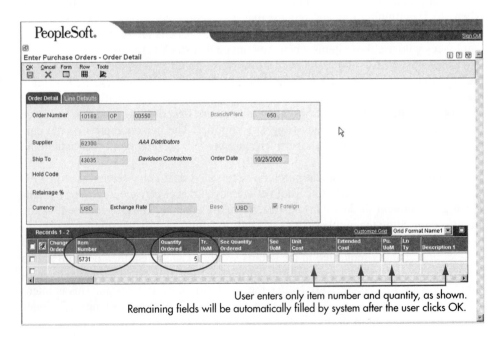

User enters only item number and quantity, as shown.
Remaining fields will be automatically filled by system after the user clicks OK.

In terms of quality and dependability, supplier reliability is important, especially to JIT systems, because a late delivery or defective parts can bring the entire system to a halt. Consequently, supplier certification is a key component of most JIT systems, and many companies require that their suppliers meet ISO 9000 quality standards.

Once a supplier has been selected for a product, the supplier's identity should become part of the product inventory master record to avoid repeating the supplier selection process for every subsequent order. (In some cases, however, such as for the purchase of high-cost and low-usage items, management may explicitly want to reevaluate all potential suppliers each time that product is ordered.) A list of potential alternative suppliers for each item should also be maintained, in case the primary supplier is out of stock of a needed item.

It is important to track and periodically evaluate supplier performance. Properly evaluating suppliers requires more than just maintaining data about purchase prices. Companies also incur costs, such as rework and scrap, related to the quality of the products purchased. There are also costs associated with supplier delivery performance. The AIS can be designed to capture and track this information. For example, AOE can measure the quality of a supplier's products by tracking how often its items fail to pass inspection in the receiving department. Data on the amount of production that had to be reworked or scrapped because of substandard materials also can be collected. AOE can measure supplier dependability by matching and tracking actual delivery dates versus those promised. Finally, to ensure that purchasing agents consider all these factors, the purchasing function should be evaluated and rewarded by how well it minimizes the total costs, not just the purchase price, of the items acquired.

A **purchase order** (Figure 11-5) is a document or electronic form that formally requests a supplier to sell and deliver specified products at designated prices. It is also a promise to pay and becomes a contract once the supplier accepts it. The purchase order includes the names of the supplier and purchasing agent, the order and requested delivery dates, the delivery location and shipping method, and information about the items ordered. Frequently, several purchase orders are generated to fill one purchase

Alpha Omega Electronics				**No. 2463**
Billing Address: **2431 Bradford Lane** **St. Louis, MO 63105–2311** **(314) 467-2341**			Reference the above number on all invoices and shipping documents	
PURCHASE ORDER				

To: Best Office Supply 4567 Olive Blvd. St. Louis, MO 63112–2345		**Ship To:** AOE, Inc. 1735 Sandy Dr. Dayton, OH 33421–2243		
Vendor Number: 121	**Order Date:** 07/03/2009	**Requisition Number:** 89010	**Buyer:** Fred Mozart	**Terms:** 1/10, n/30
F.O.B. Destination	**Ship Via:** Your choice	**Delivery Date:** 07/15/2009	**Remarks:**	

Item	**Item Number**	**Quantity**	**Description**	**Unit Price**
1	32047	15 boxes	Xerox 4200 paper, 20 wt., 10 ream box	$33.99
2	80170	5 boxes	Moore 2600 continuous form, 20 lb.	$31.99
3	81756	20 boxes	CD cases, box of 10	$ 6.49
4	10407	100	700 MB CDs, 1 box	$19.99

Approved by: *Susan Beethoven*

Figure 11-5
Sample AOE Purchase Order (items in bold are preprinted)

requisition, because different vendors may be the preferred suppliers for the various items requested. The quantity ordered may also differ from that requested, in order to take advantage of quantity discounts.

Many companies maintain special purchasing arrangements with important suppliers. One such arrangement is using blanket purchase orders. A **blanket purchase order** is a commitment to purchase specified items at designated prices from a particular supplier for a set time period, often one year. Blanket purchase orders reduce the buyer's uncertainty about reliable sources of raw materials and help the supplier plan its capacity and operations more effectively.

Improving Efficiency and Effectiveness

The major cost driver in the purchasing function is the number of purchase orders processed. Thus, finding ways to reduce the number of orders processed and to streamline the steps involved can yield significant savings. Using EDI is one way to improve the purchasing process. EDI reduces costs by eliminating the clerical work associated with printing and mailing paper documents. The time between recognizing the need to reorder an item and subsequently receiving it also is reduced. Consequently, the risk of running out of stock is diminished, which can significantly increase profitability. In the past, EDI was expensive because it required the use of proprietary third-party networks and software. However, the development of standards for EDI over the Internet (EDINT), such as AS2, which is a protocol that governs the secure electronic exchange of documents like purchase orders, has drastically cut the costs of EDI. By 2003 major companies like Wal-Mart and Albertson's had switched from proprietary EDI systems to EDINT and AS2 to exchange purchase orders with their suppliers.

Vendor-managed inventory programs provide another means of reducing purchase and inventory costs. Vendor-managed inventory essentially outsources much of the inventory control and purchasing function. Suppliers are given access to point-of-sales and inventory data and are authorized to automatically replenish inventory when stocks fall to predetermined reorder points. This arrangement cuts carrying costs by reducing the amount of inventory on hand and lowers processing costs by eliminating the need to generate and exchange formal purchase orders. To achieve these benefits, however, requires good controls to ensure the accuracy of inventory records. Focus 11-1 describes some common types of inventory errors.

Reverse auctions provide yet another technique to reduce purchasing-related expenses. In reverse auctions, suppliers compete with one another to meet demand at

11-1 FOCUS Why Inventory Data Is Often Inaccurate

When Britain's Defense Department began the task of merging three different inventory systems that contained 1.7 million records, each of which had more than 100 attributes, they found a number of inaccuracies. Some problems represented definite errors. For example, almost 10% of the part numbers in the various systems were invalid. One cause was failure to follow a standard numbering scheme, with the result that two different systems used the same part number to identify two different items. Correcting this problem required changing the part numbers stored in the system and manually relabeling the corresponding inventory items in the warehouse.

Other problems were more subtle, such as different systems using different units of measurement for the same item. For example, a military unit might track oil in 1-liter cans but the centralized procurement system might track oil in 250-liter drums. Even though neither measurement was "wrong," this inconsistency could create serious problems when units were requested to be resupplied. Correcting these and other types of data inaccuracies is not a trivial exercise. It requires the cooperation of various data owners in order to identify discrepancies and arrive at an appropriate solution. This takes time and costs money. The British Department of Defense has spent $11 million over four years to clean up its inventory data but estimates that the new system has helped save $36 million in purchasing and inventory management costs.

the lowest price. Although reverse auctions can yield significant cost savings, because the primary focus is on price, they are probably best suited to the purchase of commodity items rather than critical components for which quality, vendor reliability, and delivery performance are important.

One other way to reduce purchasing-related costs is to conduct a pre-award audit. Pre-award audits are typically used for large purchases that involve formal bids by suppliers. The internal auditor visits each potential supplier who has made the final cut in the contracting process to verify the accuracy of its bid. Pre-award audits often identify simple mathematical errors in complex pricing formulas and other discrepancies that, when corrected, can provide considerable savings.

EDI, vendor-managed inventory, reverse auctions, and pre-award audits are techniques for reducing the purchasing-related costs of raw materials and finished goods inventory. New IT developments can also change how companies account for their inventory. Traditionally, most companies have used the LIFO, FIFO, or weighted-average approaches to allocate costs to inventory and cost of goods sold. RFID, however, provides the capability to track individual inventory items. Thus, RFID makes it possible for companies to more accurately account for actual inventory-related costs by switching to the specific identification method for accounting for inventories.

Receive and Store Goods

The second major business activity in the expenditure cycle (circle 2.0 in Figure 11-2) is the receipt and storage of ordered items. The receiving department is responsible for accepting deliveries from suppliers. It usually reports to the warehouse manager, who in turn reports to the vice president of manufacturing. The inventory stores department, which also reports to the warehouse manager, is responsible for storage of the goods. Information about the receipt of ordered merchandise must be communicated to the inventory control function to update the inventory records.

Figure 11-6 shows that the receiving department has two major responsibilities: deciding whether to accept a delivery and verifying the quantity and quality of the goods delivered. The first decision is made based on information provided by the purchasing function: The existence of a valid purchase order indicates that the delivery should be accepted. This decision is important because the acceptance of unordered goods would result in wasted time and space in handling and storing those items until they can be returned. Verifying the quantity of goods delivered is important to ensure that the company pays only for usable goods actually received and that inventory records are accurately updated.

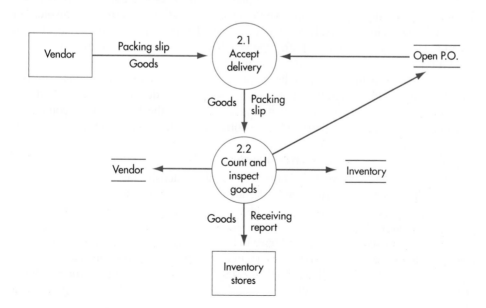

Figure 11-6
Level 1 DFD of the Receiving Function

Figure 11-7
Sample AOE Receiving Report
(items in bold are preprinted)

Alpha Omega Electronics		
RECEIVING REPORT		**No. 3113**
Vendor: Best Office Supply		**Date Received:** 07/13/2009
Shipped via: UPS		**Purchase Order Number:** 2463

Item Number	**Quantity**	**Description**
32047	15	Xerox 4200 paper, 20 wt., 10 ream box
80170	5	Moore 2600 continuous form, 20 lb.
81756	20	Box of CD cases, 10 per box
10407	100	700 MB CDs, 1 box of 100

Remarks:
Two boxes of Moore 2600 paper received with water damage on outside, but the paper appears to be okay

Received by: Nathan Hale	**Inspected by:** Nathan Hale	**Delivered to:** Harold Brown

The **receiving report** is the primary document used in the receiving subsystem of the expenditure cycle; it documents details about each delivery, including the date received, shipper, supplier, and purchase order number (see Figure 11-7 above). For each item received, it shows the item number, description, unit of measure, and quantity. It also contains space to identify the persons who received and inspected the goods as well as for remarks concerning the quality of the items received. A receiving report is typically not used to document the receipt of services, such as advertising and cleaning. Instead, receipt of such services is usually documented by supervisory approval of the supplier's invoice.

When a delivery arrives, a receiving clerk compares the purchase order number referenced on the supplier's packing slip with the open purchase order file to verify that the goods were ordered. The receiving clerk then counts the quantity of goods delivered. Before routing the inventory to the warehouse or factory, the receiving clerk also should examine each delivery for signs of obvious damage. The three possible exceptions to this process are (1) receiving a quantity of goods different from the amount ordered, (2) receiving damaged goods, or (3) receiving goods of inferior quality that fail inspection. In all three cases, the purchasing department must resolve the situation with the supplier. Usually the supplier will give the buyer permission to correct the invoice for any discrepancies in quantity. In the case of damaged or poor-quality goods, a document called a debit memo is prepared after the supplier agrees to take back the goods or to grant a price reduction. The **debit memo** records the adjustment being requested. One copy of the debit memo is sent to the supplier, who subsequently creates and returns a credit memo in acknowledgment. The accounts payable department is notified and adjusts the account balance owed to that supplier. A copy of the debit memo accompanies the goods to the shipping department to authorize their return to the supplier.

Improving Efficiency and Effectiveness

Counting and recording inventory deliveries is a labor-intensive task. One way for companies such as AOE to improve the efficiency of this process is to require suppliers to bar-code their products. Bar-coding enables receiving clerks to scan in the product number, description, and quantity of all items received, thereby virtually eliminating data entry errors. Although the goods still have to be manually inspected to ensure they meet quality standards, bar-code scanners can significantly reduce delivery processing time.

Radio frequency identification (RFID) tags can further streamline the receiving process. These RFID tags are attached to each crate of goods and emit a signal that a

receiving unit embedded in the gates near a company's warehouse unit can read. This saves time and reduces costs by eliminating the need to ensure that the items are positioned so as to be in the line of sight of reading devices. However, it costs more to RFID tag individual items than it does to bar-code them.

EDI and satellite technology provide another way to improve the efficiency of inbound logistics. EDI advance shipping notices inform companies when products have been shipped. By using shipping companies whose trucks are equipped with data terminals linked to satellites, it is possible to track the exact location of all incoming shipments and ensure that adequate staff will be there to unload the trucks. Truck drivers also can be directed to pull up to specific loading docks closest to the place where the goods will be used.

Finally, audits may identify opportunities to cut freight costs. For example, many companies have negotiated significant savings with specific carriers. The success of such arrangements depends on suppliers using the designated carriers. Periodic audits can verify this. Internal auditors should also verify the accuracy of freight bills and invoices to ensure that suppliers are not billing for transportation costs that they are supposed to pay.

Pay for Goods and Services

The third main activity in the expenditure cycle is paying vendors (circle 3.0 in Figure 11-2). Figure 11-8 (see below) shows that this involves two steps. The accounts payable department approves vendor invoices for payment. The cashier, who reports to the treasurer, is responsible for making the payment.

Approve Vendor Invoices for Payment

A legal obligation to pay suppliers arises at the time goods are received. For practical reasons, however, most companies record accounts payable only after receipt and approval of the supplier's invoice. This timing difference is usually not important for

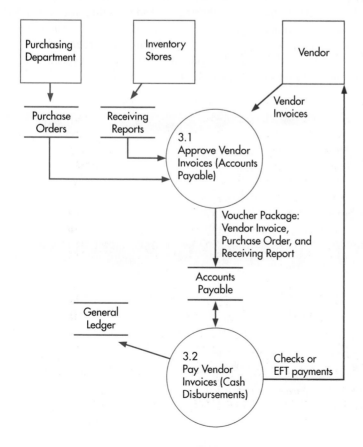

Figure 11-8
Level 1 data flow diagram of the pay for goods function

daily decision making, but it does require making appropriate adjusting entries to prepare accurate financial statements at the end of a fiscal period.

The objective of accounts payable is to authorize payment only for goods and services that were ordered and actually received. This requires internally generated information from both the purchasing and receiving functions. The existence of a valid purchase order indicates that the goods or services listed on the vendor invoice were actually ordered. The receiving report verifies that the goods were actually received.

There are two ways to process vendor invoices, referred to as nonvoucher or voucher systems. In a **nonvoucher system**, each approved invoice is posted to individual supplier records in the accounts payable file and is then stored in an open-invoice file. When a check is written to pay for an invoice, the invoice is removed from the open-invoice file, marked paid, and then stored in the paid-invoice file. In a **voucher system**, a document called a disbursement voucher is also prepared. The **disbursement voucher** (see Figure 11-9) identifies the supplier, lists the outstanding invoices, and indicates the net amount to be paid after deducting any applicable discounts and allowances. As illustrated in Figure 11-9, the employee enters the appropriate account numbers (e.g., for gross purchases, purchase discounts, returns and allowances, etc.) and the amount to be charged to each of those accounts.

Disbursement vouchers offer three advantages. First, they reduce the number of checks that need to be written, because several invoices may be included on one voucher. Second, because the disbursement voucher is an internally generated document, it can be prenumbered to simplify tracking all payables. Third, because the voucher provides an explicit record that a vendor invoice has been approved for payment, it facilitates separating the time of invoice approval from the time of invoice payment. This makes it easier to schedule both activities to maximize efficiency.

Pay Approved Invoices

The final activity in the expenditure cycle is the payment of approved invoices (circle 3.2 in Figure 11-8). The cashier, who reports to the treasurer, performs this activity, often referred to as the cash disbursements function. This segregates the custody function, performed by the cashier, from the authorization and recording functions, performed by the purchasing and accounts payable departments, respectively. The combination of a vendor invoice and supporting documentation (purchase order and receiving report) forms what is referred to as a **voucher package**. An approved voucher package authorizes disbursement of funds by check or EFT to suppliers.

Figure 11-9
Voucher Data Entry Screen

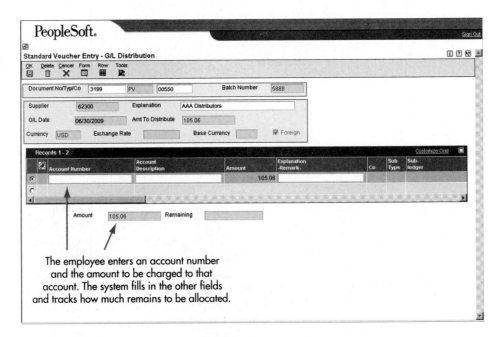

The employee enters an account number and the amount to be charged to that account. The system fills in the other fields and tracks how much remains to be allocated.

Improving Efficiency and Effectiveness

The accounts payable process, which matches vendor invoices to purchase orders and receiving reports, is a prime candidate for automation. Large global companies can process over a million vendor invoices each year. Processing efficiency can be improved by requiring suppliers to submit invoices electronically, by EDI, and having the system automatically match those invoices to the appropriate purchase orders and receiving reports. Only those vendor invoices that fail this matching process need be processed manually.

Another option is to eliminate vendor invoices. After all, for most recurring purchases, companies know the prices of goods and services at the time they are ordered. Thus, as soon as receipt of the goods or services is verified, all the information required to pay the supplier is already known. This "invoiceless" approach is called **evaluated receipt settlement (ERS)**. ERS replaces the traditional three-way matching process (vendor invoice, receiving report, and purchase order) with a two-way match of the purchase order and receiving report (see Figure 11-10 on the next page). ERS saves time and money by reducing the number of documents that need to be matched and, hence, the number of potential mismatches. In fact, ERS systems automate the two-way matching process and automatically generate payments; manual review is necessary only when there are discrepancies between the receiving report and purchase order. ERS also saves suppliers the time and expense of generating and tracking invoices. This is an example of how improvements in one company's expenditure cycle processes provide benefits to another company's revenue cycle processes.

ERS requires that suppliers quote accurate prices at the time orders are placed and that receiving dock employees accurately count and inspect merchandise received. Typically, ERS systems provide additional process improvements through timely communication: Suppliers electronically notify customers when shipments are coming, and buyers electronically acknowledge receipt of those shipments.

Noninventory purchases provide perhaps the biggest opportunity to improve the efficiency of accounts payable and cash disbursements. Noninventory purchases typically account for a large proportion of accounts payable transactions but represent a small proportion of the total dollar value of all purchases. For example, an AICPA-sponsored survey found that over 60% of all invoices processed by accounts payable departments were for amounts under $2,000. Procurement cards provide one way to eliminate the need for accounts payable to process many such small invoices. A **procurement card** is a corporate credit card that employees can use only at designated suppliers to purchase specific kinds of items. Spending limits can be set for each card. In addition, the account numbers on each procurement card can be mapped to specific general ledger accounts, such as office supplies. Procurement cards improve the accounts payable process by reducing the number of invoices that must be processed. They also simplify accounts payable because the company receives one monthly statement that summarizes noninventory purchases by account category. Procurement cards also improve the efficiency of the cash disbursement process because the company only has to make one payment for all noninventory purchases during a given time period, instead of making separate payments to various suppliers. Issuing corporate credit cards to employees who travel frequently further reduces the number of invoices that need to be processed. Procurement cards and corporate credit cards also improve the efficiency of cash disbursements because they replace the need to make individual payments for each purchase with one periodic payment to the card issuer.

It is important to take advantage of any discounts offered for prompt payment. A short-term cash flow budget is useful for making this decision. The report lists projected inflows and outflows of cash for a period of time, up to a year in advance. The information in this budget comes from a number of sources. Accounts receivable provides projections of future cash collections. The accounts payable and open purchase order files indicate the amount of current and pending commitments to suppliers, and the human resources function provides information about payroll needs. If the cash flow budget indicates that sufficient cash is available, discounts for prompt payment should be taken because they provide substantial savings. For example, a 1% discount for paying within 10 days, instead of 30 days, represents a savings of 18% annually.

Figure 11-10
Comparison of Traditional Three-way Match for Accounts Payable with Evaluated Receipt Settlement Approach (two-way match)

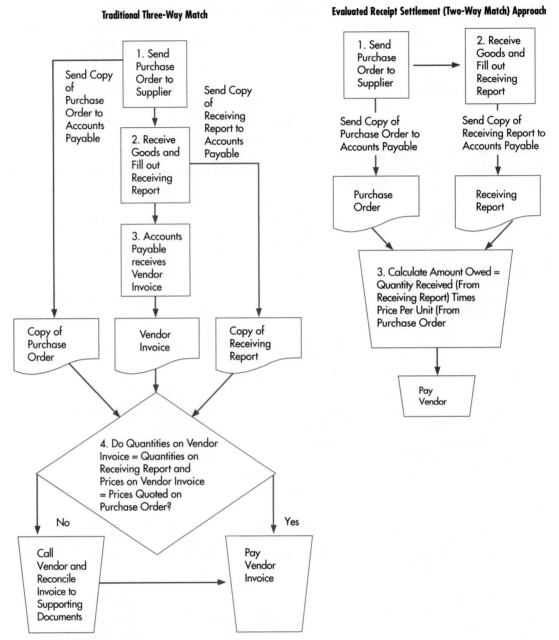

Finally, FEDI (financial data electronic interchange) can cut the costs associated with paying suppliers by eliminating the need to prepare and mail checks. FEDI also allows companies to manage more precisely the timing of cash outflows with less risk of missing due dates. The text's Web site contains a description of AOE's legacy expenditure cycle systems that were replaced by its ERP system.

Although most of the methods for improving the efficiency and effectiveness of Accounts Payable and Cash Disbursements that have been discussed involve using new IT developments, that is not always necessary. As Focus 11-2 shows, dramatic improvements can often be made simply by reengineering the process itself.

11-2 FOCUS
Applying Manufacturing Process Improvement Principles to Accounts Payable

Medtronic, Inc., a global medical technology company, is demonstrating that process improvement principles originally developed to improve manufacturing activities can also be successfully adopted to improve the finance function. Like many manufacturers, Medtronic had successfully used both Six Sigma and Lean principles to streamline its work-flow activities and improve product quality. Six Sigma is a philosophy that focuses on improving quality by reducing mistakes. Lean analysis seeks to improve efficiency by eliminating bottlenecks and redundancies. Medtronic decided to try to apply these same techniques to its finance function. The initial motivation for doing so was the insight that financial transactions, just like manufacturing a product, involved moving an item (e.g., a vendor invoice) through a sequence of steps.

Medtronic initiated a series of intensive 5-day projects, called kaizen, to apply Six Sigma and Lean principles to improve accounts payable. On day 1, a team consisting of Accounts Payable employees and manufacturing process improvement experts carefully study how vendor invoices were processed, beginning with the time when mail was first opened all the way through printing and mailing checks. On day 2, the team measured the time it took to perform each step of the process and the volume of transactions passing through each step. On days 3 and 4, the team diagrammed the physical flow of all Accounts Payable documentation. They then rearranged cubicles and desks, and added new wheeled carts and paper bins in order to slash the physical distance a vendor invoice traveled from 1,464 to 165 feet. They also modified the image-scanning process to be able to merge all vendor invoices (those for inventory purchases, with associated purchase orders, and those without purchase orders) into one queue. On day 5, the team walked the entire department through the reengineered workflow process.

Medtronic's application of process improvement techniques yielded a dramatic improvement in the efficiency and effectiveness of its Accounts Payable function:

- The time required to open the mail, sort, process, and record vendor invoices dropped from 3 days to 1 day
- The number of invoices for which discounts for prompt payment were taken increased by 15%
- Payment processing times were cut by 50%

It is important to note that these benefits were obtained with the same employees who had been working in Accounts Payable prior to the reengineering effort. This shows that when companies are seeking to improve results, they should focus first on fixing the process, rather than on replacing the people who perform it.

Information Processing Procedures

Several years ago, AOE, like many other organizations, replaced its existing AIS with an integrated ERP system. Figure 11-11 depicts the portion of AOE's new ERP system that supports its expenditure cycle activities.

The fundamental characteristics of AOE's new expenditure cycle system are the sharing of data between activities and the increased integration that results. Any department can submit a request to purchase items. Once a request has been approved, the system searches the inventory master file to identify the preferred supplier for that item. The system then creates a purchase order that is sent to the supplier via EDI. (If necessary, paper copies are printed and mailed.) The receiving department has access to the open purchase order file so that it can plan for and verify the validity of deliveries. Accounts payable is notified of orders so that it can plan for pending financial commitments. The department that generated the purchase requisition is also notified that its request has been set in motion.

Major suppliers send electronic notification of coming deliveries. When a shipment arrives, the receiving dock workers use the inquiry processing system to verify that an order is expected from that supplier. Most suppliers bar-code or RFID tag their products to facilitate the counting of the goods. Receiving dock workers also

Figure 11-11
Flowchart of AOE's Expenditure Cycle

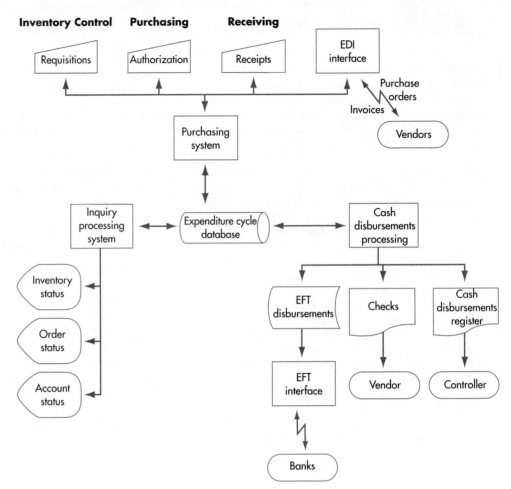

inspect the goods and use an online terminal to enter the inventory item numbers, count, and purchase order number. The exact time of the delivery also is recorded to help evaluate vendor performance. The system checks that data against the open purchase order file, and any discrepancies are immediately displayed on the screen and must be resolved.

Upon transfer of the goods to the warehouse, the inventory stores department verifies the count of the items placed into inventory and enters that data in the system. For vendors with whom ERS agreements exist, the system automatically schedules a payment according to the agreed-upon terms. Other vendors send EDI, and sometimes paper, invoices, which accounts payable clerks enter. Supplier invoices are compared with the information contained in the purchase order and receiving files to ensure accuracy and validity. For purchases of supplies or services that do not usually involve purchase orders and receiving reports, the invoice is sent to the appropriate supervisor for approval. The vendor invoice itself is also checked for mathematical accuracy. The vouchers (or approved invoices in a voucherless system) are then set up for payment by due date.

AOE, like most companies, uses batch processing to pay its suppliers. Each day, the treasurer uses the inquiry processing system to review the vouchers that are due and approves them for payment. AOE makes payments to some of its larger suppliers using FEDI but still prints paper checks for many of its smaller suppliers. When an EFT payment is authorized or a check is printed, the system updates the accounts payable, open-invoice, and general ledger files. For each supplier, the totals of all

vouchers are summed and that amount is subtracted from the balance field in that supplier's master file record. The relevant entries in the purchase order and receiving report files are flagged to mark that those transactions have been paid. The invoices that are paid are then deleted from the open-invoice file. A remittance advice is prepared for each supplier, which lists each invoice being paid and the amounts of any discounts or allowances taken. For payments made by EFT, the remittance data accompany the EFT payment as part of the FEDI package. For payments made by check, the remittance advice accompanies the signed check. After all disbursement transactions have been processed, the system generates a summary journal entry, debiting accounts payable and crediting cash, and posts that entry to the general ledger.

After reviewing checks against the voucher package, the cashier signs them. Checks above a specified amount also require the treasurer's signature. After signing them, the cashier then mails the checks and remittance advices to the suppliers. EFT transactions are also performed by the cashier and reviewed by the treasurer.

In summary, AOE's ERP system improves the efficiency and effectiveness of its expenditure cycle activities in the following ways:

1 The quantity of paper documents processed is reduced.
2 More timely and accurate information enables AOE to take advantage of discounts for prompt payment of vendor invoices.
3 Inventory records are more accurate and timely.
4 The warehouse and receiving departments can better plan activities.
5 The system compares data the receiving department entered to the purchase order file, thereby detecting and facilitating correction of any errors on a timely basis.
6 Reports and performance measures are timelier, which enhances management's ability to monitor and improve efficiency and effectiveness.

To fully appreciate these advantages of AOE's ERP system, compare the preceding discussion to the description of AOE's legacy expenditure cycle procedures (found on this book's web site). Realizing the benefits of an ERP system, however, presupposes that adequate controls exist to ensure that the information in the system is available, accurate, secure, and maintainable. The next section discusses applicable control procedures to achieve those objectives.

Control Objectives, Threats, and Procedures

Another function of a well-designed AIS is to provide adequate controls that meet the following objectives:

1 All transactions are properly authorized.
2 All recorded transactions are valid (actually occurred).
3 All valid, authorized transactions are recorded.
4 All transactions are recorded accurately.
5 Assets (cash, inventory, and data) are safeguarded from loss or theft.
6 Business activities are performed efficiently and effectively.

The documents and records described in the previous section play an important role in achieving these objectives. Simple, easy-to-complete documents with clear instructions facilitate the accurate and efficient recording of transaction data. Appropriate application controls, such as validity checks and field (format) checks, further increase the accuracy of data entry when using electronic documents. Providing space on paper and electronic documents to record who completed and who reviewed the form provides evidence that the transaction was properly authorized. Prenumbering all documents facilitates checking that all transactions have been recorded. Restricting access

to programs that create documents and to blank documents (if paper documents are still used) reduces the risk of unauthorized transactions.

Table 11-1 lists the major threats and exposures in the expenditure cycle and the applicable control procedures that should be in place to mitigate them. Every company, regardless of its line of business, faces these threats. Therefore, it is important to understand how the AIS can be designed to counter them. Our discussion will be organized around the stages of the expenditure cycle.

Order Goods

The primary objective of the purchasing process is to minimize costs associated with maintaining an adequate supply of all needed materials. The first six threats listed in Table 11-1 pertain to this objective.

Threat 1: Preventing Stockouts and/or Excess Inventory

Stockouts result in lost sales; excess inventory incurs higher than necessary carrying costs. To guard against these threats, companies need to establish an accurate inventory control system. The perpetual inventory method should be used to ensure that information about inventory stocks is always current. Companies should select suppliers that are known to meet their delivery commitments. Supplier performance reports that highlight deviations in product quality, prices, and delivery commitments should be regularly prepared. These reports should be reviewed periodically and new suppliers selected when a supplier's performance falls below acceptable levels.

Bar-code technology can improve the accuracy of perpetual inventory records by eliminating the need for human data entry. The effect on accuracy can be dramatic: Studies have found that even expert typists make one mistake for every 300 keystrokes. Bar-coding is not a panacea, however. Human error can still occur, especially when bar-code scanning is used to record the sale of assorted varieties of a product. For example, if you purchase 24 cans of store-brand soda at a grocery store, the clerk may scan only one can and then manually enter the number purchased. Since the flavors are all priced the same, the amount of the sale is correctly calculated. The perpetual inventory records will be incorrect, however, because the exact count of the flavors sold is not correctly recorded. Consequently, the grocery store may not be able to use POS data to maintain its perpetual inventory records, but must still rely on counting what is actually on the shelves. The inaccuracies in inventory records also reduce the effectiveness of vendor-managed inventory, because suppliers cannot trust the POS data to indicate when to replenish specific items. Thus, to reap the potential advantages from bar-code technology, companies must train employees to follow proper POS procedures, such as scanning every individual item being sold.

Affixing RFID tags to individual products would avoid the problems just discussed because the reader automatically record each item at the sales register. RFID technology is also more efficient than bar-codes, because there is no need for a human to align the bar-code on the product with the reader. However, RFID technology is more expensive than bar-coding.

Threat 2: Ordering Unnecessary Items

Companies must also beware of purchasing items that are not currently needed. Accurate perpetual inventory records ensure the validity of purchase requisitions that the inventory control system automatically generates. Supervisors should review and approve purchase requisitions that individual employees initiate.

A related problem is multiple purchases of the same item by different subunits of the organization. As a result, the organization may be carrying a larger inventory than desired and may fail to take advantage of volume discounts that might be available. This usually occurs because different subunits have different numbering systems for the parts they use. To overcome this problem, the AIS must be designed in a manner that facilitates integrating the databases of various subunits. Then reports linking item descriptions to part numbers can be produced.

Table 11-1
Threats and Controls in the Expenditure Cycle

Process/Activity	Threat	Applicable Control Procedures
Order goods	1. Preventing stockouts and/or excess inventory	Inventory control systems; perpetual inventory records; bar-code and RFID technology; periodic counts of inventory
	2. Ordering unnecessary items	Accurate perpetual inventory records; approval of purchase requisitions
	3. Purchasing goods at inflated prices	Price lists; soliciting competitive bids; use of approved suppliers; approval of purchase orders; budgetary controls
	4. Purchasing goods of inferior quality	Use of approved vendors; approval of purchase orders; monitoring vendor performance; budgetary controls
	5. Purchasing from unauthorized suppliers	Approval of purchase orders; restricting access to supplier master file; restrictions on procurement card usage
	6. Kickbacks	Policies against accepting gifts from vendors; training; job rotation; enforced vacations for purchasing agents; requiring purchasing employees to disclose financial interests in suppliers; supplier audits
Receive and store goods	7. Receiving unordered goods	Requiring receiving dock employees to verify existence of valid purchase order
	8. Making errors in counting goods received	Using bar-code and RFID technology; documenting employee performance; incentives for accurate counts
	9. Theft of inventory	Physical access controls; periodic counts of inventory and reconciliation of physical counts to records; documenting all transfers of inventory; proper segregation of duties
Approve and pay vendor invoices	10. Failing to catch errors in vendor invoices	Double-checking invoice accuracy; training of accounts payable staff; using ERS
	11. Paying for goods not received	Only paying invoices supported by original receiving report; using ERS; budgetary controls
	12. Failing to take available purchase discounts	Proper filing; cash flow budgets
	13. Paying the same invoice twice	Only paying invoices supported by original voucher package; cancellation of voucher package upon payment; using ERS; controlling access to supplier master file
	14. Recording and posting errors in accounts payable	Various data entry and processing edit controls discussed in Chapter 8; periodic reconciliation of accounts payable subsidiary accounts with General Ledger
	15. Misappropriating cash, checks, or EFTs	Restricting access to blank checks, check-signing machine, and EFT transfer terminals; segregation of duties of accounts payable and cashier; reconciliation of bank account by someone independent of cash disbursement process; check protection measures including Positive Pay; regular review of EFT transactions
General control issues	16. Loss, alteration, or unauthorized disclosure of data	File labels; backup and disaster recovery plans; physical and logical access controls; configuration of ERP systems to enforce proper segregation of duties; encryption; data transmission controls
	17. Performing poorly	Development and periodic review of appropriate performance reports

Threat 3: Purchasing Goods at Inflated Prices

The cost of purchased components represents a substantial portion of the total cost of many manufactured products. Therefore, companies strive to secure the best prices for the items they purchase. Several procedures can help ensure that companies do not pay too much for specific products. Price lists for frequently purchased items should be stored in the computer and consulted when ordering. The prices of many low-cost items can be readily determined from catalogs. Competitive, written bids should be solicited for high-cost and specialized products. Purchase orders should be reviewed to ensure that these policies have been followed.

Budgetary controls are also helpful in controlling expenses. Purchases should be charged to an account that is the responsibility of the person or department approving the requisition. Actual costs should be compared periodically with budget allowances. To facilitate control, these reports should highlight any significant deviations from budgeted amounts for further investigation (the principle of management by exception).

Threat 4: Purchasing Goods of Inferior Quality

In their quest to obtain the lowest possible prices, companies must beware of purchasing inferior-quality products. Substandard products can result in costly production delays. Moreover, the costs of scrap and rework often result in higher total production costs than if higher-quality, more expensive materials had been initially purchased. Through experience, buyers often learn which suppliers provide the best-quality goods at competitive prices. Such informal knowledge should be incorporated into formal control procedures so that it is not lost when a particular employee leaves the company. Establishing lists of approved suppliers known to provide goods of acceptable quality will achieve this goal. Purchase orders should be reviewed to ensure that only these approved suppliers are being used. In addition, supplier performance data should be collected and periodically reviewed to maintain the accuracy of these approved supplier lists. Finally, purchasing managers should be held responsible for the total cost of purchases, which includes not only the purchase price but also the quality-related costs of rework and scrap. Doing this requires the AIS to track the latter costs so that they can be allocated back to the purchasing department.

Threat 5: Purchasing from Unauthorized Suppliers

Purchasing from unauthorized suppliers can result in numerous problems. Items may be of inferior quality or overpriced. The purchase may even cause legal problems. Various government agencies, such as the Office of Foreign Assets Control and the Bureau of Industry and Security in the Department of Commerce, maintain lists of individuals and companies with whom it is illegal to transact business. Payments to entities on such lists can result in substantial fines and, sometimes, imprisonment. Consequently, all purchase orders should be reviewed to ensure that only approved suppliers are used. It is especially important to restrict access to the approved supplier list and to periodically review the list for any unauthorized changes. If procurement cards are used for minor purchases, the company should work with the card issuer to control which suppliers will accept the card.

Threat 6: Kickbacks

Kickbacks are gifts from suppliers to purchasing agents for the purpose of influencing their choice of suppliers. For the kickback to make economic sense, the supplier must find some way to recover the money spent on the bribe. This usually is accomplished by inflating the price of subsequent purchases or by substituting goods of inferior quality. Even if neither of these problems occurs, kickbacks impair the buyer's objectivity. Moreover, employees should not profit from performing their regular business duties.

To prevent kickbacks, companies should prohibit purchasing agents from accepting any gifts from potential or existing suppliers. (Trinkets that are clearly of inconsequential value may be allowed.) These policies should apply not only to the purchase of tangible goods, but also to services. For example, meeting planners should be informed that it is against company policy to accept frequent-traveler points from hotels for booking the company's meetings there. Training employees how to respond to unsolicited "gifts" from suppliers is also important, because many kickback schemes are initiated by unethical vendors sending such "tokens of appreciation," usually in the form of cash, to unwary employees. Once the employee accepts the gift, the supplier threatens to disclose the payment to a supervisor unless the employee makes additional purchases from that vendor.

Job rotation is also important: Purchasing agents should not deal with the same suppliers indefinitely, because that increases the risk that they may succumb to the constant temptations offered by an unethical vendor. If the organization is too small to rotate job duties across different purchasing agents, it should periodically conduct a detailed audit of the purchasing agent's activities. Purchasing agents should also be required to take their allotted vacation time each year, because many frauds are discovered when the perpetrator is absent and unable to continue covering up the illicit activity. Finally, purchasing agents should be required to sign annual conflict of interest statements, disclosing any financial interests they may have in current or potential suppliers.

Kickbacks are the most expensive form of employee corruption and are difficult to prevent, so detective controls are also necessary. Focus 11-3 discusses one particularly effective detection control: the supplier audit.

EDI-related Threats

Using EDI for purchase orders requires additional control procedures. Access to the EDI system should be controlled and limited to authorized personnel through the use of passwords, user IDs, access control matrices, and physical access controls. Procedures to verify and authenticate EDI transactions also are needed. Most EDI systems are programmed to send an acknowledgment for each transaction, which provides a rudimentary accuracy check. Further protection against transmission

11-3 FOCUS Supplier Audits: A Means to Control Purchasing

Supplier audits may be one of the best tools for assessing the effectiveness of expenditure cycle controls. A supplier audit entails visiting a supplier's office to check its records. It is designed to answer a number of questions: Who determines the business requirements for a good or service? How is the good or service consumed, and how is this documented? What is the procurement process, and how is the company assured that the best-quality goods or services were obtained at the best price? Did purchasing agents receive any gifts or favors?

The following list of red flags identify suppliers likely to represent potential problems:

1 A large percentage of the supplier's gross sales was to one company.
2 The supplier's pricing methods differ from standard industry practice.
3 The supplier does not own the equipment it rents to customers, but is itself renting that equipment from a third party.
4 Entertainment expenses are high in terms of a percentage of the supplier's gross sales.
5 The supplier submits altered or fictitious third-party invoices.
6 The supplier's address on its invoices is fictitious.

Supplier audits can yield substantial returns. One company recovered more than $250,000 for such failures as duplicate billings. Supplier audits also often uncover violations of the company's conflict of interest policy. Interestingly, many suppliers support the idea of supplier audits, because the process gives them a "good excuse" for not offering purchasing agents gifts or entertainment.

problems, which can result in the loss of orders, is provided by time-stamping and numbering all EDI transactions. Companies should maintain and periodically review a log of all EDI transactions to ensure that all have been processed and that established policies are being followed. Encryption can ensure the privacy of EDI transactions, which is especially important for competitive bids. Digital signatures should be used to ensure the authenticity of transactions.

Numerous policy-related threats also arise with EDI, each of which must be covered in the trading agreement. This is especially important when suppliers are linked to the purchasing company's POS system to automatically manage inventory. Examples of these types of issues include the following:

- At what point in the process can the order be canceled?
- Which party is responsible for the cost of return freight if contract terms are not followed?
- Which party is responsible for errors in bar-codes, RFID tags, and labels?
- What happens if errors in the purchasing company's POS system cause additional errors in the amount of goods that suppliers provide?
- Can suppliers ship more inventory than ordered if doing so reduces total freight costs by having a full, rather than partial, truckload?

Purchase of Services

Thus far, the discussion has centered on the purchase of inventory items. Different procedures are needed to control the purchase of services, such as painting or maintenance work. The major challenge in this area is establishing that the services were actually performed, which may be difficult. For example, visual inspection can indicate if a room has been painted; it does not reveal, however, if the walls were appropriately primed, unless the inspection was done during the painting process, which may not always be feasible.

One way to control the purchase of services is to hold the appropriate supervisor responsible for all such costs incurred by that department. The supervisor is required to acknowledge receipt of the services, and the related expenses are then charged to accounts for which he or she is responsible. Actual versus budgeted expenses should be routinely compared and any discrepancies investigated.

It is difficult to prevent fraudulent billing for services. Therefore, detective controls are also needed. One of the most effective techniques is for the internal audit function to periodically conduct detailed reviews of contracts for services, including audits of supplier records, as discussed in Focus 11-3.

Receive and Store Goods

The primary objectives of the receiving and storage function are to verify the receipt of ordered inventory and to safeguard it against loss or theft. Threats 7 through 9 in Table 11-1 apply to the receipt and storage of inventory.

Threat 7: Receiving Unordered Goods

Accepting delivery of unordered goods results in costs associated with unloading, storing, and later returning those items. The best control procedure to mitigate this threat is to instruct the receiving department to accept only deliveries for which there is an approved copy of the purchase order. Therefore, the receiving department needs access to the open purchase orders file.

Threat 8: Making Errors in Counting Goods Received

Accurate counting of goods received is crucial for maintaining accurate perpetual inventory records. It also ensures that the company pays only for goods actually received. As noted earlier, bar-coding and RFID technology can improve both the

efficiency and accuracy of receiving counts, although it is not foolproof. To encourage the receiving clerk to accurately count what was delivered, many companies design the inquiry processing system so that receiving-dock workers do not see the quantity ordered. (If paper documents are still used, the quantity-ordered field is blacked out on the receiving department's copy of the purchase order.) Nevertheless, the receiving clerk still knows the expected quantity of goods because suppliers usually include a packing slip with each order. Consequently, there is a temptation to do just a quick visual comparison of quantities received with those indicated on the packing slip, to quickly route the goods to where they are needed. Therefore, companies must clearly communicate to receiving clerks the importance of carefully and accurately counting all deliveries. An effective means of communication is to require receiving clerks not only to record the quantity received but also to sign the receiving report (or enter their employee ID numbers in the system). Such procedures indicate an assumption of responsibility, which usually results in more diligent work. Some companies also offer bonuses to receiving clerks for catching discrepancies between the packing slip and actual quantity received before the delivery person leaves. Additional control is provided by requiring the inventory control function, or the appropriate user department, to count the items transferred from receiving and then hold that department responsible for any subsequent shortages.

Threat 9: Theft of Inventory

Several control procedures can be used to safeguard inventory against loss. First, inventories should be stored in secure locations with restricted access. Second, all transfers of inventory within the company should be documented. For example, both the receiving department and the inventory stores department should acknowledge the transfer of goods from the receiving dock into inventory. Similarly, both the inventory stores and the production departments should acknowledge the release of inventory into production. This documentation provides the necessary information for establishing responsibility for any shortages, thereby encouraging employees to take special care to record all inventory movements accurately. Finally, it is important to periodically count the inventory on hand and to reconcile those counts with the inventory records.

One annual physical inventory count will generally not be sufficient to maintain accurate inventory records, especially for MRP and JIT systems. Instead, an ABC cost analysis should be used to classify items according to their importance: The most critical items (A items) should be counted most frequently, and the least critical items (C items) can be counted less often. If such interim counts reveal significant discrepancies with inventory records, a comprehensive count of all inventory should be immediately undertaken. This approach might have alerted management at AOE's Wichita plant in the chapter introductory case about shortages of key components early enough to avoid production delays.

Proper segregation of duties can further help minimize the risk of inventory theft. Employees who are responsible for controlling physical access to inventory should not be able to adjust inventory records without review and approval. Neither the employees responsible for custody of inventory nor those authorized to adjust inventory records should be responsible for the receiving or shipping functions.

Approve and Pay Vendor Invoices

The objective of approving and paying vendor invoices is to ensure that the company pays only for goods and services that were ordered and received. Organizations also need to safeguard cash. Threats 10 through 15 in Table 11-1 apply to these objectives.

Threat 10: Failing to Catch Errors in Vendor Invoices

Vendor invoices may contain errors such as discrepancies between quoted and actual prices charged or miscalculations of the total amount due. Consequently, the mathematical accuracy of vendor invoices must be verified and the prices and quantities

listed therein compared with those indicated on the purchase order and receiving report. For procurement card purchases, users should be required to keep receipts and verify the accuracy of the monthly statement. Adopting the ERS approach eliminates the potential for errors in vendor invoices because companies pay by matching counts of what they receive with prices quoted when the goods were ordered.

Even with ERS, freight expenses require special consideration because their complexity creates numerous opportunities for mistakes to occur. The best way to reduce freight-related threats is to provide the purchasing and accounts payable staffs with adequate training on transportation practices and terminology. For example, if the purchase contract says "full freight allowed," then the supplier is responsible for the freight costs. When the purchasing organization is responsible for freight expenses, using a designated carrier for all incoming shipments can reduce costs. The discounts will only be realized, however, if suppliers comply with requests to use that carrier. Therefore, an important detective control is to capture data on all incoming carriers, so that reports identifying suppliers who fail to comply with shipping instructions can be prepared.

Threat 11: Paying for Goods Not Received

The best control to prevent paying for goods not received is to compare the quantities indicated on the vendor invoice with the quantities entered by the inventory control person, who accepts the transfer of those goods from the receiving department. Again, the ERS approach ensures that the company pays only for goods actually received. In regard to services, budgetary controls and careful review of departmental expenses may indicate potential problems that need investigation.

Threat 12: Failing to Take Available Purchase Discounts

Failure to take advantage of purchase discounts costs money. Proper filing can significantly reduce the risk of this threat. Approved invoices should be filed by due date, and the system should be designed to track invoice due dates and print a periodic list of all outstanding invoices. A cash flow budget that indicates expected cash inflows and outstanding commitments also can help companies plan to utilize available purchase discounts.

Threat 13: Paying the Same Invoice Twice

The same invoice can be submitted for payment more than once for a variety of reasons. It may be a duplicate invoice that was sent after the company's check was already in the mail, or it may have become separated from the other documents in the voucher package. Although paying invoices a second time is usually detected by the supplier and results in a credit to the company's account, it can affect a company's cash flow needs. In addition, the financial records will be incorrect, at least until the duplicate payment is detected.

Several control procedures can mitigate this threat. First, invoices should be approved for payment only when accompanied by a complete voucher package (purchase order and receiving report). Second, only the original copy of an invoice should be paid. Most duplicate invoices that suppliers send clearly indicate that they are not originals. Payment should never be authorized for a photocopy of an invoice. Third, when the check to pay for an invoice is signed, the invoice and the voucher package should be canceled (marked "paid") in a manner that would prevent their resubmission. Although ERS eliminates vendor invoices entirely, it is still important to mark all receiving reports as paid to avoid duplicate payments.

Automating and streamlining accounts payable is not a panacea, however. Automated systems do eliminate most clerical errors associated with processing invoices, and invoiceless accounts payable systems cut costs and improve efficiency. Yet, computers can catch only the types of errors that they have been programmed to identify, whereas vendor invoices involve an infinite number of errors. In addition, unscrupulous suppliers continually devise ways to fool automated accounts payable systems. Therefore, companies must use detective controls to minimize the risk of overpayments to suppliers. Either

internal auditors or a consulting firm that specializes in helping companies to detect and recover overpayments to suppliers can do such investigative work.

Finally, in invoiceless accounts payable systems, it is important to control access to the supplier master file and monitor all changes made to it because the supplier master file now contains information about the prices of the various items being purchased. Upon entry of data about the quantity of goods received, the system uses those prices to establish the amount to be paid to suppliers. Thus, unauthorized changes to those prices can result in overpayments to suppliers.

Threat 14: Recording and Posting Errors in Accounts Payable

Errors in recording and posting payments to suppliers will result in additional errors in financial and performance reports that, in turn, can contribute to poor decision making. Various data entry and processing controls that were discussed in Chapter 8 are necessary to prevent these types of problems. One such control is comparing the difference in supplier account balances before and after processing checks with the total amount of invoices processed. The total of all supplier account balances (or unpaid vouchers, whichever exists) also should be reconciled periodically with the amount of the accounts payable control account in the general ledger.

Threat 15: Misappropriating Cash, Checks, or EFTs

Because cash is the easiest asset to steal, access to cash and blank checks should be restricted. Checks should be sequentially numbered and periodically accounted for by the cashier. Access to a check-signing machine should be restricted as well.

Fraudulent disbursements, particularly the issuance of checks to fictitious suppliers, are a common type of fraud. Proper segregation of duties can significantly reduce the risk of this threat. The accounts payable function should authorize payment, including the assembling of a voucher package; however, only the treasurer or cashier should sign checks. Checks in excess of a certain amount, such as $5,000 to $10,000, should require two signatures, thereby providing yet another independent review of the expenditure. Finally, access to the approved supplier list should be restricted and any changes to that list should be carefully reviewed and approved. In addition, internal auditors should periodically review the supplier master file to ensure that there are no duplicate entries for suppliers. Many companies who have done this have discovered that, over time, there may be three or four entries for the same supplier, each with a slightly different spelling. For example, the same supplier may be listed twice, once as AZBest Ltd. and another time as AZBest Limited.

To ensure that checks are sent to the intended recipients, the cashier should mail the signed checks rather than return them to accounts payable. The cashier also should cancel all documents in the voucher package to prevent their being resubmitted to support another disbursement. Finally, someone who did not participate in processing either cash collections or disbursements should reconcile all bank accounts. This control provides an independent check on accuracy and prevents someone from misappropriating cash and then concealing the theft by adjusting the bank statement.

Check alteration and forgery are also major problems. Check-protection machines can reduce the risk of this threat by imprinting the amount in distinctive colors, typically a combination of red and blue ink. Using special inks that change colors if altered and printing checks on special papers that contain watermarks can further reduce the probability of alteration. Many banks also provide special services to help protect companies against fraudulent checks. One such service, called Positive Pay, involves sending a daily list of all legitimate checks to the bank, which will then clear only checks appearing on that list. Finally, bank reconciliations are an important detective control for identifying check fraud. If done in a timely manner, they facilitate recovery from banks. Indeed, many banks will cover bad-check losses only if a company notifies them promptly of any such checks it discovers.

When possible, expenditures should be made by check or EFT. Nevertheless, it is often more convenient to pay for minor purchases, such as coffee or pencils, in cash.

A petty cash fund, managed by an employee who has no other cash-handling or accounting responsibilities, should be established to handle such expenditures. The petty cash fund should be set up as an imprest fund. An **imprest fund** has two characteristics: It is set at a fixed amount, such as $100, and it requires vouchers for every disbursement. At all times, the sum of cash plus vouchers should equal the preset fund balance. When the fund balance gets low, the vouchers are presented to accounts payable for replenishment. After accounts payable authorizes this transaction, the cashier then writes a check to restore the petty cash fund to its designated level. As with the supporting documents used for regular purchases, the vouchers used to support replenishment of the petty cash fund should be canceled at the time the fund is restored to its preset level.

The operation of an imprest petty cash fund technically violates the principle of segregation of duties, because the same person who has custody of the cash also authorizes disbursements from the fund and maintains a record of the fund balance. The threat of misappropriation is more than offset, however, by the convenience of not having to process small miscellaneous purchases through the normal expenditure cycle. Moreover, the risk of misappropriation can be mitigated by having the internal auditor make periodic unannounced counts of the fund balance and vouchers and by holding the person in charge of the petty cash fund responsible for any shortages discovered during those surprise audits.

Electronic funds transfer (either by itself or as part of FEDI) requires additional control procedures. Strict access controls over all outgoing EFT transactions are important. Passwords and user IDs should be used to specifically identify and monitor each employee authorized to initiate EFT transactions. The location of the originating terminal should also be recorded. EFT transactions above a certain threshold should require real-time supervisory approval. There should also be limits on the total dollar amount of transactions allowed per day per individual. All EFT transmissions should be encrypted to prevent alteration. In addition, all EFT transactions should be time-stamped and numbered to facilitate subsequent reconciliation. A control group should be established and given responsibility for monitoring EFT transactions for validity and accuracy and maintaining the adequacy of the controls outlined here. Special programs, called *embedded audit modules*, can be designed into the system to monitor all transactions and identify any that possess specific characteristics. A report of those flagged transactions then can be given to management for review and, if necessary, more detailed investigation. Finally, companies should consider placing ACH blocks, which instruct banks to not allow ACH debits (outflows) from specific accounts. For example, if a company makes all payments to its suppliers only from its main operating checking account, it may wish to instruct the bank to block all ACH debits from any of its other bank accounts.

General Control Issues

Two general objectives pertaining to all expenditure cycle activities are that accurate data be available when needed and that all activities be performed efficiently and effectively. Threats 16 and 17 in Table 11-1 are general threats that affect all phases of the expenditure cycle.

Threat 16: Loss, Alteration, or Unauthorized Disclosure of Data

Data about pending cash disbursement obligations and open orders must be safeguarded from loss or corruption. Both external and internal file labels should be used to reduce the possibility of accidentally erasing important files and to ensure that the most recent version of the master file is being updated. In addition, the purchases, receipts, master accounts payable, and cash disbursements files should be backed up regularly. Two backup copies should be made, one to be stored on-site and the other off-site. These backups should include not only the current and previous versions of the master file but also the most recent transaction file.

Access controls are also important. A system of passwords and user IDs can limit employee access to various files. For example, only the cashier should be able to alter

the field indicating if an invoice has been paid. Access controls also should exist for individual terminals. For example, the system should be programmed to accept approval of invoices only from terminals located in the accounts payable department. When image processing is used, access controls are extremely important to prevent alteration of the source document.

It is important to point out that enforcing proper access controls and segregation of duties requires that the controller or CFO review and suggest appropriate configuration of user rights in integrated AIS packages and ERP systems. The default installation of such systems typically provides every user with far too much power. For example, consider the situation where an accounts payable clerk types in the name of a supplier who is not currently on the list of approved vendors. The default configurations of most integrated AIS packages and ERP systems would respond by asking whether the clerk wants to create a new supplier record. This violates segregation of duties by permitting the person who does the recording (accounts payable) to also authorize the creation of new accounts. Similarly, the default configurations of many systems permit accounts payable staff to not only read the prices of various products and current supplier account balances but also to change the values of those data items. These examples are just some of the many areas that the controller or CFO needs to review to ensure that various users are assigned only those privileges necessary to perform their specified job duties. Properly configuring an ERP system requires both sound understanding of proper segregation of duties for different business processes and knowledge of the default manner in which those processes are configured in a particular ERP system.

Access and processing integrity controls are also needed to ensure the confidentiality and accuracy of expenditure cycle data transmissions. Sensitive data, such as purchase prices and special discounts offered by preferred suppliers, should be encrypted both while in storage and during transmission over the Internet. One way to do this is to establish VPNs with major trading partners. Parity checks and acknowledgment messages should also be used to ensure the accuracy of data transmissions. In addition, various control totals, such as the total amount of purchases or payments plus record counts indicating the number of individual purchase or payment transactions about which information is being sent, should be used to verify the accuracy of information exchanged between various offices.

Threat 17: Performing Poorly

In addition to ensuring accuracy and safeguarding assets, another objective of internal controls in the expenditure cycle is to encourage efficient and effective performance of business activities. The preparation and review of performance reports is effective in achieving this objective. The next section discusses some of the key expenditure cycle decisions and the information that the AIS must provide to enable management to make optimal choices.

Expenditure Cycle Information Needs

A third function of the AIS is to provide information useful for decision making. This means that an organization's AIS must provide the operational information needed to perform the following expenditure cycle functions:

- Determine when and how much additional inventory to order.
- Select the appropriate suppliers from whom to order.
- Verify the accuracy of vendor invoices.
- Decide if purchase discounts should be taken.
- Monitor cash flow needs to pay outstanding obligations.

In addition, the AIS must provide the following strategic and performance evaluation information:

- Efficiency and effectiveness of the purchasing department.
- Analyses of supplier performance such as on-time delivery and quality.
- Time taken to move goods from the receiving dock into production.
- Percentage of purchase discounts taken.

Notice that these decisions require both financial and operating data. For example, supplier selection should consider not only price but also information about supplier performance in meeting delivery dates and quality of goods. Traditionally, the AIS has provided the financial information needed to make expenditure cycle decisions, and other information systems have generated the operating data about expenditure cycle activities. One problem with using separate information systems, however, is that the two sets of resulting data may be inconsistent. For example, many companies are not aware that different subunits may be purchasing the same items because each unit uses a slightly different name and part number for those items. Consequently, the organization as a whole may be failing to take advantage of potential discounts for volume purchases. Moreover, the existence of multiple, overlapping systems increases costs and reduces efficiency of the systems function. Many expenditure cycle decisions also require externally generated information. For example, data about supplier financial characteristics may be useful in selecting stable suppliers that are likely to meet future commitments. A well-designed AIS facilitates the integration of such externally generated information with internally generated financial and operating data about expenditure cycle activities.

The potential number of performance reports that can be developed to monitor expenditure cycle activities is limited only by the controller's ingenuity. Several have already been discussed in this chapter, such as reports on supplier performance and lists of outstanding invoices. Other useful reports would monitor the performance of expenditure cycle employees. Examples include the number of purchase orders processed by each purchasing agent, the number of vendor invoices processed by each accounts payable clerk, the number of incoming deliveries handled by each receiving department employee, and the number of inventory transfers performed by each warehouse worker.

Because inventory represents a sizable investment of working capital, reports that help manage inventory are especially valuable. A key measure to evaluate inventory management is inventory turnover, which is the ratio of cost of goods sold divided by inventory on hand. Consider the following example: annual sales of $500 million and annual cost of goods sold of $360 million. An inventory turnover ratio of 1 means that the company is effectively carrying a year's supply of inventory, tying up $360 million. Improving the inventory turnover ratio to 3 would reduce that unprofitable investment to $120 million, thereby freeing up $240 million that could be used for other purposes.

Accountants should design other reports to help management better manage inventory. For example, it is useful to monitor the percentage of requisitions that are filled from inventory on hand. For critical items, this should be close to 100% to avoid stockouts and delays in filling customer orders. For most items, however, such a high fill rate is undesirable because it requires carrying too much inventory. Other reports can help management identify the relative importance of various inventory items. For example, it may be useful to classify items along several dimensions, such as frequency of purchase, frequency of use or resale, and contribution to profitability. Items that are frequently purchased and used and that make a significant contribution to profitability are of high importance and should be managed so as to maintain high fill rates. In contrast, management may wish to consider eliminating items that are seldom purchased, infrequently used, and that do not contribute much to profitability.

Accountants can add great value to an organization by continually looking for innovative ways to measure inventory management. Doing so can help to avoid the problems AOE encountered.

SUMMARY AND CASE CONCLUSION

The basic business activities performed in the expenditure cycle include the following:

- Ordering goods from suppliers,
- Receiving goods from suppliers,
- Approving vendor invoices for payment and paying for goods and services.

The efficiency and effectiveness of these activities can significantly affect a company's overall performance. For example, deficiencies in requesting and ordering necessary inventory and supplies can create production bottlenecks and result in lost sales due to stockouts of popular items. Problems in the procedures related to receiving and storing inventory can result in a company's paying for items it never received, accepting delivery and incurring storage costs for unordered items, and experiencing a theft of inventory. Problems in approving vendor invoices for payment can result in overpaying suppliers or failing to take available discounts for prompt payment. Weaknesses in the cash disbursement process can result in the misappropriation of cash.

IT can help improve the efficiency and effectiveness with which expenditure cycle activities are performed. In particular, EDI, bar-coding, RFID, and EFT can significantly reduce the time and costs associated with ordering, receiving, and paying for goods. In addition, a well-designed AIS can allow for the integration of internally generated financial and operating data with externally generated information so that all three types of data can be considered when making important operating and strategic decisions. Finally, proper control procedures, especially segregation of duties, are needed to mitigate various threats such as errors in performing expenditure cycle activities and the theft of inventory or cash.

At the next executive meeting, Ann Brandt and Elizabeth Venko presented their recommendations for improving AOE's expenditure cycle business activities to Linda Spurgeon. Ann indicates LeRoy Williams's plan to conduct more frequent physical counts of key raw materials components will increase the accuracy of the database and reduce the likelihood of future stockouts at the Wichita plant. She also designed a query to produce a daily supplier performance report that will highlight any negative trends before they become the types of problems that disrupted production at the Dayton plant. Ann also indicated that it would be possible to link AOE's inventory and production planning systems with major suppliers to better manage AOE's inventory levels.

Elizabeth Venko stated that she was working to increase the number of suppliers who either bar-code or RFID tag their shipments. This would not only improve both the efficiency and accuracy of the receiving process but also the accuracy of AOE's inventory records, thereby providing possible additional reductions in inventory carrying costs. In addition, Elizabeth wants to encourage more suppliers to either send invoices via EDI or agree to ERS, which should improve the efficiency and accuracy of processing invoices and reduce the costs associated with handling and storing paper invoices. Concurrently, Elizabeth plans to increase EFT as much as possible to further streamline the cash disbursements process and reduce the costs associated with processing payments by check.

KEY TERMS

expenditure cycle 440
economic order quantity
 (EOQ) 442

reorder point 442
materials requirements
 planning (MRP) 442

just-in-time (JIT)
 inventory system 443
purchase requisition 443

AIS IN ACTION

CHAPTER QUIZ

1. Which of the following inventory control methods is most likely to be used for a product like lumber (1 × 2s, 2 × 4s, etc.)
 a. JIT
 b. EOQ
 c. MRP
 d. ABC

2. Which of the following matches is performed in evaluated receipt settlement (ERS)?
 a. the vendor invoice with the receiving report
 b. the purchase order with the receiving report
 c. the vendor invoice with the purchase order
 d. the vendor invoice, the receiving report, and the purchase order

3. Which of the following is true?
 a. ERS systems use disbursement vouchers.
 b. Setting up petty cash as an imprest fund violates segregation of duties.
 c. The EOQ formula is used to identify the reorder point.
 d. A voucher package usually includes a debit memo.

4. Which document is used to establish a contract for the purchase of goods or services from a supplier?
 a. vendor invoice
 b. purchase requisition
 c. purchase order
 d. disbursement voucher

5. Which method would provide the greatest efficiency improvements for the purchase of noninventory items such as miscellaneous office supplies?
 a. bar-coding
 b. EDI
 c. procurement cards
 d. EFT

6. Which of the following expenditure cycle activities can be eliminated through the use of IT or reengineering?
 a. ordering goods
 b. approving vendor invoices
 c. receiving goods
 d. cash disbursements

7. What is the best control procedure to prevent paying the same invoice twice?
 a. Segregate check-preparation and check-signing functions.
 b. Prepare checks only for invoices that have been matched to receiving reports and purchase orders.
 c. Require two signatures on all checks above a certain limit.
 d. Cancel all supporting documents when the check is signed.

8. For good internal control, who should sign checks?
 a. cashier
 b. accounts payable
 c. purchasing agent
 d. controller

9 Which of the following procedures is designed to prevent the purchasing agent from receiving kickbacks?
 a. maintaining a list of approved suppliers and requiring all purchases to be made from suppliers on that list
 b. requiring purchasing agents to disclose any financial investments in potential suppliers
 c. requiring approval of all purchase orders
 d. prenumbering and periodically accounting for all purchase orders

10 Which document is used to record adjustments to accounts payable based on the return of unacceptable inventory to the supplier?
 a. receiving report c. debit memo
 b. credit memo d. purchase order

DISCUSSION QUESTIONS

11.1 In this chapter and in Chapter 10, the controller of AOE played a major role in evaluating and recommending ways to use IT to improve efficiency and effectiveness. Should the company's chief information officer make these decisions instead? Should the controller be involved in making these types of decisions? Why or why not?

11.2 Companies such as Wal-Mart have moved beyond JIT to VMI systems. Discuss the potential advantages and disadvantages of this arrangement. What special controls, if any, should be developed to monitor VMI systems?

11.3 Procurement cards are designed to improve the efficiency of small noninventory purchases. What controls should be placed on their use? Why?

11.4 In what ways can you apply the control procedures discussed in this chapter to paying personal debts (e.g., credit card bills)?

11.5 How can innovative uses of IT to perform expenditure cycle activities also be used to improve the efficiency and effectiveness of suppliers' revenue cycle activities? Why might a company wish to help their suppliers in this way?

11.6 Are there any limits to how little inventory a company should carry? Is it possible to entirely eliminate all inventories?

11.7 Should companies allow purchasing agents to start their own businesses that produce goods the company frequently purchases? Why? Would you change your answer if the purchasing agent's company was rated by an independent service, like Consumer Reports, as providing the best value for price? Why?

PROBLEMS

11.1 Which internal control procedure would be most cost-effective in dealing with the following expenditure cycle threats?
 a. A purchasing agent orders materials from a supplier that he partially owns.
 b. Receiving-dock personnel steal inventory and then claim the inventory was sent to the warehouse.

c. An unordered supply of laser printer paper delivered to the office is accepted and paid for because the "price is right." After jamming all of the laser printers, however, it becomes obvious that the "bargain" paper is of inferior quality.

d. The company fails to take advantage of a 1% discount for promptly paying a vendor invoice.

e. A company is late in paying a particular invoice. Consequently, a second invoice is sent, which crosses the first invoice's payment in the mail. The second invoice is submitted for processing and also paid.

f. Inventory records show that an adequate supply of copy paper should be in stock, but none is available on the supply shelf.

g. The inventory records are incorrectly updated when a receiving-dock employee enters the wrong product number at the terminal.

h. A clerical employee obtains a blank check and writes a large amount payable to a fictitious company. The employee then cashes the check.

i. A fictitious invoice is received and a check is issued to pay for goods that were never ordered or delivered.

j. The petty cash custodian confesses to having "borrowed" $12,000 over the last five years.

k. A purchasing agent adds a new record to the supplier master file. The company does not exist. Subsequently, the purchasing agent submits invoices from the fake company for various cleaning services. The invoices are paid.

l. A clerk affixes a price tag intended for a low-end flat panel TV to a top-of-the-line model. The clerk's friend then purchases that item, which the clerk scans at the checkout counter.

11.2 The following documents are used in the expenditure cycle:
Vendor invoice
Purchase order
Disbursement voucher
Purchase requisition
Packing slip
Receiving report
Check

Required

a. Identify which of these documents are internally generated and which are externally generated.

b. For each internally generated document, how many copies are needed? What is the purpose of each copy? Where does each copy go?

c. Describe the application controls that should be in place if each of these paper documents were replaced by electronic forms.

11.3 EXCEL PROJECT. This project demonstrates how Excel can be used to create a variety of useful documents for small businesses.

a. Read the article "A Do-It-Yourself Automated Invoicing System," by Jacob M. Rose, which appeared in the April 2004 issue of the *Journal of Accountancy*. A copy of the article can be downloaded from the *Journal's* archives at the AICPA's Web site (www.aicpa.org).

b. Adapt the steps described in the article to create a Purchase Order instead of a sales invoice.

c. Add appropriate input edit controls to ensure compliance with the following objectives. Your controls should display an informative error message that clearly explains the problem:
1. All product numbers should fall within the range 101–999.
2. Purchases cannot exceed 1,000 units for any item.

11.4 Modify Table 11-1 by indicating if each specific control procedure listed there is preventive (P), detective (D), or corrective (C) in nature.

11.5 Use Table 11-1 to create a questionnaire checklist that can be used to evaluate controls for each of the three basic activities in the expenditure cycle (ordering goods, receiving, and cash disbursements).

Required

 a. For each control issue, write a Yes/No question such that a "No" answer represents a control weakness. For example, one question might be "Are supporting documents, such as purchase orders and receiving reports, marked "paid" when a check is issued to the vendor?" .

 b. For each Yes/No question, write a brief explanation of why a "No" answer represents a control weakness.

11.6 EXCEL PROJECT

 a. Expand the cash budget you created in Problem 10.4 to include a row for expected cash outflows equal to 77% of the current month's sales.

 b. Also add a row to calculate the amount of cash that needs to be borrowed, in order to maintain a minimum cash balance of $50,000 at the end of each month.

 c. Add another row to show the cash inflow from borrowing.

 d. Add another row to show the cumulative amount borrowed.

 e. Add another row to show the amount of the loan that can be repaid, being sure to maintain a minimum ending balance of $50,000 each month.

 f. Add appropriate data validation controls to ensure spreadsheet accuracy.

11.7 The receiving department at Culp Electronics Company processes inventory deliveries upon arrival by means of online data terminals located on the receiving dock. Each inventory receipt entered into the system is processed to update both the inventory master file and the open purchase order file. The system then automatically generates a voucher to authorize a cash disbursement for each receipt.

Required

 a. What items of data should receiving department employees enter?

 b. Describe several application controls (refer to Chapter 8) that should be programmed into the system to check the accuracy and validity of the data the receiving department employees enter. Relate your answer specifically to the data items mentioned in part a.

11.8 The following list identifies several important control features. For each control, (1) describe its purpose and (2) explain how it could be best implemented in an integrated ERP system.

 a. Cancellation of the voucher package by the cashier after signing the check

 b. Separation of duties of approving invoices for payment and signing checks

 c. Prenumbering and periodically accounting for all purchase orders

 d. Periodic physical count of inventory

 e. Requiring two signatures on checks for large amounts

 f. Requiring that a copy of the receiving report be routed through the inventory stores department prior to going to accounts payable

 g. Requiring a regular reconciliation of the bank account by someone other than the person responsible for writing checks

 h. Maintaining an approved supplier list and checking that all purchase orders are issued only to suppliers on that list

11.9 The systems flowchart presented in Figure 11-12 and the following description summarize ConSport Corporation's cash disbursements system:

 a. The accounts payable department approves all invoices for payment by matching them with the related purchase requisitions, purchase orders, and receiving reports. The accounts payable clerks focus on matching the supplier names on all documents and skim the remaining information.

 b. The supplier file is searched daily for the disbursement vouchers of invoices due to be paid. Both copies of these vouchers are sent to the finance department, along with the other supporting documents. The cashier prepares and signs a check for each supplier and records the check in the check register.

 c. The cashier receives the monthly bank statement with canceled checks and prepares the bank reconciliation. If an adjustment is required as a consequence of the bank reconciliation, a two-copy journal voucher is prepared. A copy of the bank reconciliation is sent to the internal audit department.

Required

 a. Identify weaknesses in ConSport's expenditure cycle, explain the resulting problem, and suggest a control procedure that would best prevent or detect and correct each weakness. Use the labels next to each step to reference your answer.

 b. Describe how information technology can be used to improve the efficiency of ConSport's accounts payable and cash disbursements processes. For each process you change, also explain how to use technology to provide strong internal controls.

(CMA Examination, adapted)

11.10 Last year the Diamond Manufacturing Company recently purchased over $10 million worth of office equipment under its "special ordering" system, with individual orders ranging from $5,000 to $30,000. Special orders are for low-volume items that have been included in a department manager's budget. The budget, which limits the types and dollar amounts of office equipment a department head can requisition, is approved at the beginning of the year by the board of directors. The special ordering system functions as follows.

Purchasing

A purchase requisition form is prepared and sent to the purchasing department. Upon receiving a purchase requisition, one of the five purchasing agents (buyers) verifies that the requester is indeed a department head. The buyer next selects the appropriate supplier by searching the various catalogs on file. The buyer then phones the supplier, requests a price quote, and places a verbal order. A prenumbered purchase order is processed, with the original sent to the supplier and copies to the department head, receiving, and accounts payable. One copy is also filed in the open-requisition file. When the receiving department verbally informs the buyer that the item has been received, the purchase order is transferred from the open to the filled file. Once a month, the buyer reviews the unfilled file to follow up on open orders.

Receiving

The receiving department gets a copy of each purchase order. When equipment is received, that copy of the purchase order is stamped with the date and, if applicable, any differences between the quantity ordered and the quantity received are noted in red ink. The receiving clerk then forwards the stamped purchase order and equipment to the requisitioning department head and verbally notifies the purchasing department that the goods were received.

Accounts Payable

Upon receipt of a purchase order, the accounts payable clerk files it in the open purchase order file. When a vendor invoice is received, it is matched with the applicable

Figure 11-12
Cash Disbursement System for ConSport Corporaion

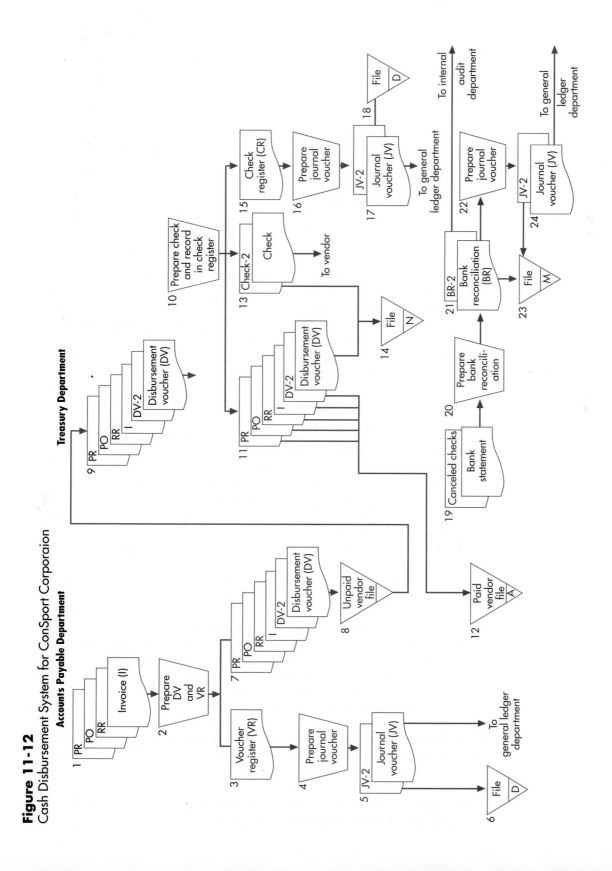

purchase order, and a payable is created by debiting the requisitioning department's equipment account. Unpaid invoices are filed by due date. On the due date, a check is prepared and forwarded to the treasurer for signature. The invoice and purchase order are then filed by purchase order number in the paid invoice file.

Treasurer

Checks received daily from the accounts payable department are sorted into two groups: those over and those under $10,000. Checks for less than $10,000 are machine signed. The cashier maintains the check signature machine's key and signature plate and monitors its use. Both the cashier and the treasurer sign all checks over $10,000.

Required

a. Describe the weaknesses relating to purchases and payments of "special orders" by the Diamond Manufacturing Company.

b. Recommend control procedures that must be added to overcome weaknesses identified in part a.

c. Describe how the control procedures you recommended in part b should be modified if Diamond reengineered its expenditure cycle activities to make maximum use of current IT (e.g., EDI, EFT, bar-code scanning, and electronic forms in place of paper documents).

(CPA Examination, adapted)

11.11 Lecimore Company has a centralized purchasing department managed by Tawanda Mason. Tawanda has established policies and procedures to guide the clerical staff and purchasing agents in daily department operations. She is satisfied that these guidelines conform to company objectives and that no major problems exist in the regular operations of the purchasing department.

Lecimore's internal audit department recently performed a routine operational audit of the purchasing department. Initial audit findings are as follows:

- All significant purchases are made on a competitive basis. The probability of timely delivery and supplier reliability is taken into account on a subjective basis.
- Quality acceptability requirements are provided to all potential suppliers.
- The materials manager of the inventory stores department (not the purchasing department) checks supplier adherence to quality specifications. The materials manager inspects the goods upon arrival and ensures that only goods meeting minimum quality standards are transferred to the storeroom.
- The materials manager prepares all purchase requests, which are based on the production schedule for the next four months.

The internal audit staff then observed the purchasing department's operations and noted the following:

- One supplier provides 90% of the crucial raw materials Lecimore uses. This supplier has a reliable delivery record and has been the low bidder for several years.
- As production plans change, rush orders are made by production directly to the purchasing department. As soon as the production department announces changes, purchasing orders the appropriate materials. Tawanda is proud of her staff's quick response time to such orders. Materials on hand are not reviewed before these orders are placed, however.
- Materials that had been ordered for cancelled production runs are placed into inventory for future use.
- The purchasing department absorbs the cost variances, if any, associated with rush orders because Tawanda believes this is a way of being a "good team player."
- The materials manager accepts partial and advance shipments and notifies the purchasing department of the receipt of the goods. The purchasing department is responsible for following up on partial shipments; no action is taken to discourage advance shipments.

Required

　　a. Identify weaknesses and inefficiencies in the purchasing procedures that Tawanda developed for Lecimore.

　　b. Suggest ways to overcome those weaknesses or inefficiencies.

(CMA Examination, adapted)

11.12　　Alden, Inc. has hired you to review its internal controls for the purchase, receipt, storage, and issuance of raw materials. You observed the following:

- Raw materials, which consist mainly of high-cost electronic components, are kept in a locked storeroom. Storeroom personnel include a supervisor and four clerks. All are well trained, competent, and adequately bonded. Raw materials are removed from the storeroom only upon written or oral authorization by a production supervisor.
- No perpetual inventory records are kept; hence, the storeroom clerks do not keep records for goods received or issued. To compensate, the storeroom clerks perform a physical inventory count each month. The clerks are supervised during this count, and other appropriate procedures are followed.
- After the physical count, the storeroom supervisor matches the quantities on hand against a predetermined reorder level. If the count is below the reorder level, the supervisor enters the part number on a materials requisition list that is sent to the accounts payable clerk. The accounts payable clerk prepares a purchase order for each item on the list and mails it to the supplier from whom the part was last purchased.
- The storeroom clerks receive the ordered materials upon their arrival. The clerks count all items and verify that the counts agree with the quantities on the bill of lading. The bill of lading is then initialed, dated, and filed in the storeroom to serve as a receiving report.

Required

　　a. Describe the weaknesses that exist in Alden's expenditure cycle.

　　b. Suggest control procedures to overcome the weaknesses noted in part a.

　　c. Discuss how those control procedures would be best implemented in an automated AIS using the latest developments in IT.

(CPA Examination, adapted)

11.13　　Branden Company, a midsize manufacturer of specialized machinery, follows these purchasing procedures:

- Materials purchase requisitions are approved by manufacturing supervisors and then forwarded to the purchasing department.
- Purchasing clerks prepare prenumbered purchase orders in triplicate. The original copy is sent to the supplier. The second copy is sent to the receiving department to notify it of an incoming shipment. The third copy is filed in the purchasing department.
- When materials are delivered, they are moved directly to the storeroom, with a copy of the receiving report. The receiving department sends another copy of the receiving report and its copy of the purchase order to the purchasing department. The third copy of the receiving report is sent to the accounting department.
- Vendor invoices are sent to the purchasing department and directed to the employee who placed that order. This employee checks the invoice for accuracy in terms of discounts, extensions, and footings. The purchasing clerk then compares the invoice with (1) the copy of the purchase order and (2) the copy of the receiving report to verify the quantities ordered and received. The clerk then approves the invoice for payment.
- The approved invoice is sent to the accounting department, where it is coded for account distribution, assigned a voucher number, entered in the voucher register, and filed according to payment due date.

Required

 a. Identify weaknesses in Branden company's expenditure cycle activities, explain the resulting problems that may occur, and recommend control procedures that should be implemented to correct those weaknesses.

 b. Describe how to use IT to improve the efficiency and effectiveness of Branden company's expenditure cycle processes. Also explain how to use IT to ensure sound internal control over those redesigned processes.

(CPA Examination, adapted)

11.14 Table 11-2 lists the various activities performed in the expenditure cycle and the journal entries, documents, data, and control issues associated with them. Complete each of the cell entries in this table.

11.15 EXCEL PROJECT

 a. Create a spreadsheet to reconcile bank statements. Organize it as follows:
 i. Ending balance, per bank statement
 ii. Deposits not included in bank statement (provide space for up to 7)
 iii. Checks outstanding that have not yet cleared (provide space for up to 20)
 iv. Fees charged, per bank statement
 v. Interest earned, per bank statement
 vi. Adjusted bank balance (this should reflect the effects of items ii–v)
 vii. Balance per books

Table 11-2
Overview of Expenditure Cycle Business Activities

			EXPENDITURE CYCLE				
	Request Purchase of Goods	**Approve Purchase**	**Receive Goods**	**Receive Invoice**	**Approve Vendor Invoice**	**Prepare Check**	**Pay Vendor**
Accounting transaction							
Journal entry					Dr. Purchases Cr. A/P		
Documents		Purchase order					
Data collected	• Name						
	• Item #						
Department					Accounting		
Control issues	Order only what is needed						
Information required							
Information generated							
Effect of automation							

Source: Adapted from teaching materials developed by Martha Eining, University of Utah.

b. Add appropriate data validation rules to ensure spreadsheet accuracy. Test your spreadsheet by entering the following data:

 i. Ending balance per bank statement = $97,525.33
 ii. Deposits not included in bank statement = $15,000 and $25,000
 iii. Checks outstanding that have not yet cleared:
 1. check number 3455 for $2,256.75
 2. check number 3487 for $13,567.95
 3. check number 3501 for $14,775.00
 iv. Fees charged by bank = $25
 v. Interest earned = $21.95
 vi. Result of your formula
 vii. Balance per books = $106,928.68

c. Tab to another blank worksheet and name it "checks cleared." Follow the instructions on the Letter to the Editor "Using VLOOKUP to do Bank Reconciliations," on page 14 of the March 2006 issue of the *Journal of Accountancy* to create a worksheet that will automatically identify any checks outstanding from last month that have not yet cleared, as well as any checks that were cashed for a different amount than originally recorded (you can access archived copies of the *Journal of Accountancy* on the AICPA's Web site at www.aicpa.org). Test your work by entering the following data:

Checks paid by bank this month:

Check number	Amount
3487	13,567.95
3502	6,500.00
3503	3,876.95
3505	18,255.95
3508	17,500.00
3510	12,000.00

Checks written this month:

Check number	Amount
3502	6,500.00
3503	3,876.95
3504	7,400.00
3505	18,255.59
3506	2,593.50
3507	11,000.00
3508	17,500.00
3509	14,500.00
3510	12,000.00

Hint: Don't forget the outstanding checks from part b when testing your worksheet.

11.16 Match threats in the first column to appropriate control procedures in the second column.

Threat	Control Procedure
_____ 1. Failing to take available purchase discounts	a. Accept only deliveries for which there is an approved purchase order.
_____ 2. Receiving unordered goods	b. Document all transfers of inventory with the company.
_____ 3. Recording and posting errors in accounts payable	c. Periodically review lists of approved vendors for unapproved changes.
_____ 4. Paying for goods not received	d. File invoices by due date.
_____ 5. Accidental loss or deletion of data	e. Compare total invoice amount processed to the difference in vendor account balances before and after check processing.
_____ 6. Kickbacks	
_____ 7. Requesting unnecessary items	
_____ 8. Making errors in counting	f. Train employees on how to properly deal with unsolicited gifts.
_____ 9. Stealing inventory	g. Maintain price lists for frequently purchased items and use competitive bids for specialized orders.
_____ 10. Purchasing goods of inferior quality	
_____ 11. Preventing stockouts and/or excess inventory	h. Install a perpetual inventory system that uses bar-code technology.
_____ 12. Paying the same invoice twice	i. Hold purchasing managers responsible for the costs of scrap and rework.
_____ 13. Purchasing goods at inflated prices	j. Require receiving clerks to sign a receiving report.
_____ 14. Misappropriating cash, checks, or EFTs	k. Design an AIS that integrates databases from various subunits.
_____ 15. Purchasing goods from unauthorized suppliers	l. Invoices should be paid only when accompanied by a purchase order and receiving report.
	m. Compare quantities on invoice to quantities received into inventory.
	n. Employ proper segregation of duties.
	o. Use external and internal data labels.
	p. Cancel all supporting documents when checks are issued.

CASE 11-1 Blackwell Industries

Blackwell Industries manufactures sporting goods. You have been asked to evaluate the proposed redesign of Blackwell's purchasing system. The new system will use a materials inventory master file, an open purchase order master file, and a supplier history file, all organized and stored in a relational database system. System inputs will include materials inventory receipts and issue transactions, which will be keyed in as they occur from online terminals located in the appropriate departments. System outputs will include batches of purchase orders and periodic reports of overdue deliveries, supplier performance, and cash flow commitments. Programs that are separate from the main update program will generate these reports. Managers can also obtain this information by creating online queries.

The main update program will begin by reading a transaction record and determining if it is a receipt or issue transaction. Then it will update the appropriate inventory master record. As each issue transaction is processed, the program will also check the quantity on hand in the master inventory record. If it falls below the reorder point, a reorder record will be written to a

temporary file on a separate disk. This file will be processed at the end of each day to prepare purchase orders. For each inventory receipt transaction, the program will update not only the quantity on hand in the inventory master record but also the corresponding open purchase order and supplier history records.

The purchase order preparation program will process the temporary reorder file by first sequencing it by supplier code number. All reorder records for the same supplier will be consolidated into one purchase order. When all reorder records for a supplier have been processed, EDI will generate and transmit a purchase order. The order will also be added to the open purchase order file.

At the end of each day, the open purchase order file will be processed to identify any purchase orders for which delivery is past due, and an overdue deliveries report will be generated. At the end of each month, the supplier history and open purchase order files will be processed to generate supplier performance and cash flow commitments reports.

Required

1 Prepare a systems flowchart of the main update program.
2 Prepare a systems flowchart of the purchase order preparation program.
3 Suggest potential ways that IT could be used to further improve the efficiency of the proposed system.
4 Identify the data that will be input on each transaction record. Suggest appropriate application controls to ensure accurate and reliable input.
5 Identify potential threats relating to the proposed system and suggest appropriate internal control procedures for mitigating them.

CASE 11-2 Boone Company

The Boone Company is looking for ways to cut costs and conserve cash. You have suggested that Boone consider taking advantage of vendor purchase discounts. But when management found that they would have to pay invoices sooner than the deadline in order to take advantage of these discounts, they scoffed at your idea as unworkable. "Who pays before they have to?" asked the director of marketing.

Currently, the Boone Company buys equipment on account from their vendors. The vendors maintain various credit terms for these purchases. To conserve their cash, Boone has maintained a long-standing policy not to pay any invoice early, but to only pay on the last day of the credit period to avoid any finance charges for late payments. Boone Company keeps its operating cash in a money market account that currently pays 4% interest annually. However, the controller is interested in your idea and has asked you to prepare an analysis of the costs and/or savings of utilizing purchase discounts. The controller has provided a list of their major vendors, Boone's average monthly purchases by vendor, and the vendor's credit terms.

Required

1 Prepare a spreadsheet to analyze Boone company's decision not to take advantage of the

Vendor	Average Monthly Purchases	Credit Terms
Quality Supply	$ 500,000	2% 10, net 30
Blaine Equipment Supply	300,000	1% 10, net 30
Standard Equipment	625,000	1% 15, net 30
National Brands	100,000	net 30
Southwestern Supply	175,000	3% 10, net 90
	$1,700,000	

purchase discounts allowed by its vendors. Calculate how much Boone could save if it took the discounts. Also calculate how much interest it could earn annually if it did not take the discounts, but left the money in a money market that earned 4% annually.

2 Based on your analysis, would you recommend to Boone management to borrow funds to take advantage of vendor purchase discounts? Explain your answer.

(CMA Exam, adapted)

AIS IN ACTION SOLUTIONS

1 Which of the following inventory control methods is most likely to be used for a product like lumber (1 × 2s, 2 × 4s, etc.)

 a. JIT (Incorrect. JIT seeks to minimize inventory by only making purchases after sales. It is used to primarily for products for which it is hard to forecast demand. Lumber is an example of a product for which demand can be forecast rather accurately.)

 b. EOQ (Incorrect. EOQ represents the optimal amount of inventory to purchase to minimize the sum of ordering, carrying, and stockout costs.)

 ✔ **c.** MRP (Correct. MRP forecasts sales and uses that information to purchase inventory to meet anticipated needs. Demand for lumber can be forecast rather accurately, including seasonal fluctuations (increased demand due to construction during spring, summer, and fall and reduced demand during winter).

 d. ABC (Incorrect. ABC is a method for stratifying inventory according to importance and scheduling more frequent inventory counts for the more important items.)

2 Which of the following matches is performed in evaluated receipt settlement (ERS)?

 a. the vendor invoice with the receiving report (Incorrect. ERS eliminates the vendor invoice.)

 ✔ **b.** the purchase order with the receiving report (Correct. ERS eliminates the vendor invoice and schedules payments based on matching the purchase order and receiving report.)

 c. the vendor invoice with the purchase order (Incorrect. ERS eliminates the vendor invoice.)

 d. the vendor invoice, the receiving report, and the purchase order (Incorrect. ERS eliminates the vendor invoice.)

3 Which of the following is true?

 a. ERS systems use disbursement vouchers. (Incorrect. Disbursement vouchers can be used in ERS systems.)

 ✔ **b.** Setting up petty cash as an imprest fund violates segregation of duties. (Correct. Technically, setting up petty cash as an imprest fund violates segregation of duties because the same person has custody of the asset (cash), authorizes its disbursement, and maintains records.)

 c. The EOQ formula is used to identify the reorder point. (Incorrect. The EOQ formula is used to determine how much to order.)

 d. A voucher package usually includes a debit memo. (Incorrect. Voucher packages consist of the purchase order, receiving report, and vendor invoice (if one is received); debit memos are used to record adjustments of accounts payable.)

4 Which document is used to establish a contract for the purchase of goods or services from a supplier?

 a. vendor invoice (Incorrect. The vendor invoice is a bill.)

 b. purchase requisition (Incorrect. A purchase requisition is an internal document.)

 ✔ **c.** purchase order (Correct. A purchase order is an offer to buy goods.)

 d. disbursement voucher (Incorrect. A disbursement voucher is used to specify which accounts to debit when paying vendor invoices.)

5 Which method would provide the greatest efficiency improvements for the purchase of noninventory items such as miscellaneous office supplies?

 a. bar-coding (Incorrect. Bar-coding's biggest payoffs come from high-volume uses.)

b. EDI (Incorrect. EDI is seldom used for miscellaneous purchases.)

✔ **c.** procurement cards (Correct. Procurement cards were designed specifically for purchase of noninventory items.)

d. EFT (Incorrect. EFT is used primarily for large purchases.)

6 Which of the following expenditure cycle activities can be eliminated through the use of IT or reengineering?

a. ordering goods (Incorrect. Even with vendor-managed inventory, the vendor's system must initiate the ordering process.)

✔ **b.** approving vendor invoices (Correct. ERS systems eliminate vendor invoices.)

c. receiving goods (Incorrect. Ordered goods must always be received and moved to the appropriate location.)

d. cash disbursements (Incorrect. IT can change the method used to make cash disbursements, such as by EFT instead of by check, but the function must still be performed.)

7 What is the best control procedure to prevent paying the same invoice twice?

a. Segregate check-preparation and check-signing functions. (Incorrect. This is a good control procedure, but its purpose is to ensure that payments are valid.)

b. Prepare checks only for invoices that have been matched to receiving reports and purchase orders. (Incorrect. This is a good control procedure, but its purpose is to ensure that organizations pay only for goods ordered and received.)

c. Require two signatures on all checks above a certain limit. (Incorrect. This is a good control procedure, but its purpose is to better control large outflows of cash.)

✔ **d.** Cancel all supporting documents when the check is signed. (Correct. This ensures that the supporting documents cannot be resubmitted to pay the same invoice again.)

8 For good internal control, who should sign checks?

✔ **a.** cashier (Correct. The cashier is responsible for managing cash and reports to the treasurer.)

b. accounts payable (Incorrect. Accounts payable maintains vendor records.)

c. purchasing agent (Incorrect. The purchasing agent authorizes acquisition of goods.)

d. controller (Incorrect. The controller is in charge of accounting, the record-keeping function.)

9 Which of the following procedures is designed to prevent the purchasing agent from receiving kickbacks?

a. maintaining a list of approved suppliers and requiring all purchases to be made from suppliers on that list (Incorrect. The purpose of this control is to minimize the risk of purchasing inferior goods at inflated prices or violating regulations.)

✔ **b.** requiring purchasing agents to disclose any financial investments in potential suppliers (Correct. The purpose of such disclosure is to minimize the risk of conflicts of interest that could result in kickbacks.)

c. requiring approval of all purchase orders (Incorrect. This control is designed to ensure that only goods that are really needed are ordered and that they are ordered from approved vendors.)

d. prenumbering and periodically accounting for all purchase orders (Incorrect. This control procedure is designed to ensure that all valid purchase orders are recorded.)

10 Which document is used to record adjustments to accounts payable based on the return of unacceptable inventory to the supplier?

a. receiving report (Incorrect. This document records quantities of goods received.)

b. credit memo (Incorrect. This document is used in the revenue cycle to adjust a customer's account.)

✔ **c.** debit memo (Correct. This document is used to adjust accounts payable.)

d. purchase order (Incorrect. This document establishes a legal obligation to purchase goods.)

CHAPTER 12

LEARNING OBJECTIVES

After studying this chapter, you should be able to:

● Describe the major business activities and related information processing operations performed in the production cycle.

● Explain how a company's cost accounting system can help it achieve its manufacturing goals.

● Identify major threats in the production cycle, and evaluate the adequacy of various control procedures for dealing with those threats.

● Discuss the key decisions that must be made in the production cycle, and identify the information required to make those decisions.

The Production Cycle

INTEGRATIVE CASE ALPHA OMEGA ELECTRONICS

LeRoy Williams, vice president for manufacturing at AOE, is concerned about problems associated with the company's change in strategic mission. Two years ago, AOE's top management decided to shift the company from its traditional position as a low-cost producer of consumer electronic products to a product differentiation strategy. Since then, AOE has increased the variety of sizes, styles, and features within each of its product lines.

To support this shift in strategic focus, AOE has invested heavily in factory automation. Top management also endorsed LeRoy's decision to adopt lean manufacturing techniques, with the goal of dramatically reducing finished goods inventory levels. AOE's cost accounting system has not been changed, however. For example, manufacturing overhead is still allocated based on direct labor hours, even though automation has drastically reduced the amount of direct labor used to manufacture a product. Consequently, investments in new equipment and machinery have resulted in dramatic increases in manufacturing overhead rates. This situation has created the following problems:.

1 Production supervisors complain that the accounting system makes no sense and that they are being penalized for making investments that improve overall efficiency. Indeed, according to the system some products now cost more to produce using state-of-the-art equipment than they did before the new equipment was purchased. Yet, the new

equipment has increased production capacity while simultaneously reducing defects.

2 The marketing and product design executives have all but dismissed the system's product cost figures as useless for setting prices or determining the potential profitability of new products. Indeed, some competitors have begun to price their products below what AOE's cost accounting system says it costs to produce that item.

3 Although a number of steps have been taken to improve quality, the cost accounting system does not provide adequate measures to evaluate the effect of those steps and to indicate areas that need further improvement. Indeed, LeRoy is frustrated by his inability to quantify the effects of the quality improvements that have occurred.

4 Performance reports continue to focus primarily on financial measures. Line managers in the factory, however, complain that they need more accurate and timely information on physical activities, such as units produced, defect rates, and production time.

5 LeRoy is frustrated because the move to lean manufacturing was successful in markedly reducing inventory levels this past year, but the traditional GAAP-based financial reports show that this has significantly lowered profitability.

LeRoy has expressed these concerns to Linda Spurgeon, AOE's president, who agrees that the problems are serious. Linda then called a meeting with LeRoy; Ann Brandt, AOE's vice president of information systems; and Elizabeth Venko, AOE's controller. At the meeting, Elizabeth and Ann agreed to study how to modify the cost accounting system to more accurately reflect AOE's new production processes. To begin this project, LeRoy agreed to take Elizabeth and Ann on a factory tour so that they could see and understand how the new technology has affected production cycle activities.

As this case suggests, deficiencies in the information system used to support production cycle activities can create significant problems for an organization. The availability of current and accurate information about product costs is crucial for effectively managing the production cycle. As you read this chapter, think about how the introduction of new technology in the production cycle may require corresponding changes in a company's cost accounting system.

Introduction

The **production cycle** is a recurring set of business activities and related information processing operations associated with the manufacture of products. Figure 12-1 shows how the production cycle is linked to the other subsystems in a company's

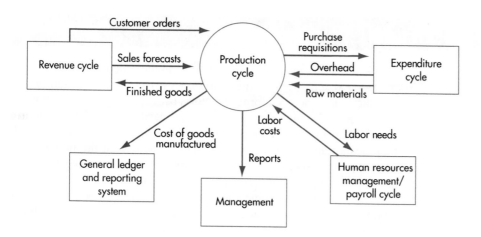

Figure 12-1
Context Diagram of the
Production Cycle

AIS. The revenue cycle information system (see Chapter 10) provides the information (customer orders and sales forecasts) used to plan production and inventory levels. In return, the production cycle information system sends the revenue cycle information about finished goods that have been produced and are available for sale. Information about raw materials needs is sent to the expenditure cycle information system (see Chapter 11) in the form of purchase requisitions. In exchange, the expenditure cycle system provides information about raw material acquisitions and also about other expenditures included in manufacturing overhead. Information about labor needs is sent to the human resources cycle (see Chapter 13), which in return provides data about labor costs and availability. Finally, information about the cost of goods manufactured is sent to the general ledger and reporting information system (see Chapter 14).

A company's AIS plays a vital role in the production cycle. Accurate and timely cost accounting information is essential input to decisions about the following:

- Product mix (what to produce),
- Product pricing,
- Resource allocation and planning (e.g., whether to make or buy a product and relative profitability of different products),
- Cost management (planning and controlling manufacturing costs and evaluting performance).

These decisions require much more detailed information about costs than the data needed to prepare financial statements in accordance with generally accepted accounting principles (GAAP). Thus, the design of a company's production cycle AIS must go beyond merely meeting external financial reporting requirements.

This chapter examines the three major functions of the AIS in the production cycle: capturing and processing data about business activities, storing and organizing the data to support decision making, and providing controls to ensure the reliability of data and the safeguarding of organizational resources. We begin by describing the basic business activities performed in the production cycle. Then we examine the methods used to collect, store, and process data about those activities. Next, we examine the major control objectives in the production cycle and discuss how to design the AIS to mitigate the threats associated with those activities. We conclude the chapter by discussing the key production cycle decisions and how accountants provide management the information needed to make those decisions.

Production Cycle Activities

Figure 12-2 (see below) shows the four basic activities in the production cycle: product design, planning and scheduling, production operations, and cost accounting. Figure 12-2 also depicts the principal information flows between each of those activities and the other AIS cycles. Although accountants are primarily involved in the fourth step, cost accounting, they also must understand the other three processes well enough to be able to help design an AIS that provides management with the information needed to manage the production cycle activities of a modern manufacturing company. For example, one popular approach to improving manufacturing performance, called Six Sigma, begins with careful measurement and analysis of current processes in order to find ways to improve them. Accountants can participate in such efforts by helping to design accurate measures; their ability to do so, however, requires an understanding of the production activities being measured.

Product Design

The first step in the production cycle is product design (circle 1.0 in Figure 12-2). The objective of this activity is to design a product that meets customer requirements in terms of quality, durability, and functionality while simultaneously minimizing production costs. Some of these criteria conflict with one another, making the product

Figure 12-2
Level 0 Data Flow Diagram of the Production Cycle

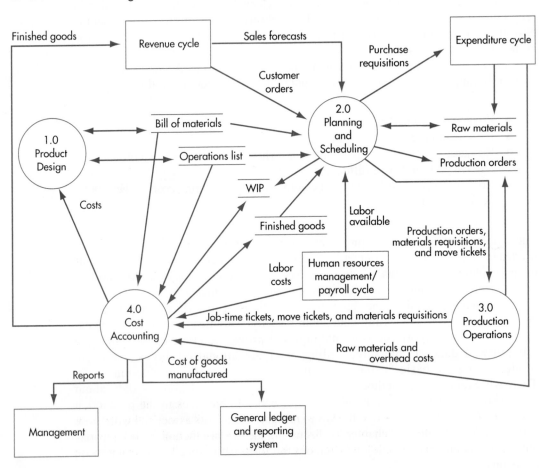

12-1 FOCUS
Using Software to Improve Product Design: The Need for Management Involvement

Product life-cycle management (PLM) software promises to dramatically improve both the design and manufacture of new products. PLM software consists of three key components: computer-aided design (CAD) software to design new products, digital manufacturing software that simulates how those products will be manufactured, and product data management software that stores all the data associated with products. CAD software enables manufacturers to design and test virtual 3-D models of products. The software facilitates collaboration by design teams dispersed around the globe. CAD software also reduces the costs associated with exchanging static copies of product designs and enables more thorough testing of those designs, while eliminating the costs associated with creating and destroying physical prototypes. Digital manufacturing software allows companies to determine labor, machine, and process requirements to optimally produce items in different facilities across the globe in order to minimize costs. Product data management software provides easy access to detailed engineering specifications and other product data to facilitate product redesign, modification, and post-sale maintenance.

The potential benefits of PLM are enormous. For example, GM estimates that it costs approximately $500,000 to run crash tests with real cars and hopes that CAD software can reduce the number of such tests by 85%. As Airbus learned, however, PLM software also has pitfalls. In 2006 it announced that production of the A380 superjumbo airliner would be delayed by up to two years, costing Airbus approximately $6 billion in lost profits. The problem? Use of different versions of the same CAD software by design teams in Germany and France resulted in incompatibilities between the front and rear fuselages. Each A380 contains over 300 miles of wires and more than 40,000 connectors to power everything in both the customer cabin and the cockpit. When workers tried to assemble the front and rear fuselages, they discovered that the wiring could not be properly connected.

How could using two editions of the same software create such problems? The answer is that each version treated drawings in different ways, resulting in different models. Engineers using the older version at the German plant had to manually tinker with the drawings to indicate where conduits should be placed, whereas the newer version of the software used at the French plant did this automatically. In addition, many technical notes containing key information about product specifications and units of measurement were lost when converting drawings between the two versions of the software.

The experience of Airbus is not unique. A survey found that almost 50% of companies using CAD software had to redesign products because of incompatibilities between CAD software used by different design teams. This underscores the importance of management involvement and support whenever companies implement complex software like PLM. Airbus executives did not force engineers at different plants to use the same versions of CAD software. This decision initially saved money by avoiding the need to purchase new software and the associated time and costs of retraining engineers. But those short-term savings were more than offset by the subsequent loss of profits due to production delays.

Properly managing the use of complex software like PLM systems, however, is neither cheap nor easy. For example, Boeing management insisted that all of its employees and business partners standardize on the same CAD software. This involved a large up-front investment: reports indicate that Boeing and its suppliers paid about $20,000 per desktop for the software. With more than 6,000 engineers worldwide, this amounted to approximately $120 million, plus additional money for training. Boeing management also actively managed version control, by mandating that all software updates to the main software and the approximately 150 related applications occur only at four specified times during the year. Boeing expects that its use of PLM software will shave at least one year off the time required to roll out its new Dreamliner and cut development costs by over $2 billion. The lesson seems clear: to reap the potential benefits and avoid the pitfalls associated with using new manufacturing software requires constant management involvement and supervision.

design task a challenging one. As Focus 12.1 explains, however, simulation software is constantly improving the efficiency and effectiveness of product design.

Key Documents and Forms

The product design activity creates two main documents. The first, a **bill of materials**, specifies the part number, description, and quantity of each component used in a finished product. The second is an **operations list**, which specifies the sequence of steps

to follow in making the product, which equipment to use, and how long each step should take.

Role of the Accountant

Accountants should participate in product design because 65% to 80% of product costs are determined at this stage of the production process. Accountants can provide information showing how various design trade-offs affect production costs and thereby profitability. For example, it is possible to significantly reduce the costs of producing a line of related products by increasing the number of common components used in each product. The AIS should be able to provide data about current component usage in various products and the projected costs of using alternative components. Similarly, aspects of product complexity, such as the number of different components and manner of assembly, can significantly affect production time and costs. Therefore, the AIS should be designed to collect and provide information about the machine setup and materials handling costs associated with alternative product designs. Data about repair and warranty costs associated with existing products can also be useful for designing better products. These costs are collected in the revenue cycle, as part of postsale customer service; the key is to design the AIS so that the information is readily available to product designers. In all these examples, accountants can add value if they not only design the AIS to measure and collect the relevant cost data but also if they help the design team to use that data proactively to improve profitability.

Planning and Scheduling

The second step in the production cycle is planning and scheduling (circle 2.0 in Figure 12-2). The objective is to develop a production plan efficient enough to meet existing orders and anticipated short-term demand while minimizing inventories of both raw materials and finished goods.

Planning Methods

Two common methods of production planning are manufacturing resource planning and lean manufacturing. **Manufacturing resource planning (MRP-II)** is an extension of materials resource planning (see Chapter 11) that seeks to balance existing production capacity and raw materials needs to meet forecasted sales demands. MRP-II systems are often referred to as *push manufacturing*, because goods are produced in expectation of customer demand.

Just as MRP-II is an extension of MRP inventory control systems, **lean manufacturing** extends the principles of just-in-time inventory systems (see Chapter 11) to the entire production process. The goal of lean manufacturing is to minimize or eliminate inventories of raw materials, work in process, and finished goods. Lean manufacturing is often referred to as *pull manufacturing*, because goods are produced in response to customer demand. Theoretically, lean manufacturing systems produce only in response to customer orders. In practice, however, most lean manufacturing systems develop short-run production plans. For example, Toyota develops monthly production plans so that it can provide a stable schedule to its suppliers. This strategy enables the suppliers to plan their production schedules so that they can deliver their products to Toyota at the exact time they are needed.

Thus, both MRP-II and lean manufacturing systems plan production in advance. They differ, however, in the length of the planning horizon. MRP-II systems may develop production plans for up to 12 months in advance, whereas lean manufacturing systems use much shorter planning horizons. If demand for a company's product is predictable and the product has a long life cycle, then an MRP-II approach may be justified. On the other hand, a lean manufacturing approach may be more appropriate if a

MASTER PRODUCTION SCHEDULE									
Product Number	120			**Description:**		DVD Player			
Lead time:[a]	**Week Number**								
1 week	**1**	**2**	**3**	**4**	**5**	**6**	**7**	**8**	
Quantity on hand	500	350[b]	350	300	350	300	450	300	
Scheduled production	150[c]	300	250	300	250	400	250	300	
Forecasted sales	300	300	300	250	300	250	400	250	
Net available	350[d]	350	300	350	300	450	300	350	

[a]Time to manufacture product (1 week for DVD player).
[b]Ending quantity on hand (net available) from prior week.
[c]Calculated by subtracting quantity on hand from sum of this week's and next week's forecasted sales, plus a 50-unit buffer stock. For example, begin week 1 with 500 units. Projected sales for weeks 1 and 2 total 600 units. Adding 50-unit desired buffer inventory yields 650 units needed by end of week 1. Subtracting beginning inventory of 500 units results in planned production of 150 units during week 1.
[d]Beginning quantity on hand plus scheduled production less forecasted sales.

Figure 12-3
Sample Master Production Schedule (MPS)

company's products are characterized by short life cycles, unpredictable demand, and frequent markdowns of excess inventory.

Key Documents and Forms

The **master production schedule (MPS)** specifies how much of each product is to be produced during the planning period and when that production should occur (see Figure 12-3). Information about customer orders, sales forecasts, and finished goods inventory levels is used to determine production levels. Although the long-range part of the MPS may be modified in response to changes in market conditions, production plans for many products must be frozen a few weeks in advance to provide sufficient time to procure the necessary raw materials, supplies, and labor resources.

The complexity of scheduling increases dramatically as the number of factories grows. Large manufacturing companies such as Motorola and General Motors must coordinate production at many different plants in different countries. Some of those plants produce basic components and others assemble the final products. The production information system must coordinate these activities to minimize bottlenecks and the buildup of partially completed inventories.

The MPS is used to develop a detailed timetable that specifies daily production and to determine if raw materials need to be purchased. To do this, it is necessary to "explode" the bill of materials to determine the immediate raw materials requirements for meeting the production goals listed in the MPS (see Table 12-1). These requirements are compared with current inventory levels and, if additional materials are needed, purchase requisitions are generated and sent to the purchasing department to initiate the acquisition process.

Figure 12-2 shows that the planning and scheduling activity produces three other documents: production orders, materials requisitions, and move tickets. A **production order** authorizes the manufacture of a specified quantity of a particular product. It lists the operations that need to be performed, the quantity to be produced, and the location where the finished product should be delivered. It also collects data about each of those activities (see Figure 12-4).

A **materials requisition** authorizes the removal of the necessary quantity of raw materials from the storeroom to the factory location where they will be used. This document contains the production order number, date of issue, and, based on the bill of materials, the part numbers and quantities of all necessary raw materials

Table 12-1
Example of "Exploding" a Bill of Materials

COMPONENTS IN EACH DVD PLAYER					
Step 1: Multiply the component requirements for ONE product by the number of products to be produced next period (from the MPS).	**Part No.**	**Description**	**Quantity**	**Number of DYD Players**	**Total Requirements**
	105	Control Unit	1	2,000	2,000
	125	Back Panel	1	2,000	2,000
	148	Side Panel	4	2,000	8,000
	173	Timer	1	2,000	2,000
	195	Front Panel	1	2,000	2,000
	199	Screw	6	2,000	12,000

COMPONENTS IN EACH CD PLAYER					
	Part No.	**Description**	**Quantity**	**Number of CD Players**	**Total Requirements**
	103	Control Unit	1	3,000	3,000
	120	Front Panel	1	3,000	3,000
	121	Back Panel	1	3,000	3,000
	173	Timer	1	3,000	3,000
	190	Side Panel	4	3,000	12,000
	199	Screw	4	3,000	12,000

	Part No.	**DVD Player**	**CD Player**	**Total**	
Step 2: Calculate total component requirements by summing products.	103	0	3,000	3,000	
	105	2,000	0	2,000	
	120	0	3,000	3,000	
	121	0	3,000	3,000	
	125	2,000	0	2,000	
	148	8,000	0	8,000	
	173	2,000	3,000	5,000	
	190	0	12,000	12,000	
	195	2,000	0	2,000	
	199	12,000	12,000	24,000	

	Part No.	**Week 1**	**Week 2**	**Week 3**	**Week 4**	**Week 5**	**Week 6**
Step 3: Repeat steps 1 and 2 for each week during planning horizon.	103	3,000	2,000	2,500	3,000	2,500	3,000
	105	2,000	2,000	2,500	2,500	2,000	3,000
	120	3,000	2,000	2,500	3,000	2,500	3,000
	121	3,000	2,000	2,500	3,000	2,500	3,000
	125	2,000	2,000	2,500	2,500	2,000	3,000
	148	8,000	8,000	10,000	10,000	8,000	12,000
	173	5,000	4,000	5,000	5,500	4,500	6,000
	190	12,000	12,000	10,000	12,000	10,000	12,000
	195	2,000	2,000	2,500	2,500	2,000	3,000
	199	24,000	20,000	25,000	27,000	22,000	30,000

Figure 12-4
Sample Production Order for AOE

								4587
Alpha Omega Engineering								
PRODUCTION ORDER								

Order No. 2289	Product No. 4430	Description: Cabinet Side Panel			Production Quantity 1000			
Approved by: PJS	Release Date: 02/24/2009	Issue Date: 02/25/2009		Completion Date: 03/09/2009	Deliver to: Assembly Department			

Work Station No.	Product Operation No.	Quantity	Operation Description	Start Date & Time		Finish Date & Time	
MH25	100	1,003	Transfer from stock	02/28	0700	02/28	0800
ML15-12	105	1,003	Cut to shape	02/28	0800	02/28	1000
ML15-9	106	1,002	Corner cut	02/28	1030	02/28	1200
S28-17	124	1,002	Turn & shape	02/28	1300	02/28	1700
F54-5	142	1,001	Finish	03/01	0800	03/01	1100
P89-1	155	1,001	Paint	03/01	1300	03/02	1300
QC94	194	1,001	Inspect	03/02	1400	03/02	1600
MH25	101	1,000	Transfer to assembly	03/02	1600	03/02	1700

Explanation of numbers in Quantity column:
1. Total of 1,003 sheets of raw material used to produce 1,000 good panels and 3 rejected panels.
2. One panel not cut to proper shape, thus only 1,002 units had operations 106 and 124 performed on them.
3. One panel not properly turned and shaped; hence only 1,001 panels finished, painted, and received final inspection.
4. One panel rejected during final inspection; thus only 1,000 good panels transferred to assembly department.

(see Figure 12-5). Subsequent transfers of raw materials throughout the factory are documented on **move tickets**, which identify the parts being transferred, the location to which they are transferred, and the time of transfer (see Figure 12-6).

Notice that many of the documents used in the production cycle track the movement and usage of raw materials. Advances in information technology continually provide opportunities to improve the efficiency of these materials handling activities. For example, bar-coding improved the speed and accuracy of recording information about material movements by eliminating the need to manually enter data. More recently, radio-frequency identification (RFID) tags further improve efficiency by eliminating the need for any human intervention in the scanning process (to align barcodes with the bar-code scanner). This makes RFID scanners up to 40 times faster than

Figure 12-5
Sample Materials Requisition for AOE

					No. 2345
MATERIALS REQUISITION					
Issued To: Assembly	Issue Date: 08/15/2009		Production Order Number: 62913		

Part Number	Description	Quantity	Unit Cost $	Total Cost $
115	Calculator Unit	2,000	2.95	5,900.00
135	Lower Casing	2,000	.45	900.00
198	Screw	16,000	.02	320.00
178	Battery	2,000	.75	1,500.00
136	Upper Casing	2,000	.80	1,600.00
199	Screw	12,000	.02	240.00
Issued by: **AKL**				10,460.00
Received by: GWS		Costed by: ZBD		

Note: Cost information is entered when the materials requisition is turned in to the cost accounting department. Other information, except for signatures, is printed by the system when the document is prepared.

Figure 12-6
Sample Move Ticket for AOE

MOVE TICKET			No. 8753

Production Order Number:	2345	Date Transferred:	08/18/2009
From: Assembly	*KLS*	**To:** Finishing	*NRC*

Operation to Perform	Completed	Date	Time
Clean	___X___	08/19/2009	0900
Polish	_____		
Package	_____		
Comments:			

bar-code scanners. Unlike bar-codes, RFID tags are also not affected by dirt, which can dramatically improve scanning accuracy in most warehouses. RFID also facilitates locating specific inventory because the scanning devices are not limited to reading only those items that are directly in line-of-sight. This can be especially useful in large warehouse and storage facilities, where items may get moved around to make room for new shipments. With bar-codes, warehouse employees must physically search for requested items. Surveys estimate that as much as 10%–20% of all materials handling costs involve time spent looking for the right product. RFID technology eliminates that non-value-added time and associated costs. With RFID tags, the scanner can broadcast a signal, locate the desired product, and transmit that information directly to the forklift driver or warehouse worker.

Role of the Accountant

The accountant must ensure that the AIS collects and reports costs in a manner consistent with the production planning techniques of the company. This may require making changes to the AIS when new planning techniques are adopted. For example, AOE is in the process of adopting the lean approach to manufacturing. Lean manufacturing emphasizes working in teams and seeks to maximize the efficiency and synergy of all teams involved in making a particular product. Consequently, Elizabeth Venko realizes that collecting and reporting labor variances at the individual or team level may create dysfunctional incentives to maximize local performance at the expense of plantwide performance. Therefore, she plans to redesign AOE's AIS so that it collects and reports costs in a manner that highlights the *joint* contributions of all teams that make a particular product.

Production Operations

The third step in the production cycle is the actual manufacture of products (circle 3.0 in Figure 12-2). The manner in which this activity is accomplished varies greatly across companies, differing according to the type of product being manufactured and the degree of automation used in the production process.

Using various forms of IT in the production process, such as robots and computer-controlled machinery, is referred to as **computer-integrated manufacturing (CIM)**. CIM can significantly reduce production costs. For example, Northrop Grumman Corporation once used 16,000 sheets of paper to record shop-floor work instructions related to the manufacture of plane fuselages. Installation of online terminals at each assembly station eliminated that paper flow and improved efficiency, reducing costs by 30%.

Accountants are not required to be experts on every facet of CIM, but they must understand how it affects the AIS. One effect of CIM is a shift from mass production to custom-order manufacturing. For example, every Northrop Grumman product is assembled to order. Each product, however, can use any of about 256,000 separate

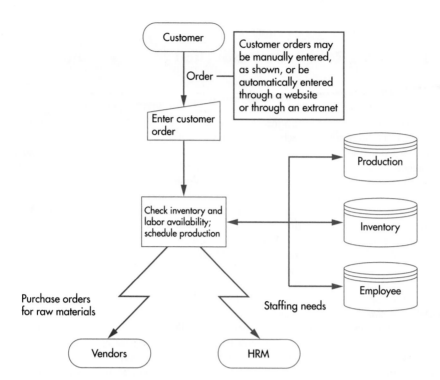

Figure 12-7
Enterprise Resource Planning
(ERP) System for
Manufacturing

components. Thus, to minimize inventory carrying costs, Northrop Grumman's AIS must maintain accurate perpetual inventory records. This requires integrating information about customer orders (from the revenue cycle) with information about purchases from suppliers (from the expenditure cycle), along with information about labor availability (from the HR/payroll cycle). As Figure 12-7 shows, ERP systems provide such integration.

Figure 12-7 illustrates how a customer order triggers other actions in a lean manufacturing environment. The system first checks inventory on hand to determine how much needs to be produced to fill the new order. It then calculates labor needs and determines whether there is a need to schedule overtime or hire temporary help in order to meet the promised fill date. At the same time, information in the bill of materials is used to determine what components, if any, need to be ordered. Any necessary purchase orders are sent to suppliers via EDI. The master production schedule is then adjusted to include the new order. Notice how this sharing of information across the revenue, production, and expenditure cycles in the manner just described enables companies to efficiently manage inventories by timing their purchases to meet actual customer demand.

Although both the nature of the production process and the extent of CIM vary across companies, for cost accounting purposes every firm requires data about the following four facets of its production operations: raw materials used, labor hours expended, machine operations performed, and other manufacturing overhead costs incurred. In the next section, we discuss the methods used to collect and process this information.

Cost Accounting

The final step in the production cycle is cost accounting (circle 4.0 in Figure 12-2). The three principal objectives of the cost accounting system are (1) to provide information for planning, controlling, and evaluating the performance of production operations; (2) to provide accurate cost data about products for use in pricing and product mix decisions; and (3) to collect and process the information used to calculate the inventory and cost of goods sold values that appear in the company's financial statements.

12-2 FOCUS — How RFID Facilitates Real-Time Production Management

Effective management of production activities requires real-time information about the status of machinery and equipment. Advances in RFID technology provide timely access to such information, thereby improving preventive maintenance and product recall decisions.

RFID capabilities embedded in new production machinery enable devices to continuously transmit information about their condition. This replaces scheduled maintenance based on predetermined time intervals with proactive maintenance to prevent problems from developing, thereby reducing downtime and improving the flow of goods through the production process. For example, Schneider Electric's Square D–brand circuit breakers alert operators when a breaker's performance indicates that it is approaching the time when it will fail. But such "smart" devices can do much more than merely signal an alarm. Built-in Internet capabilities mean that the device can automatically send e-mail requests to the manufacturer or maintenance provider to schedule service. Moreover, the service provider can use the Internet communication capabilities to monitor the device remotely,

diagnosing the problem and thereby ensuring that the technician arrives with the proper parts to service the machine. The productivity improvements made possible by such improved maintenance are tremendous. It is estimated that manufacturing plants must halt production due to machinery breakdowns almost 10% of the time. For chip manufacturing plants, the estimates are as high as 30% downtime.

RFID tags can also save manufacturers money should there be a need to recall products. Unlike bar-codes, which contain the same information for all batches of a particular product destined for a particular location, RFID tags uniquely identify each batch. Consequently, if a production problem is subsequently discovered that necessitates recalling some potentiallly defective products, only those specific units made by the equipment in question need to be recalled. Without RFID tags, every item produced at that plant on the day the problem occurred would have to be recalled. Moroever, RFID technology can record information about every movement throughout the supply chain. This saves time in locating those items that need to be recalled.

To successfully accomplish the first objective, the AIS must be designed to collect real-time data about the performance of production activities so that management can make timely decisions. As Focus 12.2 explains, RFID technology can be especially helpful in this regard. To accomplish the other two objectives, the AIS must collect costs by various categories and then assign those costs to specific products and organizational units. This requires careful coding of cost data during collection, because often the same costs may be allocated in multiple ways, for several different purposes. For example, factory supervisory costs may be assigned to departments for performance evaluation purposes but to specific products for pricing and product mix decisions.

Types of Cost Accounting Systems

Most companies use either job-order or process costing to assign production costs. **Job-order costing** assigns costs to specific production batches, or jobs, and is used when the product or service being sold consists of discretely identifiable items. For example, construction companies use job-order costing for each house being built. Similarly, public accounting and law firms use job-order costing to account for the costs of individual audits or cases, respectively. AOE currently uses job-order costing.

In contrast, **process costing** assigns costs to each process, or work center, in the production cycle, and then calculates the average cost for all units produced. Process costing is used when similar goods or services are produced in mass quantities and discrete units cannot be readily identified. For example, breweries accumulate the costs associated with the various processes (e.g., mashing, primary fermentation, filtering, and bottling) in producing a batch of a particular kind of beer and then compute the average total unit cost for that product. Similarly, mutual funds accumulate the

costs associated with handling customer deposits and withdrawals and then compute the per-unit costs of those transactions.

Accounting for Fixed Assets

Thus far, we have focused on accounting for the costs associated with the production of inventory. The AIS must also collect and process information about the property, plant, and equipment used in the production cycle. Indeed, such fixed assets represent a significant portion of total assets for many companies, so it is important to monitor this investment. At a minimum, every organization should maintain the following information about each fixed asset: identifying number, serial number, location, cost, date of acquisition, vendor name and address, expected life, expected salvage value, depreciation method, depreciation charges to date, improvements, and maintenance services performed.

Acquisitions of fixed assets represent a special type of expenditure and follow the same basic processes (order the fixed asset, receive it, and pay for it) and control procedures discussed in Chapter 11. Nonetheless, the size of fixed-asset transactions necessitates some modifications of the processes used to acquire inventory and miscellaneous supplies. One difference is that orders for machinery and equipment almost always involve a formal request for competitive bids by potential suppliers. More people may be involved in reviewing those bids and selecting the supplier than are involved in similar decisions concerning inventory sourcing. In addition, acquisitions of fixed assets often are paid for in installments, including interest. Thus, the AIS must keep accurate, detailed records of outstanding balances owed for much longer periods of time than required for routine purchases of inventory and supplies. The cost of each piece of equipment also justifies more elaborate controls to protect the investment. Indeed, companies usually maintain detailed records of each individual machine or piece of equipment. RFID tags provide an efficient method for monitoring the location of machinery and equipment. In addition, as Focus 12.2 noted, RFID sensors also provide continuous monitoring capabilities to facilitate preventive maintenance so as to maximize the useful life of each machine. Finally, because manufacturing machinery and equipment is often replaced before it is completely worn out, it is important to formally approve and accurately record its sale or disposal. The AIS also needs to maintain accurate records of acquisition cost, any improvements, and depreciation in order to properly calculate the gain or loss arising from such transactions.

Information Processing Procedures

Figure 12-8 depicts a typical online AIS for the production cycle, as used at AOE. Engineering department specifications for new products result in the creation of new records in both the bill of materials and operations list files. To develop those specifications, engineering accesses both files to examine the design of similar products. It also accesses the general ledger and inventory files for information about the costs of alternative product designs. The sales department enters sales forecasts and customer special-order information. The production planning department uses that information and data about current inventory levels to develop the master production schedule. New records are then added to the production order file to authorize the production of specific goods. At the same time, new records are added to the work-in-process file to accumulate cost data. The list of operations to be performed is displayed at the appropriate workstation. Corresponding instructions also are sent to the CIM interface to guide the operation of computerized machinery and robots. Finally, materials requisitions are sent to the inventory stores department to authorize the release of raw materials to production.

The system shown in Figure 12-8 could be used to implement either a job-order or process costing system. Both systems require accumulating data about four basic kinds of costs: raw materials, direct labor, machinery and equipment, and manufacturing

Figure 12-8
Online Production Cycle Information System

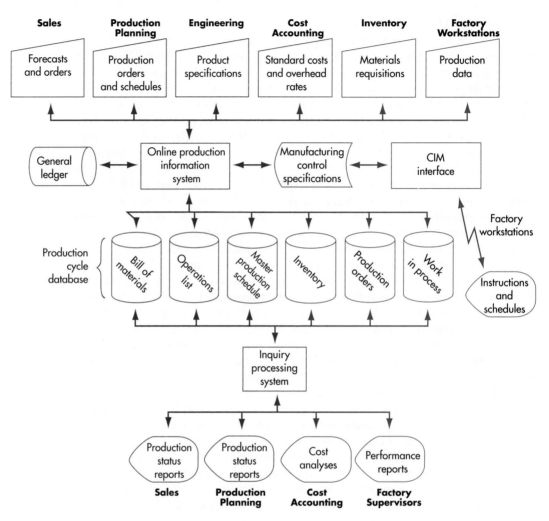

overhead. The choice of job-order or process costing affects only the method used to assign those costs to products, not the methods used for data collection. Let us now examine how these four categories of cost data are collected.

Raw Materials Usage Data

When production is initiated, the issuance of a materials requisition triggers a debit to work in process for the raw materials sent to production. If additional materials are needed, another debit is made to work in process. Conversely, work in process is credited for any materials not used and returned to inventory. Many raw materials are bar-coded so that usage data can be collected by scanning the products when released from, or returned to, inventory. Increasingly, manufacturers are using RFID tags to further improve the efficiency of tracking materials usage. RFID facilitates the use of perpetual inventory systems. In fact, if RFID tags are applied to individual products, companies may, if they desire, adopt the specific identification method for tracking inventory. It is difficult, however, to use bar-codes or RFID tags for some items, such as liquids. Inventory clerks and factory workers must use online terminals to enter usage data for such items.

Direct Labor Costs

In the past, AOE and other manufacturers used a paper document called a **job-time ticket** to collect data about labor activity. This document recorded the amount of time

a worker spent on each specific job task. Now, as shown in Figure 12-8, workers enter this data using online terminals at each factory workstation. To improve the efficiency of this process, AOE is considering switching to coded identification cards, which workers would run through a badge reader or bar-code scanner when they start and finish any task. The time savings associated with using bar-coding to automate data collection can be significant. For example, Consolidated Diesel Company, a joint venture between Cummins Engine Company and J.I. Case, found using bar-code scanners to capture data about materials usage and labor operations saved about 12 seconds per workstation, per activity. Although this may not seem like much, when multiplied by the hundreds of workstations and multiple activities performed daily by hundreds of employees, the change resulted in a permanent 15% increase in productivity.

Machinery and Equipment Usage

As companies implement CIM to automate the production process, an ever larger proportion of product costs relate to the machinery and equipment used to make that product. Data about machinery and equipment usage are collected at each step in the production process, often in conjunction with data about labor costs. For example, when workers record their activities at a particular workstation, the system can also record information identifying the machinery and equipment used and the duration of such use. Until recently, this data was collected by wiring the factory so that each piece of equipment was linked to the computer system. This limited the ability to quickly and easily redesign the layout of the shop floor to improve production efficiency. Consequently, many manufacturing companies are replacing such wired connections with wireless technology. Doing so enables them to use new 3-D simulation software to evaluate the effects of modifying shop-floor layout and workflow and to easily and quickly implement beneficial changes.

Manufacturing Overhead Costs

Manufacturing costs that are not economically feasible to trace directly to specific jobs or processes are considered **manufacturing overhead**. Examples include the costs of water, power, and other utilities; miscellaneous supplies; rent, insurance, and property taxes for the factory plant; and the salaries of factory supervisors. Most of these costs are collected by the expenditure cycle information system (see Chapter 11), with the exception of supervisory salaries, which are processed by the human resources cycle information system (see Chapter 13). The AIS must be designed to easily track and assign these costs to production activities.

Accountants can play a key role in controlling overhead costs by carefully assessing how changes in product mix affect total manufacturing overhead. They should go beyond merely collecting such data, however, and identify the underlying factors that drive the changes in total costs. This information then can be used to adjust production plans and factory layout to maximize efficiency and profitability. To do this effectively, however, requires accurate and complete information about production cycle activities. The next section discusses the necessary controls not only to ensure accurate information about production cycle activities but also to safeguard the assets used in them.

Control Objectives, Threats, and Procedures

A second function of a well-designed AIS is to provide adequate controls to meet the following production cycle objectives:

1 All production activities and fixed asset acquisitions are properly authorized.
2 Work-in-process inventories and fixed assets are safeguarded.

3 All valid, authorized production cycle transactions are recorded.
4 All production cycle transactions are recorded accurately.
5 Accurate records are maintained and protected from loss.
6 Production cycle activities are performed efficiently and effectively.

The documents and records described in the previous section play an important role in achieving these objectives. Simple, easy-to-complete documents with clear instructions facilitate the accurate and efficient recording of transaction data. Including appropriate application controls, such as validity checks and field (format) checks, further increases the accuracy of data entry when using electronic documents. Wherever feasible, use of RFID tags or bar-codes can further improve data entry accuracy. Providing space on paper and electronic documents to record who completed and who reviewed the form creates evidence that the transaction was properly authorized. Prenumbering all documents facilitates checking that all transactions have been recorded. Restricting access to programs that create documents and, if paper documents are still used, to blank documents reduces the risk of unauthorized transactions.

Table 12-2 lists the major threats and exposures in the production cycle and the additional control procedures, besides adequate documents and records, that should be in place to mitigate them. As you will see in the following discussion, every company, regardless of its line of business, faces these threats. Therefore, it is important to understand how the AIS can be designed to counter them.

Table 12-2
Threats and Controls in the Production Cycle

Process/Activity	Threat	Applicable Control Procedures
Product design	1. Poor product design	Improved information about effects of product design changes on total costs; detailed data about warranty and repair costs
Planning and scheduling	2. Over- or underproduction	Accurate production planning systems; proper approval of production orders
	3. Suboptimal investment in fixed assets	Review and approval of fixed-asset transactions; budgetary controls
Production operations	4. Theft of inventories and fixed assets	Restricted physical access to work-in-process and finished goods inventories and to fixed assets; documenting all materials movements; identification and tracking of all fixed assets; periodic counts of inventory and fixed assets; proper documentation and review of all transactions involving disposal of fixed assets; adequate insurance
	5. Disruption of operations	Backup power supplies; disaster recovery plans; evaluation of suppliers' disaster preparedness
Cost accounting	6. Inaccurate cost data	Data entry and processing controls; use of bar-code and RFID technology where feasible; periodic reconciliation of records with physical counts
General threats	7. Loss, alteration or unauthorized disclosure of data	Backup and disaster recovery plans; logical and physical access controls; configuration of ERP systems to enforce proper segregation of duties; encryption; data transmission controls
	8. Poor performance	Development and periodic review of appropriate performance reports

Product Design

Threat 1: Poor Product Design

Poor product design drives up costs in several ways. Using too many unique components when producing similar products increases the costs associated with purchasing and maintaining raw materials inventories. It also often results in inefficient production processes because of excessive complexity in changing from the production of one product to another. Poorly designed products are also more likely to incur high warranty and repair costs.

Product design can be improved with accurate data about the relationship between components and finished goods. For example, automobile manufacturers have realized significant cost savings by increasing the number of common components within and across product lines. Analysis of warranty and repair costs can identify the primary causes of product failure. That information can then be used to redesign products to improve quality.

Planning and Scheduling

Threat 2: Over- or Underproduction

Two related threats in the planning and scheduling process are overproduction and underproduction. Overproduction can result in a supply of goods in excess of short-run demands, thereby creating potential cash flow problems because resources are tied up in inventory. Overproduction also increases the risk of carrying inventory that becomes obsolete. Conversely, underproduction can result in lost sales and customer dissatisfaction because of lack of availability of desired items.

More accurate production planning can prevent over- and underproduction. Improvement requires accurate and current sales forecasts and data about inventory stocks, information that the revenue and expenditure cycle systems can provide. Investments to improve production planning, particularly the ability to quickly adjust production schedules and purchase commitments, are especially important for companies that produce new, innovative products, such as fashion clothing, because the demand for such products is much more volatile than the demand for staples and commodities, such as food or office supplies. In addition to improved forecasts, information about production performance, particularly concerning trends in total time to manufacture each product, should be regularly collected. These data sources should be used periodically to review and adjust the master production schedule.

Proper approval and authorization of production orders is another control to prevent overproduction of specific items. One means is to restrict access to the production scheduling program using passwords and an access control matrix. It is also important to ensure that the correct production orders are released. Closed-loop verification can accomplish this control: The production planner enters the product number and the system retrieves the description, order quantity, and other relevant data and requests the user to verify that the correct production order is being released.

Threat 3: Suboptimal Investment in Fixed Assets

Overinvesting in fixed assets can create excess costs; underinvestment can impair productivity. Both problems reduce profitability. Thus, proper authorization of fixed-asset transactions is important. The procedures involved in authorizing the purchase of fixed assets vary, depending on the size of the purchase request. A supervisor or manager, who provides details about expected cash flows and other costs and benefits of the proposed expenditure, should first recommend large capital expenditures. All such recommendations should be reviewed by a senior executive or by an executive committee and the various projects ranked by priority. Smaller capital expenditures (e.g., those costing $10,000 or less) usually can be purchased directly out of departmental budgets, which avoids a formal approval process. Holding managers accountable for their department's return on the fixed assets provides additional incentive to control such expenditures.

Due to the size of fixed-asset purchases, companies should invite several competing suppliers to provide bids. A document called a **request for proposal (RFP)**, which specifies the desired properties of the asset, is sent to each vendor. The capital investments committee should review the responses and select the best bid. Once a supplier has been selected, the acquisition of the asset may be handled through the regular expenditure cycle process, as described in Chapter 11. Specifically, a formal purchase order is prepared, receipt of the asset is formally documented using a receiving report, and a disbursement voucher is used to authorize payment to the supplier. The same set of processing controls and edit checks employed for other purchases also should be used for fixed-asset acquisitions (for details, refer back to the discussion in Chapter 11).

Production Operations

Threat 4: Theft of Inventories and Fixed Assets

Theft of inventories and fixed assets is a major threat to manufacturing companies. In addition to the loss of assets, thefts also result in overstated asset balances, which can lead to erroneous analyses of financial performance and, in the case of inventory, underproduction.

To reduce the risk of inventory loss, physical access to inventories should be restricted and all internal movements of inventory should be documented. Thus, materials requisitions should be used to authorize the release of raw materials to production. Both the inventory control clerk and the production employee receiving the raw materials should sign the requisition to acknowledge release of the goods to production. Requests for additional materials in excess of the amounts specified in the bill of materials should be documented and authorized by supervisory personnel. Move tickets should be used to document subsequent movement of inventory through various stages of the production process. The return of any materials not used in production also should be documented. Wherever feasible, RFID tags or bar-codes should be used to automate the tracking of inventories.

Proper segregation of duties is important to safeguard inventory. Maintaining physical custody of the raw materials and finished goods inventories is the responsibility of the inventory stores department. Department or factory supervisors have primary responsibility for work-in-process inventories. The authorization function, represented by the preparation of production orders, materials requisitions, and move tickets, is the responsibility of the production planners or, increasingly, of the production information system itself. RFID equipment, bar-code scanners, and online terminals can be used to record movement of inventory, thereby maintaining accurate perpetual inventory records. Consequently, proper access controls and compatibility tests are important to ensure that only authorized personnel have access to those records. Finally, an employee without any custodial responsibility should periodically count inventory on hand. Any discrepancies between these physical counts and recorded amounts should be investigated.

Similar controls are needed to safeguard fixed assets. As explained earlier, all fixed assets must be identified and recorded. Managers should be assigned responsibility and accountability for fixed assets under their control. Security measures should be in place to control physical access to fixed assets. Disposal of fixed assets should be properly authorized and documented. A report of all fixed-asset transactions should be printed periodically and sent to the controller, who should verify that each transaction was properly authorized and executed.

Finally, inventories and fixed assets also are subject to loss due to fire or other disasters. Therefore, adequate insurance should be maintained to cover such losses and provide for replacement of those assets.

Threat 5: Disruption of Operations

The high level of automation in production cycle activities means that disasters that disrupt the functioning of information systems can also disrupt manufacturing activities. For example, the widespread power outages in the northeastern United States and in

California affected the manufacturing operations of many businesses with factories in those states. Backup power sources, such as generators, and uninterruptible power supply devices should be acquired to ensure that critical equipment and machinery is not damaged by sudden unexpected loss of power and that important production processes can continue on schedule. Companies also need to investigate the disaster preparedness of key suppliers and identify alternative sources for critical components. This is especially important for companies that practice lean manufacturing; they maintain low inventories of both raw materials and finished goods, so any disruptions to either their manufacturing activities or those of their suppliers can quickly result in lost sales.

Cost Accounting

Threat 6: Inaccurate Cost Data

Inaccurate recording and processing of production activity data can diminish the effectiveness of production scheduling and undermine management's ability to monitor and control manufacturing operations. For example, inaccurate cost data can result in inappropriate decisions about which products to make and how to set current selling prices. Errors in inventory records can lead to either over- or underproduction of goods. Inaccuracies in financial statements and managerial reports can distort analyses of past performance and the desirability of future investments or changes in operations.

The best control procedure to ensure that data entry is accurate is to automate data collection using RFID technology, bar-code scanners, badge readers, and other devices. When this is not feasible, online terminals should be used for data entry. Passwords and user IDs should be used to restrict access to authorized employees to prevent undocumented changes to data. In addition, an access control matrix should be used to limit access to only those portions of the database that a particular employee needs to perform a given job. Check digits and closed-loop verification should be used to ensure that information about the raw materials used, operations performed, and employee number is entered correctly. Validity checks, such as comparing raw materials part numbers to those listed in the bill of materials file, provide further assurance. Finally, to verify the accuracy of database records, periodic physical counts of inventories should be made and compared with recorded quantities.

As with inventory, periodic inspections and counts of all fixed assets should be made, and those figures should be reconciled to recorded amounts. Overstated fixed assets increase expenses through extra depreciation and higher property taxes. Understated fixed assets also can cause problems; for example, inaccurate counts of the number of personal computers in use can cause a company to unknowingly violate software license requirements.

General Threats

Threat 7: Loss, Alteration, or Unauthorized Disclosure of Data

Loss or alteration of production data hinders the monitoring of inventory and fixed assets and makes it difficult to ensure that manufacturing activities are being performed efficiently and effectively. Therefore, inventory and work-in-process records must be protected from both intentional and accidental loss or damage. Regular backing up of all data files is imperative. Additional copies of key master files, such as open production orders and raw materials inventory, should be stored off-site. To reduce the possibility of accidental erasure of important files, all disks and tapes should have both external and internal file labels.

Access controls also are necessary, because the loss of production trade secrets can destroy a company. It is especially important to promptly remove all access rights of employees who quit or are fired, to prevent them from providing trade secrets and other production information to their new employers. Although companies that are victimized in this manner can sue the perpetrator, any financial compensation may come too late to restore the business.

Unauthorized access also increases the risk of damage to important data files. Using a system of passwords and user IDs can limit access to sensitive files. Moreover, access controls also should apply to terminals. For example, the system should be programmed to reject any attempts to alter inventory records from a terminal located in the engineering department. Finally, logs of all activities, especially any actions involving managerial approval, such as requests for additional raw materials or overtime, should be recorded and maintained for later review as part of the audit trail.

It is important to point out that enforcing proper access controls and segregation of duties requires that the controller or CFO review and suggest appropriate configuration of user rights in integrated AIS packages and ERP systems. The default installation of such systems typically provides every user with far too much power. For example, the default configurations of most integrated AIS packages and ERP systems may allow everyone involved in the movement of raw materials to make changes to the master data, including quantities on hand. Thus, the controller or CFO needs to review user permissions to ensure that various employees are assigned only those privileges necessary to perform their specified job duties. Although the procedures for modifying configurations vary across different software packages, knowing what changes need to be made requires only a sound understanding of proper segregation of duties for different business processes.

Access and processing integrity controls are also needed to ensure the confidentiality and accuracy of production cycle data transmissions between different factories. Sensitive data, such as the precise procedures to follow in manufacturing a given product, should be encrypted both while in storage and during transmission over the Internet. One way to do this is to use VPNs for all intracompany exchanges of production data and also for sending production information to key suppliers. Parity checks and acknowledgment messages should also be used to ensure the accuracy of data transmissions. In addition, various control totals, such as the totals of production amounts and record counts indicating the number of individual production transactions about which information is being sent, should be used to verify the accuracy of information exchanged between various offices.

Threat 8: Poor Performance

Inefficiencies in production operations result in increased expenses. Quality control problems also increase expenses and may even reduce future sales. Thus, manufacturing activities must be closely monitored and prompt action taken to correct any deviations from standards. The AIS can help control efficiency and quality by preparing appropriate performance reports. The next section discusses the key information decisions for effectively managing production cycle activities and how accountants can provide the information needed to make them.

Production Cycle Information Needs

A third function of the AIS is to provide information useful for decision making. In the modern manufacturing environment, the focus must be on total quality management. Consequently, managers need information about how well the production process is functioning, including defect rates, breakdown frequency, percentage of finished goods completed without any rework, and percentage of defects discovered by customers. Although much of this information is collected in the production cycle information system, in traditional cost accounting systems it is not integrated with cost data. Therefore, operational performance measures are not directly linked with their financial consequences.

Indeed, in many companies the cost accounting system has been separate from the production operations information system. The former collects data about the costs of production, storing that information in the work-in-process file. The latter collects

data about the physical aspects of manufacturing operations, storing that information in the open production order file. Both types of data are closely related, however, and both are needed for effectively managing the production process. For example, real-time information about production quality enables companies to spot and correct defects immediately, before additional labor and materials are used. Therefore, both cost and operational data should be integrated into one system.

In addition to failure to integrate cost and operational data, cost accounting systems have traditionally been designed to meet financial reporting requirements and only secondarily to attempt to meet the information needs of production managers. Consequently, in recent years, traditional cost systems have been criticized for not providing adequate information to manage production operations in a modern manufacturing environment. The two major criticisms of traditional cost accounting systems are reflected in the issues raised in the chapter-opening case for AOE: Overhead costs are inappropriately allocated to products, and reports do not accurately reflect the effects of factory automation.

Criticism 1: Inappropriate Allocation of Overhead Costs

Traditional cost systems use volume-driven bases, such as direct labor or machine hours, to apply overhead to products. Many overhead costs, however, do not vary directly with production volume. Purchasing costs, for example, vary with the number of purchase orders processed. Similarly, receiving costs vary with the number of shipments from suppliers. Setup and materials handling costs vary with the number of different batches that are run, not with the total number of units produced. Thus, allocating these types of overhead costs to products based on output volume overstates the costs of products manufactured in large quantities. It also understates the costs of products manufactured in small batches.

In addition, allocating overhead based on direct labor input can distort costs across products. As investments in factory automation increase, the amount of direct labor used in production decreases. Consequently, the amount of overhead charged per unit of labor increases dramatically. As a result, small differences in the amount of labor used to produce two products can result in significant differences in product costs.

Solution to Criticism 1: Activity-Based Costing

Activity-based costing[1] (ABC) can refine and improve cost allocations under both job-order and process cost systems. It attempts to trace costs to the activities that create them, such as grinding or polishing, and only subsequently allocates those costs to products or departments. An underlying objective of activity-based costing is to link costs to corporate strategy. Corporate strategy results in decisions about what goods and services to produce. Activities must be performed to produce these goods and services, which in turn incur costs. Thus, corporate strategy determines costs. Consequently, by measuring the costs of basic activities, such as materials handling or processing purchase orders, ABC provides information to management for evaluating the consequences of strategic decisions.

Activity-Based Costing versus Traditional Cost Systems

Following are three significant differences between ABC and traditional approaches to product costing:

1 ABC systems attempt to directly trace a larger proportion of overhead costs to products. Advances in IT make this feasible. For example, RFID technology and bar-coding facilitate tracking the exact quantities of miscellaneous parts used in

[1] In this section, we provide an overview of activity-based costing, its effects on the AIS, and its benefits. For additional details on the mechanics of activity-based costing, see any cost accounting textbook.

each product or process stage. When implementing ABC systems, accountants observe production operations and interview factory workers and supervisors to obtain a better understanding of how manufacturing activities affect costs.

2 ABC systems use a greater number of cost pools to accumulate indirect costs (manufacturing overhead). Whereas most traditional cost systems lump all overhead costs together, ABC systems distinguish three separate categories of overhead:

- **Batch-related overhead.** Examples include setup costs, inspections, and materials handling. ABC systems accumulate these costs for a batch and then allocate them to the units produced in that batch. Thus, products produced in large quantities have lower batch-related overhead costs per unit than products produced in small quantities.

- **Product-related overhead.** These costs are related to the diversity of the company's product line. Examples include research and development, expediting, shipping and receiving, environmental regulations, and purchasing. ABC systems try to link these costs to specific products when possible. For example, if a company produces three product lines, one of which generates hazardous waste, an ABC system would charge only that one set of products for all the costs of complying with environmental regulations. Other costs, such as purchasing raw materials, might be allocated across products based on the relative number of purchase orders required to make each product.

- **Companywide overhead.** This category includes such costs as rent or property taxes. These costs apply to all products. Thus, ABC systems typically allocate them using departmental or plant rates.

3 ABC systems attempt to rationalize the allocation of overhead to products by identifying cost drivers. A **cost driver** is anything that has a cause-and-effect relationship on costs. For example, the number of purchase orders processed is one cost driver of purchasing department costs; that is, the total costs of processing purchase orders (e.g., purchasing department salaries, postage) vary directly with the number of purchase orders that are processed. As in this example, cost drivers in ABC systems are often nonfinancial variables. In contrast, traditional costing systems often use financial variables, such as dollar volume of purchases, as the bases for allocating manufacturing overhead.

Benefits of ABC Systems

ABC systems cost more to run than traditional cost systems because they require the collection of more production-related data and in greater detail. ABC systems are also more complex, in part because more bases are used to allocate manufacturing overhead. Proponents of ABC systems argue that the increased costs and complexity provide two important benefits: More accurate cost data result in better product mix and pricing decisions, and more detailed cost data improve management's ability to control and manage total costs.

Better Decisions Traditional cost systems tend to apply too much overhead to some products and too little to others, because too few cost pools are used. This leads to two types of problems, both of which AOE experienced. First, companies may accept sales contracts for some products at prices below their true cost of production. Consequently, although sales increase, profits decline. Second, companies may overprice other products, thereby inviting new competitors to enter the market. Ironically, if more accurate cost data were available, companies would find that they could cut prices to keep competitors out of the market and still make a profit on each sale. ABC systems avoid these problems because overhead is divided into three categories and applied using cost drivers that are causally related to production. Therefore, product cost data are more accurate.

ABC also uses data to improve product design. For example, the costs associated with processing purchase orders can be used to calculate the purchasing-related overhead associated with each component used in a finished product. Engineering can use this

information, along with data on relative usage of components across products, to identify unique components that could be replaced by lower-cost, more commonly used parts.

Finally, ABC data improve managerial decision making by providing information about the costs associated with specific activities, instead of classifying those costs by financial statement category. Table 12-3 shows an example of how this rearrangement of data can improve managerial analysis by focusing attention on key processes. The traditional cost reports draws attention to the fact that travel and software costs are above budget. The ABC report, in contrast, shows which *activities* (training, testing, maintenance and systems analysis) are running over budget, and which are not.

Improved Cost Management Proponents argue that another advantage of ABC is that it clearly measures the results of managerial actions on overall profitability. Whereas traditional cost systems only measure spending to acquire resources, ABC systems measure both the amount spent to acquire resources and the consumption of those resources. This distinction is reflected in the following formula:

Cost of activity capability = Cost of activity used + Cost of unused capacity

To illustrate, consider the receiving function at a manufacturing firm such as AOE. The total monthly employee cost in the receiving department, including salaries and benefits, represents the cost of providing this function—receiving shipments from suppliers. Assume that the salary expense of the receiving department is $100,000, and assume that the number of employees is sufficient to handle 500 shipments. The cost per shipment would be $200. Finally, assume that 400 shipments are actually received. The ABC system would report that the cost of the receiving activity used is $80,000 ($200 × 400 shipments) and that the remaining $20,000 in salary expense represents the cost of unused capacity.

In this way, performance reports that ABC systems generate help direct managerial attention to how policy decisions made in one area affect costs in another area. For example, a purchasing department manager may decide to increase the minimum size of orders to obtain larger discounts for bulk purchases. This would reduce the number of incoming shipments that the receiving department must handle, thereby increasing its

TRADITIONAL COST REPORTS, BASED ON GENERAL LEDGER ACCOUNT CATEGORIES			
	Budget	**Actual**	**Variance**
Salaries	$386,000	$375,000	$11,000
Computer software	845,000	855,000	(10,000)
Travel	124,000	150,000	(26,000)
Supplies	25,000	20,000	5,000
Total	$1,380,000	$1,400,000	($20,000)
ACTIVITY-BASED COSTING ANALYSIS			
	Budget	**Actual**	**Variance**
Systems analysis	$200,000	$210,000	($10,000)
Coding	440,000	400,000	40,000
Testing	235,000	250,000	(15,000)
Maintenance	250,000	275,000	(25,000)
User support	90,000	50,000	40,000
Reports	87,000	75,000	12,000
Training	78,000	140,000	(62,000)
Total	$1,380,000	$1,400,000	($20,000)

Table 12-3
Comparison of Activity-Based Costing and Traditional Cost Allocation for the Information Systems Department

unused capacity. Similarly, actions taken to improve the efficiency of operations, such as requiring vendors to send products in bar-coded containers, increase practical capacity and create additional unused capacity. In either case, ABC performance reports highlight this excess capacity for managerial attention. Management can then try to improve profitability by applying that unused capacity to other revenue-generating activities.

Criticism 2: Misleading Reports

Modern approaches to production, such as lean manufacturing, differ significantly from traditional mass production. One major difference is a marked reduction in finished goods inventory levels, because production is scheduled in response to customer demand instead of projections based on prior years. Although this is beneficial in the long run, it often creates a short-term decline in reported profitability. The reason: Traditional financial accounting treats inventory as an asset. Thus, the costs of producing inventory are not recognized until the products are sold. When a company switches from mass production to lean manufacturing, it reduces existing inventory levels, with the result that costs incurred in prior periods to create that inventory are now expensed. In addition, since lean manufacturing seeks to minimize the creation of additional inventories, almost all labor and overhead costs are expensed in the current period, instead of being allocated to inventory and thereby treated as an asset and deferred to future periods. The combined effect of these changes often results in a marked increase in expenses in the year of transitioning to lean accounting. Although this effect is only temporary, it can create significant concern among managers, particularly if their performance evaluations are based primarily on the company's reported financial statements.

Solution to Criticism 2: Better Reports and Measures

CPAs who work for and with companies that have adopted lean manufacturing techniques advocate supplementing traditional financial reports based on GAAP with additional reports based on lean accounting[2] principles. One suggested change involves assigning costs to product lines instead of departments. For example, all the costs incurred to design, produce, sell, deliver, process customer payments, and provide post-sales support are grouped by product. Another change involves reporting overhead costs as a separate item, rather than including them in the calculation of the cost of goods sold. Lean-accounting reports also identify the change in inventory as a separate expense item, to more clearly reveal the effect of inventory levels on reported profits.

In addition to changing the structure of performance reports, accountants should also develop and refine new measures designed to focus on issues important to production cycle managers. One important concern is the level of usable output produced per unit of time. Monitoring quality is another.

Throughput: A Measure of Production Effectiveness **Throughput** represents the number of good units produced in a given period of time. It consists of three factors, each of which can be separately controlled, as shown in the following formula:[3]

$$\text{Throughput} = (\text{Total units produced/Processing time}) \times (\text{Processing time/Total time}) \times (\text{Good units/Total units})$$

Productive capacity, the first term in the formula, shows the maximum number of units that can be produced using current technology. Productive capacity can be increased by improving labor or machine efficiency, by rearranging the factory-floor layout to expedite the movement of materials, or by simplifying product design specifications.

[2]The introductory material in this section is based on an article by Karen M. Kroll, "The Lowdown on Lean Accounting," *Journal of Accountancy* (July 2004): 69–76.

[3]This formula was developed by Carole Cheatham in "Measuring and Improving Throughput," *Journal of Accountancy* (March 1990): 89–91.

Productive processing time, the second term in the formula, indicates the percentage of total production time used to manufacture the product. Productive processing time can be improved by improving maintenance to reduce machine downtime or by more efficient scheduling of material and supply deliveries to reduce wait time. *Yield*, the third term in the formula, represents the percentage of good (nondefective) units produced. Using better-quality raw materials or improving worker skills can improve yield.

Information About Quality Control Information about quality costs can help companies determine the effects of actions taken to improve yield and identify areas for further improvement. Quality control costs can be divided into four areas:

1 *Prevention costs* are associated with changes to production processes designed to reduce the product defect rate.
2 *Inspection costs* are associated with testing to ensure that products meet quality standards.
3 *Internal failure costs* are associated with reworking, or scrapping, products identified as being defective prior to sale.
4 *External failure costs* result when defective products are sold to customers. They include such costs as product liability claims, warranty and repair expenses, loss of customer satisfaction, and damage to the company's reputation.

The ultimate objective of quality control is to "get it right the first-time," by manufacturing products that meet customer specifications. This often requires trade-offs among the four quality cost categories. For example, increasing prevention costs can lower inspection costs as well as internal and external failure costs. Thus, the key management decision is to find trade-offs that minimize the sum of all four quality costs.

Some companies have found that the most important management decision involves switching from the traditional "management by exception" philosophy to a "continuous improvement" viewpoint. The change is subtle, but significant. Continuous improvement focuses on comparing actual performance to the ideal (i.e., perfection). Consequently, all variances are negative (how can you do better than perfect?). The largest variances indicate the areas with the greatest amount of "waste," and, correspondingly, the greatest opportunity for improving the bottom line. Thus, continuous improvement performance reports help companies to avoid becoming complacent by highlighting the fact that current activities can always be done better.

SUMMARY AND CASE CONCLUSION

The production cycle consists of four basic activities: product design, production planning and scheduling, production operations, and cost accounting. Companies are continually investing in IT to improve the efficiency of the first three activities. However, for a business to reap the full benefit of these changes, corresponding modifications must also be made to the cost accounting portion of the AIS. In addition, accountants need to modify financial reports and develop new measures that more accurately reflect and measure manufacturing performance.

After completing her tour of the factory, Elizabeth Venko was convinced that some major changes were required in AOE's cost accounting system. For example, although AOE's production operations were highly automated, manufacturing overhead was still being allocated based on direct labor hours. This resulted in distorted product costs due to small differences in the amount of direct labor used to assemble each item. Elizabeth decided that the solution was to do more than merely change the allocation base. Instead, AOE would implement activity-based costing. A number of different pools would be used to accumulate overhead costs, and the appropriate cost drivers would be identified for use in assigning those costs to specific

products. Based on her research, including conversations with a controller at another company that had recently implemented an ABC system, Elizabeth believed that these changes would solve AOE's problems with product pricing and mix decisions and more accurately reflect the effects of investments in factory automation.

Elizabeth also decided that three other major changes were needed in the reports the AIS produced. First, data about all the costs associated with quality control, not just those involving rework and scrap, should be collected and reported. Second, performance reports should include nonfinancial measures, like throughput, in addition to financial measures. Third, lean accounting principles, rather than GAAP, could be used to create financial reports intended for internal use. She discussed with LeRoy the likely behavioral effects of these changes. They agreed that identifying the different components of quality control costs should encourage continued investments that would be likely to improve the overall yield rate. Further, separately showing the effect of changes in inventory levels on profits would make it easier to reward efforts to reduce inventory levels. They also agreed on the need to closely monitor the effects of any new performance reports and make appropriate modifications to them.

Ann Brandt realized that Elizabeth's proposed changes would necessitate a redesign of AOE's production cycle database. In addition, the desire for more timely and accurate information would require additional investments in RFID technology to replace the use of bar-codes wherever feasible.

Elizabeth and Ann presented their plans at the next executive meeting. LeRoy Williams was satisfied that the changes would indeed address his complaints about AOE's current production cycle information system. Linda Spurgeon supported the proposal and agreed to fund the necessary changes. Peter Wu, vice president of human resources, was also impressed with Elizabeth and Ann's plans. In fact, he left the meeting resolved to secure their cooperation in helping him to revamp AOE's human resources management/payroll cycle information system.

KEY TERMS

production cycle 484
bill of materials 487
operations list 487
manufacturing resource
 planning (MRP-II) 488
lean manufacturing 488
master production
 schedule (MPS) 489
production order 489

materials
 requisition 489
move tickets 491
computer-integrated
 manufacturing
 (CIM) 492
job-order costing 494
process costing 494
job-time ticket 496

manufacturing
 overhead 497
request for proposal
 (RFP) 500
activity-based costing
 (ABC) 503
cost driver 504
throughput 506

AIS IN ACTION

CHAPTER QUIZ

1 Most costs are locked in at which stage in the production cycle?
 a. product design
 b. production planning
 c. production operations
 d. cost accounting

2 Which of the following is an advantage of bar-coding over RFID?
 a. speed
 b. accuracy
 c. cost
 d. safety

3 Which document lists the components needed to manufacture a specific product?
 a. operations list
 b. master production schedule
 c. bill of materials
 d. production order

4 Which document captures information about labor used in production?
 a. move ticket
 b. job-time ticket
 c. operations list
 d. bill of materials

5 An increase in which component of quality costs is most likely to result in a decrease in the other three components?
 a. prevention costs
 b. inspection costs
 c. internal failure costs
 d. external failure costs

6 Activity-based costing can be used to refine which of the following?
 a. job-order costing
 b. process costing
 c. both job-order and process costing
 d. neither job-order nor process costing

7 Which system is most likely to be used by a company that mass produces large batches of standard items in anticipation of customer demand?
 a. MRP-II
 b. lean manufacturing
 c. activity-based costing
 d. throughput

8 The development of an MPS would be most effective in preventing which of the following threats?
 a. recording and posting errors
 b. loss of inventory
 c. production of poor-quality goods
 d. excess production

9 Which control procedure is probably least effective in reducing the threat of inventory loss?
 a. limiting physical access to inventory
 b. documenting all transfers of inventory within the company
 c. regular materials usage reports that highlight variances from standards
 d. periodically counting inventory and investigating any discrepancies between those counts and recorded amounts

10 What is the number of good units produced in a given period of time called?
 a. productive capacity
 b. productive processing time
 c. yield
 d. throughput

DISCUSSION QUESTIONS

12.1 When activity-based cost reports indicate that excess capacity exists, management should either find alternative revenue-enhancing uses for that capacity or eliminate it through downsizing. What factors influence management's decision? What are the likely behavioral side effects of each choice? What implications do those side effects have for the long-run usefulness of activity-based cost systems?

12.2 Why should accountants participate in product design? What insights about costs can accountants contribute that differ from the perspectives of purchasing managers and engineers?

12.3 Some companies have eliminated the collection and reporting of detailed analyses on direct labor costs broken down by various activities. Instead, first-line supervisors are responsible for controlling the total costs of direct labor. The justification for this argument is that labor costs represent only a small fraction of the total costs of producing a product and are not worth the time and effort to trace to individual activities. Do you agree or disagree with this argument? Why?

12.4 Typically, McDonald's produces menu items in advance of customer orders based on anticipated demand. In contrast, Burger King produces menu items only in response to customer orders. Which system (MRP-II or lean manufacturing) does each company use? What are the relative advantages and disadvantages of each system?

12.5 How might the proportion of total quality control costs in each of the four components of quality control (prevention, inspection, internal failure, and external failure) vary for different types of products, such as operating system software versus laser printer paper?

12.6 What are the advantages and disadvantages of using RFID technology to implement the specific identification method of accounting for inventory?

12.7 What are the advantages and disadvantages of "continuous improvement" performance reports? Why do you think some companies adopt this philosophy, but others do not?

PROBLEMS

12.1 What internal control procedure(s) would best prevent or detect the following problems?
 a. A production order was initiated for a product that was already overstocked in the company's warehouse.
 b. A production employee stole items of work-in-process inventory.
 c. The "rush-order" tag on a partially completed production job became detached from the materials and lost, resulting in a costly delay.
 d. A production employee entered a materials requisition form into the system in order to steal $300 worth of parts from the raw materials storeroom.

 e. A production worker entering job-time data on an online terminal mistakenly entered 3,000 instead of 300 in the "quantity-completed" field.

 f. A production worker entering job-time data on an online terminal mistakenly posted the completion of operation 562 to production order 7569 instead of production order 7596.

 g. A parts storeroom clerk issued parts in quantities 10% lower than those indicated on several materials requisitions and stole the excess quantities.

 h. A production manager stole several expensive machines and covered up the loss by submitting a form to the accounting department indicating that the missing machines were obsolete and should be written off as worthless.

 i. The quantity-on-hand balance for a key component shows a negative balance.

 j. A factory supervisor accesses the operations list file and inflates the standards for work completed in his department. Consequently, future performance reports show favorable budget variances for that department.

12.2 What is the purpose of each of the following control activities?

 a. documenting the return of any scrapped products to inventory stores

 b. using an MPS to schedule production

 c. periodically counting fixed assets and reconciling those counts to the fixed-asset subsidiary ledger

 d. using electronic move tickets (implemented with RFID technology) to document transfers of work in process between factory departments

 e. prenumbering and periodic accounting of all materials requisitions

 f. using passwords to control access to the system that generates production orders

 g. listing and printing monthly all transactions involving the acquisition or disposal of fixed assets and having the controller review them

12.3 You have recently been hired as the controller for a small manufacturing firm that makes high-definition televisions. One of your first tasks is to develop a report measuring throughput.

Required

Describe the data required to measure throughput and the most efficient and accurate method of collecting that data.

12.4 The Joseph Brant Manufacturing Company makes athletic footwear. Processing of production orders is as follows: At the end of each week, the production planning department prepares a master production schedule (MPS) that lists which shoe styles and quantities are to be produced during the next week. A production order preparation program accesses the MPS and the operations list (stored on a permanent disk file) to prepare a production order for each shoe style that is to be manufactured. Each new production order is added to the open production order master file stored on disk.

 Each day, parts department clerks review the open production orders and the MPS to determine which materials need to be released to production. All materials are barcoded. Factory workers work individually at specially designed U-shaped work areas equipped with several machines to assist them in completely making a pair of shoes. Factory workers scan the bar-codes as they use materials. To operate a machine, the factory workers swipe their ID badge through a reader. This results in the system automatically collecting data identifying who produced each pair of shoes and how much time it took to make them.

 Once a pair of shoes is finished, it is placed in a box. The last machine in each work cell prints a bar-code label that the worker affixes to the box. The completed shoes are then sent to the warehouse.

Required

1 Prepare both a data flow diagram and a systems flowchart of all operations described.
2 Describe a comprehensive set of control procedures that should be included in each system. Organize your answer by listing the potential threats and specifying the control procedures that would best address them.
3 Describe opportunities to use information technology to further improve efficiency of operations.

12.5 The XYZ company sells approximately 900,000 gizmos annually. Each gizmo consists of 15 components. Management is currently evaluating which vendor to choose as the primary supplier of one of the components. Four vendors have been identified. Management wants you to choose the vendor that will provide the lowest total cost (purchase price plus expected warranty repairs costs). It costs $135 to repair or replace defective products returned by customers.

Required

a. Use the following information to identify which vendor to select:

Factor	Vendor A	Vendor B	Vendor C	Vendor D
Purchase price of component	$23.50	$24.00	$24.70	$26.00
Estimated failure rate of component	5.8%	5.2%	4.7%	4.2%

b. How would your decision change if marketing research indicated that product failures due to defects in this particular component were the most important factor influencing overall customer satisfaction with the company's gizmo product?

12.6 EXCEL PROBLEM
Task: Create a depreciation schedule to monitor your company's investment in fixed assets.
a. Your spreadsheet should have the following column headings:
 ● Account number (5 digits, valid range from 11000 to 19999)
 ● Description (text, valid entries = software, laptop, monitor, workstation, desk, chair)
 ● Date placed in service (mm/dd/yyyy format)
 ● Estimated useful life
 ● Acquisition cost
 ● Beginning accumulated depreciation (prior to this year)
 ● Current period depreciation (straight-line method, assume no salvage value)
 ● Ending accumulated depreciation (beginning accumulated depreciation plus current period depreciation)
 ● Net book value (acquisition cost–ending accumulated depreciation)
b. In the top rows of the spreadsheet, enter the following data:
 ● Your name (in row 1)
 ● Depreciation schedule for year (in row 2)
 ● Two cells to the right of the text "Depreciation schedule for year," a formula that returns the current year (i.e., if the date is 10/31/2009 your formula should return the value 2009)
c. Enter the following data:

Account Number	Description	Date Placed in Service	Estimated Useful Life	Acquisition Cost
11001	Desk	04/05/2006	5	500
11100	Laptop	05/02/2007	5	2400
11200	Workstation	03/25/2006	5	1900
11050	Chair	02/01/2003	5	750
11500	Software	07/01/2008	3	750
11500	Software	06/30/2007	3	2100
11500	Software	01/31/2005	3	900
11300	Monitor	02/20/2007	4	800
11300	Monitor	09/30/2003	4	1200
11300	Monitor	10/15/2006	4	600
11001	Desk	04/04/2007	5	1000
11001	Desk	08/08/2003	5	1500
11050	Chair	06/30/2008	5	1250

d. Create formulas to calculate the beginning balance of accumulated depreciation, current depreciation, ending balance, and net book value.
- Use the built-in Year(xxx) function to return the year portion of a date in mm/dd/yyyy format.
- The today() takes no arguments and returns the current date in mm/dd/yyyy format.
- Assume that assets placed in service anytime during a year can be depreciated for the entire year.

e. Include the following validation checks, with appropriate and informative error messages should any of these be violated:
- Each entry in the columns account number, description, and date contains allowable values.
- If an asset has already been fully depreciated, current depreciation should be zero.
- Ending balance of accumulated depreciation should equal beginning balance plus current depreciation.
- Net book value should equal acquisition cost minus ending balance of accumulated depreciation.
- The sum of all net book values should equal the sum of all acquisition costs minus the sum of all ending balances of accumulated depreciation.

f. Create a table at the bottom of your worksheet that consists of two columns:
- Asset name (values should be chair, desk, laptop, monitor, software, and workstation)
- New book value (use as a built-in Excel function to calculate this number)

12.7 EXCEL PROBLEM

Task: Use Excel and the Solver add-in to explore the effect of various resource constraints on the optimal product mix.

a. Read the article "Boost Profits With Excel," by James A. Weisel in the December 2003 issue of the *Journal of Accountancy* (available online at the AICPA's Web site, www.aicpa.org—navigate to the Online Journal of Accountancy pages).

b. Download the sample spreadsheet discussed in the article (http://www.aicpa.org/download/pubs/jofa/2003_12_weisel.xls), and print out the solutions discussed in the article.

c. Rerun the Solver program to determine which of the following parameter changes maximizes income (print out the results of each option):
- 2,500 additional minutes of labor for an additional $600
- 5,000 additional minutes of labor for an additional $1,500

- 7,500 additional minutes of labor for an additional $3,000
- 10,000 additional minutes of labor for an additional $5,000

d. The previous step required much manual work to repeatedly change the assumptions and rerun the simulation with Solver. Create a one-variable data table to automate this process. (The article "Hey, What If . . . ?" by Stephanie M. Bryant in the June 2000 issue of the *Journal of Accountancy* explains how to create data tables). The variable you will be modifying is additional minutes of labor, for the four increments used in step c (2,500 through 10,000 extra minutes). Change the value of the formula for total labor costs (cell J11) to equal 10,000 + 0.25 per additional minute of labor over 50,000 minutes. (*Hint:* you will want to reference cell J25 in your formula.) Your one-variable data table should look something like this (with the blank cells showing the results of the simulation—compare to your results for step c):

Additional Labor Minutes over 50,000	Operating Income
0	
2,500	
5,000	
7,500	
10,000	

12.8 The ABC Company has collected the following data concerning performance in its manufacturing plant:

Process	Actual unit costs	Budgeted unit costs	Ideal (Perfect) unit costs
Sanding	$17.50	$18.00	$16.45
Painting	$29.00	$29.00	$28.40
Polishing	$13.00	$13.20	$12.00
Packaging	$8.50	$8.00	$7.75

Required

a. Prepare a traditional performance report (comparing actual to budget). Which processes need attention? Why?

b. Prepare a continuous improvement performance report (comparing actual to perfect). Which processes need attention? Why?

12.9 Create the spreadsheet on page 515 with formulas to calculate the total depreciation expense and to display the correct values in the columns: Age, Depreciation Rate, and Depreciation Expense. Hint: You will need to use the VLOOKUP, MATCH, and ISNA functions to do this. You may also want to read the article "Double-Teaming In Excel," by Judith K. Welch, Lois S. Mahoney, and Daniel R. Brickner, in the November 2005 issue of the *Journal of Accountancy*, from which this problem was adapted.

CASE 12-1 The Accountant and CIM

Examine issues of the *Journal of Accountancy* and *Strategic Finance* for the past three years for stories about current developments in factory automation. Write a brief report that discusses the accounting implications of that development: how it affects the efficiency and accuracy of data collection and any new opportunities for improving the quality of performance reports. Also discuss how the development affects the risks of various production cycle threats and the control procedures used to mitigate those risks.

Microsoft Excel - Book1

File Edit View Insert Format Tools Data Window Help Adobe PDF

Type a question for help

100%

Reply with Changes... End Review...

L17

MACRS DEPRECIATION RATE

PROPERTY CLASS

Age	A	B	C
1	22%	16%	13%
2	30%	25%	20%
3	20%	20%	17%
4	14%	18%	15%
5	14%	16%	14%
6		5%	10%
7			7%
8			3%
9			
10			

ASSET DEPRECIATION SCHEDULE

Year for computation: 2008

Name	Year Purchased	Age	Property Class	Cost	Depreciation Rate	Depreciation Expense
Desk	2007		A	3500		
Chair	2005		B	1200		
File Cabinet	2001		B	750		
CAD software	2006		A	85000		
Copier	2005		A	1500		
Server	2002		C	6500		
Office software	2000		B	50600		
Printer	2006		C	7500		
Workstation	2005		A	2000		
Laptop	2007		B	3000		
Firewall	2003		C	10000		
IPS	2004		C	15000		
				Total		

Draw AutoShapes

Sheet1 Sheet2 Sheet3

Ready

AIS IN ACTION SOLUTIONS

1 Most costs are locked in at which stage in the production cycle?

✔ **a.** product design (Correct. Decisions made during product design determine the majority of costs.)

b. production planning (Incorrect. Decisions made during product design determine the majority of costs.)

c. production operations (Incorrect. Decisions made during product design determine the majority of costs.)

d. cost accounting (Incorrect. Decisions made during product design determine the majority of costs.)

2 Which of the following is an advantage of bar-coding over RFID?

a. speed (Incorrect. RFID technology can read information from multiple items at the same time, whereas bar-code scanners can only read one item at a time. In addition, time must be spent to align the bar-codes on each item with the reader.)

b. accuracy (Incorrect. In certain applications, RFID is more accurate than bar-coding. For example, in retail stores, checkout clerks can enter the bar-code for one item and then enter a quantity of 7, rather than scanning the bar-codes or each item, whereas an RFID reader would identify which 7 specific products were sold.)

✔ **c.** cost (Correct. Bar-coding is currently less expensive than RFID.)

d. safety (Incorrect. There is no difference in the safety of bar-coding and RFID.)

3 Which document lists the components needed to manufacture a specific product?

a. operations list (Incorrect. This document lists the sequence of steps to manufacture the product.)

b. master production schedule (Incorrect. This document is used to plan production activities.)

✔ **c.** bill of materials (Correct. The bill of materials lists the components of a finished product.)

d. production order (Incorrect. This document authorizes production activities.)

4 Which document captures information about labor used in production?

a. move ticket (Incorrect. The move ticket documents movement of materials.)

✔ **b.** job-time ticket (Correct. The job-time ticket records time spent on each activity.)

c. operations list (Incorrect. The operations list specifies the sequence of steps to manufacture a product.)

d. bill of materials (Incorrect. The bill of materials identifies the components used to manufacture a product.)

5 An increase in which component of quality costs is most likely to result in a decrease in the other three components?

✔ **a.** prevention costs (Correct. Increases in prevention costs often reduce the time and cost of inspecting products, as well as the proportion of defective products.)

b. inspection costs (Incorrect. Increasing inspection costs do not necessarily reduce the other three quality control costs.)

c. internal failure costs (Incorrect. Increasing internal failure costs do not have any effect on prevention or inspection costs.)

d. external failure costs (Incorrect. Increasing external failure costs do not reduce other components of quality costs.)

6 Activity-based costing can be used to refine which of the following?
 a. job-order costing (Incorrect. Activity-based costing can be used with either job-order or process costing.)
 b. process costing (Incorrect. Activity-based costing can be used with either job-order or process costing.)
✔ **c.** both job-order and process costing (Correct. Activity-based costing can be used with either job-order or process costing.)
 d. neither job-order nor process costing (Incorrect. Activity-based costing can be used with either job-order or process costing.)

7 Which system is most likely to be used by a company that mass-produces large batches of standard items in anticipation of customer demand?
✔ **a.** MRP-II (Correct. MRP-II is a push form of manufacturing that is appropriate for mass production of standardized items for which demand is predictable.)
 b. lean manufacturing (Incorrect. Lean manufacturing seeks to minimize inventories by producing only in response to customer orders.)
 c. activity-based costing (Incorrect. Activity-based-costing is a cost allocation system, not a production planning technique.)
 d. throughput (Incorrect. Throughput is a measure of efficiency.)

8 The development of an MPS would be most effective in preventing which of the following threats?
 a. recording and posting errors (Incorrect. Data validation and processing controls would best minimize recording and posting errors.)
 b. loss of inventory (Incorrect. Access controls and frequent physical counts of inventory would best reduce the risk of inventory theft.)
 c. production of poor-quality goods (Incorrect. Product design addresses this issue.)
✔ **d.** excess production (Correct. An MPS schedules production to satisfy demand and, therefore, reduces the chance of overproduction.)

9 Which control procedure is probably least effective in reducing the threat of inventory loss?
 a. limiting physical access to inventory (Incorrect. Physical access controls are an important method for reducing the risk of inventory theft.)
 b. documenting all transfers of inventory within the company (Incorrect. Adequate documentation is an important control to reduce the risk of inventory theft.)
✔ **c.** regular materials usage reports that highlight variances from standards (Correct. Although variances may indicate theft, they are more likely to reflect changes in efficiency.)
 d. periodically counting inventory and investigating any discrepancies between those counts and recorded amounts (Incorrect. Periodic counts of inventory are an important control for reducing the risk of inventory theft.)

10 What is the number of good units produced in a given period of time called?
 a. productive capacity (Incorrect. Productive capacity is a component of throughput that represents the total number of units, both good and bad, produced per unit of time.)
 b. productive processing time (Incorrect. Productive processing time is the component of throughput that measures the proportion of time actually spent producing output.)
 c. yield (Incorrect. Yield is the component of throughput that measures the proportion of good units produced per batch.)
✔ **d.** throughput (Correct. Throughput is the measure of the number of good units produced per unit of time.)

CHAPTER 13

The Human Resources Management and Payroll Cycle

INTEGRATIVE CASE **ALPHA OMEGA ELECTRONICS**

Like many companies, AOE did not fully implement all modules of its new ERP system at the same time. It focused first on integrating the revenue and expenditure cycles with the production cycle and continued to use its existing payroll and HRM systems. Thus, like many companies, AOE currently has separate HRM and payroll systems. The payroll system, which is under the accounting department's control, produces employee paychecks and maintains the related records as required by government regulations. The payroll system uses batch processing: Hourly employees are paid biweekly; salaried employees and those on commission are paid monthly. The HRM system, which the human resources department runs, maintains files on employee job history, skills, and benefits; these files are updated weekly. Each system maintains its own separate files, sometimes storing the same data, such as pay rates, in different formats. This practice makes it difficult for accounting personnel to prepare reports that combine HRM and payroll data.

Peter Wu, the new vice president for human resources at AOE, wants to address several problems with AOE's payroll and HRM activities. Payroll processing costs have risen and employees are unhappy with the lengthy delays required to obtain information about their benefits and retirement plans. In addition, the current HRM system makes it difficult to accurately track employee skill

development. Consequently, managers have tended to hire externally to meet new staffing needs, rather than promoting or transferring existing employees. This practice has hurt employee morale. It also impedes evaluating the effectiveness of AOE's investment in training and continuing education. Peter is certain that implementing the payroll and HRM modules of the ERP system will solve all these problems.

Peter met with Elizabeth Venko and Ann Brandt to discuss the process of migrating from AOE's current stand-alone payroll and HRM systems to integration of those functions in the new ERP system. Elizabeth and Ann agreed that such a conversion would improve both the efficiency of payroll processing and the effectiveness of HR management. They began developing a detailed timetable for the system conversions. As you read this chapter, think about the relationships between HRM and payroll activities and how an integrated database can make both functions more efficient and effective.

Introduction

The **human resources management (HRM)/payroll cycle** is a recurring set of business activities and related data processing operations associated with effectively managing the employee workforce. The more important tasks include:

1. Recruiting and hiring new employees,
2. Training,
3. Job assignment,
4. Compensation (payroll),
5. Performance evaluation,
6. Discharge of employees, due to voluntary or involuntary termination.

Tasks 1 and 6 are performed once for each employee, whereas tasks 2 through 5 are performed repeatedly for as long as an employee works for the company. In most companies, these six activities are split between two separate systems. Task 4, compensating employees, is the payroll system's primary function. (In addition, as discussed in Chapter 12, the payroll system also allocates labor costs to products and departments for use in product pricing and mix decisions.) The HRM system performs the other five tasks. In many companies, these two systems are organizationally separate: The HRM system is usually the responsibility of the director of human resources, whereas the controller manages the payroll system.

This chapter focuses primarily on the payroll system, because accountants have traditionally been responsible for this function. The payroll system must be designed to meet government regulations as well as management's information needs. Incomplete or erroneous payroll records not only impair decision making but also can result in fines and imprisonment! Thus, the design of an efficient and effective payroll system is vital.

It is also important, however, to have a well-designed HRM system. The knowledge and skills of employees are valuable assets and must be carefully managed, developed, and maintained. Companies need effective HRM systems to help assign appropriate employees to different tasks and to facilitate monitoring the continuous development of the organization's intellectual assets.

Overview

Figure 13-1 presents a context diagram of the payroll system, depicting its relationships with the HRM system and with the other parts of the AIS. This figure shows five major sources of inputs to the payroll system. The HRM department provides information about hirings, terminations, and pay-rate changes due to raises and promotions. Employees initiate changes in their discretionary deductions (e.g., contributions to retirement plans). The various departments provide data about actual hours employees work. Government agencies provide tax rates and instructions for meeting regulatory requirements. Similarly, insurance companies and other organizations provide instructions for calculating and remitting various withholdings.

Checks are the payroll system's principal output. Employees receive individual *paychecks* in compensation for their services. A *payroll check* is sent to the bank to transfer funds from the company's regular accounts to its payroll account. Checks also are issued to government agencies, insurance companies, and other organizations to meet company obligations (e.g., taxes, insurance premiums). In addition, the payroll system produces a variety of reports, which we discuss later, for internal and external use.

Organizational success depends on skilled and motivated employees because their knowledge and skills affect the quality of the goods and services provided to customers. Indeed, in professional service organizations, such as accounting and law firms, employees' knowledge and skills *are* the principal component of the company's product, and labor costs represent the major expense incurred in generating revenues. Even in manufacturing firms, where direct labor costs represent only a fraction of total direct costs, employees are a key cost driver in that the quality of their work affects both overall productivity and product defect rates. Thus, it is not surprising to find that some stock analysts believe that employee skills and knowledge may be worth several times the value of a company's tangible assets such as inventory, property, and equipment.

Nevertheless, the AIS has not traditionally been used to measure or report on the status of a company's human resources. One reason is the assets reported in financial statements represent resources the organization owns but has not yet consumed. Employees, however, are not "owned" by the company. Consequently, the value of human resources has traditionally been recognized only when they are used, at which time they are either recorded as wages and salary expenses or, in the case of direct labor in manufacturing firms, included as part of the cost of inventory.

This situation began to change in the late 1990s when companies such as Dow Chemical, created new executive positions with responsibility for developing and managing the organization's intellectual assets and human resources. Other companies, such as Skandia Group, Scandinavia's largest financial services company, even experimented with reporting human resources information in their annual reports. These efforts indicate that organizations are beginning to realize the true value of the skills and knowledge possessed by their employees.

Figure 13-1
Context Diagram of the Payroll Portion of the HRM/Payroll Cycle

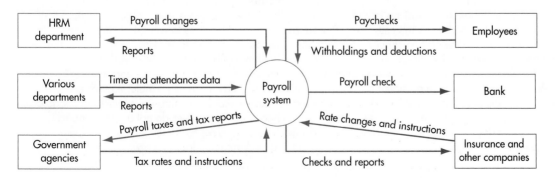

Recognizing the value of employees' knowledge and skills can help companies better understand the true costs associated with excessive turnover. Experts estimate that, on average, the costs associated with replacing an employee (recruiting and hiring expenses, training costs, and the relative inefficiency of new employees as they learn how to do the job) are 1.5 times that of an employee's annual salary. Thus, organizations that experience below-industry-average turnover rates reap considerable cost savings compared to rivals with higher turnover rates. For example, consider two companies, each with 1,500 employees earning on average $40,000. One company experiences 20% annual turnover, the other only 5%. The company with 20% annual turnover would incur costs of $18 million (300 employees times $60,000) to replace employees, compared to only $4.5 million for the company experiencing only 5% annual turnover. Of course, some turnover will always occur and may even be desirable. For example, professional consulting organizations have traditionally encouraged some level of turnover because they believe it provides an important source of new ideas. The key is to control and manage turnover rates so that they are not excessive.

Employee morale is also important. Low employee morale creates financial costs when it results in turnover. Conversely, there is increasing evidence that high employee morale provides financial benefits. For example, Sears collected detailed data on employee satisfaction, actual behavior, and customer satisfaction. Statistical analysis revealed that employee attitudes about their jobs and the company significantly predicted how they behaved with customers, which in turn affected customer satisfaction as measured by repeat sales. Sears' results are not isolated; a Gallup survey of 55,000 workers across a variety of companies found a positive correlation between employee attitudes and profitability. The survey identified four key attitudes: Employees believe they have the opportunity to do what they do best, every day; they believe their opinions count; they think that coworkers are committed to quality; and they understand the connection between their jobs and the company's mission. Focus 13-1 describes some of

13-1 FOCUS — The Value of Understanding Employee Jobs and Attitudes

A growing number of companies, including Walt Disney, Continental Airlines, Sysco, and Amazon.com, periodically require some of their upper-level executives to spend time in the trenches to better understand job duties and pressures. The experience can help executives identify needed changes in working conditions. For example, when the CEO of Loews Hotels assumed the roles of bellman, pool attendant, and housekeeper at a Florida hotel, he found that the company's polyester uniform caused him to sweat profusely. He immediately ordered that the style and material be altered for all employees. Immersion experiences also enable top executives to better empathize with rank-and-file workers. For example, after the vice president of DaVita Inc., a major dialysis-treatment provider, spent three days working in one of the company's clinics, she understood how physically demanding and stressful the work is. She also personally experienced how the need to respond to life-threatening emergencies can result in delays in completing corporate-mandated reports. Most importantly, the vice president acted on the information she learned. She now strives to ensure that new initiatives and changes in procedures are implemented in a manner that does not interfere with clinic technicians' primary patient care responsibilities.

Executive immersion experiences are important because there is a growing body of evidence that employees who have positive attitudes contribute to improved profitability by being more willing to take initiative, step in when needed to help fulfill customer requests, and promote the company when not at work. Thus, it is not surprising to find that many companies regularly survey employees to learn about their concerns. These new surveys replace traditional questions about job satisfaction with ones specially designed to better reveal employees' true attitudes about their job, coworkers, and managers. The answers can help managers take specific steps to improve employee morale and motivation. For example, such surveys informed the manager of a fast food franchise in Houston that some employees were unhappy because they were assigned too few hours to work, but others were unhappy because they had to work too many hours. The manager now makes a point to review work schedules for the following month early enough to accommodate employees' desires as much as possible. As with executive immersion experience, follow-through on such survey data is critical because if companies do not act on feedback obtained from employees by these methods, employee morale and performance drop sharply.

Figure 13-2
Integration of Payroll and HRM Functions in Typical ERP System

Notice how the ERP system integrate payroll functions (e.g., payroll, paycheck reconciliation, etc.) with HRM functions (e.g., benefits, recruitment, etc.).

the methods companies use to better understand employees' job-related concerns and how they use that information to improve working conditions and morale.

These examples illustrate why it is important that companies effectively manage and develop their intellectual capital and human resources. To do this, the AIS must be designed to do more than just record time and attendance data and prepare paychecks. Instead, the payroll system should be integrated with the HRM system so that management has easy access not only to data about employee-related costs but also to information about employees' skills and knowledge. As Figure 13-2 shows, ERP systems typically provide this level of integration.

The remainder of this chapter is organized in terms of the three basic functions the AIS provides in the HRM/payroll cycle: processing transactional data about employee activities, safeguarding the organization's assets, and providing information for decision making. We begin by describing the basic activities in the payroll cycle. Next, we discuss the control objectives of the HRM/payroll cycle and describe applicable control procedures for mitigating the major potential threats in this cycle. We conclude this chapter with a discussion of key decisions in the HRM/payroll cycle and identify the information needed to make those decisions.

Payroll Cycle Activities

Figure 13-3 (see next page) shows the seven basic activities performed in the payroll cycle. Payroll is one AIS application that continues to be processed in batch mode because (1) paychecks are prepared periodically (weekly, biweekly, or monthly) and (2) most employees are paid at the same time. Figure 13-4 (on page 525) depicts a typical batch-oriented HRM/payroll system like the one AOE uses. We will refer to Figure 13-4 as we discuss the activities depicted in Figure 13-3.

Update Payroll Master File

The first activity in the HRM/payroll cycle involves updating the payroll master file to reflect various types of payroll changes: new hires, terminations, changes in pay rates, or changes in discretionary withholdings (circle 1.0 in Figure 13-3). The HRM department provides this information. Although payroll is processed in batch mode, Figure 13-4 shows that the HRM department has online access to make these changes to the

Figure 13-3
Level 0 Data Flow Diagram for the Payroll Cycle

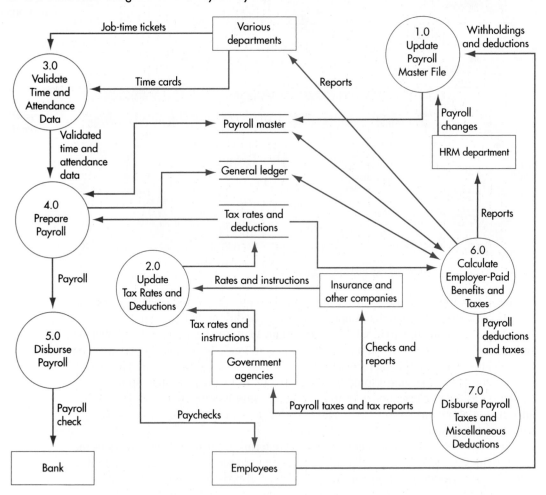

payroll master file. Appropriate edit checks, such as validity checks on employee number and reasonableness tests for the changes being made, are applied to all payroll change transactions.

It is important that all payroll changes are entered in a timely manner and are properly reflected in the next pay period. Records of employees who quit or are fired should not be deleted immediately, however, because some year-end tax reports, including W-2 forms, require data about all employees who worked for the organization at any time during the year.

Update Tax Rates and Deductions

The second activity in the HRM/payroll cycle is updating information about tax rates and other withholdings (circle 2.0 in Figure 13-3). The payroll department makes these changes, but the changes occur infrequently. They happen when the payroll department receives notification of changes in tax rates and other payroll deductions from various government units and insurance companies.

Validate Time and Attendance Data

The third step in the payroll cycle is to validate each employee's time and attendance data (circle 3.0 in Figure 13-3). This information comes in various forms, depending on an employee's pay status.

Figure 13-4
HRM/Payroll Flowchart

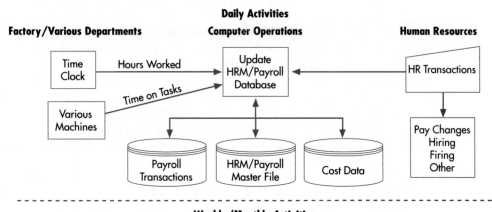

Daily Activities

Factory/Various Departments Computer Operations Human Resources

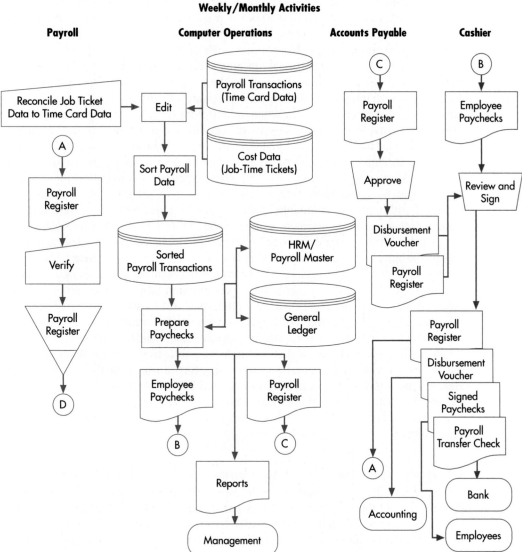

Weekly/Monthly Activities

Pay Schemes

Most employees are paid either on a fixed salary or on an hourly basis. For employees paid on an hourly basis, many companies use a **time card** to record the employee's arrival and departure times for each work shift. The time card also includes the total hours worked during a pay period. Employees who earn a fixed salary (e.g., managers and professional staff) seldom record their labor efforts on time cards. Instead, their supervisors informally monitor their presence on the job.

As discussed in Chapter 12, manufacturing companies also use job-time tickets to record detailed data about how employees use their time (i.e., which jobs they perform). The data are used to allocate labor costs among various departments, cost centers, and production jobs. Professionals in such service organizations as accounting, law, and consulting firms similarly track the time they spend performing various tasks. These data are used to accurately bill clients.

Sales staff often are paid either on a straight commission or on a salary plus commission basis. This requires the staff to carefully record the amount of their sales. In addition, some sales staff are paid bonuses for exceeding targets. An increasing number of companies in the United States are extending such incentive bonuses to employees other than sales staff, to motivate greater productivity and better work quality. For example, Nucor Corporation, one of the largest steel producers in the United States, pays its steelworkers an hourly rate set at approximately 60% of the industry average, plus a bonus based on the tons of steel they produce and ship. Companies have long used stock options to reward executives; in recent years, many companies have extended this practice to their nonexecutive employees as well. The argument is that stock options motivate employees to actively look for ways to improve service and cut costs so that the value of their compensation package rises.

Using incentives, commissions, and bonuses requires linking the payroll system and the information systems of sales and other cycles in order to collect the data used to calculate bonuses. Moreover, the bonus/incentive schemes must be properly designed with realistic, attainable goals that can be objectively measured. It is also important that goals be congruent with corporate objectives and that managers monitor goals to ensure that they continue to be appropriate. Indeed, poorly designed incentive pay schemes can result in undesirable behavior. For example, Sears Automotive experienced unintended negative effects from implementing a new incentive plan in the early 1990s that paid its repair staff a commission based on the amount of parts sold and number of hours worked. The intent was to focus employees' attention on how their efforts affected the company's bottom line. The result, however, was a scandal in which it was alleged that Sears employees recommended unnecessary repairs to boost their own pay. The alleged abuses reduced public trust in Sears Automotive and led to lower revenues. Eventually, Sears discontinued use of this incentive system. Besides the possibility of creating unintended and undesirable behaviors, poorly designed incentive pay schemes can also run afoul of legal, tax, and regulatory requirements. Thus, as Focus 13-2 explains, accountants should be involved in reviewing a company's compensation practices.

Efficiency Opportunities Using Information Technology

Payroll processing can be made more efficient by collecting employee time and attendance data electronically instead of on paper documents. This can reduce the time and potential errors associated with manually recording, verifying, and finally entering employee time and attendance data into the computer system (or payroll processing system). For example, badge readers can be used to collect job-time data for production employees. Those data are then automatically fed to the payroll processing system. Similarly, electronic time clocks can transmit time and attendance data directly to the payroll processing program. As discussed in Chapter 12, AOE is planning to implement these techniques to automate the collection of time and attendance data for its factory workers. Similar procedures can be used for professional service staff. For example,

Accountants and Compensation Policies

Recent revelations of multimillion-dollar bonuses and large severance packages for top executives of companies with declining financial performance have created the impression that some top executives are more concerned about their own compensation than shareholders' interests. As a result, regulators and Congress have begun to scrutinize executive compensation practices more closely. In particular, the use of stock options attracted a great deal of attention. The FASB issued new rules requiring that stock options be expensed, and the major U.S. stock exchanges now require companies to obtain shareholder approval of all equity-based compensation.

In the past, top executives often were involved indirectly in crafting their own compensation packages by hiring the consultants who designed those packages. Now, in response to recent scandals, the role of board compensation committees is increasing. Accountants can help these committees improve their company's compensation plans by providing advice concerning the financial and tax effects of proposed changes in executive compensation. One area where accounting expertise can be especially helpful is in identifying the appropriate metrics to use when linking compensation to performance. To be useful, those metrics need to be linked to the factors most important to a particular company's success. Obviously, this varies from company to company. For example, the key measures for a retail organization like Wal-Mart or Home Depot will be different from those used by an insurance company like Prudential, which will differ from those that are important to a basic manufacturer like Alcoa.

Accountants can also help board compensation committees comply with legal and regulatory requirements. For example, members of compensation committees may not understand all the details of tax regulations, like ERISA, which limit the allowable differences between benefit packages offered to executives and those made available to other employees. Accountants can review proposed changes for compliance with such rules. Finally, accountants can help companies improve shareholder relations by suggesting the best ways to go beyond minimum disclosure rules concerning executive compensation without revealing information vital to continued competitive success.

AT&T's internal service staff uses touch-tone telephones to log in time spent on various tasks, thereby eliminating the use of paper time sheets. The payroll program applies edit checks to verify the accuracy and reasonableness of the data at the time of entry.

Prepare Payroll

The fourth step in the payroll cycle is preparing payroll (circle 4.0 in Figure 13-3). The department in which the employee works provides data about the hours worked and a supervisor usually confirms the data. Pay-rate information is obtained from the payroll master file.

Procedures

Figure 13-4 shows the sequence of activities in processing payroll. First, the payroll transaction file is sorted by employee number so that it is in the same sequence as the payroll master file. If the organization is processing payrolls from several divisions, each of these payroll transaction files must also be merged (this step is not shown in Figure 13-4).

The sorted time-data file is then used to prepare employee paychecks. For each employee, the payroll master file record and corresponding transaction record are read and gross pay is calculated. For hourly employees, the number of hours worked is multiplied by the wage rate and then any applicable premiums for overtime or bonuses are added. For salaried employees, gross pay is a fraction of the annual salary, where the fraction reflects the length of the pay period. For example, salaried employees paid monthly would receive one-twelfth of their annual salary each pay period. Any applicable commissions, bonuses, and other incentives are also included in calculating gross pay.

Next, all payroll deductions are summed and the total is subtracted from gross pay to obtain net pay. Payroll deductions fall into two broad categories: payroll tax

withholdings and voluntary deductions. The former includes federal, state, and local income taxes, as well as Social Security taxes. Voluntary deductions include contributions to a pension plan; premiums for group life, health, and disability insurance; union dues; and contributions to various charities.

Once net pay is obtained, the year-to-date fields for gross pay, deductions, and net pay in each employee's record in the payroll master file are updated. Maintaining accurate cumulative earnings records is important for two reasons. First, because Social Security tax withholdings and other deductions have cutoffs, the company must know when to cease deductions for individual employees. Second, this information is needed to ensure that the appropriate amounts of taxes and other deductions are remitted to government agencies, insurance companies, and other organizations (such as the United Way). This information also must be included in the various reports filed with those agencies.

Finally, the payroll register and employee paychecks are printed. The **payroll register** is a report that lists each employee's gross pay, payroll deductions, and net pay in a multicolumn format. It is often accompanied by a separate **deduction register**, which lists the miscellaneous voluntary deductions for each employee. Figure 13-5 provides examples of both reports.

The payroll register also is used to authorize the transfer of funds to the company's payroll bank account. Employee paychecks also typically include an **earnings statement**, which lists the amount of gross pay, deductions, and net pay for the current period and year-to-date totals for each category.

As each payroll transaction is processed, the system also allocates labor costs to the appropriate general ledger accounts by checking the code on the job-time ticket record. The system maintains a running total of these allocations until all employee payroll records have been processed. These totals, and the column totals in the payroll register, form the basis for the summary journal entry, which is posted to the general ledger after all paychecks have been printed.

Table 13-1 describes some of the additional reports produced by the payroll system. Government agencies, in particular, require a number of detailed reports. Consequently, as Figure 13-6 shows, most payroll and HRM software provides extensive support for meeting the reporting requirements of federal, state, and local governments.

Figure 13-5
Sample Payroll and Deduction Registers

Alpha Omega Electronics				PAYROLL REGISTER					Period Ended 12/03/2009
					Deductions				
Employee No.	Name	Hours	Pay Rate	Gross Pay	Fed. Tax	FICA	State Tax	Misc.	Net Pay
37884	Jarvis	40.0	6.25	250.00	35.60	18.75	16.25	27.60	151.80
37885	Burke	43.6	6.50	295.10	42.40	22.13	19.18	40.15	171.24
37886	Lincoln	40.0	6.75	270.00	39.20	20.25	17.55	27.90	165.10
37887	Douglass	44.2	7.00	324.10	46.60	24.31	21.07	29.62	202.50

Alpha Omega Electronics			DEDUCTION REGISTER				Period Ended 12/03/2009
			Miscellaneous Deductions				
Employee No.	Name	Health Ins.	Life Ins.	Retirement	Union Dues	Savings Bond	Total Misc.
37884	Jarvis	10.40	5.50	7.50	4.20	0.00	27.60
37885	Burke	11.60	5.50	8.85	4.20	10.00	40.15
37886	Lincoln	10.40	5.20	8.10	4.20	0.00	27.90
37887	Douglass	10.20	5.50	9.72	4.20	0.00	29.62

Table 13-1
Examples of Commonly Generated HRM/Payroll Cycle Reports

Report Name	Contents	Purpose
Cumulative earnings register	Cumulative year-to-date gross pay, net pay, and deductions for each employee	Used for employee information and annual payroll reports
Workforce inventory	List of employees by department	Used in preparing labor-related reports for government agencies
Position control report	List of each authorized position, job qualifications, budgeted salary, and position status (filled or vacant)	Used in planning future workforce needs
Skills inventory report	List of employees and current skills	Useful in planning future workforce needs and training programs
Form 941	Employer's quarterly federal tax return (showing all wages subject to tax and amounts withheld for income tax and FICA)	Filed quarterly to reconcile monthly tax payments with total tax liability for the quarter
Form W-2	Report of wages and withholdings for each employee	Sent to each employee for use in preparing individual tax returns; due by January 31
Form W-3	Summary of all W-2 forms	Sent to federal government along with a copy of all W-2 forms; due by February 28
Form 1099-Misc.	Report of income paid to independent contractors	Sent to recipients of income for use in filing their income tax returns; due by January 31
Various other reports to government agencies	Data on compliance with various regulatory provisions, state and local tax reports, etc.	To document compliance with applicable regulations

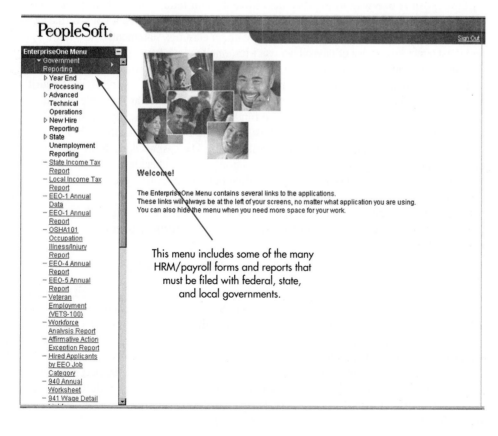

Figure 13-6
Variety of Payroll-related Reports for Federal, State, and Local Governments

Disburse Payroll

The next step is the actual disbursement of paychecks to employees (circle 5.0 in Figure 13-3). Most employees are paid either by check or by direct deposit of the net pay amount into their personal bank account. Unlike cash payments, both methods provide a means to document the amount of wages paid.

Procedures

Figure 13-4 shows that once paychecks have been prepared, the payroll register is sent to the accounts payable department for review and approval. A disbursement voucher is then prepared to authorize the transfer of funds from the company's general checking account to its payroll bank account. Payroll checks should not be drawn on the organization's regular bank account. Instead, for control purposes, a separate payroll bank account should be used. This limits the company's loss exposure to the amount of cash in the separate payroll account. It also makes it easier to reconcile payroll and to detect paycheck forgery.

The disbursement voucher and payroll register are then sent to the cashier. The cashier reviews the payroll register and disbursement voucher and then prepares and signs a check transferring funds to the company's payroll bank account. The cashier also reviews, signs, and distributes the employee paychecks. Thus, the duties of authorizing and recording payroll transactions are segregated from the actual distribution of paychecks. The cashier promptly redeposits any unclaimed paychecks in the company's bank account. To prevent the creation and distribution of fraudulent paychecks, a list of unclaimed paychecks is sent to the internal audit department for further investigation.

The payroll register is then returned to the payroll department, where it is filed by date along with the time cards and job-time tickets. The disbursement voucher is sent to the accounting clerk, who uses it to update the general ledger.

Efficiency Opportunity: Direct Deposit

Direct deposit is one way to improve the efficiency and reduce the costs of payroll processing. Employees who are paid by direct deposit generally receive a copy of the paycheck indicating the amount deposited along with an earnings statement. The payroll system must generate a series of payroll deposit files, one for each bank through which payroll deposits are made. Each file contains a record for each employee whose account is maintained at a particular bank. Each record includes the employee's name, Social Security number, bank account number, and net pay amount. These files are sent electronically, using EDI, to each participating bank. The funds are then electronically transferred from the employer's bank account to the employee's account. Direct deposit thus eliminates the need for the cashier to sign individual payroll checks. The cashier does, however, have to authorize the release of funds from the organization's regular checking account.

Direct deposit provides savings to employers by eliminating the cost of purchasing, processing, and distributing paper checks. It also reduces bank fees and postage expenses. Consequently, most companies now offer their employees the option of direct deposit payment and encourage them to elect this form of payment.

Calculate Employer-Paid Benefits and Taxes

The employer pays some payroll taxes and employee benefits directly (circle 6.0 in Figure 13-3). For example, employers must pay Social Security taxes in addition to the amounts withheld from employee paychecks. Circular E, *Employer's Tax Guide*, published by the IRS, provides detailed instructions about an employer's obligations for withholding and remitting payroll taxes and for filing various reports.

Federal and state laws also require employers to contribute a specified percentage of each employee's gross pay, up to a maximum annual limit, to federal and state unemployment compensation insurance funds. In addition, employers often contribute some or all of the amounts to pay for their employees' health, disability, and life

insurance premiums. Many companies also offer their employees **flexible benefit plans**, under which each employee receives some minimum coverage in medical insurance and pension contributions, plus additional benefit credits that can be used to acquire extra vacation time or additional health insurance. These plans are sometimes called cafeteria-style benefit plans because they offer a menu of options. Finally, many employers offer and contribute toward a choice of retirement savings plans.

Providing these additional services and benefits places increased demands on a company's HRM/payroll system. For example, the HRM staff of a large company with thousands of employees can spend a considerable amount of time just responding to 401(k) plan inquiries. Moreover, employees want to be able to make changes in their investment decisions on a timely basis. Organizations can satisfy employee demands for such services without increasing costs by providing access to HRM/payroll information on the company's intranet.

Disburse Payroll Taxes and Miscellaneous Deductions

The final activity in the payroll process is paying the payroll tax liabilities and the other voluntary deductions of each employee (circle 7.0 in Figure 13-3). An organization must periodically prepare checks or use electronic funds transfer to pay the various tax liabilities incurred. Respective government agencies specify the timing of these payments. In addition, the funds voluntarily withheld from each employee's paycheck for various benefits, such as a payroll savings plan, must be disbursed to the appropriate organizations.

Outsourcing Options: Payroll Service Bureaus and Professional Employer Organizations

In an effort to reduce costs, many organizations are outsourcing their payroll and HRM functions to payroll service bureaus and professional employer organizations. A **payroll service bureau** maintains the payroll master file for each of its clients and performs the payroll processing activities described in this section. A **professional employer organization (PEO)** not only processes payroll but also provides HRM services such as employee benefit design and administration. Because they provide a narrower range of services, payroll service bureaus are generally less expensive than PEOs.

When organizations outsource payroll processing, they send time and attendance data along with information about personnel changes to the payroll service bureau or PEO at the end of each pay period. The payroll service bureau or PEO then uses that data to prepare employee paychecks, earnings statements, and a payroll register. The payroll processing service also periodically produces employee W-2 forms and other tax-related reports.

Payroll service bureaus and PEOs are especially attractive to small and midsize businesses for the following reasons:

- **Reduced costs.** Payroll service bureaus and PEOs benefit from the economies of scale associated with preparing paychecks for a large number of companies. They can charge fees that are typically less than the cost of doing payroll in-house. A payroll service bureau or PEO also saves money by eliminating the need to develop and maintain the expertise required to comply with the constantly changing tax laws.
- **Wider range of benefits.** PEOs pool the costs of administering benefits across all their clients. Consequently, a PEO enables smaller companies to offer the same wide range of benefits that large companies typically provide.
- **Freeing up of computer resources.** A payroll service bureau or PEO eliminates one or more AIS applications (payroll and benefits management). The

freed-up computing resources can then be used to improve service in other areas, such as sales order entry.

As the basis for competitive advantage increasingly hinges on employees' skills and knowledge, the effective and efficient management of the payroll and HRM functions becomes increasingly important. Outsourcing may provide a way to reduce costs. However, companies need to be sure to carefully monitor service quality to ensure that the outsourced system effectively integrates HRM and payroll data in a manner that supports effective management of employees.

Control Objectives, Threats, and Procedures

A second major function of the AIS in the HRM/payroll cycle is to provide adequate internal controls to ensure meeting the following objectives:

1 All payroll transactions are properly authorized.
2 All recorded payroll transactions are valid.
3 All valid, authorized payroll transactions are recorded.
4 All payroll transactions are accurately recorded.
5 Applicable government regulations regarding remittance of taxes and filing of payroll and HRM reports are met.
6 Assets (both cash and data) are safeguarded from loss or theft.
7 HRM/payroll cycle activities are performed efficiently and effectively.

The various documents and records (e.g., time cards, payroll register) described in the previous section play an important role in achieving these objectives. Simple, easy-to-complete documents with clear instructions facilitate the accurate and efficient recording of payroll transactions. Appropriate application controls, such as validity checks and field (format) checks, further increase the accuracy of data entry when using electronic documents. Providing space on both paper and electronic documents to record who completed and who reviewed the form gives evidence that the transaction was properly authorized. Prenumbering all documents facilitates checking that all transactions have been recorded. Restricting access to programs that create documents and, if paper documents are still used, to blank documents reduces the risk of unauthorized transactions.

Table 13-2 lists the major threats in the HRM/payroll cycle and the applicable control procedures for mitigating those threats. Because every company, regardless of its line of business, faces these threats, it is important to understand how the AIS can be best designed to counter them. Our discussion is organized around three areas: employment practices, payroll processing, and general control issues.

Employment Practices

The objective of the HRM function is to efficiently hire, develop, retain, and dismiss employees. The two major threats to fulfilling this objective are hiring unqualified employees and violating applicable laws and regulations concerning the proper hiring and dismissal of employees.

Threat 1: Hiring Unqualified or Larcenous Employees

Hiring unqualified employees can increase production expenses, and hiring a larcenous employee can result in the theft of assets. Both problems are best dealt with by appropriate hiring procedures. Skill qualifications for each open position should be stated explicitly in the position control report. Candidates should be asked to sign a statement on the job application form that confirms the accuracy of the information

Table 13-2
Threats and Controls in the Payroll/HRM Cycle

Process/Activity	Threat	Applicable Control Procedures
Employment practices	1. Hiring unqualified or larcenous employees 2. Violation of employment law	Sound hiring procedures, including verification of job applicant's skills, references, and employment history Thorough documentation of hiring and discharge procedures; training on current developments in employment law
Payroll processing	3. Unauthorized changes to payroll master file 4. Inaccurate time data 5. Inaccurate processing of payroll 6. Theft or fraudulent distribution of paychecks	Segregation of duties: HRM, payroll calculation, and paycheck distribution; access controls; audit and review of all changes to payroll master file Automation of data collection; various edit checks; reconciliation of time card data with job-time ticket data Batch totals and other application controls; payroll clearing account; review of IRS regulations Direct deposit; paycheck distribution by someone independent of payroll process; investigation of unclaimed paychecks; restricted access to blank paychecks; prenumbering and periodic accounting for all paychecks; use of separate payroll checking account, maintained as an imprest fund; reconciliation of payroll bank account by someone not involved in payroll processing
General control issues	7. Loss, alteration, or unauthorized disclosure of data 8. Poor performance	Backup procedures; disaster recovery plans; physical and logical access controls; encryption of data and data transmission controls Development and periodic review of appropriate performance metrics; training programs

being submitted and provides their consent to a thorough background check of their credentials and employment history. It is especially important to verify a job applicant's skills and references, including college degrees earned, because research suggests that approximately 30% of resumes contain false or embellished information. It is also important to verify the actual job titles of people listed as references. Finally, when hiring for positions that involve access to financial data and assets, it may be worthwhile to hire a company that performs thorough background checks to verify that the applicant does not have a prior criminal record. Before engaging in a detailed background check, however, it is usually necessary to obtain written permission from the applicant to do so.

Threat 2: Violation of Employment Law

The government imposes stiff penalties on firms that violate provisions of employment law. In addition, organizations can also be subject to civil suits by alleged victims of employment discrimination. In this case, the best control procedure is careful documentation of all actions relating to advertising, recruiting, hiring new employees and dismissal of employees, to demonstrate compliance with the applicable government regulations. Continued training to keep current with employment law is therefore important.

Payroll Processing

The objective of payroll processing is to efficiently and effectively remunerate employees for the services they provide. Accordingly, the major threats include unauthorized changes to the payroll master file, inaccurate time data, inaccurate processing, and theft or fraudulent distribution of paychecks.

Threat 3: Unauthorized Changes to the Payroll Master File

Unauthorized changes to the payroll master file can result in increased expenses if wages, salaries, commissions, or other base rates used to determine employee compensation are falsified. These problems also result in inaccurate reports on labor costs, which in turn can lead to erroneous decisions.

Proper segregation of duties is the key control procedure for dealing with this threat. As shown in Figure 13-4, only the HRM department should be able to update the payroll master file for hirings, firings, pay raises, and promotions. HRM department employees in turn do not directly participate in payroll processing or paycheck distribution. This segregation of duties prevents someone with access to paychecks from creating fictitious employees or altering pay rates and then intercepting those fraudulent checks. In addition, all changes to the payroll master file should be reviewed and approved by someone other than the person recommending the change. Traditionally, such approval has involved reading and signing a transaction document. For changes processed through online terminals, the system must be designed to verify the identity and authority of the persons making and approving the request. A report documenting these changes should also be sent to each department supervisor for review.

Controlling access to the payroll system is also important. Indeed, in a database environment, access controls are vital because many previously separate functions are now performed solely by the system. The system should be programmed to compare user IDs and passwords with an access control matrix that (1) defines what actions each employee is allowed to perform and (2) confirms what files each employee is allowed to access. Payroll clerks, for example, should not be permitted to change employee pay rates.

Threat 4: Inaccurate Time Data

Inaccuracies in time and attendance records can result in increased labor expenses and erroneous labor expense reports. Moreover, inaccuracies can either hurt employee morale (if paychecks are incorrect or missing) or result in payments for labor services not rendered.

Automation can reduce the risk of *unintentional* inaccuracies in time data. Badge readers and bar code scanners can be used to collect data on employee time and attendance in machine-readable form. If their use is not feasible, online terminals should be used. The data entry program should include the following edit checks:

- *Field checks* for numeric data in the employee-number and hours-worked fields,
- *Limit checks* on the hours-worked field,
- A *validity check* of the employee number.

Proper segregation of duties can reduce the risk of *intentional* inaccuracies. As explained earlier, only someone not directly involved in processing payroll should make changes to the payroll master file. Moreover, the appropriate supervisors should approve all such changes.

Time card data, used for calculating payroll, also should be reconciled to the job-time ticket data, used for costing and managerial purposes, by someone not involved in generating that data. The total time spent on all tasks, as recorded on the job-time tickets, should not exceed the attendance time indicated on an employee's time card. Conversely, all time spent at work should be accounted for on the job-time tickets. Finally, to ensure the validity of the data, the employee's supervisor should approve time cards and job-time tickets.

Threat 5: Inaccurate Processing of Payroll

The complexity of payroll processing, especially the various tax law requirements, makes it susceptible to errors. Errors obviously can hurt employee morale, particularly if paychecks are late. In addition to incorrect payroll expense records and reports,

processing errors can lead to penalties if the errors result in failure to remit the proper amount of payroll taxes due the government. Similarly, failure to assess accurately garnishments on employees' wages and remit those funds to the appropriate party can also lead to financial penalties.

Three types of control procedures address the threat of payroll errors:

1 Batch totals. Even advanced HRM/payroll systems will continue to use batch processing for payroll. Consequently, batch totals should be calculated at the time of data entry and then checked against comparable totals calculated during each stage of processing. Hash totals of employee numbers, for example, are particularly useful. If the original and subsequent hash totals of employee numbers agree, it means that (1) all payroll records have been processed, (2) data input was accurate, and (3) no bogus time cards were entered during processing.

2 Cross-footing the payroll register. The total of the net pay column should equal the total of gross pay less total deductions.

3 A payroll clearing account. The **payroll clearing account** is a general ledger account that is used in a two-step process to check the accuracy and completeness of recording payroll costs and their subsequent allocation to appropriate cost centers. First, the payroll control account is debited for the amount of gross pay; cash is credited for the amount of net pay, and the various withholdings are credited to separate liability accounts. Second, the cost accounting process distributes labor costs to various expense categories and credits the payroll control account for the sum of these allocations. The amount credited to the payroll control account should equal the amount that was previously debited when net pay and the various withholdings were recorded. This particular internal check is also called a *zero-balance check*, because the payroll control account should equal zero once both entries have been posted.

Workers' tax status should be properly classified as either employee or independent contractor, because misclassification can cause companies to owe substantial back taxes, interest, and even penalties. This issue often arises when department managers attempt to circumvent a general hiring freeze by using independent contractors. The HRM department always should review any decisions to hire temporary or outside help. The IRS provides a checklist of questions that can be used to determine if a worker should be classified as an employee or an independent contractor.

Threat 6: Theft or Fraudulent Distribution of Paychecks

Another major threat is the theft of paychecks or the issuance of paychecks to fictitious or terminated employees. This can result in increased expenses and the loss of cash. The controls related to other cash disbursements, discussed in Chapter 11, also apply to payroll:

- Access to blank payroll checks and to the check signature machine should be restricted.
- All payroll checks should be sequentially prenumbered and periodically accounted for.
- The cashier should sign all payroll checks only when supported by proper documentation (the payroll register and disbursement voucher).
- Someone independent of the payroll process should reconcile the payroll bank account.

By limiting the total amount of cash at risk, a separate payroll bank account provides additional protection against forgery or alteration. This account should be operated as an imprest fund; that is, the amount of the check written to replenish the fund should equal the amount of net pay for that period. Thus, when all paychecks have been cashed, the payroll account should have a zero balance. A separate payroll checking account also makes it easier to spot any fraudulent checks when the account is reconciled.

It is also important that someone who does not authorize or record payroll should distribute paychecks and control the transfer of funds for direct deposit. To see why this segregation of duties is so important, assume that the person responsible for hiring and firing employees also distributes paychecks. This combination of duties could enable that person to conveniently forget to report an employee's termination and subsequently keep that employee's future paychecks. Requiring that the person distributing paychecks positively identify each person picking up a paycheck provides additional control over paycheck distribution. Further control is provided by having the internal audit department periodically observe, on a surprise basis, the paycheck distribution process to verify that all paychecks are picked up by valid employees.

Special procedures should be used to handle unclaimed paychecks because they indicate the possibility of a problem, such as a nonexistent or terminated employee. Unclaimed paychecks should be returned to the treasurer's office for prompt redeposit. They should then be traced back to time records and matched against the employee payroll master file to verify that they are indeed legitimate.

General Control Issues

The HRM/payroll cycle also faces the same two general threats that were discussed in previous chapters: the loss, alteration, or unauthorized disclosure of data and poor performance.

Threat 7: Loss, Alteration, or Unauthorized Disclosure of Data

The HRM/payroll database is a valuable resource that must be protected from loss or destruction. Backup and disaster-recovery procedures provide the best controls for reducing the risk of payroll data loss. Both internal and external file labels should be used to ensure that the database is not inadvertently erased or processed by the wrong program. Two backup copies of the payroll master file and recent transaction files should be created; one should be stored on-site, the other off-site.

Alteration of HRM or payroll data can lead to inefficiencies in assigning workers to tasks for which they are not adequately trained and can also result in unjustified payments. Physical and logical access controls are important preventive measures to mitigate this threat. It is important to point out that enforcing proper access controls and segregation of duties requires that the controller or CFO review and suggest appropriate configuration of user rights in integrated AIS packages and ERP systems. The default installation of such systems typically provides every user with far too much power. For example, consider the situation where a payroll clerk types in the name of an employee who is not currently in the database. The default configurations of most integrated AIS packages and ERP systems would respond by asking whether the clerk wants to create a new employee record. This violates segregation of duties by permitting the person who does the recording (payroll) to also authorize the creation of new accounts. Similarly, the default configurations of many systems permit payroll staff to not only read but also to change the salary information in the employee payroll master file. These examples are just some of the many areas that the controller or CFO needs to review to ensure that various users are assigned only those privileges necessary to perform their specified job duties. Although the procedures for modifying configurations vary across different software packages, knowing what changes need to be made requires only a sound understanding of proper segregation of duties for different business processes.

Access and processing integrity controls are also needed to ensure the confidentiality and accuracy of payroll cycle data transmissions. Sensitive data, such as employee pay and Social Security numbers, should be encrypted both while in storage and during transmission over the Internet. One way to do this is to establish VPNs with any payroll service bureau or PEO with whom data is electronically exchanged. Parity checks and acknowledgment messages should also be used to ensure the accuracy of data transmissions. In addition, various control totals, such as record counts indicating the number of employees for whom payroll information is being sent, should be used to verify the accuracy and completeness of data transmission.

Finally, protecting the privacy of employee data also is important. For example, morale may suffer if employees learn the salaries of other workers. In addition, unauthorized disclosure of performance evaluation data may subject the organization to lawsuits. The best control procedure for reducing the risk of unauthorized disclosure of payroll data is using passwords and physical security controls to restrict access to authorized persons. Encryption provides additional control by making HRM/payroll information unintelligible to anyone who succeeds in obtaining unauthorized access to the payroll master file. Use of a payroll service bureau or PEO also reduces the opportunity for employees to obtain unauthorized access to the HRM/payroll database.

Threat 8: Poor Performance

A second general threat in the payroll/HRM process is inefficient and ineffective employee performance. Preparing and reviewing performance reports is an effective means of addressing this threat, especially for employees who telecommute. Careful monitoring of these employees' productivity is necessary to ensure that they are truly working the amount of time for which they are getting paid and that they are not operating a personal business on the side, using company-provided assets. Such monitoring is also necessary to ensure that telecommuting employees do not use company-provided computing resources inappropriately (e.g., visiting pornographic Web sites, sending or forwarding offensive e-mail, or storing and using pirated copies of software).

Training is also important. For example, surveys of manufacturing companies report a direct relationship between time spent on training and performance measures such as yield rate, cycle time, and overall productivity. It is estimated that training costs represent 2% of total labor costs for manufacturing companies. Consequently, the HRM function needs to carefully evaluate and measure the benefits of such an investment. Such reports should be designed to facilitate tracking employee knowledge and skills to support optimal assignment of workers to tasks. In addition, methods for capturing and storing such knowledge, either in the form of intelligent decision aids or in the development of standard procedures, can help companies ensure continued access to those skills even when individual employees leave.

Key Decisions and Information Needs

We have discussed how the AIS fulfills the functions of processing payroll transactions and provides controls to safeguard assets. A third function of the AIS in the HRM/payroll cycle is to provide information for managing business activities. The traditional payroll system was designed primarily to meet the needs of external decision makers. Investors, creditors, and various government agencies were generally satisfied with information about a company's periodic salary expenses. Designing the payroll system to satisfy the needs of external users, however, does not ensure the production of all the information management needs to use and develop the company's human resources. Instead, the payroll system must be designed to collect and integrate cost data with other types of HR information to enable management to make the following kinds of decisions:

- **Future workforce staffing needs.** How many employees are needed in the next 5 years to accomplish the organization's strategic plans? Which employees possess the needed skills? Which skills are in short supply? Which skills are in oversupply? How effective are current training programs in maintaining and improving employee skill levels?
- **Employee performance.** Which employees should be promoted or receive pay raises? Who should be discharged? Is overall performance improving or declining? Is turnover excessive? Is tardiness or absenteeism a problem?
- **Employee morale.** What is the overall level of employee morale and job satisfaction? How can the compensation scheme be used to improve morale, satisfaction, and performance? What additional fringe benefits, if any, should be offered?

- **Payroll processing efficiency and effectiveness.** How frequently should employees be paid? Are labor costs being accurately allocated to products and other cost centers? Are all applicable tax reporting requirements being met? How easily can employee requests for information be answered?

Traditionally, the payroll system has provided some of the information needed to answer these questions, such as data about labor costs. The HRM system has normally provided other information, such as data about employee skills. Still other information, such as data about employee morale, has traditionally not been collected by either the payroll or the HRM system. Note that externally generated information, such as data about tax rates and industry averages for turnover and absenteeism, is also needed to make these decisions.

Access to current, accurate information about employee skills and knowledge can also provide an organization with strategic benefits. For example, professional services firms have databases of employee expertise. Using these databases, professional staff can quickly identify and solicit the advice of colleagues who have had prior experience in addressing a given problem. This saves staff considerable time in developing solutions to client problems and enables geographically dispersed staff to learn from each other. Well-designed and easily accessible databases help identify which employees possess specific knowledge. The proper use of communications technologies, however, is the key to effectively sharing that knowledge. For example, research on virtual collaboration indicates that the availability of easy-to-use tools that facilitate file sharing dramatically improves group performance.

A second strategic benefit of an integrated HRM/payroll data model is that staff can perform many HRM activities more efficiently, thereby reducing costs. Consider the case of hiring new employees. Online resume databases now exist for many professional fields, including accounting. That information can be downloaded and automatically stored in the job-applicant file, thereby saving considerable time and expense as compared with traditional manual collection and entry of data. Moreover, once in the system, that information can be quickly and easily accessed by any manager throughout the firm.

A well-designed HRM database also can be used to reduce recruiting costs. It is not uncommon for several related job openings to arise over a short time. If data about previous applicants are stored in an easily accessible database, much of the clerical work associated with processing applications for subsequent job openings can be avoided.

SUMMARY AND CASE CONCLUSION

The HRM/payroll cycle information system consists of two related, but separate, subsystems: HRM and payroll. The HRM system records and processes data about the activities of recruiting, hiring, training, assigning, compensating, evaluating, and discharging employees. The payroll system records and processes data used to pay employees for their services.

The HRM/payroll system must be designed to comply with a myriad of government regulations related to both taxes and employment practices. In addition, adequate controls must exist to prevent (1) overpaying employees due to invalid (overstated) time and attendance data and (2) disbursing paychecks to fictitious employees. These two threats can be best minimized by proper segregation of duties, specifically by having the following functions performed by different individuals:

1 Authorizing and making changes to the payroll master file for such events as hirings, firings, and pay raises;
2 Recording and verifying time worked by employees;
3 Preparing paychecks;
4 Distributing paychecks.

Although the HRM and payroll systems have traditionally been separated, many companies, including AOE, are trying to integrate them to manage their human resources more effectively and to provide employees with better benefits and service. Elizabeth Venko and Ann Brandt showed Peter Wu how AOE's new ERP system would facilitate integrating these two functions. Peter was impressed with how easily he could retrieve data about employee skills and attendance at training classes from this database. He agreed that this would satisfy the needs of department managers for quick and easy access to such information. Peter also realized that the HRM staff could similarly use this query capability to provide quick response to employee requests for information about their benefits, deductions, or retirement plans. He was even more impressed when Elizabeth and Ann explained that another recently implemented add-on feature would also allow employees to make direct changes in their retirement savings allocations, medical plan choices, and other benefit options. Peter realized that freeing the HRM staff from these routine clerical tasks would allow them to devote more time to helping him organize the information needed to make strategic decisions, such as planning for future workforce needs, career counseling, employee development, and negotiations with service providers to improve benefits.

Elizabeth explained that payroll processing itself could continue to be performed in batch mode, because there is no need for online processing (employees would continue to be paid only at periodic intervals). Reports, such as the payroll register, however, would be distributed electronically to improve efficiency. Elizabeth also wants to encourage more employees to sign up for direct deposit of their paychecks, thereby reducing the number of checks that need to be printed.

Elizabeth and Ann explained that an access control matrix would be created to maintain adequate segregation of duties in the new system and protect the integrity of the HRM/payroll database. For example, only HRM employees would add new employees, and only from terminals located in the HRM department.

Linda Spurgeon was pleased with Elizabeth and Ann's work on improving the company's HRM/payroll systems. She indicated that their next task would be to work with Stephanie Cromwell, AOE's chief financial officer, to improve the financial closing process and to help develop reports that would provide better insight into AOE's performance.

KEY TERMS

human resources
 management
 (HRM)/payroll
 cycle 520
time card 526
payroll register 528

deduction
 register 528
earnings statement 528
flexible benefit plans 531
payroll service
 bureau 531

professional employer
 organization
 (PEO) 531
payroll clearing
 account 535

AIS IN ACTION

CHAPTER QUIZ

1 Traditionally, accountants have been most involved with which portion of the HRM/payroll cycle?
 a. hiring
 b. payroll
 c. training
 d. performance evaluation

2 Which of the following statements is true?
a. Financial statements report the value of employee knowledge and skills.
b. Turnover and absenteeism are costly.
c. Outsourcing of HRM and payroll functions improves effectiveness of management of employees.
d. Default configurations of ERP packages typically provide good segregation of duties.

3 Which document lists the current amount and year-to-date totals of gross pay, deductions, and net pay for one employee?
a. payroll register
b. time card
c. paycheck
d. earnings statement

4 Online processing is most useful for which of these tasks?
a. preparing payroll checks
b. reconciling job-time tickets and time cards
c. paying payroll tax obligations
d. making changes in employee benefit choices

5 Use of a payroll service bureau or a PEO provides all of these benefits *except* which of the following?
a. integration of payroll and personnel data, such as job skills
b. lower cost of processing payroll
c. less need for developing and maintaining payroll tax expertise
d. fewer staff needed to process payroll

6 Which control procedure would be most effective in detecting the failure to prepare a paycheck for a new employee *before* paychecks are distributed?
a. validity checks on the employee number on each time card
b. record counts of time cards submitted and time cards processed
c. zero-balance check
d. use of a separate payroll bank account

7 Which department should have responsibility for authorizing pay-rate changes?
a. timekeeping
b. payroll
c. HRM
d. accounting

8 To maximize effectiveness of internal controls over payroll, which of the following persons should be responsible for distributing employee paychecks?
a. departmental secretary
b. payroll clerk
c. controller
d. departmental supervisor

9 Where should unclaimed paychecks be returned?
a. HRM department
b. cashier
c. payroll department
d. absent employee's supervisor

10 Which of the following is an important supporting document to authorize the transfer of funds to the payroll bank account?
a. earnings statement
b. time card
c. payroll register
d. W-2 form

DISCUSSION QUESTIONS

13.1 This chapter noted many of the benefits that can arise by integrating the HRM and payroll databases. Nevertheless, many companies maintain separate payroll and HRM information systems. Why do you think this is so? (*Hint:* Think about the differences in employee background and the functions performed by the HRM and payroll departments.)

13.2 Some accountants have advocated that a company's human assets be measured and included directly in the financial statements. For example, the costs of hiring and training an employee would be recorded as an asset that is amortized over the employee's expected term of service. Do you agree or disagree? Why?

13.3 You are responsible for implementing a new employee performance measurement system that will provide factory supervisors with detailed information about each of their employees on a weekly basis. In conversation with some of these supervisors, you are surprised to learn they do not believe these reports will be useful. They explain that they can already obtain all the information they need to manage their employees simply by observing the shop floor. Comment on that opinion. How could formal reports supplement and enhance what the supervisors learn by direct observation?

13.4 Direct deposit both reduces the costs of and improves control over payroll distribution. Does this mean that companies should require all their employees to be paid by direct deposit? Why or why not?

13.5 One of the threats associated with having employees telecommute is that they may use company-provided resources (e.g., laptop, printer, etc.) for a side business. What are some other threats? What controls can mitigate the risk of these threats?

13.6 How does use of a separate payroll checking account improve control?

PROBLEMS

13.1 What internal control procedure(s) would be most effective in preventing the following errors or fraudulent acts?
 a. An inadvertent data entry error caused an employee's wage rate to be overstated in the payroll master file.
 b. A fictitious employee payroll record was added to the payroll master file.
 c. During data entry, the hours worked on an employee's time card for one day were accidentally entered as 80 hours, instead of 8 hours.
 d. A computer operator used an online terminal to increase her own salary.
 e. A factory supervisor failed to notify the HRM department that an employee had been fired. Consequently, paychecks continued to be issued for that employee. The supervisor pocketed and cashed those paychecks.
 f. A factory employee punched a friend's time card in at 1:00 P.M. and out at 5:00 P.M. while the friend played golf that afternoon.
 g. A programmer obtained the payroll master file and increased his salary.
 h. Some time cards were lost during payroll preparation; consequently, when paychecks were distributed, several employees complained about not being paid.
 i. A large portion of the payroll master file was destroyed when the disk pack containing the file was used as a scratch file for another application.

13.2 You have been hired to evaluate the payroll system for the Skip-Rope Manufacturing Company. The company processes its payroll in-house. Prepare a list of questions to evaluate Skip-Rope's internal control structure as it pertains to payroll

processing for its factory employees. Each question should be phrased so that it can be answered with either a yes or a no; all no answers should indicate potential internal control weaknesses. Include a third column listing the potential problem that could arise if that particular control were not in place.

13.3 Although most medium and large companies have implemented sophisticated payroll and HRM systems like the one described in this chapter, many smaller companies still maintain separate payroll and HRM systems that employ many manual procedures. Typical of such small companies is the Kowal Manufacturing Company, which employs about 50 production workers and has the following payroll procedures:

- The factory supervisor interviews and hires all job applicants. The new employee prepares a W-4 form (Employee's Withholding Exemption Certificate) and gives it to the supervisor. The supervisor writes the hourly rate of pay for the new employee in the corner of the W-4 form and then gives the form to the payroll clerk as notice that a new worker has been hired. The supervisor verbally advises the payroll department of any subsequent pay raises.
- A supply of blank time cards is kept in a box near the entrance to the factory. All workers take a time card on Monday morning and fill in their names. During the week they record the time they arrive and leave work by punching their time cards in the time clock located near the main entrance to the factory. At the end of the week the workers drop the time cards in a box near the exit. A payroll clerk retrieves the completed time cards from the box on Monday morning. Employees are automatically removed from the payroll master file when they fail to turn in a time card.
- The payroll checks are manually signed by the chief accountant and then given to the factory supervisor, who distributes them to the employees. The factory supervisor arranges for delivery of the paychecks to any employee who is absent on payday.
- The payroll bank account is reconciled by the chief accountant, who also prepares the various quarterly and annual tax reports.

Required

a. Identify weaknesses in current procedures, and explain the threats that they may allow to occur.
b. Suggest ways to improve the Kowal Manufacturing Company's internal controls over hiring and payroll processing.

(CPA Examination, adapted)

13.4 Arlington Industries manufactures and sells engine parts for large industrial equipment. The company employs over 1,000 workers for three shifts, and most employees work overtime when necessary. Figure 13-7 depicts the procedures followed to process payroll. Additional information about payroll procedures follows:

- The HRM department determines the wage rates of all employees. The process begins when a form authorizing the addition of a new employee to the payroll master file is sent to the payroll coordinator for review and approval. Once the information about the new employee is entered in the system, the computer automatically calculates the overtime and shift differential rates for that employee.
- A local accounting firm provides Arlington with monthly payroll tax updates, which are used to modify the tax rates.
- Employees record time worked on time cards. Every Monday morning the previous week's time cards are collected from a bin next to the time clock, and new time cards are left for employees to use. The payroll department manager reviews the time cards to ensure that hours are correctly totaled; the system automatically determines if overtime has been worked or a shift differential is required.
- The payroll department manager performs all the other activities depicted in Figure 13-7.

Figure 13-7
Arlington Industries Flowchart of Payroll Processing

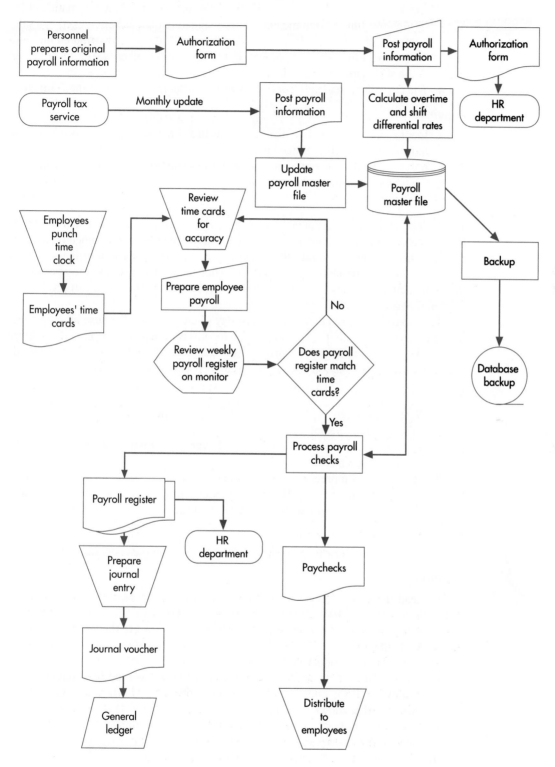

- The system automatically assigns a sequential number to each payroll check. The checks are stored in a box next to the printer for easy access. After the checks are printed, the payroll department manager uses an automatic check-signing machine to sign the checks. The signature plate is kept locked in a safe. After the checks have been signed, the payroll manager distributes the paychecks to all first-shift employees. Paychecks for the other two shifts are given to the shift supervisor for distribution.
- The payroll master file is backed up weekly, after payroll processing is finished.

Required

 a. Identify and describe five different areas in Arlington's payroll processing system where controls are inadequate.

 b. Identify and describe two different areas in Arlington's payroll processing system where controls are satisfactory.

(CMA Examination, adapted)

13.5 The Darwin Department Store pays all of its employees on a salaried basis. Payroll processing is done internally. The payroll master file is maintained on disk. At periodic intervals every month, the HRM department uses online terminals to enter batches of payroll file-change transactions. After those changes pass the appropriate data entry controls, they are posted to the payroll master file. This run produces a printed report listing all file changes processed.

 The payroll run takes place on the last day of each month. Because all employees are paid a fixed salary, there is no transaction input. This run produces printed employee paychecks, earnings registers, a printed summary report, and a payroll register file recorded on disk. The payroll register file is later processed to print a payroll register.

Required

 1 What is meant by the term "payroll file-change transactions"? Give four examples of these types of transactions.

 2 Prepare a flowchart or DFD (whichever your instructor chooses) of the processes described.

 3 Describe a comprehensive set of internal control procedures and policies for this payroll application. Relate each control procedure to a specific objective, and explain what threats it is designed to mitigate.

13.6 Excel Problem

Objective: Learn how to find and correct errors in complex spreadsheets.

Required

 a. Read the article "Ferret Out Spreadsheet Errors" by Mark G. Simkin, in the *Journal of Accountancy* (February 2004). You can find a copy online by accessing www.aicpa.org and then following the links to the Online Journal of Accountancy.

 b. Download the worksheet referenced in the article.

 c. Enter the following erroneous data: Change hours worked for Adams to 400, hours worked for Englert to 4, and hours worked for Hartford to −40. Create a chart like that shown in Exhibit 2 of the article. Which of the errors are easily found by the chart? What are the strengths and limitations of creating such charts to detect errors? Print out your chart and save your work.

 d. Create the three data validation rules described in the article (Exhibits 4–7 illustrate how to create the first rule). Print out screen shots of how you create each rule, and save your work. (Note: The article "Block That Spreadsheet Error" by Theo Callahan, in the *Journal of Accountancy* (August 2002) provides additional examples of data validation rules.)

 e. Follow the instructions for using the formula auditing tool. Print out a screen shot showing use of the tool to circle invalid data (yours should be similar to Exhibit 9 in the article).

f. Follow the instructions to run the "trace precedents" audit tool. Print screen shots that show the results, and save your work. How useful is this tool? What are its limitations, if any?

g. Enter the following data for new employees (inserting new rows in proper order to maintain alphabetical listing of employees):
- Name = Able, payrate = 11.11, regular hours = 40, overtime hours = 5
- Name = Easton, payrate = 10.00, regular hours = 40, overtime hours = 0
- Name = Johnson, payrate = 12.00, regular hours = 35, overtime hours = 10

Which audit tests and validation rules change? Why? Print screen shots, and save your work.

13.7 Excel Problem

Objective: Learn how to use the VLOOKUP function.

Required

a. Obtain the article "Make Excel a Little Smarter" by Lois S. Mahoney and Charles Kelliher in the Journal of Accountancy (July 2003). You can find a copy at www .aicpa.org by following the links to the Online Journal of Accountancy.

b. Read the section titled "Data in Different Places" and create the spreadsheet illustrated in Exhibit 6. Print a screen shot of your work, and save your spreadsheet.

c. Create a formula that calculates total bonuses. Also create a cell entry that indicates what that number represents. Print a screen shot of your work, and save it.

d. Add the following data validation controls to your spreadsheet, including explanatory error messages. Save your work.
- Sales must be positive.
- Sales cannot exceed 125.
- Amount of bonus must be nonnegative.
- Amount of bonus cannot exceed 20% of unit sales.

e. Modify your worksheet by placing the sales data and resulting bonus on a different worksheet from the bonus table. Name your table array, and modify the VLOOKUP function accordingly. Then add another employee: Johnson, who sold 150 units. Print a screen shot of your new worksheet showing the bonuses for each employee, including Johnson. Save your work.

13.8 Excel Problem

Objective: Learn how to import data into Access and Excel, and how to create and use pivot tables for detailed analyses.

Required

a. Obtain the article "Drilling for Information" by Jeff Lenning, in the *Journal of Accountancy* (August 2000 issue). You can find the article by accessing www .aicpa.org and following the links to Online Journal of Accountancy.

b. Download the text file for this problem from this course's Web site.

c. Follow the instructions in the article to do the following:
- Import the text file into Access (create a table in Access that has columns: Month, Dept_num, Account_num, Account_desc, Trans_desc, and Amount).
- Import the data from Access into Excel. The data should go into PivotTable reports that you create for each department.
- Save your work, and print screen shots of your Pivot Table for department 100.

d. Follow the instructions in the article to automate the reports. Save your work.

13.9 The local community feels that secondary school education is a necessity in our society and that lack of education leads to a number of social problems. As a result, the local school board has decided to take action to reverse the rising dropout rate. The board has voted to provide funds to encourage students to remain in school and earn their high school diplomas. The idea is to treat secondary education like a job and pay students. The board, however, could not agree on the details for implementing

this new plan. Consequently, you have been hired to devise a system to compensate students for staying in school and earning a diploma.

As you devise your compensation scheme, be sure it meets the following general control objectives for the payroll cycle:

- All personnel and payroll transactions are properly authorized.
- All employees are assigned to do productive work, and they do it efficiently and effectively.
- All transactions are accurately recorded and processed.
- Accurate records are maintained.
- All disbursements are proper.

Required

Write a proposal that addresses these five questions:

 a. How should the students be compensated (e.g., for attendance, grades)?

 b. How and by whom will the payments be authorized?

 c. How will the payments be processed?

 d. How should the payments be made (e.g., in cash or other means)?

 e. When will the payments be made?

(Adapted from Carol F. Venable, "Development of Diversity Awareness and Critical Thinking," Proceedings of the Lilly Conference on Excellence in College and University Teaching—West (Lake Arrowhead, Calif., March 1995); and American Accounting Association Teaching and Curriculum Demonstration Session (Orlando, Fla., August 1995). Reprinted with permission of Dr. Carol Venable.)

13.10 What is the purpose of each of the following control procedures (i.e., what threats is it designed to mitigate)?

 a. Compare a listing of current and former employees to the payroll register.

 b. Reconciliation of labor costs (based on job-time ticket data) with payroll (based on time card data).

 c. Direct deposit of paychecks.

 d. Validity checks on Social Security numbers of all new employees added to the payroll master file.

 e. Cross-footing the payroll register.

 f. Limit checks on hours worked for each time card.

 g. Use of a fingerprint scanner in order for employees to record the time they started and the time they quit working each day.

 h. Encryption of payroll data both when it is electronically sent to a payroll service bureau and while at rest in the HR/payroll database.

 i. Establishing a separate payroll checking account and funding it as an imprest account.

 j. Comparison of hash totals of employee numbers created prior to transmitting time-worked data to payroll provider with hash totals of employee numbers created by payroll provider when preparing paychecks.

 k. Periodic reports of all changes to payroll database sent to each department manager.

13.11 Excel Problem

 Objective: Learn how to use text and array formulas to locate potential payroll problems.

Required

 a. Download the spreadsheet for this problem from the course Web site.

 b. On the timecards data worksheet, add a column titled "Ghost Employee." Write a function for that column that compares the employee# in the timecards worksheet to the employee# in the payroll master file worksheet and displays the message: "This employee does not exist in the payroll master file" for any employee in the timecards worksheet who is not listed in the payroll master file worksheet. The function should leave the cell blank if the employee# in the

timecards worksheet does exist in the payroll master file worksheet. (*Hint:* Use the ISNA and MATCH functions.)

c. On the payroll master file worksheet, add a column titled "Invalid SSN." Write a function for that column to identify invalid Social Security numbers. Assume that Social Security numbers that begin with the digit 9 or that have the digits 00 for the middle two numbers are invalid. Your function should display a message that flags either of these two conditions or which displays nothing otherwise. (*Hint:* there are text functions that examine specific portions of a string, such as the left 3 characters, and there are also functions that convert text to numeric values.)

CASE 13-1 Research Report: HRM/Payroll Opportunities for CPAs

Payroll has traditionally been an accounting function and some CPAs have provided payroll processing services to their clients. Today, CPAs are finding additional new lucrative opportunities to provide not only payroll processing but also various HR services. Write a brief report that compares the provision of payroll and HR services by CPAs with that of national payroll providers. Perform the following research to collect the data for your report:

1 Read the articles "Be an HR Resource for Your Clients," by Michael Hayes and "Hired Help:

Finding the Right Consultant," by Joanne Sammer, both of which were published in the November, 2006 issue of the *Journal of Accountancy.*

2 Contact a local CPA firm that provides payroll and HR services and find out what types of services they perform and what types of clients they serve.

CASE 13-2 Fargo Publishing

Fargo Publishing Company serves the elementary and middle school textbook market. Their printing area is divided into eight production centers that employ approximately 250 hourly workers. Although the production workers may be involved in preparing, running, or packaging several different production runs, they are paid for the total hours worked twice a month. Each day the production employees insert their time cards into a box that prints the time of day as they arrive for work and leave work at the end of their shift. The human resource (HR) department checks the time cards on a weekly basis and manually inputs each employee's time into the payroll computer. At the end of each week, the HR department sends a report to the production departmental supervisors to review and correct. The report frequently comes back with several adjustments. The HR department then makes changes to the payroll data based on the notations on the report. Once the changes are entered, the HR department sends an updated report to the cost accounting department and a second copy to the accountant who maintains the general ledger, prints paychecks, and prepares monthly and annual

reports. The cost accounting department uses its copy of the report to prepare a monthly labor cost report.

Due to state budget cuts to education, price competition in the elementary and middle school textbook publishing business has increased steadily over the past decade. Although Fargo has been able to maintain its market share, profits have decreased. Labor costs and processes are thought to be the primary cause for the decrease in profits, but management lacks enough information to identify where the higher labor costs and process inefficiencies originate. Therefore, Fargo's management hired a consulting company to analyze their current time-keeping and payroll system and to prepare recommendations to decrease costs and to improve data collection, processing procedures, and controls.

Required

Prepare a set of recommendations to address the problems described. Explain and justify each recommendation.

(CMA exam, adapted)

AIS IN ACTION SOLUTIONS

QUIZ KEY

1 Traditionally, accountants have been most involved with which portion of the HRM/payroll cycle?

 a. hiring (Incorrect. This has traditionally been handled by the HR department.)

✔ **b.** payroll (Correct. The payroll system has traditionally been part of the AIS.)

 c. training (Incorrect. This has traditionally been handled by the HR department.)

 d. performance evaluation (Incorrect. This has traditionally been handled by supervisors.)

2 Which of the following statements is true?

 a. Financial statements report the value of employee knowledge and skills. (Incorrect. Costs associated with acquiring the use of employees' skills and knowledge have traditionally been recognized as an expense on the income statement.)

✔ **b.** Turnover and absenteeism are costly. (Correct. Turnover costs 1.5 times the departing employee's salary, and absenteeism increases overtime and short-term hiring costs.)

 c. Outsourcing of HRM and payroll functions improves effectiveness of management of employees. (Incorrect. Outsourcing improves efficiency, but not necessarily effectiveness.)

 d. Default configurations of ERP packages typically provide good segregation of duties. (Incorrect. Default configurations of ERP systems typically provide users with far too much authority.)

3 Which document lists the current amount and year-to-date totals of gross pay, deductions, and net pay for one employee?

 a. payroll register (Incorrect. The payroll register lists this information for all employees.)

 b. time card (Incorrect. Time cards collect data about time worked during a specific pay period.)

 c. paycheck (Incorrect. The paycheck is a means of transferring funds.)

✔ **d.** earnings statement (Correct. The earnings statement attached to each paycheck provides the information listed.)

4 Online processing is most useful for which of these tasks?

 a. preparing payroll checks (Incorrect. Because paychecks are issued only periodically, batch processing is appropriate.)

 b. reconciling job-time tickets and time cards (Incorrect. Because this occurs only when payroll is calculated, batch processing is appropriate.)

 c. paying payroll tax obligations (Incorrect. Payment is periodic, so batch processing is appropriate.)

✔ **d.** making changes in employee benefit choices (Correct. Employees want to be able to have access to this information and make changes whenever desired.)

5 Use of a payroll service bureau or a PEO provides all of these benefits *except* which of the following?

✔ **a.** integration of payroll and personnel data, such as job skills (Correct. Outsourcing does not ensure that such effectiveness improvements occur.)

 b. lower cost of processing payroll (Incorrect. Outsourcing usually reduces costs.)

 c. less need for developing and maintaining payroll tax expertise (Incorrect. Outsourcing does reduce the need to maintain in-house payroll tax expertise.)

 d. fewer staff needed to process payroll (Incorrect. Outsourcing typically reduces staffing requirements.)

6 Which control procedure would be most effective in detecting the failure to prepare a paycheck for a new employee *before* paychecks are distributed?

a. validity checks on the employee number on each time card (Incorrect. This control is designed to ensure that only valid employees are paid.)

✔ **b.** record counts of time cards submitted and time cards processed (Correct. Batch totals like record counts would identify failure to process all transaction records.)

c. zero-balance check (Incorrect. This control is designed to verify the accuracy of payroll disbursements.)

d. use of a separate payroll bank account (Incorrect. This control is designed to limit the amount of cash that could be lost as a result of forged or altered paychecks.)

7 Which department should have responsibility for authorizing pay-rate changes?

a. timekeeping (Incorrect. Timekeeping is a recording function.)

b. payroll (Incorrect. Payroll calculates the pay for the current period and should not also authorize changes.)

✔ **c.** HRM (Correct. HRM has no other role in the payroll process.)

d. accounting (Incorrect. Accounting maintains records related to payroll and should not authorize changes in pay rates.)

8 To maximize effectiveness of internal controls over payroll, which of the following persons should be responsible for distributing employee paychecks?

✔ **a.** departmental secretary (Correct. This person has no other payroll duties so cannot conceal theft of paychecks.)

b. payroll clerk (Incorrect. The payroll clerk prepares and records the checks and so could create checks for nonexistent employees and cash them.)

c. controller (Incorrect. The controller is in charge of the recording function and should not have custody of checks.)

d. departmental supervisor (Incorrect. The supervisor authorizes payment by reviewing time cards and should not also have custody of assets.)

9 Where should unclaimed paychecks be returned?

a. HRM department (Incorrect. Unclaimed checks should be returned to the cashier for redeposit.)

✔ **b.** cashier (Correct. This permits funds to be quickly redeposited.)

c. payroll department (Incorrect. Unclaimed checks should be returned to the cashier for redeposit.)

d. absent employee's supervisor (Incorrect. Unclaimed checks should be returned to the cashier for redeposit.)

10 Which of the following is an important supporting document to authorize the transfer of funds to the payroll bank account?

a. earnings statement (Incorrect. This is the stub attached to each paycheck, providing the employee with YTD information about pay and various deductions.)

b. time card (Incorrect. This document records time worked.)

✔ **c.** payroll register (Correct. This document summarizes the amount to be paid to each employee and is sent to the accounts payable department for use in preparing a disbursement voucher to authorize the transfer of funds to the payroll account.)

d. W-2 form (Incorrect. This is a year-end statement given to each employee summarizing net pay, taxes witheld, and other deductions.)

CHAPTER 14

LEARNING OBJECTIVES

After studying this chapter, you should be able to:

- Describe the information processing operations required to update the general ledger and to produce other reports for internal and external users.

- Understand the implications of new IT developments, such as XBRL, for internal and external reporting.

- Identify the major threats in general ledger and reporting activities, and evaluate the adequacy of various control procedures for dealing with them.

- Discuss and design a balanced scorecard for an organization.

- Explain the relationship between online transaction processing systems and data warehouses used to support business intelligence.

- Design graphs that accurately portray the data in a manner that supports decision making.

General Ledger and Reporting System

Linda Spurgeon, AOE's president and CEO, is not satisfied with the financial reporting capabilities of AOE's new ERP system. Although the monthly closing process now takes less than two days and provides management with timely information about the firm's financial performance, the new ERP system only provides information about one dimension of AOE's performance. At a recent retreat, AOE's top management developed a multidimensional report, called a *balanced scorecard*, for AOE. The proposed balanced scorecard integrates traditional financial performance measures of key business processes with several other non-financial measures. The task now is to ensure that this balanced scorecard can be produced in a timely manner.

In addition, although AOE's new system provides managers with quick and easy access to current-year financial data, trend analysis of performance over the past 5 to 10 years is much more difficult and time-consuming. Moreover, Stephanie Cromwell, AOE's chief financial officer, has received numerous requests from other managers for graphical summaries to help them better understand financial reports. Finally, Stephanie is concerned about the increased costs associated with providing financial information to interested external parties on a timely basis. Much of the increase in these costs comes from the need to copy and reenter data from AOE's general ledger into a myriad of reports and documents.

Linda calls a meeting with Elizabeth Venko, AOE's controller, and Ann Brandt, AOE's vice president of information systems, to discuss these concerns. They agree to research how AOE's new information system can be further improved to address these issues.

Introduction

This chapter discusses the information processing operations involved in updating the general ledger and preparing reports that summarize the results of an organization's activities. As shown in Figure 14-1, the general ledger and reporting system plays a central role in a company's AIS. One of its primary functions is to collect and organize data from the following sources:

- Each of the accounting cycle subsystems described in Chapters 10 through 13 provides information about regular transactions. (Only the principal data flows from each subsystem are depicted, to keep the figure uncluttered.)
- The treasurer provides information about financing and investing activities, such as the issuance or retirement of debt and equity instruments and the purchase or sale of investment securities.
- The budget department provides budget numbers.
- The controller provides adjusting entries.

This information must be organized and stored in a manner that facilitates meeting the varied information needs of internal and external users. Managers need detailed information about the results of operations in their particular area of responsibility. Investors and creditors want periodic financial statements to help them assess the organization's performance. Increasingly, they are demanding more detailed and more frequent reports. Government agencies also have periodic information requirements that must be met.

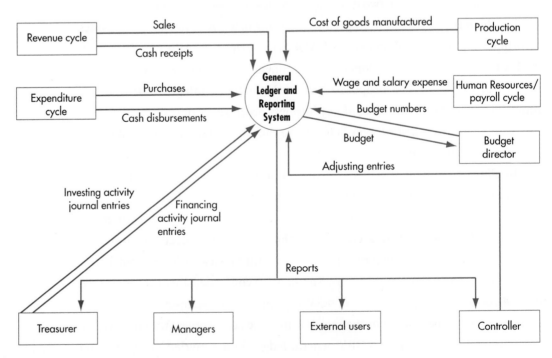

Figure 14-1
Context Diagram of the General Ledger and Reporting System

Consequently, the general ledger and reporting system must be designed to produce regular periodic reports and to support real-time inquiry needs. For example, departmental managers should be able to assess actual versus planned performance at any time so that deviations can be identified early enough to take corrective actions. Likewise, the treasurer must be able to closely monitor cash flows so that deviations from forecasts can be identified in time to adjust short-term borrowing plans.

We begin this chapter by describing the basic information processing operations performed to update the general ledger and to prepare reports for both internal management and external users. Next, we discuss major control threats in the general ledger and reporting cycle and the control procedures that can be used to mitigate them. We conclude the chapter by examining some important decisions that require information from the general ledger and discuss several new developments that improve the quality of reports produced by accounting systems.

General Ledger and Reporting System Activities

Figure 14-2 is a level 0 data flow diagram depicting the four basic activities performed by the general ledger and reporting system. Figure 14-3 (see next page) depicts a typical online system used to perform those activities.

The first three activities in Figure 14-2 represent the basic steps in the accounting cycle, which culminate in the production of the traditional set of financial statements. The fourth activity indicates that, in addition to financial reports for external users, the AIS produces reports for internal management as well. We now examine each of these activities in more detail.

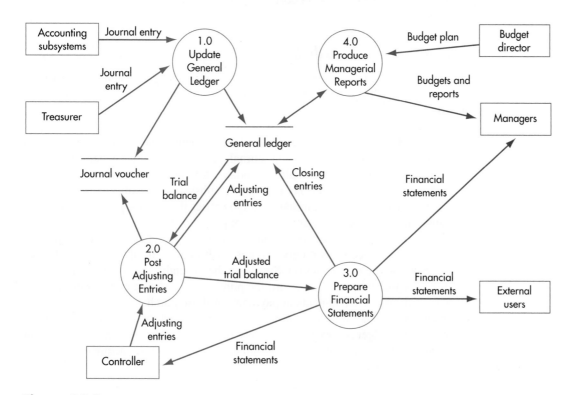

Figure 14-2
Level 0 Data Flow Diagram for the General Ledger and Reporting System

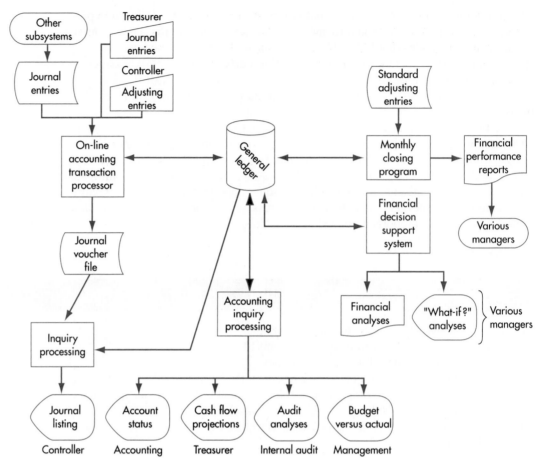

Figure 14-3
Flowchart of an Online General Ledger and Reporting System

Update General Ledger

As shown in Figure 14-2, the first activity in the general ledger system (circle 1.0) is updating the general ledger. Updating consists of posting journal entries that originate from two sources:

1 **Accounting subsystems.** Each of the accounting subsystems described in Chapters 10 through 13 creates a journal entry to update the general ledger. In theory, the general ledger could be updated for each individual transaction. In practice, however, the various accounting subsystems usually update the general ledger by means of summary journal entries that represent the results of all transactions that occurred during a given period of time (day, week, or month). For example, the revenue cycle subsystem would generate a summary journal entry debiting accounts receivable and cash and crediting sales for all sales made during the update period. Similarly, the expenditure cycle would generate summary journal entries to record the purchase of supplies and inventories and to record cash disbursements in payment for those purchases.

2 **Treasurer.** The treasurer's office creates individual journal entries to update the general ledger for nonroutine transactions such as the issuance or retirement of debt, the purchase or sale of investment securities, or the acquisition of treasury stock.

Journal entries to update the general ledger may be documented on a form called a **journal voucher**. Figure 14-2 shows that the individual journal entries used to update

the general ledger are then stored in the journal voucher file. This file therefore contains the information that would be found in the general journal in a manual AIS. Note, however, that the journal voucher file is a by-product of, not an input to, the posting process. As we will explain later, the journal voucher file forms an important part of the audit trail.

Post Adjusting Entries

The second activity in the general ledger system is posting various adjusting entries (circle 2.0 in Figure 14-2). These adjusting entries originate from the controller's office, after the initial trial balance has been prepared. The **trial balance** is a report that lists the balances for all general ledger accounts. Its name reflects the fact that if all activities have been properly recorded, the total of all debit balances in various accounts should equal the total of all credit balances. Adjusting entries fall into five basic categories:

1 *Accruals* represent entries made at the end of the accounting period to reflect events that have occurred but for which cash has not yet been received or disbursed. Examples include the recording of interest revenue earned and wages payable.

2 *Deferrals* represent entries made at the end of the accounting period to reflect the exchange of cash prior to performance of the related event. Examples include recognizing the portion of advance payments from customers earned during a specific period and expensing the portion of prepaid assets (e.g., rent, interest, and insurance) used this period.

3 *Estimates* represent entries that reflect a portion of expenses that occur over a number of accounting periods. Examples include depreciation and bad-debt expenses.

4 *Revaluations* represent entries made to reflect either differences between the actual and recorded value of an asset or a change in accounting principle. Examples include a change in the method used to value inventory, reducing the value of inventory to reflect obsolescence, or adjusting inventory records to reflect the results noted during a physical count of inventory.

5 *Corrections* represent entries made to counteract the effects of errors found in the general ledger.

As shown in Figure 14-3, information about these adjusting entries is also stored in the journal voucher file. After all adjusting entries have been posted, an adjusted trial balance is prepared. The adjusted trial balance serves as the input to the next step in the general ledger and financial reporting cycle, the preparation of financial statements.

Prepare Financial Statements

The third activity in the general ledger and reporting system is preparing financial statements (circle 3.0 in Figure 14-2). The income statement is prepared first, using data from the revenue and expense account balances in the adjusted trial balance. The balance sheet is prepared next. The third major financial statement produced is the statement of cash flows, which provides information about the cash flow effects associated with the organization's operating, investing, and financing activities. The final step is to make closing entries that zero out all revenue and expense accounts and transfer the net income or loss to retained earnings. Most organizations perform both monthly and annual closes. The former zeroes out the current month's revenue and expense account balances but leaves the year-to-date totals intact. Thus, an income statement generated immediately after a monthly closing would display all zeroes in the current month column, but would store cumulative numbers in the year-to-date column. The annual closing process zeroes out the year-to-date revenue and expense account balances.

Produce Managerial Reports

The final activity in the general ledger and reporting system (circle 4.0 in Figure 14-2) is producing various managerial reports. Examples of general ledger control reports include (1) lists of journal vouchers by numerical sequence, account number, or date, and (2) lists of general ledger account balances. These reports are used to verify the accuracy of the posting process.

A number of budgets are produced for planning and evaluating performance. The operating budget depicts planned revenues and expenditures for each organizational unit. The capital expenditures budget shows planned cash inflows and outflows for each capital project. Cash flow budgets compare estimated cash inflows from operations with planned expenditures and are used to determine borrowing needs.

Budgets and performance reports should be developed on the basis of responsibility accounting. **Responsibility accounting** is reporting financial results on the basis of managerial responsibilities within an organization. The result is a set of correlated reports that break down the organization's overall performance by specific subunits, as shown in Figure 14-4. Note that each report shows actual costs and variances from budget for the current month and the year to date, but only for those items that the manager of that subunit controls. Note also the hierarchical nature of the reports: The total cost of each individual subunit is displayed as a single line item on the next-higher-level report.

The contents of the budgetary performance reports should be tailored to the nature of the unit being evaluated. For example, many production, service, and administrative departments are treated as cost centers. Accordingly, their performance reports, as shown in Figure 14-4, should highlight actual versus budgeted performance in regard to controllable costs (those that the unit manager can affect directly). In contrast, sales departments are often evaluated as revenue centers. Consequently, their performance reports should compare actual to forecasted sales, broken down by appropriate product and geographic categories. Some departments, such as IT and utilities, charge other units for their services and are evaluated as profit centers. In this case, performance reports should appropriately compare actual revenues, expenses, and profits with their corresponding budgeted amounts. If plants, divisions, and other autonomous operating units are treated as investment centers, their performance reports also should provide data for calculating that unit's return on investment.

No matter which basis is used to prepare a unit's budgetary performance report, the method used to calculate the budget standard is crucial. The easiest approach is to establish fixed targets for each unit, store those figures in the database, and compare actual performance with those preset values. One major drawback to this approach is that the budget number is static and does not reflect unforeseen changes in the operating environment. Consequently, individual managers may be penalized or rewarded for factors beyond their control. For example, assume that the budgeted amounts in Figure 14-4 for the general superintendent are based on planned output of 2,000 units. If, however, due to greater-than-anticipated sales, actual production is 2,200 units, then the negative variances for each expense category may not really indicate inefficiency, but merely reflect the increased level of output.

A solution to such problems is to develop a flexible budget, in which the budgeted amounts vary in relation to some measure of organizational activity. In terms of our previous example, flexible budgeting would entail dividing the budget for each line item in the general superintendent's department into its fixed and variable cost components. In this way, budget standards would be automatically adjusted for any unplanned increases (or decreases) in production. Thus, any differences between these adjusted standards and actual costs can more appropriately be interpreted.

XBRL: Revolutionizing the Reporting Process

Communications technology has long been used to reduce both the time and costs of preparing and disseminating financial statements and managerial reports. For example, controllers routinely access public financial reporting databases, such as NAARS

Figure 14-4
Sample Set of Reports for a Responsibility Accounting System

and EDGAR, to find examples of how other companies disclose various items. Similarly, tax forms and instructions are available at the IRS Web site. Conversely, many companies can submit required financial and tax filings electronically to the SEC and the IRS, respectively. In addition, many companies post their financial statements on their corporate Web sites, for access by investors. Internally, management reports are usually developed in spreadsheets and disseminated either through e-mail or by posting on the company intranet.

Nevertheless, until recently, the electronic dissemination of reports containing financial and nonfinancial information was a cumbersome, inefficient process. One

Figure 14-5
Traditional Electronic Reporting
Process

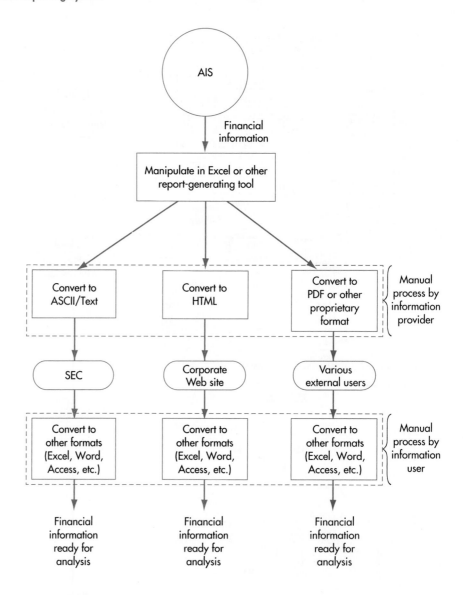

problem was that many recipients had different requirements concerning the manner in which information was to be delivered. For example, SEC filings contain much of the same information included in annual and quarterly financial statements, but organized differently. Other government agencies and regulatory bodies, like the FDIC and various state insurance commissions, specified their own unique formats for organizing information. As a result, organizations have traditionally had to devote considerable time and expense to preparing multiple reports that contain much of the same information, but presented in many different ways. Indeed, as Figure 14-5 shows, the same information often was reentered to satisfy the requirements of each external user. Not only did this incur considerable non-value-added costs but it also created numerous opportunities for error. Figure 14-5 shows that this traditional approach to electronic reporting also created significant costs and opportunities for error on the part of many external users, because they had to manually reenter much of the information into the format appropriate for their own decision analysis tools.

The underlying cause of these problems was the lack of standards for identifying the content of data. There was no way to tag a number to indicate what it represented (the amount of inventory, or accounts receivable, or any other financial item) so that the data could be automatically shared by applications. Thus, for example, there was no automated way to inform an Excel spreadsheet how to find the amount of inventory for a specific year in an HTML-formatted financial statement. Consequently, the

Panel A

ABC COMPANY (NYSE: ABC)
Condensed Consolidated Statements of Operations (unaudited)

(in thousands,	For 8 the Periods Ended September 30,			
except per share information)	Quarter		Year-to-Date	
	2008	**2007**	**2008**	**2007**
Revenue	$249,979	$214,156	$813,443	$767,107
Expenses:				
Cost of revenue	167,882	149,542	549,782	504,726
Selling and administrative	64,580	59,578	208,822	206,933
Depreciation	9,989	10,033	30,103	31,351
Amortization	893	430	2,730	1,290
Restructuring, integration	4,158	3,605	18,967	3,605
	247,502	223,188	810,404	747,905
Operating income (loss)	2,477	(9,032)	3,039	19,202
Interest expense	(3,202)	(1,844)	(8,174)	(4,951)
Gain on sale of certain printing assets	-	14,869	-	14,869
Gain on sale of building	-	4,889	-	4,889
Other income (expense), net	949	(683)	391	(224)
Income (loss) before income taxes	224	8,199	(4,744)	33,785
Income tax expense	(1,433)	(3,550)	(460)	(14,527)
Net (loss) income	$ (1,209)	$ 4,649	$ (5,204)	$ 19,258

Panel B

```
<period>
        <duration>P1Y0M0D</duration>
        <endDate>2008-09-30</endDate>
</period>
<unit>
        <measure>ISO4217:USD</measure>
</unit>
...
...
...
<usfr-pt:SalesRevenueNet numericContext="ABC_MonDur3Mths_09_2008">249979000
   </usfr-pt:SalesRevenueNet>
<usfr-pt:SalesRevenueNet numericContext="ABC_MonDur3Mths_09_2007">214156000
   </usfr-pt:SalesRevenueNet>
<usfr-pt:SalesRevenueNet numericContext="ABC_MonDurYTD_09_2008">813443000
   </usfr-pt:SalesRevenueNet>
<usfr-pt:SalesRevenueNet numericContext="ABC_MonDurYTD_09_2007">767107000
   </usfr-pt:SalesRevenueNet>
```

XBRL tags identify what the item means (e.g., that numeric values are measured in US dollars)

These entries identify the item (Net Sales Revenue), the label (2008, 2007, etc.) and the value ($249,979,000)

Figure 14-6
Panel A: Portion of Financial Statements From Excel Spreadsheet Encoded with XBRL
Panel B: Portion of XBRL Coding in Excel Spreadsheet

desired data had to be either manually reentered or copied and pasted to transfer it from one application to another.

This all changed with the development of XBRL, the extensible *b*usiness *r*eporting *l*anguage. **XBRL** is a variant of XML specifically designed for use in communicating the content of financial data. It does this by creating tags for each data item that look much like the tags used by HTML (see Figure 14-6).

The tag names in Figure 14-6 (such as usfr-pt:SalesRevenueNet) come from taxonomies that have been developed to specify which tags should be used to describe the various line items in financial statements. The other fields in each tag provide contextual information, such as what year the data represents and the units of measurement. In essence, the XBRL tags function as "bar codes" that define what a specific number or label means. Fortunately, it is not necessary to manually create these tags. Major software vendors are developing tools to automatically generate XBRL code, just as it is possible to create Web pages without having to directly write HTML code by choosing the "Save As HTML" option. Thus, accountants and systems professionals will not need to know how to write XBRL code to take advantage of the benefits it offers.

Figure 14-7 shows that XBRL provides two major benefits to the creation and electronic dissemination of financial data. First, it enables organizations to publish information only once, using standard XBRL tags. Currently, financial data may be sent to one party as an HTML document, to another as an Adobe Acrobat file, to

Figure 14-7
Electronic Reporting with XBRL

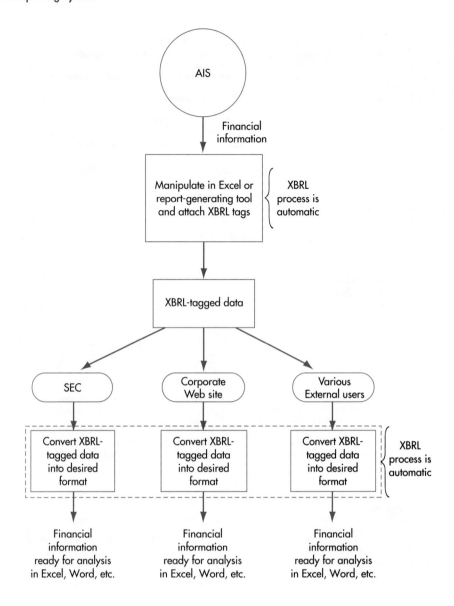

another as a text file, and to yet another party as a comma-delimited file. This process creates unnecessary costs and provides multiple opportunities to make errors when reentering data. In contrast, the same XBRL file could be sent to all external parties, who could then reformat the file as they wished. Thus, with XBRL, companies can publish their financial statements one time in a format that anyone can use.

The second benefit of XBRL is that the information the XBRL tags provide is interpretable. This means that recipients will no longer need to manually reenter data they acquired electronically so that decision support tools can analyze them. Instead, if the data contain XBRL tags, they can be fed directly into any analysis tool that understands XBRL. It also means that searching for data on the Internet will be more efficient and accurate. For example, prior to XBRL, searching the Internet for information about contingent liabilities for company X would yield hundreds of results most of which have nothing to do with the financial data being sought. With XBRL-tagged data, however, the search is limited to information about contingent liabilities reported in financial statements.

The benefits of XBRL are not limited to its use to exchange financial data with external parties. Internal reporting will also benefit because data from the organization's AIS can be exported once and then reused by different managers in different applications without the need to manually reenter it. This will improve not only efficiency but also accuracy.

14-1 FOCUS XBRL—An Accounting-Led IT Development

The origins of XBRL can be traced back to the early 1990s. At that time, a software engineer named Jon Bosak recognized that a critical shortcoming of HTML is its inability to describe the content of the data being presented. Bosak convinced the World Wide Web Consortium (W3C) to sponsor the development of a language with this capability. That project resulted in Bosak and two other software engineers creating a programming language called XML, which stands for extensible *markup language*. XML is a general-purpose tool that can tag any data with identifying markers.

XML was a step in the right direction. Charlie Hoffman, a CPA who worked for a local accounting firm in Tacoma, Washington realized, however, that XML did not go far enough to be a general-purpose language for communicating financial information. What was needed was the ability not only to identify what each piece of data was but also how to process it and how to relate it to other data items. Hoffman started work on adding the desired

capabilities to XML but realized that the project required additional support. He sought and obtained the AICPA's help to pursue the development of a prototype set of XML-enhanced financial statements.

As the work progressed, the results were shared with major software companies, who recognized the value of such a common business language and joined the project. Eventually, many leading software companies, and important user groups, cooperated in the venture with the AICPA. The result: XBRL. Vendors are currently working on making a wide range of financial and decision support software capable of supporting XBRL. Industry-specific coding taxonomies have been developed in many countries. XBRL is on its way to becoming the global computer language for communicating financial data. And it all started with one CPA who was looking for a better way to disseminate financial data on the Internet!

Post-script: In December 2006 the AICPA formally recognized Charlie Hoffman's pioneering work in developing XBRL with a special award.

The power of XBRL lies in the information provided by its tags. XBRL taxonomies define what those tags represent. There are two basic types of taxonomies. Financial reporting taxonomies, which have been developed for different industries and countries, define summary measures like accounts payable, inventory, and accounts receivable that appear in financial statements and reports. In contrast, the XBRL-GL taxonomy (the GL stands for "global ledger") defines the underlying data elements in an AIS, thereby tagging each individual piece of business data prior to its aggregation in reports.

XBRL is certainly an important IT development. It is also noteworthy because the accounting profession spearheaded its development (see Focus 14-1). The XBRL development process provides an outstanding illustration of how accountants can actively participate in the ongoing development of IT. XBRL is a work in progress. Visit the xbrl.org Web site to keep abreast of the continuing development of this revolutionary tool.

Control Objectives, Threats, and Procedures

The control objectives in the general ledger and reporting system are similar to those in the other AIS cycles discussed in previous chapters:

1 All updates to the general ledger are properly authorized.
2 All recorded general ledger transactions are valid.
3 All valid, authorized general ledger transactions are recorded.
4 All general ledger transactions are accurately recorded.
5 General ledger data are safeguarded from loss or theft.
6 General ledger system activities are performed efficiently and effectively.

Table 14-1
Threats and Controls in the General Ledger and Reporting Systems

Process/Activity	Threat	Applicable Control Procedures
All general ledger and reporting activities (posting, updating, and report generation)	1. Errors in updating the general ledger and generating reports 2. Financial statement fraud	Input and processing controls; reconciliations and control reports; audit trail Independent testing of all special journal entries to the general ledger
General control issues	3. Loss or unauthorized disclosure or alteration of financial data 4. Poor performance	Access controls, including proper configuration of ERP system; creation of audit trail; backup and disaster-recovery plans; encryption; data transmission controls XBRL and other innovative IT solutions

Well-designed documents and records play an important role in achieving these objectives. Online data entry of transactions by the treasurer and the controller, as depicted in Figure 14-3, facilitates the accurate and efficient recording of general ledger journal entries. In such situations, using appropriate application controls, such as validity checks and field (format) checks, enhances the accuracy of data entry. Recording who completed and reviewed the form provides evidence that the journal entry was properly authorized. Prenumbering all journal entries facilitates checking that all transactions have been recorded. Restricting access to the general ledger program further reduces the risk of unauthorized transactions.

Table 14-1 lists the major threats and exposures in the general ledger and financial reporting system, along with applicable control procedures for mitigating them. Let us now examine the control procedures that can be used to deal with these threats.

Threat 1: Errors in Updating the General Ledger and Generating Reports

Errors made in updating the general ledger (either through regular or adjusting journal entries) can lead to poor decision making based on erroneous information in financial performance reports. Poorly designed reports also impair decision quality. The control procedures for dealing with this threat fall into three categories: input edit and processing controls, reconciliations and control reports, and maintenance of an adequate audit trail.

Input Edit and Processing Controls

Figure 14-3 shows two sources of journal entries for updating the general ledger: summary journal entries from the other AIS cycles and direct entries made by the treasurer or controller. The former are themselves the output of a series of processing steps, each of which was subject to a variety of application control procedures designed to ensure accuracy and completeness, as described in the preceding four chapters. Consequently, the primary input edit control for summary journal entries is checking to ensure that they represent activity for the most recent time period.

Journal entries made by the treasurer and controller, however, are original data entry. Consequently, the following types of input edit and processing controls are needed to ensure that they are accurate and complete:

1 A *validity check* to ensure that general ledger accounts exist for each account number referenced in a journal entry.
2 *Field (format) checks* to ensure that the amount field in the journal entry contains only numeric data.

3 *Zero-balance checks* to verify that total debits equal total credits in a journal entry.

4 A *completeness test* to ensure that all pertinent data are entered, especially the source of the journal entry.

5 *Closed-loop verification* matching account numbers with account descriptions, to ensure that the correct general ledger account is being accessed.

6 Creating a standard adjusting entry file for recurring adjusting entries made each period, such as depreciation expense. (Input accuracy is improved by eliminating the need to repeatedly key in these entries. The possibility of forgetting to make a recurring adjusting entry is also reduced, thereby ensuring input completeness.)

7 A *sign check* of the general ledger account balance, once updating is completed, to verify that the balance is of the appropriate nature (debit or credit).

8 Calculating *run-to-run totals* to verify the accuracy of journal voucher batch processing. (The computer calculates the new balance of the general ledger account, based on its beginning balance and the total debits and credits applied to that account, then compares that with the actual account balance in the updated general ledger. Any discrepancies indicate a processing error that must be investigated.)

Reconciliations and Control Reports

Reconciliations and control reports can detect whether any errors were made during the process of updating the general ledger. One form of reconciliation is the preparation of a trial balance. It indicates if the total debit balances in the general ledger equal the total credit balances; if not, a posting error has occurred. Clearing and suspense accounts provide a means to ensure that the general ledger is always in balance. At the close of a fiscal period, these special accounts should have zero balances; otherwise, an error was made in updating the general ledger.

To illustrate how these types of special accounts are used, assume that one clerk is responsible for recording the release of inventory to customers and another clerk is responsible for recording the billing of customers. The first clerk would make the following journal entry:

Unbilled shipments	x x x	
Inventory		x x x

The second clerk would make this entry:

Accounts receivable	y y y	
Unbilled shipments		y y y

Once both entries have been completed, the special clearing account, unbilled shipments, should have a zero balance. If not, an error has been made and must be investigated and corrected.

Another important reconciliation is comparing the general ledger control account balances to the total balance in the corresponding subsidiary ledger. If these two totals do not agree, the difference must be investigated and corrected. It is also important to examine all transactions occurring near the end of an accounting period to verify that they are recorded in the proper time period.

ERP systems provide a number of control reports to help identify the source of any errors that occurred in the general ledger update process. Listing journal vouchers by general account number facilitates identifying the cause of errors affecting a specific general ledger account. Listing the journal vouchers by sequence can indicate the absence of any journal entry postings. Finally, the **general journal listing** shows the details (account number, source reference code, description, and amount debited or credited) of each entry posted to the general ledger. This report indicates if the total debits equal the total credits posted to the general ledger.

The Audit Trail

The **audit trail** depicts the path of a transaction through the accounting system (refer to Figure 2-4). Specifically, it provides the information needed to trace all changes made to the general ledger. In particular, an audit trail facilitates the following tasks:

1 Tracing any transaction from its original source document (whether paper or electronic) to the general ledger and to any report or other document using that data;
2 Tracing any item appearing in a report back through the general ledger to its original source document (whether paper or electronic);
3 Tracing all changes in general ledger accounts from their beginning balance to their ending balance.

The business workflow features provided by ERP systems make it easy to trace every step performed in processing a transaction. In legacy AIS, the journal voucher file provides information about the source of all entries made to update the general ledger. In addition, various master files or databases discussed in prior chapters contain detailed information that can be used to verify the accuracy of the general ledger. For example, the account balances of individual customers in the customer master file or database can be summed and compared with the accounts receivable control account in the general ledger. A similar process can be performed to reconcile accounts payable, inventory, and equipment balances.

The usefulness of the audit trail depends on its integrity. Therefore, it is important to periodically make backups of all audit trail components and to control access to them to ensure that they cannot be altered. ERP systems provide secure audit trails. SAP, for example, creates prenumbered records (called documents) for every action that is performed and which cannot be erased.

Threat 2: Financial Statement Fraud

Financial statement fraud often involves journal entries by upper-level management that either overstate revenues or understate liabilities. It is difficult to prevent such journal entries because upper-level management inherently has the ability to override most internal controls. Therefore, the best control to mitigate the threat of financial statement fraud is regular, detailed testing of all special journal entries to the general ledger (i.e., all entries other than the summary journal entries automatically generated by a subsystem of the AIS). Although Statement of Auditing Standards number 99 requires external auditors to "test the appropriateness of journal entries recorded in the general ledger and other adjustments," internal auditors should also regularly review all adjustments to the general ledger. To be effective, however, such testing requires proper configuration of the AIS, so that every change to general ledger accounts is captured and recorded as part of the audit trail.

Threat 3: Loss or Unauthorized Disclosure or Alteration of Financial Data

The general ledger is a key component of the organization's accounting information system. Unauthorized access to the general ledger can result in confidential data leaks to competitors or corruption of the general ledger. It can also provide a means for concealing the theft of assets. Consequently, it is important to have adequate controls to prevent unauthorized access to the general ledger.

User IDs and passwords should be used to control access to the general ledger and to enforce the proper segregation of duties by limiting the functions that each

legitimate user may perform. For example, employees who have custody of assets or the ability to authorize the release of assets should be prevented from updating the general ledger (the recording function). Similarly, management should be given read-only access to the general ledger, as depicted at the bottom of Figure 14-3. The access control matrix should also limit the functions that can be performed at various terminals. Adjusting entries, for example, should be allowed only from terminals in the controller's office.

Controls over the creation of journal voucher records also are important because they authorize changes to general ledger account balances. Thus, the system should check for the existence of a valid authorization code for each journal voucher record before posting that transaction to the general ledger. Otherwise, the integrity of the general ledger may be compromised. Note that this authorization code also forms a part of the audit trail. Indeed, inspection of the audit trail provides a means to detect unauthorized access to the general ledger.

As noted in previous chapters, enforcing proper access controls and segregation of duties requires that the controller or CFO review and suggest appropriate configuration of user rights in integrated AIS packages and ERP systems. The default installation of such systems typically provides every user with far too much power. For example, clerks with authority to record specific transaction cycle activities, such as sales order entry, may also be given access to the general ledger. Additionally, employees with programming or system administration responsibilities should not also be able to perform business processes. For example, if an employee with database administration responsibilities also had authority to perform business processes such as cash disbursements, that person could alter the database tables to conceal fraudulent activities. It is important that internal auditors be involved during the implementation process to prevent these types of weaknesses in the segregation of duties.

It is also important to provide adequate backup and disaster-recovery procedures to protect the information contained in the general ledger. At least two backup copies of the general ledger should exist. One copy should be kept on-site where it can be immediately accessed; the other copy should be stored off-site to provide protection against a major disaster such as a fire or an earthquake. In addition, organizations need to develop and practice a disaster-recovery plan.

Access and processing integrity controls are also needed to ensure the confidentiality and accuracy of any financial data transmitted electronically to branch offices or external parties. General ledger data should be encrypted both while in storage and during transmission over the Internet. Parity checks and acknowledgment messages should also be used to ensure the accuracy of data transmissions. In addition, various control totals should be used to verify the accuracy of information transmitted electronically.

Threat 4: Poor Performance

Organizations must provide information to a multitude of external parties, including government agencies, regulatory bodies, investors, and creditors. Organizations also generate a myriad of internal reports for use in managing operations. New tools, particularly XBRL, provide a means to significantly improve both the efficiency and accuracy of these processes. Redesigning business processes provides additional opportunities to improve efficiency and effectiveness. For example, adopting a standard chart of accounts to be used by all business units and subsidiaries facilitates consolidating financial statements and can speed the closing process. Accountants should also seek to redesign the metrics used to report the results of business activities as well as the manner in which such financial information is displayed in order to improve the usefulness of internal reports generated by the organization's AIS.

The next section discusses three topics that are particularly relevant to helping accountants and information systems professionals improve the quality of information provided to management.

Supporting Management's Information Needs

As noted throughout this book, a primary function of an AIS is to provide management with the information it needs to make decisions. This section discusses three important topics regarding the use of general ledger information for decision making: (1) the balanced scorecard, (2) data warehouses to support business intelligence, and (3) the proper design of graphs of financial data. These topics relate to the issues raised in the introductory case concerning the utility of an organization's information systems.

The Balanced Scorecard*

A **balanced scorecard** is a report that provides a multidimensional perspective of organizational performance. A balanced scorecard contains measures reflecting four perspectives of the organization: financial, customer, internal operations, and innovation and learning. The financial section contains lagging indicators of the organization's past performance, whereas the other three sections provide leading indicators about likely future performance. For each dimension, the balanced scorecard shows the organization's goals and specific measures that reflect performance in attaining those goals. Together, the four dimensions of the balanced scorecard provide a much more comprehensive overview of organizational performance than that provided by financial measures alone. Indeed, a properly designed balanced scorecard measures key aspects of the organization's strategy and reflects important causal links across the four dimensions. Table 14-2 shows a sample balanced scorecard for AOE.

AOE's top management, like many companies, agreed on three key financial goals: increased revenue streams through sales of new products, increased profitability as

Table 14-2
Sample Balanced Scorecard for AOE

DIMENSION GOALS	Measure	Target	Current Period	Prior Period
FINANCIAL				
New revenue streams	Sales of new products (000s)	104	103	100
Improve profitability	Return on equity (%)	12.5%	12.6%	12.2%
Positive cash flow	Cash from operations (000s)	156	185	143
CUSTOMER				
Improve satisfaction	Rating (0–100)	95	93	92
Be a preferred supplier	Percentage of key customers' electronics purchases made from us	20%	20%	18%
INTERNAL OPERATIONS				
Service quality	Orders filled without error (%)	98%	97%	95%
Speed of delivery	Order cycle time (days)	10.4	10.5	11.2
Process efficiency	Defect rate	1.0%	1.1%	1.05%
INNOVATION AND LEARNING				
New products	Number of new products	4	4	3
Employee learning	Personnel attending advanced training courses (%)	10%	25%	9%

*This section is based on two articles by Robert S. Kaplan and David P. Norton: "The Balanced Scorecard – Measures that Drive Performance," Harvard Business Review (January–February 1992): 71–79 and "Using the Balanced Scorecard as a Strategic Management System," Harvard Business Review (January–February 1996): 75–85. Additional information about the balanced scorecard can be found at www.balancedscorecard.org.

reflected in return on equity, and maintaining adequate cash flow to meet obligations. As shown in Table 14-2, specific measures and targets were developed to track the attainment of those goals. Both the choice of key metrics and the setting of target values are important management decisions. Many organizations make the mistake of setting targets that reflect industry benchmark values. The problem with such an approach is that the organization's aspirations and, hence, its performance, are limited by its competitors' performance. Although industry benchmarks may provide a useful reference point, management should set targets that take into consideration the organization's unique strengths and weaknesses.

For every organization, customers are the key to achieving financial goals. Accordingly, the customer perspective of AOE's balanced scorecard contains two key goals: improve customer satisfaction and become the preferred supplier for key customers. In turn, meeting those customer-oriented goals requires efficiently and effectively performing internal business processes. Consequently, the internal operations perspective portion of AOE's balanced scorecard focuses on those activities most likely to directly affect customer perceptions: service quality, speed of delivery, and process efficiency. Finally, AOE's top management acknowledged the importance of developing new products and training its workforce to continuously improve service and results. Therefore, measures of those two items are included in the innovation and learning perspective of AOE's balanced scorecard.

Note that the preceding discussion implied a number of hypotheses. For example, increased employee training is expected to improve service quality, as reflected in the percentage of customer orders filled correctly. In turn, improved service quality is expected to result in increased customer satisfaction and in key customers making a greater share of their electronics purchases from AOE. Finally, increased customer satisfaction is expected to result in improved profitability and cash flow. Thus, the measures in the innovation and learning internal operations, and customer perspective portions of the balanced scorecard can be thought of as leading indicators of financial measures of the organization's strategy. Analyzing trends in the actual measures allows AOE's management to test the validity of those hypotheses. If improvements in one perspective do not generate expected improvements in other areas, top management must reevaluate and probably revise hypotheses about the determinants of organizational success. Indeed, this ability to test and refine strategy is one of the major benefits the balanced scorecard provides.

Accountants and systems professionals should participate in the development of a balanced scorecard. Top management should specify the goals to be pursued in each dimension. Accountants and information systems professionals can then help management choose the most appropriate measures for tracking achievement of those goals. In addition, they can provide input concerning the feasibility of collecting the data that would be required to implement various proposed measures.

Although the balanced scorecard was initially developed as a strategic management tool, it can also be used as a vehicle to better manage enterprise risk by incorporating appropriate risk-based goals and measures in the various dimensions. For example, an organization might want to increase information security awareness among employees. One way to motivate attention to that objective is to explicitly list increased security awareness as one of the goals in the Innovation and Learning section of the scorecard and then measure employee knowledge about security best practices. Similarly, listing reduced inventory shrinkage as one of the Internal Operations Process goals and measuring it can help focus attention on reducing the risk of employee theft. External threats, such as loss of market share, can likewise be addressed by including appropriate measures (e.g., sales to repeat customers, number of new customers, etc.) in the Customer and Financial sections of the balanced scorecard. Thus, the balanced scorecard can be used as one tool to monitor and evaluate an organization's controls and risk management program.

Using Data Warehouses for Business Intelligence

Timely access to information is important. In today's fast-paced global economy, management must constantly monitor and reevaluate the organization's financial and operating performance in light of its strategic goals. Firms must be able to alter

their plans quickly in response to changes in their environment. Consequently, many organizations are adopting online general ledger systems similar to that depicted in Figure 14-3. Such systems can give management ready access to the information needed to make timely operating and tactical decisions.

ERP systems and integrated AIS are not sufficient, however, to support management's strategic decision-making needs because they are designed primarily to support the organization's transaction processing needs. Accordingly, they typically contain data for only the current fiscal year, plus perhaps one additional month to enable comparisons of the current month's activities to those of the same month a year ago. Strategic decision making, however, requires access to large amounts of historical data. For example, when evaluating marketing strategies, management may need access to data about sales broken down by products, by salesperson, and by customer for the past five years.

To provide the information needed for strategic decision making, organizations are building separate databases called data warehouses. A **data warehouse** contains both detailed and summarized data for a number of years and is used for analysis rather than transaction processing. Because they contain information for multiple years, data warehouses are enormous. Indeed, it is not unusual for them to contain tens, or even hundreds, of terabytes of data. Consequently, data warehouses are usually separate systems from the AIS used to support the organization's daily business activities so that performance of those activities is not adversely affected by the computer processing resources consumed in analyzing the data contained in the data warehouse. In addition, organizations often build separate data warehouses for various functions. For example, an organization may build one data warehouse for the finance function, another for the human resources function, and so forth. Such smaller warehouses are often referred to as **data marts**.

Data warehouses and data marts do not replace an organization's transaction processing databases. Instead, they complement those databases by providing support for strategic decision making. It is important to remember that data warehouses and data marts are not used for transaction processing. Consequently, they are not usually updated in real time, but instead are periodically updated to reflect the results of all transactions that have occurred since the last update.

Data warehouses differ from the databases used to support transaction processing not only in size but also in how they are structured. Whereas transaction processing databases are designed so as to minimize redundancy and thereby maximize the efficiency of updating them to reflect the results of current transactions, data warehouses are often designed to be purposely redundant to maximize query efficiency. Thus, data warehouses are usually designed to be dimensional in nature. The most common dimensional architecture is referred to as the star schema, which is so named because the data are arranged in a manner resembling a star (see Figure 14-8 on the next page).

At the center of the star is a *single* fact table that represents the most important variable of interest. The fact table contains multiple views or measures of a variable and a number of foreign keys that link that fact table to the various factors that influence it. Separate tables store information about each of the factors, called dimensions, which are relevant to the fact table. In Figure 14-8, the fact table contains information about purchases of raw materials, in terms of both units and dollar values. Relevant dimensions to managing and evaluating purchasing performance include the location where the material is stored, the item, the purchasing agent and department, the supplier, and the time period. A data warehouse consists of numerous such stars, one for each important set of fact data. Further information about the star schema is beyond the scope of this text but can be found in any textbook used for courses on data warehousing.

The process of accessing the data contained in a data warehouse and using it for strategic decision making is often referred to as **business intelligence**. There

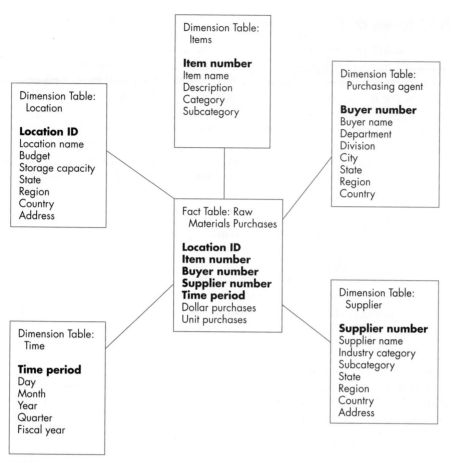

Figure 14-8
Example of a Star Schema
for a Data Warehouse

Bold attributes are the primary keys of the table.

are two main techniques used in business intelligence: online analytical processing (OLAP) and data mining. **Online analytical processing (OLAP)** is using queries in which the user guides the investigation of hypothesized relationships in the data. For example, a manager may begin with a query that breaks down purchases by supplier for the last three years. This may be followed by additional queries that "drill down" to lower levels (similar to the hierarchy of reports depicted in Figure 14-4) by, for example, grouping purchases by different items and by fiscal periods. **Data mining** is using sophisticated statistical analysis, including artificial intelligence techniques such as neural networks, to "discover" unhypothesized relationships in the data. For example, credit card companies use data mining to identify patterns of usage indicative of fraud. Similarly, data mining techniques can be used to identify previously unknown relationships in sales data that can then be used as the basis for future promotions.

Data warehousing can provide significant benefits to an organization. Proper controls are needed, however, to reap those benefits. Data quality is important; therefore, data validation controls are essential to ensure that the information input into the data warehouse is accurate. Indeed, the process of verifying the accuracy ("scrubbing") of the information to be included in a data warehouse is often one of the most time-consuming and expensive steps in creating a data warehouse. Once created, it is important to control access to the data warehouse. In addition, because of its strategic value and the insights it may provide about an organization's key activities, information in the data warehouse should probably be encrypted. Finally, it is important to regularly back up copies of the data warehouse and store them securely.

Principles of Graph Design

The typical AIS produces a multitude of reports for managers. Accountants and information systems professionals can help management deal with this information overload by preparing graphs that highlight and summarize important facts. Well-designed graphs make it easy to identify and understand trends and relationships. Poorly designed graphs, however, can impair decision making.

Although many types of graphs exist, bar charts are the most common type used to display trends in financial data. (Pie charts are used primarily to show the relative size of subcomponents, such as the proportion of product cost due to labor, materials, and overhead). Therefore, we will focus on some basic principles that make bar charts easy to read.

1 Use titles that summarize the basic message.
2 Include data values with each element instead of labeling the vertical axis, to facilitate mental calculations and analyses.
3 Use 2-D, instead of 3-D, bars because that makes it easier to accurately assess the magnitude of changes and trends.
4 Use different shades of gray or colors instead of patterns of dots or stripes to represent different variables because they are easier to distinguish.

Figure 14-9 illustrates many of these principles.

Although readability is important, the ultimate value of graphs to support decision making depends on the accuracy with which they are interpreted. The following two principles are essential for properly designing graphs of financial data so that they are accurately interpreted:

1 Begin the vertical axis at zero. Doing so ensures that the depicted magnitude of change in the data *accurately* reflects the actual change in the data. To see the importance of this rule, compare Figure 14-9, which follows this principle, to Figure 14-10 (see next page), which does not. Exception: Beginning the vertical axis at a value other than zero may be useful if there is a need to monitor minor fluctuations in the data (see Figure 14-11 on the next page).
2 For graphs that depict time-series data, order the *x*-axis chronologically from left to right. Otherwise, the viewer may form an erroneous initial impression of the nature of the change in the data (compare Figure 14-12 to Figure 14-9).

Figure 14-9
Examples of Good Graph
Design

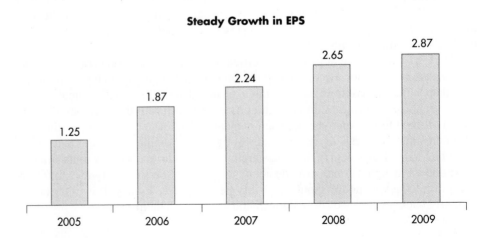

Steady Growth in EPS

2005: 1.25 2006: 1.87 2007: 2.24 2008: 2.65 2009: 2.87

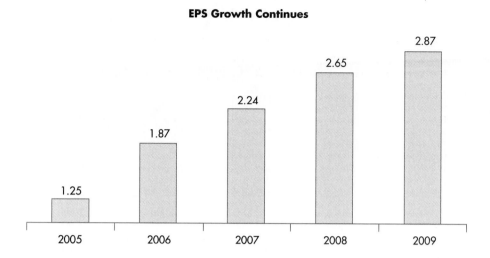

EPS Growth Continues

2.87

2.65

2.24

1.87

1.25

2005 2006 2007 2008 2009

Figure 14-10
Example of Poor Graph
Design: Vertical Axis Does Not
Start at Zero

Top graph—vertical axis starts at 35 to better show price fluctuation

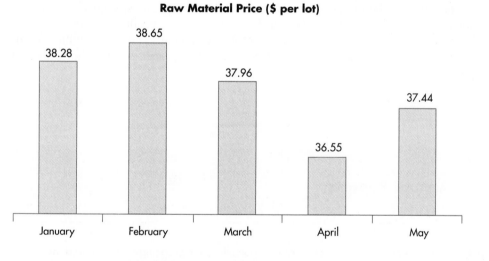

Raw Material Price ($ per lot)

38.28 38.65 37.96 36.55 37.44

January February March April May

Figure 14-11
Exception to Vertical Axis
at Zero Rule

Bottom graph—vertical axis starts at 0, price fluctuation muted

Raw Material Price ($ per lot)

38.28 38.65 37.96 36.55 37.44

January February March April May

Figure 14-12
Example of Poor Graph
Design: Reverse Chronological
Year Order

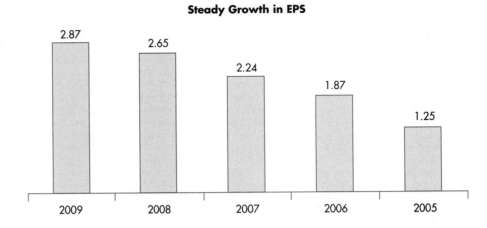

Although these rules are simple, they are easily violated. Indeed, as Focus 14-2 explains, many annual reports contain graphs that violate these design principles. Often, such violations are created automatically by the software program used to create the graph. Other times, the graph designer purposely chooses to violate these principles in order to create a special effect or to dramatize some particular aspect of the data. As the top portion of Figure 14-11 demonstrates, such violations are sometimes helpful. Usually, however, breaking the rules results in graphs that may be misleading, as in Figure 14-12. Therefore, accountants and information systems professionals should strive to follow the principles of proper graph design whenever possible.

14-2 FOCUS Graphs in Annual Reports

For more than 25 years, researchers have examined the use of graphs in published annual reports. A surprising finding is that many annual reports contain graphs that violate the principles of proper graph design. The problem has persisted over time, being documented in annual reports published during the late 1970s through those published in the 21st century. The problem is also international: improperly designed graphs have been found in annual reports published in the United States, the United Kingdom, Europe, Australia, and Asia.

By far the most common type of violation involves starting the vertical axis at a point other than zero. Most often this results in a graph that exaggerates the magnitude of an increasing trend. Sometimes, however, it smoothes the magnitude of a decreasing trend. Graphs that reverse the chronological sequence on the x-axis have also been found in annual reports.

An interesting question is why such graphs exist in annual reports. The answer is that there are no authoritative guidelines for graphing financial data, nor are there any authoritative guidelines for auditing such graphs. In the United States, SAS No. 8 discusses the auditor's responsibility for "other information" contained in annual reports. Although it requires the auditor to determine whether such information, which would include graphs, is materially consistent with the audited financial statements, no guidelines for assessing material consistency are provided. Moreover, improperly designed graphs in annual reports always include accurate data values that match the numbers in the financial statements. Therefore, the question is not whether the graphs report accurate numbers, but whether visual distortions of those accurate numbers matter. There is some research evidence that improperly designed graphs can affect decisions, but much additional work is needed before definitive conclusions can be drawn. If such evidence is forthcoming, guidelines for preparing, and auditing, graphs of financial data are likely to follow.

SUMMARY AND CASE CONCLUSION

The general ledger and financial reporting system integrates and summarizes the results of the various accounting subsystems for the revenue, expenditure, production, and human resources cycles. The general ledger is the central master file in the AIS. Consequently, it is important to implement control procedures to ensure its accuracy and security. Important controls include edit checks of the journal voucher records posted to the general ledger, access controls, an adequate audit trail, and appropriate backup and disaster-recovery procedures.

The outputs produced by the general ledger system fall into two primary categories: financial statements and managerial reports. The former are prepared periodically in accordance with GAAP and are distributed to both internal and external users. The latter are prepared for internal use only and therefore often include comparisons between actual and budgeted performance. The usefulness of these reports, whether presented in the form of tables or graphs, is affected by how well they are designed.

In addition to printed reports, the general ledger system should also support inquiry processing by decision makers. This requires adequate controls to limit access to, and permissible operations on, the data in the general ledger.

Organizations must provide information to a wide variety of users, including government agencies, industry analysts, financial institutions, and individual decision makers. XBRL provides a mechanism for improving the efficiency of generating such information, as well as for using information obtained from external sources. Elizabeth Venko and Ann Brandt proposed that AOE take advantage of the new capabilities XBRL provides to improve the efficiency and reduce the costs associated with providing financial information to external users. Linda Spurgeon and Stephanie Cromwell agreed to the acquistion of add-in tools that support XBRL.

Elizabeth and Ann also explained that although AOE's new integrated transaction processing database provides much of the data needed to create a balanced scorecard, a separate data warehouse that contains not only current but also detailed historical data will have to be built to satisfy AOE's business intelligence needs. Elizabeth also suggested that managers should be trained on how to design graphs properly to depict accurately key performance trends. Linda and Stephanie agreed with those suggestions. They asked Ann to chair a team that would develop a formal plan for building a data warehouse. Elizabeth was assigned to oversee the development of some graph design training classes.

This chapter concludes our examination of the various cycles in an AIS. You have learned that accounting information systems have three main objectives: (1) to process transactions for accountability purposes, (2) to maintain adequate controls to ensure the integrity of the organization's data and the safeguarding of its assets, and (3) to provide information to support decision making. One other theme that appears throughout this book is the need for accountants to move beyond the traditional role of scorekeeper and actively seek to add value to their organization. Accountants should participate in decisions about adopting new technology and implementing new information systems because they have the training to properly evaluate the relative costs and benefits, as well as the economic risks, underlying such investments. Effectively participating in decisions concerning technology, however, requires accountants to not only keep abreast of current accounting developments but also to stay informed about advances in IT. Thus, as an accountant, you must make a commitment to lifelong learning. We wish you well in this endeavor.

KEY TERMS

AIS IN ACTION

CHAPTER QUIZ

1 From where do adjusting entries usually come?
a. treasurer
b. controller
c. various accounting cycle subsystems, such as sales order entry
d. unit managers

2 Preparing performance reports that contain data only about items that a specific organizational unit controls is an example of which of the following?
a. flexible budget system
b. responsibility accounting system
c. closing the books
d. management by exception

3 What is the business intelligence technique designed to discover nonhypothe-sized relationships called?
a. data warehousing
b. OLAP
c. data mining
d. querying

4 Which of the following shows the implied linkages among the portions of the balanced scorecard?
a. Financial → Internal → Innovation and learning → Customer
b. Innovation and learning → Internal → Customer → Financial
c. Customer → Financial → Internal → Innovation and learning
d. Internal → Customer → Innovation and learning → Financial

5 Writing a query to identify trends in sales of a product by salesperson and by customer over the past 5 years is an example of which of the following?
a. data mining
b. responsibility accounting
c. transaction processing
d. OLAP

6 Measures of cycle time would most likely appear in which part of the balanced scorecard?
a. innovation and learning
b. customer
c. internal operations
d. financial

7 Which of the following is an important part of the audit trail?
a. journal vouchers
b. flexible budgets
c. trial balance
d. data warehouse

8 An adjusting journal entry to record interest revenue that has been earned but not yet received is an example of which of the following?
a. accrual
b. deferral
c. estimate
d. revaluation

9 What is the new common business reporting computer language developed, in part, by the accounting profession called?
a. XML
b. XBRL
c. SQL
d. HTML

10 Which of the following graph design principles is most important for ensuring that financial data are accurately interpreted?
 a. including a title that summarizes the point of the graph
 b. attaching data values to specific elements in the graph
 c. starting the *y*-axis of the graph at zero
 d. using special-purpose graphing software

DISCUSSION QUESTIONS

14.1 Although XBRL facilitates the electronic exchange of financial information, some external users do not think it goes far enough. They would like access to the entire general ledger, not just to XBRL-tagged financial reports that summarize general ledger accounts. Should companies provide external users with such access? Why or why not?

14.2 How is XBRL-GL likely to affect the role of accountants in organizations?

14.3 Compare and contrast how auditors can use OLAP and data mining techniques to evaluate internal controls.

14.4 Some companies are abandoning the practice of budgeting because they claim that the costs outweigh the benefits. They argue that instead of comparing actual performance to budgeted standards, closely monitoring trends in actual performance over time would be more effective. Deviations from historical trends would signal the need to take corrective actions. Discuss the advantages and disadvantages of this practice.

14.5 The balanced scorecard measures organizational performance along four dimensions. Is it possible that measures on the customer, internal operations, and innovation and learning dimensions could be improving without any positive change in the financial dimension? If so, what are the implications of such a pattern?

14.6 Do you think that mandatory standards should be developed for the design of graphs of financial data that are included in annual reports and other periodic communications to investors? Why or why not?

PROBLEMS

14.1 Which control procedure would be most effective in addressing the following problems?
 a. When entering a journal entry to record issuance of new debt, the treasurer inadvertently transposes two digits in the debit amount.
 b. When entering a journal entry to record the issuance of new debt, the treasurer inadvertently transposes two digits in the account code.
 c. The controller forgot to make an adjusting entry to record depreciation.
 d. The treasurer makes a journal entry authorizing the write-off of a friend's account.

 e. The general ledger master file is stored on disk. For some reason, the disk is no longer readable. It takes the accounting department a week to reenter the past month's transactions from source documents in order to create a new general ledger master file.

 f. The controller sent a spreadsheet containing a preliminary draft of the income statement to the CFO by e-mail. An analyst intercepted the e-mail and used the information to sell his stock in the company before news of the disappointing results became public.

 g. The controller made several errors when entering selected data into a spreadsheet from a report produced by the ERP system. As a result, the controller's analyses were wrong.

14.2 Give two specific examples of nonroutine transactions that may occur in processing cash receipts and updating accounts receivable. Also specify the control procedures that should be in place to ensure the accuracy, completeness, and validity of those transactions.

14.3 An important control procedure involves the periodic reconciliation of general ledger accounts with their subsidiary ledgers. Explain how this control procedure works in the context of accounts payable. Your answer should specify how to verify the accuracy, completeness, and validity of all entries involving purchases, purchase returns, purchase discounts, and cash disbursements.

14.4 Figure 14-1 is a context diagram for the general ledger and reporting cycle that shows the principal data flows to and from the general ledger.

Required

 a. List the source documents or journals underlying each data flow into the general ledger.

 b. Identify at least two additional data flows resulting from the revenue and expenditure cycle systems, and specify the source documents or journals that would support those flows.

14.5 Refer to the example of responsibility coding depicted in Figure 14-4.

Required

 a. Design a coding scheme that will support the production of this set of reports. Make and state any assumptions you believe are necessary.

 b. Write a brief (half-page) explanation of how your coding scheme works.

 c. Suggest improvements in the set of reports depicted in Figure 14-4.

14.6 As manager of a local pizza parlor, you want to develop a balanced scorecard so you can more effectively monitor the restaurant's performance.

Required

 a. Propose at least two goals for each dimension, and explain why those goals are important to the overall success of the pizza parlor. One goal should be purely performance-oriented and the other should be risk-related.

 b. Suggest specific measures for each goal developed in part a.

 c. Explain how to gather the data needed for each measure developed in part b.

14.7 Obtain the annual report of a company assigned by your professor. Read the management discussion and analysis section, and develop a balanced scorecard that reflects that company's vision, mission, and strategy. Create both performance-oriented and risk-based goals and measures for each section of the balanced scorecard.

14.8 Excel Problem
 Objective: Practice graph design principles

Required

Create bar graphs for each of the following data sets. Follow the principles for graph design presented in the chapter, or explain which rule(s) you violated and why.
 a. Sales (in 000s).

2004 = $23,456	2005 = $22,945	2006 = $24,132	2007 = $24,941	2008 = $25,655

 b. Now add the following data for COGS (in 000s) to the graph created in step a.

2004 = $17,333	2005 = $16,743	2006 = $18,500	2007 = $19,250	2008 = $20,083

14.9 Excel Problem
 Objective: Create pivot tables for what-if analysis

Required

Read the article "Make Excel an Instant Know-It-All" by Roberta Ann Jones in the March 2004 issue of the *Journal of Accountancy*. (You can find the article online by going to www.aicpa.org and following the links to Online Journal of Accountancy.)
 a. Follow the instructions in the article to create a spreadsheet with pivot tables.
 b. Print out a report that shows sales by month for each salesperson.
 c. Assume that Brown and David are in sales group 1 and the other three sales-people are in sales group 2. Print out a report that shows monthly sales for each group.

14.10 Excel Problem
 Objective: How to do what-if analysis with graphs

Required

 a. Read the article "Tweaking the Numbers," by Theo Callahan in the June 2001 issue of the *Journal of Accountancy*. (You can find the article online by going to www. aicpa. org and following the links to Online Journal of Accountancy.) Follow the instructions in the article to create a spreadsheet with graphs that do what-if analysis.
 b. Now create a spreadsheet that does graphical what-if analysis for the "cash gap." Cash gap represents the number of days between when a company has to pay its suppliers and when it gets paid by its customers. Thus, Cash gap = Inventory days on hand + Receivables collection period − Accounts payable period. For example, the cash gap for a company that carries 30 days of inventory, averages 60 days to collect from its customers, and pays its suppliers within 20 days equals 70 days (30 + 60 − 20). The purpose of your spreadsheet is to display graphically what happens to cash gap when you "tweak" policies concerning inventory, receivables, and payables. Thus, you will create a spreadsheet that looks like Figure 14-13 (see next page). The three spin buttons should have the following values set:

	Spin Button for Inventory	Spin Button for Receivables	Spin Button for Payables
Linked Cell	A2	C2	E2
Maximum	120	120	90
Minimum	0	30	20
Value	30	60	20
Small Change	10	10	10

Figure 14-13
Graphical What-if Analysis

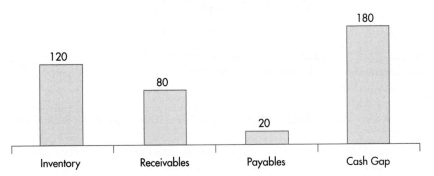

Effect of Policies on Cash Gap

Then create a bar graph that shows the effect of different policies for inventory, receivables, and payables on cash gap. Note: Unlike the tutorial example, you can do this on one page.

14.11 XBRL Problem
Objective: Learn what you can do with XBRL

Required

a. Read the article "Tap Into XBRL's Power the Easy Way" by Jeffrey W. Naumann, in the May 2004 issue of the *Journal of Accountancy* and follow the instructions to explore the use of XBRL. (You can find the article online by going to www.aicpa.org and following the links to Online Journal of Accountancy). *Note:* This requires downloading and installing the Microsoft Office Tool for XBRL, available free at www.microsoft.com/office/solutions/xbrl. Also note that the tool will only work if you have Office 2003.

b. Follow the instructions in the section of the article titled "Comparing and Analyzing Data From Different Sources" to use the XBRL tool to analyze the companies and perform the types of comparisons specified by your instructor.

CASE 14-1 Keeping Current with XBRL Developments

Like IT in general, XBRL is continually evolving. Visit xbrl.org to identify developments in the standard, the use of XBRL by companies and regulatory agencies, and XBRL-related products that have come out during the past twelve months. Write a report summarizing your findings.

CASE 14-2 Evaluating a General Ledger Package

Accounting magazines such as *Journal of Accountancy and Strategic Finance* periodically publish reviews of accounting software. Obtain a copy of a recent software review article and read its comments about a general ledger package to which you have access. Using the software, write a report that indicates whether, and why, you agree or disagree with the review's opinions about the following features of the general ledger package:

1 Ease of installation.
2 Flexibility in the initial setup of the chart of accounts and during subsequent modifications.

3 Frequency of updates from subsystems (sales, cash receipts, etc.).

4 Control procedures available to restrict access.

5 Control procedures to ensure accuracy of input and processing.

6 Report flexibility (how easy it is to design reports, etc.).

7 Adequacy of the audit trail (e.g., what reference data are automatically provided versus how much of the audit trail has to be manually constructed).

AIS IN ACTION SOLUTIONS

QUIZ KEY

1 From where do adjusting entries usually come?

 a. treasurer (Incorrect. Adjusting entries are entered by the controller after the trial balance has been prepared. The treasurer makes regular journal entries to record financing activities, such as issuing or retiring debt.)

 ✔ **b.** controller (Correct. Adjusting entries are entered by the controller after the trial balance has been prepared.)

 c. various accounting cycle subsystems, such as sales order entry (Incorrect. Subsystems send summary regular journal entries to the general ledger, not adjusting entries.)

 d. unit managers (Incorrect. Unit managers should not make any journal entries.)

2 Preparing performance reports that contain data only about items that a specific organizational unit controls is an example of which of the following?

 a. flexible budget system (Incorrect. Flexible budgets adjust targets based on actual inputs.)

 ✔ **b.** responsibility accounting system (Correct. This is the essence and purpose of responsibility accounting.)

 c. closing the books (Incorrect. Closing the books is a process performed at the end of a fiscal period to prepare financial statements.)

 d. management by exception (Incorrect. Management by exception is a reporting technique that focuses on unusual variations from standards.)

3 What is the business intelligence technique used to discover nonhypothesized relationships called?

 a. data warehousing (Incorrect. Data warehousing is the process used to collect the data needed to do business intelligence.)

 b. OLAP (Incorrect. OLAP is guided discovery of hypothesized relationships, usually by writing queries.)

 ✔ **c.** data mining (Correct. Data mining is the process used to discover new relationships in data.)

 d. querying (Incorrect. Querying is guided data exploration.)

4 Which of the following shows the implied linkages among the portions of the balanced scorecard?

 a. Financial → Internal → Innovation and learning → Customer (Incorrect.)

 ✔ **b.** Innovation and learning → Internal → Customer → Financial (Correct. The theory underlying the balanced scorecard is that learning and innovation will improve internal measures of performance, which will in turn improve customer satisfaction, which will then be reflected in better financial performance.)

 c. Customer → Financial → Internal → Innovation and learning (Incorrect.)

 d. Internal → Customer → Innovation and learning → Financial (Incorrect.)

5 Writing a query to identify trends in sales of a product by salesperson and by customer over the past 5 years is an example of which of the following?

 a. data mining (Incorrect. Writing a query is part of OLAP.)

 b. responsibility accounting (Incorrect. Writing a query is part of OLAP.)

 c. transaction processing (Incorrect. Writing a query is part of OLAP.)

✔ **d.** OLAP (Correct. Writing queries is a typical method of OLAP.)

6 Measures of cycle time would most likely appear in which part of the balanced scorecard?

 a. innovation and learning (Incorrect. Cycle time is a measure of process efficiency and, therefore, would appear in the internal operations section of the balanced scorecard.)

 b. customer (Incorrect. Cycle time is a measure of process efficiency and, therefore, would appear in the internal operations section of the balanced scorecard.)

✔ **c.** internal operations (Correct.)

 d. financial (Incorrect. Cycle time is a measure of process efficiency and, therefore, would appear in the internal operations section of the balanced scorecard.)

7 Which of the following is an important part of the audit trail?

✔ **a.** journal vouchers (Correct. Journal vouchers provide information concerning the source of changes to the general ledger accounts.)

 b. flexible budgets (Incorrect. Flexible budgets are a performance evaluation tool.)

 c. trial balance (Incorrect. The trial balance is a step in the preparation of financial statements.)

 d. data warehouse (Incorrect. A data warehouse is used for business intelligence.)

8 An adjusting journal entry to record interest revenue that has been earned but not yet received is an example of which of the following?

✔ **a.** accrual (Correct.)

 b. deferral (Incorrect. A deferral would involve postponing recognition of an event.)

 c. estimate (Incorrect. An estimate is an entry used to record the results of judgmental analysis.)

 d. revaluation (Incorrect. A revaluation entry is used to correct a prior error.)

9 What is the new common business reporting computer language developed, in part, by the accounting profession called?

 a. XML (Incorrect. XML is a general-purpose language but is not designed for financial reporting.)

✔ **b.** XBRL (Correct. The eXtensible Business Reporting Language was developed, in part, by accountants to facilitate business reporting.)

 c. SQL (Incorrect. SQL is a database query language.)

 d. HTML (Incorrect. HTML is a language for creating Web documents.)

10 Which of the following graph design principles is most important for ensuring that financial data is accurately interpreted?

 a. Including a title that summarizes the point of the graph (Incorrect. This principle improves readability but is not specifically designed to ensure accuracy of interpretation.)

 b. Attaching data values to specific elements in the graph (Incorrect. This principle improves readability but is not specifically designed to ensure accuracy of interpretation.)

✔ **c.** Starting the y-axis of the graph at zero (Correct. Starting the y-axis at zero accurately depicts the magnitude of changes in the data.)

 d. Using special-purpose graphing software (Incorrect. This principle improves readability but is not specifically designed to ensure accuracy of interpretation.)

Part IV

The REA Data Model

CHAPTER 15

Database Design Using the REA Data Model

INTEGRATIVE CASE **FRED'S TRAIN SHOP**

Fred Smith is frustrated. Business in his model train shop is booming. But the simple accounting software that he uses to run the business has only limited reporting capabilities. Consequently, he often has to manually review transaction data to prepare custom reports. The process is time-consuming and prone to error. For example, Fred spent the past weekend poring over sales records for the prior three months to try to identify which combinations of items were most frequently purchased together. He plans to use the information to offer a special sales promotion but is concerned about the quality of his analysis.

At lunch, Fred explains his frustrations to his CPA, Paul Stone. Paul mentions that he has just completed a training course on database design. He suggests that he could create a relational database for Fred that would interface with his accounting software and that would provide Fred with the ability to easily design reports to analyze his business. Fred likes the idea and hires Paul to design a relational database for his train store.

Introduction

Chapter 4 covered the fundamental principles of relational databases. The three chapters in this section will teach you how to design and document a relational database for an accounting information system. You will see that there is much more to building a database than simply learning the syntax of how to use a particular database management system (DBMS). Building accurate databases requires a great deal of careful planning and design *before* you even sit down at the computer.

This chapter introduces the topic of data modeling, one aspect of database design that accountants should understand. We discuss entity-relationship (E-R) diagrams and the REA accounting model and demonstrate how to use these tools to build a data model of an AIS. Then we discuss how such REA models can also serve as a source of documentation about an organization's business activities and policies. Chapter 16 will explain how to implement an REA data model in a database and how to query the resulting database to retrieve information needed to effectively manage an organization's business activities. Chapter 17 concludes this three-chapter section by examining a number of advanced data modeling and database design issues.

Database Design Process

Figure 15-1 shows the five basic steps in database design. The first stage (systems analysis) consists of initial planning to determine the need for and feasibility of developing a new system. This stage includes preliminary judgments about the proposal's technological and economic feasibility. It also involves identifying user information

Figure 15-1
Data Modeling in the Database Design Process

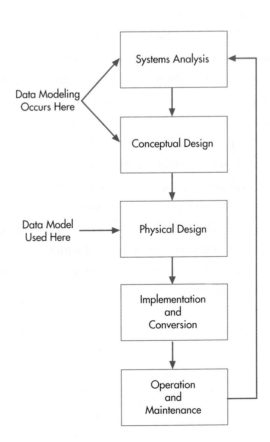

needs, defining the scope of the proposed new system, and using information about the expected number of users and transaction volumes to make preliminary decisions about hardware and software requirements. The second stage (conceptual design) includes developing the different schemas for the new system, at the conceptual, external, and internal levels. The third stage (physical design) consists of translating the internal-level schema into the actual database structures that will be implemented in the new system. This is also the stage when new applications are developed. The fourth stage (implementation and conversion) includes all the activities associated with transferring data from existing systems to the new database AIS, testing the new system, and training employees how to use it. The final stage is using and maintaining the new system. This includes carefully monitoring system performance and user satisfaction to determine the need for making system enhancements and modifications. Eventually, changes in business strategies and practices or significant new developments in information technology initiate investigation into the feasibility of developing a new system, and the entire process starts again (note the arrow returning to the systems analysis stage).

Accountants can and should participate in every stage of the database design process, although the level of their involvement is likely to vary across stages. During the systems analysis phase, accountants help evaluate project feasibility and identify user information needs. In the conceptual design stage, accountants participate in developing the logical schemas, designing the data dictionary, and specifying important controls. Accountants with good database skills may directly participate in implementing the data model during the physical design stage. During the implementation and conversion stage accountants should be involved in testing the accuracy of the new database and the application programs that will use that data, as well as assessing the adequacy of controls. Finally, many accountants are regular users of the organization's database and sometimes even have responsibility for its management.

Accountants may provide the greatest value to their organizations by taking responsibility for data modeling. **Data modeling** is the process of defining a database so that it faithfully represents all aspects of the organization, including its interactions with the external environment. As shown in Figure 15-1, data modeling occurs during both the systems analysis and conceptual design stages of database design. Next, we discuss two important tools that accountants can use to perform data modeling: entity-relationship diagramming and the REA data model.

Entity-Relationship Diagrams[1]

An **entity-relationship (E-R) diagram** is a graphical technique for portraying a database schema. It is called an E-R diagram because it shows the various *entities* being modeled and the important *relationships* among them. An **entity** is anything about which the organization wants to collect and store information. For example, Fred's Train Shop's database would include entities for inventory, business events such as sales to customers and deliveries from suppliers, employees, customers, and suppliers. In a relational database, separate tables would be created to store information about each distinct entity; in an object-oriented database, separate classes would be created for each distinct entity.

In an E-R diagram, entities are depicted as rectangles. Unfortunately, however, there are no industry standards for other aspects of E-R diagrams. Some data modelers

[1]The material in this section is based on P. Chen, "The Entity Relationship Model—Toward a Unified View of Data," *Transactions on Database Systems* (March 1976, 1:1): 9–36.

Panel A: Relationships depicted by diamonds

Sales — Line Items — Inventory

Panel B: Relationships depicted without diamonds

Sales — Inventory

Panel C: Attributes attached to entities

Invoice Number | Date | Amount — Sales

Item Number | Description | List Price — Inventory

Panel D: Attributes listed in separate table

Entity Name	Attributes
Sales	Invoice number, date, amount
Inventory	Item number, description, list price

Figure 15-2
E-R Diagram Variations

and authors use diamonds to depict relationships (Figure 15-2, panel A) whereas others do not (Figure 15-2, panel B). Sometimes the attributes associated with each entity are depicted as named ovals connected to each rectangle (Figure 15-2, panel C), whereas other times the attributes associated with each entity are listed in a separate table (Figure 15-2, panel D). In this book, we will be creating E-R diagrams with a large number of entities and relationships. Therefore, to reduce clutter and improve readability, we omit the diamonds and list the attributes associated with each entity in a separate table.

E-R diagrams can be used to represent the contents of any kind of database. For example, the E-R diagram of an intramural sports database might include students, teams, and leagues as entities, whereas an E-R diagram for a school might include students, teachers, and courses as entities. In this book, our focus is on databases designed to support an organization's business activities. Consequently, the E-R diagrams we develop not only depict the contents of a database but also graphically model an organization's business processes. In fact, E-R diagrams can be used not only to design databases but also to document and understand existing databases and to reengineer business processes. Business process reengineering is covered in Part V; in this chapter we focus on using E-R diagrams for database design and for understanding the contents of existing databases.

As noted, E-R diagrams can include many different kinds of entities and relationships among those entities. An important step in database design, therefore, entails deciding which entities need to be modeled. The REA data model is useful for making that decision.

The REA Data Model[2]

The **REA data model** was developed specifically for use in designing AIS. The REA data model focuses on the business semantics underlying an organization's value-chain activities. It provides guidance for database design by identifying what entities should be included in the AIS database and by prescribing how to structure relationships among the entities in that database. REA data models are usually depicted in the form of E-R diagrams. Consequently, in the remainder of this chapter and throughout the book, we will refer to E-R diagrams developed according to the REA data model as REA diagrams.

Three Basic Types of Entities

The REA data model is so named because it classifies entities into three distinct categories: the *r*esources the organization acquires and uses, the *e*vents (business activities) in which the organization engages, and the *a*gents participating in these events.[3] Figure 15-3 provides examples of these three types of entities.

 Resources are those things that have economic value to the organization. Figure 15-3 includes two resource entities: cash and inventory. **Events** are the various business activities about which management wants to collect information for planning or control purposes.[4] There are two event entities in Figure 15-3: Sales and Receive Cash. **Agents** are the people and organizations that participate in events and about whom information is desired for planning, control, and evaluation purposes. Figure 15-3 includes two types of agent entities: Employees and Customers.

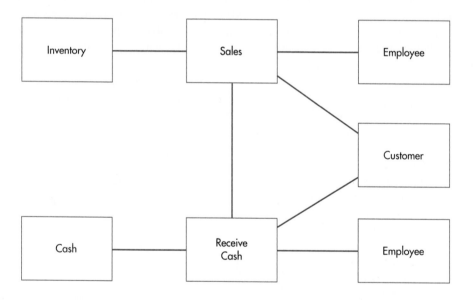

Figure 15-3
Basic Elements of an REA Diagram

[2]The material in this section is adapted from William E. McCarthy, "An Entity-Relationship View of Accounting Models," *The Accounting Review* (October 1979): 667–686; William E. McCarthy, "The REA Accounting Model: A Generalized Framework for Accounting Systems in a Shared Data Environment," *The Accounting Review* (July 1982): 554–578; and Guido L. Geerts and W. E. McCarthy, "An Ontological Analysis of the Primitives of the Extended-REA Enterprise Information Architecture," *International Journal of Accounting Information Systems* 3 (March 2002): 1–16.

[3]Recently, some researchers have proposed a fourth type of entity, which they call locations. Stores and warehouses would be examples of this fourth type of entity. Nevertheless, such "location" entities are usually also resources controlled by the organization. Therefore, the authors of this text see no compelling reason to create yet another type of entity and model locations as resources. If an organization does not want or need to store information about locations except to identify where an event occurred, location can be an attribute for each event.

Structuring Relationships: The Basic REA Template

The REA data model prescribes a basic pattern for how the three types of entities (resources, events, and agents) should relate to one another. Figure 15-4 presents this basic pattern. The essential features of the pattern are

1 Each event is linked to at least one resource that it affects.
2 Each event is linked to at least one other event.
3 Each event is linked to at least two participating agents.

Rule 1: Every Event Entity Must Be Linked to at Least One Resource Entity

Events *must* be linked to at least one resource that they affect. Some events, such as the one labeled "Get Resource A" in Figure 15-4, increase the quantity of a resource. Common examples of such "Get" events include the receipt of goods from a supplier (which increases the quantity on hand of inventory) and the receipt of payment from a customer (which increases the amount of cash). Other events, such as the one labeled "Give Resource B" in Figure 15-4, directly decrease the quantity of a resource. Common examples of such "Give" events include paying suppliers and selling merchandise, which decrease the amount of cash and quantity on hand of inventory, respectively.

Relationships that affect the quantity of a resource are sometimes referred to as *stockflow* relationships because they represent either an inflow or outflow of that resource. Not every event directly alters the quantity of a resource, however. For example, orders from customers represent commitments that will eventually result in a future sale of merchandise, just as orders to suppliers represent commitments that will eventually result in the subsequent purchase of inventory. For simplicity, Figure 15-4 does not include any such commitment events. Organizations do, however, need to track the effects of such commitments, both to provide better service and for planning purposes. For example, customer orders reduce the quantity available of the specific inventory items being ordered. Sales staff need to know this information to be able to properly

Figure 15-4
Standard REA Template

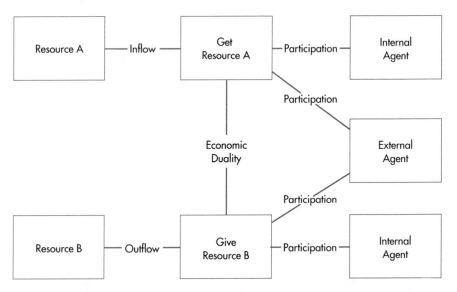

The names on the lines describe the nature of the relationship. Agents participate in events. The economic duality relationship between the "get" event and the "give" event reflects the fact that organizations must give up one resource (e.g. cash) in order to get some other resource (e.g. inventory). The stockflow relationships between an event and a resource represent either inflows or outflows of a resource.

[4]The discussion of events in this section is based on the work of Julie Smith David, "Three 'Events' That Define an REA Methodology for Systems Analysis, Design, and Implementation," Working Paper, Arizona State University, August 1997, and Guido L. Geerts and W. E. McCarthy, "An Ontological Analysis of the Primitives of the Extended-REA Enterprise Information Architecture," *International Journal of Accounting Information Systems* 3 (March 2002): 1–16.

respond to subsequent customer inquiries and orders. Manufacturing companies may use information about customer orders to plan production. Later in the chapter we will see how to add commitment events to the basic pattern shown in Figure 15-4.

Rule 2: Every Event Entity Must Be Linked to at Least One Other Event Entity

Figure 15-4 also shows that the Get Resource A event is linked to the Give Resource B event in what is labeled as an economic duality relationship. Such give-to-get duality relationships reflect the basic business principle that organizations typically engage in activities that use up resources only in the hopes of acquiring some other resource in exchange. For example, the Sales event, which requires giving up (decreasing) inventory, is related to the Receive Cash event, which requires getting (increasing) the amount of cash. Indeed, Figure 15-5 (see below) shows that each accounting cycle can be described in terms of such give-to-get economic duality relationships.

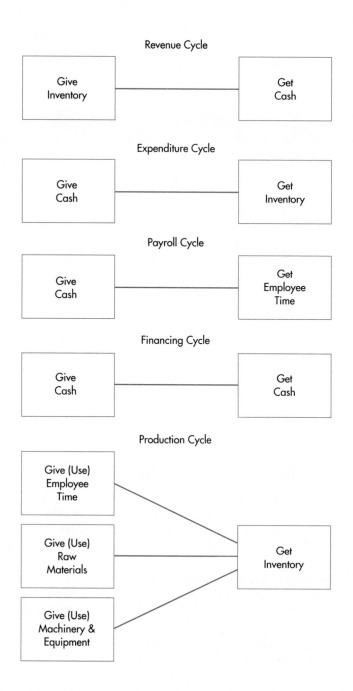

Figure 15-5
An AIS Viewed as a Set of Give-to-get Exchanges

Not every relationship between two events represents a give-to-get economic duality, however. Commitment events are linked to other events to reflect sequential cause–effect relationships. For example, the Take Customer Order event would be linked to the Sales event to reflect the fact that such orders precede and result in sales. Similarly, the Order Inventory (purchase) event would be linked to the Receive Inventory event to reflect another sequential cause–effect relationship.

Rule 3: Every Event Entity Must Be Linked to at Least Two Participating Agents

For accountability, organizations need to be able to track the actions of employees. Organizations also need to monitor the status of commitments and economic duality exchanges engaged in with outside parties. Thus, Figure 15-4 shows each event linked to two participating agent entities. For events that involve transactions with external parties, the internal agent is the employee who is responsible for the resource affected by that event and the external agent is the outside party to the transaction. For internal events, such as the transfer of raw materials from the storeroom to production, the internal agent is the employee who is giving up responsibility for or custody of the resource and the external agent is the employee who is receiving custody of or assuming responsibility for that resource.

Developing an REA Diagram

Figure 15-6 (see next page) shows the REA diagram Paul developed for the revenue cycle of Fred's Train Shop. Keep in mind that Figure 15-6 models only a subset of Fred's Train Shop's business activities. To design an REA diagram for the entire AIS, Paul not only needs to further enhance this basic model but must also develop similar models for each of the other transaction cycles and then integrate those separate diagrams into an enterprise-wide model. This chapter focuses on developing an REA diagram for an individual transaction cycle. The topics of integrating individual REA diagrams and implementing them in a database will be discussed in the next chapter.

Developing an REA diagram for a specific transaction cycle consists of the following three steps:

1 Identify the events about which management wants to collect information.
2 Identify the resources affected by each event and the agents who participate in those events.
3 Determine the cardinalities of each relationship.

Let us follow these three steps to see how Paul developed Figure 15-6 to model Fred's Train Shop's revenue cycle.

Step 1: Identify Relevant Events

The first step in developing an REA model of a transaction cycle is to identify the events of interest to management. At a minimum, every REA model must include the two events that represent the basic give-to-get economic exchange performed in that particular transaction cycle (see Figure 15-5). The "Give" event represents an activity which reduces the organization's stock of a resource that has economic value; conversely, the "Get" event represents an activity which increases the organization's stock of an economic resource. Usually there are other events that management is interested in planning, controlling, and monitoring that also need to be included in the REA model.

A solid understanding of basic business activities (see Chapters 10–14) is needed to identify which events comprise the basic give-to-get economic duality relationships.

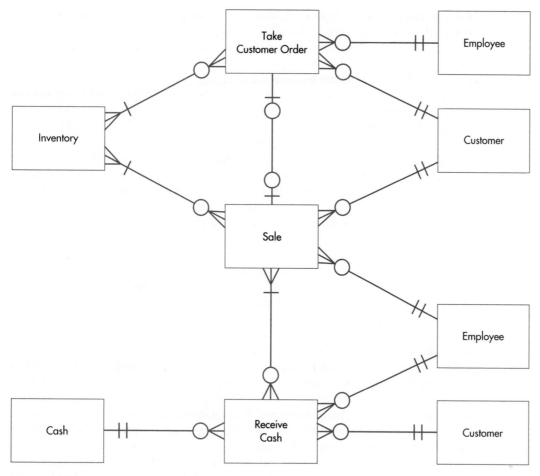

Figure 15-6
Partial REA Diagram for Fred's Train Shop Revenue Cycle

For example, Chapter 10 explained that the revenue cycle typically consists of four sequential activities:

1 Take customer orders
2 Fill customer orders
3 Bill customers
4 Collect payment from customers

Analysis of the first activity, taking customer orders, indicates that it does not involve either the acquisition of resources from or provision of resources to an external party. It is only a commitment to perform such actions in the future. The second activity, fill customer orders, does reduce the organization's stock of a resource that has economic value (inventory) by delivering it to an external party (the customer). Thus, it represents an example of the prototypical Give Resource event depicted in Figure 15-4. The third activity, billing customers, involves the exchange of information with an external party but does not directly increase or reduce the quantity of any economic resource. Finally, analysis of the fourth activity, collect payments from customers, indicates that it results in an increase in the organization's supply of an economic resource (the entity labeled "Cash" in Figure 15-6) as a result of receiving it from an external party (the customer). Thus, it is an example of the prototypical Get Resource event depicted in Figure 15-4. Consequently, analysis of the basic business activities performed in the revenue cycle indicates that the basic give-to-get economic exchange consists of two events: fill customer orders (usually referred to as the Sales event) and collect payments from customers (often called the Receive Cash event). Similar analyses of the business activities performed in the other

transaction cycles results in identification of the other give-to-get economic duality relationships depicted in Figure 15-5.

In drawing an REA diagram for an *individual* transaction cycle, it is useful to divide the paper into three columns, one for each type of entity. Use the left column for resources, the center column for events, and the right column for agents. Readability is further enhanced if the event entities are drawn from top to bottom corresponding to the sequence in which they occur. Thus, Paul begins to draw Figure 15-6 by placing the Sales event entity above the Receive Cash event entity in the center column of the paper.[5]

After identifying the economic exchange events, it is necessary to determine which other business activities should be represented as events in the REA model. This, too, requires understanding what each activity entails because only those activities that involve the acquisition of new information need to be included in the model. Returning to our example, Paul notes that the economic duality of Sales and Receive Cash accurately reflects most in-store sales transactions in which the customer selects one or more items and pays for them. Sometimes, however, customers call the store and ask if specific items can be set aside for pickup later that week. Fred needs to not only set those items aside but record such orders in the system in order to reorder popular items on a timely basis. Therefore, Paul decides to add the commitment event Take Customer Order to the REA diagram, placing it above the Sales event because customer orders precede the Sales event.

Paul then considers the other revenue cycle business activity, billing customers. He knows that in-store sales are paid for immediately and, therefore, do not involve a separate "billing" step. But Fred also sells model trains to shopping centers, hotels, and other institutions that want to set up seasonal displays for their customers. Such sales are made on credit, and Fred does subsequently prepare and mail invoices to those customers. However, printing and mailing invoices does not directly increase or decrease any economic resource. Nor does the billing activity represent a commitment to a future economic exchange: The customer's legal obligation to pay arises from the delivery of the merchandise, not from the printing of an invoice. Consequently, as noted in Chapters 10 and 11, many organizations are beginning to realize that billing is a non-value-added activity that can be eliminated entirely. Moreover, the activity of printing an invoice does not add any new information to the database. The prices and quantities of items sold were recorded at the time of the sale, at which time the terms of payment were also agreed upon. Thus, the billing activity is simply an information processing event that merely *retrieves* information from the database, similar to writing a query or printing an internal report. Since such information retrieval events do not alter the contents of the database, they need not be modeled as events in an REA diagram. For all the foregoing reasons, Paul realizes that he does not need to include a billing event in his revenue cycle REA diagram for Fred's Train Shop.

But what about accounts receivable? If there is no billing event, how can Fred's Train Shop monitor this balance sheet item? The solution lies in understanding that accounts receivable is merely a timing difference between the two components of the basic economic exchange in the revenue cycle: sales and the receipt of payment. In other words, accounts receivable simply equals all sales for which customers have not yet paid. Consequently, accounts receivable can be calculated and monitored by simply collecting information about Sales and Receive Cash events. The next chapter will illustrate several different ways for extracting information about accounts receivable from a database built using the REA data model.

Finally, notice that there are no events that pertain to the entry of data. The reason for this is that the REA data model is used to design transaction processing databases. The objective is to model the basic value-chain business activities of an organization: what it does in order to generate revenues and how it spends cash and uses its other

[5]Placement conventions, such as the use of columns and sequential ordering of events, are not *required* to use the REA model to design a database. We suggest these rules only because following them often simplifies the process of drawing an REA diagram and produces REA diagrams that are easy to read.

resources. Entering data about those events and about the resources and agents associated with them is not usually considered a primary value-chain activity. Thus, just like writing queries and printing reports, data entry activities are not considered important events about which detailed data needs to be collected. Moreover, as discussed in the preceding five chapters, there is a continuous trend to use technology to eliminate routine clerical information processing activities, including data entry. Thus, it is possible to conceive of business events (such as the sale of merchandise) being performed without the need for any separate data entry activities. Indeed, much data entry already occurs as a by-product of performing the business events that are included in the REA diagram. For example, whenever a sale, purchase, receipt of cash, or payment occurs, information about that event is entered in the database. Thus, what gets modeled in the REA diagram is the business event (e.g., the sale transaction) and the facts that management wants to collect about that event, not the entry of that data.

Step 2: Identify Resources and Agents

Once the relevant events have been specified, the resources that are affected by those events need to be identified. This involves answering three questions:

1 What economic resource is reduced by the "Give" event?
2 What economic resource is acquired by the "Get" event?
3 What economic resource is affected by a commitment event?

Again, a solid understanding of business processes makes it easy to answer these questions. To continue our example, Paul observed that the Sales event involves giving inventory to customers and that the Cash Receipts event involves receiving cash (whether in the form of money, checks, credit card, or debit card) from customers. Therefore, he added an Inventory resource entity to the REA diagram and linked it to the Sales event entity. Then he added a Cash resource entity to the diagram. Although organizations typically use multiple accounts to track cash and cash equivalents (e.g., operating checking account, petty cash, and short-term investments), these are all summarized in one balance sheet account called Cash. Similarly, the Cash resource contains information about every individual cash account. Thus, in a relational database, the "cash" table would contain a separate row for each specific account (e.g., petty cash, checking account, etc.). Paul then linked the "Cash" resource entity to the Receive Cash event entity. Finally, the Take Customer Order event involves setting aside merchandise for a specific customer. To maintain accurate inventory records, and to facilitate timely reordering to avoid stockouts, each Take Customer Order event should result in reducing the quantity available of that particular inventory item. Therefore, Paul added a link between the Inventory resource entity and the Take Customer Order event entity in the REA diagram he was developing for Fred's Train Shop revenue cycle.

In addition to specifying the resources affected by each event, it is also necessary to identify the agents who participate in those events. There will always be at least one internal agent (employee) and, in most cases, an external agent (customer or vendor) who participate in each event. In the case of Fred's Train Shop's revenue cycle, a customer and a salesperson participate in each sales event. The customer and a cashier are the two agents participating in each Receive Cash event. Both the salesperson and the cashier are employees of Fred's. Thus, both revenue cycle economic exchange events involve the same two general types of agents: employees (the internal party) and customers (the external party). The Take Customer Order event also involves both customers and employees. Therefore, Paul added both types of agents to the diagram and drew relationships to indicate which agents participated in which events. To reduce clutter, he sometimes linked one copy of a particular agent entity to two adjacent event entities.[6]

[6]Deciding how many copies of the same entity to include in an REA diagram is a matter of personal taste. Including too many copies clutters the diagram with redundant rectangles, but too few copies can result in a confusing tangled web of lines connecting entities to one another.

Step 3: Determine Cardinalities of Relationships

The final step in drawing an REA diagram for one transaction cycle is to add information about relationship cardinalities. **Cardinalities** describe the nature of the relationship between two entities by indicating how many instances of one entity can be linked to each specific instance of another entity. Consider the relationship between the customer agent entity and the sales event entity. Each entity in an REA diagram represents a set. For example, the Customer entity represents the set of the organization's customers, and the Sales entity represents the set of individual sales transactions that occur during the current fiscal period. Each individual customer or sales transaction represents a specific instance of that entity. Thus, in a relational database, each row in the "Customer" table would store information about a particular customer and each row in the "Sales" table would store information about a specific sales transaction. Cardinalities define how many sales transactions (instances of the Sales entity) can be associated with each customer (instance of the Customer entity) and, conversely, how many customers can be associated with each sales transaction.

Unfortunately, no universal standard exists for representing information about cardinalities in REA diagrams. In this text, we adopt the the graphical "crow's feet" notation style for representing cardinality information because it is becoming increasingly popular and is used by many software design tools. Table 15-1 explains the meaning of the symbols used to represent cardinality information, and Focus 15-1 (see next page) compares the notation used in this book with other commonly used conventions.

As shown in Table 15-1, cardinalities are represented by the pair of symbols next to an entity. The four rows in Table 15-1 depict the four possible combinations of minimum and maximum cardinalities. The **minimum cardinality** can be either zero (0) or one (1), depending upon whether the relationship between the two entities is optional (the minimum cardinality is zero, see rows one and three) or mandatory (the minimum

Table 15-1
Graphical Symbols for Representing Cardinality Information

Symbol	Cardinalities	Example	Meaning
─○┼─	Minimum = 0; Maximum = 1	Entity A ─○┼ Entity B	Each instance of entity A may or may not be linked to any instances of entity B, but can be linked to at most one instance of entity B.
─┼┼─	Minimum = 1; Maximum = 1	Entity A ─┼┼ Entity B	Each instance of entity A must be linked to an instance of entity B, and can only be linked to at most one instance of entity B.
─○<─	Minimum = 0; Maximum = many	Entity A ─○< Entity B	Each instance of entity A may or may not be linked to any instances of entity B, but could be linked to more than one instance of entity B.
─┼<─	Minimum = 1; Maximum = many	Entity A ─┼< Entity B	Each instance of entity A must be linked to at least one instance of entity B, but can be linked to many instances of entity B.

15-1 FOCUS

Alternative Methods to Represent Cardinality Information

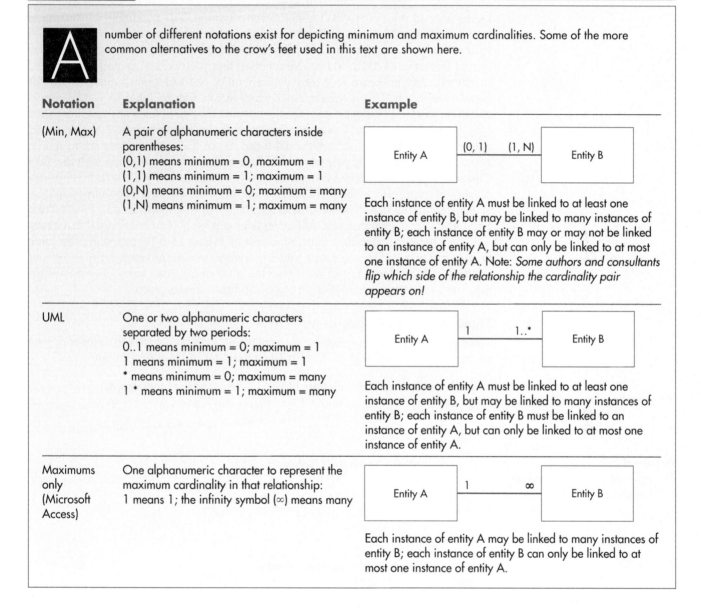

A number of different notations exist for depicting minimum and maximum cardinalities. Some of the more common alternatives to the crow's feet used in this text are shown here.

Notation	Explanation	Example
(Min, Max)	A pair of alphanumeric characters inside parentheses: (0,1) means minimum = 0, maximum = 1 (1,1) means minimum = 1; maximum = 1 (0,N) means minimum = 0; maximum = many (1,N) means minimum = 1; maximum = many	Entity A — (0, 1) (1, N) — Entity B Each instance of entity A must be linked to at least one instance of entity B, but may be linked to many instances of entity B; each instance of entity B may or may not be linked to an instance of entity A, but can only be linked to at most one instance of entity A. Note: *Some authors and consultants flip which side of the relationship the cardinality pair appears on!*
UML	One or two alphanumeric characters separated by two periods: 0..1 means minimum = 0; maximum = 1 1 means minimum = 1; maximum = 1 * means minimum = 0; maximum = many 1 * means minimum = 1; maximum = many	Entity A — 1 1..* — Entity B Each instance of entity A must be linked to at least one instance of entity B, but may be linked to many instances of entity B; each instance of entity B must be linked to an instance of entity A, but can only be linked to at most one instance of entity A.
Maximums only (Microsoft Access)	One alphanumeric character to represent the maximum cardinality in that relationship: 1 means 1; the infinity symbol (∞) means many	Entity A — 1 ∞ — Entity B Each instance of entity A may be linked to many instances of entity B; each instance of entity B can only be linked to at most one instance of entity A.

cardinality is one, as in rows two and four). The **maximum cardinality** can be either one or many (the crow's feet symbol), depending upon whether each instance of entity A can be linked to at most one instance (as in the top two rows) or potentially many instances of entity B (as in the bottom two rows).

Let us now use the information in Table 15-1 to interpret some of the cardinalities in Figure 15-6. Look first at the Sale-Customer relationship. The minimum and maximum cardinalities next to the Customer entity are both one. This pattern is the same as that in row two in Table 15-1. Thus, the minimum cardinality of one next to the Customer entity in Figure 15-6 indicates that each sale transaction (entity A) *must* be linked to some specific customer (entity B). The maximum cardinality of one means that each sale transaction can be linked to at most *only one* specific customer. This reflects normal business practices: only one legally identifiable customer (which could be an individual or a business) is held responsible for a sale and its subsequent

payment. Now look at the cardinality pair next to the Sale entity: as in row three in Table 15-1, the minimum cardinality is zero and the maximum cardinality is many. The zero minimum cardinality means that the relationship is optional: a customer does not have to be associated with any specific sale transaction. This allows Fred's Train Shop to enter information about prospective customers to whom it can send advertisements prior to their every having purchased anything. The maximum cardinality is many, indicating that a specific customer may, and Fred hopes will, be associated with multiple sale transactions (i.e., become a loyal customer who makes repeated purchases from Fred's Train Shop). Now notice that the cardinality pairs next to the Inventory entity in Figure 15-6 have a minimum of one and a maximum of many for every relationship. This is the same pattern as in row four in Table 15-1. This means that every customer order or sale transaction *must* involve at least one inventory item (you cannot sell "nothing"), but *may* involve multiple different items (e.g., a customer could purchase both a locomotive and a rail car in the same transaction). Finally, notice that the cardinality pair next to the Sale entity in its relationship with the Take Customer Order entity is like the pattern in row one of Table 15-1. The minimum cardinality of zero reflects the fact that an order may not *yet* have been turned into an actual sale transaction. The maximum cardinality of one indicates that Fred's Train Shop fills all customer orders in full rather than making a number of partial deliveries.

You should be able to interpret the rest of Figure 15-6 by following the same process just presented by comparing the cardinality pairs next to each entity to the four patterns in Table 15-1. Let us now examine what the various types of relationships mean and what they reveal about an organization's business practices.

Three Types of Relationships

Three basic types of relationships between entities are possible, depending on the *maximum* cardinality associated with each entity (the minimum cardinality does not matter):

1 A **one-to-one (1:1) relationship** exists when the maximum cardinality for each entity in that relationship is 1 (see Figure 15-7, panel A).

Figure 15-7
Examples of Different Types of Relationships

Panel A: A one-to-one (1:1) relationship

Sale — Receive Cash

Panel B: A one-to-many (1:N) relationship

Sale — Receive Cash

Panel C: Opposite one-to-many (1:N) relationship (sometimes referred to as N:1)

Sale — Receive Cash

Panel D: A many-to-many (M:N) relationship

Sale — Receive Cash

2 A **one-to-many (1:N) relationship** exists when the maximum cardinality of one entity in the relationship is 1 and the maximum cardinality for the other entity in that relationship is many (see Figures 15-7, panels B and C).

3 A **many-to-many (M:N) relationship** exists when the maximum cardinality for both entities in the relationship is many (Figure 15-7, panel D).

Figure 15-7 shows that any of these possibilities *might* describe the relationship between the Sales and Receive Cash events. The data modeler or database designer cannot arbitrarily choose which of these three possibilities to use when depicting various relationships. Instead, the cardinalities *must* reflect the organization's business policies. Let us now examine what each of the possibilities depicted in Figure 15-7 means. Figure 15-7, panel A, depicts a one-to-one (1:1) relationship between the Sales and Receive Cash events. The maximum cardinality of 1 associated with the Receive Cash entity means that each Sales event (transaction) can be linked to *at most* one Receive Cash event. This would be appropriate for an organization that had a business policy of not allowing customers to make installment payments. At the same time, the maximum cardinality of 1 associated with each Sale event means that each payment a customer submits is linked to *at most* one sales event. This would be appropriate for an organization that had a business policy of requiring customers to pay for each sales transaction separately. Thus, the 1:1 relationship depicted in Figure 15-7, panel A, represents the typical revenue cycle relationship for business-to-consumer retail sales: Customers must pay, in full, for each sales transaction before they are allowed to leave the store with the merchandise they purchased. Note that it does not matter *how* customers pay for each sales transaction (i.e., with cash, check, credit card, or debit card). Regardless of the method used, there is one, and only one, payment linked to each sales transaction and, conversely, every sales transaction is linked to one, and only one, payment from a customer (payments made by debit and credit cards also involve the card issuer; for simplicity, that transfer agent is not included in Figure 15-6). If management is interested in tracking the frequency of different payment methods, this fact might be recorded as an attribute of the Sales event.

Panels B and C of Figure 15-7 depict two ways that one-to-many (1:N) relationships can occur. Panel B shows that each Sales event may be linked to *many* Cash Receipt events. This indicates that the organization has a business policy that allows customers to make installment payments *to the selling organization*. If the customer uses a third-party source of credit, the selling organization receives *one* payment in full from that third party for that particular sales transaction; the customer may be making installment payments to the credit agency, but those payments would not be modeled in an REA diagram for the selling organization. (Think about it: The selling organization has no way of tracking when one of its customers pays a portion of a credit card bill or makes a monthly payment on a bank loan). The situation depicted in Figure 15-7, panel B, does not, however, mean that *every* sales transaction is paid for in installments: The maximum cardinality of N simply means that some sales transactions may be paid in installments. Panel B of Figure 15-7 also shows that each Receive Cash event is linked to *at most* one Sale event. This indicates that the organization has a business policy that requires customers to pay for each sales transaction separately and are not allowed to build up an account balance over a period of time. Thus, Figure 15-7, panel B, represents the revenue cycle of an organization that probably sells big-ticket items. Should a customer return and make another purchase, a separate set of installment payments would be created in order to separately track how much has been paid for each sales transaction.

Figure 15-7, panel C, shows another type of 1:N relationship between Sale and Cash Receipts. In this case, each Sale event can be linked to *at most* one Cash Receipt event. This indicates that the organization has a business policy that does not permit customers to make installment payments. Figure 15-7, panel C, also shows that each Receive Cash event *may* be linked to many different Sale events. This indicates the existence of a business policy allowing customers to make a number of purchases during a period of time (e.g., a month) and then pay off those purchases with one payment. The situation depicted in Figure 15-7, panel C, is quite common, especially for business-to-business sales of nondurable goods.

Figure 15-7, panel D, depicts a many-to-many (M:N) relationship between the Sale and Cash Receipt events. It shows that each Sales event may be linked to *one or more* Cash Receipt events and that each Cash Receipt event may in turn be linked to *one or more* Sale events. This reflects an organization that has business policies that allow customers to make installment payments and also permits customers to accumulate a balance representing a set of sales transactions over a period of time. Keep in mind, however, that maximum cardinalities of N do not represent mandatory practices: Thus, for the relationship depicted in panel D, some sales transactions may be paid in full in one payment and some customers may pay for each sales transaction separately. The situation depicted in Figure 15-7, panel D, is quite common.

Business Meaning of Cardinalities

As noted, the choice of cardinalities is not arbitrary, but reflects facts about the organization being modeled and its business practices. This information is obtained during the systems analysis and conceptual design stages of the database design process. Thus, Paul Stone had to clearly understand how Fred's Train Shop conducts its business activities to ensure that Figure 15-6 was correct.

Let us now examine Figure 15-6 to see what it reveals about Fred's Train Shop's revenue cycle processes. First, note that all of the agent–event relationships are 1:N. This is typical for most organizations: A particular agent often participates in many events. For example, organizations expect that over time a given employee will repeatedly perform a particular task. Organizations also desire their customers to make repeat orders and purchases, just as they typically place orders with the same suppliers. However, for accountability purposes, events are usually linked to a specific internal agent and a specific external agent; hence, the maximum cardinality on the agent side of the agent–event relationships in Figure 15-6 is always 1. If, however, a particular event required the cooperation of a team of employees, the maximum cardinality on the agent side of the relationship would be many.

The minimum cardinalities associated with the agent-event relationships in Figure 15-6 also reflect typical business processes followed by most organizations. The figure shows that each event *must* be linked to an agent (e.g., a sale must involve a customer, a payment must come from a customer, etc.); hence the minimum cardinality of 1 on the agent side of the relationship. In contrast, Figure 15-6 shows that the minimum cardinality on the event side of the agent–event relationship is 0. There are several reasons why a particular agent need not have participated in any events. The organization may wish to store information about potential customers and alternate suppliers with whom it has not yet conducted any business. Information about newly hired employees will exist in the database prior to their first day on the job. Finally, there is a fundamental difference in the nature of agent entities and event entities. Organizations usually desire to maintain information about agents indefinitely but typically only store information about events that have occurred during the current fiscal year. Thus, agent entities are analogous to master files, whereas event entities are analogous to transaction files. At the end of a fiscal year, the contents of event entities are typically archived and the next fiscal year begins with no instances of that event. Thus, at the beginning of a new fiscal year, agents are not linked to any current events.

Figure 15-6 depicts M:N relationships between the inventory resource and the various events that affect it. This is the typical situation for organizations, like Fred's Train Shop, that sell mass-produced items. Most organizations track such inventory by an identifier such as part number, item number, or stock-keeping unit (SKU) number and do not attempt to track each physical instance of that product. When a sale occurs, the system notes which product number(s) were sold. Thus, the same inventory item may be linked to many different sales events. For example, Fred's Train Shop uses product number 15734 to refer to a particular model of a steam locomotive. At a given point in time, it may have five of those locomotives in stock. If, during the course of a weekend, five different customers each purchased one of those locomotives, the system would link product number 15734 to five separate sales events. Hence, the maximum cardinality on the

event side of the relationship is many. Of course, Fred's Train Shop, like most organizations, permits (and desires) that customers purchase many different products at the same time. For example, a customer who purchases a steam locomotive (product number 15734) may also purchase a box of curved track (product number 3265). Thus, the system would link one sales event to multiple inventory items; hence the maximum cardinality on the inventory side of the relationship is also many.

But what if an organization sells unique, one-of-a-kind inventory, such as original artwork? Such items can only be sold one time; consequently, the maximum cardinality on the event side of the inventory–sales event would be 1. The maximum cardinality on the inventory side of the relationship would still be many, however, because most organizations will be happy to sell as many different one-of-a-kind items as a customer wants and can afford to buy.

The minimum cardinalities on each side of the inventory–event relationships depicted in Figure 15-6 also reflect typical business practices. Fred's Train Shop, like many retail organizations, only sells physical inventory. Therefore, every order or sales event *must* be linked to at least one inventory item; hence, the minimum cardinality on the inventory side of the inventory–event relationships is 1. The minimum cardinality on the event side of those relationships, however, is 0, for the same reasons that it is 0 in agent–event relationships.

Now consider the relationship between the cash resource and the Receive Cash event. Figure 15-6 depicts this as being a 1:N relationship, which reflects a best practice followed by most organizations with good internal controls. Each cash receipt from a customer is deposited into one cash account (most often the organization's general checking account); the treasurer subsequently transfers money from that account to other cash accounts (e.g., payroll, checking, investments, etc.) as necessary. Over time, payments received from many different customers will all be deposited into that same cash account. The minimum cardinalities on each side of this relationship are also typical. Each customer payment must be deposited into some account; hence the minimum cardinality of 1 on the resource side of the relationship. Conversely, the minimum cardinality on the event side of the relationship is 0 for the same reasons that it is 0 in the agent-event and inventory–event relationships as discussed previously.

Finally, let us examine the event–event relationships depicted in Figure 15-6. Fred's Train Shop ships each business customer order individually and waits until all items are in stock before filling an order. Thus, each order is linked to only one sales transaction and each sales transaction is related to only one order. Therefore, Paul modeled the relationship between the Take Customer Order and Sales events as being 1:1. The minimum cardinality on the sales side of the relationship is 0, meaning that orders may exist which are not linked to sales. This reflects the temporal sequence between the two events: Orders precede sales, so at any given point in time, Fred's Train Shop may have orders that it has not yet filled. Fred's Train Shop does not, however, require that every sale be preceded by an order; indeed, while many sales to corporate customers are preceded by orders, walk-in sales to consumers are not. Therefore, Paul Stone modeled the minimum cardinality on the order side of the sales–order relationship as 0.

Paul also learned that Fred's Train Shop extends credit to its business customers and mails them monthly statements listing all unpaid purchases. He also found out that many business customers send Fred one check to cover all their purchases during a given time period. Thus, one Cash Receipt event could be linked to many different Sale events. However, Fred's Train Shop also allows its business customers to make installment payments on large purchases; thus, a given Sale event could be connected to more than one Cash Receipt event. That is why Paul modeled the relationship between the Sale and Cash Receipt events as being many-to-many.

Because Fred's Train Shop extends credit to some of its customers, at any point in time there can be Sale events that are not yet linked to any Receive Cash events. Therefore, Figure 15-6 shows the minimum cardinality on the Receive Cash side of the relationship as 0. Paul also learned that Fred's Train Shop never requires customers to pay in advance for special orders. Thus, every Receive Cash event must be linked to

a previous Sale event; consequently, Figure 15-6 shows the minimum cardinality on the sales side of the Sale–Receive Cash relationship is 1.

Uniqueness of REA Diagrams

The preceding discussion indicates that each organization will have its own unique REA diagram. At a minimum, because business practices differ across companies, so will relationship cardinalities. In fact, an REA diagram for a given organization will have to change to reflect changes to existing business practices. For example, if Fred's Train Shop decides to begin making partial shipments to fill customer orders, then Figure 15-6 would have to be changed to show the relationship between the Take Customer Order and Sales events as being 1:N, instead of the 1:1 relationship currently depicted. Similarly, if Fred's Train Shop also decided to adopt a policy of combining several orders from one customer into one large shipment, then Figure 15-6 would have to be modified to depict the relationship between those two events as being M:N. Sometimes, differences in business practices can result in different entities being modeled. For example, if Fred's Train Shop only made sales to walk-in customers and did not take any orders from businesses, then Figure 15-6 would not need to include the Take Customer Order commitment event.

Although the development of the REA diagram for Fred's Train Shop's revenue cycle may seem to have been relatively straightforward and intuitive, data modeling is usually a complex and repetitive process. Frequently, data modelers develop an initial REA diagram that reflects their understanding of the organization's business processes, only to learn when showing it to intended users that they had omitted key dimensions or misunderstood some operating procedures. Thus, it is not unusual to erase and redraw portions of an REA diagram several times before finally producing an acceptable model. One common source of misunderstanding is the use of different terminology by various subsets of the intended user groups. Focus 15-2 highlights the importance of involving the eventual users of the system in the data modeling process so that terminology is consistent.

15-2 FOCUS Why Should Users Participate in Data Modeling?

Data modeling is not an easy task, as Hewlett-Packard learned when it began designing a new database for its accounting and finance function. A major problem was that the same term meant different things to different people. For example, accounting used the term orders to refer to the total dollar amount of orders per time period, whereas the sales department used the term to refer to individual customer orders. Moreover, such confusions existed even within the accounting and finance function. For example, the reporting group used the term product to refer to any good currently sold to customers. Thus, the primary key for this entity was product number. In contrast, the forecasting group used the term product to refer to any good that was often still in the planning stage and had no product number assigned yet.

To solve these problems, Hewlett-Packard asked the different user groups to actively participate in the data modeling process. The first step was to convince all users of the need for and benefits of creating a data model for their function. Then it was necessary to carefully define the scope of the modeling effort. Hewlett-Packard found that the time invested in these early steps was worthwhile, because it facilitated the activities of clarifying definitions and developing attribute lists that took place later in the process. The latter activity was an iterative affair that included many revisions. Documentation was critical to this process. Each member of the modeling team and user groups had copies of the proposed lists, which made it easier to spot inconsistencies in definitions.

Hewlett-Packard credits the data modeling approach as contributing significantly to the project's overall success. Data modeling allowed the participants to concentrate first on understanding the essential business characteristics of the new system, instead of getting bogged down in specifying the contents of relational tables. This helped them to identify and resolve conflicting viewpoints early in the process and paved the way for eventual acceptance of the resulting system. The key step, however, was in getting the different user groups to actively participate in the data modeling process. Otherwise, it is likely that the resulting data model would not have been accurate or widely accepted.

SUMMARY AND CASE CONCLUSION

The database design process has five stages: systems analysis, conceptual design, physical design, implementation and conversion, and operation and maintenance. Because of their extensive knowledge of transaction processing requirements and general business functions, accountants should actively participate in every stage.

One way to perform the activities of systems analysis and conceptual design is to build a data model of the AIS. The REA accounting data model is developed specifically for designing a database to support an AIS. The REA model classifies entities into three basic categories: resources, events, and agents. An REA model can be documented in the form of an entity-relationship (E-R) diagram, which depicts the entities about which data are collected as rectangles and represents the important relationships between entities by connecting lines. The cardinalities of the relationships depicted in REA diagrams specify the minimum and maximum number of times an instance of one entity can be linked to an instance of the other entity participating in that relationship. Cardinalities also provide information about the basic business policies an organization follows.

Developing an REA diagram involves three steps. First, identify the basic events of interest (any activity about which management wants to collect information in order to plan, control, and evaluate performance). Second, identify the resources affected by and the agents who participate in those events. Third, use knowledge about the organization's business practices to add relationship cardinality information to the diagram.

Paul Stone followed these steps to develop an REA diagram for Fred's Train Shop's revenue cycle. He interviewed Fred to understand the store's business policies and used his general knowledge of revenue cycle activities to draw Figure 15-6. Paul showed the diagram to Fred and explained what each portion represented. Fred indicated that the diagram correctly reflected his store's revenue cycle activities. Paul then explained that he would proceed to use the model to design a relational database that Fred could use to automate the analyses he currently did by hand.

KEY TERMS

data modeling 585
entity-relationship (E-R)
 diagram 585
entity 585
REA data model 587
resources 587

events 587
agents 587
cardinalities 594
minimum
 cardinality 594
maximum cardinality 596

one-to-one (1:1)
 relationship 596
one-to-many (1:N)
 relationship 597
many-to-many (M:N)
 relationship 597

AIS IN ACTION

CHAPTER QUIZ

1 Accounts Receivable would appear in an REA diagram as an example of which kind of entity?

a. resource

c. agent

b. event

d. none of the above

2 Which of the following is not likely to be depicted as an entity in the REA data model?

a. customers

b. sales

c. invoices

d. delivery trucks

3 In most cases, the relationship between agent entities and event entities is

a. 1:1

b. 1:N

c. M:N

d. 0:N

4 If customers pay for each sales transaction with a separate check and are not permitted to make installment payments on any sales, then the relationship between the Sales and Cash Receipt events would be modeled as being which of the following?

a. 1:1

b. 1:N

c. M:N

d. 0:N

5 Which of the following most accurately models the sales of low-cost, mass-produced items by a retail store?

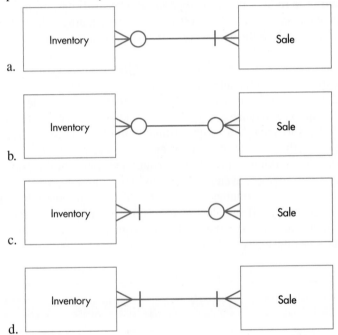

a.

b.

c.

d.

6 Data modeling occurs during which stages of database design?

a. systems analysis and physical design

b. systems analysis and conceptual design

c. conceptual design and implementation and conversion

d. physical design and implementation and conversion

7 A company has five different cash accounts (checking, money market, petty cash, payroll, and investments). It deposits all payments received from customers into its checking account. Which of the following accurately depicts the relationship between the Cash entity and the Receive Cash event?

a.

b.

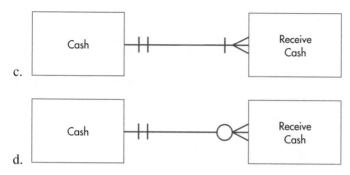

c.

d.

8 EZ Construction Company builds residential houses. It sells only homes that it
built. Most of its homes are sold to individuals, but sometimes an investor may
purchase several homes and hold them for subsequent resale. Which of the fol-
lowing is the correct way to model the relationship between Sale and Inventory
for EZ Construction Company?

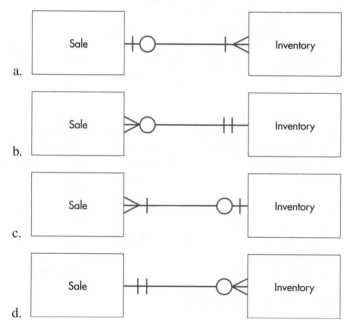

a.

b.

c.

d.

9 Which of the following statements about the REA data model is true?
a. Every event must be linked to at least two agents.
b. Every resource must be linked to at least one agent.
c. Every event must be linked to at least two resources.
d. Every agent must be linked to at least two events.

10 A business operates by always collecting payments from customers in advance.
Customers pay for the entire amount of the sale. It then orders the items from
its suppliers, and when they all arrive it ships the entire order to the customer.
Which of the following describes the relationship between Sale and Receive
Cash for this company?

a.

b.

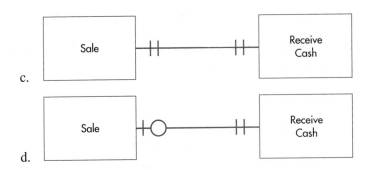

c.

d.

Expenditure Cycle for Fred's Train Shop

In order for Fred to sell trains and train accessories, he first needs to have inventory to sell. Thus, as part of his overall engagement, Paul Stone also prepared an REA model for the expenditure cycle of Fred's Train Shop. The following paragraph describes the expenditure cycle business processes of Fred's Train Shop:

> *Fred deals with more than one supplier and often places orders for multiple items at the same time. Fred takes inventory and places orders every Monday. Fred's suppliers strive to provide outstanding service. Therefore, they never consolidate multiple orders into one shipment, but always ship merchandise the day after receiving an order. Usually, Fred's suppliers can fill his entire order in one shipment. Occasionally, however, a supplier may be temporarily out of stock of a particular item. In such cases, the supplier ships as much of the order as possible and then ships the out-of-stock item separately as soon as it becomes available. Fred pays for each order in full at one time; that is, he does not make partial payments on orders received. Some suppliers offer discount terms for early payments; Fred always takes advantage of such offers, paying individual invoices, in full, on the appropriate date. Suppliers who do not offer such discounts send Fred monthly statements listing all orders placed the prior month. Fred pays the entire balance indicated on the statement in one check by the specified due date.*

Required

Prepare an REA diagram for Fred's Train Shop's expenditure cycle.

15.1 Why is it not necessary to model activities such as mailing invoices to customers and recording invoices received from suppliers as events in an REA diagram?

15.2 Why doesn't Figure 15-6 include an event for "entering information about customers"?

15.3 How can REA diagrams help an auditor understand a client's business processes?

15.4 Which parts of Figure 15-6 would accurately depict almost every organization's revenue cycle? Which parts would change?

15.5 What is the relationship between the things that would be represented as resources in an REA diagram and the different categories of assets found on an organization's balance sheet? (*Hint:* Are there any assets that would not be modeled as resources? Are there any resources in an REA diagram that are not listed as assets on a balance sheet?)

15.6 How would accounts payable be reflected in an REA diagram? Why?

PROBLEMS

15.1 Joe's is a small ice-cream shop located near the local university's baseball field. Joe's serves walk-in customers only. The shop carries 26 flavors of ice cream. Customers can buy cones, sundaes, or shakes. When a customer pays for an individual purchase, a sales transaction usually includes just one item. When a customer pays for a family or group purchase, however, a single sales transaction includes many different items. All sales must be paid for at the time the ice cream is served. Joe's maintains several banking accounts but deposits all sales receipts into its main checking account.

Required

Draw an REA diagram, complete with cardinalities, for Joe's revenue cycle.

15.2 Joe, the owner of the ice-cream shop, purchases ice cream from two vendors. Over the years, he has developed good relationships with both vendors so that they allow Joe to pay them biweekly for all purchases made during the preceding two-week period. Joe calls in ice-cream orders on Mondays and Thursdays. The orders are delivered the next day. Joe buys ice-cream toppings from one of several local stores and pays for each such purchase at the time of sale with a check from the company's main checking account.

Required

Draw an REA diagram, complete with cardinalities, for Joe's expenditure cycle.

15.3 Sue's Gallery sells original paintings by local artists. All sales occur in the store. Sometimes customers purchase more than one painting. Individual customers must pay for purchases in full at the time of sale. Corporate customers, such as hotels, however, may pay in installments if they purchase more than 10 paintings. Although Sue's Gallery has several bank accounts, all sales monies are deposited intact into the main checking account.

Required

Draw an REA diagram for the gallery's revenue cycle. Be sure to include cardinalities.

15.4 Sue's Gallery only purchases finished paintings (it never commissions artists). It pays each artist 50% of the agreed price at the time of purchase, and the remainder after the painting is sold. All purchases are paid by check from Sue's main checking account.

Required

Draw an REA diagram, complete with cardinalities, of the gallery's expenditure cycle.

15.5 Develop a data model of Fred's Train Shop's expenditure cycle activities related to the acquisition of office equipment and other fixed assets. Assume that Fred

makes installment payments for most fixed-asset acquisitions, but occasionally pays for some equipment in full at the time of purchase.

Required

Draw an REA diagram of your data model. Be sure to include cardinalities.

15.6 Provide an example (in terms of companies with which you are familiar) for each of the business situations described by the following relationship cardinalities:

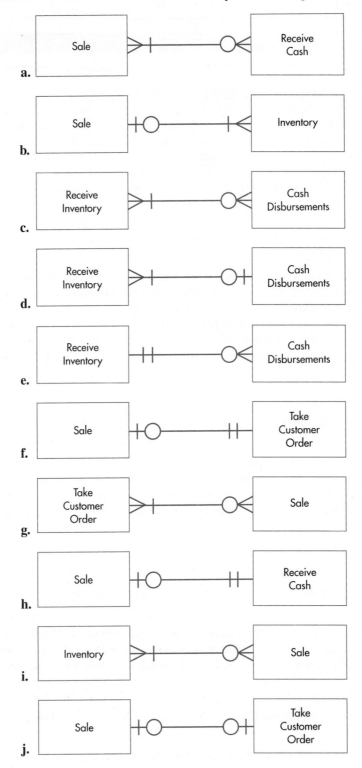

15.7 Model the cardinalities of the following business policies:

a. The relationship between the Sale and Receive Cash events for installment sales.

b. The relationship between the Sale and Receive Cash events at a convenience store.

c. The Take Customer Order–Sale relationship in a situation when occasionally several shipments are required to fill an order because some items were out of stock.

d. The Sale-Inventory relationship for a custom homebuilder.

e. The relationship between the Sale and Receive Cash events for Dell computers.

f. The relationship between the Sale and Receive Cash events for a retail store that has some in-store sales paid in full by customers at the time of the sale but that also makes some in-store sales to customers on credit, billing them later and permitting them to make installment payments.

g. The relationship between the Receive Inventory and Cash Disbursements events in the case where suppliers require payment in advance, in full.

h. The relationship between the Call on Customers event (i.e., the visit by a salesperson to a potential customer) and the Take Customer Order event for a business that is only conducted door-to-door (e.g., kitchen knives, certain books, etc.) so that the only way to order the items is when a salesperson visits the customer. (*Hint:* do you think every call results in an order?)

i. The relationship between the Call on Customers and Take Customer Orders events for a manufacturer which also accepts orders on its Web site.

j. The relationship between the Receive Inventory and Cash Disbursements events for a company which receives monthly bills from its suppliers for all purchases made the previous month; some suppliers require payment of the entire bill, in full, within 30 days or they will not accept any subsequent orders, but other suppliers accept installment payments.

15.8 The Computer Warehouse sells computer hardware, software, and supplies (such as paper). Individual customers just walk into the store, select merchandise, and must pay for their purchases in full before leaving the store. Corporate customers, however, call in orders in advance, so that the items are waiting to be picked up. Corporate customers may charge their purchases to their account. The Computer Warehouse mails corporate customers monthly statements that summarize all purchases made the prior month. Corporate customers pay the entire balance, as listed on the monthly statement, with one check or EFT transaction.

Required

Draw an REA diagram of the Computer Warehouse's revenue cycle, complete with cardinalities.

15.9 The Computer Warehouse purchases its inventory from more than a dozen different vendors. Orders are placed via telephone, fax, or on the supplier's Web site. Most orders are delivered the next day. Most orders are filled completely in one shipment, but sometimes a supplier is out of stock of a particular item. In such situations, the bulk of the order is shipped immediately and the out-of-stock item is shipped separately as soon as it arrives (such shipments of back orders are never combined with any new orders placed by the Computer Warehouse). The Computer Warehouse pays for some of its purchases COD but usually pays by the 10th of the month for all purchases made the prior month. None of its suppliers allow it to make installment payments.

Required

Draw an REA diagram of the Computer Warehouse's expenditure cycle, complete with cardinalities.

15.10 Stan's Southern Barbeque Supply Store orders mass-produced barbecue products from various suppliers. Stan's maintains information about a contact person at each supplier along with all required address information. Each purchase order has the order number, date, tax, and total. Purchase orders also contain the following information for each product ordered: stock number, description, and price. The manager of Stan's places orders by fax several times a day, whenever he notices that an item is running low. Some suppliers fill each individual order separately. Others, however, consolidate orders and fill all of them in one weekly delivery. Some suppliers require payment at the time of delivery, but others send Stan's a monthly statement detailing all purchases during the current period. Two suppliers allow Stan's to make installment payments for any individual purchase orders that exceed $20,000.

Required

Draw an REA diagram with cardinalities for the expenditure cycle of Stan's Southern Barbeque Supply Store.

CASE 15-1 REA Data Modeling Extension

An important analytical and problem-solving skill is the ability to adapt and transfer patterns learned in one setting to other situations. This chapter explained how to develop an REA diagram for a business that sells tangible inventory. Yet some businesses provide only a service. For example, the following narrative describes Sparky's Amusement Park's revenue cycle.

Sparky's Amusement Park is an entertainment park run by recent college graduates. It caters to young people and others who are young at heart. The owners are very interested in applying what they have learned in their information systems and marketing classes to operate a park better than any other in the area.

To accomplish these goals, guests of the park are given a personal "membership card" as they enter. This card will be used to identify each guest. Assume that a new card is issued each time a guest comes to the park. As a result, the system does not have to track one person over a period of time.

As at other parks, guests pay a flat fee for the day and then are able to ride all of the attractions (such as a double-looping roller coaster and the merry-go-round) for no extra charge. The owners, however, want to track the rides each guest takes and the attractions the guests use. They plan to have guests swipe their membership card through a computerized card reader, which automatically enters information into the computer system. This should allow the owners to gather data about the following:

- Number of people who use each piece of equipment. (How many people rode the Ferris wheel today?)
- Number of times each piece of equipment is operated daily.
- Times of day the attraction is busy or slow. (When was the carousel the busiest?)
- Number of attractions each guest uses. (How many different pieces of equipment did customer 1122 ride?)
- Number of rides each guest enjoys. (How many different rides did customer 1122 enjoy? Did each guest go on any rides more than once?)

Required

Draw an REA diagram for Sparky's *revenue* cycle only. Be sure to include cardinalities. State any assumptions you had to make.

(This problem is adapted from one developed for classroom use by Dr. Julie Smith David at Arizona State University.)

AIS IN ACTION SOLUTIONS

QUIZ KEY

1 Accounts Receivable would appear in an REA diagram as an example of which kind of entity?
 a. resource (Incorrect. Accounts Receivable is not a resource as defined in the REA model, but simply equals the difference between the sales and Receive Cash events.)
 b. event (Incorrect. Accounts Receivable is not an event, but represents the difference between two events.)
 c. agent (Incorrect. Agents are people or organizations.)
 ✔ **d.** none of the above (Correct. Accounts Receivable would not appear as an entity in an REA diagram because it represents the difference between two events.)

2 Which of the following is not likely to be depicted as an entity in the REA data model?
 a. customers (Incorrect. Customers are an agent entity.)
 b. sales (Incorrect. Sales are an event entity.)
 ✔ **c.** invoices (Correct. Invoices are paper outputs of a database—they do not meet the definition of being either a resource, an event, or an agent and, therefore, are not modeled as an entity in a REA diagram.)
 d. delivery trucks (Incorrect. Delivery trucks are an economic resource entity.)

3 In most cases, the relationship between agent entities and event entities is
 a. 1:1 (Incorrect. Over time, agents can participate in many events.)
 ✔ **b.** 1:N (Correct. Over time, agents usually participate in many events. Usually, for accountability purposes, an event is linked to only one specific internal agent and one specific external agent. Occasionally, a complex task may be linked to a team of internal agents, but this is not the norm.)
 c. M:N (Incorrect. This pattern may occasionally occur, but it is not the norm.)
 d. 0:N (Incorrect. There is no such thing as a 0:N relationship.)

4 If customers pay for each sales transaction with a separate check and are not permitted to make installment payments on any sales, then the relationship between the Sale and Cash Receipt events would be modeled as being which of the following?
 ✔ **a.** 1:1 (Correct. Each sales transaction is linked to only one payment (no installments) and each payment is linked to only one sales transaction (separate checks).)
 b. 1:N (Incorrect. This indicates that each sale event could be linked to multiple cash receipts, implying installment payments.)
 c. M:N (Incorrect. This not only indicates the possibility of installment payments but also the use of one check to pay for multiple sales.)
 d. 0:N (Incorrect. There is no such thing as a 0:N relationship.)

5 Which of the following most accurately models the sales of low-cost, mass-produced items by a retail store?

a.

(Incorrect. This indicates that every inventory item must be linked to at least one sale, but that a sales transaction may consist of no inventory.)

b.

(Incorrect. This shows that a sales transaction can consist of no inventory items.)

✔ **c.**

(Correct. Each sale must involve at least one item of inventory, but possibly many; conversely, each inventory item may not be linked to any sales transaction, but a given item could be linked to many sale events.)

d.

(Incorrect. This says that every inventory item must be linked to at least one sales transaction—this is not true at the beginning of a fiscal year and also precludes storing information about new products prior to their being sold.)

6 Data modeling occurs during which stages of database design?
 a. system analysis and physical design (Incorrect. Data modeling occurs during the system analysis and conceptual design stages of the database design process.)
✔ **b.** system analysis and conceptual design (Correct.)
 c. conceptual design and implementation and conversion (Incorrect. Data modeling occurs during the system analysis and conceptual design stages of the database design process.)
 d. physical design and implementation and conversion (Incorrect. Data modeling occurs during the system analysis and conceptual design stages of the database design process.)

7 A company has five different cash accounts (checking, money market, petty cash, payroll, and investments). It deposits all payments received from customers into its checking account. Which of the following accurately depicts the relationship between the cash entity and the receive cash event?

a.

(Incorrect. This says that every Cash account must be linked to at least one Receive Cash event and that a Receive Cash event could be linked to multiple cash accounts.)

b.

(Incorrect. Same problems as in a.)

c.

(Incorrect. This says that every Cash account must be linked to at least one Receive Cash event, which is not true: At the beginning of a new fiscal year, there are no Receive Cash events and four of the company's five Cash accounts never directly receive funds collected from customers.)

✔ **d.**

(Correct. This shows that some Cash accounts may not be linked to any Receive Cash events, whereas others may be linked to many events. Conversely, this shows that each Receive Cash event must be linked to a Cash account, and to only one Cash account.)

8 EZ Construction Company builds residential houses. It sells only homes that it has built. Most of its homes are sold to individuals, but sometimes an investor may purchase several homes and hold them for subsequent resale. Which of the following is the correct way to model the relationship between Sales and Inventory for EZ Construction Company?

✔ **a.**

(Correct. Each sale must involve at least one home from inventory but could involve many; conversely, each home may or may not be sold (yet) but can be sold at most one time.)

b.

(Incorrect. This shows that a sale can only involve at most one home from inventory and it shows that a given home can be sold multiple times.)

c.

(Incorrect. This shows that a sale could involve no homes or at most one home, and it shows that every home must be sold but could be sold more than once.)

d.

(Incorrect. This shows that every home must be sold and it also shows that a sale could involve no homes.)

9 Which of the following statements about the REA data model is true?

✔ a. Every event must be linked to at least two agents. (Correct.)

b. Every resource must be linked to at least two agents. (Incorrect. Resources and agents are not usually directly linked to one another.)

c. Every event must be linked to at least two resources. (Incorrect. Every event must be linked to at least one resource.)

d. Every agent must be linked to at least two events. (Incorrect. Some agents may only need to be linked to one event.)

10 A business operates by always collecting payments from customers in advance. Customers pay for the entire amount of the sale. It then orders the items from its suppliers, and when they all arrive it ships the entire order to the customer. Which of the following describes the relationship between sales and cash receipts for this company?

a.

(Incorrect. This shows that a Sale event might not be linked to any Receive Cash events, which means that the merchandise is delivered prior to the customer's payment. Another problem is that this shows that every Receive Cash event must be linked to a Sale event, but the company receives payment prior to delivering the merchandise.)

b.

(Incorrect. Same problems as in a.)

c.

(Incorrect. This shows that every Receive Cash event must be linked to a Sale event, but this is not true because the company receives cash prior to shipping the merchandise.)

✔ d.

(Correct. This shows that each Sale event must be linked to a prior Receive Cash event but that a Receive Cash event may not (yet) be linked to any Sale event.)

COMPREHENSIVE PROBLEM SOLUTION

REA Diagram of Expenditure Cycle for Fred's Train Shop

To create an entity-relationship diagram using the REA model, follow the three basic steps outlined in the chapter.

1 Identify Events

As explained in the chapter, the first step is to identify all relevant events or transactions using the basic "give-to-get" exchange. After talking to Fred about how he buys the inventory he needs, Paul identifies three basic events that occur:

1 Order Inventory
2 Receive Inventory
3 Pay for Inventory, which Paul decides to call "Disburse cash"

2 Identify Resources and Agents

Next, identify the resources involved with these events. Paul determines that there are two resources involved with these events:

1 Inventory
2 Cash

Then identify the agents or people needed to make these events happen, remembering that there are usually two agents for each event, one internal to Fred's store (i.e., an employee) and one external to Fred's store (i.e., the supplier). Paul lists the following agents as being involved in the Order Inventory event:

1 Purchasing Clerk
2 Supplier

The agents involved in the Receive Inventory event are

3 Receiving Clerk
4 Supplier

The agents involved in the Disburse Cash event are

5 Supplier
6 Cashier

3 Determine Cardinalities of Relationships

After identifying all events, resources, and agents, the next step is to determine how all of these entities interact by determining the cardinalities of all of the relationships between and among the entities. The involves three steps:

1 Specify cardinalities of event-agent relationships
2 Specify cardinalities of event-resource relationships
3 Specify cardinalities of event-event relationships

1 Event–Agent Relationship Cardinalities

After talking with Fred, Paul understands that any employee can order merchandise from suppliers. However, one and only one employee is involved in each order event. Similarly, any employee can check in deliveries from suppliers. Because model train merchandise is not heavy or bulky, each delivery is checked in by only one employee. Fred, or his wife, sign all checks to suppliers and only one signature is ever required. Thus, the *maximum* cardinality on the agent side of relationships between events and internal agents (employees) is always 1. Obviously, an employee must participate in each event: There must be some employee who places an order, some employee who checks in a delivery, and either Fred or his wife must sign each check. Thus, the *minimum* cardinality on the agent side of relationships between events and internal agents is also 1.

Orders, receipts of inventory, and payments all involve suppliers. Each event must be linked to a particular supplier: A purchase order must identify and be sent to a supplier, a delivery comes from some supplier, and a payment is made to some identifiable supplier. Moreover, each event can be linked to *only one* supplier: Each order is placed with a *specific* supplier, each delivery comes from a *specific* supplier, and each payment is made to a *specific* supplier (e.g., each check is made payable to one, and only one, supplier). Thus, the minimum and maximum cardinalities on the agent side of relationships between events and external agents is 1.

Paul also knows that information about both internal and external agents is maintained indefinitely but that information about events is only maintained for the current

fiscal year. Therefore, at the beginning of each fiscal period, every internal agent and every external agent is not linked to any order, inventory receipt, or payment events. Thus, the *minimum* cardinality on the event side of relationships between events and agents is 0. During the course of the year, however, the same employee may place many different orders or may check in many different deliveries of merchandise. In addition, both Fred and his wife will sign many different checks that are sent to suppliers. Conversely, during the year many orders may be placed with the same supplier; many deliveries may be received from the same supplier; and many payments may be made to the same supplier. Thus, the *maximum* cardinality on the event side of relationships between events and agents is N.

2 Event–Resource Relationship Cardinalities

Each order must involve at least one inventory item but could be for many different items. Similarly, each delivery of merchandise from a supplier must involve at least one inventory item but may include many different items. Consequently, Paul depicts the minimum cardinality as 1 and the maximum cardinality as N on the inventory side of all relationships between the inventory resource and various events.

Information about inventory is maintained indefinitely, but only orders and inventory receipts that occurred during the current fiscal year are maintained in the database. Thus, at the beginning of each fiscal year the inventory entity is not linked to any order or receive inventory events. During the course of the year, however, a particular inventory item may be ordered and received many times. Thus, Paul depicts the minimum cardinality as 0 and the maximum cardinality as N on the event side of all relationships between the Inventory resource and various events affecting it.

Each payment must be made from some general ledger cash account. In addition, each payment can be made from only one specific account. For example, a check can be linked to either the operating checking account or the payroll checking account, but it cannot be linked to both accounts. Therefore, Paul sets the minimum and maximum cardinalities to 1 on the resource side of the relationship between the Cash resource and the Disburse Cash event.

Information about the various cash accounts in the general ledger (operating checking, payroll, investment, etc.) is maintained indefinitely, but the Disburse Cash event entity only contains information about payments made during the current fiscal year. Therefore, at the beginning of each fiscal year, the cash resource is not linked to any Disburse Cash events. During the course of the year, however, a given cash account may be linked to many different Disburse Cash events. Thus, the minimum cardinality is 0 and the maximum cardinality is N on the event side of the relationship between the Cash resource and the Disburse Cash event.

3 Event–Event Relationship Cardinalities

Orders occur before deliveries. Some orders, however, may include items that are out of stock; when that happens, the merchandise in stock is sent immediately and one or more additional shipments are made for any items that the supplier had to back order. Thus, one order can be linked to multiple Receive Inventory events. Consequently, Paul assigns a minimum cardinality of 0 and a maximum cardinality of N on the Receive Inventory side of the relationship between the Order Inventory and Receive Inventory events.

Fred's employees have been trained to accept only deliveries for which a valid purchase order exists. Thus, each Receive Inventory event must be linked to an order. Fred's suppliers never consolidate multiple orders into one delivery; thus, each Receive Inventory event can be linked to at most one order event. Therefore, Paul depicts the minimum and maximum cardinalities on the Order Inventory side of the relationship between the Receive Inventory and Order Inventory events as both being 1.

Often, Fred pays for deliveries in the following month. Thus, there may be Receive Inventory events that are not yet linked to any Disburse Cash events. Fred always pays for deliveries in full; he never makes installment payments. Therefore,

each Receive Inventory event is linked to at most one Disburse Cash event. Consequently, Paul assigns a minimum cardinality of 0 and a maximum cardinality of 1 to the Disburse Cash side of the relationship between the Receive Inventory and Disburse Cash events.

Fred's only pays for deliveries after the merchandise has been received and inspected. Thus, every Disburse Cash event must be linked to a preceding Receive Inventory event. Oftentimes, Fred or his wife will write one check to pay for several deliveries received during the preceding month. Therefore, Paul draws the minimum cardinality as 1 and the maximum cardinality as N on the Receive Inventory side of the relationship between the Receive Inventory and Disburse Cash events.

After completing the three steps, Paul produced the following REA diagram of the expenditure cycle of Fred's Train Shop.

CHAPTER 16

LEARNING OBJECTIVES

After studying this chapter, you should be able to:

● Integrate separate REA diagrams for individual transaction cycles into a single comprehensive organization-wide REA diagram

● Build a set of tables to implement an REA model of an AIS in a relational database.

● Explain how to write queries to retrieve information from an AIS relational database built according to the REA data model.

Implementing an REA Model in a Relational Database

INTEGRATIVE CASE FRED'S TRAIN SHOP

Paul Stone showed Fred the set of REA diagrams that he had developed to model the business activities for the revenue, expenditure, and payroll cycles of Fred's Train Shop. Fred verified that Paul had correctly represented his company's business processes. He then said that although the diagrams "looked nice," he wondered why Paul had spent so much time developing them, instead of building Fred the database he had promised. Paul responded that the time spent up front in thoroughly understanding Fred's Train Shop's business processes was necessary to properly design a database that would satisfy Fred's needs.

Paul asked Fred whether he had a database program. Fred replied that a relational database was part of the "business applications" he had purchased as part of an office productivity package. Fred said that although he knew how to use the program, he had not been able to figure out how to import data to it from his AIS and store it in a manner that would allow him to analyze his store's business activities. Paul said that he would do so by following these steps:

1 First, he would integrate the separate REA diagrams he had developed into a single, comprehensive enterprise-wide data model.

2 Second, he would use the integrated data model to design a set of relational database tables.

3 Third, he would show Fred how he could query the resulting database to generate both traditional financial statements as well as any custom performance reports.

Introduction

The previous chapter introduced the topic of REA data modeling and explained how to develop REA diagrams for an individual transaction cycle. This chapter shows how to implement an REA diagram in a database. We focus on relational databases because they are commonly used to support transaction processing systems and are likely to be familiar to most business students. Nevertheless, REA data modeling is not limited for use only in designing relational databases, but can also be used to design object-oriented databases.

We begin by showing how to integrate separate REA diagrams developed for individual transaction cycles into a single, comprehensive enterprise-wide data model. Next, we explain how to implement the resulting model in a relational database. We then describe how to use the REA diagram to query the database to produce traditional financial statements as well as a variey of management reports.

Integrating REA Diagrams Across Cycles

Figures 16-1,16-2, and 16-3 present REA diagrams of Fred's Train Shop's revenue, expenditure, and payroll cycles, respectively. These separate diagrams should be integrated to provide a single comprehensive enterprise-wide model of the organization. Doing so requires understanding what the cardinalities in each separate diagram reveal about the organization's business policies and activities. Figures 16-1 and Figure 16-2 were explained in Chapter 15, so we focus here on Figure 16-3.

Figure 16-3 depicts the payroll portion of Fred's Train Shop's HR/payroll cycle activities. The basic economic exchange involves acquiring the use of each employee's time and skills in exchange for which the employee receives a paycheck. Like many

Figure 16-1
Fred's Train Shop
Revenue Cycle

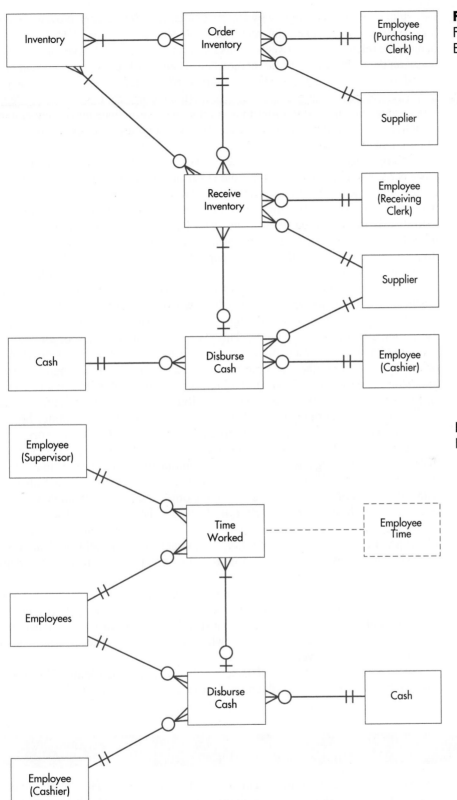

Figure 16-2
Fred's Train Shop
Expenditure Cycle

Figure 16-3
Fred's Train Shop Payroll Cycle

small businesses, Fred's Train Shop uses an electronic time clock to record the hours worked by each employee each day. Thus, each Time Worked event records the time an employee began and ended working on a specific day. Each such event must be linked to a particular employee and his or her supervisor; each employee or supervisor, however, may be linked to many different events. Similarly, a paycheck is issued to a

particular employee and signed by a particular cashier, but each employee and cashier may be associated with many different Disburse Cash events over time. Hence, Figure 16-3 depicts the relationships between agents and events as being 1:N The minimum cardinality on the agent side of those relationships is always 1, because each event *must* be linked to a specific employee. (For example, Fred would not want to issue a paycheck and leave the payee name blank.) The minimum cardinality on the event side of the relationships is always 0 in order to accommodate storing data about new employees prior to their beginning work and because the event entities are empty at the beginning of each new fiscal year.

The relationship between the Time Worked and Disburse Cash events reflects the basic economic exchange of getting the use of an employee's time and paying for it. Figure 16-3 shows that the relationship between these two events is 1:N. This is because Fred's Train Shop, like most businesses, pays employees periodically but records their time worked daily. Thus, each Disburse Cash event is linked to many daily Time Worked events. Like most businesses, however, Fred's Train Shop does not divide one day into two different pay periods, nor does it pay employees in installments; thus, each Time Worked event is linked to only 1 Disburse Cash event. The minimum cardinalities on each side of the relationship reflect the normal business practice of paying employees after they have worked, rather than in advance.

The Employee Time entity requires some explanation. It represents the fact that the resource being acquired by the Time Worked event is the use of an employee's skills and knowledge for a particular period of time. Time, however, is different from inventory, cash, and other tangible resources, as well as from intangible resources like trade secrets or other forms of intellectual property, in that it cannot be stored. In addition, there are only a few relevant attributes about employee time: the hours worked and how that time was used. Every organization needs to monitor how much time each employee works, in order to calculate payroll. The Time Worked event, which is an example of a "Get" resource event, serves this purpose. Chapter 17 will discuss how some organizations, such as manufacturers and professional services firms (e.g., law firms, consulting organizations, and accounting firms) also collect detailed records of how employees use their time, which is an example of a "Give" resource event, in order to properly bill clients for those services. These two events (Time Worked and Time Used) capture all of the information about employee time that is practical to collect and monitor. Consequently, the Employee Time resource entity is almost never implemented in an actual database. Therefore, it is depicted with dotted lines in Figure 16-3.

Finally, the cardinalities of the relationship between the cash disbursement event and the cash resource are identical to those in the expenditure cycle (Figure 16-2): Each check or electronic funds transfer must be linked to at least one cash account and can be linked to only one cash account, whereas the same cash account may be linked to many disbursement events.

Now that we understand the business policies underlying Figures 16-1, 16-2, and 16-3 we can proceed to merge them into one integrated REA diagram.

Rules for Combining REA Diagrams

You have probably noticed that Figures 16-1, 16-2, and 16-3 each contain some of the same entities. For example, the inventory resource appears in both Figures 16-1 and 16-2. The cash disbursements event appears in both Figures 16-2 and 16-3. Both the employee agent and the cash resource appear in all three diagrams. Such redundancies provide the basis for combining REA diagrams depicting individual transaction cycles into a single, comprehensive, enterprise-wide REA model. Figure 16-4 shows such a model for Fred's Train Shop. Notice that the integrated diagram merges multiple copies of resource and event entities but retains multiple copies of agent entities. This maximizes the legibility of the comprehensive REA diagram by avoiding the need to

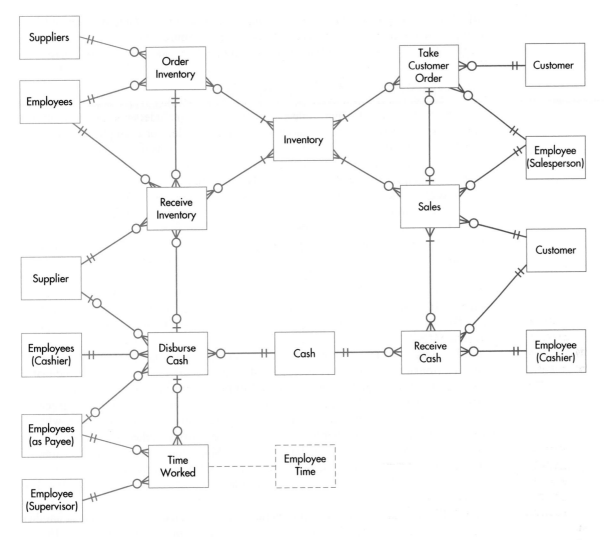

Figure 16-4
Integrated REA Diagram for Fred's Train Shop

have relationship lines cross one another. Let us now examine how to combine redundant resource and event entities.

Merging Redundant Resource Entities

Recall that REA diagrams for individual transaction cycles are built around basic give-to-get economic exchanges. Such economic duality relationships explain why a resource is either acquired or disposed of. They provide only a part of the story about each resource, however. For example, Figure 16-1 shows that inventory is reduced (the Sales event) in exchange for cash (the Receive Cash event). But Figure 16-1 does not show how that inventory was initially acquired. Nor does it show how the organization uses the cash it receives from customers. Conversely, Figure 16-2 shows how inventory was acquired (the Receive Inventory event) by giving up cash (the Disburse Cash event). Yet, Figure 16-2 does not show what the organization does with the inventory or how it acquired the cash used to pay suppliers.

Thus, REA diagrams for individual cycles provide only partial information about the resources controlled by an organization. The complete picture would show how each resource is acquired and how it is used. As shown in Figure 16-4, this can be done by redrawing an REA diagram to place common resources between the events that

affect them. Doing so reflects another important duality that must be depicted in a complete REA model of any organization: Every resource must be connected to at least one event that increases that resource and to at least one event that decreases it.

Merging Redundant Event Entities

REA diagrams for individual transaction cycles may include some events that also appear in the REA diagrams of another transaction cycle. For example, Figures 16-2 and 16-3 both contain the Disburse Cash event entity. As was the case with resources, merging these multiple occurrences of the same event improves the legibility of the resulting comprehensive REA diagram. Thus, Figure 16-4 shows that the Disburse Cash event is linked to both the Receive Inventory and the Time Worked events.

Close examination of Figure 16-4 reveals an important difference, however, between merging redundant events and merging redundant resources: Merging redundant resources does not affect any cardinalities, but merging redundant events alters the minimum cardinalities associated with the other events that are related to the merged event. Thus, in Figure 16-4 the cardinalities between the inventory resource and each of the four events to which it is related are the same as those depicted in Figures 16-1 and 16-2. In contrast, the cardinalities between the Disburse Cash event and the other events with which it is linked are different in Figure 16-4 than in Figures 16-2 and 16-3.

The reason for this difference lies in the underlying semantics about the nature of the relationship between the merged entity and other entities. An instance of a resource entity can, and usually is, linked to multiple events. For example, a given inventory item carried by Fred's Train Shop can be linked not only to a Receive Inventory event, when it is acquired from a supplier, but also to a Sales event, when it is sold to a customer. In other words, the resource entity is linked to event entities in one cycle *and* to event entities in the other cycle. Since both links are possible, none of the cardinalities in the individual REA diagrams needs to change.

The situation is different when merging an event across transaction cycles. The event that appears in both individual transaction cycle REA diagrams may be linked to *either* an event that is part of one transaction cycle *or* to an event that is part of another transaction cycle *but cannot be linked to both* events. For example, in Figure 16-4, a particular Disburse Cash event (i.e., a particular check or EFT transaction) could be associated with a prior receipt of inventory from a supplier or with time worked by an employee, but the same check (or EFT transaction) cannot be used *both* to pay a supplier for receipt of inventory *and* to pay an employee for working the previous week. Consequently, the minimum cardinality associated with the other events *must* be 0 in the integrated REA diagram, regardless of what it was in each of the individual transaction cycle REA diagrams. To understand why, recall that a minimum of 1 means that each instance of that entity has to be associated with at least one instance of the other entity. In terms of cash disbursements in Figure 16-4, retaining the minimum 1 with the Time Worked event, for example, would mean that every cash disbursement must be linked to a time card transaction—which is clearly not true, because Fred may make a cash disbursement to pay a supplier. For similar reasons, the minimum cardinality from the Disburse Cash event to the Receive Inventory event must also change from 1 to 0.

In addition, merging two transaction cycles on a common event may also affect the minimum cardinalities between the merged event and the agents participating in that event. For example, in Figure 16-4 the minimum cardinality between the Disburse Cash event and the Supplier entity is now 0, instead of 1. The reason is that a given check (cash disbursement) may be written *either* to a supplier as payee or to an employee as payee, but the same check *cannot* be written to *both* agents simultaneously. That is also why the minimum cardinality between the Disburse Cash event and the Employee (payee) agent is also 0. Thus, whenever a merged event involves different agents in each of the individual transaction cycles being merged, the minimum cardinalities between that event and those agents change from the usual 1 to 0, because the event may now be linked to either of the two types of agents, but not both.

Validating the Accuracy of Integrated REA Diagrams

Chapter 15 presented three basic principles for drawing REA diagrams for individual transaction cycles; the preceding discussion for combining such diagrams into a single, enterprise-wide model adds two more rules. Thus, a correctly drawn, integrated REA diagram must satisfy these five rules:

1 Every event must be linked to at least one resource.
2 Every event must be linked to two agents who participate in that event.
3 Every event that involves the disposition of a resource must be linked to an event that involves the acquisition of a resource. (This reflects the economic duality underlying "give-to-get" economic exchanges.)
4 Every resource must be linked to at least one event that increments that resource and to at least one event that decrements that resource.
5 If event A can be linked to more than one other event, but cannot be linked simultaneously to all of those other events, then the REA diagram should show that event A is linked to a minimum of 0 of each of those other events.

Notice that these five rules can be used not only to develop an integrated REA diagram but also as "check figures" to validate the accuracy of a completed REA diagram. Technically, Figure 16-4 is not complete because rule 4 is not satisfied for the Employee Time resource. We will correct this shortcoming in Chapter 17. For now, let us ignore it and proceed to the next step in the database design process: implementation of an REA data model in a relational database.

Implementing an REA Diagram in a Relational Database

Once an REA diagram has been developed, it can be used to design a well-structured relational database. In fact, creating a set of tables from an REA diagram automatically results in a well-structured relational database that is not subject to the update, insert, and delete anomaly problems discussed in Chapter 4.

There are three steps to implementing an REA diagram in a relational database:

1 Create a table for each *distinct* entity in the diagram and for each many-to-many relationship.
2 Assign attributes to appropriate tables.
3 Use foreign keys to implement one-to-one and one-to-many relationships.

Recall that even though REA diagrams for different organizations may include the same entities, differences in business policies are likely and will result in differences in relationship cardinalities. For example, the REA diagram for one organization may show a 1:1 relationship between the Sales and Receive Cash events, whereas the REA diagram for another organization may model that same pair of events as being involved in a M:N relationship. Thus, the design of a database (number of tables, placement of attributes) is specific to the organization being modeled.

Step 1: Create Tables for Each Distinct Entity and M:N Relationship

A properly designed relational database has a table for each distinct entity and for each many-to-many relationship in an REA diagram. Figure 16-4 has 13 distinct entities, but as previously discussed, one, Employee Time, will not be implemented in the database. The remaining 12 distinct entities that are depicted in Figure 16-4

need to be implemented as tables in a relational database. Seven tables will represent the event entities in the diagram: Order Inventory, Receive Inventory, Disburse Cash, Time Worked, Take Customer Order, Sales, and Receive Cash. There are two tables for resource entities: Inventory and Cash. Three tables are needed to implement the distinct agent entities: Employees, Customers, and Suppliers (supervisors are labeled separately to make the diagram easier to read, but are themselves employees).

Figure 16-4 also depicts five M:N relationships. Three are from the revenue cycle: Take Customer Orders–Inventory, Sales–Inventory, and Sales–Receive Cash. Two others are from the expenditure cycle: Inventory–Order Inventory and Inventory–Receive Inventory. Therefore, the 17 tables listed in Table 16-1 must be created to accurately implement Figure 16-4 in a relational data base. Notice that the suggested table names in Table 16-1 (see next page) correspond to the names of entities in the REA diagram or, in the case of tables for M:N relationships, are hyphenated concatenations of the entities involved in the relationship. This makes it easier to verify that all necessary tables have been created and also makes it easier to use the REA diagram as a guide when querying the database.

Step 2: Assign Attributes to Each Table[1]

The next step is to determine which attributes should be included in each table. The database designer needs to interview users and management to identify which facts need to be included in the database. The database designer must use the REA diagram to help determine in which table(s) to place those facts, depending upon whether that fact is a primary key or is just a descriptive attribute.

Identify Primary Keys

As explained in Chapter 4, every table in a relational database must have a primary key, consisting of an attribute, or combination of attributes, that uniquely identifies each row in that table. Companies often create numeric identifiers for specific resources, events, and agents. These numeric identifiers are good candidates for primary keys. For example, Table 16-1 shows that Fred's Train Shop uses invoice number as the primary key of the sales table and customer number as the primary key of the customer table.

Usually the primary key of a table representing an entity is a single attribute. The primary key for M:N relationship tables, however, always consists of two attributes that represent the primary keys of each entity linked in that relationship. For example, the primary key of the sales–inventory table consists of both the invoice number (the primary key of the sales entity) and product number (the primary key of the inventory entity). Such multiple-attribute primary keys are called **concatenated keys**.

Assign Other Attributes to Appropriate Tables

Additional attributes besides the primary key are included in each table to satisfy transaction processing requirements and management's information needs. As discussed in Chapter 4, any other attribute included in a relational database table must either be a fact about the object represented by the primary key or a foreign key. Thus, information about customers, such as their name and address, belongs in the customer table, because those attributes describe the object represented by the primary key (customer number) of the customer table; those attributes do not belong in the sales table, because they do not describe some property of the object represented by the primary key (invoice number) of that table.

[1]As explained in Chapter 15, some designers prefer to include attributes as part of the REA diagram itself. We choose to list them in a separate table to reduce the clutter on the diagram.

Table 16-1
Table Names and Attribute Placement for Figure 16-4

TABLES	ATTRIBUTES		
	Primary Key	**Foreign Keys**	**Other Attributes**
Order Inventory	Purchase order number	Supplier number, employee number	Date, time, reason
Receive Inventory	Receiving report number	Supplier number, employee number, purchase order number, check number	Date, time, remarks, vendor invoice number
Disburse Cash	Check number	Supplier number, employee number (payee), employee number (signer), account number	Amount, description, date
Take Customer Order	Sales order number	Customer number, employee number	Date, time, special remarks
Sales	Invoice number	Customer number, employee number	Date, time, invoice sent (Y/N)
Receive Cash	Remittance number	Customer number, employee number, account number	Date, time
Record Time Worked	Timecard number	Employee number, supervisor number, paycheck number	Date, time in, time out
Inventory	Product number		Description, list price, standard cost, quantity-on-hand, quantity-available, reorder quantity, reorder point
Cash	Account number		Beginning-balance, type of account
Employees	Employee number		Name, date hired, date of birth, pay rate, job title
Customers	Customer number		Name, address[a], beginning account balance, credit limit
Suppliers	Supplier number		Name, address[a], beginning account balance, performance rating
Order Inventory— Inventory	Purchase order number, product number		Quantity ordered, actual unit cost
Receive Inventory— Inventory	Receiving report number, product number		Quantity received, condition
Take Customer Order—Inventory	Sales order number, product number		Quantity ordered
Sales—Inventory	Invoice number, product number		Quantity sold, actual sale price
Sales—Receive Cash	Invoice number, remittance number		Amount applied to invoice

[a]Actually, only the street address and Zip code would be stored in these tables. In both tables Zip code would be a foreign key. Zip code would also be the primary key of an "address table," which would also include city and state as non-key attributes.

Table 16-1 shows some of the attributes that Paul Stone assigned to the various tables he created to implement Figure 16-4 in a relational database. Some of these attributes, such as the date of each sale and the amount remitted by a customer, are necessary for complete and accurate transaction processing and the production of financial statements and managerial reports. Other attributes are stored because they facilitate the effective management of an organization's resources, events, and agents. For example, Fred can use data about the time of day when each sales transaction occurs to design staff work schedules.

Table 16-1 also includes nonkey attributes in some of the M:N relationship tables. Let us examine the placement of the nonkey attributes in some of the M:N tables to see why they must be stored in those particular tables. Consider first the sales-receive cash table. Recall that Fred's train shop allows its customers to make multiple purchases on credit and to make installment payments on their outstanding balances. Thus, one customer payment may need to be applied to several different invoices (sales transactions). Therefore, the attribute "amount applied" cannot be placed in the receive cash table because it could take on more than one value (one for each invoice being paid), thereby violating the basic requirement of relational databases that every attribute in every row be single-valued (i.e., the requirement that every table be a flat file). Nor can the attribute "amount applied" be placed in the sales table, because the possibility of installment payments also creates a situation in which that attribute can have multiple values (i.e., one entry for each installment payment related to that particular sale). Thus, analysis of the underlying business process indicates that the attribute "amount applied" is a fact about both a specific customer payment (remittance) and a specific sales transaction and, therefore, belongs in the M:N table linking those two events.

Now examine the Sales–Inventory table. Each row in this table contains information about a line item in an invoice. Although many of Fred's Train Shop's customers buy just one of each kind of product it sells, some sales to customers involve larger quantities. For example, a department store may buy five identical coal cars (product number 31125) for its window display. Consequently, Fred's Train Shop must record the quantity sold of each item. Each sales event, however, may include more than one inventory item. Thus, the attribute "quantity sold" may have several values on a single sales invoice, one for each different item (product number) sold. Consequently, the attribute "quantity sold" cannot be an attribute in the Sales table, because there can be more than one "quantity sold" value associated with a given invoice number. In addition, recall that Fred's Train Shop, like most retail stores, tracks inventory by kinds of items, each of which is identified by product number, not by specific identification. Therefore, a given item, such as an orange diesel locomotive, product number 14887, may be sold as part of many different sales transactions. Consequently, "quantity sold" cannot be an attribute in the Inventory table because it can take on multiple values. Instead, the preceding analysis makes it clear that the attribute "quantity sold" pertains to a specific product number on a specific sales invoice. Therefore, it belongs in the M:N relationship table that links the inventory and sales entities.

Price and Cost Data In Table 16-1, notice that information about prices and costs are stored as an attribute in several different tables. For example, the Inventory table stores the suggested list price for the item, which generally remains constant for a given fiscal period. The Sales–Inventory table stores the actual sales price, which varies during the course of the year as a result of sales promotions. Similarly, the standard and actual purchase costs of each item are stored in different tables. The general rule is that time-independent data should be stored as an attribute of a resource or agent, but data that varies across time should be stored with event entities or M:N relationships that link a resource and an event.

Cumulative and Calculable Data Notice that Table 16-1 does not contain cumulative data, such as "quantity-on-hand" in the inventory table, or calculable data, such as "total amount of sale" in the sales table. The reason is that neither type of data item is

needed because those values can be derived from other attributes that are stored. For example, the quantity-on-hand of a given inventory item equals the quantity-on-hand at the beginning of the current fiscal period (an attribute of the Inventory table) plus the total quantity purchased this period (which is itself calculated by summing the quantity received attribute in the Inventory–Receive Inventory table) minus the total quantity sold (which is calculated by summing the quantity sold attribute in the Sales–Inventory table) in this period. Similarly, the total amount of a sales transaction can be calculated by multiplying the quantity sold by the actual sale price of each item sold and summing that result for every row in the Sales–Inventory table that has the same invoice number.

Step 3: Use Foreign Keys to Implement 1:1 and 1:N Relationships

Although 1:1 and 1:N relationships also can be implemented as separate tables, it is usually more efficient to implement them by means of foreign keys. Recall from Chapter 4 that a foreign key is an attribute of one entity that is itself the primary key of another entity. For example, the attribute "customer number" might appear in both the customer and the sales tables. It would be the primary key of the customer table, but a foreign key in the sales table.

Using Foreign Keys to Implement 1:1 Relationships

In a relational database, 1:1 relationships between entities can be implemented by including the primary key of either entity as a foreign key in the table representing the other entity. For purposes of designing a well-structured database, the choice of which table to place the foreign key in is arbitrary. Careful analysis of the minimum cardinalities of the relationship, however, may suggest which approach is likely to be more *efficient*.

 Consider the case of a 1:1 relationship between sales and customer payments (see Figure 15-7, panel A). The minimum cardinality for the Receive Cash event is 0, indicating the existence of credit sales, and the minimum cardinality for the Sale event is 1, indicating that customer payments only occur after a sale has been made (e.g., there are no advance deposits). In this case, including invoice number (the primary key of the sales event) as a foreign key in the Receive Cash event may be more efficient because then only that one table would have to be accessed and updated when processing each customer payment. Moreover, for 1:1 relationships between two sequential events, including the primary key of the event that occurs first as a foreign key in the event that occurs second may improve internal control, because the employee given access to update the table containing data about the second event need not access the table used to store information about the first event. However, the internal control benefits of doing this must be weighed against a possible increase in difficulty of querying the database.

Using Foreign Keys to Implement 1:N Relationships

As with 1:1 relationships, 1:N relationships also can be implemented in relational databases with foreign keys. There is only one way to do this: The primary key of the entity that can be linked to multiple instances of the other entity *must* become a foreign key in that other entity. Thus, in Table 16-1, the primary keys of the Salesperson and Customer tables are included as foreign keys in the Sales table. Similarly, the primary keys of the Cash, Customer, and Cashier tables are included as foreign keys in the Receive Cash table. Notice that reversing this procedure would violate one of the fundamental rules of relational database design. For example, placing invoice number as a foreign key in the Customer table would not work because it can have more than one value (i.e., a given customer may be, and one hopes is, associated with multiple invoice numbers because of participation in many sales transactions).

Note that this is why M:N relationships *must* be implemented as separate tables: Since each entity can be linked to multiple occurrences of the entity on the other side of the relationship, it is not possible to make either entity's primary key a foreign key in the other entity. Consider the M:N relationship between the Sales event and the Inventory resource. Each Sales event may be linked to many different inventory items. Therefore, product number cannot be used as a foreign key in the Sales table because it would be multivalued. Conversely, each product may be involved in many different sales transactions. Therefore, invoice number cannot be used as a foreign key in the Inventory table because it would be multivalued. Thus, the only way to link the Sales and Inventory tables is to create a new table which has separate rows for each actual combination of invoice number and product number. Moreover, notice that in the resulting M:N table a particular invoice number (e.g., 787923) will appear in many different rows, one for each different item that was part of that sales transaction. Conversely, a particular product number (e.g., 12345) will appear in many different rows, once for each different sales transaction in which it was sold. Thus, neither attribute, by itself, uniquely identifies a given row. However, there will be only one row that contains the combination of a particular invoice number and product number (e.g., invoice number 787923 and product number 12345); thus, both attributes together can serve as a primary key for the M:N table.

Completeness Check

The list of attributes that users and management want included in the database provides a means to check and validate the implementation process. Every attribute in that list should appear in at least one table, as either a primary key or "other" attribute.

Checking this list against the table column names may reveal not only the fact that a particular attribute has not been assigned to the appropriate table in the database but may even indicate the need to modify the REA diagram itself. For example, when Paul Stone double-checked the list of desired attributes, he found that he did not have any table in which to place the attribute "product discussed during sales call." In such a situation, the database designer needs to revisit users and management to understand the purpose for collecting that particular attribute. In this case, Fred explains that he plans to have one of his employees call on corporate customers to set up sample displays. Fred wants to collect information about such demonstrations to evaluate their effectiveness.

Paul realizes that this necessitates creating another event entity, Call on Customers, which would be linked to both the Customer and Employee agent tables, the Inventory table, and the Take Customer Order table (see Figure 17-1 on p. 623). The primary key of this new event would be "appointment number." Employee number and customer number would be foreign keys in the table, which would also include attributes for the date and time of the demonstration, along with a text field for comments. Since each demonstration could involve multiple items and each item could be demonstrated in many different calls, there would be a M:N relationship between the Call on Customer event and the Inventory table. The set of rows in that table with the same appointment number would identify which products were shown during a particular sales call. Some calls would result in orders, but others would not. In addition, some orders would occur without any sales call (e.g., because the customer saw an advertisement). Therefore, the minimum cardinality is 0 on each side of the relationship between the Call on Customer and Take Customer Order events. The maximum cardinality on each side of the relationship is 1 to simplify tracking the effect of sales calls.

Paul's need to modify his REA diagram to accommodate additional facts is not unusual. Indeed, it is often useful to create tables and assign attributes to them even before completely finishing an REA diagram. This helps clarify exactly what each entity represents, which often resolves dilemmas about the correct cardinalities for various relationships. The database designer can then modify and refine the REA diagram to include additional entities and relationships to accommodate other facts that are supposed to be in the database but that have not yet been assigned to existing tables.

Once all attributes have been assigned to tables, the basic requirements for designing well-structured relational databases that were discussed in Chapter 4 can be used as a final accuracy check:

1 Every table must have a primary key.
2 Other nonkey attributes in each table must be either a fact about the thing designated by the primary key or foreign keys used to link that table to another table.
3 Every attribute in every table is single-valued (i.e., each table is a flat file).

Note how the set of relational tables listed in Table 16-1 satisfy these three basic requirements. Moreover, they also correspond to Figure 16-4 and, therefore, reflect Fred's Train Shop's business policies. This correspondence also facilitates using the REA diagram to guide the design of queries and reports to retrieve and display information used to evaluate the performance of the organization's business activities.

Using REA Diagrams to Retrieve Information from a Database

Thus far, we have shown how to use the REA data model to guide the design of an AIS that will efficiently store information about an organization's business activities. In this section we refer to Figure 16-4 and Table 16-1 to show how to use completed REA diagrams to facilitate the retrieval of that information to evaluate performance.

At first glance, it may appear that a number of elements found in traditional AIS, such as journals, ledgers, and information about such claims as accounts receivable, are missing. In reality, that information is present but stored in a different format.

Creating Journals and Ledgers

AIS have traditionally included a number of journals and ledgers. Although neither journals nor ledgers appear explicitly in an REA diagram, each can be created through appropriate queries.

Deriving Journals from Queries

In traditional AISs, journals provide a chronological listing of transactions. In a relational database designed according to the REA data model, event entities store information about transactions. Thus, the information normally found in a journal is contained in the tables used to record data about events. For example, the Sales and Sales–Inventory tables contains information about a particular sales transaction. Thus, a sales journal can be produced by writing a query that calculates the amount of sales made during a given period.

Doing so, however, would not necessarily create the traditional sales journal because it would produce a list of *all* sales transactions, including both credit and cash sales. Traditionally, however, sales journals are used to record only *credit* sales. In a relational database built on the REA model, such as the one in Figure 16-4, customer payments are recorded in the Receive Cash event table. Consequently, a query to produce a traditional sales journal (i.e., listing only those sales made on credit) would have to also include both the Receive Cash and the Sales–Receive Cash tables. A database built on the REA model would create a row in the Sales table for each sale of merchandise to a customer and a row in the Receive Cash table to record receipt of payment from a customer. For cash sales,

both rows would have the same values in the date and customer number columns. Therefore, the logic of a query to produce a traditional sales journal would restrict the output to display only those sales that are *not* linked to a corresponding customer payment event (i.e., the same customer number appears in both tables and the amount of the Receive Cash event equals the amount of the sale) that occurred *on the same day* as the Sale event. (Rows in the Receive Cash table with dates later than the date of the corresponding sales transaction represent payments on credit sales.) Similar processes can be followed to write queries to produce other special journals, such as all credit purchases or all cash disbursements not related to payroll.

Ledgers

In traditional AISs, ledgers are master files that contain cumulative information about specific accounts. In a relational database designed according to the REA data model, resource and agent entities contain permanent information that is carried over from one fiscal year to the next. Thus, much of the information about an organization's assets that is traditionally recorded in ledgers is stored in resource tables in an REA-based relational database. For example, each row in the Equipment resource table would contain information about a specific piece or class of machinery, such as its acquisition cost, useful life, depreciation method, and estimated salvage value. Similarly, each row in the Cash resource table contains information about a specific account that holds the organization's cash and cash equivalents, and each row in the Inventory resource table stores information about a specific inventory item.

Each of these resource accounts is affected by increment and decrement events: Equipment is purchased and used; cash is received and disbursed; inventory is purchased and sold. Thus, queries to display the current cumulative balance for these accounts must reference not only the appropriate table for that resource entity but also the event tables that affect it. For example, a query to display the current balance in a specific bank account would reference not only the Cash resource table, to identify the account number and the balance as of the beginning of the current fiscal period, but also the Receive Cash and Disburse Cash tables, to find the inflows and outflows affecting that account during the current fiscal period.

Many financial statement accounts are represented as resources in the REA model. An important exception, however, are claims: Figure 16-4 includes neither an entity called Accounts Receivable nor one called Accounts Payable. As explained in Chapter 15, the reason is that both of these accounts merely represent an imbalance between two related events. Accounts receivable represents sales transactions for which customer payments have not yet been received, and accounts payable represents purchases from suppliers that have not yet been paid for. Therefore, neither accounts receivable nor accounts payable needs to be explicitly stored as separate tables in an REA database. Instead, queries can be written that calculate the amount of each claim as the difference between the sums of the two related events: accounts receivable equals total sales minus total cash received from customers, and accounts payable equals total purchases from suppliers minus total cash disbursements to those suppliers. Moreover, these queries need only be developed one time. They can then be stored and rerun whenever desired.

Table 16-2 (see next page) describes various ways to calculate accounts receivable, depending upon the nature of the relationship between the Sales and Receive Cash events. (Similar logic can be used to write queries to calculate accounts payable.) The query logic presented in Table 16-2 derives the *total* amount of accounts receivable. To derive account balances for each customer, the query logic must be expanded to reference the Customer table and to include the appropriate command (e.g., "group by" in SQL) to perform the calculations separately for each customer. The result of such a query would be a table with a row for each customer and a column showing the

Table 16-2
Query Logic for Calculating Total Accounts Receivable Under Various Relationship Cardinality Scenarios

SITUATION 1: A 1:1 RELATIONSHIP BETWEEN THE SALES AND RECEIVE CASH EVENTS

If the primary key of the Receive Cash event (remittance number) is used as a foreign key in the Sales table, then total accounts receivable can be calculated by querying only the Sales and Sales–Inventory tables. The query logic involves two steps: First identify sales invoice numbers for which there is no remittance number (because a null value for that foreign key indicates that the sale is not linked to any payments from customers, and since all sales are paid for in full by one cash receipt, the entire amount of the sale is still outstanding). Then, for each row in the Sales–Inventory table with a sales invoice number identified in step 1, multiply the quantity sold by the actual sales price.

If the primary key of the Sales table is placed as a foreign key in the Receive Cash table, then the Receive Cash table must also be referenced to calculate total accounts receivable. The first step in the query logic would then involve identifying all sales events whose invoice numbers do not appear as foreign keys in the Receive Cash table. Then, for each row in the Sales–Inventory table with a sales invoice number that does not appear in the Receive Cash table, multiply the quantity sold by the actual sales price.

SITUATION 2: A 1:N RELATIONSHIP BETWEEN THE SALES AND RECEIVE CASH EVENTS

In this situation, invoice number appears as a foreign key in the Receive Cash table. Because customers may make installment payments, at least three queries are required: (1) computing total sales by multiplying the quantity sold and actual sales price columns in the Sales–Inventory table, (2) summing the amount column in the Receive Cash table to calculate total payments received from customers, and (3) a query that calculates the difference between the two previous queries.

SITUATION 3: A 1:N RELATIONSHIP BETWEEN THE RECEIVE CASH AND SALES EVENTS

In this situation, remittance number is a foreign key in the Sales table. Since each sale is paid in full by one customer remittance, the query logic is the same as for situation 1.

SITUATION 4: A M:N RELATIONSHIP BETWEEN THE SALES AND RECEIVE CASH EVENTS

In this case, customers may make installment payments for a particular sales transaction or they may pay for multiple sales transactions in one payment. The amount applied to any particular invoice would be an attribute of the M:N table linking the Sales and Receive Cash events; the total amount remitted would be an attribute of the Receive Cash table. Total accounts receivable can be calculated using the same three queries used in situation 2.

customer's outstanding balance. Another query could be written to sum the account balances in this table, thereby calculating total accounts receivable. A similar set of queries would be needed to display the current balances owed to individual suppliers (i.e., individual accounts payable balances).

Generating Financial Statements

A completed REA diagram can also be used to guide the writing of queries to produce the information that would be included in financial statements. Knowledge about the structure of financial statements and the meaning of individual accounts indicates the desired output of those queries. It is also necessary to understand the REA data model, however, especially the meaning of various cardinality pairs, to know which tables need to be included in each query to generate the correct answers.

Creating Managerial Reports

A major advantage of the REA data model is that it integrates nonfinancial and financial data in the AIS and makes both types of data easily accessible to management. For example, Table 16-1 shows that the Sales table in Figure 16-4 includes an attribute to record the *time* that the sale occurred. Fred can use this data to track sales activity during different times of the day to better plan staffing needs at the Train Shop. Other useful nonfinancial attributes could be included in other tables. For example, the Customer table could be modified to include an attribute that identifies whether a customer has an indoor or outdoor train layout. If Fred can collect this information from his customers, he may be able to better target his advertising to meet each individual customer's interests. In addition, Table 16-1 can be modified easily to integrate data from external sources. For example, to better evaluate the creditworthiness of business customers, Fred may decide to collect information from a credit rating agency, such as Dun & Bradstreet. This information could be added to the database by creating an additional column in the Customer table to store the customer's credit rating. A similar process could be used to store information about suppliers that could be used in the vendor selection process.

In contrast to the REA data model, the general ledger in traditionally designed AISs uses the chart of accounts to store and organize data based on the structure of financial statements. Consequently, nonfinancial information that may be of use to management, such as the time of day a sale occurred or the reason why a customer was purchasing a specific item, is stored apart from the financial data about those transactions. This makes it more difficult for management to easily and quickly access the information it needs. Thus, a major benefit of using the REA model as the basis for designing an AIS is the ability to easily integrate information that traditionally appears in financial statements with other, nonfinancial information necessary to effectively manage operations and evaluate performance.

SUMMARY AND CASE CONCLUSION

REA diagrams for individual transaction cycles depict basic give-to-get economic duality relationships but usually provide only a partial view of resources, showing either how they are acquired or how they are used, but not both. Therefore, individual transaction cycle REA diagrams need to be combined in order to provide a comprehensive enterprise-wide data model. This is usually done by merging resource and event entities that appear in two or more individual REA diagrams. Merging two or more REA diagrams that contain the same resource entity does not require any changes to the cardinality pairs in the individual diagrams. Merging two or more diagrams that contain a common event entity, however, often requires changing the minimum cardinalities associated with the other events to 0, to reflect the fact that the merged event may be connected to any one of several different events, but not to all of them simultaneously. The minimum cardinalities associated with the agents participating in those merged events may also have to be changed to 0.

A data model documented in an REA diagram can be implemented in a relational DBMS in three steps. First, tables are created for all unique entities and M:N relationships in the REA diagram. Second, primary keys and nonkey attributes are assigned to each table. Third, 1:1 and 1:N relationships are implemented by means of foreign keys.

Paul Stone followed these steps to implement a database AIS for Fred's Train Shop based on Figure 16-4. He first created separate tables for each of the 12 distinct entities and 5 M:N relationships in the figure. Next, Paul identified primary keys for each table and used some of them as foreign keys to implement the 1:1 and 1:N relationships in Figure 16-4. He then assigned the remaining attributes that Fred wanted to monitor to the appropriate tables. Paul then demonstrated how easy it was to write queries to retrieve a variety of managerial reports and financial statements from the relational DBMS. Fred was quite impressed and immediately began to use the new system to provide detailed information about the business activities of Fred's Train Shop.

KEY TERMS

concatenated keys 624

AIS IN ACTION

CHAPTER QUIZ

1 Which of the following types of entities *must* become a separate table in a relational database?

 a. resources
 b. events
 c. agents
 d. all of the above

2 How many tables are needed to implement an REA data model that has seven distinct enities, three M:N relationships, and five 1:N relationships in a relational database?

 a. 7
 b. 10
 c. 12
 d. 15

3 Which type of relationship cardinality *must* be implemented in a relational database as a separate table?

 a. 1:1 relationship
 b. 1:N relationship
 c. M:N relationship
 d. all of the above

4 Combining two REA diagrams by merging entities common to both will necessitate changes in cardinality pairs associated with the merged entity if it is a(n)

 a. resource
 b. event
 c. agent
 d. all of the above

5 Information traditionally found in journals is stored in which type of entity in an REA database?

 a. resource
 b. event
 c. agent
 d. all of the above

6 Which of the following tables would most likely have a concatenated primary key?

a. inventory c. inventory-sales

b. sales d. none of the above

7 An REA diagram contains four instances of the Employee entity. How many tables does this require in a relational database?

a. 1 c. 3

b. 2 d. 4

8 The primary key of a M:N relationship between the Receive Inventory and Cash Disbursement events would be

a. receiving report number

b. check number

c. both receiving report number and check number

d. none of the above

9 Which of the following statements is only true about an integrated REA data model?

a. Every event must be linked to at least two agents.

b. Every increment (Get) event must be linked to a decrement (Give) event.

c. Every resource must be linked to at least one increment event and at least one decrement event.

d. Every resource must be linked to at least one agent.

10 In a relational database designed according to the REA data model, information traditionally stored in ledgers can be obtained by querying

a. resources c. agents

b. events d. all of the above

COMPREHENSIVE PROBLEM

Trailspan Travel Club

The Trailspan Travel Club markets travel books across the United States and Canada. Members of the travel club place orders online through Trailspan's Web site, over the phone by calling an 800 number, or by mail. Online orders are entered into the club's computer system automatically. Telephone and mail orders are entered into Trailspan's computer system by the club's sales representatives. Once the orders have been entered, an order notification is sent to the shipping department. A shipping clerk then retrieves the ordered items from inventory and then packs and ships each order. Trailspan only ships complete orders; if an item is temporarily out of stock, it notifies the customer that the entire shipment will be delayed. Once an order has been shipped, the computer system sends an invoice to the member and sends a notification to accounts receivable. Members who do not pay within 30 days are charged 6% interest on their outstanding balance. When making payments, members may pay part or all of their remaining balance. A clerk in the cash receipts department processes all cash receipts and makes deposits into the company's bank account.

When a particular inventory item meets its reorder point, Trailspan's computer system generates a purchase order and the purchasing agent sends the purchase order to the appropriate vendor. Suppliers fill each order individually; sometimes, however, they are out of stock of an item. In such cases, they immediately ship what is in stock and then make a second delivery for items that they had to back order. Once an inventory order is received by the receiving clerk, it is counted and sent to inventory. The cash disbursements clerk pays all vendor invoices individually as they become due to take advantage of any purchase discounts.

Required

 a. Prepare an integrated REA diagram for the revenue and expenditure cycles of Trailspan Travel Club.

 b. Prepare a set of tables to implement your data model in a relational database. Assign every attribute mentioned in the narrative to the appropriate table(s).

DISCUSSION QUESTIONS

16.1 How would the process of generating a cash disbursements journal from the REA data model presented in Figure 16-4 and Table 16-1 differ from the process for creating a sales journal?

16.2 Why take the time to develop separate REA diagrams for each transaction cycle if the ultimate objective is to combine them into one integrated enterprise-wide data model? Why not just focus on the integrated model from the start?

16.3 Building separate tables for every relationship (1:1, 1:N, and M:N) does not violate any of the rules for building a well-structured database. Why then do you think that REA data modelers recommend building separate tables only for M:N relationships and using foreign keys to implement 1:1 and 1:N relationships?

16.4 Assume that there exists a 1:1 relationship between the Receive Inventory and Disburse Cash events. How does the manner in which the relationship between the two events is implemented (i.e., in which table a foreign key is placed) affect the process used to record payments made to suppliers?

16.5 Refer to Figure 16-4 and Table 16-1. How would you determine the amount of cash that Fred's Train Shop has at any point in time?

16.6 Why does Figure 16-4 show only one cash disbursement entity if Fred's Train Shop uses a general operating checking account for purchases of inventory, supplies, and operating expenses such as rent but also uses a separate checking account for payroll?

16.7 Examine Figure 16-4 and Table 16-1. Why do the Inventory, Customers, and Suppliers tables all have an attribute that contains data about the balance at the beginning of the current fiscal period?

PROBLEMS

16.1 Refer to Problems 15.1 and 15.2 for information about the revenue and expenditure cycle activities for Joe's ice-cream shop in order to draw an integrated REA diagram of both cycles.

16.2 Develop a set of tables to implement the integrated REA diagram you developed in Problem 16.1 for Joe's ice-cream shop in a relational database. Specify a primary key for each table, and suggest at least one other attribute that should be included in each table.

16.3 Refer to Problems 15.3 and 15.4 for information about Sue's Gallery's revenue and expenditure cycle activities in order to draw an integrated REA diagram of both cycles.

16.4 Develop a set of tables to implement the integrated REA diagram you developed in Problem 16.3 for Sue's Gallery in a relational database. Specify a primary key for each table, and suggest at least one other attribute that should be included in each table.

16.5 The following tables and attributes exist in a relational database:

Table	Attributes
Vendor	Vendor #, name, street address, city, state
Purchases	P.O. #, date, amount, vendor #, purchasing agent
Inventory Receipts	Receiving report #, date, receiving clerk, remarks, P.O. #
Cash Disbursed	Check #, date, amount
Inventory Receipts—Cash Disbursed	Check #, receiving report #, amount applied to invoice

Required

Draw an REA diagram for this database. State any additional assumptions you need to make about cardinalities.

16.6 Refer to Problems 15.8 and 15.9 for information about the revenue and expenditure cycles for the Computer Warehouse and use that information to draw an integrated REA diagram for both cycles.

16.7 Develop a set of tables to implement the integrated REA diagram you developed in Problem 16.6 for the Computer Warehouse in a relational database. Specify a primary key for each table, and suggest at least one other attribute that should be included in each table.

16.8 The ABC Company sells mass-produced items to retail stores on credit. At the beginning of each month, ABC sends each customer a monthly statement that lists all sales transactions for the previous month. Customers must pay by the 20th of the month. If they have not paid by then, they will not be allowed to make any additional purchases on credit, but will have to pay for all subsequent deliveries at the time of the delivery (C.O.D.). The database for ABC Company's revenue cycle includes the following tables and attributes:

Table Name	Attributes
Inventory	Item #, quantity-on-hand, quantity-available, standard cost, list price, discount allowed (Y/N), description, weight
Customer	Customer #, name, zip code, account balance, credit limit
Take Customer Order	Order #, date, total amount of order, instructions
Customer Order–Inventory	Order #, item #, quantity ordered, price per unit

Required

a. List the control procedures that should be applied to every new customer order. (*Hint:* you may wish to review Chapter 10 for a description of common threats and control procedures, and Chapter 8 for a description of various input controls.) Identify the attribute(s) to which a particular control applies, explain the purpose of the control, and explain how the control accomplishes that purpose.

b. Design a form in Access (or any DBMS to which you have access) to record customer orders. Implement the controls you listed in step a in your form.

16.9 Refer to Figure 16.4 and Table 16-1 to write the query logic needed to answer the following questions. (Optional: If requested by your instructor, write your queries in SQL or a Query-By-Example graphical interface.) Some answers may require more than one query—try to write the most efficient queries possible.

a. Total accounts payable
b. Accounts payable for all suppliers in Arizona
c. Total amount of a sale to a customer named Smith

d. Total wages payable
e. Total wage expense
f. Net increase (decrease) in quantity-on-hand for a particular inventory item
g. The proportion of sales made to walk-in customers (i.e., no order)
h. The salesperson who made the largest amount of sales in October
i. The salesperson who made the most sales in October
j. The most popular item, in terms of total units sold

16.10 Refer to Problem 15.10 and develop a set of tables to implement the REA diagram you developed for Stan's Southern Barbeque Supply Store. Identify the primary and foreign keys for each table, and don't forget to address any M:N relationships.

CASE 16-1 Practical Database Design

Hands-on practice in database design is important. Use a relational DBMS to implement the integrated REA data model presented in this chapter, or one of the integrated data models from the homework problems, or a model provided by your instructor. Then, perform the following tasks:

1 Write a query to calculate total accounts receivable.
2 Write a query to calculate accounts receivable for a specific customer.
3 Create a sales invoice form that references the appropriate tables and inputs data about attributes into the proper tables.
4 Write queries to develop an income statement and a balance sheet from your database (or at least those portions of each statement that are included in your data model).
5 Design appropriate input controls to ensure the validity of data entered in the form created in step 3.

AIS IN ACTION SOLUTIONS

QUIZ KEY

1 Which of the following types of entities *must* become a separate table in a relational database?
 a. resources (Incorrect. All three types of entities become separate tables.)
 b. events (Incorrect. All three types of entities become separate tables.)
 c. agents (Incorrect. All three types of entities become separate tables.)
 ✔ **d.** all of the above (Correct. All three types of entities become separate tables.)

2 How many tables are needed to implement an REA data model that has seven distinct enities, three M:N relationships, and five 1:N relationships in a relational database?
 a. 7 (Incorrect. There must be 10 tables, one for each distinct entity and one for each M:N relationship.)
 ✔ **b.** 10 (Correct. There must be 10 tables, one for each distinct entity and one for each M:N relationship.)
 c. 12 (Incorrect. There must be 10 tables, one for each distinct entity and one for each M:N relationship.)
 d. 15 (Incorrect. There must be 10 tables, one for each distinct entity and one for each M:N relationship.)

3 Which type of relationship cardinality *must* be implemented in a relational database as a separate table?
 a. 1:1 relationship (Incorrect. Only M:N relationships must be implemented as separate tables in a relational database. Foreign keys can be used to implement 1:N and 1:1 relationships.)
 b. 1:N relationship (Incorrect. Only M:N relationships must be implemented as separate tables in a relational database. Foreign keys can be used to implement 1:N and 1:1 relationships.)
 ✔ **c.** M:N relationship (Correct. Only M:N relationships must be implemented as separate tables in a relational database. Foreign keys can be used to implement 1:N and 1:1 relationships.)
 d. All of the above (Incorrect. Only M:N relationships must be implemented as separate tables in a relational database. Foreign keys can be used to implement 1:N and 1:1 relationships.)

4 Combining two REA diagrams by merging entities common to both will necessitate changes in cardinality pairs associated with the merged entity if it is a(n)
 a. resource (Incorrect. The minimum cardinality may need to be changed when merging events common to two REA diagrams, but not when merging resources or agents.)
 ✔ **b.** event (Correct. The minimum cardinality may need to be changed when merging events common to two REA diagrams, but not when merging resources or agents.)
 c. agent (Incorrect. The minimum cardinality may need to be changed when merging events common to two REA diagrams, but not when merging resources or agents.)
 d. all of the above (Incorrect. The minimum cardinality may need to be changed when merging events common to two REA diagrams, but not when merging resources or agents.)

5 Information traditionally found in journals is stored in which type of entity in an REA database?
 a. resource (Incorrect. Journals are transaction files. Event entities store information about transactions. Resource tables store some of the information that would be contained in ledgers.)
 ✔ **b.** event (Correct. Journals are transaction files. Event entities store information about transactions. Therefore, information found in journals is stored in event tables.)
 c. agent (Incorrect. Journals are transaction files. Event entities store information about transactions. Therefore, information found in journals is stored in event tables.)
 d. all of the above (Incorrect. Journals are transaction files. Event entities store information about transactions. Therefore, information found in journals is stored in event tables.)

6 Which of the following tables would most likely have a concatenated primary key?
 a. inventory (Incorrect. Although any entity may have a concatenated key, few do except for M:N relationships, which must have concatenated primary keys.)
 b. sales (Incorrect. Although any entity may have a concatenated key, few do except for M:N relationships, which must have concatenated primary keys.)
 ✔ **c.** inventory-sales (Correct. Although any entity may have a concatenated key, few do except for M:N relationships, which must have concatenated primary keys.)

d. none of the above (Incorrect. Although any entity may have a concatenated key, few do except for M:N relationships, which must have concatenated primary keys.)

7 An REA diagram contains four instances of the Employee entity. How many tables does this require in a relational database?

✔ **a.** 1 (Correct. Multiple occurrences of the same entity in an REA diagram improve readability, but only one table is needed for each distinct entity.)

b. 2 (Incorrect. Multiple occurrences of the same entity in an REA diagram improve readability, but only one table is needed for each distinct entity.)

c. 3 (Incorrect. Multiple occurrences of the same entity in an REA diagram improve readability, but only one table is needed for each distinct entity.)

d. 4 (Incorrect. Multiple occurrences of the same entity in an REA diagram improve readability, but only one table is needed for each distinct entity.)

8 The primary key of a M:N relationship between the Receive Inventory and Cash Disbursement Events would be

a. receiving report number (Incorrect. M:N relationships have concatenated primary keys that consist of the primary key of each entity participating in that relationship.)

b. check number (Incorrect. M:N relationships have concatenated primary keys that consist of the primary key of each entity participating in that relationship.)

✔ **c.** both receiving report number and check number (Correct. M:N relationships have concatenated primary keys that consist of the primary key of each entity participating in that relationship.)

d. none of the above (Incorrect. M:N relationships have concatenated primary keys that consist of the primary key of each entity participating in that relationship.)

9 Which of the following statements is only true about an integrated REA data model?

a. Every event must be linked to at least two agents. (Incorrect. This is true of any REA model.)

b. Every increment (Get) event must be linked to a decrement (Give) event. (Incorrect. This is true of any REA diagram.)

✔ **c.** Every resource must be linked to at least one increment event and at least one decrement event. (Correct. This is a unique feature of, and is the reason for, integrating multiple REA diagrams.)

d. Every resource must be linked to at least one agent. (Incorrect. This is not true of any REA diagram.)

10 In a relational database designed according to the REA data model, information traditionally stored in ledgers can be obtained by querying

a. resources (Incorrect. To obtain the information traditionally found in a ledger often involves querying not only resource tables but also event and agent tables as well.)

b. events (Incorrect. To obtain the information traditionally found in a ledger often involves querying not only resource tables but also event and agent tables as well.)

c. agents (Incorrect. To obtain the information traditionally found in a ledger often involves querying not only resource tables but also event and agent tables as well.)

✔ **d.** all of the above (Correct. To obtain the information traditionally found in a ledger often involves querying not only resource tables but also event and agent tables as well.)

Part a Prepare an integrated REA diagram for Trailspan Travel Club's revenue and expenditure cycles.

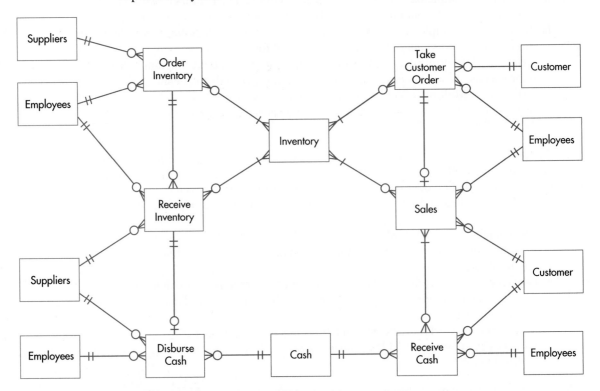

Explanation of Relationships and Cardinalities

The relationships between the agent and event entities are all modeled as 1:N with 0 minimums from the agent to the event and 1 minimums in the reverse direction. This reflects standard practice: Every event must involve at least one agent, but a given agent may or may not be involved in any particular event. Moreover, for accountability purposes, every event is linked to only one specific internal and one specific external agent, but both types of agents may be linked to many different events.

The cardinalities of the relationships between the Cash resource and the Disburse Cash and Receive Cash events are also standard. Each event must be linked to a cash account (hence the minimum of 1) and for accountability purposes is linked to only one cash account (hence the maximum of 1). Conversely, some cash accounts may never be linked to any Disburse Cash or Receive Cash events (hence the minimum cardinality is 0), but other cash accounts may be linked to many such events (hence the maximum cardinality is N).

The cardinalities of the relationships between the Inventory resource and the four events that affect it are also standard for retail organizations that sell mass-produced goods: They are all M:N. This reflects the fact that a given product number may be linked to many different events, and any given event may involve multiple products. The minimums are 0 going to the event entities for two reasons: (1) to allow the organization to add information about new products prior to engaging in any transactions involving those products and (2) because the event tables are empty at the beginning of each new fiscal year. The minimum cardinalities are 1 in the reverse direction because every event must involve at least one inventory item.

The relationship between the Order Inventory and Receive Inventory events is 1:N because Trailspan's suppliers sometimes are out of items ordered and therefore must make more than one delivery to fill a particular order. Trailspan's suppliers do not hold

and aggregate its orders, however, which is why each Receive Inventory event is linked to at most one Order event. The minimum cardinalities reflect the fact that orders precede deliveries from suppliers.

The relationship between the Receive Inventory and Disburse Cash events is 1:1 because Trailspan's policy is to pay for each vendor invoice separately, in order to take advantage of discounts for prompt payment. Thus, it cuts separate checks for each delivery received, and each check pays for only one specific delivery. The minimum cardinalities reflect the fact that Trailspan does not pay for its purchases in advance.

The relationship between Take Customer Orders and Sales is 1:1 because Trailspan fills each customer order separately but does not do so until it can completely fill each order. The minimum cardinalities reflect the fact that orders precede sales.

The relationship between the Sales and Receive Cash events is M:N because Trailspan allows its customers to make installment payments on any given sale and also allows them to periodically pay for multiple sales transactions that occurred during the prior months. The minimum cardinalities reflect the fact that Trailspan does not require customers to ever pay in advance for sales.

Part b Prepare tables for each entity. The following table lists the tables that would be created to implement this data into a relational database. Note that each entity and M:N relationship has a table and that primary keys (the unique identifiers for each table), foreign keys (the fields that each table holds in common), and table attributes (the characteristics of each table) are also identified.

Table	Primary Key	Foreign Keys	Attributes
Employee	Employee number		Name, address, data hired
Customer	Customer number		Name, address, credit limit, account balance beginning current period
Supplier	Supplier number		Name, address, account balance beginning current period
Order Inventory	Purchase order number	Supplier number, employee number	Date, comments
Receive Inventory	Receiving report number	Supplier number, employee number, purchase order number	Remarks, vendor's invoice number
Disburse Cash	Check number	Supplier number, employee number, account number, receiving report number	Amount, description
Inventory	Item number		Description, list price
Cash	Account number		Balance beginning current period, type of account
Take Customer Order	Sales order number	Customer number, employee number	Date, comments
Sale	Invoice number	Customer number, employee number, sales order number	Date, time
Receive Cash	Remittance number	Customer number, employee number, account number	Date, total amount
Inventory—Order Inventory	Item number, purchase order number		Quantity ordered
Inventory—Receive Inventory	Item number, receiving report number		Quantity received
Inventory—Take Customer Order	Item number, sales order number		Quantity ordered, price
Inventory—Sales	Item number, invoice number		Quantity sold, actual sales price
Sales—Receive Cash	Invoice number, remittance number		Amount applied to invoice

CHAPTER 17

LEARNING OBJECTIVES

After studying this chapter, you should be able to:

- Develop REA data models for a variety of organizations besides retail stores.

- Develop REA data models for the HR/payroll, manufacturing, and capital assets transaction cycles.

Special Topics in REA Modeling

INTEGRATIVE CASE PAUL STONE, CONSULTING

Paul Stone had enjoyed designing a database for Fred's Train Shop so much that he decided he wanted to do similar work for other local businesses. First, however, he realized that he needed to acquire some additional skills. Although he felt confident of his ability to model the activities of retail businesses like Fred's Train Shop, Paul knew that he needed to learn more about how to model other types of businesses, such as manufacturing and those that provided services.

Paul began searching the Internet for information about data modeling and database design. He found a link to a workshop on REA data modeling that was being offered by the American Accounting Association. After reading about it, Paul was certain that it was exactly what he was looking for. He registered for the class. He then prepared a list of the situations that he wanted to learn how to model:

- ▶ How do you model the revenue cycle activities of a business that provides services, such as computer or automotive repairs? What about a business that rents items instead of selling them?
- ▶ How do you model the production cycle activities of a manufacturer?
- ▶ How do you integrate payroll activities with other HR processes, such as hiring and training employees?
- ▶ How do you model financing transactions, such as the issuance of stock or debt?

Introduction

The previous two chapters introduced the topic of REA data modeling and explained how to implement an REA model in a relational database. Both chapters focused primarily on the revenue and expenditure cycle activities for a typical retail organization. This chapter extends those basic concepts to a variety of other types of businesses and transaction cycles. We begin by examining more complex models of the revenue and expenditure cycles, including some additional activities typically performed by manufacturers and distributors and other special situations. Then we discuss how to model basic business activities in the production, HR, and financing cycles. We conclude by presenting a comprehensive integrated REA model that incorporates many of the topics presented in this chapter.

Additional Revenue Cycle Modeling Topics

The revenue cycle REA models developed in Chapters 15 and 16 focused on the activities performed by a typical retail store: taking customer orders, filling those orders, and collecting payment for sales from customers. Manufacturers, distributors, and other types of businesses often engage in additional activities, such as sales calls on customers and the picking and packing of orders by warehouse staff, that management wants to monitor. Figure 17-1 presents a revenue cycle REA diagram that includes these additional events. Table 17-1 (see page 646) lists the tables that would be required to implement this model in a relational database and also lists many of the attributes that would likely be stored in each of those tables.

Additional Events

Many of the entities and relationships depicted in Figure 17-1 have already been discussed in previous chapters, so we will focus only on those aspects that are new. Figure 17-1 separates the warehouse activity of filling an order from the activity of actually shipping or delivering that order to the customer. Thus, each instance of the Fill Customer Order event represents the picking and packing of an order by a warehouse employee. The meaning of the cardinality pairs between that event and the inventory resource and participating agents should be understood from discussions in the previous two chapters. The relationship between the Take Customer Order and Fill Customer Order events is represented as being one-to-many (1:N). The minimum cardinalities reflect the fact that two events occur sequentially. The maximum cardinalities reflect the fact that sometimes the company may be out of stock of one or more items that were ordered. Therefore, it may take multiple warehouse activities to completely fill a particular order. Each customer order has to be individually picked and packed, however. The relationship between the Fill Customer Order and Ship Order events is 1:1. The minimum cardinalities reflect the fact that the two events are sequential. The maximum cardinalities are typical best practices followed by most companies. Once all the items that were ordered and in stock have been picked and packed, that entire package is shipped intact to the customer. Note that the Ship Order event occurs when the merchandise is given to the customer (i.e., it is the Sale event). Thus, if formal sales invoices are prepared, there would be a separate invoice for each filled order. Thus, for proper accountability each Ship Order event is linked to one, and only one, Fill Customer Order event. It is true that oftentimes many different orders are placed on the same truck or railroad car. However, producing accurate financial records requires tracking each individual "shipment" (sale) on that truckload/carload separately.

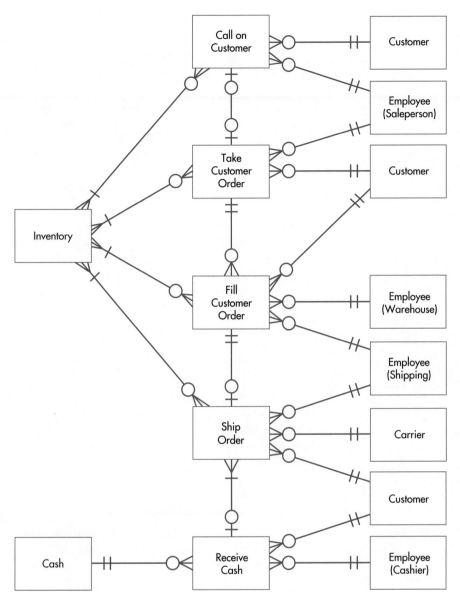

Figure 17-1
Extended Partial Revenue Cycle REA Diagram

Attribute Placement

Table 17-1 shows that the primary key of the Ship Order event is the shipment number. The bill of lading number is another attribute, but it is not the primary key because it may be null for deliveries made using the company's own trucks. Sales invoice number is another attribute of the shipment event. It is not the primary key, however, because as discussed in Chapters 10 and 11, many companies are moving to eliminate the printing of paper invoices and even the creation of electronic ones. Moreover, even when invoices are still used, they may not be generated at the time the merchandise is shipped. Therefore, if invoice number were the primary key, information about the shipment could not be recorded until the invoice was generated. For companies that do still use invoices, however, the invoice number attribute serves an important internal control function: Examination of the value of this attribute provides an easy means of verifying whether all shipments have indeed been billed and recorded (a null value means that an invoice has not yet been prepared).

Also notice that Table 17-1 shows that information about prices and costs is stored in several places. The Inventory table contains information about the standard (list) price and standard cost of each item because those values are typically constant for the

Table 17-1
Attributes for Relational Tables in Figure 17-1

Table Name	Primary Key	Foreign Keys	Other Attributes
Inventory	Product number		Description, unit standard cost, unit list price, weight, reorder point, quantity-on-hand at beginning of current fiscal period
Cash	General ledger account number		Name, balance at beginning of current fiscal period, type of account
Call On Customer	Call number	Customer number, salesperson (employee) number	Date, time, purpose
Take Customer Order	Sales order number	Customer number, salesperson (employee) number, call number	Date, time, terms, desired delivery date
Fill Customer Order	Picking ticket number	Sales order number, customer number, warehouse employee number, shipping employee number	Date, time, comments
Ship Order	Shipment number	Picking ticket number, customer number, shipping employee number, carrier number, remittance number	Date, time, bill-of-lading number, invoice number
Receive Cash	Remittance number	Customer number, employee number, cash account number	Date, time, amount received
Employees	Employee number		Name, date hired, date of birth, number of dependents, pay rate, other tax/withholding information, job title
Customers	Customer number		Name, address, credit limit, balance at beginning of current fiscal period
Carriers	Carrier number		Name, contact phone
Inventory—Call_on_Customers	Product number, Call number		Comments
Inventory—Take_Customer_Order	Product number, sales order number		Quantity ordered, price per unit
Inventory—Fill_Order	Product number, picking ticket number		Quantity picked
Inventory—Ship_Order	Product number, shipment number		Quantity shipped

entire fiscal year. The Take_Customer_Order–Inventory table, however, contains information about not only the quantity ordered but also the actual price and accounting cost assigned to each item. This reflects the fact that companies may change prices several times during the year. Thus, although the list price is constant, the actual sales price depends on when the sale occurs. Similarly, although the standard cost for each

item is constant during the year, the calculated cost (which may be determined using either FIFO, LIFO, weighted-average, or specific identification) will vary throughout the year, especially if a perpetual inventory system is used.

New REA Feature—Employee Roles

Finally, notice that Figure 17-1 explicitly identifies the different employees who participate in each event by their job functions. This makes it easier to use the REA diagram itself as a guide to verify whether duties are properly segregated. However, as shown in Table 17-1, only one employee table is required, which includes the attribute "job title" to identify each employee's primary function.

Sale of Services

Thus far, all our modeling examples have focused on businesses that sell tangible inventory. Businesses like automotive repair shops, however, generate revenue from both the sale of products and the provision of services. Figure 17-2 presents a partial REA model of the revenue cycle for such a company.

The Services entity in Figure 17-2 contains information about the organization's revenue-generating activities. Each row identifies a specific type of service the company provides. For example, the Services table for an automotive repair shop might include individual rows for oil changes and brake replacement. Each row would include information about the standard ("book") time it should take to complete the service and the standard (regular) price charged for that type of repair.

Figure 17-2 includes relationships between the Sales event and both the Services and Inventory Resource entities. The nature of the cardinality of those relationships depends on the specific business, but usually both relationships will be modeled as being M:N because most businesses provide the same types of services to many different customers, using standard mass-produced parts. The minimum and maximum cardinalities in Figure 17-2 are typical for businesses like automotive and appliance repairs. For such businesses, every sales transaction must involve at least one specific type of service but may include several services (e.g., a customer may require an oil change and brake repairs). However, some repair services, such as fixing a flat tire, may not involve the use of any identifiable inventory parts, requiring only labor.

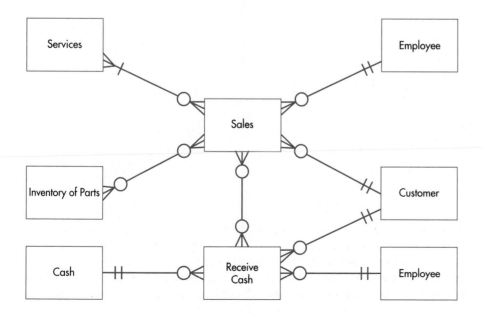

Figure 17-2
Partial Revenue Cycle
for Sale of Services

Digital Assets

What about digital assets? Companies that sell software, music, or digital photographs over the Internet give up a digital copy of those resources, but not the actual resource itself. How does this affect the REA model of the revenue cycle? It doesn't. Such companies still need to collect information about orders for and delivery of those digital assets, along with receipt of payments from their customers. Those companies also need an Inventory table so that customers can see what products are available for sale. The structure of that Inventory table is almost identical to that of mass-produced merchandise. The only difference is that because sales involve only a digital copy of the resource, there is no need for attributes such as quantity-on-hand, quantity-available, reorder point, and standard reorder quantity. However, the Inventory table will still include information about the standard list price of each item and its description.

Rental Transactions

Some businesses generate revenue through rental transactions, rather than sales. Thus, the basic give-to-get economic exchange involves the temporary use of a resource in return for both the receipt of cash and the subsequent return of the resource being rented. Figure 17-3 shows how to model such transactions.

Businesses that rent equipment or other resources want to track each physical item separately. Therefore, the primary key for the rental inventory table is some kind of unique serial number, rather than a part number. Each Rent Item event records information about the rental of one specific item, such as the date and time it was rented, the rental price, and any specific terms of the agreement. If a customer rents multiple items, the system treats this as a set of rental events, each for one particular inventory item. This facilitates tracking the status of each piece of Rental Inventory. For example, a query to determine whether an item is still outstanding needs to reference only the Rental and Return events; in contrast, if the rental of five items had been recorded as one event, then the preceding query would also have to include the M:N relationship table linking the Rental event and Rental

Figure 17-3
Partial Revenue Cycle for
Rental Transactions

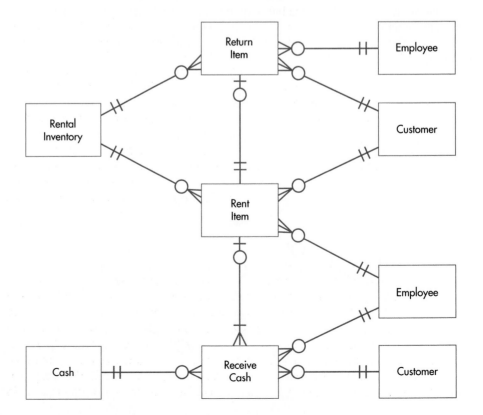

Inventory entity. (Note: this is transparent to the customer. The customer simply completes the required paperwork and pays the specified amount and neither knows, nor cares, that the system created several rows in the database, instead of one, to record the transaction.)

Figure 17-3 shows that the Rent Item event is linked to both the Receive Cash and Return Item events. Examine the relationship from the Rent Item to the Receive Cash event. The minimum cardinality of 1 reflects the fact that customers typically pay first, prior to taking possession of the item. The maximum cardinality is many because there may be additional charges imposed when the item is returned. The cardinality pair associated with the Rent Item event has a 0 minimum and 1 maximum because the Receive Cash event occurs first and is linked to one, and only one, specific rental event. The relationship between the Rent Item and Return Item events is 1:1 to reflect the fact that the rental of each specific item is individually tracked, as is its return; moreover, each item rented can be returned at most one time. The minimum cardinalities on each side of the relationship reflect the temporal sequence of the two events (i.e., an item is rented before it is returned).

Additional Expenditure Cycle Modeling Topics

Figure 17-4 (see next page) presents an expanded expenditure cycle REA diagram that includes internal requests for purchases. Table 17-2 (see page 651) lists the tables that would be required to implement this model in a relational database and also lists many of the attributes that would likely be stored in each of those tables.

Additional Events

Most of the entities and relationships depicted in Figure 17-4 have been explained in the previous two chapters. One new entity is the Request Inventory event. Many larger organizations want to formally approve requests to purchase goods; the Request Inventory event provides a way to collect data about such activities. Each instance of this event represents a request to purchase one or more items. Both cardinality pairs linking the Request Inventory event to the Order Inventory event have a minimum cardinality of 0 and a maximum of many. The 0 minimum associated with the Order Inventory event reflects the fact that requests occur before actual orders; in addition, some requests are denied and thus are never linked to an order. The 0 minimum associated with the Request Inventory event reflects the fact that some orders are generated automatically by the inventory control system, rather than as a result of a specific request. The maximum associated with the Order Inventory event is many because some requests may be for several different items, each of which may be normally obtained from different sources. Separate purchase orders are needed for each different supplier. Therefore, an approved request may be linked to several different orders. The maximum cardinality associated with the Request Inventory event is many to reflect the common practice of combining different requests for items provided by the same supplier into one larger order to obtain better terms.

Attribute Placement

Table 17-2 shows that cost information is stored in several tables. Standard cost is stored as an attribute of the Inventory table because it is the same for all units of a given inventory item for a fiscal year. In contrast, the actual cost of inventory is stored in the Inventory–Order_Inventory table. This reflects the fact that purchase prices can vary over time. By storing the cost of each order with the quantity purchased, the system can calculate the actual cost of ending inventory and the cost of goods sold according to any accepted inventory valuation method (LIFO, FIFO, weighted-average, or specific identification). If, on the other hand, actual cost were stored as an

Figure 17-4
Extended REA Diagram for
Expenditure Cycle

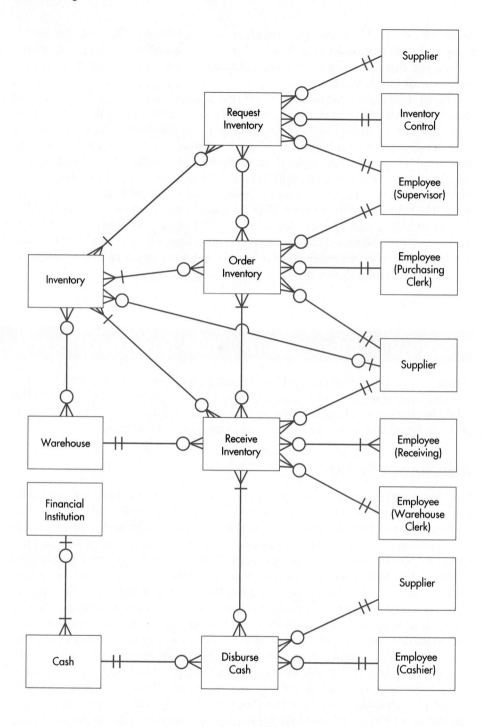

attribute of the Inventory table, it would necessitate using the weighted-average
method because all units of a given inventory item would be assigned the same cost. In
addition, cost data would be available only in this format; it would be impossible to
compute alternative values for inventory because the detailed data about the cost asso-
ciated with each purchase would not be stored in the database.

New REA Feature—M:N Agent-Event Relationships

Figure 17-4 depicts the relationship between the Receive Inventory event and employ-
ees as being M:N. This reflects the fact that many deliveries are so large that several
employees must work together to unload and store the items. M:N agent-event rela-
tionships occur whenever an activity is performed by more than one employee, yet
management wants to retain the ability to monitor each individual's performance.

Table 17-2
Attributes for Relational Tables in Figure 17-4

Table Name (Entity)	Primary Key	Foreign Keys	Other Attributes
Inventory	Product number		Description, unit standard cost, unit list price, weight, reorder point, quantity-on-hand at beginning of fiscal period
Warehouse	Warehouse number		Name, address, capacity
Financial Institution	Institution number		Name, contact phone, type of institution
Cash	General ledger account number	Financial institution number	Name, balance at beginning of fiscal period, type of account
Request Inventory	Purchase requisition number	Supplier number, employee (inventory control) number, employee (supervisor) number	Date, reason
Order Inventory	Purchase order number	Supplier number, employee (purchasing clerk) number, employee (supervisor) number	Date, comments
Receive Inventory	Receiving report number	Warehouse number, supplier number, employee (receiving) number, employee (warehouse) number	Date, time, remarks, vendor's invoice number
Disburse Cash	Check number	Supplier number, employee number, cash account number	Date, amount, memo
Suppliers	Supplier number		Name, contact phone, rating
Employees	Employee number		Name, date hired, date of birth, number of dependents, pay rate, other tax/withholding information
Inventory—Request_Inventory	Product number, purchase requisition number		Quantity requested
Inventory—Order_Inventory	Product number, purchase order number		Quantity ordered, cost per unit
Inventory—Receive_Inventory	Product number, receiving report number		Quantity received, condition
Inventory—Warehouse	Product number, warehouse number		Quantity stored
Request_Inventory—Order_Inventory	Purchase requisition number, purchase order number		
Order_Inventory—Receive_Inventory	Purchase order number, receiving report number		
Receive_Inventory—Disburse_Cash	Receiving report number, check number		Amount applied to invoice

New REA Feature—Locations

Figure 17-4 introduces two new entities: Warehouses and Financial Institutions. These entities store information about the location where resources are stored and where certain events take place. Many companies have multiple warehouses. The cardinality pairs linking the warehouse and inventory entities reflect several common situations. A warehouse can, occasionally, be empty but usually stores many different inventory items. Conversely, the same inventory items may be stored in several different warehouses. Sometimes companies may also want to maintain information about inventory that they do not normally carry.

Note also that linking the Receive Inventory event to the Warehouse entity makes it possible to evaluate performance at different locations. Events, such as Receive Inventory, can only occur at a specific location; conversely, many events can occur at the same location. Therefore, Figure 17-4 depicts the relationship between Warehouses and Receive Inventory as 1:N.

Examination of Table 17-2 shows that the Financial Institution entity clarifies the nature of the Cash entity. Each row in the Cash table corresponds to a specific general ledger account that is aggregated in the balance sheet under the heading "Cash and Cash equivalents." The cardinality pairs associated with the Financial Institution and Cash entities reflect common business practices. A specific cash account can only be located at one financial institution and some accounts, like "Petty Cash," are not on deposit anywhere. Companies also typically only keep information about financial institutions with which they have accounts but may have more than one account at the same financial institution.

New REA Feature—Relationships Between Resources and Agents

Figure 17-4 also includes a relationship between the Inventory entity (a Resource) and the Supplier entity (an Agent). This relationship reflects the common best practice of identifying preferred and alternative suppliers for specific inventory items. Similar relationships between resources and employees can be used to model responsibility and accountability.

Acquisition of Intangible Services

In addition to purchasing inventory, equipment, and buildings, organizations also acquire various intangible services, such as Internet access, telephone service, and utilities. Figure 17-5 shows how to model such activities.

The basic give-to-get economic exchange involves acquiring various services and paying for them. Payments for those services are included in the Disburse Cash table. A separate event, Acquire Services, is used to collect data about the acquisition of those services. This event entity stores information about the actual amount of the service consumed and the actual price charged. In Figure 17-5, this event is linked to a resource labeled "General and Administrative Services" that reflects the financial accounting treatment for these items. That resource entity includes information about the intangible resource, such as the length of the contract, if any, its starting date, the budgeted cost for that service, the budgeted or standard amount to be provided each period, and a description of any limitations or special requirements associated with its use.

The relationship between the acquisition event and the resource entity is modeled as 1:N in Figure 17-5 because in most cases each service (telephone, electricity, etc.) is acquired separately, usually from a different supplier. The relationship between the Acquire Services and Disburse Cash events is modeled as 1:1 to reflect the common situation in which the organization obtains the use of a specific service for a particular

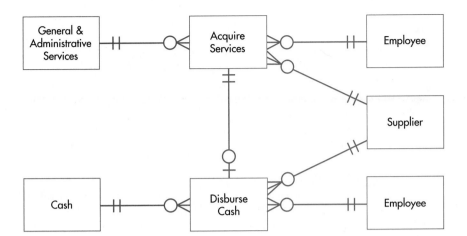

Figure 17-5
Partial Expenditure Cycle for Acquisition of Services

period of time and makes a payment each month for the services it acquired and used that month.

Rental Transactions

Organizations sometimes rent, rather than purchase, resources. For example, many organizations rent office spaces and warehouses. The basic economic give-to-get exchange involves payments to the supplier for the right to use a resource for a specific period of time. Information about the payment event is included in the Disburse Cash table. A separate Rent Resource event may be created to represent the acquisition of the resource, because that event will probably collect information about different attributes than those that are relevant to the receipt of inventory. Although it is rented and not owned, the resource itself would also be included in the model as a separate entity because organizations will likely need to maintain much of the same kind of information (e.g., location, description, etc.) about rented resources as they do for resources that are owned. Rented and owned resources may be represented in separate entities, however, because each may contain a number of attributes not relevant to the other (e.g., information about rental contract terms, acquisition cost, depreciation method, etc.). In addition, if the rented resource must be returned (e.g., rental of equipment), then another event will need to be included in the REA diagram to record that activity. In that case, the Rent Resource event would be linked to two events: Disburse Cash and the Return of the resource, forming a mirror image of the REA model of the renting organization's revenue cycle activities discussed earlier.

Production Cycle REA Model

Figure 17-6 is a data model for the basic production cycle activities of a manufacturing company and Table 17-3 lists the tables required to implement that model in a relational database, along with the placement of various attributes. Accurate product cost management and performance evaluation of production cycle activities requires collecting detailed information about the use of raw materials, labor, and machinery to produce finished products. Thus, there are four main events of interest included in a typical production cycle REA diagram:

1 Issuance of raw materials
2 Use of labor in production
3 Use of machinery and equipment in production
4 Production of new finished products, represented by the work-in-process event

Figure 17-6
Partial REA Diagram for
Production Cycle

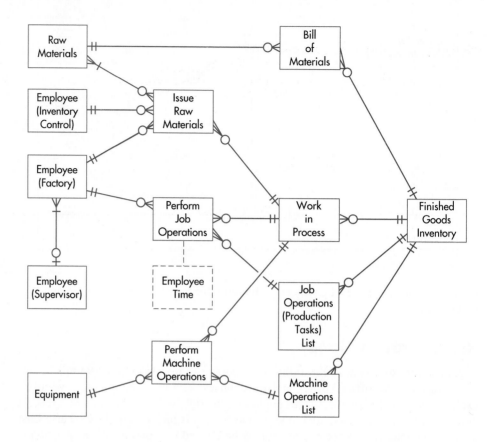

Additional Entities—Intellectual Property

Figure 17-6 includes three special types of entities—the Bill of Materials, the Job Operations List, and the Machine Operations List—that store important portions of a manufacturing company's intellectual property. The Bill of Materials entity contains information about the raw materials used to make a finished product. As Table 17-3 shows, this includes data about the *standard* quantity of each raw material that should be used to make that product. Thus, the bill of materials can be thought of as the list of ingredients in a recipe. By itself, however, such a list is not sufficient to manufacture a product—instructions concerning how to combine those components, including the proper sequence of steps, are also needed. The Job Operations List entity stores the instructions concerning labor activities, and the Machine Operations List entity stores the instructions for actions to be performed using various pieces of equipment. Both entities also store data about the *standard* time it should take to perform those operations.

Figure 17-6 shows 1:N relationships between the Bill of Materials entity and both the Raw Materials and Finished Goods inventory entities. Each row in the Bill of Materials entity specifies how much of a specific raw material is needed to make a particular finished good; thus, each row represents the information that would be found on one line of a Bill of Materials list. This reflects the fact that the same raw material (e.g., 12-gauge wire) may be used in five different products, with a different amount used to make each product. The relationship between the Raw Materials entity and the Issue Raw Materials event is M:N because the same raw materials can be related to many different events of issuing that raw material; conversely, often all of the different materials needed to manufacture a product are issued at the same time; hence, one Issue Raw Materials event can be linked to many different lines in the Raw Materials table.

The relationships between the Finished Goods Inventory resource and both the Job Operations List and Machine Operations List entities are 1:N. This reflects the fact that each row in the list entities represents information about a specific activity

Table 17-3
Attributes for Relational Tables in Figure 17-6

Table Name (Entity)	Primary Key	Foreign Keys	Other Attributes
Raw Materials[a]	RM item number		Description, standard unit cost, reorder point, quantity on hand at beginning of current fiscal period
Employees	Employee number		Name, date hired, date of birth, number of dependents, pay rate, other tax/withholding information, job title
Equipment	Equipment ID number		Description, acquisition cost, depreciation method, depreciation life, salvage value
Issue Raw Materials	RM issue number	Employee (inventory control) number, employee (factory) number, WIP job number	Date, time, comments
Perform Job Operations	Job operation number	Employee number, WIP job number, job operations list number	Date, time started, time finished
Perform Machine Operations	Machine operation number	Equipment ID number, WIP job number, machine operations list number	Date, time started, time finished
Bill of Materials	Bill of materials number	Finished good product number, raw materials item number	Standard quantity needed
Work in Process	WIP job number	Finished good product number	Date/time started, date/time completed, target completion date, quantity ordered, quantity produced, production order number
Job Operations List	Job operations list number	Finished good product number	Instructions, standard time for operation
Machine Operations List	Machine operations list number	Finished good product number	Instructions, standard time for operation
Finished Goods Inventory[a]	Product number		Description, unit standard cost, unit list price, weight, quantity-on-hand at beginning of current fiscal period
Raw Materials—Issue Raw Materials	RM item number, RM issue number		Quantity issued

[a]Some organizations may combine Finished Goods and Raw Materials into one inventory table

required to make a specific product. For example, there would be separate rows for polishing brass for each product that included brass parts; each row would store information about the standard time it should take to polish the brass when making a particular product. Often, multiple steps are required to make a single product. Thus, one finished good would be linked to many different rows in the Job Operations List and Machine Operations List entity tables.

Figure 17-6 also includes an entity labeled "Employee Time." We saw that entity in Chapter 16 when we discussed payroll activities and will discuss it in more detail in the section of this chapter that covers the HR/Payroll cycle activities.

Production Cycle Events

Data about *actual* raw materials used in production is stored in the Issue Raw Materials entity. Similarly, information about the *actual* labor and machine operations performed, including the actual amount of time each activity took, are stored in the Job Operations and Machine Operations entities, respectively. Performance can be evaluated by comparing the data in these three event entities with the information about standards that is stored in the corresponding information entities (Bill of Materials, Job Operations List, and Machine Operations List).

The Job Operations event entity is an example of a Give Resource event: It records the use of employee time. Each row in that table records information about how much time an employee spent working on a particular job. Thus, there can be many rows in this table for each employee every day. For example, on July 7, employee 727 may spend three hours on WIP job 2234, two hours on WIP job 2235, and three hours on WIP job 2236. Collecting this kind of detailed information about how factory employees use their time enables manufacturing companies to accurately assign labor costs to different production batches and product lines.

The Machine Operations event is similar to the Job Operations event, except that it records information about the use of a specific piece of machinery or equipment. This information is useful not only to assign costs to products but also for scheduling maintenance. Note that the Machine Operations event is *not* used to record depreciation. Depreciation expenses seldom correspond to actual use of the equipment. Depreciation is not modeled as an event in the REA diagram because it is an accounting concept that arbitrarily allocates the cost of an acquired resource to different fiscal periods. Periodic depreciation is simply a calculation based on a formula (depreciation method) and a set of assumptions (estimated useful life, salvage value, etc.). Information about the formula and assumptions is stored in the resource entity for use in calculating periodic depreciation charges, but the calculation process itself is not an event, just as the processes of calculating the total amount of a particular sales transaction or the amount of an employee's paycheck are not modeled as events.

Figure 17-6 models the relationships between the Job Operations event and the Job Operations List entity, and between the Machine Operations event and the Machine Operations List entity, as being 1:N. The list entities store information about the standard time it should take to perform each individually identifiable activity; the operations events record the actual time used to perform that activity. Thus, each actual event can be linked to only one entry in the standards table, but each entry in the standards table is likely to be linked to many actual performances of that activity.

The Work-in-Process entity is used to collect and summarize data about the raw materials, labor, and machine operations used to produce a batch of goods. The relationships between Work-in-Process and those three event entities are all 1:N, reflecting the fact that each production run may involve a number of raw materials issuances, labor operations, and machine operations. Each of those activities, however, is linked to a specific production run. These links reflect an internal give-to-get exchange that is the essence of the production cycle: Raw materials, labor, and equipment are all used in order to produce finished goods inventory. Thus, three Give Resource events are related to one Get Resource event.

Notice that Figure 17-6 differs from previous REA diagrams in that it shows only one agent associated with the Job Operations (and Machine Operations) events. These internal events differ from the other events discussed throughout this book in that they do not involve an exchange or transfer of resources. Instead, they represent the consumption or use of individual resources, such as a specific employee's time or the use of a specific piece of equipment. Therefore, the event is linked to that agent (employee or piece of machinery) for which management wants to collect information for product costing and performance evaluation purposes.

New REA Feature—Relationships Between Agents

Figure 17-6 also depicts a 1:N relationship between employees and supervisors. This reflects the typical situation where each employee is assigned to a specific supervisor, but each supervisor is responsible for many employees. In contrast, a matrix style of organization, where each employee reports to several supervisors, would be modeled as an M:N relationship between factory employees and supervisors. Relationships between internal agents may be created to model lines of responsibility. Relationships between internal and external agents can also occur. For example, some organizations that provide primarily services, such as banks and insurance companies, may assign customers to specific employees who are responsible for effectively managing the overall quality of the ongoing association with each customer. Relationships between external agents are rare but may sometimes be implemented to satisfy the requirements for a well-structured database. For example, if an insurance company needed to collect and maintain detailed information about each of a customer's dependents, it could do so by creating a separate entity called "Dependents" and establishing a 1:N relationship between that entity and the Customer entity.

Combined HR/Payroll Data Model

Figure 17-7 integrates payroll and HR activities. The Time Worked event is necessary to calculate payroll. The Time Used event is used for cost accounting, to properly assign labor costs (in manufacturing companies, this event entity is often called "Job Operations"). All of the other events represent important HR activities.

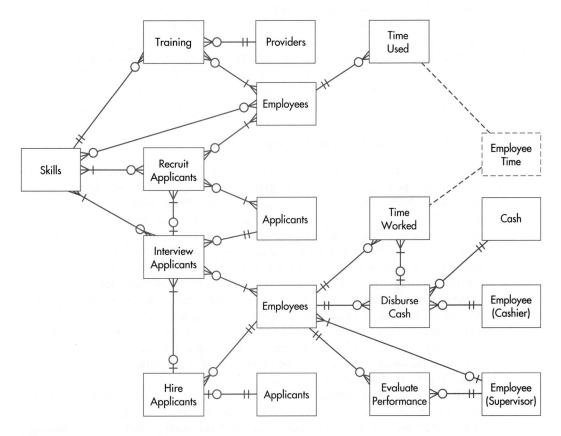

Figure 17-7
Integrated REA Diagram for HRM/Payroll Cycles

HR Cycle Entities

Notice that in Figure 17-7 the Employee entity is linked to almost every other entity in the diagram, reflecting the importance of employees to the organization. The Employee entity stores much of the data typically found in the employee (payroll) master file: name, date hired, date of birth, pay rate, job title, supervisor, number of dependents, withholding allowances, and information about any voluntary deductions, such as 401(k) plans.

The Skills entity contains data about the different job skills of interest to the organization. There would be a row in this table for each major job skill. For example, a software developer may list different programming languages and application programs in this table. The relationship between Skills and Employees is modeled as being M:N because one employee may possess a number of job skills (i.e., one programmer may be proficient in several different languages) and, conversely, several employees may possess the same skill.

The Training event entity represents the various workshops, training programs, and other opportunities provided for employees to develop and maintain their skills. Thus, this entity stores data that can be used to evaluate the effectiveness and cost of training and development efforts. The relationship between the Employees and Training entities is M:N, because a given employee will, over time, attend numerous training courses and, conversely, several employees may attend the same specific training class. The relationship between the Skills and Training entities is 1:N, because each course is designed to develop a specific skill, but each skill may be taught many different times.

The Recruiting event entity stores data about activities performed to notify the public of job openings. The data recorded in this entity are useful for documenting compliance with employment laws and also for evaluating the effectiveness of various methods used to announce job opportunities. The M:N relationship between Skills and Recruiting reflects the fact that each advertisement may seek several specific skills and that, over time, there may be several advertisements for a given skill. The relationship between the Recruiting event and Job Applicants is modeled as being M:N because many people typically apply for each job opening, but a given individual may also respond to more than one recruiting event. Also, more than one employee may participate in each recruiting event, and, over time, a given employee may participate in many such events.

The Interview event stores detailed data about each job interview. It is linked to the Hire Employees event in a 1:N relationship. This reflects the fact that the Hiring event occurs only once but may result from either one or a number of preceding interviews.

Tracking Employees' Time

The section on the Production Cycle discussed the use of a Perform Job Operations event to track how factory workers spent their time so that labor costs can be allocated to products. Professional services firms, such as law firms, consulting organizations, and accounting firms, similarly need to track how their members use their time in order to accurately bill each client. Figure 17-7 uses the Time Used event for this purpose. The structure of this table is similar to that of the Perform job operations table described earlier (we use a different name here because "perform job operations" has a manufacturing connotation). Thus, each row in this table includes the following attributes: the employee, the job (client) to which that employee's time should be charged, a description of the task performed (e.g., prepare will, telephone consultation, court appearance, etc.), and the time when that task was started and ended. Information about the nature of the task needs to be collected in order to evaluate performance and because sometimes the rate billed for a particular employee may vary depending on the task being performed.

It is instructive to compare the information provided by the Time Used event to that provided by linking specific business events to the employee agent who performed that task. Regular event-agent relationships, such as that between sales and employees, collect data that can be used to answer such questions as "How much did salesperson X sell this week?" or "How many sales did each salesperson make?" In

contrast, the Time Used event provides the information needed to answer such questions as "How much time did a particular salesperson spend calling on customers, as opposed to providing customer service support via the telephone?" Each instance of a regular event entity (e.g., each row in the call on customer, sales, or provide customer support tables) captures data about discrete activities, such as a particular sales transaction. In contrast, each row in the Time Used event captures data about what an employee did during a block of time. Hence, each row in the Time Used table can, and often is, linked to many rows in a business event table. For example, employee 007 may spend five hours making sales calls to customers, during which time she visited five customers. That would be represented as one row in the track time used table, but five separate rows in the call on customer table. Thus, there is a 1:N relationship between the two types of events. It is not necessary to link the Time Used entity to specific business events, however, but doing so facilitates evaluating performance at a very detailed level (i.e., to answer questions such as during which block of time on which days of the week is a particular salesperson most effective).

Not every organization collects detailed data about their employees' use of time, in which case there is no need for a Time Used entity. Moreover, even when such an event is included, the resource that is used (Employee Time) is seldom implemented as a table in the database because there are no meaningful attributes to describe it.

Financing Activities Data Model

Most organizations issue stock and debt to finance their operations. Figure 17-8 is an REA diagram of these two financing activities.

The event Issue Debt is a special kind of cash receipt; hence, it is connected to the Cash resource entity. It is often modeled as a separate event entity because it contains distinctly different attributes from those associated with cash receipts that arise from the Sales event, such as the face amount of debt issued, total amount received, date issued, maturity date, and interest rate. Usually, most companies do not deal directly with individual creditors. Instead, they sell their debt instruments through a financial intermediary, which is depicted in Figure 17-8 as the Transfer Agent. The transfer agent maintains the necessary information about individual creditors, to properly direct both the periodic interest payments and eventual repayment of principal. Therefore, each occurrence of an Issue Debt event contains data about the *aggregate* amount received from issuing a set of debt instruments. For example, the issuance of $10,000,000 of 5% bonds, which were ultimately purchased by several thousand different individuals for a total of $9,954,000, constitutes one Issue Debt event.

Debt-related payments (whether periodic interest payments or repayment of principal at maturity) are cash disbursements. Usually, the organization writes one check for the total amount of interest owed for a particular bond or note and sends that to the transfer agent, who then handles the distribution of individual checks to each creditor. Thus, to continue our example, the company would send $125,000 to the transfer agent to make the first quarterly payment on that $10,000,000 of bonds. The transfer of funds would be recorded as *one* row in the Disburse Cash table. Note that if a company has issued different series of bonds at different points in time, it would normally make separate transfers of funds to the transfer agent for payments linked to each debt issue. Thus, Figure 17-8 shows each Disburse Cash event linked to a maximum of 1 Issue Debt events. The minimum cardinality is 0 because a particular Disburse Cash event may be linked to either an Issue Debt event or an Issue Stock event.

Equity transactions are modeled in a manner similar to debt transactions. The Issue Stock event is a special kind of cash receipt associated with the issuance of stock, and the dividend payments are another type of cash disbursement. As with debt, most companies do not deal directly with individual stockholders. Thus, Figure 17-8 shows that both types of equity transactions involve participation by an employee (the treasurer) and the external transfer agent. The relationship between the Disburse Cash and Issue Stock events is

Figure 17-8
Partial Financing Activities
Diagram

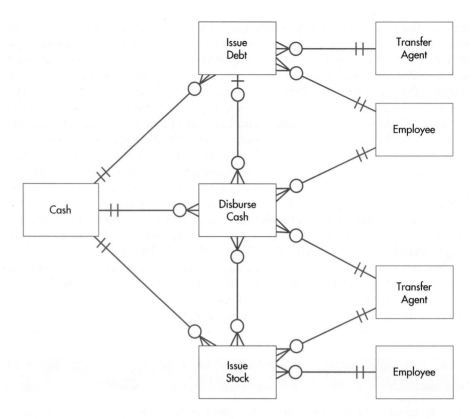

modeled as being M:N because each stock issuance may be linked to many dividend payments and, conversely, a particular dividend payment may be related to multiple different issuances of stock (i.e., *all* shareholders, regardless of which issue they bought, will receive a portion of each dividend). The minimum cardinalities are 0 in both directions because there is a temporal sequence between the two events and because a given Disburse Cash event might be linked to an Issue Debt event instead of to an Issue Stock event.

SUMMARY AND CASE CONCLUSION

Figure 17-9 (see pp. 662–663) presents an integrated enterprise-wide data model that includes most of the situations discussed in this and the previous two chapters. Note how the figure shows the linkages among different subsystems of the organization's AIS. For example, a customer order for finished goods may, if there is insufficient inventory on hand to fill the order, trigger the scheduling of a production run to produce those goods. In turn, this production run may necessitate ordering additional raw materials. ERP systems are designed to automatically trigger these types of related actions across subsystems by linking each subsystem to a common enterprise-wide database. Thus, even though the databases used in many ERP systems may not be explicitly based on the REA data model, a model like that depicted in Figure 17-9 provides useful documentation about the business activities supported by the ERP system.

Indeed, one of the benefits of an integrated enterprise-wide data model like Figure 17-9 is that auditors can use it to guide the development of queries to validate the completeness and accuracy of transaction processing. To illustrate the possibilities, let us examine the process for validating the updates to the sales account in the general ledger. Referring to Figure 17-9, the first step would be writing queries against the data model for the revenue cycle. One such query would sum the amount of all sales during the time period of interest. Other queries would link the Sales and Take Customer Order tables to verify the completeness and validity of all recorded sales. Additional queries could be written to trace sales to specific customers and sales staff. In fact, the

number of such cross-table links that can be easily generated is limited only by the auditor's imagination. In addition, the system can be configured to create extensive log files that make it possible to identify who authorized a transaction. Thus, integrated data models make it possible to write a set of queries that creates a rich, complex audit trail of an organization's business activities.

An integrated enterprise-wide data model like that depicted in Figure 17-9 can also significantly improve the support provided for managerial decision making. To appreciate this fact, consider how the chart of accounts in a traditional general ledger system limits subsequent analyses of expense data. Expenses are typically recorded and stored in an account that reflects either the nature of the expense, such as travel, or its function, such as campus recruiting visits. With the first alternative, it is easy to prepare reports of total travel expenses but difficult to identify how much travel expense is associated with campus recruiting. With the second alternative, it is easy to prepare reports that show the costs associated with campus recruiting but difficult to prepare reports that track total travel costs.

A common response to this problem in file-based general ledger systems is to create more detailed account numbers that identify both the nature and purpose of each expense; thus, there would be separate accounts for campus recruiting travel expenses, sales travel expenses, and so on. The drawback of this approach, however, is that it results in an exponential expansion of the chart of accounts and an increase in the length of each account code. Both of these factors make it more difficult for coding clerks and managers to learn the chart of accounts and apply it correctly. In addition, the ability to further analyze the data remains limited to those categories that were established when the chart of accounts was designed.

In contrast, an integrated, enterprise-wide data model avoids these problems and provides greater flexibility for analyzing data. Tables can be created for basic account categories, such as travel expenses. These tables also can include a text attribute for describing the purpose of that expenditure. Managers can then use queries to extract travel expenses by category, such as campus recruiting or trade shows. Moreover, simply changing the condition specified in the query can easily change these categories over time in response to different needs. Thus, users are not limited to predetermined expense classification schemes. Yet eliminating a clause that restricts the query's scope also can easily generate reports of total travel expenses for all purposes. Moreover, as Focus 17-1 explains, this flexibility not only facilitates managerial decisions, but can also provide tax benefits.

17-1 FOCUS — Tax Benefits of Well-Designed Databases

A well-designed database efficiently and effectively supports an organization's transaction processing requirements while also providing management with easy access to the information it needs to plan, control, and evaluate performance. A properly designed database can also yield tax benefits. This can be illustrated easily when considering business travel and entertainment expenses.

The IRS generally allows organizations to deduct 50% of the meals and entertainment expenses incurred when dealing with customers or prospective customers. Many organizations simply accumulate all meal and entertainment expenses in one general ledger account. This makes it easy to calculate the tax deduction at the end of the year: Just multiply the total amount in the meals and entertainment account by 50%. Although this approach is simple, efficient,

and logical, it can cause an organization to miss out on additional tax deductions. The IRS has established several exceptions in which meals and entertainment expenses are 100% deductible. To take advantage of these exceptions, organizations need to design their databases to be able to identify tax-relevant characteristics of specific meals and entertainment expenses. This can be as simple as adding another attribute to the table used to record those expenses.

Is it worth the effort? Consider the following examples: (a) Four tickets to an NBA game, plus refreshments, can cost over $400; (b) four tickets to a concert by a major symphony with dessert and coffee afterwards can cost over $300. When you multiply such examples by the number of times your sales staff entertains clients during the course of a year, the potential tax benefits of deducting an additional 50% of such costs can be huge.

Figure 17-9
Integrated, Enterprise-wide REA Diagram

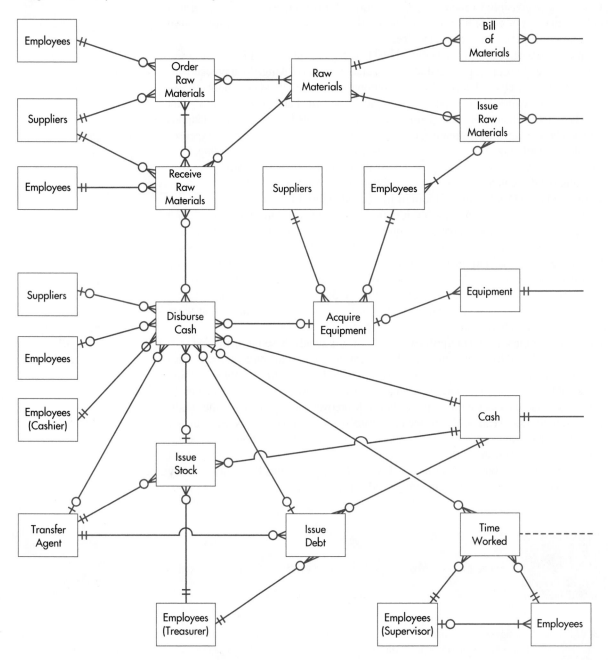

Creating an integrated, enterprise-wide data model also facilitates the amalgamation of financial and nonfinancial information in the same database, which can improve internal reporting. Traditionally, internal reports have focused primarily on financial performance measures. Effective management of an organization, however, requires measuring performance on multiple dimensions because no single measure is sufficient. Instead, top management must have reports that provide a multidimensional perspective on performance. An integrated, enterprise-wide data model like that depicted in Figure 17-9 facilitates the development of multidimensional performance reports, such as the balanced scorecard discussed in Chapter 14.

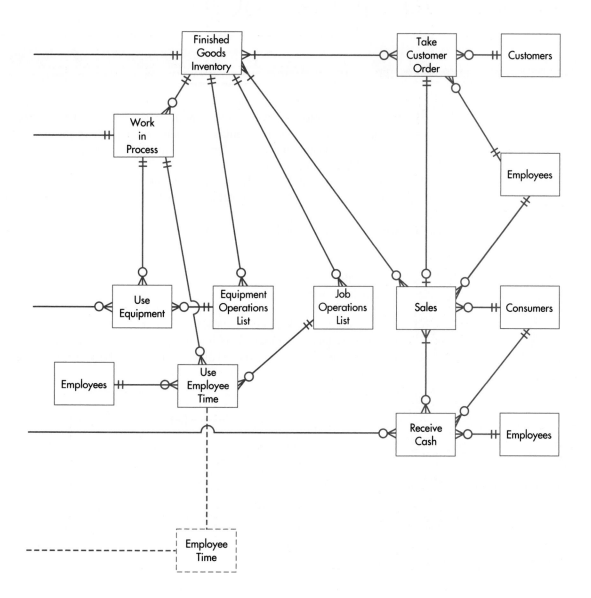

Paul Stone reflected on what he had learned at the REA workshop. He realized that although a number of different types of businesses and transactions had been covered, he was likely to encounter clients with yet other situations. Nevertheless, he felt confident that he now understood a wide enough variety of situations that he could use that knowledge to develop solutions to enable him to model almost any type of business activity he was likely to encounter. After all, as a CPA, Paul's entire career had involved continuous learning and refinement of his skills.

AIS IN ACTION

CHAPTER QUIZ

1 Which of the following events represent the basic give-to-get economic exchange for a business that rents equipment and machinery for use by others?
 a. Rent Equipment and Return Rented Equipment
 b. Rent Equipment and Receive Cash
 c. Rent Equipment, Return Rented Equipment, and Receive Cash
 d. Rent Equipment and either Return Rented Equipment or Receive Cash

2 Which resource in the HR/payroll cycle is seldom implemented in a database?
 a. skills
 b. employee time
 c. applicants
 d. cash disbursements

3 Joe's Computers makes service calls to repair computer equipment. Some calls involve only labor charges, others involve both labor and parts. Which of the following correctly models the relationship between the Service Calls event and Parts Inventory?

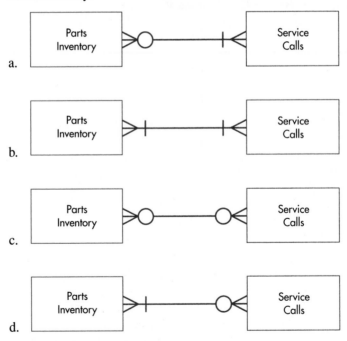

4 Which entity contains information about the components used to manufacture a particular product?
 a. Inventory
 b. Job Operations List
 c. Bill of Materials
 d. Machine Operations List

5 Which of the following production cycle events involves the *acquisition* of a resource (i.e., is a Get event)?
 a. Machine Operations
 b. Job Operations

 c. Work in Process

 d. Issue Raw Materials

6 Acme manuafacturing tracks information about customer calls by sales repre-
sentative. Although many calls involve demonstrations of products, some are
purely to build relationships. What is the correct way to model the relationship
between Inventory and the Call on Customers event?

a.

b.

c.

d.

7 Which production cycle event collects the data used to calculate payroll?

 a. Job Operations

 b. Time Worked

 c. Time Used

 d. Disburse Cash

8 The give-to-get economic exchange associated with debt financing involves
which two events?

 a. Issue Debt and Receive Cash

 b. Issue Debt and Disburse Cash

 c. Receive Cash and Disburse Cash

 d. None of the above

9 Acme manufacturing wants to track post-sales customer service by collect-
ing information about each customer service call: who called, when the call
happened, which customer service representative handled the call, how long
the call lasted, which sales transaction prompted the call, and which
inventory items were discussed. The relationship between the Sales and
Post-sales Service Call events should most likely be modeled as which of
the following?

 a. 1:1

 b. 1:N

 c. M:N

 d. 0:N

10 Which of the following is most likely to be modeled as being a 1:1 relationship?

 a. the relationship between Sales and Customers

 b. the relationship between Sales and Inventory

 c. the relationship between Sales and Receive Cash

 d. none of the above

DISCUSSION QUESTIONS

17.1 Often it takes several sales calls to obtain the first order from a new customer. Why then does Figure 17-1 depict the relationship between the Call on Customer and Take Customer Orders events as being 1:1?

17.2 How could an automobile dealer model the use of loaner cars, which it gives to customers for free whenever they drop off a vehicle for maintenance that will take longer than one day to complete?

17.3 How can service companies (accounting, law, consultants, etc.) use technology to track how their employees use time?

17.4 Why is depreciation not represented as an event in the REA data model?

17.5 How would you model the acquisition of a digital asset, such as the purchase of software online (the software is downloaded and then installed on the purchaser's computer)?

17.6 How are the similarities and differences between the purchase of services, such as telephone service, and the purchase of raw materials reflected in an REA data model?

17.7 How would you modify the expenditure cycle REA diagram depicted in Figure 17-4 to include the return of defective products to suppliers for credit?

PROBLEMS

17.1 We-Fix-Computers, Inc., provides spare parts and service for a wide variety of computers. Customers may purchase parts to take home for do-it-yourself repairs, or they may bring their systems in for repair, in which case they pay for both the parts and the labor associated with the type of service required. Some services do not include any new parts, just a labor charge for that service. Individual customers must pay for all parts purchases in full at the time of sale. Individual customers must pay 50% down when they bring their computers in for servicing and pay the balance at pickup. Corporate customers, however, are billed monthly for all sales (parts or service). Although We-Fix-Computers, Inc., has several different banking accounts, all sales are deposited intact into its main checking account.

We-Fix-Computers, Inc. purchases its inventory of parts from more than a dozen different vendors. Orders are usually delivered the next day; sometimes, however, suppliers ship only partial orders. We-Fix-Computers pays for some of its purchases COD, but usually pays by the 10th of the month for all purchases made the prior month. None of its suppliers allows it to make installment payments.

Required

Draw an integrated REA diagram for We-Fix-Computers' revenue and expenditure cycles.

17.2 The Mesa Veterinary Hospital is run by Dr. Brigitte Roosevelt. She has two employees in the office and has asked you to develop a database to help better track

her data. Dr. Roosevelt currently uses her personal computer only for word processing, but she is interested in also using it to maintain pet histories and accounting information. She is excited about the transition and is counting on you to help her through the process. She describes her daily activities as follows:

When new customers come to Mesa Veterinary Hospital, the "owners" of the pets are required to complete an introductory form. This form includes the following:
- *Owner name*
- *Address*
- *Day phone*
- *Night phone*

They are also required to provide the following information about each pet, as some people own many pets:
- *Pet name*
- *Breed*
- *Color*
- *Birth date*

Dr. Roosevelt would like to enter this information once, and then have the system retrieve it for all subsequent visits.

When customers call to make appointments, one of the office clerks asks what kind of services they require (i.e., is it a routine exam, a surgery, etc.). Dr. Roosevelt sees only one pet during each appointment. If she is going to see one owner's two pets, then two separate appointments are necessary (but scheduled back-to-back). For each appointment, Dr. Roosevelt records the pet's weight, notes the reason for the appointment, and records her diagnosis. Depending on the diagnosis, the doctor will possibly prescribe any number of medications to cure the pet. Owners are charged $25 for each appointment and must pay additionally for any medications prescribed for their pets. Dr. Roosevelt requires all pets to be brought back for another examination prior to refilling any prescriptions. Customers must pay for services and medication in full at the conclusion of their visits.

You also learn that Dr. Roosevelt orders drugs and medications from several different suppliers. She places orders weekly, on Fridays. Suppliers usually make one shipment to fill each order, but sometimes have to make additional shipments if they are currently out of stock of one or more items. In such cases, they always ship the back-ordered item as soon as they receive it from the manufacturer; they never combine such back orders with subsequent orders by Dr. Roosevelt. Suppliers bill Dr. Roosevelt monthly and expect payment in full by the 15th of the following month. A few suppliers do permit Dr. Roosevelt to make installment payments. The prices charged by suppliers for a given product may change several times during the year, so it is important to accurately store the cost of each item each time it is purchased.

Dr. Roosevelt concludes the interview by requesting that in addition to the facts mentioned, she wants the system to store the following attributes:

- Number of pets owned by each customer
- Total charge for the appointment
- Prescription price
- Drug name
- Length of appointment
- Diagnosis
- Date of appointment
- Service requested

Required

a. Given this brief overview, draw an integrated REA diagram for the Mesa Veterinary Hospital and include cardinalities.

b. As directed by your instructor, either draw the tables necessary to implement the integrated REA diagram you developed for the Mesa Veterinary Hospital or build the tables in a relational DBMS to which you have access. Be sure to

include all attributes from the narrative plus the additional ones explicitly listed by Dr. Roosevelt at the conclusion of the interview. Create additional attributes only if necessary.

(This problem is adapted from one created by Dr. Julie Smith David for classroom use at Arizona State University.)

17.3 Your university hires you to implement a database system for the library network. You have interviewed several librarians, and the following summarizes these discussions:

- The library's main goal is to provide students and professors with access to books and other publications. The library, therefore, maintains an extensive collection of materials that are available to anyone with a valid university identification card.

- The standard procedure for loaning materials is that the student or faculty member comes to one of the three campus libraries and locates the book or journal on the shelves.

- Each book is assigned three unique numbers. First, the book is assigned a number by the publisher, called the International Standard Book Number (ISBN). This number allows the publishers to track each title and the number changes with each new edition. The second number is the Dewey decimal number, which is assigned to the title and written on the outside spine of the book. This number is used to organize the library shelves and is thus helpful to the students and faculty. It is therefore critical that this number be available to users on the online inquiry screens. The last number is a university book ID number. A different number is assigned to every book that is received so the library can track all copies of each book. This number is different from the other two numbers in that if the library has three copies of one book, each will have a unique university book ID number.

- When students or faculty check out books, the system must be able to track the specific copy that is being borrowed. Each book has a magnetic strip inserted in its spine, which is used as a security measure. If someone tries to take a book without checking it out, an alarm sounds.

- In general, students and faculty have equal clout in the library. Both are able to check out most books and to check out several books at one time. No one is allowed to remove periodicals from any library. The length of time that the book may be borrowed varies, however, depending on who checks it out. Students are allowed to check out a book for several weeks; faculty may borrow books for several months.

- When patrons check out books, they take their materials to the circulation desk. At that time, the librarian scans in each item's university book ID number and the borrower's ID number. The system records a separate loan event for each book being checked out, assigning each a separate loan number. At this time, each book's due date is calculated and marked on a slip located inside each book's front cover. Simultaneously, the magnetic strip is deactivated so the book may be removed from the library.

- After borrowers check out a book, they are expected to return it by its due date. In reality, everyone is allowed 30 days after the due date recorded on the checkout slip before the book is officially overdue. At that point, the book must be returned, and the borrower is assessed a $10 fine. If the book is permanently lost, then the borrower is fined $75 for the book's replacement. All fines must be paid in cash, in full. Students are not allowed to enroll for subsequent semesters until all library fines are paid; they also do not receive a diploma until all library fines are paid. Faculty must pay all outstanding fines by June 30 of each year.

- When a book is returned, the return must be entered into the system, and a unique return number is used to log the transaction. At that time, the loan record is updated to show that the book has been returned.

The following attributes have been identified as critical for the new system:

University book ID	Actual return date	Book return number
Book publisher	Borrower ID	Dewey decimal number
Due date	Borrower name	Borrower address
Loan number	Book title	Book copyright date
Checkout date	Fine receipt number	Borrower e-mail address
Borrower phone number	Amount received	Library borrowed from
Cash account number	Library name	Librarian number
Librarian name	Amount of fine	Account balance
Book status (on the shelf or checked out)	Default library where book is shelved	Total number of books in a specific library
Type of borrower (faculty or student)	Borrower's fine balance owed	Loan status (still outstanding, or returned)
Librarian college degree	ISBN number	Author name

Required

 a. Draw an REA diagram for the library system. Remember to include cardinalities.
 b. As directed by your instructor, either create the tables on paper that would be required to implement your REA diagram or actually build those tables in a relational DBMS to which you have access. Only use the attributes listed, unless others are absolutely necessary.

(This problem is adapted from one developed by Dr. Julie Smith David for classroom use at Arizona State University.)

17.4 The XYZ Company sells tools and parts to automotive repair shops. Shops call in orders; all orders received by noon are delivered the same day. Between 12:00 and 1:00, the system prints out schedules. From 1:00 to 5:00, drivers make deliveries according to the printed schedules. Typically, each driver makes between 25 and 30 deliveries each day. Each delivery is signed for by a repair shop manager; the portable laptop then uses wireless communications to transmit information about the delivery back to the XYZ company and the information is recorded as another row in the sales event table. The XYZ Company uses its own trucks to make local deliveries to its customers. It wants to track information about the use of those trucks: which employee drove which truck, to which customers did a particular truck make deliveries, which deliveries are made on which days, what was the starting and stopping mileage each day?

Required

 a. Draw a partial REA diagram of the XYZ Company's revenue cycle to model these events: Taking Customer Orders, Deliveries, and the Use of Vehicles. Be sure to include cardinalities.
 b. Create a set of tables (either on paper or in a relational DBMS to which you have access) to implement the REA model you developed for the XYZ Company.

17.5 Assume that Stained Glass Artistry, a new shop that specializes in making stained glass artwork, has hired you to design an integrated database that will provide the owners with the accounting information they need to effectively manage the business. Stained Glass Artistry makes a wide variety of stained glass windows for sale in its store.

A unique job order is assigned to each production run, which includes creating multiple copies of the same basic design. When raw materials are issued to employees, the issuance is documented on a prenumbered raw material issue form. The different kinds of glass needed for the product, and other materials such as copper foil or lead, are issued at one time, so that employees can efficiently produce the design.

Creating a piece of stained glass art involves several different steps, including cutting, foiling, and soldering. The owners want to track how much time each employee spends each day performing each of those various tasks.

The owners have developed raw material and direct labor standards for each design they offer. They want their AIS to track actual costs and standard costs so that they can generate reports that provide price and quantity variance information.

The owners also have provided you with the following list of facts that they want stored in the database. (*Note:* You must create appropriate primary keys for each table; this is the list of other attributes.)

Attributes in Stained Glass Artistry AIS

Date hired	Time started task	Time completed task
Style of glass (name or description)	Quantity on hand	Color of glass
	Quantity to be produced	Actual cost of design
Design name	Standard quantity of glass to use in design	Quantity issued
Standard hours to make design	Date design produced	Standard cost of design
Wage rate	Employee name	Date of birth
		Standard cost of glass

Required

1 Draw an integrated REA diagram for Stained Glass Artistry. Include both minimum and maximum cardinalities.
2 Create the set of relational tables required to implement your REA diagram for Stained Glass Artistry in a relational database.

17.6 Bernie's Pet Store sells pet food, toys, and supplies. Bernie, the owner, is the only person who places orders with suppliers. He is also the only person who writes checks. Suppliers ship each order individually; if they are out of an item, they back order it and ship it separately as soon as it arrives. Bernie pays each supplier monthly for all purchases made the previous month. Suppliers do not allow him to make installment payments.

Bernie has eight employees, each of whom can check in materials received from suppliers and sell merchandise to customers. Bernie pays his employees weekly from a separate checking account used only for payroll purposes.

All sales are made in-store and are paid for immediately by cash, check, or credit card.

When employees are not working the cash register or checking in merchandise, they restock shelves and clean up the premises. Bernie does not want to track each *individual* restock or clean-up event, but does want to know how much time each employee spends each day doing those tasks. He also wants to track how much time each employee spends each day receiving inventory and how much time they spend working at the cash register. He wants to be able to write queries that would show time spent by job task (restocking, cleaning, receiving, or sales) for each employee. It is not practical, however, to try to measure the time spent on individual tasks (e.g., Bernie does not want employees to track the time they start and finished unloading a shipment from supplier X, then repeat for supplier Y; similarly, he does not want to track how long it takes to ring up each individual customer at the cash register). All he wants is to know how much time each day (e.g., 3.75 hours) each employee spent performing each different type of job.

Required

Draw an integrated REA diagram for Bernie's Pet Shop. Be sure to include both payroll processing and the ability to track how employees use their time.

17.7 At Big Time University (BTU) students are allowed to purchase two basketball tickets for each home game. Each ticket contains the date of the game, and the seat

information, such as section, row, and individual seat number. Students pay for each game individually; that is, student sporting event passes are not used at BTU. BTU deposits the proceeds from each game into its bank.

Required

a. Prepare an REA diagram with cardinalities for the revenue cycle for BTU's basketball games. State any assumptions you may have to make concerning BTU's business policies and practices.

b. Implement your model in a set of relational tables. Be sure to specify primary keys, foreign keys, and identify at least one other attribute that should be included in each table.

17.8 Small contractors often rent special equipment for specific jobs. They need to track the equipment that is rented, when it is returned, and payments made to the rental company.

Required

a. Draw a partial REA diagram for the acquisition, payment, and return of rental equipment. Be sure to include cardinalities and state any assumptions you made when specifying those cardinalities.

b. Create a set of tables (either on paper or in a relational DBMS to which you have access) to implement the REA model you developed.

CASE 17-1 Practical Database Assignment

This case involves creating a database from an integrated REA diagram and then using the REA diagram to guide the writing of queries to prepare financial statements.

Required

a. Create the tables necessary to implement Figure 17-9 in a relational database. Be sure to include primary keys and other relevant attributes in each table.

b. Write the query, or set of queries, necessary to generate each financial statement element. For example, write the query or set of queries that would be used to calculate the amount of cash on hand, the total of accounts receivable, the total value of raw materials inventory on hand, etc.

AIS IN ACTION SOLUTIONS

QUIZ KEY

1 Which of the following events represent the basic give-to-get economic exchange for a business that rents equipment and machinery?

a. Rent Equipment and Return Rented Equipment (Incorrect. The Give event (Rent Equipment) is linked to two Get events: Return Rented Equipment and Receive Cash.)

b. Rent Equipment and Receive Cash (Incorrect. The Give event (Rent Equipment) is linked to two Get events: Return Rented Equipment and Receive Cash.)

✔ **c.** Rent Equipment, Return Rented Equipment, and Receive Cash (Correct. The Give event (Rent Equipment) is linked to two Get events: Return Rented Equipment and Receive Cash.)

 d. Rent Equipment and either Return Rented Equipment or Receive Cash (Incorrect. The Give event (Rent Equipment) is linked to two Get events: Return Rented Equipment and Receive Cash.)

2 Which resource in the HR/payroll cycle is seldom implemented in a database?

 a. skills (Incorrect. Information about skills is important to record.)

✔ **b.** employee time (Correct. The employee time represents the right to use an employee's time—but time is a noninventoriable asset and is consumed when it is acquired, so this resource is seldom if ever implemented as a table in a database.)

 c. applicants (Incorrect. Applicants are agents and information about them must be recorded.)

 d. cash disbursements (Incorrect. Cash disbursements is an event about which information must be recorded.)

3 Joe's Computers makes service calls to repair computer equipment. Some calls involve only labor charges, others involve both labor and parts. Which of the following correctly models the relationship between the Service Calls event and Parts Inventory?

a.

(Incorrect. This shows that every part must be linked to use on at least one service call.)

b.

(Incorrect. This shows that every part must be linked to at least one service call and that every service call must involve use of at least one part.)

✔ **c.**

(Correct. This shows that some parts may not be linked to any service call, but others could be linked to many service calls. It also shows that some service calls do not involve the use of any parts, although other service calls may involve the use of multiple parts.)

d.

(Incorrect. This shows that every service call must involve the use of at least one part.)

4 Which entity contains information about the components used to manufacture a particular product?

 a. Inventory (Incorrect. The Bill of Materials entity stores the list of ingredients (components) used to manufacture a given product.)

 b. Job Operations List (Incorrect. The Job Operations list entity identifies the steps required to manufacture the product, but the list of components used is stored in the Bill of Materials entity.)

 ✔ **c.** Bill of Materials (Correct. The Bill of Materials entity stores the list of components used to manufacture a given product.)

 d. Machine Operations List (Incorrect. The Machine Operations List entity stores the steps and processes involving machinery used to manufacture a product.)

5 Which of the following production cycle events involves the *acquisition* of a resource (i.e., is a Get event)?

 a. Machine Operations (Incorrect. The Machine Operations event records information about the use of machinery and equipment; i.e., it is a Give event.)

 b. Job Operations (Incorrect. The job operations event records information about the use of labor to manufacture a product; i.e., it is a Give event.)

 ✔ **c.** Work in Process (Correct. The Work in Process event collects and aggregates all the costs associated with creating a finished product.)

 d. Issue Raw Materials (Incorrect. The Issue Raw Materials event records information about the raw materials used to manufacture a product; it is an example of a Give event.)

6 Acme manufacturing tracks information about customer calls by sales representative. Although many calls involve demonstrations of products, some are purely to build relationships. What is the correct way to model the relationship between Inventory and the Call on Customer event?

 a.

 (Incorrect. This shows that every call must involve demonstration of at least one product.)

 ✔ **b.**

 (Correct. This shows that a call may not involve the demonstration of any products, although it could demonstrate multiple products. At the same time, it correctly shows that some products may not be linked to any sales calls, whereas others may be linked to many different sales calls.)

 c.

 (Incorrect. This shows that every product must be linked to a sales call.)

 d.

 (Incorrect. This both shows that every product must be linked to a sales call and that every sales call must involve the demonstration of at least one product.)

7 Which production cycle event collects data used to calculate payroll?

 a. Job Operations (Incorrect. The Job Operations event collects data about the use of labor; it is used to calculate product costs.)

✔ **b.** Time Worked (Correct. This event captures the acquisition of time from employees, in return for which they must be paid.)

 c. Time Used (Incorrect. This event collects data about the use of labor; it is used to calculate product costs.)

 d. Disburse Cash (Incorrect. This event records the paying of wages, but not their calculation.)

8 The give-to-get economic exchange associated with debt financing involves which two events?

 a. Issue Debt and Receive Cash (Incorrect. The Issue Debt is a special instance of the Receive Cash Event.)

✔ **b.** Issue Debt and Disburse Cash (Correct. Issuing debt results in receipt of cash and subsequent repayments of that debt.)

 c. Receive Cash and Disburse Cash (Incorrect. The Issue Debt event is used to record the facts about borrowing events, which differ from the facts collected about cash receipts for sales.)

 d. none of the above (Incorrect.)

9 Acme manufacturing wants to track post-sales customer service by collecting information about each customer service call: who called, when the call happened, which customer service representative handled the call, how long the call lasted, which sales transaction prompted the call, and which inventory items were discussed. The relationship between the Sales and Post-sales Service Call events should most likely be modeled as which of the following?

 a. 1:1 (Incorrect. Some customers may make more than one service call related to a specific sales transaction and they may also discuss several sales transactions during the same service call.)

 b. 1:N (Incorrect. Some customers may make more than one service call related to a specific sales transaction and they may also discuss several sales transactions during the same service call.)

✔ **c.** M:N (Correct. Some customers may make more than one service call related to a specific sales transaction and they may also discuss several sales transactions during the same service call).

 d. 0:N (Incorrect. There is no such thing as a 0:N relationship).

10 Which of the following is most likely to be modeled as being a 1:1 relationship?

 a. The relationship between Sales and Customers (Incorrect. One hopes most customers will participate in many sales events (i.e., make repeat purchases).)

 b. The relationship between Sales and Inventory (Incorrect. Most organizations sell mass-produced inventory, which means the same product number can be linked to many different sales transactions. In addition, even organizations that sell unique products usually allow a customer to purchase more than one such item as part of a single sales transaction.)

✔ **c.** The relationship between Sales and Receive Cash (Correct. Although this may often be modeled as being 1:N or M:N, it is a 1:1 relationship for cash-and-carry type businesses, which do not extend credit.)

 d. None of the above (Incorrect. Answer c does occur).

Appendix: Extending the REA Model to Include Information About Policies[1]

Chapters 15–17 have explained how the REA model can be used to describe the contents of a database used to support an organization's transaction processing requirements. The various REA diagrams presented in those three chapters depicted the actual resources, events, and agents involved in carrying out the organization's business processes. The basic rules presented for developing an REA diagram are designed to ensure the accurate recording of things that exist, the events that occurred, and the specific agents who participated in those events. The REA model can be extended to also explicitly represent information about an organization's business policies. Doing so provides the opportunity to model information about such things as standards and internal controls. This Appendix provides a brief introduction to this topic.

Extending the REA model to incorporate information about policies that represent what should, could, or must happen involves the use of two new data modeling concepts: Type and Group entities. Type entities are used to depict "is-a-kind-of" relationships and Group entities are used to represent "is-a-member-of" relationships. Figure 17A-1 shows that both types of entities exist at the policy level and that they are mapped to entities at the operational level. For example, each individual sales transaction represents a specific kind of sale (e.g., Internet, In-store, Mail Catalog, etc.). Similarly, each individual employee is linked to one, and only one, specific class of employees (e.g., buyers, cashiers, salespeople, etc.); in other words, each individual employee is a kind of employee. In addition, Figure 17A-1 shows that employees are also assigned to (members of) specific divisions in the organization.

Type and Group entities are similar in that both are abstractions that represent sets of objects. They differ in terms of semantics and attributes. Type entities depict "is-a-kind-of" relationships and, therefore, contain attributes that apply to every individual entity of that type. For example, Table 17A-1 shows that the Employee Type entity

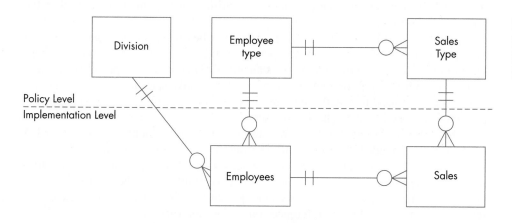

Figure 17A-1
Extending the REA Model to Include Policy-Level Information

[1]The material in this Appendix is based on the article, "Policy-Level Specification in REA Enterprise Information Systems" by Guido L. Geerts and William E. McCarthy, in the *Journal of Information Systems* 20:2 (Fall 2006): 37–63.

Table 17A-1
Policy-level Entities and
Relationships

Policy Level Entities	Primary Key	Foreign Keys	Other Attributes
Division	Division number		Budgeted sales this period
Employee Type	Employee type number		Role description, permissible salary range
Sales Type	Sales type number	Employee type number	Venue (Internet, Mail-order, In-store, etc.), collect sales tax (Y/N)

Operational Level Entities	Primary Key	Foreign Keys	Other Attributes
Employees	Employee number	Division number, employee type number	Name, date hired, salary, etc.
Sales	Invoice number	Employee number, sales type number	Date, time, comments

contains the attributes Role, Base Pay, and Salary Range and the Sales Type entity contains attributes about whether to charge for shipping, sales tax, etc. In contrast, Group entities are used to depict "is-a-member-of" relationships; consequently, Group entities contain attributes that apply to the set as a whole and are often derived values. Thus, Table 17A-1 shows that the Group entity called Division contains attributes such as average salary and the number of employees, which represent properties of the entire set that are calculated from the values of every entity that belongs to that group.

The attributes of Type entities provide a way to specify policy information (e.g., valid salary ranges, shipping charges, etc.) so that the system can enforce and validate adherence to the organization's business policies. For example, an individual employee's salary can be compared to the permissible salary range for that class of employee. Similarly, the system can decide whether to collect sales tax on a particular sales transaction by checking the stated policy for that type of sale. The attributes of Group entities provide a way to represent budgetary information, such as sales goals for each division, in a manner that facilitates creating reports that compare actual results (data stored in the operational–level entities) with plans (data stored in the policy-level entities).

Finally, Figure 17A-1 also shows that there can be relationships among Type entities. This provides another means to specify business policies and internal controls. For example, including employee type as an attribute in the Sales Type entity provides a mechanism for specifying that only sales staff can make sales to customers; similar linkages can be used to specify that only buyers can order inventory from suppliers, that only cashiers can write checks, and so on.

The objective of this Appendix was to provide an introduction to how the REA model can be extended to incorporate information about organizational policies and internal controls. If you take a database course, you will learn more about abstractions like Type and Group entities and the concepts of typification, generalization, and aggregation. You may also learn more about policy-level REA issues on your own, by reading the article cited as the reference source for this Appendix.

Part V

The Systems Development Process

CHAPTER 18

LEARNING OBJECTIVES

After studying this chapter, you should be able to:

- Explain the five phases of the systems development life cycle.

- Discuss the people involved in systems development and the roles they play.

- Explain the importance of systems development planning and describe planning techniques.

- Discuss the various types of feasibility analysis and calculate economic feasibility.

- Explain why systems change triggers behavioral reactions, what form this resistance to change takes, and how to avoid or minimize the resulting problems.

- Discuss the key issues and steps in systems analysis.

Introduction to Systems Development and Systems Analysis

INTEGRATIVE CASE SHOPPERS MART

Several months ago, Ann Christy, a successful accountant, was promoted to controller of Shoppers Mart, a small but rapidly growing regional chain of discount stores. Since her promotion, she has been assessing how the accounting function could better serve Shoppers Mart. She has held meetings with the president and CEO and with other key managers at headquarters. She has also spent several weeks visiting various Shoppers Mart stores and talking one on one with store managers and employees. Her findings are as follows:

1 Store managers cannot obtain information other than what is contained in Shoppers Mart's periodic, preformatted reports. As soon as they request information from several functional areas, the system bogs down.
2 The sales and purchasing department cannot get timely information about what products are or are not selling well. As a result, stores are often out of popular items and overstocked with products that customers are not buying.
3 Top management is concerned that Shoppers Mart is losing market share to larger rivals with better prices and selection. The current system cannot provide management with the information it needs to analyze and solve this problem.

After analyzing the situation, Ann is convinced that Shoppers Mart needs a new information system that is flexible, efficient, and responsive to user needs.

Ann knows that a new system will never be successful unless it has top management's complete support. Before she asks for approval and funding for the new system, Ann schedules a meeting with the head of systems development. She has the following questions:

1 What process must the company go through to obtain and implement a new system?

2 What types of planning are necessary to ensure the system's success? Who will be involved and how? Do any special committees need to be formed? What resources need to be planned for? How should all of the planning be documented?

3 How will employees react to a new system? What problems might this changeover cause, and how can they be minimized?

4 How should the new system be justified and sold to top management? How can expected costs and benefits be quantified to determine if the new system will indeed be cost-effective?

Introduction

Because we live in a highly competitive and ever-changing world, organizations continually face the need for new, faster, and more reliable ways of obtaining information. To meet this need, an information system must continually undergo changes, ranging from minor adjustments to major overhauls. Occasionally, the needed changes are so drastic that the old system is scrapped and replaced by an entirely new one. Change is so constant and frequent that at any given time most organizations are involved in some system improvement or change. A recent study estimates that each year corporate America spends almost $300 billion on more than 200,000 software projects.

Companies usually change their systems for one of the following reasons:

- **Changes in user or business needs.** Increased competition, business growth or consolidation, mergers and divestitures, new regulations, or changes in regional and global relationships can alter an organization's structure and purpose. To remain responsive to company needs, the system must change as well.

- **Technological changes.** As technology advances and becomes less costly, an organization can make use of the new capabilities or existing ones that were previously too expensive.

- **Improved business processes.** Many companies have inefficient business processes that require updating. For example, the ordering system at Nashua, an office supply manufacturer, caused customer frustration and dissatisfaction. When a customer called, a clerk would take information and promise to call back. Before doing so, the clerk had to access two separate systems: a mainframe system to verify customer information and perform a credit check and a PC-based system to calculate pricing. If the customer was still interested, the clerk accessed another centralized system to determine inventory availability. When the system was redesigned, it took three minutes to process a telephone order instead of two days.

- **Competitive advantage.** Increased quality, quantity, and speed of information can result in an improved product or service and may help lower costs.

For example, Wal-Mart invests heavily in technology to provide information about customers and their purchases to increase sales. This is a shift in management focus, since previously 90% of new systems were designed to automate labor and reduce expenses.

- **Productivity gains.** Computers automate clerical and repetitive tasks and significantly decrease the performance time of other tasks. Information systems can also place specialized knowledge at the disposal of many company employees. For example, Carolina Power and Light was able to eliminate 27% of its information systems staff when it installed a new system that significantly outperformed the old one.
- **Growth.** Companies outgrow their systems and must either upgrade or replace them entirely.
- **Downsizing.** Companies often move from centralized mainframes to networked PCs or to Internet-based systems to place decision making and its corresponding information as far down the organizational chart as possible. For example, a large utility in New York downsized from a mainframe-based system to a client/server system and eliminated 100 clerical positions. The new system does much more than the old one, including handling workflow management, user contact, database queries, automatic cash processing, and voice/data integration.
- **Systems integration.** Organizations often have many adequate and serviceable systems that are incompatible—that is, they do not communicate well with each other because they were developed over many years using different technologies and data formats. These systems often are rewritten to remove the incompatibilities and consolidate databases. For example, the U.S. Department of Defense is in the process of trying to integrate more closely over 700 separate systems.
- **Systems age and need to be replaced.** As systems age and are repaired numerous times, they become less stable and eventually need to be replaced. Focus 18-1 describes how the Internal Revenue Service is trying to replace its aged information system.

Developing quality, error-free software is a difficult, expensive, and time-consuming task. In fact, it is almost always the case that software development projects deliver less than one expects and take more time and money to develop than one expects. To make matters worse, most companies that want to implement a new system want it immediately. As developers feel the pressure to perform system miracles, they begin skipping systems development steps and just start writing code. Omitting basic systems development steps only leads to disaster, as developers create well-structured systems that fail to meet user needs or solve any of their business problems. This is illustrated by the following statistics:

- An American Management Systems study revealed that 75% of all large systems are not used, not used as intended, or generate meaningless reports or inaccurate data. For example, nine months after Nike implemented a much-anticipated forecasting system, the company had to admit that the system did not work properly. Nike took a huge, multimillion-dollar inventory write-down because the system was so inaccurate. The system told Nike to order $90 million worth of shoes, such as Air Garnett II, that did not sell. At the same time, Nike had almost $100 million worth of orders on popular models, such as Air Force One, that it could not meet because demand for them had been misestimated.
- The Gartner Group estimates the following:
 1 Over 40% of information technology (IT) projects do not produce a satisfactory outcome,
 2 The average company spends over $1 million a year for these unsatisfactory outcomes,
 3 Ten percent of a typical organizations's IT staff worked on projects that have no business value.

18-1 FOCUS
The IRS Attempts to Replace Its Aging Information System

The IRS has concluded it needs to modernize its computer systems and operations to provide better customer service, improve compliance with the nation's tax laws, and reduce the volume of paper tax returns. The system is responsible for processing and storing all taxpayer records and currently takes in over $2 *trillion* a year. The decision to update the system was an obvious no-brainer, as the computer system is now more than 40 years old.

Critics claim that the fragile and antiquated system has been updated, fixed, and improved so many times that not only is a software meltdown a very real possibility but the odds of that meltdown occurring rise significantly every day. And what effect would this collapse have on the U.S. government? In the worst-case scenario:

- The IRS would not be able to tell who had paid their taxes.
- Tax revenues, hundreds of billions of dollars worth, would not be collected.
- To meet its obligation, the government would have to borrow money, throwing the financial markets into a panic.

It is not that the need to modernize has been a secret or that the IRS has not tried to improve its computer systems. The IRS has been trying to modernize the system for some time. A number of years ago, the IRS spent $3.3 billion on an upgrade effort that failed. In the late 1990s the IRS decided to try again. It embarked on an $8 billion effort called the Business Systems Modernization (BSM) program.

The BSM program, a huge undertaking that involves more than 20,000 major tasks and scores of organizations, is one of the largest and most complex information system challenges in history. At the same time, the IRS is trying to change its management culture and the way it is organized, both of which, some critics claim, are even more out of date than its information system.

There is no way the IRS could change the entire system at once; instead, the replacement will occur in stages and is scheduled to take over 15 years. One person compared the effort to trying to replace the foundation of a building brick by brick. Someone else said it was like trying to rebuild New York City, including all of its buildings, streets, sewers, and communication and transportation systems, all while its inhabitants do not notice the changes as they go about their daily lives.

So how is the IRS doing? Recent reports are not encouraging. The BSM spent almost $4 million on a project that was never finished and was eventually canceled. The effort has had a number of significant cost overruns, a number of management delays and performance shortfalls, and several missed project completion dates. One report indicated that the project ran a "significant risk of not succeeding." Unfortunately, reports and problems like these erode the public's confidence in the agency's ability to deliver the new and up-to-date systems the IRS needs to dramatically improve both taxpayer services and internal operations.

- A Standish Group International study found that more than 70% of software development projects are delivered late, 54% were over budget, 66% were unsuccessful, and 30% were canceled before they were completed.
- A KPMG survey found that 35% of all major information systems projects were classified as runaways—hopelessly incomplete and over budget.

Skipping or skimping on systems development processes is a major cause of runaways. Runaways can consume a great deal of time and money and in the end produce no usable results, as illustrated by the following examples:

- Pacific Gas & Electric (PG&E) pulled the plug on a client/server information system for all of its residential and commercial customers. People in and out of the utility labeled the system, five years in development, a financial disaster with no end product.
- California's Department of Motor Vehicles decided to overhaul its system, which was originally developed in 1965. The system was so difficult to maintain that it took the equivalent of 18 programmers working for an entire year to add a Social Security number file to the drivers' license and vehicle registration file. After seven years, $44 million, and not a single usable application, the state canceled the project. The state of Washington canceled a similar project after wasting seven years and $40 million.

This chapter discusses five topics. The first is the systems development life cycle, the process that organizations follow to obtain and implement a new and well-designed AIS. The second is the planning activities that are necessary during the development life cycle. The third is preparing a feasibility analysis to demonstrate that a new AIS is feasible. The fourth is the behavioral aspects of change that companies must deal with to successfully implement a new system. The fifth topic is a discussion of systems analysis, the first step in the systems development life cycle.

Systems Development

Whether systems changes are major or minor, most companies go through a systems development life cycle. The steps in that cycle and the people involved in systems development are discussed in this section.

The Systems Development Life Cycle

Ann Christy asked the manager of systems development to explain the process Shoppers Mart would use to design and implement a new system. He sketched out a five-step process, known as the **systems development life cycle (SDLC)**, that is shown in Figure 18-1 and briefly explained here.

Systems Analysis

Do initial investigation
Do systems survey
Do feasibility study
Determine information needs and
systems requirements
.Deliver systems requirements

Conceptual Design

Identify and evaluate design alternatives
Develop design specifications
Deliver conceptual design requirements

Physical Design

Design output
Design database
Design input
Develop programs
Develop procedures
Design controls
Deliver developed system

Implementation and Conversion

Develop an implementation and
conversion plan
Install hardware and software
Train personnel
Test the system
Complete documentation
Convert from old to new system
Deliver operational system

Operations and Maintenance

Fine-tune and do post-implementation
review
Operate system
Modify system
Do ongoing maintenance
Deliver improved system

* Feasibility analysis and
decision points
Economic feasibility
Technical feasibility
Legal feasibility
Scheduling feasibility
Operational feasibility

Throughout the life cycle, planning must be done and behavioral aspects of change must be considered.

Figure 18-1
The Systems Development Life Cycle

Systems Analysis

As organizations grow and change, management and employees recognize the need for more or better information and request a new or improved information system. The first step in systems development is systems analysis. During **systems analysis**, the information needed to purchase or develop a new system is gathered. Requests for systems development are prioritized to maximize the use of limited development resources. If a project passes the initial screening, the current system is surveyed to define the nature and scope of the project and to identify its strengths and weaknesses. Then an in-depth study of the proposed system is conducted to determine its feasibility.

If the proposed system is feasible, the information needs of system users and managers are identified and documented. This is the most important part of systems analysis, as these needs are used to develop and document systems requirements. Systems requirements are used to select or develop a new system. To summarize the work done during systems analysis, a report is prepared and submitted to the information systems steering committee.

Conceptual Design

During **conceptual design**, the company decides how to meet user needs. The first task is to identify and evaluate appropriate design alternatives. There are many different ways to obtain a new system, including buying software, developing it in-house, or outsourcing system development to someone else. Detailed specifications outlining what the system is to accomplish and how it is to be controlled must be developed. This phase is complete when conceptual design requirements are communicated to the information systems steering committee.

Physical Design

During **physical design**, the company translates the broad, user-oriented requirements of the conceptual design into detailed specifications that are used to code and test the computer programs. Input and output documents are designed, computer programs are written, files and databases are created, procedures are developed, and controls are built into the new system. This phase is complete when physical system design results are communicated to the information systems steering committee.

Implementation and Conversion

Implementation and conversion constitute the capstone phase during which all the elements and activities of the system come together. Because of the complexity and importance of this phase, an implementation and conversion plan is developed and followed. As part of implementation, any new hardware or software is installed and tested. New employees may need to be hired and trained, or existing employees relocated. New processing procedures must be tested and perhaps modified. Standards and controls for the new system must be established and system documentation completed. The organization must convert to the new system and dismantle the old one. After the system is up and running, any fine-tuning adjustments needed are made and a post-implementation review is conducted to detect and correct any design deficiencies. The final step in this phase is to deliver the operational system to the organization, at which time the development of the new system is complete. A final report is prepared and sent to the information systems steering committee.

Operations and Maintenance

The new—and now operational—system is used as needed in the organization. During its life, the system is periodically reviewed. Modifications are made as problems arise or as new needs become evident and as the organization uses the improved system. This process is referred to as the **operations and maintenance** phase. Eventually, a major modification or system replacement is necessary and the SDLC begins again.

In addition to these five phases, three activities (planning, managing the behavioral reactions to change, and assessing the ongoing feasibility of the project) are performed throughout the life cycle. These three activities, as well as systems analysis, are discussed in this chapter. The different approaches to obtaining an AIS are discussed in Chapter 19. The last four SDLC phases are explained in Chapter 20.

The Players

Many people must cooperate to successfully develop and implement an AIS. This section discusses the roles of those involved.

Management

One of the most effective ways to generate systems development support is a clear signal from top management that user involvement is important. With respect to systems development, top management's most important roles are providing support and encouragement for development projects and aligning information systems with corporate strategies. Other key roles include establishing system goals and objectives, reviewing the performance and leadership of the information system department, establishing policies for project selection and organizational structure, and participating in important system decisions. The principal roles of user management are to determine information requirements for departmental projects, to assist systems analysts with project cost and benefit estimates, to assign key staff members to development projects, and to allocate appropriate funds to support systems development and operation.

Accountants

Accountants may play three roles during systems design. First, as AIS users they must determine their information needs and system requirements and communicate them to system developers. Second, as members of a project development team or information systems steering committee, they help manage systems development. Third, accountants should take an active role in designing system controls and periodically monitoring and testing the system to verify that the controls are implemented and functioning properly. All systems should contain sufficient controls to ensure the accurate and complete processing of data. The system also should be easy to audit. If addressed at the start of development, auditability and control concerns can be minimized. Trying to achieve them after a system has been designed is inefficient, time-consuming, and costly. Control and audit issues are discussed in depth in Chapters 6 through 9.

Information Systems Steering Committee

Because AIS development spans functional and divisional boundaries, organizations usually establish an executive-level **information systems steering committee** to plan and oversee the information systems function. The committee often consists of high-level management people, such as the controller and systems and user-department management. The steering committee sets policies that govern the AIS and ensures top-management participation, guidance, and control. The steering committee also facilitates the coordination and integration of information systems activities to increase goal congruence and reduce goal conflict.

Project Development Team

Each development project has a team of systems specialists, managers, accountants and auditors, and users that guides its development. Team members plan each project, monitor it to ensure timely and cost-effective completion, make sure proper consideration is given to the human element, and communicate project status to top management and the steering committee. They should communicate frequently with users and hold regular meetings to consider ideas and discuss progress so there are no surprises upon project completion. A team approach usually produces more effective results and facilitates user acceptance of the implemented system.

Systems Analysts and Programmers

Systems analysts study existing systems, design new ones, and prepare specifications that are used by computer programmers. Analysts interact with information technology and systems employees throughout the organization to successfully bridge the gap between the user and technology. Analysts are responsible for ensuring that the system meets user needs.

Computer programmers write programs using the specifications developed by the analysts. They also modify and maintain existing computer programs.

External Players

Many people outside an organization play a role in systems development, including customers, vendors, auditors, and governmental entities. For example, Wal-Mart has told its vendors that they must implement and use electronic data interchange (EDI) if they want to do business with the company.

Planning Systems Development

As shown in Figure 18-1, several activities must be performed at various times throughout the SDLC. One such activity is planning. The organization must have a long-range plan, each systems development project requires a plan, and each phase of each development plan must also be planned. This section discusses these plans and a number of techniques used to develop them.

Imagine that you built a two-bedroom house. Several years later you add a bedroom, then another bedroom and a bathroom. Over the years you add a family room, recreation room, deck, and two-car garage. In addition, you expand the kitchen and the dining area. Without prior thought to what you would eventually want in a home, your house will end up as a poorly organized patchwork of rooms surrounding the original structure. In addition, the cost of the house can end up greatly exceeding its value. This scenario also applies to an AIS that is not properly planned. The result is a costly and poorly integrated system that is difficult to operate and maintain.

Systems development planning is an important step for the following key reasons:

- **Consistency.** Planning enables the system's goals and objectives to correspond to the organization's overall strategic plan.
- **Efficiency.** Systems are more efficient, subsystems are coordinated, and there is a sound basis for selecting new applications for development.
- **Cutting edge.** The company remains abreast of the ever-present changes in information technology.
- **Lower costs.** Duplication, wasted effort, and cost and time overruns are avoided. The system is less costly and easier to maintain.
- **Adaptability.** Management is better prepared for future resource needs, and employees are better prepared for the changes that will occur.

When development efforts are poorly planned, a company must often return to a prior phase and correct errors and design flaws, as shown in Figure 18-2. Such a process is costly and results in delays, frustration, and low morale.

Two types of systems development plans are needed: individual project plans prepared by project teams and a master plan developed by the information systems steering committee.

1 **Project development plan.** The basic building block of information systems planning is the **project development plan**. Each project development plan contains a cost/benefit analysis, developmental and operational requirements (including

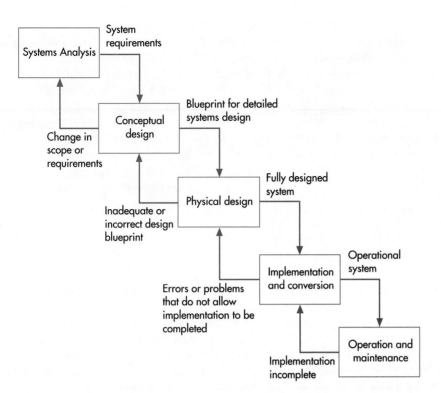

Figure 18-2
Reasons for Returning to a
Prior SDLC Phase

human resource, hardware, software, and financial resource requirements), and a
schedule of the activities required to develop and operate the new application.

2 **The master plan.** A **master plan** is a long-range planning document that spec-
ifies what the system will consist of, how it will be developed, who will develop
it, how needed resources will be acquired, and where the AIS is headed. The
master plan also should describe the status of projects in process, prioritize
planned projects, describe the criteria used for prioritization, and provide
timetables for development. The projects with the highest priority should be the
first to be developed. The importance of this decision dictates that it be made by
top management and not by computer specialists. A planning horizon of
approximately three years is reasonable, and the plan should be updated at least
two to three times a year. Many companies, because of the rapid and constant
changes in IT, update the plan quarterly or monthly.

It is important for the person fulfilling the role of the chief information officer to
gauge how soon new technologies will become widely used, whether the company
should be an early or late adopter of the technology, and to keep an eye out for busi-
ness opportunities that arise from new technologies.

The table of contents of the master plan used at Shoppers Mart is shown in
Table 18-1.

As explained in Focus 18-2, inadequate planning was one of the reasons why EDS
lost a significant amount of money in its contract with the U.S. military.

Planning Techniques

Two techniques for scheduling and monitoring systems development activities are
PERT and the Gantt chart. The **program evaluation and review technique (PERT)**
requires that all activities and the precedent and subsequent relationships among them
be identified. The activities and relationships are used to draw a PERT diagram, which
consists of a network of arrows and nodes representing, respectively, project activities
that require an expenditure of time and resources and the completion and initiation of
activities. Completion time estimates are made, and the **critical path**—the path
requiring the greatest amount of time—is determined. If any activity on the critical

Table 18-1
Components of the Master Plan at Shoppers Mart

Organizational goals and objectives	**Status of systems being developed**
Company mission statement and goals	Proposed systems priorities
Information systems strategic plan and goals	Approved systems development
Organizational constraints	Proposals under consideration
Organizational approach to AIS	Development timetables and schedules
Organizational and AIS priorities	**Forecast of future developments**
Inventory and assessments	Forecasts of information needs
Current systems	Technological forecasts
Approved systems	Environmental/regulatory forecasts
Current hardware	Audit and control requirements
Current software	External user needs
Current AIS staff	
Assessment of strengths and weaknesses	

path is delayed, then the whole project is delayed. If possible, resources are shifted to critical path activities to reduce project completion time.

A **Gantt chart** (Figure 18-3) is a bar chart with project activities listed on the left-hand side and units of time (days or weeks) across the top. For each activity, a bar is drawn from the scheduled starting date to the ending date, thereby defining expected project completion time. As activities are completed, they are recorded on the Gantt chart by filling in the bar; thus, at any time it is possible to determine quickly which activities are on schedule and which are behind. The capacity to show, in graphical

18-2 FOCUS — EDS Stands to Lose Billions in Its Contract with the Navy

The U.S. military hired Electronic Data Systems (EDS), the computer consulting firm, to develop a secure, hacker-proof network to link almost 350,000 computers at over 4,000 Navy sites. Unfortunately, the almost $10 billion contract has resulted in significant headaches and losses at one point estimated to total almost $1.7 billion. Inadequate planning was a major contributor to the problems. EDS made the following mistakes:

- Had little previous experience with the military and did not adequately plan for some of the requests. For example, Congress delayed the project for 18 months by asking for network-performance tests EDS was not used to handling. EDS also failed to plan for the more than 200 technical hurdles the military imposed.
- Did not verify Navy estimates. For example, the Navy said it had 5,000 software programs that needed to be installed on the new PCs; in reality, there were 67,000. EDS had only planned and budgeted for the 5,000 and had to absorb the costs of installing the additional software. Even worse, EDS found out it had to revamp the Navy's old software before it could be installed on the new computers.

- Did not properly plan and coordinate project tasks. For example, when EDS personnel went to the Navy bases to install the computers, they found out they did not have proper military clearances. In other cases, sailors and officers were busy (overseas in some cases) when the teams arrived.
- Underestimated the cost and time requirements to customize computers for individuals.
- Did not give the Navy adequate instructions. For example, the EDS system could not complete an order without a serviceman's rank, but EDS did not tell the Navy to send it the rank.
- Did not track the inventory of computers. For example, some servicemen ordered PCs and then changed their orders to laptops. EDS did not require them to cancel the first order, so two computers were prepared for these servicemen. These duplicate and incomplete orders sat in warehouses for months.

EDS made some changes to get the project back on track. Rather than try to install computers at many different locations simultaneously, it concentrated on installing computers at the largest bases. It began reusing expensive hardware and installing the warehoused computers before buying new ones. It also began customizing computers by job function rather than by individual.

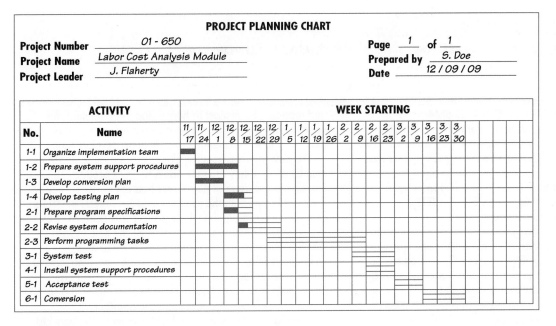

Figure 18-3
Sample Gantt Chart

form, the entire schedule for a large, complex project, including progress to date and current status, is the primary advantage of the Gantt chart. The charts do not show, however, the relationships among various project activities.

Feasibility Analysis

As shown in Figure 18-1, a **feasibility study** (also called a "business case") is prepared during systems analysis and updated as necessary during the remaining steps in the SDLC. The extent of these studies varies, depending on the size and nature of the system. For example, the study for a large-scale system is generally quite extensive, whereas one for a desktop system might be conducted informally. The feasibility team should include management, accountants skilled in controls and auditing, systems personnel, and users.

At major decision points (see Figure 18-1), the steering committee uses the study to decide whether to terminate a project, proceed unconditionally, or proceed if specific problems are resolved. Although a project can be terminated at any time, the early go/no-go decisions are particularly important as each subsequent SDLC step requires more time and monetary commitments. As the project proceeds, the study is updated and the project's viability is reassessed. The further along a development project is, the less likely it is to be canceled if a proper feasibility study has been prepared and updated.

Although uncommon, systems have been scrapped after implementation because they did not work or failed to meet an organization's needs. For example, Bank of America hired a software firm to replace a 20-year-old batch system used to manage billions of dollars in institutional trust accounts. After two years of development, the new system was implemented despite warnings that it was not adequately tested. Ten months later the system was scrapped, the bank's top systems and trust executives had resigned, and the company had taken a $60 million write-off to cover expenses related to the system. During the 10 months the system was in place, the company lost 100 institutional accounts with $4 billion in assets. Focus 18-3 describes a project at Blue Cross/Blue Shield that was scrapped after six years of work and a $120 million investment.

18-3 FOCUS — Blue Cross/Blue Shield Abandons Runaway

BLUE CROSS/BLUE SHIELD of Massachusetts hoped that its new information system would usher in a new era. After six years and $120 million, however, the System 21 project was behind schedule and significantly over budget. The project was canceled, and Blue Cross turned its computer operation over to Electronic Data Systems (EDS) Corporation, an outside contractor.

Although information system failures of this magnitude are unusual, they happen more often than one would expect. According to a KPMG survey, 35% of all major information system projects become a runaway—a project that is millions of dollars over budget and months or years behind schedule. Other surveys show that almost every Fortune 200 company has had at least one runaway.

One major reason for the development problems was Blue Cross's failure to properly supervise the project. Blue Cross hired an independent contractor to develop the software but neglected to appoint someone to coordinate and manage the project in-house. Top management did not establish a firm set of priorities regarding essential features and the sequence of application development.

The developers presented claims processing software to Blue Cross that they thought was a finished product. The managers and users at Blue Cross had other ideas. They were not happy with the software and requested numerous changes. As a result, the whole project was delayed. This led to ever-increasing cost overruns. By the time System 21 was launched, Blue Cross had fallen far behind its competitors in its ability to process an ever-swelling load of paperwork. In fact, during a six-year period it lost one million subscribers and came close to bankruptcy. It also had a poorly integrated system—nine different claims processing systems, some of which were over 20 years old.

The lesson Blue Cross learned was painful. The system it spent six years building was abandoned, and it turned its hardware over to EDS. Fortunately, although the system died, the patient survived.

Five important aspects to be considered during a feasibility study are as follows:

1 **Economic feasibility.** Will system benefits justify the time, money, and other resources required to implement it?
2 **Technical feasibility.** Can the planned system be developed and implemented using existing technology?
3 **Legal feasibility.** Does the system comply with all applicable federal and state laws and statutes, administrative agency regulations, and the company's contractual obligations?
4 **Scheduling feasibility.** Can the system be developed and implemented in the time allotted? If not, it will have to be modified, postponed, or replaced by an alternative selection.
5 **Operational feasibility.** Does the organization have access to people who can design, implement, and operate the proposed system? Can people use the system, and will they use it?

Economic feasibility, the most important and frequently analyzed of the five aspects, is now discussed in greater depth. The feasibility analysis that Ann performed for Shoppers Mart is shown in Table 18-8 on page 704 at the end of this chapter.

Calculating Economic Feasibility Costs and Benefits

In a recent survey, 9 out of 10 executives agreed that information technology could greatly enhance their competitive edge; however, only 6 out of 10 agreed that the necessary IT spending would be justified. Too often, companies overspend on information technology without any economic rationale to back it up. This occurs because IT payoffs are not measured and evaluated as thoroughly as other corporate investments. A much better business strategy is to spend only on IT projects where the expected benefits exceed the costs. This requires management to measure the economic feasibility of any proposed system.

Determining economic feasibility requires a careful investigation of the costs and benefits of a proposed system. Because accountants are familiar with cost concepts, they make a significant contribution to this evaluation. The basic framework for feasibility analysis is the **capital budgeting model**, in which cost savings and other benefits, as well as initial outlay costs, operating costs, and other cash outflows, are translated into dollar estimates. The estimated benefits are compared with the estimated costs to determine if the system is cost beneficial. When possible, benefits and costs that are not easily quantifiable should be estimated and included in the feasibility analysis. If they cannot be accurately estimated, they should be listed and the likelihood of their occurring and the expected impact on the organization evaluated.

Some of the tangible and intangible benefits a company might obtain from a new system are cost savings; improved customer service, productivity, decision making, and data processing; better management control; and increased job satisfaction and employee morale.

Equipment costs are an initial outlay cost if the system is purchased and an operating cost if rented or leased. Equipment costs vary from $1,000 for PC systems to millions of dollars for enormous mainframes. Equipment costs are usually less than the cost of acquiring software and maintaining, supporting, and operating the system. Software acquisition costs include the purchase price of software, as well as the time and effort required to design, program, test, and document software. The human resource costs associated with hiring, training, and relocating staff can be substantial. Site preparation costs may also be incurred for large computer systems. In addition, there are costs involved in installing the new system and converting files to the appropriate format and storage media.

The primary operating cost is maintaining the system. Studies show that between 65% and 75% of an organization's systems efforts are spent in maintaining current information systems. In addition, there may be significant annual cash outflows for equipment replacement and expansion, as well as software updates. Human resource costs include the salaries of systems analysts, programmers, operators, data entry operators, and management. Costs are also incurred for supplies, overhead, and financial charges. Initial outlay and operating costs are summarized in Table 18-2.

Capital Budgeting

During systems design, several alternative approaches to meeting system requirements are developed. Various feasibility measures are then used to narrow the list of alternatives. Almost all large organizations use one or more capital budgeting return-on-investment techniques to evaluate the economic merits of the alternatives. For example, Merrill Lynch had to overcome a number of significant philosophical and bureaucratic obstacles to implement a return-on-investment program for information technology expenditures. Merrill Lynch now requires a 15% cash return on equity investment within five years, and all IT spending decisions are made by business, finance, and IT professionals working together.

The following are three commonly used capital budgeting techniques:

1　**Payback period**. This is the number of years required for the net savings to equal the initial cost of the investment. The project with the shortest payback period is usually selected.
2　**Net present value (NPV)**. With the NPV method, all estimated future cash flows are discounted back to the present, using a discount rate that reflects the time value of money. The initial outlay costs are deducted from the discounted cash flows to obtain the NPV. A positive NPV indicates the alternative is economically feasible. When comparing projects, the one with the highest positive NPV is usually accepted.
3　**Internal rate of return (IRR)**. The IRR is the effective interest rate that results in an NPV of zero. A project's IRR is compared with a minimum acceptable

Table 18-2
Initial Outlay and Operating
Costs

Hardware
 Central processing unit
 Peripherals
 Communications hardware
 Special input/output devices
 Upgrade and expansion costs
Software
 Application, system, general-purpose, utility,
 and communications software
 Updated versions of software
 Application software design, programming,
 modification, and testing
Staff
 Supervisors
 Analysts and programmers
 Computer operators
 Input (data conversion) personnel
 Recruitment and staff training
 Consultants
Supplies and overhead
 Preprinted forms
 Data storage devices
 Supplies (paper, toner)
 Utilities and power

Maintenance/backup
 Hardware/software maintenance
 Backup and recovery operations
 Power supply protection
Documentation
 Systems documentation
 Training program documentation
 Operating standards and
 procedures
Site preparation
 Air-conditioning, humidity,
 and dust controls
 Physical security (access)
 Fire and water protection
 Cabling, wiring, and outlets
 Furnishings and fixtures
Installation
 Freight and delivery charges
 Setup and connection fees
Conversion
 Systems testing
 File and data conversions
 Parallel operations
Financial
 Finance charges
 Legal fees
 Insurance

rate to determine acceptance or rejection. When comparing projects, the proposal with the highest IRR is usually selected.

Payback, NPV, and IRR are illustrated in the feasibility analysis for Shoppers Mart shown in Table 18-8 (see page 704).

Behavioral Aspects of Change

Individuals participating in systems development are agents of change who are continually confronted by people's reactions and resistance to change. The **behavioral aspects of change** are crucial, because the best system will fail without the support of the people it serves. Niccolo Machiavelli discussed resistance to change some 400 years ago:[1]

> *It must be considered that there is nothing more difficult to carry out, nor more doubtful of success, nor more dangerous to handle, than to initiate a new order of things. For the reformer has enemies in all those who could profit by the old order, and only lukewarm defenders in all those who could profit by the new order. This lukewarmness arises partly from fear of their adversaries, who have the laws in their favor, and partly from the incredulity of mankind, who do not truly believe in anything new until they have had an actual experience of it.*

[1]Niccolo Machiavelli, *The Prince*, translated by Luigi Rice, revised by E.R.P. Vincent (New York: New American Library, 1952).

Organizations must be sensitive to and consider the feelings and reactions of persons affected by change. They also should be aware of the type of behavioral problems that can result from changes, as discussed in this section.

Why Behavioral Problems Occur

Individuals' views of change as good or bad will usually depend on how they are personally affected by it. For example, management views change positively if it increases profits or performance or reduces costs. Employees, on the other hand, will view the same change as bad if their jobs are terminated or adversely affected.

To minimize adverse behavioral reactions, one must first understand why resistance takes place. Some of the more important factors include the following:

- **Personal characteristics and background.** Generally speaking, the younger and more highly educated people are, the more likely they are to accept change. Likewise, the more comfortable people are with technology, the less likely they are to oppose changes in an AIS.
- **Manner in which change is introduced.** Resistance is often a reaction to the methods of instituting change rather than to change itself. For example, the rationale used to sell the system to top management may not be appropriate for lower-level employees. The elimination of menial tasks and the ability to advance and grow are often more important to users than are increasing profits and reducing costs.
- **Experience with prior changes.** Employees who had a bad experience with prior changes are more reluctant to cooperate when future changes occur.
- **Top-management support.** Employees who sense a lack of top-management support for change wonder why they themselves should endorse it.
- **Communication.** Employees are unlikely to support a change unless the reasons behind it are explained.
- **Biases and natural resistance to change.** People with emotional attachments to their duties or coworkers may not want to change if those elements are affected.
- **Disruptive nature of the change process.** Requests for information and interviews are distracting and place additional burdens on people. These disturbances can create negative feelings toward the change that prompted them to occur.
- **Fear.** Many people fear the unknown and the uncertainty accompanying change. They also fear losing their jobs, losing respect or status, failure, technology, and automation.

How People Resist AIS Changes

Behavioral problems may begin as soon as people find out that a system change is being considered. Initial resistance is often subtle, manifested by tardiness, subpar performance, or failure to provide developers with information. Major behavioral problems often occur after the new system has been implemented and the change has become a reality. Focus 18-4 explains the resistance to change that the U.S. Department of Defense has experienced in trying to update its information systems.

Major resistance often takes one of three forms: aggression, projection, or avoidance.

Aggression

Aggression is behavior that is usually intended to destroy, cripple, or weaken the system's effectiveness. It may take the form of increased error rates, disruptions, or deliberate sabotage. One organization introduced an online AIS only to discover soon

18-4 FOCUS Resistance to Change at the Department of Defense

The U.S. Department of Defense (DoD) has a budget of $417 billion, 3.3 million employees, and over $1 trillion in assets. It also has one of the world's most antiquated and inefficient information systems, is unable to produce accurate accounting information, and cannot get a clean audit. The DoD has over 4,000 systems, and only a few of them are integrated and communicate effectively with other systems. Most systems still require data that are transferred between systems to be manually reentered.

The DoD has been trying to modernize its AIS for over 20 years, at a cost of over $35 billion. It has had three notable failures and is trying a fourth time with the creation of the Business Management Modernization Project (BMMP). BMMP's goal is to integrate the DoD's systems and business processes and produce a system that is transparent to the users. Unfortunately, many people would rather not see the DoD realize this transparency.

One of the main reasons past reforms have failed is resistance to change. System developers could not break through the barriers the armed forces and other DoD agencies created to protect their processes, procedures, and chains of command.

Users resist integration because what is optimal for one user is often suboptimal for the DoD. For instance,

legislation requires all DoD business or financial-system purchases over $1 million to be approved by the DoD comptroller, in accordance with BMMP standards. DoD personnel ignored the mandate and in one 10-month period purchased over $863 million of systems. No one was ever reprimanded or punished for the violations.

Government bureaucrats and members of Congress resist transparency because an integrated, transparent system might bring to light the many unnecessary or obsolete programs that further personal agendas. An example is promoting managers for their ability to generate, receive funding for, and operate programs, regardless of how effective they are.

Senators and congressional representatives resist transparency because a new system could adversely affects their ability to steer contract spending to constituents, resulting in the loss of their support and the possibility that they might not be reelected.

The DoD is trying to overcome these behavioral problems by trying to convince the armed forces to rid themselves of their "program protection" mindset. One notable success is the Air Force promoting personnel based on actions that improve the Air Force as a whole, rather than on actions that defend a specific turf or program.

thereafter that the data input devices were inoperable; some had honey poured into them, others had been mysteriously run over by forklifts, and still others had paper clips inserted in them. Employees had also entered erroneous data into the system. More subtle forms of aggression can also undermine the system's intended use. In another organization, disgruntled workers used the new system to gang up on an unpopular foreman. Instead of clocking in and out as they moved from one station to another, they punched in at the foreman's department for the entire day and proceeded to work in different areas. This adversely affected the foreman's performance evaluation, as he was charged for hours that did not belong to his operation.

Projection

Projection involves blaming the new system for any and every unpleasant occurrence. For example, a new system is blamed for missing and incorrect data until the actual cause is determined. In essence, the system becomes the scapegoat for all real and imagined problems and errors. If these criticisms are not controlled or answered, the integrity of the system can be damaged or destroyed.

Avoidance

Dealing with problems through **avoidance** is a common human trait. For example, a person who cannot decide between two job offers may delay a decision until one company withdraws its offer and the decision is made for him. Likewise, one way for employees to deal with a new AIS is to avoid using it in the hope that the problem (the system) can be ignored or that it will eventually go away.

Davis Controls, a struggling manufacturer, processed its orders using e-mail but pertinent information was frequently lost or forgotten. Recognizing it had to improve

its customer service to survive, Davis invested $300,000 in software that efficiently captured customer information, properly handled purchase orders, performed other complex business processes, and helped managers make better daily decisions. It also allowed the company to process three to four times as many transactions as before. However, the CEO could not get many employees to use it, even though he explained the system's benefits and efficiencies and told the employees that the company survival, and their jobs, were at stake. Finally, the CEO disabled the uncooperative employees' e-mail accounts. When his chief technology officer and another employee continued to avoid the system, the CEO finally decided to terminate them.

Preventing Behavioral Problems

The human element is often thought to be the most significant problem a company encounters in designing, developing, and implementing a system. Although there is no one best way to overcome behavioral problems, people's reactions can be improved by observing the following guidelines:

- **Meet users' needs.** It is essential that the form, content, and volume of system output be designed to satisfy user needs.
- **Keep communication lines open.** Managers and users should be fully informed of system changes as soon as possible. They should be told what changes are being made and why, and they should be shown how the new system will benefit them. The objective is to help employees identify with the company's efforts to improve the system. This helps ensure that employees feel they are key players in the company's future goals and plans. Open communication also helps prevent damaging and inaccurate rumors and misunderstandings. Employees should be told who they can contact if they have questions or concerns.
- **Maintain a safe and open atmosphere.** It is vital that everyone affected by systems development have an attitude of trust and cooperation. If employees become hostile, it will be difficult to change their attitude or to implement the system successfully.
- **Obtain management support.** When possible, a powerful champion, who can provide resources for the system and motivate others to assist and cooperate with systems development, should be appointed.
- **Allay fears.** The organization should provide assurances (to the extent possible) that no major job losses or responsibility shifts will occur. These goals can be achieved through relocation, attrition, and early retirement. If employees are terminated, severance pay and outplacement services should be provided.
- **Solicit user participation.** Those who will use or be affected by the system should participate in its development by providing data, making suggestions, and helping make decisions. Participation is ego enhancing, challenging, and intrinsically satisfying. Users who participate in development are more knowledgeable, better trained, and more committed to using the system.
- **Provide honest feedback.** To avoid misunderstandings, users should be told which suggestions are being used and how, which suggestions are not being used and why, and which ones will be incorporated at a later date.
- **Make sure users understand the system.** Effective use or support cannot be obtained if users are confused about or do not understand the system. Generally, those who have a working knowledge of computers often underestimate user training needs.
- **Humanize the system.** System acceptance is unlikely if individuals believe the computer is controlling them or has usurped their positions.
- **Describe new challenges and opportunities.** System developers should emphasize important and challenging tasks that can be performed with the

new system. That the system may provide greater job satisfaction and increased opportunities for advancement also should be emphasized.

- **Reexamine performance evaluation.** Users' performance standards and criteria should be reevaluated to ensure that they are satisfactory in view of changes brought on by the new system.
- **Test the system's integrity.** The system should be properly tested prior to implementation to minimize initial bad impressions.
- **Avoid emotionalism.** When logic vies with emotion, it rarely stands a chance. Emotional issues related to change should be allowed to cool, handled in a nonconfrontational manner, or sidestepped.
- **Present the system in the proper context.** Users are vitally interested in how system changes affect them personally. Relevant explanations should be presented that address their concerns, rather than the concerns of managers or developers.
- **Control users' expectations.** A system is sold too well if users have unrealistic expectations of its capabilities and performance. Be realistic when describing the merits of the system.
- **Keep the system simple.** Avoid complex systems that cause radical changes. Make the change seem as simple as possible by conforming to existing organizational procedures.

Observing these guidelines is time-consuming and expensive, and workers may skip difficult steps to speed systems development and installation. However, the problems caused by not following these guidelines are usually more expensive and time-consuming to fix than preventing behavioral problems in the first place.

Systems Analysis

When a new or improved system is needed, a written **request for systems development** is prepared. The request describes the current system's problems, the reasons for the change, and the proposed system's goals and objectives, as well as its anticipated benefits and costs. The project development team conducts the analysis. The five steps in the analysis phase and their objectives are shown in Figure 18-4 and discussed in this section.

Initial Investigation

An **initial investigation** is conducted to screen projects. The person conducting an initial investigation must gain a clear picture of the problem or need, determine the project's viability and expected costs and payoffs, evaluate the project's scope and the nature of the new AIS, and recommend whether the development project should be initiated as proposed, modified, or abandoned.

During the initial investigation, the exact nature of the problem(s) under review must be determined. In some instances, what is thought to be the cause of the problem is not the real source. For example, a government accountant once asked a consultant to develop an AIS to produce the information he needed on fund expenditures and available funds. Further investigation showed that the agency's system already provided the information. The accountant simply did not understand the reports he was receiving.

The project's scope (what it should and should not seek to accomplish) also must be determined. A new AIS is useful when problems are a result of lack of information, inaccessibility of data, and inefficient data processing. However, a new AIS is not the answer to organizational problems, such as the controller managing too many employees. Likewise, if a manager lacks organizational skills or if a failure to enforce existing procedures causes control problems, a new AIS is not the answer.

Figure 18-4
Steps in Systems Analysis

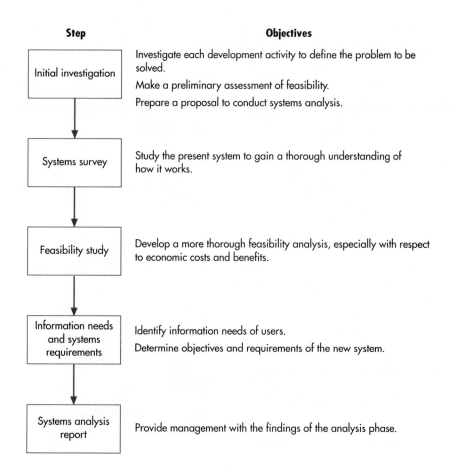

Step	Objectives
Initial investigation	Investigate each development activity to define the problem to be solved. Make a preliminary assessment of feasibility. Prepare a proposal to conduct systems analysis.
Systems survey	Study the present system to gain a thorough understanding of how it works.
Feasibility study	Develop a more thorough feasibility analysis, especially with respect to economic costs and benefits.
Information needs and systems requirements	Identify information needs of users. Determine objectives and requirements of the new system.
Systems analysis report	Provide management with the findings of the analysis phase.

If a project is approved, a **proposal to conduct systems analysis** is prepared. It is assigned a priority and added to the master plan, and the development team begins the survey of the existing AIS. As the investigation progresses, the proposal will be modified as more information becomes available. The table of contents for the Shoppers Mart proposal, shown in Table 18-3, is representative of the information in a proposal to conduct systems analysis.

Systems Survey

During the **systems survey**, an extensive study of the current AIS is undertaken. This survey may take weeks or months, depending on the complexity and scope of the system. The objectives of a systems survey are as follows:

- Gain a thorough understanding of company operations, policies, and procedures; data and information flow; AIS strengths and weaknesses; and available hardware, software, and personnel.
- Make preliminary assessments of current and future processing needs, and determine the extent and nature of the changes needed.
- Develop working relationships with users and build support for the AIS.
- Collect data that identify user needs, conduct a feasibility analysis, and make recommendations to management.

Data about the current AIS can be gathered internally from employees, as well as from documentation such as organizational charts and procedures manuals. External sources include consultants, customers and suppliers, industry associations, and government agencies. The advantages and disadvantages of four common methods of gathering data are summarized here and in Table 18-4.

Table 18-3
Table of Contents for Reports Prepared During Systems Analysis at Shoppers Mart

SHOPPERS MART PROPOSAL TO CONDUCT SYSTEMS ANALYSIS	SHOPPERS MART SYSTEMS SURVEY REPORT	SHOPPERS MART SYSTEMS ANALYSIS REPORT
Table of Contents	**Table of Contents**	**Table of Contents**
I. Executive Summary	I. Executive Summary	I. Executive Summary
II. System Problems and Opportunities	II. System Goals and Objectives	II. System Goals and Objectives
III. Goals and Objectives of Proposed System	III. System Problems and Opportunities	III. System Problems and Opportunities
IV. Project Scope	IV. Current System Operations	IV. Project Scope
V. Anticipated Costs and Benefits	A. Policies, Procedures, and Practices Affecting System	V. Relationship of Project to Overall Strategic Information Systems Plan
VI. Participants in Development Project	B. System Design and Operation (Intended and Actual)	VI. Current System Operations
VII. Proposed System Development Tasks and Work Plan	C. System Users and Their Responsibilities	VII. User Requirements
VIII. Recommendations	D. System Outputs, Inputs, and Data Storage	VIII. Feasibility Analysis
	E. System Controls	IX. System Constraints
	F. System Strengths, Weaknesses, and Constraints	X. Recommendations for New System
	G. Costs to Operate System	XI. Proposed Project Participants and Work Plan
	V. User Requirements Identified	XII. Summary
		XIII. Approvals
		XIV. Appendix of Documents, Tables, Charts, Glossary of Terms

An *interview* helps gather answers to "why" questions: Why is there a problem? Why does the AIS work this way? Why is this information important? Care must be taken, however, to ensure that interviewees' personal biases, self-interest, or desire to say what they think the interviewer wants to hear do not produce inaccurate information.

Ann Christy's interviews at Shoppers Mart were successful because of her approach and preparation. For each interview, she made an appointment, explained the purpose beforehand, indicated the amount of time needed, and arrived on time. Before each session she studied the interviewee's responsibilities and listed the points she wanted to cover. She put each interviewee at ease by being friendly, courteous, and tactful. Her questions dealt with the person's responsibilities, how the person interacted with the AIS, how the system might be improved, and the person's information needs. She let the interviewee do most of the talking and paid special attention to nonverbal communication, because subtle overtones and body language can be as significant as direct responses to questions. She took notes and augmented them with detailed impressions shortly after the interview. She asked permission to tape especially important interviews.

Questionnaires are used when the amount of information to be gathered is small and well defined, is obtained from many people or from those who are physically removed, or is intended to verify data from other sources. Questionnaires take relatively little time to administer, but developing a quality questionnaire can be challenging and requires significant time and effort.

Observation is used to verify information gathered using other approaches and to determine how a system actually works, rather than how it should work. It can be difficult to interpret observations properly because observed people may change their normal behavior or make mistakes. Observation effectiveness is maximized by identifying what is to be observed, estimating how long it will take, obtaining permission, and

Table 18-4
Advantages and Disadvantages of Data-Gathering Methods

	Advantages	**Disadvantages**
Interviews	Can answer "why" questions Interviewer can probe and follow up Questions can be clarified Builds positive relationships with interviewee Builds acceptance and support for new system	Time-consuming Expensive Personal biases or self-interest may produce inaccurate information
Questionnaires	Can be anonymous Not time-consuming Inexpensive Allows more time to think about responses	Does not allow in-depth questions or answers Cannot probe or follow up on responses Questions cannot be clarified Impersonal; does not build relationships Difficult to develop Often ignored or completed superficially
Observation	Can verify how system *actually* works, rather than how it *should* work Results in greater understanding of system	Time-consuming Expensive Difficult to interpret properly Observed people may alter behavior
Systems Documentation	Describes how system should work Written form facilitates review, analysis	Time-consuming May not be available or easy to find

explaining what will be done and why. The observer should not make value judgments, and notes and impressions should be formally documented as soon as possible. For example, a systems analyst could observe a customer representative interacting with customers to better understand what customer representatives do and what information they need.

Systems documentation describes how the AIS is intended to work. Throughout the systems survey, the project team should be alert to differences between intended and actual systems operation. These differences provide important insights into problems and weaknesses. If documentation is unavailable or incomplete, it may be worthwhile to develop it.

Document Findings and Model the Existing System

The information gathered during the analysis phase must be documented so it can be used throughout the systems development project. Documentation consists of questionnaire copies, interview notes, memos, and document copies. Another way of documenting a system is to model it. **Physical models** illustrate *how* a system functions by describing the flow of documents, the computer processes performed and the people performing them, the equipment used, and any other physical elements of the system. **Logical models** illustrate *what* is being done, regardless of how the flow is actually accomplished. The logical model focuses on the essential activities and the flow of information, not on the physical processes of transforming and storing data. Table 18-5

CASE (Chapter 19)	Gantt charts (Chapter 18)
Data dictionary (Chapter 4)	PERT charts (Chapter 18)
Data flow diagrams (Chapter 3)	Prototyping (Chapter 19)
Document flowcharts (Chapter 3)	REA data models (Chapter 15)
E-R diagrams (Chapter 15)	Record layouts (Chapter 4)
Forms design checklist (Chapter 20)	System flowcharts (Chapter 3)

Table 18-5
Systems Analysis and Design
Tools and Techniques

lists the analysis and design tools and techniques accountants and system developers use to create an AIS and identifies the chapter where each is discussed in this text.

Analyze the Existing System

Once data gathering is complete, the survey team evaluates the AIS's strengths and weaknesses to develop ideas for designing and structuring the new AIS. When appropriate, strengths should be retained and weaknesses corrected. For example, if output is being duplicated, consolidating reports might produce cost savings.

Prepare Systems Survey Report

The systems survey culminates with a **systems survey report**. Table 18-3 shows the table of contents for the Shoppers Mart systems survey report. The report is supported by documentation such as memos, interview and observation notes, questionnaire data, file and record layouts and descriptions, input and output descriptions, copies of documents, flowcharts, and data flow diagrams.

Feasibility Study

At this point in systems analysis, a more thorough feasibility analysis is conducted to determine the project's viability. Especially important is economic feasibility, as discussed previously in this chapter. The feasibility analysis is updated regularly as the project proceeds and costs and benefits become clearer.

Information Needs and Systems Requirements

Once a project is deemed feasible, the company identifies the information needs of AIS users and documents systems requirements. Table 18-6 is an example of systems requirements.

Determining information needs can be a challenging process due to the sheer quantity and variety of information that must be specified, even for a relatively simple AIS. In addition, it may be difficult for employees to articulate their information needs or they may identify them incorrectly. According to *CIO* magazine, when development projects fail, about 70% of the time it is because of insufficient, inaccurate, or outdated systems requirements. Figure 18-5 is a humorous view of the types of communication problems associated with this process.

Table 18-6
Possible Contents of System Requirements

Processes	A description of all business processes, including what is to be done and by whom
Data elements	A description of the data elements needed, including their name, size, format, source, and significance
Data structure	A preliminary data structure, showing how the data elements will be organized into logical records
Outputs	A copy of system outputs and a description of their purpose, frequency, and distribution
Inputs	A copy of system inputs and a description of their contents, source, and who is responsible for them
Documentation	A description of how the new system and each subsystem will operate
Constraints	A description of constraints such as deadlines, schedules, security requirements, staffing limitations, and statutory or regulatory requirements
Controls	Controls to ensure the accuracy and reliability of inputs, outputs, and processing
Reorganizations	Organizational reorganization needed to meet users' information needs, such as increasing staff levels, adding new job functions, restructuring, or terminating existing positions or jobs

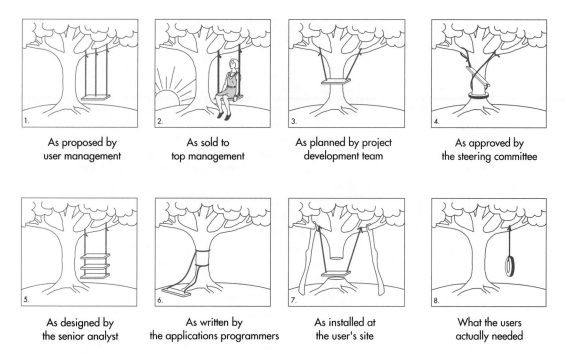

As proposed by user management	As sold to top management	As planned by project development team	As approved by the steering committee
As designed by the senior analyst	As written by the applications programmers	As installed at the user's site	What the users actually needed

Figure 18-5
Communications Problems in Systems Analysis and Design

To illustrate the importance of accurately determining systems requirements, consider the example of Corning Corporation. When the company began investigating the quality of the ophthalmic pressings it manufactures and sells to the makers of prescription lenses, it found that 35% of its drafting documents contained errors. Corning also found that the drafting errors became increasingly expensive to correct at each subsequent stage of the manufacturing process. It cost $250 if the errors were discovered before the toolmakers cut the tools, $20,000 if discovered before the assembly line began production, and up to $100,000 after the tools were sent to the customer. As a result of the study, several corrective actions were implemented that reduced the error rates from 35% to 0.2%. The same type of cost relationship exists in information systems development. The cost to correct an error increases as development proceeds through the SDLC phases.

Systems Objectives and Constraints

Many organizations take a **systems approach** to determining information needs and system requirements Problems and alternatives are viewed from the standpoint of the entire organization, rather than from any single department or interest group.

It is important to determine system objectives so that analysts and users can focus on those elements most vital to the AIS's success (see Table 18-7); however, it is difficult for a system to satisfy every objective. For example, designing adequate internal controls must be viewed as a trade-off between the objectives of economy and reliability. Similarly, cutting clerical costs must balance the objectives of capacity, flexibility, and customer service.

Organizational constraints usually make it impossible to develop all parts of a new AIS simultaneously. Therefore, the system is divided into smaller subsystems, or modules, that are analyzed, developed, and installed independently. When changes are made to the system, only the affected module needs to be changed. Great care should be taken to ensure that the modules are properly integrated into a workable system.

A system's success often depends on the project team's ability to cope with the constraints the organization faces. Common constraints include governmental agency requirements, management policies and guidelines, lack of sufficiently qualified staff,

Table 18-7
AIS Objectives

Usefulness	Information output should help management and users make decisions.
Economy	The benefits of the system should exceed the cost.
Reliability	The system should process data accurately and completely.
Availability	Users should be able to access the system at their convenience.
Timeliness	Crucial information should be produced first, and less important items as time permits.
Customer service	Courteous and efficient customer service should be provided.
Capacity	System capacity should handle periods of peak operation and future growth.
Ease of use	The system should be user-friendly.
Flexibility	The system should accommodate reasonable operating or system requirements changes.
Tractability	The system should be easily understood by users and designers and facilitate problem solving and future systems development.
Auditability	Auditability should be built into the system from the beginning.
Security	Only authorized users should be granted access or allowed to change system data.

the capabilities and attitudes of system users, available technology, and limited financial resources. To maximize system performance, the effects of these constraints on system design must be minimized.

Strategies for Determining Requirements

One or more of the following four strategies are used to determine AIS requirements:

1 **Ask users what they need.** Though this is the simplest and fastest strategy, many people do not realize or understand their true needs. Although they may know how to do their jobs, they may not be able to break them down into the individual information elements they use. It is sometimes better to ask users questions pertaining to what decisions they make and what processes they are involved in and then help them design systems to address their answers. Users must think beyond their current information needs so that new systems do not simply replicate the current information in new and improved formats.

2 **Analyze existing systems.** Both internal and external systems should be analyzed. A partial solution may already exist, thus eliminating the problem of reinventing the wheel.

3 **Examine existing system use.** This strategy differs from the previous one by taking into account that certain modules may not be used as intended, may be augmented by manual tasks, or may be avoided altogether. This approach helps determine if a system can be modified or must be replaced.

4 **Create a prototype.** When it is difficult to identify a usable set of requirements, a developer can quickly rough out a system for users to critique. Once users see something on the screen, they can begin to identify what they like and dislike and request changes. This iterative process of looking at what is developed and then improving it continues until users agree on their needs. Prototyping is discussed in Chapter 19.

Documentation and Approval of User Requirements

Detailed requirements for the new AIS that explain exactly what the system must produce should be created and documented. How to produce the required features is determined during the design phase of the SDLC. The requirements list should be

supported by sample input and output forms, as well as charts, to make it easier for readers to conceptualize the system. A nontechnical summary that captures important user requirements and development efforts to date is often prepared for management.

When user requirements have been determined and documented, the project team meets with the users, explains the requirements, and obtains their agreement and approval. When an agreement is reached, user management should sign the appropriate system requirements documents to indicate approval.

Systems Analysis Report

Systems analysis is concluded by preparing a **systems analysis report** to summarize and document the analysis activities and serve as a repository of data from which systems designers can draw. The report shows the new system's goal and objectives, the scope of the project and the new system, how the new system fits into the company's master plan, the user's processing requirements and information needs, the feasibility analysis, and recommendations for the new system. The Shoppers Mart report, shown in Table 18-3, shows in more detail the information typically contained in the report.

A go/no-go decision may be made up to three times during systems analysis: (1) during the initial investigation, to determine whether to conduct a systems survey; (2) at the end of the feasibility study, to determine whether to proceed to the information requirements phase; and (3) at the completion of the analysis phase, to decide whether to proceed to the next phase.

After systems analysis is completed, projects developed using the SDLC approach move to the conceptual design phase and then to physical design, implementation and conversion, and operation and maintenance. These topics are discussed in the next two chapters.

 SUMMARY AND CASE CONCLUSION

After conducting an extensive analysis of Shoppers Mart's current system and core business processes, Ann Christy, in consultation with the information systems steering committee, decided she wanted the corporate office to gather daily sales data from each store. Analyzing the prior day's sales will help Shoppers Mart adapt quickly to customer needs. Providing sales data to suppliers will help avoid stockouts and overstocking.

Coordinating buying at the corporate office will help Shoppers Mart to minimize inventory levels and negotiate lower wholesale prices. Stores will send orders electronically the day they are prepared. Based on store orders, the previous day's sales figures, and warehouse inventory, Shoppers Mart will send purchase orders to suppliers. Suppliers will process orders and ship goods to regional warehouses or directly to the stores the day orders are received. Each store will have the flexibility to respond to local sales trends and conditions by placing local orders. Accounts payable will be centralized so the firm can make payments electronically.

Ann reviewed the system with the legal department and the AIS staff and was assured that it complied with all legal considerations and was technologically feasible. Top management and the information systems steering committee will decide how to allocate time and resources for this massive project and will communicate all staff assignments to systems management and personnel.

Ann's team conducted an economic feasibility study and determined that the project makes excellent use of funds. As shown in Table 18-8, the team estimated that initial outlay costs for the system are $5 million (new hardware and initial systems design $2 million each; software $400,000; and training, site preparation, and conversion $200,000 each).

Table 18-8
Economic Feasibility of Shoppers Mart's New Information System

	Initial Outlay	Year 1	Year 2	Year 3	Year 4	Year 5	Year 6
INITIAL OUTLAY COSTS							
Hardware	$2,000,000						
Software	400,000						
Training	200,000						
Site preparation	200,000						
Initial systems design	2,000,000						
Conversion	200,000						
Total initial outlays	$5,000,000						
Recurring costs							
Hardware expansion			$260,000	$300,000	$340,000	$380,000	$400,000
Software			150,000	200,000	225,000	250,000	250,000
Systems maintenance		$60,000	120,000	130,000	140,000	150,000	160,000
Personnel costs		500,000	800,000	900,000	1,000,000	1,100,000	1,300,000
Communication charges		100,000	160,000	180,000	200,000	220,000	250,000
Overhead		300,000	420,000	490,000	560,000	600,000	640,000
Total costs		$960,000	$1,910,000	$2,200,000	$2,465,000	$2,700,000	$3,000,000
Savings							
Clerical cost savings		$600,000	$1,200,000	$1,400,000	$1,600,000	$1,800,000	$2,000,000
Working capital savings		900,000	1,200,000	1,500,000	1,500,000	1,500,000	1,500,000
Profits from sales increases			500,000	900,000	1,200,000	1,500,000	1,800,000
Warehousing efficiencies			400,000	800,000	1,200,000	1,600,000	2,000,000
Total savings		$1,500,000	$3,300,000	$4,600,000	$5,500,000	$6,400,000	$7,300,000
Savings minus recurring costs		$540,000	$1,390,000	$2,400,000	$3,035,000	$3,700,000	$4,300,000
Less income taxes (34% rate)		(183,600)	(472,600)	(816,000)	(1,031,900)	(1,258,000)	(1,462,000)
Cash savings (net of tax)		$356,400	$917,400	$1,584,000	$2,003,100	$2,442,000	$2,838,000
Savings on taxes due to depreciation deduction		340,000	544,000	326,400	195,500	195,500	98,600
Net savings	($5,000,000)	$696,400	$1,461,400	$1,910,400	$2,198,600	$2,637,500	$2,936,600

Payback occurs in the fourth year when the savings net of taxes of $6,266,800 exceed the costs of $5,000,000.

Net present value (interest rate of 10%):

	($5,000,000)
696,400 × 0.9091 =	633,097
1,461,400 × 0.8265 =	1,207,847
1,910,400 × 0.7513 =	1,435,284
2,198,600 × 0.6830 =	1,501,644
2,637,500 × 0.6209 =	1,637,624
2,936,600 × 0.5645 =	1,657,711
Net present value is	$3,073,207
Internal rate of return is	25.04%

Depreciation on initial investment of $5,000,000:
Tax Rate 34%

Year	Rate (%)	Depreciation	Tax Savings
1	20.00	$1,000,000	$340,000
2	32.00	1,600,000	544,000
3	19.20	960,000	326,400
4	11.50	575,000	195,500
5	11.50	575,000	195,500
6	5.80	290,000	98,600

The team estimated what it would cost to operate the system for its estimated six-year life, as well as what the system would save the company. The following recurring costs were identified: hardware expansion, additional software and software updates, systems maintenance, added personnel to operate the system, communication charges, and overhead. The system will also save Shoppers Mart money by eliminating clerical jobs, generating working capital savings, increasing sales and profits, and decreasing warehouse costs. The costs and savings for years 1 through 6, which are expected to rise from year to year, are shown in Table 18-8.

Ann calculated the annual savings minus the recurring additional costs and then calculated the after-tax cash savings for each year. The $5 million system can be depreciated over the six-year period (see Table 18-8 for the rates). For example, the depreciation in year 1 of $1 million reduces net income by that amount. Because the company does not have to pay taxes on the $1 million at its tax rate of 34%, it ends up saving an additional $340,000 in year 1. Finally, Ann calculated the net savings for each year.

Shoppers Mart has a 10% cost of capital. Ann used this rate to calculate the NPV of the investment, which is over $3 million. The internal rate of return is a lofty 25%. Ann realized how advantageous it would be for the company to borrow the money (at a 10% interest rate) to produce a 25% return on that borrowed money. In addition, payback occurs in the fourth year.

Ann presented the system to top management and described its objectives. Challenges to her estimates were plugged into the spreadsheet model so that management could see the effect of the changed assumptions. Even the stiffest challenges to Ann's numbers showed a positive return. As a result of the meeting, top management was supportive of the new system, requested some changes, and told Ann to proceed.

Ann soon found management's enthusiastic support crucial to the system's success. Several employees with vested interests in the current system believed it was adequate and were critical of her ideas. Some employees remembered the problems Shoppers Mart had when the current system was implemented years ago. Ann concluded that those who resisted the new system were afraid of the change and its effect on them personally. To counter the negative behavioral reactions, Ann took great pains to explain to all employees how the new system would benefit them individually and the company as a whole. With management's approval, she assured employees they would not lose their jobs and that all affected employees would be retrained. She involved the two most vocal opponents to the system change in planning activities, and soon they became two of its biggest advocates.

Ann set up a steering committee and was granted approval to put the managers of all affected departments on the committee. A master plan for developing the system was formulated, and the system was broken down into manageable projects. The projects were prioritized, and project teams were formed to begin work on the highest-priority projects. Documentation standards were developed and approved.

KEY TERMS

systems development life cycle (SDLC) 683
systems analysis 684
conceptual design 684
physical design 684
implementation and conversion 684
operations and maintenance 684

information systems steering committee 685
systems analyst 686
computer programmer 686
project development plan 686
master plan 687

program evaluation and review technique (PERT) 687
critical path 687
Gantt chart 688
feasibility study 689
economic feasibility 690
technical feasibility 690
legal feasibility 690

AIS IN ACTION

CHAPTER QUIZ

1. Which of the following is *not* one of the reasons why companies make changes to their AISs?
 a. gain a competitive advantage
 b. increase productivity
 c. keep up with company growth
 d. downsize company operations
 e. All of the above are reasons why companies change an AIS.

2. The planning technique that identifies implementation activities and their relationships, constructs a network of arrows and nodes, and then determines the critical path through the network is referred to as which of the following:
 a. Gantt chart
 b. PERT diagram
 c. physical model
 d. data flow diagram

3. The purchasing department is designing a new AIS. Who is best able to determine departmental information requirements?
 a. steering committee
 b. controller
 c. top management
 d. purchasing department

4. Which of the following is the correct order of the steps in systems analysis?
 a. initial investigation, determination of information needs and system requirements, feasibility study, system survey
 b. determination of information needs and system requirements, system survey, feasibility study, initial investigation
 c. system survey, initial investigation, determination of information needs and system requirements, feasibility study
 d. initial investigation, system survey, feasibility study, determination of information needs and system requirements

5. Which of the following is the long-range planning document that specifies what the system will consist of, how it will be developed, who will develop it, how needed resources will be acquired, and its overall vision?
 a. steering committee agenda
 b. master plan
 c. systems development life cycle
 d. project development plan

6. Resistance is often a reaction to the methods of instituting change rather than to change itself.
 a. true
 b. false

7 Increased error rates, disruptions, and sabotage are examples of which of the following?

a. aggression c. projection
b. avoidance d. payback

8 What is the most significant problem a company encounters in designing, developing, and implementing a system?

a. the human element c. legal challenges
b. technology d. planning for the new system

9 Determining whether the organization has access to people who can design, implement, and operate the proposed system is referred to as which of the following?

a. technical feasibility d. scheduling feasibility
b. operational feasibility e. economic feasibility
c. legal feasibility

10 Which of the following is *not* one of the tangible or intangible benefits a company might obtain from a new system?

a. cost savings
b. improved customer service and productivity
c. improved decision making
d. improved data processing
e. All are benefits of a new system.

COMPREHENSIVE PROBLEM

Riverbend Software Support Administrators (RSSA) provides online and telephone help desk services to a wide variety of customers. However, RSSA has seen its labor costs steadily increase over the past three years and is considering outsourcing its call center operations to an Eastern European firm. RSSA maintains an executive-level committee that oversees the information systems function of the company. RSSA's management selected a project development team to create an information system that would facilitate moving the help desk, as well as monitor and manage the help desk from corporate headquarters.

During the conversion to the new help desk system, a server was damaged when an unidentified person from within the company put a hot coffeepot on it. In another incident, some backup data tapes were found floating in a company restroom sink. These incidents delayed the conversion date by 15 days.

The proposed five-year contract requires an immediate payment of $1,750,000. The contract will save $750,000 per year in salary, benefits, and equipment costs, as well as $360,000 per year for the current call center's building lease. However, there will be a $150,000 one-time charge for breaking the building lease. The contract will cost $525,000 per year for the call center's operations. RSSA's cost of capital, or discount rate, is 11%.

Required

 a. What is the executive-level committee mentioned in the problem narrative commonly called, who typically serves on this committee, and what is the committee's primary function?

 b. Who typically serves on the systems development team?

 c. What steps would the development team take during the system analysis phase of the project?

 d. What is one possible reason the server and data tapes were damaged?

 e. Calculate the following capital budgeting metrics for RSSA's outsourcing plan:
 1. payback period
 2. net present value (NPV)
 3. internal rate of return (IRR)

DISCUSSION QUESTIONS

18.1 The approach to long-range AIS planning described in this chapter is important for large organizations with extensive investments in computer facilities. Should small organizations with far fewer information systems employees attempt to implement planning programs? Why or why not? Be prepared to defend your position to the class.

18.2 Assume you are a consultant advising a firm on the design and implementation of a new system. Management has decided to let several employees go after the system is implemented. Some have many years of company service. How would you advise management to communicate this decision to the affected employees? To the entire staff?

18.3 While reviewing a list of benefits from a computer vendor's proposal, you note an item that reads, "Improvements in management decision making—$50,000 per year." How would you interpret this item? What influence should it have on the economic feasibility and the computer acquisition decision?

18.4 This chapter suggests that an organization should make special efforts to ease fears among its employees about potential job or seniority loss. One advantage of mechanizing a system, however, is a reduction of clerical costs, which often results in job losses. Are these two concepts inconsistent? What policies should be consistent with both concepts?

18.5 The president of Monteer Signature Homes is perplexed by requests for computers from three different areas of the firm. The EDP manager wants $4.5 million to upgrade the mainframe computer. The vice president of engineering wants $450,000 to buy a client/server system. The vice president of finance wants $200,000 to purchase laptop computers. Rapid growth is putting a strain on computer resources and keeping profits down. Payroll, accounting, inventory, and engineering functions are computerized, while some other tasks are manual. The firm is organized by business functions, with vice presidents for manufacturing, marketing, engineering, finance, and human resources. The president wonders if a steering committee is needed. Discuss the objectives, responsibilities, and composition of an information systems steering committee. Justify your recommendations concerning its membership and the selection of a chairperson.

(CIA Examination, adapted)

18.6 Describe some examples of systems analysis decisions that involve a trade-off between each of the following pairs of objectives:

 a. economy and usefulness **e.** simplicity and reliability
 b. economy and reliability **f.** economy and capacity
 c. economy and customer service **g.** economy and flexibility
 d. simplicity and usefulness

18.7 For years, Jerry Jingle's dairy production facilities led the state in total sales volume. However, recent declines left Jerry wondering what his company was doing wrong. When he asked several customers to rate his products, they seemed satisfied but did note several areas of concern. First on the list was the dairy company's record of late deliveries and incomplete orders. Further discussion with some of the company's production employees (not the cows) revealed several problems, including bottlenecks in milk pasteurization and homogenization due to a lack of coordination in job scheduling, mix-ups in customers' orders, and improperly labeled products. How would you suggest Jerry address the company's problems? What types of data-gathering techniques would be helpful at this early stage?

18.8 The following problem situations could arise in any manufacturing firm. What questions should you ask to understand the problem?
- Customer complaints about product quality have increased.
- Accounting sees an increase in the number and dollar value of bad-debt write-offs.
- Operating margins have declined each of the past four years due to higher-than-expected production costs from idle time, overtime, and reworking products.

18.9 For each of the following items, discuss which data-gathering method(s) are most appropriate and why:
- **a.** Surveying the adequacy of internal controls in the purchase requisition procedure
- **b.** Identifying the controller's information needs
- **c.** Determining how cash disbursement procedures are actually performed
- **d.** Surveying the opinions of employees concerning the move to a total quality management program
- **e.** Investigating an increase in uncollectible accounts

 PROBLEMS

18.1 Yuping Chai has seen the future, and so far she wants no part of it. The offices at Sierra Manufacturing Company, where Chai is vice president, have just been automated. Sitting at her desk in Sacramento, Chai can push buttons on a computer keyboard and staff memos will appear on the screen. She can respond with her own memos, which will instantly be sent to colleagues, either for immediate viewing or for storage and later retrieval. By pressing a few other buttons, she can view company financial data stored in the corporate computer. Chai can do all that and more, but instead she has unplugged her computer. "I think most managers, including me, are talkers," she states. "I would much rather talk than send electronic messages." Chai's resistance exemplifies the reaction of some professionals and executives who are being forced to make major psychological and behavioral adjustments as they begin to move into a paperless world.

Required
- **a.** What do you believe is the real cause of Chai's resistance to computers?
- **b.** As a colleague of Chai, how could you help her realize the benefits of computerization and overcome her computer phobia?

18.2 Mary Smith is the bookkeeper for Dave's Distributing Company, a distributor of soft drinks and juices. Because the company is rather small, Mary performs all the daily accounting tasks herself. Dave, the president and owner of the company, supervises the warehouse/delivery and front office staff, but he also spends much of his time jogging and skiing.

For several years profits were good and sales grew faster than industry averages. Although the accounting system was working well, bottlers were pressuring Dave to computerize. With a little guidance from a CPA friend and with no mention to Mary, Dave bought a new computer system and some accounting software. Only one day was required to set up the hardware, install the software, and convert the files. The morning the vendor installed the computer system, Mary's job performance changed dramatically. Although the software company provided two full days of training, she had trouble learning the new system. As a result, Dave decided she should run both the manual and computer systems for a month to verify the new system's accuracy.

Mary continually complained that she lacked the time and expertise to run both systems by herself. She also complained that she did not understand how to run the new computer system. To keep accounts up to date, Dave spent two to three hours a day running the new system himself. Dave found that much of the time spent running the system was devoted to identifying discrepancies between the computer and manual

results. When the error was located, it was almost always in the manual system. This significantly increased Dave's confidence in the new system.

At the end of the month Dave was ready to scrap the manual system, but Mary said she was not ready. Dave went back to skiing and jogging, and Mary went on with the manual system. When the computer system fell behind, Dave again spent time catching it up. He also worked with Mary to make sure she understood how to operate the computer system.

Months later Dave was still keeping the computer system up to date and training Mary. He was at the height of frustration. "I'm sure Mary *knows* how to run the system, but she doesn't seem to *want* to. I can do all the accounting work on the computer in two or three hours a day, but she can't even do it in her normal eight-hour workday. What should I do?"

Required

 a. What events may have contributed to the new system's failure?
 b. In retrospect, how should Dave have handled the computerization of the accounting system?
 c. At what point in the decision-making process should Mary have been informed? Should she have had some say in whether the computer was purchased? If so, what should have been the nature of her input? If Mary had not agreed with Dave's decision to acquire the computer, what should Dave have done?
 d. A hard decision must be made regarding Mary. Significant efforts have been made to train her, but they have been unsuccessful. What would you recommend at this point? Should she be fired? Threatened with the loss of her job? Moved somewhere else in the business? Given additional training?

18.3 Wright Company's computer system was developed in stages over the past five years. During the design process, department heads and company management were asked to specify the types of information and reports they would need. By the time the development stage began, there were several staff changes and the new department heads requested additional reports. The information systems department complied with these changes, and reports were discontinued only upon the request of a department head. Few reports were actually discontinued, and a large number of reports are generated each period.

Company management is concerned about the number of reports the system automatically produces. Internal auditing was asked to evaluate the system's effectiveness and determined that more information was being generated than could be used effectively. The auditors noted the following reactions to this information overload:

 ● Many department heads did not act on certain reports during periods of peak activity. They let them accumulate in the hope of catching up later.
 ● Some department heads had so many reports they did not act at all or misused the information.
 ● Frequently, no action was taken until another manager needed a decision made. Department heads did not develop a priority system for acting on the information.
 ● Department heads often developed information from alternative, independent sources. This was easier than searching the reports for the needed data.

Required

 a. Indicate if each of the observed reactions is a functional or dysfunctional behavioral response. Explain your answer in each case.
 b. Recommend procedures to eliminate any dysfunctional behavior and prevent its recurrence.

(CMA Examination, adapted)

18.4 The controller of Tim's Travel (TT), a rapidly growing travel corporation, is deciding between upgrading the company's existing computer system or replacing it with a new one. The present system is four years old. Upgrading will cost $97,500 and

will extend its useful life for another seven years. The book value is $19,500, although it would sell for $24,000. Upgrading will eliminate one employee at a salary of $19,400; the new computer will eliminate two employees. Annual operating costs are estimated at $15,950 per year. Upgrading is expected to increase profits 3.5% above last year's level of $553,000.

The BetaTech Company has quoted a price of $224,800 for the new computer, which has a useful life of seven years. Annual operating costs are estimated to be $14,260. The average processing speed of the new computer is 12% faster than that of other systems in its price range, which would increase TT's profits by 4.5%.

Tim's present tax rate is 35%, and the cost of financing is 11%. Also assume that after seven years the salvage value, net of tax, would be $12,000 for the new computer and $7,500 for the present system. For tax purposes, computers are depreciated over five full years (six calendar years; a half year the first and last years), and the depreciation percentages are as follows:

Year	Percent (%)
1	20.00
2	32.00
3	19.20
4	11.52
5	11.52
6	5.76

Required

Using a spreadsheet package, prepare an economic feasibility analysis to determine if TT should rehabilitate the old system or purchase the new computer. As part of the analysis, compute the after-tax cash flows for years 1 through 7 and the payback, NPV, and IRR of each alternative.

18.5 Rossco Incorporated is considering purchasing a new computer to maximize office efficiency. The proposal estimates that initial systems design would cost $54,000; hardware, $74,000; and new software, $35,000. One-time initial training costs are expected to be $11,000, an additional $20,000 will be required to install the system, and $12,000 will be required to convert the files. A net reduction of three employees, whose average salaries are $40,000 per year, is expected if the new machine is acquired. A just-completed special study found that computerization could decrease average yearly inventory by $150,000. Annual operating costs, other than employee wages, are expected to be $30,000 per year higher than those for the current manual system.

The expected life of the machine is four years, with an estimated salvage value of zero. The effective tax rate is 40%. For purposes of the feasibility study, assume that all costs associated with the computer purchase will be depreciated equally over its four-year life using the straight-line method. Assume that Rossco can invest money made available from the reduction in inventory at 11% annually. Also, assume that all cash flows, except for the initial investment and start-up costs, are at the end of the year. Assume 365 days in a year.

Required

Use a spreadsheet to perform a feasibility analysis to determine if Rossco should purchase the computer. Compute the following as part of the analysis:

 a. initial investment
 b. after-tax cash flows for years 1 through 4
 c. payback period
 d. net present value
 e. internal rate of return

18-6 XYZ Conglomerate Company has completed a feasibility study to upgrade its computer system. Management received the information in Table 18-9, which shows the benefits of the new system.

Table 18-9
Benefits to Be Derived from the
New System

1. Production

 a. Market forecasting is presently in dollars per product line. Calculation of units by product line takes an estimated two man-days, a total of $800. This saving would be repeated each time the market forecast was updated, presumably monthly. The program to calculate the forecast in units would be more accurate than the present method of applying factors to dollar value. $ 9600

 b. More effective inventory control would permit an overall reduction in inventory. The ability to quickly establish total requirements would help to overcome parts stockout situations. For this calculation we estimate a 10% inventory reduction. As the cost of capital at XYZ Conglomerate Company approximates 20%, the benefit approximates 20% of $1,000,000. $200,000

 c. Evaluation of changes to plans will be possible in detail. This is not so under our manual system. Parts explosions are time-consuming and can only be done monthly. The impact here would be increased production flexibility and the reduction of sales losses due to finished goods stockouts. We estimate that this can be valued as the equivalent of hiring two clerks. $150,000 $359,600

2. Engineering

 a. Use of the computer in filing and updating bills of material would save 40% of the industrial engineer's time. $ 40,000

 b. The improved updating of files, which includes the bills of material and product structure files, which affect many areas, should save a minimum 25% of one clerk (if we took all areas, this would probably be closer to 50%). $ 15,000

 c. Estimated clerical savings in labor calculations, rates, and bonus detail is two days per week, or 40% of one person. $ 20,000 $ 75,000

3. Sales

 a. Improved reporting will enable sales staff and sales management to react more quickly to prevailing conditions. The implied benefit would be sales increases, especially during promotions, and a better sales/expense ratio. We are assuming an improvement in sales of only $10,000 per person, for a total of $50,000. $ 50,000

4. Marketing

 Revised reports and an improved forecasting system will help establish sales trends and will help the production department in flexibility and inventory control.

5. Accounting

 a. Standard costing of all bills of material. The side effect of being able to cost new products quickly can be expressed as the equivalent of saving 30%–40% of the plant accountant's time. $ 30,000

 b. A revised incentive earnings and payroll system installed on the computer should reduce payroll department clerical labor from three days to one day—possible benefit of 40% of one clerk. $24,000 $ 54,000

 Total $ 538,600

Required

As a board member, which of the benefits would you accept as relevant to the cost justification of the system? Defend your answer.

(SMAC Examination, adapted)

18.7 The Alkin Chemical Company manufactures and sells chemicals for agricultural and industrial use. The company has grown significantly over the past five years. However, the company's AIS is the original one developed and installed by the former president's son while he was in college. Much of the information generated by the system is irrelevant, and more appropriate and timely information is needed.

The controller is concerned that actual monthly cost data for most production processes are compared with actual costs of the same processes for the previous year. However, the production supervisors contend that the system is adequate because it accounts for discrepancies. The current year's costs seldom vary from the previous year's costs when adjusted for inflation; thus, the supervisors feel that costs are under control.

The vice president of manufacturing has found that preparing even the simplest of cost analyses requires that she spend days compiling information generated by the current system. She believes the system should be flexible enough for managers to quickly develop their own recurring reports.

As a result of these concerns, the new president has appointed a committee to review the system. It will determine management's information needs for cost control and decision purposes and ensure that the company's and employees' behavioral needs are met. The vice president of finance and administration chairs the committee.

Shortly after announcing the formation of this committee, the vice president of finance overheard a cost accountant say, "I've been doing it this way since the company began, and now this committee plans to make my job redundant." Several employees in the general accounting department also assumed that their positions would be eliminated or changed significantly. Several days later, the vice president of finance and administration overheard one production manager state that he believed the system was in need of revision because the most meaningful information he was receiving came from a junior salesperson.

Required

 a. Identify and explain the problems employees have with the AIS.
 b. Identify policies or practices the company could follow during systems implementation that would reduce costs without laying off employees.

(SMAC Examination, adapted)

18.8 Recent years have brought an explosive growth in electronic communication. Computers, personal digital assistants, cellphones, photocopiers, fax machines, word processors, electronic mail, teleconferencing, and sophisticated management information systems have changed the way information is received, processed, and transmitted. With the decreasing costs of computer equipment and the increasing power of automation, the full impact of computerization has yet to be felt. Although the development of computer applications is directed at being user-friendly or user oriented, the integration of computers into the organization has had both positive and negative effects on employees.

Required

 a. Describe the benefits that companies and their employees can receive from electronic communication.
 b. Discuss the organizational impact of introducing new electronic communication systems.
 c. Explain (1) why an employee might resist the introduction of electronic communication systems and (2) the steps an organization can take to alleviate this resistance.

(CMA Examination, adapted)

18-9 PWR Instruments manufactures precision nozzles for fire hoses. The president, Ronald Paige, an engineer, started the corporation, which has been successful and has experienced steady growth. Reporting to Ronald are six vice presidents representing the company's major functions—marketing, production, research and development, information services, finance, and human resources. The information services department was just established during the past fiscal year, when PWR began developing a new information system. The new system employs a server connected to personal computers in each of the six departments. The personal computers can both download data from and upload data to the main computer. PWR is still in the process of designing and developing applications for its new system.

Ronald has recently received a letter from the company's external audit firm and has called a meeting with his vice presidents to review the recommendations. One major item that Ronald wants to discuss is the recommendation that PWR form an information systems steering committee.

Required

 a. Explain why the external auditor would recommend that PWR establish an information systems steering committee, and discuss its specific responsibilities. What advantages can such a steering committee offer PWR?

 b. Identify the PWR managers who would be most likely to serve on the committee.
 (CMA Examination, adapted)

18-10 In the process of developing a new drug, pharmaceutical companies perform clinical trials to test the drug. The collection and processing of clinical trials' data accounts for 40% of the total cost of developing a new drug. This is no small amount, given that the average cost of drug development is $800 million. To capture data from clinical trials more effectively and efficiently, Big Pharma decided to convert to an online system.

The problem is that trial clinicians and vendors had been using a paper-based system since the company's founding. The research and development teams feared that going to the standardized and automated format required by the online format would significantly hinder their creative processes. They feared that the online system would significantly stifle their flexibility to explore new ways to provide pharmaceutical-based medical care.

(Adapted from Todd Datz, *"No small change,"* CIO
(February 15, 2004): 66–72)

Required

 a. Identify as many system analysis and design problems as you can in the case.

 b. What can the company do to allay the clinician's fear of the new system?

18.11 Don Richardson, vice president of marketing for the JEM Corporation, has just emerged from another strategic planning session aimed at developing a new line of business. The company's management team has been discussing these plans for several months, since major organizational changes will be required to implement the strategic plan. Rumors about the plans have been circulating in the office for months, and several employees who are anxious about the expected changes have already confronted Don. His only response has been to tell them that an official announcement of this new business plan is expected shortly.

When he returns to his office, Don is met by an ad hoc committee composed of his department managers. The sales manager, Susan Williams, has been the most vocal of the group and, as expected, is acting as spokesperson. "Mr. Richardson, it is imperative that we speak to you right away. The employees are becoming very apprehensive about the proposed changes, and lately their job performance has slacked off."

"That's right," adds George Sussman, accounting manager. "My subordinates are asking me all sorts of questions concerning this new line of business, and I don't have any answers for them. They're not buying the 'official announcement' line any longer. I suspect that some of them are already looking for jobs in the event that department 'changes' phase out their positions."

Implementing organizational change is one of the most demanding assignments that any executive faces. It has been suggested that every change requires three steps: unfreezing the current situation, implementing the change, and refreezing the effected change. This view, however, lacks the specific details needed by an operating manager who must initiate the change.

Required

a. Explain why employees generally resist organizational change.

b. Discuss ways JEM Corporation can alleviate employee resistance to change.

(CMA Examination, adapted)

18.12 Remnants, Inc., is a large company that manufactures and markets designer clothing throughout the United States. From its St. Louis headquarters, Remnants has developed a regional system for marketing and servicing its products. Each region functions as a profit center because of the authority given to regional managers within their territories.

Each regional organization consists of an accounting and a budget department, a human resources and training department, and several area offices to market and service the products. Each area office consists of sales, service, and administrative departments, the managers of which ultimately report to one area manager.

The New York area office departed from the standard organizational structure by establishing a branch office to market and service the firm's products in the Boston area. A branch manager who reports directly to the area manager heads the local office.

In recent years, the Boston branch manager has encouraged the area manager to consider a new information system to handle the local branch's growing information needs. The New York area manager and the eastern regional manager have concluded that they should establish a project team with employees from the regional office, the area office, and the branch office to (1) assess the information needs at the Boston branch office and (2) develop system recommendations, if necessary. The following employees have been appointed to the project team, with Keith Nash acting as chairperson:

Eastern Region Office
Kurt Johnson, Budget Supervisor
Sally Brown, Training Director
New York Office
Keith Nash, Administrative Director
Boston Branch
Heidi Meyer, Branch Manager and Sales Manager
Bobby Roos, Assistant Branch Manager and Service Manager
Joe Gonzalez, Salesperson
Juana Martinez, Serviceperson

Required

a. A project team, similar to the one organized at Remnants, Inc., is organized to contribute its skills to accomplish a given objective. Characteristics of group members can influence the functioning and effectiveness of a project team. Identify some of these characteristics.

b. Due to the team's composition, what sources of conflict can you see arising among its members? Do you think the group will succeed in its objective to develop an information system for the Boston branch office? Why or why not?

 c. What contribution would a person who holds a position as budget supervisor make in a project team such as this one?

18.13 Managers face a continual crisis in the systems development process: Information systems departments develop systems that businesses cannot use. At the heart of the problem is a proverbial "great divide" that separates the world of business from the world of information systems. Few departments seem able or ready to cross this gap.

 A major reason for the resulting information systems development crisis is that many large systems currently handling corporate information needs are seriously out of date. As a result, companies are looking for ways to improve existing systems or to build new ones.

 Another reason for the crisis is the widespread use of PC-based systems that has spawned a high level of user expectation that IS departments are not meeting. As computer usage increases, users are seeking more powerful applications that are not available on many older systems.

 The costs of the great divide can be devastating for unprepared companies. An East Coast chemical company spent more than $1 million on a budgeting and control system that was never used. The systems department created an administrative budgeting system; the department's expertise was technical excellence, not budgets. As a result, the new system completely missed the mark when it came to meeting business needs.

 Another example of poor systems development comes from a Midwestern bank. It used an expensive computer-aided software engineering (CASE) tool to develop a system that users ignored because there had been no design planning. A senior analyst for Franklin Savings Association said, "They built the system right, but, unfortunately, they didn't build the right system."

 So what is the solution? The first step in effective systems design is a thorough business analysis, not a systems analysis. A business analysis includes a thorough review of how a business operates and how the functions of the business relate. Only with this understanding can systems professionals and business managers communicate effectively when developing an integrated system.

 In addition, businesses are seeking managers who have a systems background, because they provide a liaison between the systems department and the finance and accounting departments, helping business managers to communicate their needs clearly.

 What is still missing is more involvement between systems staff and end users. Systems designers must take more time to interact with end users. In addition, business managers must provide their employees with the training time required to make the system work right.

Required

 a. What is the great divide in the systems development process? What are the reasons for this gap?

 b. What are the suggested solutions to the information crisis? How will the systems approach to development help?

 c. Discuss the role that a systems designer, a business manager, and an end user can take to narrow the great divide.

 d. Who plays the most vital role in the effective development of the system?

18.14 Joanne Grey, a senior consultant, and David Young, a junior consultant, were assigned by their firm to conduct a systems analysis for a client. The objective of the study was to consider the feasibility of integrating and automating certain clerical functions. Joanne had previously worked on jobs for this client, but David had been hired only recently.

 During the first morning on the job, Joanne directed David to interview a departmental supervisor and learn as much as he could about the department's operations. David went to the supervisor's office, introduced himself, and made the following statement: "Your company has hired my firm to study the way your department works

and to make recommendations as to how its efficiency could be improved and its cost lowered. I would like to interview you to determine what goes on in your department."

David questioned the supervisor for about 30 minutes but found him to be uncooperative. David then gave Joanne an oral report on how the interview had gone and what he had learned about the department.

Required

Describe several flaws in the approach taken to obtain information about the operation of the department under study. How should this task have been performed?

18.15 Business organizations often are required to modify or replace a portion or all of their financial information system to keep pace with their growth and take advantage of improved IT. The process involved in modifying or replacing an AIS requires a substantial commitment of time and resources. When an organization undertakes a change in its AIS, a systems analysis takes place.

Required

 a. Explain the purpose and reasons for surveying an organization's existing system during a systems study.
 b. Identify and explain the general activities and techniques that are commonly used during systems analysis.
 c. Systems analysis is often carried out by a project team composed of a systems analyst, a management accountant, and other persons in the company who would be knowledgeable and helpful in the systems study. What would be the management accountant's role in systems analysis?

(CMA Examination, adapted)

18-16 The following list presents specific project activities and their scheduled starting and completion times:

Activity	Starting Date	Ending Date
A	Jan. 5	Feb. 9
B	Jan. 5	Jan. 19
C	Jan. 26	Feb. 23
D	Mar. 2	Mar. 23
E	Mar. 2	Mar. 16
F	Feb. 2	Mar. 16
G	Mar. 30	Apr. 20
H	Mar. 23	Apr. 27

Required

 a. Using a format similar to that illustrated in Figure 18-3, prepare a Gantt chart for this project. Assume that each activity starts on a Monday and ends on a Friday.
 b. Assume today is February 16 and activities A and B have been completed, C is half completed, F is a quarter completed, and the other activities have not yet commenced. Record this information on your Gantt chart. Is the project behind schedule, on schedule, or ahead of schedule? Explain.
 c. Discuss the relative merits of the Gantt chart and PERT as tools for project planning and control.

18.17 A large manufacturing firm needed a specialized software program to identify and monitor cost overruns for one of its specialty processing plants. After an extensive search and analysis of potential vendors and considering writing the software in-house, the firm decided to purchase prepackaged software with the intent of

modifying it in-house to fit the program to its own individual circumstances and processes. Management assigned the program modification to a team of three programmers, who worked on the project for nearly six months. Near the end of the project, and during their final testing phase, the programmers' manager came to them one morning and told them to stop all testing on the program until further notice. The manager explained that the firm's manufacturing manager had been reading over the sales agreement with the software vendor and found a clause that stated the software package could not be changed without the prior written consent of the vendor. The manufacturing firm then went to the software vendor and paid an additional fee so that it could implement the modified software in its manufacturing process.

Required

Identify and explain which aspect(s) of feasibility the manufacturing firm failed to consider prior to starting the software modification project.

18.18 Ajax Manufacturing installed a new inventory tracking system in its warehouse that includes bar code scanners. Warehouse personnel must scan each item in the warehouse on a monthly basis. To properly close the books each month on a timely basis, the inventory must be scanned in a 36-hour period. The warehouse employs six workers who, in addition to their normal jobs, must perform the inventory count (scan). During certain months, the inventory is allowed to expand to meet seasonal demands. During these months, the inventory scan requires the warehouse personnel to work as many as 30 hours to scan all items in inventory. In addition, the scanners do not always record all inventory items due to the low operating temperatures required for Ajax's inventory. From a recent audit, it has come to the attention of Ajax's management that the inventory records are not always accurate.

Required

Identify and explain which aspect(s) of feasibility Ajax failed to consider prior to installing the inventory tracking system.

18.19 How do you get a grizzled veteran police officer who is used to filling out paper forms to process his arrest and case work to convert to completing these forms on a computer, especially when he has little or no experience using a computer? That was the problem facing the Chicago Police Department, the second largest in the nation, when it decided to implement a relational database that churns through massive amounts of data intended to give officers the information they needed to fight crime more effectively.

Initially, the department rolled out the case component of the CLEAR (Citizen Law Enforcement Analysis and Reporting) system. The case component provided criminal history and arrest records. The only problem is that the officers hated it. They complained that the system was not user-friendly, approval from supervisors was complex and involved multiple screens, and they did not feel properly trained on the system. After listening to the officers' complaints for a year, the department clearly had to do something.

(Adapted from Todd Datz, *"No small change,"* CIO
(February 15, 2004): 66–72)

Required

 a. Identify as many system analysis and design problems as you can.
 b. What could the department have done differently to prevent the officers' complaints?
 c. What principles of system analysis and design were violated in this case?

CASE 18-1 Audio Visual Corporation

Audio Visual Corporation (AVC) manufactures and sells visual display equipment. The company's headquarters are outside Boston. The majority of sales are made through seven geographical sales offices located in Los Angeles, Seattle, Minneapolis, Cleveland, Dallas, Boston, and Atlanta. Each sales office has a warehouse located nearby that carries an inventory of new equipment and replacement parts. The remainder of the sales are made through manufacturers' representatives.

AVC has a single manufacturing plant, which is highly departmentalized. In addition to the assembly department there are several departments responsible for the components used in the visual display equipment. The plant also has maintenance, engineering, scheduling, and cost accounting departments.

Management decided that its AIS needed upgrading. As a result, the company installed a mainframe at corporate headquarters and local area networks at each of the seven sales offices. The integration of the new computer and the LANs into the AVC AIS was carried out by the information systems staff. The systems manager and the four systems analysts who had the major responsibility for the integration were hired by the company shortly before the project was begun. The department's other employees have been with the company for several years.

During its early years, AVC had a centralized decision-making organization. Top management formulated all plans and directed all operations. As the company expanded, some of the decision making was decentralized, although the information processing was still highly centralized. Departments had to coordinate their plans with the corporate office, but they had more freedom in developing their sales programs. However, information problems developed, and the information systems department was assigned the task of improving the company's information processing system once the new equipment was installed.

The systems analysts reviewed the current AIS prior to the acquisition of the new computer and identified its weaknesses. They then designed new applications to overcome these problems. During the 18 months since the acquisition of the new equipment, the following applications have been redesigned or developed and are now operational: payroll, production scheduling, financial statement preparation, customer billing, raw material use in production, and finished goods inventory by warehouse. The operating departments of AVC affected by the systems changes were rarely consulted or contacted until the system was operational and the new reports were distributed to the operating departments.

AVC's president is very pleased with the information systems department's work. During a recent conversation with an individual who was interested in AVC's new system, the president stated, "The systems people are doing a good job and I have full confidence in their work. I touch base with them frequently, and they have encountered no difficulties in doing their work. We paid a lot of money for the new equipment and the systems people certainly cost enough, but the combination of the new equipment and new information systems staff should solve all of our problems."

Recently, two additional conversations regarding the computer and the AIS have taken place. One was between Jerry Adams, plant manager, and Bill Taylor, the information systems manager; the other was between Jerry Adams and Terry Williams, the new human resources manager.

BILL TAYLOR–JERRY ADAMS CONVERSATION

JERRY: Bill, you're trying to run my plant for me. I'm supposed to be the manager, yet you keep interfering. I wish you would mind your own business.

BILL: You've got a job to do, but so does my department. As we analyzed the information needed for production scheduling and by top management, we saw where improvements could be made in the workflow. Now that the system is operational, you can't reroute work and change procedures, because that would destroy the value of the information we're processing. And while I'm on that subject, it's getting to the point where we can't trust the information we're getting from production. The documents we receive from production contain a lot of errors.

JERRY: I'm responsible for the efficient operation of production. Quite frankly, I think I'm the best judge of production efficiency. The system you installed has reduced my workforce and increased the workload of the remaining employees, but I don't see that this has improved anything. In fact, it might explain the high error rate in the documents.

BILL: This new computer costs a lot of money, and I'm trying to ensure that the company gets its money's worth.

JERRY ADAMS–TERRY WILLIAMS CONVERSATION

JERRY: My best production assistant, the one I'm grooming to be a supervisor when the next opening occurs, came to me today and said he was thinking of quitting. When I asked him why, he said he didn't enjoy the work anymore. He's not the only one who is unhappy. The supervisors and department heads no

longer have a voice in establishing production schedules. This new computer system has taken away the contribution we used to make to company planning and direction. We seem to be going back to the days when top management made all the decisions. I have more production problems now than I used to. I think it boils down to a lack of interest on the part of my management team. I know the problem is within my area, but I thought you might be able to help me.

TERRY: I have no recommendations for you now, but I've had similar complaints from purchasing and shipping. I think we should explore your concerns during tomorrow's plant management meeting.

Questions

Evaluate the preceding information, and answer the following questions:

1. Apparently the development of and transition to the new computer-based system has created problems among AVC's staff. Identify and briefly discuss the apparent causes of these problems.
2. How could the company have avoided these problems in the first place? How could they prevent them from happening in the future?

(CMA Examination, adapted)

AIS IN ACTION SOLUTIONS

QUIZ KEY

1. Which of the following is *not* one of the reasons why companies make changes to their AISs?
 a. gain a competitive advantage [While this answer is correct, it is not the only correct answer. Changes in an AIS can help a company increase the quality, quantity, and speed of information, which leads to improved decision making and a greater competitive advantage.]
 b. increase productivity [While this answer is correct, it is not the only correct answer. Computers used in an AIS can automate repetitive tasks, which allows more work to be done in the same amount of time. This increases productivity.]
 c. keep up with company growth [While this answer is correct, it is not the only correct answer. As a company grows, its old system will likely not be able to handle the increase in demand and thus will require changes to the AIS to accommodate the growth.]
 d. downsize company operations [While this answer is correct, it is not the only correct answer. A smaller company requires a smaller AIS. For instance, due to downsizing a company may move from centralized decision making to decentralized decision making. As a result, the AIS would most likely shift from using a mainframe computer to a set of networked workstations.]
 ✔ e. All of the above are reasons why companies change an AIS. [Correct]

2. The planning technique that identifies implementation activities and their relationships, constructs a network of arrows and nodes, and then determines the critical path through the network is referred to as which of the following:
 a. Gantt chart [Incorrect. A Gantt chart is basically a bar chart that displays dates and stages of completion for each project task. See Figure 18-3.]
 ✔ b. PERT diagram [Correct.]
 c. physical model [Incorrect. A physical model illustrates how a system functions by describing document flows, computer processes, equipment used, and other physical elements of the system.]

 d. data flow diagram [Incorrect. A data flow diagram is used to document a system with four basic symbols—i.e., squares, circles, parallel lines, and arrows.]

3 The purchasing department is designing a new AIS. Who is best able to determine departmental information requirements?

 a. steering committee [Incorrect. The steering committee is a high-level executive committee that oversees the information systems function and they probably do not understand purchasing department information requirements.]

 b. controller [Incorrect. The controller is the manager of the accounting department and probably does not understand purchasing department information requirements.]

 c. top management [Incorrect. The role of top management in such cases is to provide direction and resources, not detailed analysis of purchasing department information requirements.]

✔ **d.** purchasing department [Correct. The people who will actually be using the new system are in the best position to determine the system's information requirements.]

4 Which of the following is the correct order of the steps in systems analysis?

 a. initial investigation, determination of information needs and system requirements, feasibility study, system survey [Incorrect. See Figure 18-4.]

 b. determination of information needs and system requirements, system survey, feasibility study, initial investigation [Incorrect. See Figure 18-4.]

 c. system survey, initial investigation, determination of information needs and system requirements, feasibility study [Incorrect. See Figure 18-4.]

✔ **d.** initial investigation, system survey, feasibility study, determination of information needs and system requirements [Correct. See Figure 18-4.]

5 Which of the following is the long-range planning document that specifies what the system will consist of, how it will be developed, who will develop it, how needed resources will be acquired, and its overall vision?

 a. steering committee agenda [Incorrect. The steering committee's agenda would involve discussing all aspects of the IS, not just system development.]

✔ **b.** master plan [Correct.]

 c. systems development life cycle [Incorrect. The systems development life cycle is not a long-range planning document but a conceptual framework that applies to systems development in general.]

 d. project development plan [Incorrect. The project development plan is used for individual projects and includes such items as cost/benefit analyses, developmental and operational requirements, and a schedule of activities for developing and operating the new system.]

6 Resistance is often a reaction to the methods of instituting change rather than to change itself.

✔ **a.** true [Correct. Although change is generally difficult, the way change is instituted can either facilitate the change or hinder the change.]

 b. false [Incorrect.]

7 Increased error rates, disruptions, and sabotage are examples of which of the following?

✔ **a.** aggression [Correct. These are classic symptoms of aggression as a reaction to change.]

 b. avoidance [Incorrect. Avoidance is best illustrated by the statement that if a person does not use the new system, maybe it will go away.]

 c. projection [Incorrect. Projection refers to blaming the new system for any and all problems.]

 d. payback [Incorrect. Payback is an economic feasibility metric.]

8 What is the most significant problem a company encounters in designing, developing, and implementing a system?

✔ a. the human element [Correct. A system will fail without the support of the people it is designed to serve—for a variety of reasons, including fear of change, poor communication and training, disruption of work, and lack of top-management support.]

 b. technology [Incorrect. The technology a system employs is normally tested for functionality prior to its implementation in a new system.]

 c. legal challenges [Incorrect. With proper system planning and design, systems can meet all laws and regulations.]

 d. planning for the new system [Incorrect. Proper planning can actually prevent problems from occurring.]

9 Determining whether the organization has access to people who can design, implement, and operate the proposed system is referred to as which of the following?

 a. technical feasibility [Incorrect. Technical feasibility refers to whether the system can be developed and implemented with existing technology.]

✔ b. operational feasibility [Correct. Operational feasibility refers to whether the organization and its people can actually design, implement and operate the system.]

 c. legal feasibility [Incorrect. Legal feasibility refers to whether the system complies with all applicable laws and regulations.]

 d. scheduling feasibility [Incorrect. Scheduling feasibility refers to whether the system can be analyzed, planned, designed, and implemented in the time allocated.]

 e. economic feasibility [Incorrect. Economic feasibility refers to whether the system's benefits outweigh its costs.]

10 Which of the following is *not* one of the tangible or intangible benefits a company might obtain from a new system?

 a. cost savings [While this answer is correct, there are other correct answers. Automated systems can reduce clerical costs, as well as other related costs.]

 b. improved customer service and productivity [While this answer is correct, there are other correct answers. New systems can integrate data from several sources to provide fast, reliable information to assist customers and also increase productivity.]

 c. improved decision making [While this answer is correct, there are other correct answers. Better information greatly increases the likelihood of better decisions.]

 d. improved data processing [While this answer is correct, there are other correct answers. Better-designed systems using newer technology improve data processing and reduce the likelihood of human error.

✔ e. All are benefits of a new system. [Correct.]

COMPREHENSIVE PROBLEM SOLUTION

 a. Management typically selects a set of executives to sit on the information systems steering committee. Generally, the department heads from information systems and user departments, the controller, and other executives sit on this committee.

b. The systems development team generally consists of the systems analyst, other systems specialists, managers, accountants, systems auditors, and users.

c. RSSA's development team would normally do an initial assessment of management's plans for moving the help desk. Next they would survey the existing system to determine what it does, what the company should continue to use, and what should be changed for the new system. A feasibility analysis is completed to determine the technical, operational, legal, scheduling, and economic feasibility of the new system. Lastly, the team will determine the system's information needs and requirements.

d. Change is usually difficult for people and organizations. When operations are outsourced, employees can lose their jobs. Based on the situations described, it looks like some employees exhibited aggressive behavior toward the new system.

e. To answer the economic feasibility questions, Table 18-10—an analysis of cash spent or saved for each year during the life of RSSA's proposed project—was prepared. The first column is the contents of each row, and subsequent columns show when the funds are saved or spent.

Some costs, such as the initial contract payment of $1,750,000 and the lease cancellation penalty, occur at the very beginning of the project, which we refer to as year 0. For simplicity's sake, cash flows that take place during the year are assumed to take place at the end of the year. Therefore, we assume that the $525,000 expenditure each year for operations occurs at the end of years 1 through 5.

The savings, or cash inflows, from the new system all occur each year. Accordingly, we enter $750,000 each year for savings in personnel and $360,000 each year for savings from canceling the building lease.

The last line of the table shows the net cash flows for each time period, which is total cash inflows less total cash outflows.

1. Payback

The payback period is determined by using the net cash flows calculated in Table 18-10 to determine when cash inflows equal cash outflows. To help in this analysis, a cumulative net cash flow total is shown in Table 18-11. Cumulative cash flows go to zero, or breakeven, during year 4. To determine how far into year 4, divide the last negative cumulative cash flow balance (−$145,000) by the net cash flows for the following year ($585,000 from the year 4 column) In this case, it took 25% of the year (145,000/585,000), or 3.25 years, or 3 years and 3 months, to get to payback. Therefore, to reach breakeven or payback, it required $145,000 of the year 4 net cash flow of $585,000.

Table 18-10
Cash Flows for RSSA

Year	0	1	2	3	4	5
CASH OUTFLOWS						
Initial Contract	−$1,750,000					
Lease Cancellation Penalty	−$150,000					
Center Operations Cost		−$525,000	−$525,000	−$525,000	−$525,000	−$525,000
Total Cash Outflows	−$1,900,000	−$525,000	−$525,000	−$525,000	−$525,000	−$525,000
CASH INFLOWS						
Personnel Savings		$750,000	$750,000	$750,000	$750,000	$750,000
Lease Cancellation Savings		$360,000	$360,000	$360,000	$360,000	$360,000
Total Cash Inflows	$0	$1,110,000	$1,110,000	$1,110,000	$1,110,000	$1,110,000
NET CASH FLOWS	−$1,900,000	$585,000	$585,000	$585,000	$585,000	$585,000

Table 18-11
Payback for RSSA's Proposed Project

Year	0	1	2	3	4	5
Net Cash Flows	−$1,900,000	$585,000	$585,000	$585,000	$585,000	$585,000
Cumulative Cash Flows	−$1,900,000	−$1,315,000	−$730,000	−$145,000	$440,000	$1,025,000
Payback	3 years + 0.25 years = 3.25 years or 3 years, 3 months					

2. Net Present Value

A limitation of the payback period is that it does not take into consideration the time value of money (a dollar received today is worth more than the same dollar received tomorrow). As a result, net present value (NPV) techniques are also used to evaluate projects. NPV is calculated using the net cash flows calculated in Table 18-10 and a company's cost of capital, more commonly known as its discount rate. This rate is unique to each company and can be thought of as the company's average cost of borrowing capital.

The present value of funds is determined by multiplying each year's net cash flow by a discount factor. The discount factor is calculated using the formula $1/(1+r)^n$, where r = the company's discount rate and n = the number of time periods between time 0 and the designated cash flow. For example, if the cash flow occurred at the end of year 4, n would equal 4. The discount factor is calculated for each time period and multiplied by the net cash flow for that period.

When all net cash flows have been discounted to their present value, they are totaled to determine the project's NPV. If the total is positive, the project is earning an estimated return in excess of the company's discount rate and would probably be an acceptable project. If NPV is negative, the project will return less than the company's discount rate and would likely be rejected by the company. If NPV is equal to zero, the project is earning an estimated rate equivalent to the discount rate. As shown in Table 18-12, RSSA's NPV is $262,100 and would likely be acceptable to management. Most business calculators and spreadsheets have built-in NPV functions that are relatively easy to use.

3. Internal Rate of Return

The limitation of the NPV calculation is that it does not calculate an estimated rate of return. It only indicates whether a project is estimated to earn more or less than the discount rate used in the NPV calculation. This limitation is resolved using an internal rate of return (IRR) calculation. To calculate IRR, one must perform a series of calculations to find the discount rate that forces NPV to zero. In other words, it is a trial-and-error approach that keeps varying the discount rate until NPV equals zero. Since this is so tedious, IRR is rarely calculated without using a business calculator or the IRR function in a spreadsheet program such as Excel. As shown in Table 18-13, the internal rate of return for this project is 16.35% (rounded).

Table 18-12
The Net Present Value of RSSA's Proposed Project

NET CASH FLOWS	−$1,900,000	$585,000	$585,000	$585,000	$585,000	$585,000
Present Value Factors	1	0.9009	0.8116	0.7312	0.6587	0.5935
Present Value Amounts	−$1,900,000	$527,027	$474,786	$427,752	$385,340	$347,198
Net Present Value	$262,103					

Table 18-13
The Internal Rate of Return of RSSA's Proposed Project

Year	0	1	2	3	4	5
Net Cash Flows	−$1,900,000	$585,000	$585,000	$585,000	$585,000	$585,000
Present Value Factors	1	0.85948828	0.7387201	0.6349213	0.5457074	0.4690291
Present Value Amounts	−$1,900,000	$502,801	$432,150	$371,429	$319,239	$274,381
Net Present Value	$0					
IRR	.1634833 ⇒ 16.35%					

CHAPTER 19

LEARNING OBJECTIVES

After studying this chapter, you should be able to:

- **Describe how organizations purchase application software, vendor services, and hardware.**

- **Explain how information system departments develop custom software.**

- **Explain how end users develop, use, and control computer-based information systems.**

- **Explain why organizations outsource their information systems, and evaluate the benefits and risks of this strategy.**

- **Explain the principles and challenges of business process reengineering.**

- **Describe how prototypes are used to develop an AIS, and discuss the advantages and disadvantages of doing so.**

- **Explain what computer-aided software engineering is and how it is used in systems development.**

AIS Development Strategies

INTEGRATIVE CASE **SHOPPERS MART**

Ann Christy was elated that the new system Shoppers Mart so badly needed was approved and that she and her team had accurately assessed the company's needs. Ann realized she needed to determine if it would be better to purchase a software system from an outside vendor, develop the system in-house, or hire a company that specialized in systems like the one she envisioned to develop and operate the new system. More specifically, she needed answers to the following questions:

1 Could Ann buy the software she needed? If so, how should she approach the process of buying hardware and software and selecting a vendor?

2 How do companies go about developing software in-house? Is this the best approach for Shoppers Mart?

3 How extensively should the system make use of end-user–developed software?

4 Should Shoppers Mart make the needed improvements to its existing system, or should it consider reengineering its business processes and then develop a system to support the new processes?

5 Was outsourcing the information system a viable alternative to obtaining a new system? Did the benefits of outsourcing outweigh its risks?

6 If the company decides to develop the system in-house, should it speed up the development process by using advanced techniques, such as prototyping or computer-assisted software engineering?

Ann decided to investigate the various design alternatives to determine what course of action was best for Shoppers Mart.

Introduction

Traditionally, companies have experienced the following difficulties in developing an AIS:

- Demands for development resources are so numerous that AIS projects can be backlogged for several years.
- A newly designed AIS does not always meet user needs. The problem may not be discovered until the system is in use, often after a lengthy development process. It is hard for users to visualize how the AIS will look or how it will operate by reviewing design documentation. In addition, when systems developers do not understand the company's business needs or user needs, it is hard for them to make meaningful suggestions for improvement.
- The development process can take so long that the system no longer meets company needs. For example, Fannie Mae spent eight years and $100 million developing the largest loan accounting system in the world. Unfortunately, when the system was finally completed, it no longer met most of Fannie Mae's business needs.
- Users are unable to specify their needs adequately. Often they do not know exactly what they need, and when they do, they sometimes cannot communicate these ideas to systems developers.
- Changes to the AIS are often difficult to make after requirements have been frozen into specifications. If users are allowed to keep changing the requirements, the AIS may take forever to finish and costs increase each time the AIS is reworked.

In today's fast-changing world, many companies find themselves in the position of Shoppers Mart. They must meet user information needs quickly and efficiently. In this chapter, you will learn three ways to obtain a new information system: purchasing software, developing software in-house, and hiring an outside company (outsourcing) to develop and operate the system. You will also learn three ways to hasten or improve the development process: business process reengineering, prototyping, and computer-aided software engineering (CASE) tools.

Purchasing Software

In the early days of computers it was rare that a company was able to buy software that could meet its needs. As the software industry has matured, however, most companies now purchase software. Because of software's easy availability and lower cost, a Deloitte & Touche survey found that most chief information officers expect to replace their current systems with commercially available packages rather than use custom-developed software. Consider the following examples:

- Hard Rock Café International wanted to get its customers to visit its cafés and Web site more often. It purchased customer relationship software from E.piphany, obtained 225,000 customer names from its fan club, and mailed

special promotional offers. In less than a year, the profits from the increased traffic had more than paid for the hardware and software it purchased to run the promotions.

- WellPoint Health Networks installed PeopleSoft's payroll, benefits, and human resources software to allow its employees to manage their own benefit enrollments and changes. The new system is saving the company $400,000 a year.
- Pacific Gas & Electric had to respond to the deregulation of California's power industry. Rather than try and update its 37-year-old customer information system, it spent three years and invested $204 million in software. This project was the largest installation of customer information system software in the history of the utility industry.

Written by software development companies, **canned software** is sold on the open market to a broad range of users with similar requirements. Some companies combine software and hardware and sell them as a package. These are called **turnkey systems** because the vendor installs the entire system and the user needs only to "turn the key." Many turnkey systems are written by vendors who specialize in a particular industry. For example, specific systems are geared toward doctors and dentists, automobile repair and service companies, full-service restaurants, fast-food outlets, video rental businesses, and other retail stores.

A major problem with canned software is that it often does not meet all of a company's information or data processing needs. This disadvantage can often be overcome by modifying the software. Generally, the best way to accomplish this is to have the software vendor, rather than the in-house programming staff, make the modifications. Modifications that are unauthorized by the vendor may not be supported and may make the program unreliable and unstable. Some companies have used this approach quite successfully. For example, about 90% of Dow Chemical's software consists of software that has been modified to match its business processes. The rest is custom software written in-house.

The Internet has given companies a new way to acquire software. **Application service providers (ASPs)** host Web-based software on their computers and deliver the software to their clients over the Internet. In this case, companies do not have to buy, install, and maintain software. Instead, they "rent" the software they need from an ASP. The advantages of doing this include a reduction of software costs and administrative overhead, automated software upgrades, scalability as the business grows, global access to information, access to skilled IT personnel, and the ability to focus on core financial competencies rather than IT requirements.

Purchasing Software and the SDLC

Companies that buy rather than develop AIS software still follow the SDLC process, as follows:

- **Systems analysis.** Companies must conduct an initial investigation, system survey, and feasibility survey. They must also determine AIS requirements.
- **Conceptual systems design.** An important part of conceptual design is determining if software that meets AIS requirements is already available. If so, a make-or-buy decision must be made.
- **Physical design.** If software is purchased, some of the physical design phase, such as designing and coding the program, can be omitted. However, it may be necessary to modify the purchased software to better meet company needs. Even when software is purchased, companies often design output, input, files, and control procedures.

- **Implementation and conversion.** Companies must plan implementation and conversion activities, select and train personnel, install and test the hardware and software, document procedures, and convert from the old to the new AIS. They do not, however, develop and test software modules or document the computer program itself.
- **Operation and maintenance.** The AIS is operated like any other software, and the vendor usually maintains the software.

Selecting a Vendor

Decisions to make or purchase software can be made independently of the decision to acquire hardware, service, maintenance, and other AIS resources. Likewise, these resources can be purchased independently of the software, although the hardware and vendor decisions may depend on the software decision.

Vendors can be found by looking in the phone book, obtaining referrals, scanning computer or trade magazines, attending conferences, or using search organizations. Some vendors flourish for a while and then go out of business. In addition, many companies offer computer services but have little experience or capital. When vendors go out of business, they often leave the companies that use their products high and dry. As a result, it is important to be selective when choosing a vendor.

Acquiring Hardware and Software

Once AIS requirements have been defined, an organization is ready to purchase software and hardware. Companies requiring only a PC, a word processor, and a spreadsheet usually complete their own research and make a selection. Companies that are buying large or complex systems, however, send vendors a **request for proposal (RFP)**, which is an invitation to propose a system that meets the company's needs by a specified date. Each proposal is evaluated, with the best systems investigated in depth to verify that company requirements can be met. A formal approach to acquiring system resources, such as an RFP, is important for the following reasons:

1 **Saves time.** The same information is provided to all vendors, eliminating repetitive interviews and questions.
2 **Simplifies the decision-making process.** All responses are in the same format and based on the same information.
3 **Reduces errors.** The chances of overlooking important factors are reduced.
4 **Avoids potential for disagreement.** Both parties possess the same expectations, and pertinent information is captured in writing.

When an RFP is solicited based on exact hardware and software specifications, the total costs are usually lower and less time is required for vendor preparation and company evaluation. However, this does not permit the vendor to recommend alternative technology. In contrast, a generalized RFP contains a problem definition and requests a system that meets specific performance objectives and requirements. This allows the requesting company to leave the technical issues to the vendor. Disadvantages of this approach include a greater difficulty in evaluating proposals and the potential for more costly bids.

Generally speaking, the more information a company provides to a vendor, the better the company's chances of receiving a system that meets its requirements. Vendors need detailed specifications for the new AIS, including the required applications, inputs and outputs, files and databases, frequency and methods of file updating and inquiry, and unique characteristics or requirements. It is also essential to distinguish between mandatory and desirable requirements.

Evaluating Proposals and Selecting a System

Proposals that are missing important information, fail to meet minimum requirements, or are ambiguous should be eliminated. Proposals that pass this preliminary screening should be carefully compared with the proposed AIS requirements to determine (1) if they meet all mandatory requirements and (2) how many of the desirable requirements they meet. The top vendors can be invited to demonstrate their system using company-supplied data. This measures the system's performance and validates the vendor's claims. Table 19-1 presents criteria that can be used to evaluate hardware, software, and vendors.

Table 19-1

Hardware, Software, and Vendor Evaluation Criteria

Hardware evaluation	Is the cost of the hardware reasonable, based on its capabilities and features?
	Can the hardware run the desired software?
	Are the CPU's processing speed and capabilities adequate for the intended use?
	Are the secondary storage capabilities adequate?
	Are the input and output speeds and capabilities adequate?
	Does the system have adequate communication capabilities?
	Is the system expandable?
	Is the hardware based on the most recent technology, or on technology that is old or soon to be out-of-date?
	Is the hardware available now? If not, when?
	Is the system under consideration compatible with existing hardware, software, and peripherals?
	How do evaluations of the system's performance compare with those of its competitors?
	What are the availability and cost of support and maintenance?
	What guarantees and warranties come with the system?
	Are financing arrangements available (if applicable)?
Software evaluation	Does the package meet all mandatory specifications?
	How well does the package meet desirable specifications?
	Will program modifications be required to meet company needs?
	Does the software contain adequate control capabilities?
	Is the performance (speed, accuracy, reliability) adequate?
	How many other companies use the software?
	Are other users satisfied with the package?
	Is the package well documented?
	Is the software compatible with existing corporate software?
	Is the software user-friendly?
	Can the software be demonstrated and test driven?
	Does the software have an adequate warranty?
	Is the software flexible and easily maintained?
	Is online inquiry of files and records possible?
	Will the vendor keep the package up-to-date?
Vendor evaluation	How long has the vendor been in business?
	Is the vendor financially stable and secure?
	How much experience does the vendor have with the hardware and software?
	How well does the vendor stand behind its products? How good is its guarantee?
	Does the vendor regularly update its products?
	Does the vendor provide financing?
	Will the vendor put promises in a contract?
	Will the vendor supply a list of customers as references?
	Does the vendor have a reputation for reliability and dependability?
	Does the vendor provide hardware and software support and maintenance?
	Does the vendor provide implementation and installation support?
	Does the vendor have high-quality, responsive, and experienced personnel?
	Does the vendor provide training?
	How responsive and timely is vendor support?

One way to compare system performance is to use a **benchmark problem**—a data-processing task with input, processing, and output jobs typical of those the new AIS will be required to perform. Processing times are calculated and compared, and the AIS with the lowest time is judged the most efficient.

Another approach is **point scoring**, which is illustrated in Table 19-2. For each system evaluation criterion, a weight is assigned based on its relative importance. Vendors are assigned a score for each criterion based on how well their proposals measure up to the standard. The total of the weighted scores provides a basis for comparing and contrasting the various systems. Based on the point-scoring approach in this example, vendor 3 offers the best system. Its system scored 190 points more than vendor 2, the second-place candidate.

Requirements costing estimates the cost of purchasing or developing features that are not present in a particular AIS. The total cost for each AIS is computed by adding the acquisition cost and the purchasing or developing costs. The resulting totals represent the costs of systems with all required features and provide an equitable basis for comparison.

Neither point scoring nor requirements costing is totally objective. In points scoring, the weights and the points used are assigned subjectively and dollar estimates of costs and benefits are not included. Requirements costing overlooks intangible factors such as reliability and vendor support. In any event, the final choice among vendor proposals is not likely to be clear-cut, because it must rely to some extent on subjective factors and cost considerations.

Once the best AIS has been identified, the software should be thoroughly test-driven, other users contacted to see how satisfied they are, vendor personnel evaluated, and proposal details confirmed. The company wants to verify that the AIS that appears to be the best on paper actually is the best in practice. The lessons that Geophysical Systems Corporation learned from its vendor selection process highlight the importance of a thorough vendor evaluation (see Focus 19-1).

Despite the availability of good software packages, many organizations meet their information needs by writing their own software. The next section discusses in-house software development by IT professionals. The subsequent section then discusses software that users develop themselves.

Table 19-2
Point Scoring Evaluation of Vendor Proposals

Criterion	Weight	VENDOR 1		VENDOR 2		VENDOR 3	
		Score	Weighted Score	Score	Weighted Score	Score	Weighted Score
Hardware compatibility	60	6	360	7	420	8	480
Hardware speed	30	6	180	10	300	5	150
Memory expansion	60	5	300	7	420	8	480
Hardware current	30	9	270	9	270	6	180
Software compatibility	90	7	630	7	630	9	810
Online inquiry capabilities	40	9	360	10	400	8	320
Controls	50	7	350	6	300	9	450
Positive references	40	10	400	8	320	6	240
Documentation	30	9	270	8	240	7	210
Easily maintained; updated regularly	50	7	350	8	400	9	450
Network capabilities	50	8	400	7	350	8	400
Vendor support	70	6	420	9	630	10	700
Totals			4,290		4,680		4,870

19-1 FOCUS A Software Purchase That Went Awry

Geophysical Systems Corporation (GSC), which specializes in developing drilling equipment, developed a device that uses sonar to analyze the production potential of oil and gas discoveries. GSC needed a software program to analyze the data generated by the company's sonar device. GSC hired Seismograph Service Corporation and paid it $20 million to write the computer system. To its dismay, GSC found that the Seismograph system could not accurately process the massive volume of data and perform the complex computations needed. When this failing became apparent, GSC's clients canceled their contracts. As a result, the company went from yearly sales of $40 million and profits of $6 million to filing for bankruptcy two years later.

GSC sued Seismograph, claiming that the supplier's system failed to perform as promised. In addition, it claimed that Seismograph knew the system would not be able to perform as desired before it began the development project. The jury agreed, awarding GSC over $48 million as compensation for lost profits and the cost of the computer system. Seismograph appealed on the basis that its system did work and that GSC's sales decline resulted from a slump in oil prices.

GSC's experience is not uncommon; many systems development projects do not produce the intended results.

Development by In-House IS Departments

Despite the availability of good software packages, many organizations develop their own software because their requirements are unique or their size and complexity necessitate a custom package. Developing **custom software** is difficult and error-prone, and it consumes a great deal of time and resources. The most difficult hurdles a company must overcome to develop quality software are lack of time, the complexity of the desired system, poor requirement and systems planning, inadequate communication and cooperation between affected departments and users, lack of qualified staff, and poor senior executive support. All these problems have contributed to the U.S. Government Accountability Office (GAO) reporting that 31% of the information system projects of the federal government, costing $12 billion (19% of its annual IT budget), are either poorly planned or not living up to their intended objectives. An additional 9% are listed as high risk.

After end users define their requirements, analysts work with them to determine the format of paper and screen outputs. The analysts then identify the data required for each input and the data to be retained in the files. Analysts also develop detailed program specifications to be interpreted and coded by a programmer. Because of the many and varied development tasks, the process requires a significant amount of discipline and management supervision. Accountants often help develop custom software, either as project supervisors, users, or development team members.

Custom software is usually developed and written in-house. Chapter 20 discusses in more depth the process used to develop software. Alternatively, organizations may engage an outside company, such as Accenture or EDS, to develop a package or assemble one from its inventory of program modules. These modules are adapted, combined, and organized to form a customized product that meets a company's specific requirements. When contracting with an outside organization, a company should maintain control over the development process. The following guidelines are recommended:

- **Carefully select a developer.** The outside developer should have experience in the company's industry, a good understanding of business in general, and an in-depth understanding of how the company conducts its business.

- **Sign a contract.** The contract should place responsibility for meeting the company's requirements on the developer and should allow the company to discontinue the project if certain key conditions are not met.
- **Plan and monitor each step.** All aspects of the project should be designed in detail, and there should be frequent checkpoints for monitoring the project.
- **Maintain effective communication.** The relationship between the company and the developer should be rigorously defined. Frequent communication is necessary.
- **Control all costs.** Costs should be tightly controlled and cash outflows minimized until the project has been completed and accepted.

Arthur D. Little and other information systems consultants tell clients to develop custom software only if it provides a significant competitive advantage. For example, there is usually no measurable benefit to having a custom-written payroll or accounts receivable system. On the other hand, there may be significant benefits to sophisticated, just-in-time inventory management software, product manufacturing software, or software for other core corporate functions. If a software application will not provide a competitive advantage, Little advises its clients to buy software from an outside supplier. As a result, spending on in-house software development has plunged by up to two-thirds in recent years, while spending on software packages has more than doubled.

An example of a company trying to develop software that will provide it with a significant competitive advantage is Fannie Mae. Its new system will encompass the entire life cycle of a loan, from providing potential lenders with information on all the different types of home loans, to helping them apply for the loans, to granting the loans, to informing the borrowers they have been accepted or rejected for a loan, to packaging loans into mortgage-backed securities for sale to investors. This will provide Fannie Mae with unique customer service and cost advantages.

There is no single right answer to the build-or-buy decision. Different companies come to different conclusions. For example, Gillette once developed its own software but then decided to move from proprietary systems to off-the-shelf software when possible. Its rationale is that it gains a greater competitive advantage from deciding *how* software should be used than from determining *what* software should be used and then creating it. If canned software does not meet all of Gillette's needs, it is modified using high-level development tools.

Pepsi, on the other hand, moved in the opposite direction. It once bought most of its mainframe software but, after moving to a client/server architecture, it could not find software sophisticated enough to meet its needs. Although Pepsi still buys software when it can find it, it had to create most of its newly installed software.

This section has discussed why many organizations have information systems staff develop their software. Organizations also are finding it productive to allow users to develop systems to meet their own information needs. The next section discusses this approach.

End-User-Developed Software

End-user computing (EUC) is the hands-on development, use, and control of computer-based information systems by users. In other words, EUC is people using IT to meet their information needs rather than relying on systems professionals. For example, a savings and loan in California wanted a system to track loan reserve requirements. Its information systems department said the system would take 18 months to develop. Rather than wait, the loan department used a PC and a database program to develop a functional program in a single day. Enhancing the program took several

more days. Not only did the loan department cut the development time from 18 months to a few days, it ended up with the exact information it needed because users developed the system themselves.

After the automobile was introduced, a famous sociologist predicted that the automobile market would not exceed 2 million cars because only that many people would be willing to serve as chauffeurs. Instead, tens of millions of cars are sold annually to people who drive themselves. It was once predicted that the telephone system would collapse because the geometric growth in calls would require everyone to be telephone operators. Instead, equipment was developed that automated many of the functions previously performed by operators.

Since the introduction of the computer, the demand for information systems has grown astronomically. If a company wanted to eliminate its information backlogs, almost everyone would have to become a programmer. Does this sound similar to the automobile and the telephone examples? The solution involves end users who meet their own information needs. As with telephones, technology is being developed to automate much of the process for us. Just as most people learn to drive automobiles, increased computer literacy and easier-to-use programming languages will allow almost everyone to operate powerful computers.

With the advent of inexpensive PCs and a wide variety of powerful and inexpensive software, users began developing their own systems to create and store data, access and download company data, and share data and computer resources in networks. As end users began to meet their initial needs, two things happened. First, users realized computers could be used to meet more and more information needs. Second, increased access to data created many new uses and needs for information. The result has been a tremendous growth in end-user computing, a growth that is expected to continue accelerating.

The growth in end-user computing has significantly altered the information system staff's role. They continue to develop and maintain the transaction processing systems and companywide databases on which end users draw to meet their information needs. In addition, the staff provides users with technical advice and operational support and makes as much information available to end users as possible. Although this has resulted in more work for the systems staff, it has been counterbalanced by a decreased demand for their traditional services.

If the end-user computing trend continues, it will represent 75% to 95% of all information processing by the end of this decade. Because you will be an end user or have a significant involvement with end-user computing no matter where you work, it is essential to have an understanding of end-user computing concepts.

Appropriate End-User Development and Use

End-user development (EUD) occurs when information users, such as managers, accountants, and internal auditors, develop their own applications using computer specialists as advisors. End-user development is inappropriate for complex systems, such as those that process a large number of transactions or update database records. Therefore, it is not used for processing payroll, accounts receivables and payables, general ledger, or inventory. Following are examples of appropriate end-user developments:

- Retrieving information from company databases to produce simple reports or to answer one-time queries,
- Performing "what-if," sensitivity, or statistical analyses,
- Developing applications using prewritten software, such as a spreadsheet or a database system,
- Preparing schedules and lists, such as depreciation schedules, accounts receivable aging, and loan amortizations.

Benefits of End-User Computing

One reason end-user computing has increased so significantly is that it offers the following advantages:

- **User creation, control, and implementation.** Accountants and other end users, rather than the information systems department, control the development process. They decide what information needs are important and if a system should be developed. The sense of ownership that comes with end-user development helps users develop better systems.
- **Systems that meet user needs.** When end users develop their own systems, the systems are more likely to meet the users' needs. Users also can discover flaws that the systems people would not catch. The user-analyst-programmer communication problems inherent in traditional program development are avoided.
- **Timeliness.** Much of the lengthy delay inherent in the traditional systems development process is avoided, such as expensive and time-consuming cost/benefit analysis, detailed requirements definitions, and the inevitable delays and red tape inherent in the approval process.
- **Freeing up systems resources.** The more information needs users can meet, the more time the information systems department can spend on other information and maintenance activities. This reduces both the visible and the invisible backlog of systems development projects.
- **Versatility and ease of use.** Most end-user computing software is easy to understand and use. Users can change the information they produce or modify their application anytime their requirements change. With a laptop computer, work can be completed at home, on a plane, or almost anywhere.

Risks of End-User Computing

There are some significant drawbacks to end-user computing and to eliminating analyst/programmer involvement in the development process.

- **Logic and development errors.** End users have little experience in systems development and are more likely to make errors and less likely to recognize when errors have occurred. The user-developer may solve the wrong problem, poorly define system requirements, apply an inappropriate analytical method, use the wrong software, or use incomplete or outdated information. Often the error is caused by faulty logic or by incorrectly using formulas or software commands. For example, employees at an oil and gas company developed a complex spreadsheet to analyze a proposed acquisition. Based on the results, management scheduled a meeting to propose the acquisition to the board of directors. Before the presentation, consultants from the company's CPA firm tested the model to see if they agreed with its results and gave their approval. Shortly before his speech, one of the presenters performed his own tests so he would understand how the model worked and could answer any tough questions the board threw at him. He discovered a few formulas he thought distorted the projections. He called in the group that developed the spreadsheet and several CPA firm partners. When the formulas were corrected, they showed that the acquisition would have led to significant losses. The presentation to the board was canceled, the person who developed the spreadsheet was fired, and the CPA firm no longer does any audit or consulting work for the company.
- **Inadequately tested applications.** Users are not as likely to rigorously test their applications, either because they do not recognize the need to do so or because of the difficulty or time involved. They also have grossly inflated opinions of how error-free their systems are. For example, one study showed

that users estimated only an 18% chance of there being errors in the spreadsheets they had built. In reality, 86% of them had errors. As another example, one of the Big Four CPA firms found that 90% of the spreadsheet models it tested had at least one calculation error.

- **Inefficient systems.** Most end users are not programmers and have not been trained in systems development. Although the systems they develop get the job done, they are not always efficient. For example, a bank clerk spent three weeks developing a program that examined each cell in a spreadsheet and changed its value to zero if it was a negative amount. When the 60-page program began returning a "too many nested ifs" error message, the clerk called in a computer consultant. Within five minutes the consultant developed a finished application using a built-in spreadsheet function.

- **Poorly controlled and documented systems.** Many end users do not implement controls to protect their systems. User-created systems are often poorly documented because the user considers the task boring or unimportant. Users fail to realize that without documentation, others cannot understand how their system works.

- **System incompatibilities.** Some companies add end-user equipment without considering the technological implications. As a result, they have a diversity of hardware and software that is difficult to support or to network. For example, Aetna Life & Casualty spent more than $1 billion a year on IT in an attempt to gain a competitive advantage. The result was 50,000 PCs from a few dozen manufacturers, 2,000 minicomputers and servers, 108 word processing systems, 19 incompatible e-mail systems, and 36 different communications networks. Aetna Life & Casualty finally realized it needed to shift its emphasis from trying to own the latest technology to the effective use of technology. Aetna standardized its systems and now uses only a few different types of PCs, Microsoft software products, two electronic mail systems, and one network. The result is compatibility across all systems and significantly less cost.

- **Duplication of systems and data and wasted resources.** If end users are unaware that other users have similar information needs, duplicate systems occur. Inexperienced users also may take on more than they are able to accomplish, which ends up wasting time and resources.

- **Increased costs.** A single PC purchase is inexpensive, but buying PCs for hundreds or thousands of workers is costly. Updating the hardware and software every few years is also expensive. End-user computing also has a high opportunity cost if it diverts users' attention from their primary jobs. In addition, it increases time and data demands on the company mainframe and on information systems people use for support and assistance.

A proper balance between maximizing the benefits and minimizing the risks of end-user systems is achieved by using systems analysts as advisers and requiring user-created systems to be reviewed and documented prior to use. In addition, users can be trained in the systems analysis process so they can identify and adequately meet their needs and review the work of other users.

Managing and Controlling End-User Computing

Organizations use several different approaches to manage and control end-user computing. Giving the systems department control over end-user computing discourages end-user computing's growth, denies the organization of most of its benefits, and is not in the company's best long-term interests. However, if there are no controls over end users, such as what end-user computing tools are purchased or how they are used, then chaos can easily result. It also can be difficult to support the system. It is best to provide enough guidance and standards to adequately control the system yet allow users the flexibility they need.

For instance, a **help desk** can encourage, support, coordinate, and control end-user activities. The 60 help desk analysts and technicians at Schering-Plough handle more than 9,000 calls a month. The front-line analysts use expert system software to quickly find the answers to users' questions and then provide callers with scripted answers. The second-line technicians handle the more complicated queries. Other companies use multimedia software with animation or videos to help first-line staffers walk callers through a complicated process. Duties of the help desk include the following:

- Providing hotline assistance to help resolve problems,
- Serving as a clearinghouse for information, coordination, and assistance,
- Training end-users how to use specific hardware and software and providing corresponding technical maintenance and support,
- Evaluating new end-user hardware and software products,
- Assisting with application development,
- Developing and implementing standards for (1) hardware and software purchase to ensure compatibility; (2) documentation and application testing; and (3) controlling security issues such as fraud, software piracy, and viruses,
- Controlling corporate data so (1) authorized end users can access and share it; (2) it is not duplicated; and (3) access to confidential data is restricted.

Outsourcing the System

We have discussed two approaches to obtaining software: buying it and developing it in-house. A third way to acquire software is to outsource the information system.

Outsourcing is hiring an outside company to handle all or part of an organization's data processing activities. In a mainframe outsourcing agreement, the outsourcers buy their client's computers and hire all or most of the client's employees. They then operate and manage the entire system on the client's site, or they migrate the system to the outsourcer's computers. Many mainframe outsourcing contracts are in effect for 10 years or more and cost from hundreds of thousands to millions of dollars a year. For example, several years prior to its bankruptcy filing Enron signed a $750 million agreement with EDS to outsource its entire information system. EDS bought Enron's computers, software, and transmission network. It also hired all 550 of Enron's information systems staff at comparable wages and benefits. Enron paid EDS a fixed annual fee, plus additional fees based on processing volume. During the 10-year life of the contract, Enron expected to save $200 million, which was almost 25% of its computing costs.

In a client/server or a PC outsourcing agreement, an organization outsources a particular service, a segment of its business, a particular function, or PC support. Most Fortune 500 companies outsource anywhere from 10% to 80% of their PC support functions. For example, Taco Bell outsourced its PC help desk services. Royal Dutch Shell, the international oil company, has 80,000 PCs worldwide and has outsourced most of its installation, maintenance, training, help desk, and technical support.

The Growth in Outsourcing Applications

Outsourcing was initially used for standardized applications such as payroll, accounting, and purchasing or by companies that were struggling to survive and wanted a quick infusion of cash from selling their hardware. However, in 1989 Eastman Kodak surprised the business world by hiring three different companies to operate its computer systems. Kodak outsourced its data processing operations and sold its mainframes to IBM. It outsourced its telecommunications functions to DEC and its PC operations to Businessland (and later Entek Information Services). When the

performance of DEC and Entek began to slip, Kodak opened those services to new bids. Kodak continues to perform its own information systems strategic planning and development, but the responsibility of system implementation and operation belongs to the outsourcers. The results have been dramatic. Capital expenditures for computers fell 90% while operating expenses decreased between 10% and 20%. Kodak expected the annual information systems savings to reach approximately $130 million over the 10-year period of the agreement.

Several years ago, Xerox signed what was then the largest outsourcing deal in history: a $3.2 billion, 10-year contract with EDS to outsource its computing, telecommunications, and software management in 19 countries. The company moved to outsourcing to cut costs, to speed up the move from a mainframe architecture to client/server computing, and to free management to focus on strategic management issues rather than on day-to-day concerns. However, Xerox retained control over its systems functions, such as strategic planning and new application development, to support its reengineering efforts.

The success of Kodak and Xerox motivated other organizations to outsource their information systems. For example, many Fortune 500 companies outsource some or all of their information systems. Most of them have found it more efficient to use several different outsourcing companies to increase flexibility, foster competition, and reduce costs, rather than outsource their entire system to a single outsourcer. Most companies do not outsource the strategic management of their IT environment, business process management, or IT architecture.

Outsourcing business processes is the fastest-growing information technology trend, with outsourcing services valued at well over $1 trillion. Business executives no longer look at outsourcing as just a way to meet short-term financial objectives; instead, it is a great way for companies to improve their competitive advantages. Interviewed executives in one survey said 73% of their companies outsource one or more business processes.

Outsourcing is no longer confined to large organizations. As prices have come down, smaller companies are jumping on the outsourcing bandwagon. For example, one small company with annual revenues of less than $1 million dollars used to do all its own accounting. Now it outsources all accounting functions to a local CPA for $800 a month. Whenever they want, the owners can go online to the CPA's Web site, view all their transactions, and produce a myriad of reports on demand. They have also outsourced all their IT processes, including Web site design and maintenance.

The Benefits of Outsourcing

There are a number of significant advantages to outsourcing:

- **A business solution.** Outsourcing is a viable strategic and economic business solution because it allows companies to concentrate on their core competencies. Kodak believes in focusing its efforts on what it does best and leaving data processing to more qualified computer companies. Kodak treats outsourcers as partners and works closely with them to meet its strategic and operational data processing objectives.
- **Asset utilization.** Organizations with millions of dollars tied up in IT can improve their cash position and reduce expenses by selling those assets to an outsourcer. For example, Health Dimensions, a hospital management company, outsourced the data processing functions of its four hospitals so it could use its limited monetary resources for revenue-generating purchases.
- **Access to greater expertise and more advanced technology.** Many companies cannot afford to retain a staff to manage and develop the increasingly complex networks required in today's businesses. Continental Bank and Del Monte Foods turned to outsourcing because the cost and time

involved in staying at the cutting edge of technology were rising significantly. Washington Water Power Company began outsourcing when the prospect of upgrading and replacing its obsolete computer system seemed too daunting a task.

- **Lower costs.** Many companies outsource because skilled overseas providers can perform needed work at dramatically lower labor rates, resulting in significant savings. For example, IBM is outsourcing programming and project management tasks to Chinese companies, whose labor costs are less than one-third of what they are in the United States. Outsourcers can also passa-long some of the savings achieved from standardizing users' applications, buying hardware at bulk prices, splitting development and maintenance costs-between projects, and operating at higher volumes. Continental Bank will save $100 million (20% of IT costs) during the life of its 10-year contract. However, companies such as Occidental Petroleum have rejected outsourcing as costing more than internal AIS development and operation.

- **Improved development time.** Experienced industry specialists often can develop and implement a system faster and more efficiently than can in-house staff. Outsourcers also can help a company cut through much of the internal politics surrounding systems development.

- **Elimination of peaks-and-valleys usage.** Many companies have seasonal businesses that require heavy computer power during part of the year but very little the remainder of the year. For example, from January to March, W. Atlee Burpee & Company processes mail-order and wholesale requests for its seeds and gardening products. During this period its IBM mainframe operated at 80% capacity. It functioned at 20% the rest of the time. Systems personnel were underused most of the time. Burpee turned to outsourcing and now pays Computer Science Corporation (CSC) according to how much the system is used. In doing so, Burpee cut its processing costs in half.

- **Facilitation of downsizing.** Companies that downsize are often left with an unnecessarily large AIS function. General Dynamics downsized dramatically a few years ago due to reduced spending in the defense industry. It sold its data centers to CSC for $200 million and transferred 2,600 employees to CSC. It signed a $3 billion, 10-year outsourcing contract even though its information systems function was rated number one in the aerospace industry.

Risks of Outsourcing

While many outsourcing agreements are great success stories, studies show that anywhere from 25% to 50% of outsourcing agreements either fail or do not live up to significant agreement objectives. In one survey, 17% of outsourcing agreements were labeled as disasters by company executives. Almost 50% of companies have brought work back in-house after outsourcing it. There have been a number of significant outsourcing failures, including the problems EDS has with its U.S. Navy contract (see Focus 18-2). Another example is JPMorgan Chase canceling its $5 billion, seven-year deal with IBM.

There are many reasons why outsourcing projects fail, including not preparing properly, lukewarm executive and company buy-in, thinking outsourcing will gloss over deeper problems, and entering into agreements so large and ill-defined that there is a great deal of room for disappointment and unmet expectations. Other reasons are entering into agreements to blindly imitate competitors, to shift responsibility for a bad process to someone else, and to use the latest and greatest business model, even though it is not the right model for the company or the project. Finally, many projects do not meet their intended objectives because companies do realize that a technical, in-house job becomes a much more complex management challenge when performed by outsiders.

Companies that outsource often experience one or more of the following drawbacks:

- **Inflexibility.** Many outsourcing contracts are for 10 years. If during this time problems arise, if the company is dissatisfied, or if the company goes through extensive structural changes, the contract is difficult or costly to break. Before they merged, Integra Financial Corp. and Equimark Corp. held contracts with different outsourcers. After the merger, one of the contracts had to be eliminated, at a cost of $4.5 million.
- **Loss of control.** A company that outsources runs the risk of losing control of its system and data and of its confidential data being shared with others. For that reason, Ford's outsourcing agreement with Computer Sciences Corporation excludes CSC from taking on other automobile manufacturers as clients.
- **Reduced competitive advantage.** Companies can lose a fundamental understanding of their information systems needs and how the system can provide it with competitive advantages. Outsourcers are not as motivated as their clients to try to meet a particular industry's competitive challenges. This can be mitigated significantly by outsourcing the 80% of a company's business processes considered standard (payroll, cash disbursements, accounts receivable, etc.) and customizing the 20% that provide competitive advantage.
- **Locked-in system.** It is expensive and difficult to reverse outsourcing. If the company is unable to buy back the data-processing facilities, it will have to buy new equipment and hire a new data-processing staff, often at prohibitive costs. Blue Cross of California decided that the performance of its outsourcer, EDS, was so poor that it would end the agreement. However, when Blue Cross started to initiate the change it realized that it knew virtually nothing about its system and could not afford to discharge EDS. In contrast, LSI Logic terminated its agreement with IBM and brought its system back in-house at significant dollar and personnel savings when it installed an ERP system.
- **Unfulfilled goals.** Critics point out that many outsourcing goals and benefits are never realized. One study showed that some benefits, such as increased efficiency, are a myth. USF&G Corporation canceled its $100-million contract with Cigna Information Services after 18 months because Cigna could not implement the changes needed to make the system work properly.
- **Poor service.** Some companies complain of receiving poor service from their outsourcing company. Common complaints are that responsiveness to changing business conditions is slow or nonexistent and migration to new technologies is poorly planned.
- **Increased risk.** Outsourcing business processes can expose a company to significant risks, including operational, financial, technology, strategy, market position, human capital (personnel), legal, regulatory, and reputation impairment risks.

A problem with some systems is that they are simply automated ways of doing business the same way it was done before computers. Business process reengineering, a radical approach to introducing massive changes into information systems and improving the development process, is discussed in the next section.

Business Process Reengineering

Business process reengineering (BPR) is the analysis and redesign of business processes and information systems to achieve significant performance improvements. BPR reduces a company to its essential business processes and reshapes organizational work practices and information flows to take advantage of technological

advancements. This simplifies the system, makes it more effective, and improves a company's quality and service. **Business process management (BPM)** software has been developed to help organizations automate many BPR tasks. Michael Hammer set forth several principles that help organizations successfully reengineer business processes.[1]

- **Organize around outcomes, not tasks.** Often parts of a business process are assigned to different people, which results in numerous handoffs, delays, and errors. In a reengineered system, each person's job is designed around an objective, outcome, or process rather than a task necessary to complete the process.
- **Require those who use the output to perform the process.** Companies are often organized into departments, each specializing in a separate task. Each department passes its completed product off to someone else. It is often better to require those who use the output to perform the process.
- **Require those who produce information to process it.** Ford Motor used to have 500 people matching 14 data items on purchase orders, receiving reports, and vendor invoices before processing payments. Much time was spent reconciling mismatches, resulting in delayed payments and unhappy vendors. In Ford's reengineered system, a computer compares items received with items purchased. If they do not match, the goods are returned. If they match, the goods are accepted and the computer prepares and sends the vendor's payment. This saves a significant amount of money, much of it achieved through a 75% reduction of accounts payable staff.
- **Centralize and disperse data.** To achieve economies of scale and eliminate redundant resources, companies centralize operations. To be more responsive to their customers and provide better service, they decentralize operations. Using technology, companies no longer have to choose between these two approaches. Corporate-wide databases can centralize data, and telecommunications technology can disburse it to the organization.
- **Integrate parallel activities.** Chrysler had separate departments that worked on designing engines, transmissions, frames, and so on. Unfortunately, the departments did not communicate well. At the integration and testing phase, they often found that components did not fit together properly and had to be redesigned at considerable expense. Chrysler reengineered its product development to place at least one person from each department on the team in charge of a particular automobile. This reduced product development times and costly redesigns significantly.
- **Empower workers, use built-in controls, and flatten the organizational chart.** Most organizations have a layer of employees who do the work and several layers that record, manage, audit, or control processes. In a reengineered system, the people who do the work have decision-making responsibility, and information technology helps them make correct decisions and avoid mistakes. Controls are built into the process itself.
- **Capture data once, at its source.** Historically, functional areas designed and built their own AIS. Each functional area collected the same data and entered it into its application. This is inefficient, expensive, and results in data discrepancies. It is better to use technology such as EDI and source data automation devices like bar codes to capture data electronically at the source and enter it in the database. This reduces errors, eliminates data processing delays, and reduces clerical and other costs.

Underlying reengineering is the efficient and effective use of the latest information technology. For example, in the future radio- and satellite-based communications

[1]Much of this section is adapted from Michael Hammer, "Reengineering Work: Don't Automate, Obliterate," *Harvard Business Review* (July–August 1990): 104–112.

technology, coupled with powerful handheld computers, will have a significant impact on the way companies do business. With image processing, multiple users can use a document simultaneously. Active documents that automatically know where to go will also have an impact.

Challenges Faced by Reengineering Efforts

BPR is challenging and many efforts fail or do not accomplish all they set out to do. To successfully complete the BPR process, a company must face and overcome the following obstacles:

- **Tradition.** Old ways of doing things do not die easily, especially practices associated with the organization's culture. Successful reengineering requires changes in employee culture and beliefs.
- **Resistance.** Change is always met with a great deal of resistance. Managers must continually reassure, persuade, and provide support to those affected so that the necessary changes will work.
- **Time and cost requirements.** BPR is costly and almost always takes two or more years to complete.
- **Lack of management support.** Many top managers are afraid of the "big hype, few results" syndrome. Without top-management support, reengineering has little chance of succeeding.
- **Skepticism.** Some people view BPR as traditional systems development in a new wrapper with a fancy name.
- **Retraining.** Employees must be retrained, which is time-consuming and expensive.
- **Controls.** Important controls that ensure system reliability and integrity cannot be deleted.

Sometimes systems under development do not need to be reengineered, but the development team would like to hasten the development process significantly. Prototyping, as discussed next, is a good way to do just that.

Prototyping

Prototyping is an approach to systems design in which a simplified working model of a system is developed. This **prototype**, or first draft, is quickly and inexpensively built and provided to users for testing. Experimenting with the prototype allows users to determine what they do and do not like about the system. Based on their reactions and feedback, the developers modify the system and again present it to the users. This iterative process of trial usage and modification continues until the users are satisfied that the system adequately meets their needs. The basic premise of prototyping is that it is easier for people to express what they like or dislike about a prototype than to imagine what they want in a system. In other words, if users can try out an actual application, they can provide feedback as to what they do and do not like about it. Even a simple system that is not fully functional demonstrates features far better than diagrams, drawings, verbal explanations, or volumes of documentation.

UNUM Life Insurance used prototyping to show how a new system using image processing would work. UNUM wanted to use new technologies to link its system with all external and internal systems and their users. However, top management had a hard time getting middle managers to envision how they wanted to use image processing and to understand the issues involved in the change. After viewing a prototype, the managers caught on to the possibilities and issues associated with image processing.

Up to that point, these managers thought image processing only meant replacing file cabinets. Only after viewing the prototype did they realize its business potential.

Developers who use prototyping still go through the systems development life cycle discussed in Chapter 18, but prototyping allows them to condense and speed up parts of the analysis and the design phases. For example, prototyping does a good job of capturing user needs and helps developers and users make many of the conceptual and physical design decisions. As a result, current practice leans heavily toward prototyping so that projects can be completed as quickly as possible before planned systems become obsolete.

Steps in Developing a Prototype

As shown in Figure 19-1, four steps are involved in developing a prototype. The first step is to identify basic system requirements by meeting with users to agree on the size and scope of the system and to decide what the system should include and exclude. The developer and users also determine decision-making and transaction-processing outputs, as well as the inputs and data needed to produce these outputs. The emphasis is on what output should be produced rather than *how* it should be produced. The developer must ensure that users' expectations are realistic and that their basic information requirements can be met. The designer uses the information requirements to develop cost, time, and feasibility estimates for alternative AIS solutions.

The second step is to develop an initial prototype that meets the agreed-on requirements. The emphasis is on speed and low cost rather than efficiency of operation. The goal is to implement the prototype within a short time period, perhaps days

Figure 19-1
The Steps for Developing a System from a Prototype

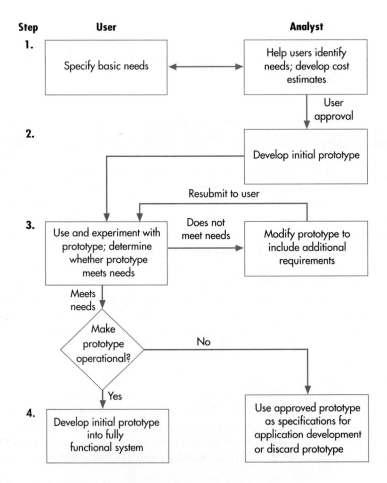

or weeks. Because of these time limitations, some aspects of the system are sacrificed in the interests of simplicity, flexibility, and ease of use. Therefore, nonessential functions, system controls, exception handling, validation of input data, processing speed, and efficiency considerations are ignored at this point. It is critical, however, that users see and use tentative versions of data entry display screens, menus, input prompts, and source documents. They must also respond to prompts, query the system, judge response times, and issue commands.

When the prototype is finished, the developer returns to the users and demonstrates the system. The users are instructed to experiment with the system and comment on what they do and do not like about its content and performance.

The third step is an iterative process in which users identify changes, developers make changes, and the system is again turned over to the users for evaluation and experimental use. This iterative process continues until the users are satisfied with the system. A typical prototype will go through four to six iterations.

The fourth step is to use the system approved by the users. As shown in Figure 19-1, an approved prototype is typically used in one of two ways. Half of all prototypes are turned into fully functional systems, referred to as **operational prototypes**. To make the prototype operational, the developer must incorporate needed controls, improve operational efficiency, provide backup and recovery, and integrate the prototype with the systems with which it interfaces. Changes may be necessary to allow the program to accept real input, access real data files, process data, make the necessary computations and calculations, and produce real output.

In many instances it is not practical to modify the prototype to make it a fully functional system. These **nonoperational (throwaway) prototypes** can be used in several ways. The prototype may be discarded, and the system requirements identified during the prototyping process can be used to develop a new system. The system development life cycle is followed to develop the system, with the prototype as the model for development. The prototype also can be used as the initial prototype for an expanded system designed to meet the needs of many different users. Finally, if the users and the developer decide that the system under consideration is unsalvageable, the prototype can be discarded completely. In this instance, the company has saved itself years of development work and a lot of money by avoiding the much more costly traditional SDLC process.

When to Use Prototyping

In most cases, prototyping supports rather than replaces the SDLC. Prototyping is appropriate when there is a high level of uncertainty about the AIS, it is unclear what questions to ask, the final AIS cannot be clearly visualized because the decision process is still unclear, speed is an issue, or there is a high likelihood of failure. Systems that are especially good candidates for prototyping are decision support systems, executive information systems, expert systems, and information retrieval systems. Prototyping is also appropriate for systems that involve experimentation and trial-and-error development or when the requirements evolve as the system is used. Prototyping is not usually appropriate for large or complex systems that serve major organizational components or cross a number of organizational boundaries. Nor is it commonly used for developing standard AIS components such as accounts receivable and payable or inventory management. A summary of the conditions that make prototyping an appropriate design methodology is presented in Table 19-3.

Advantages of Prototyping

Prototyping has the following advantages:

- **Better definition of user needs.** Because of intensive end-user involvement, prototyping usually results in a good definition of user needs.

Table 19-3
Conditions That Favor the Use
of Prototyping

Users lack a full understanding of their needs, or their needs change rapidly.
System requirements are hard to define.
System inputs and outputs are not known.
The task to be performed is unstructured or semistructured.
Designers are uncertain about what technology to use.
The system to be developed is crucial and needed quickly.
The risk associated with developing the wrong system is high.
The users' reactions to the new system are important development considerations.
Many design strategies must be tested.
The design staff has little experience developing the system or application under
consideration.
The system will be used infrequently (and therefore processing efficiency is not a major
concern).

- **Higher user involvement and satisfaction.** When user requirements are met, the results are greater user satisfaction and less risk that the AIS will not be used. Early user involvement helps to build a climate of acceptance rather than skepticism and criticism about the new AIS.
- **Faster development time.** It takes only a few days or weeks to get a prototype system up and running, which allows users to immediately evaluate significant changes in the way business is transacted. In contrast, it may take a year or more under the traditional approach before the new system can be evaluated. John Hancock Mutual Life Insurance developed the prototype of an executive information system in only one month, as described in Focus 19-2.

19-2 FOCUS — Prototyping: The Third Dimension

An architect develops two-dimensional blueprints that show how a custom home will look. However, a look at the third dimension, walking through the home, lets you actually see the rooms and get a feel for the layout. Creating customized software provides a similar challenge. Users must try to visualize the look and feel of their software from written specifications. Prototypes help users who have ideas or plans but do not know how to turn them into reality, as well as users who have a problem but do not know how to begin solving it. A prototype lets them walk through the proposed system and experiment with its look and feel before committing to the expense of application development.

John Hancock Mutual Life Insurance Company was dissatisfied with the traditional development process: determining user specifications (getting information from high-level executives was especially difficult), writing them up, developing the system, and presenting it to the end users. The typical reaction from a user was, "I may have said that this is what I wanted, but it isn't."

To counter these problems, Hancock used a prototyping approach to develop an executive information system (EIS).

The EIS was needed because the company was dissatisfied with its inability to obtain data quickly and easily from the existing system.

Hancock formed a team that included systems development consultants from IBM, user representatives, systems analysts, and programmers. The prototyping process was highly interactive, and the continual involvement of the end users eliminated a great deal of misunderstanding. The programmers on the team started programming almost immediately. They prepared sample screens for the first interview session with users. The development staff sat down with users and showed them how the system would work. Users were then given a chance to try the screens. Almost immediately, users could determine if what they said they wanted was really what they needed.

The result was a prototype for an EIS that took only one month to build. The prototype allows top management at Hancock to access and query current and historical financial data and measurements. Top managers who had been skeptical when the project began were impressed by how much the team was able to accomplish in a single month.

- **Fewer errors.** Because the user experiments with and uses each version of the prototype, errors are detected and eliminated early in the development process. In addition, it is much easier to identify and terminate an infeasible AIS before a great deal of time and expense is incurred.
- **More opportunity for changes.** Under the traditional SDLC approach, the design team is responsible for identifying AIS requirements the first time around. These requirements are then frozen so that the team can complete the AIS. With prototyping, users can continue to suggest changes until the system is exactly what they want.
- **Less costly.** Some prototype systems can be developed for 10% to 20% of the cost of traditional systems. For example, one utility company claimed a 13-to-1 improvement in development time over traditional methods when prototyping was used to develop 10 major applications.

Disadvantages of Prototyping

Prototyping has the following disadvantages:

- **Significant user time.** Prototyping requires users to devote significant time to working with the AIS and providing the developer with feedback and suggestions. Prototyping may require a greater involvement and commitment than busy users are willing to give.
- **Less efficient use of system resources.** The shortcuts that make rapid prototyping iterations possible do not always allow for efficient use of computer resources. As a result, poor performance and reliability and high maintenance and support costs may be incurred.
- **Incomplete system development.** In large or complex systems with many users, prototyping may not lead to a comprehensive and thorough requirements analysis.
- **Inadequately tested and documented systems.** Because prototypes are used heavily before acceptance, developers are often tempted to shortchange the testing and documentation process.
- **Negative behavioral reactions.** If a prototype is a throwaway, users may react negatively to learning the system and then not being able to use it. They may also become dissatisfied if all their demands for improvements are not met or if they have to go through too many iterations.
- **Never-ending development.** If prototyping is not managed properly, it may never be completed. Unending iterations and revisions may be proposed because changes are simple to make.

Another tool for improving the development process is a set of software tools referred to as CASE, which is discussed in the next section.

Computer-Aided Software Engineering

Software developers have been compared with the shoemaker whose children had to go barefoot: They develop software for others, yet fail to create software to simplify their own work. The development of powerful **computer-aided software (or systems) engineering (CASE)** tools, an integrated package of computer-based tools that automate important aspects of the software development process, has changed that. CASE tools are used to plan, analyze, design, program, and maintain an information system. They also are used to enhance the efforts of managers, users, and programmers to understand information needs.

Many companies are currently using CASE tools. For example, Florida Power's $86 million customer information system was created using a CASE tool sold by Accenture. The system has been so successful that Accenture packaged it for other utility companies. America West Airlines has more than half of its 90 programmers developing applications using a PC-based CASE tool. Its employees use the tool to model data and business processes, and then the tool uses this information to design and construct a system.

CASE tools do not replace skilled designers. Instead, they are a host of well-integrated tools that give developers effective support for all phases of the SDLC. CASE software typically has tools for strategic planning, project and system management, database design, screen and report layout, and automatic code generation.

Advantages and Disadvantages of CASE Technology

CASE tools provide the following important advantages:

- **Improved productivity.** Sony reported that CASE tools increased productivity by over 600%. CASE can generate bug-free code from system specifications and can automate repetitive tasks. Using an integrated CASE tool, a programmer at Baptist Medical System developed a system in one week that was estimated to take four months.
- **Improved program quality.** CASE tools simplify the enforcement of structured development standards, thus improving the quality of development and reducing the threat of serious design errors. CASE tools also can check the internal accuracy of the design and detect inconsistencies.
- **Cost savings.** Savings of 80% to 90% are possible. At DuPont, an application estimated to require 27 months at a cost of $270,000 was finished in 4 months for $30,000. Over 90% of the code was generated directly from design specifications.
- **Improved control procedures.** CASE tools encourage the development of system controls, security measures, and system auditability and error-handling procedures early in the design process.
- **Simplified documentation.** CASE tools automatically document the system as the development process progresses.

Some of the more serious problems with CASE technology include the following:

- **Incompatibility.** Some CASE tools do not interact effectively with other systems.
- **Cost.** CASE technology is expensive, with some packages in excess of $300,000. As a result, many small companies cannot afford integrated CASE tools.
- **Unmet expectations.** According to a Deloitte & Touche survey, only 37% of the chief information officers using CASE believe they achieved the expected benefits.

SUMMARY AND CASE CONCLUSION

A company can use many different strategies to obtain a new AIS. First, as the quality and quantity of vendor-written software increase, more and more companies are purchasing software. Second, they can use their information systems departments to develop their software or allow end users to develop their own software. When vendor-written software does not meet all of a company's needs, some companies buy the

software and then modify it themselves or, preferably, ask the vendor to make the needed modifications. Third, companies can hire an outsourcing company to handle data processing activities.

There are many ways to speed up or improve the development process. One way is business process reengineering, which is the thorough analysis and redesign of business processes and information systems to achieve dramatic performance improvements.

A second way is to design a prototype, a simplified working model of a system. A prototype is quickly and inexpensively built and is given to users to test drive so they can decide what they like and dislike about the system. Their reactions and feedback are used to modify the system, which is again given to the users to test. This iterative process of trial usage and modification continues until the users are satisfied that the system adequately meets their needs.

A third way to improve the development process is to use computer-aided software engineering tools to automate important aspects of the software development process. CASE tools are used to plan, analyze, design, program, and maintain an information system. They are also used to enhance the efforts of managers, users, and programmers in understanding information needs.

Ann considered the different strategies discussed in this chapter and eliminated several of them. She decided against outsourcing the AIS because she did not feel that option would provide Shoppers Mart with the type of system that management wanted. She also believed her team could do a better and faster job developing the system than an outsourcer could. Ann did not think that prototyping would be effective because Shoppers Mart needed a large and complex system that would serve the needs of many users in many functional areas. Ann discussed the new system with top management and the systems staff and decided that the company's business processes did not need to be radically overhauled—that is, the system did not need to be reengineered.

Ann narrowed her options down to purchasing a system or designing one in-house. If Shoppers Mart decides to develop its own software, Ann will investigate the various CASE packages on the market to see if they will add value to the development process.

No matter which approach she chooses, Ann wants to facilitate as much end-user development as is practical and useful. Ann will make the final decision during the conceptual design phase (Chapter 20). To gather the information she needs to decide whether to purchase software, Ann prepares and sends an RFP to vendors. The RFP asks the vendors to propose software and hardware to meet the company's needs as identified during systems analysis.

KEY TERMS

canned software 729
turnkey systems 729
application service
 provider (ASP) 729
request for proposal
 (RFP) 730
benchmark
 problem 732
point scoring 732
requirements
 costing 732
custom software 733

end-user computing
 (EUC) 734
end-user development
 (EUD) 735
help desk 738
outsourcing 738
business process
 reengineering
 (BPR) 741
business process
 management
 (BPM) 742

prototyping 743
prototype 743
operational prototype 745
nonoperational
 (throwaway)
 prototype 745
computer-aided software
 (or systems)
 engineering
 (CASE) 747

AIS IN ACTION

CHAPTER QUIZ

1 Which of the following is *not* one of the difficulties accountants have experienced using the traditional systems development life cycle?
 a. AIS development projects are backlogged for years.
 b. Changes are not usually possible after requirements have been frozen.
 c. The AIS that is developed may not meet their needs.
 d. All are difficulties with the SDLC.

2 Companies that buy rather than develop an AIS must still go through the systems development life cycle.
 a. True.
 b. False.

3 Which of the following statements is false?
 a. As a general rule, companies should buy rather than develop software if they can find a package that meets their needs.
 b. As an AIS increases in size and complexity, there is a greater likelihood that canned software can be found that meets user needs.
 c. A company should not attempt to develop its own custom software unless experienced, in-house programming personnel are available and the job can be completed less expensively on the inside.
 d. As a general rule, a company should develop custom software only when it will provide a significant competitive advantage.

4 When buying large and complex systems, vendors are invited to submit systems for consideration. What is such a solicitation called?
 a. request for quotation
 b. request for system
 c. request for proposal
 d. good-faith estimate

5 To compare system performance, a company can create a data processing task with input, processing, and output jobs. This task is performed on the systems under consideration and the processing times are compared. The AIS with the lowest time is the most efficient. What is this process called?
 a. benchmarking
 b. requirements costing
 c. point scoring
 d. performance testing

6 Which of the following statements is true?
 a. Because the AIS is so crucial, companies never outsource parts of the AIS.
 b. Most mainframe outsourcing contracts are for two to three years and cost thousands of dollars a year.
 c. Outsourcers often buy the client's computers and hire all or most of its information systems employees.
 d. Only companies struggling to survive and wanting a quick infusion of cash from selling their hardware use outsourcing.

7 Which of the following is *not* a benefit of outsourcing?
 a. It offers a great deal of flexibility because it is relatively easy to change outsourcers.

b. It can provide access to the expertise and special services provided by outsourcers.
c. It allows companies to move to a more sophisticated level of computing at a reasonable cost.
d. It is a cost-effective way to handle the peaks and valleys found in seasonal businesses.

8 Which of the following is a true statement with respect to prototyping?
a. In the early stages of prototyping, system controls and exception handling may be sacrificed in the interests of simplicity, flexibility, and ease of use.
b. A prototype is a scaled-down, first-draft model that is quickly and inexpensively built and given to users to evaluate.
c. The first step in prototyping is to identify system requirements.
d. All of the statements are true.

9 Which of the following is *not* an advantage of prototyping?
a. better definition of user needs
b. adequately tested and documented systems
c. higher user involvement and satisfaction
d. faster development time

10 When is it most appropriate to use prototyping?
a. when there is little uncertainty about the AIS
b. when it is clear what user needs are
c. when the final AIS cannot be clearly visualized because the decision process is still unclear
d. when there is a very low likelihood of failure

CHAPTER CASE Freedom from Telemarketers—The Do Not Call List

In 1991, telemarketers placed an average of 18 million calls per day; by 2003, telemarketers were placing 104 million calls per day. Fed up with telemarketer's intrusions, citizens complained to Congress.

In 1994, Congress enacted a law directing the Federal Trade Commission (FTC) to find a way to stop deceptive and abusive telemarketing practices. In 1995, the FTC created the Telemarketing Rule that did not allow telemarketers to call consumers after they had told them not to call again. In 2000, the FTC found that the Telemarketing Rule did not deter telemarketers from calling back.

In January 2002, the FTC proposed a rule that required all telemarketers to sign up on a national Do Not Call registry and barred them from calling consumers who had placed their phone number on that list.

In February 2003, Congress appropriated $18.1 million to create and enforce the Do Not Call Registry. As part of the $18.1 million, $5.5 million was set aside to cover redesigning the FTC Web site, internal IT infrastructure upgrades, and the cost of the registry itself.

On June 27, 2003, President Bush announced the official launch of the Do Not Call Registry. President Bush was quoted as saying, "Unwanted telemarketing calls are intrusive, they are annoying, and they're all too common. When Americans are sitting down to dinner, or a parent is reading to his or her child, the last thing they need is a call from a stranger with a sales pitch."

After the president's announcement, consumers began accessing the www.donotcall.gov Web site and calling the toll-free number to place their phone numbers on the Do Not Call list. Within 72 hours, more than 10 million phone numbers were added to the list, making it a federal offense for telemarketers to call at any time. The Do Not Call Registry was hailed as one the most successful IT projects in the history of government.

Identify the benefits and risks of the FTC purchasing a prewritten software system, developing the system in-house, and outsourcing the system to an external vendor. What approach do you think the FTC should have used?

(*Source:* Adapted from Alice Dragoon, "How the FTC rescued the dinner hour," *CIO* (June 1, 2004): 59–64.)

DISCUSSION QUESTIONS

19.1 What is the accountant's role in the computer acquisition process? Should the accountant play an active role, or should all the work be left to computer experts? In what aspects of computer acquisition might an accountant provide a useful contribution?

19.2 A city in the Midwest with a population of 45,000 purchased a computer and began developing application programs with in-house programmers. Four years later, only one major application had been developed, and it was neither complete nor functioning properly. Moreover, none of the application software running on the system met the users' minimum requirements. Both the hardware and the software frequently failed. A similarly configured system, fully programmed with software, would have saved the city nearly $500,000. Moreover, the city's annual data processing costs exceeded the annual costs of a new turnkey system with packaged software.

Why do you think the city was unable to produce quality, workable systems? Would the city have been better off purchasing software? Do you think the city would have been able to find software to adequately meet its needs? Why or why not?

19.3 You are a systems consultant for Cooper, Price, and Arthur, CPAs. During your country club's annual golf tournament, your partner is Frank Fender, owner of an automobile dealership. He describes a proposal he received from Turnkey Systems and asks for your opinion. The system will handle inventories, receivables, payroll, accounts payable, and general ledger accounting. Turnkey personnel would install the $40,000 system and train Fender's employees. Identify the major themes you would touch on in responding to Fender. Identify the advantages and disadvantages of using a turnkey system to operate the organization's accounting system.

19.4 Sara Jones is the owner of a rapidly growing department store and faces stiff competition. The store is using an out-of-date AIS, resulting in poor customer service, late and error-prone billing, and inefficient control and monitoring of inventory. If the store is to continue growing, its AIS must be upgraded. However, the company is not exactly sure what it wants the AIS to accomplish. Sara has heard about prototyping, but she does not know what it is and whether it would help her. What would you tell Sara if she asked you to define and explain prototyping? Include an explanation of the advantages and disadvantages of prototyping and the circumstances in which it would be most appropriate.

19.5 Clint Grace is the owner of a chain of regional department stores and has been in the business for more than 30 years. He has definite ideas about how department stores should be run. He is financially conservative and is reluctant to make expenditures that do not have a clear financial payoff.

In recent years, the stores' profitability has declined sharply, and customer dissatisfaction is at an all-time high. Store managers never know exactly how much inventory is on hand and when purchases are needed until a shelf is empty. Clint asks you to study the reason for the profitability decline and to recommend a solution. During your research you find that the current AIS is inefficient and unreliable and that the company's processes and procedures are out of date.

You believe the solution is to reengineer the business processes at the department stores and in the central office. What are some challenges you might face in reengineering Clint's stores? Knowing what you do about Clint's personality, how will you present your recommendation?

19.1 Don Otno is confused. He has been researching software options but cannot decide among three alternatives. He has come to you for help.

Don started his search at Computers Made Easy (CME), a computer store in his office complex. He almost wished he had looked no further. Steve Young, the manager of CME, appeared to be knowledgeable and listened attentively as Don explained his problems, needs, and concerns. Steve stated that he had a series of software packages that would, with a few exceptions, come close to meeting Don's needs. He could fix Don up with both hardware and software, and Don could start implementing the package almost immediately. The system's price was unexpectedly reasonable.

Impressed but wanting to shop around, Don visited Custom Designed Software (CDS). After three hours, he left convinced that CDS could produce a program that was exactly what he needed. Cost and time estimates had not been established, but CDS assured him that the cost would be reasonable and that the programs would only take a few months to complete.

Seeking a third opinion, Don visited Modified Software Unlimited (MSU). The MSU representative said customized packages were very good but expensive, whereas canned software was inexpensive but rarely met more than a few needs. The best of both worlds could be achieved by having MSU modify the package that came closest to meeting Don's needs.

On the way back to his office, Don stopped by CME and asked Steve about customized and modified software. Steve expressed enough concerns about both that Don came full circle, and he began thinking canned software was best. Late that night Don realized that he was not able to make an objective decision. He was swayed by whichever vendor he was talking with at the time. The next morning he called you for help.

Required

 a. At Don's request you agree to conduct a study and submit a report showing the advantages and disadvantages of each vendor's approach. Outline the report's contents, identifying the advantages and disadvantages of each approach.

 b. Recommend the course of action that you feel would be best for Don, and support your decision.

19.2 One unhappy federal agency spent almost $1 million on a development contract for an integrated human resources/payroll system that produced no usable software. The original contract was for $445,158 and 15 months. The agency terminated the contract after 28 months and $970,000. The agency had not fully developed user requirements or system specifications for the proposed software when it issued the RFP. There were a number of problems:

- The contractor did not understand the software systems desired.
- User requirements were never adequately defined and frozen. Changes delayed completion schedules and caused disagreements about whether new requirements were included in the original scope of work.
- The contract did not specify systems requirements or performance criteria and the terminology was vague. The contract was amended 13 times to add or delete requirements and to reimburse the contractor for the extra costs resulting from agency-caused delays. The amendments increased the cost of the contract to $1,037,448.
- The contractor complained of inexcusable agency delays, such as taking too much time to review items submitted for approval. The agency blamed the delays on the poor quality of the documentation under review.

- The agency did not require each separate development phase to be approved before work continued. When the agency rejected the general system design, the contractor had to scrap work already completed.

The agency eventually became convinced that the contractor could not deliver the software at an acceptable time and cost; the agency then canceled the contract and tried to withhold payment for poor performance. A negotiated settlement price of $970,000 was agreed on. None of the software was ever used by the agency.

Required

a. Who is to blame for the agency's problems? How could the agency have done a better job of managing the systems development project? What could the contractor have done differently?

b. Can we generalize from this case that organizations and governmental agencies should not try to have custom software written for them? Explain your answer.

19.3 Wong Engineering Corporation (WEC) operates in 25 states and three countries. WEC faced a crucial decision: choosing a network operating system and software that would maximize functionality, manageability, and acceptance of the system by end users. WEC developed and followed a four-step approach:

Step 1 Develop the evaluation criteria. WEC organized a committee to develop proper evaluation criteria. Committee members interviewed users and developed the following criteria:
- Menu or graphical user interface
- Ease of use
- Scope of vendor support
- Ease of network management and administration
- Cost, speed, and performance
- Wide-area communications abilities
- Ability to access other computing platforms
- Security
- Fault tolerance and recovery abilities
- Ability to connect workstations to the network
- Global naming services
- Printing capabilities
- Upgrade and enhancement options
- Stability of the vendor

WEC organized the criteria into the following four categories and prioritized them.

1. Business criteria refer to overall business, economic, and competitive issues.

2. Operational criteria refer to tactical issues and operating characteristics.

3. Organizational criteria refer to people issues such as the networks' impact on the information systems structure.

4. Technical criteria refer to hardware, software, and communications issues.

The evaluation committee used a weighting scale of 1 to 5, with 5 as the highest, to select the top three evaluation criteria for each category. Criteria vital to short-term and long-term business goals were given a 5. "Wish list" criteria were weighted a 3. Inapplicable criteria were given a 1.

Step 2 Define the operating environment. A number of data-gathering techniques were used to collect information from which an information systems model was developed. The model revealed the need to share accounting, sales, marketing, and engineering data at three organizational levels: the district, division, and home office. In addition, district offices needed access

to centralized financial information to handle payroll. WEC decided it needed a distributed network that allowed users throughout the organization access to company data.

Step 3 Identify the operating alternatives. Using the criteria developed in step 1, WEC evaluated each package identified. Each committee member established personal matrices for each product, and then members compared notes during a roundtable discussion.

Step 4 Test and prototype products. The highest-scoring products were tested further using prototypes. Finally, WEC selected the product that fit the organization's needs most completely.

Required

a. Discuss the evaluation committee's role in the selection process. How should members of the committee be selected? What advantages and problems result from using a committee to make the selection?

b. What data-gathering techniques could WEC use to assess user needs? To select a vendor?

c. What is the benefit of analyzing the operating environment before selecting the software? What data-gathering techniques should a company employ in understanding the operating environment?

d. In selecting a system using the point-scoring method, how should the committee resolve scoring disputes? List at least two methods.

e. Assume the point-scoring approach narrowed the process to three candidates. Should a purchase decision be made on the point-scoring process alone? What other procedure(s) should the committee employ in making the final selection?

19.4 Mark Mitton is the accountant acting as liaison to the information systems department for a midsize retail firm in Salem, Oregon. Mark has been investigating several computer systems and has narrowed the selection to the best three systems. Mark developed a shopping list of features the system needs. He carefully reviewed each system, talked to other users, and interviewed appropriate systems representatives. Using a point-scoring system, Mark assigned weights to each factor to coincide with his evaluation. Mark developed Table 19-4 to help him select the best system.

Required

a. Use a spreadsheet program to develop a point-scoring matrix, and determine which of the three systems Mark should select.

b. Mark's coworker, Susan Shelton, did not agree with Mark's weightings. Susan suggested the following changes:

Flexibility	60
Reputation and reliability	50
Quality of support utilities	10
Graphics capability	10

On the basis of the changes, which vendor should Mark recommend?

c. Mark's manager suggested the following changes to Susan's weightings:

Reputation and reliability	90
Installation assistance	40
Experience with similar systems	40
Training assistance	65
Internal memory size	10

Will the manager's changes affect the decision about which system to buy?

d. What can you conclude about point scoring from the changes made by Susan and Mark's manager? Develop your own weighting scale to evaluate the selection of

Table 19-4
An Evaluation Matrix

Selection Criteria	Weight	SYSTEM 1	SYSTEM 2	SYSTEM 3
SOFTWARE				
Fulfillment of business needs	100	6	8	9
Acceptance in marketplace	30	6	7	6
Quality of documentation	50	7	9	8
Quality of warranty	50	4	8	7
Ease of use	80	7	6	5
Control features	50	9	7	9
Flexibility	20	4	5	9
Security features	30	4	4	8
Modularity	30	8	5	4
Integration with other software	30	8	9	6
Quality of support utilities	50	9	8	5
VENDOR				
Reputation and reliability	10	3	9	6
Experience with similar systems	20	5	5	6
Installation assistance	70	9	4	6
Training assistance	35	4	8	6
Timeliness of maintenance	35	5	4	4
HARDWARE				
Internal memory size (RAM)	70	5	6	8
Hard-drive capacity	40	9	9	5
Graphics capabilities	50	7	7	8
Processing speed	30	8	8	5
Overall performance	40	9	4	4
Expandability	50	7	2	5
Support for network technology	30	3	4	7

the three software packages. What other selection criteria would you use? Be prepared to discuss your results with the class.

e. What are the weaknesses of the point-scoring method?

19.5 Nielsen Marketing Research USA (NMR), with operations in 29 countries, is the recognized world leader in the production and dissemination of marketing information. Nielsen was a pioneer in the development of the decision support information business and has been the primary supplier for more than 70 years. NMR's most recognizable product is the Nielsen television ratings.

Nielsen is one of the largest users of computer capacity in the United States. Its information system has consistently ranked above average in efficiency for its industry. However, NMR commissioned IBM to evaluate outsourcing its information processing. NMR wanted to know if outsourcing would allow it to concentrate on giving its customers value-added services and insights and if it could increase its flexibility, promote rapid growth, and provide it with more real-time information.

Required

What are the benefits and risks of outsourcing for NMR? Do you think the benefits of outsourcing outweigh the risks? Explain your answer.

19.6 A state department of licensing needed a new system to handle registration and license applications. After conducting a thorough systems analysis, the department estimated that the project would cost approximately $40 million and take five years to complete. But after seven years and $40 million, the project was finally discontinued with no system in place.

The system design called for a mix of in-house development and private industry contractors. Although this mix was designed to merge the best of both worlds—that is, detailed internal knowledge and external perspective and expertise—what resulted were countless delays and cost overruns due to inadequate communication and poor management. In addition, politics reared its ugly head. Since this was a government project, elected officials and political appointees could not resist sticking their noses into the project to advance their own personal agendas and siphon off critical resources to fund pet projects. In addition, the project development plan called for too few milestones for a project of this size.

Required

a. Identify and discuss the reasons for this system failure.
b. How could end-user computing have helped this project be successful?
c. What risks could have been incurred by using end-user computing for this particular project?

> (*Source: Adapted from Tom Field, "Lessons Learned: Lights Out on LAMP,"*
> *CIO (December 1, 1998): 50.)*

19.7 Meredith Corporation publishes books and magazines, owns and operates television stations, and provides a real estate marketing and franchising service. Meredith is dissatisfied with its ability to retrieve correct and timely inventory information from its AIS. Each division either developed its own inventory system or already had one in place when Meredith acquired the AIS. As a result, Meredith has 11 different inventory systems, which are unable to communicate with each other. Management wants to tie the systems together and have one consistent inventory pool from which to extract the information needed for making good business decisions. Meredith has decided to use prototyping to develop the system.

Required

a. When interviewing Meredith's personnel, what three key questions would you ask to determine systems requirements? What type of information are you attempting to elicit from each question?
b. What do you think are Meredith's basic information needs?
c. Explain how the prototyping process would work for Meredith. What would the system developer do during the iterative process step? Why would you want the fewest iterations possible?
d. Would you want this prototype to be operational or nonoperational? Why? If it were an operational prototype, what would have to happen? If it were a nonoperational prototype, how would the prototype be used?
e. Suppose the company decides the prototyped system is not practical, abandons the system, and takes some other approach to solving its inventory problem. Does that mean prototyping is not a valid systems development approach? Explain your answer.

19.8 The following list outlines the activities a company may perform in the process of reengineering its business. Match each activity with one of the seven principles of reengineering.

Reengineering Activities

a. One person processes an employment application from beginning to end.
b. The department manager using the yearly budget is also the one who prepared it.
c. The purchasing manager has the authority to handle every aspect of making purchases.
d. Each plant issues its own purchase orders, and a new corporate department coordinates purchasing across all the plants.
e. All customer service representatives share a corporatewide database that contains customer sales data.

f. A sales clerk enters a customer's order into a computer terminal. The order is then automatically sent over the network to shipping, inventory control, and the credit manager. In addition, the database is updated immediately.

Seven Principles of Reengineering

1 Organize the business and information system around outcomes, not individual tasks.
2 Have output users perform the process.
3 Have those who produce information process it.
4 Use IT to achieve the benefits of both centralization and decentralization of data.
5 Integrate parallel processes instead of performing them separately and trying to integrate them at the end of the process.
6 Flatten the organizational chart by giving workers the power to make decisions, and use built-in controls
7 Capture data only once, at its source, using source data automation.

19.9 The management of Quickfix would like to decrease costs and increase customer service by reengineering its computer repair procedures. Currently, when a defective or broken computer needs servicing, the customer calls one of five regional customer service centers. A customer service representative manually logs in the relevant customer information and then searches through a list to find the closest qualified technician. That technician is then contacted by phone to see if the repair fits into his or her schedule. If not, the representative finds the next closest technician. When a technician who can perform the service is located, the customer and repair information is provided over the phone. The technician then calls the customer and makes arrangements to pick up the broken computer and replace it with a loaner. Making these arrangements takes one to two days and sometimes more if technicians are not available or do not promptly return calls.

The broken computer is sent to a repair depot. Typically, the entire repair process takes another four to seven days. Overall, it can take up to three weeks for an item to be repaired. When a customer calls to see if the computer is ready, the customer service representative must then call the technician, find out the status of the item, and call the customer back. Throughout the entire repair process, usually five phone calls take place between the customer, the customer service representative, and the technician.

There are three main problems with this process: (1) it is time-consuming; (2) it is inconvenient for a customer to have a computer removed, a new one installed, and then the old one reinstalled; and (3) customer service representatives do not have immediate access to information about items currently being repaired.

Required

a. Identify the basic activities that occur when an item is repaired and around which the reengineered process should be developed.
b. Describe how the current repair process can be reengineered to achieve the goal of more timely repair and increased customer service.
c. What will be the specific benefits of reengineering the repair process?

19.10 Conduct a search (using written materials, the Internet, electronic databases, etc.) for successful and failed implementations of information systems. Per your professor's instructions, prepare an oral or written summary of a successful and a failed implementation. Include in your summary the approach used to acquire or develop the system (purchase software, develop it, modify it, outsource it).

19.11 Norcom, a division of a large manufacturer, needed a new distribution and customer service system to replace its old system. The project was to take 18 months to complete and cost approximately $5 million. The project team was comprised of 20 business and IT staff members. After two years, the CIO was fired and the company

hired a new CIO who was known as an expert in saving troubled projects. The new CIO found that management had committed three grave errors from the start.

1 It picked the wrong software using a very naïve Request For Proposal process.

2 It did not formulate a project plan.

3 No one "owned" the project. The information systems staff assumed the users owned the project, while the users were under the assumption that the information systems staff owned it. Management believed the vendor owned it.

The CIO developed a 2,000 line-item plan to bring order and direction to the project and set to work. However, three months later, the system failed completely, even with the best IT staff and consultants working on it day and night. The failed system was supposed to be the company's preeminent system, but it could not even process customer orders correctly, resulting in complaints about late shipments and receiving the wrong goods.

After three years and $4 million the new CIO polled the staff anonymously. All but two said the project was beyond saving, and they were holdouts who had staked their careers on the project . So the CIO had to tell his boss, the president of the division, that the project was not worth saving. It was a very difficult message for the CIO to give and for the division president to receive. At first, the president would not accept the idea of killing a project that had cost so much money. In the end, however, he accepted the decision and all the ramifications involved. The ramifications included corporate IT taking control of all IT operations at his division.

Required

 a. List the primary components of an RFP.

 b. Based on the information given in the narrative, identify possible components or deficiencies in Norcom's RFP that could have led the new CIO to claim that it was naïve or insufficient.

 c. Identify possible approaches Norcom could have used to evaluate this RFP.

19.12 A large organization needed a new system to replace its old customer database within 18 months. The new customer system was built at an estimated cost of $1 million and installed by the company's internal information systems staff. One important feature of the new system was that it needed to differentiate among customer levels and provide appropriate products and services on demand.

The good news was that the system was delivered on time. The bad news was that the system did not work properly. Although it could handle normal transactions, complex transactions were error-prone. Some transactions were canceled and others were put on hold. In addition, the new system could not differentiate among customers.

Finally, the database was shut down and transactions were processed manually. New IS management was hired to build a new system and mend the strained relationship between the operational and the IS units.

So what went wrong? IS couldn't—or wouldn't—say no. Eager to please top management, IS directors were confident that they could build a system that was scalable, on time, and on budget. In reality, IS was unable to deliver the system. Another big mistake was confining the project to a strict schedule, with little flexibility for problems and unforeseen challenges. Developers only looked at the schedule and never spoke up about any glitches they saw along the way. More than a dozen people (including the CIO) lost their jobs because of their roles in this disaster.

Required

 a. What could the IS directors have done differently to help this project be successful?

 b. What in-house development issues are demonstrated in this case?

 c. How could the in-house issues you identified have been addressed to prevent the system failure?

CASE 19-1 Professional Salon Concepts

Steve Cowan is the owner of Professional Salon Concepts (PSC), a distribution company for hair salon products, in Joliet, Illinois. Steve started working for his father, a distributor of barber and beauty salon products, at age 16, and a decade later he decided to start his own business. He rented a small warehouse, hired four people, and began selling products carrying the name of famous hairstylist Paul Mitchell. Unfortunately, hairstylists ignored the products and did not buy them. Steve eventually had to let his people go and moved his products to an inexpensive basement location.

The tables turned for Steve when he conducted a free two-hour seminar at a local hair salon demonstrating how hairstylists could successfully use his products. He left with a $1,000 order and the realization that he had found his niche. He decided to sell only to salons that allowed him to run a seminar in which he could demonstrate his products.

PSC has done very well using Steve's strategy. Sales reached $7 million as PSC grew to 45 employees and 3,000 salon customers. Warehouse operations ran smoothly due to Paul Mitchell's specialized product line, which was 75% of PSC's business. PSC carried 1,000 products, compared with 10,000 for the average salon distributor. This more focused product line enabled PSC to achieve a 24-hour turnaround on orders, in contrast to more than two days for the competition. To achieve this quick turnaround, Steve sometimes worked late packing orders so he could drive them to the UPS hub a few towns away by the 2:00 A.M. deadline.

Steve bought PSC's first computer and installed a $3,000 accounting package, which served his accounting needs very well. In fact, Steve thought everything was going great until Terri Klimko, a consultant from PSC's second-largest supplier, stopped by. Terri asked Steve the following questions designed to reveal how well he knew his business:

- Do you know exactly to whom you ship each month?
- Do you know how much each customer bought, by supplier?
- Can you rank your customer sales?
- Can you break your sales down by product?
- Do you know how the profit per client breaks down into product lines?
- Do you know how revenues per salesperson vary over the days of the week?

Steve's answer was an uncomfortable "no" to each question. Terri told him that people who cannot answer these questions are losing money. That upset Steve and he terminated the session, politely dismissing Terri. Although Steve was unimpressed with Terri's advice, he was impressed with her. They started dating and were soon married. Shortly after the marriage, she joined the company.

Steve realized that Terri's skills could be used either to help PSC's business grow or to help PSC internally. Believing it was more important to expand the business, he asked Terri to help make the salons more profitable. With PSC's help, she developed a template to break down and analyze every aspect of their business. The template helped salon owners determine such statistics as how much each hairstylist brings in per client, how many clients receive extra services, and how many clients, and which ones, buy hair products. The Cowans soon became more like partners to their customers than trainers and educators. If a salon had employee problems, the Cowans would help settle the issues. If a salon fell behind in a grand opening, the Cowans lent a hand. The only catch was the salons had to buy PSC's products. The better the customer, the more time the Cowans gave.

PSC began selling turnkey systems and support services at cost to help salons answer questions like those Terri posed to Steve. Unfortunately, PSC's computer could not answer those same questions. Steve asked Mike Fenske, a consultant, for help, and sent to Mike as much raw data as could be extracted from his PC-based accounting system. Mike entered it into a database and wrote programs to produce the information Steve wanted. The system worked, but it was very slow—so slow that accounts payable and purchasing information was handled manually. The system also failed to answer all of Terri's questions, and her list was getting longer. To make matters worse, only a few months of detailed information were available at any time. To partially alleviate some of these problems, Steve hired Mike, his brother-in-law, as the company's controller.

After reading a special industry report, Steve realized that his company was well positioned in every aspect except investment in technology. Steve and Mike knew it was time to purchase a new system. They considered outside consultants but felt they would take too much time trying to understand PSC's special needs. In addition, Mike believed consultants knew little about the detailed workings of the software they recommended. They decided to evaluate and select the software themselves and rely on the vendor for installation help.

Steve and Mike spent months researching software and attending demonstrations before settling on a generic AIS software program. They paid the $20,000 price tag, and the vendor began installing the system and training PSC

personnel. Three days prior to conversion, Steve met a distributor from North Dakota at a social gathering. The distributor described how his system not only provided the detailed accounting and customer reporting features but also met his distributorship's inventory management and order fulfillment needs. Steve was so impressed that he excused himself and called Mike, telling him to halt the conversion. They immediately went to North Dakota to check out the system, then flew to Minneapolis to visit DSM, the software developer.

DSM did a great job of demonstrating the software and provided Steve and Mike with several great references. The only hitch was DSM's inability to demonstrate two features that were particularly important to Steve. The first was the ability to adjust orders automatically to reflect outstanding customer credits and back orders. The second was the ability to determine the least expensive way to pack and ship each order. DSM's salespeople assured Steve and Mike that those features would be up and running on the package by the time it was delivered to PSC.

Before committing to the system, Steve and Mike sat down to determine if it was economically feasible. They estimated $234,000 in yearly savings in the following manner:

$144,000 Most of PSC's orders consisted of several boxes, 95% of which were sent COD. PSC's old system had no way of writing orders for shipments of more than one box. In other words, an order shipped in five boxes had required five sales invoices and five separate COD tickets. The new system would allow PSC to generate one sales order and ship one box COD. The other four would be shipped by regular delivery, which was much less costly than COD delivery. Eliminating the need to ship every box COD would save the company $144,000 a year.

$50,000 PSC paid an outside accounting firm $50,000 a year to prepare its financial statements. The new software would prepare most of those statements automatically.

$40,000 Because the old system did not have credit-managing capabilities, it was hard to detect past-due accounts. Steve believed earlier detection of past-due accounts would result in faster collections, fewer lost customers, and fewer write-offs.

Unknown The major reason for acquiring the system was to improve customer service by making more detailed customer information available.

Steve and Mike estimated annual maintenance costs of $10,000 and an annual return on investment of $224,000. Because the system would pay for itself in less than a year, Steve bought it and wrote off his $20,000 investment in the other system.

Finally, DSM technicians arrived at PSC to install the software. To Steve's dismay, the promised features were not part of the package and there was no immediate plan to add them. Although Steve and Mike were upset, they realized they had to shoulder some of the blame for not insisting on seeing the two features before signing the deal. A subsequent search found a program that automatically determined the cheapest way to pack and ship an order. DSM agreed to pay half of the $10,000 cost to integrate it into the program. DSM also offered to create the module to reflect customer credits and back orders for another $20,000, but Steve declined. These problems pushed the conversion date back several months.

PSC spent three months preparing to implement the new system. Training PSC employees to use the new system was particularly important. For example, adding a customer to the database required only one screen with the old system, whereas the new software required six screens. Employees were taught to shout "Fire!" if they came upon a problem they could not handle. Mike, or one of the DSM programmers, would come to their assistance and explain the error and the proper method of correction. During implementation, the new system was tested for glitches by processing real data. Looking back, Mike admits three months were not nearly enough for the training and testing. They should have used twice as much time to identify and eliminate glitches.

PSC dismantled the old system and converted to the new one. Before long, telephone operators grew confused and forgot how to move from one part of the system to another. They began bumping up against unfamiliar error messages and getting themselves into situations they had not been trained to handle. Soon everyone was yelling "Fire!" at the same time. In less than one hour, so many people were waiting for help that the programmers stopped explaining the correct procedures and simply ran from operator to operator correcting problems. Mistakes were repeated numerous times, and the situation intensified. Some employees, feeling embarrassed and ashamed at their inability to work the new system, broke down and cried openly.

Steve was running the warehouse area and was not having much fun either. On a normal day, PSC has 200 to 300 boxes ready for 3:30 p.m. shipment. On conversion day, a lone box sat ready to go. Facing the first default on his 24-hour turnaround promise since he started PSC, Steve, Terri, Mike, and a few others stayed long after midnight packing boxes and loading them on trucks. They just barely made it to the nearest UPS hub on time.

The next day, order entry and shipping ran much smoother. However, when Steve sat down to retrieve the data he needed to monitor sales, he could not figure out how to get the information from the system. Needless to say, he was not feeling too kindly toward his $200,000 system or the company that sold it to him.

It took Steve several weeks to figure out how to get the data he needed to monitor sales. When he did, he was horrified that sales had dropped nearly 15%. They had focused so hard on getting the system up and running that they had taken their eyes off the customers. To make matters worse, Steve could not get information on sales by customer, salesperson, or product, and he could not figure out why or where sales were falling.

However, things quickly improved after "Hell Week." Orders were entered just as quickly as before, and printed copies were not needed for filing purposes. Warehouse operations improved, thanks to the integrated add-in program. The new system provided pickers with the most efficient path to follow when picking orders. It also told them which items to pack in which boxes based on destination and weight. The system selected a carrier and printed out labels for the boxes. Order turnaround time was shaved to 20 minutes from five hours.

Months after the system was installed, it still did not do everything Steve needed it to do, including some things the old system did. Nor did it answer all of Terri's questions. Steve is confident, however, that the system will eventually provide PSC with a distinct competitive advantage. He is negotiating with DSM to write the credit and back-order module.

With all that has happened, Steve believes that the step up to the new system was necessary, even the right move, for his growing company. With the exceptions of taking the DSM salesperson's word and not taking enough time to practice with the system, Steve feels PSC did as good a job as it could have in selecting, installing, and implementing a new system.

Required

Write a memo to address the following questions. Be prepared to defend your position to the class.

1. Do you agree with Steve's assessment that PSC did a good job selecting, installing, and implementing the new system considering the exceptions he noted? If so, why? Or do you feel PSC could have done a better job? If so, what did it do wrong, and what should it have done differently?
2. How could PSC have avoided the problem of the missing features?
3. How could PSC have avoided some of the conversion and reporting problems it faced?
4. Based on what you read about economic feasibility in Chapter 18, evaluate Steve's analysis. Do you agree with his numbers and his conclusions? Explain your answer.
5. How could PSC's customers use the new multi-box shipping approach to defraud PSC?
6. On a scale of 1 to 5, with 1 being the best, how would you rate the service that PSC received from DSM? Could it have been improved? If so, how?

(*Source:* Adapted from David H. Freeman, "Computer Upgrade: To Hell and Back," *INC. Technology* (June 15, 1994): 46–53.)

AIS IN ACTION SOLUTIONS

QUIZ KEY

1. Which of the following is *not* one of the difficulties accountants have experienced using the traditional systems development life cycle?
 a. AIS development projects are backlogged for years. [Incorrect. This is one of the difficulties accountants have experienced using the traditional SDLC, but there is more than one correct answer.]
 b. Changes are not usually possible after requirements have been frozen. [Incorrect. This is one of the difficulties accountants have experienced using the traditional SDLC, but there is more than one correct answer.]
 c. The AIS that is developed may not meet their needs. [Incorrect. This is one of the difficulties accountants have experienced using the traditional SDLC, but there is more than one correct answer.]
 ✔ d. All are difficulties with the SDLC. [Correct.]

2 Companies that buy rather than develop an AIS must still go through the systems development life cycle.

✔ **a.** True. [Correct. Purchasing a system still requires a company to follow the systems development life cycle of analyzing, designing (conceptual and physical), and implementing a new system. Otherwise, the company risks not purchasing the right system for its needs.]

 b. False. [Incorrect.]

3 Which of the following statements is false?

 a. As a general rule, companies should buy rather than develop software if they can find a package that meets their needs. [Incorrect. This is a true statement, not a false statement. Purchasing software is generally less expensive than developing software in-house.]

✔ **b.** As an AIS increases in size and complexity, there is a greater likelihood that canned software can be found that meets user needs. [Correct. This is a false statement. Large and complex systems need greater customization than smaller systems and thus are less likely to lend themselves to the canned software one-size-fits-all approach.]

 c. A company should not attempt to develop its own custom software unless experienced, in-house programming personnel are available and the job can be completed less expensively on the inside. [Incorrect. This is a true statement, not a false statement. Skilled in-house programmers and the promise of lower costs are essential if companies decide to develop their own custom software.]

 d. As a general rule, a company should develop custom software only when it will provide a significant competitive advantage. [Incorrect. This is a true statement, not a false statement. According to Arthur Little, companies should pursue custom software only when it provides a distinct competitive advantage.]

4 When buying large and complex systems, vendors are invited to submit systems for consideration. What is such a solicitation called?

 a. request for quotation [Incorrect. A request for quotation asks for dollar bids on proposed systems and should follow a request for proposal.]

 b. request for system [Incorrect. A request for system is not the terminology used to refer to vendors being invited to submit systems for consideration.]

✔ **c.** request for proposal [Correct. A request for proposal invites vendors to propose solutions to a company's needs.]

 d. good-faith estimate [Incorrect. A good-faith estimate provides a vendor's best guess on the cost of a proposal based on reliable parameters.]

5 To compare system performance, a company can create a data processing task with input, processing, and output jobs. This task is performed on the systems under consideration and the processing times are compared. The AIS with the lowest time is the most efficient. What is this process called?

✔ **a.** benchmarking [Correct. Benchmarking measures system performance by comparing processing times.]

 b. requirements costing [Incorrect. Requirements costing estimates the costs of purchasing or developing features that are not present in a particular AIS.]

 c. point scoring [Incorrect. Point scoring measures system performance by comparing each system based on weighted criteria.]

 d. performance testing [Incorrect. Performance testing is a general term applied to many types of comparison testing.]

6 Which of the following statements is true?

 a. Because the AIS is so crucial, companies never outsource parts of the AIS. [Incorrect. AIS functions are routinely outsourced.]

 b. Most mainframe outsourcing contracts are for two to three years and cost thousands of dollars a year. [Incorrect. Most mainframe outsourcing contracts are longer term (averaging 10 years) and cost hundreds of thousands to millions of dollars.]

✔ **c.** Outsourcers often buy the client's computers and hire all or most of its information systems employees. [Correct. Many large outsourcing deals involve purchasing the client's hardware and hiring the client's employees.]

 d. Only companies struggling to survive and wanting a quick infusion of cash from selling their hardware use outsourcing. [Incorrect. Many large and financially sound companies use outsourcing as a way to decrease costs and become even more profitable.]

7 Which of the following is *not* a benefit of outsourcing?

✔ **a.** It offers a great deal of flexibility because it is relatively easy to change outsourcers. [Correct. This is *not* a benefit of outsourcing. Due to long-term contracts, outsourcers can be very inflexible, as well as difficult and costly to change.]

 b. It can provide access to the expertise and special services provided by outsourcers. [Incorrect. This is a benefit of outsourcing. Many companies cannot afford to retain information systems expertise on their payroll; therefore, outsourcing provides a less expensive way to acquire that expertise.]

 c. It allows companies to move to a more sophisticated level of computing at a reasonable cost. [Incorrect. This is a benefit of outsourcing. Many companies cannot afford to maintain the most effective and sophisticated hardware; therefore, outsourcing provides a less expensive way to gain access to that hardware.]

 d. It is a cost-effective way to handle the peaks and valleys found in seasonal businesses. [Incorrect. This is a benefit of outsourcing. For companies in cyclical industries, outsourcing provides an effective way to meet company needs during the busy times and to lower costs during the slow times of their business cycle.]

8 Which of the following is a true statement with respect to prototyping?

 a. In the early stages of prototyping, system controls and exception handling may be sacrificed in the interests of simplicity, flexibility, and ease of use. [Correct. This is a true statement. Prototyping provides simplicity, flexibility, and ease of use by sacrificing controls and exception handling. However, this is not the only true statement.]

 b. A prototype is a scaled-down, first-draft model that is quickly and inexpensively built and given to users to evaluate. [Correct. This is a true statement. Prototypes are essentially rough-draft models. However, this is not the only true statement.]

 c. The first step in prototyping is to identify system requirements. [Correct. This is a true statement. The first step in prototyping is to identify system requirements. However, this is not the only true statement.]

✔ **d.** All of the statements are true. [Correct.]

9 Which of the following is *not* an advantage of prototyping?

 a. better definition of user needs [Incorrect. This is an advantage of prototyping. Since users can test-drive the model, they can give better feedback to the developers of their needs and requirements.]

✔ **b.** adequately tested and documented systems [Correct. This is not an advantage of prototyping. Since prototypes are developed so quickly developers often neglect documentation and a full testing before the system becomes operational.]

 c. higher user involvement and satisfaction [Incorrect. This is an advantage of prototyping. Prototyping success depends on high user involvement, which generally leads to greater user satisfaction.]

 d. faster development time [Incorrect. This is an advantage of prototyping. Prototypes can be developed in a matter of days or weeks, whereas a more traditional approach can take a year or longer.]

10 When is it most appropriate to use prototyping?
 a. when there is little uncertainty about the AIS [Incorrect. Prototyping is more effective when there is substantial uncertainty about how an AIS should work.]
 b. when it is clear what user needs are [Incorrect. Prototyping is more effective when users are uncertain of their needs and benefit from working on models to help them identify and solidify their needs.]
 ✔ **c.** when the final AIS cannot be clearly visualized because the decision process is still unclear [Correct. Prototyping is more effective when there is substantial uncertainty about how an AIS should work, look, and feel.]
 d. when there is a very low likelihood of failure [Incorrect. Prototyping is the most effective when there is substantial uncertainty about whether a new system will work.]

CHAPTER CASE SOLUTION

Identify the benefits and risks of the FTC purchasing a prewritten software system, developing the system in-house, and outsourcing the system to an external vendor.

Purchasing Software
The primary benefit of purchasing software is cost and availability. Since the software package is designed to be used by many customers, the vendor can sell the product at a lower price. The downside of purchasing software is that, since it is designed for as wide an audience as possible, it may not meet all the specific needs of the purchaser. In addition, software support could be difficult to get if the vendor goes out of business.

Developing the System In-House
The primary benefit of in-house systems development is that the system can be built to meet the individual needs of the entity. However, there are many drawbacks to in-house development. In-house development takes a significant commitment of time and resources from the entity, and it is usually a very complex process. Problems such as poor requirements planning, inadequate communication, and a lack of cooperation between the developers and users can easily derail a project. Insufficient staff and a lack of top-management support can also create problems for a system developed in-house.

Outsourcing the System
Outsourcing frees up entity time and resources to be applied to core competencies instead of diverting attention to systems development. Outsourcing also allows companies access to expertise at a much lower cost than maintaining it in-house. Indeed, outsourcing can save 15% to 30% in overall systems development costs due to quicker development time, smoothing usage peaks and valleys, and facilitating corporate restructuring (downsizing). The risks involve a loss of control over the project and inflexibility due to outsourcing contracts. Entities can also lose some of their competitive advantage by not maintaining proprietary systems. Poor service from the outsourcing company can also create problems for the company.

What the FTC Did
Given the very short time frame the FTC was given to analyze, design, and implement the Do Not Call Registry, the FTC decided to go with AT&T, an outside vendor. AT&T had the expertise and staff to tackle such a large task in a short amount of time. The FTC could not have built this system on its own, but with AT&T's help, the project became one of the most successful in the history of government IT projects.

CHAPTER 20

LEARNING OBJECTIVES

After studying this chapter, you should be able to:

- Discuss the conceptual systems design process and the activities in this phase.

- Discuss the physical systems design process and the activities in this phase.

- Discuss the systems implementation and conversion process and the activities in this phase.

- Discuss the systems operation and maintenance process and the activities in this phase.

Systems Design, Implementation, and Operation

INTEGRATIVE CASE SHOPPERS MART

Ann Christy, the controller at Shoppers Mart, presented the results of her systems analysis to top management and received permission to develop a new AIS (Chapter 18 conclusion). Shortly thereafter, she planned the rest of the project. Ann is concerned because many development projects bog down during the design and implementation phases. She certainly does not want to have a runaway project on her hands—one that she cannot control. She believes that her staff has adequately determined the requirements for the new system and wants to be sure that the rest of the development process is completed correctly. She decides to schedule another meeting with the head of systems development to discuss the following questions:

1 She must determine what type of system will best meet Shoppers Mart's needs and then make a proposal to management. Should her team develop what it considers to be the best approach to meeting Shoppers Mart's needs? Should it develop several approaches?

2 What can be done to ensure that system output will meet user needs? When and how should input, such as accounting transactions, be captured, and who should capture it? Where should AIS data be stored, and how should the data be organized and accessed?

3 How should Shoppers Mart convert from its current to its new AIS? How much time and effort will be needed to maintain the new AIS? In what capacity should Ann's accounting staff participate?

Introduction

Accountants must understand the entire systems development process, as they are involved in it in several ways—as users helping to specify their needs, as members of the development team, and as auditors after the system is complete. Accountants should help keep the project on track by evaluating and measuring benefits, monitoring costs, and ensuring that the project stays on schedule.

Effective systems analysis and design can ensure that developers correctly define the business problem and design the appropriate solution. As discussed in Chapter 18, systems analysis is a crucial phase in the systems development life cycle (SDLC), whose goal is to define the new system's requirements. This chapter discusses the other four steps (see Figure 18-1) in the systems development life cycle: conceptual systems design, physical systems design, systems implementation and conversion, and operation and maintenance. Chapter 19 discusses how some of the steps in the SDLC can be shortened or made more effective.

Conceptual Systems Design

In the **conceptual systems design** phase, the developer creates a general framework for implementing user requirements and solving problems identified in the analysis phase. As shown in Figure 20-1, there are three main steps in conceptual design: evaluating design alternatives, preparing design specifications, and preparing the conceptual systems design report. The following sections explain these in more detail.

Evaluate Design Alternatives

There are many ways to design an AIS, so accountants and others involved in systems design must continually make design decisions. For example, should the company mail hard-copy purchase orders, use EDI, or enter orders over the Internet? Should the company have a large centralized mainframe and database or distribute computer power to the stores using a network of servers and PCs? Should data entry be through keyboard, optical character recognition, point-of-sale devices, barcodes, RFID tags, using the Internet, or some combination of these?

In addition, there are many different ways that a company can approach the systems development process. It could purchase software from a vendor, ask that the in-house information systems staff develop the software, request that the people who are going to use the system design it, or hire an outside company to develop and manage the information system. The company could modify, enhance, or replace existing software or completely reengineer all of its business processes and develop software to support these new processes. These alternatives, which must be considered in conceptual systems design, are discussed in more detail in Chapter 19.

The design team should identify a variety of design alternatives and evaluate each with respect to the following standards: (1) how well it meets organizational and system objectives, (2) how well it meets user needs, (3) whether it is economically feasible, and (4) what its advantages and disadvantages are. The steering committee evaluates the alternatives and selects the one that best meets the organization's needs.

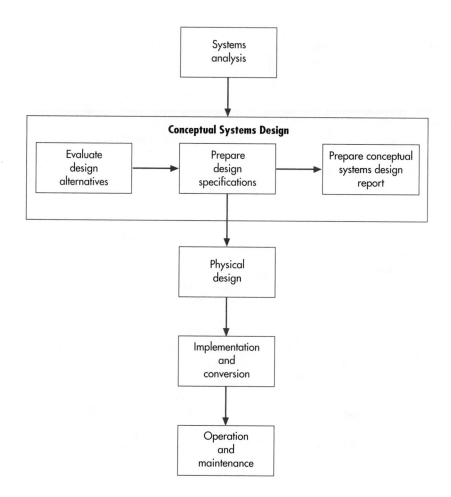

Figure 20-1
Design Considerations
and Alternatives

Table 20-1 presents examples of conceptual and physical design considerations and their corresponding design alternatives.

Prepare Design Specifications

Once a design alternative has been selected, the project team develops the **conceptual design specifications** for the following elements:

1 **Output.** Because the system is designed to meet users' information needs, output specifications must be prepared first. For example, to evaluate store sales using a sales analysis report, Shoppers Mart must decide (a) how often to produce the report (daily or weekly), (b) what the report should contain (store number, sales volume, etc.), (c) what the report will look like, and (d) if users require a hard-copy or screen (or both) output.

2 **Data storage.** Development decisions for Shoppers Mart include which data elements must be stored to produce the sales report, how the data should be stored and what type of file or database to use.

3 **Input.** Design considerations for Shoppers Mart include which sales data to enter, sale location and amount, and where, when, and how to collect data. Inputs are considered only after the desired output is identified.

4 **Processing procedures and operations.** Design considerations for Shoppers Mart include how to process the input and stored data to produce the sales report and the sequence in which the processes must be performed.

Table 20-1
Design Considerations
and Alternatives

Design Considerations	Design Alternatives
Communications channels	Telephone lines, coaxial cable, fiber optics, microwave, or satellite
Communications network	Centralized, decentralized, distributed, or local area
Data storage medium	Tape, disk, hard drive, CD, or paper
Data storage structure	Files or database
File organization and access	Random, sequential, or indexed-sequential access
Input medium	Keying, OCR, MICR, POS, EDI, or voice
Input format	Source document, turnaround document, source data automation, or screen
Operations	In-house or outsourcing
Output frequency	Instantaneous, hourly, daily, weekly, or monthly
Output medium	Paper, screen, voice, CD, or microfilm
Output scheduling	Predetermined times or on demand
Output format	Narrative, table, graph, file, or electronic communication
Printed output	Preprinted forms, turnaround document, or system-generated forms
Processing mode	Manual, batch, or real time
Processor	Personal computer, server, or mainframe
Software acquisition	Canned, custom, or modified
Transaction processing	Batch or online
Update frequency	Instantaneous, hourly, daily, weekly, or monthly

Prepare the Conceptual Systems Design Report

At the end of the conceptual design phase, a **conceptual systems design report** is prepared to (1) guide physical systems design activities, (2) communicate how management and user information needs will be met, and (3) help the steering committee assess system feasibility. The main component is a description of one or more recommended system designs. This description contains the contents of each output, database, and input; processing flows and the relationships among the programs, files, inputs, and outputs; hardware, software, and resource requirements; and audit, control, and security processes and procedures. Any assumptions or unresolved problems that may affect the final systems design should be discussed. The table of contents of the Shoppers Mart report is shown in Table 20-8, in this chapter's summary.

Physical Systems Design

During the **physical systems design** phase, the company determines how the conceptual AIS design is to be implemented. Physical design translates the broad, user-oriented AIS requirements of conceptual design into detailed specifications that are used to code and test the computer programs. As shown in Figure 20-2, physical system design phases include designing output, creating files and databases, designing input, writing computer programs, developing procedures, and building controls into the new AIS. The following subsections describe these activities in detail.

Figure 20-2
Physical Systems Design

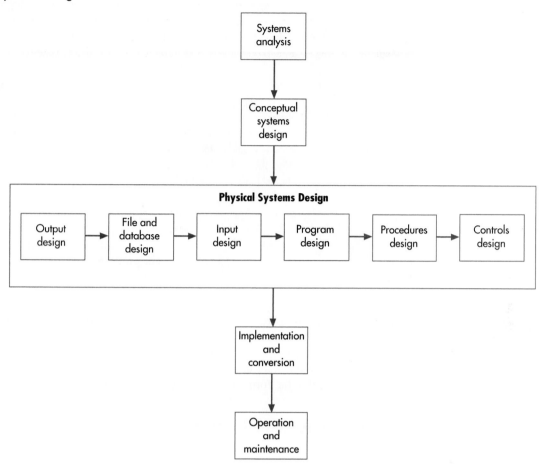

Output Design

The objective of output design is to determine the nature, format, content, and timing of printed reports, documents, and screen displays. Tailoring the output to user needs requires cooperation between users and designers. Some important output design considerations are summarized in Table 20-2.

Output usually fits into one of the following four categories:

1 **Scheduled reports** have a prespecified content and format and are prepared on a regular basis. Examples include monthly performance reports, weekly sales analyses, and annual financial statements.

2 **Special-purpose analysis reports** have no prespecified content or format and are not prepared on a regular schedule. They are prepared in response to a management request to evaluate an issue, such as which of three new products would provide the highest profits.

3 **Triggered exception reports** have a prespecified content and format but are prepared only in response to abnormal conditions. Excessive absenteeism, cost overruns, inventory shortages, and situations requiring immediate corrective action trigger such reports.

4 **Demand reports** have a prespecified content and format but are prepared only on request. Both triggered exception reports and demand reports can be used effectively to facilitate the management process.

Table 20-2
Output Design Considerations

Consideration	Concern
Use	Who will use the output, why and when do they need it, and what decisions will they need to make based on it?
Medium	Should output be paper, screen, voice response, e-mail, or some combination of these?
Format	What format can best convey the most information (table, narrative, graphic)?
Preprinted	Should paper output be on a preprinted form? Should turnaround documents be used?
Location	Where should output be sent?
Access	Who should have access to hard-copy and computer screen output?
Detail	Should lengthy output be preceded by an executive summary and a table of contents?
	Should headings and legends organize data and highlight important items?
	Should detailed information be placed in an appendix?
Timeliness	How often should AIS output be produced?

AIS developers prepare an output sample and users evaluate it to ensure that it is complete, relevant, and useful. Unacceptable output is modified and reviewed as many times as necessary to make it acceptable. To avoid the expense and time delays resulting from changes made later in the SDLC, many organizations require users to sign a document stating that the form and content are acceptable.

File and Database Design

It is important that various company units store data in compatible formats to help avoid the problem AT&T faced: 23 business units and a jumble of incompatible systems. It was difficult for some of the units to communicate with the other units. Perhaps more important, the business units did not maintain customer records in formats that allowed them to be easily shared. AT&T undertook a five-year project to create a "single view" of each customer so that customer data could be shared across all business units.

In Chapter 4 you learned about files and databases and how to design them. Some of the more important file and database design considerations are summarized in Table 20-3.

Table 20-3
File and Database Design Considerations

Consideration	Concern
Medium	Should data be stored on hard drive, disk, CD, tape, or paper?
Processing mode	Should manual, batch, or real-time processing be used?
Maintenance	What procedures are needed to maintain data effectively?
Size	How many records will be stored in the database, and how large will they be? How fast is the number of records expected to grow?
Activity level	What percentage of the records will be added or deleted each year? What percentage will need to be updated?

Input Design

Systems designers must identify the different types of data input as well as optimal input methods. Two types of data input, forms and computer screens, are discussed in the next two subsections. Considerations for input design are shown in Table 20-4.

Forms Design

Although more and more systems are moving away from the use of paper documents and toward source data automation techniques, forms design is still an important topic. The important forms design principles summarized in Table 20-5 are a useful tool for evaluating existing forms and designing new ones.

Designing Computer Screens

It is more efficient to enter data directly into the computer than onto paper for subsequent entry. As a result, it is important to understand how to design computer screens for input as well as output. Computer input screens are most effective when these procedures are followed:

- Organize the screen so data can be entered quickly, accurately, and completely. Minimize data input by retrieving as much data as possible from the system. For example, entering a customer number could automatically cause the system to retrieve the customer's name, address, and other key information.
- Enter data in the same order as displayed on paper forms used to capture the data.
- Complete the screen from left to right and top to bottom. Group together logically related data.
- Design the screen so users can jump from one data entry location to another or use a single key or go directly to screen locations.
- Make it easy to correct mistakes. Clear and explicit error messages that are consistent across all screens are essential. There should be a help feature to provide online assistance.
- Restrict the amount of data on a screen to avoid clutter. Limit the number of menu options on a single screen.

Table 20-4
Input Design Considerations

Consideration	Concern
Medium	Should data be entered using a keyboard, OCR, MICR, POS terminal, barcodes, RFID tags, EDI, or voice input?
Source	Where do data originate (computer, customer, remote location, etc.), and how does that affect data entry?
Format	What format (source or turnaround document, screen, source data automation) efficiently captures the data with the least effort and cost?
Type	What is the nature of the data?
Volume	How much data are to be entered?
Personnel	What are the data entry operators' abilities, functions, and expertise? Is additional training necessary?
Frequency	How often must data be entered?
Cost	How can costs be minimized without adversely affecting efficiency and accuracy?
Error detection and correction	What errors are possible, and how can they be detected and corrected?

Table 20-5
Principles of Good Forms
Design

GENERAL CONSIDERATIONS
- Are preprinted data used to the maximum extent possible?
- Are the weight and grade of the paper appropriate for the planned use?
- Are bold type, double-thick lines, and shading used appropriately to highlight different parts of the form?
- Is the form a standard size?
- Is the size of the form consistent with requirements for filing, binding, or mailing?
- If the form is mailed to external parties, is the address positioned so that the form can be used in a window envelope?
- Are copies of the form printed in different colors to facilitate proper distribution?
- Are there clear instructions on how to complete the form?

INTRODUCTORY SECTION OF FORM
- Does the name of the form appear at the top, in bold type?
- Is the form prenumbered consecutively?
- If the form is distributed to external parties, are the company's name and address preprinted on the form?

MAIN BODY OF FORM
- Is logically related information (e.g., customer name, address) grouped together?
- Is there sufficient room to record each data item?
- Is data item ordering consistent with the sequence in which the items are most likely to be acquired?
- Are standardized explanations preprinted so codes or checkoffs can be used instead of written user entries?

CONCLUSION SECTION OF FORM
- Is space provided to record the final disposition of the form?
- Is space provided for a signature(s) to indicate final transaction approval?
- Is space provided to record the final disposition or approval date?
- Is space provided for a dollar or numeric total?
- Is the distribution of each copy of the form clearly indicated?

Program Design

Program development is one of the most time-consuming activities in the SDLC. Programs should be subdivided into small, well-defined modules to reduce complexity and enhance reliability and modifiability, a process called **structured programming**. Modules should interact with a control module rather than with each other. To facilitate testing and modification, each module should have only one entry and exit point.

To improve software quality, organizations should develop programming standards (rules for writing programs). This contributes to consistency among programs, making them easier to read and maintain. Organizations should also conduct a structured program walk-through to find incorrect logic, errors, omissions, or other problems. Program preparation time may range from a few days to a few years, depending on program complexity.

Although accountants need not be computer programmers, they should understand how software is created. Following are eight steps for developing software. Step 1 is performed as a part of the systems analysis phase of the SDLC. Step 2 is done during conceptual systems design and may carry over to the beginning of physical design. Most of the tasks in steps 3 and 4 are done during systems design and are completed during systems implementation. Steps 5 and 6 are begun in systems design, but most of the work is done during systems implementation. Step 7 is

completed during systems implementation and conversion. Step 8 is part of the operation and maintenance phase.

1 **Determine user needs.** Systems analysts consult with users and agree on software requirements.
2 **Develop a plan.** A development plan is produced and documented.
3 **Write program instructions (code).** This is when the computer code (or program instructions) is written. Designing a program from the top down to more detailed levels is referred to as **hierarchical program design**.
4 **Test the program. Debugging** is discovering and eliminating program errors. After a program is coded, a visual and mental review, referred to as **desk checking**, is conducted to discover programming errors. During program compilation, syntax errors are uncovered. A program is tested for logic errors using test data that simulate as many real processing situations or input data combinations as possible. Test data should include all valid transactions and all possible error conditions. Large programs are often tested in three stages: individual program modules, the linkages between modules and a control module, and interfaces between the program being tested and other application programs. It is important to find errors as soon as possible during the development process.

 The Gartner Group estimates that bugs that are not discovered until later in the SDLC cost 80% to 1,000% more to fix than those discovered earlier. Focus 20-1 discusses the difficulty of testing software and the consequences of releasing software with undetected errors. Software developers state that 20% to 30% of software development costs should be allocated to testing, debugging, and rewriting software.
5 **Document the program.** Documentation explains how programs work and is used to help correct and resolve errors. Flowcharts, data flow diagrams, record layouts, E-R diagrams, REA data models, narrative descriptions of the system, and related items should be developed as part of program documentation and organized into a meaningful documentation manual.
6 **Train program users.** Program documentation is often used to train users.
7 **Install the system.** All system components, including the programs, are combined and the company begins to use the system.
8 **Use and modify the system.** Factors that require existing programs to be revised, referred to as **program maintenance**, include requests for new or revised reports; changes in input, file content, or values such as tax rates; error detection; and conversion to new hardware.

Procedures Design

Everyone who interacts with a newly designed AIS needs procedures that answer the who, what, when, where, why, and how questions related to all AIS activities. Procedures should cover input preparation, transaction processing, error detection and correction, controls, reconciliation of balances, database access, output preparation and distribution, and computer operator instructions. Procedures may take the form of system manuals, user instruction classes, training materials, or online help screens. Development teams, users, or teams representing both groups may write procedures.

Controls Design

The often-heard computer adage "garbage in, garbage out" emphasizes that improperly controlled input, processing, and database functions produce information of little value. Controls must be built into an AIS to ensure its effectiveness, efficiency, and accuracy. They should minimize errors and detect and correct them when they do occur. Accountants play a vital role in this area. Some of the more important control concerns that must be addressed are summarized in Table 20-6. Controls are discussed in greater detail in Chapters 6 through 9.

20-1 FOCUS

Software Bugs Take Their Toll

An $18.5 million rocket explodes seconds after liftoff. Telephone networks mysteriously crash in three cities, leaving 10 million customers without service. A nuclear plant releases hundreds of gallons of radioactive water near Lake Huron. These three events have one disturbing fact in common: They were caused by tiny errors (bugs) buried in computer programs. The term "bug" was coined during World War II when a researcher, puzzled by a computer shutdown, removed a moth stuck between two electric relays. Some examples of these electronics pests follow:

- Without warning, Washington, D.C., Los Angeles, and Pittsburgh residents lost local phone service at almost the same time each morning. The culprit was three missing digits in several million lines of programming that control the phone companies' call-switching computers.
- During the Persian Gulf War, a software error prevented a Patriot missile from destroying an incoming Iraqi Scud missile that killed 28 people.
- The American Airlines reservations system shut down for almost 12 hours, crippling 14,000 travel agencies nationwide and forcing American's agents to write tickets by hand.
- A bug in a linear accelerator—a device that uses X-rays to treat cancer victims—caused the accelerator to deliver a radiation overdose, killing one patient and leaving two others deeply burned and partly paralyzed.
- Ferrari North America had to recall 353 of its high-performance sports cars because of software errors in their braking system that threatened the lives of those driving the cars.

Where do these bugs originate? To create software, a programmer writes millions of lines of code. One incorrect letter or punctuation mark in a line of code—even a missing period—can cause a computer to issue an incorrect command or no command at all. For instance, a flaw in DSC's call-switching computers sent hundreds of erroneous messages to other DSC computers, asking for assistance in rerouting calls when no help was necessary. The flood of messages shut down the computers and gave callers busy signals for hours.

Bugs exist in most software and it is almost impossible to eliminate all of them. A program containing bugs can work adequately for quite some time until suddenly, with no warning, the bug triggers something and the computer suddenly goes haywire.

Programmers go to great pains to detect and eliminate bugs before software is shipped, but no one has the time or money to find every bug or to simulate the exact situations the computer program will encounter in the real world. Instead, software is tested with assumptions about how it will be used. Only a certain amount of information—for instance, the number of paychecks to be sent out each Friday—is used to test the program. No one can predict that a few enterprising customers will add more information than the software can handle.

A former product manager estimated that his company often found 5,000 bugs in each product. The company would fix serious flaws before shipping the product and ignore minor or cosmetic flaws and those that were highly unlikely to ever cause a problem. If software developers took the time to find every one of these flaws, they would miss getting their product out to market on a timely basis and thus lose market share to competitors able to get their products out on time. However, if developers made feasible improvements in their software products, software users in the United States could save an estimated $22 billion in lost productivity a year.

Software developers also cannot predict if computer users will work faster than the software itself. The linear accelerators that killed and maimed cancer patients were controlled by an operator who typed extremely fast. She accidentally selected the X-ray mode and then switched to the electron beam. The software was not quick enough to recognize the change and the machine beamed radiation at full power to a tiny spot on the patients' bodies. The bug was so subtle it took programmers a year to detect and eliminate it.

The sheer volume of software code needed in a complex program makes finding bugs difficult. There are over 2.5 million lines of code in systems that check for cracks in the engine wheel of a space shuttle and 12 million in a phone company's call-switching computer. Finding a flaw in this code is as difficult as looking for one misspelled name in the New York City phone book.

It is estimated that flawed or bug-ridden software cost businesses worldwide over $175 billion last year. Over one-third of that, or over $60 billion, is a cost that is borne by U.S. businesses.

Source: Adapted from John Schneidawind, "Getting the Bugs Out," *USA Today* (August 29, 1991): 1–2.

Table 20-6
Controls Design Considerations

Consideration	Concern
Validity	Are all system interactions valid? For example, how can the AIS ensure that cash disbursements are made only to legitimate vendors?
Authorization	Are input, processing, storage, and output activities authorized by the appropriate managers? For example, how can the AIS ensure that payroll additions have been authorized?
Accuracy	Is input verified to ensure accuracy? What controls are in place to ensure that data passed between processing activities are not lost?
Security	Is the system protected against (a) unauthorized physical and logical access to prevent the improper use, alteration, destruction, or disclosure of information and software and (b) the theft of system resources?
Numerical control	Are documents prenumbered to prevent errors or intentional misuse and to detect when documents are missing or stolen?
Availability	Is the system available for operation and use at times set forth in service-level statements or agreements? Can users enter, update, and retrieve data during the agreed-upon times?
Maintainability	Can the system be modified as required without affecting system availability, security, and integrity? Are only authorized, tested, and documented changes made to the system and related data? Are resources available to manage, schedule, document, and communicate the changes to management and authorized users?
Integrity	Is data processing complete, accurate, timely, and authorized? Is data processing free from unauthorized or inadvertent system manipulation?
Audit trail	Can transaction data be traced from source documents to final output (and vice versa)? For example, if a customer calls with a question, can transaction details be easily accessed?

Physical Systems Design Report

At the end of this phase, the team prepares a **physical systems design report** that summarizes what was accomplished and serves as the basis for management's decision whether or not to proceed to the implementation phase. Table 20-8 later in the chapter shows a table of contents for the report prepared at Shoppers Mart.

Systems Implementation

Systems implementation is the process of installing hardware and software and getting the AIS up and running. This process generally consists of developing a plan, preparing the site, installing and testing hardware and software, selecting and training personnel, completing the documentation, and testing the system. These activities are illustrated in Figure 20-3 and are discussed in this section. Systems conversion is discussed later in this chapter.

The state of Virginia has been especially successful in designing and implementing its AIS. In fact, it served as a model for other governmental agencies. Focus 20-2 describes the improvements the state made to its AIS.

Implementation Planning

An **implementation plan** consists of implementation tasks, expected completion dates, cost estimates, and the person or persons responsible for each task. The plan specifies when the project should be complete and when the AIS is operational. The implementation team should identify risk factors that decrease the likelihood of successful implementation, and the plan should contain a strategy for coping with each of the identified risk factors.

Figure 20-3
Systems Implementation

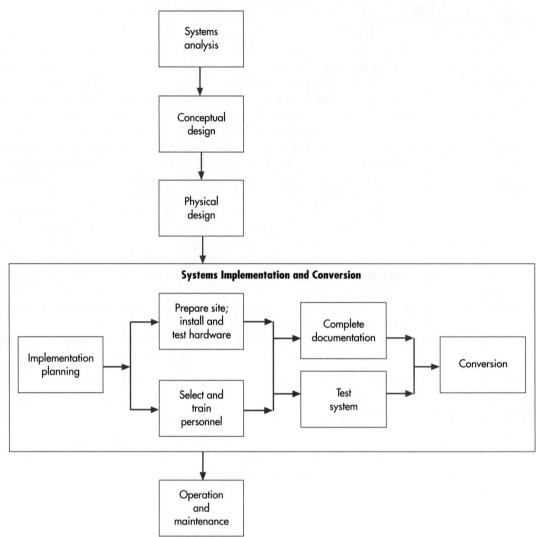

AIS changes may require adjustments to a company's existing organizational structure. New departments may be created and existing ones eliminated or reduced in size. The structure and status of the data processing department itself may change. For example, Blue Cross and Blue Shield of Wisconsin contracted for a new $200 million system. The system—initiated by technical staff who did not understand the company's business or vision—did not work properly. It sent hundreds of checks to a nonexistent town, made $60 million in overpayments, and resulted in the loss of 35,000 clients. One reason the system failed was that its implementation should have included an organizational restructuring.

Site Preparation

A large computer may require extensive changes, such as additional electrical outlets, data communications facilities, raised floors, humidity controls, special lighting, and air-conditioning. Security measures, such as fire protection and an emergency power supply, also may be necessary. Space is needed for equipment, storage, and offices.

20-2 FOCUS Stars Saves Virginia $80 Million

Most Virginia taxpayers receive tax refunds within a week of filing instead of the usual two to three months. They owe the quick turnaround to Jane Bailey, director of AIS at the Department of Taxation. Jane managed the development of the State Tax Accounting and Reporting System (STARS), a multisystem project that took nine years to complete. STARS has been so successful that the IRS, 27 states, and a Canadian province sent teams to Richmond to see if they could improve their systems development and implementation efforts.

The state's IT group strongly recommended that the department engage outside contractors for the job, saying Jane's six-person staff was far too small and unsophisticated to overhaul the vast and motley collection of manual and batch systems formerly in place. Jane insisted, however, on going with an inside job. She was able to convince management by stating that once the system was developed, she would maintain it and respond quickly to tax law changes.

Jane's staff eventually swelled to 45 people. She insisted that these employees be first-rate individuals. If she could not hire the experts and specialists she needed, she retained them as consultants and then used them to train her existing staff. In addition, she recruited five management analysts to redesign business processes, write user documentation, and train users. Ten people from her staff are management analysts who work full-time on user procedures and issues. Seeing user involvement as crucial, Jane succeeded in getting six managers from user areas assigned full-time to the project.

Over the years, the scope of STARS expanded to encompass more functions and more users, and its budget climbed from its original $3 million to $11 million. A major new piece of software was installed every three to six months. Users had to adapt, often getting 15 new screens at a time. The megaproject eventually involved putting together 1,500 programs, 40 IBM databases, and 350 online screens in 25 applications for 1,800 users.

The state, which asked for a Chevrolet, got a Cadillac; and the payoff has been impressive. STARS users estimate that it saved the state $80 million over five years, most of it from added collections from would-be tax cheats.

Site preparation is a lengthy process and should begin well in advance of the installation date.

Select and Train Personnel

Employees can be hired from outside the company or transferred internally. Hiring from within is the less costly, more effective alternative, because employees already understand the firm's business and operations. Transferring employees who are displaced as a result of the new system could boost employee loyalty and morale.

Because effective training is time-consuming and expensive, companies take shortcuts. In addition, those who understand the system are so busy trying to maintain and upgrade it that they lack the time to provide training. When users are not adequately trained, the company will not achieve the expected benefits and return on its investment. The hidden cost of inadequate training is that users turn for help to coworkers who have mastered the system, resulting in less productive coworkers and increased company costs.

Effective AIS training must consist of more than just hardware and software skills. Employees must be oriented to new policies and operations, and training should be planned and scheduled so it occurs just before systems testing and conversion. Many types of training programs are available to companies, such as technical training from vendors, self-study manuals, computer-assisted instruction, videotape presentations, role-playing, case studies, and experimenting with the AIS under the guidance of experienced users.

Boots the Chemists, a London-based international pharmacy chain with more than 1,000 stores, developed a novel approach to training. Store employees, nervous about a forthcoming computer system, were invited to a party at a store where a new POS

system had been installed. They were asked to try to harm the system by pushing the wrong buttons or fouling up a transaction. Employees quickly found they could not harm the system and that it was easy to use.

Complete Documentation

Three types of documentation must be prepared for new systems:

1 **Development documentation** describes the new AIS. It includes a system description; copies of output, input, and file and database layouts; program flowcharts; test results; and user acceptance forms.
2 **Operations documentation** includes operating schedules; files and databases accessed; and equipment, security, and file-retention requirements.
3 **User documentation** teaches users how to operate the AIS. It includes a procedures manual and training materials.

Test the System

Inadequate system testing was one reason for the Blue Cross and Blue Shield system failure. The developers underestimated the complexity of the system and promised an overly optimistic delivery time of 18 months. One shortcut they took to meet that deadline was to deliver an untested system. Documents and reports, user input, operating and control procedures, processing procedures, and computer programs should all be given a trial run in realistic circumstances. In addition, capacity limits and backup and recovery procedures should be tested. Following are three common forms of testing:

1 **Walk-throughs** are step-by-step reviews of procedures or program logic. The development team and system users attend walk-throughs early in system design. The focus is on the input, files, outputs, and data flows of the organization. Subsequent walk-throughs, attended by programmers, address logical and structural aspects of program code.
2 **Processing test transactions** determines if a program operates as designed. Valid and erroneous data are processed to determine if transactions are handled properly and errors are detected and dealt with appropriately. To evaluate test results, the correct system response for each test transaction must be specified in advance.
3 **Acceptance tests** use copies of real transactions and files rather than hypothetical ones. Users develop the acceptance criteria and make the final decision whether to accept the AIS.

Chemical Bank suffered the consequences of not adequately testing an upgrade to its ATM system. Shortly after its installation, New York customers who withdrew cash from one of the bank's 900 ATMs found their accounts were debited twice. Before the problem could be corrected, 150,000 withdrawals with a total value of $8 million were posted twice to customer accounts. Thousands of small accounts were overdrawn or emptied, which annoyed and angered customers. Chemical Bank lost a great deal of credibility with its customers as a result of the glitch.

Even software purchased from an outside vendor must be tested thoroughly before being installed. Kane Carpets learned this lesson after it installed an AIS custom tailored to the floor covering industry. No sooner was the software up and running than Kane began experiencing serious problems. For example, its inventory control system told its salespersons that orders could not be filled when the product was in fact available, and vice versa. As a result, Kane lost many of its customers.

Systems Conversion

Conversion is the process of changing from the old to the new AIS. Many elements must be converted: hardware, software, data files, and procedures. The process is complete when the new AIS has become a routine, ongoing part of the system.

Conversion Approaches

Four conversion approaches are used to change from an old to a new system:

- **Direct conversion** immediately terminates the old AIS when the new one is introduced. For example, Shoppers Mart could discontinue its old system on Saturday night and use its new AIS on Monday morning. Direct conversion is appropriate when the old AIS has no value or the new one is so different that comparisons between the two are meaningless. The approach is inexpensive, but it provides no backup AIS. Unless a system has been carefully developed and tested, therefore, direct conversion carries a high risk of failure. Focus 20-3 discusses the problems at Sunbeam Corp., in part caused by attempting a direct conversion with no backup system.
- **Parallel conversion** operates the old and new systems simultaneously for a period of time. For example, Shoppers Mart could process transactions with both systems, compare the output, reconcile the differences, and correct problems with the new AIS. After the new system proves itself, Shoppers Mart would discontinue the old system. Parallel processing protects companies from errors, but it is costly and stressful for employees to process all transactions twice. However, because companies often experience problems during conversion, parallel processing has gained widespread popularity.
- **Phase-in conversion** gradually replaces elements of the old AIS with the new one. For example, Shoppers Mart could implement its inventory system, then disbursements, followed by sales collection, and so forth, until the whole system is functional. These gradual changes mean that data processing resources can be acquired over time. The disadvantages are the cost of creating the temporary interfaces between the old and the new AIS and the time required to make the gradual changeover.
- **Pilot conversion** implements a system in just one part of the organization, such as a branch location. For example, Shoppers Mart could install its new POS system at one of its stores using a direct, parallel, or phase-in approach. When problems with the system are resolved, the new system could be implemented at the remaining locations. This approach localizes conversion problems and allows training in a live environment. The disadvantages are the long conversion time and the need for interfaces between the old and the new systems, which coexist until all locations have been converted. Owens-Corning Fiberglass implemented its accounts payable, travel and expense, and payroll systems by getting the system up and running in one plant and then moving it to all the others one by one.

Data Conversion

Data conversion can be time-consuming, tedious, and expensive. The difficulty and magnitude of the task can be easily underestimated. Data files may need to be modified in three ways. First, files may be moved to a different storage medium—for example, from tapes to disks. Second, data content may be changed—for example, fields and records may be added or deleted. Third, file or database format may be changed.

The first step in the data conversion process is to decide which data files need to be converted. Then they must be checked for completeness and any data inaccuracies and inconsistencies removed. Actual data conversion is next. Validating the new files, to

20-3 FOCUS

Sunbeam Corp. and the Price of Direct Conversion

Sunbeam Corp., a consumer products company, hired new CEO Al Dunlap to turn the company around. While turning Scott Paper Company around, Al made such drastic cost cuts that he was nicknamed Chainsaw Al.

At Sunbeam, Al also made drastic cost-cutting moves, many of which went too far and ended up hurting the company much more than they helped. His restructuring plan called for eliminating 87% of the company's products and half of its 6,000 employees. Included in the cost-cutting plan were the information systems staff, as the systems function was to be outsourced. Al terminated computer personnel who were making $35,000 a year only to discover they could earn $125,000 a year elsewhere! He then had to replace them with contract workers who had to be paid significantly more than $35,000. Ironically, some of the contract workers turned out to be terminated employees.

During the turnaround effort, the company decided to modernize its information system. To minimize costs, Sunbeam used a direct conversion approach. Unfortunately, the new system did not work, and since there was no backup system, the entire system was down for months. The result was total chaos. Orders were lost and some customers did not receive their shipments. Other customers received their orders two or three times, while others received the wrong order.

Customers were very upset and began calling at all hours about their orders. Unfortunately, Sunbeam had no way to respond to them, as employees could not track orders or shipments. With no system, customers who did receive their orders could not be billed automatically. As a result, Sunbeam had to manually bill its customers.

Imagine the headache this was for large customers such as Wal-Mart.

Due to poor management and the lack of an AIS for such a long period of time, the price of Sunbeam's stock plummeted, and in the summer of 1998 Al Dunlap was fired. Shareholder lawsuits were filed and governmental entities, including the SEC, began investigating the company. Claiming that Al perpetrated an accounting fraud at Sunbeam, the SEC contended that at least $62 million of the $189 million in income that Sunbeam reported in 1997 did not comply with accounting rules. Arthur Andersen, Sunbeam's auditors, paid out $110 million in damages to settle a shareholder class-action suit filed against the accounting firm. In February 2001, Sunbeam filed for Chapter 11 bankruptcy protection.

Two years later, after a lengthy investigation, the SEC closed the Sunbeam case on January 27, 2003. During those two years, several Sunbeam executives paid fines to settle charges of participating in a scheme to inflate the worth of the company before putting it up for sale. In his settlement, former CEO Al Dunlap agreed to pay a half-million-dollar fine without admitting or denying the SEC's accusations. Additionally, Phillip Harlow, the Arthur Andersen partner in charge of auditing Sunbeam's 1996–1997 year-end financial statements, was barred from practicing public accounting before the SEC for at least three years in exchange for the SEC withdrawing all related fraud charges.

(Adapted from John A. Byrne, "Chainsaw," *Business Week* [October 18, 1999]: 128–149.)

ensure data were not lost during conversion, follows. If the file conversion is lengthy, the new files must be updated with the transactions that occurred during data conversion. Once the files and databases have been converted and tested for accuracy, the new system is functional. The system should be monitored for a time to make sure it runs smoothly and accurately. The final activity is to document the conversion activities.

Operation and Maintenance

The final step in the SDLC is to operate and maintain the new system. A **post-implementation review** should be conducted on a newly installed AIS to ensure it meets its planned objectives. Some important factors to consider and questions to answer during the postimplementation review are listed in Table 20-7. Any problems uncovered during the review should be brought to management's attention and the necessary adjustments made. When the review has been completed, a **post-implementation review report** is prepared. The table of contents in Table 20-8 illustrates what this

Table 20-7
Factors to Investigate During
Postimplementation Review

Factors	Questions
Goals and objectives	Does the system help the organization meet its goals, objectives, and overall mission?
Satisfaction	Are users satisfied with the system? What would they like changed or improved?
Benefits	How have users benefited from the system? Were the expected benefits achieved?
Costs	Are actual costs in line with expected costs?
Reliability	Is the system reliable? Has it failed and, if so, what caused its failure?
Accuracy	Does the system produce accurate and complete data?
Timeliness	Does the system produce information on a timely basis?
Compatibility	Are hardware, software, data, and procedures compatible with existing systems?
Controls and security	Is the system safeguarded against unintentional errors, fraud, and unauthorized intrusion?
Errors	Do adequate error-handling procedures exist?
Training	Are systems personnel and users adequately trained to support and use the system?
Communications	Is the communications system adequate?
Organizational changes	Are any organizational changes brought about by the system beneficial or harmful? If harmful, how can they be resolved?
Documentation	Is system documentation complete and accurate?

report should contain. User acceptance of the postimplementation review report is the final activity in the systems development process. Control of the AIS is passed to the data processing department. Work on the new system is not finished, however. Studies show that, over the life of a system, only 30% of the work takes place during development. The remaining 70% is spent maintaining the system. Most maintenance costs relate to software modifications and updates.

The experience of the Hartford Insurance Group illustrates the cost of maintenance. Approximately 70% of its personnel resources are devoted to maintaining existing systems. Hartford must maintain an inventory of 34,000 program modules containing 24 million lines of code. The job is even more difficult because recent changes in insurance regulations and business strategies have reduced the structure of the code and increased its complexity.

SUMMARY AND CASE CONCLUSION

Ann Christy tackled the sales processing portion of the AIS first. She gave the project development team her systems analysis report and accompanying data. During conceptual systems design, the team visited stores with similar operations and identified ways to meet AIS requirements. Alternative approaches were discussed with users, management, and the steering committee and were narrowed down to Ann's original approach. Ann considered buying software but did not find any that did what she and the company wanted to accomplish. The team developed conceptual design specifications for the output, input, processing, and data storage elements.

The company decided to use screen-based output as much as possible and to capture data electronically using point-of-sale (POS) devices. Data that cannot be

Table 20-8
Table of Contents for Shoppers Mart Reports

CONCEPTUAL SYSTEMS DESIGN REPORT	PHYSICAL SYSTEMS DESIGN REPORT	POSTIMPLEMENTATION REVIEW REPORT
Table of Contents	**Table of Contents**	**Table of Contents**
I. Executive Summary of Conceptual Systems Design II. Overview of Project Purpose and Summary of Findings to Date III. Recommended Conceptual Design(s) of Proposed System A. Overview of Recommended Design(s) B. Objectives to Be Achieved by Design(s) C. Impact of Design(s) on Information System and Organization D. Expected Costs and Benefits of Design(s) E. Audit, Control, and Security Processes and Procedures F. Hardware, Software, and Other Resource Requirements G. Processing Flows: Relationships of Programs, Databases, Inputs, and Outputs H. Description of System Components (Programs, Databases, Inputs, and Outputs) IV. Assumptions and Unresolved Problems V. Summary VI. Appendixes, Glossary	I. Executive Summary of Physical Systems Design II. Overview of Project Purpose and Summary of Findings to Date III. Major Physical Design Recommendations A. Output Design B. Input Design C. Database Design D. Software (Processing) Design E. Hardware Design F. Controls Design G. Procedures Design IV. Assumptions and Unresolved Problems V. Summary VI. Appendixes, Glossary	I. Executive Summary of Postimplementation Review II. Overview of Development Project III. Evaluation of the Development A. Degree to Which System Objectives Were Met B. Analysis of Actual Versus Expected Costs and Benefits C. User Reactions and Satisfaction IV. Evaluation of Project Development Team V. Recommendations A. Recommendations for Improving the New System B. Recommendations for Improving the System Development Process VI. Summary

captured electronically will be entered using PCs. Each store will have a network that connects all its PCs and POS devices to a local database. The POS cash registers will be used to capture and feed sales data electronically to this database. Each store will be linked electronically to the central office using a wide area network. All sales data, store orders, and other summary-level information will be uploaded to the corporate database daily. The corporate database will download the information needed to manage the store. The central office will use electronic data interchange to order goods and pay suppliers. The table of contents for the conceptual systems design report is shown in Table 20-8.

During physical design, the development team designed each report identified during conceptual design in screen or hard-copy format. The reports were shown to users and reworked until everyone involved was satisfied. The team then designed all files, databases, and input screens. Next came the detailed design of the software programs needed to collect and process data and produce the output. The team also developed new procedures for handling data and operating the AIS. The accountants and the internal audit staff were especially helpful during the design of the controls needed to protect the system against errors and fraud. The physical systems design report table of contents is shown in Table 20-8.

Ann and her staff started implementation planning early. A location for the new mainframe was identified, and site preparation began during the design phase. First the hardware and then the software were installed and tested, followed by testing of the entire AIS. The new AIS was staffed almost exclusively with existing employees trained as the system was tested. System documentation was completed before data from the old AIS were converted to the new one.

Ann and her staff used a variety of conversion approaches. Because corporatewide mainframe data were vitally important, Ann used a parallel conversion strategy. The new and old systems were operated together for a month, and the results were compared. When the bugs in the new AIS were ironed out, the old AIS was discontinued. A pilot approach was used for the store's AIS. The AIS was installed at several stores, and all problems were resolved before implementing the system at the remaining Shoppers Marts. Conversion was not easy and required a fair amount of overtime and duplicate processing. After a few months, Ann and her staff conducted a postimplementation review and made some adjustments to enhance the already high user acceptance of and satisfaction with the new AIS. The table of contents for the postimplementation report is shown in Table 20-8.

Ann made a final presentation to top management after the AIS was installed and operating. She was widely congratulated and even heard the president mention to an executive vice president that she "was worth keeping an eye on" for even more responsibility in the firm.

KEY TERMS

conceptual systems
 design 768
conceptual design
 specifications 769
conceptual systems design
 report 770
physical systems
 design 770
scheduled report 771
special-purpose analysis
 report 771
triggered exception
 report 771
demand report 771

structured
 programming 774
hierarchical program
 design 775
debugging 775
desk checking 775
program
 maintenance 775
physical systems design
 report 777
systems
 implementation 777
implementation plan 777
walk-through 780

processing test
 transactions 780
acceptance test 780
conversion 781
direct conversion 781
parallel conversion 781
phase-in conversion 781
pilot conversion 781
post-implementation
 review 782
post-implementation
 review report 782

AIS IN ACTION

CHAPTER QUIZ

1 The developers of your new system have proposed two different AIS designs and have asked you to evaluate them. This evaluation process is most likely to be a part of which SDLC step?
 a. systems analysis
 b. conceptual design

 c. physical design

 d. implementation and conversion

 e. operation and maintenance

2 What is the purpose of the conceptual systems design report?

 a. to guide physical systems design activities

 b. to communicate how management and user information needs are met

 c. to help the steering committee assess system feasibility

 d. a and b

 e. a, b, and c

3 Which of the following is the correct order of the steps in physical systems design?

 a. input, file and database, output, controls, procedures, program

 b. file and database, output, input, procedures, program, controls

 c. output, input, file and database, procedures, program, controls

 d. output, file and database, input, program, procedures, controls

4 A monthly payroll register showing all hourly employees, the number of hours they worked, their deductions, and their net pay is most likely which of the following?

 a. scheduled report

 b. special-purpose analysis

 c. triggered exception report

 d. demand report

5 Which of the following is *not* a consideration in input design?

 a. Which errors are possible and how can they be detected and corrected?

 b. How can data be entered (keyboards, OCR, or POS terminal)?

 c. Which format efficiently captures the input data with the least effort and cost?

 d. How often should the system produce reports?

6 Which of the following is most likely to help improve program development?

 a. physical model

 b. IT strategic plan

 c. walk-through

 d. record layout

7 Which of the following statements is true?

 a. The Gartner Group estimates that programming bugs not found until later in the SDLC cost 25% to 30% more to correct than if they were found earlier in the SDLC.

 b. Direct system conversion is the least risky of the system conversion methods.

 c. Many software developers state that 5% to 10% of software development costs should be allocated to testing, debugging, and rewriting software.

 d. Over the life of a system, only 30% of information systems work takes place during development; the remaining 70% is spent maintaining the system.

8 Which of the following describes the systems testing approach that uses real transactions and files rather than hypothetical ones?

 a. walk-through

 b. processing of test transactions

 c. acceptance test

 d. parallel conversion test

9 What is the process of discontinuing an old system as soon as a new one is introduced?

 a. direct conversion

 b. parallel conversion

 c. phase-in conversion

 d. pilot conversion

10 Which of the following describes designing a program from the top down to more detailed levels?
 a. hierarchical program design
 b. top-down program design
 c. parallel program design
 d. unstructured program design

CHAPTER CASE Hershey's Big Bang ERP

Triggering approximately $1.8 billion in sales, Halloween is the biggest candy season of them all. But for Hershey's, the Halloween of 1999 became the scariest Halloween of all time. A three-year, $112-million ERP system was implemented in July of that year and promptly gummed up the order-distribution system. Many distributors who placed orders in September were still waiting for their shipment in late October. However, the problem was not in inventory. Hershey had plenty of candy in inventory, it just could not move the candy from its warehouses to its customers.

The new ERP system employed over 5,000 PCs, network hubs, and servers. The software for the massive ERP was supplied by three firms and implemented by one very large consulting firm. Despite the size and complexity of the new system, Hershey chose to implement a major portion of it in one step. It called the implementation the big bang. In case anything went wrong, Hershey built a cushion of eight days of inventory. However, by August it had exhausted the eight days and was fifteen days behind in orders. Unfortunately, by the end of October, the shelves of large candy distributors were still void of Hershey candy. Executives were hopeful they could meet Easter orders, since it was later than usual that year.

Required

What steps should Hershey have taken to properly design, implement, and operate this new ERP?

DISCUSSION QUESTIONS

20.1 Prism Glass Company is converting from a manual data processing system to a computerized one. To expedite the implementation of the system, the CEO has asked your consulting team to postpone establishing standards and controls until after the system is fully operational. How should you respond to the president's request?

20.2 When a company converts from one system to another, many areas within the organization are affected. Explain how conversion to a new system will affect the following groups, both individually and collectively.
 a. Personnel
 b. Data storage
 c. Operations
 d. Policies and procedures
 e. Physical facilities

20.3 The following notice was posted in the employee cafeteria on Monday morning:

To:	All Accounting and Clerical Employees
From:	I.M. Krewel, President
Subject:	Termination of Employee Positions

Effective this Friday, all accounting and clerical employees not otherwise contacted will be terminated. Our new computer system eliminates the need for most of these

*jobs. We're grateful for the loyal service you've rendered as employees and wish you
success. You may wish to pick up your final checks on Friday before you go.*

Discuss the president's approach to human resource management. What are the
possible repercussions of this episode? Assuming that job termination is the best alter-
native available, how would you approach the situation?

20.4 In which phase of the systems development cycle would each of the following
positions be most actively involved? Justify your answers.
- **a.** Managerial accountant
- **b.** Programmer
- **c.** Systems analyst
- **d.** Financial vice president
- **e.** Information systems manager
- **f.** Auditor

20.5 During which of the five SDLC stages is each task, labeled a through m,
performed? More than one answer may apply for each activity.

1 Systems analysis	**a.**	Writing operating procedures manuals
2 Conceptual (general) systems design	**b.**	Developing program and process controls
3 Physical (detailed) systems design	**c.**	Identifying alternative systems designs
4 Implementation and conversion	**d.**	Developing a logical model of the system
5 Operation and maintenance	**e.**	Identifying external and administrative controls
	f.	Testing the system
	g.	Training personnel
	h.	Evaluating the existing system
	i.	Analyzing the achievement of systems benefits
	j.	Modifying and altering programs
	k.	Analyzing total quality management (TQM) performance measures
	l.	Conducting a feasibility analysis
	m.	Aligning AIS development plans with business objectives

PROBLEMS

20.1 The Glass Jewelry Company manufactures costume jewelry. You have just
been hired as the management accountant in charge of the accounting and control
functions. During your introductory meeting with the president, he outlined your first
project: the design and implementation of a new AIS. He stated that the new system
must be fully implemented within six months. Total company sales for the past year
were $10 million. Sales are expected to double within the next 18 months.

Required
- **a.** Outline the procedures you would follow to complete the assigned project.
 Your response should include a description of the following:
 - **1.** Various sources of information
 - **2.** Methods of documenting information collected
 - **3.** Methods of verifying the information collected

b. One of the subsystems that you plan to design is the accounts payable system. This system will contain a number of programs, two of which include Enter Invoices and Print Payable Checks. For each of these programs, describe its purpose and outline the application control considerations.

(SMAC Examination, adapted)

20.2 Chaotic order processing at Wang Laboratories had long been accepted by its customers as the cost of doing business with the computer giant. The tremendous growth of Wang left the company with a serious revenue tracking problem: Customers would often wait months for Wang to fill orders and process invoices. Repeated attempts by Wang's understaffed AIS department to solve these problems always met with failure.

Finally, Wang Laboratories hired a small consulting organization to solve its revenue tracking problems and expedite prompt receipt of payments. The 18-month project turned into a doubly long nightmare. After three years and $10 million, the consultants were dismissed from the unfinished project.

The reasons for the project failure were clear. First, the project was too large and far too complex for the appointed consulting team. According to one consultant, the systems development process was so dynamic that the failure to complete the project quickly was self-defeating, as modifications took over the original design.

Second, management had no clear vision of the new AIS and lacked a strong support staff. As a result, a number of incompatible tracking systems sprang up throughout the company's distributed computer system.

Third, the consulting firm had little experience with the desired technology: a complex database that represented the heart of the new system.

Finally, the project had too many applications. Interdependencies among subprograms and subroutines left consultants with few completed programs. Every program was linked to several subprograms, which in turn were linked to several other programs. Programmers would begin an initial program only to find that several subroutines were necessary. They eventually found themselves lost in a morass of subroutines with no completed program.

Wang's ultimate solution to the crisis came from the internal AIS department. However, the revenue tracking system that the internal staff developed suffered quality problems for years.

Required

The president of Wang Laboratories has asked you, as a member of the AIS staff, to write a memo explaining the failure of the systems development project.
 a. Outline the specific reasons for the development failure. What role did the consultants play in the project's failure?
 b. Identify the organizational issues that management must address in the future.
 c. Recommend any future steps the company could take to guarantee the quality of consulting services.

20.3 Tiny Toddlers Company, a large multinational manufacturer of children's toys and furniture, is planning the design and implementation of a distributed data processing system to assist its sales force. The company has 10 sales offices in Canada and 20 in the United States. The company's sales departments have been set up in a regional structure: Each sales office maintains its own customers and is responsible for granting credit and collecting receivables.

The proposed system will not only permit inquiries but will also allow entry of daily sales and maintenance of the customer master file. Reports used by each sales office to maintain the customer master file and to enter the daily sales orders are shown in Figures 20-4 and Figure 20-5.

Figure 20-4
Customer Maintenance Form
for Tiny Toddlers

CUSTOMER MAINTENANCE FORM	
New Customer?	☐
	Yes _____
	☑
	No _____ 24671 _____
Name	The Little Ones Furniture Store
New Address	5 St. Antoine Street N.
	Quebec City
Old Address	305 St. Antoine Street S.
	Quebec City
Salesperson #	02
Requested Credit Limit	50,000
Sales Office	Eastern Canada
Pricing Code	25
Estimated Sales	300,000
Credit Limit	10,000
Currency	U.S.A. ☐, Canada ☐
Bank	Canadian Credit Bank
	50 St. Antoine Street
	Quebec City
Bank Line	
Rating	Satisfactory

Sales Manager	

Credit Manager	

Required

Evaluate the reports shown in Figures 20-4 and 20-5 using the following format:

Report Weakness	Explanation	Recommendation(s)

(SMAC Examination, adapted)

Figure 20-5
Sales Order Form for Tiny
Toddlers

SALES ORDER FORM		
Customer: 24671		Date: _____
The Little Ones Furniture Store		
5 St. Antoine Street N.		
Quebec City		

Product Code	Description	Quantity
24571	Crib	4
M0002	Mattress	102
HG730	High chair—white	32
HG223	High chair—natural wood	22
CT200	Changing table	300
D0025	Desk—modern design	2
C9925	Chair—modern design	5
BP809	Bumper pads	1200

Salesperson No.: _____

Entered by: _____

20.4 Mickie Louderman is the new assistant controller of Pickens Publishers, a growing company with sales of $35 million. She was formerly the controller of a smaller company in a similar industry, where she was in charge of accounting and data processing and had considerable influence over the entire computer center operation. Prior to Mickie's arrival at Pickens, the company revamped its entire computer operations center, placing increased emphasis on decentralized data access, personal computers with mainframe access, and online systems.

John Richards, the controller of Pickens, has been with the company for 28 years and is near retirement. He has given Mickie managerial authority over both the implementation of the new system and the integration of the company's accounting-related functions. Her promotion to controller will depend on the success of the new AIS.

Mickie began to develop the new system by using the same design characteristics and reporting format she had used at her former company. She sent details of the new AIS to the departments that interfaced with accounting, including inventory control, purchasing, human resources, production control, and marketing. If they did not respond with suggestions by a prescribed date, she would continue the development process. Mickie and John determined a new schedule for many of the reports, changing the frequency from weekly to monthly. After a meeting with the director of computer operations, Mickie selected a programmer to help her with the details of the new reporting formats.

Most of the control features of the old system were maintained to decrease the initial installation time, while a few new ones were added for unusual situations. However, the procedures for maintaining the controls were substantially changed. Mickie appointed herself the decisive authority for all control changes and program testing that related to the AIS, including the screening of control features related to payroll, inventory control, accounts receivable, cash deposits, and accounts payable.

As each module was completed, Mickie told the corresponding department to implement the change immediately, to take advantage of the labor savings. However, incomplete instructions accompanied these changes, and specific implementation responsibility was not assigned to departmental personnel. Mickie believes that operations people should learn as they go, reporting errors as they occur.

Accounts payable and inventory control were the initial areas of the AIS to be implemented, and several problems arose in both. Mickie was disturbed that the semimonthly runs of payroll, which were weekly under the old system, had abundant errors and, consequently, required numerous manual paychecks. Frequently, the control totals of a payroll run would take hours to reconcile with the computer printout. To expedite matters, Mickie authorized the payroll clerk to prepare journal entries for payroll processing.

The new inventory control system failed to improve the carrying level of many stock items, causing several critical raw material stockouts that resulted in expensive rush orders. The new system's primary control procedure was the availability of ordering and user information. The information was available to both inventory control and purchasing personnel so that both departments could issue purchase orders on a timely basis. Because the inventory levels were updated daily, Mickie discontinued the previous weekly report.

Because of these problems, system documentation is behind schedule and proper backup procedures have not been implemented in many areas. Mickie has requested budget approval to hire two systems analysts, an accountant and an administrative assistant, to help her implement the new system. John is disturbed by her request because her predecessor had only one part-time assistant.

Required

a. List the steps Mickie should have taken during the design of the AIS to ensure that end-user needs were satisfied.

b. Identify and describe three areas where Mickie has violated the basic principles of internal control during the implementation of the new AIS.

 c. Refer to Mickie's approach to implementing the new AIS.
 1. Identify and describe its weaknesses.
 2. What recommendations do you have that would improve the situation and allow development to continue on the remaining areas of the AIS?

(CMA Examination, adapted)

20.5 Columbia Corporation is a midsize, diversified manufacturing company. Ryon Pulsipher has been promoted recently to manager of the company's property accounting division. Ryon has had difficulty responding to requests from other departments for information about the company's fixed assets. Five of the requests and problems Ryon has been involved with follow:

1 The controller has requested schedules of individual fixed assets to support the balance in the general ledger. Although Ryon has furnished the necessary information, it has always been late. The manner in which the records are organized makes it difficult to obtain information easily.

2 The maintenance manager wishes to verify the existence of a punch press that he thinks was repaired twice. He has asked Ryon to confirm the asset number and location of the press.

3 The insurance department wants data on the cost and book values of assets to include in its review of current insurance coverage.

4 The tax department has requested data that can be used to determine when Columbia should switch depreciation methods for tax purposes.

5 The company's internal auditors have spent a significant amount of time in the property accounting division in a recent attempt to confirm the annual depreciation expense.

The property account records that are at Ryon's disposal are maintained in an Excel spreadsheet. These records show the date the asset was acquired, the account number to which the asset applies, the dollar amount capitalized, and the estimated useful life of the asset for depreciation purposes.

After many frustrations, Ryon realized that his records are inadequate and that he cannot supply data easily when requested. He has decided to discuss his problems with the controller, Gig Griffith.

RYON: Gig, something has to give. My people are working overtime and can't keep up. You worked in property accounting before you became controller. You know that I can't tell the tax, insurance, and maintenance people everything they need to know from my records. Also, the internal auditing team is living in my area and that slows down the work pace. The requests of these people are reasonable, and we should be able to answer their questions and provide the needed data. I think we need an automated property accounting system. I would like to talk with the AIS people to see if they can help me.

GIG: Ryon, I think you have a great idea. Just be sure you are personally involved in the design of any system so that you get all the information you need. Keep me posted on the project's progress.

Required

 a. Identify and justify four major objectives Columbia Corporation's automated property accounting system should possess to respond to departmental requests for information.

 b. Identify the data that should be included in the data base for each asset included in the property account.

(CMA Examination, adapted)

20.6 A savings and loan association has decided to develop a new AIS. The internal auditors have suggested planning the systems development process in accordance with the SDLC concept. The following nine items have been identified as major systems development activities that will have to be completed.

 1 System test
 2 User specifications

3 Conversion
4 System planning study
5 Technical specifications
6 Postimplementation planning
7 Implementation planning
8 User procedures and training
9 Programming

Required

a. Arrange the nine items in the sequence in which they should logically occur.
b. One major subactivity that will occur during system implementation is the conversion of data files from the old system to the new one. Indicate three types of documentation for a file conversion work plan that would be of particular interest to an auditor.

(CMA Examination, adapted)

20.7 Create a form in Microsoft Access or another software package of your choosing for data input. If you choose to use Microsoft Access, open the program and open a database that you have previously prepared or use the sample database provided by Microsoft Access. To find the sample database, click on Help, Sample Databases, Northwind Sample Database. To create a form in MS Access, perform the following steps:

a. Select Forms from the Objects Column.
b. Double-click on Create Form Using Wizard.
c. Select various fields of your choosing from the Available Fields list, then click Next.
d. Select a Layout for your form, then click Next.
e. Select a Style for your form, then click Next.
f. Click on Open the form to view or enter information, and then click Finish.

20.8 Create a report in Microsoft Access or another software package of your choosing for data output. If you choose to use Microsoft Access, open the program and open a database that you have previously prepared or use the sample database provided by Microsoft Access. To find the sample database, click on Help, Sample Databases, Northwind Sample Database. To create a report in MS Access, perform the following steps:

a. Select Report from the Objects column.
b. Double-click on Create Report using wizard.
c. Select various field of your choosing from the Available Fields list, then click Next.
d. Select fields for grouping levels, that is, subtotals that you would like on your report, then click Next.
e. To display sorted records in your report, select the fields that you would like to present as sorted, and then click Next.
f. Select a Layout for your report, then click Next.
g. Select a Style for your report, then click Next.
h. Click on Preview the report, and then click Finish.

20.9 MetLife, an insurance company, spent $11 billion to acquire Travelers Life and Annuity from Citicorp in one of the largest insurance company mergers of all time. The Metlife CIO estimated it would take three years to integrate the two systems. Since the integration project was especially critical, he figured he could accomplish the integration in 18 months if he pulled out all the stops. The MetLife CEO gave him 9 months to complete the task. To pull off the integration in 9 months, he had to:

● Integrate over 600 IS applications, all with their own infrastructure and business processes. The new systems had to be transformed to comply with "One

MetLife," a company policy that stated that all information systems had to have a common look and feel companywide and be able to function seamlessly with other MetLife systems.

- Work with over 4,000 employees located in 88 offices scattered all over the globe, including five countries where MetLife did not operate.
- Supervise an oversight team and 50 integration teams located in seven project management offices.
- Work with hostile, uncooperative Travelers employees for the six months it took to get regulatory approval and close the deal. The systems had to be integrated three months after the deal closed.
- Identify all the integration deliverables (144 in total) and manage the process needed to deliver them.
- Negotiate with Citicorp for hundreds of transition services that would not be immediately converted to MetLife's systems

Required

- **a.** What tasks do you think MetLife would have to perform to successfully integrate the Traveler systems into MetLife's?
- **b.** Conduct an Internet search to find articles that describe the integration process and write a two-page summary of the problems and success that MetLife experienced while trying to integrate the two systems

20.10 During final testing directly before the launch of a new payroll system, the project managers found a problem. The prepackaged payroll system started doing the following:

- Writing checks for negative amounts
- Printing checks with names and employee numbers that did not match
- Making errors such as $8 per hour becoming $800 per hour if a decimal point was not entered
- Writing checks for amounts greater than a full year's salary

Fortunately, payroll was still delivered on time and only 1.5% of the checks had to be manually reissued due to the problems with the system. Still, the 1.5% of the payroll checks had to be manually reissued every payday until the problem was solved.

Other problems were that no one made sure the new system was compatible with the existing payroll database, and there appeared to be no formal transition between the development of the project and the implementation of the project. Also, the system was never run in parallel.

Although the programming manager lost his job, the payroll problems helped raise awareness of the company's growing dependence on IT. Lacking a major problem, there was a perception that the information system did not affect operations.

Required

- **a.** What does "the system was never run in parallel" mean?
- **b.** If the company had run the system in parallel, what should have occurred?
- **c.** What other testing methodologies could have been used by the firm?
- **d.** What other types of problems are evident from reading the case?

Source: Adapted from Polly Schneider, "Lessons Learned: Payroll on the Loose,"
CIO (December 1, 1998): 56–58.

20.11 A new program at Signal Enterprises was supposed to track customer calls. Unfortunately, it took 20 minutes to load on a PC, and it crashed frequently. Management hired a new consultant to fix the application, but after three months the project was discontinued after $200,000 had been spent.

The project did not have a traditional reporting structure. For this project, it appeared that no one was actually in charge. The lead project manager quit halfway through, the in-house programmers were reassigned to other projects or let go, and the two other layers of management loosely supervised the systems analyst.

Worse yet, the company did not check the references of the consulting firm it had hired to write the program for the new system. The outside consultants, who were located two states away, made many programming errors. Although the systems analyst caught some of the consultant's mistakes, the programming consultants grew increasingly distant and difficult to work with. They would not even furnish the source code to the project managers for fear of revealing their incompetence.

Required

a. Identify potential causes for the system implementation failure.
b. What steps should Signal have taken to successfully design and implement the call tracking system?

Adapted from Tom Field, "Too Many Cooks in the Kitchen," CIO, (December 1, 1998): 54–56.

CASE 20-1 Citizen's Gas Company

Citizen's Gas Company is a midsize gas distribution company that provides natural gas service to approximately 200,000 customers. The customer base is divided into three revenue classes. Data by customer class is as follows:

Class	Customers	Sales in Cubic Feet	Revenues
Residential	160,000	80 billion	$ 160 million
Commercial	38,000	15 billion	$ 25 million
Industrial	2,000	50 billion	$ 65 million
Totals		145 billion	$250 million

Residential customer gas use is primarily for residential heating and is thus highly correlated with the weather. Commercial and industrial customers, on the other hand, may use gas for heating purposes, but consumption does not necessarily depend on the weather.

The largest 25 of the company's 2,000 industrial customers account for $30 million of the industrial revenues. Each of these 25 customers uses gas for both heating and industrial purposes and has a consumption pattern governed almost entirely by business factors.

The company obtains its gas supply from 10 major pipeline companies. The pipeline companies provide gas in amounts specified in contracts that extend over periods ranging from 5 to 15 years. For some contracts, the supply is in equal monthly increments, whereas for others the supply varies in accordance with the heating season. Supply over and above the contract amounts is not available, and some contracts contain take-or-pay clauses—that is, the company must pay for the volumes specified in the contract, regardless of the amount of gas it uses.

To assist in matching customer demand with supply, the company maintains a gas storage field. Gas can be pumped into the storage field when supply exceeds customer demand; likewise, gas can be withdrawn when demand exceeds supply. There are no restrictions on the use of the gas storage field except that the field must be filled to capacity at the beginning of each gas year (September 1). Consequently, when the contractual supply for the remainder of the gas year is less than that required to satisfy projected demand and replenish the storage field, the company must curtail service to the industrial customers (except for quantities that are used for heating). The curtailments must be carefully controlled so that an oversupply does not occur at year-end. Similarly, care must be taken to ensure that curtailments are adequate during the year to protect against the need to curtail commercial or residential customers, to replenish the storage field at year-end.

In recent years, the company's planning efforts have not provided a firm basis for the establishment of long-term contracts. The current year has been no different. Planning efforts have not been adequate to control the supply during the current gas year. Customer demand has been projected only as a function of the total number of customers. Commercial and industrial customers' demand for gas has been curtailed. This has resulted in lost sales and caused an excess of supply at the end of the gas year.

In an attempt to correct the problems at Citizen's Gas, the president has hired a new director of corporate planning. The director has been presented with a conceptual design for a system to assist him in the analysis of the supply and demand of natural gas. The system should provide a monthly gas plan for each year for the next five years, with particular emphasis on the first year. The plan should provide a set of reports that assists in the decision-making process and that contains all necessary supporting schedules. The system must provide for the use of actual data during the course of the first year to project demand for the rest of the year and the year in total. The president has indicated to the director that he

will base his decisions on the effect alternative plans have on operating income.

Required

1 Discuss the criteria that must be considered in specifying the basic structure and features of Citizen's Gas Company's new system to assist in planning its natural gas needs.

2 Identify the major data items that should be incorporated into Citizen's Gas Company's new system to provide adequate planning capability. For each item identified, explain why the data item is important, and describe the level of detail that would be necessary for the data to be useful.

(*CMA Examination, adapted*)

AIS IN ACTION SOLUTIONS

QUIZ KEY

1 The developers of your new system have proposed two different AIS designs and have asked you to evaluate them. This evaluation process is most likely to be a part of which SDLC step?
 a. systems analysis [Incorrect. During systems analysis, analysts identify user requirements and establish objectives and specifications for the design phases of the SDLC.]
 ✔ b. conceptual design [Correct. During conceptual design users develop and evaluate appropriate design alternatives.]
 c. physical design [Incorrect. During physical design the company translates the broad, user-oriented requirements of the conceptual design into detailed specifications that are used to develop and test computer programs.]
 d. implementation and conversion [Incorrect. During implementation and conversion the company installs and tests hardware, software, and procedures, as well as converts from the old system to the new system.]
 e. operation and maintenance [Incorrect. During operation and maintenance the company runs the system and performs ongoing maintenance and minor modifications.]

2 What is the purpose of the conceptual systems design report?
 a. to guide physical systems design activities [Incorrect. The conceptual design report also includes communicating how management and users' needs are met and helping the steering committee assess system feasibility.]
 b. to communicate how management and user information needs are met [Incorrect. The conceptual design report also includes guiding physical systems design activities and helping the steering committee assess system feasibility.]
 c. to help the steering committee assess system feasibility [Incorrect. The conceptual design report also includes communicating how management and users' needs are met and guiding physical systems design activities.]
 d. a and b [Incorrect. The conceptual design report also includes helping the steering committee assess system feasibility.]
 ✔ e. a, b, and c [Correct. The conceptual design report guides physical systems design activities, communicates how management and users' needs are met, and helps the steering committee assess system feasibility.]

3 Which of the following is the correct order of the steps in physical systems design?

 a. input, file and database, output, controls, procedures, program [Incorrect. See Figure 20-2.]

 b. file and database, output, input, procedures, program, controls [Incorrect. See Figure 20-2.]

 c. output, input, file and database, procedures, program, controls [Incorrect. See Figure 20-2.]

 ✔ **d.** output, file and database, input, program, procedures, controls [Correct. See Figure 20-2.]

4 A monthly payroll register showing all hourly employees, the number of hours they worked, their deductions, and their net pay is most likely which of the following?

 ✔ **a.** scheduled report [Correct. Scheduled reports have a specified content, format, and delivery time. A monthly payroll register exhibits these characteristics.]

 b. special-purpose analysis [Incorrect. A special-purpose analysis has no specified content, format or delivery schedule.]

 c. triggered exception report [Incorrect. A triggered exception report has specified content and format but is only generated if a certain event occurs.]

 d. demand report [Incorrect. A demand report has specified content and format but is only generated on request.]

5 Which of the following is *not* a consideration in input design?

 a. Which errors are possible and how can they be detected and corrected? [Incorrect. Error identification and correction should be considered during input design. See Table 20-4.]

 b. How can data be entered (keyboards, OCR, or POS terminal)? [Incorrect. Data entry methods should be considered during input design. See Table 20-4.]

 c. Which format efficiently captures the input data with the least effort and cost? [Incorrect. Data format should be considered during input design. See Table 20-4.]

 ✔ **d.** How often should the system produce reports? [Correct. Report generation frequency is not normally considered during input design. See Table 20-4.]

6 Which of the following is most likely to help improve program development?

 a. physical model [Incorrect. A physical model is most commonly used to describe the physical characteristics of a database.]

 b. IT strategic plan [Incorrect. An entity's strategic plan provides a roadmap for achieving long-range goals.]

 ✔ **c.** walk-through [Correct. During walk-throughs those associated with designing the project review it step by step so any problems can be identified and corrected.]

 d. record layout [Incorrect. A record layout illustrates how data items are stored in a file.]

7 Which of the following statements is true?

 a. The Gartner Group estimates that programming bugs not found until later in the SDLC cost 25% to 30% more to correct than if they were found earlier in the SDLC. [Incorrect. The correct estimate is 80% to 1,000% more.]

 b. Direct system conversion is the least risky of the system conversion methods. [Incorrect. Direct conversion is the most risky rather than the least risky method for converting from an old system to a new system.]

 c. Many software developers state that 5% to 10% of software development costs should be allocated to testing, debugging, and rewriting software. [Incorrect. Software developers recommend that 20% to 30% of software development costs be allocated to testing, debugging, and rewriting software.]

 ✔ **d.** Over the life of a system, only 30% of information systems costs are incurred during development; the remaining 70% is spent maintaining the system. [Correct.]

8 Which of the following describes the systems testing approach that uses real transactions and files rather than hypothetical ones?

 a. walk-through [Incorrect. Walk-throughs are step-by-step reviews of procedures or programs so any problems can be identified and corrected.]

 b. processing of test transactions [Incorrect. Processing of test transactions uses valid and erroneous data to test for the proper handling of transactions, as well as the proper detection and handling of errors.]

 ✔ **c.** acceptance test [Correct. An acceptance test uses real transaction data to test a new system.]

 d. parallel conversion test [Incorrect. Parallel conversion is a system conversion method, not a testing method.]

9 What is the process of discontinuing an old system as soon as a new one is introduced?

 ✔ **a.** direct conversion [Correct. In direct conversion the old system is discontinued as soon as the new one is activated.]

 b. parallel conversion [Incorrect. A parallel conversion involves operating both the old and the new system in parallel until the users accept the new system.]

 c. phase-in conversion [Incorrect. Phase-in conversion gradually replaces elements of the old system with the new one.]

 d. pilot conversion [Incorrect. A pilot conversion activates and tests the new system in one or a few locations.]

10 Which of the following describes designing a program from the top down to more detailed levels?

 ✔ **a.** hierarchical program design [Correct. Hierarchical program design is the process of programming from the general level to the detailed level.]

 b. top-down program design [Incorrect. This is not a program design method described in the text.]

 c. parallel program design [Incorrect. This is not a program design method described in the text.]

 d. unstructured program design [Incorrect. This is not a program design method described in the text.]

CHAPTER CASE SOLUTION

To properly design, implement, and operate this new ERP system, Hershey should have taken the following steps.

Conceptual Design

In designing its new ERP system, Hershey should look at all possible designs and evaluate the strengths and weaknesses of each design and then select the best one. Once the design is selected, the design specifications need to be addressed, such as what distribution output will be needed to meet customer demands, how the order and shipping data will be stored, how the order and shipping data will be entered into the system, and how the system will process the inputs and data to produce the outputs. Hershey should also prepare a detailed report to guide the physical design phase and communicate with management and the steering committee the project's progress, requirements, and feasibility.

Physical Design

Once the conceptual design has been approved, the physical design should begin. Detailed plans for the nature, format, content, and timing of output for the orders and shipments should be prepared. In addition, specific data and data storage requirements are needed, as well as designs for the forms and computer screens that will be needed to capture order and shipment data. Hershey must choose which ERP modules to implement and decide how to structure and modify those modules to meet its needs. Hershey must also decide how employees will interact with the system and must develop policies and procedures to formalize that interaction. Controls must be designed to make sure those procedures and the system in general perform as intended and to prevent fraud and abuse. All of the physical design elements must also be put into a report to guide Hershey in the actual implementation of the system.

Systems Implementation

Once the new ERP system has been planned and designed, the actual hardware, software, procedures, and controls must be implemented. A plan for installing the ERP system consists of a schedule for completion and the project budget. Hershey should prepare the physical location of the new ERP system and train managers and users of the system. To train the users and operate the ERP system, adequate system documentation is needed. Last, the ERP system must be tested to make sure it works. Based on the information in the case, Hershey failed to adequately test its new ERP system before converting from the old system.

System Conversion

There are four primary system conversion approaches. Hershey, unfortunately, chose the highest-risk approach—direct conversion. Hershey called it the big bang and, in essence, turned on a major portion of the new system and turned off the old system. The result was loss of orders, loss of supplier confidence, a drop in market capitalization (stock price), and a damaged reputation. Hershey should have used one of the other three approaches—parallel, phase-in, or pilot—with the parallel approach probably being the most effective. If Hershey had been able to convert to the new ERP system more successfully, it could have then focused on operating and maintaining the new system and making improvements to make it more effective and efficient.

This page is too faded and degraded to produce a reliable transcription.

A

acceptance tests Tests of new systems using specially developed transactions and acceptance criteria. The test results are evaluated to determine if the system is acceptable.

access-based strategic position A strategic position that serves a subset of customers who differ from other customers in terms of factors such as geographic location or size.

access control list (ACL) A set of rules that determine which packets of information transmitted over a network, such as the Internet, are allowed entry and which are dropped.

access control matrix An internally maintained table specifying which portions of the system users are permitted to access and what actions they can perform. The matrix contains a list of user codes, a list of all files and programs maintained on the system, and a list of the accesses each user is authorized to make.

accounting information system (AIS) A system that collects, records, stores, and processes data to produce information for decision makers. An AIS has six components: people, procedures and instructions, data, software, information technology infrastructure, and internal controls and security measures.

accounts receivable aging schedule A report listing customer account balances by length of time outstanding. The report provides useful information for evaluating current credit policies, for estimating bad debts, and for deciding whether to increase the credit limit for specific customers.

activity-based costing (ABC) A cost system designed to trace costs to the activities, such as grinding or polishing, that create them. Once the costs are traced to their specific activities, the costs are then allocated to their corresponding products or departments.

ad hoc queries Nonrepetitive requests for reports or answers to specific questions about the contents of the system's data files.

adware A type of spyware that 1) causes banner ads to pop up on your monitor as you surf the Net, and 2) collects information about the user's Web-surfing and spending habits and forwards it to the company gathering the data, often an advertising or media organization. Adware usually comes bundled with freeware and shareware downloaded from the Internet.

agents In the REA data model, the people and organizations that participate in events and about whom information is desired.

aggression A way of resisting change that is intended to destroy, cripple, or lessen the effectiveness of a system. Aggression may take the form of increased error rates, disruptions, or deliberate sabotage.

analytical review The examination of the relationships between different sets of data.

application The problem or data processing task to which a computer's processing power is applied.

application controls Controls that prevent, detect, and correct transaction errors and fraud. They are concerned with the accuracy, completeness, validity, and authorization of the data captured, entered into the system, processed, stored, transmitted to other systems, and reported. Contrast with *general controls*.

application programmer A person who writes an application program using a programming language.

application service provider (ASP) A company that provides access to and use of application programs via the Internet. The ASP owns and hosts the software; the contracting organization accesses the software remotely via the Internet.

application software The programs that perform the data or information-processing tasks required by the user. Common types of application software include accounts receivable and payable, inventory control, and payroll.

archive A copy of a database, master file, or software that is retained indefinitely as an historical record, usually to satisfy legal and regulatory requirements.

asymmetric encryption systems See *public key infrastructure (PKI)*.

asynchronous transmission Data transmission in which each character is transmitted separately. A start bit is required before the character and a stop bit after it because the interval of time between transmission of characters can vary. Contrast with *synchronous transmission.*

attributes Characteristics of interest in a file or database; the different individual properties of an entity. Examples of attributes are employee number, pay rate, name, and address.

audit committee The committee responsible for overseeing a corporation's internal control structure, financial reporting process, and compliance with related laws and regulations. It is usually comprised of outside members of the board of directors.

audit hooks A concurrent audit technique that embeds audit routines into application software to flag certain kinds of transactions that might indicate an error or fraud.

audit log A log of all transactions that have audit significance.

audit trail A traceable path of a transaction through a data processing system from point of origin (whether paper or electronic) to final output or backwards from from final output to point of origin. An audit trail provides a means to check the accuracy and validity of ledger postings and to trace all changes in general ledger accounts from their beginning balance to their ending balance.

auditing A systematic process of (1) objectively obtaining and evaluating evidence regarding assertions about economic actions and events to ascertain the degree of correspondence between those assertions and established criteria; and (2) communicating the results to interested parties.

authentication Verifying the identity of the person or device attempting to access the system.

authenticity Being able to determine who sent a message or who created a document with almost absolute certainty.

authorization The empowerment of an employee to perform certain functions within an organization, such as to purchase or sell on

behalf of the company. Authorization can be either general or specific. *General* authorization is when regular employees are authorized to handle routine transactions without special approval. *Specific* authorization is when an employee must get special approval before handling a transaction.

automated decision table programs Programs that generate a decision table representing the program's logic.

automated flowcharting program A program that interprets the source code of a program and generates a flowchart of the logic used by the program.

avoidance A way of resisting change by not using the new system.

B

back order A document authorizing the purchase or production of items for which sufficient quantity is not available to meet customer orders.

background check When a potential or current employer verifies educational and work experience data on resumes, talks to references, checks to see if the person has a criminal record, checks credit records, and checks other publicly available data about an individual.

backup An exact copy of the most current version of a database, file, or software program.

balance-forward method Method of maintaining accounts receivable in which customers typically pay according to the amount shown on a monthly statement, rather than by individual invoices. Remittances are applied against the total account balance, rather than against specific invoices.

balanced scorecard A management report that measures four dimensions of performance: financial, internal operations, innovation and learning, and customer perspectives of the organization.

bandwidth The difference between the highest and the lowest frequencies of a communications channel. Usually expressed in cycles per second (hertz).

bar code Special identification label found on most merchandise. A code includes vertical lines of differing widths that represent binary information that is read by an optical scanner.

batch processing Accumulating transaction records into groups or batches for processing at some regular interval such as daily or weekly. The records are usually sorted into some sequence (such as numerically or alphabetically) before processing.

batch totals Sums of the instances of numerical items, calculated for a batch of documents. These totals are calculated prior to processing the batch and are compared with machine-generated totals at each subsequent processing step to verify that the data was processed correctly.

behavioral aspects of change Systems development causes changes in organizations that may result in people changing their behavior. Organizations must be sensitive to and consider the feelings and reactions of persons affected by such changes.

belief system A corporate attitude enstilled by upper management that communicates company core values to employees and inspires them to live by them. It should draw attention to how the organization creates values and help employees understand the direction management wants the company to take.

benchmark problem A data processing task that is executed by different computer systems. The results are used to measure systems performance and to make comparative evaluations among systems.

bill of lading A legal contract that defines responsibility for goods while they are in transit. It identifies the carrier, source, destination, any special shipping instructions, and indicates which party (customer or vendor) must pay the carrier.

bill of materials A document that specifies the part number, description, and quantity of each component used in a product.

biometric identification Using unique physical characteristics such as fingerprints, voice patterns, retina prints, and signature dynamics to identify people.

biometric identifier A physical characteristic (fingerprint, voice, etc.) used to authenticate the identity of a user.

bits Binary digits are the smallest storage location in a computer. A bit may be either "on" or "off," or "magnetized" or "nonmagnetized." A combination of bits (usually eight) is used to represent a single character of data.

bits per second (BPS) A unit of measurement describing the number of bits of data transmitted electronically in one second.

blanket purchase order or **blanket order** A commitment to purchase specified items at designated prices from a particular supplier for a set time period, often one year.

block code Blocks of numbers within a numerical sequence reserved for categories having meaning to the user.

border router A device that connects an organization's information system to the Internet.

boundary system An established system that helps employees act ethically by setting limits beyond which an employee must not pass. Employees are encouraged to think and act creatively to solve problems and meet customer needs as long as they operate within certain limits, such as meeting minimum standards of performance, shunning activities that are off limits, and avoiding courses of action that would damage the company's reputation.

broadband lines Communications channels that are capable of handling high-speed data transmissions, usually data transmissions between computer systems.

budget The formal expression of goals in financial terms. Budgets are financial planning tools. Contrast with *performance report*.

buffer overflow attack When an attacker sends a program more data than it can handle. Buffer overflows may cause the system to crash or, even worse, may provide a command prompt that gives the attacker full administrative privileges and control of the device.

business cycle A group of related business processes. The major business cycles are sales and marketing, purchasing and inventory control, production, human resources and payroll, and finance.

business intelligence The process of accessing the data contained in a data warehouse and using it for strategic decision making. There are two main techniques used in business intelligence: online analytical processing (OLAP) and data mining.

business process management (BPM) Managing the process of improving business processes. Software has been developed to help organizations automate business process improvement tasks.

business process reengineering (BPR) The thorough analysis and redesign of business processes and information systems to achieve dramatic performance improvements.

byte A group of adjacent bits (usually 8) treated as a single unit by the computer. An 8-bit byte can be used to represent an alphabetic, numeric, or special character, or even two numeric characters "packed" into a single 8-bit byte.

C

callback system A routing verification procedure. After the user dials in and is authenticated, the computer disconnects and calls the user back as an additional security precaution.

canned software Programs written by computer manufacturers or software development companies for sale on the open market to a broad range of users with similar needs.

capital budgeting model An estimate of funds to be appropriated for the acquisition of major capital assets and for investment in long-term projects. The estimated benefits are compared with the costs to determine if the system is cost beneficial.

cardinality A property of a database relationship indicating the number of occurrences of one entity that may be associated with a single occurrence of the other entity. Three types of cardinalities are one-to-one, one-to-many, and many-to-many.

carrying costs The costs associated with holding inventory.

cash budget A budget that shows projected cash inflows and outflows. A cash budget can provide advance warning of cash flow problems so corrective action can be taken.

CD-ROM A storage device that uses laser optics for reading data rather than magnetic storage devices. Some CD-ROM discs are "read only." The discs are useful for storing large volumes of data.

central processing unit (CPU) The hardware that contains the circuits that control the interpretation and execution of instructions and that serves as the principal data processing device. Its major components are the arithmetic-logic unit, the memory, and the control unit.

centralized system or network A centralized computer system that handles a company's data processing needs. User terminals are linked to the centralized host computer so that users can send data to the host computer for processing and access data as needed. It requires complex software and is designed to provide a company with an "economy of scale" advantage in data processing operations.

certificate authority An independent organization that issues public and private keys and records the public key in a digital certificate.

change management The process of making sure that changes to the system do not negatively affect systems reliability, security, confidentiality, integrity, and availability.

character Letters, numeric digits, or other symbols used for representing data to be processed by a computer.

chart of accounts A listing of all balance sheet and income statement account number codes for a particular company.

check digit A digit in a data field that provides information about the other digits in the data field. It is used to check for errors or loss of characters in the data fields as a result of data transfer operations. If data are lost or erroneously changed, the fact that the check digit does not match the other data in the field will signal that an error has occurred.

check digit verification The edit check in which a check digit is recalculated to verify that an error has not been made. This calculation can be made only on a data item that has a check digit.

checkpoint Any one of a series of points during a long processing run at which an exact copy of all the data values and status indicators of a program are captured. Should a system failure occur, the system could be backed up to the most recent checkpoint and processing could begin again at the checkpoint rather than at the beginning of the program.

choiceboards Interactive sales order entry systems that allow customers to customize the products that they are ordering.

ciphertext Plaintext that has been transformed into unreadable gibberish through the process of encryption.

client/server system A system where information requested by a user is first processed as much as possible by the server and then transmitted to the user.

closed-loop verification An input validation method that uses data entered into the system to retrieve and display other related information so the accuracy of the input data can be verified.

coding (1) The systematic assignment of numbers or letters to items to classify and organize them. (2) Writing program instructions that direct a computer to perform a specific data processing task.

cold site A location that provides everything necessary to quickly install computer equipment in the event of a disaster.

collusion Cooperation between two or more people in an effort to thwart internal controls.

commitments Promises to engage in future economic exchanges.

Committee of Sponsoring Organizations (COSO) A private sector group consisting of the American Accounting Association, the AICPA, the Institute of Internal Auditors, the Institute of Management Accountants, and the Financial Executives Institute.

compatibility check (or **compatibility test**) Checking to see whether a person attempting to access a particular information system resource is authorized to do so. The computer matches the user's authentication credentials against the access control matrix to determine whether the employee should be allowed to access that resource and perform the requested operation.

compensating controls Control procedures that will compensate for the deficiency in other controls.

completeness test (check) An on-line data entry control in which the computer checks if all data required for a particular transaction have been entered by the user.

compliance objectives Objectives to help the company comply with all applicable laws and regulations.

computer audit software (CAS) See *generalized audit software.*

computer crime Any illegal act for which knowledge of a computer is essential for the crime's perpetration, investigation, or prosecution.

computer emergency response team (CERT) A team responsible for dealing with major security incidents.

computer forensics specialists Computer experts whose job entails discovering, extracting, safeguarding, and documenting computer evidence so that its authenticity, accuracy, and integrity will not succumb to legal challenges.

computer fraud See *computer crime.*

computer-integrated manufacturing (CIM) A manufacturing approach in which much of the manufacturing process is performed and monitored by computerized equipment, in part through the use of robotics and real-time data collection of manufacturing activities.

computer operators People who run software on the company's computers. They ensure that data are properly input to the computer, processed correctly, and needed output is produced.

computer program See *program*.

computer programmers Persons who develop, code, and test computer programs.

computer security The policies, procedures, tools, and other means of safeguarding information systems from unauthorized access or alteration and from intentional or unintentional damage or theft.

computer security officer An employee independent of the information system function who monitors the system and disseminates information about improper system uses and their consequences.

concatenated key Two or more primary keys of other database tables that, together, become a unique identifier or primary key of another table. A multiple-attribute primary key.

conceptual design specifications Once a conceptual design alternative has been selected, systems requirements are specified for systems output, data storage, input, processing procedures, and operations.

conceptual systems design The systems development life cycle phase where a general framework is created to implement user requirements and solve problems identified in the analysis phase.

conceptual systems design report A document specifying the findings and results of the conceptual systems design. The report is used by physical systems designers to identify the hardware, software, and procedures necessary to deliver the system.

conceptual-level schema The organization-wide view of the entire database. It lists all data elements in the database and the relationships between them. Contrast with *external-level schema* and *internal-level schema*.

concurrent audit techniques A software routine that continuously monitors an information system as it processes live data in order to collect, evaluate, and report to the auditor information about the system's reliability.

concurrent update controls Controls that lock out one user to protect individual records from potential errors that could occur if two users attempted to update the same record simultaneously.

context diagram The highest level of a data flow diagram. It provides a summary-level view of a system. It shows the data processing system, the input(s) and output(s) of the system, and the external entities that are the sources and destinations of the system's input(s) and output(s).

continuous and intermittent simulation (CIS) A concurrent audit technique that embeds an audit module into a database management system, rather than the application software.

control account A general ledger account that summarizes the total amounts recorded in a subsidiary ledger. Thus, the accounts payable control account in the general ledger represents the total amount owed to all vendors. The balances in the subsidiary accounts payable ledger indicate the amount owed to each specific vendor.

control activities Policies, procedures, and rules that provide reasonable assurance that management's control objectives are met and their risk responses are carried out.

control environment The organization's environment relating to controls. It consists of many factors including management's philosophy, the audit committee, and the organizational structure.

Control Objectives for Information and related Technology (COBIT) A framework of generally applicable information systems security and control practices for IT control. The framework allows (1) management to benchmark the security and control practices of IT environments, (2) users of IT services to be assured that adequate security and control exist, and (3) auditors to substantiate their opinions on internal control and to advise on IT security and control matters.

control risk The risk that a significant control problem will fail to be prevented or detected by the internal control system.

control totals Batch totals used to ensure that all data are processed correctly. Examples are the number of transactions processed and the dollar amount of all updates.

conversion The process of changing from one form or format to another.

cookie A text file created by a Web site and stored on a visitor's hard drive. Cookies store information about who the user is and what the user has done on the site.

corrective controls Procedures established to remedy problems that are discovered through detective controls.

cost driver Anything that has a cause-and-effect relationship on costs. For example, the number of purchase orders processed is one cost driver of purchasing department costs.

cracking See *hacking*.

credit limit The maximum allowable account balance for each customer, based on past credit history and ability to pay.

credit memo A document authorizing the billing department to credit the customer's account. Usually issued for sales returns, allowances granted for damaged goods kept by the customer, or to write off uncollectible accounts. Approved by the credit manager.

critical path The path requiring the greatest amount of time to complete a project. If any of the activities on the critical path are delayed, the whole project is delayed. If possible, resources are shifted to critical path activities to reduce project completion time.

cross-footing balance test A procedure in which worksheet data are totaled both across and down. Then, the total of the horizontal totals is compared to the total of the vertical totals to ensure that the worksheet balances.

cryptography See *data encryption*.

custom software Computer software that is developed and written in-house to meet the unique needs of a particular company.

cycle billing A procedure for producing monthly statements for subsets of customers at different times. For example, the customer master file might be divided into four parts, and each week monthly statements would be prepared for one-fourth of the customers.

D

data Facts that are collected, recorded, stored, and processed by an information system to produce information.

data administrator (DA) The person responsible for developing general policies and procedures governing all organizational data, not just what is stored in the database. The DA is ultimately responsible for understanding the information needs of the organization and deciding what should be included in the database.

data communications The transmission of data from a point of origin to a point of destination.

data communications network A communication system that bridges geographical distances, giving users immediate access to a company's computerized data. It also allows multiple companies or computer services to be linked for the purpose of sharing information.

data control group The group charged with ensuring that source data have been properly approved, monitoring the flow of work through the computer, reconciling input and output, maintaining a record of input errors to ensure their correction and resubmission, and distributing systems output.

data definition language (DDL) A database management system language that ties the logical and physical views of the data together. It is used to build the data dictionary, initialize or create the database, describe the logical views for each individual user or programmer, and specify any limitations or constraints on security imposed on database records or fields.

data destination A component of data flow diagrams that represents an entity outside of the system who receives data produced by the system.

data dictionary An ordered collection of data elements that contain information about the structure of the database. For each data element stored in the database, such as the customer number, there is a corresponding record in the data dictionary describing it.

data diddling Changing data before, during, or after it is entered into the system. The change can be made to add, delete, or alter system data.

data flow A component of a data flow diagram that represents data flowing into or out of a process.

data flow diagram (DFD) A diagram that graphically describes the flow of data within an organization. It is used to document existing systems and to plan and design new ones.

data independence A data organization approach in which the data and the application programs that use the data are independent. This means that one may be changed without affecting the other.

data leakage The unauthorized copying of company data, often without leaving any indication that it was copied.

data maintenance The periodic processing of transactions to update stored data. The four types of data maintenance are additions, deletions, updates, and changes.

data manipulation language (DML) A database management system language used for data maintenance, which includes such operations as updating, inserting, and deleting portions of the database.

data mart A smaller data warehouse that is built by an organization for various functions such as finance and human resources.

data mining Accessing information stored in a data warehouse through statistical analysis or artificial intelligence techniques to "discover" unhypothesized relationships in the data.

data model An abstract representation of the contents of a database.

data modeling Defining a database so that it faithfully represents all key components of an organization's environment. The objective is to explicitly capture and store data about every business activity the organization wishes to plan, control, or evaluate.

data processing center The room that houses a company's computer system (the hardware, software, and people who operate the system).

data processing cycle The operations performed on data in computer-based systems to generate meaningful and relevant information. The data processing cycle has four stages: data input, data storage, data processing, and information output.

data processing schedule A schedule of data processing tasks designed to maximize the use of scarce computer resources.

data query language (DQL) A high-level, English-like command language that is used to interrogate a database. The DQL retrieves, sorts, orders, and presents subsets of the database in response to user queries.

data redundancy The storage of the same item of data in two or more files within an organization.

data source A component of a data flow diagram that represents the people and organizations that send data that the system being modeled uses or produces.

data store A component of a data flow diagram that represents the storage of data within a system.

data transmission controls Methods of monitoring the network to detect weak points, maintain backup components, and ensure that the system can still communicate if one of the communications paths should fail.

data value The actual value stored in a field. It describes a particular attribute of an entity.

data warehouses Very large databases that contain both detailed and summarized data for a number of years and that are used for analysis rather than transaction processing.

database A set of interrelated, centrally controlled data files that are stored with as little data redundancy as possible. A database consolidates many records previously stored in separate files into a common pool of data records and serves a variety of users and data processing applications.

database administrator The person responsible for coordinating, controlling, and managing the data in the database.

database management system (DBMS) The specialized computer program that manages and controls the data and interfaces between the data and the application programs.

database query language Easy-to-use programming language that lets the user ask questions about the data stored in a database.

database system The combination of the database, the database management system, and the application programs that access the database through the database management system.

debit memo A document used to record a reduction to the balance due to a vendor.

debugging The process of checking for and correcting the errors found in a computer program.

decentralized system An information processing system that has an independent CPU and data processing manager at each location.

decision support system (DSS) An interactive computer system designed to help with the decision-making process by providing access to a computer-based database or decision-making model.

decryption Transforming ciphertext back into plaintext.

deduction register A report listing the miscellaneous voluntary deductions for each employee.

deep packet inspection When the firewall examines the data in the body of an IP packet rather than only looking at the information in the IP header.

default value A control that helps preserve the integrity of data processing and stored data by leaving a field blank if a standard value is to be used.

defense-in-depth Employing multiple layers of controls in order to avoid having a single point-of-failure. The use of overlapping, complementary, and redundant controls buys time for the organization to detect and react to attacks; it also increases effectiveness because even if one procedure fails or is circumvented, another may function as planned.

delete anomaly A problem that can arise in a poorly designed relational database when attributes that are not characteristics of the primary key of a relation are stored in that table. Deleting a row from that table may result in the loss of all information about those attributes that are not characteristics of the primary key. For example, if customer addresses are only stored in the sales invoice table, then deleting the row representing the only sale to a particular customer results in the loss of all information about that customer.

demand reports Reports that have a prespecified content and format but are prepared only in response to a request from a manager or other employee.

demilitarized zone (DMZ) Placing the organization's Web servers and e-mail servers in a separate network that sits outside the corporate network but is accessible from the Internet.

denial-of-service attack An attacker sends so many e-mail bombs (thousands per second), often from randomly generated false addresses, that the Internet service provider's e-mail server is overloaded and shuts down. Another denial-of-service attack is sending so many requests for Web pages that the Web server crashes.

desk checking A visual and mental review of a newly coded program to discover keying or program errors.

detection risk The risk that the auditors and their audit procedures will not detect a material misstatement.

detective controls Controls designed to discover control problems soon after they arise.

diagnostic control system A performance measurment system that compares actual performance to planned performance.

dictionary attack Using special software to guess company addresses and send them blank e-mail messages. Unreturned messages are usually valid e-mail addresses that can be added to spammer e-mail lists.

differential backup Copying all changes made since the last full backup. Thus, each new differential backup file contains the cumulative effects of all activity since the last full backup.

digital certificate An electronic document, created and digitally signed by a trusted third party, that certifies the identity of the owner of a particular public key. The digital certificate contains that party's public key. Thus, digital certificates provide an automated method for obtaining an organization's or individual's public key.

digital fingerprint A hash number that identifies and validates a digital certificate.

digital signature (1) A piece of data signed on a document by a computer. A digital signature cannot be forged and is useful in tracing authorization. (2) Information encrypted with the creator's private key.

direct access An access method that allows the computer to access a particular record without reading any other records. Because each storage location on a direct access storage device has a unique address, the computer can find the record needed as long as it has the record's address.

direct access storage device (DASD) A storage device (such as a disk drive) that can directly access individual storage locations to store or retrieve data.

direct conversion An approach to converting from one system to another in which the old system is discontinued, after which the new system is started (also known as "burning the bridges" or "crash conversion").

disaster recovery plan A plan that prepares a company to recover its data processing capacity as smoothly and quickly as possible in response to any emergency that could disable the computer system.

disbursement voucher A document that identifies the vendor, lists the outstanding invoices, and indicates the net amount to be paid after deducting any applicable discounts and allowances.

discretionary information Information that is available only to certain internal users. Contrast with *mandatory* and *essential information*.

diskette A round piece of flexible magnetic film enclosed within a protective cover. It used to be a popular storage medium for PCs.

distributed data processing (DDP) A system in which computers are set up at remote locations and then linked to a centralized mainframe computer.

document flowchart Document flowcharts trace a document from its cradle to its grave. They show where each document originates, its distribution, the purposes for which it is used, its ultimate disposition, and everything that happens as it flows through the system. They illustrate the flow of documents and information among areas of responsibility within an organization.

documentation The narratives, flowcharts, diagrams, and other writen materials that explain how a system works. It covers the who, what, when, where, why, and how of data entry, processing, storage, information output, and system controls.

documents Records of transaction or other company data such as checks, invoices, receiving reports, and purchase requisitions.

download Transmitting data or software maintained on an internet server or a large host (mainframe) computer to a personal computer.

downsizing Shifting data processing and problem solving from mainframes to smaller computer.

dumpster diving See *scavenging*.

E

earnings statement A report listing the amount of gross pay, deductions, and net pay for the current period; the report also lists year-to-date totals for each category.

eavesdropping Observing data transmissions intended for someone else. One way unauthorized individuals can intercept signals is by setting up a wiretap.

e-business All uses of advances in information technology, particularly networking and communications technology, to improve the ways an organization performs its business processes.

echo check A hardware control that verifies transmitted data by having the receiving device send the message back to the sending device so that the message received can be compared with the message sent.

e-commerce The electronic execution of business transactions such as buying and selling.

economic espionage The theft of information and intellectual property.

economic exchange An event in which one agent gives a resource to another agent in exchange for some other resource.

economic feasibility The dimension of feasibility concerned with whether the benefits of a proposed system will exceed the costs.

economic order quantity (EOQ) The optimal order size so as to minimize the sum of ordering, carrying, and stockout costs. Ordering costs include all expenses associated with processing purchase transactions. Carrying costs are the costs associated with holding inventory. Stockout costs represent costs, such as lost sales or production delays, which result from inventory shortages.

edit checks Accuracy checks performed by an edit program.

edit programs Computer programs that verify the validity and accuracy of input data.

electronic commerce The use of advances in networking and communications technology to improve the ways in which a company interacts with its suppliers and customers.

electronic data interchange (EDI) The use of computerized communication to exchange business data electronically in order to process transactions.

electronic data processing (EDP) Processing data utilizing a computer system.

electronic funds transfer (EFT) The transfer of funds between two or more organizations or individuals using computers and other automated technology. With EFT, customers can send their remittances electronically to the company's bank and thus eliminate the delay associated with the time the remittance is in the mail.

electronic lockbox A lockbox arrangement in which the bank electronically sends the company information about the customer account number and the amount remitted as soon as it receives and scans those checks. This enables the company to begin applying remittances to customer accounts before the photocopies of the checks arrive.

electronic vaulting Electronically transmitting backup copies of data to a physically different location. Electronic vaulting permits online access to backup data when necessary.

e-mail bomb A denial-of-service attack in which the receiver's e-mail server is bombarded with hundreds of e-mail messages per second.

e-mail forgery Altering e-mail to make it appear that it came from a different source.

e-mail threats Threats sent to victims by e-mail. The threats usually require some follow-up action, often at great expense to the victim.

embedded audit modules Special portions of application programs that track items of interest to auditors, such as unauthorized attempts to access the data files.

embezzlement The fraudulent appropriation of business property by an employee to whom it has been entrusted. It is often accompanied by falsification of records.

employee fraud An internal fraud in which an employee or group of employees use or steal company resources for personal gain.

encryption The process of transforming normal text, called plaintext, into unreadable gibberish, called ciphertext. Encryption is particularly important when confidential data is being transmitted from remote terminals because data transmission lines can be electronically monitored without the user's knowledge.

end-user computing (EUC) The creation, control, and implementation by end users of their own information system.

end-user development (EUD) When information users develop applications on their own, rather than going through the information systems department.

end-user system (EUS) An information system developed by the users themselves, rather than professionals in the information systems department, to meet their own operational and managerial information needs. An EUS draws upon the information in existing corporate databases to meet users' information needs.

enterprise resource planning (ERP) system A system that integrates all aspects of an organization's activities into one accounting information system.

Enterprise Risk Management Integrated Framework (ERM) A COSO developed internal framework that expands on the elements of COSO's Internal Control Integrated Framework and provides an all-encompassing focus on the broader subject of enterprise risk management.

entity The item about which information is stored in a record. Examples include an employee, an inventory item, and a customer.

entity integrity rule A design constraint in a relational database, requiring that the primary key have a non-null value. This ensures that a specific object exists in the world and can be identified by reference to its primary key value.

entity-relationship (E-R) diagram A graphical depiction of a database's contents. It shows the various entities being modeled and the important relationships among them. An entity is any class of objects about which data are collected. Thus, the resources, events, and agents that comprise the REA data model are all entities. An E-R diagram represents entities as rectangles; lines and diamonds represent relationships between entities.

error log The record of data input and data processing errors.

error message A message from the computer indicating that it has encountered a mistake or malfunction.

error report A report summarizing errors by record type, error type, and cause.

essential information Information required to conduct business with external parties (such as purchase orders and customer billings). Contrast with *mandatory* and *discretionary information*.

evaluated receipt settlement (ERS) An "invoiceless" approach to the accounts payable process. ERS replaces the traditional three-way matching process (vendor invoice, receiving report, and purchase order) with a two-way match of the purchase order and receiving report. ERS saves time and money by reducing the number of potential mismatches. ERS also saves suppliers the time and expense of generating and tracking invoices.

event (1) In the REA data model, a business activity about which management wants to collect information for planning or control purposes. (2) An incident or occurrence emanating from internal or external sources that affects the implementation of strategy or the achievement of objectives.

expected loss The mathematical product of the potential dollar loss that would occur should a threat become a reality (called exposure) and the risk or probability that the threat will occur (called likelihood).

expenditure cycle A recurring set of business activities and related data processing operations associated with the purchase of and payment for goods and services.

exploit The set of instructions for taking advantage of a vulnerability.

exposure The potential dollar loss should a particular threat become a reality.

external label A label on the outside of a storage medium that identifies the data it contains.

external-level schema An individual user's or application program's view of a subset of the organization's database. Each of these individual user views is also referred to as a subschema. Contrast with *conceptual-level schema* and *internal-level schema*.

extranet Linked intranets of two or more companies.

F

fault tolerance The capability of a system to continue performing when there is a hardware failure.

feasibility study An investigation to determine if the development of a new application or system is practical. This is one of the first steps in the systems evaluation and selection process.

field The part of a data record that contains the data value for a particular attribute. All records of a particular type usually have their fields in the same order. For example, the first field in all accounts receivable records may be the customer account number.

field check An edit check in which the characters in a field are examined to ensure they are of the correct field type (e.g., numeric data in numeric fields).

file A set of logically related records, such as the payroll records of all employees.

file maintenance The periodic processing of transaction files against a master file. This maintenance, which is the most common task in virtually all data processing systems, includes creating, reading, updating, and deleting records. After file maintenance, the master file will contain all current information.

file organization The way data are stored on the physical storage media. File organization may be either sequential or direct (random) access.

financial audit A review of the reliability and integrity of financial and operating information and the means used to identify, measure, classify, and report such information.

financial electronic data interchange (FEDI) The combination of EFT and EDI that enables both remittance data and funds transfer instructions to be included in one electronic package.

financial total The total of a dollar field, such as total sales, in a set of records. It is usually generated manually from source documents prior to input and compared with machine-generated totals at each subsequent processing step. Any discrepancy may indicate a loss of records or errors in data transcription or processing.

financial value-added network (FVAN) An independent organization that offers specialized hardware and software to link various EDI networks with the banking system for EFT.

financing cycle The business activities and related data processing operations associated with obtaining the necessary funds to run the operations, repay creditors, and distribute profits to investors.

firewall A combination of security algorithms and router communications protocols that prevent outsiders from tapping into corporate databases and e-mail systems.

flexible benefits plan A plan under which each employee receives some minimum coverage in medical insurance and pension contributions, plus additional benefit "credits" that can be used to acquire extra vacation time or additional health insurance. These plans are sometimes called cafeteria-style benefit plans because they offer a menu of options.

flowchart An analytical technique used to describe some aspect of an information system in a clear, concise, and logical manner. Flowcharts use a standard set of symbols to describe pictorially the transaction processing procedures a company uses and the flow of data through a system.

flowcharting symbols A set of objects that are used in flowcharts to show how and where data move. Each symbol has a special meaning that is easily conveyed by its shape.

flowcharting template A piece of hard, flexible plastic on which the shapes of flowcharting symbols have been die cut.

Foreign Corrupt Practices Act (1977) Among other things, requires all publicly owned corporations subject to the Securities Exchange Act of 1934 to keep reasonably detailed records and maintain a system of internal accounting controls.

foreign key An attribute appearing in one table that is itself the primary key of another table. Foreign keys are used to link tables.

forensic accountants Accountants who specialize in fraud auditing and investigation. Upon qualification, forensic accountants may receive a Certified Fraud Examiner (CFE) certificate.

fraud Any and all means a person uses to gain an unfair advantage over another person.

fraud hot line A telephone number employees can call to anonymously report abuses such as fraud.

fraudulent financial reporting Intentional or reckless conduct, whether by act or omission, that results in materially misleading financial statements.

G

Gantt chart A bar graph used for project planning and control. Project activities are shown on the left, and units of time are shown across the top. The time period over which each activity is expected to be performed is represented with a horizontal bar on the graph.

general authorization When regular employees are authorized to handle routine transactions without special approval.

general controls Controls designed to make sure an organization's control environment is stable and well-managed. General controls apply to all sizes of systems, from large and complex mainframe systems to client/server systems to desktop and laptop computer systems. Contrast with *application controls*.

general journal The general journal is used to record infrequent or nonroutine transactions, such as loan payments and end-of-period adjusting and closing entries.

general journal listing A report showing the details (account number, source reference code, description, and amount debited or credited) of each entry posted to the general ledger. This report indicates if the total debits equal the total credits posted to the general ledger.

general ledger Contains summary-level data for every asset, liability, equity, revenue, and expense account of the organization.

general ledger and reporting system The information-processing operations involved in updating the general ledger and preparing reports that summarize the results of the organization's activities.

generalized audit software (GAS) A software package that can be used to perform audit tests on the data files of a company.

give-get exchange An event where two entities exchange items such as cash for goods or services.

goal conflict Occurs when a decision or action of a subsystem is inconsistent with another subsystem or the system as a whole.

goal congruence Is achieved when a subsystem achieves its goals while contributing to the organization's overall goal.

grandfather-father-son concept A method for maintaining backup copies of files on magnetic tape or disk. The three most current copies of the data are retained, with the son being the most recent.

group codes Two or more subgroups of digits that are used to code an item. A group code is often used in conjunction with a block code

H

hacking Unauthorized access and use of computer systems, usually by means of a personal computer and telecommunications networks.

hardening The process of turning off unnecessary program features.

hash Plaintext that has been transformed into short code.

hashing A process that takes plaintext of any length and transforms it into a short code called a hash.

hash total A total generated from values for a field that would not usually be totaled, such as customer account numbers. It is usually generated manually from source documents prior to input and compared with machine-generated totals at each subsequent processing step. Any discrepancy may indicate a loss of records or errors in data transcription or processing.

header label or header record Type of internal label that appears at the beginning of each file and contains the file name, expiration date, and other file identification information.

help desk An in-house group of analysts and technicians who answers employees' questions with the purpose of encouraging, supporting, coordinating, and controlling end-user activity.

hierarchical program design The process of designing a program from the top level down to more detailed levels.

hijacking Gaining control of someone else's computer to carry out illicit activities, such as sending spam without the computer user's knowledge.

home page A "storefront" or site on the Internet set up by individuals and firms to provide useful and interesting information.

hosts The workstations, servers, printers, and other devices that comprise the organization's network.

hot site Completely operational data processing facility configured to meet the user's requirement that can be made available to a disaster-stricken organization on short notice.

human resources management (HRM)/(payroll) cycle The recurring set of business activities and related data processing operations associated with effectively managing the employee workforce.

I

identity theft Assuming someone's identity, almost always for economic gain, by illegally obtaining confidential information such as a social security number.

impact See *exposure*.

impersonation See *masquerading*.

implementation The process of installing a computer system. It includes selecting and installing the equipment, training personnel, establishing operating policies and control procedures, testing and documenting the system, and getting the software onto the system and functioning properly.

implementation and conversion phase The capstone phase in the systems development life cycle where the elements and activities of the system come together.

implementation plan A written plan that outlines how the new system will be implemented. The plan includes a timetable for completion, who is responsible for each activity, cost estimates, and task milestones.

imprest fund A cash account with two characteristics: (1) It is set at a fixed amount, such as $100, and (2) vouchers are required for every disbursement. At all times, the sum of cash plus vouchers should equal the preset fund balance.

incremental backup Copying only the data items that have changed since the last backup. This produces a set of incremental backup files, each containing the results of one day's transactions.

information Data that have been organized and processed to provide meaning to a user. Information can be classified as mandatory, essential, or discretionary.

information overload The state in which additional information cannot be used efficiently and has no marginal value.

information processing The process of turning data into information. This process has four stages: data input, data processing, data storage, and information output.

information system An organized way of collecting, processing, managing, and reporting information so that an organization can achieve its objectives and goals. Formal information systems have an explicit responsibility to produce information. In contrast, an informal information system is one that arises out of a need that is not satisfied by a formal channel. It operates without formal designation of responsibility.

information systems audit Reviews the general and application controls of an AIS to assess its compliance with internal control policies and procedures and its effectiveness in safeguarding assets.

information system library A collection of corporate databases, files, and programs in a separate storage area.

information systems steering committee Plans and oversees the information systems function. The committee often consists of high-level management people, such as the controller and systems and user-department management. The steering committee sets policies that govern the AIS and ensures top-management participation, guidance, and control.

inherent risk The susceptibility of a set of accounts or transactions to significant control problems in the absence of internal control.

initial investigation A preliminary investigation to determine if a proposed new system is both needed and possible.

input Data entered into the computer system either from an external storage device or from the keyboard of the computer.

input controls Controls that ensure that only accurate, valid, and authorized data is entered into the system.

input controls matrix A matrix that shows the control procedures applied to each field of an input record.

input validation routines Computer programs or routines designed to check the validity or accuracy of input data.

inquiry processing Processing user information queries by searching data bases for the desired information and then organizing the information into an appropriate response.

insert anomaly A problem that can arise in a poorly designed relational database when attributes that are not characteristics of the primary key of a relation are stored in that table. The problem arises because new information about those attributes cannot be entered in the database without violating integrity rules. For example, assume that information about vendors is only stored as part of the purchases table. Data about potential new vendors, or about alternate suppliers, could not be added until a purchase from them was made. Otherwise, the purchase order number column, the primary key of the purchases table, would have a null value, violating the entity integrity rule.

integrated test facility A testing technique in which a dummy company or division is introduced into the company's computer system. Test transactions may then be conducted on these fictitious records without affecting the real records. Test transactions may be processed along with real transactions, and the employees of the computer facility need not be aware that testing is being done.

integration Eliminating duplicate recording, storage, reporting, and other processing activities in an organization. For example, companies that used to have separate programs to prepare customer statements, collect cash, and maintain accounts receivable records now combine these functions into a single application.

integrity Protecting data from unauthorized tampering.

interactive control system Helps top-level managers with high-level activities that demand frequent and regular attention such as developing company strategy, setting company objectives, understanding and assessing threats and risks, monitoring changes in competitive conditions and emerging technologies, and developing responses and action plans to proactively deal with these high-level issues.

internal control flowchart A document flowchart that describes and evaluates internal controls. Often used by auditors in the planning stage of an audit.

Internal Control Integrated Framework A framework developed by COSO to define internal controls as well as to provide guidance for evaluating and enhancing internal control systems. It is widely accepted as the authority on internal controls.

internal controls Controls within a business organization that ensure information is processed correctly.

internal control structure The plan of organization and the methods and measures adopted within a business to safeguard its assets, maintain records that accurately and fairly reflect company assets, check the accuracy and reliability of its accounting data, provide assurance that financial reporting is prepared in accordance with GAAP, promote operational efficiency, comply with applicable laws and regulations, and encourage adherence to prescribed managerial policies.

internal environment The tone or culture of a company that helps determine the risk consciousness of employees. It is the foundation for all other ERM components, providing discipline and structure. It is essentially the same thing as the control environment in the internal control framework.

internal labels Labels written in machine-readable form on a magnetic storage medium that identify the data contained on the storage medium. Internal labels include volume, header, and trailer labels.

internal rate of return (IRR) The effective interest rate that equates the present value of total costs to the present value of total savings.

internal-level schema A low-level view of the entire database describing how the data are actually stored and accessed. It includes information about record layouts, definitions, addresses, indexes, and so forth. Contrast with *external-level schemas* and *conceptual-level schemas.*

Internet misinformation Using the Internet to spread false or misleading information. This can be done in a number of ways, including inflammatory messages in online chats, setting up Web sites, and spreading urban legends.

Internet Protocol (IP) Protocol that specifies the structure of the TCP packets and how to route them to the proper destination.

Internet service providers (ISPs) Companies that provide connections to the Internet for individuals and other companies.

Internet terrorism Hackers using the Internet to disrupt electronic commerce and destroy company or individual communications.

intranet An internal network that can connect to the main Internet and be navigated with browser software. It is usually closed off from the general public.

intrusion detection systems (IDS) A system that creates logs of all network traffic that was permitted to pass the firewall and then analyzes those logs for signs of attempted or successful intrusions.

intrusion prevention systems (IPS) A new type of filter designed to identify and drop packets that are part of an attack.

inventory control The function of determining what, when, and how much inventory to purchase.

J

job-order costing A cost system that assigns costs to specific production batches or jobs; it is used when the product or service being sold can be distinctly identified.

job-time ticket A document used to collect data about labor activity by recording the amount of time a worker spent on each specific job task.

journal voucher A form used to document one or more journal entries such as those made to update the general ledger.

just-in-time (JIT) inventory system A system that minimizes or virtually eliminates manufacturing inventories by scheduling inventory deliveries at the precise times and locations needed. Instead of making infrequent bulk deliveries to a central receiving and storage facility, suppliers deliver materials in small lots at frequent intervals to the specific locations that require them.

just-in-time (JIT) manufacturing Manufacturing systems with short planning horizons whose goal is to minimize or eliminate inventories of raw materials, work in process, and finished goods. JIT is often referred to as pull manufacturing because goods are produced in response to customer demand. Theoretically, JIT manufacturing systems produce only in response to customer orders. In practice, however, most JIT manufacturing systems develop short-run production plans.

K

key A unique identification code assigned to each data record within a system.

key escrow The process of storing a copy of an encryption key in a secure location.

key logger Using spyware to record a user's keystokes, e-mails sent and received, Web sites visited, and chat session participation.

key verification Checking the accuracy of data entry by having two people enter the same data using a key-operated device. The computer then compares the two sets of keystrokes to determine if the data were entered correctly.

key-to-disk encoder Several keying stations linked to a computer. Data may be entered simultaneously from each of the key stations and pooled on a disk file.

key-to-tape encoder A device for keying in data and recording the data on magnetic tape.

kickbacks Gifts given by vendors to purchasing agents for the purpose of influencing their choice of suppliers.

kiting A fraud scheme where the perpetrator conceals a theft of cash by creating cash through the transfer of money between banks. For example, suppose a fraud perpetrator opens checking accounts in banks A, B, and C. Then the perpetrator "creates" cash by depositing a $1,000 check from bank A into bank B and then withdraws the $1,000 from bank B. Since there are insufficient funds in bank A to cover the $1,000 check, the perpetrator deposits a $1,000 check from bank C to bank A before his check to bank B clears the bank A. Since bank C also has insufficient funds, $1,000 must be deposited to bank C before the check to bank A clears. The check to bank C is written from bank B, which also has insufficient funds. The scheme continues, with checks and deposits occurring as needed to keep the checks from bouncing.

L

LAN See *local area network*.

lapping Concealing the theft of cash by means of a series of delays in posting collections to accounts. For example, a perpetrator steals customer A's accounts receivable payment. Funds received at a later date from customer B are used to pay off customer A's balance. Funds from customer C are used to pay off B's balance, and so forth.

lean manufacturing The goal of lean manufacturing is to minimize or eliminate inventories of raw materials, work in process, and finished goods. Lean manufacturing is often referred to as *pull manufacturing* because goods are produced in response to customer demand.

legal feasibility The dimension of feasibility that determines if there will be any conflicts between the system under consideration and the organization's ability to discharge its legal obligations.

likelihood The probability that a threat to an AIS will come to pass.

limit check An edit check to ensure that a numerical amount in a record does not exceed some predetermined limit.

line count Total number of lines entered during a data processing session.

local area network (LAN) A network that links computers, printers, and other electronic equipment located within a limited geographical area, such as a single building.

lockbox A postal address to which customers send their remittances. This post office box is maintained by the participating bank, which picks up the checks each day and deposits them to the company's account. The bank sends the remittance advices, an electronic list of all remittances, and digital copies of all checks to the company.

log analysis The process of examining logs to monitor security.

logic errors Errors that occur when the instructions given to the computer do not accomplish the desired objective. Contrast with *syntax errors*.

logic time bomb A program that lies idle until some specified circumstance or a particular time triggers it. Once triggered, the program sabotages the system by destroying programs or data.

logical access The ability to use computer equipment to access company data.

logical models Descriptions of a system that focus on the essential activities and flow of information in the system irrespective of how the flow is actually accomplished.

logical view The manner in which a user or programmer conceptually organizes, views, and understands the relationships among data items. Contrast with *physical view*.

low-cost strategy Striving to be the most efficient producer of a product or service.

M

magnetic disks Magnetic storage media consisting of one or more flat round disks with a magnetic surface on which data can be written.

magnetic ink character recognition (MICR) The recognition of characters printed by a machine that uses special magnetic ink.

magnetic tape A secondary storage medium that is about 1/2 inch in width and that has a magnetic surface on which data can be stored. The most popular types are seven-track and nine-track tapes.

mainframe computers Large digital computers, typically with a separate stand-alone CPU.

management audit A review of how well management is utilizing company resources and how well company operations and programs follow established objectives.

management by exception A method for interpreting variances displayed on performance reports. If the performance report shows actual performance to be at or near budgeted figures, a manager can assume that the item is under control and that no action needs to be taken. On the other hand, significant deviations from budgeted amounts, in *either* direction, signal the need to investigate the cause of the discrepancy and take appropriate action to correct the problem.

management control Activities by management designed to motivate, encourage, and assist officers and employees in achieving corporate goals and objectives as effectively and efficiently as possible.

management information system The set of human and capital resources in an organization that are dedicated to collecting and processing data so that all levels of management have the information they need to plan and control the activities of the organization.

mandatory information Information required by a governmental entity (such as a report to the IRS on taxable income and withholdings). Contrast with e*ssential* and *discretionary information*.

manual information system Information system in which most data processing is completed by people without the use of computers.

manufacturing overhead All manufacturing costs that are not economically feasible to trace directly to specific jobs or processes.

manufacturing resource planning (MRP-II) An extension of materials resource planning that seeks to balance existing production capacity and raw materials needs to meet forecasted sales demands. Also referred to as "push manufacturing" because goods are produced in expectation of customer demand.

many-to-many (M:N) relationship A relationship between two entities where each entity can be associated with many instances of the other entity. For example, each inventory item can be sold to many different customers and each customer can order many different inventory items.

mapping programs Programs activated during regular processing that provide information as to which portions of the application program were not executed.

masquerading When a perpetrator gains access to a system by pretending to be an authorized user. This approach requires that the perpetrator know the legitimate user's identification numbers and passwords.

master file A permanent file of records that stores cumulative information about an organization's resources and the agents with whom it interacts. As transactions take place, individual records within a master file are updated to keep them current.

master plan A long-range planning document that specifies the overall information system plan of an organization. It shows what the system will consist of, how it will be developed, who will develop it, how needed resources will be acquired, and where the AIS is headed.

master production schedule (MPS) Specifies how much of each product is to be produced during the planning period and when that production should occur.

materiality The concept that an auditor should focus on detecting and reporting only those errors, deficiencies, and omissions that could possibly have a significant impact on decisions.

materials requirements planning (MRP) An approach to inventory management that seeks to reduce required inventory levels by improving the accuracy of forecasting techniques to better schedule purchases to satisfy production needs.

materials requisition Authorizes the removal of the necessary quantity of raw materials from the storeroom to the factory location in which production operations are to begin.

maximum cardinality The maximum number of instances that an entity can be linked to the other entity in the relationship.

message The data transmitted over a data communication system.

message acknowledgment techniques Techniques that let the sender of an electronic message know that a message was received. They include echo checks, trailer records, and numbered batches.

minimum cardinality The minimum number of instances that an entity can be linked to the other entity in the relationship.

misappropriation of assets See *employee fraud*.

modular conversion An approach for converting from an old system to a new system in which parts of the old system are gradually replaced by the new until the old system has been entirely replaced.

monthly statement A document summarizing all transactions that occurred during the past month and informing customers of their current account balance.

move tickets Documents that identify the internal transfer of parts, the location to which they are transferred, and the time of the transfer.

multifactor authentication The use of two or more authentication methods (passwords, ID badges, biometrics, etc.) in conjunction to achieve a greater level of security.

mutual authentication scheme A routing verification procedure that requires both computers to exchange their passwords before communication takes place.

N

narrative description Written, step-by-step explanation of system components and how the components interact.

needs-based strategic position Trying to serve most or all of the needs of a particular group of customers in a target market.

net present value (NPV) A value determined by discounting all estimated future cash flows back to the present, using a discount rate that reflects the time value of money to the organization.

network A group of interconnected computers and terminals; a series of locations tied together by communications channels.

network administrator One who installs, manages, and supports a network. The network administrator also controls access to the network and maintains the shared software and data.

network interface card (NIC) The device needed to connect a computer or peripheral to a data communications network.

network managers Responsible for ensuring that all applicable devices are linked to the organization's internal and external networks and that the networks operate continuously and properly.

neural networks Computing systems that imitate the brain's learning process by using a network of interconnected processors that perform multiple operations simultaneously and interact dynamically. Neural networks recognize and understand voice, face, and word patterns much more successfully than do regular computers and humans.

nonoperational (or **throwaway**) **prototypes** Prototypes that are discarded, but the system requirements identified from the prototypes are used to develop a new system.

nonvoucher system A method for processing accounts payable in which each approved invoice is posted to individual vendor records in the accounts payable file and is then stored in an open invoice file. When a check is written to pay for an invoice, the invoice is removed from the open invoice file, marked paid, and stored in the paid invoice file. Contrast with *voucher system*.

normalization The process of following the guidelines for properly designing a relational database that is free from delete, insert, and update anomalies.

O

off-line devices Devices that are not connected to or controlled by a computer or network. Off-line devices are used to prepare data for entry into the computer system (e.g., key-to-tape encoder, keypunch/verification equipment). Contrast with *on-line devices*.

one-to-many (1:N) relationship A relationship between two entities where one entity in the relationship can be associated with many instances of the other entity in that relationship.

one-to-one (1:1) relationship A relationship between two entities where one entity in the relationship is associated with only one instance of the other entity in the relationship.

on-line analytical processing (OLAP) Tools that provide access to information stored in a data warehouse by using queries to investigate hypothesized relationships.

on-line batch processing Processing in which the computer captures data electronically and stores it so that it can be processed later.

on-line devices Hardware devices that are connected directly to the CPU by a cable or telephone line.

on-line processing Processing individual transactions as they occur and from their point of origin rather than accumulating them to be processed in batches. Online processing requires the use of on-line data entry terminals and direct access file storage media so that each master record can be accessed directly.

on-line, real-time processing The computer system processes data immediately after capture and provides updated information to the user on a timely basis.

open-invoice method Method for maintaining accounts receivable in which customers typically pay according to each invoice. Usually, two copies of the invoice are mailed to the customer, who is requested to return one copy with the payment.

operating budget A report that projects an organization's revenues and expenses for a given time period, usually a month or a year. Typically, operating budgets are structured along the lines of financial statements.

operating system A software program that controls the overall operation of a computer system. Its functions include controlling the execution of computer programs, scheduling, debugging, assigning storage areas, managing data, and controlling input and output.

operational audit See *management audit.*

operational control Decisions that are concerned with the efficient and effective performance of specific tasks in an organization.

operational document A document that is generated as an output of transaction processing activities. Examples include purchase orders, customer statements, and employee paychecks. Contrast with *source document.*

operational feasibility The dimension of feasibility concerned with whether a proposed system will be used by the people in an organization. It also is concerned with how useful the system will be within the operating environment of the organization.

operational prototypes Prototypes that are further developed into fully functional systems.

operations and maintenance The last phase of the system development life cycle where follow-up studies are conducted to detect and correct design deficiencies. Minor modifications will be made as problems arise in the new system.

operations list A document that specifies the labor and machine requirements needed to manufacture a product. It indicates how a product moves through the factory, specifying what is done at each step and how much time each operation should take.

operations objectives Objectives that deal with the effectiveness and efficiency of company operations, such as performance and profitability goals and safeguarding assets.

opportunity The condition or situation that allows a person or organization to commit and conceal a dishonest act and convert it to personal gain.

Optical Character Recognition (OCR) The use of light-sensitive hardware devices to convert characters readable by humans into computer input. Since OCR readers can read only certain items, a special machine-readable font must be used.

output The information produced by a system. Output is typically produced for the use of a particular individual or group of users.

ordering costs All expenses associated with processing purchase transactions.

output controls Controls that regulate system output.

outsourcing Hiring an outside company to handle all or part of the data processing activities.

P

packet sniffers Programs that capture data from information packets as they travel over the Internet or company networks. Captured data is sifted to find confidential or proprietary information that can be sold or otherwise used.

packing slip A document listing the quantity and description of each item included in a shipment.

parallel conversion A systems conversion approach in which the new and old systems are run simultaneously until the organization is assured that the new system is functioning correctly.

parallel simulation An approach auditors use to detect unauthorized program changes and data processing accuracy. The auditor writes his or her own version of a program and then reprocesses data. The output of the auditor's program and the client's program are compared to verify that they are the same.

parity bit An extra bit added to a byte and magnetized as needed to ensure that there is always an odd (or even) number of magnetized bits. The computer uses the odd (or even) parity scheme to check the accuracy of each item of data.

parity checking As a computer reads or receives a set of characters, it verifies that there are the proper number of magnetized bits in each character received. If not, the corresponding character may contain an error.

password A series of letters, numbers, or both that must be entered to access and use system resources. Password use helps prevent unauthorized tampering with hardware, software, and the organization's data.

password cracking Occurs when an intruder penetrates a system's defenses, steals the file containing valid passwords, decrypts them, and uses them to gain access to system resources such as programs, files, and data.

patch Code released by software developers that fixes a particular vulnerability.

patch management The process of regularly applying patches and updates to software used by the organization.

payback period The number of years required for the net savings to equal the initial cost of an investment.

payroll clearing account A general ledger account used to check the accuracy and completeness of recording payroll costs and their subsequent allocation to appropriate cost centers.

payroll register A listing of payroll data for each employee for a payroll period.

payroll service bureau An organization that maintains the payroll master file for each of its clients and performs their payroll processing activities for a fee.

penetration test An authorized attempt by either an internal audit team or an external security consulting firm to break into the organization's information system.

performance evaluations A project development control that requires evaluating each module or task as it is completed.

performance objectives The overall performance goals that an entity wishes to achieve.

performance report A report that compares standard, or expected, performances with actual performance and also shows the variances, or differences, between the two. Used for financial control. Contrast with *budget*.

peripherals The hardware devices (input, output, processing, and data communications) that are connected to a CPU.

personal digital assistant (PDA) A handheld computer that has had a significant impact on personal productivity.

personal identification number (PIN) A confidential code that allows an individual to gain access to a system and the data or resources stored in that system.

phase-in conversion See *modular conversion*.

phishing Sending an e-mail pretending to be a legitimate company, usually a financial institution, and requesting information. The recipient is asked to either respond to the e-mail request or visit a Web page and submit the data. The request is bogus, and the information gathered is used to commit identity theft or to steal funds from the victim's account.

phreaker A hacker who attacks phone systems.

physical access Ability to physically use computer equipment.

physical design A phase of the system development life cycle where the broad, user-oriented requirements of the conceptual design are implemented by creating a detailed set of specifications that are used to code and test the computer programs.

physical model The description of how a system functions by describing the flow of documents, the computer processes performed and the people performing them, the equipment used, and other physical elements of the system.

physical systems design The phase of the systems development life cycle in which the designer specifies the hardware, software, and procedures for delivering the conceptual systems design.

physical systems design report A report prepared at the end of the physical design phase that describes the system and summarizes what was accomplished. Management uses this report to decide whether or not to proceed to the implementation phase.

physical view The way data are physically arranged and stored in the computer system. Contrast with *logical view*.

picking ticket A document authorizing the inventory control function to release merchandise to the shipping department. The picking ticket is often printed so that the item numbers and quantities are listed in the sequence in which they can be most efficiently retrieved from the warehouse.

piggybacking When a perpetrator latches on to a legitimate user who is logging in to a system. The legitimate user unknowingly carries the perpetrator with him as he is allowed into the system.

pilot conversion The implementation of a system in just one part of the organization, such as a branch location. This approach localizes conversion problems and allows training in a live environment. Disadvantages are the long conversion times and the need to interface the old system with the new system.

plaintext Normal text that has not been encrypted.

point scoring An objective procedure in which weighted selection criteria are used to evaluate the overall merits of vendor proposals.

point-of-sale (POS) devices Electronic devices used to record sales information at the time of the sale and to perform other data processing functions.

policies The rules that provide a formal direction for achieving performance objectives and that enable performance.

policy and procedures manual A management tool for assigning authority and responsibility. It explains proper business practices, describes the knowledge and experience needed by key personnel, spells out management policy for handling specific transactions, and documents the systems and procedures employed to process those transactions.

post-implementation review Review made after a new system has been operating for a brief period. The purpose is to ensure that the new system is meeting its planned objectives, to identify the adequacy of system standards, and to review system controls.

post-implementation review report A report that analyzes a newly delivered system to determine if the system achieved its intended purpose and was completed within budget.

preformatting An on-line data entry control in which the computer displays a form on the screen and the user fills in the blanks on the form as needed.

pressure A person's incentive or motivation for committing fraud.

preventive controls Controls that deter problems before they arise. Hiring qualified accounting personnel; appropriately segregating employee duties; and effectively controlling physical access to assets, facilities, and information are effective preventive controls.

preventive maintenance A program of regularly examining the hardware components of a computer and replacing any that are found to be weak.

primary activities Activities in the value chain that are performed to create, market, and deliver products and services to customers and provide post-delivery service and support. Primary activities include production, shipping and receiving, and marketing.

primary key The attribute, or combination of attributes, that uniquely identifies a specific row in a database table. The primary key is used to distinguish, order, and reference records in a database.

private key system An encryption system in which both the sender and the receiver have access to the key but do not allow others access to the same key.

process A set of actions, automated or manual, that transform data into other data or information.

process costing A cost system that assigns costs to each process, or work center, in the production cycle, and then calculates the average cost for all units produced. Process costing is used when masses of similar goods or services are produced or sold.

processing controls Controls that ensure that all transactions are processed accurately and completely and that all files and records are properly updated.

processing test transactions Running hypothetical transactions through a new system to test for processing errors.

procurement card A corporate credit card that employees can use to purchase specific kinds of items.

product differentiation strategy Adding features or services not provided by competitors to a product to be able to charge customers a premium price.

production cycle The recurring set of business activities and related data processing operations associated with the manufacture of products.

production order A document authorizing the manufacture of a specified quantity of a particular product. It lists the operations to be performed, the quantity to be produced, and the location to which the finished product is to be delivered.

professional employer organization (PEO) An organization that processes payroll and also provides human resource management services such as employee benefit design and administration.

profitability analysis report Reports used to assess overall marketing performance by breaking down the marginal profit contribution made by each territory, customer, distribution channel, salesperson, product, or other basis. Contrast with *sales analysis report.*

program A set of instructions that can be executed by a computer.

programmer The person that takes the design provided by systems analysts and creates an information system by writing the computer programs.

programming The process of writing software programs to accomplish a specific task or set of tasks.

program evaluation and review technique (PERT) A commonly used technique for planning, coordinating, controlling, and scheduling complex projects such as systems implementation.

program flowchart A diagrammatical representation of the sequence of logical operations performed by a computer in executing a program. A program flowchart describes the specific logic to perform a process shown on a system flowchart.

program maintenance The revision of a computer program to meet new program instructions, satisfy system demands such as the need for a new report, to correct an error, or make changes in file content.

program tracing A technique used to obtain detailed knowledge of the logic of an application program as well as to test the program's compliance with its control specifications.

project development plan A document that shows how a project will be completed, including the modules or tasks to be performed and who will perform them, the dates they should be completed, and project costs.

project development team A group of people consisting of specialists, management, and users that develop a project's plan and direct the steps of the systems development life cycle. The team monitors costs, progress, employees, and gives status reports to top management and to the steering committee.

project milestones Significant points in a development effort where a formal review of progress is made.

projection A way of resisting change by blaming anything and everything on the new system. The system becomes the scapegoat for all real and imagined problems and errors.

prompting An on-line data entry control that uses the computer to control the data entry process. The system displays a request to the user for each required item of input data and then waits for an acceptable response before requesting the next required item.

proposal to conduct systems analysis A document calling for the analysis of either an existing or a proposed system. This document is prepared by a user or department and requests the information systems function to analyze the feasibility of developing a system to perform a specific function.

protocol The set of rules governing the exchange of data between two systems or components of a system.

prototype A simplified working model of an information system used in prototyping.

prototyping An approach to systems design in which a simplified working model, or prototype, of an information system is developed. The users experiment with the prototype to determine what they like and do not like about the system. The developers make modifications until the users are satisfied with the system.

Public Company Accounting Oversight Board (PCAOB) A five member board that regulates the auditing profession. The PCAOB was created as part of the Sarbanes-Oxley Bill and its members are appointed and overseen by the SEC.

public key infrastructure (PKI) An approach to encryption that uses two keys: a public key that is publicly available and a private key that is kept secret and known only by the owner of that pair of keys. With PKI, either key (the public or private) can be used to encode a message, but only the other key in that public-private pair can be used to decode that message.

purchase order A document that formally requests a vendor to sell and deliver specified products at designated prices. It is also a promise to pay and becomes a contract once the vendor accepts it.

purchase requisition A document or electronic form that identifies the requisitioner; specifies the delivery location and date needed; identifies the item numbers, descriptions, quantity, and price of each item requested; and may suggest a vendor.

Q

query A request for specific information from a computer. When the information is found, it is retrieved, displayed, or analyzed as requested. Queries are often used with a database management system to extract data from the database.

query languages Languages used to process data files and to obtain quick responses to questions about those files.

query-by-example (QBE) languages Graphical query languages for retrieving information from a relational database.

R

random access memory (RAM) A temporary storage location for computer instructions and data.

random surveillance Way of detecting fraud by having auditors periodically audit the system and test system controls. Informing employees that the auditors will conduct random surveillance is a deterrent to computer crime.

range check An edit check designed to verify that a data item falls within a certain predetermined range of acceptable values.

rationalization The excuse that fraud perpetrators use to justify their illegal behavior.

REA data model A data model used to design AIS databases. REA is an acronym signifying that the data model contains information about three fundamental objects: resources, events, and agents. Resources represent identifiable objects that have economic value to the organization. Events represent an organization's business activities. Agents represent the people or organizations about which data are collected.

real-time notification A variation of the embedded audit module in which the auditor is notified of each transaction as it occurs by means of a message printed on the auditor's terminal.

real-time system A system that is able to respond to an inquiry or provide data fast enough to make the information meaningful to the user. Real-time systems are usually designed for very fast response.

reasonable assurance The concept that an auditor cannot seek complete assurance that an item is correct, since to do so would be prohibitively expensive. Instead, the auditor accepts a reasonable degree of risk that the audit conclusion is incorrect.

reasonableness test An edit check of the logical correctness of relationships among data items. For example, a journal entry that debits inventory and credits wages payable is not reasonable.

receiving report A document that records details about each delivery, including the date received, shipper, vendor, and purchase order number.

record A set of logically related data items that describe specific attributes of an entity, such as all payroll data relating to a single employee.

record count A total of the number of input documents in a process or the number of records processed at a given time.

record layout A document that illustrates the arrangement of items of data in input, output, and file records.

recovery point objective (RPO) The length of time between the last backup and the time that an incident occurred. The RPO represents the period of time for which management is willing to have to reenter, if possible, data about past transactions.

recovery procedures A set of procedures that is followed if the computer quits during data processing. The procedures allow the user to recover from hardware or software failures.

recovery time objective (RTO) The time by which the organization's information system must be available again following a disaster.

redundant data check An edit check that requires the inclusion of two identifiers in each input record (e.g., the customer's account number and the first five letters of the customer's name). If these input values do not match those on the record, the record will not be updated.

reengineering See *business process reengineering.*

referential integrity rule A constraint in relational database design requiring that any non-null value of a foreign key must correspond to a primary key in the referenced table. For example, if vendor number is a foreign key in the inventory table, to indicate the preferred source of that item, then any vendor number appearing in that table must appear as a primary key value in the vendor table. This constraint ensures consistency in the database. Note, however, that the foreign key can be null, if there is no existing relationship between the two tables. For example, a null value for vendor number in any row in the inventory table would indicate that there is no preferred vendor for that inventory item.

relational data model A database model in which all data elements are logically viewed as being stored in the form of two-dimensional tables called "relations." In these tables each row represents a unique entity or record. Each column represents a field where the record's attributes are stored. The tables serve as the building blocks from which data relationships can be created.

relational database A database management system that uses the relational data model developed by Dr. E. F. Codd in 1970.

relations The tables used to store data in a relational database.

remittance advice An enclosure included with a customer's payment that indicates the invoices, statements, or other items paid.

remittance list A document listing all checks received in the mail.

remote batch processing Accumulating transaction records in batches at some remote location and then transmitting them electronically to a central location for processing.

Remote Authentication Dial-In User Service (RADIUS) A standard method for verifying the identity of users attempting to connect via dial-in access. Users connect to a remote access server and submit their login credentials. The remote access server passes those credentials to the RADIUS server, which performs compatibility tests to authenticate the identity of that user.

reorder point The level to which the inventory balance of an item must fall before an order to replenish stock is initiated.

report System output organized in a meaningful fashion. Used by employees to control operational activities, by managers to make decisions and design strategies, and by investors and creditors to gather information about a company's business activities. Prepared for both internal and external use.

reporting objectives Objectives to help ensure the accuracy, completeness, and reliability of internal and external company reports, of both a financial and non-financial nature. They also improve decision making and monitor company activities and performance more efficiently.

report writers A language that simplifies report creation. Typically, users need only specify which data elements they want printed and how the report should be formatted. The report writer searches the database, extracts the specified data items, and prints them according to the user-specified format.

reprocessing An approach auditors use to detect unauthorized program changes. The auditor verifies the integrity of an application program and then saves it for future use. At subsequent intervals, and on a surprise basis, the auditor uses the previously verified version of the program to reprocess transaction data. The output of the two runs is compared and discrepancies are investigated.

request for proposal (RFP) A request by an organization or department for vendors to bid on hardware, software, or services.

request for systems development A written request for a new or improved system. The request describes the current system's problems, why the change is needed, and the proposed system's goals and objectives as well as its anticipated benefits and costs.

requirements costing A system evaluation method in which a list is made of all required features. If a proposed system does not have a desired feature, the cost of developing or purchasing that feature is added to the basic cost of the system. This method allows different systems to be compared and evaluated based on the costs of providing the required features.

residual risk The risk that remains after management implements internal controls or some other form of response to risk.

resources Those things that have economic value to an organization such as cash, inventory, supplies, factories, and land.

response time The amount of time that elapses between making a query and receiving a response.

responsibility accounting A system of reporting financial results on the basis of managerial responsibilities within an organization.

restoration The process of installing the backup copy of a data base of file for use in data processing.

revenue cycle The recurring set of business activities and information-processing operations associated with providing goods and

services to customers and collecting cash in payment for those sales.

risk The likelihood that a threat or hazard will actually come to pass.

risk appetite The amount of risk a company is willing to accept to achieve its goals and objectives.

rollback A process whereby a log of all pre-update values is prepared for each record that is updated within a particular interval. If there is a system failure, the records can be restored to the pre-update values and the processing restarted.

round-down technique A fraud technique used in financial institutions that pay interest. The programmer instructs the computer to round down all interest calculations to two decimal places. The fraction of a cent rounded down on each calculation is put into the programmer's own account.

routers Special purpose devices that are designed to read the destination address fields in IP packet headers to decide where to send (route) the packet next.

routing verification procedures Controls to ensure that messages are not routed to the wrong system address. Examples are header labels, mutual authentication schemes, and dial-back.

run-to-run totals Comparison of the new balance of an updated general ledger account to its prior balance plus the sum of all current period debits and credits.

S

sabotage An intentional act where the intent is to destroy a system or some of its components.

salami technique A fraud technique in which tiny slices of money are stolen from many different accounts.

sales analysis report Reports used to assess the efficiency and effectiveness of the sales force by breaking down sales by salesperson, region, or product. Contrast with *profitability analysis report.*

sales invoice A document notifying customers of the amount of a sale and where to send payment.

sales order The document created during sales order entry listing the item numbers, quantities, prices, and terms of the sale.

Sarbanes-Oxley Act (SOX) A law passed by Congress in 2002. SOX applies to publicly held companies and their auditors and is intended to prevent financial statement fraud, make financial reports more transparent, provide protection to investors, strengthen the internal controls at public companies, and punish executives who perpetrate fraud.

scanning routines Software routines that search a program for the occurrence of a particular variable name or other combinations of characters.

scavenging Searching for corporate or personal records to gain unauthorized access to confidential information. Scavenging methods include searching garbage cans, communal trash bins, and city dumps to find documents or printouts with confidential personal or company information.

scheduled reports Reports that are generated by a system at specified time intervals.

scheduling feasibility The dimension of feasibility that determines if the system being developed can be implemented in the time allotted.

schema A description of the types of data elements that are in the database, the relationships among the data elements, and the structure or overall logical model used to organize and describe the data.

secondary key A field that can be used to identify records in a file. Unlike the primary key, it does not provide a unique identification.

security management Ensures that all aspects of the system are secure and protected from all internal and external threats.

segregation of accounting duties Separating the accounting functions of authorization, custody, and recording so as to minimize an employee's ability to comitt fraud.

segregation of duties The separation of assigned duties and responsibilities in such a way that no single employee can both perpetrate and conceal errors or irregularities.

segregation of systems duties Implementing control procedures to clearly divide authority and responsibility within the information system function to prevent employees from perpetrating and concealing fraud.

semistructured decisions Decisions that require subjective assessment and judgment to supplement formal data analysis.

sequence check An edit check that determines if a batch of input data is in the proper numerical or alphabetical sequence.

sequence codes Documents are numbered consecutively to account for them, Any gaps in the sequence code indicate missing documents that should be investigated. Examples of documents that are given sequence codes include prenumbered checks, invoices, and purchase orders.

sequential access An access method that requires data items to be accessed in the same order in which they were written.

sequential file A way of storing numeric or alphabetical records according to a key (e.g., customer numbers from 00001 to 99999). To access a sequential file record, the system starts at the beginning of the file and reads each record until the desired record is located.

sequential file processing Processing a master file sequentially from beginning to end. The master and transaction files are processed in the same predetermined order, such as alphabetically.

server High-capacity computer that contains the network software to handle communications, storage, and resource-sharing needs of other computers in the network. The server also contains the application software and data common to all users.

shoulder surfing Watching people enter telephone calling card or credit card numbers or listen as they give credit-card numbers over the telephone or to a clerk.

sign check An edit check that verifies that the data in a field have the appropriate arithmetic sign.

size check An edit check that ensures the input data will fit into the assigned field.

smart cards Plastic cards containing a microprocessor, memory chips, and software that can store up to three pages of text. Used in Europe as a credit or ATM card.

snapshot technique An audit technique that records the content of both a transaction record and a related master file record before and after each processing step.

social engineering Using deception to obtain unauthorized access to information resources. Access is usually obtained by fooling an employee.

software agents Computer programs that learn how to do often-performed, tedious, timeconsuming, or complex tasks.

software piracy The unauthorized copying of software.

source code (or **source program**) A computer program written in a source language such as BASIC, COBOL, or assembly language. The source program is translated into the object (machine language) program by a translation program such as a compiler or assembler.

source data automation (SDA) The collection of transaction data in machine-readable form at the time and place of origin. Examples of SDA devices are optical scanners and ATMs.

source documents Contain the initial record of a transaction that takes place. Examples of source documents, which are usually recorded on preprinted forms, include sales invoices, purchase orders, and employee time cards. Contrast with *operational document.*

Spamming Simultaneously e-mailing the same unsolicited message to many people, often in an attempt to sell them some product.

special-purpose analysis reports Reports that have no prespecified content or format and are not prepared according to any regular schedule; rather, they are generally prepared in response to a management request to investigate a specific problem or opportunity.

specialized journals Journals where large numbers of repetitive transactions—such as credit sales, cash receipts, purchases on account, and cash disbursements—are recorded.

specific authorization When an employee must get special approval before handling a transaction.

spoofing Altering an e-mail message to make it look as if someone else sent it.

spyware Software that monitors computing habits and sends the data to someone else, often without the computer user's permission.

standards The required procedures implemented to meet the policies.

stateful packet filtering A technique employed by firewalls in which a table is maintained that lists all established connections between the organization's computers and the Internet. The firewall consults this table to determine whether an incoming packet is part of an ongoing communication initiated by an internal computer.

static packet filtering A process that screens individual IP packets based solely on the contents of the source and/or destination fields in the IP packet header.

steering committee An executive-level committee to plan and oversee the information systems function. The committee typically consists of management from the systems department, the controller, and other management affected by the information systems function.

strategic master plan An organization's multiple-year plan that serves as a technological road map and lays out the projects the company must complete to achieve its long-range goals.

strategic objectives High-level goals that are aligned with and support the company's mission.

strategic planning Decisions that establish the organization's objectives and policies for accomplishing those objectives.

structured decisions Decisions that are repetitive, routine, and understood well enough that they can be delegated to the lower-level employees of an organization.

structured programming A modular approach to programming in which each module performs a specific function, stands alone, and is coordinated by a control module.

structured query language (SQL) A text-based query language provided by most relational DBMSs. Powerful queries can be built using three basic keywords: SELECT, FROM, and WHERE.

structured relationships Relationships in program design in which every event entity is linked to a resource entity and two agent entities.

structured walkthrough A formal program design review process. One or more programmers walk through another programmer's logic and code to detect weaknesses and errors in program design.

subschema (1) A subset of the schema that includes only those data items used in a particular application program or by a particular user. (2) The way the user defines the data and the data relationships.

subsidiary ledgers Used to record the detailed data for any general ledger account that has many individual subaccounts. Subsidiary ledgers are commonly used for accounts receivable, inventory, fixed assets, and accounts payable.

subsystems Smaller systems that are a part of the entire information system. Each subsystem performs a specific function that is important to and that supports the system of which it is a part.

superzapping The unauthorized use of a special system program to bypass regular system controls and perform illegal acts. The superzap utility was originally written to handle emergencies, such as restoring a system that had crashed.

supply chain An extended system that includes an organization's value chain as well as its suppliers, distributors, and customers.

support activities Activities in the value chain that enable the primary activities to be performed efficiently and effectively. Examples include administration, purchasing, and human resources.

symmetric encryption systems Encryption systems that use the same key both to encrypt and to decrypt.

synchronous transmission Data transmission in which start and stop bits are required only at the beginning and end of a block of characters. Contrast with *asynchronous transmission.*

synergy When an entire system of organizational activities is greater than the sum of each individual part.

syntax errors Errors that result from using the programming language improperly or from incorrectly typing the source program.

system (1) An entity consisting of two or more components or subsystems that interact to achieve a goal. (2) The equipment and programs that comprise a complete computer installation. (3) The programs and related procedures that perform a single task on a computer.

systems administrator Ensures that an information system operates smoothly and efficiently.

system control audit review file (SCARF) A concurrent audit technique that embeds audit modules into application software to continuously monitor all transaction activity and collect data on transactions having special audit significance.

system flowchart A diagrammatical representation that shows the flow of data through a series of operations in an automated data processing system. It shows how data are captured and put into the system, the processes that operate on the data, and system outputs.

system performance measurements Measurements used to evaluate and assess a system. Common measurements include

throughput (output per unit of time), utilization (percentage of time the system is being productively used), and response time (how long it takes the system to respond).

system review A step in internal control evaluation in which it is determined if the necessary control procedures have been prescribed.

systems analysis (1) A rigorous and systematic approach to decision making, characterized by a comprehensive definition of available alternatives and an exhaustive analysis of the merits of each alternative as a basis for choosing the best alternative. (2) Examination of user information requirements in an organization to establish objectives and specifications for the design of an information system.

systems analysis report Comprehensive report prepared at the end of the systems analysis and design phase that summarizes and documents the findings of analysis activities.

systems analysts The people who help users determine their information needs and then design an information system to meet those needs.

systems approach Way of handling systems change by recognizing that every system must have an objective, a set of components, and a set of interrelationships among the components. The systems approach proceeds step by step, with a thorough exploration of all implications and alternatives at each step.

systems concept A systems analysis principle that states that changes in subsystems cannot be made without considering the effect on other subsystems and the system as a whole.

systems design The process of preparing detailed specifications for the development of a new information system.

systems development life cycle (SDLC) Five procedures and steps that a company goes through when it decides to design and implement a new system. The five steps are systems analysis, conceptual design, physical design, implementation and conversion, and operation and maintenance.

systems documentation A complete description of all aspects of each systems application, including narrative material, charts, and program listings.

systems implementation The task of delivering a completed system to an organization for use in day-to-day operations.

systems integrator A vendor who uses common standards and manages a cooperative systems development effort involving its own development personnel and those of the client and other vendors.

systems software Software that interfaces between the hardware and the application program. Systems software include operating systems, database management systems, utility programs, language translators, and communications software.

systems survey The systematic gathering of facts relating to the existing information system. A systems analyst generally carries out this task.

systems survey report The culmination of the systems survey. It contains documentation such as memos, interview and observation notes; questionnaire data; file and record layouts and descriptions; input and output descriptions; and copies of documents, flowcharts, and data flow diagrams.

T

tagging An audit procedure in which certain records are marked with a special code before processing. During processing, all data relating to the marked records are captured and saved so that the auditors can verify them later.

technical feasibility The dimension of feasibility concerned with whether a proposed system can be developed given the available technology.

terminal An input/output device for entering or receiving data directly from the computer.

test data Data that have been specially developed to test the accuracy and completeness of a computer program. The results from the test data are compared with hand-calculated results to verify that the program operates properly.

test data generator program A program that takes the specifications describing the logic characteristics of the program to be tested and automatically generates a set of test data that can be used to check the logic of the program.

test of control A test whose objective it is to determine if control procedures are being followed correctly.

threats Any potential adverse occurrence or unwanted event that could be injurious to either the AIS or the organization. Also referred to as an *event*.

throughput (1) The total amount of useful work performed by a computer system during a given period of time. (2) A measure of production efficiency representing the number of "good" units produced in a given period of time.

time-based model of security Implementing a set of preventive, detective, and corrective controls that enable an organization to recognize that an attack is occurring and take steps to thwart it before any assets have been compromised.

time card A document that records the employee's arrival and departure times for each work shift. The time card records the total hours worked by an employee during a pay period.

trailer label (record) Type of internal label that appears at the end of each file and serves as an indicator that the end of the file has been reached. The trailer label contains the batch totals calculated during input.

transaction An agreement between two entities to exchange goods or services. Any exchange that can be measured in economic terms by an organization.

transaction cycles A group of related business activities (e.g., the set of business activities consisting of sales order entry, shipping, billing, and cash receipts constitutes the revenue cycle). The four major transaction cycles covered in the text are revenue, expenditure, production, and human resource management/payroll.

transaction file. Transaction files contain records of the individual business transactions that occur during a specific fiscal period. A transaction file is conceptually similar to a journal in a manual AIS.

transaction log A detailed record of every transaction entered in a system.

transaction processing A process that begins with capturing transaction data and ends with an informational output.

transcription error An error in which one digit of a number is written incorrectly (e.g., a "4" in the tens position transcribed as a "9," which would cause an error of 50 in the value of the number).

Transmission Control Protocol/Internet Protocol (TCP/IP) The protocol enabling communications on the Internet. It creates what is called a packet-switching network. When a message is ready to be sent over the Internet, the TCP breaks it up into small packets.

Each packet is then given a header, which contains the destination address, and the packets are then sent individually over the Internet. The IP uses the information in the packet header to guide the packets so that they arrive at the proper destination. Once there, the TCP reassembles the packets into the original message.

transposition error An error that results when numbers in two adjacent columns are inadvertently exchanged (for example, 64 is written as 46).

trap door A set of computer instructions that allows a user to bypass the system's normal controls.

trial balance A report listing the balances of all general ledger accounts. It is so named because one of its purposes is to allow the accountant to verify that the total debit balances in various accounts equal the total credit balances in other accounts.

triggered exception reports Preformatted reports generated only when certain conditions exist (e.g., the amount of raw materials on hand falls below the safety stock amount). The reports bring the information about the existing conditions to the attention of a decision maker.

Trojan horse A set of unauthorized computer instructions in an authorized and otherwise properly functioning program. It performs some illegal act at a preappointed time or under a predetermined set of conditions.

tuple (rhymes with *couple*). A row in a relation. A tuple contains data about a specific occurrence in a database table. For example, each row in the inventory table contains all the pertinent data about a particular inventory item.

turnaround document Records of company data sent to an external party and then returned to the system as input. Turnaround documents are prepared in machine-readable form to facilitate their subsequent processing as input records. An example is a utility bill.

turnkey system A system that is delivered to customers ready (theoretically) to be turned on. A turnkey system supplier buys hardware, writes application software that is tailored both to that equipment and to the specific needs of its customers, and then markets the entire system.

U

uninterruptible power system (UPS) An alternative power supply device that protects against the loss of power and fluctuations in the power level by using battery power to enable the system to operate long enough to back up critical data and safely shut down.

Universal Product Code (UPC) A machine-readable code that is read by optical scanners. The code consists of a series of bar codes and is printed on most products sold in grocery stores.

UNIX A flexible and widely used operating system for 16-bit machines.

unstructured decisions Nonrecurring and nonroutine decisions that require considerable judgment and intuition. No framework or model exists to solve such problems.

update anomaly A problem that can arise in a poorly designed relational database. If attributes that are not characteristics of the primary key of a relation are stored in that table, then that data item is stored in many different rows. For example, if customer addresses are stored in the sales invoice table, then the address for a given customer is stored many times (once for each sale). Consequently, if the value of that data item is not changed in every row in which it is stored, inconsistencies in the database will result.

updating Changing stored data to reflect more recent events (e.g., changing the accounts receivable balance because of a recent sale or collection).

user ID A knowledge identifier such as an employee number or account number that users enter to identify themselves when signing on to a system.

user identification (ID) and authentication system A system that requires users to identify themselves by entering a unique user ID when they sign on to the system.

users All people who interact with the system. Users are those who record data, manage the system, and control the system's security. Those who use information from the system are end users.

utility programs A set of prewritten programs that perform a variety of file and data-handling tasks (e.g., sorting or merging files) and other housekeeping chores.

utilization The percentage of time a system is being productively used.

V

validity check An edit test in which an identification number or transaction code is compared with a table of valid identification numbers or codes maintained in computer memory.

value chain The linking together of all the primary and support activities in a business. Value is added as a product passes through the chain.

value of information The benefit produced by the information minus the cost of producing it.

value system The combination of several value chains into one system. A value system includes the value chains of a company, its suppliers, its distributors, and its customers.

value-added network (VAN) A public network that adds value to the data communications process by handling the difficult task of interfacing with the multiple types of hardware and software used by different companies.

variety-based strategic position Producing or providing a subset of the industry's products or services.

vendor-managed inventory (VMI) When manufacturers and distributors manage a retail customer's inventory using an EDI.

virtual private network (VPN) A network that controls access to an extranet by encryption and authentication technology.

virus A segment of executable code that attaches itself to an application program or some other executable system component. When the hidden program is triggered, it makes unauthorized alterations to the way a system operates.

volume label A type of internal label that identifies the contents of each separate data recording medium, such as a tape, diskette, or disk pack.

voucher A document that summarizes the data relating to a disbursement and represents final authorization of payment.

voucher package The set of documents used to authorize payment to a vendor. It consists of a purchase order, receiving report, and vendor invoice.

voucher system A method for processing accounts payable in which a disbursement voucher is prepared instead of posting invoices directly to vendor records in the accounts payable subsidiary ledger. The disbursement voucher identifies the vendor, lists the outstanding invoices, and indicates the net amount to be paid

after deducting any applicable discounts and allowances. Contrast with *nonvoucher system.*

vulnerabilities Flaws in programs which can be exploited to either crash the system or take control of it.

vulnerability scans Automated tools designed to identify whether a given system possesses any well-known vulnerabilities.

W

walk-throughs Meetings, attended by those associated with a project, in which a detailed review of systems procedures and/or program logic is carried out in a step-by-step manner.

war dialing Searching for an idle modem by programming a computer to dial thousands of phone lines. Finding an idle modem often enables a hacker to gain access to the network to which it is connected.

war chalking The practice of drawing chalk symbols on sidewalks to mark unprotected wireless networks.

war driving The practice of driving around in cars looking for unprotected home or corporate wireless networks.

white-collar criminals Typically businesspeople who commit fraud. White-collar criminals usually resort to trickery or cunning and their crimes usually involve a violation of trust or confidence.

wide area network (WAN) A telecommunications network that covers a large geographic area anywhere in size from a few cities to the whole globe. A WAN uses telephone lines, cables, microwaves, or satellites to connect a wide variety of hardware devices in many different locations.

wiretap To listen (eavesdrop) in on an unprotected communications line.

worm Similar to a virus except that it is a program rather than a code segment hidden in a host program. A worm also copies itself automatically and actively transmits itself directly to other systems.

X

XBRL eXtensible Business Reporting Language is a variant of XML (eXtensible Markup Language) specifically designed for use in communicating the content of financial data. It does this by creating tags for each data item that look much like the tags used by HTML.

Z

zero-balance check An internal check that requires the balance of an account to be zero after all entries to it have been made.